Street by Street

HAMPSHIRE

Enlarged areas ALDERSHOT, ANDOVER, BASINGSTOKE, BOURNEMOUTH, FAREHAM, GOSPORT, HAVANT, NEWBURY, PORTSMOUTH, SOUTHAMPTON, WINCHESTER

Plus Canford Heath, Christchurch, Farnham, Ferndown, Haslemere, Tidworth, Poole, Sandhurst, Verwood, Wimborne Minster

3rd edition August 2008
© Automobile Association Developments Limited 2008

Original edition printed May 2001

 This product includes map data licensed from Ordnance Survey® with the permission of the Controller of Her Majesty's Stationery Office. © Crown copyright 2008. All rights reserved. Licence number 100021153.

The copyright in all PAF is owned by Royal Mail Group plc.

RoadPilot® Information on fixed speed camera locations provided by RoadPilot © 2008 RoadPilot® Driving Technology.

All rights reserved. No part of this publication may be reproduced, stored in a retrieval system, or transmitted in any form or by any means – electronic, mechanical, photocopying, recording or otherwise – unless the permission of the publisher has been given beforehand.

Published by AA Publishing (a trading name of Automobile Association Developments Limited, whose registered office is Fanum House, Basing View, Basingstoke, Hampshire RG21 4EA. Registered number 1878835).

Produced by the Mapping Services Department of The Automobile Association. (A03663)

A CIP Catalogue record for this book is available from the British Library.

Printed by Oriental Press in Dubai

The contents of this atlas are believed to be correct at the time of the latest revision. However, the publishers cannot be held responsible or liable for any loss or damage occasioned to any person acting or refraining from action as a result of any use or reliance on any material in this atlas, nor for any errors, omissions or changes in such material. This does not affect your statutory rights. The publishers would welcome information to correct any errors or omissions and to keep this atlas up to date. Please write to Publishing, The Automobile Association, Fanum House (FH12), Basing View, Basingstoke, Hampshire, RG21 4EA. E-mail: *streetbystreet@theaa.com*

Ref: ML011y

Key to map pages	ii-iii
Key to map symbols	iv-1
Enlarged map pages	2-23
Main map pages	24-339
Index – towns & villages	340-342
Index – streets	343-392
Index – featured places	392-401
Acknowledgements	401

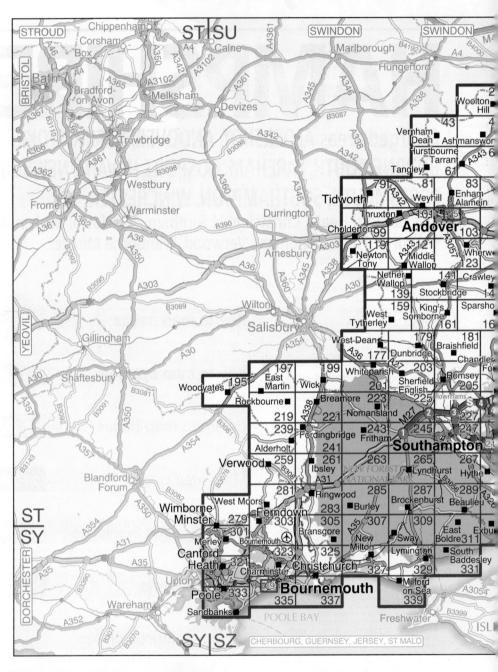

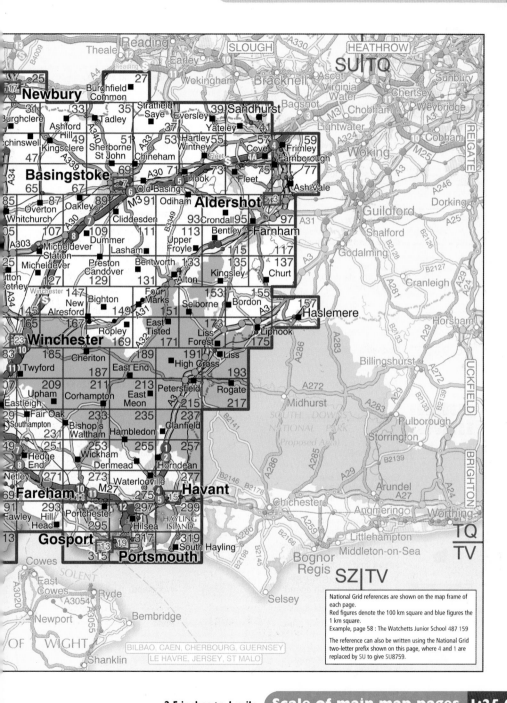

National Grid references are shown on the map frame of each page.
Red figures denote the 100 km square and blue figures the 1 km square.
Example, page 58 : The Watchetts Junior School 487 159

The reference can also be written using the National Grid two-letter prefix shown on this page, where 4 and 1 are replaced by SU to give SU8759.

Junction 9 — Motorway & junction	Railway & minor railway station
Services — Motorway service area	Underground station
Primary road single/dual carriageway	Light railway & station
Services — Primary road service area	Preserved private railway
A road single/dual carriageway	LC — Level crossing
B road single/dual carriageway	Tramway
Other road single/dual carriageway	Ferry route
Minor/private road, access may be restricted	Airport runway
One-way street	County, administrative boundary
Pedestrian area	Mounds
Track or footpath	17 — Page continuation 1:25,000
Road under construction	3 — Page continuation to enlarged scale 1:10,000
Road tunnel	River/canal, lake, pier
30 — Speed camera site (fixed location) with speed limit in mph	Aqueduct, lock, weir
V — Speed camera site (fixed location) with variable speed limit	465 ▲ Winter Hill — Peak (with height in metres)
40 — Section of road with two or more fixed camera sites; speed limit in mph or variable	Beach
50 ⟶ ⟵ 50 — Average speed (SPECS™) camera system with speed limit in mph	Woodland
P — Parking	Park
P+🚌 — Park & Ride	Cemetery
Bus/coach station	Built-up area
Railway & main railway station	IKEA — IKEA store

Symbol	Description	Symbol	Description
	Industrial/business building		Abbey, cathedral or priory
	Leisure building		Castle
	Retail building		Historic house or building
	Other building	Wakehurst Place NT	National Trust property
	City wall		Museum or art gallery
A&E	Hospital with 24-hour A&E department		Roman antiquity
PO	Post Office		Ancient site, battlefield or monument
	Public library		Industrial interest
i	Tourist Information Centre		Garden
i	Seasonal Tourist Information Centre		Garden Centre Garden Centre Association Member
	Petrol station, 24 hour Major suppliers only		Garden Centre Wyevale Garden Centre
†	Church/chapel		Arboretum
	Public toilet, with facilities for the less able		Farm or animal centre
PH	Public house AA recommended		Zoological or wildlife collection
	Restaurant AA inspected		Bird collection
Madeira Hotel	Hotel AA inspected		Nature reserve
	Theatre or performing arts centre		Aquarium
	Cinema		Visitor or heritage centre
	Golf course		Country park
▲	Camping AA inspected		Cave
	Caravan site AA inspected		Windmill
	Camping & caravan site AA inspected		Distillery, brewery or vineyard
	Theme park	•	Other place of interest

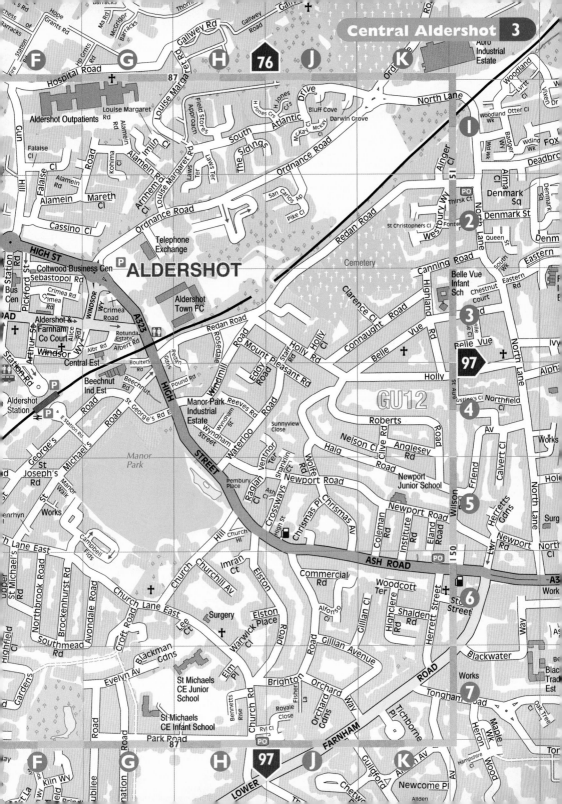

West March Business Centre

Hayles Ct

Itchen Court

Court

Court

Tyne Court

Wye Ct

Icknield School

River Way

Walworth

Walworth Road

Industrial Estate

Water

Central Way

South Way

Industrial Estate

F

G

82

H

J

K

I

37

Pilgrims W

Pilgrims Wy

Pilgrims W

Pilgrims Way

Pilgrims Way

Pilgrims

Walworth Road

West Way

West Way

West Way

West Way

Duke

Focus

38

A3093

Superstore

Pilgrims Way

CHURCHILL WAY

Walworth Road Industrial Estate

Focus 303 Business Cen

I

Watery Lane

Colenzo

Majorca Av

Toledo Gv

Madrid Rd

Vigo Rd

Granada Place

WALWORTH ROUNDABOUT

A3093

CHURCHILL WY

Industrial Estate

2

Central Way

Magellan Close

Columbus Way

Dou

March Cl

Colenzo Drive

Drive

Seville Crs

Vigo Road

Bilbao Ct

London

Nelson Walk

Rodney Ct

Tovey Court

Way

Main

Barcelona Close

Seville Crs

Vigo Rd

Vigo J&I School

Napier Walk

Jervis Court

Admirals

Somerville Court

Hawke Close

46

3

Road

Works

Valencia Way

Vigo Road

Vigo Rd

Norman Gate School

Road

Mountbatten Court

Admirals

Drake Court

Hood

Duncan Court

London

103

A3093

OVER

Sports Centre

Batchelors Barn Road

Borsberry Close

The Mark Way School

Winton School

Admirals Way

Admirals Way

Collingwood Walk

Beatty Court

Byng Walk

Admirals Way

Admirals Way

Boscowen Close

Fisher Close

Charlotte

& The n Age

Recreation Road

Acre Path

Sports Centre

London Road

Stiles Drive

Harvey Pl

Springfield Close

Springfield Close

Springfield Close

Springfield Close

Springfield Close

4

Acre Ct

Eastfield Rd

Eastfield Close

Tyrells Croft

London Road

Winton Chase

Pearman Drive

Palmer Drive

Springfield

eld Cl

Road

Walled Meadow

Woodlands Way

London Road

Sheep Fair Close

Sheep Fair close

Sidmouth Rd

5

Walled Garden Close

Clover Mews

Meadow

Lamb Cl

Bell Road

Wool

Grove

Pen

Highlands Rd

CE Stn

street

vincent rive

Micheldever Road

Bell Rd

shepherds

Row

Highlands Road

Micheldever Road

6

The Gr

Lane

Wolverdene School

Colvin Close

Dene Path

Cummins

Hill

Beech Gdns

Greenhaven Close

Wolversdene Road

Wolversdene Close

Leigh Cl

Wolversdene Gdns

Wolversdene Rd

Quality Hotel

Leigh Gdns

Leigh

View Gdns

Road Belmont

Farrs Avenue

Leigh Road

Bere Hill Crs

Hedge End Road

Hedge Ed Rd

Charnwood Cl

45

7

Dunmow

South Road

End Road

Herons

Cornfields

37

F

G

H

J

103

K

38

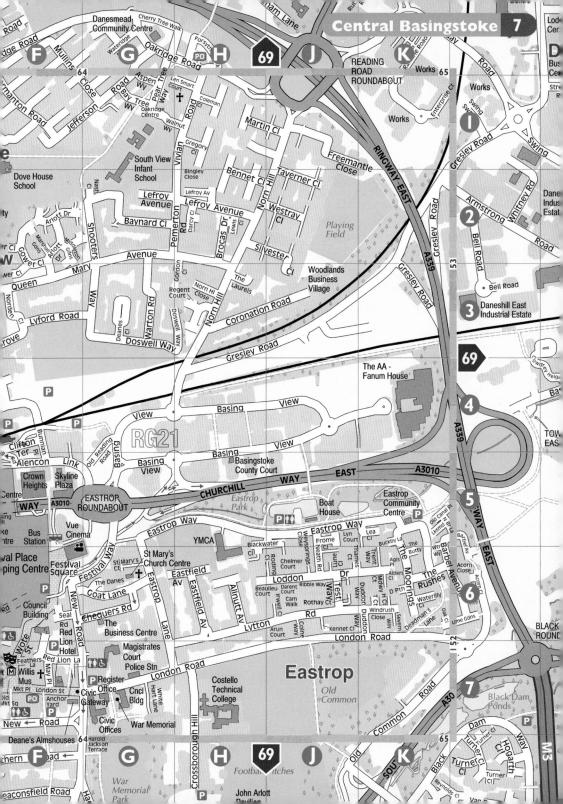

F G H 335 J K

Cavendish Road

Surgery

Dean Park
Cricket
Ground

Coach House Pl

Bourne
Station

Parkway
Retail Park

10

Cooper Dean
Pavilion

Park
Rd

Surg

Corporation Road

Northcote Road

BH1

Southcote Road

Cavendish Road

P

Lansdowne Gdns

ST PAULS
ROUNDABOUT

ST PAULS RD A35

Travel
Interchange

Superstore

Superstore

Works

Gardens
View

I Carlton Road

Dean Park Road

Madeira Road

Lansdowne Road

50 WESSEX WAY

P

St Paul's Lane

Cncl
Bldg

St Paul's Pl

BOURNEMOUTH
STATION
ROUNDABOUT

St Oxford Road

HOLDENHURST RD

ST SWITHUN'S RD S

St Swithun's Rd

Knyveton
Gardens

Frances Road

Elstead
Hotel

Works

Spencer Road

The Bournemouth
& Poole College

Knyveto

Trinity Rd

The
Firs

Stafford Rd

Police
Stn

Council
Building

Surgery

Bournemouth
Business Cen

Cotlands Rd

York
Road

A35

Council
Building

Woodford
Road

Annerley Rd

A35

The
Bournemouth
& Poole College

Langtry Manor
Lovenest of
a King Hotel

Derby Road

2

Lorne
Pk
Cumnor
Road

Surgery Rd

Magistrates
Court
Coroners
Court

Inst of Health
& Community
Studies

Bournemouth
University

PO

30 CHRISTCHUR

Christchurch Road

3

335

Glen Fern Rd

Wootton Gdns

Christchurch Road

Wootton Mt

THE LANSDOWNE
ROUNDABOUT

Meyrick Rd

Christchurch
Road

Chrstchrch
Road

Anglo-Swiss
Hotel

Bournemouth
University

Weston Drive

Gervis Rd

Manor

Jewish
Day School

Synagogue

P

BATH ROAD

Burley
Court
Hotel

The Bournemouth
& Poole College

Surg

GERVIS ROAD

Hinton
Firs Hotel

4 30

Belvedere
Hotel

Parsonage Rd

ST PETERS
ROUNDABOUT

Hotel
Piccadilly

Quality Hotel

Queens
Hotel

Heathlands
Hotel

Grove

Suncliff
Hotel

Weston Road

Ocean View
Hotel

Manor Rd

East Overcli

Bay View
Court Hotel

E O Dr

Ocean View

Underc

BOURNEMOUTH

Hotel
Miramar

BATH RD

Cumberland
Hotel

Cliffside
Hotel

5

HILL
DABOUT

Russell Cotes Rd

Marsham
Court Hotel

East Overcliff Drive

Meyrick Rd

East Cliff
Lift

East Cliff

D066

P

De Vere
Royal Bath
Hotel

Russell Cotes
Art Gallery &
Museum

Undercliff Drive

6

erfront

Poole Bay

7

F G H J 10 K

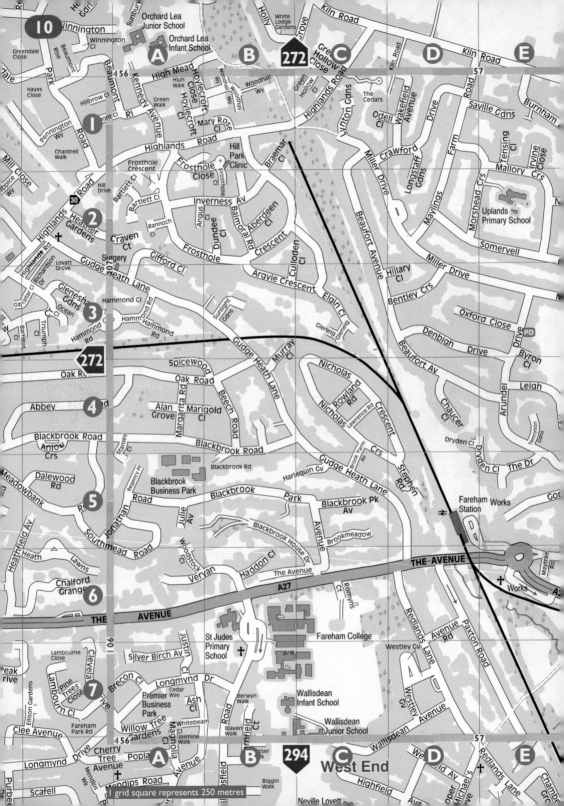

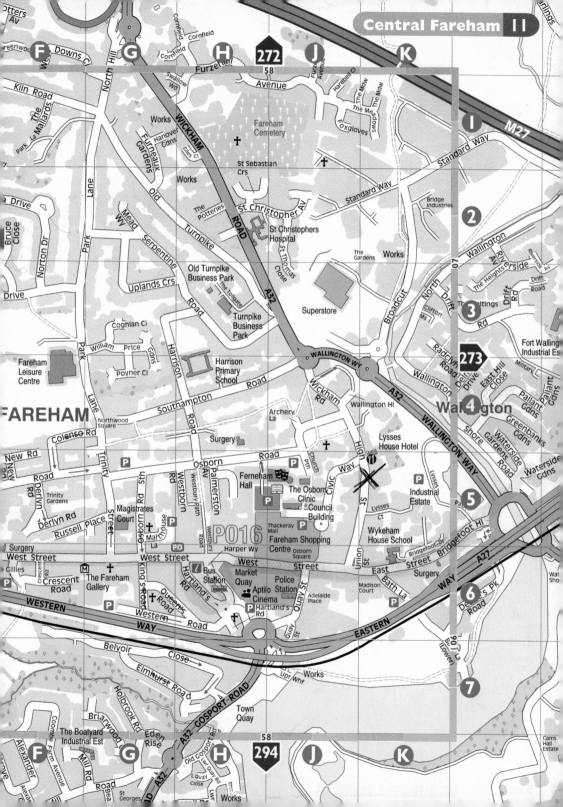

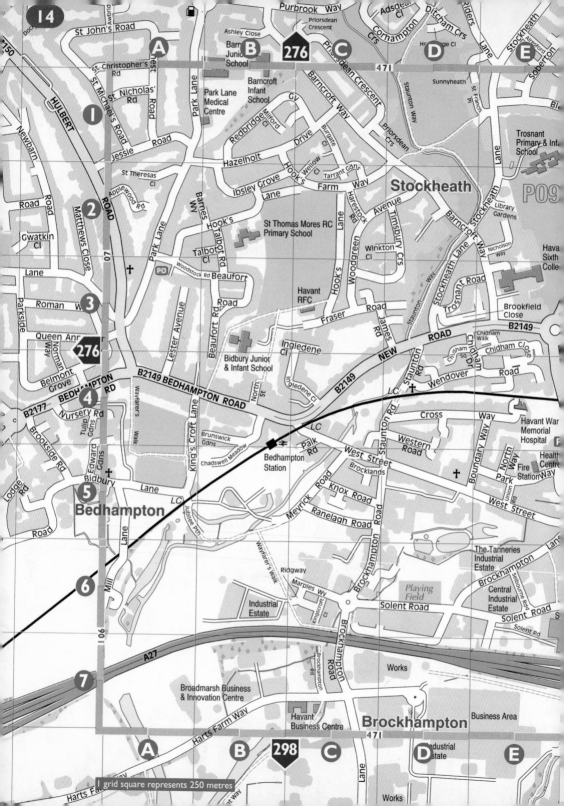

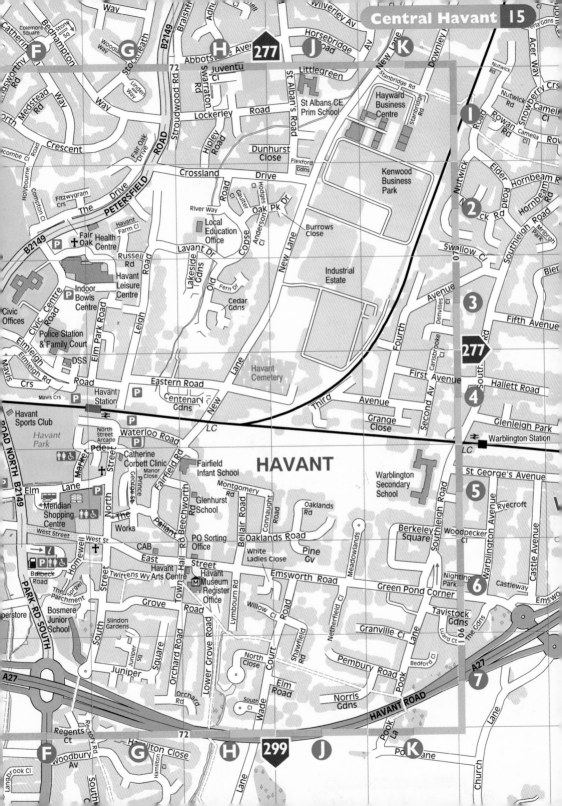

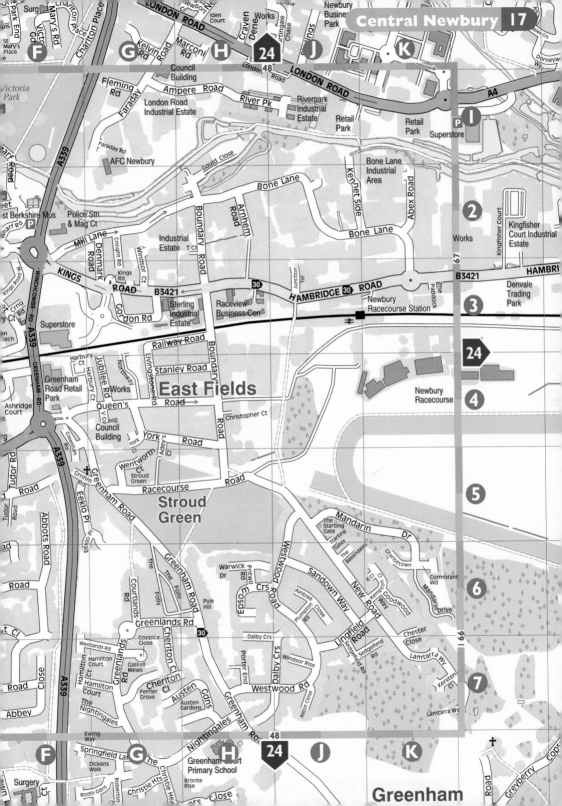

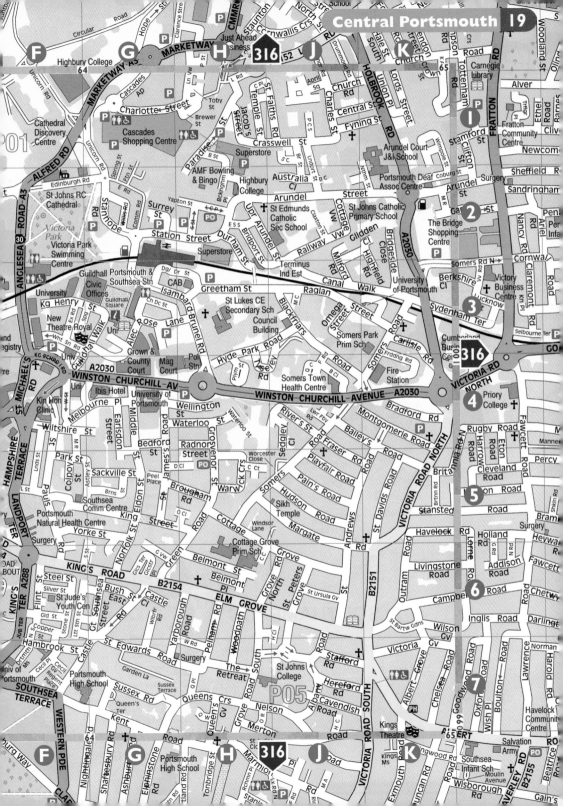

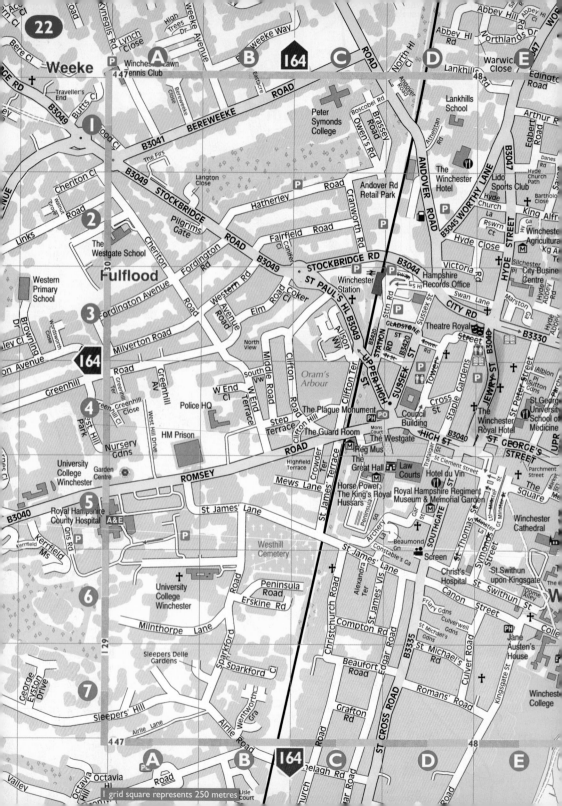

A   B   C   D   E   F   G

461   62   63   64

I

Sulhamstead

Kingston

Sulhamstead
Bannister Upp

2

Lower Padworth

Ufton Green

Ufton Lane

Hart's Lane

Works

3

Middle Farm

Church Lane

Sulhamstead & Ufton Nervet
Primary School

Ufton Nervet

Shortheath

4

Padworth Lane

Wise's Firs

5

Lodge Farm

RG7

Benham Farm

Firlands

6

Padworth

The Ark School

Old Farm

School Road

Padworth College

Camp Road

Island Farm Road

7

The Old Rectory

Four Corne

8

Silver Lane

Rectory Road

West Berkshire County
Hampshire County

9

Court Farm

Raghill Farm

Hatch Farm House

Padworth Common

Mary's Lane

Baughurst Road

Ramptons Lane

461   62   63   64

A   **34**   B   C   D   E   **35**   F   G

Chapel Road

Welshman's Road

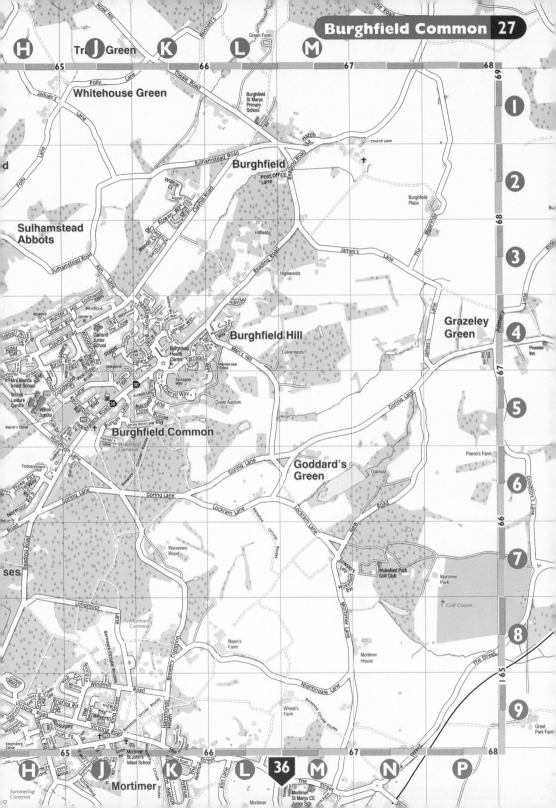

H   J   K   L   M

65   66   67   68   69

I
2
3
4
5
6
7
8
9

Whitehouse Green

Tr... Green

Folly Lane
Hose Hill
Bennett's
Green Farm
Theale Road

Burghfield St Marys Primary School

Church Lane
Hatch La

Sulhamstead Road

Burghfield

Post Office Lane

Willow Cl
Hazel Close
Clayhill Road
Rowan Way
Reading Road

Burghfield Place

The Marlings

Burghfield Place
Bu

Sulhamstead Abbots

Sulhamstead Road
Ash La

Beech Croft
Chestnut Cr

Hillfields

James's Lane

Highwoods

Reading Road

Hillside

Palmers Lane

Ride

Grazeley Green

Hunter's Hill
Pinchcut
Omer's
Bluebell Cl
Omer's Rd
Clayhill Road
Iuebell Rd
Alder Cld
Woodman Rd
Garland Junior School
Annister
R d
Mrs Blands Infant School
Birch
Goodwood
Warren Rd
Willink Leisure Centre
Willink School
Bland's Close
Recreation Gd
Reading Road
Burges Lane
Auckland Rd
Valley Rd
Stable
Oakdene
Lamden Way
Hammonds Way
Man's Hill
Tarragon
Tarragon Way
Chervil Way
First Fruit
Auckland Lane
Russet Cld
Goring Wood Lane
Auckland Close

Burghfield Hill

Burghfield Health Centre
Pembroke Close
Great Auckium

Culverlands

James's Lane

Premier Inn

Goring Lane

Pierce's Farm

Burghfield Common

Palmer's Lane
Wokefield Common

Goddard's Green

Oakfield

Goring Lane

Totterdown
Three Firs Way
Firs
Normoor Rd
Goring Lane
Road

Goring Lane

Lockram Lane

Lockram Lane

New Road

Crosby's Lane

Warennes Wood

Berkshire Circular Routes

Wokefield Park Golf Club

Sawyer's Lay
Wokefield Pk

Mortimer Park

Longmoor
Mortimer Common
Berkshire Circular Routes

Golf Course

The Street

Windmill

Reading Road
Brewery Common Road
Mann's Farm

Mortimer Lane

Mortimer House

Nightingale Lane

ses

The C of E
Briarlea Rd
The Beve's
The Devers
Victoria Road
Stephens
Firs
Inn Street
Victoria Road
Stephen's Close
Surgery
Croft Rd
Hammonds Heath
Berkshire Circular Routes
Wheat's Farm

Great Park Farm

65   66   67   68

H   J   K   L   **36**   M   N   P

Mortimer

Garth Rd
St John's Infant School
Mortimer St Marys CE Junior Sch
Kiln Road
The Street
Kiln Lane
The Avenue
The Street
The Street

Summerlug Common
Loves
Wood

A B C D E F G

438 39 40

New Mill

Holt Lodge

Waterman's

1
The Old
The Firs
Post Office Road
Lane

Inkpen
Common

Heads
Lane

Roudnert Lane

Hell Corner

Burgess Lane

Holt Manor Farm

Watery Lane

Nature
Reserve

64

Trapshill

PH

Malt House

2

63

3

Kirby House

West
Woodhay

Fishponds Farm

Hazelby

No
En

Park House

✝

Hatch
House Farm

4

62

5

Highwood Farm

Hayes

West
Woodhay
Down

6

Test Way

Walbury
Hill

7

61

Lower Farm

Wayfarer's Walk

East Woodhay

✝

8

Hampshire County
West Berkshire County

Eastwick

Wayfarer's Walk

9

160

Wayfarer's
Walk

438 39 40

A B C   D E F G

Hogs Hole

Wayfarer's Walk

1 grid square represents 500 metres

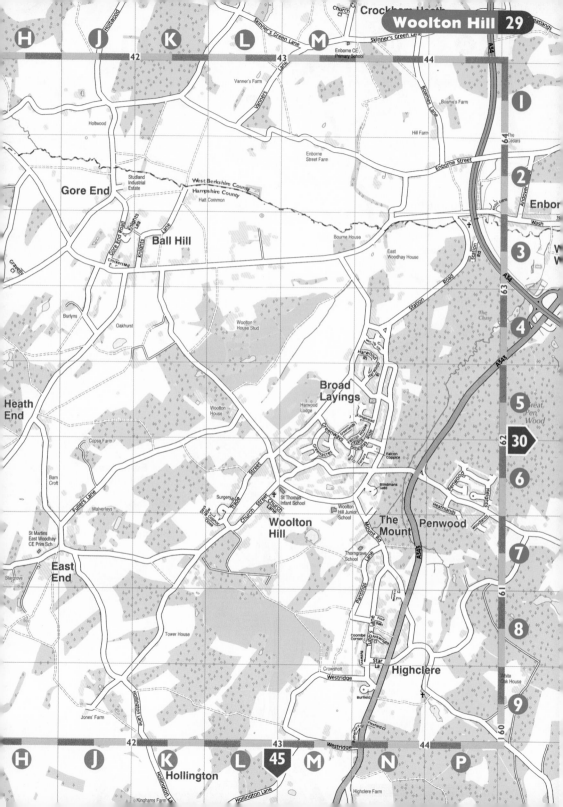

A   **25** B   C   D   E   F   G

452   Thornford Park Track   Crookham House

Crookham Common Road   53   54

Poplar Close   Azalea Rd

Laurel Avenue   Birch Avenue   Oaktree Avenue

1 Goldfinch Bottom

Crookham Common

RG19

Foxhold

Little Park House

Hyde E

Stone House

64

2 Ford

Folly Farm

Thornford Road

3 Thornfield

West Berkshire County

Hampshire County

63

Works

Mill Green

Goose Hill

Riddings Farm

Works

Ashford Hill Road

Marigold Lane

Riddings Lane

4 Ashford Hill Road

Thornford Road

Works

Old Farm

Headley

Common Road

Hillhouse Lane

62

Headley Stud

Ashford Hill Road

Tucker's Hill Stud

5

Galley Lane

31 Cheam Haettreys

Schoolhouse

Kingsclere Woodlands

Barn Alley

6 Cheam School

Catt's Place

Scarlett's Farm

61

Plastow Green

Hillhouse Lane

7

Galley Lane

Watts Farm

Works

Strattons

Dairy House Farm

8

KNOWL

60

Upper House Farm

B3051

9

Pitchorn Farm

Hall's Farm

Union Lane

LITTLE KNOWL HILL

A339

452   53   **48**   54

A   B   C   D   E   F   G

Stanton's Farm   Hamdens Farm

1 grid square represents 500 metres

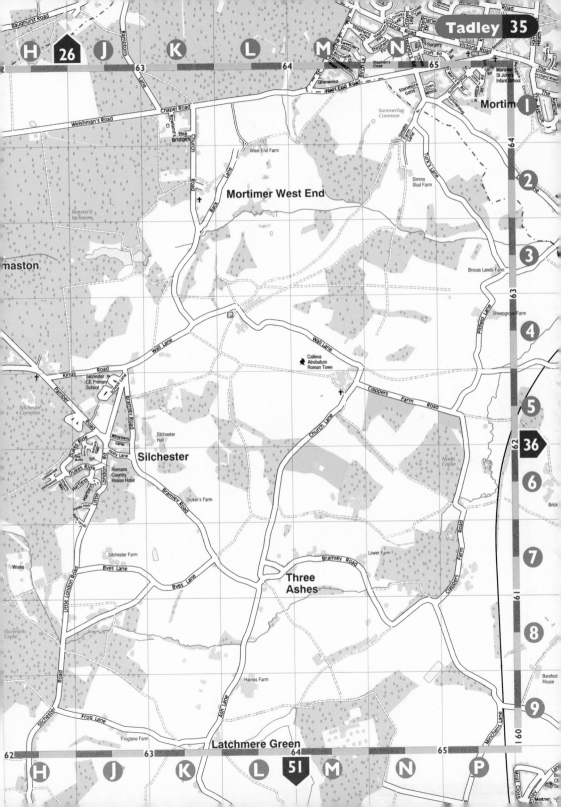

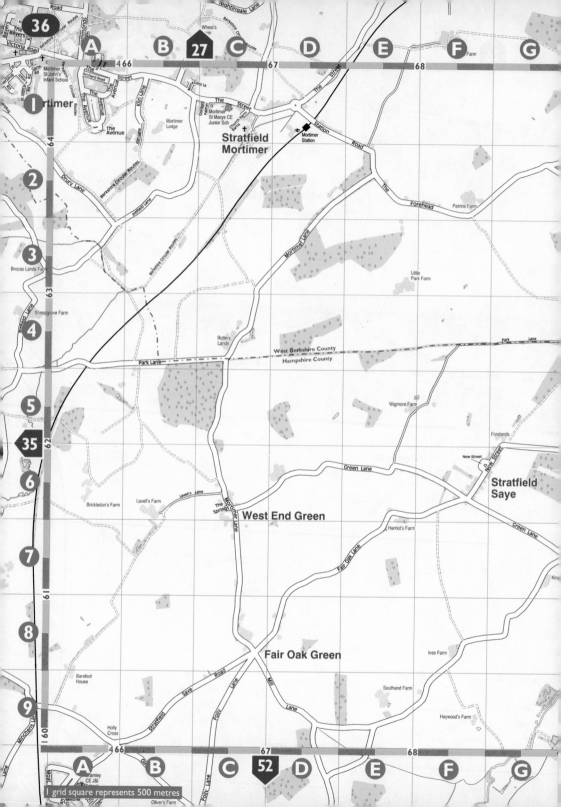

Mortimer

Stratfield Mortimer

Mortimer Station

The Forehead

Perrins Farm

Little Park Farm

Brocas Lands Farm

Sheepgrove Farm

Butlers Lands

West Berkshire County
Hampshire County

Park Lane

Wigmore Farm

Forelands

New Street

Green Lane

Stratfield Saye

Brickledon's Farm

Lavell's Farm

Lavell's Lane

West End Green

The Springs

Mortimer Lane

Herriot's Farm

Fair Oak Lane

Green Lane

Ives Farm

Barefoot House

Fair Oak Green

Southend Farm

Mill Lane

Heywood's Farm

Holly Cross

Stratfield Saye Road

Folly Lane

Bramley CE J&I

Oliver's Farm

River Loddon

A B C D E F G

438 39 40

1

Hogs
Hole

West Berkshire County
Hampshire County

2

59

3

4

58

Arthur's
Lane

Faccombe

Curzon
Street Farm

Netherton

Privet
Copse

5

43

6

57

7

Kimmer Farm

Faccombes
Wood

Lower Manor
Farm

8

56

9

Sidley's
Wood

438 39 40

A B C D E F G

62

Doyley
Manor

Wayfarer's Walk

Wayfarer's
Walk

1 grid square represents 500 metres

White
Oak House

H   J   K   L   **29**   M

Westridge

Flexford Cl

42   **43**   44

60

1

Hollington Lane

Hollington

Highclere Farm

Kinghams Farm Lane

Hollington Lane

Blakes Farm

**Highclere
Street**

A343

2

59

**Hollington
Cross**

PH

Maple
Farm

3
& Gardens

Zell House
Farm

Coles
Wood

4

Wayfarer's Walk

58

Manor Farm

5

Wayfarer's Walk

46

Barn Close Lane

Cross Lane

Three Legs House

Wayfarer's Walk

Grotto
Copse

6

RED

HILL

A343

57

Ashmansworth

Mopper's Barn

Steeles
Farm

Rabbit
Warren

7

Alexander
Farm

Farm

Upper
Woodcott
Down

8

Crux Easton

56

9

Beech
Hanger
Copse

Hook
Copse

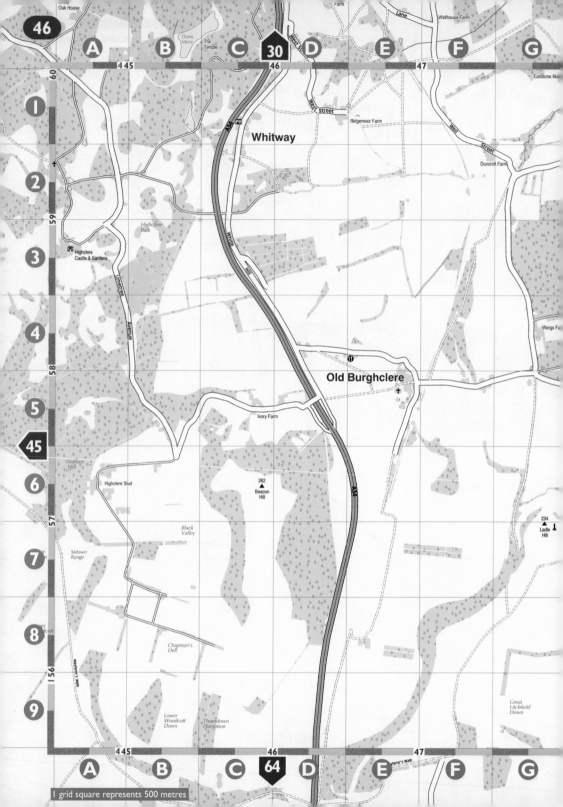

H J K L **33** M N

56 57 58 60

I

Brown
Green

59

2

3

Hollybush La

Old Vyne Lane

4

58

5

57

50

6

7

56

8

9

H J K L **67** M N P

5 56 57 58

Frith Farm

Ham Farm House

Chapel Lane

Holt Lane

Wolverton Common

Wolverton Road

Wolverton Wood

Wordford Woods

Baughurst House

Brown's Farm

Pound Green

Hillside

Stratton

Towns End

Wolverton Road

Townsend

Wolverton

Hill Lane

Wolverton House

Ramsdell Road

Ramsdell Road

Wolverton Lane

Wolverton

Stony Heath

Povey's Farm

The Firs

Baughurst Road

Foscot Farm

A339

Ewhurst Park

Ewhurst

Ro

Slyer's Farm

Dorrel Wood

Home Farm

Ewhurst House

Slyer's Wood

Pitt Hall Farm

Lloyd's Lane

Folly Dairy

A339

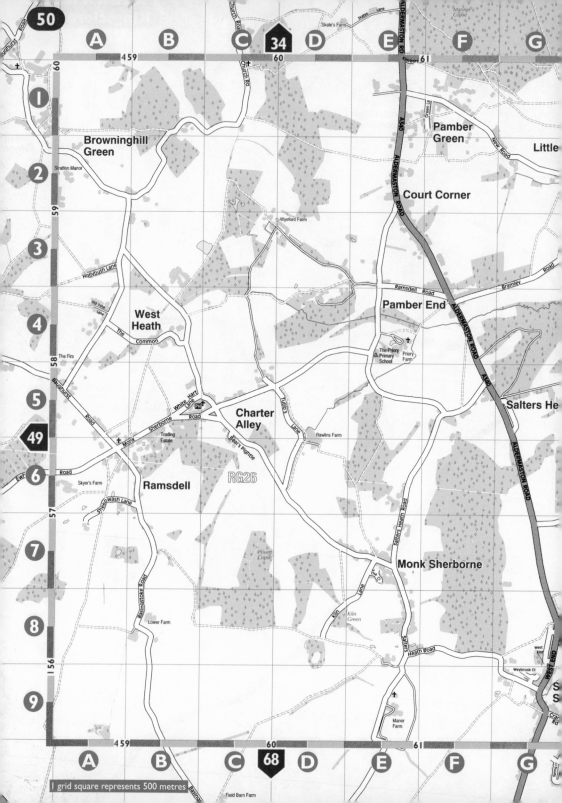

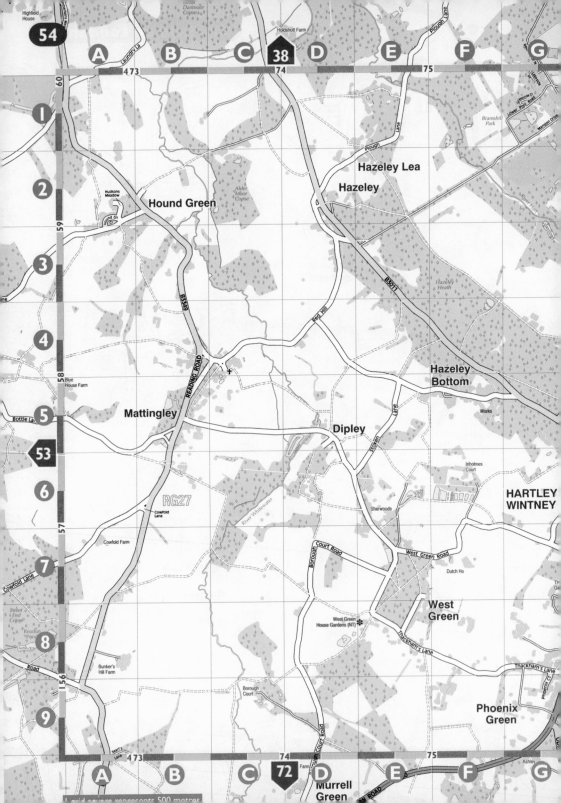

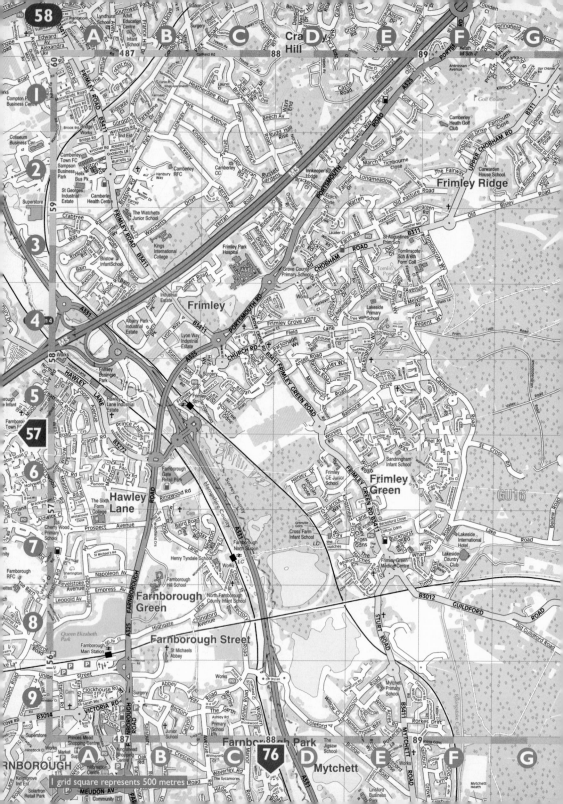

A   B   C   42   D   E   F   G

431   32   33

Conholt Hill

Conholt Lane

1

Little Down

Chute Causeway

Middle Conholt Farm

55

Du... Lane

Conholt House

Barn

2

Conholt Park

Hungerford Lane

3

54

Hampshire Gate

Wiltshire County
Hampshire County

Catharijer Wood

Standen House

4

Chute
Standen

Upstreet

Dummer Lane

Holt Lane

Dowlands Farm

Chute
Cadley

5

Lower Chute

✝

Tangley
Bottom

53

6

Forest House

Jolly's Farm

Clark Lane

Tangley

✝

Hungerford Lane

7

52

✝

Lodge Lane

...well B...

8

Coach Hill

Chute
Lodge

Ph

...gbottom F

9

51

Lodge Lane

431   32   33

A   B   C   81   D   E   F   G

Roundaway Lane

Roundaway Farm

Redhouse Farm

I grid square represents 500 metres

H **J** **K** **L** `45`
42 43 44

I

Hook
Copse

Lye Farm

Woodcott

Lower Woodcott

2

Easton Park
Wood

✝ Upper Woodcott
Farm

Woodcott House

3

Sladen
Green

Paul's
Copse

Stubb's
Copse

Suggeaston
Copse

54

'Highfield House'

Buckets Down Farm

4

Binley

Hollycroft
Copses

5

Wadwick
House

Binley Bottom

53 **64** ►

Wadwick

Wadwick Bottom

6

ade Bottom Farm

Elm Farm

Egbury
Farm

Egbury

7

Downhams Farm

52

Copper's
Wood Far

8

Egbury Castle Farm

om

Cold Harbour

Wakeswood

9

Swampton

Wadwick Bottom

ane

✝
St Mary Bourne

Spring Hill Lane

H **J** **K** **L** `84` **M** **N** **P**
42 43 44

Road

Newbam

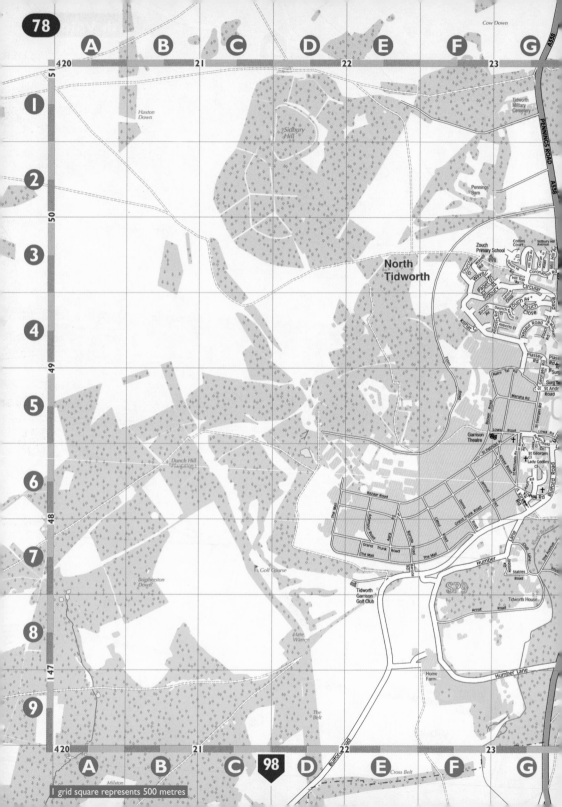

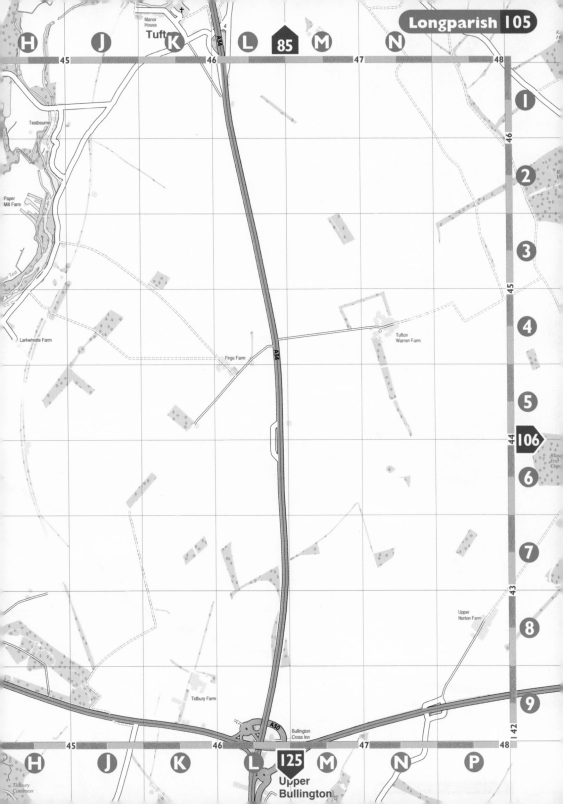

H   J   K   L   **85**   M   N

45   46   47   48

Manor House

Tuft

Testbourne

Paper Mill Farm

Larkwhistle Farm

Firgo Farm

Tufton Warren Farm

A34

1

46

2

3

45

4

5

44 **106**

Blue End Gap

6

7

43

Upper Norton Farm

8

Tidbury Farm

9

42

A30

Bullington Cross Inn

Upper Bullington

Tidbury Common

88

A   B   C No   alt   D   E   F   G

Waltham

Manor Farm

Stevenson

North Waltham School

55   56   57   58

1

Folly Farm

Maldenthorn   Lane

Waltham Cross Centre

Wyevale Garden Centre

Lane

Church Road

Coldharbour

2

PH

Popham Lane

A30

M3

Premier Inn

3

Basingstoke Crematorium

STOCKBRIDGE ROAD   A30

Dummer Down Farm

Dummer   Down

4

Waltham Trinleys

Junction 8

5

West Farm

107

The Holt

6

A33

Popham Court Farm

Popham

Walmer's Walk

7

College Wood

8

Bradley Farm

9

Rownest Wood

Woodmancott

55   56   57   58

A   B   C   **128**   D   E   F   G

46   45   44   43   42

1 grid square represents 500 metres

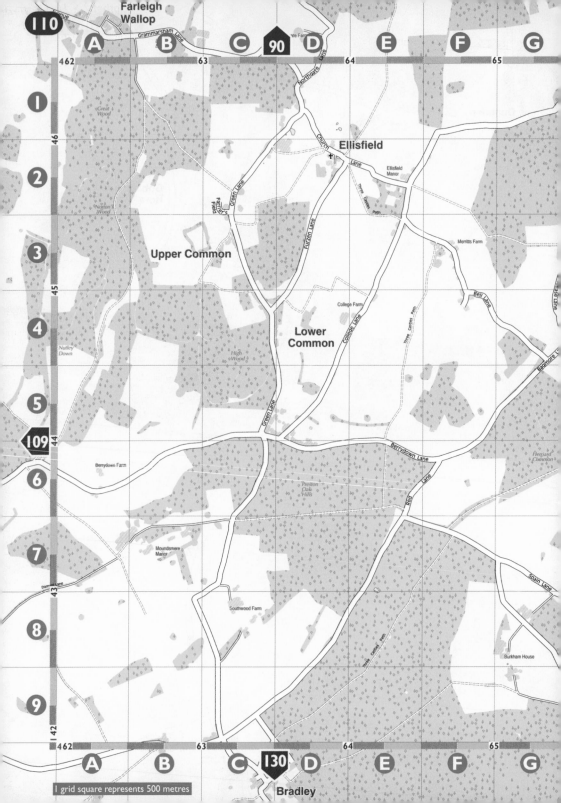

Farleigh
Wallop

110

A   B   C   90   D   E   F   G

462   63   64   65

Grammarsham Lane

Northgate Lane

1

Great
Wood

46

2

Norton's
Wood

Green Lane

Farrier's
Field

Church Lane

Ellisfield

Ellisfield
Manor

Three Castles Path

3

Upper Common

45

Furzen Lane

Merritts Farm

Bell Lane

4

Nutley
Down

High
Wood

College Farm

Lower
Common

College Lane

Three Castles Path

5

44

109

Green Lane

Berrydown Lane

Bagmore Lane

Fleugard
Common

6

Berrydown Farm

Preston
Oak
Hills

Red Lane

7

Moundsmere
Manor

43

Spain Lane

Damson Lane

8

Southwood Farm

Three Castles Path

Burkham House

9

42

462   63   64   65

A   B   C   130   D   E   F   G

1 grid square represents 500 metres

Bradley

Weston Patrick

A B C 92 D E F G

469 70 71 72

1

46

2

Little
Wood

3

45

High
Wood

4

Great
Park

5

Weston
Common

111

44

6

Shalden Green

Avenue Road

7

43

Lasham
Wood

8

9

42

469 70 71 72

Little Park
Copse

New Farm

Humbly Grove
Copse

Humbly
Grove

Blounce

Dean
Copse

Pickaxe Lane

B3349

Powntley
Copse

Swainshill Farm

Pickaxe Lane

Sowgate Lane

Swaines
Hill Manor

Golden
Pot

Shalden
Park Farm

B3349

Old Odiham Road

Brockham Hill Lane

NEW ODIHAM ROAD

Shalden Park
Wood

Stancombe Lane

Alton
Golf Club

Golf Course

Fiddlers
Field

Shalden

1 grid square represents 500 metres

H   J   K   L   93   M

73   74   75   76

Lord Wandsworth College
Hyde Farm
Lord Wandsworth College

New Farm

Virney Copse
Froyle Lane

Sutton Common

Ighnham Copse

Sheephouse Copse

Crest Hill Farm

Well Lane

Yarnhams

Hawkins Wood

Lower Froyle

114

Park Lane

Lane

Barnet

Ham Wood

Spellycombe Copse

Holybourne Down

Upper Froyle

Treloar School

A31

Lane

Beech

River Wey

W

1
2
3
4
5
6
7
8
9

PH

PH

H   J   K   L   133   M   N   P

73   74   75   76

Brockhd

Bonha Farm

Mill Court

H   J   K   L   99   M

24   25   26   27   42   Grate

Cholderton Lodge

Cholderton Road

Cholderton Road

Quarley Down Farm

Grateley Grove

I

Portway Farm

CHOLDERTON ROAD

Station

2

Grateley Business Park

Station Rd

Campbell Cl

Streetway Road

B3084

Station Ap

Grateley Station

Streetway Road

3

Mount Hermon Road

Palestine Road

Zion Road

Palestine

Salisbury Road

Bournemouth Road

4

Orange Grove

orange Grove

olive Grove

Peach Grove

olive Grove

Peach Grove

Mount Carmel Road

40

5

WALLOP R

120

Castle Farm

6

Hampshire County Wiltshire County

39

Martin's Clump

7

Pott

Croft Farm

8

I 38

9

H   J   K   L   138   M   N   P

24   25   26   27

H   J   K   L   101   M

31   32   33   34

42

Stockbridge Road

SALISB

Red
e

1

Farleigh
School

41

Stonehanger
Copse

Prospect Farm

A343

Down Farm

Dipden
Bottom

2

3

Road

Saxley Farm

40

4

Kentsboro

Stockbridge Road

Clatford
Oakcuts

5

122

The Green
The Avenue
Paddock
Fields
Farriers
Lane
Old Park La
The Fox Cover
The Furrows

6

Middle Wallop
Airfield

39

7

Down Farm

8

Works

38

P
i

9

143
Danebury Hill
Danebury
Ring

The
Turret

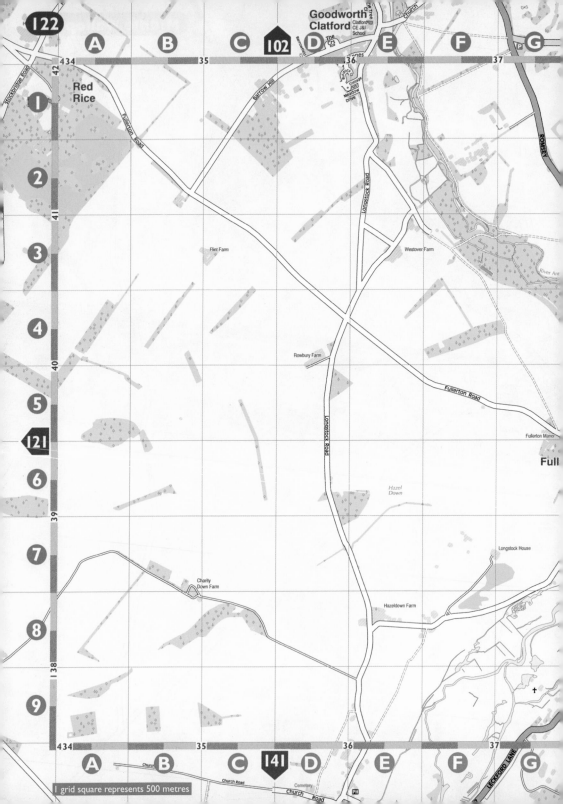

122

A   B   C **102** D   E   F   G

Goodworth
Clatford

Clatford
CE J&I
School

Red
Rice

Stockbridge Road

Fullerton Road

Barrow Hill

The

Jones

Cottage

Meadow
Drive

Church

P

ROMSEY

1

42

434   35   36   37

2

41

3

Flint Farm

Westover Farm

River Ant

Longstock Road

4

40

Rowbury Farm

Fullerton Road

5

121

Longstock Road

Fullerton Manor

6

39

Hazel
Down

Full

7

Charity
Down Farm

Longstock House

8

38

Hazeldown Farm

9

434   35   36   37

A   B   C **141** D   E   F   G

Church Road

Church Road

Cemetery

Church Road

PH

LECKFORD LANE

1 grid square represents 500 metres

H J K L 103 M N

38 39 40 41 42

LONGPARISH

LONGPARISH ROAD

B3048

River Test

1

2

Newt

3

4

5

124

6

7

8

9

WINCHESTER ROAD

B3420

New Barn

Wherwell J&I School

B3048

Dublin Farm

Wherwell

Church St

Beech Gr

B3420

WINCHESTER ROAD

B3420

A3057

Fullerton

Road

River Test

Test Way

Winchester

Martins Lane

PO

Joy's Lane

Village Street

Peacock Field

Cottonworth

ROMSEY ROAD

River Test

Testcombe

Station Road

Coley Lane

Branscombe Avenue

Chilbolton

Eastmans Field

Grove Hill

Little Drove Road

Drove Road

Martins Lane

Birch Grove

West Down

Ivy Farm

River Anton

A3057

Thirt Way

Leckford

Works

ford Abba

38 39 40 41

H J K L 142 M N P

Martins Lan

Middlebar

Mari

124

LONGPARISH

A **B** **C** **104** **D** **E** **F** **G**

Bransbury

441 42 43 44

River Dever

Roberts Road

Barton Stacey
CE Primary
School

Roman Way

The Green

Pleasant Cl

West Road East Rd

Bullir

Barton Stacey

Ashfields

Greenacre

Gravel Lane

Kings End

Works

Bransbury
Common

River Test

Newton Stacey

Manor Farm

123

B3420

Cocum Farm

Newton Down Farm

Moody's Down Farm

B3420

Middlebarn Farm

Drift Road

Hill Farm

A272

441 42 43 44

A **B** **143** **C** **D** **E** **F** **G**

Mullens Lane

A30

1 grid square represents 500 metres

H J K L M

A 105 on Cross Inn

Tidbury Farm

Tidbury Common

Upper Bullington

Lower Bullington

Norton Park Hotel

Cranbourne Grange

Hill Barn

BULLINGTON LANE

A34

A30

Egypt

Travelodge
Sutton Scotney Service Area
Travelodge

Wonston Grange

BY PASS ROAD A30

Surgery

Sutton Scotney

Stockbridge Road

Sutton Manor

Hunton Lane

River Dever

Wonston

Wonston Lane

WINCHESTER BY-PASS A34

Christmas Hill

Beggars Drove

A30

Wonston Manor Farm

Sutton Down Farm

West Stoke Farm

H J K L M N P

A 144

125 · 126 grid references along right edge: 1 2 3 4 5 6 7 8 9

45 46 47 48

42 41 40 39 38

130

A   B   C   110   D   E   F   G

462   63   64   65
42

1

+
Bradley

Preston
Down

2

41

Berrywood Lane

3

Outrow Way

Three Castles Path

Lower
Wield

4

40

Ashley Farm

5

129

PH

Gaston
Wood

6

39

Three Castles Path

Wield Road

Outrow Way

Gaston
Grange

Holt

Upper Wield

Jenkin Green Lane

7

+
+   Home Close

Pound
Cd

8

38

Barton
Copse

Barton
Industrial
Estate

Red
Barn Farm

Trinity

Ferney Lane

9

Newmer Farm

Trinity

Ferney
La

462   63   64   65

A   B   C   149   D   E   F   G

Hoggs
Lodge

Upper Lenten Lane

Hattingley

Hattingley Road

Wield Road

Castle St

Heath

1 grid square represents 500 metres

H · J · K · L · M · N

66 · 67 · 68 · 69 · 42

Powells Farm

Wadgell's Copse

Shalden Lane

1

2

41

3

Bentworth Lodge

4

Thedden Copse

40

5

Drury Lane

Crabe Close

Bentworth CE Primary School

PH

Church St

PH

Summerley

PH

Bentworth

Holt End Lane

Village Street

Stanley Road

Childer Hill Farm

Heathcroft Farm

132

6

Lode Hill

Wivelrod Road

Thedden Grange

Holt End

Bentworth Hall

39

7

Church Lane

Lane

Jennie Green Lane

Medstead Grange

Wivelrod

King's Hill

Wivelrod Road

Medstead Road

Wellhouse

Be

8

Bushy Leaze Wood

38

9

King's Hill

The Abbey

Clim

Jennie Green Lane

Rosewood Lane

Old Park Farm

66 · 67 · 68 · 69

H · J · K · L · **150** · M · N · P

Abbey

Road

Sprat Lane

The Oak

138

A 424 B C 119 25 D E 26 F G

combe wn

37

1

2

36

3
Roche Court Down

Easton Down

4

Lopcombe Corner

Hampshire County
Wiltshire County

A343

Hollom Down Farm

Jack's Bush Farm

35

5
A30
A30

A30

6

Gutteridge Farm

Ashley's Copse

7

Roche Court

Burretts Grove

34

East Winterslow

8

Warren Farm

Mill Lane

Hill Farm

9

Clough La

The Frood

Roman

Middleton Road

PO

Middle Winterslow

1 33

A 424 B 158 25 C D 158 E 26 F G

Yew Tree

Surgery

Saxon Leas

Gunville Rd

The Causeway

Easton Common Hl

Irving Hill

School

The Common

1 grid square represents 500 metres

140

A B C **121** D E F G

431 32 33

1

37

Neth
Wall
The Square
an Street
Church Hill

2

Church Hill

3

36

Berry
rt Farm

4

Garlogs

Wallop Brook

5

A30 Darfield Farm A30 Works

Houghton
Down

Spitfire Lane

Chattis
Hill Ho

Houghton
Down Farm

139

35

6

Nine Mile
Water Farm

Broughton Road

7

34

Wallop Brook

8

Water
Works

Manor Farm

SALISBURY

9

Broughton
Primary
School

School Lane High St

Dixons Lane

whiteshoot

ROAD 133 Rectory Lane

431 Broughton

Church Farm

A B C **160** D E F G

32 33

Danebury
Down

Danebury

143
ebury Hill
Danebury
Ring

Houghton
Down

Eveley Farm

S020

1 grid square represents 500 metres

H J K L **124** M N

Hill Farm

A3M

Marlols Lane

A30

42 **43** 44

I

37

Brockley Warren

2

ilbolton Down

Crawley Down

3

36

4

Warren Wood

Hacks Lane

5

35 **144**

Crawley Court

Cricket Close

Crawley

New Barn

6

Cemetery

PH

7

B3049

Beeches Farm

34

Folly Farm

8 Littleton House

STOCKBRIDGE ROAD B3049

Long Park

Folly Farm Touring Caravan Park

Kirton Farm

9

33

H J K L **163** M N P

42 **43** 44

A B C 125 D E F G

4 45   46   47

1

37

2

3

Larkwhistle Farm

36

West Stoke Farm

SO21

South Wonston Farm

South Wonston

4

Stavedown Road Wrights Close Wrights Way Downs Road
Downs Road
Blackthorn Cl
Christmas Hill
Orchard Road
Downlands
Wonston Primary School
Lower Road

A272

Ox Drove

Airesford Drove

A34

5

143

35

Worthy Down

Connaught Road
Coopers Close Cowley Dr
Connaught Rd
Connaught Road

6

34

7

A272

8

Long Park

Littleton House

A272

Down Farm

Down Farm Lane
WINCHESTER BY-PASS A34

9

33

ANDOVER ROAD NORTH

Church Lane

4 45   46   47

A B C **164** D E F G

Littleton Barrows

1 grid square represents 500 metres

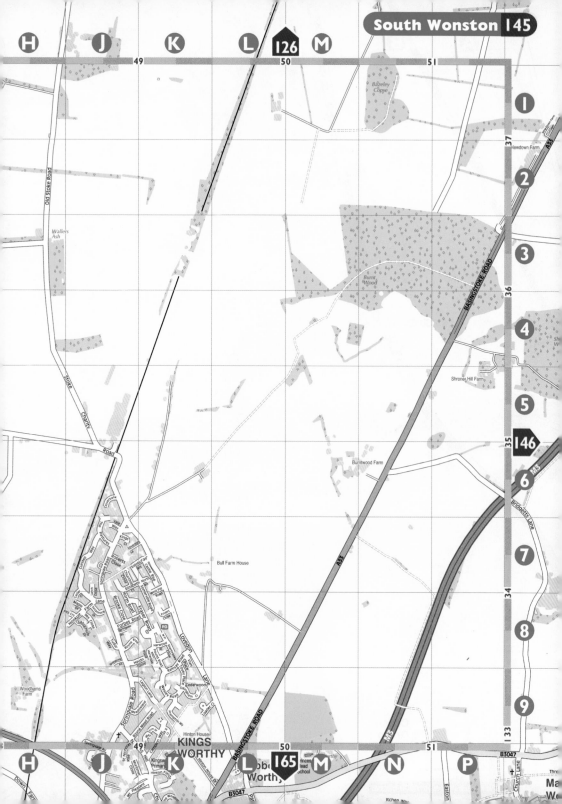

H   J   K   L   126   M

49   50   51

I

1

37

Newdown Farm

2

Bazeley
Clope

A33

3

36

Burnt
Wood

Basingstoke Road

4

She
W

Shroner Hill Farm

5

Walters
Ash

Old Stoke Road

35   146

M3

6

Bridgetts Lane

Burntwood Farm

Stoke

Charity

Road

7

Bull Farm House

A33

34

8

Woodhams
Farm

9

I 33

H   J   49   K   L   50   165   M   N   P

KINGS
WORTHY

Springvale Road

Hinton House

Basingstoke Road

Lober
Worthy

Princes
head
School

Church Lane

Ma
We

B3047

Itchen Wa

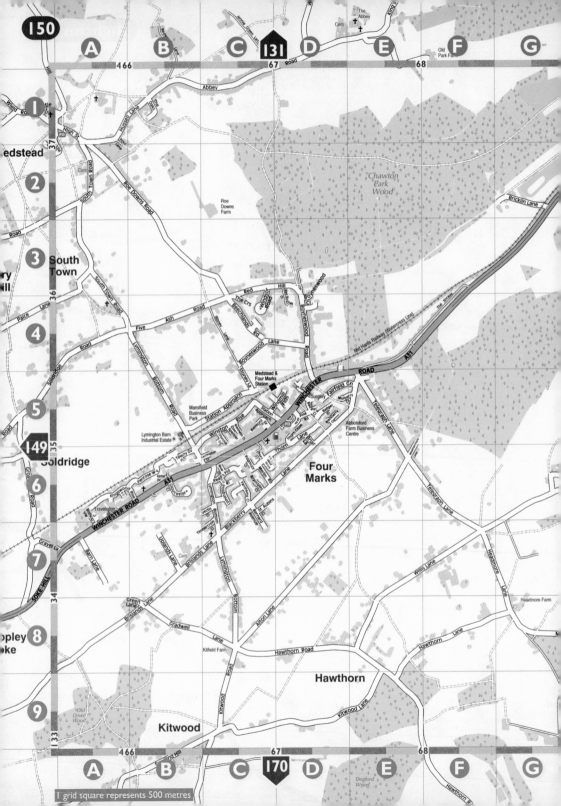

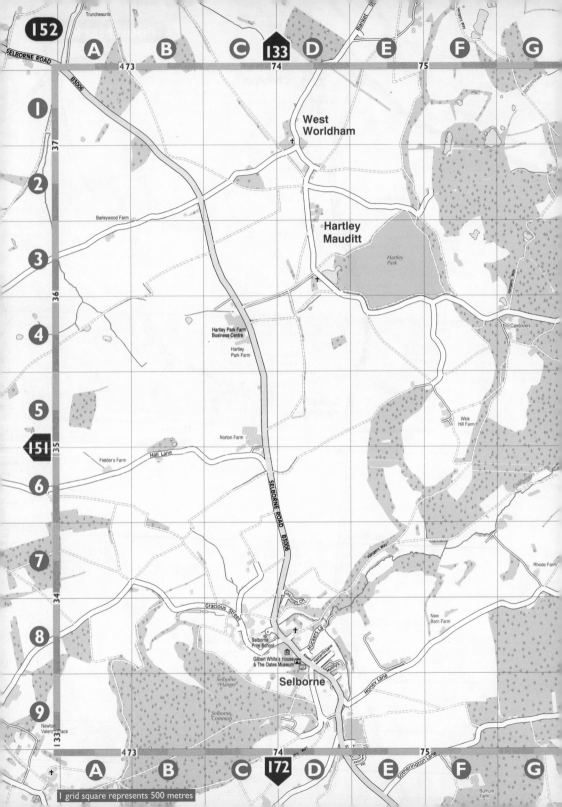

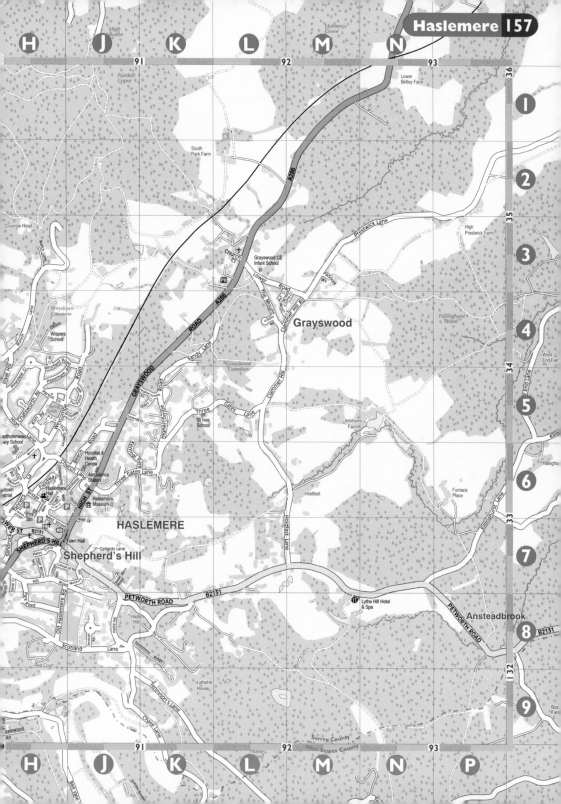

H J K L 139 M

28 29 30

Broughton Primary
High St
Dixons La
Hazelwood
Daphne La
Whiteshoot
Mount

ROMSEY ROAD 33

1

Queenwood Rd
Queenwood Rise
Beechcroft Cottages

Church Farm

Buckholt Road

Clarendon Way
Monarch's Way

2

32

B3084

3

Aven

Clarendon Way
Monarch's Way

Buckholt Farm

Queenwood

4

Queenwood Farm

31

Yew Tree Lane

5

160

6

30

North Lane

Rectory Hill
Chalk Pit Lane

West Tytherley
Primary School

West
Tytherley

Stony Batter

7

Pug's Hole

Dean Road

The Coach Road

Stride's Farm

Manor Farm

The Coach Road

Manor Rd

East
Tytherley

8

Cedars Vw

29

The
Green

Red Lane

Pug's Hole

9

Bulls Drove

Pug's Hole

Lockerley Hall

Larm Copse

H J K L 178 M N P

28 29 30

Home Farm
Business

160

A   B   C   140   D   E   Eveley Farm   F   G

32   33

Broughton Primary School
High St.
Dixon's Lane
Whiteshoot
431
Broughton
Queenwood Rd
High Street
Queenwood Rise

1   Church
Cucknolt
Beechcroft Cottages

Coolest Farm
Rookery Lane
Monxton's Way

2   ROMSEY ROAD
South Road

The Hollow
Roake Farm
Faithfulls Drove

3   Avenue
B3084
Horsebridge Road   Wallop Brook

4   Beech Tree Walk
Queenwood Farm   Horsebridge Road   Bossington

5
159

6   Crown Farm
River Test

7   Pittleworth Farm

8   Bentley Farms
B3084

9

A   B   C   179   D   E   F   G
431   32   33

1 grid square represents 500 metres

H J K L 141 M

35 36 37 33

1

2 New Lease Farm

3

4

5

162

6

30

7

8

9

Houghton Lodge & Garden

Church Lane

River Test

Stevens Grove

Drove

Houghton

Clarendon Way

Test Way

Cow Drove Hill

Hoopers Farm

Works

Cemetery

Stockbridge Road

New Lane

Winchester Road

King's Somborne

The Old Iron Foundry

Frogmole Lane

Old Vicarage Lane

The Cross

Church Rd

Muss Lane

King's Camp Fld

King Acre

A3057

Kings Somborne CE Prim Sch

Hayes Close

Romsey Road

Scott Close

Old Manor Farm

The Gorings

Eldon Close

Scowith Close

Eldon Road

Furzedown Road

Humbers View

Hunter Close

orsebridge

Pit

Test Way

Horsebridge Road

Romsey Road

Compton Park

Clarendon

Hoplands

Furzedown Road

Compton Manor

Humbers Wood

Compton

Works

Brook

Furzedown

29

H J K L 180 M N P

35 36 37

H J K L **143** M N

42 43 44

33

I

Northwood Park

2

STOCKBRIDGE ROAD B

32

Garstons Track

Westley Lane

Sparsholt College Hampshire

Hillside

Long Barn
Farm Rd

Library Lane

Westley Road

Westley Lane

3

Lainston House Hotel

Witley Lane

Moor Court Farm

Lock's Lane
Lock's Lane

Durt Lane

Home Lane
Lambourne Close

Church Lane

PH

Woodman Lane

Dean

4

Moor Court Lane

Sparsholt

Sparsholt CE Primary School

Dean Lane

31

5

Littleton Lane

164

6

Well Copse

Burrow Road

30

West Wood

Farley Mount Country Park

Crab Wood

Crabwood Farm House

Lanham

7

Lanham Lane

Clarendon Way

Clarendon Way

Sarum Road

8

29

Farley Mount Road

Pitt Down

Sparsholt Road

9

H J K L **182** M N P

42 43 44

Enmill Farm

Enmill Road

A   B   C   144   D   E   F   G

445   46   47

I

Littleton Barrows

Littleton

Northwood Park

2

Headb

Well House Lane

STOCKBRIDGE ROAD B3049

Well

3

Laing House Hotel

Harestock

Henry Beaufort School

Harestock Prim Sch

Barton Farm

4

Dean

Woodman Lane

Dean Lane

Rowlings Road

Taplings

Stoney Lane

Wychwood Place

Weeke

Stoney

Vernham Road

Lynford Av

Lynford Way

Winchester Lawn Tennis Club

Primary School

Butts Close

Bereweeke Way

BEREWEEKE ROAD   B3041

22

5

163

6

SO22

STOCKBRIDGE RD B3049

Andover Road Retail Park

The Winche Hotel

Winchester Station

The Westgate School

Fulflood

7

Teg Down

Golf Course

CHILBOLTON AVENUE   B3041

Western Primary Sch

Byron Avenue

Greenhill

West End Close

Police HQ

HM Prison

B3040

The Great Hall

Courts Reg Mus

Cinema

8

Royal Winchester Golf Club

Sarum Road Hospital

Sarum Road

ROMSEY   ROAD

Univ College

Garden Centre

Royal Hampshire County Hospital

St James' Lane

Westhill Cemetery

9

Kings School

Kilham Lane

ROMSEY   ROAD

University College Winchester

Minthorpe Lane

Sleepers Dell Gardens

Beaufort Road

Compton Road

CROSS   ST

Sleepers' Hill

445   46   47

A   B   C   183   D   E   F   G

Stanmore

A   B   C   146   D   E   F   G

452   53   B3047   54

1   Three Castles Path

Martyr Worthy   Chilland   Chilland Lane

Station CI
Hazeldene Gardens Works

Station CI
STATION   HILL
Shelley CI

Itchen Abbas CP School

School La

Lt Hayes Lane

Park Farm

King's Way

Itchen Abbas

River Itchen   Itchen   Way

2   PH

Easton   Avington Park   Avington

3

4   Gospel Oak

Mud Farm

5   Hampage Wood

165   Hampage Farm

6   Larkwhistle Farm

Chapel Lane   Fair Lane

Avington Manor Farm

7   A31

Pits Farm

ROAD   B3404   A31   ALRESFORD ROAD

8   Telegraph Way
Magdalen Cemetery
INTECH - Family Science Centre

PETERSFIELD ROAD   Chilcomb Down

King's Way

9   A272

452   53   185   54

A   B   C   185   D   E   F   G

1 grid square represents 500 metres

A B C D E F G

148

Gun

Pinglestone Farm
THE SOKE
Old Alresford Pond

459 60 61 Northlaide Farm
33 Bighton Bottom Farm
Northlaide Farm

I
Arle Cl
Arle Gdns
Industrial
The George Yard
BROAD ST

Bighton Lane

POUND HILL
WEST ST EAST ST
Sun Hill
Swan Hill
Surgery
Station Rd
Haig Rd
Perins Community School
Nursery Road
Alresford Station
B3047

2
Grange
Lime Rd
Hawthorn
Langtons Ct
Mid Hants Railway (Watercress Line)
Western Court
Mill Lane
North Street
Green Lane
Home Close

Belley Ter
Russell
Alresford County Junior School
Beneden Cl
Oak Hill Junior School
Oak Hill
B3047
Church
School
Riverhead
Hobbs Cl
Water Lane
B3047

JACKLYNS LANE
32
Culley VW
Lindley Gdns
Corfe Cl
Derwent Gdns
Crescent
Bishop's Sutton

3
Prospect Business Ct
Fair Vw
Paddock Wy
Sparrow
Appledown
Tichborne Down

Tichborne
Down
A31
Whitehill Lane
A31

4
Alresford Golf Club
Golf Course
Appledown Lane
Scrubbs Lane
Manor House Farm

31

5
167

6
Haydock Walk
Scrubb Farm
Dark Lane
Cheriton Lane
Common Farm

30

7
Lane
Baghheat

8
North End
North End Lane
Middle Farm
Cheriton Wood
Marine

129

9
Cheriton Primary School
Crichen Way
Upper Lamborough La
Alresford Lane
The Spinney

459 60 61
Cheriton
A B C D E F Gamdean
187
The Cheriton
rewhouse
Lwr Lamborough
Dark Lane
Wood Lane

1 grid square represents 500 metres

A   **B**wood   **C**   150   **D**   **E**   **F**   **G**

466   67   68

Old Down Wood

Kirwood

Kirwood Lane

1   33

Street

Swelling Hill

Boxford Wood

Hawthorn Road

Gilbert Street

Andrew's Lane

2   32

Lyeway Rd

Lyeway Lane

Lyeway Farm

Winchester Wood

Ro

3

Green Lane

Charlwood Lane

Lane

Plain Farm

Plaindell

Lyewood Ho

Charlwood

Plaindell

4   31

Soame's Lane

Smugglers Lane

Petersfield Road

Monkwood

5

Soames Farm

Hill Farm Road

Petersfield Road

169

Soame's Lane

Hill Farm Road

6   30

Merryfield Farm

West Tisted Common

Brewers Lane

Woodside Farm

7

8   29

Brick Kiln Lane

Brick Kiln Farm

Brick Kiln Lane

Lane End

Brewers Lane

West Tisted

RD

Bur.. re

Basing Park

9

The Jumps

A32

Basing Home Farm

466   67   68

A   **B**   **C**   189   **D**   **E**   **F**   **G**

Ashen Wood House

Lane

1 grid square represents 500 metres

A B C D E F G

4 20 21 22 23

I

28

Clarendon Road

Whitehouse Farm

Nightwood Copse

Coachworks

Grimstead Road

Long Drove

East
Grimstead

2

Common Plantation

Green Drove

Long Drove

Walden House

Manor Farm

Works

3

Butter Furlong Road

River Dunn

Dean Road

27

Whaddon Common

Crockford Road

Chapel Hill

Greenfields

4

Grimstead Road

Church St

West
Grimstead

5

Windwhistle Lane

26

A36

Rentbury Caravan Camping Park

6

Windwhistle Lane

7

25

8

Witherington Down

9

24

Brickworth Ho

Whelpley Farm

A36

4 20 21 22 23

A B C D E F G

200

A36

A27

BRICK

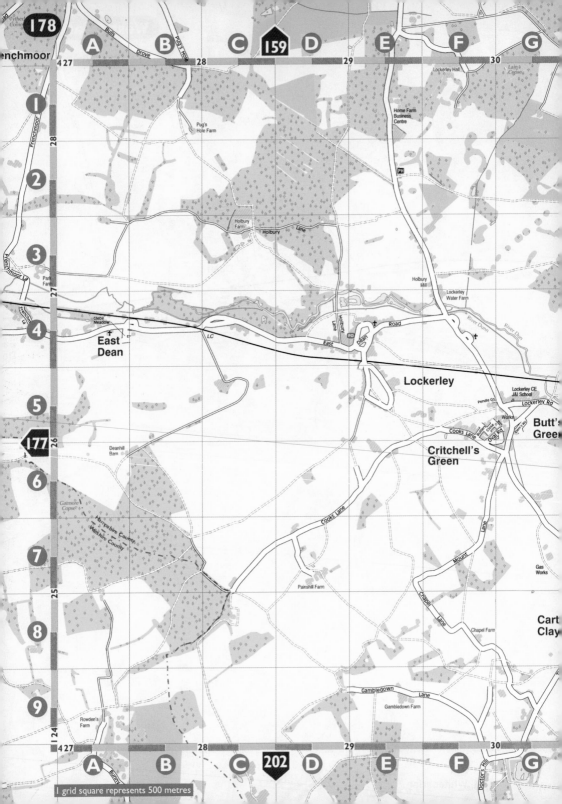

H J K L 162 M N

38 39 40 41

1
28
2
3
27
4
5
182 26
6
7
25
8
9
24

Pamhol Wood
Farley Down
Bailey Down
Fishponds Fm
Farley Fm
Berrydown Farm
Farley Ho
Oakfield
Dores Lane
Merdon Manor
Furzedown Road
Farley Lane
Dores Lane
Gudge Copse
Pitt Fm
Kings Somborne Road
Farley Lane
Fern Hill Lane
Dores Lane
Upper Slackstead
Lower Slackstead
Monarch's Way
Dores Lane
Woolley Green Fm
Monarch's Way
Dores Lane
Amfield Wood
Summers Rd
Blackthorn Close
Monarch's Way
Common Hill Road
Pucknall
Braishfield Primary School
Dores Lane
Dores Lane
Monarch's Way

H J K L 205 M N P

38 39 40 41

Hillier
Jermyns House
Monarch's Way
Knapp

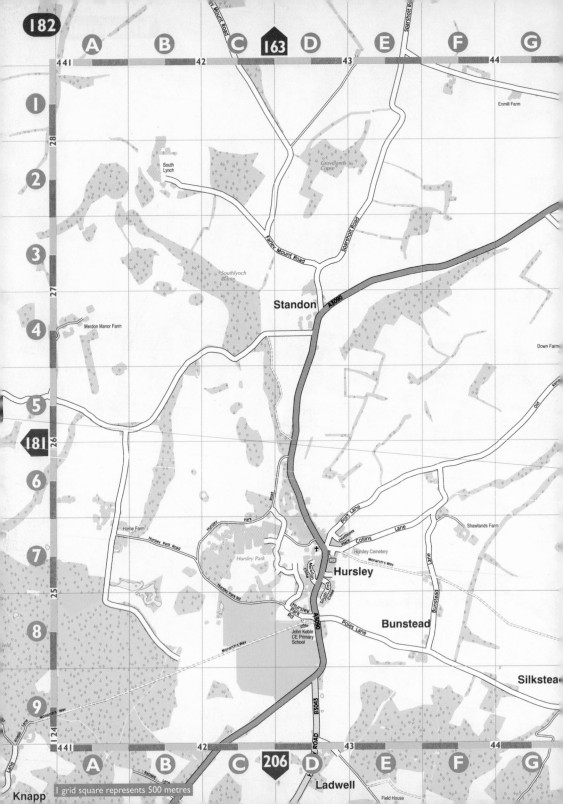

H Upper J ough La **J** **K** **L** 168 **M** **N**

59 60 61 62

I

Cheriton

Lwr Lamborough

La Seborn Cl

Mansel Cl

B3046

28

Bramdean

The Spinney

Wood Lane

Woodlane Close

A272

I

PETERSFIELD ROAD

Hinton Ampner

Cem

Hinton Hill

Church Lane

A272

2

New Cheriton

Greys Farm Cl

Kilmeston Rd

Source of the River Itchen

Hinton Ampner

Hinton Ampner Garden (NT)

3

27

Joan's Acre

Brockwood Bottom

4

Brock Park

Wayfarer's Walk

Westwood View

Joan's Acre Wood

5

Brockwood Bottom

Kilmeston

Dean House

26 188

6

Wayfarer's Walk

Black House Farm

7

Bere

25

College Down Farm

Riversdown House

Wheely Farm

8

9

24

Lomer Farm

Rooksg

W Down

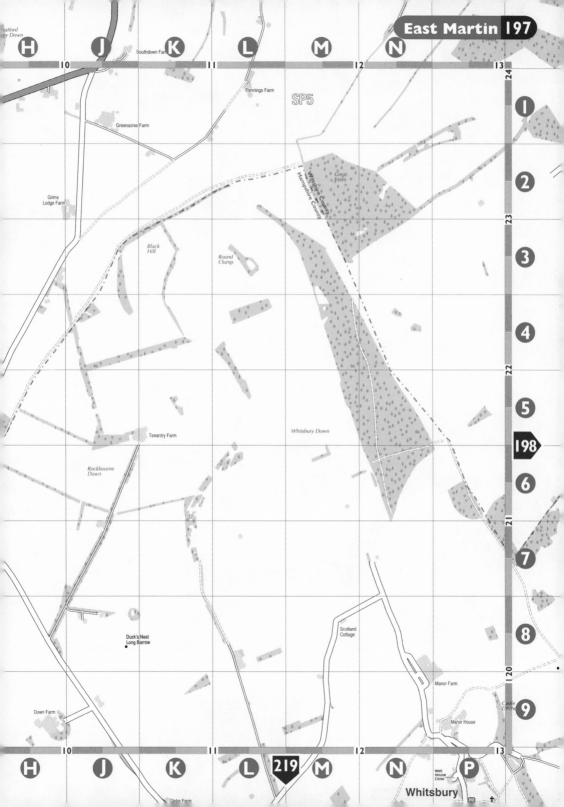

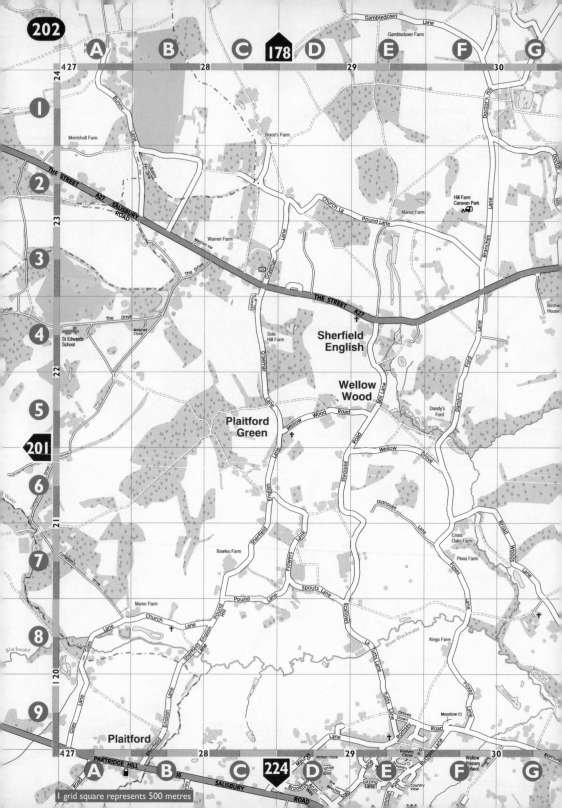

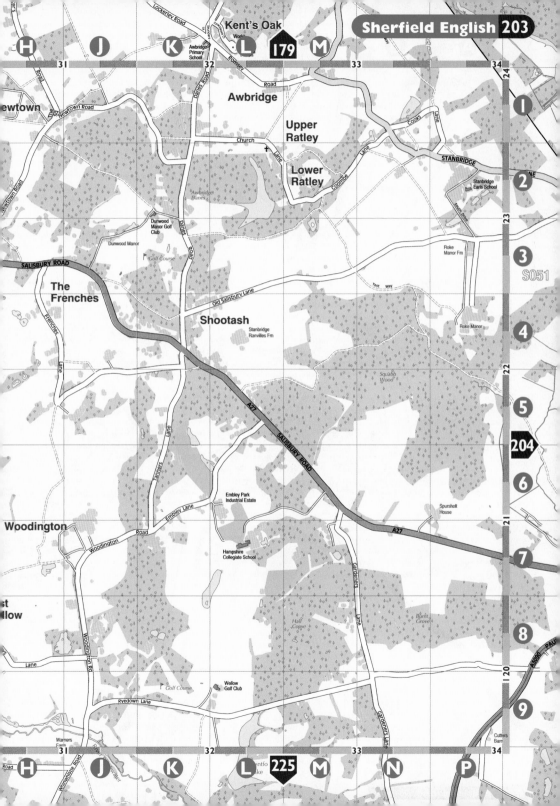

H J K L 179 M

31 32 33 34

24

Lockerley Road

Kent's Oak

Works

Awbridge Primary School

Romsey

Road

I

Newtown

The

Newtown Road

Awbridge

2

Upper Ratley

STANBRIDGE

Church Lane

Lower Ratley

Cooks Lane

Stanbridge Earls School

Beech Drive

23

Danes Road

Coombe Lane

Awbridge Danes

Dunwood Manor Golf Club

Dunwood Manor

Golf Course

Roke Manor Fm

3

S051

SALISBURY ROAD

Danes Road

Test Way

Roke Manor

4

The Frenches

Old Salisbury Lane

Shootash

Stanbridge Ranvilles Fm

22

Squabb Wood

5

Frenches Lane

Lane

A27

SALISBURY ROAD

204

6

Tanners Lane

Embley Lane

Embley Park Industrial Estate

Spursholt House

21

Woodington

Woodington Road

A27

7

Hampshire Collegiate School

Gardeners Lane

st llow

Woodington Road

Hall Copse

Burnt Grove

8

PAU

Lane

20

Golf Course

Wellow Golf Club

9

Ryedown Lane

Gardeners Lane

Warners Farm

Cutlers Barn

31 32 33 34

Whitenap Road

Road

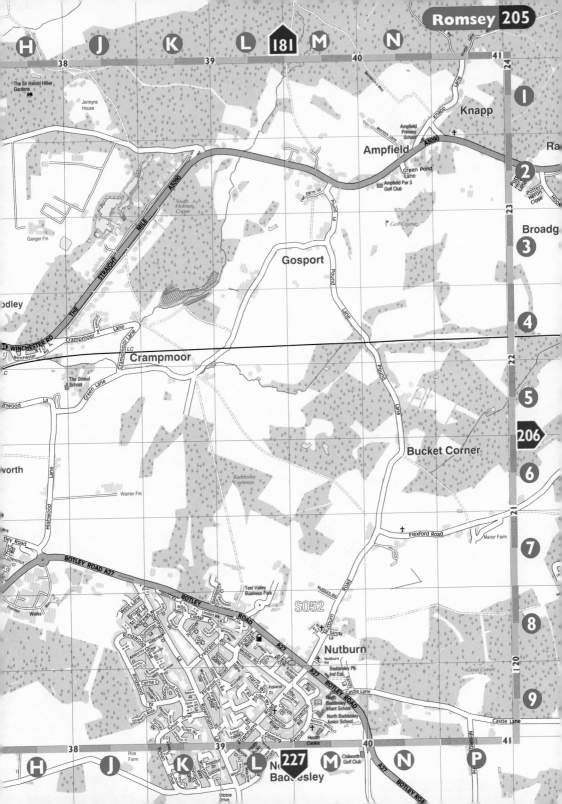

H J K L 185 M N

52 53 54 55

Bottom Fa

Longwood Road

Belmore Lane

Main Rd

Hilly Ct

'Baybridge House

Longwood Dean Farm

Doe Wood

I

2

3

4

5

210

6

7

8

9

24

23

22

21

20

Baybridge

Lower Baybridge Lane

Baybridge Lane

King's Way

Rowhay Wood

Woodlock's Down Farm

Monarch's Way

Roughay Farm

Hatchley Lane

Rowhay Lane

Blackdown Farm

High Wood

Woodcote

Belmore Lane

Woodcote Lane

Ower P

Monarch's Way

Bigpath Farm

Upham

Cem

Widley's La

Shore Lane

Church Street

Upham St

Clews Way

West Hall

Upham C E Primary School

Upham Street

King's Way

Stakes Lane

Peak Lane

Peak Lane

Monarch's Way

Street E

Popes Lane

Upham Farm

Stroudwood Farm

PORTSMOUTH ROAD

Upham Street

B3037

WINC

52 53 54 55

H J K B2177 L 231 M Farm N P

Stakes Lane

Cross Lane

Lower Upham

Ashton

A   B   C   186   D   E   F   G

455   56   57   58

Longwood Dean Farm

Oll Wood

1

2   Drive   The Holt   Salt Lane   South Downs Wy   Wind Fa

Farm

23

Stony Hard Farm

Preshaw House

3

4   Belmore House   Preshaw

22

5   Ower Farm   Stephen's Castle Down   Corhampton Forest

209

6   Borepath Farm   Monarch's Way   Stake's Lane   St Clair's Farm   Sale's

21

7   Dean Farm   Franklin Farm   Corhampton Down   Corhampton Lane   Bottom Copse

8   Mo   Hazel Holt

20

Street End

9

455   56   57   58

A   B   Highfield Fa   C   Dea   232   D   E   F   G

hton

Little Ashto   Limekiln   Lane

1 grid square represents 500 metres

Monarch's Way   Sil Lane   Salt Lane   Monarch's Way   Lower Preshaw Lane   Dean Lane   B3035   Galley Down

H   J   K   L   189   M   N

66   67   68   69

24

1

GU32

2

23

3

Pidham

4

22

5

214

Oxenbourne House

6

21

7

8   Stonyland

20

9

H   J   K   L   235   M   N   P

66   67   68   69

Westbury House

River Meon

Riplington

Drayton

Bereleigh House

Park Farm

Hen Wood

The Cross
School
Workhouse Lane
Chapel St
Church St
Duncombe Rd
The Glebe
Chapel St
Temple Lane
High Street
Glenthorne Meadow

Coombe   Road

East Meon

Duncombe Farm

Lower House Farm

South Downs Way

South Downs Way

Coombe Cross

Coombe

Monarch's   Way

South Downs Way

South Farm

233
▲
Salt Hill

Chidden Down

Farm

A   B   C   190   D   E   F   G

469   70   71   72

24

GU32

23

1

2

3

4

22

5

213

6

21

7

8

120

9

469   70   71   72

A   B   C   236   D   E   F   G

Bordean House

A272

WINCHESTER ROAD

Langrish

The Close

Home Farm

Langrish House

Langrish
House
Hotel

Pidham Farm

Ramsdean

North
Stroud Farm

North Stroud Lane

Ramsdean Road

Rotherombe Lane

Willowdale Cl

Langrish Primary
School

St

Ramsdean Road

Stroudbridge
Farm

Leythe House

Harroway Farm

Limekiln Lane

Swanbourne House

Harvesting Lane

Stonylands Farm

Harvesting Lane

Ramsdean
Down

271
Butser Hill

National
Nature Reserve

South Downs Way

A3

Wale Do

South Downs Way

1 grid square represents 500 metres

A   B   C   D   E   F   G

196 in

4 06   07   Martin   08   09

1

19

Allen River

Tidpit

Toyd
Down

Knoll
Down

2

195

Grans
Barrow

18

3

North Allenford Farm

Darnell
Knoll

Tidpit
Common
Down

4

Blackheath
Down

South Allenford Farm

Kites
Nest Farm

5

17

6

Martin
Wood

7

Boulsbury
Farm

16

Hampshire County
Dorset County

8

9

15

Boulsbury
Woods

Stapleton Farm

4 06   07   08   09

Boveridge

Philip Green
Memorial School

1 grid square represents 500 metres

197

H J K L M

10 11 12 13

Down Farm

Manor House

Glebe Farm

Well House Close

Whitsbury

I

Lower Grove

2

New Rd

3

Whitsbury Common

Rockbourne

Western Downland CE Primary School

Knoll Farm

4

Rockstead Farm

Rockbourne Lane

Marsh Farm

West Park

Rockbourne Roman Villa

Radnall

Green Lane

5

Clack Lane

220

6

Allen River

Littlemill La

North End

West Park Lane

West Park Drive

Walks

7

Pound Lane

High Street

Damerham

Court Farm

Court Hill

West Park Farm

Allen's Farm

Browns Lane

Browns Lane

Wilkins County

8

Steels La

Church Lane

Lower Court Wood

9

Cornpits Lane

Mill End

South End

The Common

Lower Court Wood

Tanners Lane

10 11 12 13

H J K L M N P

239

Sandleheath

Sandle Manor

Station Road

Ashridge Copse

H   J   K   L **199**   M   N

17   18   19   20

N Charford Crossing

River Avon

Wiltshire County
Ham?

Searchfield Farm

North Charford Manor House

North Charford

Whiteshoot

Firs

Hatchet Green

Carter's Close

Tethering Drove

FOR

Tethering Drove

1

Hatchet Cl

Hale Lane

South Charford Farm

Hale Primary School

2

Hale

Avon Valley Path

Queen Street

3

Hale Lane

Hale Road

18

Dodgson Cl

Woodgreen

Lwr Densome Wd

Higherend Farm

Millersford Plantation

4

Crack Lane

High St
Trimm?
Love Lane
Green
Drove

PO

5

The Shallows

Avon Valley
Love Lane
Green
Drove

Brook Lane

222

Millersford Bottom

6

Godshill
Inclosure

B3078

7

Stone Quarry Bottom

16

New Forest

8

Millersford Bottom

Brune's Purlieu

ROGER PENNY WAY

Ditchend Brook

9

115

Field Wy

Purlieu Lane

H   J   K   L **241**   M   N   P

17   18   19   20

Sandy Balls Holiday Centre

Godshill

Well Lane

B3078

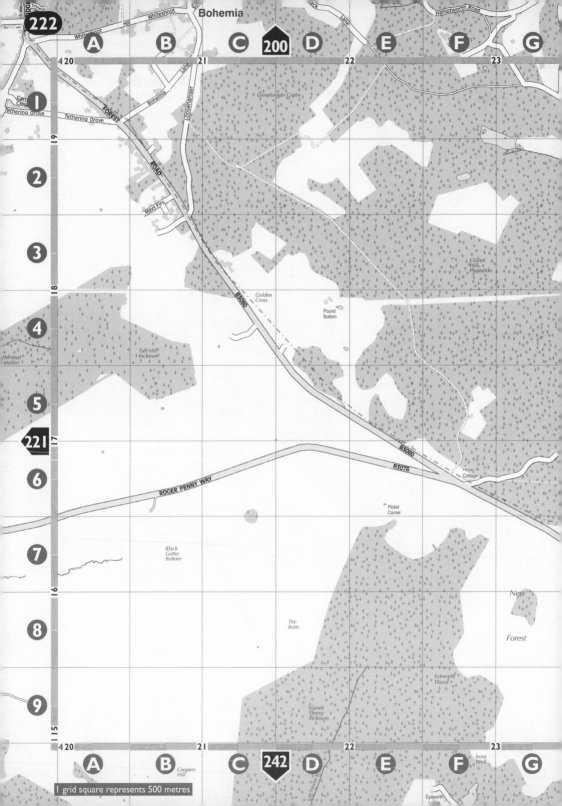

Bohemia

222

200

221

242

I grid square represents 500 metres

A B C D E F G

Whiteshoot Hill   Whiteshoot   Hamptworth Road

420   21   22   23

Tethering Drove

FOREST

Tethering Drove

Bohemia Lane

Loosehanger Lane

Looshanger Copse

Mays Firs

ROAD

Cliven Hills Plantation

B3080

Golden Cross

Pound Bottom

Tuff Hill Inclosure

Hersford Plantation

B3080

B3078

Hope Cottage

ROGER PENNY WAY

Picket Corner

Black Gutter Bottom

New Forest

The Butts

Eyeworth Wood

Islands Thorns Inclosure

Eyeworth Lodge

Irons Well

Coopers Hill

420   21   22   23

19

18

17

16

15

H   J   K   L   ⌂ 211   M

59   60   61   62

WARNFORD
ROAD

Meonstoke
CE School

New   Road

Chapel

I   Pondside Fi

19

Golf Course   Golf Club

Shepherds
Farm

Wayfarer's Walk

Sheep Pond   Lane

Sheep   Pond   Lane

Sheep
Pond

Hacketts   Lane

Shepherds Down

Lane

Cem   Garston Thorpe

GARSTON HILL

A32

Watton Lane   2   Wat

B2150   **Brockbridge**

Northend   Lane

Waltham
Close

Union   Lane

The   PK

Surgery

Cowslet Fd

Mill Lane

18

Droxford   High St   Mill La

PO

3   Bushy
Down F

Wayfarer's

Wayfarer's   Walk

Droxford
Junior
School

Station Road

Walk

South Hill

Mayhill Lane

MIDLINGTON ROAD

Crookhorn
La

4

Oxford   Lane

Swanmore   Road

Midlington Ho

5

Mayhill Farm

Midlington   Hill

Cutts

Station Road

234

17

Mayhill Lane

Swanmore   Road

A32

ROAD

Arch

Soberton
Towers

Long   Road

6

Hill Place

River Meon

Hill Loops

Soberton

WICKHAM

Green   Lane

West Street

West
St

Wayfarer's   Walk

7

King's Way

Meon
Valley

Cole

Chalk   Hill

High St

16   Wayfarer's Walk

Cott   Tower   Lane

High Street

8

Cott Street

Cott
Street Farm

Peststead   Lane

Dirty
Copse

Cott   Street

Green   Lane

Seoforth   Lane

9   Broom

St Clair's Fm

Webbs Green
Fm

Holywell House

Meon
Valley

115

H   J   K   L   ⌄ 253   M   N   P

59   60   61   62

Hambledon Lane

Taplands

Hons   Lane

Plough Lane

Roy's Lane

Arnsworth Lane

Chapel Ro

H 73 J K L **215** M N 75 76

1

19

2

3
West
Harting
Down

18

4

5

17

6
Eckensfield

7

16

8
Cowdown Fm

9

115

Hangers Way
South Downs Way
Coulters
Dean Fm
Sunwood Fm
Forty Acre
Lane

Newbarn Road
Head
Down Plantation

Hampshire County
West Sussex County

Queen
Elizabeth
Forest

Newbarn Road

Oakham
Bottom

Downley

Ditcham Park
School

Glass
Brow

Sussex Border Path

Ladyholt

Sussex Border Path

Chalton Lane
Old
Farm

Chalton
PH
South La

South Lane

Harris La
Sussex Border Path

Woodcroft
Fm

South Lane

Sussex Border Path

220

A **B** **C** **D** **E** **F** **G**

1

Industrial Estate

Sandle Manor

Forres Sandle Manor School

Station Road

Peasham Gardens

Hertford Close

Fordingbridge J&I School

Farm Centre

Waverley Road

River Avon

2

Manor Farm Rd

Jubilee Rd

Elmwood Av

Fordingbridge Business Park

Marbrean Close

Mayfield

Victoria Gdns

Bowerwood Road

Marl Lane

Willow Av

Meadow Court

Stephen Martin Gdns

Fire Stn

Green Lane

Lesser Bartons

Fordingbridge Hospital

Park Rd

Works

Alexandra Rd

Addison Road

St Georges Rd

FORDINGBRIDGE

SOUTHAMPTON ROAD

Criddlestyle

Ashford

Station Road

Ashford Works Industrial Estate

Beechwood

Flaxfields End

Reeds Close

Shaftesbury St

Provost St

High St

Bridge St

Market Place

Town Hall

B3078

Stuckton Road

Cemetery

3

BOWERWOOD ROAD

B3078

Padstow Pl

Church St

Works

Church Farm

Frog Lane

The Merrie Thought

Stuckton

Stuckton Road

Works

DINGBRIDGE ROAD

Dorset County / Hampshire County

Avon Valley Path

Redbrook

Ditchend Brook

Flaxfields

Hyde Lane

4

5

Midgham Farm

Bickton

RINGWOOD ROAD

A338

Hern Lane

Hye

239

Gilbert Close

6

Harbridge Drove

Drove End Farm

North End Lane

Avon Valley Path

Hung

Ringwood Road

7

Lomer Lane

Buckle Hill

Lawrence Lane

8

Bleak Hill

North End Farm

River Avon

North Gorley

9

Harbridge Green

Churchfield Lane

Huckles Brook

Hucklesbrook Farm

South Gorley

A **B** **C** **D** **E** **F** **G**

260

Kent Lane

Harbridge

Salisbury Road

Blind La

Ibsley

Newtown La

Drove

H J K L **221** M

17 18 19 20 15

I

Brune's Purlieu

PENNY WAY

Ditchend Brook

Butts Lane

Field Wy

Works

Sandy Balls Holiday Centre

Godshill

Well Lane

B3078

Newgrounds

Pitts Wood Inclosure

2

Crystal Hollow

14

Long Bottom

Hampton Ridge

3

Blissford Road

Broadhill Lane

Blissford

Alderhill Inclosure

4

Ditchend Brook

Blissford Cross

Abbots Well Road

Blissford Hill

13

Bartletts Common

Frogham

The Paddock

Abbots Well Road

Abbots Well

Latchmore Bottom

Latchmoor Brook

5

Pentons Hill

Blissford Hill

Hyde Common

Gorley Lynch

Ogdens Farm

242

Hyde Primary School

6

Gorley Lynch

Ogdens

Halsey Inclosure

12

7

ord

New

8

Forest

Furze Hill

Ogden's Purlieu

11

9

Black Barrow

High Corner Inn

H 17 J K L **261** M 18 N 19 P 20

Ibsley Common (NT)

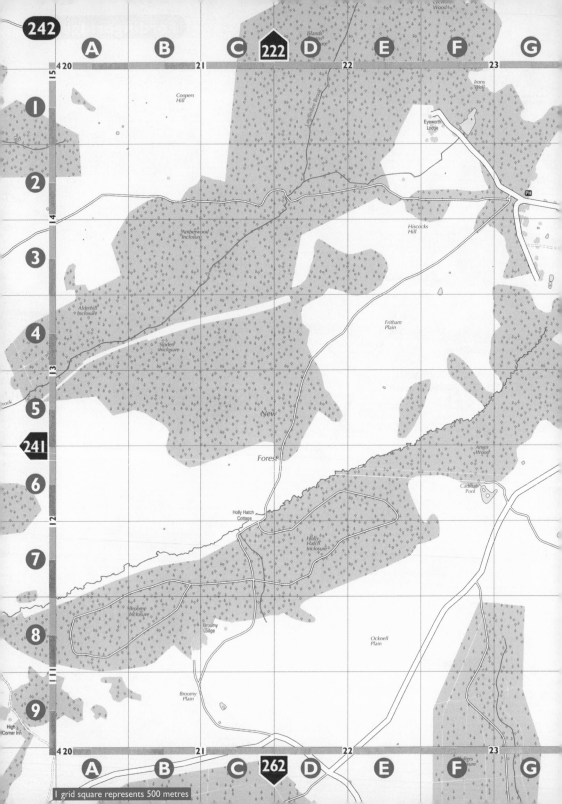

A   B   C   **222**   D   E   F   G

4 20   21   22   23

15

1

Coopers
Hill

Blands
Lane

Latchmore Brook

Irons
Well

Eyeworth
Lodge

2

14

PH

Amberwood
Inclosure

Hiscocks
Hill

3

Alderhill
Inclosure

Fritham
Plain

4

Sloden
Inclosure

13

5

New

Anses
Wood

241

Forest

6

Cadman's
Pool

12

Holly Hatch
Cottage

Holly
Hatch
Inclosure

7

8

Broomy
Inclosure

Broomy
Lodge

Ocknell
Plain

11

9

Broomy
Plain

High
Corner Inn

4 20   21   22   23

A   B   C   **262**   D   E   F   G

1 grid square represents 500 metres

223

244

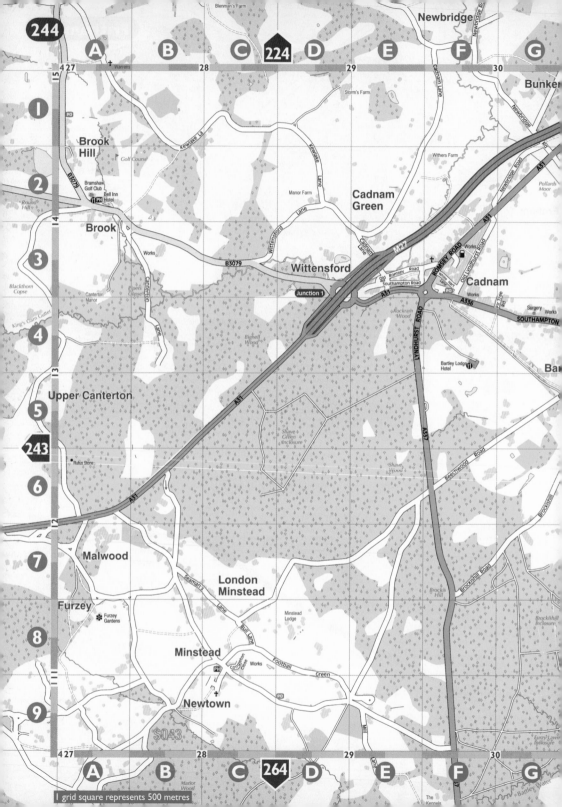

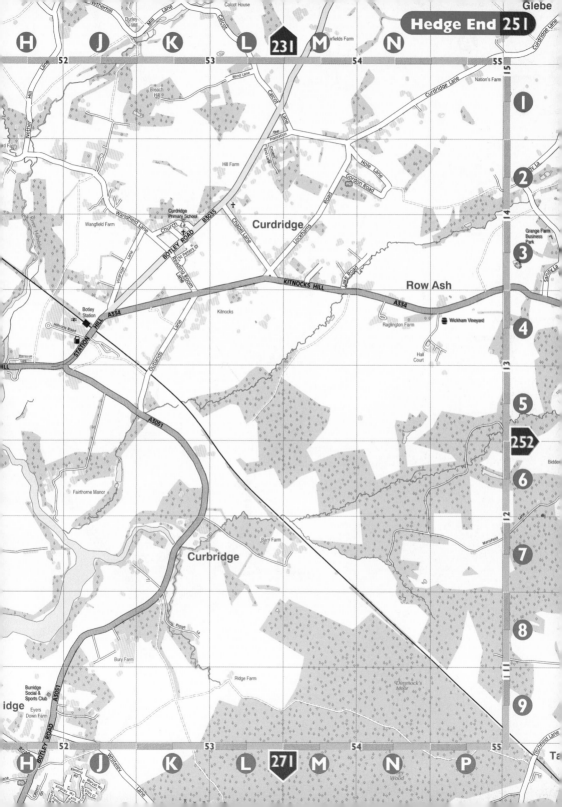

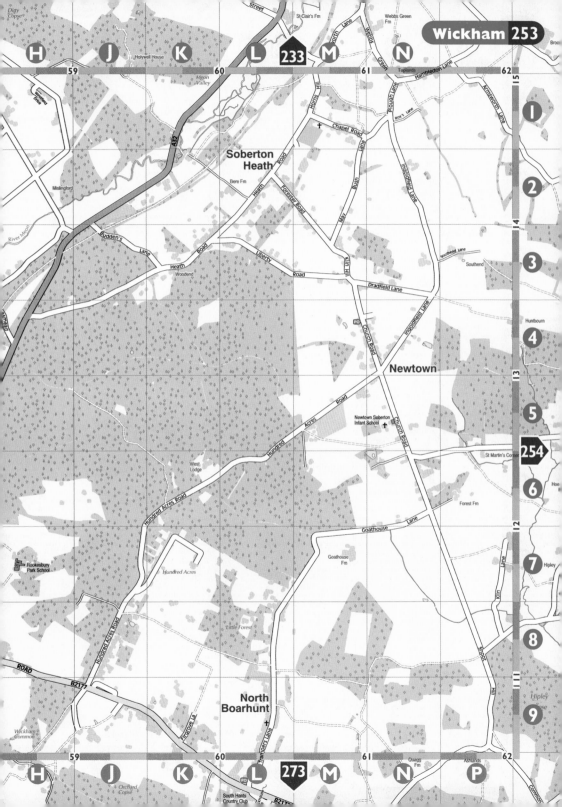

H J K L 239 M N

10 11 12 13

1

2

3

4

5

260

6

7

8

9

H J K L 281 M N P

10 11 12 13

Sleep Brook

Dorset County
Hampshire County

North Plumley
North Plumley Farm

Mount Ararat

Boveridge Heath

Wild Church Bottom

Plumley Woods

Plumley Farm

Harefield Plantation

Starlight Farm Close

Strathmore Dr

Ebblake

Ringwood Forest

Home Farm

Shepherds Lane

The Forestside

Roseberry Close

Enterprise Park

Virginia Close

Cemetery

Ebblake Ind Est

Forest Close

B3081

Ringwood Road

River Crane

Golf Course

Moors Valley Golf Club

Hampshire County
Dorset County

Verwood Road

B3081

Hanging

H J K L **241** M N

Black Barrow

High Corner Inn

17 18 19 20

I

1

Ibsley Common (NT)

Dockeny Water

Toms Lane

Linwood

Toms Lane

10

2

Whitefield Plantn

Toms Lane

Linwood Farm

3

ockbeggar

Digden Bottom

Dockeny Water

Red Shoot Camping Park

Red Shoot Brewery

4

Appleslade Inclosure

Red Shoot Wood

60

Rockford Common (NT)

Linford Brook

5

08

262

Highwood

Great Linford Inclosure

Pinnick Wood

6

Handy Cross Plain

7

07

A31

Lin Brook

Highwood Lane

8

North Poulner

wpitts Lane

Linford

Little Linford Inclosure

Works

Hangersley

St Aubyns Lane

9

06

Road

Burcombe Lane

Shobley

Picket Post

BH24

17 18 19 20

H ner

J K L **283** M N P

A31

HILL A31

POULNER

Picket

Inn

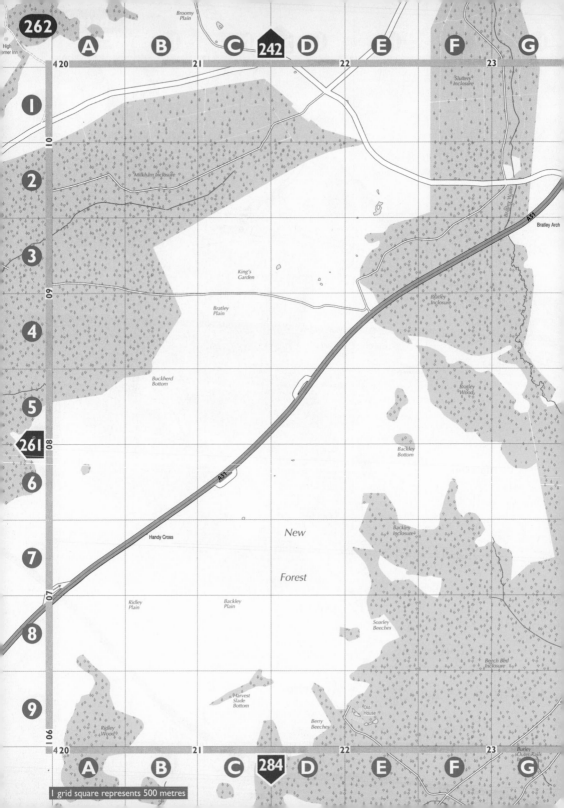

Ashurs

H J K L 245 M N

31 32 33 34

Basketts
Lawn
Inclosure

Ironshill
Lodge

Ironshill
Inclosure

Rushpole
Wood

Lodgehill
Cottage

A35

Mallard
Wood

New Forest
Golf Club

Dunces Arch

Knightwood
Lodge
Hotel

SOUTHAMPTON

ROAD

White
Moor

Beaulieu River

Ormonde House
Hotel

Cemetery

BEAULIEU ROAD

B3056

Pondhead Inclosure

Keeping Lane

Little
Pignal hill
Inclosure

Denny
Inclosure

Park Hill

Park
Ground
Inclosure

Elm
Tree
Pl

Prince's
Rd

LYNDHURST

Works

Ashurst
Hospital

Ashurst (New Forest)
Station

Ashurst
Wood

Ashurst Lodge

Churchpl
Inclosure

Matley
Wood

Matley
Heath

Matley
Passage

Denny
Wood

1
2
3
4
5
266
6
7
8 56
9

10
09
08
07
06

H J K L 287 M N P

31 32 33 34

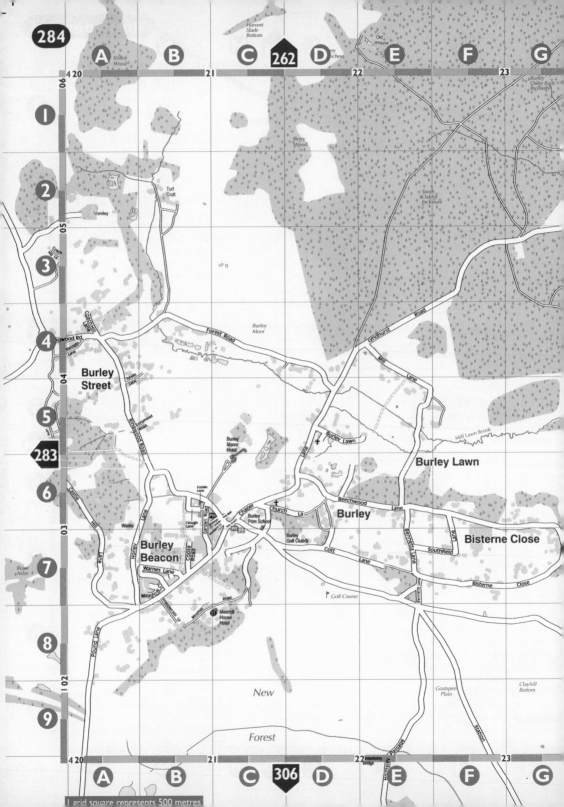

A B C **262** D E F G

4 20 21 22 23

1

06

2

05

Vereley

3

Coach Hill La

4

Burley
Street

04

Forest Road

Burley
Moor

Lyndhurst
Road

Mill
Lane

Ridley
Wood

Turf
Croft

Harvest
Slade
Bottom

Betty
Wood

Old
House

Burley
Outer Rails
Inclosure

South
Oakley
Inclosure

5

283

Burley
Manor
Hotel

Burley Lawn

Mill Lawn Brook

Burley Lawn

6

03

Castle
Hill
Lane

Ringwood Road

Longwood
Road

Works

Eudale
Lane

Clough
Lane

Garden Road

Chapel
Lane

Burley
Prim School

Church La

Beechwood Lane

Burley

Burley

Burley
Golf Club

Cott
Lane

Bennetts Lane

Southfield

Burn

Bisterne Close

Bisterne Close

7

Bratt
Axon

Honey
Lane

Castle Hill Lane

**Burley
Beacon**

Warnes Lane

Mead La

Bisterne Close

8

02

Pound
Lane

Moorhill
House Hotel

road

Morhill

Golf Course

Goatspen
Plain

Clayhill
Bottom

9

New

Forest

Burbush
Bridge

Hensley

Passage

Station

4 20 21 22 22 23

A B C **306** D E F G

H   J   K   L   263   M   N

24   25   26   27   06

I

2   Nev

Fores

3

4

5

286

6

7

8

9

H   J   K   L   307   M   N   P

24   25   26   27

Burley Road

Burley Lodge

Lyndhurst Road

Danes Slough Inclosure

Vinney Ridge Inclosure

Fletchers Thorns Inclosure

Pound Hill Inclosure

Rhinefield Ornamental Drive

Rhinefield Sandy's Inclosure

Burley Old Inclosure

Red Rise

Rhinefield House Hotel

Aldridge Inclosure

A35

Markway Inclosure

Ober Water

Crab Tree Earth

Duck Hole

Wilverley Post

White Moor

Naked Man

Wilverley Plain

Hincheslea Moor

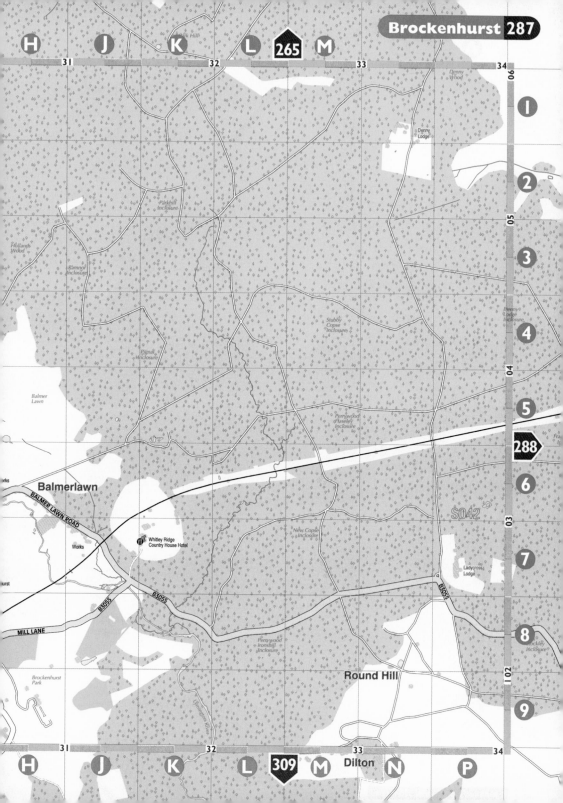

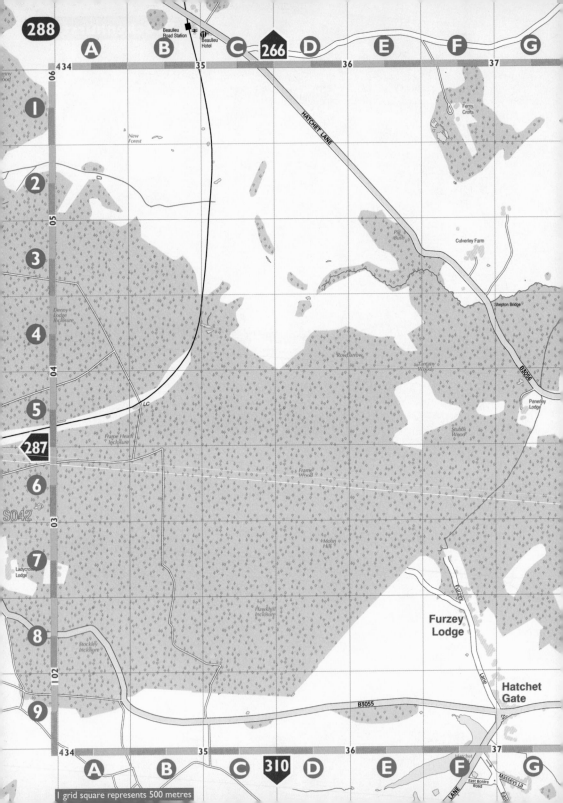

288

A B C 266 D E F G

434 35 06 36 37

Beaulieu
Road Station

Beaulieu
Hotel

HATCHET LANE

I

New
Forest

Ferny
Crofts

2

05

Pig
Bush

Culverley Farm

3

Denny
Lodge
Inclosure

Shepton Bridge

4

04

Rowbarrow

Tantany
Woods

B3056

5

LC

Penerley
Lodge

287

Frame Heath
Inclosure

Stubbs
Wood

6

Frame
Wood

SO42

03

7

Ladycross
Lodge

Mobn
Hill

FURZEY LANE

**Furzey
Lodge**

8

Stockley
Inclosure

02

Hawkhill
Inclosure

**Hatchet
Gate**

9

B3055

HATCHET LANE

434 35 06 36 37

A B C 310 D E F G

East Boldre
Road

Masseys La

Hatchet

I grid square represents 500 metres

H J K L **269** M N

45 46 47 48

06

1

2

05

3

4

04

5

292

6

03

7

8

02

9

Calshot

H J K L **313** M N P

45 46 47 48

Cadland Creek

Foreshore

J Av.

H Avenue

Avenue

E Avenue

4th Street

5th Street

6th Street

2nd St

1st Street

Fawley
Oil Refinery

SO45

Avenue

South

ROAD

B3053

Fawley
Business
Centre

School Rd

Ashmere

Foreshore
South

North Trestle Road

Burnah
Road

Burmah
Road

P.L.P.H.

Cadland
Road

Burmah
Road

South

South

Trestle
Road

Road

Old Agwi Road

Agwi Road

Agwi Road

Flume Rd

Road

Marsh Lane

Bryn Paddock
Ct

Bryn
Ln

Coquina
Lane

Chatham
Cl

Sherel
Cl

Church
Lane

Wordsworth
Cl

Garden Cl

Church
Rd

School Lane

Fawley
Infant
School

Cl

Coptnorne
Lane

Ashlett
Cl

Ashlett

Ashlett
Road

Southill

Ashlett Creek

Fawley

FAWLEY BY-PASS

B3053

Stonehills

Ashdown
Road

Blackfield
Road

The
Pentagon

Chapel Ln

Blackfield Road

Heather
Road

Thornhill
Road

Furzey
Road

Heathet

Hill

Slades

Northern Access
Road

Northern Access Road

Fields Heath

Fields Farm

Badminston Farm

Badminston Lane

Holbury
Road

Mopley
Pond

Tom's Down

Badminston
Drove

Badminston
Common

B3053

Ower

Mopley

Green Lane

Walker Lane South

Holbury Avenue

Calshot

Stanswood Road

Bob Dln

Calshot
Cl

Tristan Cl

Castle
Lane

Jack

Hillhead

Hamble
Common

P

Sylvan La

Way

Heath

Titchfield
Common

H J K L M N Catisfield

SOUTHAMPTON ROAD A27

271

Titchfield Primary School

West Hill Park School

Common Lane

Titchfield

West Street

Coach Hill

Bridge Street

Hookgate Coppice

Brownwich Lane

Occupation Lane

Posbrook Lane

Heath Lane

Hook Lane

Warsash Road

Singledge

Little Posbrook

PO14

Triangle Lane

River Meon

Meon

Brownwich Farm

Solent Way

Titchfield Haven

Cliff Road

Hill Head

The Solent

H J K L M N P

52 53 54 55

1 2 3 4 5 6 7 8 9

THE AVENUE

Ranvilles Lane

TITCHFIELD ROAD

B3354

Frogmore

294

Crofton Anne Dale J&I School

Crofton Hammond Infant School

Crofton Hammond Junior School

Hill Head Prep School

Park Road

Monks Way

Solent Way

A   B   C   284   D   E   F   G

420   21   22   23

284

Plain

Cres

Greenberry
Bridge

1

Holmsley
Ridge

Whitten
Bottom

Holmsley
Lodge

2

Thorney
Hill
Holms

Holmsley
Inclosure

3

Forest
Rd
Ernco
Road
Forest Road
School
Lane

4

Valley
Lane

Whitsthall Rd

Thorney Hill

Willow Lane

Wootton
Old Fa

Brownhill   Road

5

Hill Farm

305

Rhinefield Road

Plain
Heath

HOLMSLEY

Wootton Farm

R

6

Poors
Common

Manor Farm

7

Forest
Lodge

Ossemsley

Heathfield

Lyndhurst Road

green
Lane

North Drive

8

Beech House

North Hinton
Farm

Ham   Hill   Lane

9

arrow Ro
Harrow
Lodge

hurst Road

Ossemsley
Manor

420   21   326   22   23

A   B   C   326   D   E   F   G

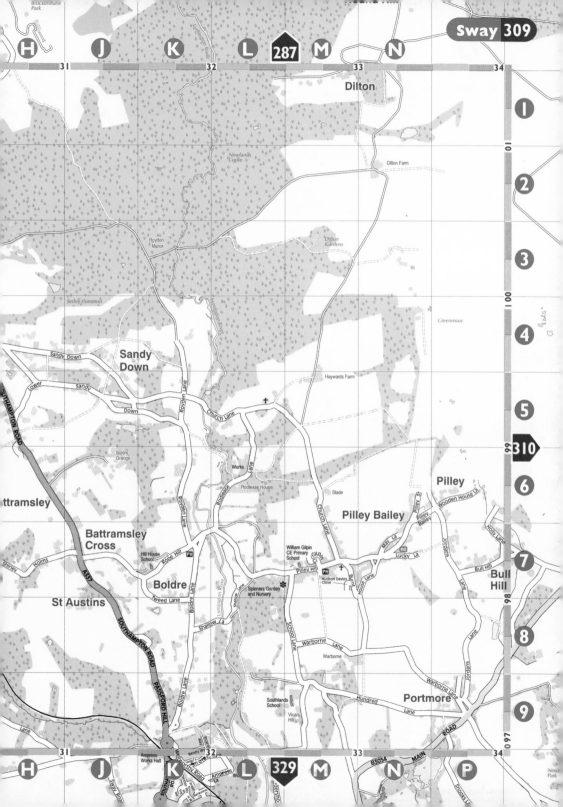

H J K L 291 M N

45 46 47 48

1
2
3
4
5
6
7
8
9

010
100
99
98
097

Tom's Down
Mopley Pond
Sprat's Down
Mopley
Clare Gdns
Forge Road
Whitefield Farm
Dark Water
Lepe Road
Stanswood Farm
Stanswood Road
Stanswood Road
Hillhead
Eaglehurst
Nelson's Place
Stanswood Bay
Cadland House
Stone Farm
Stanswood Road
Lepe Road
Lepe
Lepe Country Park
Stansore Point
Castle Lane
B3053
Beaulieu Road

H J K L M N P

45 46 47 48

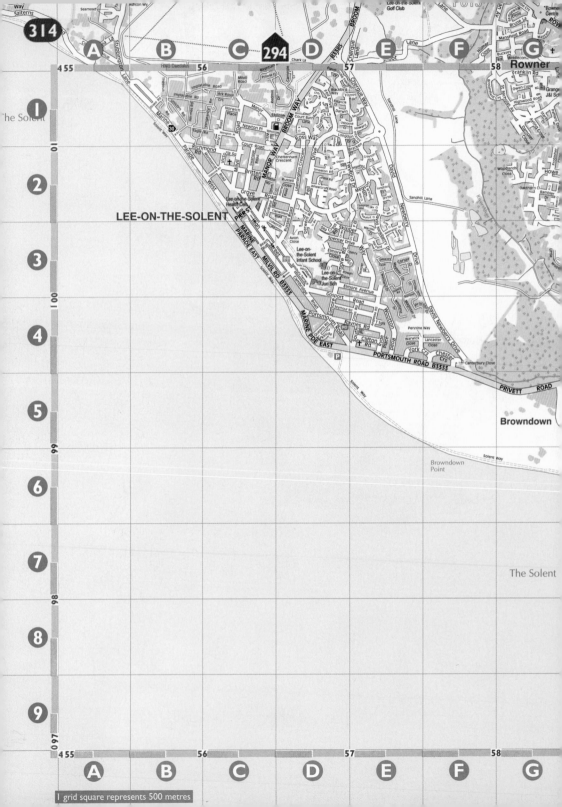

299

H J K L M

73 74 75 76

1

Mill Rythe

2

Mill Rythe
Holiday Village

Mill Rythe
J&I School

3

Pilsey
Sand

100

4

West Sussex County
Hampshire County

Stocker's Lake

Eastwood

99

5

Black Point

Mengham
Salterns

Mengham

Salterns
Lane

Marine
Road

Seaview
Road

Bracklesham
Rd

Selsmore

6

North Crs

Norman Rd

Harold Road

Blackthorn Dr

Kings Rd

Selsmore Avenue

Foreland
Ct

St Hermans Rd

Eastoke

Avenue

Farnier

Bosmere Rd

Seafarers

Bracklesham

Rd

St Andrew's Road

Old School Dr

Southwood

Mengham Rd

Sea
Front

Bembridge Drive

Eastoke
Creek

Avenue

Haven Road

Haven
Road

Sandy
Point
Road

Treloar
Rd

7

Winner Cl

Wheatlands

Avenue

Southwood Road

Eastoke Point

98

8

97

9

H J K L M N P

73 74 75 76

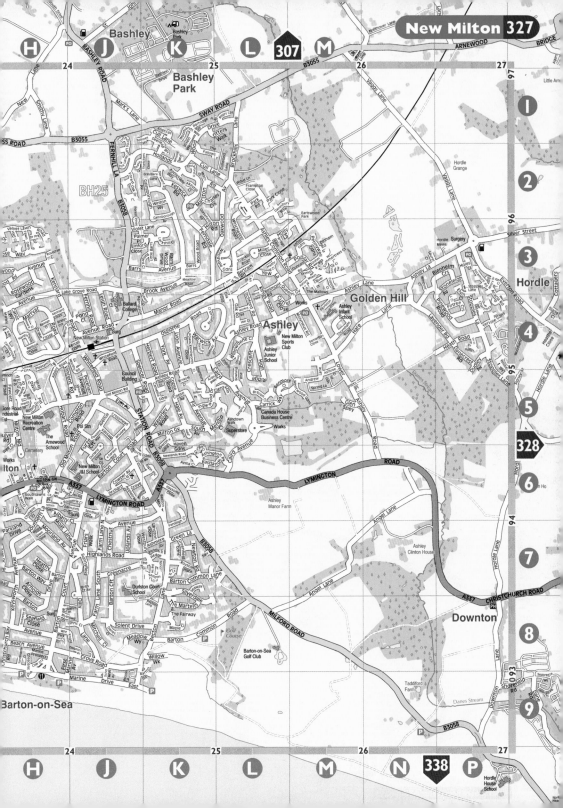

Warren

H J K L 311 M

38 39 40 41
97

1

Sowley Lane

Thorns Lane

Park Lane

Sowley Pond

Park Farm

Thorns Beach

Little Marsh

Park Shore

2

96

Sandpit Lane

Works

Colgrims

3

95

4

5

94

6

7

93

8

9

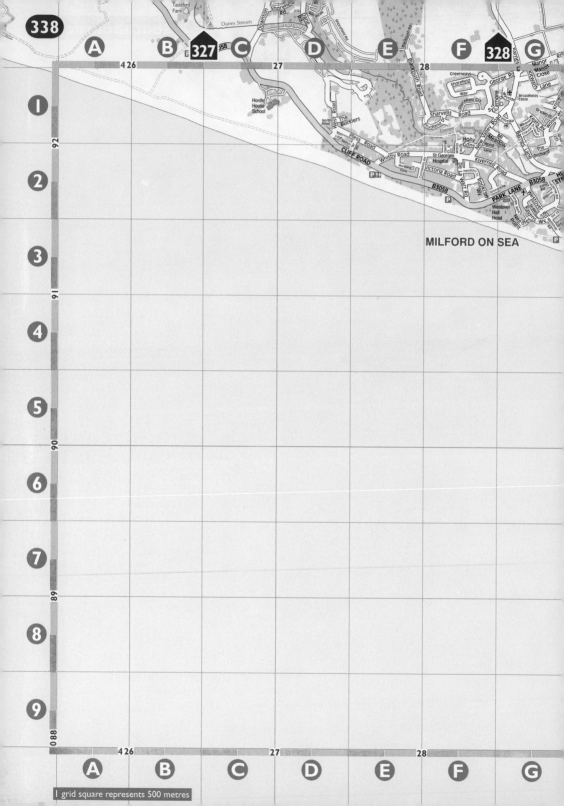

338

A B 327 J58 C D E F 328 G

4 26   27   28

1

92

Hordle House School

North Head The Bucklers
Bless Road
CLIFF ROAD Whitby Road
2

St Georges Hospital
Victoria Road
B3058

MILFORD ON SEA

3

91

4

5

90

6

7

89

8

9

0 88

4 26   27   28

A B C D E F G

I grid square represents 500 metres

Abbotstone 147 L6
Abbotswood 204 E2
Abbots Worthy 165 L1
Abbotts Ann 101 L7
Abshot 292 G1
Alderholt 239 M5
Aldermaston Soke 34 G3
Aldermoor 227 L9
Alderney 321 L2
Aldershot 3 G3
Allbrook 207 J7
Allington 118 B6
Alton 132 E6
Alverstoke 315 J6
Amesfield 280 C8
Ampfield 205 N2
Amport 100 F5
Anchorage Park 297 K5
Andover 4 E4
Andover Down 5 J4
Andwell 71 H7
Anmore 255 K7
Anna Valley 102 B5
Ann's Hill 315 K3
Ansteadbrook 157 P8
Anthill Common 254 F5
Applemore 267 L6
Appleshaw 81 H5
Arford 154 F2
Ash 76 F9
Ashe 87 L3
Ashfield 204 F9
Ashford 240 B2
Ashford Hill 33 H5
Ashington 300 C4
Ashlett 291 L6
Ashley 282 A4
Ashley 162 C4
Ashley 327 L4
Ashley Heath 281 N3
Ashmansworth 45 J6
Ashton 231 P1
Ashurst 246 A9
Ashurst Bridge 246 A6
Ash Vale 76 F6
Avington 166 D2
Avon 304 D6
Avon Castle 282 B7
Awbridge 203 L1
Axford 109 N7
Axmansford 33 M7
Badshot Lea 97 H5
Baffins 317 K1
Bagmore 111 J4
Bailey Green 189 L3
Ball Hill 29 K3
Balmerlawn 287 H6
Bank 264 D7
Bar End 165 J9
Barford 136 E9
Barrow Hill 245 K1
Bartley 244 G4
Barton-on-Sea 327 H9
Barton Stacey 124 F3
Bashley 307 J9
Bashley Park 327 K1
Bassett 6 C4
Bassett 228 C7
Bassett Green 228 C7
Battramsley 308 G6
Battramsley Cross 309 J7
Batt's Corner 135 M2
Baughurst 33 N7
Baybridge 209 J2
Bear Cross 301 P7
Bearwood 301 P7
Beaulieu 289 J9
Beauworth 186 E6
Beckley 326 E2
Bedhampton 276 C9
Beech 132 A8
Beech Hill 37 H1
Bell Hill 191 L9
Bentley 114 D5
Bentworth 131 H4
Bickton 240 D5
Bidden 92 D4
Bighton 148 F7
Binley 63 J4
Binsted 134 C2
Birchy Hill 308 C7
Bishop's Green 31 M3
Bishop's Sutton 168 E3
Bishopstoke 229 L1
Bishop's Waltham 232 A3
Bisterne 304 D2
Bisterne Close 304 F7
Bitterne 248 C4
Bitterne Park 248 F2
Black Dam 69 N9
Blackfield 290 F8
Blackhill 134 C2
Blackmoor 153 L9
Blacknest 135 H2
Blackwater 57 L1
Blackwater 323 P2
Blashford 260 E7
Bleak Hill 240 A8
Blendworth 256 E4
Blissford 241 J3
Blounce 112 E3
Boarhunt 273 M5
Bohemia 200 B9
Boldre 289 H7
Booley Green 250 E1
Borden 193 P8
Bordon 154 B6
Boscombe 118 A7
Boscombe 335 L3
Bossington 160 F4
Botley 250 C4
Boundstone 116 B6
Bournemouth 9 F4
The Bourne 116 C4
Bourne Valley 322 B9
Boveridge 238 A1
Bowling Alley 94 G3

Bowling Green 328 E1
Boyatt Wood 207 H8
Bradley 130 D1
Braishfield 180 G2
Brambridge 207 M5
Bramdean 187 N1
Bramley 51 P1
Bramley Corner 51 L2
Bramley Green 51 P1
Bramshaw 223 P8
Bramshill 38 E7
Bramshott 175 K1
Branksome 321 P7
Branksome Park 333 P1
Bransbury 104 C9
Bransgore 305 M8
Breamore 220 E3
Bridgemary 294 F6
Brighton Hill 90 A3
Brimpton Common 33 M4
Broadgate 28 A3
Broad Layings 29 M5
Broadmere 89 P7
Broadoak 250 E4
Broad Oak 72 F8
Broadstone 300 D3
Brockbridge 233 P2
Brockenhurst 286 E7
Brockhampton 14 C7
Brockhurst 315 H2
Brock's Green 31 M6
Brook 244 A5
Brook 161 H9
Brooke's Hill 225 P8
Brook Hill 244 A1
Broom Hill 279 K4
Broughton 160 B1
Brown Candover 128 F6
Browndown 314 G5
Brown Heath 231 J7
Browninghill Green 50 A2
Bucket Corner 205 N6
Buckland 329 J2
Bucklers Hard 311 N3
Bucks Horn Oak 135 J1
Buckskin 68 D8
Bull Hill 309 P7
Bunker's Hill 244 G1
Bunstead 182 E8
Burgates 173 K9
Burghclere 30 E7
Burghclere Common 30 F5
Burghfield 27 L2
Burghfield Common 27 J5
Burghfield Hill 27 L4
Buriton 215 L8
Burley 284 D6
Burley Beacon 284 B7
Burley Lawn 284 E6
Burley Street 284 A4
Burridge 250 G9
Bursledon 270 A2
Burton 325 H5
Bury's Bank 25 H8
Butlocks Heath 269 M3
Buttsash 290 D1
Butt's Green 178 G5
The Butts 132 E7
Cadnam 244 F3
Cadnam Green 244 E2
Calmore 246 A2
Calshot 291 P9
Camel Green 239 P5
Camelsdale 156 F8
Canada 224 D3
Canford Cliffs 333 M4
Canford Heath 320 G3
Canford Magna 301 J4
Carter's Clay 178 C8
Catherington 256 A2
Catisfield 271 N9
Causeway 256 B6
Causeway 215 L3
Chalton 257 H7
Chandler's Ford 206 F5
Chandlers Green 53 L3
Charleshill 117 N5
Charlton 82 C9
Charlton-All-Saints 199 K1
Charlwood 170 D4
Charminster 323 J6
Charter Alley 50 C5
Chawton 151 L1
Cheriton 187 H1
Chidden 235 H4
Chidden 123 L5
Chilbolton 143 H2
Chilbolton Down 143 H2
Chilcomb 184 F1
Chilton Candover 129 J4
Chilworth 227 P3
Chilworth Old Village 227 N2
Chineham 70 A1
Choiderton 198 A9
Christchurch 336 F1
Church Common 191 H6
Church End 52 C7
Church Oakley 88 C1
Churt 136 F8
Chute Cadley 60 C5
Chute Standen 60 A4
Clanfield 236 B7
Clanville 81 K4
Clapgate 278 E5
Clarken Green 88 B1
Clatford Oakcuts 121 N5
Clayhall 315 L5
Clayhill 264 C2
Cliddesden 90 B4
Cobley 239 L9
Colbury 246 B9
Cold Ash Hill 175 M2
Colden Common 208 A4
Cole Henley 64 E9
Colehill 279 H7
Colemore 171 L5
College Town 41 M5

Colt Hill 72 E9
The Common 158 B1
Compton 116 F1
Compton 161 H8
Compton 183 M7
Compton End 183 L5
Conford 154 C9
Cookham 213 H7
Coombe 297 J8
Copythorne 245 J1
Corhampton 211 M8
Cosham 297 J1
Cottonworth 123 J5
Couch Green 146 B9
Cove 50 E2
Cove 57 M7
Cowesfield Green 201 L2
Cowplain 255 P8
Coxford 247 L1
Crab Orchard 258 E8
Crampmoor 205 N4
Cranbourne 90 B1
Crawley 143 L6
Creekmoor 320 C4
Crendell 238 F4
Cricket Hill 38 C8
Criddlestyle 240 F2
Cripplestyle 238 G6
Critchell's Green 178 F6
Critchmere 156 D6
Crockerhill 272 C3
Crondall 94 C4
Crookham 92 E1
Crookham Village 73 P6
Crosswater 136 E5
Crossways 136 E8
Crow 285 H5
Crowdhill 208 C8
Crowthorne 40 F1
Crux Easton 45 K8
Cuckoo's Corner 133 L1
Cufaude 51 P6
Cupernham 206 B3
Curbridge 251 K7
Curdridge 251 L3
Custards 264 C5
Daggons 239 J6
Damerham 219 K7
Daneshill 69 P4
Darby Green 41 H8
Deadwater 154 C5
Dean 232 C1
Dean 163 P4
Deane 87 N2
Deanland 194 A8
Deanlane End 257 K6
Deepcut 59 H7
The Dene 62 C4
Denmead 255 H6
Denvilles 277 J8
Dewlands Common 258 D5
Dibden 267 P5
Dibden Purlieu 267 N9
Dilton 309 M1
Dipley 54 D5
Dippenhall 95 M9
Dockenfield 135 F3
Dogmersfield 54 A7
Donnington 24 A1
Dora's Green 95 L6
Downton 199 M6
Downton 327 P8
Drayton 297 L1
Droxford 233 L5
Dry Hill 149 P3
Dudsbury 302 C7
Dummer 109 H1
Dunbridge 179 J5
Dundridge 232 F2
Dunley 64 B4
Durleighmarsh 216 E2
Durley 231 H6
Durley Street 231 J4
Durns Town 308 C6
Durrants 277 H2
Earlstone Common 30 E6
East Anton 82 C7
East Boldre 311 H3
East Cholderton 100 F4
East Dean 178 A4
East End 300 A4
East End 188 F9
East End 310 F9
East End 29 H7
East Fields 29 H7
East Green 114 G4
East Grimstead 176 E2
East Howe 322 C4
Eastland Gate 255 M6
Eastleigh 229 K1
East Liss 183 L6
East Martin 196 C9
East Meon 213 M5
Eastney 317 L5
East Oakley 88 G1
Eastoke 319 J6
Easton 165 P2
East Parley 303 L8
Eastrop 7 J7
East Stratton 127 N5
East Tisted 171 K2
East Tytherley 159 N8
East Wellow 202 G8
East Winterslow 188 A8
East Woodhay 28 F7
East Worldham 133 L8
Ebbtake 259 K5
Ecchinswell 47 L1
Edmondsham 258 B2
Egbury 63 N6
Egypt 125 M4
Eling 246 F6
Ellingham 260 C5
Ellisfield 110 D2
Elson 295 L9
Eisted 217 L9

Elvetham 55 N8
Elvetham Heath 56 B9
Emery Down 264 D4
Empshott 172 F4
Empshott Green 172 E4
Emsworth 299 L2
Enborne Row 30 A2
Enham Alamein 82 C4
Ensbury 322 E1
Ensbury Park 322 C5
Eversley 39 L5
Eversley Centre 39 N6
Eversley Cross 40 A6
Everton 328 E6
Ewshot 95 L5
Exbury 312 D3
Exton 211 N6
Faberstown 80 B2
Faccombe 44 C4
Fairmile 324 D6
Fair Oak 230 C2
Fair Oak 33 H7
Fair Oak Green 36 C8
Fareham 11 F4
Farleigh Wallop 90 A9
Farley Hill 38 C1
Farlington 297 M1
Farnborough 75 P1
Farnborough Green 58 B8
Farnborough Park 76 C1
Farnborough Street 58 B8
Farnham 96 B9
Farringdon 171 H1
Fawley 291 K7
Ferndown 302 B3
Filmore Hill 189 J2
Finchampstead 39 N3
Finchdean 257 J5
Fisher's Pond 208 D7
Fleet 74 D3
Fleet 298 F9
Fleetend 270 F9
Fleetlands 294 G4
Flexford 206 B5
Flood Street 220 D5
Folly Hill 96 A6
Fordingbridge 240 E2
Forest Gate 254 F4
Forestside 257 P5
Forton 104 B6
Forton 315 M2
Fosbury 42 C4
Foulford 283 L2
Four Houses Corner 26 G7
Four Marks 150 D6
Foxdown 87 J1
Foxhills 86 B8
Fox Lane 57 N4
Foyers 245 J8
Fratton 316 G2
Freefolk 85 P5
Freemantle 247 N5
The Frenches 203 H3
Frenchmoor 158 D9
Frensham 136 B2
Friars Cliff 325 N9
Frimley 58 B4
Frimley Green 58 B6
Frimley Ridge 58 F2
Fritham 243 H2
Frithend 135 K5
Frogham 241 J5
Frogmore 41 J8
Frostlane 268 E8
Froxfield Green 190 C6
Fryern Hill 206 F7
Fulfood 164 E7
Fullerton 122 G6
Funtley 272 C5
Furzedown 161 N8
Furze Hill 278 E5
Furzey Corner 275 H1
Furzey 244 A8
Furzey Lodge 288 F8
Furzley 224 D7
Fyfield 80 E9
Fyning 193 L9
Gilbert Street 170 A1
Glebe 232 A9
Gobley Hole 109 N2
Goddard's Green 180 A5
God's Blessing Green 279 J5
Godshill 241 J1
Godswinscroft 325 M2
Goldenhayes 245 H7
Golden Hill 327 M4
Golden Pot 112 C7
Goldfinch Bottom 31 P1
Goodworth Clatford 102 D9
Goose Green 264 C6
Goose Hill 32 E3
Gore End 29 J2
Gosport 205 L3
Gotham 238 E8
Grange 278 F2
Grange Estate 281 M9
Grateley 100 A9
Grayshott 157 H4
Graywood 157 M4
Grazeley Green 27 P4
Greatham 173 K6
Great Shoddesden 80 A5
Green Cross 157 H8
Greenham 24 F7
Greenham Common 31 J1
The Green 159 J8
Greywell 74 D3
Griggs Green 174 G3
Gundleton 168 G5
Hablin 217 K3
Hale 96 D6
Hale 221 N2
Halecommon 193 J9
Halterworth 206 D6
Hambledon 234 D9
Hamble-le-Rice 269 P7
Hammer 156 B8

Hammer Bottom 156 A8
Hampreston 301 N3
Hampton Park 228 E9
Hamptworth 201 N5
Hamworthy 320 A9
Hangersley 261 J8
Hannington 48 E9
Harbridge 260 C1
Harbridge Green 240 B9
Hardley 290 E3
Hardway 315 M1
Harefield 249 L4
Harestock 164 D4
Hartfordbridge 55 L5
Hartley Mauditt 152 D3
Hartley Wespall 53 H4
Hartley Wintney 54 C6
Haslemere 157 J7
Hatch 70 D7
Hatch Bottom 249 M1
Hatchet Gate 288 C9
Hatchet Green 221 N1
Hatch Warren 89 L5
Hatherden 82 A2
Hatt Hill 179 K5
Hattingley 148 M1
Haughurst Hill 33 M5
Havant 15 L5
Hawkley 172 D3
Hawley 57 M2
Hawley Lane 58 A6
Hawthorn 150 D9
Hayling Island 299 H7
Hazeley 54 D2
Hazeley Bottom 54 E4
Hazeley Lea 54 E2
Headbourne Worthy 164 C2
Headley 32 B5
Headley 154 E3
Headley Down 155 J4
Hearn 155 J1
Heath End 34 A5
Heath End 96 D4
Heath End 29 H5
Heather Row 54 F1
Heatherside 58 C1
Heathfield 272 A9
Heath Green 149 K1
Heckfield 37 P8
Hedge End 250 B4
Hell Corner 28 C1
Henley 42 D2
Hensting 208 D4
Hermitage 277 N9
Herriard 111 H1
Hides Close 289 K5
Highbridge 207 M6
Highbury 297 H3
Highclere 29 N9
Highclere Street 45 L2
Highcliffe 326 C7
High Cross 190 F4
Higher Row 283 H2
Highfield 248 C1
Hightown 283 H2
Hightown 249 N7
Highwood 286 D6
Hillbourne 320 C2
Hill Brow 192 C4
Hillbutts 278 B7
Hill Head 293 M8
Hill Park 272 B7
Hillside 192 G2
Hill Side 192 D2
Hillside 93 N1
Hillstreet 225 P7
Hill Top 289 N5
Hillyfields 226 C8
Hiltingbury 206 F3
Hindhead 156 E1
Hinton 326 C5
Hinton Ampner 187 J2
Hinton Parva 278 B1
Hocombe 206 D3
Hoe 206 D3
Hoe Gate 254 B4
Hog Hatch 95 P5
Holbury 290 E6
Holdenhurst 323 N4
Hollington 45 K1
Hollington Cross 45 L2
Hollywater 154 C7
Holt 72 C3
Holt 279 H2
Holt End 131 J6
Holt Heath 280 A3
Holt Pound 115 M6
Holybourne 133 J2
Hook 72 A3
Hook Park 292 E2
Hordle 328 A3
Horndean 256 D4
Horsebridge 161 H6
Horton Common 258 C3
Horton Heath 258 A9
Horton Heath 230 C4
Houghton 161 H2
Hound 269 N4
Hound Green 54 B2
Hound Hill 115 N6
Houndmills 69 H5
Hounsdown 246 C7
Hungerford 24 A3
Hunton 126 A5
Hurn 303 P9
Hursley 182 D7
Hurstbourne Priors 84 E9
Hurstbourne Tarrant 61 J7
Hyde 63 E5
Hyde 240 C5
Hyde End 33 N2
Hythe 268 D6
Ibsley 260 E3
Ibthorpe 61 P4
Ibworth 67 L2

Iford....324 B8
Inhurst....33 M6
Inkpen Common....28 A1
Isington....114 C9
Itchen....248 G8
Itchen Abbas....166 D1
Itchen Stoke....167 J1
Jumpers Common....324 C7
Kempshott....89 J7
Kempshott Park....89 J7
Kent's Oak....179 L9
Keyhaven....339 K3
Kilmeston....187 H5
Kimbridge....179 L6
Kimpton....80 B9
Kingsclere....48 B4
Kingsclere Woodlands....32 D6
Kings Furlong....69 H8
Kingsley....134 E8
Kingsmead....252 C5
King's Somborne....161 L4
Kingston....282 D8
Kingston....317 H1
Kings Worthy....165 K1
Kinson....322 B2
Kitwood....187 J3
Knapp....205 P1
Knighton....301 M6
Knights Enham....82 E6
Knowle Village....272 C3
Ladwell....206 D1
Lambs Green....300 A3
Landford....201 M9
Landfordwood....201 M6
Lane End....186 A6
Lane End....136 D2
Lane End....170 E8
Landown....268 D7
Langley....174 C9
Langley....312 F1
Langrish....214 C1
Langstone....298 E3
Lasham....91 M6
Latchmere Green....35 K9
Laverstoke....86 C6
Leagreen....328 A7
Leckford....123 H9
Lee....226 E4
Lee Ground....271 N5
Lee-on-the-Solent....314 A2
Leigh....301 H1
Leigh Park....276 D6
Lepe....313 J6
Liliput....333 L4
Linchmere....175 N6
Lindford....154 C4
Linford....261 L8
Linkenholt....43 N4
Linwood....261 M2
Liphook....175 H4
Liss....143 P8
Liss Forest....173 L8
Litchfield....64 D4
Little Ann....101 N6
Little Canford....301 L1
Littledown....43 J5
Littledown....323 N8
Little Hoddington....92 C6
Little Holbury....290 D4
Little London....50 G2
Little London....83 H3
Little Posbrook....293 L4
Little Sandhurst....41 H4
Little Shoddesden....80 C5
Little Somborne....162 A1
Littleton....164 C2
Lockerley....178 E5
Locks Heath....270 F7
London Minstead....244 C7
Long Common....250 F2
Longfleet....320 E8
Longham....302 B7
Longparish....104 D4
Long Park....143 P8
Longstock....141 K1
Long Sutton....93 L8
Lord's Hill....227 L8
Lordswood....227 P8
Lovedean....255 N5
Lover....200 B8
Lower Bordean....190 A0
Lower Bourne....116 E4
Lower Brook....179 P2
Lower Buckland....329 L2
Lower Bullington....125 J2
Lower Burgate....220 D8
Lower Chute....60 A5
Lower Common....110 D4
Lower Common....39 J5
Lower Daggons....238 G4
Lower Farringdon....151 L5
Lower Froyle....114 A5
Lower Hamworthy....332 C2
Lower Holwell....238 D5
Lower Mannington....280 B1
Lower Pennington....329 J7
Lower Ratley....203 M2
Lower Slackstead....181 K7
Lower Swanwick....270 C2
Lower Turmer....260 B3
Lower Upham....209 K9
Lower Wield....130 D3
Lowford....270 A1
Lumley....277 N9
Lychpit....69 K6
Lyde Green....53 M6
Lymington....329 L4
Lymore....328 F9
Lynch....86 E3
Lynch Hill....85 M6
Lyndhurst....264 E5
Malwood....244 A7
Mannington....280 A1
Mapledurwell....70 F9
Marchwood....247 L9
Marnel Park....69 L2
Martin....218 C1

Martin Drove End....195 L2
Martyr Worthy....166 A1
Mattingley....54 A5
Maybush....247 J1
Mead End....307 N7
Medstead....149 P2
Mengham....319 H5
Meon....293 L6
Meonstoke....211 P9
Merley....300 C4
Merritown....303 L9
Merry Field Hill....278 C6
Merry Oak....248 G6
Merton Rise....69 H5
Meyrick Park....334 D1
Micheldever....127 H6
Micheldever Station....107 H8
Michelmersh....180 A5
Midanbury....249 H3
Middle Bockhampton....325 K1
Middle Bourne....116 C3
Middleton....104 C5
Middle Wallop....120 E9
Middle Winterslow....138 B9
Milford on Sea....338 F5
Millbridge....116 D9
Millbrook....247 J4
Mill Green....32 C3
Mill Lane....94 E2
Milton....317 L4
Minstead....244 B8
The Mint....192 E1
Mockbeggar....261 H5
Monk Sherborne....50 E7
Montgomery Lines....76 B8
Monxton....101 H5
Moorcourt....268 A5
Moorgreen....322 C6
Moorgreen....229 P9
Moor Park....117 H1
Moortown....282 F4
Morestead....184 F6
Morgan's Vale....199 N6
Mortimer....35 P1
Mortimer West End....35 L2
Mottisfont....179 L4
The Mount....29 N7
Mudeford....337 L1
Mullenspond....100 E2
Murrell Green....72 D1
Muscliff....323 H2
Mytchett....76 D1
Mytchett Place....76 G2
Nash's Green....111 L3
Nately Scures....71 K5
Neacroft....325 M1
Neatham....133 L3
Netherton....44 A5
Nether Wallop....139 P2
Netley....269 K4
Netley Hill....249 P7
Netley Marsh....245 N5
New Alresford....167 P1
Newbridge....224 E9
New Brighton....277 N7
Newbury....16 C2
New Cheriton....187 H2
Newfound....67 N9
Newgrounds....241 L1
New Milton....326 G3
Newnham....71 J4
Newton....201 H3
Newton....244 B9
Newton....292 D2
Newton....132 D6
Newton....30 G2
Newtown....203 H1
Newtown....143 P8
Newtown....321 K5
Newtown....231 M4
Newtown....253 N4
Newtown....269 J1
No's Crook....208 A6
Nomansland....223 M5
No Man's Land....165 N7
Normandy....310 D8
Normandy....77 N8
Northam....21 H1
North Baddesley....227 L1
North Boarhunt....253 L9
North Bockhampton....305 J9
Northbourne....322 D3
Northbrook....232 A3
Northbrook....126 F5
North Camp....76 A6
North Charford....199 N9
North End....28 C4
North End....297 H7
North End....219 J7
North End....167 P8
Northfields....184 A7
North Gorley....240 F8
North Hayling....299 H6
North Houghton....141 J8
Northington....128 D9
North Kingston....282 G7
Northney....299 J5
North Oakley....66 D3
North Poulner....261 H8
North Ripley....305 H4
North Stoneham....228 F5
North Street....227 J5
North Street....149 M9
North Tidworth....78 E3
North Town....97 M1
North Waltham....88 C9
North Warnborough....72 B8
North Weirs....286 C8
Nursling....246 A6
Nursted....216 A6
Nutburn....205 H3
Nutcombe....156 C3

Nutley....109 N5
Nyewood....217 J5
Oakdale....320 C6
Oakhanger....153 J4
Oakley....88 E2
Oakley....300 F4
Oakridge....6 E1
Oakshott....191 K2
Ocean Village....248 D9
Odiham....93 L1
Ogdens....241 K6
Old Alresford....147 P7
Old Basing....70 B6
Old Burghclere....48 D5
Old Milton....326 G6
Old Netley....269 N1
Old Portsmouth....18 C4
Old Shirley....247 L2
Oliver's Battery....183 J3
Ossemsley....324 B1
Otterbourne....207 K1
Otterwood....289 P9
Outwick....220 C4
Overton....87 H4
Over Wallop....120 C7
Ovington....167 K5
Ower....225 M6
Owlsmoor....41 L4
Owslebury....208 F2
Oxenwood....42 A2
Padworth....26 A6
Padworth Common....26 C8
Palestine....119 N3
Pamber End....50 E4
Pamber Green....50 F1
Pamber Heath....34 E4
Pamphill....278 A8
Pardown....88 F5
Park Gate....271 H5
Parkstone....333 K1
Parley Green....323 J1
Passfield....154 G7
Paulsgrove....296 C1
Peartree Green....248 F7
Peel Common....294 D7
Pennington....329 J5
Penton Corner....101 N1
Penton Grafton....81 M8
Penton Mewsey....81 N7
Pentridge....195 K9
Penwood....29 N7
Perham Down....79 L4
Petersfield....215 N3
Phoenix Green....54 F9
Picket Hill....283 L1
Picket Piece....83 L9
Pig Oak....278 C3
Pikeshill....264 E4
Pilford....279 J6
Pilley....309 P6
Pilley Bailey....309 M6
Pitch Place....137 N6
Pitt....183 J1
Plaitford....202 A9
Plaitford Green....202 C5
Plastow Green....32 D7
Pokesdown....335 N2
Pondtail....74 G4
Pooksgreen....247 H9
Poole....320 D9
Popham....108 C6
Popley....69 M3
Portchester....295 M1
Portmore....309 N9
Portsea....18 E2
Portsea Island....297 K9
Portsmouth....18 C1
Port Solent....296 B2
Portswood....248 D2
Potbridge....72 F4
Poulner....283 H1
Pound Green....49 N2
Pound Street....30 B7
Powntley Copse....112 D5
Preston Candover....129 L1
Priddy's Hard....315 J5
Prince's Marsh....192 D4
Privett....315 J5
Privett....189 L4
Pucknall....181 K8
Purbrook....275 M5
Purewell....324 G5
Pylehill....230 C1
Pyott's Hill....70 B3
Quarley....100 A6
Quidhampton....87 H2
Racedown....136 B1
Ratbrough....75 M1
Ragged Appleshaw....81 J5
Rake....193 J2
Ramsdean....214 C4
Ramsdell....50 B6
Ratlake....206 C6
Redbridge....246 C5
Redenham....80 F4
Red Hill....322 F3
Red Hill....277 H1
Redlynch....200 B8
Red Rice....122 A1
Ridge....226 A3
Ridge Common....191 J9
The Ridges....40 C2
Ringwood....282 C1
Ripley....304 G6
Riseley....57 P5
Rockbourne....219 L3
Rockford....260 C5
Rogate....217 J2
Romford....258 B3
Romsey....204 C6
Ropley....169 N3
Ropley Dean....169 K2
Ropley Soke....149 P8
Rossmore....321 N5
Rotherwick....53 M7
Rotten Green....56 A8
Round Hill....287 M9

Row Ash....251 N3
Rowland's Castle....257 K9
Rowledge....115 P7
Rowner....294 D9
Rownhams....227 K5
Runfold....97 J8
Rushcombe Bottom....300 A6
Rushington....246 D5
Rushmere....254 C4
Rushmoor....137 J2
St Catherine's Hill....324 C4
St Cross....183 P1
St Denys....248 E3
St Giles's Hill....23 H5
St Ives....281 N4
St Leonards....281 L4
St Mary Bourne....84 C2
Salters Heath....50 G5
Sandbanks....333 L8
Sandford....243 J8
Sandhurst....41 J5
Sandleheath....239 M1
The Sands....97 L9
Sandy Cross....97 M7
Sandy Down....309 J4
Sarisbury....270 C5
Sarson....101 H4
Seale....97 P7
Selborne....152 D9
Selsmore....319 K6
Setley....308 C3
Shalden....132 A1
Shalden Green....112 A6
Shaw....24 E2
Shawford....183 N7
Shedfield....252 B4
Sheet....191 P8
Shepherd's Hill....157 H7
Sherborne St John....50 C9
Sherfield English....202 D4
Sherfield on Loddon....52 F5
Sherfield Park....52 B8
Shipton Bellinger....98 F5
Shirley....305 L6
Shirley....247 P3
Shirley Holms....308 C7
Shirley Warren....247 M1
Shirrell Heath....252 C2
Shobley....261 L9
Sholing....249 K7
Sholing Common....249 J6
Shootash....203 K4
Shorley....186 F5
Shorn Hill....225 N9
Shortfield Common....116 B8
Shortheath....116 B4
Shortheath....153 K2
Shottermill....156 D7
Silchester....35 J6
Silkstead....182 C9
Sladen Green....63 J9
Sleaford....135 J8
Sleepers' Hill....164 E9
Smannell....83 J5
Soake....255 K8
Soberton....253 L2
Soberton Heath....253 L2
Soldridge....149 P6
Somerford....325 J8
Sopley....304 F9
Southampton....20 A6
South Baddesley....330 C1
South Bockhampton....336 C3
Southbourne....183 M9
South Down....219 J9
South Gorley....240 F9
South Ham....68 G9
South Harting....216 E9
South Hayling....318 E6
Southington....86 F4
Southrope....111 J4
Southsea....316 E7
South Tidworth....79 J7
South Town....149 P3
South View....6 E3
South Warnborough....92 G8
South Weirs....286 D9
Southwick....244 D3
South Wonston....144 D5
Southwood....75 J1
Spanish Green....52 G2
Sparsholt....163 M4
Spearywell....179 K3
Spreakley....136 B1
Springbourne....323 L9
Stamshaw....296 E8
Stanbridge....278 C2
Standford....154 D6
Standon....182 C4
Stanford End....57 N5
Stanley Green....320 D5
Stanmore....183 M1
Stanpit....325 J9
Stapehill....279 N9
Steep....191 M5
Steep Marsh....191 N5
Sterte....320 D9
Steventon....87 P2
Stockbridge....141 L5
Stockheath....14 D2
Stoke....62 F8
Stoke....298 C7
Stoke Charity....126 A6
Stoke Common....207 L8
Stonehills....291 L7
Stoner Hill....191 H6
Stoney Cross....243 N7
Stony Batter....225 M8
Stonyford....320 C3
Stony Heath....49 N4
Stonymarsh....179 N5
The Straits....134 E7
Stratfield Mortimer....36 C1
Stratfield Saye....36 G6

Stratfield Turgis....53 H1
Street End....210 A9
Stroud....214 C1
Strouden....323 K6
Stroud Green....17 G5
Stubbermere....277 N2
Stubbington....294 B6
Stuckton....240 G4
Sulhamstead....26 D1
Sulhamstead Abbots....27 H3
Sulhamstead Bannister
Upper End....26 F2
Sutton Scotney....125 M5
Swampton....63 J9
Swanmore....232 F7
Swanwick....270 C3
Swarraton....147 L1
Sway....308 A7
Swaything....228 G9
Sydmonton....47 J5
Tadley....34 E7
Talbot Heath....322 B8
Talbot Village....322 C7
Talbot Woods....322 E8
Tangley....60 D6
Tapnage....272 A1
Terwick Common....193 M9
Testwood....246 C2
Thatcham....25 M3
Thorney Hill....306 A4
Thornhill....249 M4
Thornhill Park....249 M1
Thorns Beach....331 M1
Three Ashes....35 L7
Three Legged Cross....280 E1
Throop....323 K3
Thruxton....100 D2
Tichborne....167 M6
Tidpit....218 D2
Tidworth....79 J5
Tilford....117 K7
Tilford Common....117 H9
Tilford Reeds....117 H7
Tilly Down....81 H4
Timsbury....180 A7
Tipner....296 D6
Tiptoe....307 M8
Titchfield....293 L1
Titchfield Common....271 K9
Titchfield Park....271 K6
Tongham....97 M5
Toothill....227 J3
Totford....128 E9
Tot Hill....30 D5
Totton....246 E3
Townhill Park....249 H1
Towns End....49 K5
Trickett's Cross....302 C1
Trotten Marsh....193 N7
Trotts....246 G8
Tuckton....336 D1
Tufton....85 K9
Tullecombe....193 J6
Tunworth....91 L5
Turbary Common....321 P2
Turgis Green....53 H2
Turkey Island....252 D4
Turmer....260 B2
Twyford....184 A8
Tye....299 J8
Ufton Green....26 D2
Ufton Nervet....26 F3
Up Green....39 P8
Upham....209 M7
Up Nately....71 J8
Upper Bullington....125 L1
Upper Burgate....220 E6
Upper Canterton....243 P5
Upper Clatford....102 C6
Upper Common....110 B3
Upper Enham....82 F3
Upper Farringdon....151 N5
Upper Froyle....113 N8
Upper Hale....96 B5
Upper Pennington....328 G4
Upper Ratley....203 M1
Upper Shirley....247 P1
Upper Slackstead....181 L5
Upper Street....220 D2
Upper Swanmore....232 G4
Upper Wield....130 B7
Upper Wootton....67 P2
Up Somborne....162 D2
Upton....227 H5
Upton....61 L1
Upton Grey....92 A6
Upwood....194 B7
Vernham Bank....42 F7
Vernham Dean....42 G7
Vernham Row....42 G5
Vernham Street....43 J5
Verwood....258 F4
Wadwick....65 M6
Walhampton....329 N5
Walkford....326 D6
Wallington....11 K4
Wallisdown....322 A6
Waltham Chase....232 B8
Walton Heath....275 N5
Warblington....277 J9
Warnborough Green....72 A7
Warnford....212 A1
Warren Corner....190 G1
Warren Corner....95 L4
Warsash....270 D9
Wash Common....30 C1
Wash Water....30 A3
Wasing....33 N1
Waterditch....325 L2
Water End....71 J6
Waterford....329 N5
Waterloo....320 C3
Waterlooville....275 L2
Wecock....255 N8
Weeke....164 E5
Well....94 A9
Wellow Wood....202 D5

Westbourne	334 B4	West Meon	212 D1	Whitchurch	85 L6	Winklebury	68 E6	Woodyates	195 H6
Westbourne	277 P5	West Meon Woodlands	188 E4	Whitehall	72 E6	Winkton	324 G2	Woolmer Hill	156 B6
West Cliff	8 A6	West Moors	280 G7	Whitehill	155 P6	Winnall	23 J5	Woolsbridge	280 G2
West Common	312 G2	Weston	268 G1	Whitehouse Green	27 J1	Winslade	91 H6	Woolston	248 C9
West Dean	177 M3	Weston	215 H5	Whiteley	271 K2	Winsor	245 K2	Woolton Hill	29 L7
West Down	123 K7	Weston Colley	126 E5	Whitenap	204 G6	Wintershill	231 K3	Wootton	307 J6
West End	294 C1	Weston Common	249 K7	Whiteparish	201 J1	Winton	322 F8	Wootton St Lawrence	68 A5
West End	149 L4	Weston Corbett	91 P9	Whitsbury	219 N1	Wittensford	244 D3	Worlds End	254 C6
West End	249 N2	Weston Patrick	92 A9	Whitway	46 C1	Wivelrod	131 L8	Worting	68 D7
West End	135 P1	West Parley	302 F8	Wick	336 F2	Wolverton	49 J4	Wrecclesham	115 P4
West End Green	36 C6	West Southbourne	336 B1	Wick	199 H5	Wolverton Common	49 K1	Wyck	133 N5
Westfield	318 E6	West Stratton	127 L4	Wickham	252 D7	Wonston	125 P6	Wyke	77 L9
West Fields	16 B3	West Tisted	169 P8	Widley	275 L8	Woodcot	294 E6	Wymering	296 C1
West Green	54 E8	West Town	318 E5	Wildern	250 C4	Woodcott	63 N2	Yateley	40 E8
West Grimstead	176 C5	West Tytherley	159 J7	Wildhern	82 C1	Woodfalls	199 N8	York Town	57 P1
West Ham	68 F7	West Wellow	224 E1	Wildmoor	52 F8	Woodgreen	221 H4		
West Harting	216 E6	West Woodhay	28 D5	Wilsom	132 C6	Woodhouse	82 G5		
West Heath	50 B4	West Worldham	152 D1	Wimble Hill	95 J9	Woodington	203 H7		
West Heath	57 M8	Weybourne	96 F5	Wimborne Minster	278 E9	Woodlands	245 L8		
West Howe	301 N9	Weyhill	81 J9	Wimpson	247 J2	Woodlands Common	258 A4		
West Hurn	323 M1	Wheat Hold	33 H8	Winchester	22 E6	Woodley	204 G4		
West Leigh	276 G5	Wheatley	134 E4	Winchfield	73 H2	Woodmancott	108 C9		
West Liss	192 D1	Wherwell	123 J3	Winchfield Hurst	73 K4	Woodside	329 L6		

USING THE STREET INDEX

Street names are listed alphabetically. Each street name is followed by its postal town or area locality, the Postcode District, the page number, and the reference to the square in which the name is found.

Standard index entries are shown as follows:

Aaron Cl *CFDH* BH17 ....**321** H5

Street names and selected addresses not shown on the map due to scale restrictions are shown in the index with an asterisk:

Abbeywood *ASHV* GU12 * **76** G8

GENERAL ABBREVIATIONS

ACC	ACCESS	CTYD	COURTYARD	HLS	HILLS	MWY	MOTORWAY	SE	SOUTH EAST
ALY	ALLEY	CUTT	CUTTINGS	HO	HOUSE	N	NORTH	SER	SERVICE AREA
AP	APPROACH	CV	COVE	HOL	HOLLOW	NE	NORTH EAST	SH	SHORE
AR	ARCADE	CYN	CANYON	HOSP	HOSPITAL	NW	NORTH WEST	SHOP	SHOPPING
ASS	ASSOCIATION	DEPT	DEPARTMENT	HRB	HARBOUR	O/P	OVERPASS	SKWY	SKYWAY
AV	AVENUE	DL	DALE	HTH	HEATH	OFF	OFFICE	SMT	SUMMIT
BCH	BEACH	DM	DAM	HTS	HEIGHTS	ORCH	ORCHARD	SOC	SOCIETY
BLDS	BUILDINGS	DR	DRIVE	HVN	HAVEN	OV	OVAL	SP	SPUR
BND	BEND	DRO	DROVE	HWY	HIGHWAY	PAL	PALACE	SPR	SPRING
BNK	BANK	DRY	DRIVEWAY	IMP	IMPERIAL	PAS	PASSAGE	SQ	SQUARE
BR	BRIDGE	DWGS	DWELLINGS	IN	INLET	PAV	PAVILION	ST	STREET
BRK	BROOK	E	EAST	IND EST	INDUSTRIAL ESTATE	PDE	PARADE	STN	STATION
BTM	BOTTOM	EMB	EMBANKMENT	INF	INFIRMARY	PH	PUBLIC HOUSE	STR	STREAM
BUS	BUSINESS	EMBY	EMBASSY	INFO	INFORMATION	PK	PARK	STRD	STRAND
BVD	BOULEVARD	ESP	ESPLANADE	INT	INTERCHANGE	PKWY	PARKWAY	SW	SOUTH WEST
BY	BYPASS	EST	ESTATE	IS	ISLAND	PL	PLACE	TDG	TRADING
CATH	CATHEDRAL	EX	EXCHANGE	JCT	JUNCTION	PLN	PLAIN	TER	TERRACE
CEM	CEMETERY	EXPY	EXPRESSWAY	JTY	JETTY	PLNS	PLAINS	THWY	THROUGHWAY
CEN	CENTRE	EXT	EXTENSION	KG	KING	PLZ	PLAZA	TNL	TUNNEL
CFT	CROFT	F/O	FLYOVER	KNL	KNOLL	POL	POLICE STATION	TOLL	TOLLWAY
CH	CHURCH	FC	FOOTBALL CLUB	L	LAKE	PR	PRINCE	TPK	TURNPIKE
CHA	CHASE	FK	FORK	LA	LANE	PREC	PRECINCT	TRL	TRACK
CHYD	CHURCHYARD	FLD	FIELD	LDG	LODGE	PREP	PREPARATORY	TRL	TRAIL
CIR	CIRCLE	FLDS	FIELDS	LGT	LIGHT	PRIM	PRIMARY	TWR	TOWER
CIRC	CIRCUS	FLS	FALLS	LK	LOCK	PROM	PROMENADE	U/P	UNDERPASS
CL	CLOSE	FM	FARM	LKS	LAKES	PRS	PRINCESS	UNI	UNIVERSITY
CLFS	CLIFFS	FT	FORT	LNDG	LANDING	PRT	PORT	UPR	UPPER
CMP	CAMP	FTS	FLATS	LTL	LITTLE	PT	POINT	V	VALE
CNR	CORNER	FWY	FREEWAY	LWR	LOWER	PTH	PATH	VA	VALLEY
CO	COUNTY	FY	FERRY	MAG	MAGISTRATE	PZ	PIAZZA	VIAD	VIADUCT
COLL	COLLEGE	GA	GATE	MAN	MANSIONS	QD	QUADRANT	VIL	VILLA
COM	COMMON	GAL	GALLERY	MD	MEAD	QU	QUEEN	VIS	VISTA
COMM	COMMISSION	GDN	GARDEN	MDW	MEADOWS	QY	QUAY	VLG	VILLAGE
CON	CONVENT	GDNS	GARDENS	MEM	MEMORIAL	R	RIVER	VLS	VILLAS
COT	COTTAGE	GLD	GLADE	MI	MILL	RBT	ROUNDABOUT	VW	VIEW
COTS	COTTAGES	GLN	GLEN	MKT	MARKET	RD	ROAD	W	WEST
CP	CAPE	GN	GREEN	MKTS	MARKETS	RDG	RIDGE	WD	WOOD
CPS	COPSE	GND	GROUND	ML	MALL	REP	REPUBLIC	WHF	WHARF
CR	CREEK	GRA	GRANGE	MNR	MANOR	RES	RESERVOIR	WK	WALK
CREM	CREMATORIUM	GRG	GARAGE	MS	MEWS	RFC	RUGBY FOOTBALL CLUB	WKS	WALKS
CRS	CRESCENT	GT	GREAT	MSN	MISSION	RI	RISE	WLS	WELLS
CSWY	CAUSEWAY	GTWY	GATEWAY	MT	MOUNT	RP	RAMP	WY	WAY
CT	COURT	GV	GROVE	MTN	MOUNTAIN	RW	ROW	YD	YARD
CTRL	CENTRAL	HGR	HIGHER	MTS	MOUNTAINS	S	SOUTH	YHA	YOUTH HOSTEL
CTS	COURTS	HL	HILL	MUS	MUSEUM	SCH	SCHOOL		

POSTCODE TOWNS AND AREA ABBREVIATIONS

ALDT	Aldershot	CHOB/PIR	Chobham/Pirbright	HAV	Havant	NMIL/BTOS	New Milton/	STHA	Thatcham south
ALTN	Alton	CWTH	Crowthorne	HEND	Hedge End		Barton on Sea	STOK	Stockbridge
AMSY	Amesbury	DEAN	Deane/Oakley	HISD	Hayling Island	NTHA	Thatcham north	SWGE	Swanage
AND	Andover	ELGH	Eastleigh	HLER	Hamble-le-Rice	NWBY	Newbury	TADY	Tadley
ASH VALE	Ash Vale	EMRTH	Emsworth/	HORN	Horndean	ODIM	Odiham	TDWTH	Tidworth
BDST	Broadstone		Southbourne	HSEA	Hilsea	OVTN	Overton/	THLE	Theale/Rural Reading
BH/HW/K	Brighton Hill/	ENEY	Eastney	HTWY	Hartley Wintney		Rural Basingstoke	TOTT	Totton
	Hatch Warren/	EPSF	Petersfield east	HUNG	Hungerford/	PLE	Poole	TWDS	Talbot Woods
	Kempshott	EWKG	Wokingham east		Lambourn	PSEA	Portsea	UPTN	Upton
BKME/WDN	Branksome/	FARN	Farnborough	ITCH	Itchen	PSF	Petersfield	VWD	Verwood
	Wallisdown	FAWY	Fawley/Hythe	KSCL	Kingsclere/	PSTN	Parkstone	WBNE	Westbourne
BLKW	Blackwater	FBDG	Fordingbridge		Rural Newbury	RAND	Rural Andover	WCLF	West Cliff
BMTH	Bournemouth	FERN	Ferndown/	LIPH	Liphook	RCCH	Rural Chichester	WEND	West End
BOR	Bordon		West Moors	LISS	Liss	RDGW/BURGH	Reading west/	WHAM	Wickham
BOSC	Boscombe	FHAM	Fareham	LSOL/BMARY	Lee-on-the-Solent/		Burghfield	WHCH	Whitchurch
BPWT	Bishop's Waltham	FHAM/PORC	Fareham/		Bridgemary	RFNM	Rural Farnham	WIMB	Wimborne Minster
BROC	Brockenhurst		Porchester	LTDN	Littledown	RGUW	Rural Guildford west	WINC	Winchester
BSTK	Basingstoke	FHAM/STUB	Fareham/	LYMN	Lymington	RGWD	Ringwood	WSHM	Southampton west
BWD	Bearwood		Stubbington	LYND	Lyndhurst	ROMY	Romsey	WVILLE	Waterlooville/
CBLY	Camberley	FLEETN	Fleet north	MARL	Marlborough	ROWN	Rownhams		Denmead
CCLF	Canford Cliffs	FLEETS	Fleet south	MFD/CHID	Milford/	RSAL	Rural Salisbury	YTLY	Yateley
CFDH	Canford Heath	FNM	Farnham		Chiddingfold	RWIN	Rural Winchester		
CHAM	Cosham	FRIM	Frimley	MIDH	Midhurst	SBNE	Southbourne		
CHAR	Charminster	FUFL	Fulflood/	MOOR/WNTN	Moordown/Winton	SD/PW	St Denys/Portswood		
CHCH/BSGR	Christchurch/		Winchester west	NARL	New Alresford	SELS	Selsey		
	Bransgore	GPORT	Gosport	NBAD	North Baddesley	SHAM	Southampton		
CHFD	Chandler's Ford	GSHT	Grayshott	NBNE	Northbourne	SHST	Sandhurst		
CHIN	Chineham	HASM	Haslemere	NEND	North End	SSEA	Southsea		

1

1st St FAWY SO45 .... 291 J6
2nd St FAWY SO45 .... 291 J4
3rd St FAWY SO45 .... 291 H5
4th St FAWY SO45 .... 291 H5
5th St FAWY SO45 .... 291 H4
6th St FAWY SO45 .... 290 G4
7th St FAWY SO45 .... 290 G6
8th St FAWY SO45 .... 290 F5
9th St FAWY SO45 .... 290 G4
10th St FAWY SO45 .... 290 F4
11th St FAWY SO45 .... 290 F4
12th St FAWY SO45 .... 290 F3
13th St FAWY SO45 .... 290 F3

A

Aaron Cl CFDH BH17 .... 321 H5
Aaron Ct TOTT SO40 .... 247 K9
A Av FAWY SO45 .... 290 F4
Abbatt Cl RAND SP11 .... 80 B1
Abbetts La CBLY GU15 .... 58 A2
Abbey Cl FAWY SO45 .... 268 C7
  NWBY RG14 .... 17 F7
Abbey Ct CHIN RG24 .... 69 K3
Abbeydore Cl BOR GU35 .... 154 F3
Abbeydore Rd CHAM PO6 .... 274 E9
Abbeyfield Dr FHAM PO15 .... 272 A3
Abbeyfields Cl HLER SO31 .... 269 M4
Abbey Gdns WIMB BH21 .... 279 M9
Abbey Hill Cl WINC SO23 .... 269 H3
Abbey Hill Cl WINC SO23 .... 31 G5
Abbey Hill Rd WINC SO23 .... 164 C5
Abbey Pk THLE RG7 .... 27 H4
Abbey Pas WINC SO23 .... 23 F5
Abbey Rd ALTN GU34 .... 150 C1
  FARN GU14 .... 69 K4
  FERN BH22 .... 280 G9
  FHAM PO15 .... 272 B8
Abbey Spring La BROC SO42 .... 289 L5
Abbey Water ROMY SO51 .... 204 C6
Abbeywood Av FARN GU14 .... 58 B9
Abbeywood ASHV GU12 * 76 C8
Abbotsbury Rd ELGH SO50 .... 229 P2
  FLEETN GU51 .... 74 D3
Abbots Cl CHCH/BSGR BH23 .... 326 E8
Abbotsfield TOTT SO40 .... 246 C3
Abbotsfield Cl ROWN SO16 .... 227 N7
Abbotsford TOTT SO40 .... 245 H5
Abbot's Ride FLEETN GU51 .... 116 E2
Abbots Rd NWBY RG14 .... 17 F5
  THLE RG7 .... 27 H5
Abbotstone Av NWBY RG14 .... 276 G6
Abbots Wy FHAM PO15 .... 272 B9
  HLER SO31 .... 269 M4
Abbots Well Rd FBDG SP6 .... 241 J5
Abbotswood Cl ROMY SO51 .... 204 C4
Abbotswood Cl BH/HW/K RG22 .... 89 N1
  MOOR/WNTN BH9 .... 322 C7
Abbott Rd MOOR/WNTN BH9 .... 322 C7
Abbotts Ann Rd FUFL SO22 .... 164 C4
  RAND SP11 .... 101 J5
Abbotts Cl RAND SP11 .... 101 N6
Abbotts Dro ROMY SO51 .... 224 E3
Abbotts Hl RAND SP11 .... 101 N6
Abbotts Rd ELGH SO50 .... 228 G3
  TDWTH SP9 .... 78 G4
Abbotts Wy FERN BH22 .... 280 C9
  SD/PW SO17 .... 248 D2
Abbottswood Cl TADY RG26 .... 34 C7
A'Becket Ct PSEA PO1 .... 18 D5
Abercrombie Gdns
  ROWN SO16 .... 227 J4
Aberdare Av CHAM PO6 .... 275 K9
Aberdare Rd NBNE BH10 .... 322 B4
Aberdeen Cl FHAM PO15 .... 10 B2
Aberdeen Rd SD/PW SO17 .... 248 E2
Aberdeen Ter GSHT GU26 .... 156 C2
Aberdour Cl WEND SO18 .... 249 K3
Abex Rd NWBY RG14 .... 17 K2
Abingdon Cl GPORT PO12 .... 12 D3
Abingdon Dr
  CHCH/BSGR BH23 .... 326 E7
Abingdon Gdns ROWN SO16 .... 228 E9
Abingdon Rd CFDH BH17 .... 320 C4
  SHST GU47 .... 41 K6
Abinger Rd ITCH SO19 .... 323 N9
Abney Rd NBNE BH10 .... 322 B4
Aborn Pk THLE RG7 * 27 H6
Above Bar St SHAM SO14 .... 20 D4
Above Town RAND SP11 .... 102 C6
Abraham Cl HEND SO30 .... 248 E2
Acacia Av HAV PO9 .... 283 H4
Acacia Gdns HORN PO8 .... 256 B6
Acacia Rd ITCH SO19 .... 249 H6
  LYMN SO41 .... 327 F3
Academy Pl SHST GU47 .... 41 M7
Acanthus Cl FHAM PO15 .... 271 K1
Accentors Cl ALTN GU34 .... 132 F3
Ace Wy HAV PO9 .... 277 H6
Acheulian Cl FNM GU9 .... 116 C3
Achilles Cl CHIN RG24 .... 52 A9
Ackender Rd ALTN GU34 .... 132 E6
Ackrells Md SHST GU47 .... 40 C5
Ackworth Rd HSEA PO3 .... 297 J4
Acland Rd MOOR/WNTN BH9 .... 323 H7
Acorn Av PLE BH15 .... 332 E1
Acorn Cl BSTK RG21 .... 69 P7
  CHAM PO6 .... 297 N1
  CHCH/BSGR BH23 .... 324 D7
  LSOL/BMARY PO13 .... 295 H8
  NMIL/BTOS BH25 .... 327 J3
  RGWD BH24 .... 203 J6
  TOTT SO40 .... 267 L1
Acorn Ct HLER SO31 .... 269 P7

Acorn Dr CHFD SO53 .... 206 E6
  NTHA RG18 .... 25 N2
  ROWN SO16 .... 227 J5
Acorn Gdns THLE RG7 .... 26 C5
Acorn Gv CHFD SO53 .... 206 B9
Acorn Keep FNM GU9 .... 96 D3
Acorn Rd BLKW GU17 .... 41 J9
The Acorns HLER SO31 .... 269 P2
  RGWD BH24 .... 281 H9
  WIMB BH21 .... 301 J1
Acorn Wy VWD BH31 .... 258 G4
Acre Cl AND SP10 .... 5 F4
Acre La WVILLE PO7 .... 276 C1
Acre Pth AND SP10 .... 5 G4
Acres Rd BWD BH11 .... 322 B5
Acton Rd NBNE BH10 .... 322 B6
Adair Rd ENEY PO4 .... 317 J6
Adam Cl TADY RG26 .... 33 P5
Adames Rd PSEA PO1 .... 316 G2
Adampur Rd TDWTH SP9 .... 78 F6
  RAND SP11 .... 79 M1
Adams Cft CHOB/PIR GU24 .... 59 P6
Adams Dr FLEETN GU51 .... 74 E3
Adamsfield Gdns NBNE BH10 .... 322 C5
Adams Ms LIPH GU30 .... 181 K5
Adamson Cl CHFD SO53 .... 206 C5
Adams Ter CHAM PO6 * 297 L3
Adams Wy ALTN GU34 .... 132 C5
  FHAM PO15 .... 271 J5
Adams Wood Dr TOTT SO40 .... 267 K1
Adastral Rd CFDH BH17 .... 321 H4
  PLE BH15 .... 320 C5
Adbury Holt KSCL RG20 .... 30 F4
Adderbury Av EMRTH PO10 .... 277 M6
Addington Pl
  CHCH/BSGR BH23 * 325 H9
Addiscombe Rd
  CHCH/BSGR BH23 .... 324 E8
  CWTH RG45 .... 41 K2
Addison Cl FUFL SO22 .... 183 L1
Addison Gdns ODIM RG29 .... 72 D9
Addison Rd BROC SO42 .... 286 F9
  ELGH SO50 .... 207 K8
  FRIM GU16 .... 58 D5
  HLER SO31 .... 270 F4
  SSEA PO5 .... 19 J6
Addison Sq RGWD BH24 .... 282 F2
Adelaide Cl CHCH/BSGR BH23 .... 324 D7
Adelaide Rd FHAM/PORC PO16 .... 11 J6
  SHAM SO14 .... 4 E4
  SD/PW SO17 .... 248 E3
Adela Verne Cl ITCH SO19 .... 249 N8
Adeline Rd BMTH BH1 .... 335 L2
Adey Cl ITCH SO19 .... 249 K9
Adey's Cl NWBY RG14 * 17 G5
Adlityard Rd HAV PO9 .... 276 G6
Adlam's La LYMN SO41 .... 307 P5
Adlington Pl FARN GU14 .... 76 D2
Admers Crs LIPH GU30 .... 175 K5
The Admiral Pk HSEA PO3 * 297 K6
Admirals Cl FAWY SO45 .... 291 K6
Admirals Rd HLER SO31 .... 271 H6
Admiral's Wk PSEA PO1 * 18 B1
Admirals Wk WCLF BH2 * 8 A6
Admiralty Cl GPORT PO12 .... 315 N1
  SBNE BH6 .... 336 D5
Admiralty Wy CBLY GU15 .... 57 N1
  TOTT SO40 .... 247 K8
Adrian Cl HTWY RG27 .... 55 J3
Adsdean Cl HAV PO9 .... 276 E6
Adstone La HSEA PO3 .... 297 L5
Adur Cl GPORT PO12 .... 315 K1
  WEND SO18 .... 249 K2
Adwood Ct STHA RG19 .... 25 P4
Aerial Rd CHAM PO6 .... 274 D8
Aerodrome Rd
  LSOL/BMARY PO13 .... 295 N5
Aerospace Bvd FARN GU14 .... 75 N5
Africa Dr TOTT SO40 .... 267 K1
Agars La LYMN SO41 .... 308 A9
Agarton La LYMN SO41 .... 328 F9
Aggis Farm Rd VWD BH31 .... 258 E4
Aghemund Cl CHIN RG24 .... 69 P1
Agincourt Rd NEND PO2 .... 316 F1
Agitator Rd FAWY SO45 .... 291 L4
Agnew Rd LSOL/BMARY PO13 .... 294 G6
Agra Rd TDWTH SP9 .... 78 E7
Agravaine Cl AND SP10 .... 82 E8
Agricola Wk AND SP10 .... 82 F8
Aikman La TOTT SO40 .... 245 P4
Ailsa La ITCH SO19 .... 248 F7
Ainger Cl ASHV GU12 .... 3 K1
Ainsdale Rd CHAM PO6 .... 275 M9
Ainsley Gdns ELGH SO50 .... 207 J8
Aintree Cl ELGH SO50 .... 230 D5
  FRIM GU16 .... 17 J6
Aintree Dr WVILLE PO7 .... 276 B1
Aintree Rd TOTT SO40 .... 246 A2
Aircraft Esp FARN GU14 .... 76 B3
Aird Cl KSCL RG20 .... 30 C6
Airetons Cl BDST BH18 .... 320 E1
Airfield Rd CHCH/BSGR BH23 .... 325 K8
Airfield Wy CHCH/BSGR BH23 .... 325 K8
Airlie Cnr FUFL SO22 .... 164 F9
Airlie La FUFL SO22 .... 22 A7
Airlie Rd FUFL SO22 .... 22 B7
Airport Service Rd HSEA PO3 .... 297 K6
Airspeed Rd
  CHCH/BSGR BH23 .... 325 M8
Aisne Rd FRIM GU16 .... 59 K4
Ajax Cl CHIN RG24 .... 52 A9
  FHAM/STUB PO14 .... 294 B8
Akeshill Cl NMIL/BTOS BH25 .... 327 K2
Alameda Rd WVILLE PO7 .... 275 M6
Alameda Wy WVILLE PO7 .... 275 M6
Alamein Rd ALDT GU11 .... 3 F2
Alanbrooke Cl HTWY RG27 .... 55 H1
Alanbrooke Rd ALDT GU11 .... 76 C6
Alandale Rd ITCH SO19 .... 249 M7

Alan Drayton Wy ELGH SO50 .... 229 M3
Alan Gv FHAM PO15 .... 10 A4
Albacore Av HLER SO31 * 270 E9
Albacore Cl
  LSOL/BMARY PO13 .... 314 E3
Albany Cl FLEETN GU51 .... 74 E4
  NMIL/BTOS BH25 .... 327 H6
Albany Ct BPWT SO32 .... 231 N4
Albany Dr BPWT SO32 .... 231 N4
  WIMB BH21 .... 280 E1
Albany Gdns PLE BH15 .... 332 B1
Albany Pk FRIM GU16 .... 58 B4
Albany Rd AND SP10 .... 102 C2
  FAWY SO45 .... 290 E5
  FLEETN GU51 .... 74 D4
  ROMY SO51 .... 204 C6
  SSEA PO5 .... 19 J7
  WSHM SO15 .... 247 N5
Albatross Wk
  LSOL/BMARY PO13 .... 294 F7
Albemarle Av GPORT PO12 .... 315 M1
Albemarle Rd TWDS BH3 .... 322 F8
Albert Cl HLER SO31 .... 269 L5
Albert Gv SSEA PO5 .... 19 K7
Albert Rd ALDT GU11 .... 3 G5
  ALTN GU34 .... 132 E7
  BKME/WDN BH12 .... 321 M7
  BMTH BH1 .... 8 E3
  BPWT SO32 .... 231 P5
  CHAM PO6 .... 297 H2
  CWTH RG45 .... 41 L2
  ELGH SO50 .... 207 K8
  ENEY PO4 .... 316 G6
  FARN GU14 .... 76 B2
  FERN BH22 .... 280 D6
  FHAM/STUB PO14 .... 294 D7
  HEND SO30 .... 230 D6
  NMIL/BTOS BH25 .... 327 H5
  NWBY RG14 .... 16 D1
Albert Rd North SHAM SO14 .... 21 H6
Albert Rd South SHAM SO14 .... 21 H7
Albert St FLEETN GU51 .... 74 C3
  GPORT PO12 .... 13 G2
Albion Cl BKME/WDN BH12 .... 321 J5
  FHAM/PORC PO16 .... 295 M3
Albion Pl SHAM SO14 .... 20 D5
  SHST GU47 .... 41 J7
Albion Wy VWD BH31 .... 258 D3
Albright La BKME/WDN BH12 .... 321 J6
Albury Pl CHFD SO53 .... 206 D4
Albury Wy STHA RG19 .... 25 J2
Alby Rd BKME/WDN BH12 .... 321 P7
Alcantara Crs SHAM SO14 .... 21 H7
Alcester Rd BKME/WDN BH12 .... 321 M6
Alchorne Pl HSEA PO3 .... 297 L6
Alcot Cl CWTH RG45 .... 41 J2
Alderbrook Cl CWTH RG45 .... 40 F1
Alder Cl ALTN GU34 .... 132 E4
  ASHV GU12 .... 76 F5
  CHCH/BSGR BH23 .... 325 H6
  FAWY SO45 .... 267 N7
  NWBY RG14 .... 24 G3
  ROMY SO51 .... 205 H5
  ROWN SO16 .... 208 A5
  TOTT SO40 .... 247 K9
Alder Crs BKME/WDN BH12 .... 321 N5
Alder Hangar Cl AND SP10 .... 82 A8
Alderfield PSF GU32 .... 215 L2
Alder Gld THLE RG7 .... 27 H6
Alder Gv YTLY GU46 .... 40 D9
Alder Hts BKME/WDN BH12 .... 322 A9
Alderholt Rd FBDG SP6 .... 239 N2
Alder La NBNE BH10 .... 322 A8
Alderley Rd NBNE BH10 .... 322 D3
Aldermaston Rd CHIN RG24 .... 68 C2
  TADY RG26 .... 34 B4
Aldermaston Road Rbt
  BSTK RG21 .... 69 J4
Aldermaston Rd South
  BSTK RG21 .... 6 A2
Aldermoor Av ROWN SO16 .... 227 L8
Aldermoor Cl ROWN SO16 .... 227 N8
Aldermoor Rd
  LSOL/BMARY PO13 .... 315 H1
  ROWN SO16 .... 227 L8
  WVILLE PO7 .... 275 M6
Aldermoor Rd East
  WVILLE PO7 .... 275 M6
Alderney Av BH/HW/K RG22 .... 89 M4
  BKME/WDN BH12 .... 321 M6
Alderney Cl ROWN SO16 .... 227 J8
Alder Rd BKME/WDN BH12 .... 321 P6
  BOR GU35 .... 182 F3
  ROWN SO16 .... 227 K9
Alders Cl BDST BH18 .... 319 P1
Aldersey Flds ALTN GU34 .... 132 F4
Aldershot Rd ASHV GU12 .... 97 M2
  FLEETS GU52 .... 74 C8
Alders Rd FHAM/PORC PO16 .... 294 F2
The Alders FNM GU9 .... 96 G5
  NTHA RG18 .... 25 N3
Alderwood CHIN RG24 .... 69 N1
Alderwood Av CHFD SO53 .... 206 C7
Alderwood Cl HAV PO9 .... 276 A7
Alder Wood Dr HTWY RG27 .... 72 A2
Aldis Gdns PLE BH15 .... 332 A1
Aldrich Rd PSEA PO1 .... 316 E1
Aldridge Cl HORN PO8 .... 236 C7
Aldridge Rd BKME/WDN BH12 .... 302 D5
  CHAM PO6 .... 274 D1
Aldridge Wy FERN BH22 .... 302 F5
Aldrin Cl AND SP10 .... 82 C8
Aldrin Pl FARN GU14 .... 57 L9
Aldsworth Cl CHAM PO6 .... 297 L1
Aldsworth Ct CHAM PO6 .... 297 L1
Aldsworth Gdns CHAM PO6 .... 297 L1
Aldwell St SSEA PO5 .... 19 J4
Aldwick Cl FARN GU14 .... 59 L9
Aldworth Crs BH/HW/K RG22 .... 69 H8
Aldworth Gdns CWTH RG45 .... 41 H1
Alec Rose La PSEA PO1 .... 18 E3
Alecto Rd GPORT PO12 .... 12 C5

Alencon Cl GPORT PO12 .... 295 N9
Alencon Link BSTK RG21 .... 6 E5
Alexander Cl
  CHCH/BSGR BH23 .... 325 J9
  SHST GU47 .... 41 M7
  STOK SO20 .... 160 G2
  TOTT SO40 .... 246 B3
  WVILLE PO7 * 275 M5
Alexander Gv
  FHAM/PORC PO16 .... 294 E1
Alexander Rd OVTN RG25 .... 86 G4
  STHA RG19 .... 25 P5
Alexandra Av CBLY GU15 .... 11 F9
  HISD PO11 .... 318 F6
Alexandra Cl FAWY SO45 .... 268 C6
Alexandra Ct BOR GU35 .... 154 A7
  FARN GU14 .... 76 B3
Alexandra Pk NEND PO2 .... 296 F6
Alexandra Rd ALDT GU11 * 2 A1
  ALTN GU34 .... 132 F4
  AND SP10 .... 4 C3
  ASHV GU12 .... 97 M2
  BSTK RG21 .... 6 B6
  CHFD SO53 .... 207 H5
  FARN GU14 .... 76 B3
  FAWY SO45 .... 268 C6
  FBDG SP6 .... 240 D1
  HEND SO30 .... 250 B6
  LYMN SO41 .... 329 J2
  PSEA PO1 .... 316 F2
  SBNE BH6 .... 335 P1
  WSHM SO15 .... 247 P5
Alexandra St GPORT PO12 .... 315 L2
Alexandra Ter ALDT GU11 * 2 D3
  ODIM RG29 * 72 B8
  WINC SO23 .... 22 C6
Alexandra Wy HEND SO30 .... 250 C4
Alexandria Rd RWIN SO21 .... 125 M4
Alex Wy NEND PO2 .... 296 F6
Alfonso Cl ASHV GU12 .... 3 J6
Alford Cl SHST GU47 .... 41 H7
Alford Rd TWDS BH3 .... 322 D8
Alfred Cl FLEETN GU51 .... 74 A1
  TOTT SO40 .... 246 A4
Alfred Gdns AND SP10 .... 82 D9
Alfred Rd FHAM/STUB PO14 .... 294 B6
  FNM GU9 .... 116 C1
  PSEA PO1 .... 19 F2
Alfred Rose Ct WEND SO18 * 228 G3
Alfred St SHAM SO14 .... 21 G1
Alfriston Gdns ITCH SO19 .... 249 K8
Alfriston Rd FRIM GU16 .... 59 H6
Algiers Rd HSEA PO3 .... 297 K9
Alhambra Rd ENEY PO4 .... 316 C7
Alice Rd ALDT GU11 .... 3 F3
Alington Cl FARN GU14 .... 75 N1
Alington Ri HTWY RG27 .... 52 B8
Alington Rd BMTH BH1 .... 333 L4
  TWDS BH3 .... 322 G9
Alipore Cl PSTN BH14 .... 321 M9
Alison Cl FARN GU14 .... 75 N1
Alison Wy ALDT GU11 * 2 B3
  FUFL SO22 .... 22 C3
Alladin Av ROMY SO51 .... 204 F6
Allaway Av CHAM PO6 .... 296 B1
Allbrook Cl HAV PO9 .... 276 D4
Allbrook Hl ELGH SO50 .... 207 K6
Allbrook Knoll ELGH SO50 .... 207 J6
Allbrook Wy ELGH SO50 .... 207 J5
Allcot Rd HSEA PO3 .... 297 H7
Allee Dr LIPH GU30 .... 175 J2
Allenby Cl CFDH BH17 .... 320 D2
Allenby Gv FHAM/PORC PO16 .... 295 N2
Allenby Rd CBLY GU15 .... 41 P8
  CFDH BH17 * 320 D3
  GPORT PO12 .... 315 J2
Allen Cl ALTN GU34 .... 132 G4
  BSTK RG21 .... 69 J9
Allen Ct WIMB BH21 .... 278 E9
Allendale Av EMRTH PO10 .... 277 L7
Allendale Cl SHST GU47 .... 41 H4
Allen Rd HEND SO30 .... 250 C4
  WIMB BH21 .... 300 E1
Allen's Cl AND SP10 .... 82 D9
Allen's Rd SSEA PO5 .... 316 G6
Allenview Rd WIMB BH21 .... 278 E9
Allen Water Dr FBDG SP6 .... 240 C1
Allerton Cl TOTT SO40 .... 246 B1
Alliance Cl
  LSOL/BMARY PO13 .... 295 H9
Allington La HEND SO30 .... 229 K9
Allington Rd WSHM SO15 .... 247 N4
Allison Wy BH/HW/K RG22 .... 68 E9
  WHCH RG28 .... 87 J5
Allmara Dr WVILLE PO7 .... 275 N5
Allnutt Av BSTK RG21 .... 7 H6
Allotment Rd HLER SO31 .... 270 E5
  HLER SO31 .... 247 H2
All Saints Crs FARN GU14 .... 57 M4
All Saints Gdns FARN GU14 .... 57 M4
All Saints Rd LYMN SO41 .... 329 G5
All Saint's Rd PSEA PO1 .... 316 F1
Alma Cl ASHV GU12 .... 76 C9
Alma La FNM GU9 .... 59 J5
Alma La BPWT SO32 .... 232 C1
  FNM GU9 .... 96 C4
Alma Rd BOR GU35 .... 154 B5
  MOOR/WNTN BH9 .... 322 G6
  ROMY SO51 .... 204 D6
  SHAM SO14 .... 4 E1
Alma St GPORT PO12 .... 315 L2
Almatade Rd WEND SO18 .... 249 J4
Alma Ter ENEY PO4 .... 317 J5
Alma Wy FNM GU9 .... 96 C4
Almer Rd PLE BH15 .... 320 A9
Almond Av NWBY RG14 .... 24 D2
Almond Cl CHIN RG24 .... 70 B6
  FARN GU14 .... 96 G2
  HAV PO9 .... 297 P1
  HORN PO8 .... 256 C7
Almond Dr NTHA RG18 .... 25 M2
Almond Gv BKME/WDN BH12 .... 321 N5
Almond Rd WSHM SO15 .... 248 A3
Almondsbury Rd CHAM PO6 .... 274 B8

Almondside
  LSOL/BMARY PO13 .... 295 J8
Almswood Rd TADY RG26 .... 34 B4
The Aloes FLEETN GU51 .... 74 E4
Alphage Rd GPORT PO12 .... 295 K8
Alpha Rd ASHV GU12 .... 97 K2
Alphington Av FRIM GU16 .... 58 E4
Alphington Gn FRIM GU16 .... 58 D4
Alpine Cl FARN GU14 .... 75 L1
  WEND SO18 .... 249 K3
Alpine Ct BH/HW/K RG22 .... 68 D9
Alpine Rd BOR GU35 .... 154 A7
  RCWD BH24 .... 282 A7
Alpine St TOTT SO40 .... 245 M8
Alresford Dro RWIN SO21 .... 144 G3
Alresford La NARL SO24 .... 168 D9
Alresford Rd HAV PO9 .... 276 E6
  NARL SO24 .... 167 M3
  RWIN SO21 .... 165 N8
  WINC SO23 .... 23 F5
Alsford Rd WVILLE PO7 .... 275 M5
Alston Ms STHA RG19 .... 25 M5
Alswitha Ter WINC SO23 * 22 E2
Althorpe Dr HSEA PO3 .... 297 L5
Altona Gdns AND SP10 .... 82 D8
Alton Cl ELGH SO50 .... 230 B2
Alton Gv FHAM/PORC PO16 .... 295 N3
Alton La ALTN GU34 .... 150 C8
Alton Ride BLKW GU17 .... 41 K8
Alton Rd FLEETN GU51 .... 74 F3
  NBNE BH10 .... 322 D6
  ODIM RG29 .... 71 J9
  PSTN BH14 .... 321 K9
  RFNM GU10 .... 115 M3
Alton Rd East PSTN BH14 .... 333 M1
Alum Chine Rd WBNE BH4 .... 334 D3
Alum Cl FAWY SO45 .... 290 F5
Alumdale Rd WBNE BH4 .... 334 B4
Alumhurst Rd WBNE BH4 .... 334 C5
Alum Rd FHAM/PORC PO16 .... 275 J9
  SWTH BH6 .... 335 H2
Alvara Rd GPORT PO12 .... 12 B6
Alver Bridge Vw GPORT PO12 .... 12 C5
Alverclilfe Dr GPORT PO12 .... 315 K6
Alver Rd GPORT PO12 .... 12 C4
  PSEA PO1 .... 316 G2
Alverstoke Gdns ALDT GU11 .... 2 A5
Alverstone Rd ENEY PO4 .... 317 J4
Alverton Av PLE BH15 .... 321 H9
Alveston Av
  FHAM/STUB PO14 .... 294 A1
Alwin Pl FNM GU9 .... 96 C1
Alyth Rd TWDS BH3 .... 322 C9
Amarylis Cl FHAM PO15 .... 271 L6
Amazon Cl BSTK RG21 .... 6 A3
Ambarrow Crs SHST GU47 .... 40 G5
Ambarrow La SHST GU47 .... 40 E4
Ambassador Cl
  CHCH/BSGR BH23 .... 325 L9
Amber Cl BOR GU35 .... 154 B6
Amber Gdns AND SP10 .... 102 B2
Amber Hl CBLY GU15 .... 58 C1
Amberley Cl
  CHCH/BSGR BH23 .... 326 A7
  HEND SO30 .... 250 F3
  NBNE BH10 .... 322 B3
  NWBY RG14 .... 24 C3
Amberley Ct SD/PW SO17 .... 246 C5
Amberley Gra ALDT GU11 .... 2 B6
Amberley Rd GPORT PO12 .... 295 L9
  HORN PO8 .... 236 D7
  NEND PO2 .... 297 H6
Ambersdale Wk FAWY SO45 .... 268 B9
Amberwood Cl TOTT SO40 .... 246 A1
Amberwood Dr
  CHCH/BSGR BH23 .... 326 C5
Amberwood Gdns
  CHCH/BSGR BH23 .... 326 C5
Ambleside HLER SO31 .... 270 E6
  CWTH RG45 .... 41 K2
  HLER SO31 .... 250 D6
Ambleside Cl BDST BH18 .... 319 M9
  FARN GU14 .... 57 M9
  FRIM GU16 .... 76 F2
Ambleside Crs FNM GU9 .... 96 A5
Ambleside Gdns ITCH SO19 .... 249 J8
Ambleside Rd LYMN SO41 .... 329 L5
Ambrose Rd TADY RG26 .... 34 B4
Ambury La CHCH/BSGR BH23 .... 325 K7
Amersham Cl GPORT PO12 .... 315 J4
Amery Hl ALTN GU34 .... 132 F5
Amery St ALTN GU34 .... 132 E6
Amesbury Rd AMSY SP4 .... 118 E3
  RAND SP11 .... 100 C1
  SBNE BH6 .... 324 A9
Amethyst Gv WVILLE PO7 .... 276 B2
Amethyst Rd
  CHCH/BSGR BH23 .... 325 K8
Amey Gdns CHAM PO6 .... 297 P2
Ameysford Rd FERN BH22 .... 302 C1
Ameys La FERN BH22 .... 302 F1
Amherst Rd BOR GU35 .... 153 P2
Amoy St WSHM SO15 .... 248 B5
Ampere Rd NWBY RG14 .... 17 C1
Ampfield Cl HAV PO9 .... 276 A7
Ampfield Rd CHAM PO6 .... 274 D1
Amport Cl CHIN RG24 .... 70 B4
  FUFL SO22 .... 164 C4
Amport Ct HAV PO9 .... 276 D4
Ampress La LYMN SO41 .... 329 L1
Ampthill Rd WSHM SO15 .... 247 M4
Amsterdam Sq
  CHCH/BSGR BH23 .... 325 H8
Amyas Ct FNNY SO41 .... 317 L4
Ancasta Rd SHAM SO14 .... 248 C4
Ancells Rd FLEETN GU51 .... 56 E8
Anchorage Rd HSEA PO3 .... 297 J6
The Anchorage GPORT PO12 .... 13 F5
Anchorage Wy LYMN SO41 .... 329 L2
Anchor Cl BWD BH11 .... 301 P8
Anchor Cl BDST BH18 .... 337 L1
  RGUW GU3 .... 77 P8
Anchor Gate Rd PSEA PO1 .... 316 C2
Anchor La PSEA PO1 .... 18 B1

Anchor Meadow *FARN* GU14 57 N9
Anchor Ms *LYMN* SO41 329 L3
Anchor Rd *BWD* BH11 301 P8
KSCL RG20 48 C3
Anchor Yd *BSTK* RG21 7 F7
KSCL RG20 48 C3
Andalusian Gdns *FHAM* PO15 271 H2
Andeferas Rd *AND* SP10 82 D8
Anderby Rd *ROWN* SO16 247 H1
Andersen Cl *FHAM* PO15 271 J2
Anderson Cl *HAV* PO9 15 H2
ROMY SO51 204 G3
Anderson Gdns *TADY* RG26 34 C5
Andersons Rd *SHAM* SO14 21 H6
Anders Rd *RWIN* SO21 144 F4
Anderwood Dr *LYMN* SO41 308 B6
Andes Cl *SHAM* SO14 21 J7
Andes Rd *ROWN* SO16 226 F9
Andlers Ash Rd *LISS* GU33 192 C4
Andover Cl *CHCH/BSGR* BH23 325 M8
Andover Dro *KSCL* RG20 30 A2
Andover La *RAND* SP11 80 A4
Andover Rd *BLKW* GU17 41 K8
DEAN RG23 67 L9
ENEY PO4 317 H6
FUFL SO22 164 G5
KSCL RG20 30 A4
NWBY RG14 16 C6
OVTN RG25 87 N3
RAND SP11 79 P1
RAND SP11 81 H8
RWIN SO21 107 H8
WINC SO23 22 D1
WSHM SO15 247 P5
Andover Rd North *RWIN* SO21 144 D9
Andover Wy *ALDT* GU11 97 H4
Andrew Bell St *PSEA* PO1 316 E2
Andrew Cl *FAWY* SO45 268 C9
HSEA PO3 317 H2
TOTT SO40 246 B4
Andrew Crs *WVILLE* PO7 275 M1
Andrewes Cl *BPWT* SO32 232 A4
Andrew La *NMIL/BTOS* BH25 327 M5
Andrew Pl *FHAM/STUB* PO14 293 P7
Andrews Cl *BWD* BH11 322 A4
FLEETS GU52 74 D6
Andrew's La *NARL* SO24 170 A2
ODIM RG29 93 M8
Andrews Rd *FARN* GU14 57 M8
Andromeda Rd *ROWN* SO16 227 J8
Andwell La *HTWY* RG27 71 H6
Anfield Cl *ELGH* SO50 230 C3
Angel Ct *NWBY* RG14 24 D3
Angel Crs *ITCH* SO19 249 H5
Angelica Gdns *ELGH* SO50 230 C5
Angelica Wy *FHAM* PO15 271 L2
Angeline Cl *CHCH/BSGR* BH23 326 B7
Angel La *FERN* BH22 302 B5
NMIL/BTOS BH25 327 M7
Angel Mdw *ODIM* RG29 72 D9
Angelo Cl *WVILLE* PO7 276 A2
Angelus Cl *FHAM/STUB* PO14 294 A7
Angerstein Rd *NEND* PO2 296 F8
Anglers Pl *BSTK* RG21 7 K6
Anglers Wy *HLER* SO31 270 D2
Anglesea Rd
LSOL/BMARY PO13 314 E4
PSEA PO1 19 F3
WSHM SO15 247 M2
Anglesea Ter *SHAM* SO14 21 H6
Anglesey Arms Rd
GPORT PO12 12 A7
Anglesey Av *FARN* GU14 57 N6
Anglesey Cl *AND* SP10 102 E5
CHIN RG24 69 M2
Anglesey Rd *ASHV* GU12 3 K4
GPORT PO12 12 A7
Anglesey Vw *GPORT* PO12 * 12 D4
Angora Wy *FLEETN* GU51 56 E9
Angus Cl *FHAM* PO15 10 A2
Anjou Cl *BWD* BH11 301 M8
Anjou Crs *FHAM* PO15 272 B8
Anker La *FHAM/STUB* PO14 294 A5
Ankerwyke
LSOL/BMARY PO13 294 F8
Anmore Cl *HAV* PO9 276 D6
Anmore Dr *WVILLE* PO7 255 M9
Anmore La *WVILLE* PO7 255 L7
Anmore Rd *WVILLE* PO7 255 J7
Anna La *CHCH/BSGR* BH23 304 E4
Annandale Dr *RFNM* GU10 116 D4
Anne Armstrong Cl
ALDT GU11 76 C7
Anne Cl *CHCH/BSGR* BH23 324 E6
Anne Crs *WVILLE* PO7 275 N4
Annerley Rd *BMTH* BH1 9 K2
Annes Wy *FLEETS* GU52 74 E6
Annet Cl *PLE* BH15 332 A1
Annettes Cft *FLEETS* GU52 74 B8
Ann's Hill Rd *GPORT* PO12 12 A3
Ansell Rd *FRIM* GU16 58 D5
Anson Cl *ALDT* GU11 2 B1
CHCH/BSGR BH23 325 K9
LSOL/BMARY PO13 315 H3
RGWD BH24 282 G1
Anson Dr *ITCH* SO19 249 L6
Anson Gv *FHAM/PORC* PO16 273 P9
Anson Rd *ELGH* SO50 230 C5
ENEY PO4 317 H3
Anstey Cl *BSTK* RG21 90 C1
BWD BH11 322 A1
Anstey La *ALTN* GU34 132 F2
Anstey Mill Cl *ALTN* GU34 133 H4
Anstey Mill La *ALTN* GU34 133 H4
Anstey Pl *THLE* RG7 27 J4
Anstey Rd *ALTN* GU34 132 G4
BWD BH11 322 A2
ROMY SO51 204 F4
Antar Cl *BSTK* RG21 6 A7
Antell's Wy *FBDG* SP6 239 N5
Anthill Cl *WVILLE* PO7 254 E5
Anthony Gv *GPORT* PO12 295 K8
Anthony Pl *GSHT* GU26 * 156 E4
Anthony's Av *PSTN* BH14 333 L2
Antler Dr *NMIL/BTOS* BH25 326 G3
Anton Cl *DEAN* RG23 88 F2
ROMY SO51 204 G6
Anton La *RAND* SP11 82 F5
Anton Mill Rd *AND* SP10 4 B7
Anton Rd *AND* SP10 4 C7
Antrim Cl *BH/HW/K* RG22 68 E9
Anvil Cl *TADY* RG26 52 A2
WVILLE PO7 276 C1
Anvil Crs *BDST* BH18 300 A8
Anvil Wy *TADY* RG26 52 A2
Anzac Cl *FHAM/STUB* PO14 294 A5
Anzio Cl *ALDT* GU11 2 E2
Apex Dr *FRIM* GU16 58 C4
Apless La *WVILLE* PO7 254 B7
Apollo Cl *BKME/WDN* BH12 321 M5
Apollo Dr *BOR* GU35 154 B6
WVILLE PO7 275 P7
Apollo Pl *WEND* SO18 * 249 J4
Apollo Ri *FARN* GU14 57 K9
Apollo Rd *CHFD* SO53 207 H6
Appelford Cl *STHA* RG19 25 N5
Apple Cl *BKME/WDN* BH12 334 A2
Apple Dene *TADY* RG26 52 A3
Appledore Ms *FARN* GU14 57 P6
Appledown Cl *NARL* SO24 168 A3
Appledown La *NARL* SO24 168 B4
Applegarth Cl *BSTK* RG21 69 M9
Applegate Pl *HORN* PO8 * 256 C6
Apple Gv *CHCH/BSGR* BH23 324 C5
EMRTH PO10 277 P9
Applelands Cl *RFNM* GU10 116 A6
Applemore Hl *FAWY* SO45 267 M5
Appleshaw Cl *FUFL* SO22 164 E3
TADY RG26 34 C7
Appleshaw Gn *HAV* PO9 276 C6
Appleshaw Wy *RAND* SP11 79 M5
Appleslade Wy
NMIL/BTOS BH25 327 K2
Appleton Cl *STOK* SO20 120 C8
Appleton Dr *CHIN* RG24 69 L2
Appleton Ms *AND* SP10 4 E7
Appleton Rd *FHAM* PO15 272 A9
WEND SO18 248 G2
Appleton Vw *ALTN* GU34 171 L2
Apple Tree Cl *NWBY* RG14 24 B8
RSAL SP5 199 P6
Appletree Cl *DEAN* RG23 88 F3
NMIL/BTOS BH25 327 J6
SBNE BH6 336 A1
TOTT SO40 246 A3
Appletree Ct *HEND* SO30 250 G4
LYND SO43 264 G6
Apple Tree Gv *AND* SP10 102 B1
FERN BH22 302 E3
Appletree Md *HTWY* RG27 72 B3
Apple Tree Rd *FBDG* SP6 239 M6
Appletree Rd *RSAL* SP5 199 P6
Apple Tree Wy *SHST* GU47 41 L5
Apple Wy *CHIN* RG24 70 C7
Applewood Gv *WVILLE* PO7 275 L8
Applewood Pl *TOTT* SO40 246 A5
Applewood Rd *HAV* PO9 14 A2
Approach Rd *FNM* GU9 116 C1
PSTN BH14 321 K9
The Approach *HSEA* PO3 * 297 J8
April Cl *BWD* BH11 322 A3
CBLY GU15 58 B3
WEND SO18 249 K4
April Gdns *FAWY* SO45 290 G8
April Gv *HLER* SO31 270 E7
April Sq *PSEA* PO1 19 J1
Apron Rd *STHA* RG19 31 M1
Apsley Cl *AND* SP10 102 D5
Apsley Crs *CFDH* BH17 320 E3
Apsley Pl *CHFD* SO53 206 D4
Apsley Rd *ENEY* PO4 317 J4
Aquarius Cl *RFNM* GU10 94 F2
Aquila Wy *HLER* SO31 269 P8
Arabian Gdns *FHAM* PO15 271 J3
Aragon Rd *YTLY* GU46 56 D1
Aragon Wy *MOOR/WNTN* BH9 323 H2
Arakan Crs *TOTT* SO40 267 K1
The Arboretum *OVTN* RG25 92 B5
Arbour Ct *FHAM* PO15 271 K1
The Arcade *ALDT* GU11 * 2 E3
BMTH BH1 8 D4
LISS GU33 192 C1
Arcadia Av *CHAR* BH8 323 H8
Arcadia Cl *BH/HW/K* RG22 89 L7
ROWN SO16 227 M9
Arcadia Rd *CHCH/BSGR* BH23 324 D6
Archdale Cl *NBNE* BH10 322 D5
Archers *WSHM* SO15 * 248 B4
Archers Cl *TOTT* SO40 246 A1
Archers Rd *ELGH* SO50 207 J9
WSHM SO15 248 A5
Archery Flds *ODIM* RG29 72 D9
Archery Gdns *ITCH* SO19 249 H9
Archery Gv *ITCH* SO19 248 G9
Archery La *FHAM/PORC* PO16 11 J4
WINC SO23 22 C5
Archery Ri *ALTN* GU34 132 E7
Archery Rd *ITCH* SO19 268 G1
Archway Rd *PSTN* BH14 321 N8
Arcot Rd *TDWTH* SP9 78 F8
Arden Cl *GPORT* PO12 315 K4
WEND SO18 249 K2
Arden Rd *MOOR/WNTN* BH9 322 F4
Arden Wk *NMIL/BTOS* BH25 327 K5
Ardglen Rd *WHCH* RG28 85 K6
Ardingly Crs *HEND* SO30 250 D1
Ardington Ri *WVILLE* PO7 275 N7
Ardmore Rd *PSTN* BH14 321 K8
Ardwell Cl *CWTH* RG45 40 F1
Arena La *ALDT* GU11 75 M8
Arenal Dr *CWTH* RG45 41 J3
Arford Common *BOR* GU35 154 G2
Arford Rd *BOR* GU35 154 G2
Argente Cl *FLEETN* GU51 56 E9
Argent Ter *SHST* GU47 * 41 M6
Argosy Cl *HLER* SO31 270 F9
Argyle Cl *BOR* GU35 154 A6
Argyle Crs *FHAM* PO15 10 B3
Argyle Rd *CHCH/BSGR* BH23 337 J1
NWBY RG14 16 D4
SHAM SO14 21 F2
Argyle St *CHOB/PIR* GU24 59 M7
Argyll Rd *BKME/WDN* BH12 321 M6
BOSC BH5 335 L2
Ariel Cl *SBNE* BH6 336 F2
Ariel Dr *SBNE* BH6 336 F2
Ariel Rd *PSEA* PO1 316 G3
Ark Dr *FERN* BH22 302 F5
Arkle Av *STHA* RG19 25 J4
Ark Royal Crs
LSOL/BMARY PO13 314 C1
Arkwright Cl *KSCL* RG20 29 N8
Arle Cl *HORN* PO8 236 C8
NARL SO24 167 P1
Arle Gdns *NARL* SO24 168 A1
Arley Rd *PSTN* BH14 333 J1
Arlington Ct *NMIL/BTOS* BH25 327 K7
Arlington Pl *WINC* SO23 * 22 E3
Arlington Ter *ALDT* GU11 2 C3
Arliss Rd *ROWN* SO16 247 L2
Arlott Ct *WSHM* SO15 248 A4
Arlott Dr *BSTK* RG21 7 F2
Armada Cl *ROWN* SO16 227 J5
Armada Dr *FAWY* SO45 268 B8
Arminers Cl *GPORT* PO12 315 M7
Armitage Av *FAWY* SO45 268 B9
Armitage Dr *FRIM* GU16 58 E4
Armory La *PSEA* PO1 18 D5
The Armoury *TOTT* SO40 * 247 L8
Armstrong Cl *BROC* SO42 286 E8
GPORT PO12 315 N2
RWIN SO21 144 F4
WVILLE PO7 255 M9
Armstrong Ct *ROWN* SO16 227 K7
Armstrong La *BROC* SO42 286 E8
Armstrong Ml *FARN* GU14 57 L9
Armstrong Ri *AND* SP10 82 C8
Armstrong Rd *BROC* SO42 286 E8
CHIN RG24 69 P5
Armstrong Wy *FARN* GU14 75 J3
Armsworth La *BPWT* SO32 253 P1
Arnaud Cl *NEND* PO2 316 F1
Arne Av *BKME/WDN* BH12 321 N5
Arne Cl *BH/HW/K* RG22 89 P4
Arne Crs *BKME/WDN* BH12 321 N5
Arnewood Av *TADY* RG26 34 E5
Arnewood Bridge Rd
LYMN SO41 307 P9
Arnewood Rd *SBNE* BH6 336 A1
Arnheim Cl *ROWN* SO16 227 N8
Arnheim Rd *ROWN* SO16 227 P8
Arnhem Cl *ALDT* GU11 3 G2
Arnhem Rd *NWBY* RG14 17 H2
Arnold Cl *FERN* BH22 280 E6
Arnold Rd *ELGH* SO50 229 J4
FERN BH22 280 E6
SD/PW SO17 248 E1
Arnolds Cl *NMIL/BTOS* BH25 327 H7
Arnside Rd *WVILLE* PO7 275 N2
Arnwood Av *FAWY* SO45 290 B1
Arragon Ct *WVILLE* PO7 276 A2
Arran Cl *CHAM* PO6 275 H9
DEAN RG23 88 E1
Arran Wy *CHCH/BSGR* BH23 326 D6
Arreton *HLER* SO31 269 L4
Arrow Cl *ELGH* SO50 207 J9
ITCH SO19 268 F1
Arrow La *HTWY* RG27 54 G6
Arrow Rd *FARN* GU14 75 N2
Arrowsmith La *WIMB* BH21 300 G6
Arrowsmith Rd *CFDH* BH17 300 F7
Arters Lawn *TOTT* SO40 266 F4
Arthur Cl *FNM* GU9 116 B1
WCLF BH2 334 F1
Arthur La *CHCH/BSGR* BH23 324 E8
Arthur Rd *CHCH/BSGR* BH23 324 E8
ELGH SO50 207 J9
FNM GU9 116 B2
NWBY RG14 16 B4
WINC SO23 22 E1
WSHM SO15 247 P4
Arthurs Gdns *HEND* SO30 230 B9
Arthur's La *RAND* SP11 44 D4
Arthur St *ALDT* GU11 3 F4
NEND PO2 316 G1
Artillery Cl *CHAM* PO6 296 E1
Artillery Dr *STHA* RG19 25 P6
Artillery Rd *ALDT* GU11 76 C5
Artillery Ter *ENEY* PO4 * 317 K4
Artists Wy *AND* SP10 82 D9
Arun Cl *EPSF* GU31 215 L3
Arun Ct *BSTK* RG21 7 J6
Arundel Cl *FLEETN* GU51 74 E4
LIPH GU30 154 E8
NARL SO24 168 A3
NMIL/BTOS BH25 326 G4
Arundel Dr *FHAM/PORC* PO16 10 E4
Arundel Gdns *DEAN* RG23 68 E5
Arundel Pl *FNM* GU9 * 96 B9
Arundel Rd *CBLY* GU15 59 H1
ELGH SO50 207 J7
GPORT PO12 315 K3
TOTT SO40 246 E3
Arundel St *PSEA* PO1 19 J2
Arundel Wy
CHCH/BSGR BH23 326 B8
Arun Rd *WEND* SO18 249 K1
Arun Wy *ROMY* SO51 224 D1
Ascension Cl *CHIN* RG24 69 M3
Ascham Rd *CHAR* BH8 335 H1
Ascot Cl *ALTN* GU34 132 G7
FHAM/STUB PO14 271 J8
NWBY RG14 17 J7
Ascot Ct *ALDT* GU11 2 E4
Ascot Rd *BDST* BH18 300 C9
ELGH SO50 230 D5
HSEA PO3 317 J1
Ascott Wy *NWBY* RG14 24 G3
Ascupart St *SHAM* SO14 21 G4
Asford Gv *ELGH* SO50 207 L9
Ashbarn Crs *FUFL* SO22 183 M1
Ashbourne Cl *ASHV* GU12 77 H9
Ashbourne Rd *BOSC* BH5 335 P1
Ashbourne Wy *STHA* RG19 25 L4
Ashbridge Ri *CHFD* SO53 206 C4
Ashburn Garth *RGWD* BH24 283 H3
Ashburnham Cl *ITCH* SO19 248 F6
Ashburn Pl *FBDG* SP6 240 C2
Ashburton Cl *FAWY* SO45 267 P7
NARL SO24 167 P2
Ashburton Gdns *NBNE* BH10 322 D6
Ashburton Rd *GPORT* PO12 315 K6
NARL SO24 167 P2
SSEA PO5 316 E6
Ashbury Dr *BLKW* GU17 57 P4
Ashbury Rd *BOR* GU35 154 A6
Ashby Rd *ITCH* SO19 249 K8
TOTT SO40 246 B4
Ash Church Rd *ASHV* GU12 97 P1
Ash Cl *ASHV* GU12 3 H5
BLKW GU17 41 K9
FAWY SO45 290 C1
FBDG SP6 239 N6
FHAM/STUB PO14 10 A7
GPORT PO12 12 C3
HLER SO31 269 P2
HORN PO8 255 N8
ITCH SO19 249 L5
NBAD SO52 205 K8
ROMY SO51 204 G7
RWIN SO21 207 P5
TDWTH SP9 79 J4
Ash Copse *HORN* PO8 255 P6
Ash Crs *STHA* RG19 32 D1
Ashcroft La *HORN* PO8 257 K5
Ashdell Rd *ALTN* GU34 132 G6
Ashdene *WSHM* SO15 247 M3
Ashdene Cl *WIMB* BH21 278 F9
Ashdene Crs *ASHV* GU12 76 F9
Ashdene Rd *ASHV* GU12 76 F9
TOTT SO40 245 P9
Ashdown *FAWY* SO45 291 H6
LSOL/BMARY PO13 295 H8
Ashdown Av *FARN* GU14 76 D2
Ashdown Cl *CFDH* BH17 320 G3
CHFD SO53 206 E3
Ashdown Dr *CHFD* SO53 206 E3
Ashdown Rd *CHFD* SO53 206 E4
FAWY SO45 291 H7
Ashdown Ter *TDWTH* SP9 79 H6
Ashdown Wk
NMIL/BTOS BH25 327 L5
Ashdown Wy *ROMY* SO51 204 F6
Ashen Cl *CHFD* SO53 206 E5
Ashe Rd *HAV* PO9 277 H5
Ashfield *CHIN* RG24 70 A1
Ashfield Gn *YTLY* GU46 40 G9
Ashfield Rd *AND* SP10 102 B2
Ashfields *RWIN* SO21 124 F3
Ashfield Vw *NBAD* SO52 205 L8
Ashford Cl *CHAM* PO6 274 G9
FBDG SP6 240 B2
Ashford Crs *FAWY* SO45 268 D7
Ashford Hill Rd *STHA* RG19 32 A4
Ashford Rd *FBDG* SP6 240 A3
SBNE BH6 324 B8
Ash Green La West
RFNM GU10 97 M3
Ash Gv *CHIN* RG24 70 D6
KSCL RG20 48 C3
LIPH GU30 175 L4
LYMN SO41 328 D7
RGWD BH24 282 G2
TOTT SO40 246 A9
Ash Hill Rd *ASHV* GU12 76 G9
Ashington Cl *HORN* PO8 256 A8
Ashington Gdns *WIMB* BH21 300 B5
Ashington La *WIMB* BH21 300 C4
Ashington Pk
NMIL/BTOS BH25 327 K6
Ash La *TADY* RG26 33 P5
TADY RG26 35 L9
THLE RG7 27 J3
Ashlawn Gdns *AND* SP10 4 E7
Ashlea *HTWY* RG27 72 A2
Ashlea Cl *ELGH* SO50 230 D2
Ashleigh Cl *FAWY* SO45 290 C1
Ashleigh Ri *NBNE* BH10 322 D5
Ashlet Gdns
NMIL/BTOS BH25 327 M3
Ashlett Cl *FAWY* SO45 291 L6
Ashlett Rd *FAWY* SO45 291 L6
Ashley Cl *BMTH* BH1 323 L9
FRIM GU16 58 E7
FUFL SO22 164 D4
HAV PO9 276 D6
HLER SO31 271 H3
HORN PO8 255 P6
RFNM GU10 95 H4
RGWD BH24 283 H3
Ashley Common Rd
NMIL/BTOS BH25 327 L3
Ashley Ct *HLER* SO31 250 A9
Ashley Crs *ITCH* SO19 249 L9
Ashleycross Cl *FAWY* SO45 290 F6
Ashley Dr *BLKW* GU17 57 K1
RGWD BH24 282 A1
Ashley Dr North *RGWD* BH24 281 M3
Ashley Dr South *RGWD* BH24 281 M4
Ashley Dr West *RGWD* BH24 281 M4
Ashley Dro *MARL* SN8 42 C1
Ashley Gdns *BPWT* SO32 232 C9
CHFD SO53 206 G8
DEAN RG23 88 F1
Ashley La *NMIL/BTOS* BH25 327 M3
Ashley Mdw *ROMY* SO51 204 E5
Ashley Meads
NMIL/BTOS BH25 327 M3
Ashley Pk *RGWD* BH24 281 N3
Ashley Rd *ALTN* GU34 131 H4
BMTH BH1 323 L9
FARN GU14 58 C9
NMIL/BTOS BH25 327 K5
PSTN BH14 321 L7
Ashling Cl *CHAR* BH8 323 J7
WVILLE PO7 255 H7
Ashling Gdns *WVILLE* PO7 255 H7
Ashling La *NEND* PO2 296 F9
Ashling Park Rd *WVILLE* PO7 255 H7
Ash Lodge Cl *ASHV* GU12 97 N2
Ash Lodge Dr *ASHV* GU12 97 N2
Ashlyn Cl *FHAM* PO15 271 P9
Ashmead *BOR* GU35 154 A5
Ashmead Rd *ROWN* SO16 227 K9
Ashmeads Cl *WIMB* BH21 279 J8
Ashmeads Wy *WIMB* BH21 279 J8
Ashmoor La *CHIN* RG24 70 F6
Ashmore *WIMB* BH21 300 F1
Ashmore Av
NMIL/BTOS BH25 327 K7
PLE BH15 332 B2
Ashmore Cl *RSAL* SP5 201 K1
Ashmore Crs *PLE* BH15 332 B2
Ashmore Gv
CHCH/BSGR BH23 326 A6
Ashmore La *RSAL* SP5 177 L4
Ashmore Rd *FUFL* SO22 164 D6
Ashridge *FARN* GU14 57 N6
Ashridge Av *NBNE* BH10 322 D2
Ashridge Cl *WSHM* SO15 248 B3
Ashridge Ct *NWBY* RG14 17 F4
Ashridge Gdns *NBNE* BH10 * 322 D2
Ash Rd *ASHV* GU12 3 K6
KSCL RG20 31 L3
TOTT SO40 245 P9
Ash St *ASHV* GU12 97 N2
Ashtead Cl *FHAM/PORC* PO16 295 L1
Ashton Cl *BPWT* SO32 231 N3
Ashton Cross *ROMY* SO51 224 G2
Ashton La *BPWT* SO32 231 N2
Ashton Pl *CHFD* SO53 * 206 D4
Ashton Rd *MOOR/WNTN* BH9 322 F5
Ashton Wy *FHAM/STUB* PO14 294 B9
Ash Tree Cl *DEAN* RG23 88 E3
FARN GU14 75 K1
HASM GU27 157 L4
Ashtree Cl *NMIL/BTOS* BH25 327 M5
Ash Tree Rd *AND* SP10 102 A2
WEND SO18 248 G2
Ashurst Bridge Rd *TOTT* SO40 246 A5
Ashurst Cl *FUFL* SO22 164 E4
ITCH SO19 269 J1
TADY RG26 34 B6
TOTT SO40 245 P9
Ashurst Rd *ASHV* GU12 76 E8
CHAM PO6 296 G1
CHAR BH8 323 K4
FERN BH22 280 D6
Ashwood *FHAM* PO15 271 L5
HLER SO31 271 J8
Ashwood Cl *HAV* PO9 276 B7
HISD PO11 318 G5
Ashwood Dr *BDST* BH18 300 E9
NWBY RG14 24 G3
Ashwood Gdns *ROWN* SO16 228 A9
TOTT SO40 246 A5
Ashwood Wy *DEAN* RG23 68 G5
Ashworth Dr *STHA* RG19 25 M5
Aspen Av *HLER* SO31 292 D1
Aspen Cl *BOR* GU35 154 A7
HEND SO30 250 D4
RWIN SO21 208 A5
Aspen Dr *VWD* BH31 259 H4
Aspen Gdns *BKME/WDN* BH12 321 P5
HTWY RG27 72 A2
Aspen Gv *ASHV* GU12 97 L3
Aspengrove
LSOL/BMARY PO13 295 J8
Aspen Holt *ROWN* SO16 228 C7
Aspen Pl *NMIL/BTOS* BH25 327 K6
Aspen Rd *BKME/WDN* BH12 321 P5
Aspen Wk *TOTT* SO40 245 P3
Aspen Wy *BKME/WDN* BH12 321 P5
BSTK RG21 69 M4
HORN PO8 256 A6
Aspin Wy *BLKW* GU17 41 J9
Asquith Cl *CHCH/BSGR* BH23 337 H1
Astbury Av *BKME/WDN* BH12 322 A7
Aster Ct *AND* SP10 * 102 B4
Aster Rd *BH/HW/K* RG22 89 L4
ROWN SO16 228 E8
Astley St *SSEA* PO5 19 G5
Aston Md *CHCH/BSGR* BH23 324 C3
Aston Rd *ENEY* PO4 317 H5
WVILLE PO7 275 M1
Astor Crs *RAND* SP11 79 N1
Astra Ct *FAWY* SO45 268 C5
Astral Gdns *HLER* SO31 269 P7
Astra Wk *GPORT* PO12 13 G3
Astrid Cl *HISD* PO11 319 J5
Asturias Wy *SHAM* SO14 21 J7
Asylum Rd *WSHM* SO15 20 E1
Atalanta Cl *ENEY* PO4 317 L3
Atbara Rd *FLEETS* GU52 74 D8
Atheling Rd *FAWY* SO45 268 C6
Athelstan Rd *ITCH* SO19 248 G4
SBNE BH6 336 C1
WINC SO23 22 D1
Athena Av *WVILLE* PO7 275 P7
Athena Cl *ELGH* SO50 230 A1
Atherfield Rd *ROWN* SO16 227 J9
Atherley Ct *WSHM* SO15 248 A3
Atherley Rd *HISD* PO11 318 E3
WSHM SO15 247 P5
Athlone Cl *RAND* SP11 82 F3
Athoke Cft *HTWY* RG27 72 C3
Atholl Ct *AND* SP10 82 E8
Atholl Rd *BOR* GU35 154 A7
Atkinson Cl *GPORT* PO12 12 B7
Atkins Pl *FHAM* PO15 272 A7
Atlantic Cl *SHAM* SO14 248 D9
Atlantic Park Vw *WEND* SO18 249 J1
Atlantis Av *WVILLE* PO7 275 P8
Atrebatti Rd *SHST* GU47 41 K5
Attenborough Cl *FLEETN* GU51 74 E1
Attfield Cl *ASHV* GU12 97 M2
Attlee Gdns *FLEETS* GU52 74 C8
Attwood Cl *BSTK* RG21 6 A7
FBDG SP6 239 M6
Attwoods Dro *RWIN* SO21 183 L6
Aubrey Cl *HISD* PO11 318 E4
LYMN SO41 339 J2
Auchinleck Wy *ALDT* GU11 2 A3
Auckland Pl *BROC* SO42 286 F8
Auckland Rd
CHCH/BSGR BH23 325 N8
WSHM SO15 247 K4
Auckland Rd East *SSEA* PO5 316 E6
Auckland Rd West *SSEA* PO5 316 E6
Auclum Cl *THLE* RG7 27 K5
Auclum La *THLE* RG7 27 J5
Audemer Ct *RGWD* BH24 282 G1
Audley Cl *NWBY* RG14 24 G2
Audley Pl *ELGH* SO50 * 229 P2
Audret Cl *FHAM/PORC* PO16 295 M3

Augustine Rd *CHAM* PO6 ...... 275 L9
 SHAM SO14 ...... 21 H1
Augustus Dr *AND* SP10 ...... 82 B8
Augustus Dr *DEAN* RG23 ...... 68 F5
Augustus Wk *AND* SP10 ...... 82 F8
Augustus Wy *CHFD* SO53 ...... 206 C6
Aukland Av *WEND* SO2 ...... 286 C8
Auklet Cl *BH/HW/K* RG22 ...... 89 K4
Auriol Dr *HAV* PO9 ...... 298 A1
Aurora Dr *FUFL* SO22 ...... 183 L3
Austen Av *FUFL* SO22 ...... 183 L3
 NBNE BH10 * 322 D1
Austen Cl *TOTT* SO40 ...... 246 B5
 WINC SO23 ...... 165 H5
Austen Gdns *FHAM* PO15 ...... 271 J2
 NWBY RG14 ...... 17 G7
Austen Gv *BH/HW/K* RG22 ...... 90 A1
Austen Rd *FARN* GU14 ...... 57 P7
Austerberry Wy
 LSOL/BMARY PO13 ...... 295 H9
Auster Cl *CHCH/BSGR* BH23 ...... 325 M8
Austin Cl *BMTH* BH1 ...... 335 K1
Austin Cl *CHAM* PO6 ...... 274 D9
Australia Cl *PSEA* PO1 ...... 19 J2
Aust Rd *FHAM/STUB* PO14 ...... 294 B1
Autumn Rd *BWD* BH11 ...... 321 M1
 TOTT SO40 ...... 267 L1
Avalon *PSTN* BH14 ...... 333 L3
Avebury Av *WEND* BH10 ...... 322 E1
Avebury Gdns *CHFD* SO53 ...... 206 C4
Aveley La *FNM* GU10 ...... 116 B5
Avenger Cl *CHFD* SO53 ...... 206 D8
Avens Cl *ELGH* SO50 ...... 230 C6
Avenue C *FAWY* SO45 ...... 290 C1
Avenue Cl *AND* SP10 ...... 102 C2
 LIPH GU30 ...... 175 J3
Avenue Ct *GPORT* PO12 ...... 12 A6
Avenue D *FAWY* SO45 ...... 290 C1
Avenue De Caen *SSEA* PO5 ...... 316 E6
Avenue E *FAWY* SO45 ...... 290 C1
Avenue La *WCLF* BH2 ...... 8 C4
Avenue Rd *ALTN* GU34 ...... 112 C7
 BROC SO42 ...... 286 F8
 CHCH/BSGR BH23 ...... 324 D8
 CHCH/BSGR BH23 ...... 326 E6
 FARN GU14 ...... 58 C9
 FHAM/STUB PO14 ...... 10 D6
 FLEETS GU51 ...... 74 C2
 FUFL SO22 ...... 22 B3
 GPORT PO12 ...... 12 E1
 GSHT GU26 ...... 156 C2
 HISD PO11 ...... 298 F6
 LYMN SO41 ...... 329 K3
 NMIL/BTOS BH25 ...... 327 J4
 OVTN RG25 ...... 111 N6
 SHAM SO14 ...... 248 C3
 WCLF BH2 ...... 8 B4
 WIMB BH21 ...... 300 F1
Avenue Sucy *CBLY* GU15 ...... 57 P1
The Avenue *AND* SP10 ...... 102 C2
 BPWT SO32 ...... 231 P4
 CBLY GU15 ...... 58 A1
 CCLF BH15 ...... 334 A6
 CWTH RG45 ...... 41 H1
 EPSF GU31 ...... 215 M2
 FERN BH22 ...... 280 D6
 FHAM/STUB PO14 ...... 10 B6
 FLEETS GU51 ...... 74 B3
 GPORT PO12 ...... 12 A4
 GSHT GU26 ...... 156 C2
 LIPH GU30 ...... 175 L3
 MOOR/WNTN BH9 ...... 322 F4
 NARL SO24 ...... 129 J5
 NARL SO24 ...... 167 N2
 OVTN RG25 ...... 89 P8
 RAND SP11 ...... 82 C1
 RAND SP11 ...... 104 E7
 RFNM GU10 ...... 115 N7
 RGWD BH24 ...... 281 H9
 RWIN SO21 ...... 184 A8
 SD/PW SO17 ...... 240 B7
 STOK SO20 ...... 121 H5
 TDWTH SP9 ...... 78 C7
 THLE RG7 ...... 36 A1
Avery La *GPORT* PO12 ...... 315 N4
Aviary Ct *CHIN* RG24 * 69 P4
Aviemore Dr *DEAN* RG23 ...... 88 E2
Avington Cl *ELGH* SO50 ...... 207 N8
Avington Ct *ROWN* SO16 ...... 228 B8
Avocet Cl *ENEY* PO4 ...... 317 K3
Avocet Crs *SHST* GU47 ...... 41 L6
Avocet Quay *EMRTH* PO10 ...... 299 N2
Avocet Wk
 LSOL/BMARY PO13 ...... 294 E7
Avon Av *RGWD* BH24 ...... 282 B6
Avonborne Wy *CHFD* SO53 ...... 206 D5
Avon Blds *CHCH/BSGR* BH23 ...... 324 F8
Avon Castle Dr *RGWD* BH24 ...... 282 B5
Avon Cswy *CHCH/BSGR* BH23 ...... 304 C8
Avoncliffe Rd *SBNE* BH6 ...... 336 C3
Avon Cl *ASHV* GU12 ...... 97 M2
 CHAR BH8 ...... 323 K9
 EPSF GU31 ...... 215 L4
 FARN GU14 ...... 57 M6
 LSOL/BMARY PO13 ...... 314 D3
 LYMN SO41 ...... 329 J4
Avon Ct *AND* SP10 ...... 82 F9
Avon Crs *ROMY* SO51 ...... 204 G6
Avondale *ASHV* GU12 ...... 76 E5
Avondale Rd *ALDT* GU11 ...... 54 B6
 FLEETS GU51 ...... 74 D2
 PSEA PO1 ...... 317 H1
 WVILLE PO7 ...... 275 D7
Avondyke *RSAL* SP5 ...... 199 K7
Avon Gn *CHFD* SO53 ...... 206 F8
Avon Meade *FBDG* SP6 ...... 240 C1
Avon Ms *CHAR* BH8 ...... 323 J9
Avon Pk *RGWD* BH24 ...... 282 B3
Avon Rd *CHAR* BH8 ...... 323 J9
 DEAN RG23 ...... 87 K9
 FERN BH22 ...... 280 E8
 FNM GU9 ...... 116 C1
 TDWTH SP9 ...... 78 G6

WEND SO18 ...... 249 H2
Avon Rd East
 CHCH/BSGR BH23 ...... 324 E7
Avon Rd West
 CHCH/BSGR BH23 ...... 324 D7
Avon Run Cl
 CHCH/BSGR BH23 ...... 337 M1
Avon Run Rd
 CHCH/BSGR BH23 ...... 337 M1
Avon Valley Pth
 CHCH/BSGR BH23 ...... 304 F9
 RGWD BH24 ...... 282 C9
 RGWD BH24 ...... 241 H2
Avon Vw *FBDG* SP6 ...... 241 H2
Avon View Rd
 CHCH/BSGR BH23 ...... 324 G4
Avon Wk *BSTK* RG21 * 7 J6
Avon Wy *THLE* RG7 ...... 26 A1
 HEND SO30 ...... 249 N1
Avorway *NWBY* RG14 ...... 24 G3
Avon Whf *CHCH/BSGR* BH23 * 324 C9
Avro Cl *WSHM* SO15 ...... 247 L4
Avro Ct *HLER* SO31 ...... 269 P8
Award Rd *FLEETS* GU51 ...... 74 C7
 WIMB BH21 ...... 279 P9
Awbridge Rd *HAV* PO9 ...... 276 C6
Axford Cl *CHAR* BH8 ...... 323 K4
Ayerswood *HEND* SO30 ...... 250 B7
Ayesgarth *FLEETS* GU52 ...... 74 E7
Aylen Cl *ALDT* GU11 * 97 H4
Aylen Rd *HSEA* PO3 ...... 297 J7
Aylesbury Rd *BMTH* BH1 ...... 335 K2
 HEND SO30 ...... 297 H9
Aylesham Wy *YTLY* GU46 ...... 40 C8
Ayling Cl *LSOL/BMARY* PO13 ...... 314 C1
Ayling Ct *FNM* GU9 ...... 96 F4
Ayling La *HLDT* GU11 ...... 2 C6
Aylings Cl *DEAN* RG23 ...... 68 E8
Aylward's Dr *ALTN* GU34 ...... 151 K5
Aylward St *PSEA* PO1 ...... 18 D2
Aylwin Cl *BSTK* RG21 ...... 7 J4
Aylwin Cl *BSTK* RG21 ...... 90 C1
Ayres La *KSCL* RG20 ...... 30 E6
Ayrshire Gdns *FLEETS* GU51 ...... 56 E9
Aysgarth Rd *NMIL/BTOS* BH25 ...... 327 K6
Aysha Cl *WIMB* BH25 * 309 J5
Azalea Av *BOR* GU35 ...... 154 D3
Azalea Cl *HAV* PO9 ...... 277 J6
 RGWD BH24 ...... 281 N4
Azalea Dr *HASM* GU27 ...... 156 E5
Azalea Gdns *FLEETS* GU52 ...... 74 E7
Azalea Rd *STHA* RG19 ...... 32 D1
Azura Cl *WIMB* BH21 ...... 281 H5

B

Babbs Md *FNM* GU9 ...... 116 A1
Babs Flds *RFNM* GU10 ...... 114 E5
Bach Cl *BH/HW/K* RG22 ...... 89 P4
Back Down La *RGWD* BH24 ...... 283 H2
Back La *LYMN* SO41 ...... 308 C6
 OVTN RG25 ...... 111 M5
 RAND SP11 ...... 42 G7
 RAND SP11 ...... 81 J4
 RFNM GU10 ...... 135 K1
 ROWN SO16 ...... 179 K1
 THLE RG7 ...... 33 L5
 THLE RG7 ...... 35 K2
 WHAM SO17 ...... 274 A4
Back of The Walls *SHAM* SO14 * 9 F5
Back St *WINC* SO23 ...... 183 P2
Bacon Cl *ITCH* SO19 ...... 249 H9
 SHST GU47 ...... 41 L8
Bacon La *HISD* PO11 ...... 318 D5
 RFNM GU10 ...... 136 C7
Badajos Rd *ALDT* GU11 ...... 2 B1
Badbury Cl *BDST* BH18 ...... 320 E1
Badbury Vw *WIMB* BH21 ...... 278 F9
Baddesley Cl *NBAD* SO52 ...... 205 K8
Baddesley Rd *NBAD* SO52 ...... 206 C4
Baddesley Rd *NMIL/BTOS* BH25 ...... 327 K6
Baden Powell Rd *LISS* GU33 ...... 175 P5
Bader Cl *HEND* SO30 ...... 250 C3
Bader Rd *CFDH* BH17 ...... 320 A8
Bader Wy *FHAM* PO15 ...... 271 L5
Badger Brow *WVILLE* PO7 ...... 276 A4
Badger Cl *ALTN* GU34 ...... 150 D5
 ELGH SO50 ...... 229 P2
 FHAM PO15 ...... 272 B8
Badger Farm Rd *FUFL* SO22 ...... 183 L3
Badger's Bank *CHIN* RG24 ...... 70 A4
Badgers Cl *FLEETS* GU52 ...... 74 C4
 LYMN SO41 ...... 308 C6
 RGWD BH24 ...... 281 M4
Badgers Copse *CBLY* GU15 ...... 58 D2
 HLER SO31 ...... 271 H5
 NMIL/BTOS BH25 ...... 327 L1
Badgers Cft *THLE* RG7 * 27 J3
Badgers Gld *THLE* RG7 ...... 27 J5
Badgers Holt *YTLY* GU46 ...... 40 C9
Badgers Rdg *NWBY* RG14 ...... 30 B2
Badgers Sett *CWTH* RG45 ...... 40 C1
The Badgers *HLER* SO31 ...... 269 L4
Badgers Wk *FAWY* SO45 ...... 268 B8
 FERN BH22 ...... 302 E1
Badger Wy *ASHV* GU12 ...... 76 C9
Badgerwood Dr *FRIM* GU16 ...... 58 C3
Badminton La *NARL* SO24 ...... 168 B8
Badshot Lea Rd *FNM* GU9 ...... 96 G5
Badshot Pk *FNM* GU9 ...... 96 G5
Baffins Rd *HSEA* PO3 ...... 317 J2
Bagmore La *OVTN* SO23 ...... 110 C5
Bagnum Rd *NWBY* RG14 ...... 16 B8
Bagshot La *WVILLE* PO7 ...... 249 H8
Bagshot Ms *ITCH* SO19 ...... 249 H8
Bagwell La *HTWY* RG27 ...... 73 H5

Baigent Cl *WINC* SO23 ...... 23 J6
Bailey Cl *FRIM* GU16 ...... 58 C5
 HEND SO30 ...... 250 F5
 NMIL/BTOS BH25 * 327 M3
Bailey La *PLE* BH15 ...... 320 E5
Bailey Dr *CHCH/BSGR* BH23 ...... 324 D8
Baileys Cl *BLKW* GU17 ...... 57 J1
Bailey's Rd *SSEA* PO5 ...... 19 J4
Baily Av *NTHA* RG18 ...... 25 L3
Bain Av *CBLY* GU15 ...... 58 A3
Baird Av *BH/HW/K* RG22 ...... 90 A1
Baird Rd *FARN* GU14 ...... 58 B7
Baiter Gdns *PLE* BH15 ...... 332 E2
Bakehouse Gdns
 FLEETS GU52 ...... 74 E7
Bakehouse Ms *ALDT* GU11 * 2 E2
Bakers Dro *ROWN* SO16 ...... 227 J7
Bakers Farm Rd *VWD* BH31 ...... 258 E3
Bakers Fld *LISS* GU33 ...... 175 L5
Baker St *PSEA* PO1 ...... 316 F1
Balaclava Rd *WEND* SO18 ...... 249 J4
Balcombe Rd *CCLF* BH13 ...... 334 A5
Balderton Cl *NEND* PO2 ...... 297 H5
Baldreys *FNM* GU9 ...... 116 A2
Baldwin Cl *CHCH/BSGR* BH23 ...... 325 H9
Balena Cl *CFDH* BH17 ...... 320 C4
Balfour Cl *CHCH/BSGR* BH23 ...... 325 P7
Balfour Cl *RWIN* SO21 ...... 315 H2
Balfour Crs *NWBY* RG14 ...... 30 B1
Balfour Dr *LISS* GU33 ...... 192 C2
Balfour Rd *ITCH* SO19 ...... 249 K6
 MOOR/WNTN BH9 ...... 322 F6
Balintore Ct *SHST* GU47 ...... 41 L7
Baksbury Rd *AND* SP10 ...... 102 B5
Baksbury Rd *AND* SP10 ...... 102 C5
Ballantyne Rd *FARN* GU14 ...... 57 P7
Ballard Cl *BH/HW/K* RG22 ...... 68 F7
 NMIL/BTOS BH25 ...... 327 K3
 ROWN SO16 ...... 228 B3
 ROWN SO16 ...... 246 G2
Ballard Rd *PLE* BH15 ...... 332 E2
Balliol Cl *FHAM/STUB* PO14 ...... 271 J2
Balliol Rd *NEND* PO2 ...... 316 G1
Balliol Wy *SHST* GU47 ...... 41 M5
Ball & Wicket La *FNM* GU9 ...... 96 C4
Balmer Lawn Rd *BROC* SO42 ...... 287 H6
Balmoral Cl *CHAR* BH8 ...... 323 L6
Balmoral Cl *ALTN* GU34 ...... 132 D6
 CHFD SO53 ...... 206 B6
 LSOL/BMARY PO13 ...... 295 H6
 ROWN SO16 ...... 227 N7
Balmoral Ct *BH/HW/K* RG22 * 68 F7
Balmoral Crs *FNM* GU9 ...... 96 B5
Balmoral Dr *FRIM* GU16 ...... 58 D5
 WILLE PO7 ...... 275 L6
Balmoral Ri *AND* SP10 ...... 4 C4
 ASHV GU12 ...... 76 F8
 PSTN BH14 ...... 321 L9
Balmoral Wk
 NMIL/BTOS BH25 ...... 327 H4
Balmoral Wy *BH/HW/K* RG22 ...... 89 L4
 PSF GU32 ...... 215 M1
 ROWN SO16 ...... 227 H6
Balsan Cl *FHAM/STUB* PO14 ...... 68 F4
Balston Rd *PSTN* BH14 ...... 321 J7
Balston Ter *PLE* BH15 * 332 D1
Baltic Rd *HEND* SO30 ...... 249 N2
Bamber La *ALTN* GU34 ...... 113 P6
Bampton Rd *ROWN* SO16 ...... 247 H3
Banbury Av *ITCH* SO19 ...... 249 L1
Banbury Cl *FRIM* GU16 ...... 58 A5
Banbury Rd *CFDH* BH17 ...... 320 E5
Band Hall Pl *HTWY* RG27 ...... 72 A3
Bangor Rd *WSHM* SO15 ...... 247 M5
Banister Gdns *WSHM* SO15 ...... 248 B4
Banister Ms *WSHM* SO15 * 248 B4
Banister Rd *WSHM* SO15 ...... 248 B4
Bankhill Dr *LYMN* SO41 ...... 321 J7
Bank Pde *BNKH/BH12* 322 A6
Bank Rd *ALDT* GU11 ...... 76 C7
Banks Cl *AND* SP10 ...... 102 C3
Bankside *FNM* GU9 ...... 96 F4
 LYMN SO41 ...... 329 K1
Bank Side *WEND* SO18 ...... 228 F8
Bankside Rd
 MOOR/WNTN BH9 ...... 323 K8
Banks Rd *CCLF* BH13 ...... 333 K8
The Banks *ROMY* SO51 ...... 178 G9
Bank St *BPWT* SO32 ...... 232 B5
Bankview *LYMN* SO41 ...... 329 K1
Bannerman Rd *PSF* GU32 ...... 215 M1
Banning Rd *ROMY* SO51 ...... 204 C7
Bannister Gdns *HTWY* RG27 ...... 39 P6
Bannister Rd *THLE* RG7 ...... 27 H5
Banstead Rd *BDST* BH18 ...... 306 C8
Bapaume Rd *HSEA* PO3 ...... 297 H4
Baptist Hl *RAND* SP11 ...... 84 E1
Barbara Cl *FLEETS* GU51 ...... 74 E6
Barbara Ct *BPWT* SO32 ...... 210 F2
Barbe Baker Av *HEND* SO30 ...... 249 L1
Barber Av *BSTK* RG21 ...... 7 H5
Barberry Cl *FLEETS* GU52 ...... 74 D6
Barberry Dr *TOTT* SO40 ...... 245 P2
Barberry Wy *BLKW* GU17 ...... 57 N2
 VWD BH31 ...... 256 F2
Barbers Piles *PLE* BH15 ...... 332 D2
Barbour Cl *ODIM* RG29 ...... 93 J4
Barcelona Cl *AND* SP10 ...... 5 F2
Barclay Ms *FAWY* SO45 ...... 290 C1
Bardon Av *FHAM/STUB* PO14 ...... 294 B1
Bardsley Dr *FNM* GU9 ...... 116 A2
Bardwell Cl *BH/HW/K* RG22 ...... 89 P4
The Baredown *HTWY* RG27 ...... 71 L5
Bar End Rd *WINC* SO23 ...... 23 G7
Barfield Cl *WINC* SO23 ...... 23 G7
Barfield Rd *NTHA* RG18 ...... 25 K3
Barfields *NMIL* SO41 ...... 329 L3
Barfleur Cl *FHAM* PO15 ...... 271 J2
Barfleur Rd *FHAM/STUB* PO14 ...... 294 E4
Barford Cl *CHFD* SO53 ...... 205 M3
 FLEETS GU51 ...... 74 G4

Barford La *RSAL* SP5 ...... 199 L5
Bargates *CHCH/BSGR* BH23 ...... 324 E8
Bargate St *SHAM* SO14 ...... 20 D5
Barge Cl *ALDT* GU11 ...... 76 D8
Barge La *THLE* RG7 ...... 37 L2
Barham Cl *GPORT* PO12 ...... 315 M2
Barham Rd *WINC* SO23 ...... 215 M2
Barham Wy *NEND* PO2 ...... 296 F5
Baring Cl *RWIN* SO21 ...... 127 N5
 RWIN SO21 ...... 146 F9
Baring Rd *SBNE* BH6 ...... 336 E2
 WINC SO23 ...... 23 H6
Barker Mill Cl *ROWN* SO16 ...... 227 J6
Barkis Md *SHST* GU47 ...... 41 M4
Barlands Cl *CHCH/BSGR* BH23 ...... 324 G5
Barle Cl *WEND* SO18 ...... 249 K2
Barley Down Dr *FUFL* SO22 ...... 183 M2
Barley Flds *ELGH* SO50 ...... 230 C6
Barley Mow Cl *HTWY* RG27 ...... 73 L4
Barley Mow Hl *BOR* GU35 ...... 155 L4
Barley Vw *OVTN* RG25 ...... 108 D1
Barlow Cl *FHAM/STUB* PO14 ...... 294 D7
Barnard Cl *FRIM* GU16 ...... 58 E5
Barnard Wy *ALDT* GU11 ...... 2 C1
Barnbrook Cl *HLER* SO31 ...... 270 E6
Barn Cl *NWBY* RG14 ...... 24 A8
Barn Close La *KSCL* RG20 ...... 45 J5
Barncroft *FNM* GU9 ...... 116 C1
 RAND SP11 ...... 80 G6
Barncroft Wy *HAV* PO9 ...... 14 C1
Barnes La *FARN* GU14 ...... 58 C9
 HLER SO31 ...... 270 D6
Barnes La *FRIM* GU16 ...... 58 E5
 NBNE BH10 ...... 322 D4
 WINC SO23 ...... 183 N1
Barnes Rd *FRIM* GU16 ...... 58 E5
 ITCH SO19 ...... 249 L5
 NBNE BH10 ...... 322 D4
 PSEA PO1 ...... 316 G2
Barnes Wallis Rd *FHAM* PO15 ...... 271 K5
Barnet La *NBAD* SO52 ...... 14 A2
Barnetts Wood La *NARL* SO24 ...... 149 K8
Barney Evans Crs *HORN* PO8 ...... 255 M8
Barneyhayes La *TOTT* SO40 ...... 244 D8
Barnfield *CHCH/BSGR* BH23 ...... 325 P7
 YTLY GU46 ...... 40 E9
Barnfield Cl *ALTN* GU34 ...... 114 A6
 ITCH SO19 ...... 268 C1
Barnfield Ct
 FHAM/STUB PO14 ...... 294 C1
 ITCH SO19 ...... 269 H1
Barnfield Ri *AND* SP10 ...... 102 C8
Barnfield Wy *ITCH* SO19 ...... 269 H1
Barn Fold *WVILLE* PO7 ...... 276 B1
Barn Green Cl *WVILLE* PO7 ...... 255 H7
Barn La *ALTN* GU34 ...... 132 C1
 DEAN RG23 ...... 87 J4
Barn Meadow Cl *FLEETS* GU52 ...... 74 C9
Barn Owl Wy *THLE* RG7 ...... 36 A2
Barn Piece *CHFD* SO53 ...... 206 B7
Barnsfield Crs *TOTT* SO40 ...... 245 H4
Barnsfield Rd *RGWD* BH24 ...... 281 N7
Barnside Wy *LISS* GU33 ...... 192 D3
Barnsland *ROWN* SO16 ...... 249 L1
Barnsley Cl *ASHV* GU12 ...... 76 C3
Barnsley Dro *WIMB* BH21 ...... 278 D2
The Barns *OVTN* RG25 ...... 109 H2
Barn Wood Rd *FHAM* PO15 ...... 272 B9
Baroda Rd *GPORT* PO12 ...... 13 K2
Baron Cl *HLER* SO31 ...... 269 P7
Barons Rd *BWD* BH11 ...... 301 M7
Barracane Dr *CWTH* RG45 ...... 41 J3
Barrack La *RGWD* BH24 ...... 283 H5
Barrack Rd *CHCH/BSGR* BH23 ...... 324 C8
 FERN BH22 ...... 302 C6
Barracuda Rd *ALDT* GU11 ...... 75 M5
Barrie Cl *FHAM* PO15 ...... 271 J2
Barrie Rd *FNM* GU9 ...... 96 B4
 MOOR/WNTN BH9 ...... 322 F4
Barrington Cl *ELGH* SO50 ...... 207 H8
Barrington Dr *CHIN* RG24 ...... 69 L3
Barron Pl *CHIN* RG24 ...... 68 C2
Barrow Down Gdns
 ITCH SO19 ...... 249 N8
Barrow Dr *CHAR* BH8 ...... 323 M5
Barrowfield *RAND* SP11 ...... 102 D9
Barrowgate Rd *CHAR* BH8 ...... 323 K5
Barrowgate Wy *CHAR* BH8 ...... 323 K5
Barrow Hl *RAND* SP11 ...... 122 C1
Barrow Hill Rd *TOTT* SO40 ...... 245 K1
Barrow Rd *CHAR* BH8 ...... 323 L5
Barrs Av *NMIL/BTOS* BH25 ...... 327 J5
Barrs Wood Dr
 NMIL/BTOS BH25 ...... 327 K3
Barrs Wood Rd
 NMIL/BTOS BH25 ...... 327 K3
Barry Gdns *BDST* BH18 ...... 300 D4
Barrys Meadow
 FHAM/STUB PO14 ...... 293 M1
Barry Wy *BH/HW/K* RG22 ...... 88 G5
Barter Rd *BKME/WDN* BH12 ...... 322 A4
Barters La *BDST* BH18 ...... 300 D8
Bartholomew St *NWBY* RG14 ...... 16 D4
Bartlemy La *NWBY* RG14 ...... 16 A7
Bartlemy Rd *NWBY* RG14 ...... 16 A7
Bartlett Cl *FHAM* PO15 ...... 10 A2
 TADY RG26 ...... 52 C3
Bartlett Dr *LTDN* BH7 ...... 323 P7
Bartlett Pl *FHAM* PO15 ...... 10 A2
Bartletts Common *FBDG* SP6 ...... 241 J4
The Bartletts *HLER* SO31 ...... 270 A8
Bartley Av *TOTT* SO40 ...... 246 C5
Bartley Rd *TOTT* SO40 ...... 245 J8
Bartley Wy *HTWY* RG27 ...... 72 B4
Bartok Cl *BH/HW/K* RG22 ...... 90 A2
Barton Cha
 NMIL/BTOS BH25 * 327 H8
Barton Cl *ALDT* GU11 ...... 96 E2
 AND SP10 ...... 82 B8
 ROMY SO51 ...... 204 F5
Barton Common La
 NMIL/BTOS BH25 ...... 327 K7
Barton Common Rd
 NMIL/BTOS BH25 ...... 327 K8
Barton Court Av
 NMIL/BTOS BH25 ...... 327 H7
Barton Court Rd
 NMIL/BTOS BH25 ...... 327 J6
Barton Cft *NMIL/BTOS* BH25 ...... 327 J8
Barton Cross *HORN* PO8 ...... 256 B4
Barton Dr *HEND* SO30 ...... 269 P7
Barton Dro *RWIN* SO21 ...... 125 J5
Barton Gn *NMIL/BTOS* BH25 ...... 327 J9
Barton Gv *HSEA* PO3 ...... 297 K6
Barton La *NMIL/BTOS* BH25 ...... 327 J9
Barton Pk *ELGH* SO50 ...... 229 L2
Bartons Cl *NMIL/BTOS* BH25 ...... 229 L1
Bartons Ct *ODIM* RG29 * 72 C9
Barton's Dr *YTLY* GU46 ...... 56 E1
Bartonside Rd
 NMIL/BTOS BH25 ...... 326 E7
Bartons La *CHIN* RG24 ...... 70 A5
Bartons Rd *FBDG* SP6 ...... 240 D2
 HAV PO9 ...... 276 C5
The Bartons *FBDG* SP6 ...... 240 D2
 HEND SO30 ...... 250 A5
Barton Wy *FARN* GU14 ...... 57 K6
Barton Wd *NMIL/BTOS* BH25 ...... 327 H7
Barton Wood Rd
 NMIL/BTOS BH25 ...... 326 G8
Bartram Rd *TOTT* SO40 ...... 246 E5
Barwell Cl *CWTH* RG45 ...... 40 C2
Barwell Gv *ASHV* GU12 ...... 76 A4
Bascott Cl *BWD* BH11 ...... 322 A6
Bascott Rd *BWD* BH11 ...... 321 P5
Bashley Common Rd
 NMIL/BTOS BH25 ...... 307 J8
Bashley Cross Rd
 NMIL/BTOS BH25 ...... 326 D2
Bashley Dr *NMIL/BTOS* BH25 ...... 327 K1
Bashley Rd *NMIL/BTOS* BH25 ...... 307 J9
Basingbourne Cl
 FLEETS GU52 ...... 74 C6
Basingbourne Rd
 FLEETS GU52 ...... 74 C7
Basing Dr *ALTN* GU34 ...... 109 N1
Basing Ms *BDST* BH23 * 97 H4
Basing Ms *BDST* BH23 * 232 A5
Basing Rd *HAV* PO9 ...... 276 E5
Basingstoke Rd *ALTN* GU34 ...... 132 B5
 HTWY RG27 ...... 51 J2
 KSCL RG20 ...... 48 D3
 RWIN SO21 ...... 165 L1
 TADY RG26 ...... 68 B1
Basing Vw *BSTK* RG21 ...... 7 G5
Basing Wy *CHFD* SO53 ...... 206 C9
Basingwell Street Lower
 BPWT SO32 ...... 232 A5
Basingwell Street Upper
 BPWT SO32 ...... 232 A5
Basin St *NEND* PO2 ...... 296 F9
Baslow Rd *BWD* BH11 ...... 321 M4
Basset Cl *ALTN* GU34 ...... 189 N1
Bassett Av *ROWN* SO16 ...... 58 D5
 ROWN SO16 ...... 228 D8
Bassett Crs East *ROWN* SO16 ...... 228 D8
Bassett Crs West *ROWN* SO16 ...... 228 C8
Bassett Dr *ROWN* SO16 ...... 228 D8
Bassett Gdns *ROWN* SO16 ...... 228 A8
Bassett Green Cl *ROWN* SO16 ...... 228 D7
Bassett Green Ct *ROWN* SO16 ...... 228 D6
Bassett Green Dr *ROWN* SO16 ...... 228 D7
Bassett Green Rd *ROWN* SO16 ...... 228 D6
Bassett Heath Av *ROWN* SO16 ...... 228 C5
Bassett Meadow *ROWN* SO16 ...... 228 D8
Bassett Ms *ROWN* SO16 ...... 228 D7
Bassett Rd *BKME/WDN* BH12 ...... 321 K6
Bassett Rw *ROWN* SO16 ...... 228 C6
Bassett Wood Dr *ROWN* SO16 ...... 228 C6
Bassett Wood Rd *ROWN* SO16 ...... 228 D6
Basswood Dr *CHIN* RG24 ...... 68 C4
Bastins Cl *HLER* SO31 ...... 271 H4
Bat & Ball La *RFNM* GU10 ...... 116 A5
Batchelor Crs *BWD* BH11 ...... 321 L4
Batchelor Dr *RSAL* SP5 ...... 199 D7
Batchelor Gn *HLER* SO31 ...... 269 P2
Batchelor Rd *HLER* SO31 ...... 269 P2
Batchelors Barn Rd *AND* SP10 ...... 5 J3
Batcombe Cl *BWD* BH11 ...... 321 N1
Bateman Gv *ASHV* GU12 ...... 97 M3
Bath Hill Rbt *BMTH* BH1 ...... 8 J5
Bathing La *PO4* PO1 ...... 18 E5
Bath Lane (Lower)
 FHAM/PORC PO16 ...... 11 K7
Bath Rd *BMTH* BH1 ...... 8 F5
 EMRTH PO10 ...... 299 M1
 ENEY PO4 ...... 317 H5
 ITCH SO19 ...... 249 L1
 LYMN SO41 ...... 329 M4
 NWBY RG14 ...... 25 J3
 NWBY RG14 ...... 16 E3
 WCLF BH2 ...... 8 E5
Bath Sq *PSEA* PO1 ...... 18 B5

Bath St SHAM SO14.... 248 C4
Bathurst Cl HISD PO11.... 318 E5
Bathurst Wy NEND PO2.... 296 D7
Batsford RAND SP11.... 84 B1
Batstone Wy FERN BH22.... 302 B2
Battalion Wy STHA RG19.... 25 P6
Battenburg Av NEND PO2.... 197 H7
Battenburg Rd GPORT PO12.... 12 E1
Batten Cl CHCH/BSGR BH23.... 325 H7
Batten Rd RSAL SP5.... 199 J3
Battens Av OVTN RG25.... 87 H3
Battens Wy HAV PO9.... 276 F6
Batterley Dro WIMB BH21.... 238 F7
Battery Cl GPORT PO12.... 286 E3
Battery End NWBY NW14.... 24 A9
Battery Hl BPWT SO32.... 231 P4
Battery Rd PSEA PO1.... 18 C7
Battery Rw PSEA PO1.... 18 C7
Battle Cl HLER SO31.... 270 F6
Baughurst Rd TADY RG26.... 49 P5
  THLE RG7.... 26 C9
B Av FAWY SO45.... 290 F4
Baverstock Rd
  BKME/WDN BH12.... 322 B7
Baverstock Av ALTN GU34.... 132 G3
The Baxendales NWBY RG14.... 17 J6
Baxter Rd ITCH SO19.... 249 N7
Baybridge La RWIN SO21.... 209 L3
Baybridge Rd HAV PO9.... 277 H5
Bay Cl ITCH SO19.... 249 J8
  WIMB BH21.... 280 E1
Bayfield Av FRIM GU16.... 58 D3
Bayford Cl BLKW GU17.... 57 P4
Bay Hog La PLE BH15.... 332 D1
Bayly Av FHAM/PORC PO16.... 295 P3
Baynum Cl BSTK RG21.... 7 G2
Baynum Dr
  LSOL/BMARY PO13.... 314 C1
Bay Rd GPORT PO12.... 315 K5
Bays Rd LYMN SO41.... 249 J8
Baythorn Cl NEND PO2.... 316 F1
Bay Tree Gdns TOTT SO40.... 267 K1
Bay Trees ITCH SO19.... 249 N5
Bay Tree Wy BSTK RG21.... 7 G1
Baywood Cl FARN GU14.... 57 K8
  CHCH/BSGR BH23.... 325 P6
Bazaar Rd TDWTH SP9.... 78 E6
Beach Av NMIL/BTOS BH25.... 327 H8
Beach Dr CHAM PO6.... 296 B1
Beach Rd CCLF BH13.... 334 A6
  EMRTH PO10.... 161 H1
  HISD PO11.... 318 E5
  LSOL/BMARY PO13.... 314 C3
  SSEA PO5.... 316 F7
Beach's Crs CHAM PO6.... 51 L2
Beachway FHAM/PORC PO16.... 295 P3
Beacon Bottom HLER SO31.... 270 C4
Beacon Cl HLER SO31.... 270 C4
  LYMN SO41.... 328 D6
  RFNM GU10.... 116 A5
Beaconhill La BPWT SO32.... 211 N4
Beacon Hill La BPWT SO32.... 211 L6
Beacon Ms HLER SO31.... 249 M5
Beacon Mt HLER SO31.... 270 C4
Beacon Rd FARN GU14.... 76 A4
  HEND SO30.... 249 M3
  WCLF BH2.... 8 D6
Beaconsfield Av CHAM PO6.... 297 J2
Beaconsfield
  BKME/WDN BH12.... 321 M7
  BSTK RG21.... 69 L8
  CHCH/BSGR BH23.... 324 F8
  FHAM/PORC PO16.... 294 F1
  WVILLE PO7.... 275 N2
Beacon Sq EMRTH PO10.... 299 J2
Beacon Wy BDST BH18.... 320 A1
  HLER SO31.... 270 C4
Beagon Cl ROWN SO16.... 227 H6
Beale's Cl AND SP10.... 4 E4
Beales La RFNM GU10.... 135 N3
Bealeswood La RFNM GU10.... 135 N5
Bealing Cl ROWN SO16.... 228 D8
Beal's Pightle TADY RG26.... 50 C6
Beam Hollow FNM GU9.... 96 C4
Beamish Rd CFDH PH17.... 321 H4
Beancroft Rd STHA RG19.... 25 N5
Bear Cross Av BWD BH11.... 301 N7
Beard Ct RAND SP11.... 80 A1
Bear Hl KSCL RG20.... 48 B4
Bear La FNM GU9.... 96 B8
  NWBY RG14.... 16 E2
Bearslane Cl TOTT SO40.... 246 D2
Bearwood Cots RFNM GU10.... 115 P3
Bearwood Gdns FLEETN GU51.... 74 D3
Beasant Cl FHAM PO15.... 317 K2
Beatrice Rd ENEY PO4.... 316 C6
  WSHM SO15.... 247 N4
Beattie Rd HEND SO30.... 250 C1
Beatty Cl HLER SO31.... 271 H6
  RGWD BH24.... 282 C1
Beatty Ct AND SP10.... 5 J3
Beatty Dr GPORT PO12.... 315 K6
Beatty Rd MOOR/WNTN BH9.... 323 H6
Beauchamp Av
  LSOL/BMARY PO13.... 294 C7
Beauchamp Pl
  CHCH/BSGR BH23.... 324 E8
Beauchamps Gdns LTDN BH7.... 323 N7
Beauclerk Gn HTWY RG27.... 73 H3
Beaucroft La WIMB BH21.... 278 C8
Beaucroft Rd BDST BH18.... 320 C9
  WIMB BH21.... 278 C9
Beaufighter Rd FARN GU14.... 75 P4
Beaufort Av
  FHAM/PORC PO16.... 295 P3
Beaufort Cl CHCH/BSGR BH23.... 325 M8
  LSOL/BMARY PO13.... 314 D3
Beaufort Dr BPWT SO32.... 232 A4
  WIMB BH21.... 278 E9

Beaufort Rd ASHV GU12.... 76 E6
  BOR GU35.... 154 A3
  FLEETS GU52.... 74 E5
  FNM GU9.... 96 C8
  HAV PO9.... 14 B3
  SBNE BH6.... 336 A1
  SSEA PO5 *.... 316 F7
  WINC SO23.... 22 C7
Beaufoys Av FERN BH22.... 302 C1
Beaufoys Cl FERN BH22.... 302 C1
Beaulieu Av
  CHCH/BSGR BH23.... 324 C8
  FHAM/PORC PO16.... 295 L1
  HAV PO9.... 276 D4
Beaulieu Cl FUFL SO22.... 164 E3
  NMIL/BTOS BH25.... 326 C4
  ROWN SO16.... 227 M7
Beaulieu Gdns BLKW GU17.... 41 K9
Beaulieu Pl
  LSOL/BMARY PO13.... 294 C7
Beaulieu Rd BROC SO42.... 289 N5
  CHCH/BSGR BH23.... 324 C8
  ELGH SO50.... 207 J9
  HAV PO9.... 14 B5
  LYND SO43.... 268 A9
  LYND SO43.... 265 H6
  NEND PO2.... 296 C8
  TOTT SO40.... 267 H5
  WBNE BH4.... 334 B5
Beaumaris Cl AND SP10.... 102 C4
Beaumaris Gdns FAWY SO45.... 268 B6
Beaumaris Rde FERN GU16.... 58 E5
Beaumond Gn WINC SO23.... 22 D5
Beaumont Cl FHAM PO15.... 272 B7
  ROWN SO16.... 228 A9
Beaumont Ct GPORT PO12 *.... 295 L9
Beaumont Gv ALDT GU11.... 2 A2
Beaumont Ri FHAM PO15.... 272 B6
Beaumont Rd CCLF BH13.... 333 N4
  TOTT SO40.... 246 D4
Beaumont Ter CADNM SO40 *.... 51 N2
Beauworth Av WEND SO18.... 249 L3
Beaver Dr ELGH SO50.... 230 A2
Beaver La YTLY GU46.... 40 F9
Beavers Cl ALTN GU34.... 132 C5
  FNM GU9.... 96 A9
  TADY RG26.... 34 A5
Beavers Hl FNM GU9.... 95 P9
Beavers Ms BOR GU35.... 154 B4
Beavers Rd FNM GU9.... 96 A9
Beccles Cl PLE BH15.... 332 B1
Bechin Cl FLEETS GU52.... 74 A9
Beck Cl HLER SO31.... 270 E7
Beckett Rd AND SP10.... 102 C2
Beckford La WHAM PO17.... 274 A1
Beck Gdns FHAM PO15.... 96 A5
Beckham La PSF GU32.... 215 K1
Beckhampton Rd PLE BH15.... 320 A8
Beckley Copse
  CHCH/BSGR BH23.... 326 C5
Beck St PSEA PO1.... 18 E2
Becton La NMIL/BTOS BH25.... 327 J9
Becton Md NMIL/BTOS BH25.... 327 K6
Bedale Wy PLE BH15.... 321 H7
Beddington Cl CHIN RG24.... 70 B4
Bede Dr AND SP10.... 82 F8
Bedenham La
  LSOL/BMARY PO13.... 295 J6
Bedfield La WINC SO23.... 165 J2
Bedford Av BOR GU35.... 154 A7
  ITCH SO19.... 248 G9
Bedford Crs FRIM GU16.... 58 D7
  LTDN BH7.... 324 A8
Bedford La FRIM GU16.... 58 E7
Bedford Pl WSHM SO15.... 21 K2
Bedford Rd BOR GU35.... 154 A7
  HEND SO30.... 250 D5
  NWBY RG14.... 30 B1
Bedford Rd North
  BKME/WDN BH12.... 321 L2
Bedford Rd South
  BKME/WDN BH12.... 321 L2
Bedford St GPORT PO12.... 315 L2
  SSEA PO5.... 19 G4
Bedhampton Hl HAV PO9.... 276 A9
Bedhampton Rd HAV PO9.... 14 A4
  NEND PO2.... 297 H8
Bedhampton Wy HAV PO9.... 276 F6
Bedser Sq AND SP10.... 82 F8
Bedwell Cl ROWN SO16.... 227 K7
Beecham Berry
  BH/HW/K RG22.... 89 P4
Beecham Rd PSEA PO1.... 316 C1
Beech Av CBLY GU15.... 58 F7
  CHCH/BSGR BH23.... 324 B7
  RFNM GU10.... 116 C5
  SBNE BH6.... 336 A2
  STOK SO20.... 121 H5
  WEND SO18.... 248 G4
Beechbank Av CFDH BH17.... 320 A5
Beechbrook Av YTLY GU46.... 97 L3
Beech Cl ASHV GU12.... 97 J3
  CHFD SO53.... 206 F5
  FBDG SP6.... 239 N6
  FUFL SO22.... 183 K3
  HLER SO31.... 270 E7
  HORN PO8.... 255 P9
  LYMN SO41.... 328 D2
  OVTN RG25.... 87 H1
  RAND SP11.... 100 E2
  RAND SP11.... 101 N1
  RGWD/BURGH RG30.... 277 G1
  STHA RG19.... 32 E1
  TADY RG26.... 52 B3
  VWD BH31.... 258 E5
Beech Copse FUFL SO22.... 164 C6
  HEND SO30 *.... 249 M2
  RGWD BH24.... 265 N2
Beech Crs AND SP10.... 290 C1
Beechcroft Cl AND SP10.... 4 C1

CHFD SO53.... 206 F7
FHAM PO15.... 272 A9
LIPH GU30.... 174 E4
Beechcroft Cots STOK SO20.... 160 A1
Beechcroft Rd GPORT PO12.... 282 F1
Beechcroft Rd GPORT PO12.... 12 B5
Beechcroft Wy CHFD SO53.... 206 F7
Beechdale Cl TOTT SO40.... 246 A1
Beech Dr BLKW GU17.... 57 L1
Beechen Hl BPWT SO32.... 232 B2
Beeches Hl BPWT SO32.... 232 B2
The Beeches AND SP10.... 102 C2
  ASHV GU12.... 76 E3
  BH/HW/K RG22.... 89 P5
  ELGH SO50.... 230 D3
  LTDN BH7.... 323 N7
  ROMY SO51.... 224 D1
Beechey Rd CHAR BH8.... 335 H1
Beechfield AMSY SP4.... 118 C3
Beechfield Ct WSHM SO15.... 247 L3
Beech Gdns HLER SO31.... 269 N8
Beech Gra RSAL SP5.... 223 M2
Beech Gv ALTN GU34.... 115 P7
  CHOB/PIR GU24.... 59 P6
  FHAM/PORC PO16.... 12 B4
  RAND SP11.... 123 K3
  RWIN SO21.... 208 G1
Beech Hanger AMSY SP4.... 98 F9
Beech Hanger End
  GSHT GU26.... 156 A2
Beech Hl BOR GU35.... 155 J3
Beech Hill Rd BOR GU35.... 154 G2
  TDWTH SP9.... 79 J4
Beeching Cl ASHV GU12.... 76 G9
Beechlands Rd ALTN GU34.... 156 A1
Beech La GSHT GU26.... 156 A1
  RCWD BH24.... 281 L7
Beechleigh Pl RGWD BH24 *.... 282 E1
Beechmount Rd ROWN SO16.... 228 B7
Beechnut Dr BLKW GU17.... 41 J8
Beechnut Rd ASHV GU12.... 3 G4
Beech Ride FLEETS GU52.... 74 C5
  SHST GU47.... 42 F4
Beech Rd CHFD SO53.... 206 F5
  FARN GU14.... 10 B4
  FHAM PO15.... 10 B4
  HASM GU27.... 158 E7
  HEND SO30.... 250 D4
  HORN PO8.... 236 D7
  KSCL RG20.... 31 M4
  NARL SO24.... 168 A2
  ROMY SO51.... 204 G7
  TOTT SO40.... 245 P9
  WSHM SO15.... 247 M5
Beech Tree Cl DEAN RG23.... 88 E3
Beech Tree Dr FNM GU9.... 96 G6
Beech Tree Wk STOK SO20.... 160 B4
Beech Wy AND SP10.... 102 B4
Beech Wy DEAN RG23.... 88 E5
  HORN PO8.... 256 B6
Beechwood Cl CHIN RG24.... 69 P1
  FBDG SP6.... 240 B2
Beechwood Av BOSC BH5.... 335 M2
  NMIL/BTOS BH25.... 326 C3
  WVILLE PO7.... 255 N2
Beechwood Cl LISS GU33.... 173 M9
Beechwood Crs CHFD SO53.... 206 C3
Beechwood Gdns BOSC BH5.... 335 N2
  WEND SO18.... 248 C3
Beechwood La RGWD BH24.... 284 D6
Beechwood Ri WEND SO18.... 249 L2
Beechwood Rd ALTN GU34.... 132 D7
  FAWY SO45.... 290 E6
  FERN PO2.... 280 F8
  NEND PO2.... 296 D2
  TOTT SO40.... 267 M8
Beechwood Wy FAWY SO45.... 267 N8
Beechworth Rd HAV PO9.... 15 H5
Beehive Wk PSEA PO1.... 18 D5
Beethoven Rd BH/HW/K RG22.... 90 A3
Beeton's Av HAV PO9.... 276 F8
Beggars Dro RWIN SO21.... 189 J5
Beggar's La WINC SO23.... 23 G4
Beggarwood La DEAN RG23.... 89 K6
Begonia Cl AND SP10.... 82 F8
Begonia Rd ROWN SO16.... 228 D8
Behrendt Cl GPORT PO12.... 315 L2
Belben Cl BKME/WDN BH12.... 321 J4
Belben Rd BKME/WDN BH12.... 321 J4
Belbins ROMY SO51.... 204 D1
Beldham Rd FNM GU9.... 115 P3
Belfairs Dr LTDN BH7.... 324 B7
Belfry Ms SHST GU47.... 40 G6
Belfry Sq BH/HW/K RG22.... 89 L6
Belfry Wk FHAM/STUB PO14.... 271 J8
Belgrave Ct BLKW GU17.... 57 L2
Belgrave Rd CCLF BH13.... 334 A4
  SD/PW SO17.... 248 E1
Belgravia Rd NEND PO2.... 297 H8
Belinair Rd HAV PO9.... 15 H6
Belland Dr ALDT GU11.... 2 A4
Bell Cha ALDT GU11.... 2 C3
Bell Cl FARN GU14.... 58 B7
Bell Crs WVILLE PO7.... 275 N4
Bell Davies Rd
  FHAM/STUB PO14.... 293 P8
Bellemoor Rd WSHM SO15.... 247 L5
Bellevue WHCH RG28.... 85 L6
Belle Vue Cl SBNE BH6.... 336 B2
Belle Vue Crs SBNE BH6.... 336 D2
Belle Vue Gv FERN BH22.... 280 F7
Belle Vue La EMRTH PO10.... 277 M8
Belle Vue Rd CHIN RG24.... 70 C6
  AND SO10.... 4 E7
  PSTN BH14.... 321 L9
  SBNE BH6.... 336 B3
  ASHV GU12.... 3 J1
Bellevue Rd ELGH SO50.... 229 J1
  WSHM SO15.... 20 E1

Belle Vue Wk FERN BH22.... 302 E6
Bellew Rd FRIM GU16.... 58 G7
Bellflower Cl
  CHCH/BSGR BH23.... 325 M7
Belliflower Wy CHFD SO53.... 206 B6
Bell Hl PSF GU32.... 191 L9
Bell Hill Rdg PSF GU32.... 191 L9
Bell Holt NWBY RG14.... 30 B1
Bellingham Cl HLER SO31.... 59 H1
Bell La BLKW GU17.... 41 K9
  OVTN RG25.... 110 F4
  RFNM GU10.... 135 L9
Bell Meadow Rd HTWY RG27.... 72 A3
Bell Ms WHCH RG28.... 85 L6
Bell Rd AND SP10.... 5 G4
  CHAM PO6.... 296 F1
  CHIN RG24.... 69 P5
Bells La FHAM/STUB PO14.... 294 A7
Bell St RAND SP11.... 80 A1
  ROMY SO51.... 204 C6
  SHAM SO14.... 21 F6
  WHCH RG28.... 85 L6
Bell Vale La HASM GU27.... 158 G8
Belmont Av CHAR BH8.... 323 J6
Belmont Cl AND SP10.... 5 F7
  FARN GU14.... 57 N6
  FAWY SO45.... 268 C8
  FHAM/STUB PO14.... 294 B6
  HORN PO8.... 256 C1
Belmont Dr BH31.... 258 G5
Belmont Gv HAV PO9.... 276 D8
Belmont Hts BH/HW/K RG22.... 89 N6
Belmont La AND SP10.... 5 C6
Belmont Pl SSEA PO5.... 19 H6
Belmont Rd AND SP10.... 5 F7
  CBLY GU15.... 58 B1
  CHFD SO53.... 228 F1
  LYMN SO41.... 329 J3
  PSTN BH14.... 321 P9
  SD/PW SO17.... 248 E5
Belmore La LYMN SO41.... 329 L4
  NARL SO24.... 168 A2
Belney La FHAM PO15.... 274 C2
Belsize Rd FNM GU9.... 74 E3
Belstone Rd TOTT SO40.... 246 C4
Belton Rd ITCH SO19.... 249 K8
Belvedere Cl FLEETN GU51.... 73 P5
Belvedere Ct BLKW GU17 *.... 57 L2
Belvedere Dr NWBY RG14.... 16 E7
Belvedere Gdns CHIN RG24.... 52 B9
Belvedere Rd
  CHCH/BSGR BH23.... 324 E8
  FARN GU14.... 58 A7
  TWDS BH3.... 322 C9
Belverdere Cl PSF GU32.... 215 M1
Belvidere Rd SHAM SO14.... 21 J3
Belvidere Ter SHAM SO14.... 21 J2
Belvoir Cl FHAM/PORC PO16.... 58 E4
Bembridge HLER SO31.... 269 L4
Bembridge Cl ROWN SO16.... 228 E7
Bembridge Crs ENEY PO4.... 316 C7
Bembridge Dr HISD PO11.... 319 J7
Bemister Rd
  MOOR/WNTN BH9.... 322 G7
Bemisters La GPORT PO12.... 13 J2
Benbow Cl HORN PO8.... 256 C4
Benbow Ct AND SP10 *.... 5 J3
Benbow Crs
  BKME/WDN BH12.... 321 N3
Benbow Pl PSEA PO1.... 18 C2
Benbridge Av BWD BH11.... 301 P8
Bendeng Cl FLEETN GU51.... 74 A1
Bendigo Rd CHCH/BSGR BH23.... 324 C7
Beneden Gn NARL SO24.... 168 A2
Benedict Cl ROMY SO51.... 204 G6
Benedict Wy
  FHAM/PORC PO16.... 274 A8
Beneficial St PSEA PO1.... 18 C5
Benellen Av WBNE BH4.... 334 C2
Benellen Gdns WBNE BH4.... 334 C1
Benellen Rd WBNE BH4.... 334 C1
Benenden Gn NARL SO24.... 168 A2
Benett Cl RSAL SP5.... 199 P7
Benett Gdns NWBY RG14.... 24 C2
Benett Rd MOOR/WNTN BH9.... 322 G6
Bengers La AND SP10.... 79 J8
Benham Dro PROS *.... 297 H5
Benham Dro STOK SO20.... 139 L2
Benham Gv
  FHAM/PORC PO16.... 295 P3
Benhams La LISS GU33.... 173 L3
Benhams Rd WEND SO18.... 249 J1
Benin Rd RAND SP11.... 79 M5
Benmoor Rd CFDH BH17.... 320 C4
Benmore Cl NMIL/BTOS BH25.... 327 L1
Benmore Gdns CHFD SO53.... 206 D3
Benmore Rd
  MOOR/WNTN BH9.... 322 G6
Bennet Cl WVILLE PO7.... 275 N4
Bennett Rd CHAR BH8.... 323 J9
Bennetts La RGWD BH24.... 284 E7
Bennetts Ri ALDT GU11.... 3 G4
Bennion Rd NBNE BH10.... 322 C4
Benny Hill Cl ELGH SO50.... 229 H1
Benson Cl CHCH/BSGR BH23.... 305 M7
Benson Rd CFDH PH17.... 320 F5
  CWTH RG45.... 40 G1
  WSHM SO15.... 247 M5
Bentall Pl AND SP10.... 5 G4
Bentham Rd GPORT PO12.... 12 C5
Bentham Wy HLER SO31.... 270 D2

Bentley Cl HORN PO8.... 256 C3
  WINC SO23.... 165 J1
Bentley Copse CBLY GU15.... 58 G1
Bentley Ct HAV PO9.... 277 H5
Bentley Crs FHAM/PORC PO16.... 10 D5
Bentley Gn WEND SO18.... 249 L3
Bentley Rd MOOR/WNTN BH9.... 322 F4
Bentley Wy RSAL SP5.... 158 C2
Bent St HLER SO31.... 329 K1
Bent St STOK SO20.... 139 M2
Benville Dr FERN BH22.... 276 D6
Benwell Cl ODIM RG29.... 93 J5
Bepton Down EPSF GU31.... 215 N2
Berber Cl FHAM PO15.... 271 J3
Bercotte Cl FUFL SO22.... 164 C2
Bere Cl CFDH BH17.... 320 C5
  FUFL SO22.... 164 E5
Bere Farm La WHAM PO17.... 273 K2
Bere Hl WHCH RG28.... 85 L5
Bere Hill Cl WHCH RG28.... 85 M5
  AND SP10.... 5 C6
Bere Vale ALTN GU34.... 132 F7
Bere Rd WVILLE PO7.... 255 H7
Beresford Cl AND SP10.... 102 C5
  BKME/WDN BH12.... 321 M6
  FRIM GU16.... 58 E7
  WVILLE PO7.... 275 N4
Beresford Gdns
  CHCH/BSGR BH23.... 325 J9
  CHFD SO53.... 206 C5
Beresford Ga AND SP10 *.... 103 J1
Beresford Rd
  BKME/WDN BH12.... 321 M6
  CHFD SO53.... 206 C5
  FHAM/STUB PO14.... 294 B6
  LYMN SO41.... 329 J3
  NEND PO2.... 296 C7
  SBNE BH6.... 335 P2
Bereweeke Cl FUFL SO22.... 22 A1
Bereweeke Rd FUFL SO22.... 164 C5
Bereweeke Wy FUFL SO22.... 164 D5
Bergen Crs HEND SO30.... 250 C6
Berkeley Av
  BKME/WDN BH12.... 321 L4
Berkeley Cl FHAM/STUB PO14.... 293 P7
  FLEETN GU51.... 74 E3
  VWD BH31.... 258 E3
  WSHM SO15.... 248 A4
Berkeley Crs FRIM GU16.... 58 F5
Berkeley Dr BH/HW/K RG22.... 90 B5
Berkeley Gdns HEND SO30.... 250 C6
Berkeley Rd NWBY RG14.... 16 C3
  TWDS BH3.... 322 E8
Berkeley Sq HAV PO9.... 15 K5
Berkley Av FRIM GU16.... 58 D1
Berkshire Circular Routes
  THLE RG7.... 26 A1
Berkshire Cl PSEA PO1.... 19 K3
Berkshire Corpse Rd
  ALDT GU11.... 75 M5
Bermuda Cl CHIN RG24.... 69 L2
Bernard Av ALTN GU34.... 150 C6
  CHAM PO6.... 297 J1
Bernards Ct CHCH/BSGR BH23.... 324 C7
Bernard St SHAM SO14.... 20 E6
Bernersh Rd SHST GU47.... 41 K5
Berney Rd ENEY PO4.... 317 L4
Bernina Av WVILLE PO7.... 255 L9
Bernina Cl WVILLE PO7.... 255 L9
Bernstein Rd BH/HW/K RG22.... 89 N3
Bernwood Gv FAWY SO45.... 312 C1
Berrans Av BWD BH11.... 322 B1
Berrington Wy CHIN RG24.... 69 P4
Berry Cl HEND SO30.... 250 D5
Berrydown La OVTN RG25.... 87 J4
  OVTN RG25.... 110 E6
Berrydown Rd HAV PO9.... 276 C3
Berryfield Rd LYMN SO41.... 328 A5
Berryl Hl NARL SO24.... 168 K2
Berrylands LISS GU33.... 173 M8
Berry La FHAM/STUB PO14.... 293 N7
  RWIN SO21.... 184 A1
Berry Wy AND SP10.... 102 B3
Berrywood Gdns HEND SO30.... 250 B3
Berrywood Rd HEND SO30.... 250 B3
Bertie Rd ENEY PO4.... 317 K4
Bertram Rd NMIL/BTOS BH25.... 327 L3
Berwick Cl ROWN SO16.... 227 L7
Berwick Rd TWDS BH5.... 322 E9
Berwyn Cl BH/HW/K RG22.... 68 D9
Berwyn Wk FHAM/STUB PO14.... 293 N7
Beryl Av GPORT PO12.... 295 K9
Beryton Cl GPORT PO12.... 315 L2
Beryton Rd GPORT PO12.... 315 L2
Besomer Dro RSAL SP5.... 200 B9
Bessborough Rd CCLF BH13.... 333 N4
Bessemer Cl STHA RG19.... 25 N9
Bessemer Rd BSTK RG21.... 90 B1
Beswick Av NBNE BH10.... 322 D5
Beta Rd FARN GU14.... 57 N8
Bethel Cl FNM GU9.... 96 D5
Bethia Cl CHAR BH8.... 323 K9
Bethia Rd CHAR BH8.... 323 K9
Betjeman Wk YTLY GU46.... 40 D9
Betsy Cl CHCH/BSGR BH23.... 305 M7
Betsy La CHCH/BSGR BH23.... 305 M7
Betteridge Dr ROWN SO16.... 316 C1
Bettesworth Rd PSEA PO1.... 19 J2
Betticombe Cl CFDH BH17.... 320 F2
Betula Cl CHCH/BSGR BH23.... 276 A4
Beulah Rd ROWN SO16.... 247 L2
Bevan Cl ITCH SO19.... 268 C1
Bevans Cl PSEA PO1.... 19 H6
Beveren Cl FLEETN GU51.... 56 E9
Beverley Cl ASHV GU12.... 97 M2
  BH/HW/K RG22.... 90 D2
  HLER SO31.... 271 J6
  NTHA RG18.... 15 H2
Beverley Crs FARN GU14.... 75 N1
  HEND SO30.... 250 B3
Beverley Gdns BPWT SO32.... 232 F7
  HLER SO31.... 269 N1
  NBNE BH10.... 322 D4
  ROMY SO51.... 204 A9

Beverley Gv *CHAM* PO6.......... 275 P9
Beverley Hts *WEND* SO18.......... 229 H9
Beverley Rd *FAWY* SO45.......... 290 A5
  FHAM/STUB PO14.......... 294 A8
Bevers Cl *LSOL/BMARY* PO13.... 295 H7
The Bevers *THLE* RG7.......... 27 J9
Beverston Rd *CHAM* PO6.......... 274 A8
Bevis Cl *FAWY* SO45.......... 291 H7
  HLER SO31.......... 292 D1
Bevis Rd *GPORT* PO12.......... 12 D1
  NEND PO2.......... 296 F8
Bevis Gdns *SHAM* SO14.......... 248 C4
Bevois Hl *SD/PW* SO17.......... 248 D3
Bevois Valley Rd *SHAM* SO14.... 248 D4
Bexington Cl *BWD* BH11.......... 321 N1
Bexmoor *THLE* RG7.......... 70 B6
Bexmoor Wy *CHIN* RG24.......... 70 A6
Beyne Rd *FUFL* SO22.......... 183 K3
Bible Fids *OVTN* RG25.......... 108 C2
Bicester Cl *WHCH* RG28.......... 85 L6
Bickerley Gdns *RING* BH24...... 282 D5
Bickerley Rd *RGWD* BH24.......... 282 D5
Bicknell Rd *FRIM* GU16.......... 58 D3
Bicton Rd *BWD* BH11.......... 322 B4
Bidbury La *HAV* PO9.......... 202 E9
Biddenfield La *WHAM* PO17.... 252 B7
Bidden La *RAND* SP11.......... 80 B1
Biddlecombe Cl
  LSOL/BMARY PO13.......... 294 G9
Bideford Cl *FHAM/STUB* PO14.... 294 C1
  ROWN SO16.......... 247 J2
Biggin Wk *FHAM/STUB* PO14...... 294 C1
Bighton Dean La *NARL* SO24.... 148 G3
Bighton Hl *NARL* SO24.......... 169 K1
Bighton La *NARL* SO24.......... 148 F7
Bighton Rd *ALTN* GU34.......... 149 M3
Bilbao Cl *AND* SP10.......... 5 J2
Bilberry Cl *HLER* SO31.......... 270 F4
Bilberry Dr *TOTT* SO40.......... 247 J9
Billesden Rd *CHOB/PIR* GU24.... 59 P7
Billett Av *WVILLE* PO7.......... 275 P1
Billing Cl *ENEY* PO4.......... 317 K5
Billington Gdns *HEND* SO30...... 250 D2
Billington Wy *NTHA* RG18.......... 84 B3
Bill Sargent Crs *PSEA* PO1...... 316 C2
Billy Lawn Av *HAV* PO9.......... 276 F5
Billys Copse *HAV* PO9.......... 276 F5
Bilton Rd *CHIN* RG24.......... 69 P3
Bilton Wy *HSEA* PO3.......... 297 L7
Bindon Cl *ROWN* SO16.......... 247 L1
Binfields Cl *CHIN* RG24.......... 70 A3
Bingham Av *PSTN* BH14.......... 333 N4
Bingham Dr *LYMN* SO41.......... 329 L4
Bingham Rd
  CHCH/BSGR BH23.......... 325 J8
  MOOR/WNTN BH9.......... 322 F2
  WVD BH31.......... 258 C6
Bingley Cl *ALTN* GU34.......... 132 E5
  BSTK RG21.......... 7 H2
Binley Bottom *RAND* SP11...... 62 C8
Binnacle Wy *CHAM* PO6.......... 296 D1
Binness Wy *CHAM* PO6.......... 297 N2
Binnie Rd *BKME/WDN* BH12.... 321 K7
Binsey Cl *ROWN* SO16.......... 247 J3
Binstead Rd *ROWN* SO16.......... 228 E2
Binstead Rd *ALTN* GU34.......... 135 J1
Binsted Dr *BLKW* GU17.......... 41 L9
Binsteed Rd *NEND* PO2.......... 296 D9
Binton La *RFNM* GU10.......... 97 L9
Birch Av *CHCH/BSGR* BH23.... 324 C4
  FERN BH22.......... 302 F7
  FLEETN GU51.......... 74 C3
  NMIL/BTOS BH25.......... 326 F1
  STHA RG19.......... 15 K4
Birch Cl *BOR* GU35.......... 154 B6
  HORN PO8.......... 255 N8
  LISS GU33.......... 192 C2
  RFNM GU10.......... 321 N9
  RGWD BH24.......... 281 K6
  ROWN SO51.......... 204 C7
  RWIN SO21.......... 207 P5
Birch Dl *FAWY* SO45.......... 268 D8
Birchdale Cl *HLER* SO31.......... 292 D1
Birchdale Rd *WIMB* BH21...... 278 F9
Birch Dr *BLKW* GU17.......... 57 L2
  CHAR BH8.......... 323 N5
  LSOL/BMARY PO13.......... 294 C5
Birchen Cl *HLER* SO31.......... 271 J6
The Birches *NBAD* SO52.......... 205 K8
Birches Crest *BH/HW/K* RG22.... 89 P5
The Birches *BLKW* GU17.......... 41 L9
  FARN GU14.......... 57 L9
Birchett Rd *ALDT* GU11.......... 2 D3
  FARN GU14.......... 57 M7
Birchfields Cl *FLEETN* GU51.... 58 B1
Birch Gv *BOR* GU35.......... 154 A7
  ELGH SO50.......... 207 H7
  FERN BH22.......... 280 D7
  HTWY RG27.......... 72 A2
  STOK SO20.......... 123 H7
Birchland Cl *THLE* RG7.......... 26 C9
Birchlands *TOTT* SO40.......... 246 B6
Birch La *THLE* RG7.......... 35 N1
Birchmore Cl
  LSOL/BMARY PO13.......... 294 C7
Bircholt Rd *LIPH* GU30.......... 174 E3
Birch Rd *BOR* GU35.......... 155 J2
  HEND SO30.......... 250 D4
  RGWD BH24.......... 281 P5
  ROWN SO16.......... 228 C4
  THLE RG7.......... 33 P4
  THLE RG7.......... 27 J7
Birch Tree Cl *EMRTH* PO10...... 277 M6
Birch Tree Dr *EMRTH* PO10...... 277 M6
Birchview Cl *YTLY* GU46.......... 56 D1
Birch Wk *FERN* BH22.......... 302 F5
Birch Wy *ASHV* GU12.......... 76 F5
Birchwood *CHIN* RG24.......... 70 A1
Birch Wd *ITCH* SO19.......... 249 N6
Birchwood Cl
  CHCH/BSGR BH23.......... 326 A7

Birchwood Dr *FBDG* SP6.......... 239 N6
Birchwood Gdns *HEND* SO30.... 250 C3
Birchwood Rd *NWBY* RG14...... 24 G3
  PSTN BH14.......... 321 N9
Birchy Hl *LYMN* SO41.......... 308 C7
Bird Fld *CHFD* SO53.......... 206 A7
Birdham Rd *HISD* PO11.......... 319 L6
Birdhaven *RFNM* GU10.......... 116 A5
Birdlip Cl *HORN* PO8.......... 256 A5
Birdlip Rd *CHAM* PO6.......... 274 D9
Birds Hill Gdns *PLE* BH15...... 320 G9
Bird's Hill Rd *PLE* BH15.......... 320 G8
Birdwood Gv
  FHAM/PORC PO16.......... 295 K1
Birdwood Rd *CBLY* GU15.......... 41 N8
Birinus Rd *WINC* SO23.......... 23 F2
Birkbeck Pl *SHST* GU47.......... 41 M5
Birkdale Av *CHAM* PO6.......... 275 L9
Birkdale Cl *BDST* BH18.......... 300 C8
Birkdale Rd *BDST* BH18.......... 300 C8
Birkenholme Cl *BOR* GU35...... 155 K4
Birmingham Ct
  LSOL/BMARY PO13 *.......... 315 H3
Biscay Cl *FHAM/STUB* PO14.... 295 P6
Bishearne Gdns *LISS* GU33.... 192 C1
Bishop Cl *BKME/WDN* BH12.... 322 C8
Bishop Ct *RGWD* BH24.......... 282 E2
Bishop Rd *MOOR/WNTN* BH9.... 322 G7
Bishops Cl *FLEETS* GU52.......... 74 D5
  LTDN BH7.......... 323 M9
  TADY RG26.......... 34 B5
  TDWTH SP9.......... 79 H7
  TOTT SO40.......... 246 C3
Bishops Ct *ELGH* SO50.......... 207 M8
Bishops Crs *PSTN* SO19.......... 249 H7
Bishopsfield Rd
  FHAM/STUB PO14.......... 294 C2
Bishops Ga
  FHAM/STUB PO14.......... 271 J7
Bishops La *BPWT* SO32.......... 252 F2
Bishop's La *BPWT* SO32.......... 232 A5
Bishop's Md *FNM* GU9.......... 96 B5
  ITCH SO19.......... 248 G8
Bishopstoke La *ELGH* SO50.... 207 H7
Bishopstoke Mnr *ELGH* SO50 *.. 229 M1
Bishopstoke Rd *ELGH* SO50...... 229 L1
  HAV PO9.......... 276 E5
Bishop St *PSEA* PO1.......... 18 D2
Bishop Sumner Dr *FNM* GU9.... 96 F5
Bishop's Vw *ALTN* GU34.......... 150 A6
Bishop's Wy *AND* SP10.......... 4 A3
Bishopswood La *TADY* RG26.... 33 P5
Bishop's Wood Rd
  BPWT SO32.......... 232 F3
Bishopswood Rd *TADY* RG26.... 34 A5
Bisley Ct *ITCH* SO19.......... 249 K8
Bittacy Cl *RCWD* BH24.......... 284 F7
Bittern Cl *ALDT* GU11.......... 96 A1
  BH/HW/K RG22.......... 89 K3
  GPORT PO12.......... 315 M1
  SHST GU47.......... 41 L6
Bitterne Cl *HAV* PO9.......... 276 F4
Bitterne Crs *ITCH* SO19.......... 249 J5
Bitterne Rd *WEND* SO18.......... 249 H4
Bitterne Rd East *WEND* SO18.. 249 K4
Bitterne Rd West
  WEND SO18.......... 248 G4
Bitterne Village *WEND* SO18.... 249 J5
Bitterne Wy *LYMN* SO41.......... 329 K5
  LYMN SO41.......... 258 G5
Blackberry Cl *ALTN* GU34.......... 150 D5
Black Berry Cl *HORN* PO8...... 236 D8
Blackberry Cl *THLE* RG7 *........ 27 J5
Blackberry La *ELGH* SO50...... 230 C3
Blackberry La *ALTN* GU34.......... 150 C7
  CHCH/BSGR BH23.......... 325 K9
Blackberry Ter *SHAM* SO14.... 248 D4
Blackbird Cl *BH/HW/K* RG22.... 89 K3
  CFDH BH17.......... 320 A4
  HORN PO8.......... 255 P7
  SHST GU47.......... 41 M6
  THLE RG7 *.......... 27 K4
Blackbird Ct *AND* SP10.......... 82 F9
Blackbird Rd *ELGH* SO50.......... 228 F2
Blackbird Wy
  BKME/WDN BH12.......... 305 N8
  LSOL/BMARY PO13.......... 314 D1
Blackbrook House Dr
  FHAM/STUB PO14.......... 10 B5
Blackbrook Park Av
  FHAM PO15.......... 10 B5
Blackbrook Rd *FHAM* PO15.... 10 A4
Blackburn Ct
  LSOL/BMARY PO13 *.......... 315 H3
Blackburn Rd
  BKME/WDN BH12.......... 321 K6
Blackbushe Cl *ROWN* SO16.... 227 K7
Blackbushe Pk *YTLY* GU46 *.... 40 D8
Blackbushes Rd *FLEETN* GU51.. 56 B7
  HTWY RG27.......... 55 P4
Blackbush Rd *LYMN* SO41...... 328 B9
Blackcap Cl *HAV* PO9.......... 276 C1
Blackcap Pl *SHST* GU47.......... 41 M6
Black Dam Wy *BSTK* RG21...... 69 H9
Blackdown Cl *BH/HW/K* RG22.. 68 D9
  FAWY SO45.......... 267 P9
Blackdown Crs *HAV* PO9.......... 276 C6
Blackdown La *FRIM* GU16.......... 59 H6
Blackdown Wy *STHA* RG19.... 25 M5
Blackfield La *FRIM* GU16.......... 280 E6
Blackfield Rd *CHAR* BH8.......... 323 K4
  FAWY SO45.......... 290 C8
Blackfriars Cl *SSEA* PO5.......... 19 J4
Blackfriars Rd *SSEA* PO5.......... 19 J3
Black Hill *NWBY* RG14.......... 32 D2
Black Hill Rd *ROMY* SO51...... 224 F4
Black Horse La *BPWT* SO32.... 252 C2
Blackhouse La *WHAM* PO17.... 273 L2
Black La *RSAL* SP5.......... 200 C8
Blackman Gdns *ALDT* GU11.... 3 G7
Blackmoor Rd *LISS* GU33...... 173 M1
Black Moor Rd *WHCH* BH31.... 259 J6
Blackmore La *PSF* GU32.......... 190 E2
Blacknest La *ALTN* GU34.......... 114 G9

Black Pond La *RFNM* GU10...... 116 C4
Blackstocks La *HTWY* RG27.... 71 J7
Blackstone Cl *FARN* GU14.......... 57 L7
Black Swan Yd *AND* SP10...... 4 E4
Blackthorn Cl *ITCH* SO19.......... 249 H6
  ROMY SO51.......... 181 H7
  RWIN SO21.......... 144 D4
Blackthorn Crs *FARN* GU14.... 57 N5
Blackthorn Dr *GPORT* PO12.... 295 L8
Blackthorn Gn *ROWN* SO21.... 255 M7
Blackthorne Cl *BOR* GU35...... 154 B5
Blackthorn Gn *HORN* SO21.... 208 A5
Blackthorn Rd *HISD* PO11...... 319 H6
  ITCH SO19.......... 249 H6
  VWD BH31.......... 259 H5
Blackwater Cl *ASHV* GU12...... 97 N2
  BSTK RG21.......... 7 H6
  CHAM PO6.......... 296 F1
  DEAN RG23.......... 88 F2
Blackwater Dr *TOTT* SO40...... 246 B2
Blackwater Gv *RGWD* BH24...... 300 F6
Blackwater Ms *TOTT* SO40...... 246 B2
Blackwater Pk *ASHV* GU12...... 97 L2
Blackwater Vw *EWKG* RG40.... 40 F2
Blackwater Wy *ASHV* GU12...... 97 K3
Blackwell Rd *RWIN* SO21...... 144 D6
Bladon Cl *HAV* PO9.......... 277 J7
Bladon Rd *ROWN* SO16.......... 247 N1
Blagdon Cl *STHA* RG19.......... 24 C8
Blagdon Rd *CHAM* PO6.......... 296 C1
Blaire Pk *YTLY* GU46.......... 40 C6
Blair Av *PSTN* BH14.......... 321 L8
Blair Cl *NMIL/BTOS* BH25.... 326 C4
Blaire Pk *YTLY* GU46.......... 40 C6
Blaise Cl *FARN* GU14.......... 76 C1
Blake Cl *CWTH* RG45.......... 41 P1
  FHAM PO15.......... 271 H1
  ODIM RG29.......... 93 J3
  ROWN SO16.......... 226 D7
Blake Ct *AND* SP10.......... 4 D1
Blakedene Rd *PSTN* BH14.......... 333 K2
Blake Hill Av *PSTN* BH14.......... 333 L2
Blake Hill Crs *PSTN* BH14...... 333 K2
Blakemere Crs *CHAM* PO6.......... 274 E9
Blakeney Rd *ROWN* SO16.......... 247 H1
Blake Rd *CHAM* PO6.......... 275 M9
Blake's La *TADY* RG26.......... 34 C5
Blakesley La *HSEA* PO3.......... 297 L5
Blakes Ride *YTLY* GU46.......... 40 C8
Blanchard Rd *BPWT* SO32.......... 231 P4
Blandford Cl *PLE* BH15.......... 332 B1
Bland's Cl *THLE* RG7.......... 27 H5
Blanket St *ALTN* GU34.......... 153 J6
Blankney Cl
  FHAM/STUB PO14.......... 295 P7
Blann Cl *ROWN* SO16.......... 226 C7
Blaven Wk *FHAM/STUB* PO14.. 10 B7
Bleaklow Cl *ROWN* SO16.......... 247 K3
Blechynden Ter *WHAM* SO15.. 20 B3
Bledlow Cl *NWBY* RG14.......... 30 C1
Blencowe Dr *CHFD* SO53.......... 206 A8
Blendon Dr *AND* SP10.......... 102 B1
Blendworth Crs *HAV* PO9.......... 14 E1
Blendworth La *HORN* PO8.......... 256 D8
  WEND SO19.......... 249 L4
Blendworth Rd *ENEY* PO4 *...... 317 J4
Blenheim Av *SD/PW* SO17.......... 248 C2
Blenheim Cl *ALTN* GU34.......... 132 G6
  ALTN GU34.......... 150 C5
  CHFD SO53.......... 206 B9
  FARN GU14.......... 97 L4
  TOTT SO40.......... 246 B5
Blenheim Ct *ENEY* PO4.......... 317 J5
  FARN GU14.......... 76 C2
Blenheim Crs *FNM* GU9.......... 96 A5
  LYMN SO41.......... 327 N3
Blenheim Dr
  CHCH/BSGR BH23.......... 325 M8
Blenheim Gdns *FAWY* SO45.... 267 P8
  GPORT PO12.......... 295 M9
  HAV PO9.......... 277 H8
Blenheim Pk *ALDT* GU11.......... 76 E5
Blenheim Rd *ALDT* GU11.......... 76 A5
  CHIN RG24.......... 70 D7
  ELGH SO50.......... 229 J2
  HORN PO8.......... 256 A6
Blenheim Pl *CBLY* GU15.......... 58 A2
Bleriot Crs *FHAM* PO15.......... 10 C9
Blighmont Crs *WSHM* SO15.... 247 M5
Blighton La *RFNM* GU10.......... 97 K9
Blind La *BPWT* SO32.......... 251 L1
  FBDG SP6.......... 240 C7
  HEND SO30.......... 230 D2
  WHAM PO17.......... 252 D6
  WIMB BH21.......... 278 D8
Blindmans Ga *KSCL* SO20...... 29 N6
Bliss Cl *BH/HW/K* RG22.......... 90 A2
  WVILLE PO7.......... 201 M4
Blissford Cl *HAV* PO9.......... 277 H4
Blissford Cross *FBDG* SP6...... 241 J3
Blissford Hl *FBDG* SP6.......... 241 J5
Blissford Rd *FBDG* SP6.......... 241 J5
Blissmore La *RAND* SP11.......... 81 K9
Bloomfield Av
  MOOR/WNTN BH9.......... 322 F5
Bloomsbury Wk *ITCH* SO19.... 248 G9
Bloomsbury Wy *BLKW* GU17.... 57 K2
Blossom Sq *PSEA* PO1 *.......... 18 D2
Bloswood Dr *WHCH* RG28.......... 85 K6
Bloswood La *WHCH* RG28.......... 85 J3
Blount Rd *PSEA* PO1.......... 18 E6
Bloxworth Rd
  BKME/WDN BH12.......... 321 M6
Blue Ball Cnr *WINC* SO23 *...... 23 G4
Blue Ball Hl *WINC* SO23.......... 23 G4
Bluebell Cl *AND* SP10.......... 102 A3
  CHCH/BSGR BH23.......... 325 M7
  WVILLE PO7.......... 275 P4

Bluebell Copse *HLER* SO31...... 270 F8
Bluebell Dr *THLE* RG7.......... 27 H4
Bluebell La *CFDH* BH17.......... 320 A3
  BOR GU35.......... 154 A6
  ROWN SO16.......... 228 D8
Bluebell Wy *FHAM* PO15.......... 271 K2
  NTHA RG18.......... 25 N2
Blueberry Gdns *AND* SP10...... 102 A3
Bluecoats *NTHA* RG18.......... 25 N3
Bluehaven Wk *HTWY* RG27.... 71 N3
Blue Hayes Cl *AND* SP10.......... 4 E8
Blueprint Portfield Rd
  HSEA PO3.......... 297 J7
Blue Prior Ct *FLEETS* GU52...... 74 B9
Bluestar Gdns *HEND* SO30...... 250 C1
Bluethroat Cl *SHST* GU47.......... 41 M6
Blue Timbers Cl *BOR* GU35.... 154 A6
Bluff Cove *ALDT* GU11.......... 3 J3
Blundell La *BPWT* SO32.......... 250 C9
Blunden Rd *FARN* GU14.......... 57 J8
Blunt Rd *BH/HW/K* RG22.......... 89 K7
Blyth Av *STHA* RG19.......... 25 P5
Blyth Cl *CHCH/BSGR* BH23.... 324 B3
  ROWN SO16.......... 247 H1
Blythe Cl *SPN* SP11.......... 82 F5
Blythswood Ct
  NMIL/BTOS BH25.......... 327 H8
Blythwood Dr *FRIM* GU16...... 58 G1
Boakes Pl *TOTT* SO40.......... 246 A9
Boames La *KSCL* SO20.......... 29 L1
Boardwalk Wy *TOTT* SO40...... 247 L7
Boarhunt Cl *PSEA* PO1.......... 18 E3
Boar's Br *TADY* RG26.......... 51 J3
Bob Hann Cl
  BKME/WDN BH12.......... 321 N7
Bockhampton Rd
  CHCH/BSGR BH23.......... 325 J2
Bodin Gdns *NWBY* RG14.......... 24 D7
Bodley Rd *CCLF* BH13.......... 333 N4
Bodmin Cl *BH/HW/K* RG22...... 68 E9
  STHA RG19.......... 25 M5
Bodmin Rd *CHAM* PO6.......... 296 C1
  ELGH SO50.......... 229 N1
Bodorgan Rd *WCLF* BH2.......... 8 D2
Bodowen Cl
  CHCH/BSGR BH23.......... 325 H5
Bodowen Rd
  CHCH/BSGR BH23.......... 325 J5
Bodycoats Rd *CHFD* SO53...... 206 A8
Bofors Rd *FARN* GU14.......... 75 P4
Bogmoor Cl *ALTN* GU34.......... 150 C6
Bognor Rd *BDST* BH18.......... 300 C9
Bohemia La *RSAL* SP5.......... 222 D1
Boiler Rd *FAWY* SO45.......... 291 N8
  PSEA PO1.......... 316 B2
Bolde Cl *HSEA* PO3.......... 297 K6
Boldens Rd *GPORT* PO12.......... 315 M7
Bolderford Br *BROC* SO42.......... 286 C6
Bolderwood Arboretum
Ornamental Dr *LYND* SO43.... 263 J6
Bolderwood Cl *ELGH* SO50...... 230 C2
Boldre Cl *BKME/WDN* BH12.... 321 M7
  HAV PO9.......... 276 C6
Boldre La *LYMN* SO41.......... 309 K3
Boldrewood Pl *FARN* GU14...... 57 M6
Boldrewood Rd *ROWN* SO16.. 228 A4
Boleyn Crs *MOOR/WNTN* BH9.. 322 F5
Bolhinton Av *TOTT* SO40.......... 245 J8
Bolle Rd *ALTN* GU34.......... 132 D7
Bolley Av *BOR* GU35.......... 153 N5
Bolton Crs *BH/HW/K* RG22...... 69 H5
  FERN BH22.......... 302 G2
Bolton Dr *GPORT* PO12.......... 315 M7
Bolton Rd *SBNE* BH6.......... 336 C3
The Boltons *LYMN* SO41.......... 328 G2
  WVILLE PO7.......... 275 N7
Bonchurch Cl *ROWN* SO16...... 228 E7
Bonchurch Rd *ENEY* PO4.......... 317 J5
Bond Av *FERN* RG24.......... 280 D5
Bond Rd *FARN* GU14.......... 96 A3
  LYMN SO41.......... 308 D5
  TADY RG26.......... 34 B5
Bondfields Crs *HAV* PO9.......... 203 H6
Bond Rd *PLE* BH15.......... 321 H7
  WEND SO18.......... 248 G2
Bond St *SHAM* SO14.......... 21 K1
Bone La *NWBY* RG14.......... 17 H2
Bonemill La *KSCL* SO20.......... 215 K8
Bonfire Cnr *PSEA* PO1.......... 18 C1
Bonham Rd
  MOOR/WNTN BH9 *.......... 322 F8
Bonhams Cl *ALTN* GU34.......... 133 J2
Boniface Cl *TOTT* SO40.......... 246 B3
Boniface Crs *ROWN* SO16...... 227 J9
Bonington Cl
  CHCH/BSGR BH23.......... 325 N2
Bonners Fld *RFNM* GU10.......... 114 E5
Boon Wy *DEAN* RG23.......... 88 D1
Boothby Cl *TOTT* SO40.......... 246 E5
Bordean La *PSF* GU32.......... 190 C9
Borden Gates *AND* SP10.......... 4 C5
Borden La *LIPH* GU30.......... 193 P8
Border Dr *NBAD* SO52.......... 205 L9
Border End *HASM* GU27.......... 156 C7
Border Rd *HASM* GU27.......... 156 C7
Borderside *YTLY* GU46.......... 40 E8
Bordon Cl *TADY* RG26.......... 34 B5
Bordon Rd *HAV* PO9.......... 276 F6
The Boreen *BOR* GU35.......... 155 J3
Boreham Rd *SBNE* BH6.......... 336 B1
Borelli Ms *FNM* GU9.......... 96 C5
Borkum Cl *AND* SP10.......... 82 D8
Borley Rd *CFDH* BH17.......... 320 C4
Borman Wy *RWIN* SO21.......... 143 N3
Borodin Cl *BH/HW/K* RG22...... 90 B3
Borough Court Rd *HTWY* RG27.. 72 C1
Borough Gv *PSF* GU32.......... 215 L3
Borough Hl *PSF* GU32.......... 215 L3
The Borough *FNM* GU9.......... 96 B5
  RFNM GU10.......... 116 A5
  RSAL SP5.......... 199 J5
Borovere Cl *ALTN* GU34.......... 132 C7
Borovere Gdns *ALTN* GU34.... 132 C7

Borovere La *ALTN* GU34.......... 132 E7
Borrowdale Rd *ROWN* SO16.... 247 J2
Borsberry Cl *AND* SP10.......... 5 F3
Borthwick Rd *BMTH* BH1.......... 335 L1
Boscobel Rd *FUFL* SO22.......... 22 C1
Boscombe Cliff Rd *BOSC* BH5.. 335 L3
Boscombe Grove Rd
  BMTH BH1.......... 335 K1
Boscombe Overcliff Dr
  BOSC BH5.......... 335 M3
Boscombe Spa Rd *BOSC* BH5.. 335 L2
Boscowen Cl *AND* SP10.......... 5 K3
Bosham Rd *NEND* PO2.......... 297 H9
Bosham Wk
  LSOL/BMARY PO13.......... 294 G9
Bosley Cl *CHCH/BSGR* BH23.... 324 C5
Bosley Wy *CHCH/BSGR* BH23.. 324 C5
Bosmere Rd *EMRTH* PO10...... 319 L6
Bosmere Rd *HISD* PO11.......... 319 L6
Bossington Cl *ROWN* SO16...... 227 J7
Bostock Cl *RWIN* SO21.......... 163 N4
Boston Rd *CHAM* PO6.......... 274 C9
Bosville *ELGH* SO50.......... 207 J7
Boswell Cl *HEND* SO30.......... 250 F4
Bosworth Ms
  MOOR/WNTN BH9.......... 323 H3
Botany Bay Rd *ITCH* SO19...... 249 J3
Botany Rd *RFNM* GU10.......... 117 K8
Botisdone Cl *RAND* SP11.......... 42 C7
Botley Dr *HAV* PO9.......... 276 D5
Botley Gdns *ITCH* SO19.......... 249 N8
Botley La *WHAM* PO17.......... 274 C5
Boulters Rd *ALDT* GU11.......... 3 G4
Boulton La *WHAM* PO17.......... 274 C3
Boulton Rd *SSEA* PO5.......... 316 C5
Boundary Acre *HLER* SO31...... 250 B7
Boundary Cl *WSHM* SO15.......... 247 K5
Boundary La *RGWD* BH24...... 281 K8
Boundary Rd *FARN* GU14.......... 76 B2
  CSHT GU26.......... 156 C2
Boundary Wy *CHAM* PO6.......... 275 K8
  MOOR/WNTN BH9.......... 322 D6
  NWBY RG14.......... 17 H2
  RFNM GU10.......... 135 M3
Boundary Wy *WHAM* PO17...... 272 C3
Bound La *HISD* PO11.......... 318 C6
Bound Cl *ALDT* GU11.......... 2 D6
  AND SP10.......... 82 C9
  BSTK RG21 *.......... 7 J5
  WIMB BH21.......... 278 F9
Bourne Dene *RFNM* GU10...... 116 A5
Bourne Fld *CHIN* RG24.......... 51 H9
Bourne Fld *RWIN* SO21.......... 184 B7
Bourne Firs *RFNM* GU10.......... 116 C5
Bourne Gv *RFNM* GU10.......... 116 E5
Bourne Grove Cl *RFNM* GU10.. 116 E5
Bourne Grove Dr *RFNM* GU10.. 116 C5
Bourne Hts *FNM* GU9.......... 116 C2
Bourne La *RWIN* SO21.......... 184 A7
  TDWTH SP9.......... 79 H5
  TOTT SO40.......... 245 K6
Bourne Meadow *RAND* SP11.... 81 J7
Bournemouth Av
  GPORT PO12.......... 315 L1
Bournemouth International
Centre Rbt *WCLF* BH2.......... 8 D5
Bournemouth Rd *CHFD* SO53.. 228 D1
  LYND SO43.......... 264 E5
  PSTN BH14.......... 333 M8
  RFNM GU10.......... 119 N4
Bournemouth Road Castle
  HI *PSTN* BH14.......... 321 K8
Bournemouth Station
  Rbt *CHAR* BH8.......... 9 H2
Bourne Rd *CHAM* PO6.......... 296 D1
  TDWTH SP9.......... 79 H5
  TDWTH SP9.......... 79 H5
  TOTT SO40.......... 245 J6
  WSHM SO15.......... 247 P6
The Bourne *FLEETS* GU52.......... 74 D6
Bourne Valley Rd
  BKME/WDN BH12.......... 334 A1
Bourne Vw *AMSY* SP4.......... 118 A7
  RAND SP11 *.......... 84 D3
  TDWTH SP9.......... 79 H4
Bournewood Dr *WBNE* BH4.... 334 C2
Bourton Gdns *CHAR* BH7.......... 323 P7
Bouverie Cl *NMIL/BTOS* BH25.. 327 H6
Boveridge Gdns
  MOOR/WNTN BH9.......... 323 H5
Bovington Cl *CFDH* BH17.......... 321 H5
Bowater Cl *TOTT* SO40.......... 246 A2
Bowater Wy *TOTT* SO40.......... 246 A3
Bowcombe *BKME/WDN* BH12.... 321 K3
Bowden Cl *SD/PW* SO17.......... 248 E1
Bowden La *SD/PW* SO17.......... 248 E1
Bowden Rd *BKME/WDN* BH12.. 321 L2

Bow Dr HTWY RG27 .... 52 E5
Bowenhurst Gdns
  FLEETS GU52 .... 74 D8
Bowenhurst La FLEETN GU51 .. 73 P9
  RFNM GU10 .... 94 F2
Bowenhurst Rd FLEETS GU52 .. 74 D7
Bowen La EPSF GU31 .... 215 M2
Bower Av FAWY SO45 .... 290 E6
  ITCH SO19 .... 269 H1
Bower Rd CHAR BH8 .... 323 K7
  RFNM GU10 .... 116 A5
Bowers CI HORN PO8 .... 256 A7
Bowers Grove La NARL SO24 .. 149 M9
Bowers Hl RSAL SP5 .... 200 A6
Bowers La RAND SP11 .... 42 F6
Bowerwood Rd FBDG SP6 ..... 240 A3
Bowes HI HAV PO9 .... 257 J8
Bowes-Lyon Ct HORN PO8 .... 256 B4
Bow Fld HTWY RG27 .... 25 N5
Bow Gdns HTWY RG27 .... 52 E5
Bow Gv HTWY RG27 .... 52 E4
Bowland Ri CHFD SO53 ...... 206 C6
  NMIL/BTOS SO41 .... 327 L5
Bowland Wy FAWY SO45 ...... 312 C7
Bowler Av HAV PO9 .... 317 H2
Bowler Ct HSEA PO3 .... 317 H2
Bowling Aly HTWY RG27 ..... 71 N5
Bowling Court Gn FRIM GU16 . 58 D6
Bowling Green Dr HTWY RG27 . 71 N5
Bowling Green La RSAL SP5 .. 195 H8
Bowling Green Rd HAV PO9 .. 40 F2
Bowman Ct CWTH RG45 .... 40 F2
  ITCH SO19 .... 249 K8
Bowman Rd CHIN RG24 .... 52 A9
Bowmonts Rd TADY RG26 ..... 34 E6
Bow St ALTN GU34 .... 132 E7
Bowyer Ct BSTK RG21 * 69 K8
Boxall's Ct ALDT GU11 ..... 96 C4
Boxall's La ALDT GU11 ..... 96 G4
Box CI CFDH BH17 .... 320 C5
Boxwood CI WVILLE PO7 ..... 275 N4
Boyatt Crs BLOT SO50 ...... 207 J5
Boyatt La BLOT SO50 .... 207 J6
Boyce CI BH/HW/K RG22 ..... 89 N3
Boyd CI FHAM/STUB PO14 .... 293 P8
Boyd Rd BKME/WDN BH12 ..... 321 P6
  LSOL/BMARY PO13 .... 295 H4
Boyes La RWIN SO21 .... 208 A4
Boyle Crs WVILLE PO7 ...... 275 M5
Boyne Mead Rd WINC SO23 ... 145 J9
Boyne Ri WINC SO23 .... 145 J8
Boyneswood CI ALTN GU34 ... 150 D4
Boyneswood La ALTN GU34 ... 150 D4
Boyneswood Rd ALTN GU34 ... 150 D4
Boynton CI CHFD SO53 ...... 206 D5
Brabant CI FHAM PO15 ...... 271 H3
Brabazon Dr
  CHCH/BSGR BH23 .... 325 M8
Brabazon Rd FHAM PO15 ..... 271 K5
  WIMB BH21 .... 901 H4
Brabon Rd FARN GU14 .... 57 N8
Braborne Av FERN BH22 ..... 302 C4
Bracebridge CBLY GU15 ..... 41 P9
Bracher CI AND SP10 .... 4 E3
Bracken Bank CHIN RG24 .... 70 A4
Brackenbury AND SP10 ...... 102 B1
Bracken CI
  LSOL/BMARY PO13 .... 314 C2
  NBAD SO52 .... 227 L1
  RGWD BH24 .... 281 K5
Brackens Crs ELGH SO50 .... 230 C6
Brackendale CI WIMB BH21 .. 280 D1
Brackendale Rd CBLY GU15 .. 58 C1
  CHAR BH8 .... 323 J7
Brackendene ASHV GU12 ..... 77 H9
Bracken Gln PLE BH15 ...... 320 C8
Bracken Heath WVILLE PO7 .. 276 B1
Brackenhill CCLF BH13 ..... 334 A5
Brackenhill Rd WIMB BH21 .. 279 J7
Bracken La BOR GU35 .... 153 M8
  ROWN SO16 .... 247 L2
  YTLY GU46 .... 40 B8
Bracken Pl ROWN SO16 ...... 228 C5
Bracken Rd EPSF GU31 ...... 216 A3
  FERN BH22 .... 302 B1
  NBAD SO52 .... 227 L1
  SBNE BH6 .... 336 A2
The Brackens BH/HW/K RG22 . 89 M5
  FAWY SO45 .... 267 P7
  HLER SO31 .... 271 H8
Brackens Wy LYMN SO41 ..... 329 N5
Bracken Wy
  CHCH/BSGR BH23 .... 326 D6
  THLE RG7 .... 35 J2
Brackenway Rd CHFD SO53 ... 206 B5
Bracklesham CI FARN GU14 .. 57 P6
  ITCH SO19 .... 249 H8
Bracklesham Pl
  NMIL/BTOS SO41 .... 327 H8
Bracklesham Rd HISD PO11 .. 319 M7
  LSOL/BMARY PO13 .... 295 H9
Brackley Av ELGH SO50 ..... 230 B2
  HTWY RG27 .... 54 C7
Brackley CI CHCH/BSGR BH23 303 N8
Brackley Wy BH/HW/K RG22 .. 89 N2
  TOTT SO40 .... 246 E3
Bracknell La HTWY RG27 .... 52 C2
Bracknell Rd CWTH RG45 .... 41 K1
Bradburne Rd WCLF BH2 ..... 8 B3
Bradbury CI WHCH RG28 ..... 85 K6
Bradford Ct
  LSOL/BMARY PO13 * 314 C2
Bradford Rd
  MOOR/WNTN BH9 .... 323 J3
  SSEA PO5 .... 19 K4
Brading Av ENEY PO4 .... 19 L7
Brading CI ROWN SO16 ...... 228 E7
Bradley CI HAV PO9 .... 277 H5
Bradley Gn ROWN SO16 ...... 227 M8
Bradley-Moore Sq NTHA RG18 25 P2
Bradley Peak FUFL SO22 .... 164 D6
Bradley Rd FUFL SO22 ...... 164 D4
Bradly Rd FHAM PO15 .... 272 A9
Bradman Sq AND SP10 * 82 F8

Bradpole Rd CHAR BH8 ...... 323 L6
Bradshaw CI ELGH SO50 ..... 230 E2
Bradstock CI
  BKME/WDN BH12 .... 321 P4
Bradwell CI AND SP10 ...... 82 B8
Braehead FAWY SO45 .... 268 B8
Braemar Av CHAM PO6 .... 297 K2
  SBNE BH6 .... 336 E2
Braemar CI FHAM PO15 ...... 10 B1
  FRIM GU16 .... 58 E5
  LSOL/BMARY PO13 .... 295 H7
  SBNE BH6 .... 336 E2
Braemar Dr CHCH/BSGR BH23 . 326 B6
  DEAN RG23 .... 88 E1
Braemar Rd
  CHCH/BSGR BH23 .... 295 H6
Braemore CI STHA RG19 ..... 25 N6
Braeside CI FUFL SO22 ..... 183 K2
Braeside Crs ITCH SO19 .... 156 E5
  ITCH SO19 .... 248 G6
Braeside Rd FERN BH22 ..... 248 G6
Brahms Rd BH/HW/K RG22 .... 90 A5
Braidley Rd WCLF BH2 ...... 8 C1
Brailswood Rd PLE BH15 .... 320 F8
Braine L'Alleud Rd BSTK RG21 7 F5
Braintree Rd CHAM PO6 ..... 274 F9
Brairwood Gdns HISD PO11 .. 318 F9
Braishfield CI ROWN SO16 .. 247 K2
Braishfield Gdns CHAR BH8 . 323 K5
Braishfield Rd HAV PO9 .... 276 G6
Brake Rd FARN GU14 .... 75 M3
Brakes Ri SHST GU47 .... 41 M6
Bramber Rd GPORT PO12 ..... 315 L1
Bramble Bank FRIM GU16 .... 58 F7
  FAWY SO45 .... 290 E6
  FBDG SP6 .... 239 N6
Bramble Cl FERN BH22 ...... 293 N8
  HAV PO9 .... 277 J7
Bramble Ct FERN BH22 ...... 280 D7
Bramble Dr ROMY SO51 ...... 204 G4
Bramblegate ELGH SO50 * ... 230 D3
Bramble Hl CHFD SO53 ...... 206 A8
  NARL SO24 .... 168 A2
Bramble La CHCH/BSGR BH23 . 326 D6
  HLER SO31 .... 270 E5
  HORN PO8 .... 236 B5
Bramble Ms WEND SO18 ...... 249 J3
Bramble Rd ENEY PO4 .... 19 L4
  EPSF GU31 .... 216 A2
Brambles CI ALTN GU34 ..... 150 C6
  ASHV GU12 .... 97 P2
Brambles Rd
  LSOL/BMARY PO13 .... 314 B1
The Brambles NWBY RG14 .... 24 B7
Brambleton Av FNM GU9 ..... 116 B3
Bramble Wk LYMN SO41 ...... 329 J3
Bramble Wy
  CHCH/BSGR BH23 .... 305 M7
  DEAN RG23 .... 70 D6
  LSOL/BMARY PO13 .... 294 E7
Brambling Pl BH/HW/K RG22 . 89 K4
  ROWN SO16 .... 227 M6
Brambling Rd HAV PO9 ...... 277 J7
The Bramblings TOTT SO40 .. 246 A4
Bramblys Ct BSTK RG21 ..... 6 D7
Bramblys Dr BSTK RG21 ..... 6 C7
Bramdean CI TADY RG26 ..... 34 C7
Bramdean Rd HAV PO9 .... 276 D5
Bramdean Rd WEND SO18 ..... 249 M4
Bramdown Hts
  BH/HW/K RG22 .... 89 M5
Bramham Moor
  FHAM/STUB PO14 .... 293 P7
Bramley CI ALTN GU34 ...... 132 C6
  LYMN SO41 .... 329 L5
  WVILLE PO7 .... 275 P2
Bramley Crs ITCH SO19 ..... 249 K9
Bramley Gdns ELGH SO50 .... 230 C6
  EMRTH PO10 .... 299 P1
  GPORT PO12 .... 315 L7
Bramley Green Rd TADY RG26 52 B5
Bramley Gv CWTH RG45 ...... 40 E1
Bramley La BLKW GU17 ...... 41 J9
  TADY RG26 .... 52 A1
Bramley Rd CBLY GU15 ...... 50 B2
  FERN BH22 .... 302 C2
  NBNE BH10 .... 322 C2
  TADY RG26 .... 50 G4
  THLE RG7 .... 35 J5
The Bramleys RSAL SP5 ..... 201 K2
Bramley Wk BOR GU35 .... 153 N6
Bramling Av YTLY GU46 ..... 40 C8
Brampton Gdns
  BH/HW/K RG22 .... 89 M6
Brampton La HSEA PO3 ...... 297 L5
Brampton Rd PLE BH15 ...... 320 F6
Bramshaw FUFL SO22 .... 164 D4
Bramshaw CI WINC SO23 ..... 277 H5
Bramshaw Gdns CHAR BH8 .... 323 H4
Bramshaw Wy
  NMIL/BTOS SO41 .... 326 F7
Bramshot Dr FLEETS GU51 ... 74 D2
Bramshot La FLEETN GU51 ... 55 H2
Bramshott Cl FARN GU14 .... 57 P6
Bramshott Dr HTWY RG27 .... 72 A3
Bramshott Pl FLEETN GU51 .. 74 D1
Bramshott Rd ENEY PO4 ..... 317 H4
  ITCH SO19 .... 269 H2
Bramston Rd WSHM SO15 ..... 247 N3
Bramwell Ct ITCH SO19 ..... 249 K5
Brancaster Av AND SP10 .... 82 B8
Branches La ROMY SO51 ..... 202 F3
Branders CI SBNE BH6 ...... 336 E2
Branders La SBNE BH6 ...... 336 E2
Brandon Cl ALTN GU34 ...... 132 D5
  CBLY GU15 .... 59 J1
Brandon Rd CHAM PO6 .... 297 N1

SSEA PO5 .... 316 F6
Brandy Bottom YTLY GU46 * . 56 F2
Brandy Mt NARL SO24 .... 168 A1
Branewick Cl FHAM PO15 .... 271 K7
Branksea CI PLE BH15 ...... 332 A2
Branksome Av STOK SO20 .... 123 L6
Branksome Dene Rd
  WBNE BH4 .... 334 B1
Branksome Hill Rd SHST GU47 41 M6
  WBNE BH4 .... 334 B1
Branksome Towers
  CCLF BH13 .... 334 A2
Branksome Wood Gdns
  WBNE BH4 .... 8 A1
Branksome Wood Rd
  WBNE BH4 .... 334 C1
  WCLF BH2 .... 8 A2
Bransbury Cl ROWN SO16 .... 227 N8
Bransbury Rd ENEY PO4 ..... 317 K5
Bransgore Av HAV PO9 ...... 276 C6
Bransgore Gdns
  CHCH/BSGR BH23 .... 305 M7
Bransley Cl ROMY SO51 ..... 204 F4
Branson Rd BOR GU35 .... 154 G5
Branton CI BH/HW/K RG22 ... 68 F9
Branwell CI CHCH/BSGR BH23 324 E6
Branwood CI LYMN SO41 ..... 328 E6
Brasenose CI
  FHAM/STUB PO14 .... 271 H9
Brasher CI ELGH SO50 ...... 230 A2
Brassey CI MOOR/WNTN BH9 .. 322 G6
Brassey Rd FUFL SO22 ...... 22 C1
  MOOR/WNTN BH9 .... 322 F6
Brassey Ter
  MOOR/WNTN BH9 * 322 F6
Brasted Ct ENEY PO4 .... 317 K3
Braunfels Wk KSCL SO20 .... 24 A5
Braye CI SHST GU47 .... 41 K5
Breachfield KSCL SO20 ..... 30 E7
Breach La ELGH SO50 .... 207 M8
  NWBY RG14 .... 16 A3
Breadells Fld BH/HW/K RG22 89 L7
Breamore CI ELGH SO50 ..... 207 J7
  NMIL/BTOS SO41 .... 326 G4
Breamore Rd RSAL SP5 ...... 199 H7
  WEND SO18 .... 249 M4
Brean CI ROWN SO16 .... 227 J9
Brecon Av CHAM PO6 .... 275 K9
Brecon CI CHFD SO53 .... 228 D1
  FARN GU14 .... 57 L6
  FAWY SO45 .... 268 A7
  FHAM/STUB PO14 .... 10 A7
  NBNE BH10 .... 322 E1
  NMIL/BTOS SO41 .... 327 L1
Brecon Rd ITCH SO19 .... 249 L6
Bredenbury Crs CHAM PO6 ... 274 E9
Bredon Wk FHAM/STUB PO14 .. 294 C1
Bre CI CFDH BH17 .... 320 F3
Breech CI HSEA PO3 .... 297 H5
The Breech SHST GU47 ...... 41 M7
Bremble CI BKME/WDN BH12 .. 321 L2
Bremen Gdns AND SP10 ...... 82 D9
Brenchley CI
  FHAM/PORC PO16 .... 295 L2
Brendon CI CHAR BH8 * 323 L5
  FAWY SO45 .... 267 P8
Brendon Gn ROWN SO16 ...... 247 K3
Brendon Rd FARN GU14 ...... 57 L6
  FHAM/STUB PO14 .... 294 D1
Brent CI STHA RG19 .... 25 N5
Brent CI EMRTH PO10 .... 299 J9
Brentwood Crs WEND SO18 ... 249 J2
Bret Harte Rd FRIM GU16 ... 58 D4
Breton CI FHAM PO15 .... 271 H3
Brewells La LISS GU33 ..... 174 B9
Brewer CI BH/HW/K RG22 .... 68 F9
  HLER SO31 .... 271 H6
Brewers Ct FARN GU14 ...... 57 P8
Brewers La
  LSOL/BMARY PO13 .... 294 C5
  NARL SO24 .... 170 C8
  RWIN SO21 .... 183 P9
Brewer St PSEA PO1 .... 19 H1
Brewery Common THLE RG7 ... 27 K9
Brewery La ROMY SO51 ...... 204 C5
Brewhouse La HTWY RG27 .... 55 J2
Brewhouse Sq GPORT PO12 ... 315 P3
Brewster CI HORN PO8 ...... 256 A8
Briar CI CHCH/BSGR BH23 ... 325 K9
  GPORT PO12 .... 315 J7
  HORN PO8 .... 256 B6
  HLER SO31 .... 271 L7
Briardene Ct TOTT SO40 .... 246 C4
Briarfield Gdns HORN PO8 .. 256 C5
Briar La ALTN GU34 .... 150 D5
Briarlea Rd THLE RG7 ...... 12 H9
Briars CI FARN GU14 .... 75 L1
Briars Cft AND SP10 .... 4 C6
The Briars ASHV GU12 ...... 97 P2
  FLEETS GU52 .... 74 D4
  WVILLE PO7 .... 275 L1
Briarswood RI FAWY SO45 ... 267 P8
Briar Wy ROMY SO51 .... 204 G4
Briarwood CI
  FHAM/PORC PO16 .... 11 G7
Briarwood Rd TOTT SO40 .... 246 A5
Brickfield La CHFD SO53 ... 206 D8
  LYMN SO41 .... 329 H5
Brickfield Rd SD/PW SO17 .. 248 E1
Brickfields CI CHIN RG24 .. 70 A4
Brick Kiln La ALTN GU34 ... 132 C5
  NARL SO24 .... 132 C5
Brick La CHCH/BSGR BH23 ... 306 A4
  FLEETN GU51 .... 74 D2
Bricklin La ALTN GU34 ..... 150 G2

Brickmakers Rd RWIN SO21 .. 207 P5
Brick Quarters ALDT GU11 * . 76 C7
Bricksbury HI FNM GU9 ..... 96 C4
Brickwoods Ct RWIN SO21 ... 204 F5
Brickworth La RSAL SP5 .... 200 G1
Brickworth Rd RSAL SP5 .... 200 G1
Brickyard La WIMB BH21 .... 302 A2
Brickyard Rd BPWT SO32 .... 232 D9
Bridefield CI ROWN SO16 ... 245 H3
Bridefield Crs HORN PO8 ... 255 N8
Bridge Ap PLE BH15 .... 332 D2
Bridge Cl HLER SO31 .... 270 D1
Bridge Ct RFNM GU10 .... 115 P3
Bridge End CBLY GU15 ...... 58 A1
Bridge Industries
  FHAM/PORC PO16 .... 11 K2
Bridge La RWIN SO21 .... 183 N7
Bridgemary Av
  LSOL/BMARY PO13 .... 295 H6
Bridgemary Gv
  LSOL/BMARY PO13 .... 294 C4
Bridgemary Wy
  LSOL/BMARY PO13 * 294 C4
Bridge Md BPWT SO32 .... 211 P8
Bridgemead FNM GU9 .... 58 C5
Bridge Mdw LISS GU33 ...... 192 D2
Bridge Rd NBNE BH10 .... 302 D9
  CBLY GU15 .... 58 A2
  EMRTH PO10 .... 277 M9
  HASM GU27 .... 157 H6
  HLER SO31 .... 270 D1
  ITCH SO19 .... 248 F8
  LYMN SO41 .... 329 M4
  NARL SO24 .... 167 N2
Bridgers CI ROWN SO16 ..... 227 J7
Bridges Av CHAM PO6 .... 274 B9
Bridges CI ELGH SO50 ...... 229 H1
  FERN BH22 .... 280 F6
Bridgeside CI PSEA PO1 .... 19 K2
Bridge Sq FNM GU9 .... 116 C1
The Bridges RGWD BH24 ..... 282 C2
  THLE RG7 .... 35 K1
Bridge St AND SP10 .... 4 D5
  CHCH/BSGR BH23 .... 324 G9
  FBDG SP6 .... 240 D2
  FHAM/STUB PO14 .... 293 N1
  NWBY RG14 .... 16 C5
  OVTN RG25 .... 86 C3
  WHAM PO17 .... 252 E7
  WHAM PO17 .... 273 P4
Bridge Ter SHAM SO14 * 21 H7
Bridget CI HORN PO8 .... 256 C4
Bridge Wk YTLY GU46 .... 40 E7
Bridgewater Rd
  BKME/WDN BH12 .... 321 M6
The Bridgeway ITCH SO19 * . 248 G8
Bridgwater Ct WSHM SO15 ... 247 P6
Bridle Ct ALTN GU34 .... 171 L2
  GSHT GU26 .... 155 P5
Bridle Ct ALDT GU11 .... 2 A3
Bridle CI LTDN BH7 .... 324 A7
Bridle Wy WIMB BH21 .... 279 K8
Bridleways VWD BH31 .... 258 E4
Bridlington Av WSHM SO15 .. 247 P3
Bridport Rd FHAM/STUB PO14 293 P4
  VWD BH31 .... 258 F4
Bridport St PSEA PO1 ...... 19 H7
Brierley Av FERN BH22 ..... 302 E7
Brierley Cl NBNE BH10 ..... 322 C2
Brierley Rd NBNE BH10 ..... 322 C2
Brigantine Rd HLER SO31 ... 270 E9
Brighstone Ct ROWN SO16 .. 228 E7
Brighstone Rd CHAM PO6 .... 296 D2
Brightlands Av SBNE BH6 ... 336 D2
Brighton Av GPORT PO12 .... 295 K9
  LTDN BH7 .... 324 A5
Brighton Rd ASHV GU12 ..... 3 J7
  LYMN SO41 .... 308 A5
  WSHM SO15 .... 248 B4
Brighton Wy BH/HW/K RG22 .. 89 P3
Bright Rd PLE BH15 .... 320 F6
Brightside Av FHAM/STUB PO14 294 C1
Brightside Rd ROWN SO16 ... 247 K1
Brights La HISD PO11 ...... 318 F3
Brightstone La ALTN GU34 .. 151 H6
Brightwells Rd FNM GU9 .... 116 D2
Brightwire Crs ELGH SO50 .. 229 H2
Brimley Hill Ct KSCL SO20 . 48 C3
Brimpton La THLE RG7 ...... 33 L3
Brimpton Rd TADY RG26 ..... 33 H4
Brindle CI ALDT GU11 ...... 97 H4
  ROWN SO16 .... 228 C7
Brinksway FLEETN GU51 ..... 74 D4
Brinn's La BLKW GU17 ...... 41 K9
Brinsons CI CHCH/BSGR BH23 324 G2
Brinton La HAV PO9 .... 14 E6
Brinton Rd CHAM PO6 .... 275 H1
Brintons Rd SHAM SO14 ..... 21 J2
Brintons Ter SHAM SO14 .... 21 H7
Brisbane Rd
  CHCH/BSGR BH23 .... 324 C6
Brislands La NARL SO24 .... 149 N9
Bristol Ct CBLY GU15 * 314 C2
Bristol Rd ENEY PO4 .... 316 G5
Bristow Rd CBLY GU15 ...... 58 A2
Britain St PSEA PO1 .... 18 F3
Britannia Av RWIN SO21 .... 207 P1
Britannia Ct ASHV GU12 .... 97 P1
Britannia Gdns HEND SO30 .. 250 D2
Britannia Rd BH/HW/K RG22 . 89 P3
Britannia Rd BOR GU35 ..... 154 B5
Britannia Rd PSTN BH14 .... 321 J9
  SHAM SO14 .... 21 J2
  SSEA PO5 .... 19 K5
Britannia Rd North SSEA PO5 19 K5

Britannia St EPSF GU31 .... 191 N9
Britannia Wy
  CHCH/BSGR BH23 .... 325 M8
  GPORT PO12 .... 315 N1
Briton St SHAM SO14 .... 20 D7
Brittany CI TOTT SO40 ..... 267 K1
Britten CI ASHV GU12 ...... 97 P1
Britten Wy WVILLE PO7 ..... 275 N6
Brixey CI BKME/WDN BH12 ... 321 L5
Brixey Rd BKME/WDN BH12 ... 321 L5
Broadacre Pl
  FHAM/STUB PO14 .... 294 E1
Broadacres FLEETS GU51 .... 74 A4
Broad Av CHAR BH8 .... 323 J2
Broadbent CI ROWN SO16 .... 227 H6
Broad Chalke Down
  FUFL SO22 .... 183 L2
Broad Cft HAV PO9 .... 257 J9
Broadcut FHAM/PORC PO16 ... 11 K6
Broadfields CI LYMN SO41 .. 328 C1
Broad Gdns CHAM PO6 .... 297 N1
Broad Gn SHAM SO14 .... 21 F3
Broadhalfpenny La
  TADY RG26 .... 34 D6
Broad Ha'Penny RFNM GU10 .. 116 A5
Broadhill La FBDG SP6 ..... 241 H3
Broadhurst Av NBNE BH10 ... 322 E1
Broadhurst Gv CHIN RG24 ... 76 D2
Broadlands Av ELGH SO50 ... 207 J8
  SBNE BH6 .... 336 D2
  WVILLE PO7 .... 275 N4
Broadlands CI CHAR BH8 .... 323 K4
  CHCH/BSGR BH23 .... 326 D5
  RFNM GU10 .... 114 F5
Broadlands Rd BROC SO42 ... 286 E7
  SD/PW SO17 .... 228 D9
Broad La BPWT SO32 .... 232 E7
  LYMN SO41 .... 329 M4
  NBAD SO52 .... 205 J8
Broadlaw Wk FHAM/STUB PO14 294 C2
Broad Leaze HTWY RG27 ..... 71 P2
Broadley CI FAWY SO45 ..... 290 E5
Broadly CI LYMN SO41 ...... 329 H5
Broadmayne Rd ITCH SO19 ... 321 P1
Broadmead CI FARN GU14 .... 75 L1
Broadmead Rd WIMB BH21 .... 258 E9
Broadmeadow La WVILLE PO7 . 276 F5
Broadmeadows La
  WVILLE PO7 .... 276 A3
Broadmead Rd BH/HW/K RG22 . 89 L6
Broadmere Av HAV PO9 ...... 276 F5
Broad Oak HEND SO30 .... 250 D4
Broadoak TADY RG26 .... 34 E6
Broadoak CI FAWY SO45 ..... 290 E6
Broad Rd ODIM SO29 .... 101 H7
Broadsands Dr GPORT PO12 .. 315 H5
Broadshard La RGWD BH24 ... 260 E9
The Broads WIMB BH21 ...... 278 B8
Broadstone Wy BDST BH18 ... 320 B5
Broad St NARL SO24 .... 168 A1
  PSEA PO1 .... 18 B6
Broadview CI ALTN GU34 .... 134 C2
Broad View La FUFL SO22 ... 183 J3
Broad Wk FNM GU10 .... 58 D3
Broadwater Av PSTN BH14 ... 321 K1
Broadwater Rd WEND SO18 ... 229 H9
  FARN GU14 .... 57 J3
  HLER SO31 .... 269 N5
Broad Wy THLE RG7 .... 37 H7
Broadway SBNE BH6 .... 336 E2
  STHA RG19 .... 25 N4
  WHCH RG28 .... 85 M7
Broadway La CHAR BH8 ...... 323 J4
  HORN PO8 .... 255 M5
Broadway Pk EPSF GU31 * ... 215 M6
The Broadway AND SP10 ..... 4 C5
  NBNE BH10 .... 322 D1
  SD/PW SO17 .... 248 D2
  SHST GU47 .... 41 J7
  WINC SO23 .... 23 F5
Brocas Dr BSTK RG21 .... 7 H2
Brocas Ter FARN GU14 ...... 27 H6
Brock CI FRIM GU16 .... 59 J5
Brockenhurst Av HAV PO9 ... 276 D4
Brockenhurst Dr YTLY GU46 . 40 E9
Brockenhurst Rd ALDT GU11 . 3 H5
  MOOR/WNTN BH9 .... 323 H5
Brockhampton La HAV PO9 ... 14 E6
Brockhampton Rd HAV PO9 ... 14 C6
Brockhills La
  NMIL/BTOS SO41 .... 327 L2
Brockhurst Ldg FNM GU9 .... 116 B3
Brockhurst Rd GPORT PO12 .. 315 K1
Brockishill Rd TOTT SO40 .. 244 F7
Brocklands HAV PO9 .... 14 C5
  YTLY GU46 .... 40 C8
Brockley Rd NBNE BH10 ..... 322 E3
  STOK SO20 .... 121 H5
Brocks CI FAWY SO45 .... 267 P8
Brocks Pine RGWD BH24 ..... 281 M6
Brockway WEND SO18 .... 249 H2
Brockwood RGWD BH24 .... 258 E3
Brockwood Bottom
  NARL SO24 .... 187 M4
Brodrick Av GPORT PO12 .... 12 B5
Brokenford Av TOTT SO40 ... 246 E4
Brokenford La TOTT SO40 ... 246 D4
Broken Wy KSCL SO20 .... 30 D5
Brokle CI TADY RG26 .... 34 B8
Bromelia CI TADY RG26 ..... 52 A1
Bromley Rd WEND SO18 ...... 249 H2
Brompton CI ENEY PO4 ...... 317 H6
Bromyard Crs CHAM PO6 ..... 296 E1

Bronte Av CHCH/BSGR BH23 324 E6
Bronte Cl TOTT SO40 246 B5
Bronte Gdns FHAM PO15 271 J2
Bronte Ri NWBY RG14 24 E7
Bronte Wy ITCH SO19 248 G5
Bronze Cl BH/HW/K RG22 89 L7
Brook Av FNM GU9 96 F4
HLER SO31 270 C7
NMIL/BTOS BH25 327 K3
Brook Cl CHFD SO53 206 E9
FLEETN GU51 74 D4
HLER SO31 270 D7
NBAD SO52 227 L1
NBNE BH10 322 C3
SHST GU47 41 M5
Brookdale Cl BDST BH18 300 C9
WVILLE PO7 275 N2
Brook Dr VWD BH31 259 H6
Brooke Cl WINC SO23 145 J8
Brooke Ri AND SP10 102 C1
Brookers Cnr CWTH RG45 41 K1
Brookers La
LSOL/BMARY PO13 294 E6
Brook Farm Av FHAM PO15 10 C5
Brookfield Cl CHIN RG24 70 B1
HAV PO9 14 E3
Brookfield Gdns
HLER SO31 270 F6
Brookfield Pl SD/PW SO17 * 248 D1
Brookfield Rd ASHV GU12 76 D9
ELGH SO50 230 B2
PSEA PO1 316 G2
Brookfields ROMY SO51 224 D1
Brook Gdns EMRTH PO10 299 K1
FARN GU14 75 N2
Brook Gn TADY RG26 34 E6
Brook Hl LYMN SO41 310 C9
Brookhouse Rd FARN GU14 75 N1
Brookland Cl LYMN SO41 329 J4
Brooklands ALDT GU11 2 A4
Brooklands Cl FNM GU9 96 D4
Brooklands Rd BPWT SO32 232 A4
FNM GU9 96 E4
HAV PO9 276 B8
Brooklands Wy FNM GU9 96 E4
Brook La CHCH/BSGR BH23 305 L9
FBDG SP6 221 J5
HEND SO30 250 F6
HLER SO31 270 C9
WVILLE PO7 234 D6
Brookley Cl RFNM GU10 97 H8
Brookley Rd BROC SO42 286 F8
Brookly Gdns FLEETN GU51 74 E3
Brooklyn Cl RWIN SO21 207 L2
Brooklyn Ct NMIL/BTOS BH25 327 H4
Brooklyn Dr WVILLE PO7 275 P2
Brooklynn Cl BPWT SO32 252 C1
Brookmead Ct FNM GU9 116 B1
Brookmeadow FHAM PO15 10 C5
Brookmead Wy HAV PO9 298 F2
Brook Rd BKME/WDN BH12 321 L7
CBLY GU15 58 A1
ELGH SO50 230 C2
LYMN SO41 329 M5
NBNE BH10 322 C3
WEND SO18 249 J4
WIMB BH21 300 G2
Brook Rw FAWY SO45 * 268 D8
Brooksby Cl BLKW GU17 41 J9
Brooks Cl RGWD BH24 282 F3
WHCH RG28 85 M7
Brookside FBDG SP6 240 G9
FNM GU9 96 C5
LSOL/BMARY PO13 294 F4
SHST GU47 41 K7
TOTT SO40 246 D6
Brookside Av WSHM SO15 247 K4
Brookside Cl
CHCH/BSGR BH23 305 L7
WVILLE PO7 255 H7
Brookside Pk FARN GU14 * 57 P4
Brookside Rd BROC SO42 286 F7
CHCH/BSGR BH23 305 L8
HAV PO9 276 C8
WIMB BH21 301 H1
Brookside Wk TADY RG26 34 D6
Brookside Wy
CHCH/BSGR BH23 326 A6
HEND SO30 229 N9
WEND SO18 228 G8
Brooks Rd NTHA RG18 25 P3
The Brooks WINC SO23 * 23 F4
Brook St BPWT SO32 232 A5
Brook Ter FBDG SP6 240 D3
The Brook NARL SO24 148 A8
Brookvale Cl BSTK RG21 6 C6
Brookvale Rd SD/PW SO17 248 C2
Brook Va ROWN SO16 247 L1
Brookview Cl
FHAM/STUB PO14 293 P1
Brook Wy ROMY SO51 204 E4
CHCH/BSGR BH23 325 N8
Brookway NWBY RG14 25 H4
RAND SP11 102 A6
Brookwood Av ELGH SO50 229 H1
Brookwood Rd FARN GU14 58 C9
ROWN SO16 247 H3
Broom Acres FLEETS GU52 74 C6
SHST GU47 41 J5
Broom Cl ENEY PO4 317 M4
WVILLE PO7 276 A5
Broome Cl YTLY GU46 40 D7
Broomfield Crs
LSOL/BMARY PO13 314 F1
Broomfield Dr FBDG SP6 239 N6
Broomfield La LYMN SO41 329 L3
RFNM GU10 116 A9
Broomfield Pl FLEETN GU51 74 B1
Broomfield Rd BOR GU35 153 N6
Broom Hl LYMN SO41 310 F9
Broomhill RFNM GU10 95 M3
RSAL SP5 223 M3
Broomhill Cl LYMN SO41 329 H5
Broomhill Rd FARN GU14 57 L8
Broomhill Ter RSAL SP5 * 223 M2
Broom Hill Wy ELGH SO50 207 H6
Broomhurst La FLEETN GU51 74 B1
Broom La SBNE BH6 335 P2
Broomleaf Cnr FNM GU9 96 D9
Broomleaf Rd FNM GU9 96 D9
Broomrigg Rd FLEETN GU51 74 A2
Broom Rd BKME/WDN BH12 321 L3
EPSF GU31 216 A3
Brooms Gv ITCH SO19 249 M8
Broom Sq ENEY PO4 317 M4
Broom Wy BLKW GU17 57 L1
LSOL/BMARY PO13 314 D1
Broomwood Wy RFNM GU10 116 C4
Broomy Cl FAWY SO45 267 N6
Brougham La GPORT PO12 315 L2
Brougham Pl FNM GU9 96 B4
Brougham Rd SSEA PO5 19 G5
Brougham St GPORT PO12 * 315 L2
Broughton Av NBNE BH10 322 E3
Broughton Cl NBNE BH10 322 E4
ROWN SO16 247 L2
Broughton Ms FRIM GU16 58 E4
Broughton Rd LYND SO43 264 F4
STOK SO20 140 D6
Brown Cft HTWY RG27 71 N3
Browndown Rd
LSOL/BMARY PO13 314 G5
Brownen Rd
MOOR/WNTN BH9 323 H7
Brownhill Cl CHFD SO53 206 E6
Brownhill Ct ROWN SO16 227 J9
Brownhill Gdns CHFD SO53 206 E6
Brownhill Rd CHFD SO53 206 E6
NBAD SO52 205 L9
NMIL/BTOS BH25 306 F5
Brownhill Wy ROWN SO16 226 G9
Browning Av BOSC BH5 335 M2
CHAM PO6 274 A9
ITCH SO19 249 M5
Browning Cl CBLY GU15 59 H1
CHIN RG24 69 M4
ELGH SO50 229 H1
FHAM PO15 271 J1
NTHA RG18 25 M3
TOTT SO40 246 B4
Browning Dr FUFL SO22 164 E7
Browning Rd
BKME/WDN BH12 321 M6
FLEETS GU52 74 B8
Brownings Cl LYMN SO41 328 G3
Brownlow Av ITCH SO19 249 J5
Brownlow Gdns ITCH SO19 249 J5
Browns Cl TADY RG26 51 P1
Brownsea Cl
NMIL/BTOS BH25 326 G4
Brownsea Rd CCLF BH13 333 K8
Brownsea View Av
PSTN BH14 333 K2
Brownsfield Rd NTHA RG18 25 M4
Browns La FBDG SP6 219 H7
LYMN SO41 330 G2
Brownsover Rd FARN GU14 57 K9
Browns Wk RFNM GU10 115 P5
Brownwich La
FHAM/STUB PO14 293 J5
The Brow WVILLE PO7 275 L8
Broxburn Cl CHFD SO53 206 G4
Broxhead Farm Rd BOR GU35 135 J9
Broxhead Rd HAV PO9 276 G4
Bruan Rd NWBY RG14 24 C7
Bruce Cl FHAM/PORC PO16 11 F2
Bruce Rd ENEY PO4 317 H6
Brudenell Av CCLF BH13 333 M4
Brudenell Rd CCLF BH13 333 M4
Brue Cl CHFD SO53 206 D6
Bruna La LSOL/BMARY PO13 294 E8
Brunel Cl HEND SO30 250 D2
RWIN SO21 107 H8
VWD BH31 259 J6
Brunel Rd BSTK RG21 69 H6
NEND PO2 296 G6
TOTT SO40 226 B9
WSHM SO15 246 G4
Brunel Wy FHAM PO15 271 K5
Brune Wy FERN BH22 302 D5
Brunstead Pl
BKME/WDN BH12 334 B2
Brunstead Rd
BKME/WDN BH12 334 A2
Brunswick Cl ELGH SO50 230 B2
Brunswick Gdns HAV PO9 14 B4
Brunswick Pl BH/HW/K RG22 90 B2
LYMN SO41 329 L3
WSHM SO15 20 D1
Brunswick Rd ELGH SO50 230 B1
FRIM GU16 59 H7
Brunswick Sq SHAM SO14 20 E7
Brunswick St SSEA PO5 19 G5
Bruntile Cl FARN GU14 76 C3
Bruyn Rd FBDG SP6 240 E2
Bryanstone Cl FLEETS GU52 74 D6
Bryanstone Rd TWDS BH3 322 E8
Bryanston Rd ITCH SO19 248 F7
Bryant Rd BKME/WDN BH12 322 A7
Bryces La NARL SO24 128 E6
Brydes Rd RAND SP11 79 P1
Bryher Island CHAM PO6 296 D2
Brympton Cl FBDG SP6 240 A1
Bryn Rd RFNM GU10 115 P3
Bryon Rd WIMB BH21 278 E8
Bryony Cl BDST BH18 320 B1
HLER SO31 * 270 F8
Bryony Gdns ELGH SO50 230 C6
Bryony Wy WVILLE PO7 276 A4
Bryson Cl LSOL/BMARY PO13 314 E2
Bryson Rd CHAM PO6 296 F1
Bubb La HEND SO30 230 B9
Bub La CHCH/BSGR BH23 325 J9
Buccaneers Cl
CHCH/BSGR BH23 325 H9
Buccaneer Wy FARN GU14 75 K4
Buccleuch Rd CCLF BH13 334 A5
Bucehayes Cl
CHCH/BSGR BH23 326 C7
Buchanan Av LTDN BH7 323 L9
Buchanan Rd ROWN SO16 227 K7
Buchan Av FHAM PO15 271 J2
Buchan Ct FAWY SO45 267 N8
Buckby La BSTK RG21 7 K5
HSEA PO3 297 L5
Bucketts Farm Cl BPWT SO32 232 F7
Buckfast Cl CHIN RG24 69 K3
Buckholt Rd STOK SO20 159 P1
Buckhurst Rd FRIM GU16 58 E7
Buckingham Cl ALTN GU34 132 D6
Buckingham Ct
BH/HW/K RG22 89 L3
Buckingham Ga
WSHM SO15 248 A3
Buckingham Gn PSEA PO1 316 F1
Buckingham Pde
BH/HW/K RG22 89 L2
Buckingham Pl PSEA PO1 19 H2
Buckingham Rd
BKME/WDN BH12 321 M5
NWBY RG14 16 B5
PSF GU32 215 K2
Buckingham St PSEA PO1 19 H1
Buckingham Wy FRIM GU16 58 E5
Buckland Av
BH/HW/K RG22 89 P2
Buckland Cl ELGH SO50 207 J8
FARN GU14 58 B6
WVILLE PO7 255 M9
Buckland Dene LYMN SO41 329 K2
Buckland Gdns TOTT SO40 246 A1
Buckland Gv
CHCH/BSGR BH23 326 A5
Buckland Pth NEND PO2 316 F1
Buckland Rd
BKME/WDN BH12 321 L7
Buckland St NEND PO2 316 G1
Buckland Ter
BKME/WDN BH12 321 L7
Bucklers Ct HAV PO9 276 D3
Bucklers Rd GPORT PO12 295 N9
The Bucklers LYMN SO41 338 D1
Bucklers Wy CHAR BH8 323 K4
Buckmore Av PSF GU32 215 K1
Buckner Croke Wy STHA RG19 31 L1
Bucksey Rd
LSOL/BMARY PO13 294 G9
Bucks Head Hl BPWT SO32 211 N8
Buckskin La BH/HW/K RG22 89 L1
Buckstone Cl LYMN SO41 328 E6
Buckthorn Cl CFDH BH17 320 B3
TOTT SO40 245 N3
Budden's La WHAM PO17 253 J3
Buddens Rd WHAM PO17 252 E7
Buddle Hl FBDG SP6 240 G7
Buddlesgate RWIN SO21 125 M6
Budd's Cl BSTK RG21 6 C7
Budds La BOR GU35 153 P4
ROMY SO51 204 C4
Bude Cl CHAM PO6 274 B9
Buffbeards La HASM GU27 156 D6
Buffins Cnr ODIM RG29 93 J1
Buffins Rd ODIM RG29 93 J1
Bugdens La VWD BH31 258 F4
Bugkingham Wy FRIM GU16 58 E4
Bugle St SHAM SO14 20 D7
Bulbeck Rd HAV PO9 15 F6
Bulbery RAND SP11 101 M7
Buldowne Wk LYMN SO41 308 B5
Bulford Rd TDWTH SP9 98 D1
Bullar Rd WEND SO18 248 G4
Bullar St SHAM SO14 21 G1
Bull Dro WINC SO23 184 B1
Buller Ct FARN GU14 76 B3
Buller Rd ALDT GU11 76 A8
Bullers Rd FNM GU9 96 E5
Bullfinch Cl CFDH BH17 320 B3
SHST GU47 41 M6
TOTT SO40 246 A4
Bull Hl LISS GU33 193 J2
LYMN SO41 309 P7
Bullington La RWIN SO21 124 G2
Bull La BPWT SO32 232 B9
HTWY RG27 37 M4
LYND SO43 244 C8
Bullrush Cl FAWY SO45 268 B9
Bulls Bushes HTWY RG27 71 N4
Bulls Copse La HORN PO8 256 A5
Bulls Copse Rd TOTT SO40 246 D7
Bulls Down Cl HTWY RG27 52 D4
Bulls Dro RSAL SP5 159 H9
Bulpits Hl RAND SP11 43 H7
Bulwark Rd
FHAM/STUB PO14 293 P8
Bunces La THLE RG7 27 J5
Bunch La HASM GU27 156 F6
Bunch Wy HASM GU27 156 F7
Bungalow Rd FARN GU14 76 A2
Bunkers Hl NWBY RG14 30 B1
WVILLE PO7 254 F8
Bunnian Pl BSTK RG21 7 F4
Bunns La WVILLE PO7 254 A6
Bunny La ROMY SO51 180 D8
ROMY SO51 202 A1
Bunstead La RWIN SO21 182 F8
Bunting Gdns HORN PO8 255 P7
Bunting Ms BH/HW/K RG22 89 K4
Bunting Rd FERN BH22 280 B9
Buntings ALTN GU34 132 F3
The Buntings FNM GU9 115 P2
Burbidge Gv ENEY PO4 317 J6
Burbridge Cl CFDH BH17 320 G4
Burbush Cl FAWY SO45 290 E6
Burchell Rd NWBY RG14 24 B2
Burcombe La RGWD BH24 261 J9
Burcombe Rd NBNE BH10 322 C2
Burcote Dr HSEA PO3 297 K5
Burdale Dr HISD PO11 319 K5
Burdock Cl CHCH/BSGR BH23 325 M6
RAND SP11 122 D1
THLE RG7 27 K5
Bure Cl CHCH/BSGR BH23 325 M9
Bure Haven Dr
CHCH/BSGR BH23 325 L9
Bure Homage Gdns
CHCH/BSGR BH23 325 M9
Bure Homage La
CHCH/BSGR BH23 325 L9
Bure La CHCH/BSGR BH23 337 M1
Bure Pk CHCH/BSGR BH23 325 M9
Bure Rd CHCH/BSGR BH23 325 M9
Burfield KSCL RG20 29 N9
Burford Cl CHCH/BSGR BH23 324 B6
Burford La BROC SO42 286 G7
Burford Rd CBLY GU15 58 A1
Burgage Fld WHCH RG28 85 M5
Burgate Cl HAV PO9 14 C1
Burgate Flds FBDG SP6 220 E9
Burge Cl FARN GU14 57 K9
Burgess Cl BWD BH11 301 P9
HISD PO11 319 K7
ODIM RG29 93 J1
Burgess Fld WIMB BH21 258 A4
Burgess Gdns ROWN SO16 228 A9
Burgess La KSCL RG20 28 D1
Burgess Rd BSTK RG21 6 D3
ROWN SO16 247 P1
Burghclere Rd HAV PO9 277 H4
ITCH SO19 269 H2
Burghead Cl SHST GU47 41 L7
Burgh Hill Rd LIPH GU30 154 G9
Burgoyne Rd ITCH SO19 249 N7
SSEA PO5 316 F7
Burgundy Cl HLER SO31 270 F8
Buriton Cl
FHAM/PORC PO16 273 P9
Buriton Rd FUFL SO22 164 E3
Buriton St PSEA PO1 19 J1
Burkal Dr AND SP10 82 E7
Burke Dr ITCH SO19 249 L5
Burleigh Rd FRIM GU16 58 C5
NEND PO2 297 H9
SBNE BH6 324 B9
Burley Cl CHFD SO53 206 D9
HAV PO9 277 H4
NMIL/BTOS BH25 326 F7
TOTT SO40 245 P4
VWD BH31 258 E5
Burley Down CHFD SO53 228 D1
Burley La OVTN RG25 107 K1
Burley Lawn RGWD BH24 284 D5
Burley Rd BKME/WDN BH12 321 L6
BROC SO42 308 A1
CHCH/BSGR BH23 324 G2
FUFL SO22 164 E3
Burley Wy BLKW GU17 41 K8
Burlington Ar BMTH BH1 * 8 E3
Burlington Ct ALDT GU11 2 C5
BLKW GU17 57 K2
Burlington Gra ODIM RG29 72 B9
Burlington Rd NEND PO2 296 G8
WSHM SO15 248 A5
Burlington Wk TDWTH SP9 79 H5
Burmah Rd North
FAWY SO45 291 L3
Burmah Rd South
FAWY SO45 291 K4
Burma Wy TOTT SO40 267 K2
Burmese Cl FHAM PO15 271 J3
Burnaby Cl BH/HW/K RG22 68 F9
Burnaby Rd PSEA PO1 18 E3
WBNE BH4 334 C5
Burnbake Rd VWD BH31 258 F5
Burnbank Gdns TOTT SO40 246 C4
Burnbrae Rd FERN BH22 302 D7
Burn Cl VWD BH31 259 H6
Burne Cl RWIN SO21 144 E6
Burne-Jones Dr SHST GU47 41 L8
Burnett Av CHCH/BSGR BH23 324 C8
Burnett Cl FAWY SO45 268 D8
FUFL SO22 164 D5
WEND SO18 248 G2
Burnett Rd CHCH/BSGR BH23 324 D8
GPORT PO12 315 K2
Burnetts Flds ELGH SO50 230 C5
Burnetts Gdns ELGH SO50 230 D5
Burnetts La HEND SO30 230 B8
Burney Bit TADY RG26 34 F6
Burney Rd GPORT PO12 315 J5
Burngate Rd PLE BH15 332 A1
Burnham Beeches CHFD SO53 207 D7
Burnham Cha WEND SO18 249 K4
Burnham Dr CHAR BH8 323 J8
Burnham Rd ALTN GU34 132 C8
CHAM PO6 275 M9
CHCH/BSGR BH23 324 G5
FBDG SP6 220 D9
TADY RG26 34 A4
Burnhams Cl AND SP10 82 E8
Burnhams Wk GPORT PO12 13 H1
Burnham Wd
FHAM/PORC PO16 10 E1
Burnleigh Gdns
NMIL/BTOS BH25 327 L3
Burnley Cl TADY RG26 34 C7
Burnmoor Meadow
EWKG RG40 39 P4
Burnsall Cl FARN GU14 58 A7
Burns Av FLEETS GU52 74 E6
Burns Cl CHIN RG24 69 M4
ELGH SO50 228 G2
FARN GU14 57 N7
RWIN SO21 144 F4
Burnside CHCH/BSGR BH23 325 P7
FLEETN GU51 74 D3
LSOL/BMARY PO13 294 F4
WVILLE PO7 276 A1
Burns Pl ROWN SO16 247 L1
Burns Rd ELGH SO50 229 H3
ITCH SO19 249 M6
SBNE BH6 324 B8
Burnt Hill Rd RFNM GU10 116 A4
Burnt Hill Wy RFNM GU10 116 B5
Burnt House La
CHCH/BSGR BH23 305 M7
FHAM/STUB PO14 294 B6
LYMN SO41 309 M7
Burrard Gv LYMN SO41 329 M5
Burr Cl RWIN SO21 207 P5
Burrell Rd FRIM GU16 58 B5
Burrfields Rd HSEA PO3 297 J8
Burridge Rd HLER SO31 250 G9
Burrill Av CHAM PO6 297 J1
Burrowfields
BH/HW/K RG22 89 M5
Burrow Rd RWIN SO21 163 M6
Burrows Cl HAV PO9 15 J2
Burrows La VWD BH31 258 F1
The Burrows TADY RG26 34 B5
Burrwood Gdns ASHV GU12 76 F8
Bursledon Hts HLER SO31 270 B1
Bursledon Pl WVILLE PO7 275 M5
Bursledon Rd HEND SO30 250 B6
WVILLE PO7 275 M5
Bursledon Ter TDWTH SP9 * 98 G2
Burtley Rd SBNE BH6 336 C3
Burton Cl CHCH/BSGR BH23 324 G6
RGWD BH24 281 K4
Burtoncroft
CHCH/BSGR BH23 324 G4
Burton Hall Pl C
HCH/BSGR BH23 324 G4
Burton Rd CCLF BH13 334 A3
CHCH/BSGR BH23 325 J7
WSHM SO15 248 A4
Burton's Gdns CHIN RG24 70 B5
Burt's Hl WIMB BH21 278 E8
Burt's La WIMB BH21 280 A1
Burwood Gv HISD PO11 318 G4
Bury Brickfield Pk
TOTT SO40 * 246 G7
Bury Cl GPORT PO12 12 C3
Bury Crs GPORT PO12 12 C3
Burydown Md OVTN RG25 108 D1
Buryfields ODIM RG29 93 L1
Bury Hall La GPORT PO12 315 K5
Bury Hill Cl RAND SP11 102 B6
Bury La TOTT SO40 246 F6
Bury Rd CCLF BH13 333 N2
DEAN RG23 68 G6
GPORT PO12 12 A3
TOTT SO40 247 H8
Bury's Bank Rd STHA RG19 24 G8
Bus Dro FAWY SO45 291 N9
Bushell Rd PLE BH15 320 E5
Bushells Farm FBDG SP6 240 C3
Bushey La ALTN GU34 * 132 E1
Bushey Rd CHAR BH8 323 J6
Bushmead Dr RGWD BH24 281 L4
Bushnells Dr KSCL RG20 48 B2
Bush St West SSEA PO5 * 19 G6
Bush St East SSEA PO5 19 G6
Bushy Md WVILLE PO7 275 L7
Bushywarren La OVTN RG25 111 H1
Busk Crs FARN GU14 75 N1
Busket La WINC SO23 23 F5
Busketts Wy TOTT SO40 245 N9
Butcher St PSEA PO1 18 C3
Bute Dr CHCH/BSGR BH23 326 D8
Butler Cl BH/HW/K RG22 68 F8
Butlers Cl ROMY SO51 178 F5
Butlers La RGWD BH24 260 G9
Butser Wk FHAM/STUB PO14 294 C1
Butson Cl NWBY RG14 16 A2
Buttercup Cl BOR GU35 154 D3
FAWY SO45 268 C9
HEND SO30 250 A5
Buttercup Dr
CHCH/BSGR BH23 325 M6
Buttercup Pl NTHA RG18 25 N3
Buttercup Wy HLER SO31 270 E7
Butterfield CBLY GU15 58 A1
Butterfield Rd ROWN SO16 228 A8
Butterfly Dr CHAM PO6 274 C9
Butter Furlong Rd RSAL SP5 176 B3
Butteridge Ri ROMY SO51 179 L8
Buttermer Cl RFNM GU10 115 N3
Buttermere Cl BOR GU35 154 A3
FARN GU14 57 M9
ROWN SO16 247 J1
Buttermere Ct ASHV GU12 * 76 E8
Buttermere Dr BH/HW/K RG22 89 L2
Buttermere Gdns NARL SO24 168 A3
The Buttery
CHCH/BSGR BH23 325 H8
Button's La ALTN GU34 172 A5
Buttons La ROMY SO51 224 E1
Buttsash Av FAWY SO45 290 C1
Butts Ash Gdns FAWY SO45 268 C9
Butts Ash La FAWY SO45 290 B1
Butts Bridge Hl FAWY SO45 268 C8
Buttsbridge Rd FAWY SO45 268 C9
Butts Cl FUFL SO22 164 E6
Butt's Cl ITCH SO19 249 M7
Butt's Crs ITCH SO19 249 L7
Butts Farm La BPWT SO32 232 B4
Butts Lawn BROC SO42 286 F7
Butts Meadow HTWY RG27 71 P3
Butts Ms ALTN GU34 132 F7
Butts Paddock BROC SO42 286 F7
Butts Rd ALTN GU34 132 E7
Butt's Rd ITCH SO19 249 K9
Butt's Sq ITCH SO19 249 L7
The Butts BPWT SO32 211 N7
THLE RG7 35 J6
Butt St RAND SP11 79 N1
The Butty BSTK RG21 7 K5
Byerley Cl EMRTH PO10 277 P5
Byerley Rd PSEA PO1 317 H2
Byes La THLE RG7 35 J7
Byeways FAWY SO45 268 B8
KSCL RG20 29 N8
Byfields Rd KSCL RG20 48 B3
Byfleet Av CHIN RG24 70 C7
The Byfrons FARN GU14 61 K6
Byng Wk AND SP10 5 K3
By-Pass Rd ROMY SO51 204 C7
RWIN SO21 125 K5
Byrd Cl WVILLE PO7 275 N5
Byrd Gdns BH/HW/K RG22 89 N4
Byron Av CBLY GU15 58 G2
FUFL SO22 164 E7
Byron Cl BPWT SO32 232 C4
CHIN RG24 69 M3
FHAM/PORC PO16 10 E3
NWBY RG14 24 C8
RAND SP11 79 P1
YTLY GU46 56 C1
Byron Dr CWTH RG45 41 H2
Byron Rd BOSC BH5 335 M2
ELGH SO50 207 J9
ITCH SO19 249 M5
NEND PO2 297 H9
NMIL/BTOS BH25 326 G7
Byways YTLY GU46 40 C9

Byworth Cl FNM GU9 ..... 95 P9
Byworth Rd FNM GU9 ..... 95 P9

C

Cable St ELGH SO50 ..... 229 J2
  SHAM SO14 ..... 21 J2
Cabot Cl AND SP10 ..... 82 E9
Cabot La CFDH BH17 ..... 320 C4
Cabrol Rd FARN GU14 ..... 57 P8
Cadet Wy FLEETS GU52 ..... 74 E8
Cadgwith Pl CHAM PO6 ..... 296 D2
Cadhay Cl NMIL/BTOS BH25 ..... 326 C4
Cadland Rd FAWY SO45 ..... 290 E9
Cadnam Cl BEAN BH23 ..... 88 F1
Cadnam La TOTT SO40 ..... 244 E3
Cadnam Rd ENEY PO4 ..... 317 K5
Cadnam Wy CHAR BH8 ..... 323 K4
Cadogan Rd ALDT GU11 ..... 76 C5
  RGWD BH24 ..... 282 F2
Cador Dr FHAM/PORC PO16 ..... 295 M3
Caerleon Av ITCH SO19 ..... 249 L5
Caerleon Dr AND SP10 ..... 82 E7
  ITCH SO19 ..... 249 K5
Caernarvon Cl ELGH SO50 ..... 58 E5
Caernarvon Gdns CHFD SO53 ..... 206 C4
Caer Peris Vw
  FHAM/PORC PO16 ..... 273 N8
Caesar Cl AND SP10 * 82 E8
Caesar Ct ALDT GU11 ..... 2 A3
Caesar Rd AND SP10 ..... 82 E8
Caesar's Wy BDST BH18 ..... 300 A9
  WHCH RG28 ..... 85 K5
Caigers Gn HLER SO31 ..... 271 H1
Cains Cl FHAM/STUB PO14 ..... 294 C6
Caird Av NMIL/BTOS BH25 ..... 327 K4
Cairn Cl CBLY GU15 ..... 58 C2
Cairngorm Cl RFNM GU10 ..... 68 E8
Cairngorm Pl FARN GU14 ..... 57 M6
Cairns Cl CHCH/BSGR BH23 ..... 324 D7
Cairo Ter NEND PO2 ..... 316 F1
Caister Cl FARN GU14 ..... 302 C2
Caistor Cl ROWN SO16 ..... 227 L8
Caithness Cl DEAN RG23 ..... 88 E1
Caker's La ALTN GU34 * 133 K7
Caker Stream Rd ALTN GU34 ..... 133 H5
Calabrese Wk HLER SO31 ..... 271 K3
Calard Dr NTHA RG18 ..... 25 K2
Calbourne HLER SO31 ..... 269 L3
Calcot Hi BPWT SO32 ..... 251 L3
Calcot La BPWT SO32 ..... 251 L1
Calcott Pk YTLY GU46 ..... 40 D8
Calder Cl ROWN SO16 ..... 247 J3
Calder Ct AND SP10 ..... 82 G9
Calder Rd BCFDH BH17 ..... 321 H4
Calderwood Dr ITCH SO19 ..... 249 J7
Caledonian Cl
  CHCH/BSGR BH23 ..... 325 M8
Caledon Rd PSTN BH14 ..... 321 M9
Calender Cl ALTN GU34 ..... 133 G7
California Cl TOTT SO40 ..... 245 P2
Calleva Cl BH/HW/K RG22 ..... 89 M4
Callowing Cl RWIN SO21 ..... 207 P5
Calluna Rd BKME/WDN BH12 ..... 321 K3
Calmore Av FARN GU14 ..... 323 K4
Calmore Crs TOTT SO40 ..... 245 P2
Calmore Dr TOTT SO40 ..... 245 P2
Calmore Gdns TOTT SO40 ..... 246 A4
Calmore Rd TOTT SO40 ..... 245 P3
Calpe Av LYND SO43 ..... 264 F4
Calshot Cl FAWY SO45 ..... 290 E3
Calshot Dr CHFD SO53 ..... 206 C9
Calshot Rd FAWY SO45 ..... 291 K6
  HAV PO9 ..... 276 C3
Calshot Wy FRIM GU16 ..... 58 F6
  LSOL/BMARY PO13 ..... 294 F8
Calvecroft LIPH GU30 ..... 175 K3
Calvert Cl ASHV GU12 ..... 97 K2
Calvin Cl FHAM PO15 ..... 272 A1
Calvin Rd MOOR/WNTN BH9 ..... 322 F7
Camber Pl PSEA PO1 ..... 14 C6
Camberry Cl BSTK RG21 ..... 69 M9
Cambria Dr FAWY SO45 ..... 267 P7
Cambrian Cl HLER SO31 ..... 250 A9
Cambrian Wk FLEETS GU52 * 19 J6
Cambrian Wk
  FHAM/STUB PO14 ..... 294 D2
Cambridge Dr CHFD SO53 ..... 228 E1
Cambridge Gdns
  CHCH/BSGR BH23 ..... 324 D5
Cambridge Gn
  FHAM/STUB PO14 ..... 271 J8
Cambridge Rd ALDT GU11 ..... 2 B3
  CWTH RG45 ..... 41 K2
  LSOL/BMARY PO13 ..... 314 D3
  PSEA PO1 ..... 18 C5
  SHAM SO14 ..... 248 C3
  SHST GU47 ..... 41 M5
  WCLF BH2 ..... 8 A3
Cambridge Rd East
  FARN GU14 ..... 76 B3
Cambridge Rd West
  FARN GU14 ..... 76 B3
Camcross Cl CHAM PO6 ..... 274 D9
Camden St GPORT PO12 ..... 315 L2
Camden Wk FLEETS GU52 ..... 74 F3
Camel Green Rd FBDG SO46 ..... 239 N5
Camelia Cl HAV PO9 .....
  NBAD SO52 ..... 205 L8
Camelia Dr WEND SO18 ..... 249 J1
Camelia Gv ELGH SO50 ..... 230 C2
Camellia Cl WIMB BH21 ..... 258 E9

Camellia Gdns
  NMIL/BTOS BH25 ..... 327 K5
Camelot Cl AND SP10 ..... 82 E9
Camelot Crs
  FHAM/PORC PO16 ..... 273 M9
Camelsdale Rd HASM GU27 ..... 156 E8
Cameron Cl
  LSOL/BMARY PO13 ..... 294 G6
Cameron Rd ALDT GU11 ..... 76 C5
  CHCH/BSGR BH23 ..... 325 H8
Camfield Cl BSTK RG21 ..... 69 M9
Camford Cl BH/HW/K RG22 ..... 89 L7
Camilla Cl TOTT SO40 ..... 245 G2
Camlea Cl BSTK RG21 ..... 69 M9
Camley Cl ITCH SO19 ..... 268 C1
Cammel Rd FERN BH22 ..... 302 D6
Camomile Dr RAND SP11 ..... 79 P1
Campbell Cl ALDT GU11 ..... 74 B3
  FLEETN GU51 ..... 74 B3
  RAND SP11 ..... 119 N2
  YTLY GU46 ..... 40 G8
Campbell Ct TADY RG26 ..... 52 C3
Campbell Flds ALDT GU11 ..... 3 F5
Campbell Pl FRIM GU16 ..... 58 E2
Campbell Rd ALDT GU11 ..... 2 C1
  BMTH BH1 ..... 335 L1
  CHCH/BSGR BH23 ..... 324 C4
  RWIN SO21 ..... 104 EB
  SSEA PO5 ..... 19 K6
  TADY RG26 ..... 52 C3
Camp Cl SE SHAM SO14 ..... 21 J1
Camp Hi ELGH SO50 ..... 230 C2
Camp Farm Rd ALDT GU11 ..... 76 C7
Camp Hl STOK SO20 ..... 161 M4
Campion Cl BLKW GU17 ..... 57 N2
  BOR GU35 ..... 154 D4
  HLER SO31 ..... 230 C6
  LYMN SO41 ..... 329 L2
  WVILLE PO7 ..... 161 N4
Campion Dr ROMY SO51 ..... 204 G4
Campion Rd ITCH SO19 ..... 249 M6
Campion Wy HTWY RG27 ..... 55 J6
  LYMN SO41 ..... 329 L2
  WINC SO23 ..... 165 A5
Camp Rd BOR GU35 ..... 154 A5
  FARN GU14 ..... 76 B4
  LSOL/BMARY PO13 ..... 295 H6
  THLE RG7 ..... 26 E6
Campsie Cl RWIN SO21 ..... 68 E8
Camrose Wy BSTK RG21 * 69 M9
Cams Bay Cl
  FHAM/PORC PO16 ..... 273 K9
Cams Hall Est
  FHAM/PORC PO16 ..... 295 H1
Cams Hi FHAM/PORC PO16 ..... 273 H9
Camus Cl FLEETS GU52 ..... 74 A7
Cam Wk BSTK RG21 * 7 J6
Camwood Cl BSTK RG21 ..... 69 J5
Canada Rd FRIM GU16 ..... 59 J5
  ITCH SO19 ..... 248 G9
  ROMY SO51 ..... 224 D4
Canada Wy ROMY SO51 ..... 224 D4
Canadian Wy CHIN RG24 ..... 68 F4
Canal Cl ALDT GU11 ..... 76 C7
Canal Reach HTWY RG27 ..... 71 N3
Canal View Rd NWBY RG14 ..... 24 C4
Canal Wk NWBY RG14 ..... 16 J2
  PSEA PO1 ..... 15 J3
  ROMY SO51 ..... 204 D5
  SHAM SO14 ..... 20 E6
Canberra Cl GPORT PO12 ..... 315 K4
  YTLY GU46 * 40 B7
Canberra Rd
  CHCH/BSGR BH23 ..... 324 C6
  EMRTH PO10 ..... 299 N6
  ROWN SO16 ..... 228 G1
Canberra Wy BH/HW/K RG22 ..... 89 L7
  FARN GU14 ..... 75 N4
Candleford Ga LISS GU33 * 175 J3
Candlemas Pl SD/PW SO17 * 248 C3
Candover Cl TADY RG26 ..... 34 C7
Candover Ct BH/HW/K RG22 ..... 89 L7
Candy La WEND SO18 ..... 249 N4
Candys Cl WIMB BH21 ..... 300 A3
Candys La WIMB BH21 ..... 300 A3
Canes La BOR GU35 ..... 154 C3
Canford Av BWD BH11 ..... 321 P5
Canford Bottom WIMB BH21 ..... 259 J8
Canford Cliffs Av PSTN BH14 ..... 333 M1
Canford Cliffs Rd CCLF BH13 ..... 333 N5
Canford Cl BPWT SO32 ..... 252 C4
  ROWN SO16 ..... 247 H1
Canford Crs CCLF BH13 ..... 333 N4
Canford Gdns BWD BH11 ..... 322 A6
Canford Heath Rd CFDH BH17 ..... 320 C2
Canford Magna WIMB BH21 ..... 301 H5
Canford Rd BWD BH11 ..... 322 A6
  PLE BH15 ..... 320 FB
Canford View Dr WIMB BH21 ..... 279 K8
Canford Wy
  BKME/WDN BH12 ..... 321 L2
Canhouse La LISS GU33 ..... 193 K3
Canning Rd ENEY PO4 ..... 3 K3
Cannock Wk
  FHAM/STUB PO14 ..... 294 C2
Cannon Cl BDST BH18 ..... 320 B3
  SHST GU47 ..... 41 N6
Cannon Hill Gdns WIMB BH21 ..... 279 K7
Cannon Hill Rd WIMB BH21 ..... 279 J7
Cannon St LYMN SO41 ..... 329 M3
  WSHM SO15 ..... 247 N3
Cannon's Barn Cl
  FHAM/PORC PO16 ..... 273 N9
Canons Cl RWIN SO21 ..... 79 H7
Canon's Ct KSCL RG20 ..... 48 B3
Canon St WINC SO23 ..... 22 D6

Cansfield End NWBY RG14 ..... 16 D1
Canterbury Cl BH/HW/K RG22 ..... 89 M3
  FERN BH22 ..... 280 C8
  LSOL/BMARY PO13 ..... 314 F4
Canterbury Dr FAWY SO45 ..... 267 N7
Canterbury Gdns FARN GU14 ..... 76 C2
Canterbury Rd ASHV GU12 ..... 76 F9
  ENEY PO4 ..... 317 H5
  FHAM/STUB PO14 ..... 294 A6
Canterbury Wk FARN GU14 ..... 76 C2
Canterton La LYND SO43 ..... 244 A5
Canton St WSHM SO15 ..... 248 C3
Canute Rd ALDT GU11 ..... 21 J7
  WINC SO23 ..... 23 H7
Capella Gdns FAWY SO45 ..... 267 P7
Capel Ley WVILLE PO7 ..... 275 N6
Capers End La BPWT SO32 ..... 251 L2
Capesthorne
  CHCH/BSGR BH23 ..... 337 M1
Capper Rd CBLY GU15 ..... 41 P7
Capstone Pl CHAR BH8 ..... 323 K9
Capstone Rd CHAR BH8 ..... 323 J9
Captains Cl GPORT PO12 ..... 295 K9
Captains Pl SHAM SO14 ..... 21 J4
Captains Rw LYMN SO41 ..... 329 K5
Captains Rw PSEA PO1 ..... 18 C6
Caradon Pl VWD BH31 ..... 258 D3
Carbery Dr
  FHAM/PORC PO16 ..... 295 M2
Carbery Av SBNE BH6 ..... 336 D2
Carbery Cl HAV PO9 ..... 276 D5
Carbery Gdns SBNE BH6 ..... 336 C1
Carbery La SBNE BH6 * 336 A2
Carbis Cl CHAM PO6 ..... 296 C2
Carbonel Cl DEAN RG23 ..... 87 M3
Carcary Cl FLEETS GU52 ..... 74 C5
Cardiff Rd NEND PO2 ..... 296 F7
Cardigan Rd
  BKME/WDN BH12 ..... 321 P6
  MOOR/WNTN BH9 ..... 322 F7
Cardinal Dr WVILLE PO7 ..... 276 B1
Cardinal Wy RFNM GU10 ..... 97 M4
Cardinal Wy HLER SO31 ..... 271 H7
The Cardinals RFNM GU10 ..... 97 M4
Carey Rd ITCH SO19 ..... 249 L6
  MOOR/WNTN BH9 ..... 322 F5
Careys Cots BROC SO42 ..... 286 F7
Cargate Av ALDT GU11 ..... 2 D4
Cargate Gv ALDT GU11 ..... 2 C5
Cargate Hl ALDT GU11 ..... 2 C5
Cargate Ter ALDT GU11 ..... 2 C5
Carina Cl HLER SO31 ..... 269 L3
Carisbrooke Av
  FHAM/STUB PO14 ..... 293 N7
Carisbrooke Cl DEAN RG23 ..... 68 F6
  HAV PO9 ..... 15 K4
  NARL SO24 ..... 168 A3
Carisbrooke Ct
  NMIL/BTOS BH25 ..... 327 H4
  ROMY SO51 ..... 204 E4
Carisbrooke Crs CHFD SO53 ..... 206 D5
Carisbrooke Dr ITCH SO19 ..... 249 H5
Carisbrooke Rd ENEY PO4 ..... 317 H4
  LSOL/BMARY PO13 ..... 294 F8
Carisbrooke Wy
  CHCH/BSGR BH23 ..... 326 A6
Carless Cl LSOL/BMARY PO13 ..... 315 H1
Carlin Cl HTWY RG27 ..... 71 N3
Carlisle Cl DEAN RG23 ..... 68 F6
Carlisle Rd RFNM GU10 ..... 137 H2
  ROWN SO16 ..... 247 M3
  SSEA PO5 ..... 19 K3
Carlton Av NMIL/BTOS BH25 ..... 326 F8
Carlton Cl CBLY GU15 ..... 58 C2
Carlton Crs FLEETS GU52 ..... 248 B5
  WSHM SO15 ..... 248 B5
Carlton Gv PSTN BH14 ..... 321 M7
Carlton Pl WSHM SO15 ..... 20 D1
Carlton Rd BMTH BH1 ..... 335 J2
  BOR GU35 ..... 154 C4
  FHAM/PORC PO16 ..... 273 P9
  GPORT PO12 ..... 15 F1
  WSHM SO15 ..... 248 B4
Carlton Wy GPORT PO12 ..... 15 F1
Carlyn Dr CHFD SO53 ..... 206 F6
Carlyon Cl FARN GU14 ..... 58 B9
  FRIM GU16 ..... 58 B9
Carmans La RWIN SO21 ..... 183 M7
Carmarthen Av CHAM PO6 ..... 275 K9
Carmarthen Cl FARN GU14 ..... 57 N6
Carmichael Wy
  BH/HW/K RG22 ..... 89 N3
Carmine Cl
  LSOL/BMARY PO13 ..... 314 C2
Carminc Ter LIPH GU30 ..... 175 J3
Carnac Ct FHAM/PORC PO16 * 295 H1
Carnarvon Rd BMTH BH1 ..... 335 L2
  GPORT PO12 ..... 12 A1
  NEND PO2 ..... 297 H9
Carnation Rd ROWN SO16 ..... 227 P8
Carne Cl CHFD SO53 ..... 206 E5
Carnegie Cl BKME/WDN BH12 ..... 321 M1
  LSOL/BMARY PO13 ..... 314 D1
Carnegie Rd NWBY RG14 ..... 17 F3
Caroline Av CHCH/BSGR BH23 ..... 337 J1
Caroline Gdns CHAM PO6 ..... 272 A8
Caroline Pl GPORT PO12 ..... 315 H1
Caroline Rd BWD BH11 ..... 322 B4
Caroline Wy FRIM GU16 ..... 58 F2
Carolyn Cl ITCH SO19 ..... 248 G9
Carpathia Cl WEND SO18 ..... 249 J1
Carpathia Dr SHAM SO14 ..... 21 J1
Carpenter Cl ENEY PO4 * 317 J5
  FAWY SO45 ..... 291 K2
  LYMN SO41 ..... 329 K2
Carpenter Dr RWIN SO21 ..... 104 EB
Carpenters NARL SO24 ..... 168 A2
Carpenters Cl ALTN GU34 ..... 133 K2

HEND SO30 ..... 250 B7
HTWY RG27 ..... 52 E4
Carpenter's Ct BH/HW/K RG22 * 89 P1
Carpenter's Down CHIN RG24 ..... 69 L2
Carran Wk FHAM/STUB PO14 ..... 294 C2
Carraway FHAM PO15 ..... 271 K3
Carrbridge Cl TWDS BH3 ..... 322 D8
Carrbridge Rd TWDS BH3 ..... 322 D8
Carrick La YTLY GU46 ..... 40 F8
Carrick Wy NMIL/BTOS BH25 ..... 327 L5
Carrington Cl LYMN SO41 ..... 339 H2
Carrington Crs TADY RG26 ..... 34 C6
Carrington La ASHV GU12 ..... 76 E4
  LYMN SO41 ..... 339 H1
Carroll Av FERN BH22 ..... 302 D5
Carroll Cl BKME/WDN BH12 ..... 322 A9
  ELGH SO50 ..... 230 D3
Carronade Wk HSEA PO3 ..... 297 N4
Carshalton Av FERN BH22 ..... 297 K1
Carsworth Wy CFDH BH17 ..... 321 J2
Carter's Clay Rd ROMY SO51 ..... 179 H9
Carter's La FBDG SO46 ..... 221 P1
Carter's La FLE BH15 ..... 332 E1
  TOTT SO40 ..... 267 J5
Carter's Meadow AND SP10 ..... 82 B9
Carters Wk CHAR PO6 ..... 96 D3
Carthage Cl CHFD SO53 ..... 206 D4
Carthagena RWIN SO21 ..... 125 M5
Carthona Dr FLEETS GU52 ..... 74 C5
Cartref Cl VWD BH31 ..... 258 F4
Cartwright Cl NBNE BH10 ..... 322 C3
Cartwright Dr FHAM PO15 ..... 271 M8
Carvers La ALDT GU11 ..... 3 F2
Carvers La BOR GU35 ..... 282 E2
Carysfort Rd BMTH BH1 ..... 335 K2
Cascades Ap PSEA PO1 ..... 19 G1
Cases Bakery Cl WHAM PO17 ..... 252 E7
Cashmoor Cl
  BKME/WDN BH12 ..... 321 P5
Caspian Cl HLER SO31 ..... 271 H3
Cassel Av CCLF BH13 ..... 333 J1
Cassino Cl ALDT GU11 ..... 3 F2
Casterbridge La RAND SP11 ..... 81 K9
Casterbridge Rd FERN BH22 ..... 302 B5
  HAV PO9 ..... 277 H9
Castle Cl LYMN SO41 ..... 339 H2
  SSEA PO5 ..... 19 G6
Castle Ct WSHM SO15 ..... 247 L5
Castlecraig Cl SHST GU47 ..... 41 L7
Castledene Crs PSTN BH14 ..... 333 J1
Castle Farm La WHAM PO17 ..... 252 F9
Castle Gate Cl CHAR BH8 ..... 323 J5
Castle Gv FHAM/PORC PO16 ..... 295 P2
  NWBY RG14 ..... 24 C2
Castle Hill La RGWD BH24 ..... 284 A6
Castle La FAWY SO45 ..... 291 K5
  NBAD SO52 ..... 205 M9
  NWBY RG14 ..... 24 B1
  SHAM SO14 ..... 20 D5
Castle La East LTDN BH7 ..... 323 P7
Castle La West
  MOOR/WNTN BH9 ..... 322 C3
Castlemain Av SBNE BH6 ..... 336 A1
Castlemans La HISD PO11 ..... 298 C8
Castleman Trailway
  CFDH BH17 ..... 320 A4
  WIMB BH21 ..... 279 N3
Castleman Wy RGWD BH24 ..... 282 E5
Castlemews RGWD BH24 ..... 282 A4
Castle Point CHAR BH8 * 323 L5
Castle Rd ODIM RG29 ..... 72 B8
  WINC SO23 ..... 145 K7
Castle Rw GPORT PO12 * 13 J2
Castleshaw Cl ROWN SO16 ..... 247 K4
Castle Sq SHAM SO14 ..... 20 D6
Castle Vw GPORT PO12 ..... 13 F1
Castleway HAV PO9 ..... 277 H9
Castlewood CHFD SO53 ..... 206 E9
  RGWD BH24 ..... 282 B4
Castle Woods RSAL SP5 ..... 199 P7
Castle St CFDH BH17 ..... 320 A4
Castle Vw HSEA PO3 ..... 317 K1
Catalina Rd CHCH/BSGR BH23 ..... 325 L9
Catalina Dr PLE BH15 ..... 332 C2
Catamaran Cl HLER SO31 ..... 269 P2
Catchmoor RSAL SP5 ..... 199 K1
Cateran Cl ROWN SO16 ..... 247 K3
Catesby Gdns YTLY GU46 ..... 40 E7
Cathay Gdns FAWY SO45 ..... 267 N7
Cathedral Vw WINC SO23 ..... 23 G7
Catherine Cl HEND SO30 ..... 250 C4
Catherine Gdns HEND SO30 ..... 199 H6
Catherine Rd NWBY RG14 ..... 249 N1
Catherines Wk RAND SP11 ..... 101 M7
Catherington La HORN PO8 ..... 256 A2
Catherington Wy HAV PO9 ..... 256 B3

Catisfield La FHAM PO15 ..... 271 P9
Catisfield Rd ENEY PO4 ..... 317 K3
  FHAM PO15 ..... 272 A9
Catkin Cl CHAR RG24 ..... 70 A1
Catmint Cl CHFD SO53 ..... 206 B6
Caton Cl BKME/WDN BH12 ..... 322 B7
Cattistock Rd CHAR BH8 ..... 323 L4
Cattle La RAND SP11 ..... 101 N6
Caunter Rd NWBY RG14 ..... 24 B3
Causeway ROMY SO51 ..... 204 B7
Causeway Crs TOTT SO40 ..... 246 E3
Causeway Farm HORN PO8 ..... 256 B5
The Causeway EPSF GU31 ..... 215 G5
  FHAM/PORC PO16 ..... 273 J9
  HTWY RG27 ..... 57 P7
  PSF GU32 ..... 215 L3
  RSAL SP5 ..... 158 D1
  STOK SO20 ..... 139 N2
Causton Gdns ELGH SO50 ..... 229 J1
Causton Rd BH/HW/K RG22 ..... 89 M7
Cavalier Cl CHIN RG24 ..... 70 C6
  NWBY RG14 ..... 24 F2
Cavalier Rd CHAR RG24 ..... 267 N7
Cavalry Cl ALDT GU11 ..... 3 H3
Cavan Crs CFDH BH17 ..... 320 D3
Cavanna Cl
  LSOL/BMARY PO13 ..... 294 F6
Cavell Dr NBNE BH10 ..... 322 C3
Cavell Cl CHIN RG24 ..... 70 B4
Cavell Dr CHAM PO6 ..... 274 C9
Cavendish Cl ROMY SO51 ..... 204 G2
Cavendish Ct BLKW GU17 * 57 L2
  NWBY RG14 ..... 25 H2
Cavendish Dr WVILLE PO7 ..... 275 P5
Cavendish Gdns FLEETS GU52 ..... 73 P7
Cavendish Gv SD/PW SO17 * 248 B3
  WINC SO23 ..... 165 A3
Cavendish Ms ALDT GU11 ..... 2 D5
  WSHM SO15 ..... 248 B3
Cavendish Pl BMTH BH1 ..... 334 C1
  SSEA PO5 ..... 19 J7
  WCLF BH2 ..... 334 F2
Cavendish Rd FLEETS GU52 ..... 74 C8
  SSEA PO5 ..... 19 J7
Caversham Cl HEND SO30 ..... 249 K9
  ITCH SO19 ..... 249 J7
  PLE BH15 ..... 332 A9
Caves Farm Cl SHST GU47 ..... 41 H6
Cawdor Rd TWDS BH3 ..... 322 D8
Cawte Rd WSHM SO15 ..... 247 P5
Caxton Av ITCH SO19 ..... 249 H9
Caxton Cl AND SP10 ..... 102 A1
  CHCH/BSGR BH23 ..... 325 K8
Cayman Cl CHIN RG24 ..... 69 M3
Cecil Av CHAR BH8 ..... 323 J7
  ROWN SO16 ..... 247 M2
  TOTT SO40 ..... 267 P8
Cecil Cl WIMB BH21 ..... 300 A7
Cecil Gv SSEA PO5 ..... 19 F7
Cecil Hl CHAR BH8 ..... 323 H7
Cecil Pl SSEA PO5 ..... 19 J7
Cecil Rd BKME/WDN BH12 ..... 321 M6
  BOSC BH5 ..... 335 L2
  ITCH SO19 ..... 249 H8
Cedar Av BLKW GU17 * .....
  CHCH/BSGR BH23 ..... 324 B7
  NBNE BH10 ..... 322 D1
  RGWD BH24 ..... 281 K6
Cedar Cl ASHV GU12 ..... 97 L3
  GPORT PO12 ..... 295 L8
  HEND SO30 ..... 250 C4
  HLER SO31 ..... 269 P2
  TADY RG26 ..... 34 EB
  WINC SO23 ..... 145 J8
  WVILLE PO7 ..... 275 N4
Cedar Crs HORN PO8 ..... 256 C6
  NBAD SO52 ..... 205 K8
Cedar Dr FLEETN GU51 ..... 73 P5
  KSCL RG20 ..... 48 B5
  LYMN SO41 ..... 329 K3
  WIMB BH21 ..... 279 K9
Cedar Gdns HAV PO9 ..... 15 H3
  SHAM SO14 ..... 248 C3
Cedar Gv HSEA PO3 ..... 317 K1
  STHA RG19 ..... 25 M4
Cedar Lawn AND SP10 ..... 82 G4
Cedar Ldg HASM GU27 * 157 K8
Cedarmount LYND SO43 ..... 264 F6
Cedar Mt NWBY RG14 ..... 17 F7
Cedar Rd CHCH/BSGR BH23 ..... 305 M7
  FARN GU14 ..... 76 B1
  FAWY SO45 ..... 290 C2
  HEND SO30 ..... 250 C4
  ITCH SO19 ..... 249 H9
Cedars Cl SHST GU47 ..... 40 G6
The Cedars FHAM/PORC PO16 ..... 10 C1
  FLEETN GU51 ..... 74 F8
  NWBY RG14 ..... 24 F8
  RWIN SO21 ..... 304 D2
Cedars Vw RSAL SP5 ..... 159 M8
Cedar Ter HTWY RG27 * 54 G8
Cedar Tree Cl DEAN RG23 ..... 88 E3
Cedar Vw FLEETS GU52 ..... 74 E6
Cedar Wk AND SP10 ..... 102 B4
  FUFL SO22 ..... 22 B5
Cedarways FRIM GU16 ..... 116 B3
  WINC SO23 ..... 145 K9
Cedar Wood Cl ELGH SO50 ..... 230 C2
  TOTT SO40 ..... 246 A3
Cedric Cl FAWY SO45 ..... 291 H9
Celandine Av HLER SO31 ..... 271 H3
  HORN PO8 ..... 256 A7
Celandine Cl
  CHCH/BSGR BH23 ..... 325 M7

CHFD SO53 .... 206 B8
Celandine Ct YTLY GU46 .... 40 B7
Celia Ct WVILLE PO7 .... 276 B2
Cellars Farm Rd SBNE BH6 .... 336 E3
Celtic Dr AND SP10 .... 102 C4
Cement Ter SHAM SO14 .... 20 D6
Cemetery Av PLE BH15 .... 321 H6
Cemetery HI ODIM RG29 .... 93 L2
Cemetery La OVTN RG25 .... 92 B6
WVILLE PO7 .... 255 H6
Cemetery Rd FLEETN GU51 .... 74 B5
WIMB BH21 .... 278 D9
WSHM SO15 .... 248 A3
Centaur St NEND PO2 .... 296 F9
Centenary Gdns ELGH SO50 .... 230 C5
Centenary Cl LYMN SO41 .... 308 C6
Centenary Gdns HAV PO9 .... 15 G4
Central Av BKME/WDN BH12 .... 321 N6
Central Br SHAM SO14 .... 21 C6
Central Dr RCWD BH24 .... 281 H9
WCLF BH2 .... 8 C2
Central Rd BOR GU35 .... 154 A2
CHAM PO6 .... 297 L2
FHAM/PORC PO16 .... 295 M2
SHAM SO14 .... 248 C9
Central Sq WHAM PO17 .... 272 C3
Central Station Br
WSHM SO15 .... 20 A3
Central St PSEA PO1 .... 19 J1
RAND SP11 .... 79 P1
Central Wy AND SP10 .... 103 J1
Centre Dr CHIN RG24 .... 70 A3
Centre La LYMN SO41 .... 328 E6
Centre PI RCWD BH24 .... 282 D2
Centre Terrace Rd FARN GU14 .... 75 P4
Centre Wy HLER SO31 .... 270 C7
Centurion CI SHST GU47 .... 41 L6
Centurion Ct ENEY PO4 .... 317 M5
Centurion Wy BH/HW/K RG22 .... 89 M4
Century CI OVTN RG25 .... 90 C4
Cerdic Ms HLER SO31 .... 270 A6
Cerne Abbas CCLF BH13 .... 334 A4
Cerne CI MOOR/WNTN BH9 .... 323 H5
NBAD SO52 .... 205 J9
WEND SO18 .... 249 K2
Chadderton Gdns PSEA PO1 .... 18 E6
Chaddesley Gln CCLF BH13 .... 333 M5
Chaddesley Pines CCLF BH13 .... 333 N5
Chaddesley Wood Rd
CCLF BH13 .... 333 N6
Chadswell Meadow HAV PO9 .... 14 B5
Chadwell Av ITCH SO19 .... 249 M1
Chadwick Rd ELGH SO50 .... 228 G2
Chadwick Wy HLER SO31 .... 269 P8
Chafen Rd WEND SO18 .... 248 F3
Chaffers CI ODIM RG29 .... 93 K9
Chaffey Cl RCWD BH24 .... 282 C1
Chaffinch CI BH/HW/K RG22 .... 89 L3
CFDH BH17 .... 320 B3
NMIL/BTOS BH25 .... 327 H5
SHST GU47 .... 41 M6
TOTT SO40 .... 246 A3
Chaffinch Gn HORN PO8 .... 255 N7

Chaffinch Wy
FHAM/PORC PO16 .... 295 K1
Chalbury CI CFDH BH17 .... 321 J2
Chalcraft Cl LIPH GU30 .... 175 H3
Chalcrafts ALTN GU34 .... 132 C4
Chaldecott Gdns NBNE BH10 .... 322 C3
Chaldon Rd CFDH BH17 .... 321 H2
Chale Cl LSOL/BMARY PO13 .... 294 C7
Chalet HI BOR GU35 .... 154 B5
Chalewood Rd FAWY SO45 .... 312 C1
Chalfont Av CHCH/BSGR BH23 .... 324 B4
Chalfont Dr FARN GU14 .... 76 B2
Chalford Gra FHAM PO15 .... 272 B9
Chalford Rd NWBY RG14 .... 16 A3
Chalice CI HEND SO30 .... 250 C4
Chalice Cl ALTN GU34 .... 150 C6
Chalk Hill Rd HORN PO8 .... 256 C5
Chalk La WHAM PO17 .... 272 F3
Chalkpit La RAND SP11 .... 101 K5
Chalk Pit La RSAL SP5 .... 159 J6
Chalkpit Rd CHIN RG24 .... 274 D8
Chalk Rdg HORN PO8 .... 236 D9
WINC SO23 .... 23 K6
Chalkridge Rd CHAM PO6 .... 275 J9
Chalk's Cl RSAL SP5 .... 199 P6
Chalk V CHIN RG24 .... 70 D7
Chalky Copse HTWY RG27 .... 71 P2
Chalky HI ALTN GU34 .... 149 K2
Chalky La BPWT SO32 .... 232 B4
HTWY RG27 .... 73 L9
Challenger Wy FAWY SO45 .... 267 P7
Challis CI BH/HW/K RG22 .... 89 N1
Challis CI RAND SP11 .... 79 M1
SHAM SO14 .... 21 F6
Challoner CI BH/HW/K RG22 .... 68 F9
Chalmers Wy HLER SO31 .... 269 N7
Chaloner Crs FAWY SO45 .... 268 C9
Chalton Crs HAV PO9 .... 276 D5
Chalton La HORN PO8 .... 256 C6
Chalvington Rd CHFD SO53 .... 206 F3
Chalybeate CI ROWN SO16 .... 247 M1
Chamberlain Gv
FHAM/STUB PO14 .... 294 E1
Chamberlain Rd SD/PW SO17 .... 228 C3
Chamberlains Meadow
HTWY RG27 .... 37 P8
Chamberlain La RFNM GU10 .... 115 J2
Chamberlayne HLER SO31 .... 269 P2
Chamberlayne Rd ELGH SO50 .... 229 J3
HLER SO31 .... 269 J4
Chambers CI ROWN SO16 .... 226 G1
Chambers Rd ASHV GU12 .... 76 G6
Chamomile Gdns FARN GU14 .... 57 K8
Champion CI LYMN SO41 .... 339 L9
Champion Wy FLEETS GU52 .... 74 D7
Champ La BOR GU35 .... 153 N7

Chancellors La BPWT SO32 .... 230 E9
Chancel Rd HLER SO31 .... 271 H7
Chander CI FERN BH22 .... 302 E4
Chandler Rd BSTK RG22 .... 90 C1
Chandlers CI HISD PO11 .... 319 J5
LTDN BH7 .... 325 P7
Chandlers Ga CHFD SO53 .... 206 E7
Chandlers La YTLY GU46 .... 40 D7
Chandlers Rd ASHV GU12 .... 76 G8
Chandlers Wy HLER SO31 .... 271 H4
Chandos Av
BKME/WDN BH12 .... 322 A7
Chandos Ri PSEA PO1 * 19 K7
Chandos Rd NWBY RG14 .... 24 C7
Chandos St SHAM SO14 .... 21 F6
Channels Farm Rd
ROWN SO16 .... 228 F7
Channel Wy SHAM SO14 .... 21 H7
Chant Cl CHCH/BSGR BH23 .... 325 H8
RAND SP11 .... 123 K3
Chantrell Wk FHAM PO15 .... 272 B7
Chantreys FLEETN GU51 .... 74 A4
Chantry CI CHCH/BSGR BH23 .... 326 B6
HTWY RG27 .... 71 P4
Chantry Ms BH/HW/K RG22 .... 89 M4
Chantry Rd GPORT PO12 .... 315 K1
HORN PO8 .... 256 B3
SHAM SO14 .... 21 H6
Chantry St AND SP10 .... 4 D4
The Chantrys FNM GU9 .... 95 P9
The Chantry
FHAM/STUB PO14 .... 271 J7
Chantry Wk HLER SO31 .... 269 L4
Chantry Wy AND SP10 .... 4 D4
Chapel CI CHIN RG24 .... 70 C5
OVTN RG25 .... 109 H1
RAND SP11 .... 101 H4
RAND SP11 .... 181 H8
STOK SO20 .... 161 H2
Chapel Ct NTHA RG18 .... 25 P3
Chapel Crs ITCH SO19 .... 249 J7
Chapel Dro ELGH SO50 .... 230 C5
HEND SO30 .... 250 B5
Chapel Gdns BOR GU35 .... 154 C3
Chapel Gv RWIN SO21 .... 207 P4
Chapel Hl BSTK RG21 .... 6 F7
RSAL SP5 .... 176 B4
Chapel La BPWT SO32 .... 251 L3
BROC SO42 .... 310 C2
CHCH/BSGR BH23 .... 303 J7
FARN GU14 .... 57 N5
FAWY SO45 .... 290 C9
LYND SO43 .... 264 F6
PLE BH15 .... 332 E1
RAND SP11 .... 79 N1
RAND SP11 .... 82 F5
RAND SP11 .... 120 B1
RGWD BH24 .... 284 C6
ROMY SO51 .... 180 B6
ROMY SO51 .... 180 B6
RSAL SP5 .... 200 A7
RSAL SP5 .... 223 L5
RWIN SO21 .... 165 P5
RWIN SO21 .... 207 K4
STHA RG19 .... 13 J5
STOK SO20 .... 140 A3
TADY RG26 .... 49 J1
THLE RG7 .... 34 C1
THLE RG7 .... 37 P3
WIMB BH21 .... 278 D9
Chapel Md HTWY RG27 .... 39 P6
Chapel Pond Dr ODIM RG29 .... 72 B9
Chapel Ri RGWD BH24 .... 282 B7
Chapel River Cl AND SP10 .... 102 C3
Chapel Rd BPWT SO32 .... 232 F7
BPWT SO32 .... 233 N1
HEND SO30 .... 249 N1
HLER SO31 .... 270 E4
PSTN BH14 .... 321 J8
RFNM GU10 .... 115 N7
SHAM SO14 .... 21 G5
THLE RG7 .... 35 K1
Chapel Rw HTWY RG27 .... 39 P6
Chapelside
FHAM/STUB PO14 .... 293 N1
Chapel Sq CBLY GU15 .... 41 N8
Chapel St FARN GU14 .... 58 C7
GPORT PO12 .... 295 M9
NEND PO2 .... 296 D9
NTHA RG18 .... 25 P4
OVTN RG25 .... 108 C1
PSF GU32 .... 213 M5
PSF GU32 .... 215 M1
SSEA PO5 * 18 C9
Chaplains Av HORN PO8 .... 255 M8
Chaplains CI HORN PO8 .... 255 M7
Chaplins HI CWTH RG45 .... 41 L2
Chaplins Ter TDWTH SP9 * 79 H4
Chappell CI LIPH GU30 .... 175 K3
Chapter Ter HTWY RG27 .... 71 P3
Charborough Rd BDST BH18 .... 320 D1
Charden Rd ELGH SO50 .... 230 A3
LSOL/BMARY PO13 .... 295 H9
Charing CI RGWD BH24 .... 282 E3
Charity Vw WHAM PO17 .... 272 C3
Chark La LSOL/BMARY PO13 .... 294 D9
Charlbury La CHIN RG24 .... 69 K3
Charlcot CI WHCH RG28 .... 85 L8
Charlecote Dr CHFD SO53 .... 206 A4
Charlecote Cl FARN GU14 .... 76 C1
Charledown Cl OVTN RG25 .... 86 G4
Charledown Rd OVTN RG25 .... 86 G4
Charlesbury Av GPORT PO12 .... 315 K4
Charles CI HTWY RG27 .... 71 P3
WINC SO23 .... 165 H5
WVILLE PO7 .... 275 M4
Charles Crs NMIL/BTOS BH25 .... 327 K2
Charles Daiton Ct AND SP10 * 4 C5
Charles Dickens St PSEA PO1 .... 19 G3
Charles Gdns NBNE BH10 .... 322 C5

Charles HI RFNM GU10 .... 117 L4
Charles Keightley Ct
WSHM SO15 * 300 F2
Charles Knott Gdns
WSHM SO15 .... 248 B4
Charles Richards Cl
BSTK RG21 .... 6 D6
Charles Rd CHCH/BSGR BH23 .... 325 K7
PLE BH15 .... 320 F8
Charles's La RGWD BH24 .... 283 H7
Charles St BH/HW/K RG22 .... 68 C8
NWBY RG14 .... 24 B8
PSEA PO1 .... 19 J1
PSF GU32 .... 215 L2
SHAM SO14 .... 21 F6
Charleston CI HISD PO11 .... 318 E4
Charleston Rd NWBY RG14 .... 24 D9
Charles Watts Wy HEND SO30 .... 249 N4
Charlesworth Dr WVILLE PO7 .... 275 L1
Charlesworth Gdns
WVILLE PO7 .... 275 M1
Charliejoy Gdns SHAM SO14 .... 21 J1
Charlock CI NTHA RG18 .... 25 P2
Charlotte CI AND SP10 .... 5 K3
BKME/WDN BH12 .... 322 C8
CHCH/BSGR BH23 .... 326 D5
Charlotte Dr GPORT PO12 .... 315 N1
Charlotte PI WSHM SO15 .... 20 E1
Charlotte St PSEA PO1 .... 19 G1
Charlottown NWBY RG14 .... 17 K6
Charlton CI DENM SO41 .... 327 H6
MARLOW/WNTN BH9 .... 323 J3
Charlton Ct SHST GU47 .... 41 L5
Charlton Dr EPSF GU31 .... 191 N9
Charlton La THLE RG7 .... 37 P1
Charlton PI NWBY RG14 .... 24 D3
Charlton Rd AND SP10 .... 4 A2
WSHM SO15 .... 247 P4
Charlwood La NARL SO24 .... 170 D3
Charminster
MOOR/WNTN BH9 .... 323 H6
Charminster CI CHAR BH8 .... 323 H5
WVILLE PO7 .... 275 M2
Charminster PI CHAR BH8 * 323 J5
Charminster Rd CHAR BH8 .... 322 G9
Charmouth Gv PSTN BH14 .... 321 J8
Charmouth Ter ROWN SO16 * 247 L2
Charmus Rd TOTT SO40 .... 245 P1
Charnwem Crs WEND SO18 .... 249 K3
Charnwood CI NWBY RG14 .... 24 C2
Charnock CI LYMN SO41 .... 327 P4
Charnwood
LSOL/BMARY PO13 .... 295 H7
Charnwood Av
MOOR/WNTN BH9 .... 323 H4
Charnwood CI AND SP10 .... 5 F7
BH/HW/K RG22 .... 68 E9
CHFD SO53 .... 206 B3
FERN BH22 .... 280 E7
TOTT SO40 .... 246 A1
Charnwood Crs CHFD SO53 .... 206 E3
Charnwood Dr FBDG SP6 .... 240 C1
Charnwood Gdns CHFD SO53 .... 206 E3
Charnwood Wy FAWY SO45 .... 312 G1
Charterhouse Wy HEND SO30 .... 250 C2
Charter Wk HASM GU27 * 157 H7
Chart House Rd ASHV GU12 .... 76 F5
Chartwell FNM GU9 .... 115 P4
FHAM/STUB PO14 .... 271 J8
Chartwell Dr HAV PO9 .... 277 J7
Chartwell CI GPORT PO12 .... 315 K4
FHAM/STUB PO14 .... 271 J8
Chase CI LISS GU33 .... 192 E2
Chase Farm CI BPWT SO32 .... 232 C9
Chase Fld ALTN GU34 .... 151 L6
Chase Gv BPWT SO32 .... 232 C9
Chase La HASM GU27 .... 157 K9
Chase Pln GPORT GU26 * 156 B4
Chase Rd BOR GU35 .... 154 C3
LISS GU33 .... 192 E2
Chaseside LTDN BH7 .... 325 N1
The Chase FARN GU14 .... 58 C7
FHAM/STUB PO14 .... 271 K8
GPORT PO12 .... 315 K4
RGWD BH24 .... 282 B4
VWD BH31 .... 259 J4
Chasewater Av HSEA PO3 .... 317 J1
Chatburn Av HORN PO8 .... 255 P8
Chatfield Av NEND PO2 .... 296 C8
Chatfield CI FARN GU14 .... 76 D1
Chatfield Rd
BH/HW/K RG22 .... 89 N5
Chatsworth Av FNM GU9 .... 96 B5
Chatsworth Rd CHAR BH8 .... 323 H9
FARN GU14 .... 76 D1
ITCH SO19 .... 249 J6
PSTN BH14 .... 321 K7
Chatsworth Wy
NMIL/BTOS BH25 .... 326 G4
Chaucer Av AND SP10 .... 5 G4
Chaucer Av BSTK RG21 .... 6 A6
CHAM PO6 .... 296 G4
Chaucer CI CHIN RG24 .... 69 M3
FHAM/PORC PO16 .... 10 D4
RWIN SO21 .... 144 F3
WVILLE PO7 .... 255 N9
Chaucer Crs NWBY RG14 .... 24 B2
Chaucer Dr LYMN SO41 .... 338 C1
Chaucer Rd CCLF BH13 .... 333 N3
CWTH RG45 .... 41 M1
FARN GU14 .... 57 N7
ITCH SO19 .... 249 M5

Chaucombe PI
NMIL/BTOS BH25 .... 327 H6
Chaundler Rd WINC SO23 .... 165 H5
Chaundlers Cft RFNM GU10 .... 95 H6
Chauntsingers Rd ALTN GU34 .... 132 F5
Chavasse Wy FARN GU14 .... 57 L8
Chaveney CI FAWY SO45 .... 268 B9
Chavy Water ROMY SO51 .... 204 C7
Chawton CI FLEETN GU51 .... 73 P1
FUFL SO22 .... 164 E3
WEND SO18 .... 249 M3
Chawton Park Rd ALTN GU34 .... 132 C9
Cheam Rd BDST BH18 .... 300 B9
Cheam Rd TOTT SO40 .... 246 B2
Cheap St NWBY RG14 .... 16 E2
Cheater's La FBDG SP6 .... 239 J3
Cheavley CI AND SP10 .... 102 A2
Cheddar CI ITCH SO19 .... 248 G8
Cheddington Rd
MOOR/WNTN BH9 .... 323 G3
Chedington CI CFDH BH17 .... 320 C2
Chedworth Crs CHAM PO6 .... 274 C9
Cheesecombe Farm La
LISS GU33 .... 172 E9
Cheetah Rd FARN GU14 .... 76 A2
Chelmarsh Gdns ELGH SO50 .... 230 D4
Chelmer CI BSTK RG21 .... 7 J6
Chelmsford Rd NEND PO2 .... 297 H7
Chelsea Rd SSEA PO5 .... 18 D7
Cheltenham Crs
LSOL/BMARY PO13 .... 314 D2
Cheltenham Gdns HEND SO30 .... 230 C9
Cheltenham Rd
BKME/WDN BH12 .... 321 L7
CHAM PO6 .... 296 E1
Chelveston Crs ROWN SO16 .... 227 K8
Chelwood Dr SHST GU47 .... 40 C5
Cheping Gdns NEND SO18 .... 250 C5
Chepstow CI CHFD SO53 .... 206 D7
TOTT SO40 .... 246 A3
Chepstow CI WVILLE PO7 .... 276 B1
Chequer La THLE RG7 .... 37 K4
Chequers Wy LYMN SO41 .... 329 H4
Chequers La HTWY RG27 .... 39 P7
Chequers Rd BSTK RG21 .... 7 F6
Cherberry CI FLEETN GU51 .... 56 E9
Cherbourg Rd ELGH SO50 .... 228 H3
Cherford Rd BWD BH11 .... 321 H6
Cherita Ct FUFL SO22 .... 279 N8
Cheriton Av LTDN BH7 .... 324 F4
WEND SO18 .... 249 L4
Cheriton CI FUFL SO22 .... 164 E6
HAV PO9 .... 276 D5
HORN PO8 .... 256 A4
NWBY RG14 .... 17 G6
TADY RG26 .... 34 C7
Cheriton La NARL SO24 .... 168 D6
Cheriton Rd ELGH SO50 .... 229 H4
ENEY PO4 .... 317 L4
GPORT PO12 .... 315 K4
Cheriton Wy BLKW GU17 .... 41 L9
WIMB BH21 .... 278 E8
Cherque La
LSOL/BMARY PO13 .... 294 B7
Cherque Wy
LSOL/BMARY PO13 .... 314 C1
Cherrett CI BWD BH11 .... 301 P9
Cherries Dr MOOR/WNTN BH9 .... 322 E6
Cherrimans Orch HASM GU27 .... 156 E7
Cherry CI HTWY RG27 .... 72 A2
NWBY RG14 .... 24 C3
PSTN BH14 .... 321 K8
RWIN SO21 .... 144 E4
Cherry Dro ELGH SO50 .... 230 C6
Cherry Gdns BPWT SO32 .... 232 B5
Cherrygarth Rd FHAM PO15 .... 272 A9
Cherry Gv FERN BH22 .... 302 C2
Cherryhill Gv ALDT GU11 .... 2 B5
Cherry Ldg ASHV GU12 * 3 J4
Cherry Orch WHCH RG28 .... 85 M8
Cherryton Gdns FAWY SO45 .... 290 D6
Cherry Tree Av
FHAM/STUB PO14 .... 294 B1
HASM GU27 .... 158 A6
HORN PO8 .... 256 A4
TDWTH SP9 .... 79 H4
Cherry Tree Dr
NMIL/BTOS BH25 .... 326 G2
Cherry Tree Rd AND SP10 .... 102 C1
HORN PO8 .... 115 N7
Cherry Tree Wk BSTK RG21 .... 69 M4
Cherry Wk WSHM SO15 .... 248 C2
Cherryway ALTN GU34 .... 132 C4
Cherrywood CHIN RG24 * 69 P1
HEND SO30 .... 250 B5
Cherrywood Gdns
TOTT SO40 .... 246 A4
HISD PO11 .... 318 F4
Cherrywood Rd FARN GU14 .... 57 N2
Chertsey St FLEETN GU51 .... 74 B1
Chervil CI CFDH BH17 .... 320 B2
Cherville St ROMY SO51 .... 204 B5
Chervil Wy THLE RG7 .... 27 L5
Cherwell CI ROWN SO16 .... 247 J5
Cherwell Gdns CHFD SO53 .... 206 B3
Cherwell Rd BSTK RG21 .... 7 J8
Cheshire CI CHAM PO6 .... 271 M5
Cheshire Dr CHAR BH8 .... 323 N5
Cheslbourne Gv CHAR BH8 .... 323 M5
Chesildene Av CHAR BH8 .... 323 M5
Chesildene Dr CHAR BH8 .... 323 M5
Chesil St WINC SO23 .... 25 G5
Cheslton Crs FLEETS GU52 .... 74 D7
Chessel Av ITCH SO19 .... 13 N3
Chessel Crs ITCH SO19 .... 248 G4
Chessel Wd WINC SO23 .... 25 H4
Cheslyn Rd HSEA PO3 .... 317 K2
Chessel Av BOSC BH5 .... 335 M2
ITCH SO19 .... 13 N3
Chester CI ASHV GU12 .... 97 P1

NWBY RG14 .... 17 K7
Chester Crs
LSOL/BMARY PO13 .... 314 F4
Chester Rd SSEA PO5 .... 18 E5
Chesterfield CI CCLF BH13 .... 333 P3
Chesterfield Rd BSTK RG21 .... 69 M9
HSEA PO3 .... 317 J1
NWBY RG14 .... 16 E5
Chester Pl BSTK RG21 .... 69 K8
SSEA PO5 .... 18 E5
Chester Rd ASHV GU12 .... 76 G9
CCLF BH13 .... 334 A4
WEND SO18 .... 249 J2
WINC SO23 .... 23 G5
Chesterton Gdns HORN PO8 .... 255 N8
Chesterton PI FHAM PO15 .... 272 C4
Chesterton Rd RTHA RG18 .... 25 M2
Chesterton Wy BKME/WDN BH12 .... 97 M5
Chestnut Av ASHV GU12 .... 97 L4
CHCH/BSGR BH23 .... 324 B7
ELGH SO50 .... 229 N2
ENEY PO4 .... 317 H4
FNM GU9 .... 116 A2
FUFL SO22 .... 164 C3
HASM GU27 .... 157 H6
HAV PO9 .... 276 B7
HORN PO8 .... 236 M8
NMIL/BTOS BH25 .... 327 J7
RGWD BH24 .... 259 P4
RWIN SO21 .... 207 P4
SBNE BH6 .... 336 A2
TDWTH SP9 .... 79 H4
TOTT SO40 .... 246 A8
Chestnut Bank CHIN RG24 .... 70 A3
Chestnut CI ALTN GU34 .... 132 E4
BLKW GU17 * 41 M9
CHFD SO53 .... 228 E2
FLEETN GU51 .... 56 F9
HEND SO30 .... 250 A2
LIPH GU30 .... 175 L4
ROMY SO51 .... 205 H7
WVILLE PO7 .... 255 H7
Chestnut Ct ASHV GU12 .... 97 K1
SHST GU47 * 154 B6
Chestnut Crs NWBY RG14 .... 16 C3
Chestnut Dr EPSF GU31 .... 215 M4
RDGW/BURGH RG30 .... 27 K3
Chestnut End BOR GU35 .... 154 C4
Chestnut Gv FLEETN GU51 .... 74 E2
WIMB BH21 .... 279 N8
Chestnut PI STOK SO20 .... 121 H5
Chestnut Ri BPWT SO32 .... 233 L3
ELGH SO50 .... 228 F3
Chestnut Rd BROC SO42 .... 286 G8
Chestnut Wk GPORT PO12 .... 295 L9
Chestnut Wy
CHCH/BSGR BH23 .... 324 C4
FHAM/STUB PO14 .... 271 J9
Cheswell Gdns FLEETN GU51 .... 74 B6
Chetnole CI CFDH BH17 .... 321 H5
Chettle Rd ITCH SO19 .... 249 N6
Chetwode Ter ALDT GU11 .... 96 E2
Chetwynd Dr ROWN SO16 .... 228 B8
Chetwynd Rd ROWN SO16 .... 228 B8
SSEA PO5 .... 316 G5
Chevening Ct ENEY PO4 * 317 K3
Cheviot CI BH/HW/K RG22 .... 68 E9
CBLY GU15 .... 59 H1
FARN GU14 .... 96 A1
HAV PO9 .... 30 B1
Cheviot Dr FAWY SO45 .... 267 P7
Cheviot Gn HLER SO31 .... 292 C1
Cheviot Rd ROWN SO16 .... 247 J3
SHST GU47 .... 40 C5
Cheviot Wk FHAM/STUB PO14 .... 294 D2
Chevron CI BWD BH11 .... 258 F5
Chewter CI ENEY PO4 .... 316 G2
Chewton Common Rd
CHCH/BSGR BH23 .... 326 C6
Chewton Farm Rd
CHCH/BSGR BH23 .... 326 E6
Chewton Ldg
CHCH/BSGR BH23 .... 326 D7
Chewton Wy
CHCH/BSGR BH23 .... 326 C6
Cheyne Dr FARN GU14 .... 59 J2
Cheyne Wy FARN GU14 .... 57 N6
LSOL/BMARY PO13 .... 314 C3
Chichester Av HISD PO11 .... 318 F6
Chichester CI AND SP10 .... 102 C2
HEND SO30 .... 250 C2
HLER SO31 .... 270 E7
LSOL/BMARY PO13 .... 294 F7
ROMY SO51 .... 225 P2
Chichester PI BH/HW/K RG22 .... 90 A1
Chichester Rd ASHV GU12 .... 77 G9
HISD PO11 .... 299 J8
NEND PO2 .... 296 C9
RGWD BH24 .... 282 G1
WEND SO18 .... 249 J4
Chickenhall La ELGH SO50 .... 229 L2
Chickerell CI
MOOR/WNTN BH9 .... 323 H4
Chicklade CI PSF GU32 .... 213 M8
Chideock Ct BKME/WDN BH12 .... 321 N6
Chidham CI HAV PO9 .... 14 E3
Chidham Dr HAV PO9 .... 14 D3
Chidham Rd CHAM PO6 .... 275 J9
Chilbolton Av FUFL SO22 .... 164 E7
Chilbolton Ct HAV PO9 .... 15 H5
Chilcomb CI
LSOL/BMARY PO13 .... 314 D2
Chilcombe Rd SBNE BH6 .... 335 N4

Chilcombe Rd SBNE BH6 * 335 P1
Chilcomb La WINC SO23 184 B1
Chilcomb Rd WEND SO18 249 L3
Chilcote Rd HSEA PO3 317 J1
Chilcroft Rd HASM GU27 156 E6
Childerstone Cl LIPH GU30 175 J3
Childe Sq NEND PO2 296 E7
Chilfrome Cl CFDH BH17 320 E3
Chilgrove Rd CHAM PO6 297 L1
Chilham Cl ELGH SO50 207 J6
FRIM GU16 58 E5
Chillandham La RWIN SO21 146 B5
Chilland La RWIN SO21 166 B1
Chillenden Ct TOTT SO40 246 A5
Chillerton HLER SO31 269 L3
Chillingham Wy CBLY GU15 58 B1
Chilling La HLER SO31 292 E4
Chillington Gdns CHFD SO53 206 D4
Chilmark Ct LISS GU33 * 192 D2
Chilsdown Wy WVILLE PO7 275 N5
Chiltern Av FARN GU14 57 L9
Chiltern Cl FARN GU14 57 K9
FLEETS GU52 74 E6
HASM GU27 156 G8
NMIL/BTOS BH25 327 H6
NWBY RG14 30 B1
TOTT SO40 246 B6
WBNE BH4 334 B1
Chiltern Dr NMIL/BTOS BH25 326 G7
VWD BH31 258 F4
Chiltern Gn ROWN SO16 247 J3
Chiltern Rd SHST GU47 40 G5
Chiltern Wk FHAM/STUB PO14 294 D2
Chiltern Wy BH/HW/K RG22 68 D9
Chitlee Cl LIPH GU30 175 K3
Chitlee Mnr LIPH GU30 175 K3
Chitley La LIPH GU30 175 L5
Chitley Wy LIPH GU30 175 K5
Chilton Farm Pk FARN GU14 * 57 K9
Chilton Rdg BH/HW/K RG22 89 M6
Chilworth Cl ROWN SO16 227 P3
Chilworth Dro ROWN SO16 227 N4
Chilworth Gdns HORN PO8 236 D8
Chilworth Gra ROWN SO16 228 B4
Chilworth Gv GPORT PO12 315 L3
Chilworth Rd ROWN SO16 228 A3
Chine Av ITCH SO19 248 G5
Chine Cl HLER SO31 270 G6
Chine Crs WCLF BH2 8 A5
Chine Crescent Rd WCLF BH2 8 A5
Chineham Cl FLEETN GU51 73 P1
Chineham Farm Cots
CHIN RG24 69 N3
Chineham La CHIN RG24 69 K2
Chineham Park Ct CHIN RG24 69 N4
The Chine LSOL/BMARY PO13 295 J8
RFNM GU10 115 P5
Chine Wk FERN BH22 302 E6
Chingford Av FARN GU14 58 B8
Chinham Rd TOTT SO40 245 H5
Chinnock Cl FLEETS GU52 74 C5
Chippendale Cl TADY RG26 33 P5
Chipstead Rd CHAM PO6 297 H1
Chirk Pl ROMY SO51 204 E6
Chisels La CHCH/BSGR BH23 325 M1
Chisholm Cl ROWN SO16 227 K7
Chislett Gdns SHST GU47 40 G6
Chiswell Rd CFDH BH17 320 F3
Chitty Rd ENEY PO4 317 J6
Chivers Cl BH/HW/K RG22 68 E9
SSEA PO5 19 H6
Chloe Gdns BKME/WDN BH12 321 M5
Chobham Rd FRIM GU16 58 D3
Cholderton Rd AMSY SP4 118 C2
Chopin Rd BH/HW/K RG22 89 P3
Chorley Cl PLE BH15 320 E6
Chrismas Av ASHV GU12 3 J5
Chrismas Pl ASHV GU12 3 J5
Christchurch Bay Rd
NMIL/BTOS BH25 327 H8
Christchurch By-Pass
CHCH/BSGR BH23 324 F8
Christchurch Cl FLEETS GU52 74 C8
Christchurch Dr BLKW GU17 41 K8
Christchurch Gdns
WINC SO23 183 N1
WVILLE PO7 275 K8
Christchurch Rd BMTH BH1 9 H3
CHCH/BSGR BH23 323 P1
FERN BH22 302 B6
LTDN BH7 335 N1
LYMN SO41 327 P8
NMIL/BTOS BH25 326 F7
RGWD BH24 282 D2
WINC SO23 22 C7
Christie Av FHAM PO15 271 J2
Christie Hts NWBY RG14 24 E7
Christie Wk YTLY GU46 56 D1
Christine Cl ASHV GU12 97 M2
Christmas Hl RWIN SO21 125 L7
Christopher Ct NWBY RG14 17 H4
Christopher Crs PLE BH15 320 E6
Christopher Wy EMRTH PO10 277 M8
Christy Ct TADY RG26 34 D7
Christy Est ASHV GU12 * 97 L1
Chubb Ms BKME/WDN BH12 321 L7
Church Av FARN GU14 76 B2
Church Bank Rd RWIN SO21 127 M4
Church Brook TADY RG26 34 B8
Church Cir FARN GU14 76 B3
Church Cl AND SP10 4 E3
ELGH SO50 207 L9
HASM GU27 157 L3
HLER SO31 271 H7
HORN PO8 236 B6
NBAD SO52 205 L9
RAND SP11 101 M7
STHA RG19 25 N4
Church Ct FLEETN GU51 * 74 B2
Church End WSHM SO15 247 N4
Churcher Cl GPORT PO12 315 H5
Churcher Rd EMRTH PO10 277 P6
Church Farm FBDG SP6 240 D3
Church Farm Barns THLE RG7 36 C1
Church Farm Cl FAWY SO45 267 M4
OVTN RG25 88 C9
Churchfield VWD BH31 258 E4
Churchfield Crs PLE BH15 320 G8
Churchfield La RGWD BH24 260 C1
Churchfield Rd EPSF GU31 215 P1
PLE BH15 320 G9
Church Flds BOR GU35 154 E3
Churchfields BOR GU35 134 F8
FAWY SO45 291 K6
Churchfields Rd RWIN SO21 183 P8
Church Ga STHA RG19 25 N4
Church Green Cl WINC SO23 165 K2
Church Green Cots
HASM GU27 * 157 H6
Church Gv FLEETN GU51 74 B3
Church Hatch RSAL SP5 199 L5
Church Hl ASHV GU12 3 H5
HEND SO30 249 L2
LYMN SO41 339 H1
RSAL SP5 200 B8
STOK SO20 139 P3
VWD BH31 258 E4
Church Hill Ter RFNM GU10 * 95 H5
Churchill Av ASHV GU12 3 H6
BPWT SO32 231 N3
ODIM RG29 93 K3
Churchill Cl ALTN GU34 132 F7
ALTN GU34 150 C5
FBDG SP6 239 L6
FHAM/STUB PO14 271 J9
HTWY RG27 54 G6
ODIM RG29 93 K3
TADY RG26 34 E7
TDWTH SP9 78 F3
WINC SO23 145 J7
Churchill Ct HORN PO8 * 256 A5
Churchill Crs
BKME/WDN BH12 321 L6
BOR GU35 154 G4
FARN GU14 58 A5
Churchill Dr EMRTH PO10 277 M6
Churchill Gdns
BKME/WDN BH12 321 L7
Churchill Ms GPORT PO12 * 315 L2
Churchill Plaza BSTK RG21 * 7 F5
Churchill Rd
BKME/WDN BH12 321 L7
BMTH BH1 335 K1
WIMB BH21 300 F2
Churchill Sq ENEY PO4 317 K6
Churchill Wy AND SP10 5 G1
BSTK RG21 6 E5
Churchill Wy East BSTK RG21 7 H5
Churchill Wy West AND SP10 82 B9
BH/HW/K RG22 68 G7
BSTK RG21 6 A6
Church Lands TADY RG26 51 N2
Church La ALTN GU34 131 H7
ALTN GU34 133 J2
ALTN GU34 189 L3
ASHV GU12 97 P1
BOR GU35 154 E2
BPWT SO32 230 F6
BPWT SO32 232 F6
BPWT SO32 251 K3
BROC SO42 286 G9
BROC SO42 311 H3
CHCH/BSGR BH23 324 F9
CHIN RG24 70 C6
DEAN RG23 68 D8
ELGH SO50 207 N5
FARN GU14 57 M9
FAWY SO45 291 J6
FBDG SP6 219 K8
FERN BH22 302 F9
FUFL SO22 164 B1
GSHT GU26 156 B2
HASM GU27 157 H6
HAV PO9 299 H1
HEND SO30 250 B6
HLER SO31 270 B2
HTWY RG27 37 P8
HTWY RG27 55 J9
KSCL RG20 29 L6
KSCL RG20 30 E7
LIPH GU30 175 J1
LISS GU33 172 G4
LYMN SO41 308 B7
LYMN SO41 309 K5
LYMN SO41 329 L4
LYND SO43 264 F5
NARL SO24 168 E3
NARL SO24 169 M3
NARL SO24 187 N2
NWBY RG14 24 A3
OVTN RG25 90 C4
OVTN RG25 110 D1
PSF GU32 188 D9
RAND SP11 42 F5
RAND SP11 79 N1
RAND SP11 102 E9
RDGW/BURGH RG30 27 N1
RFNM GU10 95 M4
RFNM GU10 114 E4
RFNM GU10 115 N7
RGWD BH24 284 C6
ROMY SO51 179 M5
ROMY SO51 180 G7
ROMY SO51 202 B8
ROWN SO16 226 D7
RWIN SO21 163 M4
RWIN SO21 165 N2
RWIN SO21 184 A6
RWIN SO21 207 P5
SD/PW SO17 248 D1
STHA RG19 25 N4
STOK SO20 139 P3
STOK SO20 161 H1
TADY RG26 48 G3
TDWTH SP9 79 H7
THLE RG7 26 D3
THLE RG7 35 M5
WINC SO23 165 K1
WVILLE PO7 234 D7
Church Lane Cnr LYMN SO41 * 309 M7
Church La East ALDT GU11 2 E5
Church La West ALDT GU11 2 C5
Church Leat RSAL SP5 199 K5
Church Md LYMN SO41 329 L5
Church Mdw TDWTH SP9 98 G2
Church Ms RAND SP11 * 102 A6
Churchmoor Rd WIMB BH21 279 J9
Church Pth ASHV GU12 76 F9
EMRTH PO10 299 M1
FHAM/PORC PO16 11 J5
FHAM/STUB PO14 293 N1
GPORT PO12 13 H3
HORN PO8 256 D5
HTWY RG27 71 N4
Church Pth North PSEA PO1 * 19 H1
Church Rd ALDT GU11 3 H7
ALTN GU34 151 M5
BPWT SO32 232 F6
BPWT SO32 252 B4
CBLY GU15 41 N7
ELGH SO50 207 M8
EMRTH PO10 277 P7
FERN BH22 302 C3
FHAM/PORC PO16 296 A3
FLEETN GU51 74 B2
FRIM GU16 58 C5
GPORT PO12 12 A6
HASM GU27 157 H6
HISD PO11 318 G4
HLER SO31 292 D1
ITCH SO19 268 F1
LIPH GU30 175 K1
NWBY RG14 24 D2
OVTN RG25 86 G3
OVTN RG25 108 C1
PSEA PO1 19 J1
PSF GU32 191 L7
PSTN BH14 321 J8
ROMY SO51 180 B4
ROMY SO51 204 C6
SBNE BH6 336 D3
SHST GU47 40 G5
STOK SO20 139 P3
STOK SO20 141 J1
STOK SO20 161 M4
TADY RG26 34 C9
THLE RG7 35 K1
WHAM PO17 253 M4
WIMB BH21 258 E9
Church Rd East CWTH RG45 41 J1
FARN GU14 76 C3
Church Rd West CWTH RG45 41 J2
FARN GU14 76 B3
Church Sq BSTK RG21 6 E6
Church St ALDT GU11 2 B4
ALTN GU34 131 J4
ALTN GU34 132 F5
BPWT SO32 209 M7
BSTK RG21 6 E5
CHCH/BSGR BH23 324 F9
CWTH RG45 41 J1
FBDG SP6 240 C3
FHAM/STUB PO14 293 M1
KSCL RG20 29 L7
LISS GU33 173 J9
NARL SO24 169 M3
ODIM RG29 93 K1
PLE BH15 332 D2
PSF GU32 213 M4
RAND SP11 62 B5
RAND SP11 123 L3
RFNM GU10 94 G5
ROMY SO51 204 C6
RSAL SP5 176 C4
RWIN SO21 126 F5
WHCH RG28 85 L7
WIMB BH21 278 D9
WSHM SO15 247 M3
Church Street Rbt PSEA PO1 316 E1
Church Vw ASHV GU12 97 N1
BPWT SO32 252 D4
EMRTH PO10 * 277 P7
ENEY PO4 317 J4
HTWY RG27 55 H9
HTWY RG27 72 A3
ODIM RG29 92 F8
YTLY GU46 40 E7
Church View Cl ITCH SO19 249 J8
Church Wk RSAL SP5 200 C8
Churchward Gdns HEND SO30 250 C1
Churn Cl CHIN RG24 70 C5
Churt Rd BOR GU35 155 H1
Chute Cl TADY RG26 52 A1
Chute Hl RWIN SO21 163 K3
Cibbons Rd CHIN RG24 70 A1
Cinderford Cl CHAM PO6 274 D9
Cinnamon La PLE BH15 332 D2
Circle Hill Rd CWTH RG45 41 K1
The Circle MOOR/WNTN BH9 * 322 G3
SSEA PO5 * 316 F6
WHAM PO17 252 D7
Circular Rd NEND PO2 316 E1
PSEA PO1 18 E1
The Circus CHAM PO6 274 C8
Cirrus Gdns HLER SO31 269 P8
City Rd WINC SO23 22 D3
Civic Centre Rd HAV PO9 15 F3
SHAM SO14 20 D3
Civic Wy FHAM/PORC PO16 11 J5
Clack La FBDG SP6 219 N6
Clacton Rd CHAM PO6 296 F1
Claire Gdns HORN PO8 256 C1
Clammer Hl HASM GU27 157 L5
Clammer Hill Rd HASM GU27 157 L4
Clandon Ct FARN GU14 76 C1
Clandon Dr ELGH SO50 207 H7
Clanfield Cl CHFD SO53 206 F7
Clanfield Dr CHFD SO53 206 F7
Clanfield Ride BLKW GU17 41 L9
Clanfield Rd WEND SO18 249 L4
Clanfield Wy CHFD SO53 206 F7
Clanwilliam Rd
LSOL/BMARY PO13 314 C2
Clappers Farm Rd THLE RG7 35 N5
Clapps Gate Rd TADY RG26 34 F5
Clare Cl FHAM/STUB PO14 271 J8
Clare Gdns EPSF GU31 216 A2
FAWY SO45 313 H1
Clare Lodge Cl
CHCH/BSGR BH23 305 L7
Clare Md RFNM GU10 115 P7
Claremont Av
MOOR/WNTN BH9 323 H5
Claremont Cl ELGH SO50 207 J7
Claremont Crs NWBY RG14 24 G3
WSHM SO15 247 L4
Claremont Gdns WVILLE PO7 275 N6
Claremont Rd
MOOR/WNTN BH9 323 H5
PSEA PO1 * 316 G3
WSHM SO15 247 L4
Clarence Cl ASHV GU12 3 J3
RAND SP11 79 N1
Clarence Esp SSEA PO5 316 D6
Clarence Gdns BDST BH18 320 C2
Clarence Pde SSEA PO5 316 E6
Clarence Park Rd LTDN BH7 323 N9
Clarence Rd FLEETN GU51 74 C4
GPORT PO12 13 H1
LYND SO43 264 F5
PSTN BH14 * 321 J9
SSEA PO5 316 F7
Clarence St PSEA PO1 316 E2
Clarence Whf GPORT PO12 * 13 H1
Clarendon Av AND SP10 102 C4
Clarendon Cl BDST BH18 300 C9
ROMY SO51 204 F4
WVILLE PO7 255 H6
Clarendon Ct BLKW GU17 57 L2
Clarendon Crs
FHAM/STUB PO14 271 H9
Clarendon Gdns NWBY RG14 24 D3
Clarendon Ms SSEA PO5 * 316 F7
Clarendon Pk LYMN SO41 329 K5
Clarendon Pl PSEA PO1 316 F2
Clarendon Rd BDST BH18 320 A1
CHCH/BSGR BH23 324 E8
ENEY PO4 316 F7
ROWN SO16 247 L3
RSAL SP5 176 A2
SSEA PO5 316 E6
WBNE BH4 334 D4
Clarendon St PSEA PO1 316 F2
Clarendon Wy RWIN SO21 163 K8
STOK SO20 159 N1
STOK SO20 161 H3
WINC SO23 183 P2
Clarke Crs SHST GU47 41 M7
Clarke's La RAND SP11 60 E6
Clarke's Rd PSEA PO1 317 H2
Clark Ms WHCH RG28 85 L6
Clark's Cl RGWD BH24 282 E2
Clarks Hl RFNM GU10 95 L9
Clatford Ldg RAND SP11 * 102 A5
Claude Ashby Cl WEND SO18 228 G8
Claudeen Ct WEND SO18 228 G7
Claudia Ct GPORT PO12 315 K2
Claudius Cl AND SP10 82 F7
CHFD SO53 207 H6
Claudius Dr DEAN RG23 68 F5
Claudius Gdns CHFD SO53 207 H7
Clausentum Cl CHFD SO53 206 G6
Clausentum Rd SHAM SO14 248 C4
WINC SO23 183 P1
Clausen Wy LYMN SO41 329 J6
Claxton St PSEA PO1 19 J2
Claybank Sp HSEA PO3 297 J8
Claydon Av ENEY PO4 317 J4
Claydon Gdns BLKW GU17 57 P4
Clayford Av FERN BH22 302 B1
Clayford Cl CFDH BH17 320 F2
Clayhall Rd GPORT PO12 12 B7
Clay Hl LYND SO43 264 G9
Clayhill Cl BPWT SO32 232 B8
Clay Hill Crs NWBY RG14 24 G2
Clayhill Rd THLE RG7 27 H4
Claylake Dr VWD BH31 258 G5
Claylands Ct BPWT SO32 231 P4
Claylands Rd BPWT SO32 231 P4
Claypit Rd ROMY SO51 181 P9
Claypits La FAWY SO45 267 N7
Claypitt La PSF GU32 171 K9
Clay's La ALTN GU34 133 L8
Clay St RSAL SP5 201 J2
Claythorpe Rd BH/HW/K RG22 68 E9
Clayton Barracks ALDT GU11 76 C8
Clayton Cl HTWY RG27 55 H8
Clayton Ct FNM GU9 * 96 B9
Clayton Rd FARN GU14 57 N4
Cleasby Cl ROWN SO16 247 J4
Clease Wy RWIN SO21 183 L7
Cleaver Rd BH/HW/K RG22 68 F9
Clee Av FHAM/STUB PO14 294 B1
Cleek Dr ROWN SO16 228 B7
Cleethorpes Rd ITCH SO19 249 K7
Cleeve Cl CHAM PO6 274 D9
Cleeve Rd CHIN RG24 69 L2
Cleeves Cl BKME/WDN BH12 321 M2
The Cleeves TOTT SO40 246 A5
Clegg Rd ENEY PO4 317 J5
Clematis Cl CHCH/BSGR BH23 325 N7
Clement Attlee Wy
CHAM PO6 296 D1
Clements Cl ALTN GU34 134 C2
Clements Gdns WHCH RG28 85 L6
Clem's Wy ROMY SO51 178 G5
Clench St SHAM SO14 21 G6
Clere Gdns CHIN RG24 70 A2
Clerewater Pl STHA RG19 25 J4
Cleric Ct FHAM/STUB PO14 271 J7
Clevedge Wy ODIM RG29 72 B8
Clevedon Ct FARN GU14 76 C1
FRIM GU16 58 F5
Cleveland Cl BH/HW/K RG22 68 E9
NMIL/BTOS BH25 326 F8
Cleveland Ct WEND SO18 249 J2
Cleveland Dr FAWY SO45 267 P8
FHAM/STUB PO14 294 B1
Cleveland Gdns BMTH BH1 335 J1
Cleveland Gv NWBY RG14 16 C1
Cleveland Rd BMTH BH1 335 K1
GPORT PO12 12 D4
SSEA PO5 316 G4
WEND SO18 249 H1
Clevelands Cl CHFD SO53 206 D4
Cleves La OVTN RG25 92 B5
Clewers Hl BPWT SO32 232 B8
Clewers La BPWT SO32 232 B8
Cliddesden Ct BSTK RG21 90 D1
Cliddesden La BH/HW/K RG22 89 M6
Cliddesden Rd BSTK RG21 69 L9
Cliff Crs NMIL/BTOS BH25 327 H8
Cliff Dr CCLF BH13 333 P5
CHCH/BSGR BH23 325 N9
Cliffe Av HLER SO31 269 N7
Cliffe Rd NMIL/BTOS BH25 326 G8
Clifford Dibben Ms
SHAM SO14 248 B3
Clifford Pl ELGH SO50 230 C2
Clifford Rd MOOR/WNTN BH9 322 G6
Clifford St SHAM SO14 21 G3
Cliff Rd FHAM/STUB PO14 293 M8
LYMN SO41 338 D2
WSHM SO15 247 P6
Cliff Ter NMIL/BTOS BH25 * 327 H9
Cliff Wy RWIN SO21 183 M8
Clifton Cl RFNM GU10 116 A6
Clifton Crs WVILLE PO7 255 K7
Clifton Gdns FERN BH22 302 C4
FRIM GU16 58 E7
WEND SO18 249 L2
Clifton Hl FUFL SO22 22 C4
Clifton Ms FHAM/PORC PO16 11 K3
Clifton Rd FUFL SO22 22 B3
LSOL/BMARY PO13 314 E4
NWBY RG14 16 A3
PSTN BH14 333 M1
SBNE BH6 336 B3
SSEA PO5 316 E6
WSHM SO15 247 L3
Clifton St GPORT PO12 315 K2
Clifton Ter BSTK RG21 7 F4
FUFL SO22 22 C4
SSEA PO5 * 316 E6
Clingan Rd SBNE BH6 324 B9
Clinton Cl CHCH/BSGR BH23 326 D5
Clinton Rd LYMN SO41 329 L2
WVILLE PO7 255 L8
Clipper Cl HLER SO31 270 E9
Clitheroe Rd BLKW GU17 56 G4
Cliveden Cl FERN BH22 302 C1
Clive Gv FHAM/PORC PO16 295 N2
Clive Rd ASHV GU12 3 K5
CHCH/BSGR BH23 326 A5
MOOR/WNTN BH9 322 F6
PSEA PO1 316 G2
Clock House Ct HASM GU27 * 157 H7
Clockhouse Rd FARN GU14 58 A9
Clock St PSEA PO1 18 C3
Clocktower Dr ENEY PO4 317 K6
The Cloisters ALTN GU34 * 132 F5
FHAM PO15 272 A8
FRIM GU16 58 C4
LYMN SO41 * 329 L4
RGWD BH24 282 G3
ROMY SO51 204 C5
ROWN SO16 228 C8
The Close Bellfield
FHAM/STUB PO14 293 M2
The Close BDST BH18 320 A1
CHAM PO6 297 J2
DEAN RG23 * 68 G5
ELGH SO50 * 207 M4
FAWY SO45 290 F6
FHAM/PORC PO16 295 N1
FNM GU9 116 D1
FRIM GU16 58 B5
HEND SO30 250 B5
LYMN SO41 308 A6
NMIL/BTOS BH25 327 J7
NTHA RG18 25 L3
PSF GU32 214 B2
RAND SP11 82 A1
RGWD BH24 281 N5
RSAL SP5 199 P6
SHST GU47 41 M6
TADY RG26 50 E7
THLE RG7 27 J4
WEND SO18 249 M4
WINC SO23 22 E6
Closewood Rd WVILLE PO7 275 J1
Closeworth Rd FARN GU14 76 D4
Clough La RGWD BH24 284 B6
RSAL SP5 138 A9
Clough's Rd RGWD BH24 282 F2
Clouston Rd FARN GU14 57 N8
Clovelly Rd EMRTH PO10 299 L1
ENEY PO4 317 J4
HISD PO11 299 J5
SHAM SO14 21 F1
Cloverbank WINC SO23 145 J6
Clover Cl BOR GU35 154 D3
CHCH/BSGR BH23 325 M7
HLER SO31 270 E8
LSOL/BMARY PO13 294 G7
Clover Ct NMIL/BTOS BH25 327 M3
Clover Dr CFDH BH17 320 B3
Clover Fld CHIN RG24 70 A4
Clover Gdns RAND SP11 79 P1
Clover La YTLY GU46 40 B8
Cloverleaf Wy CHIN RG24 70 C8
Clover Ms AND SP10 5 F5
The Clovers BKME/WDN BH12 322 A7
Clover Wy HEND SO30 250 A5
ROMY SO51 204 G5
Clowes Av SBNE BH6 336 F3
Club House La BPWT SO32 232 C9
Clubhouse Rd ALDT GU11 75 N7
Club La CWTH RG45 41 L1
TDWTH SP9 78 G7
Clump Hl WIMB BH21 258 A9
Clumps Rd RFNM GU10 116 E6
Clydebank Rd NEND PO2 296 F9
Clyde Ct AND SP10 82 G9
GPORT PO12 315 K2
Clyde Rd CFDH BH17 320 D2
GPORT PO12 315 K2
Clydesdale Dr TOTT SO40 * 245 P3
Clydesdale Rd FHAM PO15 271 H3
Clydesdale Wy TOTT SO40 245 P3
Coach Hl FHAM/STUB PO14 293 M1
RAND SP11 60 A8
Coach Hill Cl CHFD SO53 206 D6
Coach Hill La RGWD BH24 283 P3
Coach House Cl FRIM GU16 58 D2

Coach House Gdns
FLEETN GU51 74 D1
Coach House Ms ENEY PO4 * 317 L4
FERN BH22 302 F1
Coach House Pl BMTH BH1 334 G1
Coachmans Copse
WEND SO18 249 J1
Coachman's Ct NWBY RG14 24 E2
Coachmans Halt
WVILLE PO7 * 254 E1
Coach Rd HLER SO31 269 N8
The Coach Rd RSAL SP5 159 J7
Coachways AND SP10 4 C7
Coal Park La HLER SO31 270 D2
Coalville Rd ITCH SO19 249 K7
Coastguard Cl GPORT PO12 315 K6
Coastguard Wy
CHCH/BSGR BH23 337 J2
Coate Dr RWIN SO21 144 D6
Coates Cl BH/HW/K RG22 90 B2
Coates Rd ITCH SO19 249 M7
Coates Wy WVILLE PO7 275 N5
Coat Gdns FAWY SO45 268 C7
Cobalt Ct LSOL/BMARY PO13 * 314 G2
Cobbets Rdg RFNM GU10 117 J2
Cobbett Cl FUFL SO22 183 L1
Cobbett Gn BH/HW/K RG22 90 A1
Cobbett Rd WEND SO18 248 G4
Cobbett's La BLKW GU17 56 G1
Cobbetts Ms FNM GU9 * 96 B9
Cobbetts Wy FNM GU9 115 P4
Cobbett Wy HEND SO30 250 E4
Cobblers Cnr LYMN SO41 308 G5
Cobblewood EMRTH PO10 277 M7
Cobb Ms RAND SP11 101 H4
Cobbs La PLE BH15 320 G6
Cobb's Rd WIMB BH21 278 G8
Cobden Av HSEA PO3 297 J9
WEND SO18 248 F3
Cobden Ct WEND SO18 248 G3
Cobden Crs WEND SO18 249 H3
Cobden Gdns WEND SO18 248 G2
Cobden La HASM GU27 157 J6
Cobden Ri WEND SO18 * 248 G2
Cobden St GPORT PO12 315 M3
Cobham Rd FERN BH22 280 B9
MOOR/WNTN BH9 322 G4
WIMB BH21 279 P7
Cobham Wy WIMB BH21 300 G4
Coblands Av TOTT SO40 246 B4
Cobley Cl RSAL SP5 195 H6
Coburg St PSEA PO1 19 K2
SHAM SO14 21 J1
Cochcrane Cl
LSOL/BMARY PO13 315 H2
Cochrane Cl STHA RG19 25 P4
Cock-a-Dobby SHST GU47 41 H5
Cockerell Cl FHAM PO15 271 J5
WIMB BH21 301 H4
Cockleshell Cl HLER SO31 270 E9
Cockleshell Gdns ENEY PO4 317 L5
Cockleshell Sq GPORT PO12 313 G1
Cocklydown La TOTT SO40 246 C6
Cockshott La PSF GU32 191 J4
Cody Cl ASHV GU12 76 E7
Cody Rd FARN GU14 75 N1
Coe Cl ALDT GU11 2 D4
Cogdean Cl WIMB BH21 300 A5
Cogdeane Rd CFDH BH17 320 F2
Cogdean Wk WIMB BH21 300 A5
Cogdean Wy WIMB BH21 300 A5
Coghlan Cl FHAM/PORC PO16 11 G3
Cokenor Wd RFNM GU10 115 P4
Coker Cl FUFL SO22 22 B3
Colbeck FLEETS GU52 74 E8
Colborne Av WIMB BH21 279 H9
Colborne Cl LYMN SO41 329 L2
PLE BH15 332 F2
Colbourne Cl
CHCH/BSGR BH23 305 L8
Colbred Cnr FLEETN GU51 56 F9
Colburn Cl ROWN SO16 247 H1
Colbury Gv HAV PO9 276 C6
Colchester Av ELGH SO50 207 N9
Colchester Rd CHAM PO6 274 F9
Cold Ash Hl NTHA RG18 25 M1
Cold East Cl HLER SO31 270 E5
Coldeast Wy HLER SO31 270 F5
Colden La NARL SO24 148 B7
Coldharbour OVTN RG25 108 C1
Cold Harbour Cl WHAM PO17 252 D7
Coldharbour Farm Rd
EMRTH PO10 277 M9
Cold Harbour La FARN GU14 57 M5
Coldharbour La ROMY SO51 226 F4
Coldhill La HORN PO8 255 N4
Cole Av ALDT GU11 2 B1
Colebrook Av HSEA PO3 317 K1
WSHM SO15 247 N2
Colebrook Pl WINC SO23 23 G6
Colebrook St WINC SO23 23 F6
Colebrook Wy AND SP10 102 B3
Cole Cl AND SP10 82 E7
Coleford Bridge Rd FARN GU14 58 C9
Coleford Cl FRIM GU16 76 E1
Coleford Paddocks FRIM GU16 58 E9
Cole Hl BPWT SO32 233 M7
Colehill Crs MOOR/WNTN BH9 323 H4
Colehill Gdns BPWT SO32 231 N4
Colehill La WIMB BH21 278 G8
Coleman Cl BSTK RG21 7 H1
Coleman Rd ASHV GU12 3 K5
BWD BH11 322 A4
Coleman St SHAM SO14 21 G4
Colemere Gdns
CHCH/BSGR BH23 326 B6
Colemore Rd LTDN BH7 324 A8
Colemore Sq HAV PO9 * 276 F6
Colenso Rd FHAM/PORC PO16 11 F4
Colenzo Dr AND SP10 5 F1
Coleridge Av YTLY GU46 40 F9
Coleridge Cl CWTH RG45 41 K2
HLER SO31 270 D9
Coleridge Dr FHAM PO15 271 J1
Coleridge Gdns HORN PO8 255 P7
Coleridge Gn
CHCH/BSGR BH23 325 K7
Coleridge Rd CHAM PO6 274 B9
Coles Av PLE BH15 332 A1
Colesbourne Rd CHAM PO6 274 D9
Coles Cl ELGH SO50 229 K1
RWIN SO21 184 A7
Coles Gdns PLE BH15 332 A1
Coles Mede RWIN SO21 207 K2
Coleson Hill Rd RFNM GU10 115 P5
Coleson Rd WEND SO18 248 G3
Coles's La RSAL SP5 200 G8
Coleville Av FAWY SO45 291 K6
Coleville Rd FARN GU14 57 N8
Coley La STOK SO20 123 K5
Colinton Av
FHAM/PORC PO16 273 P9
Collards Ga HASM GU27 * 157 J7
Collards La HASM GU27 157 J7
Collard Wy LISS GU33 192 D2
College Cl HAV PO9 277 J1
HLER SO31 269 P8
College Crs SHST GU47 41 M6
College Gdns FNM GU9 96 B9
College Hl HASM GU27 157 H7
College Hill Ter HASM GU27 157 H7
College La OVTN RG25 110 D4
PSEA PO1 18 C3
College Ms AND SP10 4 D3
College Piece THLE RG7 27 H9
College Pl WSHM SO15 248 C5
College Rd ASHV GU12 76 F9
BOSC BH5 335 N2
BSTK RG21 6 B5
ITCH SO19 248 G9
PSEA PO1 18 C2
RGWD BH24 282 E2
SHST GU47 41 M7
WVILLE PO7 275 N8
College St EPSF GU31 215 M2
PSEA PO1 18 C3
SHAM SO14 21 F6
WINC SO23 22 E6
College Wk WINC SO23 23 F7
Collett Cl HEND SO30 250 B1
Colley Cl WINC SO23 165 H4
Collier Cl FARN GU14 75 M3
SD/PW SO17 248 E3
Collingbourne Av SBNE BH6 324 B9
Collingbourne Dr CHFD SO53 206 C7
Collington Crs CHAM PO6 274 D9
Collingwood FARN GU14 76 D2
Collingwood Rd SSEA PO5 316 F6
WIMB BH21 280 E3
Collingwood Wk AND SP10 5 K3
Collingwood Wy EPSF GU31 191 N9
Collingworth Cl HLER SO31 271 H4
Collingworth Ri HLER SO31 271 H5
Collins Cl AND SP10 82 C8
CHFD SO53 206 B7
NWBY RG14 24 F3
Collins Ct TDWTH SP9 78 G3
Collins Gdns ASHV GU12 97 P1
Collins La EPSF GU31 216 D6
RGWD BH24 282 E2
RWIN SO21 182 E7
Collins Rd ENEY PO4 317 J6
Collis Rd HSEA PO3 297 J9
Collwood Cl PLE BH15 320 E5
Collyers Crs LIPH GU30 175 M3
Collyers Rd BROC SO42 308 F1
Colne Av ROWN SO16 227 H9
Colne Valley Wy RWIN SO21 125 K2
WHCH RG28 86 B6
Colne Wy ASHV GU12 97 N2
BSTK RG21 6 E4
Colonnade Rd BOSC BH5 335 N1
Colonnade Rd West
BOSC BH5 335 N1
The Colonnade ITCH SO19 * 248 F8
Colpoy St SSEA PO5 19 F5
Colson Cl WINC SO23 23 H3
Colson Rd WINC SO23 23 H3
Colt Cl ROWN SO16 227 K7
WIMB BH21 279 K8
Colton Copse CHFD SO53 206 B7
Coltsfoot Cl HEND SO30 250 B4
THLE RG7 27 K4
Coltsfoot Dr HLER SO31 270 E8
WVILLE PO7 275 P5
Coltsfoot Pl HTWY RG27 72 B2
Colts Foot Rd BOR GU35 154 D3
Coltsfoot Wk ROMY SO51 204 G4
Coltsmead CHAM PO6 296 B1
Colts Rd ROWN SO16 227 J5
Columbian Wy NBNE BH10 322 C5
Columbia Rd NBNE BH10 322 D5
Columbia Trees La
NBNE BH10 322 C6
Columbine Cl
CHCH/BSGR BH23 325 M6
Columbine Rd BH/HW/K RG22 89 L3
Columbus Dr FARN GU14 57 K9
Columbus Wy AND SP10 103 J2
Colville Cl BOSC BH5 335 N1
Colville Dr BPWT SO32 232 B4
Colville Rd CHAM PO6 297 J1
LTDN BH7 335 N1
Colvin Cl AND SP10 5 F6
Colvin Gdns CHFD SO53 206 D5
Colwell Cl ROWN SO16 247 H3
Colwell Rd CHAM PO6 297 H2
Colwyn Cl YTLY GU46 40 C8
Colyer Cl BH/HW/K RG22 68 F9
Combe La FARN GU14 57 P7
Combe Ri RFNM GU10 116 D5
Comber Rd MOOR/WNTN BH9 322 F4
Comet Cl ASHV GU12 76 E7
Comet Rd FARN GU14 75 K3
Comet Wy CHCH/BSGR BH23 325 L9
Comfrey Cl FARN GU14 57 K8
HORN PO8 256 C2
ROMY SO51 204 G4
Comines Wy HEND SO30 249 N5
Comley Hl HAV PO9 277 J3
Comley Rd MOOR/WNTN BH9 322 F5
Commercial Pl PSEA PO1 19 H1
Commercial Rd ASHV GU12 3 J6
PSEA PO1 19 G2
PSTN BH14 321 H8
TOTT SO40 246 E4
WCLF BH2 8 B4
WSHM SO15 20 B2
Commercial St WEND SO18 249 K4
Common Barn La
LSOL/BMARY PO13 * 314 D1
Common Cl CHFD SO53 206 E5
Common Gdns CHFD SO53 206 E5
Common Hl ALTN GU34 149 N2
Common Hill Rd ROMY SO51 181 H8
Common La
FHAM/STUB PO14 293 K1
WHAM PO17 274 A4
Common Rd CHFD SO53 206 E5
RSAL SP5 201 K5
STHA RG19 32 B6
Commonside EMRTH PO10 277 P5
Common St PSEA PO1 * 19 K1
The Common FBDG SP6 219 J9
RSAL SP5 158 C1
TADY RG26 50 A4
Communications Rd
STHA RG19 31 L1
Compass Cl ITCH SO19 249 J7
LSOL/BMARY PO13 315 H2
Compass Fld HTWY RG27 72 A3
Compass Point HLER SO31 * 269 N8
Compass Rd CHAM PO6 296 D1
Complins ALTN GU34 133 H3
Compound Rd FARN GU14 75 P2
Compton Av PSTN BH14 333 M1
Compton Beeches
RGWD BH24 281 N4
Compton Cl ELGH SO50 207 H7
FLEETS GU52 74 E7
FUFL SO22 183 K3
HAV PO9 15 F2
HTWY RG27 72 A4
LSOL/BMARY PO13 314 E2
SHST GU47 41 K5
VWD BH31 258 F4
Compton Crs FERN BH22 280 G8
Compton Dr PSTN BH14 333 L1
Compton Gdns PSTN BH14 333 L1
Compton Rd FLEETS GU52 74 E7
NEND PO2 297 H6
NMIL/BTOS BH25 327 J5
TDWTH SP9 79 H5
TOTT SO40 246 E3
WINC SO23 22 C6
Compton's Dr ROMY SO51 201 P6
Compton Sq AND SP10 82 G8
Compton St RWIN SO21 183 L6
Compton Wk SHAM SO14 20 E2
Compton Wy FUFL SO22 183 K3
HTWY RG27 52 C8
RFNM GU10 97 J9
Conan Rd NEND PO2 296 G5
Concorde Cl FHAM PO15 271 K5
Concorde Rd FARN GU14 75 K3
Concorde Wy FHAM PO15 271 L5
Conde Wy BOR GU35 154 A6
Condor Av FHAM/PORC PO16 295 K1
Condor Cl ITCH SO19 248 F8
WIMB BH21 281 H4
Condor Rd FARN GU14 76 A2
Coneygar La FERN BH22 302 A5
Coney Gn WINC SO23 165 H5
Conference Dr HLER SO31 271 H7
Conference Pl LYMN SO41 329 L5
Conford Ct HAV PO9 276 D4
Congleton Cl LYND SO43 244 C8
Conholt Hl RAND SP11 60 E1
Conholt La RAND SP11 60 G1
Conholt Rd AND SP10 102 E5
Conifer Av PSTN BH14 333 K1
Conifer Cl BOR GU35 153 P7
CHCH/BSGR BH23 324 B4
FAWY SO45 268 A7
FERN BH22 302 F7
FLEETS GU52 74 C7
FUFL SO22 22 B2
HORN PO8 * 256 A9
RGWD BH24 281 K5
TADY RG26 33 P4
Conifer Crs LYMN SO41 329 H4
Conifer Crest NWBY RG14 30 B2
Conifer Gv LSOL/BMARY PO13 294 G9
Conifer Ms FHAM/PORC PO16 273 P9
Conifer Rd ROWN SO16 227 L8
Conigar Rd EMRTH PO10 277 M7
Coniston Av BWD BH11 301 N8
Coniston Cl CBLY GU15 59 H2
FARN GU14 75 M1
STHA RG19 25 K4
VWD BH31 258 E5
Coniston Ct ASHV GU12 * 76 E8
Coniston Dr FNM GU9 96 A5
Coniston Gdns HEND SO30 250 B6
Coniston Gv NARL SO24 168 A3
Coniston Rd BH/HW/K RG22 89 L2
BOR GU35 153 P3
ELGH SO50 229 H2
RGWD BH24 * 282 F3
ROWN SO16 246 G3
Coniston Wk
FHAM/STUB PO14 294 C2
Coniston Wy FLEETS GU52 74 B7
Connaught Barracks
ALDT GU11 76 C6
Connaught Cl BOR GU35 154 A6
CWTH RG45 40 G3
NMIL/BTOS BH25 326 G7
YTLY GU46 40 C8
Connaught Crs
BKME/WDN BH12 321 N6
Connaught Gdns STHA RG19 25 P5
Connaught La CHAM PO6 296 B1
Connaught Rd ASHV GU12 3 J3
FLEETN GU51 74 C4
HAV PO9 15 H5
LTDN BH7 335 P1
NEND PO2 296 F7
NWBY RG14 17 G2
RWIN SO21 144 D6
TDWTH SP9 79 J5
Connaught Wy ALTN GU34 132 D8
The Connection NWBY RG14 24 D1
Connell Rd PLE BH15 320 E7
Connemara Crs FHAM PO15 271 H3
Connigar Cl
LSOL/BMARY PO13 314 G1
Connop Wy FRIM GU16 58 E2
Conqueror Wy
FHAM/STUB PO14 294 B7
Conrad Gdns FHAM PO15 271 J2
The Conservatory WINC SO23 * 23 G5
Consort Cl BKME/WDN BH12 321 L7
ELGH SO50 207 K8
Consort Ct FHAM/PORC PO16 * 11 J6
Consort Ms WHAM PO17 272 B3
Consort Rd ELGH SO50 207 K8
Constable Cl BSTK RG21 69 N9
FERN BH22 302 C4
GPORT PO12 315 N7
ITCH SO19 249 L9
Constable Ct AND SP10 4 C2
Constable's Ga WINC SO23 22 C5
Constable Wy SHST GU47 41 M8
Constantine Av CHFD SO53 206 G7
Constantine Cl CHFD SO53 207 H7
Constantine Sq AND SP10 * 82 F9
Constantine Wy
BH/HW/K RG22 89 L5
Constant Rd FARN GU14 75 H2
Constitution Hill Rd
PSTN BH14 321 H8
Convent La EMRTH PO10 299 M1
Conway Cl CHFD SO53 228 D1
NMIL/BTOS BH25 327 K4
Conway Dr FARN GU14 57 L8
NTHA RG18 25 L2
Conways Dr PSTN BH14 321 J8
Cook Cl RGWD BH24 282 G1
Cooke Rd BKME/WDN BH12 321 P6
Cookham Cl SHST GU47 41 K5
Cook Rw WIMB BH21 300 D1
Cooks La ROMY SO51 178 D7
ROMY SO51 203 N1
TOTT SO40 246 A1
Cook St SHAM SO14 21 F5
Coolers Farm STOK SO20 160 B1
Coombe Av NBNE BH10 322 E4
Coombe Cl FRIM GU16 58 C5
Coombe Cnr KSCL RG20 29 M8
Coombe Ct STHA RG19 25 P4
Coombedale HLER SO31 271 H8
Coombe Dr FLEETN GU51 74 F3
Coombe Farm Av
FHAM/PORC PO16 11 F7
Coombe Gdns NBNE BH10 322 D5
Coombehurst Dr BSTK RG21 90 D1
Coombe La LYMN SO41 308 D7
PSF GU32 212 G1
ROMY SO51 203 M2
Coombe Rd GPORT PO12 315 M1
LISS GU33 192 F5
PSF GU32 213 L5
YTLY GU46 40 C7
Coombe Sq STHA RG19 25 P4
Coombs Cl HORN PO8 256 C2
The Cooperage ALTN GU34 132 E6
Cooper Dean Dr CHAR BH8 323 M6
Cooper Gv FHAM/PORC PO16 295 P3
Cooper Rd HSEA PO3 317 K1
TOTT SO40 246 A8
Cooper's Cl ROMY SO51 225 H2
Coopers Cl RWIN SO21 144 E6
Cooper's Cl WEND SO18 249 L2
Coopers Ct TADY RG26 52 A2
Coopers Crs NTHA RG18 25 M3
Cooper's Hl HTWY RG27 55 N2
Coopers Hill Dr
CHOB/PIR GU24 59 P6
Cooper's La ITCH SO19 248 F8
Coopers La TADY RG26 51 P2
VWD BH31 258 F3
Coopers Ri HORN PO8 256 D4
Coopers Ter FNM GU9 * 96 C8
Copeland Dr PSTN BH14 333 K1
Copeland Rd ROWN SO16 247 H2
Copelands Cl CBLY GU15 59 J1
Copes La HTWY RG27 38 D7
Copinger Cl TOTT SO40 246 A5
Copland Cl BH/HW/K RG22 89 N3
Copnor Cl KSCL RG20 29 L7
Copnor Rd HSEA PO3 297 H9
NEND PO2 297 H5
Copper Beech Cl
BKME/WDN BH12 334 A2
Copper Beech Dr CHAM PO6 297 N1
Copper Beech Gdns
NBNE BH10 322 D5
Copperfield Av SHST GU47 41 M4
Copperfield Rd ROWN SO16 228 C7
Copperfields TOTT SO40 245 P4
Coppers Cl FBDG SP6 239 N5
Copper St SSEA PO5 19 F6
Coppice Av FERN BH22 302 B1
Coppice Cl FNM GU9 96 E5
FUFL SO22 164 D6
NMIL/BTOS BH25 327 M3
NWBY RG14 17 G7
RGWD BH24 281 M5
TADY RG26 33 N6
Coppice Gdns CWTH RG45 40 G1
YTLY GU46 40 D9
Coppice Hl BPWT SO32 232 A5
Coppice Ms DEAN RG23 68 F6
Coppice Rd KSCL RG20 48 D3
TOTT SO40 246 A1
The Coppice BROC SO42 286 D7
CHCH/BSGR BH23 325 M9
HORN PO8 256 A5
LSOL/BMARY PO13 295 H7
Coppice Vw NBNE BH10 322 E4
Coppice Wy FHAM PO15 272 B7
Coppins Gv
FHAM/PORC PO16 295 N3
Copse Av FNM GU9 96 E4
NMIL/BTOS BH25 327 K5
Copse Cl EPSF GU31 216 A1
LISS GU33 192 F2
NBAD SO52 205 K9
PSTN BH14 321 H9
RWIN SO21 207 L1
TOTT SO40 246 D5
WVILLE PO7 275 M8
Copse Fld CHIN RG24 70 B4
Copse La HISD PO11 298 G9
HLER SO31 269 P8
LSOL/BMARY PO13 295 H8
NARL SO24 128 C6
ODIM RG29 93 K8
ROWN SO16 228 B3
Copse Rd HASM GU27 156 C8
NMIL/BTOS BH25 327 K5
OVTN RG25 87 H1
RGWD BH24 284 B7
VWD BH31 258 F4
WEND SO18 249 H1
The Copse CHFD SO53 206 G8
DEAN RG23 89 H8
FARN GU14 75 L1
FHAM PO15 272 B6
RFNM GU10 115 P6
RGWD BH24 281 H9
TADY RG26 34 B6
TOTT SO40 * 245 K6
Copse Vw ITCH SO19 249 N6
Copse View Cl CHIN RG24 70 A1
Copse Wy CHCH/BSGR BH23 326 A7
RFNM GU10 115 P4
Copsewood Av CHAR BH8 323 L6
Copsewood Rd FAWY SO45 268 B7
TOTT SO40 246 A8
WEND SO18 248 G1
Copsey Cl CHAM PO6 297 M1
Copsey Gv CHAM PO6 297 M1
Copthorne La FAWY SO45 291 K6
Copythorne Cl CHAR BH8 323 K5
Copythorne Crs TOTT SO40 245 J1
Copythorn Rd NEND PO2 297 H8
Coracle Cl HLER SO31 270 F9
Coral Cl FHAM/PORC PO16 295 N3
Coral Ct LSOL/BMARY PO13 * 314 G2
Coralin Gv WVILLE PO7 276 B1
Coram Cl WINC SO23 165 H5
Coranation Rd WVILLE PO7 275 N2
Corbar Rd CHCH/BSGR BH23 324 C7
Corbett Rd WVILLE PO7 275 M4
Corbiere Av BKME/WDN BH12 321 M3
Corbiere Cl ROWN SO16 227 J9
Corbin Av FERN BH22 302 G2
Corbin Rd LYMN SO41 329 H5
Corbould Rd FAWY SO45 268 B9
Corby Crs HSEA PO3 297 K5
Cordale Rd BSTK RG21 69 K9
Cordelia Cl FAWY SO45 267 P7
Cordelia Gdns ASHV GU12 76 E4
Corfe Cl FHAM/STUB PO14 293 N7
NARL SO24 167 P3
Corfe Gdns FRIM GU16 58 E4
Corfe Halt Cl WIMB BH21 300 A4
Corfe View Rd PSTN BH14 321 K9
Corfe Wk DEAN RG23 68 F6
Corfe Wy BDST BH18 320 A1
FARN GU14 76 D3
Corfield Cl EWKG RG40 39 P3
Corhampton Crs HAV PO9 276 D6
Corhampton La BPWT SO32 210 G7
Corhampton Rd SBNE BH6 324 A9
Coriander Cl FARN GU14 57 K9
Coriander Dr TOTT SO40 245 P4
Coriander Wy FHAM PO15 271 K2
Corinna Gdns FAWY SO45 267 P7
Corinthian Cl AND SP10 82 F7
BH/HW/K RG22 89 N4
Corinthian Rd CHFD SO53 206 G6
Cork La TOTT SO40 247 K9
Cormorant Cl BH/HW/K RG22 89 K3
FHAM/PORC PO16 295 K1
Cormorant Dr FAWY SO45 268 D8
Cormorant Pl SHST GU47 41 M6
Cormorant Wk
LSOL/BMARY PO13 294 F7
Cormorant Wd NWBY RG14 17 K6
Cornaway La
FHAM/PORC PO16 295 M2
Cornbrook Gv WVILLE PO7 276 C1
Cornbunting Cl SHST GU47 41 L7
Cornelia Cl FARN GU14 * 75 L1
Cornelia Crs BKME/WDN BH12 322 A9
Cornelius Dr WVILLE PO7 276 A1
Cornel Rd ITCH SO19 249 H6
Corner Md WVILLE PO7 255 H7
Cornes Cl FUFL SO22 164 E7
Cornfield FHAM/PORC PO16 272 F6
Cornfield Cl CHFD SO53 206 B7
Cornfield Rd
LSOL/BMARY PO13 314 D2
Cornfields AND SP10 102 F4
YTLY GU46 56 C1
The Cornfields BH/HW/K RG22 89 N4
Cornflower Cl HLER SO31 270 E8
Cornflower Dr
CHCH/BSGR BH23 325 N6
Cornflower Wy RAND SP11 79 P2
Cornford Wy
CHCH/BSGR BH23 325 P7
Cornforth Rd TOTT SO40 246 A2
Cornish Cl BH/HW/K RG22 68 F9
Cornish Gdns NBNE BH10 322 D6
Corn Market ROMY SO51 204 C6
Cornpits La FBDG SP6 219 J9
Cornwall Crs WEND SO18 249 H1
Cornwallis Crs PSEA PO1 316 E2
Cornwallis Rd LYMN SO41 338 E2
Cornwall Rd BOR GU35 154 A7
CHFD SO53 228 E1
PSEA PO1 316 G3
WEND SO18 249 H1
Cornwell Cl
LSOL/BMARY PO13 315 H1
NEND PO2 296 D7
Coronado Rd GPORT PO12 315 M2
Coronation Av
MOOR/WNTN BH9 322 F5
Coronation Cl KSCL RG20 30 E7
ODIM RG29 72 F9

Coronation Pde HLER SO31....269 N7
Coronation Rd ALDT GU11....97 H4
BPWT SO32....232 F7
BSTK RG21....7 H5
HISD PO11....319 L7
RAND SP11....80 A1
TDWTH SP9....78 G3
VWD BH31....258 F5
YTLY GU46....40 E7
Corporation Rd BMTH BH1....9 J1
Correlli Rd BH/HW/K RG22....90 E5
Corringway FLEETS GU52....74 E6
Corsair Cl LSOL/BMARY PO13....314 E3
Corsair Dr FAWY SO45....267 P6
Corscombe Cl CFDH BH17....320 G2
Cortina Wy HEND SO30....250 C6
Corte Cl BKME/WDN BH12....322 A8
Cort Wy FHAM PO15....272 A6
Corunna Main AND SP11....5 F2
Corvette Av HLER SO31....270 F9
Cosford Cl ELGH SO50....230 A2
Cosham Park Av CHAM PO6....297 H2
Cossack Gn SHAM SO14....3 J5
Cossack La WINC SO23....23 F4
Coster Cl NWBY RG14....24 A2
Cosworth Dr FAWY SO45....267 P7
Cotes Av PSTN BH14....321 J7
Cotlands Rd CHAR BH8....9 J2
Cotsalls ELGH SO50....230 C3
Cotswold Cl BH/HW/K RG22....68 E8
FARN GU14....57 M6
FAWY SO45....267 P7
HAV PO9....276 L4
VWD BH31....258 B3
Cotswold Rd ROWN SO16....247 K3
SHST GU47....40 G5
Cotswold Wk
FHAM/STUB PO14....294 D2
Cottage Cl IWVILLE PO7....255 H8
Cottage Gdns
BKME/WDN BH12....321 L7
FARN GU14....57 N9
Cottage Gn HTWY RG27....55 J8
Cottage Gv GPORT PO12....12 C1
SSEA PO5....19 H5
Cottage Ms FBDG SP6....240 C1
Cottage Rd BROC SO42....282 D2
Cottage Rd STOK SO20....120 C9
Cottagers La LYMN SO41....328 A8
Cottage Vw PSEA PO1....19 J2
Cottes Wy FHAM/STUB PO14....293 N8
Cottesway East
FHAM/STUB PO14....293 N8
Cottington Cl KSCL RG20....48 D3
Cottle La RGWD BH24....284 D7
Cottle Ct BSTK RG21....C C1
Cotton Cl ALDT GU11....2 B1
BDST BH18....300 B8
Cotton Dr EMRTH PO10....277 L7
Cott St BPWT SO32....233 J8
Cotwell Av HORN PO8....256 B7
Coulmere Rd GPORT PO12....315 L2
Coulsdon Rd HEND SO30....250 C5
Coultas Rd CHFD SO53....206 G3
Council Rd BSTK RG21....69 L8
Countess Cl WIMB BH21....300 C5
Countess Gdns LTDN BH7....323 M7
Country Vw
FHAM/STUB PO14....293 P5
ROMY SO51....224 E1
County Gdns
FHAM/STUB PO14....294 A1
County Gates La WBNE BH4....334 B2
Course Park Crs
FHAM/STUB PO14....271 J8
Court Barn La
LSOL/BMARY PO13....314 C1
Court Cl CHAM PO6....297 K2
CHCH/BSGR BH23....325 J8
LIPH GU30....175 J4
LYMN SO41....329 K5
TOTT SO40....246 A1
Court Dr FLEETS GU52....74 D5
Court Dro OVTN RG25....65 N9
Courtenay Cl
FHAM/STUB PO14....271 K7
Courtenay Dr WIMB BH21....278 E8
Courtenay Pl LYMN SO41....329 K6
Courtenay Rd FNM GU9....96 E5
PSTN BH14....321 K8
WINC SO23....165 H5
Court HI FBDG SP6....219 L7
Courthill Rd PSTN BH14....321 L8
Courthouse Cl FAWY SO45....248 C6
Courtland Gdns ROWN SO16....228 D7
Courtlands Rd NWBY RG14....17 G6
Courtlands Ter HORN PO8 *....58 C4
Court La CHAM PO6....297 K2
NARL SO24....169 N1
STOK SO20....162 E1
Court Ldg LYMN SO41 *....329 L1
Court Md CHAM PO6....297 K2
Courtmoor Av FLEETS GU52....74 C5
Courtmount Gv CHAM PO6....297 J1
Court Rd ALDT GU11....2 E2
LSOL/BMARY PO13....314 C1
MOOR/WNTN BH9....323 H2
WINC SO23....165 K2
WSHM SO15....248 B3
Court Royal Ms WSHM SO15 *....248 B3
Courts Hill Rd HASM GU27....156 G7
Courts Mount Rd HASM GU27....156 G7
The Courtyard EPSF GU31....156 A1
The Court Yd STHA RG19 *....25 N4
Cousins Gv ENEY PO4....317 J4
Covena Rd SBNE BH6....324 B9
Coventry Cl BH/HW/K RG22....89 M3
Coventry Ct
LSOL/BMARY PO13 *....315 H2
Coventry Crs CFDH SO53....320 C3
Coventry Rd WSHM SO15....248 B5
Coverack Wy CHAM PO6....296 D2
Cove Rd FARN GU14....57 N9

FLEETN GU51....74 E1
NBNE BH10....322 C5
Covers La HASM GU27....156 B7
Covert Gv IWVILLE PO7....276 A5
Coverts Cl FHAM GU14....96 E7
The Coverts TADY RG26....34 C7
The Covert FARN GU14....57 M5
ROMY SO51....204 F7
Covey Cl FARN GU14....57 P5
Covey Wy NARL SO24....167 N3
Covington Rd EMRTH PO10....277 P5
Cowan Rd IWVILLE PO7....275 M5
Coward Rd GPORT PO12....315 K6
Cowdery Hts CHIN RG24....69 P6
Cowdown La AND SP11....102 F7
Cowdray Cl ELGH SO50....229 P2
Cowdray Pk ALTN GU34....227 M8
Cowdrey Gdns CHAR BH8....323 M5
Cowdrey Sq AND SP10 *....82 F8
Cow Drove HI STOK SO20....161 K1
Cowdrys Fld WIMB BH21....278 D8
Cowfold Dr LTDN BH7....323 N7
Cowfold La HTWY RG27....53 P7
Cow La EPSF GU31....216 E9
FHAM/PORC PO16....296 A2
RAND SP11....80 D8
Cowley Cl ROWN SO16....247 J1
Cowley Dr RWN SO21....144 E6
Cowley Rd CFDH BH17....320 F4
Cowleys La BROC SO42....290 A9
Cowleys Rd CHCH/BSGR BH23....324 C5
Cowper Av NMIL/BTOS BH25....327 J6
Cowper Rd ITCH SO19....249 M5
MOOR/WNTN BH9....322 E9
PSEA PO1 *....316 C1
Cowpitts La RGWD BH24....261 H8
Cowslade Dr CHIN RG24....70 A2
Cowslade NWBY RG14....24 A2
Cowslease Cl RWN SO21....179 L9
Cowslease Cots ROMY SO51....179 L9
Cowslip Bank CRAN RG24....70 A4
Cowslip Cl BOR GU35....154 D4
HLER SO31....270 E9
LSOL/BMARY PO13....294 C7
Cowslip Crs NTHA RG18....25 N2
Cowslip Rd BDST BH18....320 A2
Cox Av MOOR/WNTN BH9....323 G1
Coxbridge Mdw FNM GU9....115 P1
Cox Cl MOOR/WNTN BH9....323 H5
Cox Di FHAM/STUB PO14....271 J9
Coxes Meadow PSF GU32....191 U9
Coxeter Rd NWBY RG14....24 B3
Coxford Cl ROWN SO16....247 H1
Coxford Dr ROWN SO16....227 L9
Coxford Rd ROWN SO16....247 K1
Coxgreen SHST GU47....41 L8
Coxheath Rd CHFD SO53....58 B6
Coxmoor Cl FLEETS GU52....74 F7
Cox Gw CHFD SO53....228 F1
Cox's Dr ITCH SO19....250 B2
Coxs HI RWIN SO21....184 A6
Coxstone La RGWD BH24....282 E3
Coy Pond Rd
BKME/WDN BH12....334 A1
Cozens Cl ITCH SO19....268 F1
Crabapple Cl TOTT SO40....246 A4
Crabbe Ct SSEA PO5....19 H5
Crabbs Wy TOTT SO40....245 P4
Crabbswood La LYMN SO41....307 N8
Crabden La HORN PO8....256 E5
Crab Orchard Wy WIMB BH21....258 D6
Crabs HI TADY RG26....48 C4
Crabthorne Farm La
FHAM/STUB PO14....293 P6
Crabton Close Rd LTDN BH7....335 M1
Crabtree ROWN SO16....227 M8
Crabtree Cl CHCH/BSGR BH23....324 C5
Crabtree Gdns BOR GU35....154 F3
RFNM GU10....136 C7
Crabtree Rd CBLY GU15....58 A5
Crabtree Wy CHIN RG24....70 C8
Crabwood Dr ROWN SO16....247 K1
Crabwood Rd ROWN SO16....276 D3
Cracknore Hard TOTT SO40....247 N9
Cracknore Hard La TOTT SO40....267 M1
Cradle La BOR GU35....135 L5
Crafts La EPSF GU31....191 N9
Craigmoor Av CHAR BH8....323 L6
Craigmoor Cl CHAR BH8....323 L5
Craigmoor Wy CHAR BH8....323 L5
Craigside Rd BH/HW/K RG22....281 K5
Craigwell Rd IWVILLE PO7....275 M6
Craigwood Dr FERN BH22....302 E4
Crake PI SHST GU47....41 L6
Cramborne La ROMY SO51....205 H4
Cramptons ALTN GU34....132 A7
Cranberry Ct TOTT SO40....267 K1
Cranborne Crs
BKME/WDN BH12....321 N4
Cranborne Gdns CHFD SO53....206 D4
Cranborne Rd CHAM PO6....297 K2
FBDG SP6....238 G6
WCLF BH2....8 C5
Cranborne Wk
FHAM/STUB PO14....294 C2
Cranbourne Cl BSTK RG21....90 B1
Cranbourne Dr RWIN SO21....207 K2
Cranbrook Ct FLEETN GU51....74 D1

Cranbury Gdns HLER SO31....269 P1
Cranbury Pl SHAM SO14....248 C5
Cranbury Rd ELGH SO50....229 J2
Crane Cl LSOL/BMARY PO13....294 H8
VWD BH31....258 E3
Crane Ct SHST GU47....41 L6
Crane Dr VWD BH31....258 E5
Cranemoor Av
CHCH/BSGR BH23....326 A5
Cranemoor Cl
CHCH/BSGR BH23....326 A5
Cranemoor Gdns
CHCH/BSGR BH23....326 B5
Cranesfield CHIN RG24....51 H9
Cranes Ms BLKW GU17....72 C3
Cranes Rd CHIN RG24....51 H9
Craneswater Av ENEY PO4....316 G6
Craneswater Ga ENEY PO4....316 G6
Craneswater Pk ENEY PO4....316 G6
Crane Wy WIMB BH21....281 H5
Cranfield Av WIMB BH21....278 F9
Cranford Av FLEETS GU52....74 B7
Cranford Dr ALTN GU34....133 J3
Cranford Gdns CHFD SO53....206 D5
Cranford Park Dr YTLY GU46....40 E8
Cranford PSF GU32....215 L3
Cranleigh Av SD/PW SO17....248 C1
Cranleigh Av PSEA PO1....316 C2
Cranleigh Cl SBNE BH6....336 C1
Cranleigh Ct SSEA PO5....19 H1
Cranleigh Gdns SBNE BH6....336 C1
Cranleigh Rd
FHAM/PORC PO16....295 L2
HEND SO30....250 C5
PSEA PO1....316 C2
SBNE BH6....324 B9
Cranmer Dr ROWN SO16....226 G7
Cranmer Rd
MOOR/WNTN BH9....322 F7
Cranmore HLER SO31....269 L3
Cranmore Gdns ALDT GU11....96 E2
Cranmore La ALDT GU11....96 E2
Cranmore La ALDT GU11....96 E2
Cranshaw Cl AND SP10 *....81 P1
Crantock Gv CHAR BH8....323 H5
Cranwell Cl BWD BH11....301 N9
CHCH/BSGR BH23....305 M7
Cranworth Rd FUFL SO22....22 C2
Crasswell St PSEA PO1....19 H1
Craven Cl RFNM GU10....116 C4
Craven La CFHAM PO15....272 E7
Craven Dene NWBY RG14....24 E2
Craven Rd CHFD SO53....206 F7
NWBY RG14....16 A3
Craven St SHAM SO14....21 F3
Crawford Cl ROWN SO16....227 H7
Crawford Dr
FHAM/PORC PO16....10 C1
Crawford PI NWBY RG14....16 D1
Crawley Av HAV PO9....276 G4
Crawley HI CBLY GU15....50 G3
Crawshaw Rd PSTN BH14....333 K1
Crawte Av FAWY SO45....290 F7
Crawts Rd OVTN RG25....86 G4
Craydown La STOK SO20....120 E7
Creasey Rd BWD BH11....322 A2
Credenhill Rd CHAM PO6....274 E9
Credon Cl FARN GU14....57 M8
Creech Rd BKME/WDN BH12....321 L7
Creech Vw IWVILLE PO7....256 A7
Creedy Gdns WSD SO18....229 J9
Creek End EMRTH PO10....299 M2
Creekmoor La CFDH SO53....320 E3
Creek Rd GPORT PO12....13 G2
HISD PO11....319 K6
Creighton Rd WSHM SO15....247 K5
Cremorne PI PSF GU32 *....215 M1
Cremyll Cl FHAM/STUB PO14....72 A1
Crerar Cl FARN GU14....77 N4
Crescent Cl FUFL SO22....183 K2
Crescent Dr NMIL/BTOS BH25....327 H8
Crescent Gdns
FHAM/PORC PO16....11 F6
Crescent La ASHV GU12....76 D7
Crescent Rd
FHAM/PORC PO16....11 F6
GPORT PO12....315 G2
HLER SO31....270 F7
NBAD SO52....205 K8
PSTN BH14....321 N8
VWD BH31....258 C4
WCLF BH2....8 B3
WIMB BH21....300 E1
The Crescent ALTN GU34....150 C4
AND SP10....102 A2
BMTH BH1....333 J2
CHIN RG24....50 E8
ELGH SO50....207 J9
FARN GU14....78 B5
FLEETN GU51....75 F6
FNM GU9....96 D5
HLER SO31....269 K4
HTWY RG27....52 C8
ITCH SO19....249 J9
NMIL/BTOS BH25....326 E7
RAND SP11....102 C6
RGWD BH24....281 H9
ROMY SO51....184 A4
THLE RG7....34 C8
TOTT SO40....245 L4
WILLE PO7....267 J1
YTLY GU46....40 E7
Crescent Wk FERN BH22....302 E4
Cressey Rd ROMY SO51....204 D6
Cress Gdns AND SP10....102 A3
Cresswell Rd NWBY RG14....24 C5
Cressy Rd NEND PO2....316 F1
Cresta Gdns FERN BH22....302 E5
Crest Cl FHAM/PORC PO16....273 H4
Crestland Cl HORN PO8....256 A6

Crest Rd BKME/WDN BH12....321 L6
The Crest WVILLE PO7....275 L8
Crest Wy ITCH SO19....249 L7
Creswell HTWY RG27....72 C3
Crete Cots FAWY SO45....290 A1
Crete La FAWY SO45....268 B9
Crete Rd FAWY SO45....290 B1
Cribb Cl CFDH BH17....320 G5
Crichel Mount Rd PSTN BH14....333 L3
Crichel Rd MOOR/WNTN BH9....322 C7
Crichton Ct THLE RG7....43 L6
Cricket Cl CHCH/BSGR BH23....337 K1
RWIN SO21....143 L6
Cricket Dr HORN PO8....256 A6
Cricket Field Gv CWTH RG45....41 L2
Cricket Gn HTWY RG27....55 J7
Cricket Green La HTWY RG27....55 J7
Cricket La RFNM GU10....116 D4
Cricket Lea BOR GU35....154 C5
Cricklade Pl AND SP10 *....102 C1
Cricklemede BPWT SO32....232 B5
Cricklewood Cl BPWT SO32....232 B5
Crigdon Cl ROWN SO16....247 J3
Crimea Rd ALDT GU11....3 F7
BKME/WDN BH12....321 M7
MOOR/WNTN BH9....322 F8
Cringle Av SBNE BH6....336 E2
Crinoline Gdns ENEY PO4....317 J6
Cripley Rd FARN GU14....57 L7
Cripple Gate La BROC SO42....310 F4
Crispin Cl CHCH/BSGR BH23....326 E7
ELGH SO50....230 C6
HLER SO31....271 H6
Crispstead La WINC SO23....183 P1
Crisspyn Cl HORN PO8 *....256 B5
Critchmere La HASM GU27....156 D6
Critchmere Hill HASM GU27....156 D6
Critchmere La HASM GU27....156 C7
Criterion Ar BMTH BH1 *....8 D7
Crittall Cl ALDT GU11....308 C6
Crockers Md KSCL RG20....29 J3
Crockford Br LYMN SO41....333 L6
Crockford Rd PSTN BH14....333 K2
Crockford La CHIN RG24....51 P9
Crockford Rd EMRTH PO10....277 P6
RSAL SP5....176 A4
Crocus Md NTHA RG18....25 P3
Croft Av AND SP10....82 F8
Croft Cl CFRIM GU16....59 J4
Crofters Cl SHST GU47....41 H6
Crofters Meadow CHIN RG24....70 A4
NWBY RG14....24 B3
Croft Gdns WSD SO18....248 E1
AND SP10....102 A4
Croft Hts RSAL SP5....201 K2
Croftlands Av
FHAM/STUB PO14....294 A6
Croft La HISD PO11....298 G8
NWBY RG14....24 B3
WILLE PO7....90 C6
YTLY GU46....40 D7
Crofton Av
LSOL/BMARY PO13....294 A9
Crofton Cl CHCH/BSGR BH23....324 C7
SD/PW SO17....248 C2
WVILLE PO7....275 L5
Crofton La FHAM/STUB PO14....294 A8
Crofton Rd ENEY PO4....317 K3
NEND PO2....296 D7
Crofton Wy BPWT SO32....232 E7
HLER SO31....270 C9
Croft Rd ALDT GU11....3 G7
MOOR/WNTN BH9....293 P6
Croft Rd ROWN SO16....227 J7
Crombie Cl HORN PO8....255 P7
Cromalt Cl FHAM/STUB PO14....294 A6
Cromarty Av ENEY PO4....317 K4
Cromarty Cl
FHAM/STUB PO14....293 P6
Cromarty Rd ROWN SO16....227 J1
Crombie CI HORN PO8....255 P7
Cromer Gdns
BKME/WDN BH12....321 P7
Cromer Rd BKME/WDN BH12....321 P7
CHAR PO6....274 F9
CHAR BH8....323 H8
ROWN SO16....247 H2
Cromhall Cl FHAM/STUB PO14....294 A5
Crompton Wy FHAM PO15....271 J9
Cromwell Cl CHIN RG24....70 C6
Cromwell Pl BOSC RG15....335 P1
NWBY RG14....16 D6
Cromwell Rd
BKME/WDN BH12....321 M7
BOSC BH5....335 P1
ENEY PO4....317 K6
FUFL SO22....22 A4
NWBY RG14....16 D7
WIMB BH21....300 F1
WSHM SO15....248 B4
Cromwell Ter NWBY RG14 *....24 A2
Crondall Av HAV PO9....276 E4
Crondall End YTLY GU46....40 D7
Crondall La RFNM GU10....113 P9
Crondall Rd FLEETN GU51....73 P9
RFNM GU10....95 L6
Crooked Hays Cl TOTT SO40....245 K1
Crooked Walk La WHAM PO17....254 D6
Crookham HAV PO9....276 D6
TADY RG26....43 P8

Crookham HI STHA RG19....25 P8
Crookham Reach FLEETS GU52....74 B7
Crookham Rd FLEETS GU51....74 B6
ITCH SO19....249 H8
Crook HI HORN PO8....256 B1
Crook La FAWY SO45....204 C1
Crookhorn La BPWT SO32....233 N4
CHAM PO6....275 N9
Crooksbury Rd RFNM GU10....97 H8
Cropmark Wy BH/HW/K RG22....89 M4
Crosby Gdns YTLY GU46....40 F7
Crosby Rd BWBNE BH4....334 C5
Crosby Wy FNM GU9....116 A1
Crosfield Cl ROMY SO51....225 H2
Crossbill Cl HORN PO8 *....256 A4
Crossborough Gdns
BSTK RG21 *....7 H7
Crossborough HI BSTK RG21....69 M8
Crossfell Wk
FHAM/STUB PO14....294 C1
Cross Gdns FRIM GU16....58 E7
Crosshouse Rd SHAM SO14....21 J7
Cross Keys Pas WINC SO23 *....23 F5
Crossland Ct GPORT PO12....12 E5
Crossland Dr HAV PO9....15 H2
Cross La AND SP10....4 A3
BPWT SO32....233 N1
FRIM GU16....58 E7
KSCL RG20....45 K5
Crossley Pl WSHM SO15....248 A5
Crossmead Av
NMIL/BTOS BH25....327 J5
Cross & Pillory La ALTN GU34 *....132 F6
Cross Rd ASHV GU12....76 G9
FARN GU14....75 M3
ITCH SO19....248 G4
LSOL/BMARY PO13....314 E4
Cross St ALDT GU11....2 D3
BPWT SO32....232 A4
FARN GU14....76 B4
PSEA PO1....18 D2
SSEA PO5....22 D4
WINC SO23....22 D4
The Cross PSF GU32....215 M4
RGWD BH24....283 G8
STOK SO20....161 M4
Crosstrees HLER SO31 *....270 F4
Crosswater La RFNM GU10....136 C5
Cross Wy CHCH/BSGR BH23....324 B6
HAV PO9....14 B4
RWIN SO21....183 M9
Crossways ASHV GU12....3 J5
LYMN SO41....328 D6
RFNM GU10....116 C6
Crossways Rd GSHT GU26....156 C2
The Crossways AND SP10....4 B3
SD/PW SO17....206 B9
GPORT PO12....315 M2
The Crossway
FHAM/PORC PO16....295 N1
Crosswell Cl ITCH SO19....249 L6
Croucher's Cft FUFL SO22....164 C6
Crouch La ROWN SO16....248 B4
Crowborough Rd BH/HW/K RG22....89 N5
Crowder Ter FUFL SO22....22 C5
Crowfield Dr STHA RG19....25 L4
Crow La RGWD BH24....282 G4
Crown Cl BKME/WDN BH12....321 L7
WVILLE PO7....275 N7
Crown Dr FNM GU9....96 G6
Crownfields ODIM RG29....93 K1
Crown Gdns FLEETN GU51....74 D6
Crown La CHIN RG24....70 B6
FNM GU9....96 G6
HTWY RG27....71 J5
RAND SP11....29 N1
Crown Md NTHA RG18 *....25 M4
Crown Rd YTLY GU46....40 F8
Crown Pl PSEA PO1....316 F2
WSHM SO15....247 M3
Crown St PSEA PO1....316 F2
WSHM SO15....247 M3
Crown Wk WINC SO23 *....22 E3
Crowsbury Cl EMRTH PO10....277 L7
Crows Nest La BPWT SO32....232 D7
Crowsport HLER SO31....270 A7
Crowther Cl ITCH SO19....249 L7
Crowthorne Rd PSEA PO1....41 J6
Croyde Cl FARN GU14....57 P7
Croydon Cl ROWN SO16....227 L8
Croye CI AND SP10....4 A4
Cruikshank Lea SHST GU47....41 M8
Crummock Rd CHFD SO53....206 C6
Crundles EPSF GU31....156 C1
Crusader Ct GPORT PO12....315 N1
Crusader Rd BWD BH11....301 M9
HEND SO30....250 D6
Crusaders Wy CHFD SO53....205 M4
Cruse Cl LYMN SO41....308 B6
Crystal Hollow FBDG SP6....240 C1
Crystal Wy IWVILLE PO7....276 A6
Cucklington Gdns
MOOR/WNTN BH9....323 H4
Cuckmere La ROWN SO16....247 H3
Cuckoo Bushes La CHFD SO53....206 D5
Cuckoo Cl FARN GU14....58 C3
Cuckoo Hill Wy
CHCH/BSGR BH23....305 N7
Cuckoo La CHAM/STUB PO14....293 P5
Cuckoo La FHAM/STUB PO14....271 J9
Cuckoo Rd BKME/WDN BH12....321 J4
Cudnell Av BWD BH11....301 P7
Cudworth Md HEND SO30....250 D4
Cufaudle La TADY RG26....42 A7
Cuffelle Cl HAV PO9....276 A1
Cuffnells Cl RGWD BH24....282 F2
The Cul-de-dac
NMIL/BTOS BH25 *....326 E7
Culford Cl CHAR BH8....323 M6
Culford Ct CHAR BH8....323 M5
Culford Wy TOTT SO40....246 B5
Cull Cl BKME/WDN BH12....321 J8
Cullen Cl YTLY GU46....40 D9
Culliford Crs CHIN RG24....69 P2

Culley Vw *NARL* SO24 .... 168 A3
Culliford Crs *CFDH* BH17 .... 320 G2
Cull La *NMIL/BTOS* BH25 .... 327 K1
Culloden CI *FHAM* PO15 .... 10 B3
Culloden Rd
  FHAM/STUB PO14 .... 294 D3
Cullwood La
  NMIL/BTOS BH25 .... 327 L2
Culver CI *ROWN* SO16 .... 247 L1
Culver Ct *ROWN* SO16 .... 247 L1
Culver Dr *HISD* PO11 .... 319 J7
Culverhayes PI *WIMB* BH21 ...... 278 D8
Culverhayes Rd *WIMB* BH21 ..... 278 D8
Culverin Sq *HSEA* PO3 * 297 J6
Culverlands Crs *HAV* GU12 ...... 78 E9
Culverley CI *BROC* SO42 .... 286 F8
Culver Ms *WINC* SO23 * 2 E6
Culver Rd *BSTK* RG21 .... 69 K9
  ENEY PO4 .... 317 J6
  NMIL/BTOS BH25 .... 327 H5
  SHST GU47 .... 41 L5
  WINC SO23 .... 22 D7
Culverwell Gdns *WINC* SO23 .... 22 D6
Culvery Gdns *WEND* SO18 .... 249 K2
Cumberland Av
  BH/HW/K RG22 .... 90 A2
  CHFD SO53 .... 206 A6
  EMRTH PO10 .... 277 L6
Cumberland CI *CHFD* SO53 ...... 206 C2
Cumberland Rd *CBLY* GU15 ..... 59 H1
  SSEA PO5 .... 316 C5
Cumberland St *PSEA* PO1 .... 18 D1
  SHAM SO14 .... 21 G4
Cumberland Wy *FAWY* SO45 .... 267 P7
Cumber Rd *HLER* SO31 .... 270 E7
Cumbria Ct *FARN* GU14 .... 76 E3
Cumbrian Wy *ROWN* SO16 ...... 247 J5
Cummins CI *AND* SP10 .... 5 F5
Cummins Gn *HLER* SO31 .... 270 A1
Cumnor Rd *BMTH* BH1 .... 9 F3
Cunard Av *WSHM* SO15 .... 247 N3
Cunard La *WEND* SO18 .... 248 C9
Cundell Wy *WINC* SO23 .... 145 J7
Cunningham Av *BPWT* SO32 ..... 231 N4
Cunningham CI *BWD* BH11 .... 322 A4
  CHCH/BSGR BH23 .... 325 L9
  RGWD BH24 .... 282 G1
Cunningham Crs *BWD* BH11 ..... 322 A4
  ITCH SO19 .... 249 J7
Cunningham Dr *HLER* SO31 ..... 270 C6
Cunningham Gdns *HLER* SO31 .. 269 N2
Cunningham PI *BWD* BH11 .... 322 A4
Cunningham Rd *HORN* PO8 ..... 256 C4
  WVILLE PO7 .... 275 M5
Cunnington Rd *FARN* GU14 ..... 76 D3
Cupernham CI *ROMY* SO51 ...... 204 E5
Cupernham La *ROMY* SO51 ..... 204 E5
Curdridge CI *HAV* PO9 .... 256 C3
Curdridge La *BPWT* SO32 .... 251 N1
Curlew CI *BH/HW/K* RG22 .... 89 L1
  EMRTH PO10 .... 299 L1
  FERN BH22 .... 302 B1
  ROWN SO16 .... 227 M7
  STHA RG19 .... 25 M4
Curlew Dr *FAWY* SO45 .... 268 D8
Curlew Gdns *HORN* PO8 .... 255 P7
Curlew Rd *CHAR* BH8 .... 323 K5
  CHCH/BSGR BH23 .... 325 L9
Curlews ALTN *GU34* 132 F3
Curlew Sq *ELGH* SO50 .... 206 A2
The Curlews *VWD* BH31 .... 258 C5
Curlieu Rd *PLE* BH15 .... 320 C6
Curling Wy *NWBY* RG14 .... 24 F3
Curly Bridge CI *FARN* GU14 ..... 76 B5
Curnock Ct *NWBY* RG14 .... 25 H5
Curtis CI *BOR* GU35 .... 154 F2
Curtis La *BOR* GU35 .... 154 F2
Curtis Md *NEND* PO2 .... 297 H5
Curtis Rd *ALTN* GU34 .... 132 C5
  BMTH BH12 .... 321 L7
Curtiss Gdns *GPORT* PO12 ...... 315 K4
The Curve *HORN* PO8 .... 255 P5
  LSOL/BMARY PO13 .... 294 C1
Curzon Av *CHCH/BSGR* BH23 ... 325 J7
Cusden Dr *AND* SP10 .... 82 E9
Custards Rd *LYND* SO43 .... 264 F4
Cutbush La *WEND* SO18 .... 229 J9
Cuthbert Rd *ASHV* GU12 .... 76 F6
  PSEA PO1 .... 317 H2
Cuthburga Rd *WIMB* BH21 ...... 278 E9
Cuthbury CI *WIMB* BH21 .... 300 C1
Cuthbury Gdns *WIMB* BH21 ..... 278 C9
Cutler CI *NMIL/BTOS* BH25 ...... 345 L2
  TWDS BH3 .... 321 N1
Cutlers La *FHAM/STUB* PO14 ... 294 A6
Cutlers PI *WIMB* BH21 .... 279 J9
Cut Pound *ALTN* GU34 .... 132 E6
Cutter Av *HLER* SO31 .... 270 E9
Cut Throat La *BPWT* SO32 .... 232 D6
Cutts Arch *BPWT* SO32 .... 233 M5
Cutts Rd *ALDT* GU11 .... 76 C5
Cuxhaven Wy *AND* SP10 .... 82 D8
Cygnet CI *FHA* RG19 .... 25 L4
Cygnet Ct *FHAM/PORC* PO16 ... 295 K1
Cygnet Rd *CHAM* PO6 .... 297 J5
Cygnus Gdns *FAWY* SO45 .... 267 N7
Cynthia CI *BKME/WDN* BH12 ... 321 K5
Cypress Av *ITCH* SO19 .... 249 H6
Cypress Crs *HORN* PO8 .... 256 A6
Cypress Dr *FLEETS* GU51 .... 74 F3
Cypress Gdns *NEND* SO30 ...... 250 C4
  NEND PO2 .... 246 A4
Cypress Gv *AND* SP10 .... 102 A3
  HLER SO31 .... 76 E5

CHFD SO53 .... 206 E5
Cypress Hill Ct *FARN* GU14 ..... 57 N4
Cypress Rd *BOR* GU35 .... 153 M5
Cypress Wy *GSHT* GU26 .... 156 C5
Cyprus Rd *BH/HW/K* RG22 ...... 89 N6
  FHAM/STUB PO14 .... 271 J9
  FRIM GU16 .... 59 J5
  NEND PO2 .... 296 G9
Cyril Rd *CHAR* BH8 .... 323 J9
Cyril Vokins Rd *NWBY* RG14 ... 25 H5

D

Dacre CI *AND* SP10 .... 82 B8
Daffodil CI *BH/HW/K* RG22 ...... 89 L3
Daffodil Rd *ROWN* SO16 .... 228 E8
Daggons Rd *FBDC* SP6 .... 239 J5
Dahlia CI *BH/HW/K* RG22 .... 89 L3
Dahlia Ct *AND* SP10 * 102 B4
Dahlia Rd *ROWN* SO16 .... 228 C8
Daintree CI *ITCH* SO19 .... 249 M8
Dairy CI *CHCH/BSGR* BH23 ..... 325 H8
Dairy Gate Rd *FARN* GU14 ...... 55 P8
Dairy La *ROWN* SO16 .... 226 E8
Dairy Rd *PLE* BH15 .... 320 F6
Daisy La *ELGH* SO50 .... 206 D6
Daisy Md *WVILLE* PO7 .... 276 A4
Daisy Rd *ELGH* SO50 .... 206 D6
Dalby Crs *NWBY* RG14 .... 17 H2
Dale CI *FUFL* SO22 .... 164 B2
  PLE BH15 .... 321 H6
Dale Dr *LSOL/BMARY* PO13 ..... 294 F4
Dale Gdns *SHST* GU47 .... 41 H6
Dale Rd *FAWY* SO45 .... 268 B7
  FHAM/STUB PO14 .... 294 B6
  PLE BH15 .... 321 H6
Dales CI *WIMB* BH21 .... 279 L8
Dales Dr *WIMB* BH21 .... 279 K9
Dales La *CHCH/BSGR* BH23 .... 303 L9
Dales Wy *TOTT* SO40 .... 245 P3
The Dale *WVILLE* PO7 .... 275 L8
Dale Valley CI *ROWN* SO16 ..... 247 N1
Dale Valley Gdns *ROWN* SO16 . 247 N1
Dale Valley Rd *PLE* BH15 .... 320 C5
  ROWN SO16 .... 227 N9
Dale Vw *HASM* GU27 .... 156 E8
Dalewood *BH/HW/K* RG22 ...... 89 L1
Dalewood CI *FHAM* PO15 .... 271 L4
Dalewood Rd *FHAM* PO15 ...... 272 B9
Dalkeith Rd *CCLF* BH13 .... 334 A5
Dalkeith Steps *BMTH* BH1 * 8 E5
Dalling Rd *BKME/WDN* BH12 ... 334 A1
Dallington CI
  FHAM/STUB PO14 .... 294 A8
Dalmally Gdns *WEND* SO18 .... 248 G3
Dalmeny Rd *SBNE* BH6 .... 336 E3
Dalston CI *CBLY* GU15 .... 59 J2
Damask Gdns *WVILLE* PO7 ..... 276 B1
Damen CI *HEND* SO30 .... 250 B6
Damerham Rd *CHAR* BH8 .... 323 K4
Dampier CI
  LSOL/BMARY PO13 .... 314 C1
Damsel La *OVTN* RG25 .... 109 P7
Damsel Pth *BSTK* RG21 .... 44 C8
Damson Crs *ELGH* SO50 .... 230 A5
Damson Hl *BPWT* SO32 .... 232 F4
Danbury Ct *EMRTH* PO10 .... 277 M8
Dances CI *AND* SP10 .... 4 E2
Dances La *AND* RH28 .... 85 L5
Dances Wy *HISD* PO11 .... 318 E4
Dandelion CI
  LSOL/BMARY PO13 .... 294 F6
Dando Rd *BWD* BH11 .... 255 J7
Dandy's Ford La *ROMY* SO51 .. 202 F5
Danebury CI *HAV* PO9 .... 276 E4
Danebury Gdns *CHFD* SO53 .... 206 C9
Danebury Rd *BH/HW/K* RG22 .. 89 M5
Danebury Wy *ROWN* SO16 ..... 226 G9
Dane CI *FAWY* SO45 .... 291 H8
Danecourt CI *PSTN* BH14 .... 321 H8
Danecourt Rd *PSTN* BH14 ...... 321 H8
Danecrest Rd *LYMN* SO41 ...... 327 P4
Dane Dr *FERN* BH22 .... 302 C5
Danegeld CI *AND* SP10 .... 82 F7
Danehurst New Rd
  LYMN SO41 .... 307 L2
Danehurst PI *AND* SP10 .... 102 A1
  HLER SO31 .... 270 C8
Dane Rd *LYMN* SO41 .... 307 L3
Danesbrook La *WVILLE* PO7 .... 276 A3
Danesbury Av *SBNE* BH6 .... 336 D2
Danesbury Mdw
  NMIL/BTOS BH25 .... 327 L4
Danes CI *NMIL/BTOS* BH25 ..... 327 J8
Daneshill Ct *CHIN* RG24 .... 70 A4
Daneshill Dr *CHIN* RG24 .... 70 A4
Danes Rd *FHAM/PORC* PO16 .. 273 M9
  ROMY SO51 .... 203 K3
Danesstream CI *LYMN* SO41 ... 338 C2
Daneswood Rd
  NMIL/BTOS BH25 .... 327 L4
Daniell's La *LYMN* SO41 .... 329 L5
Daniell's Wk *LYMN* SO41 .... 329 L5
Daniel Rd *WHCH* RG28 .... 85 M7
Daniels CI *GPORT* PO12 .... 315 J4
Danley La *HASM* GU27 .... 175 P4
Dansie CI *PSTN* BH14 .... 321 K8
Danvers CI *STHA* RG19 .... 25 J4
Danvers Dr *FLEETS* GU52 ...... 74 B9
Daphne Dr *FLEETS* GU51 .... 74 B9
Dapple PI *TOTT* SO40 .... 267 L1
Darby Green La *BLKW* GU17 ... 41 H9
Darby Green Rd *BLKW* GU17 .. 41 H9
Darby's CI *PLE* BH15 .... 320 F6

Darby's Cnr *CFDH* BH17 .... 320 E2
Darby's La *PLE* BH15 .... 320 F6
Darby's La North *CFDH* BH17 .. 320 F1
Darcy CI *BSTK* RG21 * 7 H2
Dare's La *RFNM* GU10 .... 95 J2
Dark La *CHCH/BSGR* BH23 ..... 69 H1
  FAWY SO45 .... 291 H8
  NARL SO24 .... 187 H1
Darlee Ga *HLER* SO31 .... 269 P1
Darleydale CI *SHST* GU47 ...... 41 L4
Darley Rd *FERN* BH22 .... 302 C5
Darlington Gdns *WSHM* SO15 . 247 P3
Darlington Rd *BSTK* RG21 ...... 6 D2
  SSEA PO5 .... 316 C5
Darracott Rd *BOSC* BH5 .... 335 N2
Darren CI *FHAM/STUB* PO14 ... 294 B5
Darset Av *FLEETN* GU51 .... 74 D2
Dart CI *NTHA* RG18 .... 25 J1
Dart Ct *AND* SP10 .... 82 C9
Dartington Rd *ELGH* SO50 ...... 207 M8
Dartmouth CI *GPORT* PO12 .... 315 N1
Dartmouth Ms *SSEA* PO5 ...... 19 F7
Dartmouth Rd *HSEA* PO3 .... 297 J7
Dartmouth Wk *BH/HW/K* RG22 68 F9
Dart Rd *FARN* GU14 .... 57 L7
  WEND SO18 .... 229 K9
Darvill Hts *FNM* GU9 * 96 C9
Darvill Rd *NARL* SO24 .... 169 K2
Darvills La *FNM* GU9 .... 96 C9
Darwin Av *CHCH/BSGR* BH23 .. 324 C6
Darwin CI *LSOL/BMARY* PO13 . 314 D1
Darwin Gv *ALDT* GU11 .... 3 J1
Darwin Rd *ELGH* SO50 .... 207 K9
  WSHM SO15 .... 247 P4
Darwin Wy
  LSOL/BMARY PO13 .... 315 H2
Dashwood CI *ALTN* GU34 .... 132 D7
Dasna Rd *TDWTH* SP9 .... 78 F6
Daulston Rd *PSEA* PO1 .... 316 C1
Daunch CI *TDWTH* SP9 .... 78 C4
Dauntless Rd *THLE* RG7 .... 36 D1
Dauntsey Dro *RAND* SP11 ..... 80 C9
Dauntsey La *AND* SP11 .... 100 C1
Davenport CI
  LSOL/BMARY PO13 .... 314 C2
Davenport Ga *AND* SP10 .... 102 A1
Daventry La *HSEA* PO3 .... 297 L5
D Av *FAWY* SO45 .... 290 F5
David Newberry Dr
  LSOL/BMARY PO13 .... 314 F4
David's La *RGWD* BH24 .... 282 A4
Davidson CI *FAWY* SO45 .... 268 B7
Davis CI *LSOL/BMARY* PO13 ... 294 C9
Davis Rd *NMIL/BTOS* BH25 .... 327 H5
Davis Gdns *SHST* GU47 * 41 M7
Davis Wy *FHAM/STUB* PO14 ... 294 E5
Davies CI *BH/HW/K* RG22 ...... 89 L1
Dawkins Wy *NMIL/BTOS* BH25 . 327 J5
Daw La *HISD* PO11 .... 298 F9
Dawlish Av *WSHM* SO15 .... 247 P3
Dawnay CI *ROWN* SO16 .... 228 F7
Dawnay Rd *CBLY* GU15 .... 41 P6
Dawn CI *AND* SP10 .... 80 F9
Dawn Gdns *FUFL* SO22 .... 164 D9
Daws Av *BWD* BH11 .... 322 B5
Dawson Rd *ITCH* SO19 .... 249 L9
  RWIN SO21 .... 104 E7
Day La *HORN* PO8 .... 255 M4
Daylesford CI *PSTN* BH14 ...... 333 J1
Dayrell CI *TOTT* SO40 .... 245 P2
Day's Ct *WIMB* BH21 .... 300 F1
Dayshes CI *LSOL/BMARY* PO13 294 F6
Dayslondon Rd *WVILLE* PO7 ... 275 M5
Days Meadow *KSCL* SO20 ..... 29 K7
Deacon CI *ITCH* SO19 .... 248 A5
Deacon Crs *ITCH* SO19 .... 249 J5
Deacon Rd *BWD* BH11 .... 322 A2
  BWD BH11 .... 322 A2
  HLER SO31 .... 271 H8
  ITCH SO19 .... 249 J6
Deadman's La *BSTK* RG21 ..... 7 K6
Deadmans La *STHA* RG19 ..... 24 E9
Deadmoor La *KSCL* SO20 ..... 30 D4
Deal CI *FHAM/STUB* PO14 ..... 294 A5
Deal Rd *CHAM* PO6 .... 274 C9
Dean CI *FAWY* SO45 .... 268 C8
  PLE BH15 .... 320 A9
  WIMB BH21 .... 300 D2
Dean Ct *HEND* SO30 .... 250 C4
Deane Ct *HAV* PO9 * 277 H5
Deane Down Dro *FUFL* SO22 .. 164 C5
The Deanery *CHFD* SO53 .... 206 D5
Deanes CI *BSTK* RG21 .... 7 G3
Deane's Park Rd
  FHAM/PORC PO16 .... 273 H9
Deanfield CI *HLER* SO31 .... 269 P8
Dean La *BPWT* SO32 .... 232 C1
  FUFL SO22 .... 166 E2
  HORN PO8 .... 257 K6
  RSAL SP5 .... 194 A8
  RSAL SP5 .... 201 K1
  RWIN SO21 .... 163 P4
Dean Park Crs *BMTH* BH1 ..... 8 E2
Dean Park Rd *WCLF* BH2 ...... 8 D2
  BMTH BH1 .... 62 C5
Dean Rd *AND* SP11 .... 5 F6
  AND SP10 .... 4 E5
  FARN GU14 .... 75 N1
  TOTT SO40 .... 246 A9
Deanside Copse *LYMN* SO41 .. 329 H6
Deanside Gdns *LYMN* SO41 ... 329 H6
The Dene *NARL* SO24 .... 169 J5
Deneve Av *CFDH* BH17 .... 320 B1
Dene Wk *FERN* BH22 .... 302 C5
Dene Wy *NWBY* RG14 .... 24 C2
Denewood Copse *FERN* BH22 . 280 D5
Denewood Rd *FERN* BH22 ..... 280 D5
  WBNE BH4 .... 334 B2
Denewulf CI *BPWT* SO32 .... 232 A4
Denham CI *CFDH* BH17 .... 320 E2
  FHAM/STUB PO14 .... 293 P7
Denham Rd *TADY* RG26 .... 34 B6

Denham Dr *BH/HW/K* RG22 .... 89 N1
Denham Rd *BSTK* RG21 .... 326 B6
  YTLY GU46 .... 40 C9
Denham Flds *ELGH* SO50 .... 230 B1
Denham Gdns *HLER* SO31 ..... 269 K5
Denhill CI *HISD* PO11 .... 318 C3
Denholm CI *RGWD* BH24 .... 261 H9
Denison Rd *CFDH* BH17 .... 320 E3
Denmark La *FLEETS* GU51 ..... 74 F1
Denmark La *PLE* BH15 .... 320 F9
Denmark Rd
  MOOR/WNTN BH9 .... 322 F6
  NWBY RG14 .... 17 G2
  PLE BH15 .... 320 F9
Denmark St *ASHV* GU12 .... 97 K1
Denmead Rd *NMIL/BTOS* BH25 327 M3
Denmead Rd *SBNE* BH6 .... 324 D8
  TADY RG26 .... 34 C6
  WEND SO18 .... 249 L3
Denning CI *FLEETS* GU52 ...... 74 B5
Denning Md *AND* SP10 .... 4 A5
Dennistoun Av
  CHCH/BSGR BH23 .... 325 K8
Dennis Wy *LISS* GU33 .... 192 E3
Denny CI *FAWY* SO45 .... 291 K6
Denton CI *STHA* RG19 .... 25 M5
Denton Wy *FRIM* GU16 .... 59 J3
Denville Av *FHAM/PORC* PO16 . 295 P3
Denville CI *CHAM* PO6 .... 297 P1
  HAV PO9 .... 15 K3
Denzil Av *HLER* SO31 .... 269 L4
Denbden Gdns *FAWY* SO45 .... 290 D5
Deppedene CI *FAWY* SO45 ..... 290 D5
De Port Gdns *FERN* BH22 ...... 70 A3
De Port Hts *BPWT* SO32 .... 211 N7
Deptford La *ODIM* RG29 .... 71 P9
Derby CI *LSOL/BMARY* PO13 * 314 C2
Derby Flds *ODIM* RG29 .... 71 M9
Derby Rd *BMTH* BH1 .... 335 J2
  ELGH SO50 .... 229 H2
  HASM GU27 .... 156 C6
  NEND PO2 .... 296 F8
  ROWN SO16 .... 16 E5
  STHA RG19 .... 21 G2
De Redvers Rd *PSTN* BH14 .... 333 L1
Dereham Wy
  BKME/WDN BH12 .... 321 P6
Deridene Ct *TOTT* SO40 .... 246 B5
Dering Rd *FHAM/PORC* PO16 . 11 F5
Derritt La *CHCH/BSGR* BH23 .. 304 G9
Derrybrian Gdns
  NMIL/BTOS BH25 .... 327 J5
Derry Rd *ASHV* GU12 .... 76 E7
Derwent CI *FARN* GU14 .... 57 N4
  FERN BH22 .... 302 C2
  FHAM/STUB PO14 .... 294 B5
  FNM GU9 .... 96 A5
  MOOR/WNTN BH9 .... 322 C5
  WEND SO18 .... 249 K2
Derwent Ct *AND* SP10 .... 82 G9
Derwent Dr *TOTT* SO40 .... 245 P3
Derwent Gdns *NARL* SO24 .... 168 A3
  LSOL/BMARY PO13 .... 314 D3
  NMIL/BTOS BH25 .... 327 K2
  ROWN SO16 .... 247 J2
  STHA RG19 .... 25 K4
Derwentwater Rd
  WIMB BH21 .... 300 E3
Desborough CI *NWBY* RG14 ... 24 C2
Desborough Rd *ELGH* SO50 ... 229 J2
Dettingen Crs *FRIM* GU16 ..... 59 J5
Dettingen Rd *FRIM* GU16 ...... 59 K5
Devenish Rd *FUFL* SO22 .... 164 E4
Deverel CI *CHCH/BSGR* BH23 . 324 E7
Deverell PI *WVILLE* PO7 .... 275 L7
Dever Wy *BSTK* RG21 .... 88 F2
The Devil's Hwy *CWTH* RG45 .. 40 F1
Devils La *LIPH* GU30 .... 175 M4
Devine Gdns *ELGH* SO50 ...... 229 M2
Devon CI *FLEETN* GU51 .... 56 E9
  SHST GU47 .... 41 L7
Devon Dr *CHFD* SO53 .... 228 C3
Devon Rd *ALDT* GU11 .... 75 M5
  BOR GU35 .... 154 C7
  FARN GU14 .... 75 N4
  HSEA PO3 .... 297 J6
  PLE BH15 .... 320 C7
Devonshire Av *ENEY* PO4 ...... 317 J5
Devonshire Gdns *FAWY* SO45 . 290 C7
  HLER SO31 .... 269 L5
  BSTK RG21 .... 69 K8
Devonshire PI *ALDT* GU11 ..... 2 B5
Devonshire Rd *WSHM* SO15 ... 248 B5
Devonshire Sq *ENEY* PO4 ..... 317 H4
Devonshire Wy
  FHAM/STUB PO14 .... 294 A1
Dewar CI *FHAM* PO15 .... 271 J5
Deweys La *RAND* SP11 .... 79 P1
Dewlands Rd *VWD* BH31 .... 258 D4
Dewlands Wy *VWD* BH31 ...... 258 D4
Dewlish CI *CFDH* BH17 .... 320 C1
Dewpond Wk *CHIN* RG24 ...... 70 A4
Dexter Sq *AND* SP10 * 82 G8
Dexter Wy *FLEETN* GU51 .... 56 E9
Dial CI *CHCH/BSGR* BH23 ..... 305 N6
Diamond CI *ELGH* SO50 .... 240 C5
Diamond St *SSEA* PO5 * 18 D6
Diamond Wy *FERN* BH22 ...... 280 A4
Diana CI *BH/HW/K* RG22 .... 69 H9
  EMRTH PO10 .... 277 L6
  GPORT PO12 .... 315 J4
Diana Dr *WIMB* BH21 .... 300 D2
Dibben Rd *CHAR* BH8 .... 323 K4
  HAV PO9 .... 276 C6
Dibden Lodge CI *FAWY* SO45 . 268 B5
Dibles Pk *HLER* SO31 .... 270 E9
Dibles Rd *HLER* SO31 .... 270 D9
Dibley CI *BH/HW/K* RG22 ...... 89 J2

Dickens Cl NEND PO2 ... 316 F1
Dickens Dell TOTT SO40 ... 245 P4
Dickens Dr FHAM PO15 ... 271 J1
Dickens La OVTN RG25 ... 91 H1
Dickens Wk NARL SO24 ... 168 A5
Dickens Rd SBNE BH6 ... 324 B8
Dickens Wk NWBY RG14 ... 24 D7
Dicker's La ALTN GU34 ... 132 C5
Dickins La EPSF GU31 ... 191 N9
Dickinson Rd PSEA PO1 ... 317 H5
Dickson Pk WHAM PO17 ... 252 E7
Didcot Rd CFDH BH17 ... 320 F4
  WSHM SO15 ... 247 N2
Dieppe Crs NEND PO2 ... 296 C5
Dieppe Gdns GPORT PO12 ... 315 K4
Digby Rd NWBY RG14 ... 24 B3
Diligence Cl HLER SO31 ... 270 A1
Dilly La HTWY RG27 ... 55 H9
  NMIL/BTOS BH25 ... 327 J8
Dimond Cl WEND SO18 ... 248 G2
Dimond Hl WEND SO18 ... 248 G2
Dimond Rd WEND SO18 ... 248 G2
Dines Cl RAND SP11 ... 62 A5
Dingle Rd BOSC BH5 ... 335 P2
Dingle Wy PLE BH15 ... 320 F6
Dingley Rd PLE BH15 ... 320 F6
Dingley Wy HLER SO31 ... 75 N4
Dinham Rd NMIL/BTOS BH25 ... 327 M5
Dinorben Av FLEETS GU52 ... 74 B5
Dinorben Beeches
  FLEETS GU52 ... 74 B5
Dinorben Cl FLEETS GU52 ... 74 C5
Dinwoodie Dr CHIN RG24 ... 69 H4
Dippenhall Rd RFNM GU10 ... 95 H5
Dippenhall St RFNM GU10 ... 95 H5
Diprose Rd WIMB BH21 ... 300 A6
Discovery Cl
  FHAM/STUB PO14 * ... 294 A4
Disraeli Rd CHCH/BSGR BH23 ... 324 D3
Ditcham Crs HAV PO9 ... 276 E6
Ditchbury LYMN SO41 ... 329 K1
Dittany Gdns NTHA RG18 ... 25 N2
Ditton Cl FHAM/STUB PO14 ... 294 A6
Divers Cl ALTN GU34 ... 132 F5
Dixon Rd TADY RG26 ... 52 C5
Dixons La STOK SO20 ... 140 A9
Dockenfield Cl HAV PO9 * ... 276 C6
Dockenfield St RFNM GU10 ... 135 K2
Dock La BROC SO42 ... 289 M8
Dock Rd GPORT PO12 ... 13 F5
Doctors Acre HTWY RG27 ... 72 C2
Doctors Dro RAND SP11 ... 42 A5
Doctor's Hl ROMY SO51 ... 202 F1
Doctors La PSF GU32 ... 188 E9
Dodds La BPWT SO32 ... 232 F7
Dodgson Cl FBDG SP6 ... 221 J4
Doe Copse Wy
  NMIL/BTOS BH25 ... 326 C3
Doe Wk HEND SO30 ... 250 D3
Dogdean WIMB BH21 ... 278 E6
Dogflud Wy FNM GU9 ... 96 C8
Dogkennel La WVILLE PO7 ... 235 H9
Dogwood Dell WVILLE PO7 ... 275 P5
Dogwood Rd BDST BH18 ... 320 A2
Doiley Bottom RAND SP11 ... 62 G4
Doiley Hl RAND SP11 ... 62 E2
Dolbery Rd North
  BKME/WDN BH12 ... 321 M2
Dolbery Rd South
  BKME/WDN BH12 ... 321 L3
Dollis Dr FNM GU9 ... 96 D8
Dollis Gn TADY RG26 ... 52 A2
Dolman Rd GPORT PO12 ... 13 F4
Dolomans La RAND SP11 ... 42 A5
Dolphin Av NBAD SO52 ... 322 E2
Dolphin Cl ELGH SO50 ... 229 P2
  HASM GU27 ... 156 D7
Dolphin Ct FHAM/STUB PO14 * ... 295 P5
Dolphin Crs GPORT PO12 ... 12 C5
Dolphin Hl HAWK SO24 ... 108 A4
Dolphin Pl NMIL/BTOS BH25 ... 327 H8
Dolphin Wy GPORT PO12 ... 13 H7
Dolton Rd ROWN SO16 ... 227 K9
Doman Rd CBLY GU15 ... 51 P1
Dome Aly WINC SO23 ... 22 E6
Dominica Cl CHIN RG24 ... 69 M2
Dominion Rd BWD BH11 ... 321 N1
Domitian Gdns CHIN RG24 ... 68 C4
Domoney Cl STHA RG19 ... 25 P4
Domum Rd NEND PO2 ... 297 H7
  WINC SO23 ... 3 G6
Domvilles Ap NEND PO2 ... 296 D8
Donaldson Rd CHAM PO6 ... 297 H3
Doncaster Dro ELGH SO50 ... 229 H4
Doncaster Rd ELGH SO50 ... 229 J5
Donigers Dell BPWT SO32 ... 232 E6
Donkey La NEND PO2 ... 297 J5
Donkey Town HTWY RG27 ... 49 M3
Donley Dr FARN GU14 ... 75 K3
Donnelly Rd SBNE BH6 ... 336 D1
Donnelly St GPORT PO12 ... 315 L2
Donnington Cl CBLY GU15 ... 58 A1
Donnington Dr
  CHCH/BSGR BH23 ... 325 M8
  CHFD SO53 ... 220 C3
Donnington Gv SD/PW SO17 ... 248 D1
Donnington Pk NWBY RG14 ... 24 C1
Donoughmore Rd BMTH BH1 ... 335 K2
Dora's Green La RFNM GU10 ... 95 L4
Dorcas Cl WVILLE PO7 ... 276 A1
Dorcas Cl CBLY GU15 ... 58 A2
Dorchester Gdns PLE BH15 ... 320 C7
Dorchester Rd HTWY RG27 ... 72 E1
  PLE BH15 ... 320 F6
Dorchester Wy CHAM PO6 ... 297 H2
Doreen Cl FARN GU14 ... 57 L5
Dores La ROMY SO51 ... 181 K7
Doric Cl CHFD SO53 ... 207 H6
Dorking Crs CHAM PO6 ... 297 H2
Dorland Gdns TOTT SO40 ... 246 B5
Dormer Rd CWTH RG45 ... 41 H4
  NWBY RG14 ... 24 B9

Dormington Rd CHAM PO6 ... 274 E9
Dormy Cl HLER SO31 ... 270 D7
Dormy Wy LSOL/BMARY PO13 ... 294 F8
Dorneywood Wy NWBY RG14 ... 24 G3
Dornie Rd CCLF BH13 ... 333 N4
Dornmere La WVILLE PO7 ... 276 A3
Dorothy Dymond St
  PSEA PO1 * ... 19 G3
Dorrel Cl BH/HW/K RG22 ... 89 M5
Dorrita Av HORN PO8 ... 256 A7
Dorrita Av RWIN PO8 ... 256 A7
Dorrita Cl ENEY PO4 ... 317 H6
The Dorrits TOTT SO40 ... 245 P4
Dorset Av FERN BH22 ... 302 D4
Dorset Cl HORN PO8 ... 256 D5
Dorset Lake Av PSTN BH14 ... 333 K3
Dorset Rd ASHV GU12 ... 76 F7
  CHCH/BSGR BH23 ... 325 K7
  CHFD SO53 ... 228 C1
  WBNE BH4 ... 334 C1
Dorset St WSHM SO15 ... 248 C5
Dorset Wy PLE BH15 ... 320 F5
Dorstone Rd CHAM PO6 ... 274 E9
Doswell Wy BSTK RG21 ... 14 B1
Douai Cl FARN GU14 ... 58 B9
Doublet Cl STHA RG19 ... 25 K4
Doughty Wy AND SP10 ... 103 J1
Douglas Av CHCH/BSGR BH23 ... 324 D7
Douglas Crs ITCH SO19 ... 249 L5
Douglas Gdns
  BKME/WDN BH12 ... 321 N7
  HAV PO9 ... 276 D6
Douglas Gv RFNM GU10 ... 116 C5
Douglas Ms SBNE BH6 ... 336 A1
Douglas Pl FARN GU14 ... 57 P8
Douglas Ride KSCL RG20 ... 29 M6
Douglas Rd BKME/WDN BH12 ... 321 N7
  HSEA PO3 ... 317 H1
  RAND SP11 ... 101 P3
  SBNE BH6 ... 336 C5
Douglas Wy FAWY SO45 ... 268 B6
Doulton Gdns PSTN BH14 ... 333 K1
Dove Cl AND SP10 ... 82 F9
  BH/HW/K RG22 ... 89 K2
Dove Dl HORN PO8 ... 255 P7
Dove La ROMY SO51 ... 181 M7
Dover Cl CCLF BH13 ... 334 A3
  DEAN RG23 ... 68 C6
Dovedale Cl SHST GU47 ... 41 L4
Doveland Cl STHA RG19 ... 25 K4
Dover Ct HISD PO11 ... 318 E3
Dovercourt Rd CHAM PO6 ... 297 J9
Dover Rd CCLF BH13 ... 334 A3
  HSEA PO3 ... 297 J9
Dover St SHAM SO14 ... 248 C4
Doves Cl ALTN GU34 ... 132 C5
Doveshill Crs NBNE BH10 ... 322 D4
Doveshill Gdns NBNE BH10 ... 322 D4
Doves La RSAL SP5 ... 201 J2
Doveton Wy NWBY RG14 ... 24 E3
Doveys Cl RWIN SO21 ... 234 B6
Dowden Gv ALTN GU34 ... 132 H4
Dowds Cl HEND SO30 ... 250 B3
Dowlands Cl NBNE BH10 ... 322 D4
Dowlands Rd NBNE BH10 ... 322 C5
Dowland Ct
  FHAM/STUB PO14 * ... 295 M1
Down End CHAM PO6 ... 275 L9
Down End Rd CHAM PO6 ... 275 L9
Downend Rd
  FHAM/PORC PO16 ... 275 K9
Downey Cl BWD BH11 ... 321 P2
Down Farm La RWIN SO21 ... 144 D8
  WINC SO23 ... 165 H1
Down Farm Pl HORN PO8 * ... 256 C2
Down Ga NARL SO24 ... 167 P5
Downham Cl HORN SO24 ... 255 P8
Downhouse Rd HORN PO8 ... 256 A8
Downing St FNM GU9 ... 96 B9
Downland Cl HEND SO30 ... 250 G6
  HLER SO31 ... 270 G4
Downland Pl CFDH BH17 * ... 320 C4
  HEND SO30 ... 250 G6
Downlands Cl RSAL SP5 ... 199 K7
Downlands Rd FUFL SO22 ... 183 K2
Down La OVTN RG25 ... 70 G9
Downley Point HAV PO9 * ... 277 H6
Downley Rd HAV PO9 ... 277 H6
Down Lodge Cl FBDG SP6 ... 239 N5
Down Rd HORN PO8 ... 256 B2
  RAND SP11 ... 79 P8
Downs Cl FARN GU14 ... 57 M6
Downscroft Gdns HEND SO30 ... 250 B4
Downside LSOL/BMARY PO13 ... 294 C5
Downside Av ITCH SO19 ... 249 J5
Downside Rd FUFL SO22 ... 164 C5
  WVILLE PO7 ... 275 L7
Downsland Rd BSTK RG21 ... 6 B7
Down's Park Av TOTT SO40 ... 246 E5
Down's Park Crs TOTT SO40 ... 246 E5
Down's Park Rd TOTT SO40 ... 246 E5
Downs Rd RWIN SO21 ... 144 D4
  STOK SO20 ... 123 L6
Down St OVTN RG25 ... 109 H1
Downs Vw ALTN GU34 ... 132 B9
Downsview Rd BOR GU35 ... 155 K3
Downsview Wy RAND SP11 ... 79 M5
Downs Wy ALTN GU34 ... 132 D7
The Downsway
  FHAM/PORC PO16 ... 295 M1
Downton Cl CHAM PO6 ... 323 J4
Downton Hl RSAL SP5 ... 199 N6
Downton La LYMN SO41 ... 327 P9
Downton Rd WEND SO18 ... 249 H1
Downview Rd FBDG SP6 ... 196 A9
Downwood Cl FAWY SO45 ... 267 N8
  FBDG SP6 ... 240 B1
Dowrwood Wy HORN PO8 ... 256 C2
Doyle Av NEND PO2 ... 296 D7
Doyle Cl NEND PO2 ... 296 D7
Doyle Ct ITCH SO19 ... 269 H1
Doyle Gdns YTLY GU46 * ... 40 D9

Doyne Rd PSTN BH14 ... 321 N8
Dpdn La BWD BH11 ... 301 N8
Dradfield La WHAM PO17 ... 253 N5
Dragon Est CHAM PO6 * ... 297 N2
Dragonfly Dr CHIN RG24 ... 44 P3
Dragon La KNAP BD28 ... 282 E9
Dragon St EPSF GU31 ... 215 M3
Dragoon Cl ITCH SO19 ... 249 L7
Dragoon Ct ALDT GU11 ... 2 A3
Drake Av CHCH/BSGR BH23 ... 324 D8
Drake Av FRIM GU16 ... 76 F3
Drake Cl CHCH/BSGR BH23 ... 325 K9
  HLER SO31 ... 271 H5
  NMIL/BTOS BH25 ... 327 H4
  RCWD BH24 ... 260 C9
  SO40 ... 247 K9
Drake Ct AND SP10 ... 4 C4
Drake Rd ELGH SO50 ... 207 N9
  LSOL/BMARY PO13 ... 314 B1
  PLE BH15 ... 332 E2
Drakes Cl FAWY SO45 ... 268 B8
Drakes Mdw FERN BH22 ... 302 F5
Draper Cl STHA RG19 ... 25 N5
Draper Rd BWD BH11 ... 322 A3
  CHCH/BSGR BH23 ... 325 J8
Drapers Copse FAWY SO45 ... 267 P6
Draycote Rd HORN PO8 ... 236 C9
Draycott Rd NBNE BH10 ... 322 D5
Drayman's Wy ALTN GU34 ... 132 F6
Drayton Cl ITCH SO19 ... 269 H2
Drayton La CHAM PO6 ... 275 L9
Drayton Pl TOTT SO40 ... 246 B4
Drayton Rd NEND PO2 ... 296 C8
Drayton St FUFL SO22 ... 22 C3
Draytons Vw STHA RG19 ... 24 F8
Dreadnought Rd
  FHAM/STUB PO14 ... 294 C4
Dresden Dr HORN PO8 ... 255 M9
Dreswick Cl CHCH/BSGR BH23 ... 324 B3
Drew Cl BKME/WDN BH12 ... 322 C8
Drifters Dr FRIM GU16 ... 59 J4
Drift Rd BOR GU35 ... 153 N8
  FHAM/PORC PO16 ... 11 K3
  HORN PO8 ... 236 B7
The Drift HAV PO9 ... 277 H1
  RFNM GU10 ... 114 E6
Driftway Rd HTWY RG27 ... 72 B3
Driftwood Gdns ENEY PO4 ... 317 L6
  TOTT SO40 ... 246 A5
Drill Shed Rd NEND PO2 ... 296 D6
Drinkwater Cl ELGH SO50 ... 229 P2
The Drive BKME/WDN BH12 ... 321 M7
  CCLF BH13 ... 333 M4
  DEAN RG23 ... 88 F2
  FHAM/PORC PO16 ... 10 E5
  FRIM GU16 ... 59 N8
  HAV PO9 ... 116 B3
  HEND SO30 ... 229 J3
  LSOL/BMARY PO13 ... 294 E7
  NWBY RG14 ... 16 B7
  ROMY SO51 ... 181 J9
  RWIN SO21 ... 224 C2
  TOTT SO40 ... 246 D6
The Driveway ENEY PO4 ... 317 L4
Drove Cl RWIN SO21 ... 183 P9
Drove Hl STOK SO20 ... 123 L6
Drove Rd ITCH SO19 ... 167 M1
  STOK SO20 ... 123 L6
  WHAM PO17 ... 274 C6
Drovers End FLEETN GU51 ... 56 F9
Drovers Vw RAND SP11 ... 79 N2
Drovers Wy FNM GU9 ... 96 A5
The Drove AND SP10 ... 102 B2
  BPWT SO32 ... 231 K4
  BPWT SO32 ... 232 F7
  ELGH SO50 ... 230 D6
  FAWY SO45 ... 290 C8
  HEND SO30 ... 229 P9
  ROMY SO51 ... 224 E1
  RSAL SP5 ... 199 P7
  RWIN SO21 ... 183 P9
  TOTT SO40 ... 245 P2
  WEND SO18 ... 249 J4
Droxford Cl GPORT PO12 ... 315 K4
Droxford Crs TADY RG26 ... 34 B7
Droxford Rd BPWT SO32 ... 232 G8
  LTDN BH7 ... 323 P9
Druce Wy STHA RG19 ... 25 N4
Druids Cl FERN BH22 ... 302 D6
Drum Mead PSF GU32 ... 215 L2
Drum Rd ELGH SO50 ... 229 H2
Drummond Cl YTLY GU46 ... 56 D1
Drummond La ALTN GU34 ... 150 A6
Drummond Rd BMTH BH1 ... 335 L2
  FAWY SO45 ... 268 C6
  HEND SO30 ... 250 C2
  PSEA PO1 ... 316 F2
Drum Rd ELGH SO50 ... 229 H2
Drury Cl WHCH RG28 ... 104 F2
Drury La ALTN GU34 ... 131 J4
  THLE RG7 ... 36 G3
Drury Rd WBNE BH4 ... 334 B4
Dryden Av CHAM PO6 ... 274 A9
Dryden Cl CHIN RG24 ... 69 M5
  FHAM/PORC PO16 ... 10 D4
  NTHA RG18 ... 25 M2
  RCWD BH24 ... 285 M2
  WVILLE PO7 ... 255 P5
Dryden La PLE BH15 * ... 338 C1
Dryden Rd FARN GU14 ... 57 N7
Dryden Wy ITCH SO19 ... 249 N6
Drysdale Ms ENEY PO4 ... 317 K6
Duchess Cl ALTN GU34 ... 132 E6
Duchess of Kent Barracks
  ALDT GU11 ... 76 A9
Ducking Stool La
  CHCH/BSGR BH23 ... 324 F9
Duck Island La RCWD BH24 ... 282 D3
Ducklands BOR GU35 ... 154 B6
Duck La BWD BH11 ... 301 M9
Duckmead La LISS GU33 ... 173 N9
Ducks La STOK SO20 ... 139 N2

Duddon Cl WEND SO18 ... 249 K2
Dudley Cl PSEA PO1 ... 317 H1
Dudleston Heath Dr
  HORN PO8 ... 256 B9
Dudley Av FBDG SP6 ... 220 D9
  LYMN SO41 ... 327 P5
Dudley Cl BOR GU35 ... 153 P7
  DEAN RG23 ... 68 E7
Dudley Gdns NBNE BH10 ... 322 D2
Dudley Rd HSEA PO3 ... 317 J1
  NBNE BH10 ... 322 D2
Dudmoor Farm Rd
  CHCH/BSGR BH23 ... 324 D4
Dudmoor La
  CHCH/BSGR BH23 ... 324 D3
Dudsbury Av FERN BH22 ... 302 D4
Dudsbury Crs FERN BH22 ... 302 D4
Dudsbury Gdns FERN BH22 ... 302 D7
Dudsbury Rd FERN BH22 ... 302 D7
Dugald Drummond St
  PSEA PO1 ... 19 G3
Dugdell Cl FERN BH22 ... 302 F2
Duisburg Wy SSEA PO5 ... 18 E7
Duke Cl AND SP10 ... 4 A3
Duke Crs PSEA PO1 ... 316 F1
Duke of Connaughts Rd
  ALDT GU11 ... 76 C7
Duke Rd HEND SO30 ... 250 D6
Dukes Cl ALTN GU34 ... 132 D7
  FNM GU9 ... 96 A5
  PSF GU32 ... 215 K1
  SBNE BH6 ... 324 B9
Dukes Dr BWD BH11 ... 301 N8
Dukesfield CHCH/BSGR BH23 ... 324 B5
Dukes Md FLEETN GU51 ... 74 A3
Dukes Pk ALDT GU11 ... 76 C6
Duke's Ride CWTH RG45 ... 40 G2
Dukes Ride THLE RG7 ... 35 H6
Dukes Rd GPORT PO12 ... 315 L2
  SD/PW SO17 ... 248 D3
  SHAM SO14 ... 248 D3
Duke St RWIN SO21 ... 126 C7
  SHAM SO14 ... 21 G6
Dukes Walk Service Rd
  WVILLE PO7 ... 275 N3
Dukes Wd CWTH RG45 ... 41 J1
Dukeswood Dr FAWY SO45 ... 290 B6
Duke Ter HAV PO9 * ... 276 D6
Dulsie Rd TWDS BH3 ... 322 C8
Dumas Cl YTLY GU46 ... 40 D9
Du Maurier Cl FLEETS GU52 ... 74 B9
Dumbarton Cl NEND PO2 ... 296 D9
Dumbleton Cl ITCH SO19 ... 249 P6
Dummer Ct HAV PO9 ... 276 D4
Dummer Down La OVTN RG25 ... 108 F3
Dummers Dro ELGH SO50 ... 230 D8
Dumpers La EPSF GU31 ... 217 K5
Dump Rd FARN GU14 ... 75 M5
Dunbar Cl ROWN SO16 ... 227 K7
Dunbar Crs CHCH/BSGR BH23 ... 326 B5
Dunbar Rd ENEY PO4 ... 317 K4
  FRIM GU16 ... 58 F6
  TWDS BH3 ... 322 D8
Dunbridge La ROMY SO51 ... 179 L6
Duncan Cl ITCH SO19 ... 268 C2
Duncan Ct AND SP10 ... 5 K3
Duncan Rd HLER SO51 ... 271 H5
  NMIL/BTOS BH25 ... 327 M7
  SSEA PO5 ... 316 F6
Duncan's Cl RAND SP11 ... 80 E9
Duncans Dr FHAM/STUB PO14 ... 293 P1
Duncliff Rd SBNE BH6 ... 336 E2
Duncombe Rd CHAM PO6 ... 297 K7
Duncton Rd HORN PO8 ... 256 A9
Dundas La HSEA PO3 ... 297 K8
Dundas Rd CFDH BH17 ... 320 C4
Dundas Sp HSEA PO3 ... 297 K7
Dundee Cl FHAM PO15 ... 271 K2
Dundee Rd SD/PW SO17 ... 248 E2
Dundonald Cl HISD PO11 ... 318 C3
  ITCH SO19 ... 268 F1
Dundridge La BPWT SO32 ... 232 C5
Dundry Wy HEND SO30 ... 250 C4
Dunedin Cl FERN BH22 ... 302 B5
Dunedin Dr FERN BH22 ... 302 B5
Dunedin Gdns FERN BH22 ... 302 B5
Dunedin Gv CHCH/BSGR BH23 ... 325 N8
Dunford Cl NMIL/BTOS BH25 ... 338 C2
Dunford Rd BKME/WDN BH12 ... 321 N7
Dunhill La HSEA PO3 ... 297 P3
Dungannon Dr SSEA PO5 ... 317 J4
Dunkeld Rd GPORT PO12 ... 315 K1
Dunkirk Cl ROWN SO16 ... 227 P8
Dunkirk Rd ROWN SO16 ... 227 P8
Dunkirt La RAND SP11 ... 101 L7
Dunley's Hl ODIM RG29 ... 72 B9
Dunlin Cl CHCH/BSGR BH23 ... 337 M1
  ENEY PO4 ... 317 M3
Dunmow Hl FLEETN GU51 ... 74 D2
Dunmow Rd AND SP10 ... 5 F7
Dunn Cl ENEY PO4 ... 317 K5
Dunnings La NBAD SO52 ... 205 J8
Dunnock Cl FERN BH22 ... 280 B9
Dunsbury Wy HAV PO9 ... 276 B5
Dunsell's La NARL SO24 ... 169 N2
Dunsfold Crs DEAN RG23 ... 68 F5
Dunsmore Gdns YTLY GU46 ... 40 F8
Dunstable Wk
  FHAM/STUB PO14 ... 294 B2
Dunstall Pk FARN GU14 ... 57 P6
Dunstan Rd NTHA RG18 ... 25 P3
Dunstan's Dro RAND SP11 ... 61 P3
Dunstans La PSTN BH14 ... 321 H6
Dunster Cl ROWN SO16 ... 227 N7
Dunvegan Dr ROWN SO16 ... 227 N7
Dunyeats Rd BDST BH18 ... 300 D9
Dunyeats Rbt BDST BH18 ... 300 F8
Duouro Cl TADY RG26 ... 33 N6
Dupree Dr ENEY PO4 ... 317 L5

Durban Cl ROMY SO51 ... 204 E4
Durban Rd PSEA PO1 ... 317 H1
Durbidges STHA RG19 ... 32 B6
Durdells Av BWD BH11 ... 322 A2
Durdells Gdns BWD BH11 ... 322 A2
Durford Ct HAV PO9 ... 276 D4
Durford Rd EPSF GU31 ... 216 A2
Durham Dr FRIM GU16 ... 59 J4
Durham Gdns WVILLE PO7 ... 275 P5
Durham Rd SHST GU47 ... 41 M4
Durham St GPORT PO12 ... 12 C2
  PSEA PO1 ... 19 H2
Durham Wy BH/HW/K RG22 ... 89 M3
Durland Cl NMIL/BTOS BH25 ... 327 J6
Durlands Rd HORN PO8 ... 256 C5
Durley Av HORN PO8 ... 255 P8
Durley Brook Rd BPWT SO32 ... 250 F6
Durley Chine Rd WCLF BH2 ... 8 A6
Durley Chine Rd South
  WCLF BH2 ... 8 A6
Durley Cl AND SP10 ... 102 C3
Durley Gdns TOTT SO40 ... 246 B6
Durley Gdns WCLF BH2 ... 8 A6
Durley Hall La BPWT SO32 ... 231 H5
Durley Rd ELGH SO50 ... 230 E5
  GPORT PO12 ... 315 K2
  WCLF BH2 ... 8 B5
Durley Rd South WCLF BH2 ... 8 B5
Durley Rbt WCLF BH2 ... 8 B5
Durley St BPWT SO32 ... 231 K5
Durlston Crs
  CHCH/BSGR BH23 ... 324 B3
Durlston Rd PSTN BH14 ... 333 L1
  ROWN SO16 ... 246 G2
Durnford Cl STOK SO20 ... 123 L5
Durnford Rd SHAM SO14 ... 21 G1
Durngate Pl WINC SO23 ... 3 G4
Durngate Ter WINC SO23 ... 3 G4
Durnsford Av FLEETS GU52 ... 74 D5
Durnstown LYMN SO41 ... 308 C6
Durrant Rd PSTN BH14 ... 321 L9
  WCLF BH2 ... 8 C2
Durrants Gdns HAV PO9 ... 277 H2
Durrants Rd HAV PO9 ... 277 H3
Durrant Wy LYMN SO41 ... 308 B6
Durrell Wy PLE BH15 ... 332 F1
Durrington Pl LTDN BH7 ... 323 P9
Durrington Rd LTDN BH7 ... 323 P9
Dursley Crs CHAM PO6 ... 296 E1
Durt La RWIN SO21 ... 163 M4
Durweston Cl
  MOOR/WNTN BH9 ... 323 H4
Dutton La ELGH SO50 ... 229 K1
Duttons Rd ROMY SO51 ... 204 C5
Dyehouse Rd MFD/CHID GU8 ... 137 N5
Dyer Rd WSHM SO15 ... 247 N4
Dymewood Rd WHBY BH21 ... 288 E2
Dymoke Gdns ST EMRTH PO10 ... 277 L6
Dymott Cl WSHM SO15 ... 248 C4
Dyneley Gn WEND SO18 ... 249 J2
Dyram Cl ELGH SO50 ... 207 N8
Dysart Av CHAM PO6 ... 297 H3
Dyserth Cl ITCH SO19 ... 269 K1
Dyson Dr WINC SO23 ... 165 H5
Dysons Cl NWBY RG14 ... 16 B2

E

Eadens La TOTT SO40 ... 245 K4
Eagle Av HORN PO8 ... 255 M7
Eagle Cl ALTN GU34 ... 132 F3
  BH/HW/K RG22 ... 89 K3
  CHFD SO53 ... 220 C9
  FHAM/PORC PO16 ... 295 K1
Eagle Cft STOK SO20 ... 120 G4
Eagle Dean STOK SO20 ... 120 C5
Eagle Rd BKME/WDN BH12 ... 334 A4
  KSCL RG20 ... 31 M4
  LSOL/BMARY PO13 ... 314 D1
Eagles Nest SHST GU47 ... 41 H5
Eames La LISS GU33 ... 172 E7
Eardley Av AND SP10 ... 102 B1
Earle Rd WBNE BH4 ... 334 C4
Earlham Dr PSTN BH14 ... 321 L8
Earl of Chester Dr FRIM GU16 ... 59 J5
Earlsbourne FLEETS GU52 ... 74 E8
Earls Cl ELGH SO50 ... 230 A2
Earlsdon St SSEA PO5 ... 18 D5
Earlsdon Wy
  CHCH/BSGR BH23 ... 326 B7
Earls Rd FHAM/PORC PO16 ... 294 F2
  SHAM SO14 ... 248 C3
Earlswood Pk
  NMIL/BTOS BH25 ... 327 M2
Early Lands THLE RG7 ... 35 H6
Earnley Rd HISD PO11 ... 319 M6
Eastacre FUFL SO22 ... 164 C5
East Av FNM GU9 ... 96 D5
  NMIL/BTOS BH25 ... 326 G7
  TWDS BH3 ... 334 D1
East Bank Rd BROC SO42 ... 286 G9
East Bargate SHAM SO14 ... 20 E5
East Beach BMTH BH1 * ... 8 E5
East Boldre Rd BROC SO42 ... 310 F1
East Borough WIMB BH21 ... 278 D8
Eastbourne Av GPORT PO12 ... 291 P3
  WSHM SO15 ... 247 P3
Eastbourne Rd HSEA PO3 ... 297 J9
Eastbrook Cl ALTN GU34 ... 132 C5
  HLER SO31 ... 270 C5
Eastbrook Rd ALTN GU34 ... 132 C5
Eastbrook Rw WIMB BH21 * ... 278 E9
East Cams Cl
  FHAM/PORC PO16 ... 295 K9
Eastchurch Cl ROWN SO16 ... 227 K8
Eastcliff Cl LSOL/BMARY PO13 ... 314 C1
East Cliffe WINC SO23 ... 3 J5
East Cliff Wy
  CHCH/BSGR BH23 ... 325 N8
East Cl NMIL/BTOS BH25 ... 326 F7
East Cosham Rd CHAM PO6 ... 297 L1
Eastcot Cl FAWY SO45 ... 290 D6
Eastcott Cl ITCH SO19 ... 249 N5

East Ct CHAM PO6 * 297 K1
Eastcroft Rd GPORT PO12 .... 315 L3
East Dean Rd ROMY SO51 ..... 178 D4
East Dr ELGH SO50 .... 207 M9
  RGWD BH24 .... 281 H9
Eastern Av AND SP10 .... 4 E6
  ENEY PO4 .... 317 K2
Eastern Pde ENEY PO4 .... 317 H7
  FHAM/PORC PO16 .... 296 C2
Eastern Rd ASHV GU12 .... 97 K1
  CHAM PO6 .... 154 A2
  CHAM PO6 .... 297 M3
  ENEY PO4 .... 317 K2
  HAV PO9 .... 15 G4
  HEND SO30 .... 249 M2
  HSEA PO3 .... 317 K2
  LYMN SO41 .... 329 K3
  NEND PO2 .... 317 J6
Eastern Ter ENEY PO4 * 317 J6
Eastern Villas Rd ENEY PO4 * 316 F7
Eastern Wy FHAM/PORC PO16 ... 11 J6
  LYMN SO41 .... 339 J2
Easter Rd MOOR/WNTN BH9 ..... 322 C5
Eastfield Av BSTK RG21 .... 7 G6
  FHAM/STUB PO14 .... 294 D3
Eastfield CI AND SP10 .... 5 G4
Eastfield Crs RGWD BH24 ..... 282 G2
Eastfield La RGWD BH24 ...... 282 G2
Eastfield Rd AND SP10 .... 4 E4
  CHAM PO6 .... 274 D8
  ENEY PO4 .... 317 J5
Eastgate St SHAM SO14 .... 20 E6
  WINC SO23 .... 23 G5
East Gn BLKW GU17 .... 57 K1
East HI LYMN SO41 .... 329 L3
  WINC SO23 .... 23 G7
East Hill CI FHAM/PORC PO16 . 275 H8
East Hill Dr LISS GU33 ...... 192 E5
East Hoe Rd WVILLE PO7 ...... 234 C9
East House Av
  FHAM/STUB PO14 .... 294 C9
East Howe La NBNE BH10 ...... 322 C3
Eastlake Av BKME/WDN BH12 ... 321 K6
Eastland CI EPSF GU31 .... 216 A2
Eastlands NMIL/BTOS BH25 .... 326 E8
East La LYMN SO41 .... 328 E6
  NARL SO24 .... 167 K3
Eastleigh Rd ELGH SO50 ...... 230 C3
East Leigh Rd HAV PO9 .... 272 A9
East Lga FHAM PO15 .... 272 K9
East Lodge Pk CHAM PO6 ...... 297 P1
Eastlyn Rd TADY RG26 .... 34 F5
Eastman CI RSAL SP5 .... 199 L7
Eastmans Fld STOK SO20 ...... 123 L6
Eastmead FARN GU14 .... 58 A9
Eastmere Ct TOTT SO40 .... 246 A5
Eastney Farm Rd ENEY PO4 .... 317 L5
Eastney Rd ENEY PO4 .... 317 K5
Eastney St ENEY PO4 .... 317 K2
Eastoke Av HISD PO11 .... 319 K7
Easton Common HI RSAL SP5 ... 158 D1
Easton La WINC SO23 .... 165 L5
  WINC SO23 .... 23 J3
East Overcliff Dr BMTH BH1 ... 9 G5
Eastover Ct HAV PO9 .... 276 D4
East Park Ter SHAM SO14 ..... 20 L2
East Portway AND SP10 .... 4 B2
East Quay Rd PLE BH15 .... 332 E2
East Ring RFNM GU10 .... 97 M4
East Rd FAWY SO45 .... 290 F1
  RWIN SO21 .... 124 G2
  WHAM PO17 .... 274 C4
Eastrop La BSTK RG21 .... 7 G6
Eastrop Rbt BSTK RG21 .... 7 G5
Eastrop Wy BSTK RG21 .... 7 G5
East St AND SP10 .... 4 E4
  EMRTH PO10 .... 277 P7
  FHAM/PORC PO16 .... 11 K6
  FHAM/STUB PO14 .... 293 M1
  FNM GU9 .... 96 C8
  HAV PO9 .... 15 H3
  HORN PO8 .... 235 L7
  NARL SO24 .... 168 A1
  PLE BH15 .... 332 E1
  PSEA PO1 .... 18 E5
  SHAM SO14 .... 20 E5
  WIMB BH21 .... 300 D1
  WVILLE PO7 .... 205 P6
East Surrey St PSEA PO1 ..... 19 H2
East View Rd RGWD BH24 ...... 282 C3
Eastville Rd ELGH SO50 ...... 230 C3
East Wy CHAR BH8 .... 323 H6
Eastways BPWT SO32 .... 232 A5
Eastwood ROMY SO51 .... 202 C4
Eastwood Av FERN BH22 .... 302 E2
Eastwood CI HISD PO11 .... 319 H4
Eastwood CI ROMY SO51 * 204 C6
East Woodhay Rd FUFL SO22 ... 164 E3
Eastwood Rd NEND PO2 .... 296 C5
Eastworth Rd VWD BH31 .... 258 E3
Eaton Rd CBLY GU15 .... 58 A3
  CCLF BH13 .... 334 A4
E Av FAWY SO45 .... 290 G4
Ebblake CI VWD BH31 .... 259 J7
Ebble CI TDWTH SP9 .... 79 H4
Ebden Rd WINC SO23 .... 23 H3
Ebery Gv HSEA PO3 .... 317 J1
Ebor CI FERN BH22 .... 302 E6
Ebor Rd BKME/WDN BH12 .... 321 M6
Ecchinswell Rd KSCL RG20 .... 48 A3
Eccles Rd PLE BH15 .... 332 C1
Echo Barn La RFNM GU10 ...... 115 J5
Ecton La HSEA PO3 .... 297 L9
Eddeys CI BOR GU35 .... 155 J2
Eddeys La BOR GU35 .... 155 J3
Eddy Rd ASHV GU12 .... 3 H4
Eddystone Rd TOTT SO40 ...... 226 B9
Edelvale Rd WEND SO18 .... 249 K2
Eden CI AND SP10 .... 4 A3
Edenbridge Rd ENEY PO4 ...... 317 K3
Edenbridge Wy RSLY SO31 ..... 270 F4
Eden Gv WIMB BH21 .... 300 C2
Eden Ri FHAM/PORC PO16 ...... 294 F1
Eden Rd WEND SO18 .... 249 K1

Eden St PSEA PO1 * 19 H1
Eden Wk CHFD SO53 .... 206 C8
Edgar CI AND SP10 .... 82 F7
Edgar Crs FHAM/PORC PO16 .... 295 P5
Edgar Rd WINC SO23 .... 164 G9
Edgarton Rd CFDH BH17 .... 320 F1
Edgbarrowhill Star
  CWTH RG45 .... 41 H3
Edgbarrow Ri SHST GU47 ...... 41 H4
Edgcumbe Park Dr
  CWTH RG45 .... 41 H1
Edgecombe Crs
  LSOL/BMARY PO13 .... 294 C9
Edgecombe La NWBY RG14 ...... 24 F2
Edgedale CI CWTH RG45 .... 41 J2
Edgefield Gv WVILLE PO7 ..... 276 C1
Edgehill CI BH/HW/K RG22 .... 68 E9
  NWBY RG14 .... 24 C2
Edgehill Rd MOOR/WNTN BH9 ... 322 F1
  WEND SO18 .... 249 H2
Edgell Rd EMRTH PO10 .... 277 P6
Edgell Rd FERN BH22 .... 281 H8
  FRIM GU16 .... 59 H2
Edgerly Gdns CHAM PO6 .... 297 H3
The Edge CHAM PO6 .... 296 B1
Edgeware Rd ENEY PO4 .... 317 K3
Edifred Rd MOOR/WNTN BH9 .... 322 G3
Edington CI BPWT SO32 .... 231 P3
Edington Rd WINC SO23 .... 165 H5
Edison Rd BSTK RG21 .... 69 H5
Edith Haisman CI SHAM SO15 .. 247 P6
Edmondsham Rd VWD BH31 ...... 258 F2
Edmund Rd ENEY PO4 .... 316 G5
Edmunds CI HEND SO30 .... 250 D6
  NMIL/BTOS BH25 .... 327 H6
Edney CI FLEETS GU52 .... 74 E6
Edney's La WVILLE PO7 .... 255 J6
Edrich Sq AND SP10 * 5 J2
Edric's Gn AMSY SP4 .... 98 F9
Edward Av CBLY GU15 .... 41 P9
  ELGH SO50 .... 207 M9
Edward CI FAWY SO45 .... 290 G8
Edward Gv FHAM/PORC PO16 .... 295 M3
Edward Gv FHAM/PORC PO16 .... 274 A9
Edward Rd ALTN GU34 .... 132 C4
  BWD BH11 .... 322 B4
  CHCH/BSGR BH23 .... 325 K7
  FAWY SO45 .... 268 C6
  FNM GU9 .... 116 C3
  PSTN BH14 .... 333 J2
  WINC SO23 .... 183 N2
  WSHM SO15 .... 247 N4
Edwards CI CHAM PO6 .... 274 D9
  HORN PO8 .... 255 P9
  WINC SO23 .... 329 H4
  WINC SO23 .... 165 K2
Edward St ALDT GU11 .... 2 C3
Edward Ter NARL SO24 * 168 B2
Edwina CI ITCH SO19 .... 249 H5
  NBAD SO52 .... 205 L9
Edwina Dr CFDH BH17 .... 320 D2
Eeklo PI NWBY RG14 .... 17 F5
Eelmoor Br ALDT GU11 .... 75 K6
Eelmoor Plain Rd ALDT GU11 .. 75 L8
Eelmoor Rd ALDT GU11 .... 75 L7
  FARN GU14 .... 75 M9
Effingham Gdns ITCH SO19 .... 249 L7
Efford Wy LYMN SO41 .... 329 H5
Egan CI NEND PO2 .... 297 H6
Egbert Rd WINC SO23 .... 22 E1
Egbury Rd RAND SP11 .... 84 C1
Egdon CI FERN BH22 .... 302 B5
Egdon Dr WIMB BH21 .... 300 C5
Egerton Dr CHAR BH8 .... 69 L2
Egerton Gdns CHAR BH8 * 323 K9
Egerton Rd CHAR BH8 .... 323 K9
  SHST GU47 .... 41 M8
Eggars CI ALTN GU34 .... 132 C5
Eggars Fld RFNM GU10 .... 114 F5
Eggar's HI ALDT GU11 .... 2 D7
Eggleton CI FLEETS GU52 ..... 74 B7
Eglantine CI HORN PO8 .... 256 B7
Eglantine Wk HORN PO8 .... 256 B7
Eglinton Rd RFNM GU10 .... 137 H5
Egmont CI RGWD BH24 .... 282 A7
Egmont Dr RGWD BH24 .... 282 A7
Egmont Gdns RGWD BH24 .... 282 A7
Egret Gdns ALDT GU11 .... 96 G4
Eight Acres ROMY SO51 .... 204 F6
Eighth St HORN PO8 .... 256 E5
Elan CI WEND SO18 .... 249 K2
Eland Rd ASHV GU12 .... 3 K5
Elbow Cnr BSTK RG21 .... 6 E6
Elcho Rd CHOB/PIR GU24 ...... 41 P2
Elcombes CI LYND SO43 .... 264 F5
Elden St TDWTH SP9 .... 79 J2
Elderberry Bank CHIN RG24 ... 70 A1
Elderberry CI ELGH SO50 ..... 230 A3
  HORN PO8 .... 236 D8
Elderberry La
  CHCH/BSGR BH23 .... 325 K9
Elderberry Rd HORN PO8 ...... 154 D3
Elderberry Wy HORN PO8 ...... 256 B7
Elder CI FUFL SO22 .... 183 L2
  HLER SO31 .... 270 F8
Elder Crs AND SP10 .... 102 A1
Elderfield CI EMRTH PO10 .... 277 N7
Elderfield Rd HAV PO9 .... 48 D3
Elder Gn RWIN SO21 .... 208 A5
Eldergrove Farm GU14 .... 76 D2
Elder Rd CHIN RG24 .... 43 M4
  NMIL/BTOS BH25 .... 326 G7
Eldon Av NMIL/BTOS BH25 ..... 161 J5
  STOK SO20 .... 161 M5
Eldon PI WBNE BH4 .... 334 C4
Eldon Rd RFNM GU10 .... 116 D6
Eldon St SSEA PO5 .... 19 G5
Eldridge Gdns ROMY SO51 ..... 204 D5
Eleanor CI LIPH GU30 .... 154 E8
Eleanor Ct RAND SP11 .... 79 N1

Eleanor Dr BWD BH11 .... 301 M8
Eleanor Gdns
  CHCH/BSGR BH23 .... 324 C7
Eleanors Wd
  FHAM/PORC PO16 .... 275 M9
Electron Wy CHFD SO53 .... 206 E7
Elettra Av WVILLE PO7 .... 275 M1
Elfin Dr FERN BH22 .... 302 C1
Elgar CI BH/HW/K RG22 .... 90 A5
  CHAM PO6 .... 296 A1
  GPORT PO12 .... 315 K6
Elgar Rd ITCH SO19 .... 248 D1
  NBNE BH10 .... 322 D3
Elgars Ct LYMN SO41 .... 329 M3
Elgar Wk WVILLE PO7 .... 275 N5
Elgin CI FAWY SO45 .... 268 C7
  FHAM PO15 .... 10 C3
Elgin Rd BLKW GU17 .... 56 F4
  CHAM PO6 .... 333 K1
  PSTN BH14 .... 333 K1
  TWDS BH3 .... 322 D8
  WBNE BH4 .... 334 D1
  WSHM SO15 .... 247 P6
Elgin Wy FRIM GU16 .... 58 E6
Elijah CI PLE BH15 .... 332 A1
Eling CI FUFL SO22 .... 164 E4
Eling Ct HAV PO9 .... 250 F6
Eling HI TOTT SO40 .... 246 F5
Eling La TOTT SO40 .... 246 E5
Eliot CI FHAM PO15 .... 271 J1
  NTHA RG18 .... 25 M2
Eliot Dr HASM GU27 .... 156 D7
Elizabethan Ri OVTN RG25 .... 88 C9
Elizabeth Av
  CHCH/BSGR BH23 .... 324 D7
  NWBY RG14 .... 24 A8
Elizabeth CI HEND SO30 ...... 249 M2
  RSAL SP5 .... 199 N6
  WHAM PO17 .... 252 D7
  WINC SO23 .... 145 J7
Elizabeth Ct
  FHAM/STUB PO14 .... 294 D2
  FLEETS GU52 .... 74 E7
  HTWY RG27 .... 49 J3
Elizabeth Crs LYMN SO41 ..... 328 A5
Elizabeth Dr FLEETS GU52 .... 74 E7
Elizabeth Gdns ENEY PO4 ..... 317 H6
  FAWY SO45 .... 268 C9
  FHAM/STUB PO14 .... 294 B7
  PLE BH15 .... 320 F9
  WHAM PO17 .... 252 E7
  WIMB BH21 .... 278 E9
Elizabeth Wy BPWT SO32 ...... 231 P3
  ELGH SO50 .... 207 K8
Eliza PI GPORT PO12 .... 12 E1
Elkhams CI LYMN SO41 .... 328 D6
Elking Sq ELGH SO50 .... 230 A2
Elkington CI KSCL RG20 ...... 30 F7
Elkins Gv FNM GU9 .... 95 P9
Elkstone Rd CHAM PO6 .... 274 D9
Ellachie Ms GPORT PO12 ...... 315 M7
Ellachie Rd GPORT PO12 ...... 315 M7
Elland CI ELGH SO50 .... 230 C3
Elldene Ct TOTT SO40 .... 246 C6
Ellen Gdns CHFD SO53 .... 206 C8
Ellen Wy NMIL/BTOS BH25 ..... 327 N2
Ellerslie CI FHAM/STUB PO14 . 293 M8
Ellerslie Dr FHAM/STUB PO14 . 293 M8
Ellerton Wy RFNM GU10 .... 115 P3
Ellery Gv LYMN SO41 .... 329 L2
Elion CI FARN GU14 .... 76 A1
Ellesfield Dr FERN BH22 ..... 301 J3
Ellesmere Orch EMRTH PO10 ... 277 P6
Elles Rd FARN GU14 .... 75 M2
Ellingham CI NARL SO24 ...... 168 A2
Ellingham Dr RGWD BH24 ...... 260 D5
Ellingham Dro RGWD BH24 ..... 260 G5
Ellingham Rd
  NMIL/BTOS BH25 .... 326 F7
Ellington Dr BH/HW/K RG22 ... 89 N4
Elliot CI TOTT SO40 .... 246 B5
Elliot Rd HEND SO30 .... 250 C1
Elliot Ri HEND SO30 .... 250 C1
Ellisfield Rd HAV PO9 .... 276 E6
Ellison Gdns
  FHAM/STUB PO14 .... 294 B1
Ellison Wy RFNM GU10 .... 97 M4
Ellis Rd ITCH SO19 .... 249 N6
Ellwood Av ITCH SO19 .... 249 N6
Ellwood CI ITCH SO19 .... 249 N5
Elm Av CHCH/BSGR BH23 .... 324 C6
  LYMN SO41 .... 329 J6
  NMIL/BTOS BH25 .... 327 J5
Elm Bank YTLY GU46 .... 40 D7
Elm Bank Rd AND SP10 .... 4 A8
Elm CI BOR GU35 .... 154 B5
  HISD PO11 .... 318 G5
  RAND SP11 .... 80 B1
  RAND SP11 .... 100 D2
  ROWN SO16 .... 228 C5
Elm Crs BPWT SO32 .... 209 J7
  FAWY SO45 .... 290 C2
  FNM GU9 .... 96 D4
Elmcroft CI FRIM GU16 .... 58 E6
Elmdale CI HLER SO31 .... 292 D1
Elmdale Gv RWIN SO21 .... 124 A6
Elm Dr EPSF GU31 .... 215 L4
  RDGW/BURGH RG30 .... 27 K2
Elmers Wy CHCH/BSGR BH23 ... 305 M7
Elmes Dr WSHM SO15 .... 247 N4
Elmes Rd MOOR/WNTN BH9 ...... 322 E5
Elm Farm Gv KSCL RG20 .... 48 C5
Elmfield CI RSAL SP5 .... 199 P8
Elmfield Gdns NWBY RG14 ..... 24 B3
Elmfield La FAWY SO45 .... 313 N1
Elmfield West Block
  WSHM SO15 .... 247 P6
Elm Gdns AND SP10 .... 249 M1
Elmgate Dr LTDN BH7 .... 334 C1
Elm Gv ASHV GU12 .... 97 K5
  FNM GU9 .... 96 C4
  GPORT PO12 .... 315 M3

HISD PO11 .... 318 G5
KSCL RG20 .... 48 C3
NTHA RG18 .... 25 L2
SSEA PO5 .... 19 H6
Elm Grove Farm KSCL RG20 .... 48 A8
Elm Grove La FARN GU14 ...... 58 A9
Elm Grove PI NWBY RG14 ...... 16 B4
Elm Grove Rd NWBY RG14 ...... 16 B4
  NWBY RG14 .... 30 P2
Elmhurst Rd BWD BH11 .... 322 A2
  FERN BH22 .... 280 F8
  FHAM/PORC PO16 .... 11 G7
  GPORT PO12 .... 12 E2
  NTHA RG18 .... 25 L2
Elm La HAV PO9 .... 15 F5
  RFNM GU10 .... 97 M3
Elmleigh Rd HAV PO9 .... 15 F5
Elmore Av LSOL/BMARY PO13 ... 314 D5
Elmore Dr RGWD BH24 .... 281 L3
Elmore Rd LSOL/BMARY PO13 ... 314 D5
Elm Pk HAV PO9 .... 15 G4
Elm Rd BPWT SO32 .... 232 C4
  CHIN RG24 .... 96 D4
  FNM GU9 .... 96 D4
  FUFL SO22 .... 122 G7
  HAV PO9 .... 15 F5
  NARL SO24 .... 168 A2
  OVTN RG25 .... 87 H1
Elms Av PSTN BH14 .... 333 J2
  SSEA PO5 .... 25 P4
Elms CI FBDC SP6 .... 239 N1
  PSTN BH14 .... 333 J2
Elmside HTWY RG27 * 74 A8
Elmsleigh Gdns ROWN SO16 .... 228 C8
Elmsleigh Rd FARN GU14 ...... 57 P8
Elmslie Gdns HLER SO31 ...... 269 P1
Elms Rd ALDT GU11 .... 2 C4
  FHAM/PORC PO16 .... 294 F2
  FLEETN GU51 .... 74 F3
  HTWY RG27 .... 74 A8
Elmstead Rd CCLF BH13 .... 333 P3
The Elms AND SP10 .... 4 B5
  RFNM GU10 .... 97 M4
Elm St SHAM SO14 .... 21 H6
  SSEA PO5 .... 19 F6
Elm Tree CI TOTT SO40 .... 245 P9
Elmtree Gdns ROMY SO51 ...... 204 C7
Elm Tree Rd FERN BH22 .... 297 N1
Elm Tree Wk FERN BH22 .... 302 E8
Elm Vw ASHV GU12 .... 76 G9
Elmwood Av FBDC SP6 .... 240 F1
Elmwood CI RGWD BH24 .... 51 P9
Elmwood Wy
  CHCH/BSGR BH23 .... 326 E8
  DEAN RG23 .... 89 K9
Elphage Rd FLEETS GU51 ...... 74 B1
Elphinstone Rd
  CHCH/BSGR BH23 .... 326 C7
  SSEA PO5 .... 19 G5
Elsfred Rd FHAM/STUB PO14 ... 293 M8
Elsley CI FRIM GU16 .... 58 F7
Elson La GPORT PO12 .... 295 K9
Elstead Gdns WVILLE PO7 ..... 275 L6
Elstree Rd ITCH SO19 .... 248 G6
Eltham CI CFDH BH17 .... 323 P7
Elvetham CI FLEETN GU51 ..... 74 C1
Elvetham Crs FLEETS GU51 .... 74 C1
Elvetham Heath Wy
  FLEETN GU51 .... 55 L5
Elvetham La HTWY RG27 .... 55 L5
Elvetham PI FLEETN GU51 ..... 74 C1
Elvetham Rd FHAM GU34 .... 70 B3
Elvetham Rd FLEETN GU51 ..... 74 C1
Elvin CI LYMN SO41 * 327 P3
Elwell Gn HISD PO11 .... 318 F5
Elwyn Rd CHAR BH8 .... 58 F6
Ely CI CHCH/BSGR BH23 .... 324 C6
Ely Ct NBAD SO52 .... 205 L8
Ely Gv NWBY RG14 .... 25 J2
Emanuel St NEND PO2 .... 316 F1
Embankment Wy
  RGWD BH24 .... 282 F3
Emberley CI FERN BH22 .... 302 C2
Embledon Rd BOR GU35 .... 155 J2
Embley Ct TOTT SO40 .... 246 B1
Embley La ROMY SO51 .... 245 H4
Embsay Rd HLER SO31 .... 270 D2
Emden Rd AND SP10 .... 5 H1
Emerald CI ITCH SO19 .... 249 K5
Emerald Cres HLER SO31 ...... 290 F1
Emerson CI PLE BH15 .... 332 E1
Emerson Rd PLE BH15 .... 332 E1
Emily CI CHCH/BSGR BH23 ..... 325 N4
Emmanuel CI
  FHAM/STUB PO14 .... 271 J8
Emmett Rd ROWN SO16 .... 227 K7
Emmons CI HLER SO31 .... 269 P9
Empress Av FARN GU14 .... 58 A8
Empress Pk SHAM SO14 * 248 A3
Empress Rd LYND SO43 .... 264 F5
  SHAM SO14 .... 248 A3
Empress Wy RAND SP11 .... 79 P1
Empshott Rd ENEY PO4 .... 317 H4
Empson Wk
  LSOL/BMARY PO13 .... 314 D1
Emsbrook Dr EMRTH PO10 ...... 277 M8
Emsworth Common Rd
  HAV PO9 .... 277 K5
Emsworth House CI
  EMRTH PO10 .... 277 M7
Emsworth Rd EMRTH PO10 ...... 299 P7
  HAV PO9 .... 15 H5

LYMN SO41 .... 329 L3
NEND PO2 .... 296 C8
SSEA PO5 .... 247 M3
Enborne CI NWBY RG14 * 24 A4
Enborne Gv NWBY RG14 .... 24 A6
Enborne Gv NWBY RG14 .... 16 B4
Enborne PI NWBY RG14 .... 16 B4
Enborne Rd NWBY RG14 .... 24 A6
Enborne St KSCL RG20 .... 30 P2
  NWBY RG14 .... 30 P2
Encombe CI BKME/WDN BH12 .... 321 P4
Endeavour CI GPORT PO12 ..... 13 G3
  WSHM SO15 .... 247 M4
Endeavour Wy FAWY SO45 ...... 268 B5
Enderwood CI TOTT SO40 * 245 P5
Endfield CI CHCH/BSGR BH23 .. 324 D6
Endfield Rd CHCH/BSGR BH23 .. 324 C6
  MOOR/WNTN BH9 .... 322 G5
Endle St SHAM SO14 .... 21 H6
Endofield CI
  FHAM/STUB PO14 .... 294 D3
Enfield Av PLE BH15 .... 320 G6
Enfield Crs PLE BH15 .... 320 G6
Enfield Gv WVILLE PO7 .... 248 G9
Enfield Rd ASHV GU12 .... 76 G7
  PLE BH15 .... 320 G6
Engineer's Rd STHA RG19 ..... 31 M1
Englands Wy BWD BH11 .... 301 M9
Englefield Rd WEND SO18 ..... 248 F4
English Rd WSHM SO15 .... 247 M4
English Wy WINC SO23 .... 183 M4
Engvch Arm Rbt AND SP10 ...... 4 D1
Enham La AND SP10 .... 82 C8
Enmill La FUFL SO22 .... 183 H1
Ennel Copse NBAD SO52 .... 205 L9
Ennerdale CI BH/HW/K RG22 ... 89 M1
  WEND SO18 .... 249 K2
Ennerdale Gdns NARL SO24 .... 168 A3
  WEND SO18 .... 249 K2
Ennerdale Gv FNM GU9 .... 96 A5
Ennerdale Rd BOR GU35 .... 154 A3
  FHAM/STUB PO14 .... 294 B5
  WEND SO18 .... 249 K2
Ennerdale Wy STHA RG19 ...... 30 A6
Ensbury Av NBNE BH10 .... 322 D6
Ensbury Br NBNE BH10 .... 302 E9
Ensbury CI NBNE BH10 .... 322 D6
Ensbury Park Rd
  MOOR/WNTN BH9 .... 322 E5
Ensign Dr LSOL/BMARY PO13 ... 315 H2
Ensign Wy HLER SO31 .... 269 N8
Enterprise CI CHIN RG24 ...... 7 K1
Enterprise Rd HORN PO8 ...... 256 C3
  ROWN SO16 .... 227 N3
Enterprise Wy
  CHCH/BSGR BH23 .... 303 J8
  SHAM SO14 .... 248 D9
Epping CI WEND SO18 .... 249 K2
Epsom CI ELGH SO50 .... 230 C5
Epsom Crs NWBY RG14 .... 17 H6
Epsom Down ALTN GU34 .... 132 F7
Epts Rd FARN GU14 .... 75 P4
Epworth Rd NEND PO2 .... 297 H8
Equine Wy NWBY RG14 .... 24 E8
Erica Dr HORN PO8 .... 256 B7
Ericksen Rd BWD BH11 .... 322 C4
Eric Rd FHAM/STUB PO14 ...... 294 A7
Erleigh Dene NWBY RG14 ...... 16 C6
Erles Rd LIPH GU30 .... 175 K3
Ernest CI EMRTH PO10 .... 277 M9
  FRNM GU10 .... 116 B4
Ernest Rd HAV PO9 .... 276 C6
  PSEA PO1 .... 316 C1
Erpingham Rd
  BKME/WDN BH12 .... 334 A1
Erskine CI TADY RG26 .... 34 G5
Erskine Rd FUFL SO22 .... 22 B6
Escombe Rd ELGH SO50 .... 229 M1
Escur CI NEND PO2 .... 297 H5
Esdaile La RGWD BH24 .... 284 B6
Esher CI BH/HW/K RG22 .... 90 C3
Esher Gv WVILLE PO7 .... 255 L9
Eskdale CI HORN PO8 .... 256 C1
Eskdale Wy CBLY GU15 .... 59 H1
Esmond CI EMRTH PO10 .... 299 M1
Esmonde Wy
  LSOL/BMARY PO13 .... 314 D2
Esmonde Wy CFDH BH17 .... 321 H4
Esplanade CCLF BH13 .... 333 P4
  ENEY PO4 .... 316 G7
Esplanade Gdns ENEY PO4 ..... 317 L6
The Esplanade CHAR BH8 ...... 334 C1
Essex Av CHCH/BSGR BH23 ..... 324 D5
  FARN GU14 .... 58 F6
Essex PI NWBY RG14 .... 24 A2
Essex Rd BOR GU35 .... 154 A4
  BSTK RG21 .... 6 C5
  ENEY PO4 .... 317 J4
Esslemont Rd ENEY PO4 .... 316 G5
Estancia CI LSOL/BMARY PO13 . 314 D1
Estella Rd NEND PO2 .... 296 F9
Estridge CI HLER SO31 .... 269 L5
Ethelbert Dr AND SP10 .... 82 B8
Ethelbert Rd WIMB BH21 ...... 300 E1
Ethel Rd PSEA PO1 .... 316 G2
Eton Gdns WBNE BH4 .... 334 D2
Eton Rd BH/HW/K RG22 .... 89 L5
Eton Rd SSEA PO5 .... 316 C4
Ettrick Rd CCLF BH13 .... 333 P4
Etwall AND SP10 .... 100 A6
Eucalyptus Av RGWD BH24 ..... 281 N7
Europa CI TADY RG26 .... 34 F6
European Wy SHAM SO14 .... 248 C9
Euryalus Rd
  FHAM/STUB PO14 .... 294 D3
Euskirchen Wy BH/HW/K RG22 .. 89 P7
Euston Gv RGWD BH24 .... 282 F3
Euston Rd ENEY PO4 .... 316 G5

Evans Cl BWD BH11 ... 321 P3
  NEND PO2 ... 296 D7
  RGWD BH24 ... 281 L3
  STOK SO20 ... 120 C7
Evans Rd ENEY PO4 ... 317 J4
Evelegh Rd CHAM PO6 ... 297 M1
Evely Ct BOR GU35 ... 153 N8
Evelyn Av ALDT GU11 ... 3 G7
Evelyn Cl BPWT SO32 ... 232 C8
Evelyn Crs WSHM SO15 ... 247 P3
Evelyn Rd MOOR/WNTN BH9 ... 322 G6
Evelyn Woods Rd ALDT GU11 ... 76 B5
Evening Gdn FERN BH22 ... 302 E5
Evenlode Rd ROWN SO16 ... 247 J2
Evenlode Wy SHST GU47 ... 41 K6
Everdon La HSEA PO3 ... 297 L5
Everest Rd CHCH/BSGR SO ... 325 J7
Everglades Av HORN PO8 ... 255 P8
Everglades Cl FERN BH22 ... 302 D1
Evergreen Cl TOTT SO40 ... 267 K1
  WIMB BH21 ... 280 E1
Evergreen Rd FRIM GU16 ... 58 E3
Evergreens RGWD BH24 ... 265 J2
  TOTT SO40 * ... 246 E5
Evering Av BKME/WDN BH12 ... 321 M3
Evering Gdns
  BKME/WDN BH12 ... 321 L3
Everon Cl LYMN SO41 ... 328 D6
Everon Gdns
  NMIL/BTOS BH25 ... 327 K6
Eversfield Av WHCH RG28 ... 85 L5
Evershot Rd CHAR BH8 ... 323 L6
Eversley Crs HAV PO9 ... 276 D6
Eversley Pl HTWY RG27 ... 183 M1
Eversley Rd HTWY RG27 ... 40 A6
Eversley St HTWY RG27 ... 39 V5
Everton Rd LYMN SO41 ... 327 P3
Evesham Cl WCHN RG24 ... 71 H7
Evesham Wk CHIN RG24 ... 69 K4
  SHST GU47 ... 41 K5
Evingar Gdns WHCH RG28 ... 85 L5
Evingar Rd WHCH RG28 ... 85 L5
Ewart Cl FAWY SO45 ... 268 C5
Ewart Rd PSEA PO1 ... 316 C1
Ewell Wy TOTT SO40 ... 246 B2
Ewer Common GPORT PO12 ... 12 D6
Ewhurst Cl HAV PO9 ... 276 D6
Ewhurst Rd TADY RG26 ... 49 P6
Ewins Cl ASHV GU12 ... 97 N1
Ewshot La FLEETS GU52 ... 74 C9
  RFNM GU10 ... 94 C6
Exbury Cl ELGH SO50 ... 229 P2
Exbury Dr BWD BH11 ... 301 P8
Exbury Rd FAWY SO45 ... 290 C9
  HAV PO9 ... 276 C5
Exbury Wy AND SP10 ... 102 C3
Excellent Rd
  FHAM/STUB PO14 ... 294 D4
Excelsior Rd PSTN BH14 ... 333 J1
Exchange Rd PSEA PO1 ... 19 F5
Exeter Cl FARN GU14 ... 76 A4
Exeter Crs WCLF SO41 * ... 8 D5
Exeter Gdns YTLY GU46 ... 40 C7
Exeter Park Rd WCLF BH2 ... 8 D5
Exeter Rd ASHV GU12 ... 76 F9
  ENEY PO4 ... 317 H6
  WCLF BH2 ... 8 D4
  WEND SO18 ... 249 J3
Exford Av WEND SO18 ... 249 L4
Exford Dr WEND SO18 ... 249 L4
Exhibition Rd FARN GU14 ... 76 A4
Exleigh Cl ITCH SO19 ... 249 K5
Exmoor Cl BH/HW/K RG22 ... 89 M4
  ELGH SO50 ... 207 H8
  EMRTH PO10 ... 277 M7
  HLER SO31 ... 270 F7
  WEND SO18 ... 249 J2
Exmoor Rd SHAM SO14 ... 21 F1
  STHA RG19 ... 25 M4
Exmouth Gdns ELGH SO50 ... 230 C5
Exmouth Rd GPORT PO12 ... 295 L9
  SSEA PO5 ... 316 F6
Express Wy NBWY RG14 ... 25 H5
Exton Gdns
  FHAM/PORC PO16 ... 273 N9
  SBNE BH6 ... 324 B8
Exton Rd HAV PO9 ... 277 H5
Eyebright Cl FAWY SO45 ... 267 N6
Eyeworth Wk FAWY SO45 ... 267 N6
Eynham Av ITCH SO19 ... 249 L5
Eynham Cl ITCH SO19 ... 249 K5
Eynsham Wk CHIN RG24 ... 69 K3
Eyre Cl TOTT SO40 ... 246 B5

F

Faber Cl HAV PO9 ... 276 G6
Fabian Cl BSTK RG21 ... 6 C7
  WVILLE PO7 ... 185 L9
Factory Rd ELGH SO50 ... 229 J2
Fairacre KSCL RG20 ... 29 N6
Fairacre Rd FHAM/STUB PO ... 293 P11
Fairacres RFNM GU10 * ... 115 P6
Fairbairn Cl HORN PO8 ... 255 N9
Fairbourne Cl HORN PO8 ... 255 L9
Fair Cl NWBY RG14 * ... 24 B4
Fairclose Rd MERR RG ... 85 K7
Fair Cl WHCH RG28 ... 85 L7
Faircross Cl FAWY SO45 ... 290 E6
Fairdown Cl WINC SO23 ... 3 F3
Fairfax Cl FUFL SO22 ... 183 K1
Fairfax Ct ITCH SO19 ... 249 N5
Fairfax Ms FARN GU14 ... 76 C2
Fairfax Pl NWBY RG14 ... 35 H2
Fairfax Rd FARN GU14 ... 58 A6
Fairfield CHCH/BSGR BH23 ... 324 F8
Fair Fld ROMY SO51 ... 204 E4

Fairfield WHCH RG28 ... 85 L5
  WVILLE PO7 ... 255 H7
Fairfield Av FHAM/STUB PO14 ... 294 C1
Fairfield Cl CHCH/BSGR BH23 ... 324 F8
  EMRTH PO10 ... 277 M8
  FAWY SO45 ... 334 L4
  WHAM PO17 ... 329 L4
  WIMB BH21 ... 185 H2
Fairfield Dr FRIM GU16 ... 58 D2
Fairfield Gn ALTN GU34 ... 150 D5
Fairfield Pk THLE RG7 * ... 35 N1
Fairfield Rd FUFL SO22 ... 22 B2
  HAV PO9 ... 15 G5
  NMIL/BTOS BH25 ... 326 C8
  RWIN SO21 ... 183 M9
  WIMB BH21 ... 300 F1
Fairfield Sq CHAM PO6 ... 296 G1
Fairfields Rd BSTK RG21 ... 69 L9
Fairfield Ter HAV PO9 * ... 15 G5
The Fairfield FNM GU9 ... 96 C9
Fair Gn ITCH SO19 ... 249 K6
The Fairground RAND SP11 ... 81 K9
Fairholme Gdns FNM GU9 ... 116 C1
Fairhome Cl GPORT PO12 ... 315 L1
Fairies Dr FERN BH22 ... 302 D3
Fair Isle Cl FHAM/STUB PO14 ... 293 P6
Fairland Cl FLEETS GU52 ... 74 E4
Fair La RWIN SO21 ... 165 N7
Fairlawn Cl ROWN SO16 ... 227 K6
Fairlawn Rd TADY RG26 ... 34 E7
Fairlead Dr
  LSOL/BMARY PO13 ... 315 H2
Fairlea Rd EMRTH PO10 ... 277 M7
  LYMN SO41 ... 329 L3
Fairlie RGWD BH24 ... 260 G9
Fairlie Rd NEND SO30 ... 230 B9
Fairlie Pk HWY RG27 ... 260 F9
Fairlight Gdns ALTN GU34 ... 150 D5
Fairlight La LYMN SO41 ... 307 M7
Fairmead Cl SHST GU47 * ... 41 M7
Fairmead Rd WK HORN PO8 ... 256 A8
Fairmead Wy TOTT SO40 ... 246 C6
Fairmile FLEETS GU52 ... 74 D6
Fairmile Rd CHCH/BSGR BH23 ... 324 D6
Fair Oak Dr HAV PO9 ... 15 F2
Fair Oak Dr HAV PO9 ... 15 G1
Fair Oak La THLE RG7 ... 84 C7
Fairoak Rd ELGH SO50 ... 229 M2
Fairoak Wy TADY RG26 ... 33 N5
Fairthorne Gdns GPORT PO12 ... 12 B3
Fairthorne Ri CHIN RG24 ... 70 D7
Fair Vw NARL SO24 ... 167 P3
Fairview Cl FAWY SO45 ... 268 C7
  ROMY SO51 ... 204 F4
Fairview Crs BDST BH18 ... 300 C8
Fairview Dr BDST BH18 ... 300 C8
  FAWY SO45 ... 268 B8
  ROMY SO51 ... 204 F5
Fairview Gdns FNM GU9 ... 96 D5
Fairview Meadow
  DEAN RG23 ... 88 F3
Fairview Pde FAWY SO45 ... 268 C8
Fairview Rd ASHV GU12 ... 114 B6
  PSTN BH14 ... 300 C8
  RAND SP11 ... 81 J9
Fairview Ter BOR GU35 * ... 155 H2
Fairwater Cl
  LSOL/BMARY PO13 ... 294 F8
Fairway Cl LIPH GU30 ... 174 E4
Fairway Dr
  CHCH/BSGR BH23 ... 324 D9
Fairway Gdns ROWN SO16 ... 227 J7
Fairway Rd FAWY SO45 ... 268 B6
  PSTN BH14 ... 333 L3
Fairways FERN BH22 ... 302 N2
  RAND SP11 ... 81 H9
The Fairways CHAM PO6 ... 297 N2
The Fairway BOR GU35 ... 153 N7
  CBLY GU15 ... 58 F2
  FARN GU14 ... 75 H5
  FHAM/PORC PO16 ... 295 N1
  FNM GU9 ... 96 D4
  HAV PO9 ... 257 J9
  LSOL/BMARY PO13 ... 294 G8
  NMIL/BTOS BH25 ... 327 K8
Fairwood Rd VWD BH31 ... 259 J5
Fairy Crossway HORN PO8 ... 256 B9
Faithfulls Dro STOK SO20 ... 160 F3
Fakenham Wy SHST GU47 ... 41 L5
Falaise Cl ALDT GU11 ... 3 F1
  ROWN SO16 ... 227 M8
Falaise Rd STOK SO20 ... 120 C5
Falcon Cl BH/HW/K RG22 ... 89 K2
  FHAM/PORC PO16 ... 295 K1
  GPORT PO12 ... 315 N1
Falcon Coppice KSCL RG20 ... 29 N6
Falcon House Gdns KSCL RG20 ... 29 M6
Falcon Rd CHFD SO53 ... 206 F9
Falcon Rd HORN PO8 ... 256 A4
Falcon Sq ELGH SO50 ... 228 F3
Falcon Vw FUFL SO22 ... 183 L2
Falcon Wy BPWT SO32 ... 250 F2
  YTLY GU46 * ... 40 C8
Falconwood Cl FBDG SY6 ... 240 B2
Falkland Dr NBWY RG14 ... 16 C1
Falkland Garth NWBY RG14 ... 24 A8
Falkland Rd CHFD SO53 ... 228 E1
  CHIN RG24 ... 69 M2
  NEND PO2 ... 296 F5
  NWBY RG14 ... 24 A9
  WSHM SO15 ... 21 J2
Falklands Cl
  LSOL/BMARY PO13 ... 314 D1
Falklands Rd NEND PO2 * ... 296 G5
Falkner Rd FNM GU9 ... 96 A9
Falkners Cl FLEETN GU51 ... 56 F9
Fallow Crs HEND SO30 ... 250 D5
Fallowfield FLEETN GU51 ... 56 F9

Fallow Fld FUFL SO22 ... 183 L2
Fallowfield YTLY GU46 ... 40 C7
The Fallows NMIL/BTOS BH25 ... 327 K2
Falmouth Cl CBLY GU15 ... 58 F1
Falmouth Rd CHAM PO6 ... 274 B9
Falstaff Wy TOTT SO40 ... 246 C6
Fancy Rd BKME/WDN BH12 ... 321 K4
Fanshawe St SHAM SO14 ... 268 C5
Fantails ALTN GU34 ... 132 F5
Faraday Ct CHIN RG24 ... 69 N4
Faraday Rd CHIN RG24 ... 69 N4
  FARN GU14 ... 58 A3
  NWBY RG14 ... 17 G1
Farcroft Rd PSTN BH14 ... 321 K7
Farcrosse Cl SHST GU47 ... 41 K6
Fareham Dr YTLY GU46 ... 40 C7
Fareham Hts
  FHAM/PORC PO16 * ... 273 H8
Fareham Park Rd FHAM PO15 ... 272 A6
Fareham Rd FHAM/STUB PO14 ... 294 B1
Fareham Rd
  LSOL/BMARY PO13 ... 294 G4
  WHAM PO17 ... 252 E8
Faringdon Cl SHST GU47 ... 41 K5
Faringdon Rd WEND SO18 ... 249 M4
Farleigh Cl HAV PO9 ... 276 D5
Farleigh La OVTN RG25 ... 109 L1
Farleigh Ri BSTK RG21 ... 90 E1
Farleigh Rd BH/HW/K RG22 ... 90 D2
  FARM GU14 ... 90 A7
Farleigh Wallop Dr
  FLEETN GU51 ... 75 P1
Farley Cl ELGH SO50 ... 230 D3
  FUFL SO22 ... 183 G2
Farley Ct FARN GU14 * ... 76 C2
Farley La ROMY SO51 ... 188 H5
Farley Mount Rd RWIN SO21 ... 182 C5
Farley St STOK SO20 ... 139 N2
Farlington Av CHAM PO6 ... 275 L9
Farlington Rd NEND PO2 ... 296 C8
Farm Cl HLER SO31 ... 270 A8
  RGWD BH24 ... 282 E1
  YTLY GU46 ... 40 E9
Farm Ct FRIM GU16 * ... 58 E3
  WIMB BH21 ... 301 J1
Farmdene Cl
  CHCH/BSGR BH23 * ... 325 P7
Far Dr BPWT SO32 ... 210 A3
  FLEETN GU51 ... 56 E9
Far Meadow Wy
  EMRTH PO10 ... 299 K1
Farm Edge Rd
  FHAM/STUB PO14 ... 294 A8
Farmers Wk LYMN SO41 ... 328 D7
  WIMB BH21 ... 278 D8
Farmery Cl WEND SO18 ... 228 F8
Farm Ground Cl HTWY RG27 ... 72 B3
Farm House Cl
  FHAM/STUB PO14 ... 294 A8
Farmhouse Ms MTHA RG18 ... 25 P2
Farmhouse Wy HORN PO8 ... 256 A6
Farm La CHCH/BSGR BH23 ... 337 L1
  RFNM GU10 ... 94 G6
Farm Lane Cl WVILLE PO7 ... 275 M4
Farm La North
  NMIL/BTOS BH25 ... 327 J7
Farm La South
  NMIL/BTOS BH25 ... 327 J8
Farmlea Rd CHAM PO6 ... 296 B1
Farm Rd ASHV GU12 ... 76 D9
  FERN BH22 ... 280 D7
  FRIM GU16 ... 271 L8
  RAND SP11 ... 101 N4
  RWIN SO21 ... 163 L2
Farmside Gdns HSEA PO3 ... 297 H5
Farm View Av HORN PO8 ... 236 D7
Farm View Dr CHIN RG24 ... 70 B1
Farnborough Ga FARN GU14 * ... 58 B6
Farnborough Rd ALDT GU11 ... 2 B1
  FARN GU14 ... 58 A3
  FNM GU9 ... 96 D3
Farnborough St FARN GU14 ... 58 C8
Farnham By-Pass FNM GU9 ... 115 P7
Farnham La HASM GU27 ... 156 F6
Farnham Park Cl FNM GU9 ... 96 B5
Farnham Rd
  BKME/WDN BH12 ... 322 A8
  BOR GU35 ... 154 A2
  FLEETN GU51 ... 74 G3
  LISS GU33 ... 192 B5
  MFD/CHID GU8 ... 117 P5
  ODIM RG29 ... 72 E9
  PSF GU32 ... 191 P6
  RFNM GU10 ... 136 D6
Farnleys Md LYMN SO41 ... 329 L5
Faroe Cl CHIN RG24 ... 69 N3
Faroes Cl FHAM/STUB PO14 * ... 293 P6
Farrell Cl CBLY GU15 ... 58 A2
Farriers Cl FLEETS GU52 ... 95 J1
Farriers Fld OVTN RG25 ... 110 C2
Farriers La STOK SO20 ... 121 H5
Farriers Wk CGRT PO12 ... 13 H1
Farriers Wy WVILLE PO7 ... 276 C1
Farrier Wy FHAM/PORC PO16 ... 294 F3
Farringdon Rd HAV PO9 ... 276 B3
Farringdon Wy TADY RG26 ... 32 C6
Farringford Rd ITCH SO19 ... 249 M5
Farrs Av AND SP10 ... 5 F7
Farthingale Ter PSEA PO1 * ... 18 D6
Farthing Cl GPORT PO12 ... 12 B1
Farthing Flds BMT SO41 ... 154 F3
Farthing La PSEA PO1 ... 18 D6
Farthings Ga WVILLE PO7 ... 275 N7
The Farthings
  FHAM/STUB PO14 ... 293 J1
Farwell Cl CHCH/BSGR BH23 ... 324 G4
Farwell Rd BKME/WDN BH12 ... 321 L2
Fastnet Cl ROWN SO16 ... 227 J7
Fastnet Wy FHAM/STUB PO14 ... 293 P6
Fathersfield BROC SO42 ... 286 F8

Fathoms Reach HISD PO11 ... 318 E4
F Av FAWY SO45 ... 291 H3
Faversham Rd SHST GU47 ... 41 L5
Fawcett Rd ENEY PO4 ... 316 C5
  SBNE BH6 ... 327 H5
Fawconer Rd KSCL RG20 ... 48 C3
Fawley By-Pass FAWY SO45 ... 291 K6
Fawley Ct HAV PO9 ... 277 H5
Fawley Gn CHAR BH8 ... 323 K4
Fawley La ALTN GU34 ... 133 N8
  RWIN SO21 ... 184 F6
Fawley Rd FAWY SO45 ... 290 G4
  NEND PO2 ... 296 C4
  WSHM SO15 ... 247 L5
Fawn Crs HEND SO30 ... 250 D8
Fawn Dr ASHV GU12 ... 76 D9
Fawn Gdns NMIL/BTOS BH25 ... 327 K3
Fay Cl FHAM/STUB PO14 ... 294 A7
Fayre Rd FHAM/PORC PO16 ... 294 C2
Fayrewood Cha
  BH/HW/K RG22 ... 89 M4
Fearon Rd NEND PO2 ... 296 C7
Feathers La BSTK RG21 ... 7 F7
Feildon Cl KSCL RG20 ... 48 B4
Felbridge Cl FRIM GU16 ... 58 E3
Felders Mede HTWY RG27 ... 72 C3
Feld Wy CHIN RG24 ... 69 N3
Felix Rd GPORT PO12 ... 315 M1
Fell Cl HLER SO31 ... 270 C6
Fell Dr LSOL/BMARY PO13 ... 314 D2
Fellows Rd FARN GU14 ... 76 C3
Felmer Dr WINC SO23 ... 3 K6
Feltham Ct ROMY SO51 ... 204 G5
Felton Crs LYMN SO41 ... 328 D3
Felton Rd PSTN BH14 ... 321 H7
Felton Wk FHAM PO15 ... 271 J1
Fen Av FHAM/PORC PO16 ... 294 F2
Fencott Pl BSTK RG21 ... 6 E3
Fenleigh Cl NMIL/BTOS BH25 ... 327 K7
Fennel Cl CHIN RG24 ... 52 B8
  FARN GU14 ... 57 J9
  NWBY RG14 ... 24 G2
Fennel Gdns LYMN SO41 ... 329 K2
Fennell Cl WVILLE PO7 ... 275 M1
Fenton Rd SBNE BH6 ... 324 A9
Fenton Wy FRIM GU16 ... 58 B6
Ferbies FLEETS GU52 ... 74 D6
Ferguson Cl BSTK RG21 ... 90 C1
  BKME/WDN BH12 ... 322 B7
Fern Av CHCH/BSGR BH23 ... 324 C5
  EPSF GU31 ... 216 A2
  FBDG SP6 ... 239 N6
  FRIM GU16 ... 58 B6
Fern Bank WIMB BH21 ... 280 E2
Fern Barrow
  BKME/WDN BH12 ... 322 D1
Fernbrae Cl RFNM GU10 ... 116 B8
Fern Cl CHCH/BSGR BH23 ... 324 C5
  EPSF GU31 ... 216 A2
  FBDG SP6 ... 239 N6
  FRIM GU16 ... 58 B6
Ferncroft Cl
  FHAM/STUB PO14 ... 294 A8
Ferncroft Gdns NBNE BH10 ... 322 D2
Ferncroft Rd NBNE BH10 ... 322 D2
Ferndale HEND SO30 ... 250 D7
  WVILLE PO7 ... 275 P3
Ferndale Ct STHA RG19 ... 25 M4
Ferndale Ms
  LSOL/BMARY PO13 ... 294 F5
Ferndale Rd AND SP10 ... 102 C1
  FLEETS GU52 ... 74 C7
  NMIL/BTOS BH25 ... 327 K3
  TOTT SO40 ... 267 K1
Ferndene Wy WEND SO18 ... 249 H5
Ferndown Cl BH/HW/K RG22 ... 89 L7
Ferndown Gdns FARN GU14 ... 57 M9
Ferndown, Stour & Forest
  Trail WIMB BH21 ... 279 L7
  HAV PO9 ... 277 H8
Fernfield Ms LSOL/BMARY ... 294 F5
Fernham Rd ALTN GU34 * ... 151 L1
Ferney La NARL SO24 ... 130 B8
Fern Gale NMIL/BTOS BH25 ... 327 J4
Fernheath Cl BWD BH11 ... 322 A5
Fernheath Rd BWD BH11 ... 322 A4
Fernhill Cl BLKW GU17 ... 57 M4
  CFDH BH17 ... 321 J2
  FNM GU9 ... 96 B5
Fernhill Dr FNM GU9 ... 96 B5
Fernhill La BLKW GU17 ... 57 N4
  NMIL/BTOS BH25 ... 327 J1
Fern Hill La ROMY SO51 ... 181 H6
Fernhill Pl HTWY RG27 ... 52 C8
Fernhill Rd FARN GU14 ... 57 M7
  NMIL/BTOS BH25 ... 327 J3
Fernhills Rd FAWY SO45 ... 268 D9
Fernhill Wk BLKW GU17 * ... 57 N4
Fernhurst Cl HISD PO11 ... 318 D5
Fernie Cl FHAM/STUB PO14 ... 293 P7
Feriehurst CBLY GU15 ... 58 E1
Fernlea BOR GU35 ... 155 H5
Fern La HAV PO9 ... 97 H5
Fernlea Av FERN BH22 ... 302 C4
Fernlea Cl FERN BH22 ... 302 C4
  RGWD BH24 ... 281 L5
Fernlea Gdns FERN BH22 ... 302 C4
  ROWN SO16 ... 227 M7
Fernlea Wy FAWY SO45 ... 267 P7
Fernleigh Ri FERN GU16 ... 59 H6
Fern Rd FAWY SO45 ... 268 B7
  ITCH SO19 ... 249 H9
Fernside Av PSTN BH14 ... 321 H8
Fernside Rd FERN BH22 ... 302 D7
  MOOR/WNTN BH9 ... 322 D7
  PLE BH15 ... 320 G8
Ferns Md FNM GU9 ... 116 A1
The Ferns FNM GU9 ... 96 C4
Fernway Cl WIMB BH21 ... 278 G6
Fernwood Cl RGWD BH24 ... 281 P4
Fernwood Crs WEND SO18 ... 249 K6
Ferrell Fld HTWY RG27 ... 71 N3
Ferrier Gv NWBY RG14 ... 17 G7
Ferris Av CHAR BH8 ... 323 J5
Ferris Cl CHAR BH8 ... 323 J5

Ferris Pl CHAR BH8 ... 323 K5
Ferrol Rd GPORT PO12 ... 315 N2
Ferry Point LYMN SO41 * ... 329 N5
Ferry Rd FHAM/PORC PO16 ... 317 M5
  FAWY SO45 ... 268 B7
  HISD PO11 ... 318 A4
  PLE BH15 ... 332 D2
  SBNE BH6 ... 336 D3
Ferry Wy CCLF BH13 ... 333 K8
Festing Gv ENEY PO4 ... 317 H6
Festing Rd ENEY PO4 ... 317 H6
Festival Sq BSTK RG21 ... 7 F6
Feversham Av CHAR BH8 ... 323 L6
Fey Rd GPORT PO12 ... 12 E1
Fibbards Rd BROC SO42 ... 286 F8
Fiddlers Fld ALTN GU34 ... 132 B1
Field Cl FHAM/STUB PO14 ... 294 F4
  HLER SO31 ... 270 C8
  ROMY SO51 ... 204 E6
  ROWN SO16 ... 228 E7
  RWIN SO21 ... 185 L8
  THLE RG7 ... 27 K5
Fielden Cl NBAD SO52 ... 205 K9
Field End FNM GU9 ... 96 F7
  WINC SO23 ... 145 K9
Fielders Ct ALTN GU34 ... 152 N6
The Fielders HTWY RG27 ... 39 P6
Fielders Wy ROMY SO51 ... 225 H2
Fieldfare Av YTLY GU46 ... 40 B8
Fieldfare Cl HORN PO8 ... 236 C8
Fieldfare Ct TOTT SO40 ... 246 A3
Field Gate Dr KSCL RG20 ... 48 B3
Fieldhouse Dr
  LSOL/BMARY PO13 ... 294 D9
Fielding Gdns CWTH RG45 ... 41 J2
Fielding Rd FHAM PO15 ... 271 J1
  SHST GU47 ... 41 M8
Field La FRIM GU16 ... 58 D4
Fieldmore Rd GPORT PO12 ... 315 M1
Field Pl LIPH GU30 ... 175 J4
  NMIL/BTOS BH25 ... 326 F7
  VWD BH31 ... 258 E3
Fieldridge NWBY RG14 ... 14 C4
Fields Cl FAWY SO45 ... 57 N4
Fields Cl FAWY SO45 ... 290 C8
Field Stores Ap ALDT GU11 ... 3 H1
Field Vw CHFD SO53 ... 206 B7
Field Wk LYMN SO41 ... 329 K2
Fieldway FLEETN GU51 ... 74 E4
  HASM GU27 ... 157 H6
  RGWD BH24 ... 282 F1
Field Wy ASHV GU12 ... 97 L1
  CHCH/BSGR BH23 ... 325 P6
  FBDG SP6 ... 221 J9
  FRIM GU16 ... 58 D4
  ROWN SO16 ... 228 E7
  RWIN SO21 ... 185 L8
  WIMB BH21 ... 300 A5
  WVILLE PO7 ... 255 H7
Fifield La WINCH GU34 ... 116 C8
Fifth Av CHAM PO6 ... 296 G1
  HAV PO9 ... 277 H8
Fifth Rd NBWY RG14 ... 16 A6
Fifth St PSEA PO1 ... 317 H1
  STHA RG19 ... 31 L1
Filmer Cl LSOL/BMARY PO13 ... 295 H9
Filmorehill La ALTN GU34 ... 189 H5
Filnham Cl LYTON SO41 ... 206 A3
Filton Rd LYMN SO41 ... 329 K3
Fincham End Dr CWTH RG45 ... 40 G2
Finchampstead Rd EWKG RG40 ... 39 P1
Finch Cl TADY RG26 ... 34 D7
Finchdean Rd HAV PO9 ... 276 D6
Finches Gn ALTN GU34 ... 132 F5
The Finches SD/PW SO17 ... 248 D1
Finchfield Av BWD BH11 ... 301 P7
Finchleigh Pl ODIM RG29 * ... 93 L1
Finchmead La PSF GU32 ... 215 H1
Finch Rd ENEY PO4 ... 317 M5
Finch's La RWIN SO21 ... 185 P8
Finch Wy THLE RG7 ... 27 K4
Findhorn Ct SHST GU47 ... 41 L7
The Findings FARN GU14 ... 57 M5
Findon Rd GPORT PO12 ... 295 M9
Fingle Dr AND SP10 ... 102 C2
Finisterre Sq
  FHAM/STUB PO14 ... 293 P5
Finkley Rd RAND SP11 ... 83 K6
Finley Cl TOTT SO40 ... 245 P2
Fintry Pl FARN GU14 ... 249 L8
Finzi Cl ITCH SO19 ... 249 L8
Fiona Cl WINC SO23 ... 23 J5
Fir Acre Rd ASHV GU12 ... 76 F6
Fir Av NMIL/BTOS BH25 ... 327 K5
Firbank Rd MOOR/WNTN BH9 ... 323 H7
Fir Cl FERN BH22 ... 302 C4
  FLEETN GU51 ... 74 C4
  LYND SO43 ... 286 E6
  STHA RG19 ... 32 E1
Fir Copse Rd WVILLE PO7 ... 275 M7
Fir Croft Dr CHFD SO53 ... 206 F8
Fir Dr BLKW GU17 ... 57 L2
Fircrest Cl ROWN SO16 ... 227 M7
Fircrest Rd BH/HW/K RG22 ... 89 K4
Firefly Cl LSOL/BMARY PO13 ... 314 E3
Fire Station Rd ALDT GU11 ... 76 A9
Firfield Rd FNM GU9 ... 116 A3
Fir Gdn Dr YTLY GU46 ... 40 D8
Fir Gv BOR GU35 ... 153 N7
Firgrove Cl NBAD SO52 ... 205 J9
Firgrove Crs HSEA PO3 ... 297 H4
Firgrove Hl FNM GU9 ... 116 C1
Firgrove La THLE RG7 ... 32 B5
Firgrove Pde FARN GU14 * ... 58 A7
Firgrove Rd BOR GU35 ... 153 N7
  FARN GU14 ... 58 A9
  HTWY RG27 ... 40 B3
  NBAD SO52 ... 205 K9
  WSHM SO15 ... 247 N4
Firlands Ri HAV PO9 ... 276 A9
Firmain Rd BKME/WDN BH12 ... 321 M3
Firmount Cl LYMN SO41 ... 328 E6
Firmstone Rd WINC SO23 ... 3 J4
Fir Rd TOTT SO40 ... 245 P9
Firs Av HORN PO8 ... 256 A8

Firs Cl FARN GU14 76 B2
Firs Crs WINC SO23 145 H8
Firs Dr HEND SO30 250 A5
Fir's End THLE RG7 27 J5
Firs Glen Rd FERN BH22 280 E7
MOOR/WNTN BH9 322 D7
VWD BH31 258 F5
Firshill CHCH/BSGR BH23 326 A6
Firs La ODIM RG29 93 J1
PSTN BH14 333 K3
First Av CHAM PO6 297 H1
HAV PO9 15 K4
HORN PO8 236 C9
THLE RG7 34 D4
WSHM SO15 247 H4
The Firs AND SP10 102 C2
BMTH BH1 9 G2
FUFL SO22 22 A1
LIPH GU30 175 J4
LSOL/BMARY PO13 295 H8
NTHA RG18 25 L3
ROWN SO16 228 B8
First Marine Av
NMIL/BTOS BH25 327 H8
First St FAWY SO45 290 G1
STHA RG19 31 M1
First St East STHA RG19 31 M1
Firs Wy DEAN RG23 68 E5
Firsway WHCH RG28 85 L6
Firth Cl THLE RG7 35 J6
Fir Tree Av HASM GU27 156 C7
Fir Tree Cl ELGH SO50 230 C5
RGWD BH24 281 K7
Firtree Cl SHST GU47 40 G6
Fir Tree Cnr TADY RG26 33 P4
Firtree Crs LYMN SO41 327 P4
Firtree Gdns HORN PO8 256 C6
Firtree Gv FAWY SO45 * 290 C1
Fir Tree Hl FBDG SP6 239 N5
Fir Tree La CHCH/BSGR BH23 325 P6
ELGH SO50 230 B5
NWBY RG14 25 H3
Fir Tree Rd HISD PO11 318 G5
TOTT SO40 244 G4
Firtree Wy FLEETS GU52 74 E4
ITCH SO19 249 K6
Fir Vale Rd BMTH BH1 8 E3
Firway GSHT GU26 155 M3
Firwood Cl CHFD SO53 206 E5
Fisgard Rd GPORT PO12 315 M1
Fisher Cl AND SP10 5 K3
FHAM/STUB PO14 293 P6
Fisher La ALDT GU11 3 J7
Fisherman's Av BOSC BH5 335 P2
Fisherman's Bank
CHCH/BSGR BH23 337 J1
Fishermans Quay
LYMN SO41 * 329 M3
Fishermans Rd PLE BH15 332 E2
The Fishermans EMRTH PO10 299 N1
Fishermans Wk HISD PO11 319 L6
Fishermen's Cl ALDT GU11 76 D7
Fisher Rd LSOL/BMARY PO13 294 G6
Fishers Fld RAND SP11 84 B1
Fishers Gv CHAM PO6 297 N2
Fishers Hl FHAM PO15 271 N8
Fisher's Rd TOTT SO40 246 E5
Fishery La HISD PO11 319 J6
Fishlake Mdw ROMY SO51 204 D4
Fish La RWIN SO21 163 L2
Fiske Cl BH/HW/K RG22 68 F8
Fitzgerald Cl FHAM PO15 271 J2
Fitzharris Av
MOOR/WNTN BH9 322 G8
Fitzherbert Rd CHAM PO6 297 M2
Fitzherbert Sp CHAM PO6 297 N2
Fitzherbert St PSEA PO1 316 E2
Fitzhugh Dr FLEETN GU51 * 74 B1
Fitzhugh Pl WSHM SO15 248 B4
Fitzhugh St SHAM SO14 * 20 C3
Fitzmaurice Rd
CHCH/BSGR BH23 324 C7
Fitzpain Cl FERN BH22 302 D6
Fitzpain Rd FERN BH22 302 D6
Fitzpatrick Ct CHAM PO6 * 274 F9
Fitzroy Cl ROWN SO16 228 B5
Fitzroy Dr LSOL/BMARY PO13 314 D1
Fitzroy Rd FLEETN GU51 74 A3
Fitzwilliam Av
FHAM/STUB PO14 293 N7
Fitzwilliam Cl BWD BH11 301 N8
Fitzwygram Crs HAV PO9 15 F2
Five Acres Cl BOR GU35 154 C3
Five Ash Rd ALTN GU34 150 B4
Five Bells La STOK SO20 139 M3
Five Bridges Rd WINC SO23 183 N3
Five Elms Dr ROMY SO51 204 F7
Fivefields Cl WINC SO23 23 J6
Fivefields Rd WINC SO23 23 K6
Five Heads Rd HORN PO8 256 A3
Five Post La GPORT PO12 315 M2
Flaghead Chine Rd
CCLF BH13 333 N5
Flaghead Rd CCLF BH13 333 N4
Flag Staff Gn GPORT PO12 315 P2
Flagstaff Sq STHA RG19 25 P5
Flag Wk HORN PO8 255 P6
Flambard Av
CHCH/BSGR BH23 324 D6
Flambard Rd PSTN BH14 333 L1
Flamborough Cl ROWN SO16 247 H1
Flamingo Ct
FHAM/PORC PO16 295 K1
Flanders Rd HEND SO30 250 B3
The Flashett RSAL SP5 158 C1
Flathouse Rd PSEA PO1 316 E1
The Flats BLKW GU17 57 J1
Flaxfield Ct BSTK RG21 6 D6
Flaxfield Rd BSTK RG21 6 D6
Flaxfields End FBDG SP6 240 C2
Flazen Cl BWD BH11 321 M1
Flecker Cl NTHA RG18 25 M2
Fleet Cl LSOL/BMARY PO13 295 H8
Fleet End Bottom HLER SO31 292 F1
Fleetend Cl HAV PO9 276 E4
Fleet End Rd HLER SO31 292 F1
Fleet Hl EWKG RG40 39 M4
Fleet La EWKG RG40 39 L4
Fleet Rd FLEETN GU51 74 C3
HTWY RG27 55 J7
Fleet's Cnr CFDH BH17 320 D5
Fleets La PLE BH15 320 E6
Fleet Ter RWIN SO21 * 207 K4
Fleet Wy PSEA PO1 316 D2
Fleetwood Cl NWBY RG14 24 G2
Fleming Av NBAD SO52 205 L9
Fleming Cl FARN GU14 58 C7
FHAM PO15 271 K6
RAND SP11 79 P1
Fleming Pl ROMY SO51 204 D5
RWIN SO21 207 P4
Fleming Rd FUFL SO22 164 D4
NWBY RG14 17 G1
ROWN SO16 228 F8
Flensburg Cl AND SP10 82 D8
Fletcher Cl BSTK RG21 69 J8
FAWY SO45 267 P7
NBNE BH10 * 322 D4
Fletcher Rd NBNE BH10 322 D4
Fletchers Fld LIPH GU30 175 J4
Fletchwood La TOTT SO40 245 M9
Fletchwood Rd TOTT SO40 245 P5
Fleur-de-Lys Pk LYMN SO41 * 309 M7
Fleuret Cl FAWY SO45 290 C1
Flexford Cl CHFD SO53 206 C4
KSCL RG20 29 N9
Flexford Gdns HAV PO9 15 J1
Flexford La LYMN SO41 328 C1
Flexford Rd NBAD SO52 205 N7
Flinders Cl AND SP10 103 K1
Flinders Ct ENEY PO4 317 K6
Flint Cl AND SP10 102 B4
ITCH SO19 249 N7
Flint La RAND SP11 81 K3
Flint St SSEA PO5 19 F6
Floating Bridge Rd
SHAM SO14 21 J7
The Flood RSAL SP5 138 A9
Floral Farm WIMB BH21 301 H3
Floral Wy AND SP10 102 B4
NTHA RG18 25 N2
Floreat Gdns NWBY RG14 16 A5
Florence Cl ROMY SO51 225 H2
YTLY GU46 40 D8
Florence Ct AND SP10 82 F8
Florence Gdns NTHA RG18 25 K2
Florence Portal Cl WHCH RG28 86 B6
Florence Rd BOSC BH5 335 L2
FLEETS GU52 74 E6
ITCH SO19 248 F9
PSTN BH14 321 L8
SHST GU47 41 M7
SSEA PO5 316 F7
Florence Wy CHIN RG24 68 F4
Florentine Wy WVILLE PO7 276 A2
The Florins FHAM/STUB PO14 270 G9
WVILLE PO7 275 N7
Floriston Gdns
NMIL/BTOS BH25 327 M4
Florrie Pl ALTN GU34 * 151 L5
Floud La PSF GU32 188 D9
Flowerdown Cl TOTT SO40 246 A3
Flowers Cl HLER SO31 269 N7
Flowers La ROMY SO51 202 D7
Flume Rd FAWY SO45 291 L5
Flushards LYMN SO41 329 M4
Focus Wy AND SP10 5 K1
Foden Rd ALDT GU11 2 E4
Foldsgate Cl LYND SO43 264 F4
Folkestone Rd HSEA PO3 317 J1
Folland Cl NBAD SO52 205 L9
Folly Cl FLEETS GU52 74 D5
Folly Farm La RGWD BH24 282 A3
Folly Fld BPWT SO32 232 B5
Folly Hl FNM GU9 96 A6
Folly La PSF GU32 215 M2
TADY RG26 52 C1
THLE RG7 27 H2
THLE RG7 36 C9
Folly La North FNM GU9 96 B4
Folly La South FNM GU9 96 A5
Folly Rbt AND SP10 4 C2
The Folly NWBY RG14 17 G6
Font Cl FHAM/STUB PO14 271 J7
Fontley Rd FHAM PO15 271 N7
Fontmell Rd BDST BH18 320 E2
Fontwell Cl ASHV GU12 3 K2
TOTT SO40 246 A2
Fontwell Dr ALTN GU34 132 F7
Fontwell Gdns ELGH SO50 230 D5
Fontwell Ms WVILLE PO7 276 B1
Fontwell Rd NWBY RG14 17 H6
SSEA PO5 316 F6
Foord Rd HEND SO30 250 A6
Football Gn LYND SO43 244 C8
Footner Cl ROMY SO51 204 G3
Footners La
CHCH/BSGR BH23 324 G5
Forbes Cha SHST GU47 41 L7
Forbes Cl ROWN SO16 227 K6
Forbes Rd WINC SO23 145 J8
Forbury Rd SSEA PO5 19 J4
Ford Av CHFD SO53 206 F9
Ford Cl FERN BH22 302 F1
Forders Cl RSAL SP5 199 P8
Fordingbridge Rd ENEY PO4 317 K5
FBDG SP6 239 P4
Fordington Rd FUFL SO22 22 A3
Ford La FERN BH22 302 G1
HTWY RG27 38 D2
OVTN RG25 92 G4
RFNM GU10 116 B4
Ford Rd GPORT PO12 315 K2
Fore Br EPSF GU31 215 M3
Forefield Dr BH/HW/K RG22 89 L6
The Forehead THLE RG7 36 E2
Foreland Cl CHCH/BSGR BH23 324 B3
Foreland Ct HISD PO11 319 J6
Foreman Pk ASHV GU12 97 P1
Foreman Rd ASHV GU12 97 P2
Foreshore North FAWY SO45 291 K3
Foreshore South FAWY SO45 291 K4
Forest Av HORN PO8 255 P8
Forest Cl BPWT SO32 232 C9
CHCH/BSGR BH23 325 P6
CHFD SO53 206 E5
HORN PO8 255 P8
NBAD SO52 205 J8
TADY RG26 33 P4
VWD BH31 259 K6
Forest Cnr LISS GU33 173 M8
Forest Ct NMIL/BTOS BH25 327 K5
Forestdale GSHT GU26 156 C2
Forest Dean FLEETN GU51 56 F9
Forest Dr CHIN RG24 52 A9
RFNM GU10 116 C6
TDWTH SP9 79 J4
Forest Edge FAWY SO45 291 J6
Forest Edge Cl LYMN SO41 308 A5
RGWD BH24 281 K4
Forest Edge Rd RGWD BH24 283 J4
Forest End Rd FLEETS GU52 74 C6
WVILLE PO7 275 M3
Forest End Rd SHST GU47 40 G5
Forester Rd BPWT SO32 253 L2
Foresters Ga FAWY SO45 312 G1
Foresters Rd FAWY SO45 291 H7
Foresters Wy CWTH RG45 41 N3
Forest Front FAWY SO45 290 B1
Forest Gdns BPWT SO32 232 C9
LYND SO43 264 F5
Forest Ga FAWY SO45 313 H1
Forest Gate Gdns LYMN SO41 329 K6
Forest Gld RFNM GU10 115 M7
Forest Glade Cl BROC SO42 286 D8
Forest Hall BROC SO42 286 G8
Forest Hills CBLY GU15 58 A1
Forest Hills Ct RGWD BH24 283 H3
Forest Hills Dr WEND SO18 228 G9
Forest Hill Wy FAWY SO45 268 B8
Forestlake Av RGWD BH24 283 H3
Forest La BOR GU35 154 D2
FAWY SO45 290 D3
RAND SP11 103 K4
RGWD BH24 283 J3
TADY RG26 34 E8
VWD BH31 258 E3
WHAM PO17 272 F2
Forest Lane Cl LIPH GU30 175 H3
Forest Links Rd FERN BH22 280 B8
Forest Md WVILLE PO7 255 H8
Forest Meadow FAWY SO45 290 C1
Forest Oak Dr
NMIL/BTOS BH25 327 J2
Forest Park Rd BROC SO42 286 E7
Forest Pines NMIL/BTOS BH25 327 J2
Forest Ri CHCH/BSGR BH23 325 P5
LISS GU33 173 M9
Forest Rd BOR GU35 154 A7
BPWT SO32 232 D9
CCLF BH13 334 A4
CHCH/BSGR BH23 306 A3
CHFD SO53 206 F5
CWTH RG45 41 K1
FBDG SP6 222 A1
FERN BH22 280 F6
LISS GU33 173 K6
RGWD BH24 284 B4
RSAL SP5 223 M4
WVILLE PO7 254 C7
Forestside Av HAV PO9 276 G5
Forestside Gdns RGWD BH24 260 G9
The Forestside VWD BH31 259 K5
Forest Vw BROC SO42 286 D8
SHAM SO14 20 D6
Forest View Cl
MOOR/WNTN BH9 322 G5
Forest View Dr WIMB BH21 302 A2
Forest View Rd
MOOR/WNTN BH9 322 G4
Forest Wk NMIL/BTOS BH25 326 F2
Forest Wy CHCH/BSGR BH23 325 P5
LSOL/BMARY PO13 295 H7
LYMN SO41 328 D6
TOTT SO40 245 N1
WIMB BH21 302 A3
Forge Cl FNM GU9 96 D8
HLER SO31 270 A1
STOK SO20 161 M4
TADY RG26 52 B3
Forge Fld AND SP10 4 E2
Forge La ALDT GU11 75 N6
Forge Rd BOR GU35 134 E9
FAWY SO45 313 H1
Forneth Gdns FHAM PO15 293 P1
Forster Rd SHAM SO14 248 C4
Forsyth Gdns NBNE BH10 322 C6
Forsythia Cl FAWY SO45 290 C2
HAV PO9 277 H6
HEND SO30 250 B3
Forsythia Pl ITCH SO19 * 249 H6
Forsythia Wk BSTK RG21 69 M4
Fort Cumberland Rd
ENEY PO4 317 M5
Fortescue Rd
BKME/WDN BH12 321 M5
TWDS BH3 322 G9
Fort Fareham Rd
FHAM/STUB PO14 294 D3
Forth Cl CHFD SO53 206 D8
FARN GU14 57 L7
FHAM/STUB PO14 293 P6
Forth Ct AND SP10 82 G9
Fort Hl DEAN RG23 68 F6
Forthill Rd STOK SO20 120 G5
Forties Cl
FHAM/STUB PO14 * 293 P5
Forton Cl NBNE BH10 322 E3
Forton Rd GPORT PO12 315 M2
PSEA PO1 316 G2
Fort Rd GPORT PO12 315 L7
ITCH SO19 248 G8
Fortrose Cl SHST GU47 41 L7
Fortunes Wy HAV PO9 275 P9
Forty Acre La EPSF GU31 237 P1
Forum Cl DEAN RG23 68 E7
The Forum FHAM PO15 * 271 L4
Forward Dr LYMN SO41 329 J5
Fosseway CWTH RG45 40 G1
Foster Cl FHAM/STUB PO14 294 A5
Foster Rd GPORT PO12 12 B4
PSEA PO1 316 F2
Foul La ALTN GU34 150 A1
Founders Wy
LSOL/BMARY PO13 295 H7
Foundry Crs HLER SO31 269 P2
Foundry La HASM GU27 156 F7
WSHM SO15 247 M4
Foundry Rd RAND SP11 102 A6
RSAL SP5 199 P6
Fountain Ct HEND SO30 250 B5
Fountain Rd PSEA PO1 296 C9
Fountains Cl CHIN RG24 69 K3
Fountain St PSEA PO1 19 G2
Fountain Wy
CHCH/BSGR BH23 324 F9
Four Acre HEND SO30 250 G5
Four Acre Coppice HTWY RG27 72 B3
Four Lanes Cl CHIN RG24 70 B1
Four Oaks KSCL RG20 29 N8
Fourposts Hl WSHM SO15 20 A2
Fourshells Cl FAWY SO45 291 H7
Fourth Av CHAM PO6 296 G1
HAV PO9 15 K4
Fourth St PSEA PO1 317 H2
STHA RG19 31 L1
Fourways RAND SP11 * 102 F7
Four Wells Rd WIMB BH21 279 J7
Fowey Cl CHFD SO53 206 D6
Fowey Ct GPORT PO12 * 295 N9
The Fowey FAWY SO45 290 G7
Fowler Av FARN GU14 75 P2
Fowler Rd FARN GU14 75 N2
Fowler's Rd ALDT GU11 76 B6
Fowlers Rd HEND SO30 250 B3
Fowler's Wk ROWN SO16 227 P2
Foxbury Cl FAWY SO45 268 C8
Foxbury La EMRTH PO10 277 P6
LSOL/BMARY PO13 295 H5
Foxbury Rd RGWD BH24 303 L2
Fox Cl ELGH SO50 229 P2
THLE RG7 27 J4
Foxcombe Cl BPWT SO32 232 E6
Foxcote Gdns
NMIL/BTOS BH25 * 327 H4
Foxcott Cl ITCH SO19 269 H2
Foxcotte Cl AND SP10 82 B9
Foxcotte La AND SP10 81 P9
Foxcotte Rd AND SP10 82 B8
Foxcott Gv HAV PO9 276 F5
Fox Ct ASHV GU12 76 D9
The Fox Cover STOK SO20 121 H5
Fox Cft FLEETS GU52 74 D7
Foxcroft Dr FAWY SO45 290 D6
WIMB BH21 279 K9
Foxdown OVTN RG25 86 G1
Fox Dr YTLY GU46 40 E7
Foxes Cl VWD BH31 258 F5
WVILLE PO7 275 N4
Foxes La ROMY SO51 202 F9
Fox Farm RAND SP11 100 E7
Fox Fld LYMN SO41 328 D6
Foxglade FAWY SO45 313 H1
Foxglove Cl BH/HW/K RG22 89 L4
CHCH/BSGR BH23 325 N7
Foxglove Dr BOR GU35 154 B6
Foxglove Pl
NMIL/BTOS BH25 327 M3
Foxgloves FHAM/PORC PO16 11 J1
The Foxgloves HEND SO30 250 D6
Foxglove Wy NTHA RG18 25 N2
Foxhayes La FAWY SO45 313 H1
Fox Heath FARN GU14 75 K1
Foxhill Gv FHAM/PORC PO16 295 M2
Foxhills TOTT SO40 246 A7
VWD BH31 259 H4
Foxhills Cl TOTT SO40 246 A8
Fox Hills La ASHV GU12 77 H9
Foxholes Rd PLE BH15 321 H6
SBNE BH6 336 D2
Foxhunter Wy STHA RG19 25 J4
Foxhurst Rd ASHV GU12 76 F7
Foxlands FAWY SO45 313 H1
Fox La DEAN RG23 67 P9
FUFL SO22 183 L1
HTWY RG27 40 A6
WIMB BH21 279 L9
Foxlea Gdns GPORT PO12 315 M1
Foxley Cl BLKW GU17 41 K9
Foxley Dr HSEA PO3 297 K5
Foxmoor Cl DEAN RG23 67 N9
Fox Pond La LYMN SO41 329 J5
Fox Rd HASM GU27 156 D7
RFNM GU10 116 C3
Fox's Furlong CHIN RG24 52 C9
Fox's La KSCL RG20 48 B4
Fox's Wk FAWY SO45 313 H1
Foxtail Dr FAWY SO45 268 B9
Foxtail Gdns RAND SP11 79 P1
Fox Wy RFNM GU10 95 M3
Foxwood FLEETN GU51 74 F1
Foxwood Av
CHCH/BSGR BH23 337 K1
Fox Yd FNM GU9 96 B9
Foxy Paddock FAWY SO45 313 H1
Foye La FLEETS GU52 74 E7
Foy Gdns HLER SO31 270 C9
Foyle Pk BSTK RG21 90 D1
Foyle Rd CHFD SO53 206 D7
Frampton Cl
NMIL/BTOS BH25 327 L2
RWIN SO21 207 P4
Frampton Pl RGWD BH24 282 E2
Frampton Rd
MOOR/WNTN BH9 322 G7
Frampton Wy TOTT SO40 246 D5
WINC SO23 145 K9
Frances Rd BMTH BH1 9 K2
BSTK RG21 69 K8
WVILLE PO7 275 M7
The Frances NTHA RG18 25 N3
Francis Av BWD BH11 321 M1
ENEY PO4 317 H5
Francis Cl LSOL/BMARY PO13 314 E3
Francis Gdns WINC SO23 165 J5
Francis Pl FHAM/STUB PO14 294 B7
Francis Rd BKME/WDN BH12 321 N7
HORN PO8 236 C9
Frankland Crs PSTN BH14 321 N9
Frankland Ter EMRTH PO10 299 N1
Franklin Av HTWY RG27 55 H6
TADY RG26 34 A5
Franklin Rd
LSOL/BMARY PO13 314 G1
MOOR/WNTN BH9 322 G4
NMIL/BTOS BH25 327 L3
Franklyn Av ITCH SO19 249 J7
Frankston Rd SBNE BH6 336 A2
Franks Wy BKME/WDN BH12 321 K5
Frankton Wy GPORT PO12 13 G1
Fraser Cl CHIN RG24 70 C6
ROWN SO16 227 K6
Fraser Md SHST GU47 41 M8
Fraser Rd BKME/WDN BH12 321 P3
HAV PO9 14 C3
LSOL/BMARY PO13 294 G5
NEND PO2 296 D7
SSEA PO5 19 J4
WINC SO23 145 J8
Frater La GPORT PO12 295 L8
Fratton Rd PSEA PO1 316 G2
Fratton Wy ELGH SO50 230 C3
ENEY PO4 317 H3
Frayslea FAWY SO45 268 C9
Freda Rd CHCH/BSGR BH23 324 D9
Freda Routh Gdns ELGH SO50 230 D2
Frederica Rd
MOOR/WNTN BH9 322 E7
Frederick St ALDT GU11 2 D3
SHAM SO14 248 D5
Freedom Ct FAWY SO45 268 C6
Freegrounds Av HEND SO30 250 C5
Freegrounds Cl HEND SO30 250 C5
Freegrounds Rd HEND SO30 250 C5
Freelands Dr FLEETS GU52 74 B7
Freemans Cl WIMB BH21 279 K8
Freemans La WIMB BH21 279 K9
Freemantle Cl BSTK RG21 7 J1
ITCH SO19 249 H6
Freemantle Common Rd
ITCH SO19 249 H6
Freemantle Rd GPORT PO12 315 M1
Freestone Rd SSEA PO5 316 F6
Free St BPWT SO32 232 B4
Fremantle Rd RAND SP11 79 M4
Frenches La ROMY SO51 203 H4
French Gdns BLKW GU17 57 L1
Frenchies Vw WVILLE PO7 254 G7
Frenchmans Creek
FLEETS GU52 74 B8
Frenchmans Rd PSF GU32 215 L1
Frenchmoor La RSAL SP5 177 P4
French Rd CFDH BH17 320 D3
LISS GU33 174 A4
French St PSEA PO1 * 18 C6
SHAM SO14 20 D7
Frendstaple Rd WVILLE PO7 276 A5
Frensham Av FLEETN GU51 74 F3
Frensham Cl HEND SO30 250 C5
NBNE BH10 322 E4
YTLY GU46 40 C8
Frensham Ct RFNM GU10 116 B6
Frensham Heights Rd
RFNM GU10 116 A8
Frensham La BOR GU35 154 D2
RFNM GU10 136 A7
Frensham Rd ENEY PO4 317 H4
RFNM GU10 116 D7
Frensham V RFNM GU10 116 C6
Frere Av FLEETN GU51 74 B5
Frescade Crs BSTK RG21 69 K9
Freshfield Gdns WVILLE PO7 275 N2
Freshfield Rd WSHM SO15 247 M4
Freshfield Sq WSHM SO15 247 M4
Freshwater Rd CHAM PO6 296 G2
CHCH/BSGR BH23 325 N9
Freshwood Dr YTLY GU46 56 D1
Friarscroft HLER SO31 269 K3
Friars Cft TOTT SO40 245 P1
Friars Fld FNM GU9 96 B8
Friarsgate WINC SO23 23 F4
Friars Pond Rd FHAM PO15 272 A9
Friars Rd CHCH/BSGR BH23 325 M9
ELGH SO50 229 H3
NWBY RG14 16 E7
Friars Wk NMIL/BTOS BH25 327 J7
Friars Wy WEND SO18 228 F8
Friary Cl GPORT PO12 315 N7
Friary Gdns WINC SO23 22 D6
Friend Av ASHV GU12 97 K2
Friesian Cl FLEETN GU51 56 E9
Frimley Green Rd FRIM GU16 58 D6
Frimley Grove Gdns
FRIM GU16 58 C4
Frimley High St FRIM GU16 58 C4
Frimley Rd ASHV GU12 76 F3
CBLY GU15 58 A3
Frimley Sq FRIM GU16 58 D4
Fritham Cl TOTT SO40 246 A4
Fritham Gdns CHAR BH8 323 K4
Fritham Rd WEND SO18 249 L3
Frith End Rd ALTN GU34 135 J2
Frith Hill Rd FRIM GU16 58 F4
Frith La WHAM PO17 252 E5
Frithmead Cl BSTK RG21 90 C1
Frobisher Av
BKME/WDN BH12 321 P3
Frobisher Cl
CHCH/BSGR BH23 325 K9
LSOL/BMARY PO13 314 G2
RGWD BH24 282 G1
Frobisher Gdns
EMRTH PO10 299 M1
ITCH SO19 249 L7
Frobisher Gv
FHAM/PORC PO16 295 N2
Froddington Rd SSEA PO5 19 K4
Frodsham Wy SHST GU47 41 M4
Froghall FAWY SO45 268 B9
Frogham Hl FBDG SP6 240 G4
Froghole La STOK SO20 161 L4
Frog La FBDG SP6 240 C4
HTWY RG27 53 L6
OVTN RG25 70 G7
TADY RG26 35 J9

Frogmore *FHAM/STUB* PO14 .... 294 A1
Frogmore La *BLKW* GU12 .... 57 K1
Frogmore La *HORN* PO8 .... 255 P6
Frogmore Park Dr
  ROWN SO16 .... 227 H9
Frogmore Park Dr
  BLKW GU17 .... 57 L1
Frogmore Rd *BLKW* GU17 .... 41 J9
  ENEY PO4 .... 317 H4
Frogs Hole *KSCL* RG20 .... 48 B3
Frome Ct *BSTK* RG21 .... 7 J5
  DEAN RG23 .... 88 C2
  FARN GU14 .... 57 L7
  TOTT SO40 .... 247 L9
Fromond Rd *WEND* SO18 .... 229 J9
Fromond Cl *LYMN* SO41 .... 329 L2
Fromond Rd *FUFL* SO22 .... 164 D4
Fromont Dr *STHA* RG19 .... 25 N4
Frosthole Cl *FHAM* PO15 .... 10 A1
Frosthole Crs *FHAM* PO15 ...... 10 A1
Frost La *FAWY* SO45 .... 268 B5
Frost Rd *BWD* BH11 .... 301 P9
Froud Cl *HTWY* RG27 .... 71 N4
Froxfield Cl *FUFL* SO22 .... 164 E3
Froxfield Gdns
  FHAM/PORC PO16 .... 273 N9
Froxfield Rd *HAV* PO9 .... 277 H5
Froyle Ct *HAV* PO9 .... 277 H5
Froyle La *ODIM* RG29 .... 92 G8
Fry La *FAWY* SO45 .... 291 H7
  HLER SO31 .... 270 A6
Fryer Cl *BWD* BH11 .... 322 B2
Fryern Ar *CHFD* SO53 * 206 G6
Fryern Cl *CHFD* SO53 .... 206 C7
Fryern Court Rd *FBDG* SP6 .... 220 C8
Fryers Cl *WINC* SO23 .... 145 K8
Fryer's Copse *WIMB* BH21 ..... 279 L8
Fryers Rd *FAWY* SO45 .... 280 E1
Fry's La *BPWT* SO32 .... 211 P7
Frys La *LYMN* SO41 .... 328 D6
Fry Sq *AND* SP10 * 82 F9
Fugelmere Rd
  FLEETN GU51 .... 74 F2
Fulbrook Wy *ODIM* RG29 .... 93 J3
Fulford Rd *HAV* PO9 .... 276 E5
Fulford Rd *NBAD* SO52 .... 205 L9
Fullers La *KSCL* RG20 .... 29 J7
Fullers Rd *RFNM* GU10 .... 115 M6
Fullers V *BOR* GU35 .... 154 C3
Fullerton Cl *FLEETN* GU51 .... 73 P1
  HAV PO9 .... 277 H5
  ITCH SO19 .... 269 H2
Fullerton Rd *LYMN* SO41 .... 329 J3
  RAND SP11 .... 123 J4
Fullerton Wy *RAND* SP11 .... 34 D7
Fulmar Cl *BH/HW/K* RG22 ..... 89 K4
  ROWN SO16 .... 227 M7
Fulmar Rd
  CHCH/BSGR BH23 .... 337 L1
Fulmer Wk *HORN* PO8 .... 255 N7
Fulwood Av *BWD* BH11 .... 301 N8
Funtington Rd *NEND* PO2 .... 297 H9
Funtley Hl
  FHAM/PORC PO16 .... 272 C6
Funtley Rd *FHAM* PO15 .... 272 B5
Furdies *WVILLE* PO7 .... 254 C7
Furley Cl *WINC* SO23 .... 23 H4
The Furlong *HMB* BH24 .... 282 D2
Furneaux Gdns
  FHAM/PORC PO16 .... 11 G1
Furnell Rd *PLE* BH15 .... 332 F2
Furness Rd *SSEA* PO5 .... 316 F6
Furniss Wy *HISD* PO11 .... 318 D4
The Furrows *STOK* SO20 .... 121 H5
Furse Cl *CBLY* GU15 .... 58 C1
Furse Hill Rd *TDWTH* SP9 .... 79 H6
Further Vell-Mead
  FLEETS GU52 .... 74 B8
Fury Wy *FHAM/STUB* PO14 .... 293 P6
Furzebrook Cl *CFDH* BH17 .... 320 C2
Furze Cl *ASHV* GU12 .... 41 L2
  ITCH SO19 .... 249 J6
Furze Cft *NMIL/BTOS* BH25 .... 323 P4
Furzedale Gdns *FAWY* SO45 ... 268 F9
Furzedale Pk *FAWY* SO45 .... 268 D9
Furzedown Crs *HAV* PO9 .... 276 C5
Furzedown Rd *RAND* SP11 ..... 100 A5
Furzedown Ms *FAWY* SO45 .... 268 D9
Furzedown Rd *ROMY* SO51 .... 181 H3
  SD/PW SO17 .... 248 C1
  STOK SO20 .... 161 M6
Furze Dr *RAND* SP11 .... 79 M5
Furzehall Av
  FHAM/PORC PO16 .... 11 J1
Furzehill *WIMB* BH21 .... 278 F5
Furze Hill Crs *CWTH* RG45 ...... 41 L3
Furze Hill Dr *PSTN* BH14 .... 333 L2
Furze Hill Rd *BOR* GU35 .... 155 J4
Furzelands Rd *WIMB* BH21 .... 280 E1
Furze La *ENEY* PO4 .... 317 M3
Furzeley Rd *WVILLE* PO7 .... 255 H9
Furze Meadow *EPSF* GU31 ..... 217 J5
Furzen La *OVTN* RG25 .... 119 N8
Furze Rd *ITCH* SO19 .... 249 J6
  TADY RG26 .... 34 A4
Furze Vale Rd *BOR* GU35 .... 155 J4
Furze Wy *HORN* PO8 .... 256 B7
Furzey Cl *FAWY* SO45 .... 291 H8
Furzey La *BROC* SO42 .... 288 F7
Furzley Ct *HAV* PO9 .... 276 C4
Furzley Rd *LYND* SO43 .... 224 D7
Furzy Whistlers Cl
  CHCH/BSGR BH23 .... 305 M7
Fushia Cl *HAV* PO9 .... 277 J6
Fushsia Gdns *ROWN* SO16 .... 247 P1
Fuzzy Dro *BH/HW/K* RG22 ...... 89 K3
Fyeford Cl *ROWN* SO16 .... 227 K6
Fyfield Cl *BLKW* GU17 .... 41 L9
  FHAM PO15 .... 271 J2
Fyfield La *RAND* SP11 .... 78 F2
Fyfield Rd *RAND* SP11 .... 80 E9
  STHA RG19 .... 25 N5
Fyfield Rd *FUFL* SO22 .... 164 C2
  RAND SP11 .... 79 M5
Fylingdales *STHA* RG19 .... 25 M5

Fylingdales Cl *BH/HW/K* RG22 .. 68 D9
Fyning St *PSEA* PO1 .... 19 J1

Gable End *FARN* GU14 * 58 A9
Gables Cl *ASHV* GU12 .... 76 F7
  FARN GU14 .... 57 P9
Gables Ct *ROWN* SO16 .... 228 B7
Gables Rd *FLEETS* GU52 .... 74 C8
Gabriel Dr *CBLY* GU15 .... 58 G1
The Gabriels *NWBY* RG14 .... 24 A9
Gaffney Cl *ALDT* GU11 * 76 C5
Gage Cl *FARN* GU24 .... 70 A5
  TOTT SO40 .... 247 L9
Gaiger Av *HTWY* RG27 .... 52 C8
Gainsborough Av
  NMIL/BTOS BH25 * 327 K2
Gainsborough Cl *FARN* GU14 ... 76 C2
  ITCH SO19 .... 249 L9
Gainsborough Ct *AND* SP10 .... 4 B1
Gainsborough Ms
  FHAM PO15 .... 293 M1
Gainsborough Rd *BSTK* RG21 ... 90 E1
  LTDN BH7 .... 323 M8
  RGWD BH24 .... 281 L4
Gainsford Rd *ITCH* SO19 .... 248 G6
Gain's Rd *ENEY* PO4 .... 316 G6
Galahad Cl *AND* SP10 .... 82 E9
Galaxie Rd *HORN* PO8 .... 256 B7
Gale Barracks *ALDT* GU11 * 76 A8
Galileo Pk *AND* SP10 * 102 A1
Gallaghers Md *AND* SP10 .... 101 P2
Galley Av *HTWY* RG27 .... 52 C8
Galley La *STHA* RG19 .... 32 A5
The Gallops *FHAM/STUB* PO14 271 K8
The Gallop *YTLY* GU46 .... 40 E7
Gallop Wy *BKME/WDN* BH12 .. 322 C8
Galloway Cl *BH/HW/K* RG22 .... 89 K8
  FLEETN GU51 .... 74 C2
Gallows Dr *FERN* BH22 .... 302 D7
Gallwey Rd *ALDT* GU11 .... 76 A9
Gally Hill Rd *FLEETS* GU52 .... 74 B7
Galsworthy Rd *TOTT* SO40 ..... 246 B4
Galton Av *CHCH/BSGR* BH23 .. 324 D9
Galt Rd *CHAM* PO6 .... 297 M1
Galway Rd *YTLY* GU46 .... 56 D1
Gamble Cl *ITCH* SO19 .... 249 H7
Gambledown La *ROMY* SO51 .. 178 E9
Gamblins La *BPWT* SO32 .... 209 K5
Gammon Cl *EPSF* GU31 .... 191 N9
Gander Dr *CHIN* RG24 .... 68 F4
Gangbridge La *RAND* SP11 ..... 62 G9
Ganger Rd *RAND* SP11 .... 204 C3
Gannet Cl *BH/HW/K* RG22 ...... 89 K4
  FAWY SO45 .... 268 D8
  ROWN SO16 .... 227 M7
The Gannets
  FHAM/STUB PO14 .... 293 P7
Gape Mouth Rd
  CHOB/PIR GU24 .... 59 K8
Garbett Rd *WINC* SO23 .... 23 J4
Garbetts Wy *RFNM* GU10 .... 97 L5
Garbitts La *EPSF* GU31 .... 217 K2
Garden City *FAWY* SO45 .... 267 L4
Garden Cl *AND* SP10 .... 5 F5
  HISD PO11 .... 318 F4
  HTWY RG27 .... 71 N5
  KSCL RG20 .... 48 C3
  LYND SO43 .... 264 E5
  NMIL/BTOS BH25 .... 327 J6
Garden Close La *NWBY* RG14 .. 30 C2
Gardeners Gn *TDWTH* SP9 ...... 98 F3
Gardener's Hill Rd
  RFNM GU10 .... 116 B6
Gardeners La *ROMY* SO51 ..... 203 M7
Gardenia Dr *FHAM* PO15 .... 271 L7
Garden La *RGWD* BH24 .... 281 L6
  SSEA PO5 .... 19 G7
  WINC SO23 .... 23 F4
Garden Ms *HLER* SO31 .... 270 C9
Garden Rd *CHCH/BSGR* BH23 .. 324 F7
  FHAM/STUB PO14 .... 295 M2
  RGWD BH24 .... 282 F3
Gardner Wy *CHFD* SO53 .... 206 D5
Garendon Ct *FBDG* SP6 .... 240 C1
Garfield Av *BMTH* BH1 .... 335 K1
Garfield Cl *BPWT* SO32 .... 232 A4
Garfield Rd *BPWT* SO32 .... 232 A4
  HLER SO31 .... 269 J4
  ITCH SO19 .... 248 G4
Garford Crs *NWBY* RG14 .... 24 A7
Garland Av *ENEY* PO4 .... 277 M7
Garland Rd *PLE* BH15 .... 320 F8
Garland Wy *THLE* RG7 .... 27 H5
Garnet Fld *YTLY* GU46 .... 40 B9
Garnet Rd *BOR* GU35 .... 154 B6
Garnett Cl *FHAM/STUB* PO14 .. 294 B5
Garnier Pk *WHAM* PO17 .... 252 E7
Garnier Rd *WINC* SO23 .... 184 A1
Garnier St *PSEA* PO1 .... 19 K2
Garnock Rd *ITCH* SO19 .... 249 H6
Garratt Cl *HEND* SO30 .... 250 C1
Garrett Cl *ITCH* SO19 .... 269 J1

Garrick Gdns *ITCH* SO19 .... 249 K9
Garrick Wy *FRIM* GU16 .... 58 D7
Garrison Hl *BPWT* SO32 .... 233 M2
Garrow Dr *LYMN* SO41 .... 329 L2
Garsdale Cl *BWD* BH11 .... 322 A1
Garston Cl *PSF* GU32 .... 185 L2
Garston Mede *STOK* SO20 ..... 123 L5
Garstons Cl *FHAM/STUB* PO14 .. 295 M1
Garstons Rd
  FHAM/STUB PO14 .... 295 M1
Garstons Tr *RWIN* SO21 .... 163 L2
Gar St *WINC* SO23 .... 22 D5
Garth Cl *FNM* GU9 .... 116 A3
Garth Rd *MOOR/WNTN* BH9 .. 322 G6
  THLE RG7 .... 35 P1
The Garth *ALTN* GU34 .... 132 C5
  ASHV GU12 .... 97 M2
  FARN GU14 .... 58 C9
  FAWY SO45 .... 268 A8
Garton Rd *ITCH* SO19 .... 248 F8
Gascoigne La *NARL* SO24 ...... 169 L2
Gashouse Hl *HLER* SO31 .... 294 B4
Gaskell Cl *ALTN* GU34 .... 133 J3
Gaskell Ms *WBLY* RG14 .... 17 G7
Gason Hill Rd *TDWTH* SP9 ...... 78 C5
Gaston Gdns *ROMY* SO51 ..... 204 D5
Gaston La *ALTN* GU34 .... 151 M5
  OVTN RG25 .... 92 F5
Gatcombe *HLER* SO31 .... 269 L3
Gatcombe Av *HSEA* PO3 .... 297 H7
Gatcombe Dr *NEND* PO2 .... 297 H6
Gatcombe Gdns
  FHAM/STUB PO14 .... 293 P1
  WEND SO18 .... 249 J1
Gatehouse La *EPSF* GU31 ...... 193 P8
Gate House Rd
  FHAM/PORC PO16 .... 295 L2
Gatekeeper Cl *WINC* SO23 .... 23 K4
Gaters Hill *WEND* SO18 * 229 J1
The Gates *FLEETN* GU51 .... 56 F9
Gatwick Cl *BWD* BH11 .... 322 A1
Gaulter Cl *HAV* PO9 .... 15 H2
Gauvain Cl *ALTN* GU34 .... 132 C7
Gavan St *ITCH* SO19 .... 249 M6
G Av *FAWY* SO45 .... 291 H3
Gawaine Cl *AND* SP10 .... 82 E7
Gaydon Ri *BWD* BH11 .... 301 N9
Gaylyn Wy *FHAM/STUB* PO14 .. 293 P1
Gaywood Dr *NWBY* RG14 .... 34 G3
Gazebo Av *BROC* SO42 .... 310 C2
Gazelle Cl *LSOL/BMARY* PO13 .. 315 H3
Gazing La *FHAM/STUB* PO14 .. 224 E1
Geale's Crs *ALTN* GU34 .... 132 C4
Geales Wy *EPSF* GU31 .... 216 A1
Gemini Cl *ROWN* SO16 .... 227 K8
Geneva Av *SBNE* BH6 .... 336 D1
Genoa Cl *LYMN* SO41 .... 329 J6
Genoa Ct *AND* SP10 .... 82 F8
Gentles La *LIPH* GU30 .... 155 H7
Geoffrey Av *WVILLE* PO7 .... 255 J7
Geoffrey Crs
  FHAM/PORC PO16 .... 294 F3
George Byng Wy *NEND* PO2 ... 296 F3
George Curl Wy *WEND* SO18 .. 229 H6
George Denyer Cl *HASM* GU27 .. 157 H6
George Eyston Dr *FUFL* SO22 .. 164 E9
Georgeham Rd *SHST* GU47 ...... 41 L4
George Raymond Rd
  ELGH SO50 .... 229 H2
George Rd *FLEETN* GU51 .... 74 E3
  NWBY RG14 .... 338 F1
George St *BSTK* RG21 .... 6 B6
  CHOB/PIR GU24 .... 59 M7
  ELGH SO50 .... 229 K1
  GPORT PO12 .... 315 N3
  KSCL RG20 .... 48 C3
  PSEA PO1 .... 316 C1
George Vl Rd *TDWTH* SP9 .... 98 C5
George Wright Cl *ELGH* SO50 .. 229 H2
George Yd *AND* SP10 .... 4 E5
Georgia Cl *AND* SP10 .... 102 B4
Georgian Cl *AND* SP10 .... 100 E7
Georgian Ct *RGWD* BH24 .... 282 E1
Georgian Wy *NBNE* BH10 ...... 321 N1
Georgina Cl *BKME/WDN* BH12 .. 322 C7
  TOTT SO40 .... 245 P2
Georgina Gdns *TADY* RG26 ..... 34 F6
Gerald Rd *TWDS* BH3 .... 334 E1
Gerald Sq *ALTN* GU34 .... 132 C5
Geranium Gdns *WVILLE* PO7 .. 255 J7
Gerard Crs *ITCH* SO19 .... 249 M5
Germaine Cl
  CHCH/BSGR BH23 .... 326 B7
German Rd *TADY* RG26 .... 63 P7
Gershwin Cl *BH/HW/K* RG22 ... 89 N3
Gershwin Rd *BH/HW/K* RG22 .. 89 N3
Gervis Crs *PSTN* BH14 .... 321 J8
Gervis Pl *BMTH* BH1 .... 8 A4
Gervis Rd *BMTH* BH1 .... 9 H4
Gibbons Cl *SHST* GU47 .... 41 K7
Gibbs Cl *FAWY* SO45 .... 290 C1
Gibbs' La *BOR* GU35 .... 154 C2
Gibbs Rd *SHAM* SO14 .... 20 D3
Gibbs Wy *YTLY* GU46 .... 56 C1
Gibraltar Cl *FHAM/STUB* PO14 .. 295 N8
Gibraltar Rd *FHAM* PO15 ...... 272 B8
Gibraltar Rd *ENEY* PO4 .... 317 H5
  FHAM/STUB PO14 .... 294 D1
Gibson Cl *FHAM* PO15 .... 271 L5
  LSOL/BMARY PO13 .... 314 C2
Giddylake *WIMB* BH21 .... 278 E8
Gid La *ALTN* GU34 .... 115 P7
Giffard Dr *FARN* GU14 .... 77 N2
Giffard Cl *FLEETN* GU51 .... 74 B1
Giffards Meadow *FNM* GU9 .... 116 E2
Gifford Cl *FHAM* PO15 .... 272 A8
Gilbert Cl *CHIN* RG24 .... 68 F4
  FBDG SP6 .... 239 P5
  LSOL/BMARY PO13 .... 295 H9
  LYMN SO41 .... 329 K5
Gilbert Md *HISD* PO11 .... 318 E4

Gilbert Rd *CHAR* BH8 .... 323 K9
  LYMN SO41 .... 328 M4
Gilbert's Gn *TDWTH* SP9 .... 98 G3
Gilberts Mead Cl *RAND* SP11 .. 101 P6
Gilbert St *NARL* SO24 .... 169 N2
Gilbert Wy *WVILLE* PO7 .... 275 N5
Gilbert White Wy *ALTN* GU34 .. 132 F4
Gilbury Cl *ELGH* SO50 .... 229 H5
  WEND SO18 .... 228 G8
Gilchrist Gdns *HLER* SO31 ..... 292 C2
Giles Cl *FHAM/PORC* PO16 ..... 11 H1
  GPORT PO12 .... 315 L2
  HEND SO30 .... 250 D2
Giles La *RSAL* SP5 .... 202 A9
Giles Rd *FAWY* SO45 .... 291 K5
Gilkicker Rd *GPORT* PO12 ...... 315 N7
Gillam Rd *NBNE* BH10 .... 322 D3
Gillcrest *FHAM/STUB* PO14 ... 271 J6
Gillett Rd *BKME/WDN* BH12 .. 322 C8
Gillhams La *HASM* GU27 .... 175 P5
Gillian Av *ASHV* GU12 .... 3 K6
Gillies Dr *CHIN* RG24 .... 68 F4
Gilligham Cl
  MOOR/WNTN BH9 .... 323 J4
  WINC SO23 .... 145 K9
Gillingham Rd *LYMN* SO41 .... 338 C2
Gillman Rd *HSEA* PO3 .... 298 A3
Gilpin Cl *ITCH* SO19 .... 249 M6
  LYMN SO41 .... 309 M7
Gilpin Hl *LYMN* SO41 .... 308 B6
Gilpins Polly *LYMN* SO41 ...... 308 A5
Gins La *BROC* SO42 .... 311 P7
Girton Cl *FHAM/STUB* PO14 .. 271 J9
Gisors Rd *ENEY* PO4 .... 317 K4
  RFNM GU10 .... 115 K9
Gisors Rd *ENEY* PO4 .... 317 K4
Gitsham Gdns *WVILLE* PO7 .... 255 L7
Gladdis Rd *BWD* BH11 .... 301 P9
Glade Cl *CHIN* RG24 .... 70 A2
Gladeland Rd *FERN* BH22 ...... 280 F9
Gladelands Pk *FERN* BH22 .... 302 F1
Gladelands Wy *BDST* BH18 ... 300 A4
The Glades *HLER* SO31 .... 270 G6
The Glade *CHFD* SO53 .... 207 H4
  FAWY SO45 .... 312 C1
  FHAM PO15 .... 272 B6
  FNM GU9 .... 96 D4
  FRIM GU16 .... 58 E7
  HISD PO11 .... 319 J6
  NWBY RG14 .... 24 C8
  RFNM GU10 .... 115 K9
  RGWD BH24 .... 281 L4
  WILLE PO7 .... 276 A2
Gladiator Wy *FARN* GU14 .... 75 P4
Gladstone Cl
  CHCH/BSGR BH23 .... 325 H9
Gladstone Gdns
  FHAM/PORC PO16 .... 295 N2
Gladstone Rd
  BKME/WDN BH12 .... 321 L7
  ITCH SO19 .... 249 K6
  LTDN BH7 .... 335 M1
Gladstone Rd East *LTDN* BH7 .. 335 M1
Gladstone Rd West
  BKME/WDN BH12 .... 321 L7
Gladys Av *HORN* PO8 .... 256 A7
  NEND PO2 .... 296 F2
Glaisdale *STHA* RG19 .... 25 M5
Glamis Av *NBNE* BH10 .... 322 E2
Glamis Dr *CHAR* RG23 .... 88 F1
  FRIM GU16 .... 58 D6
  WVILLE PO7 .... 256 B3
Glamorgan Rd *HORN* PO8 ...... 256 B1
Glasgow Rd *ENEY* PO4 .... 317 K5
Glasslaw Rd *WEND* SO18 ...... 249 J3
Glasspool *WVILLE* PO7 .... 254 G6
Glastonbury Cl *FHAM* PO15 ... 272 B8
Glaston Hill Rd *HTWY* RG27 .... 39 K7
Glayshers Hl *BOR* GU35 .... 155 H2
Glaziers La *RGUW* GU3 .... 77 N7
Gleadowe Av
  CHCH/BSGR BH23 .... 324 D9
Glebe Cl *ALDT* GU11 .... 96 C4
  ALTN GU34 .... 131 K3
  HISD PO11 .... 318 E5
  OVTN RG25 .... 109 H1
  TADY RG26 .... 34 D7
Glebe Cnr *WHAM* PO17 .... 252 F8
Glebe Ct *ELGH* SO50 .... 230 D2
  FLEETN GU51 .... 74 C3
  HEND SO30 .... 250 C3
  SD/PW SO17 .... 248 C1
Glebefield Gdns *CHAM* PO6 ... 296 G8
Glebe Flds *ALTN* GU34 .... 131 K3
Glebeland Rd *CBLY* GU15 .... 57 N1
Glebelands *RAND* SP11 .... 102 F8
  STHA RG19 .... 8 A5
Glebe La *DEAN* RG23 .... 68 D8
  HTWY RG27 .... 55 J8
  RFNM GU10 .... 137 J4
  RSAL SP5 .... 201 M9
Glebe Meadow *OVTN* RG25 ..... 86 G5
Glebe Park Av *HAV* PO9 .... 276 A9
Glebe Rd *BOR* GU35 .... 154 F3
  EPSF GU31 .... 215 K8
  FARN GU14 .... 57 N8
  LSOL/BMARY PO13 .... 314 G3
  NWBY RG14 .... 16 B3
  PSEA PO1 .... 316 C2
  WVILLE PO7 .... 275 P6
Gloucester Sq *SHAM* SO14 ..... 20 E7
Gloucester Ter *SSEA* PO5 .... 19 G6
Gloucester Vw *ELGH* SO50 ..... 19 G6
Glyn Dr *FHAM/STUB* PO14 .... 294 A7
Glyn Gdns *CI FAWY* SO45 ...... 291 H7
Glynswood *CBLY* GU15 .... 58 B2
  RFNM GU10 .... 116 A6
Glynville Cl *WIMB* BH21 .... 279 J7
Glynville Rd *WIMB* BH21 .... 279 J7
Glynwood *FHAM/STUB* PO14 .. 293 P8

Glen Cl *AND* SP10 .... 102 C3
  NMIL/BTOS BH25 * 326 F7
Glencoe Cl *FRIM* GU16 .... 58 E5
Glencoe Rd *BKME/WDN* BH12 .. 321 M7
  LTDN BH7 .... 323 M8
  PSEA PO1 .... 317 H1
Glencoyne Gdns *ROWN* SO16 .. 247 K1
Glenda Cl *HLER* SO31 .... 292 D1
Glendale *BPWT* SO32 .... 232 F8
Glen Dl *HAV* PO9 .... 277 J1
Glendale Cl *HLER* SO31 .... 270 C8
Glendale Av *FERN* BH22 .... 302 D2
  NWBY RG14 .... 30 B1
Glendale Cl *CHCH/BSGR* BH23 .. 324 B4
  WIMB BH21 .... 278 E9
Glendale Pk *FLEETN* GU51 ...... 73 P2
Glendale Rd *SBNE* BH6 .... 336 E2
  TADY RG26 .... 51 J8
Glendeep Cl *WINC* SO23 .... 165 J1
Glendene Pk
  NMIL/BTOS BH25 * 326 C2
Glendon Av *NBNE* BH10 .... 322 C1
Glendowan Rd *CHFD* SO53 ... 206 C6
Glendrive *NMIL/BTOS* BH25 ... 326 E7
Gleneagles Cl *BH/HW/K* RG22 .. 89 L3
  FERN BH22 .... 302 F2
Gleneagles Dr *FARN* GU14 ...... 75 K1
  HORN PO8 .... 256 B2
Glenealy *FHAM* PO15 .... 10 C3
Glenesha Gdns *FHAM* PO15 .. 272 B8
Glen Eyre Cl *ROWN* SO16 ...... 228 C2
Glen Eyre Rd *ROWN* SO16 ..... 228 B7
Glen Eyre Wy *ROWN* SO16 .... 228 C2
Glenferness Av *TWDS* BH3 .... 322 D9
Glen Fl *AND* SP10 .... 102 C3
Glenfield Av *WEND* SO18 .... 249 H4
Glenfield Cl *RSAL* SP5 .... 158 C1
Glenfield Crs *WEND* SO18 ..... 249 H4
Glenfield Wy *WEND* SO18 ...... 249 H4
Glengarriff Rd *PSTN* BH14 ..... 333 L1
Glengarry *NMIL/BTOS* BH25 .. 327 J5
Glengarry Wy
  CHCH/BSGR BH23 .... 325 N9
Glenhurst Cl *BLKW* GU17 .... 57 M1
Glen Innes *SHST* GU47 .... 41 K5
Glenives Cl *RGWD* BH24 .... 281 M5
Glenlea Cl *HEND* SO30 .... 250 C2
Glenlea Dr *HEND* SO30 .... 250 M2
Glenlea Hollow *GSHT* GU26 ... 156 D5
Glenleigh Av *CHAM* PO6 .... 297 H2
Glenlyn Av *ELGH* SO50 .... 230 C4
Glenmead Cl *ITCH* SO19 .... 249 N1
Glenmoor Cl *NBNE* BH10 ...... 322 D6
Glenmoor Rd *FERN* BH22 ...... 302 C5
  MOOR/WNTN BH9 .... 322 D7
Glenmore Cl *STHA* RG19 .... 25 N5
Glenmore Gdns *HORN* PO8 ... 255 P9
Glenmount Dr *FRIM* GU16 .... 76 F2
  HLER SO31 .... 249 M1
Glenny Cl *LSOL/BMARY* PO13 .. 314 E2
Glen Rd *BOSC* BH5 .... 335 L2
  FLEETN GU51 .... 74 C4
  HLER SO31 .... 270 C8
  ITCH SO19 .... 268 F1
  PSEA PO1 .... 317 K8
Glenroyd Gdns *SBNE* BH6 ..... 336 B2
Glenside *FAWY* SO45 .... 268 B7
  HEND SO30 * 249 M2
  NMIL/BTOS BH25 .... 326 D8
Glenside Av *ITCH* SO19 .... 249 N1
Glen Spey *NMIL/BTOS* BH25 .. 327 M5
The Glen *CCLF* BH13 .... 333 N1
  FNM GU9 .... 96 C5
  LSOL/BMARY PO13 .... 295 J8
  TADY RG26 .... 34 F5
Glenthorne Cl
  FHAM/STUB PO14 .... 294 B8
Glenthorne Meadow
  PSF GU32 .... 213 N5
Glenthorne Rd *HSEA* PO3 ...... 297 J8
Glenville Cl *CHCH/BSGR* BH23 .. 326 D5
Glenville Gdns *CSHT* GU26 .... 156 E1
Glenville Rd *CHCH/BSGR* BH23 .. 326 D5
  NBNE BH10 .... 322 C5
Glenwood Av *ROWN* SO16 ..... 228 C7
Glenwood Cl *FERN* BH22 .... 280 E7
Glenwood Ct *FERN* BH22 .... 280 E7
  FARN GU14 .... 58 F3
Glenwood Gdns *HORN* PO8 ... 255 P9
Glenwood La *FERN* BH22 .... 280 E7
Glenwood Rd *FERN* BH22 ...... 280 E7
  VWD BH31 .... 258 E5
Glenwood Wy *FERN* BH22 ..... 280 E7
Globe La *WVILLE* PO7 .... 234 G9
Glidden La *WVILLE* PO7 .... 234 G9
Glissons *FERN* BH22 .... 302 A6
Globe Farm La *BLKW* GU17 ..... 41 J9
Globe Yd *AND* SP10 * 4 D5
Glorney Md *FNM* GU9 .... 96 D4
Gloster Cl *FHAM* PO15 .... 271 J5
Gloster Ct *FHAM* PO15 .... 271 J5
Gloucester Dr *BH/HW/K* RG22 .. 89 M4
Gloucester Pl *SSEA* PO5 .... 19 G6
Gloucester Rd
  BKME/WDN BH12 .... 321 N7
  LTDN BH7 .... 335 M1
  NWBY RG14 .... 16 B3
  PSEA PO1 .... 316 C2
  WVILLE PO7 .... 275 P6
Gloucester Sq *SHAM* SO14 ..... 20 E7
Gloucester Ter *SSEA* PO5 .... 19 G6
Gloucester Vw *ELGH* SO50 ..... 19 G6
Glyn Dr *FHAM/STUB* PO14 .... 294 A7
Glyn Gdns *CI FAWY* SO45 ...... 291 H7
Glynswood *CBLY* GU15 .... 58 B2
  RFNM GU10 .... 116 A6
Glynville Cl *WIMB* BH21 .... 279 J7
Glynville Rd *WIMB* BH21 .... 279 J7
Glynwood *FHAM/STUB* PO14 .. 293 P8

Goatacre Rd *ALTN* GU34 .... **149** M3
Goathouse La *WHAM* PO17 .. **253** M7
Goat La *BSTK* RG21............. **7** G6
Goch Wy *AND* SP10 .... **82** C9
Goddards Cl *HTWY* RG27 .... **52** E5
Goddards La *CBLY* GU15....... **58** A2
Goddards Md *AND* SP10 ...... **102** C3
Goddard Sq *AND* SP10........... **82** F9
Godfrey Cl *SHST* GU47 ....
Godfrey Pink Wy *BPWT* SO32 .. **232** B5
Godmanston Cl *CFDH* BH17... **321** J3
God's Blessing La *WIMB* BH21 .. **278** C3
Godshill Cl *CHAR* BH5.......... **323** K4
Godwin Cl *EMRTH* PO10 ..... **277** L7
FUFL SO22 .... **164** D4
Godwin Crs *HORN* PO8......... **236** C8
Godwit Cl *GPORT* PO12.......... **295** M9
Godwit Rd *ENEY* PO4 .... **317** L3
Gofton Av *CHAM* PO6 .... **297** K2
Gogg's La *RSAL* SP5.............. **200** B7
Goldcrest Cl
 FHAM/PORC PO16 *............ **295** J1
 HORN PO8........................... **256** A4
 YTLY GU46.......................... **40** B7
Goldcrest Gdns *ROWN* SO16... **227** L7
Goldcrest La *TOTT* SO40 ...... **246** A3
Golden Ct *HEND* SO30........... **249** P1
Golden Crs *LYMN* SO41........ **328** D6
Golden Flds *LIPH* GU30......... **175** L8
Goldenfields Cl *LYMN* SO41... **328** D5
Golden Gv *SHAM* SO14......... **21** J3
Golden Hind Pk *FAWY* SO45... **268** D8
Goldenleas Dr *BWD* BH11..... **321** N1
Golden Lion Rbt
 BH/HW/K RG22 .... **90** D2
Goldfinch Cl *ALDT* GU11...... **2** C7
 NMIL/BTOS BH25 .... **327** H5
Goldfinch Gdns
 BH/HW/K RG22.................... **89** K5
Goldfinch La
 LSOL/BMARY PO13.............. **314** D1
Goldfinch Rd *CFDH* BH17..... **320** A4
Goldfinch Wy *RWIN* SO21 .... **144** F3
Gold Hl *BOR* GU35 * **134** G8
Goldhill *RFNM* GU10 .... **116** C4
Gold La *ALDT* GU11.............. **76** D8
Gold Mead Cl *LYMN* SO41.... **329** L5
Goldney Rd *CBLY* GU15......... **58** G1
Goldring Cl *HISD* PO11 .... **318** G5
Goldsmith Av *ENEY* PO4........ **35** M2
 TOTT SO40 .... **246** B4
Goldsmith Rd *ELGH* SO50..... **229** H1
Goldsmith Wy *CWTH* RG45.... **41** J2
Gold st *SSEA* PO5 .... **18** F5
Goldwell Dr *NWBY* RG14....... **24** C3
Goldwire Dr *CHFD* SO53....... **206** B8
Golf Course Rd *ROWN* SO16... **206** B7
Golf Dr *CBLY* GU15............... **58** E1
Golf La *BDST* BH18............... **153** N7
Golf Links Rd *BDST* BH18 .... **300** D8
 FERN BH22.......................... **302** E5
Gomer La *GPORT* PO12......... **315** H5
Gondreville Gdns *FLEETS* GU52.. **74** B8
Gong Hill Dr *RFNM* GU10 .... **116** D6
Goodden Crs *FARN* GU14 ..... **75** N2
The Goodens *NARL* SO24...... **186** C1
Goodison Cl *ELGH* SO50....... **230** B5
Goodlands V *HEND* SO30...... **250** A4
Goodman Cl *BSTK* RG21....... **321** L5
Good Rd *BKME/WDN* BH12... **321** J5
Goodsell Cl *FHAM/STUB* PO14.. **293** P7
Goodwin Cl *ROWN* SO16....... **247** H1
Goodwood Cl *ALTN* GU34..... **132** F7
 FHAM/STUB PO14................ **271** J8
 GPORT PO12........................ **295** M9
 HORN PO8........................... **256** D8
 THLE RG7........................... **27** H5
Goodwood Gdns *TOTT* SO40... **246** A3
Goodwood Pl *FARN* GU14 ..... **76** D1
Goodwood Rd *ELGH* SO50..... **206** D9
 SSEA PO5 .... **18** F7
Goodworth Rd *NWBY* RG14 ... **17** K6
Goodwyns Cl *TDWTH* SP9..... **98** F3
Goodwyns Gn *ALTN* GU34..... **132** G6
Goodyers *ALTN* GU34............ **132** G6
Goose Gn *HTWY* RG27 .... **71** N2
Goose La *HTWY* RG27........... **71** P2
Gordon Av *CBLY* GU15.......... **58** A1
 TAD SO40........................... **74** E6
 SHAM SO14........................ **248** C3
 WINC SO23......................... **23** J7
Gordon Cl *BSTK* RG21.......... **7** H3
Gordon Crs *CBLY* GU15......... **58** B1
Gordon Mt
 CHCH/BSGR BH23................ **326** D6
Gordon Palmer Cl *THLE* RG7... **36** C1
Gordon Rd *ALDT* GU11 .... **2** E4
 BKME/WDN BH12............... **334** A1
 BPWT SO32.......................... **251** M2
 CBLY GU15.......................... **58** B1
 CHCH/BSGR BH23................ **326** C7
 CHFD SO53.......................... **206** A4
 CWTH RG45......................... **41** L3
 EMRTH PO10....................... **299** P2
 FARN GU14.......................... **76** C4
 FHAM/PORC PO16............... **10** E5
 GPORT PO12........................ **12** B3
 LYMN SO41......................... **329** J4
 NTHA RG18.......................... **8** F5
 NWBY RG14......................... **17** G3
 PSEA PO1............................ **18** E7
 WIMB BH21......................... **300** G1
 WINC SO23.......................... **23** F2
 WVILLE PO7........................ **275** M4
Gordon Rd South
 BKME/WDN BH12............... **334** A1
Gordon Ter *ITCH* SO19........ **249** J9
Gordon Wk *YTLY* GU46......... **40** F9
Gordon Wy *CHCH/BSGR* BH23.. **324** G6
Gore End Rd *KSCL* RG20........ **29** J3
Gore Rd *NMIL/BTOS* BH25 ... **326** A6
Gorey Av *ALTN* GU34............. **236** C8
Gorey Rd *BKME/WDN* BH12... **321** M3
Goring Fld *FUFL* SO22........... **164** D6
Goring La *THLE* RG7.............. **27** H6

Gorleston Rd
 BKME/WDN BH12............... **321** P7
Gorley Ct *HAV* PO9............... **276** C4
Gorley Lynch *FBDG* SP6........ **241** H6
Gorley Rd *RGWD* BH24......... **282** G1
Gorran Av *LSOL/BMARY* PO13.. **294** G8
The Gorrings *STOK* SO20...... **161** M5
Gorselcliff Rd *NBNE* BH10.... **322** D6
Gorse Cl *HLER* SO31 .... **270** F8
 NMIL/BTOS BH25 .... **327** M3
 RFNM GU10 .... **116** A4
 RGWD BH24......................... **284** P1
Gorsedown Cl *BOR* GU35...... **153** N7
Gorsefield Rd
 BKME/WDN BH12............... **327** K2
Gorse Hill Cl *PLE* BH15........ **320** C7
Gorse Hill Crs *PLE* BH15....... **320** C7
Gorse Hill Rd *PLE* BH15........ **320** C7
Gorse Knoll Dr *WBY* BH31.... **258** E3
Gorse La *CFERN* BH24........... **302** E5
Gorselands *NWBY* RG14 .... **30** C1
 TADY RG26........................... **34** C5
Gorselands Cl *ASHV* GU12 .... **76** F7
Gorselands Rd *WEND* SO18... **249** K2
Gorselands Wy
 LSOL/BMARY PO13.............. **295** H9
Gorse La *RFNM* GU10........... **116** A4
Gorse Rd *EPSF* GU31............. **216** A2
 FRIM GU16........................... **58** D5
Gorseway *FLEETS* GU52........ **74** D5
The Gorseway *HISD* PO11 *.. **318** D5
Gort Cl *ALDT* GU11............... **76** D5
Gort Crs *ITCH* SO19.............. **249** K7
Gort Rd *BWD* BH11............... **321** C5
Gorwell *BWD* BH11.............. **320** C5
Goscombe La *SHAM* SO14.... **21** H5
Grasdean Cl *WEND* SO18 ..... **249** J2
Gosling Cl *CFDH* BH17.......... **321** H5
Goslings Cft *ALTN* GU34 ...... **152** D7
Gosnell Cl *FRIM* GU16.......... **59** J2
Gosport La *LYND* SO43......... **264** G6
Gosport Rd *ALTN* GU34......... **151** K4
 FHAM/STUB PO14................ **294** B7
Gosport St *LYMN* SO41......... **329** M3
Gough Crs *CFDH* BH17.......... **320** D2
Gough Rd *FLEETN* GU51....... **74** B2
Gough's Meadow *SHST* GU47.. **41** J7
Gough's Way *RFNM* GU14..... **79** N1
 RAND SP11.......................... **79** N1
Government House Rd
 FARN GU14.......................... **75** P5
Governors Rd *CBLY* GU15..... **76** D8
Gover Rd *ROWN* SO16........... **246** C2
Gower Ct *BSTK* RG21............ **6** E2
Gower Crs *HTWY* RG27.......... **72** A3
Gowers Pk *SHST* GU47.......... **41** L7
Grace Bennett Cl *FARN* GU14 *.. **57** P4
Grace Dieu Gdns *HLER* SO31 *.. **269** P1
Grace La *FBDG* SP6............... **221** J4
Gracemere Crs *BH/HW/K* RG22.. **89** K4
Grace Sq *AND* SP10.............. **82** G9
Gracious St *ALTN* GU34......... **152** C8
Graddidge Wy *TOTT* SO40..... **266** E8
Gradwell La *ALTN* GU34........ **150** B8
Graemar La *ROMY* SO51........ **202** C3
Grafton Cl *BOR* GU35............ **154** B6
 CHCH/BSGR BH23................ **325** H9
 GPORT PO12........................ **315** N1
 TWDS BH3........................... **334** D2
Grafton Gdns *LYMN* SO41..... **329** J6
 ROWN SO16........................ **227** N7
Grafton Rd *TWDS* BH3........... **322** C9
 WINC SO23......................... **22** C7
Grafton St *NEND* PO2........... **316** E1
Grafton Wy *BH/HW/K* RG22... **68** G4
Graham Rd *ENEY* PO4........... **316** G5
 GPORT PO12........................ **315** L2
 PSEA PO1............................ **21** F1
Graham St *SHAM* SO14........ **21** J1
Grainger Cl *BH/HW/K* RG22... **90** A2
Grainger Gdns *ITCH* SO19.... **249** L8
Grammar School La
 WIMB BH21......................... **300** D1
Grammarsham La *OVTN* RG25.. **90** B9
Grampian Rd *SHST* GU47...... **40** G4
Grampian Wy *BH/HW/K* RG22.. **68** F9
Granada Cl *HORN* PO8.......... **256** A8
Granada Pl *AND* SP10........... **5** H2
Granada Rd *ENEY* PO4.......... **316** G7
 HEND SO30.......................... **250** A4
The Granary *NWBY* RG14 *.... **16** D2
Granby End *THLE* RG7........... **27** J4
Granby Cv *SD/PW* SO17........ **228** D9
Granby Rd *MOOR/WNTN* BH9.. **322** C3
Grand Av *SBNE* BH6.............. **336** A2
Grand Pde *FUFL* SO22........... **164** D2
 HISD PO11........................... **318** G6
 PLE BH15 * **332** D2
 PSEA PO1............................ **18** C7
Grand Trunk Rd *TDWTH* SP9.. **98** F7
Grange *WIMB* BH21.............. **278** E4
Grange Cl *GPORT* PO12........ **295** L2
 HAV PO9.............................. **15** K4
 RAND SP11........................... **328** E7
 WEND SO18......................... **228** G8
Grange Ct *HLER* SO31.......... **269** K4
 RFNM GU10......................... **97** L5
Grange Crs *GPORT* PO12 ...... **315** K2
 HEND SO30.......................... **250** D3
Grange Farm Rd *ASHV* GU12.. **76** F7
Grange Gdns
 BKME/WDN BH12............... **321** N5
Grange La *HTWY* RG27.......... **54** G8
 LSOL/BMARY PO13.............. **294** G6
Grange Ms *ROMY* SO51........ **204** G4
Grange Rd *ASHV* GU12......... **97** P2
 BDST BH18........................... **300** C9
 CHCH/BSGR BH23................ **325** M8
 FARN GU14.......................... **58** A6
 FLEETS GU52....................... **73** M6
 GPORT PO12........................ **315** H4
 HEND SO30.......................... **250** C3
 HLER SO31........................... **269** J4
 LSOL/BMARY PO13.............. **315** H3

NARL SO24........................... **167** P2
NEND PO2............................ **296** F8
PSF GU32............................. **215** L3
RFNM GU10.......................... **97** L5
RFNM GU10.......................... **137** H1
RGWD BH24.......................... **281** K7
ROWN SO16.......................... **247** M2
SBNE BH6............................ **336** B3
WINC SO23........................... **183** N2
The Grange *LYMN* SO41........ **328** E7
 NWBY RG14.......................... **30** D1
Grangewood Gdns
 ELGH SO50 .... **230** B2
Grantham Av *HLER* SO31...... **269** N7
Grantham Cl *SHST* GU47...... **41** M5
Grantham Rd *BMTH* BH1...... **335** L1
 ITCH SO19........................... **229** H2
Grantley Ct *FNM* GU9 .... **115** P4
Grantley Dr *FLEETS* GU52..... **74** C5
Grantley Rd *BOSC* BH5......... **335** M2
Grant Rd *CHAM* PO6............. **297** M1
 CWTH RG45.......................... **41** K2
Grant's Av *BMTH* BH1........... **323** K9
Grants Cl *CHAR* BH8............. **323** K9
Granville Cl *HAV* PO9............ **15** J6
Granville Pl *WINC* SO23........ **23** C7
Granville Rd
 BKME/WDN BH12............... **321** K7
 BOSC BH5............................ **335** N1
Granville St *SHAM* SO14....... **21** H5
Grasdean Cl *WEND* SO18...... **249** J2
Grasmere Cl *ELGH* SO50...... **229** H2
Grasmere Cl *BOR* GU35......... **154** A3
 CHCH/BSGR BH23................ **324** B4
 WEND SO18......................... **249** K2
Grasmere Gdns
 NMIL/BTOS BH25 .... **327** K2
Grasmere Rd *BOSC* BH5....... **335** N2
 CCLF BH13........................... **333** K8
 FNM GU9............................. **115** M1
 FNM GU9............................. **96** A5
Grasmere Wy
 FHAM/STUB PO14................ **294** B5
Graspan Rd *RAND* SP11........ **80** B2
Grassington Pl *STHA* SO19 ... **25** N5
Grassmere Wy *WVILLE* PO7... **256** D9
Grassymead
 FHAM/STUB PO14................ **271** J6
Grateley Cl *ITCH* SO19.......... **269** H2
Grateley Crs *HAV* PO9........... **276** C6
Grateley Dro *RAND* SP11...... **99** P9
Grateley Rd *AMSY* SP4.......... **99** J1
Gratton Cl *RWIN* SO21.......... **125** M5
Gravel Cl *NARL* SO24............ **128** G5
 RSAL SP5............................. **199** J3
Gravel Hl *BDST* BH18........... **320** E1
Gravel Hill Rd *RFNM* GU10 ... **115** J7
 RGWD BH24.......................... **282** D1
 RWIN SO21.......................... **124** F2
Gravelly Cl *KSCL* RG20......... **10** C1
Gravel Rd *FARN* GU14........... **76** C4
 FLEETS GU52....................... **74** E6
Graveney Sq *AND* SP10......... **82** F9
Cray Cl *CFDH* BH17.............. **321** H4
 HLER SO31........................... **270** F8
Graycot Cl *NBNE* BH10......... **322** C2
Grayland Cl *HISD* PO11........ **318** E5
Grayling Md *ROMY* SO51...... **204** D4
Graylings *WSHM* SO15 *....... **247** L3
Grays Av *FAWY* SO45............ **268** D7
Grays Ct *GPORT* PO12........... **315** J5
 HASM GU27.......................... **157** K5
 ROMY SO51.......................... **204** E6
 RSAL SP5............................. **201** P5
Grayshot Dr *BLKW* GU17...... **41** K9
Grayshott Cl *FUFL* SO22....... **164** E3
Grayshott Laurels *BOR* GU35.. **154** D2
Grayshott Rd *BOR* GU35....... **155** K1
 ENEY PO4............................ **317** H4
Grayson Cl *LSOL/BMARY* PO13.. **314** E2
Grayswood Dr *FRIM* GU16..... **76** F3
Grayswood Ms *HASM* GU27 *.. **157** L3
Grayswood Rd *HASM* GU27.... **157** J5
Gray's Yd *PLE* BH15 *............ **332** E2
Great Austins *FNM* GU9 .... **116** D2
Great Binfields Crs *CHIN* RG24.. **70** A4
Great Binfields Rd *CHIN* RG24.. **70** A4
Great Br *ROMY* SO51 .... **204** C3
Greatbridge Rd *ROMY* SO51... **204** C5
Great Copse Dr *HAV* PO9...... **276** C5
Great Elms Cl *FAWY* SO45.... **290** D6
Greater Horseshoe Wy
 WHAM PO17......................... **272** C2
Great Farm Rd *ELGH* SO50.... **229** H1
Greatfield Cl *FARN* GU14....... **58** A5
Greatfield Rd *FARN* GU14..... **57** P5
Great Field Rd *FUFL* SO22..... **164** E4
Greatfield Wy *HAV* PO9......... **257** H9
Great Gays *FHAM/STUB* PO14.. **293** M8
Great Hanger *EPSF* GU31....... **215** P2
Great La *WHCH* RG28............ **85** L6
Great Marlow *HTWY* RG27..... **72** C3
Great Mead Pk *LYND* SO43.... **264** C5
Great Minster St *WINC* SO23.. **22** E5
Great Oaks Cha *CHIN* RG24... **69** P2
Great Sheldons Coppice
 RGWD BH24.......................... **71** P2
Great Southsea St *SSEA* PO5.. **19** G6
Great Well Dr *ROMY* SO51..... **204** E5
Greatwood Cl *FAWY* SO45..... **268** C6
Greaves Cl *NBNE* BH10 *....... **322** C4
Grebe Cl *ALTN* GU34............. **132** E3
 FHAM/PORC PO16............... **295** J1
 HORN PO8........................... **256** B8
 YTLY GU46........................... **40** D7

HORN PO8............................ **255** N7
LYMN SO41.......................... **339** H2
Green Acre *ALDT* GU11......... **48** C3
Greenacre *KSCL* RG20........... **48** C3
Greenacre Gdns *WVILLE* PO7.. **275** M6
Greenacres *BOR* GU35.......... **154** C4
 KSCL RG20........................... **29** M6
 RFNM GU10.......................... **97** J9
 RSAL SP5............................. **199** H6
Green Acres *HAV* PO9........... **124** E5
Greenacres Cl *NBNE* BH10.... **302** E9
Green Acres Cl *RGWD* BH24... **282** B4
Greenacres Dr *RWIN* SO21.... **207** L2
Greenaway La *HLER* SO31..... **270** D8
The Greenaways *DEAN* RG23.. **88** F1
Greenbank Crs *ROWN* SO16... **228** B7
Greenbanks Cl *LYMN* SO41... **338** C1
Greenbanks Gdns
 FHAM/PORC PO16............... **273** H8
Greenberry Br *RGWD* BH24... **306** E1
Greenbirch Cl *BH/HW/K* RG22.. **89** K4
Green Bottom *WIMB* BH21.... **279** J7
Greenbury Cl *DEAN* RG23..... **68** E7
Green Cl *FAWY* SO45............. **268** C6
 NARL SO24........................... **148** A7
 PLE BH15............................. **332** F2
 RSAL SP5............................. **201** N1
 RWIN SO21.......................... **144** F4
 TOTT SO40........................... **245** M7
Greenclose La *WIMB* BH21.... **300** F1
Green Crs *LSOL/BMARY* PO13.. **294** G8
Greencroft *FARN* GU14......... **58** A9
Green Cft *FNM* GU9.............. **97** H5
Green Cross La *RFNM* GU10... **136** C8
Greendale Cl *FHAM* PO15..... **272** B6
The Greendale *FHAM* PO15... **272** B6
Green Dro *RAND* SP11.......... **82** F1
 RSAL SP5............................. **176** B2
Green End *FYLY* GU46........... **40** E7
Green Farm Gdns *HSEA* PO3.. **297** H5
Greenfield Cl *HEND* SO30..... **250** B7
 LIPH GU30........................... **175** K2
Greenfield Crs *HORN* PO8..... **256** D8
Greenfield Rd
 NMIL/BTOS BH25 .... **327** K7
Greenfield Rd *FNM* GU9........ **115** P3
 PLE BH15............................. **320** G6
Greenfields *EPSF* GU31......... **217** H6
 LISS SO53............................ **192** E2
 RAND SP11........................... **81** L3
 RSAL SP5............................. **176** C4
Greenfields Av *ALTN* GU34.... **132** E5
 TOTT SO40........................... **246** C2
Greenfields Cl *EPSF* GU31..... **217** J5
Greenfinch Cl *CFDH* BH17 *.. **320** B3
 NARL SO24........................... **228** E3
Greenfinch Wk *RGWD* BH24.. **282** G5
Greenham Cl *STHA* SO19...... **54** C2
Greenham Rd *NWBY* RG14.... **17** F4
Greenhanger *RFNM* GU10..... **136** F9
Greenhaven *YTLY* GU46........ **40** C9
Greenhaven Cl *AND* SP10..... **5** C5
Greenhayes *RGWD* BH24....... **284** B3
Greenhays Ri *WIMB* BH21..... **278** E2
Greenhill Av *FUFL* SO22........ **22** A4
Greenhill Cl *FNM* GU9........... **116** A3
Greenhill La *ROWN* SO16...... **227** L4
 WIMB BH21......................... **278** F8
Greenhill Rd *FNM* GU9......... **116** D2
 FUFL SO22............................ **22** A4
Greenhill Ter *FUFL* SO22...... **22** A4
Green Hollow Cl
 FHAM/PORC PO16............... **10** C1
Green Jacket Cl *FUFL* SO22... **183** N1
Greenlands *KSCL* RG20......... **29** M5
Greenlands Rd *CBLY* GU15.... **48** C3
 KSCL RG20........................... **10** G6
 NWBY RG14.......................... **17** G6
Green La *ALTN* GU34............. **150** A8
 BLKW GU17.......................... **57** J1
 BPWT SO32.......................... **232** B5
 FAWY SO45.......................... **291** H9
 FBDG SP6............................ **240** D7
 FERN BH22.......................... **302** A7
 FNM GU9............................. **96** F5
 FNM GU9............................. **116** A5
 GPORT PO12........................ **12** A6
 HASM GU27.......................... **157** K3
 HISD PO11........................... **318** E6
 HORN PO8........................... **236** N1
 HLER SO31........................... **269** J4
 NARL SO24........................... **168** F2
 NARL SO24........................... **168** P2
 NBNE BH10.......................... **322** N8
 NMIL/BTOS BH25 .... **306** G7
 NTHA RG18.......................... **25** M4
 NWBY RG14.......................... **16** B3
 OVTN RG25.......................... **110** C5
 PSF GU32............................. **190** F1
 RAND SP11........................... **101** J3
 RAND SP11........................... **117** K4
 RFNM GU10.......................... **136** F9
 RGWD BH24.......................... **284** D7
 ROMY SO51.......................... **205** J3
 ROWN SO16.......................... **247** H1
 RSAL SP5............................. **199** K5
 SHST GU47.......................... **41** K6
 TADY RG26........................... **50** F1
 THLE RG7............................ **27** H3
 TOTT SO40........................... **264** A8
 WBNE BH4 *........................ **334** C1
 WHCH RG28.......................... **85** M6
Green Wk *HASM* GU12.......... **10** A1
 RAND SP11........................... **76** D9
 BH/HW/K RG22.................... **68** F8
Greenway *HTWY* RG27.......... **52** E5
Greenway Cl *LYMN* SO41...... **329** J3
Greenway La *EPSF* GU31....... **215** J7
Greenway Rd *GPORT* PO12.... **315** M2
Greenways *BPWT* SO32......... **232** F7
 CHCH/BSGR BH23................ **325** J4
 FLEETS GU52....................... **74** C6
 KSCL RG20........................... **29** M5
 LYMN SO41......................... **338** F1
 ROWN SO16.......................... **228** F7
Greenways Av *CHAR* BH8...... **323** J4
Greenways Rd *BROC* SO42.... **286** C8
The Greenwich *FAWY* SO45... **290** C7
Greenwich Wy *FHAM/STUB* PO14.. **82** E9
Greenwood Av *CHAM* PO6..... **296** F1
 PSTN BH14........................... **333** L3
 ROWN SO16.......................... **227** H6
Greenwood Cl
 FHAM/PORC PO16............... **272** E6
 ROMY SO51.......................... **204** E5
Greenwood Copse
 RGWD BH24.......................... **281** M5
Greenwood Dr *CHIN* RG24.... **52** A9
Greenwood La *BPWT* SO32.... **230** F5
Greenwood Rd
 CHOB/PIR GU24................... **59** N7
 MOOR/WNTN BH9................ **322** E6
Greenwoods
 NMIL/BTOS BH25 .... **327** K6
 WHCH RG28.......................... **85** L5
Greenwood Wy *RGWD* BH24.. **281** M5
Greetham St *SSEA* PO5......... **19** H5
Gregory Cl *BSTK* RG21.......... **57** J1
Gregory Gdns *TOTT* SO40..... **246** A2
Gregory La *BPWT* SO32......... **231** H7
Gregson Dr
 LSOL/BMARY PO13.............. **294** G6
Greig Rd *BH/HW/K* RG22...... **90** A2
Grenadier Cl *HLER* SO31....... **271** H8
Grenadier Rd *ASHV* GU12..... **76** G8
Grenadiers Wy *FARN* GU14... **75** K1
Grendon Cl *ROWN* SO16....... **228** D7
Grenehurst Wy *EPSF* GU31.... **215** N1
Grenfell Rd *MOOR/WNTN* BH9.. **322** F4
Grensell Cl *HTWY* RG27........ **39** P6
Grenville Cl *LIPH* GU30......... **175** K3
 RGWD BH24.......................... **260** C9
Grenville Dr *FLEETS* GU51.... **74** B5
Grenville Gdns *FAWY* SO45... **268** D7
 FRIM GU16.......................... **58** D7
Grenville Rd *ENEY* PO4......... **316** G4
 FNM GU9............................. **300** F1
Gresham Rd
 MOOR/WNTN BH9................ **322** G6
Gresley Cl *HEND* SO30.......... **250** C1
Gresley Gdns *HEND* SO30..... **250** C1
Gresley Rd *BSTK* RG21......... **7** H4
Grevillea Av *FHAM* PO15...... **271** J3
Greville Cl *ALDT* GU11.......... **2** C2
Greville Gn *EMRTH* PO10..... **277** L6
Greville Rd *WSHM* SO15....... **247** P4
Greyberry Copse Rd
 STHA SO19........................... **24** G7
Greycot Cl *WIMB* BH21......... **280** E1
Greyfriars Rd *FHAM* PO15..... **272** A4
Greyhound Cl *ASHV* GU12.... **97** H2
Greyhound La *OVTN* RG25..... **86** G4
Greys Cl *ALDT* GU11............. **96** E1
Greys Farm Cl *NARL* SO24.... **187** H2
Greyshott Av
 FHAM/STUB PO14................ **294** A1

Greystead Pk RFNM GU10 ... 115 N4
Greystoke Av BWD BH11 ... 301 P7
Greystoke Ct CWTH RG45 ... 41 H2
Greywell Av ROWN SO16 ... 227 N8
Greywell Cl TADY RG26 ... 34 B6
Greywell Rd CHIN RG24 ... 70 F7
  HAV PO9 ... 276 E5
  HTWY RG27 ... 71 K8
Grieve Cl RFNM GU10 ... 97 L4
Griffen Ct SD/PW SO17 ... 248 E3
Griffin Cl LSOL/BMARY PO13 ... 314 C2
Griffin Wk PSEA PO1 ... 19 F4
Griffin Wy North HTWY RG27 ... 72 A1
Griffin Wy South HTWY RG27 ... 72 A5
Griffiths Gdns NBNE BH10 ... 322 B2
Griffon Cl FARN GU14 ... 75 L1
  HLER SO31 ... 270 A1
Grigg La BROC SO42 ... 286 C8
Grindle Cl NTHA RG18 ... 25 M2
Gritanwood Rd FAWY SO45 ... 317 K5
Grosvenor Cl BH/HW/K RG22 ... 89 M6
  RGWD BH24 ... 281 K4
  SD/PW SO17 ... 248 E1
  TDWTH SO19 ... 37 J5
Grosvenor Ct BLKW GU17 ... 57 J2
Grosvenor Dr WINC SO23 ... 165 J5
Grosvenor Gdns BMTH BH1 ... 335 J2
  HEND SO30 ... 249 M2
  SD/PW SO17 ... 248 E1
Grosvenor House
  WSHM SO15 * ... 248 B5
Grosvenor Lawn NWBY RG14 * ... 16 A3
  SD/PW SO17 * ... 329 K2
Grosvenor Ms LYMN SO41 * ... 329 K2
  SD/PW SO17 * ... 248 E1
Grosvenor Rd ALDT GU11 ... 2 D3
  ALTN GU34 ... 149 P6
  CHFD SO53 ... 206 C4
  SD/PW SO17 ... 248 E1
  WBNE BH4 ... 334 C3
Grosvenor Sq WSHM SO15 ... 20 C1
Grosvenor St SSEA PO5 ... 19 H4
Grove Av FHAM/PORC PO16 ... 295 N5
  GPORT PO12 ... 12 E1
Grovebury Rd HLER SO31 ... 270 C8
Grove Cl BSTK RG21 ... 69 M9
Grove Cross Rd FRIM GU16 ... 58 C4
Grove End Rd FNM GU9 ... 116 B2
Grove Farm Pk FRIM GU16 * ... 76 E3
Grovefields Av FRIM GU16 ... 58 B1
Grove Gdns ITCH SO19 ... 269 K1
Groveland Rd NWBY RG14 ... 24 A2
Grovelands RFNM GU10 ... 116 E3
Grovelands Rd FUFL SO22 ... 164 C6
Grove La RSAL SP5 ... 200 B6
Groveley Rd
  CHCH/BSGR BH23 ... 325 D9
  WBNE BH4 ... 334 B4
Grovely Av ROMY SO51 ... 335 M2
Grovely Wy ROMY SO51 ... 205 J8
Grove Pastures LYMN SO41 ... 329 L4
Grove Pl FUFL SO22 ... 164 F4
  ITCH SO19 ... 249 K9
  LYMN SO41 ... 329 L4
Grove Rd ALTN GU34 ... 132 F7
  ASHV GU12 ... 76 F8
  BKME/WDN BH12 ... 321 M5
  BMTH BH1 ... 9 J4
  BSTK RG21 ... 69 M9
  CHAM PO6 ... 297 L2
  FHAM/PORC PO16 ... 10 E6
  FLEETS GU52 ... 74 E7
  GPORT PO12 ... 315 M2
  HAV PO9 ... 15 K4
  LYMN SO41 ... 329 M4
  NMIL/BTOS BH25 ... 327 J8
  NWBY RG14 ... 24 A2
  RWIN SO21 ... 189 H1
  WIMB BH21 ... 300 E1
  WSHM SO15 ... 247 N4
Grove Rd East
  CHCH/BSGR BH23 ... 324 F7
Grove Rd North SSEA PO5 ... 19 H6
Grove Rd South SSEA PO5 ... 19 H7
Grove Rd West
  CHCH/BSGR BH23 ... 324 D7
Groves Cl RWIN SO21 ... 144 C4
Groves Down ROMY SO51 ... 202 E9
Groves Lea THLE RG7 ... 27 H9
Groves Orch WHCH RG28 ... 85 K4
Grove St SHAM SO14 ... 21 G5
The Grove ALDT GU11 ... 2 E4
  CHCH/BSGR BH23 ... 324 C6
  EMRTH PO10 ... 277 P7
  FARN GU14 ... 76 C3
  FERN BH22 ... 302 C4
  FHAM/STUB PO14 ... 293 P7
  FRIM GU16 ... 58 C4
  HLER SO31 ... 269 M3
  ITCH SO19 ... 269 K1
  LIPH GU30 ... 175 J5
  MOOR/WNTN BH9 ... 322 F4
  NTHA RG18 ... 15 H1
  RAND SP11 ... 81 M7
  VWD BH31 ... 258 C5
Grower Gdns BWD BH11 ... 322 A3
Gruneisen Rd NEND PO2 ... 296 E7
Guardhouse Rd PSEA PO1 ... 316 D1
Guardroom Rd NEND PO2 ... 296 D8
Gudge Heath La FHAM PO15 ... 10 B3
The Guelders WVILLE PO7 ... 275 N1
Guernsey Cl CHIN RG24 ... 69 M2
  ROWN SO16 ... 227 J9
Guernsey Dr FLEETN GU51 ... 56 E9
Guernsey Rd
  BKME/WDN BH12 ... 321 M8
Guessens La
  FHAM/STUB PO14 ... 293 N8
Guest Av BKME/WDN BH12 ... 321 P6
Guest Cl BKME/WDN BH12 ... 322 A9
Guest Rd ELGH SO50 ... 230 D1
Guildford Ct
  LSOL/BMARY PO13 * ... 315 H3
Guildford Dr CHFD SO53 ... 228 D1
Guildford Rd ASHV GU12 ... 77 J9
  ASHV GU12 ... 97 K4
  FLEETN GU51 ... 57 J8
  FNM GU9 ... 96 D8

  FRIM GU16 ... 58 F8
  PSEA PO1 ... 316 Q2
  RFNM GU10 ... 96 F8
  RGUW GU3 ... 77 N8
Guildford Rd East FARN GU14 ... 76 B3
Guildford Rd West FARN GU14 ... 76 B3
Guildford St SHAM SO14 ... 21 H2
Guildhall Sq PSEA PO1 ... 316 D3
Guildhall Wk PSEA PO1 ... 19 F4
Guildmill Rd SBNE BH6 ... 336 C2
Guillemont Flds FARN GU14 ... 57 L8
Guillemot Cl FAWY SO45 ... 268 D7
Guillemot Gdns
  LSOL/BMARY PO13 ... 294 F6
Guinea Ct CHIN RG24 ... 52 B9
Gull Cl LSOL/BMARY PO13 ... 294 F7
Culley Rd FARN GU14 ... 75 P4
Gulliver Ct PLE BH14 ... 333 L3
The Gulls TOTT SO40 ... 247 K9
Gullycroft Md HEND SO30 ... 250 B4
Gun Hl ALDT GU11 ... 3 F1
Gunners La NARL SO24 ... 128 E5
Gunners Ms BPWT SO32 ... 232 B4
Gunners Rw BPWT SO32 ... 232 C4
Gunners Rw ENEY PO4 ... 317 K6
Gunners Wy GPORT PO12 ... 295 K9
Gunns Farm LIPH GU30 ... 175 K5
Gunstore Rd HSEA PO3 ... 297 J5
Gunville Crs
  MOOR/WNTN BH9 ... 323 H4
Gunville Hl RSAL SP5 ... 158 D1
Gunville Rd RSAL SP5 ... 158 C1
Gunwharf Quays PSEA PO1 ... 18 C4
Gurnard Rd CHAM PO6 ... 296 G2
Gurnays Md ROMY SO51 ... 224 D1
Gurney Rd ENEY PO4 ... 317 K4
  WIMB BH21 ... 300 A7
  WSHM SO15 ... 247 N3
Gussage Rd BKME/WDN BH12 ... 321 N4
Gutner La HISD PO11 ... 299 J8
Guttridge Dro ROMY SO51 ... 141 K4
Guttridge La TADY RG26 ... 34 B6
Gwatkin Cl HAV PO9 ... 276 B8
Gwyn Cl NWBY RG14 ... 24 C7
Gwynne Rd BKME/WDN BH12 ... 321 N7
Gypsy La HORN PO8 ... 255 P6
  RGWD BH24 ... 282 F1

H

Haarlem Ms CHCH/BSGR BH23... 325 H8
Habershon Dr FRIM GU16... 59 J3
Habin Hl EPSF GU31... 217 K1
Haccups La ROMY SO51... 180 B5
Hack Dr RWIN SO21... 207 P5
Hacketts La BPWT SO32... 233 K1
Hackett Wy FHAM/STUB PO14... 294 E3
Hackleys La RWIN SO21... 203 H8
Hacks La RWIN SO21... 143 L5
Hackwood Cl AND SP10... 102 B3
Hackwood Cots BSTK RG21... 90 E1
Hackwood La OVTN RG25... 90 D5
Hackwood Rd BSTK RG21... 69 L8
Hackwood Road Rbt
  BSTK RG21... 69 M9
Hackworth Gdns HEND SO30... 250 C1
Hadden Rd CHAR BH8... 323 K7
Haddon Cl FHAM/STUB PO14... 10 B6
Haddon Dr ELGH SO50... 207 J8
Haddons Dr WIMB BH21... 280 D2
Hadleigh Gdns ELGH SO50... 207 J8
  FUFL GU16... 58 D7
Hadleigh Rd CHAM PO6... 296 F1
Hadley Fld FAWY SO45... 290 D4
Hadleys RFNM GU10... 115 N7
Hadley Rd BDST BH18... 320 A1
Hadow Rd NBNE BH10... 322 C4
Hadrian Cl FERN BH22... 302 D6
Hadrian Rd AND SP10... 82 E3
Hadrians Wy DEAN RG23... 68 F5
Hadrians Wy ROWN SO16... 228 A5
  WIMB BH21... 300 A5
Haflinger Dr FHAM PO15... 271 H2
Haglane Copse LYMN SO41... 329 H5
Hagley Rd FLEETN GU51... 74 B2
Hahnemann Rd WCLF BH2... 8 B5
Haig Av CCLF BH13... 333 N2
Haig La FLEETS GU52... 74 E7
Haig Rd AND SP10... 102 C2
  ASHV GU12... 3 J4
  CBLY GU15... 41 N8
  ELGH SO50... 230 A3
  NARL SO24... 168 A1
Haileybury Gdns HEND SO30... 250 B2
Hailsham Cl SHST GU47... 41 L5
Hailstone Rd BSTK RG21... 69 L4
Hainault Dr VWD BH31... 258 C4
Haining Gdns FRIM GU16... 76 F1
Haking Rd CHCH/BSGR BH23... 325 H8
Halcyon Dr RAND SP11... 100 E2
Halden Cl ROMY SO51... 206 D4
Hale Av NMIL/BTOS BH25... 327 K5
Hale Cl NARL SO24... 169 M2
Hale Gdns NMIL/BTOS BH25... 327 K5
Hale House La RFNM GU10... 136 F8
Hale La FBDG SP6... 221 K3
Hale Rd FBDG SP6... 221 J2
Hale Reeds FNM GU9... 96 D5
Hale Rd FBDG SP6... 221 J3
Halewood Wy
  Half Moon Hl HASM GU27... 324 D7
  Half Moon Hl HASM GU27... 157 H7
Halfpenny La PSEA PO1... 18 D6
Halfway Rd FAWY SO45... 291 N8
Halifax Cl AND SP10... 4 A2

  FARN GU14 ... 75 N1
Halifax Ct HEND SO30 ... 249 L1
Halifax Ri NTHA RG18 ... 25 M3
Halifax Ri WVILLE PO7 ... 275 P3
Halifax Wy CHCH/BSGR BH23... 325 M8
  FARN GU14 ... 75 N5
Hall Av ALDT GU11 ... 2 E4
Hall Cl BPWT SO32 ... 232 B4
Hall Dr FLEETS GU52 ... 74 E6
Hallet Cl WEND SO18 ... 249 H2
Hallett Rd HAV PO9 ... 277 H8
Halletts Cl FHAM/STUB PO14 ... 294 A6
Hall Farm Crs YTLY GU46 ... 40 D9
The Halliards
  FHAM/PORC PO16 ... 294 F2
Halliday Ct BSTK RG21 ... 90 C1
  GPORT PO12 ... 315 M3
Halliday Crs ENEY PO4 ... 317 L5
Hall Lands La ELGH SO50 ... 230 D2
Hall La ALTN GU34 ... 152 B6
  YTLY GU46 ... 40 D9
Hallmark Cl SHST GU47 ... 41 M6
Hall Md ALTN GU34 ... 132 C3
  BWD BH11 ... 321 P1
  FARN GU14 ... 76 A2
Halls Farm Cl FUFL SO22 ... 164 F4
Hall's Wy HTWY RG27 ... 40 B6
The Hall Wy FUFL SO22 ... 164 C2
Halsey Cl GPORT PO12 ... 315 K5
Halstead Rd CHAM PO6 ... 296 F1
Hamtun Crs TOTT SO40 ... 249 H1
Haistock Crs CFDH BH17 ... 320 F2
Halter Pth PLE BH15 ... 320 K9
Halter Ri WIMB BH21 ... 279 L8
Halters End GSHT GU26 ... 155 P5
The Halters NWBY RG14 ... 24 E7
Halterworth La ROMY SO51 ... 204 C5
Halton Cl CHCH/BSGR BH23 ... 305 M8
Halton Rd RAND SP11 ... 79 M4
Haltons Cl TOTT SO40 ... 246 B2
Halyard Cl LSOL/BMARY PO13 ... 315 H1
Hambert Wy TOTT SO40 ... 246 C6
Hamble Av BLKW GU17 ... 41 L9
Hamble Cl DEAN RG23 ... 88 F2
  HLER SO31 ... 270 C9
Hamble Ct AND SP10 ... 82 C9
  BSTK RG21 ... 7 K6
  CHFD SO53 ... 206 F8
Hambledon Cl FUFL SO22 ... 164 E3
Hambledon Gdns SBNE BH6 ... 336 C2
Hambledon La BPWT SO32 ... 253 N1
Hambledon Pde
  WVILLE PO7 ... 255 L9
Hambledon Rd HORN PO8 ... 236 A7
  LTDN BH7 ... 323 P8
  WVILLE PO7 ... 254 F3
Hambledon Wy FHAM/PORC PO16... 52 C8
Hamble Dr TADY RG26 ... 34 E6
Hamble House Gdns
  HLER SO31 ... 270 A8
Hamble La HLER SO31 ... 269 N7
  WVILLE PO7 ... 274 N5
Hamble Pk HLER SO31 * ... 270 F9
Hamble Rd GPORT PO12 ... 315 J4
  HLER SO31 ... 321 H5
Hamble Springs BPWT SO32 ... 232 B5
Hambleton Cl FRIM GU16 ... 58 C2
Hamblewood HEND SO30 ... 250 C5
Hamblin Wy CHAR BH8 ... 323 L5
Ham Br NWBY RG14 ... 25 H4
Hamesmoor Rd FRIM GU16 ... 58 D9
Hamesmoor Wy FRIM GU16 ... 58 E9
Hamfield Dr HISD PO11 ... 318 E4
Hamilton Cl BMTH BH1 ... 335 K2
  BOR GU35 ... 154 C4
  CHCH/BSGR BH23 ... 306 H5
  HAV PO9 ... 337 K2
  PLE BH15 ... 298 F1
  TOTT SO40 ... 332 A1
Hamilton Ct LYMN SO41 ... 338 F2
  NWBY RG14 ... 17 F7
Hamilton Crs PLE BH15 ... 332 A1
Hamilton Gdns BSTK RG21 ... 57 K8
Hamilton Gv
  LSOL/BMARY PO13 ... 294 F7
Hamilton Ms FAWY SO45 ... 268 D9
Hamilton Pk RSAL SP5 ... 199 L5
Hamilton Pl ALDT GU11 ... 2 C5
  LYMN SO41 * ... 329 K4
Hamilton Rd BMTH BH1 ... 335 K2
  CHAM PO6 ... 296 A1
  ELGH SO50 ... 229 M1
  FAWY SO45 ... 290 D1
  FLEETS GU52 ... 74 E6
  LISS GU33 ... 174 A5
  PLE BH15 ... 332 A1
  SSEA PO5 ... 316 F6
  WIMB BH21 ... 300 A8
Hamilton Wy
  NMIL/BTOS BH25 ... 326 G5
Ham La FERN BH22 ... 302 B6
  GPORT PO12 ... 295 L8
  HORN PO8 ... 255 P3
  TADY RG26 ... 34 C2
  WIMB BH21 ... 301 K1
Hamlash La HASM GU10 ... 116 C9
Hamlet Gdns RAND SP11 ... 82 F5
Hamlet Wy GPORT PO12 ... 295 L8
Hammer Hl HASM GU27 ... 156 D8
Hammer La HASM GU27 ... 155 M1
Hammer Rd HASM GU27 ... 156 B9
Hammersley Rd ALDT GU11 ... 76 A5
Hammer V HASM GU27 ... 156 C7
Hammerwood Copse
  HASM GU27 ... 156 C8
Ham Mi NWBY RG14 * ... 24 C4
Hammond Cl FHAM PO15 ... 272 B8

STHA RG19 ... 25 P5
Hammond Rd BSTK RG21 ... 69 K9
  FHAM PO15 ... 10 A3
Hammonds Cl TOTT SO40 ... 246 B3
Hammond's Gn TOTT SO40 ... 246 B3
Hammonds Heath THLE RG7 ... 27 K6
Hammond's La NARL SO24 ... 169 M3
Hammonds La TOTT SO40 ... 246 B3
Hammond Sq AND SP10 * ... 82 F9
Hammonds Wy TOTT SO40 ... 246 C3
Hampden La SBNE BH6 ... 335 P1
Hampshire Cl BH/HW/K RG22 ... 68 D9
  CHCH/BSGR BH23 ... 324 D5
Hampshire Hatches La
  RGWD BH24 ... 282 E5
Hampshire Rd BOR GU35 ... 154 A4
Hampshire St BSTK RG21 ... 316 C1
Hampshire Ter PSEA PO1 ... 19 F5
Hampshire Cl FAWY SO45 ... 290 C9
  FLEETS GU52 ... 74 C7
  WVILLE PO7 ... 276 A3
Hampton Cl BH/HW/K RG22 ... 260 F9
Hampton Gdns FAWY SO45 ... 290 C9
Hampton Gv FHAM PO15 ... 271 P9
Hampton Hl BPWT SO32 ... 232 F6
Hampton La DEAN RG23 * ... 68 D9
  FUFL SO22 ... 164 D6
Hampton Rd FNM GU9 ... 96 A5
  NWBY RG14 ... 16 D5
Hamptworth Rd RSAL SP5 ... 200 D8
Hamtun Crs TOTT SO40 ... 246 C2
Hamtun Gdns TOTT SO40 ... 246 C2
Hamtun Rd ITCH SO19 ... 249 L9
Hamtun St SHAM SO14 ... 20 D6
Hanbidge Crs
  LSOL/BMARY PO13 ... 295 H5
Hanbury Wy CBLY GU15 ... 58 B2
Hancombe Rd SHST GU47 ... 41 H4
Handcroft Cl RFNM GU10 ... 95 H5
Handel Cl BH/HW/K RG22 ... 89 P2
Handel Rd WSHM SO15 ... 20 B2
Handel Ter WSHM SO15 ... 20 B2
Handford La YTLY GU46 ... 40 D9
Handford Pl WSHM SO15 ... 248 B5
Handley Rd GPORT PO12 ... 315 K2
Hanger Farm Ar TOTT SO40 ... 34 C4
The Hangers BPWT SO32 ... 232 B2
Hangers Wy ALTN GU34 ... 132 C5
  HORN PO8 ... 255 L5
  LISS GU33 ... 178 C8
  PSF GU32 ... 191 L9
The Hanger BOR GU35 ... 154 F1
Hanger Wy EPSF GU31 ... 215 P2
Hanham Rd WIMB BH21 ... 278 E9
Hankinson Rd
  MOOR/WNTN BH9 ... 322 G7
Hanley Rd WSHM SO15 ... 247 P3
Hanmore Rd CHIN RG24 ... 69 P1
Hanna Cl BWD BH11 ... 322 A3
Hannah Gdns WVILLE PO7 ... 275 P2
Hannah Wy LYMN SO41 ... 330 F3
Hannam's Farm RFNM GU10 ... 94 C5
Hannay Rd ITCH SO19 ... 249 M6
Hannington Rd HAV PO9 ... 276 D3
  LTDN BH7 ... 335 N1
Hanningtons Wy THLE RG7 ... 27 L4
Hann Rd ROWN SO16 ... 227 J6
Hans Wy ELGH SO50 ... 229 J2
Hanover Bldg SHAM SO14 ... 20 E5
Hanover Cl AND SP10 ... 102 C4
  FARN GU14 ... 58 D4
  YTLY GU46 ... 40 D8
Hanover Ct PSEA PO1 * ... 18 D5
Hanover Dr FLEETN GU51 ... 56 F9
Hanover Gdns BSTK RG21 ... 90 C1
  FARN GU14 ... 57 M7
  FHAM/PORC PO16 ... 11 C1
Hanover Gn CFDH BH17 * ... 311 K6
Hanoverian Wy FHAM PO15 ... 271 J3
Hanover Md NWBY RG14 ... 24 A9
Hanover St PSEA PO1 ... 18 C2
Hanson Rd AND SP10 ... 102 C1
Hanway Rd NEND PO2 ... 296 F9
Ha'Penny Dell WVILLE PO7 * ... 275 P1
Harbeck Rd CHAR BH8 ... 323 J4
Harborough Rd WSHM SO15 ... 248 B5
Harbour Cl FARN GU14 ... 57 P5
  TOTT SO40 ... 247 N9
Harbour Crs
  CHCH/BSGR BH23 ... 337 J1
Harbour Hill Crs PLE BH15 ... 320 C7
Harbour Hill Rd PLE BH15 ... 320 C7
Harbourne Gdns WEND SO18 ... 249 K1
Harbour Pde WSHM SO15 ... 20 B4
Harbour Rd GPORT PO12 ... 295 L9
  HISD PO11 ... 318 C4
  SBNE BH6 ... 336 E5
Harbourside HAV PO9 ... 298 F3
Harbour Vw
  FHAM/PORC PO16 ... 295 N3
Harbour View Cl PSTN BH14 ... 331 P7
Harbour View Rd PSTN BH14 ... 321 J7
Harbour Wy EMRTH PO10 ... 299 N1
  NEND PO2 ... 296 E7
Harbridge Dro FBDG SP6 ... 240 A7
Harbridge Dro FBDG SP6 ... 276 D3
Harcombe Cl CFDH BH17 ... 320 C1
Harcourt Cl HORN PO8 ... 256 A7
Harcourt Rd BOSC BH5 ... 335 N1
  FHAM/STUB PO14 ... 293 P2
  GPORT PO12 ... 12 B1
  PSEA PO1 ... 316 D1
  WEND SO18 ... 248 F1
Harding La ELGH SO50 ... 230 B1
Harding Rd GPORT PO12 ... 315 K2
Hardley La HTWY RG27 ... 55 J7
Hardley La HASM GU27 ... 290 D2
The Hard PSEA PO1 ... 18 C2
Hardwicke Cl ROWN SO16 ... 247 K1
Hardwick Rd CHFD SO53 ... 206 F7
Hardy Av YTLY GU46 ... 56 D1
Hardy Cl FERN BH22 ... 280 F8
  HLER SO31 ... 271 H6
  LSOL/BMARY PO13 ... 294 D5

  NMIL/BTOS BH25 ... 327 H4
  NTHA RG18 ... 25 M2
  SO45 ... 247 M5
Hardy Crs WIMB BH21 ... 300 F1
Hardy Dr EPSF GU31 ... 191 N9
  FAWY SO45 ... 268 D9
Hardyfair Cl RAND SP11 ... 81 K9
Hardy La BCAS SO40 ... 57 K6
Hardy La BSTK RG21 ... 69 J8
Hardy Rd CHAM PO6 ... 297 N2
  ELGH SO50 ... 229 H3
  FERN BH22 ... 280 F8
  PSTN BH14 ... 321 M8
Hardys Fld KSCL RG20 ... 48 B2
Harebell Cl FHAM/PORC PO16 ... 11 J1
  HTWY RG27 ... 55 J6
Harebell Dr NTHA RG18 ... 25 P3
Harebell Gdns HTWY RG27 ... 55 J6
Harefield Ct ROMY SO51 ... 204 F5
Harefield Rd SD/PW SO17 ... 228 B5
Hare La NMIL/BTOS BH25 ... 327 M4
  RWIN SO21 ... 208 A1
Hares Gn LTDN BH7 ... 323 N7
Hare's La HTWY RG27 ... 55 K5
Harestock Cl FUFL SO22 ... 164 E3
Harestock Rd FUFL SO22 ... 164 E3
  HAV PO9 ... 14 C2
Harewood Av ELGH SO50 ... 207 J8
Harewood Cl ELGH SO50 ... 207 J8
Harewood Crs LTDN BH7 ... 323 M8
Harewood Gdns LTDN BH7 ... 323 M8
Harewood Gn LYMN SO41 ... 339 L2
Harewood Pl LTDN BH7 ... 323 P9
Harfield Cl HTWY RG27 ... 71 J5
Harford Cl LYMN SO41 ... 329 H6
Harford Rd BKME/WDN BH12 ... 321 L4
Harkwood Dr PLE BH15 ... 320 A8
Harland Crs WSHM SO15 ... 247 P2
Harland Rd SBNE BH6 ... 336 E2
Harlaxton Cl ELGH SO50 ... 207 H8
Harlech Cl DEAN RG23 ... 68 F7
Harlech Dr CHFD SO53 ... 206 B3
Harlech Rd BLKW GU17 ... 57 L1
Harlequin Gv FHAM PO15 ... 10 B5
Harleston Rd CHAM PO6 ... 274 F9
Harleston Vis WIMB BH21 ... 300 F1
Harlington Wy FLEETN GU51 ... 74 B4
Harlyn Rd ROWN SO16 ... 247 K2
Harman Rd
  LSOL/BMARY PO13 ... 294 G6
Harmes Wy ALDT GU11 ... 76 C5
Harmsworth Rd TADY RG26 ... 34 C6
Harness Cl WIMB BH21 ... 279 K8
Harold Ct TOTT SO40 ... 246 B5
Harold Gdns ALTN GU34 ... 132 C4
Harold Jackson Ter BSTK RG21 ... 69 M8
Harold Rd EMRTH PO10 ... 277 P6
  ENEY PO4 ... 316 G5
  FHAM/STUB PO14 ... 294 B6
  HISD PO11 ... 319 H6
  WSHM SO15 ... 247 N4
Harpdon Pde YTLY GU46 ... 40 E7
Harper Wy FHAM/PORC PO16 ... 11 H6
Harpton Cl YTLY GU46 ... 40 E7
Harpway La CHCH/BSGR BH23 ... 324 C1
The Harrage ROMY SO51 ... 204 D6
Harrier Cl HORN PO8 ... 256 A4
  LSOL/BMARY PO13 ... 314 D2
  ROWN SO16 ... 227 M6
Harrier Dr WIMB BH21 ... 300 F3
Harrier Gn FAWY SO45 ... 290 D9
Harriers Cl CHCH/BSGR BH23 ... 325 P7
Harrier Wy EPSF GU31 ... 216 A3
  FAWY SO45 ... 290 D3
Harriet Cl FHAM/STUB PO14 ... 293 P7
Harrington Cl NWBY RG14 ... 24 C2
Harrington La NWBY RG14 ... 16 C9
Harris Cl LIPH GU30 ... 175 J5
Harris Hl BH/HW/K RG22 ... 89 M4
Harris La HORN PO8 ... 237 K7
Harrison Av BMTH BH1 ... 323 K9
Harrison Cl CHCH/BSGR BH23 ... 324 G4
Harrison Pl BSTK RG21 ... 69 D3
Harrison Rd FHAM/STUB PO14 ... 11 G3
  SD/PW SO17 ... 228 E9
Harrison Wy FERN BH22 ... 280 E6
Harris Rd LSOL/BMARY PO13 ... 294 G6
  NMIL/BTOS BH25 ... 205 L9
Harroway RAND SP11 ... 84 C6
Harroway La RAND SP11 ... 81 N9
Harrow Cl CHCH/BSGR BH23 ... 324 B1
Harrowgate La WVILLE PO7 ... 255 H3
Harrow Rd CHCH/BSGR BH23 ... 305 L9
  FLEETN GU51 ... 74 C1
  SSEA PO5 ... 316 G4
Harrow Wy AND SP10 ... 102 B3
  DEAN RG23 ... 66 G9
  RAND SP11 ... 81 H9
The Harrow Wy
  BH/HW/K RG22 ... 90 A2
Harry Barrow Cl RGWD BH24 ... 282 E2
Hart Cl FARN GU14 ... 57 M5
  NMIL/BTOS BH25 ... 327 H3
Hartford Bridge Flats
  HTWY RG27 ... 55 M4
Hartford Ct HTWY RG27 ... 55 M3
Hartford Rd FLEETN GU51 ... 74 C1
Hartford Wy HTWY RG27 ... 55 J7
Hartfort Ter HTWY RG27 ... 55 J7
Harthill Dro RSAL SP5 ... 268 E9
Harthouse Ct HTWY RG27 ... 200 A8
Harting Cl HORN PO8 ... 236 D8
Harting Down EPSF GU31 ... 215 P2
Harting Gdns
  FHAM/PORC PO16 ... 273 N9
Harting Rd SBNE BH6 ... 324 D8
Hartington Rd GPORT PO12 ... 315 N3
  SHAM SO14 ... 21 H2
Hartland Pl FARN GU14 ... 57 N8
Hartland's Rd
  FHAM/PORC PO16 ... 11 H6

Hartley Av SD/PW SO17 .... 248 D1
Hartley Cl BLKW GU17 .... 41 J9
ELGH SO50 .... 230 A3
FAWY SO45 .... 268 C9
Hartley Gdns TADY RG26 .... 34 C7
Hartley Gv ROWN SO16 .... 228 C8
Hartley La HTWY RG27 .... 52 G3
Hartley Meadow WHCH RG28 .... 85 K6
Hartley Rd ELGH SO50 .... 230 A2
NEND PO2 .... 296 F6
Hartleys THLE RG7 .... 35 J6
Hartley Wk FAWY SO45 .... 268 B9
Hartmead Rd STHA RG19 .... 25 P4
Hart Plain Av HORN PO8 .... 255 M8
Hartsbourne Dr LTDN BH7 .... 323 P7
Hartsgrove Av FAWY SO45 .... 290 G9
Hartsgrove Cl FAWY SO45 .... 290 G9
Harts Hill Rd NTHA RG18 .... 25 P3
Hartshill Rd TADY RG26 .... 34 A6
Harts La KSCL RG20 .... 30 D8
Hart's La THLE RG7 .... 26 D2
WIMB BH21 .... 279 J3
Hartsleaf Cl FLEETN GU51 .... 74 C4
Harts Leap Cl SHST GU47 .... 41 H5
Harts Leap Rd SHST GU47 .... 41 H6
Harts Wy LYMN SO41 .... 328 D6
Hartswood CHIN RG24 .... 69 P2
The Hart FNM GU9 .... 96 B9
Hartwell Rd HSEA PO3 .... 297 K5
Hartwood Gdns HORN PO8 .... 255 N9
Harvard Cl LSOL/BMARY PO13 .. 314 E7
Harvard Rd SHST GU47 .... 41 N5
Harvest Cl FUFL SO22 .... 183 M2
YTLY GU46 .... 56 C1
Harvest Crs FLEETN GU51 .... 56 E8
Harvester Dr FHAM PO15 .... 271 P9
Harvester Wy LYMN SO41 .... 329 K1
Harvest Gn NWBY RG14 .... 16 A6
Harvesting La PSF GU32 .... 214 A7
Harvest La STOK SO20 .... 121 H5
Harvest Rd CHFD SO53 .... 206 B7
WVILLE PO7 .... 254 G7
Harvest Wy CHIN RG24 .... 70 A4
Harvey Ct FAWY SO45 .... 290 G7
Harvey Crs HLER SO31 .... 270 F8
Harvey Gdns FAWY SO45 .... 268 D7
Harvey Pl AND SP10 .... 5 J3
Harvey Rd BOSC BH5 .... 335 N1
ELGH SO50 .... 229 N1
FARN GU14 .... 57 K8
WIMB BH21 .... 300 G5
Harveys Fld OVTN RG25 .... 86 G3
Harwell Rd CFDH BH17 .... 320 F5
Harwich Rd CHAM PO6 .... 274 F9
Harwood Cl
LSOL/BMARY PO13 .... 294 G5
TOTT SO40 .... 246 B3
Harwood Pl WINC SO23 .... 145 K8
Harwood Ri KSCL RG20 .... 29 N4
Harwood Rd
LSOL/BMARY PO13 .... 294 G6
Haselbury Rd TOTT SO40 .... 246 D4
Haselfoot Gdns HEND SO30 .... 249 N4
Haselworth Dr GPORT PO12 .... 315 M7
Haskells Cl LYND SO43 .... 264 E6
Haskells Rd BKME/WDN BH12 ... 321 K5
Haslar Br GPORT PO12 .... 13 J4
Haslar Crs WVILLE PO7 .... 255 L9
Haslar Rd GPORT PO12 .... 13 G6
Hasle Dr HASM GU27 .... 156 G8
Haslemere Av
CHCH/BSGR BH23 .... 326 B7
Haslemere Cl FRIM GU16 .... 59 H2
Haslemere Gdns HISD PO11 .... 319 M6
Haslemere Pl
CHCH/BSGR BH23 .... 326 C7
Haslemere Rd ENEY PO4 .... 317 H6
LIPH GU30 .... 175 L3
Hasler Rd CFDH BH17 .... 320 E2
Haslop Rd WIMB BH21 .... 279 H7
The Hassocks WVILLE PO7 .... 276 A3
Hastards La ALTN GU34 .... 152 D8
Hasted Dr NARL SO24 .... 167 P3
Haste Hl HASM GU27 .... 157 J8
Haste Hill Top HASM GU27 * 157 J8
Hastings Av GPORT PO12 .... 295 K9
Hastings Cl DEAN RG23 .... 68 E7
FRIM GU16 .... 58 F6
Hastings Rd CFDH BH17 .... 320 D2
CHAR BH8 .... 323 M5
Hatchbury La RAND SP11 .... 43 H7
Hatch Ct HAV PO9 .... 276 C3
Hatchers La RWIN SO21 .... 184 F9
Hatchery Hl RWIN SO21 .... 163 K1
The Hatches FNM GU9 .... 115 P2
FRIM GU16 .... 58 D7
Hatchet Cl FBDG SP6 .... 221 P1
Hatchet La BROC SO42 .... 288 D1
BROC SO42 .... 310 E2
RAND SP11 .... 81 N2
Hatchetts Dr HASM GU27 .... 156 B7
Hatchgate Cl NTHA RG18 .... 25 M1
Hatch La CHIN RG24 .... 70 C7
LISS GU33 .... 192 G2
RDGW/BURGH RG30 .... 27 M1
Hatchley La BPWT SO32 .... 209 H7
Hatch Md HEND SO30 .... 249 L1
Hatchmoor Rd WVILLE PO7 .... 254 G7
Hatch Pond La CFDH BH17 .... 320 E5
Hatch Pond Rd CFDH BH17 .... 320 E4
Hatch Rw BH/HW/K RG22 .... 89 N5
Hatch Warren Gdns
BH/HW/K RG22 .... 90 A4
Hatch Warren La
BH/HW/K RG22 .... 89 M4
BH/HW/K RG22 .... 90 A4
Hatfield Ct NMIL/BTOS BH25 ...... 326 G4
Hatfield Gdns FARN GU14 .... 76 D1
LTDN BH7 .... 323 P7
Hatfield Rd ENEY PO4 .... 317 J5
Hathaway Cl ELGH SO50 .... 207 K9
Hathaway Gdns CHIN RG24 .... 69 M4
WVILLE PO7 .... 276 B1
Hathaway Rd SBNE BH6 .... 336 B2
Hatherden Av PSTN BH14 .... 321 H7
Hatherden Ct AND SP10 * 4 E4
Hatherell Cl HEND SO30 .... 249 M2
Hatherley Crs
FHAM/PORC PO16 .... 295 M1
Hatherley Dr
FHAM/PORC PO16 .... 295 M1
Hatherley Rd CHAM PO6 .... 274 C9
FUFL SO22 .... 22 B2
Hatherwood YTLY GU46 * 40 G9
Hatley Rd WEND SO18 .... 249 K3
Hattem Pl AND SP10 .... 82 D9
Hattingley Rd ALTN GU34 .... 149 M1
Hatt La ROMY SO51 .... 179 L4
Haughurst Hl TADY RG26 .... 33 L6
Havant Farm Cl HAV PO9 .... 15 G2
Havant Rd CHAM PO6 .... 297 H1
HAV PO9 .... 15 K7
HORN PO8 .... 256 D5
NEND PO2 .... 296 F8
Havant St PSEA PO1 .... 18 C3
Havelock Rd
BKME/WDN BH12 .... 334 A1
HLER SO31 .... 270 C9
SHAM SO14 .... 20 C2
SSEA PO5 .... 19 K5
Havelock Wy
CHCH/BSGR BH23 .... 325 P5
Haven Cl CHCH/BSGR BH23 .... 337 J1
Haven Crs FHAM/STUB PO14 .... 293 M8
Havendale HEND SO30 .... 250 D6
Haven Gdns NMIL/BTOS BH25 ... 327 K5
Haven Rd CCLF BH13 .... 333 N4
HISD PO11 .... 319 L7
Havenstone Wy WEND SO18 .... 228 G8
The Haven ELGH SO50 .... 207 K8
ENEY PO4 .... 317 K3
GPORT PO12 .... 12 C7
HEND SO30 * 250 B7
H Av FAWY SO45 .... 291 H3
Haven Wy FNM GU9 .... 96 D7
Haverstock Rd
MOOR/WNTN BH9 .... 323 H5
Haviland Rd BMTH BH1 .... 335 M1
WIMB BH21 .... 302 A1
Haviland Rd East LTDN BH7 .... 335 M1
Haviland Rd West BMTH BH1 .... 335 L2
Havisham Rd NEND PO2 * 316 F1
Hawden Rd BWD BH11 .... 322 A6
Haweswater Cl BOR GU35 .... 154 A3
Haweswater Ct ASHV GU12 * 76 E8
Hawfinch Cl ROWN SO16 .... 227 M6
Hawkchurch Gdns
CFDH BH17 .... 320 G2
Hawk Cl BH/HW/K RG22 .... 89 K3
FHAM/STUB PO14 .... 293 P7
WIMB BH21 .... 279 J7
Hawke Cl AND SP10 .... 5 K2
Hawker Cl WIMB BH21 .... 301 H4
Hawker Rd ASHV GU12 .... 76 E7
Hawkers Cl TOTT SO40 .... 246 C2
Hawkes Cl HTWY RG27 .... 55 H6
Hawke St PSEA PO1 .... 18 C2
Hawkeswood Rd WEND SO18 .... 248 E4
Hawkewood Av WVILLE PO7 .... 255 M9
Hawkfield La BSTK RG21 .... 69 K9
Hawkhill FAWY SO45 .... 267 N6
Hawkhurst Cl ITCH SO19 .... 269 J1
Hawkins Cl RGWD BH24 .... 260 G9
Hawkins Gv FLEETN GU51 .... 74 A6
Hawkins Rd BKME/WDN BH12 ... 321 P3
LSOL/BMARY PO13 .... 295 H7
Hawkins Wy FLEETS GU52 .... 74 F4
Hawkley Cl HAV PO9 .... 276 E4
Hawkley Dr TADY RG26 .... 34 D7
Hawkley Gn ITCH SO19 .... 269 H2
Hawkley Rd LISS GU33 .... 172 E8
Hawkley Wy FLEETN GU51 .... 73 P1
Hawkshaw Cl LIPH GU30 .... 175 L3
Hawks Lea LYMN SO41 .... 338 G2
Hawkswood Av FRIM GU16 .... 58 E3
Hawksworth Rd THLE RG7 .... 27 K4
Hawkwell FHAM/PORC PO16 .... 295 K1
FLEETS GU52 .... 74 E8
Hawkwood Rd BOSC BH5 .... 335 L2
Hawley Ct FARN GU14 .... 57 M5
Hawley Gn BLKW GU17 .... 57 M2
Hawley Gv BLKW GU17 .... 57 M3
Hawley La FARN GU14 .... 58 A5
Hawley Rd BLKW GU17 .... 57 N2
Haworth Cl CHCH/BSGR BH23 ... 324 E6
Hawswater Cl ROWN SO16 .... 247 K2
Hawthorn Cl ASHV GU12 .... 97 L3
ELGH SO50 .... 230 C2
FHAM/PORC PO16 .... 273 M9
HEND SO30 .... 250 D5
NARL SO24 .... 168 A2
NMIL/BTOS BH25 .... 327 L3
RWIN SO21 .... 127 H7
RWIN SO21 .... 208 A5
Hawthorn Ct EPSF GU31 * 216 A2
FARN GU14 .... 76 B4
Hawthorn Crs CHAM PO6 .... 297 J3
Hawthorn Dr CFDH BH17 .... 320 B3
LYMN SO41 .... 308 B6
Hawthorne Cl NTHA RG18 .... 25 N2
RAND SP11 .... 120 B1
Hawthorne Crs BLKW GU17 .... 57 M1
Hawthorne Gv HISD PO11 .... 318 G4
Hawthorne Rd TOTT SO40 .... 246 B3
Hawthorn La ALTN GU34 .... 150 E8
HLER SO31 .... 270 E5
RFNM GU10 .... 115 P7
Hawthorn Ri HTWY RG27 .... 72 A2
Hawthorn Rd ALTN GU34 .... 150 C8
CHCH/BSGR BH23 .... 325 J5
FAWY SO45 .... 268 B7
FRIM GU16 .... 58 E3
HORN PO8 .... 256 C2
MOOR/WNTN BH9 .... 322 F7
NWBY RG14 .... 24 D3
SD/PW SO17 .... 248 C1
TDWTH SP9 .... 79 H4
WVILLE PO7 .... 254 F7
Hawthorns ALTN GU34 .... 132 E4
The Hawthorns BPWT SO32 * ... 231 N3
CHCH/BSGR BH23 .... 325 K9
ELGH SO50 .... 228 G3
TADY RG26 .... 33 P6
TOTT SO40 .... 267 L1
Hawthorn Wy BOR GU35 .... 154 C3
DEAN RG23 .... 68 F6
Hayburn Rd ROWN SO16 .... 247 H1
Haydn Cl WINC SO23 .... 145 J8
Haydn Rd BH/HW/K RG22 .... 89 P3
Haydock Cl ALTN GU34 .... 132 F7
TOTT SO40 .... 246 A3
Haydock Ms WVILLE PO7 .... 276 B1
Haydon Rd CCLF BH13 .... 334 B5
Hay Down La RAND SP11 .... 100 E5
Hayes Av LTDN BH7 .... 323 L9
Hayes Cl FHAM PO15 .... 272 B7
STOK SO20 .... 161 L5
WIMB BH21 .... 279 J9
Hayes La WIMB BH21 .... 279 K9
Hayes Md FAWY SO45 .... 290 D4
Hayeswood Rd WIMB BH21 .... 279 J8
Hayle Rd CHAM PO6 .... 274 B9
WEND SO18 .... 249 K1
Hayles Ct AND SP10 .... 82 G9
Hayley Cl FAWY SO45 .... 290 B1
Hayley La ODIM RG29 .... 93 H6
Hayling Av HSEA PO3 .... 317 K1
Hayling Billy Coastal Pth
HISD PO11 .... 318 E1
Hayling Cl FHAM/STUB PO14 .... 294 B1
GPORT PO12 .... 295 N9
Haymoor Rd PLE BH15 .... 321 J5
Haynes Av PLE BH15 .... 320 F8
Haynes Rd WEND SO18 .... 249 J4
Haynes Wy FAWY SO45 .... 268 A9
Haysoms Cl NMIL/BTOS BH25 ... 327 K6
Haysoms Dr STHA RG19 .... 24 E8
Hay St PSEA PO1 .... 18 E2
Hayter Gdns ROMY SO51 .... 204 E5
Hayters Wy FBDG SP6 .... 239 N5
Hayward Cl TOTT SO40 .... 246 B4
Hayward Ct FAWY SO45 .... 290 E5
Hayward Crs VWD BH31 .... 258 E5
Haywarden Pl HTWY RG27 .... 55 J6
Haywards Farm Cl VWD BH31 .. 258 E5
The Haywards NTHA RG18 .... 25 N3
Hayward Wy VWD BH31 .... 258 D5
Haywood Dr FLEETS GU52 .... 74 D5
Hazel Av FARN GU14 .... 75 N1
Hazelbank Cl EPSF GU31 .... 215 P1
LIPH GU30 .... 175 L3
Hazel Cl AND SP10 .... 102 B4
CHCH/BSGR BH23 .... 325 N6
CHFD SO53 .... 206 E3
DEAN RG23 .... 88 F2
FBDG SP6 .... 239 N6
RDGW/BURGH RG30 .... 27 K2
RWIN SO21 .... 208 A4
Hazelcombe OVTN RG25 .... 87 H4
Hazel Coppice HTWY RG27 .... 72 A2
Hazeldean Dr HAV PO9 .... 277 H1
Hazeldene CHIN RG24 .... 70 A2
Hazeldene Gdns RWIN SO21 .... 146 D9
Hazeldene Rd LIPH GU30 .... 174 E3
Hazeldown Rd ROWN SO16 .... 227 J7
Hazel Dr FERN BH22 .... 280 D9
Hazeleigh Av ITCH SO19 .... 248 G9
Hazeley Cl HTWY RG27 .... 55 H6
Hazeley Rd RWIN SO21 .... 184 A8
Hazel Farm Rd TOTT SO40 .... 246 A4
Hazel Gn TADY RG26 .... 33 N5
Hazel Gv NTHA RG18 .... 25 N2
TOTT SO40 .... 245 M8
FUFL SO22 .... 183 M1
GSHT GU26 .... 156 D4
HLER SO31 .... 271 H8
Hazelgrove HORN PO8 .... 236 C7
Hazelholt Dr HAV PO9 .... 14 B2
Hazell Av NBNE BH10 .... 322 B5
Hazell Rd FNM GU9 .... 95 P9
Hazel Rd ALTN GU34 .... 150 D5
FRIM GU16 .... 76 F2
HORN PO8 .... 236 C7
ITCH SO19 .... 248 F8
LYMN SO41 .... 328 G3
Hazelton Cl LTDN BH7 .... 323 N7
Hazelwood CHIN RG24 .... 51 P9
FHAM/STUB PO14 .... 293 P4
Hazelwood Av HAV PO9 .... 276 B7
NMIL/BTOS BH25 .... 326 G3
Hazelwood Cl DEAN RG23 .... 68 G5
Hazelwood Dr DEAN RG23 .... 68 G5
VWD BH31 .... 259 H6
Hazelwood Rd WEND SO18 .... 249 J2
Hazely Cl HTWY RG27 .... 55 H6
Hazlebury Rd CFDH BH17 .... 320 C5
Hazlemere Dr RGWD BH24 .... 281 L6
Hazleton Int HORN PO8 * 256 C5
Hazleton Wy HORN PO8 .... 256 B8
Head Down EPSF GU31 .... 215 P2
Headington Cl BH/HW/K RG22 .. 89 P3
Headland Dr HLER SO31 .... 270 G6
Headley Cl
LSOL/BMARY PO13 * 314 D2
NARL SO24 .... 168 A3
Headley Flds BOR GU35 .... 154 F3
Headley Hill Rd BOR GU35 .... 154 G3
Headley La LIPH GU30 .... 154 F6
Headley Rd BOR GU35 .... 154 D3
LIPH GU30 .... 175 H1
Headmore La ALTN GU34 .... 150 F7
Headon Vw PSF GU32 .... 188 E9
Heads Farm Cl NBNE BH10 .... 322 E2
Heads La HUNG RG17 .... 28 B1
Head's La NBNE BH10 .... 322 E2
Headswell Av NBNE BH10 .... 322 E3
Headswell Crs NBNE BH10 .... 322 E3
Headswell Gdns NBNE BH10 .... 322 E3
Heanor Cl NBNE BH10 .... 322 C5
Hearmon Cl YTLY GU46 .... 40 E8
Hearne Gdns BPWT SO32 .... 252 E2
Hearn V BOR GU35 .... 155 H1
Hearsey Gdns BLKW GU17 .... 41 J8
Heath Av PLE BH15 .... 320 F6
Heath Cl ELGH SO50 .... 230 D3
FNM GU9 .... 96 C4
HORN PO8 .... 256 B4
WIMB BH21 .... 279 K7
Heath Cnr CBLY GU15 .... 58 F2
Heathcote Cl ASHV GU12 * 76 F9
Heathcote Pl RWIN SO21 .... 182 D7
Heathcote Rd ASHV GU12 .... 76 G9
BOR GU35 .... 154 B5
BOSC BH5 .... 335 M2
CHFD SO53 .... 206 F7
NEND PO2 .... 297 H8
Heathcourt TADY RG26 .... 33 P5
Heath End Farm TADY RG26 .... 33 P5
Heath End Rd TADY RG26 .... 33 P4
Heathen St BPWT SO32 .... 231 H8
Heatherbank Rd WBNE BH4 .... 334 C3
Heatherbrae Gdns
NBAD SO52 .... 205 K9
Heather Cha ELGH SO50 .... 230 A2
Heather Cl ALDT GU11 .... 96 E2
ASHV GU12 .... 76 G7
BOR GU35 .... 153 N7
CHAR BH8 .... 323 K3
CHCH/BSGR BH23 .... 326 C6
FNM GU9 .... 115 P4
LSOL/BMARY PO13 .... 294 F7
LYMN SO41 .... 328 A4
RGWD BH24 .... 281 L6
TOTT SO40 .... 246 C4
WIMB BH21 .... 300 A7
WVILLE PO7 .... 275 P4
Heather Ct WEND SO18 .... 249 L4
Heatherdale Rd CBLY GU15 .... 58 B1
Heatherdeane Rd
SD/PW SO17 .... 248 C1
Heatherdene Av CWTH RG45 .... 40 F2
Heatherdene Rd CHFD SO53 .... 206 G4
Heatherdown Rd FERN BH22 .... 280 G8
Heatherdown Wy FERN BH22 .. 280 G8
Heather Dr AND SP10 .... 4 B2
BOR GU35 .... 154 C3
FERN BH22 .... 302 D1
FLEETS GU52 .... 74 C7
NTHA RG18 .... 25 N2
TADY RG26 .... 34 A4
Heatherfield EPSF GU31 .... 215 K8
Heather Gdns FHAM PO15 .... 272 B7
NWBY RG14 .... 24 B8
Heather Gv HTWY RG27 .... 55 H6
Heatherlands Ri
BKME/WDN BH12 .... 321 M7
Heatherlands Rd ROWN SO16 .... 228 B4
Heather La HTWY RG27 .... 71 K7
Heatherlea Rd SBNE BH6 .... 336 B2
Heather Md FRIM GU16 .... 58 E3
Heather Rd EPSF GU31 .... 216 A2
FAWY SO45 .... 291 H7
NBNE BH10 .... 322 D4
Heather Row La HTWY RG27 .... 71 K8
The Heathers ELGH SO50 .... 228 G2
Heatherstone Av FAWY SO45 .... 290 B1
Heatherton Ms EMRTH PO10 .... 277 M7
Heatherview Cl NBAD SO52 .... 205 K8
Heather View Rd
BKME/WDN BH12 .... 321 P5
Heatherway CWTH RG45 .... 41 H1
Heather Wy BH/HW/K RG22 .... 89 L4
FERN BH22 .... 302 D1
GSHT GU26 .... 156 E1
Heath Farm Cl FERN BH22 .... 302 C5
Heath Farm Rd FERN BH22 .... 302 C5
Heath Farm Wy FERN BH22 .... 302 C5
Heathfield FAWY SO45 .... 268 B8
Heathfield Av
BKME/WDN BH12 .... 322 A7
FHAM PO15 .... 272 B9
Heathfield Cl ITCH SO19 .... 249 K8
Heathfield Ct FLEETN GU51 .... 74 B5
Heathfield Rd
BH/HW/K RG22 .... 89 P4
CHFD SO53 .... 206 E3
EPSF GU31 .... 216 A2
FERN BH22 .... 280 F8
ITCH SO19 .... 249 K8
NEND PO2 .... 296 F9
Heathfields TADY RG26 .... 33 P5
Heathfield Wy FERN BH22 .... 280 F8
Heath Gdns HLER SO31 .... 269 M3
Heath Green La NARL SO24 .... 149 K1
Heath Hl RFNM GU10 .... 135 N6
Heath Hill Rd North
CWTH RG45 .... 41 J1
Heath Hill Rd South
CWTH RG45 .... 41 J1
Heath House Cl HEND SO30 .... 250 B7
Heath House Gdns
HEND SO30 .... 250 B7
Heathhouse La HEND SO30 .... 250 B7
Heathlands KSCL RG20 .... 29 P6
Heathlands Av FERN BH22 .... 302 D6
Heathlands Cl
CHCH/BSGR BH23 .... 324 G4
CHFD SO53 .... 206 E5
VWD BH31 .... 258 G4
Heathlands Rd CHFD SO53 .... 206 E5
Heathland St ALDT GU11 .... 2 E3
Heath La BROC SO42 .... 310 G1
FHAM/STUB PO14 .... 293 L2
FNM GU9 .... 96 C4
NTHA RG18 .... 25 M2
RFNM GU10 .... 95 J5
Heath Lawns FHAM PO15 .... 272 B9
Heathman St STOK SO20 .... 139 P2
Heath Rd BPWT SO32 .... 253 L2
CHCH/BSGR BH23 .... 326 D6
EPSF GU31 .... 215 N2
HASM GU27 .... 156 C8
HLER SO31 .... 270 F7
ITCH SO19 .... 249 J6
LYMN SO41 .... 327 P4
NBAD SO52 .... 227 L1
RGWD BH24 .... 281 K5
TADY RG26 .... 34 F5
WHAM PO17 .... 253 K3
Heath Rd East EPSF GU31 .... 215 P3
Heath Rd North HLER SO31 .... 270 F7
Heath Rd South HLER SO31 .... 270 F7
Heath Rd West EPSF GU31 .... 215 N3
RGWD BH24 .... 303 L2
Heathrow Copse TADY RG26 .... 33 N6
Heathside Wy HTWY RG27 .... 55 H6
The Heath WVILLE PO7 .... 255 J7
Heath V AND SP10 .... 4 E6
Heathvale Bridge Rd
ASHV GU12 .... 76 F6
Heathview HTWY RG27 .... 72 B2
Heathwood Av
NMIL/BTOS BH25 .... 326 G7
Heathwood Cl YTLY GU46 .... 40 E7
Heathwood Rd
MOOR/WNTN BH9 .... 322 E7
Heathy Cl NMIL/BTOS BH25 .... 327 H7
Heathyfields Rd FNM GU9 .... 95 P5
Heaton Rd GPORT PO12 .... 315 K1
NBNE BH10 .... 322 B5
Heavytree Rd PSTN BH14 .... 321 K8
Hebden Cl STHA RG19 .... 25 M6
Hebrides Cl FHAM/STUB PO14 .. 293 P6
Heckfield Cl HAV PO9 .... 277 H5
Heckfield Dr FLEETN GU51 .... 73 P1
Heckford La PLE BH15 .... 320 F8
Heckford Rd PLE BH15 .... 320 F8
Hector Cl WVILLE PO7 .... 275 N8
Hector Rd FHAM/STUB PO14 .... 294 E4
Heddon Wk FARN GU14 .... 57 P6
Hedera Rd HLER SO31 .... 270 F7
Hedgecroft YTLY GU46 * 40 C8
Hedge End Rd AND SP10 .... 5 F7
Hedgehog La HASM GU27 .... 156 G8
Hedgerley NMIL/BTOS BH25 .... 327 K7
Hedgerow Cl ROWN SO16 .... 227 J6
Hedgerow Dr WEND SO18 .... 249 K2
Hedgerow Gdns EMRTH PO10 .. 277 M7
The Hedgerows CHIN RG24 .... 70 B4
The Hedge Rows HEND SO30 .... 250 C4
Hedges Cl TDWTH SP9 .... 98 F3
The Hedges ELGH SO50 * 230 D6
Hedgeway NWBY RG14 .... 24 F3
Hedley Cl FAWY SO45 .... 291 H8
Hedley Gdns HEND SO30 .... 230 B9
Heenan Cl FRIM GU16 .... 58 D6
Heidelberg Rd ENEY PO4 .... 317 H4
The Heights
FHAM/PORC PO16 .... 273 H8
HEND SO30 .... 250 A5
Hei-lin Wy RAND SP11 .... 79 N1
Heinz Burt Cl ELGH SO50 .... 229 H1
Hele Cl BSTK RG21 .... 90 C1
Helena Rd ENEY PO4 .... 317 H6
Helen Ct FARN GU14 .... 58 A9
Helford Ct AND SP10 .... 82 G9
Helford Gdns WEND SO18 .... 249 K1
Helksham Cl SHST GU47 .... 41 L5
Hellyer Rd ENEY PO4 .... 317 J5
Helm Cl LSOL/BMARY PO13 .... 315 H2
Helsby Cl FHAM/STUB PO14 .... 294 C1
Helsted Cl GPORT PO12 .... 315 J4
Helston Dr EMRTH PO10 .... 277 L7
Helston Rd CHAM PO6 .... 274 B9
Helvellyn Rd ROWN SO16 .... 247 K3
Helyar Rd CHAR BH8 .... 323 M5
Hemdean Gdns HEND SO30 .... 249 M2
Hemlock Rd HORN PO8 .... 255 N7
Hemlock Wy CHFD SO53 .... 206 B8
Hemming Cl TOTT SO40 .... 246 C5
Hemmingway Gdns
FHAM PO15 .... 271 J2
Hempland La ALTN GU34 .... 189 L2
Hempsted Rd CHAM PO6 .... 274 D9
Hemsley Wk HORN PO8 .... 255 P7
Henbest Cl WIMB BH21 .... 279 L9
Henbury Cl CFDH BH17 .... 321 J2
Henchard Cl FERN BH22 .... 302 C6
Henderson Rd ENEY PO4 .... 317 K5
Hendford Rd NBNE BH10 .... 322 D5
Hendon Rd BOR GU35 .... 154 A6
Hendren Sq AND SP10 .... 82 F9
Hendy Cl SSEA PO5 .... 19 J7
Henery St GPORT PO12 * 13 F2
Hengest Cl AND SP10 .... 82 B8
Hengistbury Rd
NMIL/BTOS BH25 .... 326 G7
SBNE BH6 .... 336 D3
Hengist Pk SBNE BH6 * 336 F2
Hengist Rd BMTH BH1 .... 335 K2
Henley Cl FARN GU14 .... 57 M5
Henley Dr FRIM GU16 .... 58 D6
Henley Gdns FHAM PO15 .... 272 B6
LTDN BH7 .... 323 N8
YTLY GU46 .... 40 E9
Henley Ga CHOB/PIR GU24 .... 77 P4
Henley Rd ENEY PO4 .... 317 H5
Henning's Park Rd PLE BH15 ... 320 F7
Henry Cl FAWY SO45 .... 290 D3
Henry Cort Dr FHAM PO15 .... 272 A7
Henry Player Av GPORT PO12 ... 315 P3
Henry Rd ELGH SO50 .... 207 M9
WSHM SO15 .... 247 N4
The Henrys NTHA RG18 .... 25 N3
Henry St WSHM SO15 * 248 B5
Henshaw Crs NWBY RG14 .... 24 A7
Henstead Rd WSHM SO15 .... 20 C1
Hensting La ELGH SO50 .... 208 C6
RWIN SO21 .... 208 E2
Henty Rd ROWN SO16 .... 247 L3
Henville Cl
LSOL/BMARY PO13 .... 295 H9
Henville Rd CHAR BH8 .... 335 J1
Henwick Cl NTHA RG18 .... 25 K1
Henwick La NTHA RG18 .... 25 K3
Henwood Down EPSF GU31 .... 215 N2
Hepplewhite Cl TADY RG26 .... 33 P5
Hepplewhite Dr
BH/HW/K RG22 .... 89 L4
Hepworth Cl AND SP10 .... 4 C1
ITCH SO19 .... 249 L9
Hepworth Cft SHST GU47 .... 41 M8
Herald Rd HEND SO30 .... 250 B2
Herbert Av BKME/WDN BH12 ... 321 N5
Herberton Rd SBNE BH6 .... 336 A1
Herbert Rd FLEETN GU51 .... 74 B3
NMIL/BTOS BH25 .... 327 K4
RSAL SP5 .... 199 P7
SSEA PO5 .... 316 G6
WBNE BH4 .... 334 B4
Herbert St PSEA PO1 .... 316 E1
Herbs End FARN GU14 .... 57 K8
Hercules St NEND PO2 .... 296 F9
Hercules Wy FARN GU14 .... 75 N4
Hereford Cl ODIM RG29 .... 93 J1

Hereford Ct
LSOL/BMARY PO13 * 314 G2
Hereford La *FHAM* GU9 ....96 B5
Hereford Md *FLEETN* GU51 ....56 E9
Hereford Rd *DEAN* RG23 ....68 F7
SSEA PO5 ....15 J7
Hereward Cl *ROMY* SO51 ....204 F6
Herewood Cl *NWBY* RG14 ....24 C3
Heritage Gdns
FHAM/PORC PO16 ....298 E2
Heritage Pk *BH/HW/K* RG22 ....89 M6
Heritage Vw *GPORT* PO12 ....295 L8
LSOL/BMARY PO13 ....295 J8
Hermes Cl *FLEETN* GU51 ....74 F5
Hermes Ct *GPORT* PO12 * 295 N9
Hermes Rd
LSOL/BMARY PO13 ....314 B1
Hermitage Cl *ALTN* GU34 ....132 E7
BPWT SO32 * 231 N4
FARN GU14 ....76 C3
FRIM GU16 ....58 E4
HAV PO9 ....276 E6
WIMB BH21 * ....
Hermitage Rd *PSTN* BH14 ....321 J6
Hermits Cl *THLE* RG7 ....27 K4
Herm Rd *CHAM* PO6 ....296 G1
EPSF GU31 ....215 N2
Hern La *FBDG* SP6 ....240 F5
Heron Cl *ALTN* GU34 ....132 F5
ENEY PO4 ....317 K3
FLEETS GU52 ....74 F7
FRIM GU16 ....58 E9
LYMN SO41 ....
Heron Court Rd *TWDS* BH3 ....322 C9
Herondale *HASM* GU27 ....156 D7
Heron Dr *WIMB* BH21 ....279 J7
Heron La *ROMY* SO51 ....180 B8
Heron Pk *CHIN* RG24 ....70 A3
Heron Quay *EMRTH* PO10 ....299 N2
Herons Cl *FHAM/STUB* PO14 ....294 A5
Heron Sq *ELGH* SO50 ....228 C3
Herons Ri *AND* SO10 ....102 F4
Heron Wy *BH/HW/K* RG22 ....89 K3
LSOL/BMARY PO13 ....
STHA RG19 ....25 L4
Heron Wood Rd *ASHV* GU12 ....97 K3
Herretts Gdns *ASHV* GU12 ....97 K2
Herrett St *ASHV* GU12 ....3 K6
Herriard Pl *BH/HW/K* RG22 ....89 K5
Herriard Wy *TADY* RG26 ....34 C7
Herrick Cl *FRIM* GU16 ....59 H2
ITCH SO19 ....249 M7
Herridge Cl *TADY* RG26 ....52 C3
Herriot Ct *YTLY* GU46 ....56 D1
Herriott Cl *HORN* PO8 ....256 A6
Herstone Cl *CFDH* BH17 ....321 H3
Hertford Pl *FBDG* SP6 ....220 D9
Hertford Pl *PSEA* PO1 ....316 F1
Hertsfield *FHAM/STUB* PO14 ....271 J6
Hesketh Cl *RGWD* BH24 ....281 N4
Hester Rd *ENEY* PO4 ....317 K4
Hesters Vw *ODIM* RG29 ....93 K9
Hestia Cl *ROMY* SO51 ....204 A6
Heston Cl *CHCH/BSGR* BH23 ....324 B3
Heston Wy *FERN* BH22 ....280 D6
Hewett Cl *FHAM/STUB* PO14 ....293 M2
NEND PO2 ....296 C7
Hewetts Ri *HLER* SO31 ....292 C1
Hewitt Rd *CHIN* RG24 ....69 J2
PLE BH15 ....320 A8
Hewitt's Rd *WSHM* SO15 ....247 P6
Hewshott Gdns *HORN* PO8 ....256 D8
Hewshott La *LIPH* GU30 ....175 M2
Hewshott La *LIPH* GU30 ....175 L2
The Hexagon *AND* SP10 * 102 B4
Hexham Cl *SHST* GU47 ....41 L4
Heyes Dr *ITCH* SO19 ....249 L8
Heysham Rd *BDST* BH18 ....320 C1
WSHM SO15 ....247 M3
Heyshott Gdns *HORN* PO8 ....256 D8
Heyshott Rd *ENEY* PO4 ....317 H4
Heytesbury Rd *SBNE* BH6 ....324 B9
Heyward Rd *ENEY* PO4 ....316 G4
Heywood Gn *ITCH* SO19 ....249 N6
Hibberd Wy *NBNE* BH10 ....322 D6
Hibiscus Crs *AND* SP10 ....102 A3
Hibiscus Dr *BOR* GU35 ....154 B6
Hickes Cl *BWD* BH11 ....301 P9
Hickory Dr *FUFL* SO22 ....164 D3
Hickory Gdns *HEND* SO30 ....229 M9
Hicks Cl *TADY* RG26 ....34 C6
Hicks La *BLKW* GU17 ....41 J9
Hides Cl *WHCH* RG28 ....47 J3
Hides Hill La *BROC* SO42 ....289 J5
Highams Cl *KSCL* RG20 ....48 D3
Highbank Av *WVILLE* PO7 ....275 K7
Highbank Gdns *FBDG* SP6 ....240 D2
High Beeches *GMAN* GU16 * 58 C5
Highbridge Rd *ELGH* SO50 ....207 M6
PSTN BH14 ....321 L9
Highbury Cl *ELGH* SO50 ....230 C3
NMIL/BTOS BH25 ....327 K4
Highbury Gv *CHAM* PO6 ....297 J3
HASM GU27 ....157 H5
Highbury Rd *RAND* SP11 ....102 B6
Highbury St *PSEA* PO1 ....18 D5
Highbury Wy *CHAM* PO6 ....297 H3
Highclere Av *HAV* PO9 ....276 D6
Highclere Rd *ASHV* GU12 ....3 K6
ROWN SO16 ....227 P9
Highclere Wy *CHFD* SO53 ....228 C1
Highcliff Av *SHAM* SO14 ....248 C3
Highcliffe Dr *ELGH* SO50 ....207 J6
Highcliffe Rd
CHCH/BSGR BH23 ....325 L7
WINC SO23 ....23 G7
High Copse *FNM* GU9 ....96 A5
Highcroft La *HORN* PO8 ....256 C3
High Cross *PSF* GU32 ....190 E4
High Cross La *PSF* GU32 ....190 C5
Highcrown Ms *SD/PW* SO17 ....248 C1
Highcrown St *SD/PW* SO17 ....248 C1
Highdown *FLEETN* GU51 ....74 D2
Highdowns *BH/HW/K* RG22 ....89 N5

High Dr *BH/HW/K* RG22 ....89 N1
LSOL/BMARY PO13 ....294 G8
Higher Blandford Rd
WIMB BH21 ....300 B7
Highercombe Rd *HASM* GU27 ....157 K5
Higher Md *CHIN* RG24 ....70 A4
Higher Merley La *WIMB* BH21 ....300 A3
Highfield *LYMN* SO41 ....329 K4
RWIN SO21 ....184 A9
Highfield Av *ALDT* GU11 ....2 E7
FHAM/STUB PO14 ....294 D1
RWIN SO21 ....184 A4
NWBY RG14 ....16 E3
RGWD BH24 ....282 E1
ROWN SO16 ....228 B9
RWIN SO21 ....184 A9
WVILLE PO7 ....275 P1
Highfield Cla *BSTK* RG21 ....6 F6
Highfield Cl *ALDT* GU11 ....3 F7
CHFD SO53 ....206 F7
FARN GU14 ....57 N9
FNM GU9 ....116 B3
SD/PW SO17 ....248 C1
WIMB BH21 ....300 A8
WVILLE PO7 ....275 P1
Highfield Crs *CSHT* GU26 ....156 D1
RSAL SP5 ....158 A1
SD/PW SO17 ....248 D1
Highfield Dr *RGWD* BH24 ....260 E9
Highfield Gdns *ALDT* GU11 ....2 F2
LISS SO48 ....192 F2
LYMN SO41 ....308 B6
Highfield La *LIPH* GU30 ....175 L5
MFD/CHID GU8 ....183 P8
RSAL SP5 ....199 P8
SD/PW SO17 ....248 C1
Highfield Pth *FARN* GU14 ....57 N9
Highfield Rd *CHFD* SO53 ....206 G7
FARN GU14 ....57 N9
FERN BH22 ....280 B6
GPORT PO12 ....315 K2
LYMN SO41 ....329 J3
MOOR/WNTN BH9 ....322 E5
NWBY RG14 ....16 D7
PSEA PO1 ....19 K2
PSF GU32 ....215 J1
RGWD BH24 ....282 E1
SD/PW SO17 ....248 B2
WIMB BH21 ....300 A8
Highfields *HLER* SO31 ....270 F9
OVTN RG25 ....87 H4
Highfield Ter *FUFL* SO22 ....2 B5
High Firs Gdns *ROMY* SO51 ....204 C6
High Firs Rd *ITCH* SO19 ....249 K6
ROMY SO51 ....204 C5
Highgate La *FARN* GU14 ....58 B8
Highgate Rd *HSEA* PO3 ....297 J8
Highgrove *FARN* GU14 ....58 A6
Highgrove Cl *TOTT* SO40 ....246 B6
Highgrove Rd *HSEA* PO3 ....297 K9
High Howe Cl *BWD* BH11 ....301 N9
High Howe Gdns *BWD* BH11 ....301 N9
High Howe La *BWD* BH11 ....321 N1
Highland Av
CHCH/BSGR BH23 ....326 D6
Highland Cl *EMRTH* PO10 ....299 L1
Highland Dr *DEAN* RG23 ....88 E1
FLEETN GU51 ....74 E1
Highland Rd *ASHV* GU12 ....3 K3
EMRTH PO10 ....277 L9
ENEY PO4 ....317 H5
PSTN BH14 ....321 K7
WIMB BH21 ....278 F8
Highlands Cl *FAWY* SO45 ....268 C8
FNM GU9 ....116 B3
NBAD SO52 ....205 J8
Highlands Crs *NBNE* BH10 ....322 C5
Highlands Rd *AND* SP10 ....5 H5
BH/HW/K RG22 ....68 D9
CHAM PO6 ....297 M1
FNM GU9 ....10 A1
FNM GU9 ....116 B3
NMIL/BTOS BH25 ....327 J7
Highland St *ENEY* PO4 ....317 J6
Highland View Cl *WIMB* BH21 ....278 F8
High La *HASM* GU27 ....157 H5
High Lawn Wy *HAV* PO9 ....276 E5
High Md *FERN* BH22 ....302 A6
FHAM PO15 ....10 A1
High Mead La *FERN* BH22 ....302 A7
High Meadow *ITCH* SO19 ....249 L5
Highmoor Rd *BWD* BH11 ....322 A6
PSTN BH14 ....321 L9
Highmoors *CHIN* RG24 ....69 P1
Highmount Cl *WINC* SO23 ....23 H6
Highnam Gdns *HLER* SO31 ....270 F6
High Oaks Cl *HLER* SO31 ....270 G7
High Oaks Gdns *BWD* BH11 ....301 N9
High Park Rd *BDST* BH18 ....300 A9
FNM GU9 ....96 B8
Highpath Wy *CHIN* RG24 ....68 F5
High Pitfold *CSHT* GU26 ....156 C3
Highridge *ALTN* GU34 ....132 D6
High Ridge Crs
NMIL/BTOS BH25 ....327 L4
High Rd *ROWN* SO16 ....228 F9
High St *ALDT* GU11 ....2 D2
ALTN GU34 ....132 E6
AND SP10 ....150 A1
AND SO10 * 4 D4
BOR GU35 ....154 F3
BPWT SO32 ....211 N9
BPWT SO32 ....232 A5
BROC SO42 ....289 K9
CHAM PO6 ....297 H1
CHCH/BSGR BH23 ....324 F9
CWTH RG45 ....41 K2
ELGH SO50 ....228 D3
EMRTH PO10 ....299 M1
EPSF GU31 ....215 K8
FARN GU14 ....76 B4

FAWY SO45 ....268 C5
FBDG SP6 ....219 J7
FBDG SP6 ....240 D2
FHAM/PORC PO16 ....11 J4
FHAM/STUB PO14 ....293 M1
GPORT PO12 ....186 F1
HASM GU27 ....157 J6
HEND SO30 ....249 M2
HEND SO30 ....250 G4
HLER SO31 ....270 A8
HTWY RG27 ....55 J7
LSOL/BMARY PO13 ....314 C2
LYMN SO41 ....329 L4
LYMN SO41 ....338 C2
LYND SO43 ....264 F5
ODIM RG29 ....93 K1
OVTN RG25 ....86 G3
PLE BH15 ....332 D2
PSEA PO1 ....18 C6
PSF GU32 ....188 E9
PSF GU32 ....213 N4
PSF GU32 ....215 M2
RAND SP11 ....79 N1
RAND SP11 ....100 B9
RFNM GU10 ....115 N7
RGWD BH24 ....281 L3
RGWD BH24 ....282 D2
RSAL SP5 ....199 K6
RWIN SO21 ....184 A9
SHAM SO14 ....20 D6
SHST GU47 ....40 G6
STHA RG19 ....25 N4
STOK SO20 ....139 P3
STOK SO20 ....141 K5
STOK SO20 ....160 A1
TADY RG26 ....49 N1
THLE RG7 ....27 L4
WHCH RG28 ....47 H5
WEND SO18 ....248 G2
WVILLE PO7 ....275 K8
High St North *PLE* BH15 ....320 F9
High Thicket Rd *RFNM* GU10 ....135 M5
Hightown Gdns *RGWD* BH24 ....282 F3
Hightown HI *BWD* BH11 ....302 B2
Hightown Rd *RGWD* BH24 ....282 E5
Hightrees *LYMN* SO41 ....329 K6
High Trees *ELGH* SO50 ....230 E2
WVILLE PO7 ....275 P2
Hightrees Av *CHAR* BH8 ....323 L6
High Trees Dr *FUFL* SO22 ....164 F5
High Trees Rd *FERN* BH22 ....302 D1
High Vw *FHAM/PORC* PO16 ....273 N9
PSF GU32 * 215 M1
Highview Cl *CHCH/BSGR* BH23 ....324 C4
High View Cl *FARN* GU14 ....57 P9
Highview Gdns
BKME/WDN BH12 ....321 L5
High View Rd *FARN* GU14 ....57 P9
High View Wy *WEND* SO18 ....249 H3
High Wk *FHAM* PO15 ....10 A1
High Wy *BDST* BH18 ....320 C2
Highway *CWTH* RG45 ....41 H1
Highways Rd *RWIN* SO21 ....183 L9
Highwood Cl *FBDG* SP6 ....239 K5
NWBY RG14 ....24 E1
YTLY GU46 ....56 D1
Highwood La *RGWD* BH24 ....260 C8
Highwood Rd *PSTN* BH14 ....205 H7
Highwood Rdg *BH/HW/K* RG22 ....89 M5
Highwood Rd *BROC* SO42 ....289 F9
LSOL/BMARY PO13 ....314 N1
PSTN BH14 ....321 N8
Higworth La *HISD* PO11 ....318 F3
Hilary Av *CHAM* PO6 ....297 J2
Hilary Cl *CFDH* BH17 ....320 C3
Hilda Gdns *WVILLE* PO7 ....255 J7
Hilda Rd *BKME/WDN* BH12 ....321 N5
Hilden Wy *FUFL* SO22 ....164 D3
Hilder Gdns *LYMN* SO41 ....76 C1
Hiley Rd *PLE* BH15 ....320 E6
Highfield *YTLY* GU46 ....40 G9
Hilland Rd *BOR* GU35 ....154 C4
Hillary Cl *FHAM/PORC* PO16 ....10 C3
FNM GU9 ....116 B3
LYND SO43 ....264 C7
Hillary Rd *BSTK* RG21 ....6 B2
CHCH/BSGR BH23 ....325 J7
FNM GU9 ....116 B3
FNM GU9 * 116 J3
Hill Barn La *RWIN* SO21 ....205 J7
Hillboroughs Crs *SSEA* PO5 ....19 J7
Hillbourne Rd *CFDH* BH17 ....320 C2
Hillbrook Ri *FNM* GU9 ....96 A5
Hillbrow Cl *FHAM/PORC* PO16 ....272 B7
Hill Brow Cl *HAV* PO9 ....277 H1
Hill Brow Rd *LISS* SO33 ....192 D3
Hillbrow Rd *SBNE* BH6 ....323 P9
Hillbury Av *AND* SP10 ....102 C4
Hillbury Rd *FBDG* SP6 * 239 P6
Hillbury Rd *FBDG* SP6 ....239 P6
Hill Cl *CHCH/BSGR* BH23 ....305 L9
ELGH SO50 ....208 C8
NWBY RG14 ....24 A8
Hill Ct *HASM* GU27 ....156 C7
Hillcrest *FLEETN* GU51 ....74 D1
FNM GU9 * 96 C5
Hillcrest Av *CHFD* SO53 ....206 F7
Hillcrest Cl *MOOR/WNTN* BH9 ....302 C1
Hillcrest Dr *CHFD* SO53 ....206 F7
Hill Crest Dr *RFNM* GU10 ....115 J2
Hill Crest Gdns *FHAM/PORC* BH12 ....321 J7
MOOR/WNTN BH9 ....322 C4
Hillcrest Rd *BKME/WDN* BH12 ....321 N7
Hillcroft *RSAL* SP5 * 199 P7
Hillcroft Cl *LYMN* SO41 ....329 L3
Hilldene Wy *HEND* SO30 ....229 N1
Hillditch *LYMN* SO41 ....329 K1
Hilldown Rd *SD/PW* SO17 ....228 C9
Hilldowns Av *NEND* PO2 ....296 E7
Hill Dr *FHAM* SO15 ....272 B7
Hill Farm Cl *HASM* GU27 * 156 E8
Hill Farm La *NARL* SO24 ....170 C5

WSHM SO15 ....248 A5
Hillgrove Rd *WEND* SO18 ....229 H9
Hill Head Rd
FHAM/STUB PO14 ....293 N8
Hillhouse HI *LIPH* GU30 ....154 G9
Hillhouse La *STHA* RG19 ....32 C7
Hill Houses La *NARL* SO24 ....165 H5
Hillier Wy *WINC* SO23 ....165 H5
Hill La *CHCH/BSGR* BH23 ....325 K5
ROWN SO16 ....227 P9
RWIN SO21 ....207 P4
RWIN SO16 ....20 A1
Hillman Rd *PSTN* BH14 ....321 M7
Hillmead Gdns *HAV* PO9 ....276 B8
Hill Meadow *OVTN* RG25 ....86 G1
Hillmeadow *VWD* BH31 ....258 G6
Hill Park Rd *FHAM* PO15 ....272 B6
GPORT PO12 ....315 K2
Hill PI *HLER* SO31 ....270 E2
Hill RI *BPWT* SO32 ....211 N8
RWIN SO21 ....184 A8
Hill Rd *DEAN* RG23 ....88 E2
FHAM/PORC PO16 ....273 P9
FNM GU9 ....96 C4
CSHT GU26 ....156 C2
HASM GU27 ....157 H7
NWBY RG14 ....24 B3
RGWD BH24 ....303 N2
RWIN SO21 ....104 D8
Hillsborough Ct *FARN* GU14 ....57 M5
Hill School *RFNM* GU10 ....115 P3
Hillside *CBLY* GU15 ....41 N7
Hillside Cl *ALTN* GU34 ....132 F4
Hillside Crs *CHAM* PO6 ....274 D9
FRIM GU16 ....58 E6
Hillside Dr *CHCH/BSGR* BH23 ....324 C5
Hillside La *FNM* GU9 ....96 D4
Hillside Ms *HLER* SO31 ....270 D4
Hillside Rd *ALTN* GU34 ....2 C7
BKME/WDN BH12 ....321 P5
FNM GU9 ....96 D4
FUFL SO22 ....164 D6
HASM GU27 ....156 E8
LYMN SO41 ....329 J4
ODIM RG29 ....93 M2
RFNM GU10 ....116 B7
RWIN SO21 ....165 K3
Hillside Vls *AND* SP10 ....82 C9
Hillsley Rd *CHAM* PO6 ....274 B8
Hillslow Rd *FHAM* PO15 ....272 A7
Hillsons Rd *HEND* SO30 ....251 H4
Hill Sq *CHIN* RG24 ....69 L3
Hillstead Ct *BSTK* RG21 * 69 L1
Hill St *PLE* BH15 ....332 E1
TOTT SO40 ....226 A6
Hill Ter *WIMB* BH21 ....301 J3
Hilltop Cl *FERN* BH22 ....302 B1
Hilltop Dr *ITCH* SO19 ....249 L7
Hilltop Gdns *HORN* PO8 ....236 D9
Hilltop Rd *CHAM* PO6 ....274 B8
FERN BH22 ....302 B1
OVTN RG25 ....86 G1
WIMB BH21 ....300 A8
Hilltop Vw *YTLY* GU46 ....40 C9
Hillview *HORN* PO8 ....256 C6
Hill Vw *PSF* GU32 ....215 M1
Hill View Pk *ELGH* SO50 * 208 B8
Hillview Rd *FAWY* SO45 ....268 B7
NBNE BH10 ....322 D3
Hill View Rd *BH/HW/K* RG22 ....69 H9
FERN BH22 ....302 C2
FHAM/PORC PO16 ....273 N9
FNM GU9 ....95 P9
ROMY SO51 ....180 A6
Hill Wk *FHAM* PO15 ....272 B7
Hill Wy *RGWD* BH24 ....281 L4
The Hillway *CHFD* SO53 ....206 F6
HAV PO9 ....276 B6
Hillyfields *ROWN* SO16 ....226 G8
Hilsea Crs *NEND* PO2 ....296 G4
Hiltingbury Cl *CHFD* SO53 ....206 F4
Hiltingbury Rd *CHFD* SO53 ....206 D4
HAV PO9 ....276 B6
Hilton Cl *PLE* BH15 ....321 J6
Hilton Rd *GPORT* PO12 ....15 F5
NMIL/BTOS BH25 ....327 K3
Hinchliffe Cl *PLE* BH15 ....332 B1
Hinchliffe Rd *PLE* BH15 ....332 B1
Hindell Cl *FARN* GU14 ....57 P5
Hindhead Rd *HASM* GU27 ....156 D5
Hines Ct *CHIN* RG24 ....68 G4
Hinkler Rd *ITCH* SO19 ....249 L6
Hinstock Cl *FARN* GU14 ....275 P5
Hinton Cl *HAV* PO9 ....276 C6
TADY RG26 ....34 C7
Hinton Crs *ITCH* SO19 ....249 N6
Hinton Flds *WINC* SO23 ....165 K1
Hinton HI *NARL* SO24 ....187 K7
Hinton House Dr *WINC* SO23 ....165 K1
Hinton Manor La *HORN* PO8 ....255 L5
Hinton Rd *BMTH* BH1 ....8 E4
Hinton Wood Av
CHCH/BSGR BH23 ....326 A5
Hintonwood La
CHCH/BSGR BH23 ....326 A5
Hinwood Cl *STOK* SO20 ....140 A9

Hipley Rd *HAV* PO9 ....15 H3
Hirst Copse *RAND* SP11 ....84 C1
Hirst Rd *FAWY* SO45 ....268 D7
Hispano Av *FHAM* PO15 ....271 J3
Hitches La *FLEETN* GU51 ....73 P5
Hitherwood Cl *WVILLE* PO7 ....276 B1
Hive Wy *WINC* SO23 ....329 K1
H Jones Crs *ALDT* GU11 ....3 H1
Hoadlands *EPSF* GU31 ....215 N1
Hoad's HI *FHAM* PO17 ....252 F9
Hobart La *HEND* SO30 ....250 D5
Hobbs Cl *NARL* SO24 ....168 F5
Hobbs Pk *RGWD* BH24 ....281 M5
Hobbs Sq *ALDT* GU11 ....3 H4
EPSF GU31 ....191 N9
Hobby Cl *HSEA* PO3 ....297 J5
Hobson Wy *FAWY* SO45 ....290 F6
Hoburne Gdns
CHCH/BSGR BH23 ....325 N6
Hoburne La *CHCH/BSGR* BH23 ....325 M7
Hockford La *THLE* RG7 ....33 K3
Hockham Ct *HAV* PO9 ....15 G4
Hockley Cl *CHAM* PO6 ....296 F1
Hockley Link *RWIN* SO21 ....183 N4
Hocombe Dr *CHFD* SO53 ....206 D3
Hocombe Park Cl *CHFD* SO53 ....206 D3
Hocombe Rd *CHFD* SO53 ....206 D3
Hocombe Wood Rd
CHFD SO53 ....206 C3
Hodder Cl *CHFD* SO53 ....206 D8
Hoddinott Rd *ELGH* SO50 ....229 H2
Hodges Cl *CFDH* BH17 ....320 C5
Hoe La *ROMY* SO51 ....226 G2
Hoe Rd *BPWT* SO32 ....232 C5
Hoe St *WVILLE* PO7 ....254 B5
The Hoe *LSOL/BMARY* PO13 ....295 J8
Hogarth Cl *BSTK* RG21 ....26 F8
ITCH SO19 ....249 K9
ROMY SO51 ....204 F4
SHST GU47 ....41 M8
Hogarth Ct *AND* SP10 ....4 A1
Hoggarth Cl *EPSF* GU31 ....215 N1
Hogmoor Rd *BOR* GU35 ....153 N6
Hog's Back *RFNM* GU10 ....97 N6
Hog Lodge La *HORN* PO8 ....236 D2
Hogue Av *NBNE* BH10 ....322 D2
Hogwood La *HEND* SO30 ....229 P5
Holbecke Cl *YTLY* GU46 ....40 B9
Holbein Cl *BSTK* RG21 ....69 N9
Holborne Cl *NWBY* RG14 ....30 B1
Holbrook Cl *FNM* GU9 ....2 C7
Holbrook Rd
FHAM/PORC PO16 ....11 G7
PSEA PO1 ....316 F2
Holbrook Vs *ALDT* GU11 ....97 H4
Holbury Cl *CHAR* BH8 ....323 L4
Holbury Ct *HAV* PO9 ....277 H5
Holbury Dro *FAWY* SO45 ....290 D5
Holbury La *ROMY* SO51 ....178 E3
Holcot La *HSEA* PO3 ....297 L5
Holcroft Rd *ITCH* SO19 ....249 N6
Holdaway Cl *WINC* SO23 ....145 K9
Holdenbury Ct *HSEA* PO3 ....297 L4
Holdenhurst Av *HAV LTDN* BH7 ....324 A8
Holdenhurst Cl *HORN* PO8 ....256 C2
Holdenhurst Rd *BMTH* BH1 ....323 K9
CHAR BH8 ....9 H2
Holden La *NARL* SO24 ....186 D7
Holder Rd *ASHV* GU12 ....97 L2
Holdfast La *HASM* GU27 ....156 B3
Hole La *BPWT* SO32 ....251 N2
RFNM GU10 ....114 E5
WVILLE PO7 ....254 B5
Holes Bay Rd *PLE* BH15 ....320 D8
Holes Cl *LYMN* SO41 ....327 P3
Holkham Cl *ROWN* SO16 ....226 D2
Hollam Cl *FHAM/STUB* PO14 ....293 P1
Hollam Crs *FHAM/STUB* PO14 ....293 P1
Hollam Dr *FHAM/STUB* PO14 ....293 P1
Hollam Rd *ENEY* PO4 ....317 K3
Holland Cl *FNM* GU9 ....116 E1
Holland Dr *HAV* PO9 ....82 D8
Holland Gdns *FLEETN* GU51 ....74 B8
Holland Pk *HLER* SO31 ....270 F7
Holland Pl *LSOL/BMARY* PO13 ....295 H7
ROWN SO16 ....247 M2
Holland Rd *ITCH* SO19 ....248 F9
SSEA PO5 ....316 G4
TOTT SO40 ....246 A4
Hollands Cl *FUFL* SO22 ....164 C2
The Hollands *STHA* RG19 ....25 P4
Hollands Wood Dr
NMIL/BTOS BH25 ....327 K2
Holland Wy *BDST* BH18 ....308 B8
Hollies Cl *LYMN* SO41 ....308 B7
Hollies Ct *CHIN* RG24 ....68 G4
The Hollies *BLKW* GU17 * 57 N4
CHIN RG24 ....70 E7
HTWY RG27 ....55 H9
HAV PO9 ....277 H2
Hollingbourne Cl *WEND* SO18 ....248 F3
Hollington La *KSCL* RG20 ....45 K1
Hollington Pl *STHA* RG19 * 25 M4
Hollist La *EPSF* GU31 ....217 H9
Hollis Wood Dr *RFNM* GU10 ....115 N5
Holman Dr *ROWN* SO51 ....204 B8
Holloway Av *BWD* BH11 ....301 P8
Hollow La *BOR* GU35 ....154 F2
HISD PO11 ....318 F5
Hollowshot La *KSCL* RG20 ....48 B4
The Hollow *KSCL* RG20 ....48 B3
STOK SO20 ....160 B5
Holly Av *FRIM* GU16 ....58 G2
Hollybank *LSOL/BMARY* PO13 ....314 D3
Holly Bank Cl *HORN* PO8 ....256 C6
Hollybank Crs *FAWY* SO45 ....268 B6
Hollybank La *EMRTH* PO10 ....277 M6
Hollybank Rd *HEND* SO30 ....250 C2
Hollybrook Av *ROWN* SO16 ....227 N9
Hollybrook Cl *ROWN* SO16 ....227 N9

Hollybrook Gdns *HLER* SO31 ...... 270 G5
Hollybrook Pk *BOR* GU35 .... 154 B5
Hollybrook Rd *ROWN* SO16 ...... 247 N1
Hollybush La *ALDT* GU11 .... 76 D7
  HTWY RG27 .... 39 P6
  TADY RG26 .... 50 A3
  THLE RG7 .... 27 H5
Hollybush Ride *EWKG* RG40 ...... 40 D1
Holly Cl *ASHV* GU12 .... 3 J5
  BOR GU35 .... 155 K5
  FARN GU14 .... 57 P9
  FAWY SO45 .... 290 C2
  FERN BH22 .... 280 D7
  FERN BH22 .... 161 J3
  RGWD BH24 .... 281 K5
  STHA RG19 .... 32 E1
  TADY RG26 .... 52 B3
Hollycombe Cl *LIPH* GU30 ...... 175 K5
Holly Ct *CWTH* RG45 * 40 C1
Hollycroft *STHA* RG19 .... 33 J6
Holly Dell *ROWN* SO16 .... 228 A7
Holly Dr *CHIN* RG24 .... 70 D6
  WVILLE PO7 .... 276 A4
Holly Gdns *CHCH/BSGR* BH23 .. 325 H6
  HEND SO30 .... 249 N3
Holly Grn *FARN* GU14 .... 338 F1
Holly Green Rd *BWD* BH11 .... 301 N9
Holly Gv *FHAM/PORC* PO16 .... 272 C6
  VWD BH31 .... 258 D5
Holly Hatch Rd *TOTT* SO40 ...... 246 C5
Holly Hedge La *FRIM* GU16 ..... 58 D5
Holly Hedge La *CFDH* BH17 ..... 320 E4
Holly Hedge Rd *FRIM* GU16 ..... 58 D5
  FHAM 272 B5
  RGWD BH24 .... 258 A7
Holly HI *ROWN* SO16 .... 228 A7
Holly Hill Cl *ROWN* SO16 .... 228 A7
Holly Hill La *HLER* SO31 .... 270 C6
Hollyhock Cl *BH/HW/K* RG22 .... 89 L6
Holly La *CHCH/BSGR* BH23 ...... 326 E5
  LYMN SO41 .... 309 P7
  NMIL/BTOS BH25 .... 327 L3
  THLE RG7 .... 35 J6
Holly Ldg *CHFD* SO53 * 228 E1
Holly Mdw *FUFL* SO22 .... 180 F8
Holly Ms *ROWN* SO16 * 228 B8
Holly Oak Rd *ROWN* SO16 ...... 227 L9
Hollyridge *HASM* GU27 .... 156 C7
Holly Rd *ASHV* GU12 .... 3 J3
  FARN GU14 .... 57 N9
  FAWY SO45 .... 290 C9
  TOTT SO40 .... 245 P9
Holly St *GPORT* PO12 .... 13 F2
Hollytree Gdns *FRIM* GU16 ...... 58 C5
Holly Tree Pk *RWIN* SO21 .... 125 L5
Hollytrees *FLEETN* GU51 * 74 B6
Holly Wk *AND* SP10 .... 52 B8
Hollywater Rd *LIPH* GU30 ...... 154 C8
Holly Wy *BLKW* GU17 .... 57 L1
Hollywell *NBAD* SO52 .... 205 K9
Hollywood Cl *NBAD* SO52 .... 205 K9
Hollywood La *LYMN* SO41 ...... 329 K2
Holm Cl *HORN* PO8 .... 256 G3
  TADY RG26 .... 52 C3
Holmbrook Cl *FARN* GU14 ...... 57 K9
Holm Cl *RGWD* BH24 .... 260 G9
Holmdale Rd *GPORT* PO12 ...... 315 K1
Holmdene *THLE* RG7 .... 27 H4
Holmefield Av
  FHAM/STUB PO14 .... 294 D3
Holme Rd *CHCH/BSGR* BH23 .... 326 D7
Holmes Cl *BH/HW/K* RG22 ...... 89 N5
  HLER SO31 .... 269 K4
Holmes Ct *AND* SP10 .... 102 C5
Holmesland Dr *HEND* SO30 .... 250 A4
Holmesland La *HEND* SO30 .... 250 F4
Holmfield Av *LTDN* BH7 .... 324 A8
Holmgrove *FHAM/STUB* PO14 .. 271 J7
Holm Hill La *CHCH/BSGR* BH23 .. 306 D9
Holmhurst Av
  CHCH/BSGR BH23 .... 326 B6
  VWD BH31 .... 258 E3
Holm Oak Cl *FUFL* SO22 .... 164 B2
Holmsley Cl *LYMN* SO41 .... 329 H5
  WEND SO18 .... 249 L4
Holmsley Ct *TOTT* SO40 * 245 P5
Holmsley Pas *ROWN* BH24 ..... 306 E1
Holmsley Rd *NMIL/BTOS* BH25 .. 306 F6
Holmwood Garth *RGWD* BH24 .. 283 H3
Holne Ct *ENEY* PO4 .... 317 L5
Holnest Rd *CFDH* BH17 .... 320 F3
  BH/HW/K RG22 .... 90 A4
Holst Wy *WVILLE* PO7 .... 275 P5
Holt Cl *FARN* GU14 .... 58 B6
  LSOL/BMARY PO13 .... 314 E2
  WHAM PO17 .... 252 D7
Holt Cots *STHA* RG19 .... 33 J6
Holt Cl *ITCH* SO19 .... 288 D2
Holt Down *EPSF* GU31 .... 215 P2
Holt End La *ALTN* GU34 .... 130 C7
Holt Gdns *HAV* PO9 .... 257 H8
Holt La *HTWY* RG27 .... 72 B2
  RAND SP11 .... 60 C4
  WIMB BH21 .... 278 C3
Holt Pound La *RFNM* GU10 ..... 115 L5
Holt Rd *BKME/WDN* BH12 .... 321 P6
  WIMB BH21 .... 279 K1
Holt Wy *HTWY* RG27 .... 72 B2
Holworth Cl *BWD* BH11 .... 321 N1
Holy Barn Cl *BH/HW/K* RG22 .... 89 L2
Holyborne Rd *ROMY* SO51 ..... 204 F6
Holybourne La *HAV* PO9 .... 15 J5
Holyrood Av *SD/OW* SO17 .... 248 D1
Holyrood Cl *WVILLE* PO7 ...... 276 A3
Holy Rood Pl *SHAM* SO14 ...... 20 E6
Holywell Cl *CFDH* BH17 .... 320 F1
  FARN GU14 .... 57 P6
Holywell Cl *STHA* RG19 .... 33 J6
Home Cl *NARL* SO24 .... 130 C7
  NARL SO24 .... 168 F2
Home Farm Cl *FARN* GU14 ...... 58 C7
  FAWY SO45 .... 268 D8
Home Farm Gdns *AND* SP10 .... 82 B8
Home Farm Rd *HTWY* RG27 .... 55 M6
Home Farm Wy *VWD* BH31 ..... 258 E4

Homefield *ROMY* SO51 .... 204 E4
Home Field Dr *ROWN* SO16 ..... 226 G7
Homefield Rd *CHAM* PO6 .... 297 L2
  EMRTH PO10 .... 277 P6
  HORN PO8 .... 236 B6
Home La *RWIN* SO21 .... 163 M4
Homelea Cl *FARN* GU14 .... 58 A5
Homeleigh Crs *ASHV* GU12 ..... 76 F4
Home Md *OVTN* RG25 .... 108 D1
  WVILLE PO7 .... 255 H8
Home Mead Cl *NWBY* RG14 .... 24 C1
Home Park Rd *YTLY* GU46 ...... 40 D8
Home Pk *ROWN* SO16 .... 255 N9
  LSOL/BMARY PO13 .... 254 F9
Homer Farm La *FAWY* SO45 .... 312 C2
Homer Rd *BWD* BH11 .... 322 B1
Homer Pk *FAWY* SO45 * 312 C2
Home Rule Rd *HLER* SO31 ...... 270 G6
Homeside Rd
  MOOR/WNTN BH9 .... 322 C5
Homestead Rd *ALTN* GU34 .... 149 N3
Homesteads Rd
  BH/HW/K RG22 .... 89 L2
Homeweald Cl *ROWN* 15 F6
Homewood Cl
  NMIL/BTOS BH25 .... 327 L4
Hone HI *SHST* GU47 .... 41 M4
Honeybottom Rd *TADY* RG26 .. 34 C5
Honeybourne Crs *SBNE* BH6 ... 336 E2
Honeycritch La *PSF* GU32 ...... 191 H5
Honey La *ALTN* GU34 .... 152 E9
  FHAM 272 B5
  RGWD BH24 .... 258 A7
Honeyleaze *BH/HW/K* RG22 .... 89 L6
Honeysuckle Cl *BH/HW/K* RG22 .. 89 L6
  FUFL SO22 .... 183 M2
  HLER SO31 .... 270 C5
  LSOL/BMARY PO13 .... 294 F6
  YTLY GU46 .... 40 B8
Honeysuckle Ct *WVILLE* PO7 ... 275 P5
Honeysuckle Gdns *AND* SP10 .. 102 A3
  LYMN SO41 .... 309 P7
  CFDH BH17 .... 320 B3
Honeysuckle Wy
  CHCH/BSGR BH23 .... 325 M7
  CHFD SO53 .... 206 C7
Honeywood Cl *HSEA* PO3 .... 297 H5
  TOTT SO40 .... 245 N8
Honeywood Cl East
  HSEA PO3 .... 297 H6
Honeywood Cl West
  HSEA PO3 .... 297 H6
Honister Cl *FLEETN* GU51 * 74 F2
Hood Cl *AND* SP10 .... 5 K3
  HLER SO31 .... 271 H6
  NBNE BH10 .... 322 B6
Hood Cl *NBNE* BH10 .... 322 B6
Hood Rd *WEND* SO18 .... 249 J3
Hook Cl *ROMY* SO51 .... 206 C3
  STHA RG19 .... 32 E4
Hook Common *HTWY* RG27 .... 71 N5
Hook Crs *ROMY* SO51 .... 206 C3
Hook Crs *CFDH* BH17 .... 321 J2
Hook La *DEAN* RG23 .... 67 M4
  FHAM/STUB PO14 .... 293 J1
  HLER SO31 .... 292 F3
  NARL SO24 .... 169 K3
  TADY RG26 .... 53 L8
Hook Park Est *HLER* SO31 * 292 D5
Hook Park Rd *HLER* SO31 ...... 292 C2
Hookpit Farm La *WINC* SO23 .. 145 J3
Hook Rd *HTWY* RG27 .... 71 P5
  KSCL RG20 .... 48 D3
  ODIH RG29 .... 71 N8
  ROMY SO51 .... 206 C3
Hook's Farm Wy *HAV* PO9 ..... 14 B2
Hook's La *HAV* PO9 .... 14 B2
Hookstile La *FNM* GU9 .... 116 C1
Hook Water Rd *CHFD* SO53 .... 206 E3
Hookwood La *ROMY* SO51 ..... 206 B3
Hoopersmead *OVTN* RG25 .... 90 C4
Hoopers Wy *DEAN* RG23 ...... 88 B1
Hope Cl *FARN* GU14 .... 57 J9
Hope Cl La *FNM* GU9 .... 96 B5
Hope Grants Rd *ALDT* GU11 ... 76 A9
Hope Grant's Rd *ALDT* GU11 ... 75 P8
Hopeman Cl *SHST* GU47 .... 40 F1
Hope Rd *HEND* SO30 .... 249 N1
Hope St *PSEA* PO1 .... 316 E2
Hopeswood *LISS* GU33 .... 173 L4
Hope Wy *ALDT* GU11 .... 2 C1
Hopfield *WVILLE* PO7 .... 275 N4
Hopfield Ms *WVILLE* PO7 ...... 275 N4
Hop Gdn *FLEETS* GU52 .... 74 B8
Hop Garden Rd *HTWY* RG27 .... 71 N3
Hopkins Cl *ENEY* PO4 .... 296 A1
  CHAR BH8 .... 323 M5
Hopkins Ct *ENEY* PO4 .... 317 K6
Hopkinson Wy *AND* SP10 ..... 101 P1
Hopton Garth *CHIN* RG24 ...... 70 B3
Hopwood Cl *NWBY* RG14 ...... 24 C3
Horace Rd *BOSC* BH5 .... 335 L2
Horder Cl *ROWN* SO16 .... 228 D9
Hordle La *LYMN* SO41 .... 327 P7
Hordle Ms *LYMN* SO41 .... 327 P3
Hordle Rd *HAV* PO9 .... 276 C6
Horlock Rd *BROC* SO42 .... 286 G7
Hornbeam Cl *FARN* GU14 ...... 57 K8
Hornbeam Cl *SHST* GU47 ...... 41 K8
Hornbeam Gdns *HEND* SO30 ... 249 M1
Hornbeam Pightle *THLE* RG7 ... 27 K4
Hornbeam Rd *CHFD* SO53 ..... 206 A8
  HAV PO9 .... 277 H7
Hornbeam Wy *WIMB* BH21 .... 251 J9
Hornby Cl *HLER* SO31 .... 291 D1
Hornchurch Rd *ROWN* SO16 ... 227 M7
Horndean Prec *HORN* PO8 .... 256 C6

Horndean Rd *EMRTH* PO10 ..... 277 K6
Horne Rd *SHAM* SO14 .... 25 F5
Hornet Cl *FHAM* PO15 .... 272 B8
  GPORT PO12 .... 13 F5
Hornet Rd *EMRTH* PO10 .... 299 N6
Horn Rd *FARN* GU14 .... 57 M8
Horns Dro *ROWN* SO16 .... 227 J6
Horns HI *BPWT* SO32 .... 253 M1
Horns Hill Cl *ROWN* SO16 ..... 227 H6
Horsa Cl *SBNE* BH6 .... 336 C2
Horsa Ct *SBNE* BH6 .... 336 C2
Horsea La *NEND* PO2 .... 296 F5
Horsea Rd *NEND* PO2 .... 296 C4
Horsebridge Rd *HAV* PO9 ...... 276 C6
  STOK SO20 .... 160 F4
Horsebridge Wy *ROWN* 227 J7
Horsecroft *ROMY* SO51 .... 204 D5
Horsefair Ms *ROMY* SO51 ...... 204 C6
Horse La *NARL* SO24 .... 149 N9
Horsepost La *HORN* PO8 .... 255 K1
Horse Sands Cl *ENEY* PO4 ..... 317 M5
Horseshoe Bend *GSHT* GU26 .. 155 P5
Horseshoe Cl
  FHAM/STUB PO14 .... 271 K8
  WIMB BH21 .... 279 K8
Horseshoe Crs *BOR* GU35 ..... 154 B5
  THLE RG7 .... 27 J4
Horseshoe Dro *ROMY* SO51 ... 204 F3
  TOTT SO40 .... 245 J1
Horseshoe End *NWBY* RG14 ... 24 F7
Horseshoe La *ASHV* GU12 ..... 76 F6
  RAND SP11 .... 62 A4
Horseshoe Ldg *HLER* SO31 .... 270 E9
Horsham Av *NBNE* BH10 .... 322 C1
Horsham Rd *SHST* GU47 .... 41 L5
Horton Cl *MOOR/WNTN* BH9 ... 323 J4
Horsham La *LSOL/BMARY* PO13 .. 294 C4
  RGWD BH24 .... 281 J3
Horton Rd *MOOR/WNTN* BH9 ... 323 J4
Horton Wy *ELGH* SO50 .... 258 D7
  VWD BH31 .... 258 D5
Horwood Gdns *BSTK* RG21 .... 90 B1
Hosker Rd *BOSC* BH5 .... 335 P1
Hospital HI *ALDT* GU11 .... 2 D2
Hospital La *STOK* SO20 .... 139 M3
Hospital Rd *ALDT* GU11 .... 76 A4
  BPWT SO32 .... 252 E2
Hostel Rd *FARN* GU14 .... 76 A4
Hotspur Cl *FAWY* SO45 .... 268 B5
Houchin St *BPWT* SO32 .... 232 A5
Houghton Cl *HAV* PO9 * 277 H4
Houghton Sq *HTWY* RG27 ..... 72 C8
Houlton Rd *PLE* BH15 .... 320 C8
Hound Green *HTWY* RG27 ..... 54 A2
Houndmills Rd *BSTK* RG21 .... 69 H6
Houndown La *MFD/CHID* GU8 .. 137 M4
Hound Rd *HLER* SO31 .... 291 K5
Hound Road Gdns *HLER* SO31 .. 269 M5
Hounds Wy *WIMB* BH21 .... 279 K9
Hounds Wy *HLER* SO31 .... 269 M4
Houndwell Pl *SHAM* SO14 ..... 21 F5
Hounsdown Av *TOTT* SO40 .... 246 D6
Hounsdown Cl *TOTT* SO40 .... 246 D6
Hounslow Cl *PLE* BH15 .... 332 A1
Hoursemoor La *HTWY* RG27 ... 89 M7
Houston Wy *CWTH* RG45 ...... 40 E1
Houseman Rd *FARN* GU14 ..... 57 N7
Hoverfly Cl
  LSOL/BMARY PO13 .... 314 E3
Hoveton Gv *CHFD* SO53 .... 206 D5
Howard Cl *CHCH/BSGR* BH23 ... 325 K9
  CHFD SO53 .... 206 F9
  ELGH SO50 .... 222 F3
  FLEETN GU51 .... 74 F3
  LSOL/BMARY PO13 .... 314 E1
  RGWD BH24 .... 284 B7
  WEND SO18 .... 228 G8
Howard Ct *FARN* GU14 .... 57 J9
Howard Rd *BSTK* RG21 .... 69 H8
  CHAR BH8 .... 323 J8
  NEND PO2 .... 296 C5
  NWBY RG14 .... 16 E5
  VWD BH31 .... 258 F4
Howard's Av *WHAM* PO15 ..... 325 N5
Howard's La *ALTN* GU34 ...... 133 J2
Howards Md *LYMN* SO41 ...... 329 H5
Howberry Cha *HASM* GU27 .... 156 C7
Howden Cl *WVILLE* PO7 .... 204 B6
Howe La *NBNE* BH10 * 337 H4
Howell Cl *SHAM* SO14 .... 21 J2
Howe Rd *LSOL/BMARY* PO13 ... 314 C2
Howerts Cl *HLER* SO31 .... 292 D2
Howes Gdns *FLEETN* GU51 * ... 74 B6
Howeth Cl *NBNE* BH10 .... 322 D4
The Howe *FARN* GU14 .... 75 J5
Howeth Rd *NBNE* BH10 .... 322 C5
Howgare Rd *RSAL* SP5 .... 195 L1
Howlett Cl *SHAM* SO14 .... 329 J3
Howton Cl *NBNE* BH10 * 322 C2
Howton Rd *NBNE* BH10 .... 322 C2
Hoxley Rd *NBNE* BH10 .... 322 C3
Hoylake Cl *LSOL/BMARY* PO13 .. 294 A8
Hoylake Rd *CHAM* PO6 .... 275 J9
Hoylecroft Cl *FHAM* PO15 .... 10 A1
Hubbard Rd *BSTK* RG21 .... 68 F4
Hubert Rd *WINC* SO23 .... 183 N2
Huckers La *ALTN* GU34 .... 152 D8
Huddington Gld *YTLY* GU46 .... 40 F8
Hudson Cl *BKME/WDN* BH12 ... 321 L2
  CFDH BH17 .... 319 P3
  LSOL/BMARY PO13 .... 314 G2
  RGWD BH24 .... 282 C1
Hudson Davies Cl *LYMN* SO41 .. 309 M7
Hugh De Port La *FLEETN* GU51 .. 74 B6
Hugh's Cl *HAV* PO9 .... 290 G8

Hugo Platt *EPSF* GU31 .... 217 J1
Huish La *CHIN* RG24 .... 91 K1
Hulbert Rd *HAV* PO9 .... 276 C7
  WVILLE PO7 .... 275 P2
Hulbert Wy *BH/HW/K* RG22 .... 89 N1
Hulfords La *HTWY* RG27 .... 55 K4
Hullam La *ALTN* GU34 .... 172 A2
Hull Crs *BWD* BH11 .... 301 M9
Hulles Wy *NBAD* SO52 .... 205 K9
Hull Rd *BWD* BH11 .... 301 M9
Hull Wy *BWD* BH11 .... 301 N9
Hulse Rd *WSHM* SO15 .... 248 B5
Hulton Cl *ITCH* SO19 .... 268 F1
Hulton Cl *FHAM/STUB* PO14 ... 295 J3
  NTHA RG18 .... 25 L2
Humber Ct *AND* SP10 .... 82 C9
Humber Gdns *HLER* SO31 ...... 270 A1
Humber La *TDWTH* SP9 .... 78 F7
Humber Rd *FERN* BH22 .... 302 C2
  BH/HW/K RG22 .... 88 A9
Humbers Vw *STOK* SO20 ...... 161 M6
The Hummicks *BROC* SO42 .... 289 N9
Humming Bird Cl
  WHAM PO17 .... 253 J8
Humphrey Pk *FLEETS* GU52 ... 74 C9
Hundred Acres Rd
  WVILLE PO7 .... 275 M1
Hundred La *LYMN* SO41 .... 309 M9
The Hundred *WVILLE* PO7 ..... 4 D7
  WVILLE PO7 .... 275 M1
Hungerfield Ct
  CHCH/BSGR BH23 .... 305 L7
Hungerford Cl *BH/HW/K* RG22 .. 88 D2
Hungerford La *BH/HW/K* RG22 .. 84 F6
  SHST GU47 .... 41 K6
Hungerford La *AND* SP10 ..... 82 C5
  RAND SP11 .... 62 C5
Hungerford Rd *CHAR* BH8 ..... 323 K4
Hunnels Cl *FLEETS* GU52 ...... 74 B9
Hunt Av *HLER* SO31 .... 269 L4
Hunt Cl *RWIN* SO21 .... 144 F4
Hunt Ct *CHCH/BSGR* BH23 .... 305 M9
  FAWY SO45 .... 290 C5
  LSOL/BMARY PO13 .... 315 H1
  STOK SO20 .... 161 M6
  WIMB BH21 .... 279 L8
Hunter Rd *EMRTH* PO10 ...... 299 N5
  ENEY PO4 .... 317 H5
  FARN GU14 .... 75 N1
Hunters Cha *BPWT* SO32 ...... 232 C9
  LIPH GU30 .... 175 J2
Hunters Cl *DEAN* RG23 .... 67 N9
Hunters Cl *HLER* SO31 * 250 B7
Hunters Crs *ROMY* SO51 ...... 204 C3
  TOTT SO40 .... 245 P5
Hunters' HI *THLE* RG7 .... 27 H4
Hunters HI *TOTT* SO40 .... 246 B8
Hunters Lage *FHAM* PO15 ..... 293 P1
Hunters Rde *WVILLE* PO7 ..... 275 N3
Hunters La *HTWY* RG27 .... 174 A5
Hunters Wy *ELGH* SO50 .... 230 A2
Huntfield Rd
  MOOR/WNTN BH9 .... 323 H4
Huntingdon Cl
  FHAM/STUB PO14 .... 271 J9
Huntingdon Dr *WIMB* BH21 ... 300 C4
Huntingdon Gdns
  CHCH/BSGR BH23 .... 324 D5
  ELGH SO50 .... 206 D5
Huntingdon House Dr
  GSHT GU26 .... 156 D1
Hunting Ga *AND* SP10 .... 102 A2
Huntley Cl *CHAM* PO6 * 277 J2
Huntly Rd *TWDS* BH3 .... 322 D9
Hunton Cl *ROWN* SO16 .... 227 P9
Hunton Down La *RWIN* SO21 .. 126 A4
Hunton La *HWY* SO21 .... 125 P5
Hunt Rd *CHCH/BSGR* BH23 .... 325 K7
  PLE BH15 .... 320 A7
Huntsbottom La *LISS* GU33 ... 192 F5
Hunts Cl *HTWY* RG27 .... 72 B3
Hunts Common *HTWY* RG27 ... 55 J6
Hunts Hill Rd *RGUW* GU3 ..... 77 M7
Huntsman Cl *HORN* PO8 ...... 255 P6
Huntsmead *ALTN* GU34 ...... 132 G6
Huntsmead Rd *TADY* RG26 .... 34 A6
Hunts Pond Rd *HLER* SO31 ... 271 J4
Huntvale Rd
  MOOR/WNTN BH9 .... 323 H4
Hurdles Md *LYMN* SO41 ...... 338 C3
The Hurdles *CHCH/BSGR* BH23 .. 305 P6
  FHAM/STUB PO14 .... 271 K8
Hurdle Wy *WINC* SO18 .... 183 M7
Hurland La *BOR* GU35 .... 154 C4
Hurlands Cl *FNM* GU9 .... 96 F1
Hurlands Pl *FNM* GU9 .... 96 F1
Hurlingham Gdns *ROWN* SO16 .. 228 C7
Hurn Br *CHCH/BSGR* BH23 .... 323 P1
Hurn Cl *RGWD* BH24 .... 282 B3
Hurn Ct La *CHCH/BSGR* BH23 .. 304 A3
  RGWD BH24 .... 282 A9
Hurn La *RGWD* BH24 .... 282 A9
Hurn Rd *CHCH/BSGR* BH23 .... 323 P1
  RGWD BH24 .... 282 A9
Huron Cl *LIPH* GU30 .... 175 J3
Huron Dr *LIPH* GU30 .... 175 J2
Hurricane Wy *FARN* GU14 .... 75 N1
Hursley Cl *LTDN* BH7 .... 324 A7
Hursley Dr *FAWY* SO45 .... 312 C1
  FLEETN GU51 .... 73 P1
Hursley Park Rd *RWIN* SO21 .. 182 D7
Hursley Rd *CHFD* SO53 .... 206 D6
  HAV PO9 .... 276 D5
  RWIN SO21 .... 206 D1
Hurstbourne Av
  CHCH/BSGR BH23 .... 326 A6
Hurstbourne Cl *HAV* PO9 ..... 276 D4
Hurstbourne Pl *ITCH* SO19 * .. 269 H2
Hurst Cl *CHCH/BSGR* BH23 ... 326 E5

  CHFD SO53 .... 206 C9
  FHAM/STUB PO14 .... 293 N8
  LIPH GU30 .... 175 N2
  NMIL/BTOS BH25 .... 326 F7
  TOTT SO40 .... 246 D5
Hurstdene Rd *CHAR* BH8 ...... 323 J5
Hurst Grn *LSOL/BMARY* PO13 .. 294 F7
Hurst Green Cl *HORN* PO8 .... 256 B9
  ITCH SO19 .... 11 J9
Hurst HI *PSTN* BH14 .... 333 L3
Hurst La *ALTN* GU34 .... 190 B3
  ELGH SO50 .... 208 G7
Hurstleigh Dr *LYMN* SO41 * .. 329 K6
Hurstmere Cl *HLER* SO31 ..... 309 H5
Hurstmere Ct *GSHT* GU26 .... 156 C2
Hurst Rd *ALDT* GU11 .... 76 E8
  FARN GU14 .... 58 A5
  LYMN SO41 .... 339 H5
  RGWD BH24 .... 260 G9
The Hurst *HTWY* RG27 .... 73 J3
Hurstville Dr *WVILLE* PO7 .... 275 M2
Hussar Cl *CHCH/BSGR* BH23 .. 324 D9
Hussar Ct *ALDT* GU11 .... 96 E1
  WVILLE PO7 .... 275 L1
Hussell La *ALTN* GU34 .... 150 A1
Hussey Cl *WINC* SO23 .... 165 H5
Hussey's La *ALTN* GU34 ..... 114 A5
Hutton Cl *NWBY* RG14 ...... 24 B4
Hutton Rd *ASHV* GU12 ...... 76 F6
Hutton Sq *AND* SP10 .... 82 G9
Hutwood Rd *ROWN* SO16 .... 228 C4
Huxley Cl *HLER* SO31 .... 270 C1
Huxley Ct *FARN* GU14 * 267 H8
Hyacinth Cl *BH/HW/K* RG22 .. 89 L3
  CFDH BH17 .... 320 A3
Hyde Abbey Rd *WINC* SO23 ... 22 E3
Hyde Church La *WINC* SO23 ... 4 D7
Hyde Church Pth *WINC* SO23 .. 22 E1
  TOTT SO40 .... 308 B6
  WINC SO23 .... 245 P4
Hyde Cl *FLEETS* GU52 * 22 D2
  TOTT SO40 .... 22 D2
  WSHM SO15 .... 247 N2
Hyde Ga *WINC* SO23 .... 22 E2
Hyde Gdns *WINC* SO23 ...... 22 E2
Hyde House Gdns *WINC* SO23 * .. 22 E2
Hyde La *FBDG* SP6 .... 240 C5
  KSCL RG20 .... 31 M8
  MFD/CHID GU8 .... 137 N7
  RFNM GU10 .... 94 H8
  RFNM GU10 .... 137 K8
Hyden Farm La *HORN* PO8 .... 235 M4
Hyde Park Rd *SSEA* PO5 ...... 19 H4
Hyde Rd *NBNE* BH10 .... 322 C2
Hydes Platt *THLE* RG7 .... 35 J6
Hyde St *SSEA* PO5 .... 19 G6
The Hyde *NMIL/BTOS* BH25 ... 326 F6
Hylton Ct *TADY* RG26 .... 34 D6
Hylton Rd *PSF* GU32 .... 215 M2
Hymans Wy *TOTT* SO40 ...... 246 C4
Hynesbury Rd
  CHCH/BSGR BH23 .... 325 N9
Hyson Crs *RAND* SP11 .... 80 B1
Hyssop Cl *FHAM* PO15 ...... 271 K3
Hythe By-Pass *FAWY* SO45 ... 267 M6
Hythe Cl *TADY* RG26 .... 34 C7
Hythe Rd *CHAM* PO6 .... 296 C1
  PLE BH15 .... 321 J5
  TOTT SO40 .... 267 J2

I

Ibberton Cl *CHAR* BH8 .... 323 M5
Ibberton Rd *CHAR* BH8 .... 323 M5
Ibbett Rd *NBNE* BH10 .... 323 J5
Ibbotson Wy *TOTT* SO40 ..... 246 B6
Ibsen Cl *FHAM* PO15 .... 271 J2
Ibsley Cl *CHAR* BH8 .... 323 J9
Ibsley Dro *RGWD* BH24 ...... 260 F1
Ibsley Gv *HAV* PO9 .... 14 B2
Ibworth La *FLEETS* GU52 ..... 73 P1
  TADY RG26 .... 66 C1
Icarus Pl *WVILLE* PO7 .... 275 P7
Icknield Wy *AND* SP10 .... 82 G8
Iddesleigh Rd *TWDS* BH3 .... 322 F9
Iden Ct *NWBY* RG14 .... 24 D3
Idsworth Cl *HORN* PO8 ...... 256 E5
Idsworth Rd *HORN* PO8 ...... 256 B9
  HSEA PO3 .... 297 J3
Iford Cl *SBNE* BH6 .... 324 B7
Iford Ct *HAV* PO9 .... 277 H4
Iford Gdns *LTDN* BH7 .... 324 A8
Iford La *SBNE* BH6 .... 324 C7
Ilex Cl *TADY* RG26 .... 34 F5
  WINC SO23 .... 145 J8
Ilex Rd *AND* SP10 .... 40 C8
Ilex Crs *HLER* SO31 .... 270 F7
Ilex Wk *NMIL/BTOS* BH25 * .. 319 J5
Iley La *LYMN* SO41 .... 329 J3
Ilford Cl *SBNE* BH6 .... 324 D1
Ilkley Wy *STHA* RG19 .... 33 H6
Illingworth Cl *TADY* RG26 ... 52 C3
Illustrious Rd
  FHAM/STUB PO14 .... 293 P8
Imadene Crs *BOR* GU35 ...... 154 C4
Imber Cl *ITCH* SO19 .... 249 L7
Imber Dr *CHCH/BSGR* BH23 .. 326 D3
Imber Rd *WINC* SO23 .... 23 J3
Imber Wy *ITCH* SO19 .... 249 L7
Imbrecourt *CHAR* BH8 .... 333 H4
Imjin Cl *ALDT* GU11 .... 2 E4
Imperial Av *WSHM* SO15 ..... 247 M4
Imperial Rd *SHAM* SO14 ..... 248 D4
Imperial Wy *STHA* RG19 ..... 25 P5
Implacable Rd
  LSOL/BMARY PO13 .... 314 B1
Impstone Rd *TADY* RG26 ..... 34 G5
Imran Cl *ASHV* GU12 .... 3 H6
Infantry Dr *STHA* RG19 ..... 25 P6
Ingersley Rd *HEND* SO30 .... 249 M2
Ingle Dell *CBLY* GU15 .... 58 C1
Ingledene Cl *GPORT* PO12 ... 12 C3

HAV PO9 14 B3
Ingle Gln FAWY SO45 268 C9
Ingle Gn TOTT SO40 245 P2
Inglesham Wy PLE BH15 320 A8
Ingleside HLER SO31 269 L3
Ingleside Cl
FHAM/STUB PO14 293 P1
Ingleton Rd ROWN SO16 247 H2
Inglewood Av CBLY GU15 59 H1
CHAR BH8 323 M6
Inglewood Dr BH/HW/K RG22 89 M5
NMIL/BTOS BH25 327 K5
Inglewood Gdns ELGH SO50 230 C1
Inglis Rd SSEA PO5 316 G5
Ingoldfield La WHAM PO17 253 N4
Ingram Wk WIMB BH21 300 F1
Ings Cl ALTN GU34 132 F7
Ingworth Rd
BKME/WDN BH12 334 A1
Inhams La WVILLE PO7 254 F7
Inhams Rd ALTN GU34 133 K3
Inhams Wy THLE RG7 35 H6
Inhurst Av WVILLE PO7 276 A1
Inhurst La TADY RG26 33 M5
Inhurst Rd NEND PO2 296 G7
Inhurst Wy TADY RG26 34 A5
Inkerman Rd ITCH SO19 248 F8
Inkpen Gdns CHIN RG24 70 B4
Inmans La PSF GU32 191 P9
Innisfail Gdns ALDT GU11 2 B6
Insley Crs BDST BH18 300 A8
Institute Rd ASHV GU12 3 K6
Instow Gdns FARN GU14 57 P6
Interchange Pk HSEA PO3 * 297 L6
International Wy ITCH SO19 268 G2
Inval Hl HASM GU27 157 H5
Inveravon CHCH/BSGR BH23 337 K1
Inverclyde Rd PSTN BH14 321 K8
Invergordon Av CHAM PO6 297 K2
Inverkip Cl
LSOL/BMARY PO13 * 314 C1
Inverleigh Rd SBNE BH6 324 A9
Inverness Av FHAM PO15 10 A2
Inverness Rd GPORT PO12 315 L3
NEND PO2 316 G1
Inverness Wy SHST GU47 41 L7
Invincible Rd FARN GU14 75 P2
FHAM/STUB PO14 293 P8
Inwood Rd LISS GU33 192 E3
Ionic Cl CHFD SO53 207 H6
Iping Av HAV PO9 276 D5
Ipley Wy FAWY SO45 268 C8
Ipswich Rd WBNE BH4 334 B2
Ireland Wy WVILLE PO7 275 N5
Iris Cl BH/HW/K RG22 89 L4
Iris Rd MOOR/WNTN BH9 322 F6
ROWN SO16 228 D8
Ironbridge Crs HLER SO31 270 G4
Ironbridge La ENEY PO4 317 L4
Iron Mill Cl FHAM PO15 272 B7
Ironmill La FHAM PO15 271 P5
Irvine Cl FHAM/PORC PO16 10 E2
Irvine Dr FARN GU14 57 M5
Irvine Wy CHCH/BSGR BH23 325 J7
Irving Rd ROWN SO16 247 K2
SBNE BH6 336 B1
Irwell Cl BSTK RG21 7 J6
CHFD SO53 206 C8
Isaacs Cl BKME/WDN BH12 322 B8
Isambard Brunel Rd PSEA PO1 19 G3
Isington La ALTN GU34 114 C7
Isington Rd ALTN GU34 134 B1
Isis Cl ROWN SO16 247 J3
Isis Wy SHST GU47 41 L6
Island Cl HISD PO11 298 G6
Island Farm Rd THLE RG7 26 G6
Island View Av
CHCH/BSGR BH23 325 M9
Island View Gdns
LYMN SO41 339 H3
Island View Rd
NMIL/BTOS BH25 326 E8
Island View Ter NEND PO2 296 E8
Islay Gdns CHAM PO6 275 H9
Isley Rd CHIN RG24 69 L2
Itchel La RFNM GU10 94 F4
Itchen Av ELGH SO50 229 P2
Itchen Br SHAM SO14 21 K7
Itchen Cl DEAN RG23 88 F2
EPSF GU31 215 L3
ROMY SO51 224 D1
Itchen Ct AND SP10 82 G9
Itchenor Rd HISD PO11 319 M6
Itchen Rd HAV PO9 277 H4
Itchenside Cl WEND SO18 229 H8
Itchen Vw NARL SO24 167 J2
Itchen Wy ELGH SO50 229 L1
ITCH SO19 268 F2
NARL SO24 167 L5
RWIN SO21 165 L2
RWIN SO21 207 N1
WEND SO18 248 F2
WINC SO23 23 F7
Itchin Cl TOTT SO40 246 B5
Ithica Cl HISD PO11 318 G4
Ivamy Pl BWD BH11 321 P2
Ivanhoe Rd WSHM SO15 247 P2
Ivar Gdns CHIN RG24 70 B3
Ively Rd FARN GU14 75 H4
Ives Cl YTLY GU46 40 C7
Ivor Cl FAWY SO45 290 E5
Ivor Rd PLE BH15 332 C2
Ivy Cl FUFL SO22 183 N1
RGWD BH24 281 K5
TOTT SO40 246 C1
Ivy Ct WVILLE PO7 275 M6
Ivy Dene ITCH SO19 249 M7
Ivydene Gdns HORN PO8 256 A7
Ivy Down La DEAN RG23 67 K9
Ivyhole Hl HTWY RG27 55 N5
Ivyhouse La PSF GU32 190 E3
Ivy La FNM GU9 96 B9
PSEA PO1 316 C2
RGWD BH24 260 F6
WEND SO18 249 K1
Ivy Rd ASHV GU12 97 L1
SD/PW SO17 248 E3
WIMB BH21 300 F5
Iwerne Cl MOOR/WNTN BH9 323 H3

J

Jacaranda Cl FHAM PO15 271 L7
Jacaranda Rd BOR GU35 154 A6
Jack Cl CHFD SO53 206 A7
Jack Cockerill Wy SSEA PO5 * 316 F7
Jackdaw Cl BH/HW/K RG22 89 K3
HORN PO8 255 N7
Jackdaw Ri ELGH SO50 228 F3
Jackie Wigg Gdns TOTT SO40 246 D4
Jacklyns Cl NARL SO24 167 P3
Jacklyns La NARL SO24 167 P3
Jackmans Cl ITCH SO19 248 F8
Jackman's Hl RWIN SO21 184 G7
Jackson Cl CHAM PO6 297 L3
Jackson Rd BKME/WDN BH12 321 L6
Jacobean Cl CHCH/BSGR BH23 326 D6
Jacob Rd CBLY GU15 41 P7
Jacobs Cl HORN PO8 236 C7
ROMY SO51 204 E6
Jacob's Gutter La TOTT SO40 246 D6
Jacobs Rd PLE BH15 332 A1
Jacob's St PSEA PO1 19 H1
Jacobs Wk TOTT SO40 246 C7
Jacomb Pl
LSOL/BMARY PO13 * 295 H7
Jacqueline Av WVILLE PO7 275 M6
Jacqueline Rd
BKME/WDN BH12 321 K5
Jade Ct LSOL/BMARY PO13 * 314 G2
Jagdalik Rd TDWTH SP9 78 G7
Jago Ct NWBY RG14 24 D7
Jago Rd PSEA PO1 18 B1
Jaguar Rd FARN GU14 76 A2
Jamaica Rd GPORT PO12 315 P3
James Callaghan Dr
CHAM PO6 274 C8
James Cl HISD PO11 318 E5
LSOL/BMARY PO13 294 G5
James Copse Rd HORN PO8 255 P6
James Grieve Av HLER SO31 270 G8
Jameson Rd
MOOR/WNTN BH9 322 E6
James Pl TADY RG26 34 D6
James Rd ALDT GU11 76 C5
BKME/WDN BH12 334 A1
CBLY GU15 58 A3
HAV PO9 14 C3
LSOL/BMARY PO13 294 G5
James's La RDGW/BURGH RG30 27 M3
James St SHAM SO14 21 G4
James Wy CBLY GU15 58 A3
Jamrud Rd TDWTH SP9 78 F6
Janaway Gdns SD/PW SO17 248 E3
Janes Cl FAWY SO45 290 G9
Jan Smuts Cl LISS GU33 174 A6
Janson Rd WSHM SO15 247 N4
Japonica Wy HAV PO9 277 J6
Jaques's La THLE RG7 27 H1
Jardine Sq AND SP10 82 G9
Jarndyce Wk NEND PO2 * 316 E1
Jarvis Cl HTWY RG27 39 P6
Jarvis Flds HLER SO31 270 B2
Jasmine Ct AND SP10 * 102 B4
FHAM PO15 271 K1
LSOL/BMARY PO13 * 314 G2
LYMN SO41 329 K3
Jasmine Gv WVILLE PO7 276 A4
Jasmine Rd BH/HW/K RG22 89 M3
HEND SO30 250 B3
Jasmine Wk
FHAM/STUB PO14 294 C1
Jasmine Wy BOR GU35 154 B6
HORN PO8 236 C7
STHA RG19 32 E1
Jasmond Rd CHAM PO6 297 J3
Jason Pl WVILLE PO7 275 N8
Jason Wy GPORT PO12 * 295 K9
Jaundrells Cl
NMIL/BTOS BH25 327 L4
Java Dr FHAM PO15 271 J3
Java Rd SHAM SO14 268 D1
Javelin Rd EMRTH PO10 299 N6
J Av FAWY SO45 291 H3
Jay Cl FHAM/STUB PO14 293 P5
HORN PO8 256 A4
Jays Cl BH/HW/K RG22 90 B3
Jay's Ct CHCH/BSGR BH23 326 D7
Jays Nest Cl BLKW GU17 57 L1
Jealous La LYMN SO41 308 G6
Jefferson Av CHAR BH8 323 K9
Jefferson Rd BSTK RG21 7 F1
CHOB/PIR GU24 59 P6
Jeffries Cl ROWN SO16 227 J7
Jellicoe Av GPORT PO12 315 K6
Jellicoe Cl PSTN BH14 321 H7
Jellicoe Ct AND SP10 * 5 J3
Jellicoe Dr CHCH/BSGR BH23 325 K9
Jenkins Gv HSEA PO3 317 K1
Jenkyns Cl HEND SO30 250 G4
Jenner Cl VWD BH31 258 E3
Jenner Wy ALTN GU34 132 G3
ROMY SO51 204 G5
Jennie Green La ALTN GU34 130 G7
Jennings Rd PSTN BH14 333 L1
TOTT SO40 246 E3
Jenny's Wk YTLY GU46 40 F8
Jenson Gdns AND SP10 102 C3
Jephcote Rd BWD BH11 301 P9
Jermyns La ROMY SO51 204 G2
Jerome Cnr CWTH RG45 41 K3
Jerome Ct ITCH SO19 249 M5
Jerram Cl GPORT PO12 315 K5
Jerrett's La ROWN SO16 227 H9
Jersey Brow Rd FARN GU14 75 P2
Jersey Cl BKME/WDN BH12 321 L3
CHIN RG24 69 M2
FHAM/STUB PO14 294 B8
FLEETN GU51 56 E9
ROWN SO16 227 J9
Jersey Rd BKME/WDN BH12 321 M3
NEND PO2 296 G9
Jervis Ct AND SP10 5 J2
Jervis Court La BPWT SO32 232 E4
Jervis Dr GPORT PO12 315 M2
Jervis Rd NEND PO2 296 E7
Jesmond Av
CHCH/BSGR BH23 326 B7
Jesmond Dene NWBY RG14 24 C3
Jesmond Gv HLER SO31 270 G9
Jessamine Rd ROWN SO16 247 M1
Jesse Cl YTLY GU46 40 G9
Jessett Dr FLEETS GU52 74 B8
Jessica Av VWD BH31 258 D3
Jessica Cl WVILLE PO7 276 B1
Jessica Crs TOTT SO40 245 P2
Jessie Rd ENEY PO4 316 G4
GPORT PO12 12 B3
HAV PO9 14 A2
Jessie Ter SHAM SO14 21 F7
Jessop Cl FAWY SO45 268 B5
Jessopp Cl NBNE BH10 322 F3
Jessopp Rd WIMB BH21 279 K8
Jesty Rd NARL SO24 167 N3
Jetty Rd FAWY SO45 291 K4
Jewell Rd CHAR BH8 323 M6
Jewry St WINC SO23 22 E4
Jex Blake Cl ROWN SO16 227 M8
Jibbs Meadow TADY RG26 52 A2
Jimmy Brown Av WIMB BH21 280 E4
Jinny La ROMY SO51 180 C9
Joanna Cl RSAL SP5 199 H6
Jobson Cl WHCH RG28 85 L6
Jockey La ELGH SO50 207 N8
Jodrell Cl HORN PO8 256 C4
Joe Bigwood Cl ROWN SO16 227 H7
John Arlott Ct NARL SO24 167 P2
John Bunyan Cl FHAM PO15 271 J2
John Childs Cl NWBY RG14 16 E5
John Cl ALDT GU11 96 E3
John Darling Ml ELGH SO50 * 207 J9
John Eggars Sq ALTN GU34 132 G4
John Hunt Cl STHA RG19 25 P5
John King Shipyard
EMRTH PO10 * 299 N1
John Morgan Cl HTWY RG27 71 P2
Johnson Rd WIMB BH21 302 A1
Johnson St SHAM SO14 21 F4
Johnson Vw FHAM PO15 271 L4
Johnson Wy FLEETS GU52 74 C6
RAND SP11 79 N2
Johns Rd FHAM/PORC PO16 294 F2
John's Rd ITCH SO19 248 F8
Johnstone Rd
CHCH/BSGR BH23 325 J9
Johnston Rd PLE BH15 320 F5
John St SHAM SO14 21 F7
Jolliffe Av PLE BH15 320 F8
Jolliffe Rd PLE BH15 320 F8
Jonas Nichols Sq SHAM SO14 21 G4
Jonathan Cl LYMN SO41 329 L2
Jonathan Hl KSCL RG20 30 G3
Jonathan Rd FHAM PO15 272 C9
Jones La FAWY SO45 268 B6
Jopps Cnr CHCH/BSGR BH23 324 G3
Jordans La LYMN SO41 308 C5
LYMN SO41 309 P9
Jordan's La THLE RG7 27 H5
Joseph St GPORT PO12 * 13 F2
Joshua Cl PLE BH15 332 A1
Josian Wk SHAM SO14 21 G3
Joslin Cl GPORT PO12 315 P2
Jouldings La THLE RG7 38 G2
Joule Rd AND SP10 101 P1
BSTK RG21 6 B2
Jowitt Dr NMIL/BTOS BH25 327 H5
Joys La LYMN SO41 310 C8
Joy's La STOK SO20 123 L5
Joys Rd WIMB BH21 280 E1
Jubilee Av CHAM PO6 296 A1
Jubilee Cl ELGH SO50 229 H3
FARN GU14 57 K9
RGWD BH24 282 G1
TADY RG26 34 F5
WIMB BH21 300 A6
Jubilee Ct FHAM/STUB PO14 294 E2
LYMN SO41 308 B7
Jubilee Crs BKME/WDN BH12 321 M7
FBDG SP6 240 B2
Jubilee Dr ASHV GU12 76 F6
Jubilee Gdns NBNE BH10 322 D5
WEND SO18 249 K4
Jubilee Hall Rd FARN GU14 58 B9
Jubilee La GSHT GU26 156 B2
RFNM GU10 116 A5
Jubilee Pth HAV PO9 14 A5
Jubilee Rd ALDT GU11 97 H4
BSTK RG21 69 L8
ENEY PO4 317 H5
EWKG RG40 40 A3
FBDG SP6 240 A2
FHAM/PORC PO16 295 P1
FRIM GU16 76 F2
GPORT PO12 315 M3
NWBY RG14 17 G4
PSTN BH14 321 M7
ROMY SO51 204 C5
WIMB BH21 300 A6
WVILLE PO7 275 M1
Jubilee Ter SSEA PO5 19 F6
Jubilee Trail RSAL SP5 195 M7
Jukes Wk HEND SO30 249 P1
Julia Cl CHCH/BSGR BH23 326 B7
Julian Cl ROWN SO16 228 B6
Julian Rd ITCH SO19 249 K8
Julian's Rd WIMB BH21 300 C1
Julian Ter BOSC BH5 * 335 P1
Julie Av FHAM PO15 10 A5
Juliet Ct WVILLE PO7 * 276 A2
Julius Cl CHFD SO53 206 G7
CHIN RG24 68 F4
Julyan Av BKME/WDN BH12 322 A7
Jumar Cl HLER SO31 292 D2
Jumpers Av CHCH/BSGR BH23 324 C7
Jumpers Rd CHCH/BSGR BH23 324 D7
Jumps Rd RFNM GU10 136 E6
Junction Rd AND SP10 4 A2
MOOR/WNTN BH9 322 F7
TOTT SO40 246 E4
Junction Ter NWBY RG14 17 J3
June Dr DEAN RG23 68 E7
Juniper Cl AND SP10 102 B3
BOR GU35 153 M6
CHIN RG24 52 B9
FERN BH22 280 C9
FUFL SO22 183 M1
LYMN SO41 329 H5
NBAD SO52 205 K8
WIMB BH21 280 E1
Juniper Rd FARN GU14 57 K8
HORN PO8 256 C2
WEND SO18 249 H4
Juniper Sq HAV PO9 15 G7
Jupiter Cl ROWN SO16 227 J8
Jupiter Ct PSEA PO1 18 C5
Jupiter Wy WIMB BH21 300 A5
Jura Cl CHAM PO6 275 H9
Jurds Lake Wy ITCH SO19 268 F1
Jurd Wy HLER SO31 269 P1
Justin Cl FHAM/STUB PO14 10 A6
Justin Gdns NBNE BH10 322 E3
Justinian Cl CHFD SO53 207 H6
Jute Cl FHAM/PORC PO16 273 M9
Jutland Cl FHAM PO15 271 H3
Jutland Crs AND SP10 82 D7
Juventu Cl HAV PO9 15 H1

K

Kamptee Copse
NMIL/BTOS BH25 327 K1
Kanes Hl ITCH SO19 249 P5
Karachi Cl TDWTH SP9 78 G4
Karen Av CHAM PO6 297 L3
Kassassin St ENEY PO4 317 J6
Kassel Cl WVILLE PO7 276 B2
Katherine Chance Cl
CHCH/BSGR BH23 324 G4
Kathleen Cl BSTK RG21 90 C1
Kathleen Rd ITCH SO19 249 K8
Kathryn Cl TOTT SO40 245 P2
Katrina Gdns HISD PO11 318 G3
Katrine Crs CHFD SO53 206 C6
Katterns Cl CHCH/BSGR BH23 324 C5
Kayak Cl HLER SO31 270 E9
Kay Cl CHCH/BSGR BH23 325 J9
Kay Crs BOR GU35 155 J2
Kayleigh Cl TOTT SO40 246 B5
Keable Rd RFNM GU10 115 P3
Kealy Rd GPORT PO12 315 L2
Kearsney Av NEND PO2 296 G7
Keats Av CHAM PO6 274 A9
LYMN SO41 338 G1
Keats Cl CHIN RG24 69 M3
FHAM PO15 271 H1
FUFL SO22 183 L2
HORN PO8 255 P7
RWIN SO21 144 E4
Keats Rd ITCH SO19 249 L5
Keats Wy YTLY GU46 56 C1
Keble Cl CHFD SO53 206 E9
Keble Rd CHFD SO53 206 E9
Keble St FUFL SO22 164 D9
Keble Wy SHST GU47 41 M4
Keeble Cl NBNE BH10 322 D1
Keeble Crs NBNE BH10 322 D1
Keeble Rd NBNE BH10 322 D1
Keel Cl HSEA PO3 297 L6
LSOL/BMARY PO13 315 H1
Keepers Cl CHFD SO53 206 D7
Keeper's Hl RAND SP11 100 G5
Keepers La ROMY SO51 179 J4
WIMB BH21 279 N9
Keepers Md KSCL RG20 48 B2
The Keep FHAM/PORC PO16 295 P2
Kefford Cl HORN PO8 * 256 B5
Keighley Av BDST BH18 320 B2
Keighley Cl STHA RG19 25 M5
Keith Cl GPORT PO12 315 M2
Keith Lucas Rd FARN GU14 75 N2
Keith Rd TWDS BH3 322 C9
Kelburn Cl CHFD SO53 206 D6
Kellaway Rd CFDH BH17 321 H4
Kellett Rd WSHM SO15 247 P3
Kelly Cl CFDH BH17 321 H4
Kellynch Cl ALTN GU34 132 E5
Kelly Rd WVILLE PO7 275 N5
Kellys Wk AND SP10 102 C3
Kelmscott Gdns CHFD SO53 206 C4
Kelsall Gdns NMIL/BTOS BH25 327 J4
Kelsey Cl FHAM/STUB PO14 271 H9
LISS GU33 192 E1
Kelsey Gv YTLY GU46 40 F9
Kelston Cl WSHM SO15 247 L4
Kelvin Cl FAWY SO45 268 C7
Kelvin Gv FHAM/PORC PO16 295 P1
HLER SO31 269 L4
Kelvin Hl BH/HW/K RG22 90 A1
Kelvin Rd ELGH SO50 229 H2
NWBY RG14 24 E3
Kembers La OVTN RG25 70 F8
Kemmel Rd RAND SP11 79 L4
Kemmitt Wy AND SP10 102 C4
Kemnal Pk HASM GU27 157 J5
Kemp Rd MOOR/WNTN BH9 322 F7
Kempshott Gdns
BH/HW/K RG22 89 L3
Kempshott Gv BH/HW/K RG22 68 D8
Kempshott La BH/HW/K RG22 89 L4
Kempton Cl ALTN GU34 132 F7
NWBY RG14 17 K6
Kempton Ct FARN GU14 75 N2
Kempton Pk WVILLE PO7 276 B1
Kemshott Ct HAV PO9 276 D4
Kemys Gdns AND SP10 4 A4
Ken Berry Ct HAV PO9 277 H4
Kenchester Cl CHAM PO6 296 E1
The Kench HISD PO11 * 318 A4
Kendal Av HSEA PO3 297 J8
ROWN SO16 247 H2
Kendal Cl CHFD SO53 206 G6
FARN GU14 * 57 M9
HORN PO8 256 A7
NTHA RG18 25 M3
Kendal Gdns BH/HW/K RG22 89 M2
Kendal Gv CBLY GU15 59 J1
Kendrick Rd NWBY RG14 30 C1
Kenilworth Cl
LSOL/BMARY PO13 314 D1
NMIL/BTOS BH25 327 K4
Kenilworth Crs FLEETN GU51 74 F2
Kenilworth Dr ELGH SO50 207 J7
Kenilworth Gdns HEND SO30 249 N2
Kenilworth Rd DEAN RG23 68 E6
FARN GU14 57 K8
FLEETN GU51 74 E3
SSEA PO5 * 316 F7
WSHM SO15 20 C1
Kenley Rd BOR GU35 155 J3
Kenmore Cl FLEETS GU52 74 E7
FRIM GU16 58 C5
TOTT SO40 246 B6
Kennard Ct NMIL/BTOS BH25 327 H4
Kennard Rd NMIL/BTOS BH25 327 H3
Kennart Rd CFDH BH17 320 C5
Kennedy Av FHAM PO15 10 A1
Kennedy Cl NWBY RG14 24 A9
WVILLE PO7 275 N6
Kennedy Crs GPORT PO12 315 J6
Kennedy Rd ROWN SO16 227 K9
Kennel La RFNM GU10 116 C8
Kennel Rd FUFL SO22 164 C3
Kennels La FARN GU14 75 J1
Kennet Cl ASHV GU12 97 N2
BSTK RG21 7 J6
FARN GU14 57 L7
GPORT PO12 315 M7
STHA RG19 25 P4
WEND SO18 229 K9
Kennet Ct AND SP10 * 82 G9
Kennet Pl THLE RG7 27 K4
Kennet Rd EPSF GU31 215 L3
NWBY RG14 16 D3
TDWTH SP9 79 J5
Kennet Side NWBY RG14 17 J2
Kennett Pl NWBY RG14 * 24 E3
Kennett Rd ROMY SO51 204 G5
Kennet Wy DEAN RG23 88 F2
Kennington La TOTT SO40 245 H4
Kennington Rd CFDH BH17 320 F4
Ken Rd SBNE BH6 336 C2
Kensington Cl ELGH SO50 207 M8
Kensington Dr WCLF BH2 8 A1
Kensington Flds FAWY SO45 267 P8
Kensington Gdns FHAM PO15 271 K2
FHAM/STUB PO14 271 J8
Kensington Pk LYMN SO41 338 F2
Kensington Rd GPORT PO12 12 E4
NEND PO2 297 H7
Kenson Gdns ITCH SO19 249 J7
Kent Gv FHAM/PORC PO16 295 N3
Kentidge Rd WVILLE PO7 275 M5
Kentigern Dr CWTH RG45 41 M1
Kentish Rd WSHM SO15 247 N4
Kent La RGWD BH24 260 C1
Kenton Cl FRIM GU16 58 E3
Kent Rd BKME/WDN BH12 321 N6
BOR GU35 154 A6
CHFD SO53 228 E1
FLEETN GU51 74 E3
LSOL/BMARY PO13 294 F5
SD/PW SO17 248 E2
SSEA PO5 19 G7
Kent St PSEA PO1 18 D3
SHAM SO14 21 J2
Kenwith Av FLEETN GU51 74 F3
Kenwood Rd
FHAM/PORC PO16 295 P4
Kenwyn Cl WEND SO18 249 K1
Kenya Rd FHAM/PORC PO16 295 M2
Kenyon Cl PLE BH15 320 G5
Kenyon Rd NEND PO2 297 H7
PLE BH15 320 G5
Keogh Barracks ASHV GU12 76 F4
Keogh Cl ASHV GU12 76 G3
Keppel Cl RGWD BH24 282 F2
Kerchers Fld OVTN RG25 86 G4
Kerfield Wy HTWY RG27 72 A3
Kerley Rd WCLF BH2 * 8 C6
Kern Cl ROWN SO16 227 K9
Kerrfield FUFL SO22 164 E8
Kerrfield Ms FUFL SO22 164 E8
Kerry Cl CHFD SO53 206 E7
FLEETN GU51 56 E8
LYMN SO41 329 J4
Kersey Crs NWBY RG14 24 B2
Kersley Crs ODIM RG29 93 J3
Kersley Gdns ITCH SO19 249 J7
Kersten Cl NWBY RG14 17 K7
Kesteven Wy WEND SO18 249 K3
Kestrel Cl ASHV GU12 76 F5
BPWT SO32 231 N4
BPWT SO32 250 F2
FERN BH22 302 B1
FHAM/STUB PO14 293 P5
FUFL SO22 183 M2
HORN PO8 236 C8
RFNM GU10 95 M4
ROWN SO16 227 M7
STHA RG19 25 L4
TOTT SO40 267 J1
Kestrel Ct CHIN RG24 * 51 J9
RGWD BH24 282 E1
Kestrel Dr CHCH/BSGR BH23 325 L9
Kestrel Pl CHAM PO6 297 P2
Kestrel Rd BH/HW/K RG22 89 K2
ELGH SO50 228 G2
FARN GU14 76 A2
HSEA PO3 297 J5
Kestrels Md TADY RG26 34 C4
The Kestrels HLER SO31 269 P2
Kestrel Wy FBDG SP6 239 P6
THLE RG7 27 K4
Keswick Av HSEA PO3 297 J9
Keswick Cl CBLY GU15 59 H1
Keswick Rd BOSC BH5 335 M2
ITCH SO19 248 F8
NMIL/BTOS BH25 327 K2
Keswick Wy VWD BH31 258 E5

Ketchers Fld ALTN GU34............172 E1
Ketelbey Ri BH/HW/K RG22.......90 B4
Kettering Ter NEND PO2............296 E9
Kevin Cl KSCL RG20.................48 E3
Kevins Dr YTLY GU46................40 F7
Kevin Gv FLEETN GU51...............74 E3
Kevlyn Crs HLER SO31..............269 P1
Kewlake La LYND SO43.............244 B2
Kew La HLER SO31..................270 A3
Kew Wk AND SP10...................102 C3
Keydell Av HORN PO8...............256 A6
Keydell Cl HORN PO8...............256 A6
Keyes Cl BKME/WDN BH12...........321 P3
 CHCH/BSGR BH23...................325 K9
 LSOL/BMARY PO13..................294 G5
Keyes Rd LSOL/BMARY PO13.........294 G5
Keyhaven Cl
 LSOL/BMARY PO13..................294 E7
Keyhaven Dr HAV PO9..............276 C5
Keynes Cl FLEETS GU52..............74 E8
Keynsham Rd ITCH SO19............249 K5
Keysham Wy SHST GU47..............41 L4
Keysworth Av
 NMIL/BTOS BH25...................327 H8
The Key FLEETS GU52................74 A1
Khandala Gdns WVILLE PO7........275 P6
Khartoum Rd SD/PW SO17..........248 C1
Khyber Rd BKME/WDN BH12.........321 M7
Kidlington Rd CHIN RG24............69 K3
Kidmore La WVILLE PO7............255 H5
Kielder Cl CHFD SO53.............206 C6
Kiel Dr AND SP11...................82 D7
Kildare Rd BOR GU35..............154 A4
Kilderkin Dr HORN PO8............256 D4
Kilford Ct HEND SO30.............250 G5
Kilham La FUFL SO22..............164 C9
Killinghurst La HASM GU27.......157 P7
Kilmarnock Rd
 MOOR/WNTN BH9....................322 F6
Kilmartin Gdns FRIM GU16..........58 E4
Kilmeston Cl HAV PO9.............276 F4
Kilmeston Rd SU24................187 H2
Kilmington Wy
 CHCH/BSGR BH23...................326 B7
Kilmiston Cl PSEA PO1............316 C1
Kilmore Dr CBLY GU15..............58 G1
Kilmuir Cl SHST GU47..............41 L7
Kiln Acre FHAM/PORC PO16 *.......11 H2
Kiln Av HASM GU27...............157 H5
Kiln Cl FAWY SO45................268 A7
Kiln Fld LISS GU33...............102 F1
Kiln Gdns HTWY RG27...............55 H7
Kiln Hl BPWT SO32...............253 M3
Kiln La EPSF GU31................215 K8
 NARL SO24........................148 A7
 RFNM GU10........................116 C4
 ROMY SO51........................180 F8
 RSAL SP5.........................206 A5
 RWIN SO21........................207 K3
 TADY RG26.........................50 DB
 THLE RG7..........................36 B1
 WVILLE PO7.......................253 P7
Kiln Rd CHIN RG24.................69 H1
 FHAM/PORC PO16...................297 J8
 HSEA PO3.........................297 J8
 NWBY RG14.........................24 F2
Kilnside WVILLE PO7..............255 H8
The Kilns ALTN GU34 *...........133 H6
 BOR GU35.........................135 J4
 FNM GU9 *.........................96 D2
Kiln Wy ALDT GU11.................97 H4
 GSHT GU26........................155 M3
 VWD BH31.........................259 J6
Kilnyard Cl TOTT SO40............246 B2
Kilpatrick Cl NEND PO2...........296 F9
Kilwich Wy FHAM/PORC PO16.......295 M5
Kilworth Ct AND SP11..............82 D7
Kimbell Rd BH/HW/K RG22...........90 B1
Kimber Cl CHIN RG24...............70 A2
Kimberley Rd AND SP10.............82 E8
 CHCH/BSGR BH23...................324 D7
 ELGH SO50........................230 D2
 HEND SO30........................250 B6
Kimberley Rd BH/HW/K RG22........69 H9
 ENEY PO4.........................317 J6
 LISS GU33........................102 G1
 PSTN BH14........................321 K9
 SBNE BH6.........................324 A9
Kimber Rd BWD BH11 *.............321 P1
Kimbers PSF GU32.................215 L1
Kimbers Cl NWBY RG14..............16 D2
Kimbers La HAM SO24..............
 TADY RG26.........................34 E9
Kimbolton Rd HSEA PO3...........317 J2
Kimbridge Crs HAV PO9...........276 G4
Kimbridge La ROMY SO51..........179 M7
Kimmeridge Av
 BKME/WDN BH12....................321 L4
Kimpton Cl
 LSOL/BMARY PO13..................314 D2
Kimpton Ct HAV PO9..............277 H4
Kimpton Dr FLEETN GU51............73 P1
Kineton Rd WSHM SO15............248 A2
King Alfred Pl WINC SO23..........22 E2
King Alfred Ter WINC SO23.........22 E2
King Arthur's Ct CHAM PO6 *.....297 N1
King Arthur's Wy AND SP10.........82 E8
King Charles St PSEA PO1..........18 C5
King Cl BKME/WDN BH12...........281 M5
King Cup Av HLER SO31...........270 F8
Kingcup Cl BDST BH18............320 A2
Kingdom Cl FHAM PO15............271 K5
King Edward Av
 MOOR/WNTN BH9....................322 F5
 ROWN SO16........................247 J1
King Edwards Crs NEND PO2.......296 F7
Kingfisher Cl BH/HW/K RG22........89 K2
 BOR GU35.........................154 B6
 FARN GU14.........................57 K7
 FERN BH22........................280 F7
 FLEETS GU52.......................74 D7

 HAV PO9..........................277 H1
 HISD PO11........................319 J6
 HLER SO31........................270 A6
 PORN PO8.........................255 N7
 SBNE BH6.........................324 C9
 WHCH RG28 *.......................85 L6
Kingfisher Copse HLER SO31......271 H7
Kingfisher Ct HSEA PO3..........297 J5
 NWBY RG14.........................24 G4
Kingfisher Dr EMRTH PO10........277 P6
 YTLY GU46.........................40 C8
Kingfisher Pk WIMB BH21 *.......280 E3
Kingfisher Rd ELGH SO50.........228 F2
 FNM GU9...........................98 C5
Kingfishers FHAM/PORC PO16......295 K1
 TDWTH SP9.........................98 G3
The Kingfishers WIMB BH31.......258 G5
Kingfisher Wk ASHV GU12..........76 E9
Kingfisher Wy
 CHCH/BSGR BH23...................337 L1
 RGWD BH24........................260 F9
 ROMY SO51........................204 D5
 TOTT SO40........................246 B2
Kingfisher Wy
 MOOR/WNTN BH9....................322 F5
 PSF GU32.........................215 M1
King George I Ct HAV PO9........322 F5
King George Ms PSF GU32.........215 M1
King George Rd AND SP10.........102 B2
 FHAM/PORC PO16...................295 N2
King George's Av WSHM SO15......247 K5
King Henry I St PSEA PO1.........19 F3
King Henry Rd FLEETN GU51........74 C1
King John Av BWD BH11...........301 M7
 FHAM/PORC PO16...................295 M2
King John Rd KSCL RG20...........48 C3
King Johns St ODIM RG29..........72 B8
King John St FLEETN GU51.........74 C1
Kings Acre STOK SO20............161 M4
Kings Apartments CBLY GU15.......58 B1
Kings Arms La RGWD BH24.........282 D2
Kings Arms Rw RGWD BH24.........282 D2
King's Av CHCH/BSGR BH23........324 D9
 FUFL SO22........................183 N1
 RAND SP11.........................84 F4
King's Rd PSF GU32..............215 K1
 RAND SP11........................
King's td Gdns 19 F6
King's Rd HASM GU27.............156 F7
King's Rd HISD PO11.............318 G5
 HORN PO8.........................255 P8
 LSOL/BMARY PO13..................314 C1
Kings Rd LYMN SO41..............329 K3
 NMIL/BTOS BH25...................327 L3
 NWBY RG14.........................17 F5
King's Rd PSEA PO1...............18 B1
King's Rd RAND SP11..............82 F4
King's Rd SSEA PO5...............19 F6
King's Rd TWDS BH3...............35 H5
King's Rd WNBY RG14.............322 J8
Kingsroad Rbt PSEA PO1...........18 E6
Kings Rd West NWBY RG14..........17 F5
Kings Saltern Rd LYMN SO41......329 N5
Kings Somborne Rd
 ROMY SO51........................181 H5
King's Ter EMRTH PO10...........299 M1
 PSEA PO1..........................19 F6
Kingston HLER SO31..............269 L3
Kingston Cl AND SP10............102 C4
Kingston Crs NEND PO2...........296 F9
Kingston Gdns FHAM PO15.........272 D6
Kingston La THLE RG7.............26 E1
Kingston Pk LYMN SO41...........329 J5
 ROMY SO51........................224 E4
King St EMRTH PO10..............299 N1
 GPORT PO12........................13 H1
 ODIM RG29.........................72 D9
 SHAM SO14..........................9 G5
 SSEA PO5..........................19 G5
 THLE RG7..........................27 J9
 WIMB BH21........................300 D1
King's Wk WCHY RG28..............85 L6
Kingsway CHFD SO53..............206 F7
 FERN BH22........................280 B9
 HISD PO11........................298 C6
 ALDT GU11..........................2 A4
 AND SP10..........................83 J9
 BLKW GU17.........................41 L9
King's Wy BPWT SO32.............231 L1
Kingsway Ct
 CHCH/BSGR BH23...................324 D6
Kingsway Gdns AND SP10...........82 E8
 CHFD SO53........................206 G5
The Kingsway
 FHAM/PORC PO16...................295 N1
Kingswell Cl NBNE BH10..........322 B5
Kingswell Gdns NBNE BH10........322 B5
Kingswell Rd NBNE BH10..........322 B5
Kingswell St PSEA PO1 *..........19 G2
Kingswood TOTT SO40.............277 K1
Kingswood Cl FHAM PO15..........271 K2
Kingswood Firs GSHT GU26........156 B5
Kingswood Ri ALTN GU34..........150 A6
Kingswood Rd FLEETN GU51.........75 P9
 HAV PO9..........................275 H9
King's Yd AND SP10...............18 D1
King William St PSEA PO1.........18 D1
Kinloss Crs CHAM PO6............297 K2
Kinross Rd CHAM PO6.............297 K2
 TOTT SO40........................246 D4
Kinsbourne Av NBNE BH10.........322 D3
Kinsbourne Cl ITCH SO19.........249 P5
Kinsbourne Ri ITCH SO19.........249 N5
Kinsbourne Wy ITCH SO19.........249 N5
Kinson Av PLE BH15..............321 J5
Kinson Gv NBNE BH10.............322 C1
Kinson Pk Rd NBNE BH10..........322 A6
Kinson Rd NBNE BH10.............322 A6
Kintyre Cl DEAN RG23.............88 E1
Kintyre Rd CHAM PO6.............275 H9
Kinver Cl ROMY SO51.............204 F4

Kipling Cl FHAM PO15............271 H1
 NTHA RG18.........................25 M2
 YTLY GU46.........................56 D1
Kipling Rd ALTN GU34............132 D8
 ELGH SO50........................229 H1
 NEND PO2.........................296 G6
 NEND PO2.........................321 K7
Kipling Wk BH/HW/K RG22..........69 H9
Kirby Cl PLE BH15...............321 H6
Kirby Rd NEND PO2...............296 G7
Kirby Wy SBNE BH6...............336 B2
Kirkby Ct FRIM GU16..............58 D4
Kirkee Rd TDWTH SP9..............98 F4
Kirkham Av CHCH/BSGR BH23.......324 G4
Kirkham Cl SHST GU47.............41 L4
Kirk Knoll BOR GU35.............154 G3
Kirkstall Rd ENEY PO4...........316 F7
Kirkstone Cl GPORT PO12...........3 J8
Kirkway BDST BH18...............300 D9
Kirkwood Crs THLE RG7............27 H4
Kirpal Rd HSEA PO3..............317 K2
Kirtlemead Gdns ASHV GU12.........7 J3
Kirtley Cl HAV PO9..............150 B6
Kirtley Cl CHAM PO6.............297 L5
Kirton Rd CHAM PO6.............297 L2
Kitcher Crs CFDH BH17...........320 D2
Kitchener Rd ALDT GU11...........76 C6
 LISS GU33........................173 P5
Kitcombe La ALTN GU34...........151 J3
Kitnocks Hl BPWT SO32 *.........251 L3
Kitscroft Rd NBNE BH10..........322 C2
Kittiwake Cl
 LSOL/BMARY PO13..................294 F7
 SBNE BH6.........................324 B9
Kitts La PSF GU32...............188 E4
Kitts La RFNM GU10..............338 C1
Kitwalls La LYMN SO41...........338 C1
Kitwood Gn HAV PO9 *............277 H5
Kitwood La NARL SO24............150 D9
Kitwood Rd NARL SO24............150 C9
Kivernell Rd LYMN SO41..........338 F2
Kiwi Cl PLE BH15................320 G9
Knapp Cl CHCH/BSGR BH23.........324 E7
Knapp La ROMY SO51..............205 P1
Knapp Mill Av
 CHCH/BSGR BH23...................324 E7
Knapps Hard PSF GU32............188 D9
Knatchbull Cl ROMY SO51.........204 D6
Knellers La TOTT SO40...........246 B7
Knight Cl FLEETS GU52............75 P6
 ROWN SO16........................165 H5
Knightcrest Pk LYMN SO41 *.......58 B8
Knight Gdns CHAM PO6............297 M2
Knighton Heath Cl BWD BH11......301 N3
Knighton Heath Rd
 BWD BH11.........................301 N9
Knighton La BWD BH11............301 M9
Knighton Rd ITCH SO19...........249 H6
Knights Bank Rd
 FHAM/STUB PO14...................293 M8
Knightsbridge Dr STHA RG19.......31 N3
Knightsbridge Rd RAND SP11.......82 G4
Knights Cl HLER SO31............270 E9
Knights Enham Dr
 FLEETN GU51.......................73 P1
Knights Lea KSCL RG20............29 K3
Knights Park Rd BSTK RG21.........6 A2
Knights Rd BWD BH11.............301 M8
 FNM GU9...........................96 E4
Knightstone Gra FAWY SO45.......268 C8
Knightstone Cl FERN BH22........280 D7
Knight St BSTK RG21...............6 B7
Knightwood Cl ALTN GU34.........132 D6
 CBLY GU15.........................59 H1
Knightwood Vw
 CHFD SO53........................206 E7
Knightwood Av HAV PO9...........276 G5
 LYND SO43........................264 F5
Knightwood Cl
 CHCH/BSGR BH23...................326 A7
 LYND SO43........................264 F5
 TOTT SO40........................245 P9
Knightwood Crs CHFD SO53........206 C7
Knightwood Gra FERN BH22........280 D7
Knightwood Rd ALTN GU34.........132 D6
Knobcrook Rd WIMB BH21..........278 D8
Knockhundred La GSHT GU26.......156 A5
Knockwood La STOK SO20..........139 M1
Knole Gdns BMTH BH1.............335 K2
Knole Rd BMTH BH1...............335 K1
Knoll Cl FLEETN GU51.............74 D1
Knoll Ct FLEETN GU51.............74 D1
Knoll Gdns KSCL RG20.............29 P2
 RGWD BH24........................281 M5
Knoll Rd FLEETN GU51.............74 D1
Knollys Rd ALDT GU11.............75 N9
The Knook SHST GU47 *............41 L7
Knottgrass Rd HLER SO31.........270 E8
Knowland Dr LYMN SO41...........338 G1
Knowle Av WHAM PO17............272 B3
Knowle Gv WHAM PO17............272 C3
Knowle Hl ELGH SO50.............207 K6
Knowle Rd BROC SO42.............286 E7
 CHIN RG24.........................68 F4
 FARN GU14.........................75 P5
Knowles Av CWTH RG45............40 C1
Knowles Cl CHCH/BSGR BH23.......325 J8
 ROWN SO16........................227 H7
Knowles Meadow LISS GU33........192 F5
The Knowle BOR GU35.............135 J2
The Knowlings WHCH RG28.........85 M7
Knowlton Gdns
 CHCH/BSGR BH23...................326 B6
 CHFD SO53........................206 D5
 TOTT SO40........................246 A8

L

Labrador Dr PLE BH15............332 F2
Laburnum Av CHAM PO6............297 L2
Laburnum Cl ALDT GU11.............2 D3
 NBAD SO52........................183 LB
 VWD BH31.........................259 J5
Laburnum Crs FAWY SO45..........290 C2
Laburnum Dr LYMN SO41...........328 D7
 HISD PO11........................145 J8
 NEND PO2.........................296 G8
 NWBY RG14.........................24 D3
Laburnum Gv ELGH SO50...........229 J1
 HISD PO11........................319 H4
 NEND PO2.........................296 G8
 NWBY RG14.........................24 D3
Laburnum Pas ALDT GU11............2 D3
Laburnum Rd FHAM/PORC PO16......294 F5
 FNM GU9...........................96 E4
 HEND SO30........................250 D5
 ROWN SO16........................228 D8
Laburnums HTWY RG27 *............52 E4
The Laburnums BLKW GU17..........41 J9
Laburnum Wy DEAN RG23............68 G6
Lacey Crs PLE BH15..............321 J6
Lackford Av TOTT SO40...........246 C5
Lacon Cl WEND SO18..............248 G3
Lacy Cl WIMB BH21...............278 F8
Lacy Dr WIMB BH21...............278 E8
Ladram Rd GPORT PO12............315 J4
Ladwell Cl NWBY RG14.............30 C1
Lady Betty's Dr FHAM PO15.......271 L4
Ladybridge Rd WVILLE PO7........275 L4
Ladycross Rd FAWY SO45..........268 C8
Lady Diana Ct RAND SP11..........79 P1
Ladygate Dr GSHT GU26...........155 P5
Lady Godley Cl TDWTH SP9.........98 F4
Lady Jane Wk RAND SP11...........79 P1
Ladysmith Cl
 CHCH/BSGR BH23...................325 J8
Ladysmith Pl BOR GU35...........153 P3
Ladywell La NARL SO24...........148 G3
Ladywood ELGH SO50..............207 H7
Ladywood Av FARN GU14............57 K9
Laffan's Rd ALDT GU11............75 K6
Laffans Rd ODIM RG29.............93 K3
Laffan Tr ALDT GU11..............75 K6
Lagado Cl PSTN BH14.............333 L3
Lagland St PLE BH15.............332 E1
Lagoon Rd PSTN BH14.............333 K3
Lahore Cl TDWTH SP9..............78 G4
Lahore Rd TDWTH SP9..............78 G6
Laidlaw Cl BKME/WDN BH12........322 B7
Laidlaw Gdns CHFD SO53..........206 D4
Lainston Cl FUFL SO22...........164 D5
Lake Cl TADY RG26................34 E6
Lake Crs PLE BH15...............154 E5
Lake Dr BOR GU35................183 J3
Lake End Wy CWTH RG45............41 H2
Lake Farm Cl HEND SO30..........250 C3
Lakeland Dr FRIM GU16............58 D4
Lakeland Gdns TOTT SO40.........247 J1
Lakelands Dr WSHM SO15..........247 N5
Lake La RFNM GU10...............135 N3
Lake Rd BH/HW/K RG22 *...........90 B1
 BWD BH11.........................322 B1
 CHFD SO53........................206 G5
 FRIM GU16.........................58 F7
 ITCH SO19........................248 F9
 PLE BH15.........................332 A1
 PSEA PO1..........................19 F2
 VWD BH31.........................258 E5
Laker Sq AND SP10...............82 G9
Lakeside AND SP10...............82 G8
 BLKW GU17.........................41 L1
Lakeside Av HSEA PO3............317 K2
 ROWN SO16.........................76 B9
Lakeside Cl FLEETS GU51..........75 L9
Lakeside Dr HTWY RG27............54 C1
Lakeside Gdns FARN GU14..........57 L6
 HAV PO9..........................275 N3
Lakeside Rd ASHV GU12............76 E9
The Lake Side BLKW GU17 *........57 L1
Lakesmere Rd HORN PO8...........256 C5
The Lakes BPWT SO32.............232 E8
Lake Vw HTWY RG27 *..............55 J6
Lakeview Dr RGWD BH24...........282 G3
Lakewood Rd ASHV GU12............76 E9
 CHCH/BSGR BH23...................326 B6
 CHFD SO53........................206 F5
 TOTT SO40........................246 A8
Lamb Cl AND SP10.................5 G5

NTHA RG18................................25 M2
Lambdens Wk TADY RG26..........34 C6
Lambdown Ap RAND SP11..........79 L5
Lambdown Ter RAND SP11.........79 K4
Lamberhurst Cl ITCH SO19.......269 J2
Lambert Cl WVILLE PO7............275 N5
Lambert Crs BLKW GU17............57 K1
Lamborne Cl SHST GU47.............41 H5
Lambourn Cl
  FHAM/STUB PO14...................294 B1
Lambourne Cl FAWY SO45........268 B9
  RAND SP11.............................100 L2
  RWIN SO21.............................165 M4
Lambourne Dr HLER SO31.........270 C7
Lambourne Rd WEND SO18.......249 K1
Lambourne Wy RAND SP11.......100 E2
  RFNM GU10.............................97 L4
Lamburn Sq CHFD SO53...........206 C7
Lambourn Valley Wy.....................16 B2
Lambs Cl CFDH BH17...............320 E3
Lambsgreen La WIMB BH21......300 B3
Lambs Rw CHIN RG24..................70 A5
Lamden Wy THLE RG7.................27 K4
Lamerton Rd BOR GU35............155 P4
Lammas Rd FAWY SO45...........268 C8
Lamp Acres WHBY RG14.............62 F4
Lampard La RFNM GU10...........136 D7
Lampards Cl HTWY RG27..........153 N7
Lampeter Av POR PO6...............297 K1
The Lamports ALTN GU34.........132 C5
Lampton Gdns
  MOOR/WNTN BH9...................322 F6
Lamtarra Wy NWBY RG14...........17 K7
Lanark Cl FRIM GU16..................58 D3
Lancaster Av FNM GU9...............29 N4
Lancaster Cl AND SP10.................4 A1
  ASHV GU12.............................74 E7
  BDST BH18............................300 B8
  CHCH/BSGR BH23..................325 N8
  FHAM/PORC PO16..................273 M9
  HLER SO31.............................270 A1
  LSOL/BMARY PO13.................314 F4
  NTHA RG18..............................25 L5
Lancaster Dr HEND SO30..........249 L1
Lancaster Dr BDST BH18...........300 A8
  VWD BH31.............................258 E4
Lancaster Rd BSTK RG21..............6 C5
  FARN GU14..............................76 D6
  ROWN SO16...........................227 K9
  WIMB BH21............................280 A9
Lancaster Wy FARN GU14............58 B6
  WVILLE PO7...........................275 P4
Lancer Cl CHCH/BSGR BH23.....324 D8
Lancer Ct ALDT GU11..................96 E1
Lancers Dr STHA RG19................25 P5
Landale Cl RAND SP11................82 F4
Lander Cl PLE BH15..................332 F2
Landford Gdns CHAR BH8..........323 K5
Landford Wy CHAR BH8............323 K5
Landguard Rd ENEY PO4............317 J5
  WSHM SO15...........................247 P5
Landon Cl GPORT PO12..............12 A7
Landon Rd LSOL/BMARY PO13...295 H9
Landport St PSEA PO1.................19 F5
Landport Ter PSEA PO1...............19 H1
Landport Vw PSEA PO1...............19 H1
Landsdowne St SSEA PO5...........19 F5
Landseer Cl AND SP10..................4 B1
Landseer Rd ITCH SO19............249 L8
  NBNE BH4.............................334 C3
Lands End La BOR GU35............154 B3
Lands End Rd HLER SO31...........270 B3
Lane End TADY RG26...................52 A3
Lane End Dr EMRTH PO10.........299 M1
Lanehays Rd FAWY SO45..........268 B7
Lanesbridge Cl TOTT SO40........245 M6
Lanes End CHIN RG24..................70 B2
  FHAM/STUB PO14...................294 A7
The Lanes NMIL/BTOS BH25......327 J2
The Lane CHAR BH8*.................335 J1
  ENEY PO4..............................317 H6
  FAWY SO45............................291 K6
  GPORT PO12..........................315 L7
  MFD/CHID GU8......................137 P5
  TADY RG26..............................34 C6
Langbar Cl ITCH SO19..............248 G5
Langbrook Cl HAV PO9.............298 F1
Langdale Av CHAM PO6............297 K2
Langdale Cl FARN GU14.............57 M9
  ROWN SO16...........................227 K9
Langdale Ct ASHV GU12 *...........76 E7
Langdon Cl CBLY GU15...............59 H1
Langdon Rd PSTN BH14............321 L8
Langdown Firs FAWY SO45.......268 C7
Langdown Lawn FAWY SO45......268 C8
Langdown Lawn Cl
  FAWY SO45............................268 C8
Langdown Rd FAWY SO45.........268 C7
Langford La RSAL SP5...............199 P5
Langford Rd NEND PO2.............317 H1
Langham Cl NBAD SO52............205 K9
Langham Rd ROWN SO16..........228 M8
Langhorn Rd ROWN SO16.........281 N4
Langley Cha RCWD BH24..........281 N4
Langley Cl FLEETS GU52.............74 C8
Langley Dr ALDT GU11.................2 E6
Langley Gdn FBDG SP6.............220 E9
Langley Lodge Gdns
  FAWY SO45............................312 C1
Langley Wy CHCH/BSGR BH23...326 A6
Langrish Cl HAV PO9................298 F5
Langrish Rd ROWN SO16...........227 M8
Langside Av
  BKME/WDN PO12...................322 A7
Langstaff Wy WEND SO18.........249 J3
Langstone Av HAV PO9.............298 F2
Langstone Br HAV PO9.............298 G4
Langstone High St HAV PO9......298 F3

Langstone Rd HAV PO9.............298 F2
  HSEA PO3..............................317 J2
Langstone Wk
  FHAM/STUB PO14...................294 A1
  LSOL/BMARY PO13.................294 F7
Langton Cl FUFL SO22...............22 A2
  LSOL/BMARY PO13.................314 E2
  NMIL/BTOS BH25...................327 K7
Langton Dr BOR GU35..............155 H1
Langton Farm Gdns
  NEND PO2.............................316 C1
Langton Rd BPWT SO32............231 P4
  LTDN BH7..............................335 M1
Langtons Ct NARL SO24............168 B2
Lanham La FUFL SO22..............163 P8
Lankhills Rd WINC SO23...........164 G5
Lansdown Av
  FHAM/PORC PO16..................295 P3
  WINC SO23.............................183 P1
  WVILLE PO7...........................275 K7
Lansdowne Cl ROWN SO16........204 C5
Lansdowne Gdns BMTH BH1........9 G1
  ROMY SO51............................204 C5
Lansdowne HI SHAM SO14..........20 D6
Lansdowne Rd ALDT GU11...........2 D4
  ALTN GU34............................132 C4
  FRIM GU16.............................58 D3
  WCLF BH2..............................334 G1
  WSHM SO15...........................247 L4
The Lansdowne Rbt BMTH BH1....9 G3
Lansley Rd BSTK RG21................69 L4
Lantana Cl WVILLE PO7............275 P4
Lanyard Dr
  LSOL/BMARY PO13.................315 H2
Lapin La BH/HW/K RG22.............89 M6
Lapthorn Cl
  LSOL/BMARY PO13.................294 F5
Lapwing Cl BH/HW/K RG22..........89 K4
  ENEY PO4..............................317 L3
  GPORT PO12..........................315 M1
  HORN PO8..............................256 A4
Lapwing Dr TOTT SO40..............246 A3
Lapwing Gv
  FHAM/PORC PO16..................295 K1
Lapwing Rd WHCH RG28............85 K5
Lapwing Rd WIMB BH21............279 J7
Lara Cl CHAR BH8.....................323 K4
Larch Av FAWY SO45................290 E4
Larch Cl CFDH BH17.................320 A3
  HEND SO30...........................250 A4
  LIPH GU30.............................175 J4
  LSOL/BMARY PO13.................314 E3
  LYMN SO41............................327 P4
  NWBY RG14............................24 A2
  RGWD/BURGH RG30...............27 K5
  WINC SO23.............................145 J8
Larchdale Cl HLER SO31............292 D1
Larch Dr AND SP10...................102 A3
  KSCL RG20.............................48 C3
Larches Gdns CHAM PO15.........272 A9
Larchfield Rd FLEETS GU52.........74 B8
Larchfield Wy HORN PO8...........256 C6
Larch Rd BOR GU35..................155 J2
  ROWN SO16...........................227 H9
Larch Rw FBDG SP6..................241 H1
Larkbarn Cl AND SP11*...............80 A1
Larkfield CHIN RG24...................70 A1
Larkfield Rd FNM GU9.................95 P8
Larkhill Hi FUFL SO22...............183 M2
Larkhill Rd HSEA PO3...............297 H5
Larkin Cl RAND SP11*.................80 A1
Lark Ri LIPH GU30....................175 H2
Lark Rd CHCH/BSGR BH23........325 L9
Lark Ri CHAR BH8....................302 B2
Larks Barrow HI WHCH SO23......85 L1
Larks Cl FERN BH22..................302 B1
Larkfield Av
  MOOR/WNTN BH9...................323 H4
Larkshill Cl NMIL/BTOS BH25....327 K3
Larkspur Cha ITCH SO19..........249 N6
Larkspur Cl ALDT GU11...............96 C4
  BPWT SO32............................232 E7
  HLER SO31.............................270 E8
  TOTT SO40.............................267 J2
Larkspur Gdns FAWY SO45.......290 D5
  HEND SO30...........................250 C5
Larks Ri FERN BH22.................302 E1
Larkswood Cl SHST GU47...........41 H5
Larkswood Dr CWTH RG45.........41 J1
Larkwhistle Farm Rd
  RWIN SO21............................107 K9
Larmer Cl FLEETN GU51.............74 A5
Larwood Sq AND SP10................82 G8
Lascelles Rd LTDN BH7.............323 P9
Laser Cl HLER SO31..................270 E9
Lasham Gn HAV PO9*................277 H5
Lasham Rd FLEETN GU51...........54 B2
Lashly Mdw FHAM/STUB PO14...294 B2
Lashly Meadow WVILLE PO7......294 F3
Latch Farm Av
  CHCH/BSGR BH23..................324 E7
Latchmoor Dr FAWY SO45.........267 N6
Latchmore Forest Gv
  WVILLE PO7...........................255 P8
Latchmore Gdns HORN PO8......255 N8
Latchwood La RFNM GU10........116 D5
Latelie Cl HLER SO31................269 K5
Latham Av FRIM GU16.................58 D3
Latham Cl ELGH SO50...............206 D3
Latham Ct WSHM SO15.............230 B2
Latham Rd BOR GU35*..............230 B2
  ROMY SO51............................204 C5
Latimer Ct HSEA PO3*..............297 K6
Latimer Rd MOOR/WNTN BH9...322 F7
Latimers Cl CHCH/BSGR BH23...326 B6
Latimer St ROMY SO51.............204 C6

SHAM SO14..............................21 F7
Laud Cl NWBY RG14....................44 C4
Lauder Cl FRIM GU16.................58 D3
Lauderdale FARN GU14...............75 L2
Launcelot Cl AND SP10................82 E8
Launcelyn Cl NBAD SO52..........227 K1
Launceston Cl GPORT PO12.......315 N1
Launceston Dr ELGH SO50.........207 H8
Laundry La HTWY RG27...............88 A9
  LYMN SO41............................339 H2
  SHST GU47.............................41 M9
Laundry Rd ROWN SO16...........247 M1
Laura Cl RWIN SO21.................183 L9
Laurel Av STHA RG19.................32 C1
Laurel Cl CBLY GU15...................58 C1
  CHCH/BSGR BH23..................325 P6
  DEAN RG23............................88 F2
  FAWY SO45.............................75 K1
  FAWY SO45............................268 A7
  GPORT PO12..........................12 C3
Laurel Ct AND SP10...................102 C4
Laurel Dr BDST BH18................300 E9
Laurel Gdns ALDT GU11..............96 C4
  BDST BH18............................300 E9
  HLER SO31.............................271 H6
Laurel Gv RFNM GU10..............115 P5
Laurel La RGWD BH24..............281 L6
Laurel Rd HLER SO31................256 C7
  HORN PO8..............................256 C7
The Laurels AND SP10...............102 C1
  BROC SO42 *..........................286 F9
  BSTK RG21..............................7 H3
  FERN BH22............................302 C2
  FLEETN GU51.........................74 D3
  FNM GU9...............................96 F4
  NTHA RG18*..........................25 M2
Laurence Ct RAND SP11..............79 P1
Lauren Wy TOTT SO40..............245 P2
Lauriston Dr CHFD SO53...........206 D4
Laurus Cl WVILLE PO7..............275 P4
Lavant Cl HORN PO8.................276 B1
Lavant Dr HAV PO9.....................15 H2
Lavantfield ALTN GU34.............132 E9
Lavant St PSF GU32..................215 L2
Lavell's La THLE RG7...................26 B6
Lavender Cl ITCH SO19.............249 H6
  VWD BH31.............................259 J5
Lavender Ct AND SP10 *............102 C4
Lavender La RFNM GU10...........271 K1
Lavender Rd BH/HW/K RG22......89 L4
  CHAR BH8..............................323 K3
  LYMN SO41............................327 N4
  WVILLE PO7...........................276 A4
Laverock Lea
  FHAM/PORC PO16..................273 N9
Laverstock Cl FLEETN GU51.......55 P9
Laverstoke La WHCH RG28........106 C2
Lavey's La FHAM PO15..............271 P4
Lavington Gdns NBAD SO52.......227 K1
Lavinia Rd BKME/WDN PO12.....321 L5
  CHCH/BSGR BH23..................324 A7
Lawday Link FNM GU9................96 A4
Lawday Pl FNM GU9....................96 A4
Lawday Place La FNM GU9..........96 A4
Lawford Crs YTLY GU46...............40 E8
Lawford Rd
  MOOR/WNTN BH9 *................322 C4
Lawford Rd
  MOOR/WNTN BH9...................322 C3
Lawford Wy TOTT SO40.............246 C3
Lawn Cl LSOL/BMARY PO13......295 H8
Lawn Dr HLER SO31..................270 C8
Lawn Rd ELGH SO50.................207 K8
  FUFL SO22.............................164 D2
  LYMN SO41............................329 H4
  LYMN SO41............................329 J4
  SD/PW SO17...........................248 D3
Lawns Cl WIMB BH21................279 L8
Lawnside Rd WSHM SO15..........247 L3
Lawns Rd WIMB BH21...............279 K8
The Lawns CHCH/BSGR BH23....326 D7
  FARN GU14.............................75 M1
  ELGH SO50.............................206 E9
  FHAM/PORC PO16..................15 G3
  HAV PO9................................15 G3
  NMIL/BTOS BH25...................327 J3
  SD/PW SO17...........................248 D3
Lawn Vw NMIL/BTOS BH25........326 F2
Lawrence Av HORN PO8.............255 N9
Lawrence Cl AND SP10.................4 D3
  CHIN RG24.............................69 M3
Lawrence Ct BSTK RG21...............6 B7
Lawrence Dr CCLF BH13............333 N2
Lawrence Gv WINC SO23..............24 C6
Lawrence Houses RAND SP11....100 B9
Lawrence La FBDG SP6..............240 F7
Lawrence Ms ROMY SO51.........204 D5
Lawrence Pl NWBY RG14.............24 F2
Lawrence Rd FHAM PO15.............10 C4
  FLEETS GU52.........................74 D6
  RGWD BH24...........................260 G8
  SSEA PO5..............................316 C5
Lawrences La NTHA RG18..........25 N1
Lawrence Wk
  LSOL/BMARY PO13 *...............315 H2
Lawson Wy CBLY GU15..............165 H5
Lawson La HLER SO31...............270 D2
Lawson Rd BKME/WDN PO12....321 K6
  SSEA PO5...............................316 C4
Laws Ter ALDT GU11..................96 D3
Laxton Cl HLER SO31................271 H7
Layard Dr WIMB BH21...............300 F4
Lay Fld HTWY RG27.....................71 N3
Layton Rd BKME/WDN PO12.....321 M7
  LSOL/BMARY PO13.................294 G6
Lea Cl ASHV GU12......................97 N2
  BSTK RG21...............................7 K5

FNM GU9.................................96 G5
Leacock Cl BPWT SO32.............232 F8
Lea Ct FNM GU9........................96 F4
Leaden Vere ODIM RG29............93 K7
Leafy La FHAM PO15..................271 L4
Lealand Gv CHAM PO6..............297 M1
Lealand Rd CHAM PO6..............297 M2
Leamington Crs
  LSOL/BMARY PO13.................314 D2
Leamington Rd
  MOOR/WNTN BH9...................322 C8
Leander Cl ELGH SO50..............207 J8
Leander Dr GPORT PO12...........315 N1
Leander Rd CHAM PO6.............272 E7
Lea-Oak Gdns FHAM PO15........10 A1
Leaphill Rd LTDN BH7...............323 N9
Lea Rd CBLY GU15.......................58 A3
  FAWY SO45............................312 G1
Learoyd Rd CFDH BH17............320 F5
Lear Rd GPORT PO12.................12 D1
Leaside Wy ROWN SO16...........228 E7
Lea Springs FLEETN GU51...........74 A5
The Lea FLEETN GU51.................74 B5
  VWD BH31.............................258 C5
Leatherhead Gdns
  HEND SO30............................250 C4
Lea Wy ASHV GU12....................76 E9
  BWD BH11.............................301 N7
Leaway FNM GU9.......................96 G6
The Leaway
  FHAM/PORC PO16..................295 P1
Leawood Rd FLEETN GU51.........74 B5
Lebanon Rd WSHM SO15..........247 H4
Le Borowe FLEETS GU52.............74 B8
Lechlade Gdns FHAM PO15.......272 A9
  LTDN BH7..............................323 N7
Leckford Cl FHAM/PORC PO16...295 P1
  WEND SO18............................249 M3
Leckford La HAV PO9................277 H4
Lecole Wk HEND SO30..............250 G4
Ledbury Rd CHAM PO6..............274 E9
  CHCH/BSGR BH23..................337 K1
Lederle La LSOL/BMARY PO13...294 G8
Ledgard Ct PSTN BH14.............321 P9
Ledwell Ct GPORT PO12............315 P2
Lee Church La ROMY SO51..........3 H6
Lee Ct ALDT GU11.......................2 A5
Leedam Rd NBNE BH10............322 D3
Lee Dro ROMY SO51..................226 E3
Lee Lands LYMN SO41..............329 K6
Lee La ROMY SO51...................226 D6
Leep La GPORT PO12.................12 D7
Lee Rd ALDT GU11.....................96 E1
  GPORT PO12..........................315 L2
Lees Cl CHCH/BSGR BH23.........324 B3
Leesland Rd GPORT PO12.........315 L3
Lees La GPORT PO12................315 M3
Lees La North GPORT PO12......315 M3
Leeson Dr FERN BH22..............280 B9
Leeson Rd LTDN BH7.................323 M8
Le Freth Dr FLEETN GU51 *.........74 B1
Lefroy Av BSTK RG21...................7 G2
Lefroy's Fld RFNM GU10.............95 H3
Leger Cl FLEETS GU52.................74 B7
Legge Crs ALDT GU11.................96 B3
Legg La WIMB BH21..................300 F1
Legion Cl PLE BH15...................332 A1
  ROWN SO16...........................228 G5
Legion La WINC SO23................145 K9
Legion Rd HISD PO11................318 G4
  PLE BH15...............................332 A1
Lehar Cl BH/HW/K RG22.............89 P3
Leicester Ct
  LSOL/BMARY PO13 *...............315 H3
Leicester Pl AND SP10.................4 C5
Leicester Rd CCLF BH13............321 P9
  WSHM SO15...........................247 P1
Leicester Wy WINC SO23............23 K1
Leigham Vale Rd SBNE BH6......336 B2
Leigh Cl AND SP10.......................5 G6
  WIMB BH21............................300 D1
Leigh Common WIMB BH21......278 C9
Leigh Fld THLE RG7....................27 H9
Leigh Gdns AND SP10..................5 G6
  WIMB BH21............................300 D1
Leigh La FNM GU9....................116 E2
Leigh Pk LYMN SO41.................329 J5
Leigh Rd AND SP10......................5 G6
  ELGH SO50.............................206 E9
  FERN BH22............................302 E1
  FHAM/PORC PO16..................15 G3
  HAV PO9................................15 G3
  NMIL/BTOS BH25...................327 J3
  SD/PW SO17...........................248 E1
Leighton Av AROWN SO16.........247 M3
Leighton Rd ITCH SO19.............248 G8
Leipzig Barracks FLEETS GU52....95 M1
Leipzig Rd FLEETS GU52.............95 M1
Leith Av FHAM/PORC PO16.......273 P9
Leith Dr ALDT GU11.....................2 A5
Le Marchant Rd FRIM GU16.......58 E2
Lemon Gv BOR GU35.................155 P3
Lemon Rd WSHM SO15.............247 M4
Lena Cl RAND SP11.....................79 N1
Lendorber Av CHAM PO6...........297 J2
Lendore Rd FRIM GU16...............58 C5
Lennel Gdns FLEETS GU52..........74 A7
Lennon Wy BH/HW/K RG22........89 N4
Lennox Cl CHFD SO53...............205 M6
  GPORT PO12..........................315 M7
  ROWN SO16...........................228 G5
Lennox Rd BH/HW/K RG22........90 A1
Lennox Rd North SSEA PO5.......316 F6
Lennox Rd South SSEA PO5.......316 F6
Len Smart Ct BSTK RG21..............7 G1
Lensyd Gdns HORN PO8............255 P5
Lenten St ALTN GU34................132 E6
Lenton Cl CFDH BH17...............320 F5
Leofric Ct ENEY PO4.................317 L5
Leominster Rd CHAM PO6.........274 D9
Leonard Rd GPORT PO12............13 F1
Leonardslee Crs NWBY RG14....24 G3

Leopold Av FARN GU14...............58 A8
Leopold Dr BPWT SO32.............231 P5
Leopold St ENEY PO4................316 G6
Le Patourel Cl
  CHCH/BSGR BH23..................325 H8
Lepe Rd FAWY SO45.................313 H2
Leroux Cl WSHM SO15..............247 J1
Lerryn Rd LSOL/BMARY PO13...295 H7
Leslie Rd MOOR/WNTN BH9.....322 E7
  PSTN BH14............................321 N9
Leslie Southern Ct NWBY RG14...24 E3
Lesser Horseshoe Cl
  WHAM PO17..........................272 C2
Lester Av HAV PO9......................14 A4
Lester Rd GPORT PO12.............315 K3
Lestock Wy FLEETN GU51..........74 F3
Letcombe Pl HORN PO8............256 D5
Levell Ct RAND SP11...................79 P1
Leven Av WBNE BH4.................334 B3
Leven Cl CHFD SO53.................206 C5
  WBNE BH4.............................334 D2
Leventhorpe Ct GPORT PO12.....12 E3
Leveret Cl GPORT PO12............295 N9
Leverette Cl ASHV GU12.............76 C9
Leveson Cl GPORT PO12...........315 K5
Levet's La PLE BH15..................332 D2
Leviathan Cl
  FHAM/STUB PO14..................294 B7
Levignen Cl FLEETS GU52..........74 A2
Levendon Rd NWBY RG14..........24 E8
Lewes Cl WIMB BH21................300 E1
Lewes Ct ELGH SO50................207 D3
Lewesdon Dr BDST BH18..........300 B9
Lewin Cl RWIN SO21.................208 A5
Lewins Wk HLER SO31..............269 P7
Lewis Cl BSTK RG21.....................7 H2
  FAWY SO45............................267 N8
Lewisham Wy SHST GU47..........41 L5
Lewis Rd EMRTH PO10..............277 N1
Lewis Silkin Wy ROWN SO16....227 L8
Lewry Cl HEND SO30.................250 A4
Lexby Rd TOTT SO40.................246 E5
Lexden Gdns HISD PO11...........318 E4
Leybourne Av NBNE BH10........322 C2
  WEND SO18............................249 H3
Leybourne Cl NBNE BH10.........322 C2
Leydene Av CHAR BH8..............323 M6
Leydene Cl CHAR BH8...............323 M5
Leydene PI PSF GU32................235 N2
Leyland Cl GPORT PO12.............12 D5
Leyland Rd BKME/WDN BH12...321 N2
Leys Gdns NWBY RG14...............24 C3
Leyside CHCH/BSGR BH23........325 K9
  CWTH RG45............................41 P5
Leyton Rd SHAM SO14...............21 J1
Liam Cl HAV PO9......................276 G6
The Liberties BPWT SO32 *........253 M1
Liberty Cl WIMB BH21..............300 E1
Liberty Rd WHAM PO17............253 L3
The Liberty WVILLE PO7...........254 G8
Library Gdns HAV PO9................14 E2
Library La RWIN SO21...............163 L3
Library Rd BKME/WDN PO12....321 N3
  FARN GU14.............................76 A2
  FERN BH22............................302 D3
  MOOR/WNTN BH9...................322 F6
  TOTT SO40.............................246 E4
Lichen Wy TOTT SO40...............247 K9
Lichfield Ct
  LSOL/BMARY PO13.................315 H3
Lichfield Dr GPORT PO12..........315 N1
Lichfield Rd FHAM/STUB PO14...271 J7
  HSEA PO3..............................317 J2
Liddel Cl EWKG RG40..................39 P5
Liddel Wy CHFD SO53...............206 C3
Liddiards Wy WVILLE PO7.........275 N7
Lidiard Gdns ENEY PO4.............317 K6
Liederbach Dr VWD BH31.........259 J6
Lightfoot Gv BSTK RG21.............20 D1
Lightsfield DEAN RG23................88 F1
Lilac Cl AND SP10.....................102 A3
  BOR GU35.............................154 A6
  HAV PO9................................277 J7
Lilac Rd BWD BH11..................282 F1
Lilac Rd ROWN SO16................228 A5
Lilac Wk STHA RG19....................32 E1
Lilac Wy DEAN RG23....................68 G6
Lilie Barracks ALDT GU11...........76 A7
The Lillies ELGH SO50..............230 D5
Lilliput Rd PSTN BH14..............333 L3
Lillymill Chine CHIN RG24.........70 B2
Lillywhite Crs AND SP10.............82 F7
Lily Av WVILLE PO7..................275 K8
Lily Cl BH/HW/K RG22................89 L4
Limberline Rd HSEA PO3...........297 J3
Limberline Sp HSEA PO3...........297 J4
Limbrey Hl OVTN RG25.............109 N6
Lime Av ALTN GU34..................132 E4
  ITCH SO19.............................248 G3
  ITCH SO19.............................249 J6
  NWBY RG14............................24 C3
  PLE BH15...............................321 H6
  RWIN SO21............................208 A5
  STHA RG19.............................32 D1
Limecroft YTLY GU46..................40 D9
Lime Cl BOR GU35....................155 J2
Lime Gdns BSTK RG21...............81 N7
  WEND SO18............................229 M9
Lime Gv ALTN GU34..................132 E4
  CHAM PO6.............................274 D9
  HISD PO11.............................318 C5
  LYMN SO41............................328 D7
Limekiln La BPWT SO32............232 D1
Lime Kiln La FAWY SO45...........290 D4
Limekiln La PSF GU32...............214 C6
Limekiln Lane Est
  FAWY SO45............................290 D4
Limekiln Rd RAND SP11..............60 A7
Limes Av KSCL RG20...................30 F7
Limes Cl LIPH GU30..................155 K9

LISS GU33 .... 192 D2
The Limes BH/HW/K RG22 .... 89 L3
  LSOL/BMARY PO13 * 295 H8
  TADY RG26 .... 52 C3
  TOTT SO40 .... 267 L1
Lime St ALDT GU11 .... 2 C3
  SHAM SO14 .... 21 F6
Limetree Av KSCL RG20 .... 46 A3
Lime Tree FBDG SP6 .... 239 M6
Limetree Wk WINC SO23 .... 23 K4
Lime Tree Wy CHIN RG24 .... 69 P1
Lime Wk AND SP10 * 102 B4
Limited Rd MOOR/WNTN BH9 .... 322 G6
Linacre Rd ITCH SO19 .... 249 M7
Lin Brook Dr RGWD BH24 .... 260 G8
Lincoln Av BMTH BH1 .... 323 K9
  CHCH/BSGR BH23 .... 324 D5
Lincoln Cl ASHV GU12 .... 96 P1
  BH/HW/K RG22 .... 89 M4
  CBLY GU15 .... 58 G1
  FHAM/STUB PO14 .... 271 J7
Lincoln Ct
  LSOL/BMARY PO13 .... 315 H3
  NEND PO2 * 296 F9
Lincoln Gn ALTN GU34 .... 132 E7
Lincoln Pl CHFD SO53 .... 206 F9
Lincoln Ri HORN PO8 .... 256 A7
Lincoln Rd BKME/WDN BH12 .... 321 M5
  FARN GU14 .... 75 H8
  PSEA PO1 .... 316 C3
Lincolns Ri ELGH SO50 .... 207 K5
Linda Gv HORN PO8 .... 255 P8
Linda Rd FAWY SO45 .... 291 K6
Linda St WCH RG28 .... 85 M5
Lindbergh Cl
  LSOL/BMARY PO13 .... 315 H3
Lindbergh Rd WIMB BH21 .... 280 M9
Lindberg Ri FHAM PO15 .... 271 L5
Lind Cl WVILLE PO7 .... 275 P7
Linden Av CHIN RG24 .... 70 C7
  ODIM RG29 .... 72 D9
Linden Cl BPWT SO32 .... 232 C9
  FERN BH22 .... 302 D7
  NWBY RG14 .... 24 C3
  RAND SP11 .... 80 A1
Linden Ct WEND SO18 .... 229 K9
Linden Dr LISS GU33 .... 192 E2
Linden Gdns HEND SO30 .... 250 C6
Linden Gv CHFD SO53 .... 206 E5
  GPORT PO12 .... 12 C4
  HISD PO11 .... 318 C5
Linden Lea FHAM/PORC PO16 .... 173 K9
Lindenmuth Wy STHA SO19 .... 85 L1
Linden Rd BKME/WDN BH12 .... 321 L6
  BOR GU35 .... 155 J3
  FERN BH22 .... 302 D7
  MOOR/WNTN BH9 .... 322 G4
  ROMY SO51 .... 206 D6
  ROWN SO16 .... 227 L8
Lindens Cl EMRTH PO10 .... 277 M7
The Lindens CHCH/BSGR BH23 .... 325 H4
  FNM GU9 .... 116 D2
Linden Wk NBAD SO52 .... 205 K8
Linden Wy HAV PO9 .... 15 C1
  HORN PO8 .... 256 B6
  LYMN SO41 .... 329 J3
Lindenwood CHIN RG24 .... 51 N9
Lindford Cha BOR GU35 .... 154 C3
Lindford Rd BOR GU35 .... 154 B2
Lindford Wey BOR GU35 .... 154 C2
Lindisfarne Cl CHAM PO6 .... 297 J2
Lindley Av ENEY PO4 .... 317 J6
Lindley Gdns NARL SO24 .... 168 A3
Lind Rd GPORT PO12 .... 315 N7
Lindsay Rd CCLF BH13 .... 334 A2
  ITCH SO19 .... 249 N5
Lindum Dene ALDT GU11 .... 2 D5
Lindway HLER SO31 .... 270 C5
Lineside CHCH/BSGR BH23 .... 324 C7
The Lines KSCL RG20 .... 48 C2
Linford Cl NMIL/BTOS BH25 .... 327 J3
Linford Ct HAV PO9 .... 256 D5
Linford Crs ROWN SO16 .... 227 P9
Linford Rd RGWD BH24 .... 261 H9
Ling Crs BOR GU35 .... 155 J2
Ling Dl ROWN SO16 .... 228 B5
Lingdale Rd SBNE BH6 .... 324 D9
Lingen Cl AND SP10 .... 132 F7
Lingfield Cl CHIN RG24 .... 70 D7
Lingfield Gdns WEND SO18 .... 229 H9
Lingmala Gv FARN GU14 .... 74 E7
Lingwood Av CHCH/BSGR BH23 .... 325 K9
Lingwood Cl ROWN SO16 .... 228 B5
Lingwood Wk ROWN SO16 .... 228 B5
Linhorns La NMIL/BTOS BH25 .... 276 C5
Linkenholt Wy HAV PO9 .... 276 C5
Linklater Pth PSEA PO1 .... 316 F1
Link Ri WIMB BH21 .... 300 A7
Link Rd ALTN GU34 .... 132 C3
  CHAM PO6 .... 274 D8
  FARN GU14 .... 75 J4
  KSCL RG20 .... 48 D5
  NWBY RG14 .... 16 E4
  RGWD BH24 .... 260 C9
  ROWN SO16 .... 227 K9
Links Dr CHCH/BSGR BH23 .... 324 B6
Linkside Av CHAR BH8 .... 323 L7
Links La HAV PO9 .... 257 H9
  HISD PO11 .... 318 C5
Links Rd FUFL SO22 .... 164 E6
  PSTN BH14 .... 333 M1
The Links BOR GU35 .... 153 H7
  LSOL/BMARY PO13 .... 294 C8
Links View HAV PO9 .... 333 N2
Links View Wy ROWN SO16 .... 228 B6
Links Wy FARN GU14 .... 75 L1
The Link AND SP10 .... 102 A2
  WVILLE PO7 .... 276 A1
  YTLY GU46 .... 40 D7
Linkway FHAM/STUB PO14 .... 294 A8
  FLEETS GU52 .... 74 C6
  CBLY GU15 .... 58 B1
  CWTH RG45 .... 40 G1
Link Wy DEAN RG23 .... 88 F2
  NTHA RG18 .... 25 L3
Linmead Dr BWD BH11 .... 322 A1
Linnet Cl BH/HW/K RG22 .... 89 L1
  EPSF GU31 .... 216 A3
  HORN PO8 .... 255 N7
  RGWD BH24 .... 282 C3
Linnet Ct GPORT PO12 .... 315 K2
  NMIL/BTOS BH25 .... 327 H4
Linnet Rd CFDH BH17 .... 320 A4
Linnet Sq ELGH SO50 .... 207 M4
Linnets Rd NARL SO24 .... 167 P5
The Linnets
  TOTT SO40 .... 246 A3
Linnets Wy ALTN GU34 .... 132 F4
Linsade La LYMN SO41 .... 308 A9
Linsford La FARN GU14 .... 76 E1
Linsted La BOR GU35 .... 154 E1
Linthorpe Rd PLE BH15 .... 320 G8
Linton Cl TADY RG26 .... 34 D7
Linwood Cl AND SP10 .... 4 B1
Linwood Ct FAWY SO45 .... 268 C8
Linwood Rd
  MOOR/WNTN BH9 .... 323 H8
The Lion Brewery
  NEND PO2 * 296 F9
Lion Cl OVTN RG25 .... 86 G4
Lionheart Cl BWD BH11 .... 301 M8
Lionheart Wy HLER SO31 .... 269 P1
Lion & Lamb Wy FNM GU9 .... 96 B9
Lion & Lamb Yd FNM GU9 * 96 B9
Lion La HASM GU27 .... 156 E6
Lion Md HASM GU27 .... 156 E7
Lion Rd FARN GU14 .... 76 A2
  PSEA PO1 .... 316 B2
Lions Hall BOR GU35 .... 153 J4
Lions Ga FBDG SP6 * 240 D2
Lions Hill Wy RGWD BH24 .... 281 J4
Lions Lane BOR GU35 .... 281 L4
Lion St PSEA PO1 .... 18 E2
Lions Wd RGWD BH24 .... 281 L5
Lion Ter PSEA PO1 .... 18 E2
Lion Wy FLEETS GU52 .... 74 E7
Liphook Rd BOR GU35 .... 154 C5
Lipizzamer Flds HLER SO31 .... 271 H2
Lippen La BPWT SO32 .... 212 B2
Lipscombe Cl NWBY RG14 .... 16 A3
Lipscombe Ri ALTN GU34 .... 132 F4
Lisbon Rd WSHM SO15 .... 247 P5
Liskeard Dr FARN GU14 .... 57 P7
Lisle Cl FUFL SO22 .... 183 J3
  LYMN SO41 .... 329 K4
  NWBY RG14 .... 24 C2
Lisle Ct FUFL SO22 .... 164 F9
Lisle Court Rd LYMN SO41 .... 329 P3
Lisle La HASM GU27 .... 177 L7
Lismoyne Cl FLEETS GU52 * 74 C2
Liss Rd ENEY PO4 .... 317 H4
Lister Rd BH/HW/K RG22 .... 90 B1
Litchfield Cl AND SP10 * 82 B8
Litchfield Crs WEND SO18 .... 249 H2
Litchfield Rd FUFL SO22 .... 164 E3
  WEND SO18 .... 249 H2
Litchford Rd
  NMIL/BTOS BH25 .... 327 L3
Lith Av HORN PO8 .... 256 C5
Lith La HORN PO8 .... 256 C5
Lile Hyden La HORN PO8 .... 236 B5
The Litter KSCL RG20 .... 48 C3
Little Abshot Rd
  FHAM/STUB PO14 .... 293 H1
Little Aldershot La THLE RG7 .... 33 M4
Little Anglesey Rd
  GPORT PO12 .... 12 A6
Little Arthur St NEND PO2 * 316 G1
Little Ashton La BPWT SO32 .... 233 G1
Little Austins Rd FNM GU9 .... 116 D2
Little Barn Pl LISS GU33 .... 192 F2
Little Basing CHIN RG24 .... 70 A5
Little Binfield CHIN RG24 .... 70 B3
Little Bull La BPWT SO32 .... 252 B1
Little Copse AND SP10 .... 102 C4
  FLEETS GU52 .... 74 C5
  YTLY GU46 .... 40 D7
Little Copse Cha CHIN RG24 .... 69 P2
Little Cnr WVILLE PO7 .... 255 H8
Littlecroft AND SP10 .... 102 C2
Little Croft Rd
  BKME/WDN BH12 .... 321 K6
Little Dean La OVTN RG25 .... 92 E6
Little Dene Copse LYMN SO41 .... 328 D5
Little Dewlands VWD BH31 .... 258 D4
Littledown Av CHAR BH8 .... 323 L8
Littledown Dr LTDN BH7 .... 323 J5
Little Dro FBDG SP6 .... 221 J5
Little Drove Rd STON SO20 .... 123 L6
Little Fallow CHIN RG24 .... 70 A4
Littlefield Cl ASHV GU12 .... 97 N2
Littlefield Crs CHFD SO53 .... 206 A7
Littlefield Gdns ASHV GU12 .... 97 N2
Littlefield Rd ALTN GU34 .... 132 C5
Little Forest Rd WBNE BH4 .... 334 D1
Little Fox Dr HLER SO31 .... 270 A2
Little Gays FHAM/STUB PO14 .... 293 M7
Little George St PSEA PO1 .... 316 C1
Little Gn Cl GPORT PO12 .... 12 A6
Littlegreen Av HAV PO9 .... 15 J1
Little Green La FNM GU9 .... 115 P3
Little Green Orch
  GPORT PO12 * 12 A6
Little Hackets HAV PO9 .... 276 E5
Little Hartleys HTWY RG27 .... 72 E8
Little Hayes La RWIN SO21 .... 146 E9
Little Hoddington Cl
  OVTN RG25 .... 92 C6
Little Knowl Hl KSCL RG20 .... 48 E1
Little Lance's Hl ITCH SO19 .... 249 J4
Little La GPORT PO12 .... 12 A6
Little London Rd THLE RG7 .... 35 H8
Little Lonnen WIMB BH21 .... 279 H6
Little Md WVILLE PO7 .... 255 J8
Littlemead Ct CFDH BH17 .... 320 C5
Littlemeads ROMY SO51 .... 204 B6
Littlemill La FLBDG SP6 .... 219 J7
Little Minster St WINC SO23 .... 22 E5
Little Moor SHST GU47 .... 41 K5
Littlemoor Av BWD BH11 .... 301 M9
Little Oak Rd ROWN SO16 .... 228 B8
Littlepark Av HAV PO9 .... 276 B7
Little Park Farm Rd
  FHAM PO15 .... 271 J5
Little Quob La HEND SO30 .... 249 N1
Little Shore La BPWT SO32 .... 232 A5
Little Southsea St SSEA PO5 .... 19 F6
Little Thurbans Cl FNM GU9 .... 116 A4
Littleton Gv HAV PO9 .... 276 F6
Littleton La RAND SP11 .... 163 N5
Little Vigo YTLY GU46 .... 56 C1
Little Wellington St ALDT GU11 .... 2 E3
Littlewood ROMY SO51 .... 230 C8
Little Woodfalls Dr RSAL SP5 .... 199 P9
Littlewoods Gdns HEND SO30 .... 249 N1
  HLER SO31 .... 270 E7
Little Woodham La
  LSOL/BMARY PO13 .... 314 G3
Littleworth Rd RFNM GU10 .... 117 M1
Litton Gdns DEAN RG23 .... 88 F2
Liverpool Ct
  LSOL/BMARY PO13 .... 315 H3
Liverpool Rd
  FHAM/STUB PO14 .... 294 D3
  PSEA PO1 .... 316 C3
Liverpool St SHAM SO14 .... 248 C4
Livery Rd RSAL SP5 .... 158 A4
Livesay Gdns HSEA PO3 .... 317 H2
Livia Cl AND SP10 .... 82 F7
Livingston Ct
  LSOL/BMARY PO13 .... 315 H3
Livingstone Rd AND SP10 .... 103 J1
  BKME/WDN BH12 .... 321 L6
  BOSC BH5 .... 335 P2
  CHCH/BSGR BH23 .... 325 H9
  NWBY RG14 .... 17 C3
  SHAM SO14 .... 248 C3
  WIMB BH21 .... 300 C1
Llangar Gv CWTH RG45 .... 41 H1
Lloyd Av TOTT SO40 .... 267 J1
Lloyd's La TADY RG26 .... 49 M8
Loader Cl WINC SO23 .... 145 K9
Loaders Cl MOOR/WNTN BH9 .... 322 G7
Loane Rd ITCH SO19 .... 249 H8
Lobelia Rd ROWN SO16 .... 228 E8
Locarno Rd HSEA PO3 .... 297 H7
Lock Appoach CHAM PO6 .... 296 C2
Locke Cl AND SP10 .... 119 N2
Lockerley Cl LYMN SO41 .... 329 L5
Lockerley Crs ROWN SO16 .... 247 K1
Lockerley Rd HAV PO9 .... 15 H1
  ROMY SO51 .... 179 K9
Locke Rd HEND SO30 .... 250 C3
  LIPH GU30 .... 175 L3
Locke's Dro RAND SP11 .... 61 K4
Locksbridge La TADY RG26 .... 51 N3
Locksheath Cl HAV PO9 .... 276 D4
Locksheath Park Rd
  HLER SO31 * 271 H9
Locks La RWIN SO21 .... 163 H4
Locksley Dr FERN BH22 .... 302 C5
Locksley Rd ELGH SO50 .... 228 G3
Locksmead BSTK RG21 .... 7 K5
Lock Sq AND SP10 .... 82 G9
Locks Rd HLER SO31 .... 270 G8
Locksway Rd ENEY PO4 .... 317 K4
Lockswood Keep
  HLER SO31 * 270 G6
Lockswood Rd HLER SO31 .... 270 D8
Lock Vw CHAM PO6 .... 296 C2
Lockwood Cl FARN GU14 .... 57 M5
Lockyers Dr FERN BH22 .... 302 F2
Lockyers Rd WIMB BH21 .... 300 A5
Loddon Ct BSTK RG21 .... 90 D1
Loddon Dr BSTK RG21 .... 7 J6
Loddon Rd FARN GU14 .... 57 L7
Lode Hl RSAL SP5 .... 199 M6
Loders Cl CFDH BH17 .... 320 E1
Lodge Av CHAM PO6 .... 297 J1
Lodge Cl AND SP10 .... 102 C2
Lodge Dr FAWY SO45 .... 268 B9
  RAND SP11 .... 81 K9
Lodge Dro RSAL SP5 .... 199 N9
Lodge Gdns GPORT PO12 .... 12 A4
Lodge Gv YTLY GU46 .... 40 G8
Lodge Hill Rd FNM GU9 .... 116 C4
Lodge Hill Rd RFNM GU10 .... 116 D4
Lodge La BROC SO42 .... 311 J2
  RAND SP11 .... 60 A9
Lodge Rd CHCH/BSGR BH23 .... 324 C7
  HEND SO30 .... 276 B9
  HLER SO31 .... 271 J6
  LYMN SO41 .... 329 H4
  SHAM SO14 .... 248 C4
  WIMB BH21 .... 279 H6
The Lodge WSHM SO15 * 248 B4
Lodsworth FARN GU14 .... 75 P1
Lodsworth Cl HORN PO8 .... 256 B6
Loewy Crs BKME/WDN BH12 .... 321 M2
Lofting Cl ELGH SO50 .... 229 N2
Logan Cl ROWN SO16 .... 227 K7
Loggon Rd BSTK RG21 .... 90 C2
Lomax Cl HEND SO30 .... 250 C2
Lomax St PSEA PO1 .... 18 C5
Lombard Av SBNE BH6 .... 336 B1
Lombard St PSEA PO1 .... 18 C5
Lombardy Cl
  LSOL/BMARY PO13 .... 295 J3
  VWD BH31 .... 259 H5
Lombardy Ri WVILLE PO7 .... 275 P5
Lomer La BH/HW/K RG24 .... 240 A7
Lomond Cl DEAN RG23 .... 88 E2
  NEND PO2 .... 296 B9
Londesborough Rd ENEY PO4 .... 316 G5
Londiandes FLEETS GU52 .... 74 B8
London La CHCH/BSGR BH23 .... 304 D6
London Rd AND SP10 .... 102 F2
  AND SP10 .... 3 K2
  NEND PO2 .... 296 F8
London Rd ALTN GU34 .... 133 H4
  AND SP10 .... 2 E5
  BLKW GU17 .... 57 M1
  BSTK RG21 .... 7 F7
  CBLY GU15 .... 41 N9
  CHAM PO6 .... 275 J9
  EPSF GU31 .... 191 P9
  HORN PO8 .... 255 P9
  HORN PO8 .... 256 C2
  HTWY RG27 .... 71 M5
  LIPH GU30 .... 175 K3
  LISS GU33 .... 193 K2
  NEND PO2 .... 296 F9
  NTHA RG18 .... 25 P4
  NWBY RG14 .... 24 D3
  ODIM RG29 .... 72 D9
  ROWN SO16 .... 87 H3
  RAND SP11 .... 105 N3
  STOK SO20 .... 141 M4
  WCH RG28 .... 85 N6
  WINC SO23 .... 165 J2
  WSHM SO15 .... 20 D1
London St AND SP10 .... 4 E5
  BSTK RG21 .... 7 F7
  WHCH RG28 .... 85 L6
Lone Barn La BPWT SO32 .... 211 J6
Lone Pine Dr FERN BH22 .... 302 E5
Lone Pine Wy FERN BH22 .... 302 E5
Lone Wa WVILLE PO7 .... 275 L7
Longacre ASHV GU12 .... 97 M1
  NWBY RG14 .... 24 A7
Longacre Cl LISS GU33 .... 192 E2
Long Acre Ct PSEA PO1 .... 316 C1
Longacre Rd ENEY PO4 .... 317 J6
Longacres FHAM/STUB PO14 .... 271 J6
Long Barn Rd RWIN SO21 .... 163 L2
Longbarrow Cl CHAR BH8 * 323 M6
Long Barrow Cl RWIN SO21 .... 144 F3
Long Beech Dr FARN GU14 .... 75 K1
  TOTT SO40 .... 266 B4
Long Br FNM GU9 .... 96 C9
Longbridge Cl HTWY RG27 .... 52 F4
Longbridge Rd TADY RG26 .... 52 A2
Long Cl RSAL SP5 .... 199 J5
Longclose Rd HEND SO30 .... 250 C4
Long Copse FAWY SO45 .... 290 C6
Long Copse Cha CHIN RG24 .... 69 P2
Long Copse La EMRTH PO10 .... 277 M6
Longcroft Av KSCL RG20 .... 48 B2
Longcroft Cl BSTK RG21 .... 6 C1
Longcroft Rd HASM GU27 .... 156 C7
  STHA SO19 .... 25 P5
Long Cross Hl BOR GU35 .... 154 F3
Long Cross La BH/HW/K RG22 .... 89 L5
Long Curtain Rd SSEA PO5 .... 18 D7
Longden Rd HASM GU27 .... 156 C7
Longdon Dr
  LSOL/BMARY PO13 .... 314 D1
Long Down EPSF GU31 .... 215 P1
Longdown FLEETS GU52 .... 74 C6
Longdown Rd RFNM GU10 .... 116 C4
  SHST GU47 .... 41 H5
Long Dr HEND SO30 .... 249 N1
  RSAL SP5 .... 158 D5
Longespee Rd WIMB BH21 .... 300 F5
Longfellow Pde CHIN RG24 .... 69 M4
Longfield DEAN RG23 .... 67 M9
Longfield Av
  FHAM/STUB PO14 .... 294 C2
Longfield Cl ENEY PO4 .... 317 C3
  FARN GU14 .... 57 P5
  OVTN RG25 .... 108 C1
Longfield Dr BWD BH11 .... 322 A1
  FERN BH22 .... 302 E8
Longfield Rd ASHV GU12 .... 97 N1
  EMRTH PO10 .... 277 L7
  LYMN SO41 .... 329 K4
  STOK SO20 .... 141 M4
Longfleet Dr WIMB BH21 .... 301 J6
Longfleet Rd PLE BH15 .... 320 G8
Longford Ct CBLY GU15 .... 50 A3
Longford Pl LYMN SO41 .... 329 K6
Long Garden Pl FNM GU9 * 96 B8
Long Garden Wk East
  FNM GU9 .... 96 B8
Long Garden Wk West
  FNM GU9 .... 96 B8
Long Garden Wy FNM GU9 .... 96 B9
Long Gv TADY RG26 .... 33 N4
Longham Br FERN BH22 .... 302 A9
Long Hl RFNM GU10 .... 117 L1
Longhope Dr RFNM GU10 .... 116 A4
Longhouse Gn WINC SO23 .... 23 K4
Long La CHIN RG24 .... 70 B2
  FAWY SO45 .... 290 E4
  HLER SO31 .... 270 A1
  ODIM RG29 .... 93 N9
  ROWN SO16 .... 228 D5
  TOTT SO40 .... 267 H1
  WIMB BH21 .... 278 F7
Long Lane Cl FAWY SO45 .... 290 F6
Longleat Gdns
  NMIL/BTOS BH25 .... 326 C4
  ROWN SO16 .... 227 M7
Longleaze Sq FARN GU14 .... 76 D1
Long Leaze La WVILLE PO7 .... 62 F8
Longley Rd FNM GU9 .... 116 D1
Longmead FLEETS GU52 .... 74 D6
  ODIM RG29 .... 92 N5
  WIMB BH21 .... 278 F7
Longmead Av ELGH SO50 .... 207 M9
Longmead Gdns HAV PO9 .... 298 F2
Longmeadow FRIM GU16 .... 58 E2
Longmeadow Gdns
  FAWY SO45 .... 268 C6
Longmeadow La CFDH BH17 .... 320 A4
Longmead Rd RGWD BH24 .... 284 A5
  WEND SO18 .... 249 J1
Long Mickle SHST GU47 .... 41 K5
Longmoor Dr LIPH GU30 .... 174 E5
Longmoor La THLE RG7 .... 27 J8
Longmoor Rd BSTK RG21 .... 90 C2
  LIPH GU30 .... 174 D3
  LISS GU33 .... 173 M5
Longmore Av ITCH SO19 .... 248 F9
Longmore Crs ITCH SO19 .... 248 F9
Longmynd Dr
  FHAM/STUB PO14 .... 10 A7
Longparish Rd RAND SP11 .... 123 L2
  WHCH RG28 .... 104 F1
Long Priors PSF GU32 .... 188 D9
Longridge Rd HEND SO30 .... 250 C5
Long Rd BPWT SO32 .... 233 N6
  NBNE BH10 .... 322 B2
  PSF GU32 .... 191 N9
The Long Rd RFNM GU10 .... 115 P7
Longs Ct WCH RG28 .... 85 L6
Longshore Wy ENEY PO4 .... 317 M3
Longs La FHAM/STUB PO14 .... 294 A6
Longstaff Gdns
  FHAM/PORC PO16 .... 10 D2
Long Steeple La FBDG SP6 .... 220 C2
Longstock Cl AND SP10 .... 102 C3
  ITCH SO19 .... 269 J2
Longstock Crs TOTT SO40 .... 246 B4
Longstock Rd HAV PO9 .... 277 H4
  RAND SP11 .... 122 D5
Longs Wk PSEA PO1 .... 316 F1
Long Wk RWIN SO21 .... 165 N5
Long Water Dr GPORT PO12 .... 315 N7
Longwater La EWKG RG40 .... 39 P4
Longwater Rd HTWY RG27 .... 40 A6
Longwood Av HORN PO8 .... 255 P8
Longwood Copse La
  DEAN RG23 .... 89 K7
Longwood Dean La
  RWIN SO21 .... 186 A8
Longwood Rd RWIN SO21 .... 209 J1
Lonnen Rd WIMB BH21 .... 279 H7
Lonnen Wood Cl WIMB BH21 .... 279 H7
Lonsdale Av CHAM PO6 .... 297 J2
  FHAM/PORC PO16 .... 295 P3
Lonsdale Rd TWDS BH3 .... 322 F8
Loosehanger FBDG SP6 .... 220 B2
Loperwood TOTT SO40 .... 245 M1
Loperwood La TOTT SO40 .... 245 M3
Loraine Av CHCH/BSGR BH23 .... 326 E1
Lord Cl CFDH BH17 .... 321 H5
Lordington Cl CHAM PO6 .... 297 J1
Lord Mountbatten Cl
  WEND SO18 .... 228 G8
Lordsfield Gdns OVTN RG25 .... 86 F3
Lord's Hill Centre East
  ROWN SO16 .... 227 K8
Lord's Hill Centre West
  ROWN SO16 .... 227 K8
Lord's Hill Wy ROWN SO16 .... 227 K8
Lords St PSEA PO1 .... 19 K1
Lordswood Cl ROWN SO16 .... 207 N6
  THLE RG7 .... 35 H6
Lordswood Cl ROWN SO16 .... 227 P9
Lordswood Gdns ROWN SO16 .... 227 P8
Lordswood La ROWN SO16 .... 227 P8
Loreille Gdns ROWN SO16 .... 227 J5
Lorne Park Rd BMTH BH1 .... 9 F3
Lorne Pl WEND SO18 * 249 J4
Lorne Rd SSEA PO5 .... 316 G5
Lothian Rd CHOB/PIR GU24 .... 59 M7
Loughwood Cl PLE BH15 .... 207 J7
Louisburg Rd BOR GU35 .... 154 D2
Louise Margaret Rd
  ALDT GU11 .... 3 G1
Loundyes Cl NTHA RG18 .... 25 L3
Lovage Gdns TOTT SO40 .... 246 A4
Lovage Rd FHAM PO15 .... 271 K3
Lovage Wy HORN PO8 .... 256 C2
Lovatt Gv FHAM PO15 .... 272 B7
Lovedean La HORN PO8 .... 256 A6
Lovedon La WINC SO23 .... 145 J7
Lovegroves CHIN RG24 .... 70 B1
Lovell Cl RAND SP11 .... 98 D3
  BPWT SO32 .... 210 F2
  EPSF GU31 .... 215 N1
  FBDG SP6 .... 221 J4
  KSCL RG20 .... 48 C3
  NWBY RG14 .... 24 C1
  PSF GU32 .... 93 K2
  ROMY SO51 .... 204 C6
  RWIN SO21 .... 184 B9
Lovell Cl RAND SP11 .... 100 D3
  FAWY SO45 .... 144 F4
Lovells Wk NARL SO24 .... 167 P2
Loveridge Cl AND SP10 .... 82 F7
  BSTK RG21 .... 90 C1
Loveridge Wy ELGH SO50 .... 229 H1
Lovers La FRIM GU10 .... 136 C2
Love's Cl THLE RG7 .... 27 H4
Loves Wd THLE RG7 .... 35 N1
Lovett Rd PSEA PO1 .... 297 H6
Lovett Wk FUFL SO22 .... 164 D4
Lovington La RWIN SO21 .... 167 H3
Lowa Cl TDWTH SP9 .... 78 G6
Lowa Rd TDWTH SP9 .... 78 G6
Lowcay Rd SSEA PO5 .... 19 K6
Lowden Cl FUFL SO22 .... 185 M2
Low La AND SP10 .... 2 B1
Lower Alfred St SHAM SO14 .... 21 H1
Lower Ashley Rd
  NMIL/BTOS BH25 .... 327 M4
Lower Banister St WSHM SO15 .... 20 D1
Lower Bartons FBDG SP6 .... 240 D2
Lower Baybridge La
  RWIN SO21 .... 209 H4
Lower Bellfield
  FHAM/STUB PO14 .... 293 M2

Lower Bere Wd WVILLE PO7 ..... 275 P3
Lower Blandford Rd
　BDST BH18 ..... 300 C9
Lower Broadmoor Rd
　CWTH RG45 ..... 41 K2
Lower Brook St BSTK RG21 ..... 6 A6
　WINC SO23 ..... 23 F4
Lower Brownhill Rd
　ROWN SO16 ..... 246 G1
Lower Buckland Rd
　LYMN SO41 ..... 329 K2
Lower Canal Wk SHAM SO14..... 20 E7
Lower Canes YTLY GU46..... 40 B8
Lower Chase Rd BPWT SO32.....232 C8
Lower Chestnut Dr BSTK RG21.. 69 J9
Lower Church La FHAM PO16 ..... 11 H5
Lower Church Pth PSEA PO1 ..... 19 H2
Lower Church Rd
　FHAM/STUB PO14 ..... 271 J7
　SHST GU47 ..... 40 F5
Lower Common La HTWY RG27 ..... 39 H5
Lower Common
　WIMB BH21 ..... 280 G2
Lower Common Rd
　ROMY SO51 ..... 224 E2
Lower Crabbick La
　WVILLE PO7 ..... 254 D7
Lower Densome Wd
　FBDG SP6 ..... 221 J4
Lower Derby Rd NEND PO2 ..... 296 E8
Lower Drayton La CHAM PO6 ..... 297 L2
Lower Duncan Rd HLER SO31.. 211 H5
Lower Evingar Rd WHCH RG28.. 85 L6
Lower Farlington Rd
　CHAM PO6 ..... 297 N1
Lower Farm Ct NWBY RG14 ..... 25 J6
Lower Farm La ROMY SO51 .....205 M2
Lower Farnham Rd FNM GU9..... 97 H5
Lower Forbury Rd SSEA PO5 ..... 19 J4
Lower Golf Links Rd
　..... 300 D8
Lower Gv FBDG SP6 ..... 219 P2
Lower Grove Rd HAV PO9..... 15 H7
Lower Hanger HASM GU27..... 156 B7
Lower Heyshott EPSF GU31..... 215 N1
Lower Lamborough La
　NARL SO24 ..... 187 H1
Lower La BPWT SO32 ..... 232 A4
Lower Md EPSF GU31..... 215 P2
　LISS GU33 * 192 D2
　STOK SO20 ..... 121 H5
Lower Mead End Rd LYMN
　SO41 ..... 307 P8
Lower Moor YTLY GU46..... 40 E9
Lower Moors Rd RWIN SO21 ..... 207 P4
Lower Mortimer Rd
　ITCH SO19 ..... 248 F8
Lower Mount St FLEETN GU51.. 73 P1
Lower Mullin's La FAWY SO45 .. 268 B6
Lower Neatham Mill La
　ALTN GU34 ..... 133 K2
Lower Nelson St ALDT GU11..... 2 D2
Lower Newport Rd
　ASHV GU12 ..... 97 K2
Lower New Rd HEND SO30 .....249 M2
Lower Northam Rd
　HEND SO30 ..... 250 C4
Lower Paice La ALTN GU34 .....149 M4
Lower Pennington La
　LYMN SO41 ..... 329 K8
Lower Pool Rd HTWY RG27 ..... 54 C1
Lower Preshaw La
　BPWT SO32 ..... 210 D5
Lower Quay Rd
　FHAM/PORC PO16 ..... 294 F1
Lower Rd HASM GU27 ..... 157 L3
　HAV PO9 ..... 276 B9
　RSAL SP5 ..... 199 K1
　RWIN SO21 ..... 144 D4
Lower St Helens Rd
　HEND SO30 ..... 250 C6
Lower Sandhurst Rd
　EWKG RG40 ..... 40 B4
Lower Sandy Down
　LYMN SO41 ..... 309 H5
Lower South Vw FNM GU9..... 96 C8
Lower Spinney HLER SO31 ..... 292 C2
Lower St HASM GU27..... 156 G7
　ROMY SO51..... 180 F7
Lower Swanwick Rd
　HLER SO31 ..... 270 D2
Lower Terrace Rd FARN GU14 .. 75 P4
Lower Turk St ALTN GU34 ..... 148 G6
Lower Vicarage Rd ITCH SO19.. 248 F8
Lower Wardown EPSF GU31..... 215 P1
Lower Wy STHA RG19 ..... 25 J4
Lower Weybourne La
　FNM GU9 ..... 96 F5
Lower William St SHAM SO14 .. 248 F5
Lower Woodside LYMN SO41..... 329 L7
Lower York St SHAM SO14 ..... 21 K1
Lowestoft Rd CHAM PO6 ..... 274 F9
Loweswater Gdns BOR GU35.. 154 A3
Lowford HI HLER SO31..... 269 P1
Lowford Hill Cl HLER SO31 .....269 P1
Lowicks Rd RFNM GU10..... 137 H3
Lowland Rd WVILLE PO7..... 254 G7
Lowlands Rd BH/HW/K RG22.. 68 D9
　BLKW GU17 ..... 57 K1
Low La FNM GU9 ..... 97 H5
Lowndes Blds FNM GU9 * 96 E7
Lowry Cl SHST GU47 ..... 41 L8
Lowry Ct AND SP10 ..... 4 D8
Lowry Gdns ITCH SO19 ..... 249 L9
Lowther Gdns CHAR BH8..... 335 J1
Lowther Rd CHAR BH8..... 322 G9
Lowton Av FLEETN GU51..... 73 N1
Loxwood Rd HORN PO8..... 255 P5
Loyalty La CHIN RG24 ..... 70 C6
Loyd-Lindsay Sq FUFL SO22 *.. 164 E5
Luard Ct HAV PO9 ..... 15 K6
Lubeck Dr AND SP10..... 82 D8
Lucas Cl ROWN SO16 ..... 42 E9
　YTLY GU46 ..... 40 E9
Lucas Fld HASM GU27..... 156 D7
Lucas Rd BKME/WDN BH12.. 321 L6
　PLE BH15 ..... 332 D2

Luccombe Pl WSHM SO15 ..... 247 P1
Luccombe Rd WSHM SO15 ..... 247 P1
Lucerne Av SBNE BH6 ..... 336 E5
　WVILLE PO7 ..... 275 L1
Lucerne Gdns HEND SO30 ..... 250 A5
Lucerne Rd LYMN SO41 ..... 329 H5
Luckham Cl MOOR/WNTN BH9.. 323 H5
Luckham Pl
　MOOR/WNTN BH9 ..... 323 H5
Luckham Rd
　MOOR/WNTN BH9 ..... 323 H5
Luckham Rd East
　MOOR/WNTN BH9 ..... 323 H5
Lucknow St PSEA PO1 ..... 316 G3
Lucky La LYMN SO41 ..... 309 N7
Ludcombe WVILLE PO7 ..... 255 H6
Ludgershall Rd TDWTH SP9 ..... 79 H4
Ludlow Cl DEAN RG23 ..... 68 F7
　FRIM GU16 ..... 58 F6
　NWBY RG14 ..... 25 H3
Ludlow Gdns DEAN RG23 ..... 68 G7
Ludlow Pl TADY RG26 ..... 34 D6
Ludlow Rd CHAM PO6 ..... 274 E9
　ITCH SO19 ..... 248 G7
Ludshott Gv BOR GU35 ..... 155 J3
Ludwell's La BPWT SO32 ..... 232 D8
Lugano Cl WVILLE PO7 ..... 275 M1
Luke Rd ALDT GU11..... 96 E3
Luke Rd East ALDT GU11..... 2 A8
Lukes Cl HLER SO31 ..... 270 A8
Lukin Dr ROWN SO16 ..... 226 C7
Lulworth Av PLE BH15 ..... 332 A2
Lulworth Cl CHFD SO53..... 228 D1
　FARN GU14 ..... 76 A4
　HISD PO11 ..... 318 C5
　PLE BH15 ..... 332 A1
　ROWN SO16 ..... 247 J1
Lulworth Crs PLE BH15 ..... 332 A2
Lulworth Gn ROWN SO16 ..... 247 J1
Lulworth Rd
　LSOL/BMARY PO13 ..... 314 C2
Lumby Dr RGWD BH24..... 282 F1
Lumby Drive Pk RGWD BH24.. 282 F1
Lumley Rd EMRTH PO10..... 277 N9
Lumsden Av WSHM SO15 .....247 N4
Lumsden Rd ENEY PO4 ..... 317 M5
Lundy Cl CHIN RG24 ..... 69 L5
　ROWN SO16 ..... 226 B2
Lune Cl BSTK RG21 ..... 7 J6
Lune Ct AND SP10..... 82 G9
Lunedale Rd FAWY SO45 ..... 290 A1
Lupin Cl AND SP10 ..... 94 A3
Lupin Gdns FUFL SO22 ..... 164 C5
Lupin Rd ROWN SO16 ..... 228 E7
Luscombe Rd PSTN BH14 ..... 333 L1
Luther Rd MOOR/WNTN BH9.. 322 F7
Lutman St EMRTH PO10..... 277 L6
Luton Rd ITCH SO19..... 249 M8
Lutyens Cl CHIN RG24 ..... 70 A4
　ITCH SO19 ..... 249 M8
Luxton Cl HEND SO30 ..... 250 F3
Luzborough La ROMY SO51.....204 F9
Lyall Pl FNM GU9 ..... 96 B9
Lyburn Cl ROWN SO16 ..... 227 N8
Lyburn Rd RSAL SP5..... 223 J2
Lych Gate Cl SHST GU47 ..... 40 G6
Lych Gate Ct RGWD BH24 ..... 282 G3
Lychgate Dr HORN PO8 ..... 256 B4
Lychgate Gn
　FHAM/STUB PO14 ..... 294 A4
Lydford Cl DEAN RG23 ..... 88 F7
Lydford Cl FARN GU14 * 57 P6
　FRIM GU16 ..... 58 F6
Lydford Gdns BWD BH11 ..... 322 A5
Lydford Rd BWD BH11 ..... 322 A5
Lydgate LYMN SO41 ..... 338 D1
　TOTT SO40 ..... 246 B4
Lydgate Cl ITCH SO19..... 249 M7
Lydgate Gn ITCH SO19 ..... 249 M7
Lydgate Rd ITCH SO19 ..... 249 M7
Lydiard Cl ELGH SO50 ..... 207 J8
Lydlinch Cl FERN BH22 ..... 302 D7
Lydlynch Rd TOTT SO40 ..... 246 C4
Lydney Cl CHAM PO6 ..... 296 E1
Lydney Rd HLER SO31 ..... 270 F8
Lydwell Cl BWD BH11 ..... 301 P8
Lye Copse Av FARN GU14 ..... 58 A5
Lyell Rd BKME/WDN BH12 ..... 321 L6
Lyeway La NARL SO24 ..... 169 N3
Lyeway Rd NARL SO24 ..... 170 B2
Lyford Rd BSTK RG21 ..... 7 F3
Lymbourn Rd HAV PO9 ..... 15 H6
Lyme Cl ELGH SO50 ..... 207 H8
Lyme Crs CHCH/BSGR BH23.. 326 B7
Lymefields LYMN SO41 ..... 328 E9
Lymer La ROWN SO16 ..... 226 G6
Lymer Vis ROWN SO16 * 226 G6
Lymington Av YTLY GU46..... 40 B8
Lymington Bottom
　..... 150 C7
Lymington Bottom Rd
　ALTN GU54 ..... 150 B4
Lymington Cl ALTN GU54 ..... 150 C6
　BH/HW/K RG22 ..... 89 M5
Lymington Rd ALTN GU54 ..... 150 C6
Lymington Rd BROC SO42 ..... 308 G2
　CHCH/BSGR BH23 ..... 326 A8
　LYMN SO41 ..... 328 E3
　LYMN SO41 ..... 330 E2
　NMIL/BTOS BH25 ..... 327 J4
Lymington Road Shelley HI
　CHCH/BSGR BH23 ..... 325 N8
Lymore La LYMN SO41 ..... 328 F8
Lymore Va LYMN SO41 ..... 328 E8
Lynams FLEETS GU52 ..... 74 B9
Lynchborough Rd LIPH SO24.. 154 E8
Lynch Cl FUFL SO22..... 164 F5
Lynchford La FARN GU14 ..... 76 B3
Lynchford Rd FARN GU14..... 76 A3
Lynch HI WHCH RG28..... 85 L6
Lynch Hill Pk WHCH RG28 ..... 85 L6
Lynch La PSF GU32..... 212 E1
Lynch Rd FNM GU9 ..... 96 D9
The Lynch OVTN RG25 ..... 86 E3
　WHCH RG28 ..... 85 L6
Lyn Ct BSTK RG21 ..... 7 J5
Lyndale Cl LYMN SO41 ..... 339 H1

Lyndale Dr FLEETN GU51..... 74 G3
Lyndale Rd HLER SO31 ..... 271 H6
Lynden Cl FHAM/STUB PO14.. 293 P1
Lynden Ga ITCH SO19 ..... 248 G9
Lyndford Ter FLEETS GU52 ..... 74 C5
Lyndhurst Av ALDT GU11 ..... 97 J5
Lyndhurst Cl BH/HW/K RG22.. 89 M5
Lyndhurst Ct BH/HW/K RG22.. 89 M5
　HISD PO11 ..... 318 G6
Lyndhurst Dr BH/HW/K RG22.. 89 M5
Lyndhurst Rd BROC SO42 ..... 286 G7
　CHCH/BSGR BH23 ..... 325 K3
　FLEETN GU51 ..... 55 P9
　GPORT PO12 ..... 12 A1
　NEND PO2 ..... 297 H7
　RSAL SP5 ..... 223 L1
　TOTT SO40 ..... 244 E4
　TOTT SO40 ..... 265 P1
Lyndock Cl ITCH SO19 * 248 G9
Lyndock Pl ITCH SO19 ..... 248 G9
Lyndsey Cl FARN GU14 ..... 57 J9
Lyndum Cl PSF GU32 ..... 215 M2
Lyndum Pl BOR GU35 * 154 C3
Lyneham Rd CWTH RG45 ..... 41 J1
Lyne Pl HORN PO8 ..... 256 B5
Lynes La RGWD BH24 ..... 282 D3
Lynford Av FUFL SO22 ..... 164 F5
Lynford Wy FUFL SO22 ..... 164 F5
Lynn Rd CFDH BH17..... 321 H4
　NEND PO2 ..... 297 H9
Lynn Wy FARN GU14 ..... 57 N6
　WINC SO23 ..... 148 D3
Lyric Cl NMIL/BTOS BH25 ..... 327 H8
Lynton Cl FNM GU9 ..... 116 A3
Lynton Ct TOTT SO40 ..... 246 C5
Lyntons
　CHCH/BSGR BH23 ..... 324 B4
Lynton Gdns
　..... 10 C1
Lynton Gdns ITCH SO19 ..... 249 K7
Lynton Gv HSEA PO3 ..... 297 J9
Lynton Meadow STOK SO20.. 123 L4
Lynton Rd BOR GU35..... 154 A5
　FUFL SO22 ..... 164 B1
　LSOL/BMARY PO13 ..... 295 H5
　LYMN SO41 ..... 329 N1
　PSEA PO1 ..... 18 D1
　RWIN SO21 ..... 207 K3
　RWIN SO21 ..... 209 H1
　TADY RG26 ..... 34 E8
　TOTT SO40 ..... 246 C7
Lynwood Av WVILLE PO7 .....255 M8
Lynwood Cl BOR GU35 ..... 154 D3
　FERN BH22 ..... 302 D1
Lynwood Dr AND SP10 ..... 102 C2
Lynx Cl FRIM GU16..... 76 F1
Lynwood Cl ELGH SO50..... 300 G5
Lynwood Gdns HTWY RG27..... 71 P5
Lynx Cl ELGH SO50..... 229 P2
Lyon Av NMIL/BTOS BH25 .....327 K4
Lyon Rd BKME/WDN BH12 .....321 N2
Lyons Pl HEND SO30 ..... 250 B6
Lyon St SHAM SO14 ..... 248 C5
Lyon Wy FRIM GU16..... 58 B4
Lysander Cl
　CHCH/BSGR BH23 ..... 325 M8
Lysander Wy FARN GU14..... 76 A3
　WVILLE PO7 ..... 276 A2
Lysons Av ASHV GU12 ..... 76 E4
Lyss Ct LISS GU33 * 192 D2
Lysses Ct FHAM/PORC PO16.. 11 K5
Lysses Pth FHAM/PORC PO16 .. 11 K5
Lyster Rd FBDG SP6 ..... 240 F1
Lystra Rd MOOR/WNTN BH9.. 322 G4
Lytchett Dr BDST BH18 ..... 320 B2
Lyteltane Rd LYMN SO41 ..... 329 K5
Lytham Rd BDST BH18 ..... 320 C1
　WEND SO18 ..... 249 J5
Lythe La PSF GU32 ..... 190 B4
Lyttell Coombe HTWY RG27 ..... 72 C3
Lytton Rd BSTK RG21..... 7 H6
　CHAR BH8 ..... 335 J1
　FAWY SO45 ..... 268 D8

M

Mabbs La HTWY RG27 ..... 55 H9
Mabelmwll Crt HTWY RG27 ..... 72 C2
Mabey Av NBNE BH10..... 322 D5
Mabey Cl GPORT PO12 ..... 12 E7
Mablethorpe Rd CHAM PO6 .. 274 C9
Macadam Wy AND SP10 ..... 101 P1
Macandrew Rd CCLF BH13.. 333 K8
Macarthur Crs WEND SO18.. 249 J5
Macaulay Av CHAM PO6 ..... 274 B9
Macaulay Rd BDST BH18 ..... 300 C9
Maccallum Rd RAND SP11..... 82 F3
Macdonald Rd FNM GU9..... 96 B4
Maclaren Rd
　MOOR/WNTN BH9 ..... 322 F4
Maclean Rd BWD BH11 ..... 321 P1
Macnaghten Rd WEND SO18.. 248 F4
Macrae Rd YTLY GU46..... 40 B8
Madden Cl GPORT PO12..... 315 K5
Maddison St SHAM SO14 ..... 20 D5
Maddoxford La BPWT SO32.. 231 J2
Maddoxford Wy BPWT SO32.. 252 C2
Madeira Cl CHIN RG24 ..... 69 N3
Madeira Pl NWBY RG14 ..... 16 E4
Madeira Rd BMTH BH1 ..... 9 F2
　NEND PO2 ..... 296 G6
　PSTN BH14 ..... 333 L2
Madeley Rd FLEETS GU52 ..... 74 E6
Madeline Crs
　BKME/WDN BH12 ..... 321 K5
Madeline Rd EPSF GU31 ..... 215 M1
Madison Av BMTH BH1 ..... 323 K9
Madison Cl LSOL/BMARY PO13.. 295 J9
Madjeston Wy HORN PO8 ..... 255 N8
Madocks Wy HORN PO8 ..... 255 N8
Madox Brown End SHST GU47.. 41 M8
Madrid Rd AND SP10 ..... 5 L6
Mafeking Rd ENEY PO4 ..... 317 H5
Magazine La TOTT SO40 ..... 247 L8
Magdala Rd CHAM PO6 ..... 297 H1
　HISD PO11 ..... 318 E5
Magdalene Rd SHST GU47 ..... 41 N4

Magdalene Wy
　FHAM/STUB PO14 ..... 271 J9
Magdalen HI WINC SO23 ..... 23 G5
Magdalen La
　CHCH/BSGR BH23 ..... 324 E9
Magdalen Ms WINC SO23 * 23 G5
Magdalen Rd NEND PO2 ..... 296 G6
Magdalen Rw PSF GU32 * 215 L2
Magellan Cl AND SP10 ..... 103 J1
Magennis Ct
　LSOL/BMARY PO13 ..... 315 H1
Magenta Ct
　LSOL/BMARY PO13 ..... 314 G2
Magister Dr
　LSOL/BMARY PO13 ..... 314 E3
Magna Cl BWD BH11..... 301 P7
Magna Gdns BWD BH11 ..... 301 P7
Magna Rd WIMB BH21 ..... 301 K5
Magnolia Cl AND SP10 ..... 102 C3
　FAWY SO45 ..... 267 N6
　FHAM/STUB PO14 ..... 10 A7
　SBNE BH6 ..... 336 E1
　SHST GU47 ..... 41 L5
　VWD BH31 ..... 259 J6
Magnolia Ct CHIN RG24 ..... 69 K3
　STHA RG19 ..... 32 E2
Magnolia Gv ELGH SO50 ..... 230 E2
Magnolia Rd ITCH SO19 ..... 249 H6
Magnolia Wy FLEETS GU52 ..... 74 D5
　HORN PO8 ..... 256 C7
Magnus Dr BH/HW/K RG22.. 89 K3
Magpie Cl BH/HW/K RG22 ..... 89 K3
　BOR GU35 ..... 154 B6
　CHAR BH8 ..... 323 J4
　FHAM/PORC PO16 ..... 295 J1
　RFNM GU10 ..... 95 M3
　STHA RG19 ..... 25 L4
Magpie Dr TOTT SO40 ..... 246 A8
Magpie Gdns ITCH SO19 ..... 249 K7
Magpie La NMIL/BTOS BH25.. 327 H5
Magpie La ELGH SO50 ..... 228 G2
Magpie Rd HORN PO8 ..... 256 C8
Magpie Wk HORN PO8 ..... 255 N8
Mag's Barrow FERN BH22 .....302 E6
Maguire Dr FRIM GU16 ..... 76 F1
Mahler Cl BH/HW/K RG22 ..... 90 B3
Maida Rd ALDT GU11 ..... 76 A8
Maiden La LYMN SO41 ..... 329 M6
Maidenthorn La OVTN RG25.. 108 D1
Maidford Gv HSEA PO3 * 297 L5
Maidment Cl BWD BH11 ..... 301 N9
Maidstone Crs CHAM PO6 ..... 274 G9
Main Dr FAWY SO45 ..... 312 C2
　WHAM PO17 ..... 274 C4
Main Gate Rd FARN GU14 ..... 76 A2
Main Rd FAWY SO45 ..... 290 E3
　FUFL SO22 ..... 164 B1
　LSOL/BMARY PO13 ..... 295 H5
　LYMN SO41 ..... 329 N1
　PSEA PO1 ..... 18 B1
　RWIN SO21 ..... 207 K3
　RWIN SO21 ..... 209 H1
　TADY RG26 ..... 34 E8
　TOTT SO40 ..... 246 C7
Mainsail Dr FHAM/PORC PO16.. 294 F1
Mainstone ROMY SO51 ..... 204 B8
Mainstone Cl FRIM GU16..... 59 H6
Mainstream Ct ELGH SO50 .....229 M1
Main St STHA RG19..... 31 L1
Maisemore Gdns
　EMRTH PO10 ..... 299 K1
Maison Belle Vue ITCH SO19 *.. 269 H1
Maitland Cl FARN GU14 ..... 76 A4
Maitlands Cl RFNM GU10 ..... 97 J3
Maitland St PSEA PO1 ..... 316 F1
Majendie Cl NWBY RG14..... 24 A2
Majestic Rd BH/HW/K RG22 ..... 89 L6
　ROWN SO16 ..... 226 A3
Majoram Wy FHAM PO15..... 271 K3
Majorca Av AND SP10..... 5 L6
Malcolm Cl CFDH BH17..... 320 G4
　HLER SO31 ..... 271 H7
Malcolm Rd CHFD SO53..... 206 D4
Malcomb Cl SBNE BH6..... 336 E3
Malcroft Ms TOTT SO40..... 267 L1
Maldive Rd CHAR BH8 ..... 69 N3
Maldon Cl ELGH SO50 ..... 229 M1
　ITCH SO19 ..... 248 G7
Malham Gdns BH/HW/K RG22.. 89 M6
Malibres Rd CHFD SO53 ..... 206 F2
Malin Cl FHAM/STUB PO14 ..... 293 P6
　ROWN SO16 ..... 227 J8
Malins Rd NEND PO2 ..... 316 F1
Mallard Cl AND SP10 ..... 94 A4
　ASHV GU12 ..... 97 M1
　BH/HW/K RG22 ..... 89 K4
　BPWT SO32 ..... 231 N4
　CHAR BH8 ..... 323 J6
　CHCH/BSGR BH23 ..... 325 L9
　HASM GU27 ..... 156 E6
　LYMN SO41 ..... 328 A4
　NARL SO24 ..... 168 A1
　ROMY SO51 ..... 204 D5
Mallard Ct NWBY RG14 * 16 C2
Mallard Gdns HEND SO30 ..... 250 B5
　LSOL/BMARY PO13 ..... 294 F7
Mallard Pl FARN GU14 ..... 57 P5
Mallard Rd CHAR BH8..... 323 K6
　ENEY PO4 ..... 317 K3
　HAV PO9 ..... 15 J2
　WIMB BH21 ..... 279 J7
Mallards
　FHAM/PORC PO16 ..... 11 L5
　FRIM GU16 ..... 58 E3
　NEND PO2 ..... 298 F2
Mallard Wy YTLY GU46 * 40 C8
The Mallards
　CHCH/BSGR BH23 ..... 325 N7
　NEND PO2 * 275 P4
Mallow Gdns NTHA RG18 ..... 25 H2
Mallow Rd HEND SO30 ..... 250 A5
The Mallows NMIL/BTOS BH25.. 327 M3
The Mall CHFD SO53 * 206 D6
　NEND PO2 ..... 296 F8
　RGWD BH24 ..... 284 C6
　TDWTH SP9 ..... 78 D6
Malmesbury Ct ELGH SO50 ..... 230 C2
Malmesbury Ct CHAR BH8..... 323 J9
Malmesbury Fld
　BH/HW/K RG22 ..... 89 P3
Malmesbury Gdns FUFL SO22.. 164 E5
Malmesbury Park Pl
　CHAR BH8 ..... 335 J1
Malmesbury Park Rd
　CHAR BH8 ..... 323 H9
Malmesbury Pl WSHM SO15 .. 247 P4
Malmesbury Rd RGWD BH24.. 281 L6
　ROWN SO16 ..... 204 C5
　WSHM SO15 ..... 247 P4
Malmsbury Cl
　CHCH/BSGR BH23 ..... 336 E1
Malmsbury Rd BOR GU35 ..... 154 A6
Maloren Wy FERN BH22..... 280 F8
Malory Ct ITCH SO19 ..... 249 J8
Malpass Rd RWIN SO21 ..... 144 D6
Malshanger La DEAN RG23 ..... 67 M9
Malta Cl CHIN RG24 ..... 69 L3
Malta Rd FRIM GU16 ..... 59 J5
　NEND PO2 ..... 296 G9
Maltby's Ml FERN BH22 * 89 P3
Malthouse Cl HLER SO31 * 332 E1
　ROMY SO51 ..... 204 C5
　RWIN SO21 ..... 165 N2
Malthouse Gdns TOTT SO40 .. 267 K1
Malt House La RAND SP11 ..... 82 G4
Malthouse La
　FHAM/PORC PO16 ..... 11 G5
　NARL SO24 ..... 148 F2
　TADY RG26 ..... 34 E8
Malthouse Mdw LIPH SO30.. 175 K3
Malthouse Ms ALTN GU34 ..... 133 K3
Malthouse Rd NEND PO2 ..... 296 F9
Maltings Cl ALTN GU34..... 132 F7
The Maltings EPSF GU31 ..... 215 M2
　FHAM/PORC PO16 ..... 273 H8
　FNM GU9 ..... 96 B9
　LISS GU33 ..... 175 L3
　NWBY RG14 ..... 16 D5
　RGWD BH24 ..... 52 A3
Malt La BPWT SO32 ..... 232 A4
Malus Cl FHAM/STUB PO14 .....294 C2
Malvern Av FHAM/STUB PO14.. 294 C2
Malvern Cl BH/HW/K RG22 ..... 89 P3
　BPWT SO32 ..... 232 B5
　MOOR/WNTN BH9 ..... 322 G4
Malvern Ct BMTH BH1..... 16 D5
Malvern Dr FAWY SO45 ..... 267 P7
Malvern Gdns HEND SO30 .....250 D1
Malvern Ms EMRTH PO10 ..... 277 L6
Malvern Rd BLKW GU17 ..... 56 G4
　FARN GU14 ..... 57 L6
　GPORT PO12 ..... 315 K3
　LISS GU33 ..... 192 F4
　MOOR/WNTN BH9 ..... 322 G4
　ROWN SO16 ..... 247 N1
　SSEA PO5 ..... 316 F7
Malvern Ter ROWN SO16 * 247 J1
Malwood Av ROWN SO16 .....227 P9
Malwood Gv HAV PO9 ..... 276 G4
Malwood Rd FAWY SO45 ..... 246 A3
Malwood Rd East FAWY SO45.. 268 B6
Malwood Rd West
　FAWY SO45 ..... 268 B6
Manaton Wy HEND SO30 ..... 250 B2
Manchester Ct
　LSOL/BMARY PO13 * 315 H3
Manchester Rd HLER SO31..... 269 P1
　LYMN SO41 ..... 308 B5
　PSEA PO1 ..... 316 C3
Mancroft Av
　FHAM/STUB PO14 ..... 294 A8
Mandale Cl BWD BH11 ..... 322 A4
Mandale Rd BWD BH11 ..... 321 P1
Mandarin Ct NWBY RG14 * 17 J3
Mandarin Dr NWBY RG14 ..... 17 J5
Mandarin Wy
　LSOL/BMARY PO13 ..... 315 H2
Manderley Cl NWBY RG14 * 20 A2
Manderley Wy WSHM SO15 .. 339 H3
Mandora Rd ALDT GU11..... 76 A8
Manfield Rd ASHV GU12 ..... 97 N1
Manica Cl BOR GU35 ..... 154 A5
Manley Bridge Rd
　RFNM GU10 ..... 115 N6
Manley James Cl ODIM RG29.. 72 F6
Manley Rd HLER SO31 ..... 269 P1
Mann Cl WHCH RG28..... 85 M7
Manners Rd ENEY PO4 ..... 316 G4
Manning Av CHCH/BSGR BH23.. 325 N6
Manningford Ct WINC SO23.. 165 H4
Mannings Heath Rd
　BKME/WDN BH12 ..... 321 K2
Mannington Rd WCLF BH2 * 8 B4
Mannington Wy FERN BH22.. 280 D7
Manns Cl WEND SO18 ..... 249 L1
Manningham Wy
　ROMY SO51 ..... 180 B7
Manor Av BKME/WDN BH12.. 321 L3
Manor Bridge Ct TDWTH SP9.. 79 J4
Manor Cl ALTN GU54 ..... 132 C3
　FBDG SP6 ..... 240 D2
　FERN BH22 ..... 302 E3
　HASM GU27 ..... 156 C7
　HAV PO9 ..... 15 G5
　HLER SO31 ..... 269 P1
　LYMN SO41 ..... 338 C1
　RAND SP11 ..... 101 N7
　RFNM GU10 ..... 97 M4
　TDWTH SP9 ..... 98 D3
　TOTT SO40 ..... 246 C5
　WHAM PO17 ..... 252 E8
　WINC SO23 ..... 23 H3

Manor Copse AND SP10 .... 82 F6
Manor Ct FLEETS GU52 .... 74 C6
  RCWD BH24 .... 282 E1
  VWD BH31 .... 258 F4
Manor Crs CHAM P06 .... 297 K2
  HASM GU27 .... 156 D7
  HLER SO31 .... 269 P1
Manor Farm CI ASHV GU12 * 97 M2
  NMIL/BTOS BH25 .... 327 H6
  RGUW GU3 .... 77 N9
Manor Farm Gn RWIN SO21 ...... 185 P9
Manor Farm Gr CI ELGH SO50 * . 229 N2
Manor Farm La ROMY SO51 ...... 180 B5
Manor Farm Rd FBDG SP6 .... 239 P2
  NBNE BH10 .... 302 C9
  WEND SO18 .... 228 C9
Manor Farmyard CHAR BH8 ...... 323 P4
Manor Flds LIPH GU30 .... 175 L3
Manor Gdns RFNM GU10 .... 116 D5
  RGWD BH24 .... 282 E1
  VWD BH31 .... 258 F4
Manor House Av WSHM SO15 ..... 347 J5
Manor La CHIN RG24 .... 26 A4
  NWBY RC14 .... 25 H3
  VWD BH31 .... 258 F5
Manor Lodge Rd HAV PO9 .... 276 C1
Manor Ms CHAM P06 .... 297 L1
Manor Park Av HSEA PO3 .... 297 J9
Manor Park Dr TYLY GU46 ...... 40 E9
Manor Park Est ASHV GU12 * ... 3 H4
Manor Pl NWBY RC14 .... 26 A2
Manor Ri RAND SP11 .... 102 C6
Manor Rd ALDT GU11 .... 2 C6
  ALTN GU34 .... 132 G5
  AND SP10 .... 4 A2
  BMTH BH1 .... 8 A4
  BPWT SO32 .... 231 K5
  CHCH/BSGR BH23 .... 324 E9
  CHIN RG24 .... 69 H1
  ELGH SO50 .... 229 N2
  FARN GU14 .... 76 C1
  FAWY SO45 .... 267 L5
  FAWY SO45 .... 96 E7
  FNM GU9 .... 96 E7
  HISD PO11 .... 318 E4
  LYMN SO41 .... 328 D9
  NMIL/BTOS BH25 .... 327 K4
  PSEA PO1 .... 316 G1
  RFNM GU10 .... 97 M3
  RGWD BH24 .... 282 E2
  ROWN SO16 .... 227 P5
  RSAL SP5 .... 158 M8
  RWIN SO21 .... 185 P9
  VWD BH31 .... 258 F6
Manor Rd North ITCH SO19 ..... 248 G7
Manor Rd South ITCH SO19 ..... 248 G8
Manorside CI RFNM GU10 .... 97 M3
Manor Wk HISD PO11 .... 318 G6
  LSOL/BMARY PO13 ... 314 C2
  VWD BH31 .... 258 F3
Mans Br WEND SO18 .... 229 H8
Mansbridge Rd WEND SO18 ...... 229 H8
Manse La TADY RG26 .... 34 E8
Mansel CI BKME/WDN BH12 ...... 322 C8
Mansel Ct ROWN SO16 .... 247 J1
Mansell CI FAWY SO45 .... 290 A1
Mansell Dr NWBY RC14 .... 30 B1
Mansel West ROWN SO16 .... 247 H1
Mansfield CI FERN BH22 .... 302 D6
  PSTN BH14 .... 321 L8
Mansfield La BPWT SO32 .... 251 P7
Mansfield Rd BH/HW/K RG22 .... 90 A1
  LSOL/BMARY PO13 ... 294 G9
  MOOR/WNTN BH9 ..... 322 E8
  PSTN BH14 .... 321 L8
  RGWD BH24 .... 282 D2
Man's HI THLE RG7 .... 27 L4
Mansion Dr HTWY RG27 .... 54 G1
Mansion House St
  NWBY RC14 .... 16 D2
Mansion Rd ENEY PO4 .... 316 G7
  WSHM SO15 .... 247 P5
Mansvid Av CHAM P06 .... 297 K2
Mantle CI LSOL/BMARY PO13 .... 315 H1
Mantle Sq NEND PO2 .... 296 D7
Manton Rd PLE BH15 .... 320 A9
Maple CI ALTN GU34 .... 132 F4
  ASHV GU12 .... 76 E5
  BLKW GU17 .... 41 K9
  CHCH/BSGR BH23 .... 326 B8
  EMRTH PO10 .... 277 M8
  FHAM PO15 .... 272 M8
  LSOL/BMARY PO13 ... 314 D3
  NARL SO24 .... 167 P3
  NMIL/BTOS BH25 .... 327 K8
  PSEA PO1 .... 316 G1
  SHST GU47 .... 40 G5
Maple Crs BSTK RG21 .... 7 H1
  HORN PO8 .... 236 C6
  NWBY RC14 .... 24 D3
  RAND SP11 .... 80 B1
Maple Dr FERN BH22 .... 302 D6
  WINC SO23 .... 145 J8
  WVILLE PO7 .... 201 K1
  YTLY GU46 .... 40 E9
Maple Gdns TOTT SO40 .... 246 A5
  YTLY GU46 .... 40 E9
Maple Gv TADY RG26 .... 34 G6
Maplehurst Cha
  CHCH/BSGR BH23 .... 89 M5
Maple Leaf CI FARN GU14 ...... 75 N1
Maple Leaf Dr BOR GU35 .... 114 B6
Maple Ldg HASM GU27 * 157 K9
Maple Rd FAWY SO45 .... 290 D1
  MOOR/WNTN BH9 ..... 322 F7
  PLE BH15 .... 320 F9
  SSEA PO5 .... 316 E6
  WEND SO18 .... 248 G4
Maplespeen Ct NWBY RC14 ...... 24 C3
Maple Sq ELGH SO50 .... 228 G3
The Maples CHFD SO53 .... 206 E5
Maple Ter TDWTH SP9 * 79 J4
Mapleton Rd HEND SO30 .... 250 C5
Mapletree Av HORN PO8 .... 256 C6
Maple Wk AND SP10 .... 102 B4
ASHV GU12 .... 97 K3
Maple Wy BOR GU35 .... 155 J2
Maple Wd HAV PO9 .... 276 B9
Maplewood CI TOTT SO40 .... 246 A5
Maplin Rd ROWN SO16 .... 247 H1
Mapperton CI CFDH BH17 .... 321 H2
Marabout CI
  CHCH/BSGR BH23 .... 325 H8
Maralyn Av WVILLE PO7 .... 275 N4
Marathon PI ELGH SO50 .... 230 B2
Marazan Rd HSEA PO3 .... 297 K7
Marbrean CI FBDG SP6 .... 240 A1
Marchant CI STHA RG19 .... 24 C8
Marchant Rd AND SP10 .... 102 C3
March CI AND SP10 .... 5 F2
Marchwood By-Pass
  TOTT SO40 .... 246 E6
Marchwood Rd HAV PO9 .... 276 E4
  NBNE BH10 .... 322 C4
  TOTT SO40 .... 246 G7
Marchwood Ter TOTT SO40 * 247 K9
Marcus CI ELGH SO50 .... 230 B2
Mardale CBLY GU15 .... 59 H1
Mardale Rd ROWN SO16 .... 247 H3
Marden Wy EPSF GU31 .... 215 N2
Mardon CI WEND SO18 .... 228 G7
Mare La RWIN SO21 .... 184 E7
Mareth CI ALDT GU11 .... 3 C2
Margam Av ITCH SO19 .... 249 H6
Margards La WVILLE PO7 .... 275 M1
Margaret CI LSOL/BMARY PO13 .. 331 D5
Margaret Rd BH/HW/K RG22 ..... 68 G8
Margarita Rd FHAM PO15 .... 19 H4
Margate Rd SSEA PO5 .... 19 J5
Margery's Ct PSEA PO1 * 18 D3
Margha Rd TDWTH SP9 .... 78 G5
Marguerite CI FBDG SP6 .... 52 A2
Marianne Rd WSHM SO15 .... 247 K5
Marianne Rd
  BKME/WDN BH12 ..... 322 C7
  WIMB BH21 .... 279 J7
Marie Av RSAL SP5 .... 199 H6
Marie CI BKME/WDN BH12 .... 321 M5
Marie Rd ITCH SO19 .... 249 L8
Marigold CI BH/HW/K RG22 ..... 89 L3
  FHAM PO15 .... 10 A4
Marina CI EMRTH PO10 .... 299 N1
Marina Dr HLER SO31 .... 270 A8
  PSTN BH14 .... 333 K2
Marina Gv FHAM/PORC PO16 ..... 295 N3
  HSEA PO3 .... 317 K2
Marina Keep CHAM P06 .... 296 C2
The Marina BOSC BH5 .... 335 L3
Marine Ct ENEY PO4 .... 317 J6
Marine Dr NMIL/BTOS BH25 ..... 326 G8
Marine Dr East
  NMIL/BTOS BH25 .... 327 J9
Marine Dr West
  NMIL/BTOS BH25 .... 326 F8
Marine Pde SHAM SO14 .... 21 H5
Marine Pde East
  LSOL/BMARY PO13 ... 314 D4
Marine Pde West
  LSOL/BMARY PO13 ... 314 B1
Marine Prospect
  NMIL/BTOS BH25 .... 327 H8
Mariners Rd SBNE BH6 .... 336 B5
Mariners CI HLER SO31 .... 270 A6
Mariners Ct TADY RG26 .... 34 E8
Mariners Dr FARN GU14 .... 58 B6
  RGUW GU3 .... 77 N9
Mariners Ms FAWY SO45 .... 268 C6
Mariners Wk ENEY PO4 .... 317 K3
Mariners Wy GPORT PO12 .... 15 G4
  HLER SO31 .... 319 K5
Marine Wk HISD PO11 .... 319 K5
Marion Rd ENEY PO4 .... 316 G6
Maritime Av SToTT SO40 .... 247 K8
Maritime Wk SHAM SO14 .... 248 D9
Maritime Wy SHAM SO14 .... 248 B9
Marjoram CI FHAM GU14 .... 57 J9
Marjoram Crs HORN PO8 .... 256 B8
Marjoram Wy FHAM PO15 .... 271 K3
Markall CI NARL SO24 .... 187 H1
Mark CI HSEA PO3 .... 297 H5
Marken CI HLER SO31 .... 270 E7
Market CI PLE BH15 .... 332 E1
Market La WINC SO23 .... 22 E5
Market Pde HAV PO9 .... 15 F5
Market PI BSTK RG21 .... 7 F7
  CFDH BH17 .... 320 B5
  LSOL/BMARY PO13 ... 314 D1
Marketway PSEA PO1 .... 316 E2
Market Wy WIMB BH21 .... 300 F1
Markham Av HAV PO9 .... 322 D1
Markham CI NBNE BH10 .... 302 D9
Markham Rd
  MOOR/WNTN BH9 ..... 322 G7
Mark's La NMIL/BTOS BH25 ..... 327 J1
Marks Rd RWIN SO21 .... 144 D4
Mark's Rd FHAM/STUB PO14 ..... 294 C7
Marks Rd MOOR/WNTN BH9 .... 322 F7
Marks Tey Rd
  FHAM/STUB PO14 .... 294 A4
Mark Wy ROMY SO51 .... 178 D3
Markway CI EMRTH PO10 .... 277 K9
Marlborough CI FLEETN GU51 ... 74 C4
  WVILLE PO7 .... 275 M5
Marlborough Ct FAWY SO45 ..... 268 A8
Marlborough Gdns DEAN RG23 ... 88 F1
  HEND SO30 .... 230 C9
Marlborough Gv
  FHAM/PORC PO16 .... 295 N2
Marlborough Pk HAV PO9 .... 277 H7
Marlborough PI LYMN SO41 ..... 329 K2
  WIMB BH21 .... 278 F9
Marlborough Rd CHFD SO53 ..... 206 G4
  GPORT PO12 .... 315 K2
  PSTN BH14 .... 321 L8
  ROWN SO16 .... 247 N3
  WBNE BH4 .... 334 C3
Marlborough Rw PSEA PO1 ...... 18 D1
Marlborough St SHAM SO14 ..... 21 F3
Marlborough Vw FARN GU14 ..... 57 K8
Maridell CI HAV PO9 .... 276 C5
Marles CI LSOL/BMARY PO13 .... 315 H1
Marley Av NMIL/BTOS BH25 ..... 326 C5
Marley Rd NMIL/BTOS BH25 ..... 327 H4
Marley Combe Rd
  HASM GU27 .... 156 E8
Marley La HASM GU27 .... 156 D8
Marlhill CI WEND SO18 .... 249 H1
Marlin CI LSOL/BMARY PO13 .... 315 H2
Marline Rd BKME/WDN BH12 ..... 321 M6
Marl La FBDG SP6 .... 220 A9
Marlott Rd PLE BH15 .... 320 E7
Marlow CI FHAM PO15 .... 272 C6
Marlow Dr CHCH/BSGR BH23 ..... 324 C4
Marlowe CI CHIN RG24 .... 49 H8
Marlowe Ct WVILLE PO7 .... 275 M1
The Marlowes NWBY RC14 .... 24 C7
Marlow Rd BPWT SO32 .... 231 N3
Marlpit Dr CHCH/BSGR BH23 .... 326 C5
Marlpit La NMIL/BTOS BH25 .... 307 J8
Marls La CHIN RG24 .... 49 H3
Maris Rd HEND SO30 .... 250 E5
Marmion Av BH/HW/K RG22 ...... 89 M7
Marmion Gn
  CHCH/BSGR BH23 .... 325 K8
Marmion Rd SSEA PO5 .... 316 D6
Marne Rd WEND SO18 .... 249 J4
Marnhull Ri FUFL SO22 .... 164 D8
Marnhull Rd PLE BH15 .... 320 F8
Marpet CI BWD BH11 .... 301 P7
Marples Wy HAV PO9 .... 14 C6
Marquis Wy BWD BH11 .... 301 M8
Marram CI LYMN SO41 .... 329 L1
Marrels Wood Gdns
  WVILLE PO7 .... 275 L6
Marrowbrook La FARN GU14 ..... 75 P1
Marrow Meade FLEETN GU51 ..... 74 B1
Marryat Rd NMIL/BTOS BH25 .... 327 H4
Marsden CI WHCH RG28 .... 86 C5
Marsden Rd WEND SO18 .... 296 D1
Marshal CI FARN GU14 .... 132 E7
Marshall La FARN GU14 .... 57 N6
Marshall Rd HISD PO11 .... 319 J6
Marshall Sq AND SP11 .... 82 G9
Marshals Ct NWBY RC14 .... 24 A2
Marshal Wy HEND SO30 .... 249 P2
Marsh CI BOR GU35 .... 154 C5
Marsh Gdns HEND SO30 .... 230 C9
Marshlands CI
  CHCH/BSGR BH23 .... 325 H9
Marshlands Rd CHAM P06 .... 297 M2
Marsh La CHCH/BSGR BH23 ...... 324 D5
  ELGH SO50 .... 291 K5
  FBDG SP6 .... 220 E4
  HTWY RG27 .... 40 A7
  LYMN SO41 .... 329 J4
  NWBY RC14 .... 16 E1
  SHAM SO14 .... 21 F5
Marsh Rd NTHA RG18 .... 25 P3
The Marsh FAWY SO45 .... 268 C5
Marshwood Av CFDH BH17 .... 321 H2
  WVILLE PO7 .... 202 B2
Marston CI NMIL/BTOS BH25 .... 327 K2
Marston Dr FARN GU14 .... 58 A6
Marston Ga WINC SO23 .... 22 G2
Marston Gv CHCH/BSGR BH23 .... 326 A6
Marston La HSEA PO3 .... 297 K8
Marston Rd FNM GU9 .... 95 P3
  ITCH SO19 .... 249 M6
  NMIL/BTOS BH25 .... 327 K2
  PLE BH15 .... 332 D1
Marsum CI AND SP10 .... 82 D7
Martello CI GPORT PO12 .... 315 H5
Martello Pk CCLF BH13 .... 333 P4
Martello Rd CCLF BH13 .... 333 N7
The Martells NMIL/BTOS BH25 .. 327 K8
Martin Av FHAM/STUB PO14 ..... 294 B7
  WVILLE PO7 .... 255 J7
Martin CI BPWT SO32 .... 232 B5
  BSTK RG21 .... 7 H1
  CFDH BH17 .... 320 B5
  LSOL/BMARY PO13 ... 314 D1
Martindale Av CBLY GU15 ...... 59 H2
Martingale CI HLER SO31 ...... 269 K9
Martingale CI ALDT GU11 ...... 2 A3
Martin Rd FHAM/STUB PO14 ..... 294 A7
  HAV PO9 .... 276 D6
  HSEA PO3 .... 297 J8
Martins CI ALTN GU34 .... 132 G4
  BLKW GU17 .... 57 L1
  FERN BH22 .... 302 E1
Martins Fids HWIN SO21 .... 183 L5
Martins Hill CI
  CHCH/BSGR BH23 .... 324 G6
Martins Hill La
  CHCH/BSGR BH23 .... 324 G6
Martins La STON SO20 .... 159 J1
Martins Pk FERN BH22 .... 157 L6
Martins Ri RSAL SP5 .... 201 H1
Martin St BROC SO42 .... 286 G7
The Martins ELGH SO50 .... 230 D3
Martin Wy BPWT SO32 .... 231 P5
Martins Wy FERN BH22 .... 302 E1
Martins Wd CHIN RG24 .... 70 A1
Martley Gdns HEND SO30 .... 250 C1
Marvic CI HAV PO9 .... 276 A4
Marvin Wy HEND SO30 .... 250 E4
  WEND SO18 .... 249 L5
Marwell CI LTDN BH7 .... 323 N8
Marwell Rd FLEETN GU51 .... 55 P9
Maryat Wy FHAM PO15 .... 271 J1
Marybridge CI TOTT SO40 ...... 246 C5
Maryfield SHAM SO14 .... 21 G4
Maryland Gdns WEND SO18 ...... 229 H9
Maryland Gdns LYMN SO41 ...... 338 E2
Mary La ALTN GU34 .... 150 G8
  ENEY PO4 .... 280 D7
  OVTN RG25 .... 88 C9
Mary Rose CI FHAM PO15 .... 10 A1
The Mary Rose St PSEA PO1 * .. 19 G3
Masefield Av CHAM P06 .... 274 B9
Masefield CI ELGH SO50 .... 230 B2
Masefield Crs HORN PO8 .... 255 P8
Masefield Gn ITCH SO19 .... 249 M5
Masefield Rd NTHA RG18 .... 25 M3
Maskell Wy FARN GU14 .... 75 K1
Mason CI BH/HW/K RG22 .... 68 M7
Mason CI YTLY GU46 .... 40 C8
Mason PI SHST GU47 .... 40 G6
Mason Rd FARN GU14 .... 57 M7
Masons Yd WINC SO23 * 22 D5
Mason Wy ALDT GU11 .... 97 H4
Masseys La BROC SO42 .... 288 C4
Masten Crs
  LSOL/BMARY PO13 ... 294 G9
Masterson CI
  CHCH/BSGR BH23 .... 325 H8
Matapan Rd NEND PO2 .... 296 F5
Matcham CI RGWD BH24 .... 303 P1
Matchams La
  CHCH/BSGR BH23 .... 303 P7
Matchlock Ms NWBY RC14 * 24 C3
Matheson Rd ROWN SO16 .... 227 K6
Mathews Ter ALDT GU11 * 3 H2
Mathias Wk BH/HW/K RG22 ...... 89 M4
Matilda Dr BH/HW/K RG22 ...... 89 M4
Matilda PI WINC SO23 * 23 F3
Matley Gdns TOTT SO40 .... 245 P4
Matlock Rd FARN GU14 .... 302 C5
Matthew Rd ALDT GU11 .... 96 B3
Matthews CI HAV PO9 .... 276 C7
  STHA RG19 .... 25 L4
Matthews La BROC SO42 .... 310 C2
Matthews PI WVILLE PO7 .... 275 N5
Matthews Wy DEAN RG23 .... 88 E2
Mattock Wy CHIN RG24 .... 49 K5
Maturin CI LYMN SO41 .... 329 K4
The Maulways CBLY GU15 .... 59 J1
Maundeville Crs
  CHCH/BSGR BH23 .... 324 C7
Maundeville Rd
  CHCH/BSGR BH23 .... 324 C7
Maunsell Wy HEND SO30 .... 230 C9
Maureen CI BKME/WDN BH12 ..... 321 K4
Maurepas Wy WVILLE PO7 .... 275 M3
Mauretania Rd ROWN SO16 ...... 227 H4
Maury's La WINC SO23 * 144 H4
Maury La ROMY SO51 .... 224 D1
Mavins Rd FNM GU9 .... 116 D2
Mavis Crs HAV PO9 .... 15 F4
Maw CI BH/HW/K RG22 .... 89 M3
Maxine CI SHST GU47 .... 41 J5
Maxstoke CI SSEA PO5 .... 19 J5
Maxwell Rd CCLF BH13 .... 333 P4
  ENEY PO4 .... 317 J5
  ITCH SO19 .... 249 J8
  MOOR/WNTN BH9 ..... 322 G8
May Av LYMN SO41 .... 329 J4
Mayray King Wy
  WEND SO18 .... 249 J4
Maybrick CI SHST GU47 .... 40 G5
Maybrook Rd CFDH BH17 .... 52 A9
Maybury CI FRIM GU16 .... 58 D4
May Bush La BPWT SO32 .... 253 M2
Maybush Rd ROWN SO16 .... 247 J1
Mayc CI BOR GU35 .... 154 F4
  CHIN RG24 .... 70 D6
  FAWY SO45 .... 41 L6
  SHST GU47 .... 41 L6
May Copse FAWY SO45 .... 290 F1
May Crs ASHV GU12 .... 97 J4
  FAWY SO45 .... 290 F6
Maycrete Rd
  CHCH/BSGR BH23 .... 303 K7
Mayday Ct TOTT SO40 .... 246 E4
Maydman Sq HSEA PO3 .... 317 J2
Mayfair Dr WEND SO18 .... 250 G4
Mayfair Gdns BWD BH11 .... 322 A3
Mayfair Gdns WSHM SO15 .... 347 J1
Mayfield RFNM GU10 .... 115 P7
Mayfield Av FERN BH22 .... 302 C2
  TOTT SO40 .... 246 C5
Mayfield CI FERN BH22 .... 302 C2
  FHAM/STUB PO14 .... 294 E7
  FNM GU9 .... 97 H5
  TDWTH SP9 .... 78 G3
Mayfield Dr FERN BH22 .... 302 C2
Mayfield Rdg BH/HW/K RG22 .... 89 M6
Mayfield Rd FARN GU14 .... 58 B4
  FBDG SP6 .... 240 A1
  GPORT PO12 .... 15 F1
  MOOR/WNTN BH9 ..... 322 G5
  NEND PO2 .... 296 C2
  SD/PW SO17 .... 149 H6
Mayfield Wy FERN BH22 .... 302 C2
Mayflower CI CHFD SO53 .... 206 E7
  CHIN RG24 .... 69 P2
  FERN BH22 .... 302 E1
  LYMN SO41 .... 329 N4
Mayflower Dr YTLY GU46 .... 40 E7
Mayflower Rd BOR GU35 .... 153 P8
  WSHM SO15 .... 247 N3
Mayflower Rbt SHAM SO14 ...... 20 C7
The Mayflowers ROWN SO16 ..... 228 C8
Mayfly CI FBDG SP6 .... 240 D1
Mayford Rd BKME/WDN BH12 ..... 322 B9
May Gdns BWD BH11 .... 321 N1
  CHCH/BSGR BH23 .... 326 D5
Mayhall Rd HSEA PO3 .... 297 J8
Mayhill La BPWT SO32 .... 233 H5
Maylands Av ENEY PO4 .... 317 J4
Maylands Rd HAV PO9 .... 276 B8
May La LYMN SO41 .... 309 N7
May Rd WSHM SO15 .... 247 N4
Mayles CI FERN BH22 .... 252 E8
Mayles Cnr WHAM PO17 .... 272 B2
Mayles La WHAM PO17 .... 272 C1
Mayles Rd ENEY PO4 .... 317 K3
Maylings Farm Rd
  FHAM/PORC PO16 .... 10 D2
Maynard CI
  LSOL/BMARY PO13 ... 294 C5
  NTHA RG18 .... 25 M2
Maynard PI HORN PO8 .... 256 D5
Maynard Rd TOTT SO40 .... 246 D4
Maynard's Wd CHIN RG24 .... 69 P2
Mayo CI PSEA PO1 .... 316 F1
Mayors La NWBY RC14 .... 16 E5
May PI BSTK RG21 .... 7 F7
Mayridge FHAM/STUB PO14 ...... 271 J7
May Rd WSHM SO15 .... 247 N4
Mays Firs FBDG SP6 .... 222 B2
Mays La FHAM/STUB PO14 .... 294 B5
May Tree CI FUFL SO22 .... 183 L2
Maytree CI HLER SO31 .... 270 C7
Maytree Gdns HORN PO8 .... 255 N8
May Tree Rd AND SP10 .... 82 G6
Maytree Rd CHFD SO53 .... 206 E3
  FHAM/PORC PO16 .... 10 E6
  HORN PO8 .... 255 N8
Mayvale CI TOTT SO40 .... 267 K1
McCartney Wk BH/HW/K RG22 .... 89 N4
McFauld Wy WHCH RG28 .... 85 C1
McIntyre Rd
  CHCH/BSGR BH23 .... 303 N8
McKay CI ALDT GU11 .... 3 J1
McKinley Rd WBNE BH4 .... 334 C4
Mc Naughton CI FARN GU14 ..... 75 K1
McWilliam CI
  BKME/WDN BH12 ..... 322 C7
McWilliam Rd
  MOOR/WNTN BH9 ..... 322 G5
Mead CI FBDG SP6 .... 240 C1
Meacher CI TOTT SO40 .... 246 C3
Meadbrooke Gdns CHFD SO53 .... 206 E7
Mead CI AND SP10 .... 4 A6
  BDST BH18 .... 320 C3
  ROMY SO51 .... 204 F6
Mead Crs WEND SO18 .... 228 F9
Meadcroft CI HLER SO31 .... 292 D1
Meadend CI HAV PO9 .... 277 H3
Mead End Rd LYMN SO41 .... 307 P6
  WVILLE PO7 .... 255 J8
Meade Rd RAND SP11 .... 80 A1
Mead Gdns HTWY RG27 .... 54 G6
Meadham La OVTN RG25 .... 71 P2
Mead Hatchgate HTWY RG27 ..... 71 P2
Mead Hawks LISS GU33 .... 192 C1
Mead Hedges AND SP10 .... 102 C4
Mead La FNM GU9 .... 116 B1
Meadow Av HLER SO31 .... 270 G6
Meadow Bank FNM GU14 .... 116 E1
Meadowbank RWIN SO21 .... 185 K8
Meadowbank Rd FHAM PO15 ...... 272 B9
Meadow CI ASHV GU12 .... 76 E3
  BLKW GU17 .... 57 L1
  BPWT SO32 .... 232 B8
  FBDG SP6 .... 240 C1
  FERN BH22 .... 302 D7
  HEND SO30 .... 249 N1
  HISD PO11 .... 298 F6
  LIPH GU30 .... 175 K3
  NARL SO24 .... 188 C9
  NEAD SO22 .... 227 L1
  RCWD BH24 .... 260 F9
  RGWD BH24 .... 284 B2
  ROMY SO51 .... 202 F9
  STHA RG19 .... 25 M4
  TOTT SO40 .... 246 D6
Meadow Court CI
  MOOR/WNTN BH9 ..... 322 G4
Meadowcroft CI RWIN SO21 ..... 207 L2
Meadow Dr RAND SP11 .... 71 P2
Meadow Edge WVILLE PO7 .... 275 K8
Meadow Gdns BPWT SO32 .... 232 C8
Meadow Gate Av FARN GU14 ..... 75 N2
Meadow Gv WVD BH31 .... 259 H5
Meadowhead Rd ROWN SO16 ...... 228 B9
Meadowland
  CHCH/BSGR BH23 .... 325 J9
  CHIN RG24 .... 69 P1
  WINC SO23 .... 145 J9
Meadow Lands PSF GU32 .... 215 L2
Meadowlands HAV PO9 .... 257 J6
  HAV PO9 .... 257 J8
  LYMN SO41 .... 329 J3
  RGWD BH24 .... 282 F6
Meadow La CHCH/BSGR BH23 ..... 324 C5
  ELGH SO50 .... 229 J2
  HLER SO31 .... 270 A8
  HTWY RG27 .... 55 H7
Meadowmead Av
  WSHM SO15 .... 247 L4
Meadowridge BH/HW/K RG22 ..... 89 N6
Meadow Ri BDST BH18 .... 300 B8
  HORN PO8 .... 236 D1
  OVTN RG25 .... 108 D1
Meadow Rd BSTK RG21 .... 90 C2
  FARN GU14 .... 58 A6
  LYMN SO41 .... 329 J5
  NMIL/BTOS BH25 .... 327 K3
  RGWD BH24 .... 282 F1
Meadowside CI WEND SO18 ...... 228 G8
The Meadows
  FHAM/PORC PO16 .... 11 J1

HTWY RG27 ... 52 E4
LYND SO43 ... 264 C6
RFNM GU10 ... 136 F8
Meadow St SSEA PO5 * ... 19 F6
Meadowsweet HORN PO8 ... 276 B1
Meadowsweet Cl NTHA RG18 ... 25 P3
Meadowsweet Rd CFDH BH17 ... 320 A4
Meadowsweet Wy CHAM PO6 ... 274 F9
ELGH SO50 ... 230 C6
Meadow Ter
FHAM/PORC PO16 * ... 11 F5
The Meadow ROMY SO51 ... 204 D4
WVILLE PO7 ... 255 H7
Meadow V HASM GU27 ... 185 J7
Meadow Vw BOR GU35 ... 154 B5
FLEETS GU52 ... 74 B7
RAND SP11 * ... 81 H9
WHCH RG28 ... 85 K6
Meadowview Cl RAND SP11 * ... 79 M5
Meadow View Rd BWD BH11 ... 268 F7
Meadow Wk LISS GU33 ... 192 D2
LSOL/BMARY PO13 ... 294 F4
Meadow Wy AND SP10 ... 102 B2
ASHV GU12 ... 76 E9
BLKW GU17 ... 41 K9
FAWY SO45 ... 291 K6
FUFL SO22 ... 183 L2
LIPH GU30 ... 175 K2
NMIL/BTOS BH25 ... 327 J8
RFNM GU10 ... 115 P7
RGWD BH24 ... 282 F1
WHCH RG28 ... 259 H6
Mead Rd AND SP10 ... 4 A6
CHFD SO53 ... 206 E7
GSHT GU26 ... 156 E1
LYMN SO41 ... 339 H5
WINC SO23 ... 183 N2
The Meads CHFD SO53 ... 206 B6
HASM GU27 ... 156 E7
ROMY SO51 ... 204 B6
The Mead CHIN RG24 ... 70 C6
FARN GU14 * ... 76 A1
FAWY SO45 ... 291 L6
LIPH GU30 ... 175 J2
LISS GU33 ... 192 D2
PSF GU32 ... 215 K3
Mead Wy FHAM/PORC PO16 ... 11 G2
Meadway FRIM GU16 ... 58 F2
HASM GU27 ... 156 E7
WVILLE PO7 ... 255 M1
The Meadway
CHCH/BSGR BH23 ... 325 P5
The Mearings
RDCW/BURGH RG30 ... 27 N3
Mears Rd ELGH SO50 ... 230 D2
Meath Cl HISD PO11 ... 319 J7
Mede Cl OVTN RG25 ... 87 H4
Medina Cl CHFD SO53 ... 206 G8
Medina Gdns DEAN RG23 ... 88 F2
Medina Rd CHAM PO6 ... 296 F1
WSHM SO15 ... 247 M2
Medina Wy CHCH/BSGR BH23 ... 325 N9
Medlar Cl CHCH/BSGR BH23 ... 325 H6
HEND SO30 ... 250 D5
Medlar Dr BLKW GU17 ... 57 N2
Medlicott Wy BPWT SO32 ... 232 F8
Medonte Cl FLEETN GU51 ... 74 E4
Medstead Rd ALTN GU34 ... 132 A7
HAV PO9 ... 15 F1
Medwall Gn ITCH SO19 ... 249 M6
Medway Av DEAN RG23 ... 88 F1
Medway Cl NTHA RG18 ... 25 L2
Medway Ct AND SP10 ... 82 C8
BSTK RG21 ... 7 K6
Medway Dr CHFD SO53 ... 206 C5
FARN GU14 ... 57 M6
Medway Rd FERN BH22 ... 302 G2
Meerut Rd BROC SO42 ... 286 F7
TDWTH SP9 ... 78 G5

ROWN SO16 ... 247 K3
VWD BH31 ... 258 F4
Mendips Rd
FHAM/STUB PO14 ... 294 B1
Mendips Wk
FHAM/STUB PO14 ... 294 B1
Mengham Av HISD PO11 ... 318 C6
Mengham La HISD PO11 ... 318 C5
Mengham Rd HISD PO11 ... 318 C5
Merlin Wy FNM GU9 ... 116 D1
Menslands La WVILLE PO7 ... 254 B3
Mentone Rd PSTN BH14 ... 321 J9
Menzies Cl ROWN SO21 ... 227 K7
Meon Cl CFARN GU14 ... 57 L7
HORN PO8 ... 256 C8
LSOL/BMARY PO13 ... 294 F7
PSF GU32 ... 215 L1
ROMY SO51 ... 204 C6
TADY RG26 ... 34 B5
Meon Ct WEND SO18 ... 249 M3
Meon Crs CHFD SO53 ... 206 F7
Meon Rd DEAN RG23 ... 88 F2
ENEY PO4 ... 317 J4
LTDN BH7 ... 323 P8
Meon Wk BSTK RG21 * ... 7 H6
Meonwara Crs PSF GU32 ... 188 F9
Mercer Cl BH/HW/K RG22 ... 88 C8
Mercer Wy ROMY SO51 ... 204 D5
Merchants Pl WINC SO23 ... 23 F4
Merchants Wk SHAM SO14 ... 20 C7
Merchistoun Rd HORN PO8 ... 256 B5
Mercia Av AND SP10 ... 82 B8
Mercury Cl BOR GU35 ... 154 B5
ROWN SO16 ... 227 K8
Mercury Gdns HLER SO31 ... 270 A6
Mercury Pl WVILLE PO7 ... 275 N8
Merdon Av CHFD SO53 ... 206 F5
Merdon Cl CHFD SO53 ... 206 F5
Mere Cft FHAM PO15 ... 271 K7
Meredith Cl CHCH/BSGR BH23 ... 325 H8
Meredith Gdns TOTT SO40 ... 246 B5
Meredith Rd NEND PO2 ... 296 D2
Merepond La ALTN GU34 ... 189 L3
Merganser Cl GPORT PO12 ... 315 M1
Meriden Cl CCLF BH13 ... 333 P4
Meriden Pk AND SP10 ... 82 E9
The Meridians
CHCH/BSGR BH23 ... 336 D1
Merino Wy FLEETN GU51 ... 74 A4
Merivale Cl FAWY SO45 ... 268 F8
Merlewood Cl WCLF BH2 ... 8 D1
Merley Dr CHCH/BSGR BH23 ... 326 C7
Merley Gdns WIMB BH21 ... 300 C4
Merley La WIMB BH21 ... 300 A5
Merley Park Rd WIMB BH21 ... 300 A5
Merleys Wy WIMB BH21 ... 300 F2
Merlin Cl AND SP10 ... 82 E8
BPWT SO32 ... 251 P4
HORN PO8 ... 255 N7
RGWD BH24 ... 282 C3
Merlin Dr HSEA PO3 ... 297 J3
Merlin Gdns
FHAM/PORC PO16 ... 273 M9
NEND SO30 ... 250 B4
Merlin Md BH/HW/K RG22 ... 89 K5
Merlin Pl ALTN GU34 ... 132 A3
Merlins Cl FNM GU9 ... 116 C1
Merlin Wy CHCH/BSGR BH23 ... 337 L1
CFDH SO53 ... 206 B6
FARN GU14 ... 75 L1

Metcalfe Av
FHAM/STUB PO14 ... 294 B6
Meteor Rd EMRTH PO10 ... 299 N6
Meteor Wy FARN GU14 ... 75 P3
Methuen Cl CHAR BH8 ... 335 J1
Methuen Rd CFDH BH17 ... 320 D2
CHAR BH8 ... 335 H1
ENEY PO4 ... 317 J5
LISS GU33 ... 173 P4
Methuen St SHAM SO14 ... 248 C4
Metuchen Wy HEND SO30 ... 250 C7
Meudon Av FARN GU14 ... 76 A1
Mews Ct RWIN SO21 ... 207 K2
Mewsey Ct HAV PO9 ... 276 D5
Mews La FUFL SO22 ... 22 B5
The Mews AND SP10 ... 5 F7
CHFD SO53 * ... 228 E1
EPSF GU31 * ... 215 N1
FAWY SO45 ... 313 H1
HORN PO8 ... 276 E6
ROWN SO16 ... 227 K6
TADY RG26 ... 52 C3
WVILLE PO7 ... 258 C6
Mey Cl WVILLE PO7 ... 275 P3
Meynell Cl ELGH SO50 ... 229 H1
Meyrick Cl CHCH/BSGR BH23 ... 325 K8
Meyrick Dr NWBY RG14 ... 30 B1
Meyrick Park Crs TWDS BH3 ... 322 F9
Meyrick Rd BMTH BH1 ... 9 H3
HAV PO9 ... 14 C5
NEND PO2 ... 296 E8
Michael Crook Cl HAV PO9 ... 276 C7
Michaelmas Cl YTLY GU46 ... 56 E1
Michaelmas Dro RAND SP11 ... 81 H9
Michaelmas Rd CHAR BH8 ... 323 K5
Michigan Wy TOTT SO40 ... 245 P3
Mickleham Cl
BKME/WDN BH12 ... 322 B7
Mickle Hl SHST GU47 ... 41 H5
Midanbury Broadway
WEND SO18 ... 249 J1
Midanbury Crs WEND SO18 ... 249 H2
Midanbury La WEND SO18 ... 248 G3
Midanbury Rd WEND SO18 ... 249 H3
Midas Cl WVILLE PO7 ... 275 P3
Middle Av HAV PO9 ... 116 D2
Middle Bourne La RFNM GU10 ... 116 B9
Middlebridge St ROMY SO51 ... 204 C7
Middlebrook BPWT SO32 ... 232 A4
Middle Church La FNM GU9 * ... 96 B9
Middle Brook St WINC SO23 ... 23 F5
Middle Common Rd
LYMN SO41 ... 328 G4
Middlecroft La GPORT PO12 ... 315 K2
Middlefield Cl FNM GU9 ... 116 A3
Middlefield Cl WIMB BH21 ... 116 A2
Middlehill Dr WIMB BH21 ... 279 K8
Middlehill Rd WIMB BH21 ... 279 J7
Middle La RGWD BH24 ... 282 E2
Middle Md FHAM/STUB PO14 ... 295 H7
HTWY RG27 ... 71 P2
Middle Meadow LISS GU33 ... 192 D2
Middlemoor Rd FRIM GU16 ... 58 D5
Middle Old Pk FNM GU9 ... 95 P7
Middle Park Wy HAV PO9 ... 276 C6
Middle Rd FUFL SO22 ... 22 B3
HLER SO31 ... 271 H5
ITCH SO19 ... 249 J8
LYMN SO41 ... 307 M8
LYMN SO41 ... 329 K4
NBAD SO52 ... 205 L8
NBNE BH10 ... 322 C2
PLE BH15 ... 320 G6
Middleton Rd ENEY PO4 ... 317 J5
Middle St CCLF BH13 ... 332 F6
SHAM SO14 ... 248 C4
SSEA PO5 ... 19 G4
Middleton RSAL SP5 ... 158 A1
Middleton Cl
FHAM/STUB PO14 ... 294 C2
WEND SO18 ... 249 J1
Middleton Ct NWBY RG14 ... 25 H2
FARN GU14 ... 57 M7
Middleton Ms
NMIL/BTOS BH25 ... 327 H6
Middleton Park Farm
RAND SP11 * ... 104 B4
Middleton Ri HORN PO8 * ... 236 D8
Middleton Rd
MOOR/WNTN BH9 ... 322 E5
RGWD BH24 ... 282 E1
RSAL SP5 ... 138 G9
The Middleway RAND SP11 ... 103 M2
Midhurst Rd HASM GU27 ... 156 G8
LIPH GU30 ... 175 K3
Midland Rd MOOR/WNTN BH9 ... 322 F6
Midlands Est HEND SO30 ... 249 L1
Midlane Cl BSTK RG21 ... 90 C1
Midlington Hl BPWT SO32 ... 233 L5
Midlington Rd BPWT SO32 ... 233 L5
Midway FAWY SO45 ... 268 F7
Midway Rd NEND PO2 ... 296 G4
Midways FHAM/STUB PO14 ... 294 A8
Midwood Av CHAR BH8 ... 323 K7
Mike Hawthorn Dr FNM GU9 * ... 96 C8
Milbeck Cl HORN PO8 ... 256 A8
Milbourne Crs
BKME/WDN BH12 ... 321 N5
Milbourne Rd FERN BH22 ... 302 C2
Milburn Cl WBNE BH4 ... 334 C2
Milburn Rd WBNE BH4 ... 334 D2
The Milburns ROMY SO51 ... 180 B1
Milbury Crs ITCH SO19 ... 249 M4
Milbury Cl FRIM GU16 ... 58 F7

Milden Gdns FRIM GU16 ... 58 F7
Mildmay St FUFL SO22 ... 93 L1
Mildmay Ct ODIM RG29 ... 93 L1
Milebush Rd ENEY PO4 ... 317 L3
Mile End Rd PSEA PO1 ... 316 E1
Miles Rd ASHV GU12 ... 76 G9
Miles's La RSAL SP5 ... 177 L7
Milestone Rd PLE BH15 ... 320 E8
Milford Cl FERN BH22 ... 280 F7
HAV PO9 ... 14 B1
Milford Ct LYMN SO41 ... 339 H2
Milford Crs LYMN SO41 ... 339 H2
Milford Dr BWD BH11 ... 301 P8
Milford Gdns LYMN SO41 ... 339 H2
Milford Rd LYMN SO41 ... 339 H2
Milford Rd LYMN SO41 ... 328 F6
NMIL/BTOS BH25 ... 327 L8
PSEA PO1 ... 19 J2
Military Dr STHA RG19 ... 25 P5
Military Rd FHAM/PORC PO16 ... 11 P6
GPORT PO12 ... 315 J4
HSEA PO3 ... 297 H4
PSEA PO1 ... 316 D1
Milkingpen La CHIN RG24 ... 70 C5
Milkwood Ct TOTT SO40 ... 245 P4
Millais Cl FHAM/STUB PO14 ... 294 B6
Milland La LIPH GU30 ... 175 H9
Milland Rd WINC SO23 ... 165 J9
Millard Cl BSTK RG21 ... 6 B1
Millbank St ITCH SO19 ... 21 K1
Millbridge Gdns ITCH SO19 ... 249 K7
Millbrook Cl CHFD SO53 ... 206 D8
LISS GU33 ... 192 E2
Millbrook Dr HAV PO9 ... 276 C4
Millbrook Point Rd
WSHM SO15 ... 247 L5
Millbrook Rd West
WSHM SO15 ... 247 J4
Mill Chase Rd BOR GU35 ... 154 B5
Mill Cl HASM GU27 ... 156 D7
HISD PO11 ... 298 F7
ROWN SO16 ... 227 K8
WVILLE PO7 ... 255 K7
Mill Copse Rd HASM GU27 ... 156 C9
Mill Cnr FLEETN GU51 ... 56 F8
Mill Ct ELGH SO50 ... 230 D2
FBDG SP6 ... 240 C2
Mill End PLE BH15 ... 219 K8
FBDG SP6 ... 219 K8
Millennium Ct BSTK RG21 ... 6 A6
Miller Cl NMIL/BTOS BH25 ... 327 L3
Miller Dr FHAM/PORC PO16 ... 10 C1
Miller La FUFL SO22 ... 21 J5
Millers Cl NMIL/BTOS BH25 ... 327 H8
Millers La FUFL SO22 ... 183 L2
Miller's Pond Gdns ITCH SO19 ... 249 H8
Millers Rd YTLY GU46 ... 34 C6
Millers Yd RWIN SO21 ... 125 L5
Millfield CFDH BH17 ... 320 C5
Millgreen La STHA RG19 ... 32 C4
Millhams Cl NBNE BH10 ... 322 B1
Millhams Rd BWD BH11 ... 302 A9
Millhams St CHCH/BSGR BH23 ... 325 L6
Millhams St North
CHCH/BSGR BH23 ... 324 F9
Mill HI HEND SO30 ... 250 C4
NARL SO24 ... 145 P9
Mill Hill Av TDWTH SP9 ... 78 C5
Mill Hill Cl FHAM/STUB PO14 ... 295 H1
Mill La ALTN GU34 ... 188 A9
Mill La FUFL SO22 ... 94 A2
Mill La LYMN SO41 ... 339 K1
BOR GU35 ... 154 D4
BPWT SO32 ... 231 K9
BROC SO42 ... 233 M2
CHCH/BSGR BH23 ... 325 P1
CHCH/BSGR BH23 ... 326 D7
EMRTH PO10 ... 277 P8
EPSF GU31 ... 217 P5
FHAM PO15 ... 272 A8
HASM GU27 ... 157 H9
HAV PO9 ... 14 A6
HTWY RG27 ... 53 J6
KSCL RG20 ... 47 M1
LISS GU33 ... 172 E7
LYMN SO41 ... 308 E9
LYMN SO41 ... 329 M3
LYND SO43 ... 244 E9
NARL SO24 ... 168 D2
NWBY RG14 ... 17 F2
PSF GU32 ... 215 L6
RAND SP11 ... 104 E5
RFNM GU10 ... 136 B2
RGWD BH24 ... 284 E4
RWIN SO21 ... 124 E3
THLE RG7 ... 36 D9
WHAM PO17 ... 252 E6
WIMB BH21 ... 203 L8
WIMB BH21 ... 278 D9
WVILLE PO7 ... 274 G6
YTLY GU46 ... 40 E7
Mill Meadow LYMN SO41 ... 338 F1
Millmere YTLY GU46 ... 40 D9
Mill Pond Rd GPORT PO12 ... 315 M2
The Mill Pond FAWY SO45 ... 291 L2
Mill Quay EMRTH PO10 ... 299 N2
Mill Reef Cl STHA RG19 ... 25 J4
Mill Rd CHCH/BSGR BH23 ... 324 F7
CHIN RG24 ... 68 F4
EMRTH PO10 ... 277 P6
FHAM/PORC PO16 ... 294 E1
GPORT PO12 ... 315 M2
LISS GU33 ... 192 E1
NMIL/BTOS BH25 ... 327 H4
TOTT SO40 ... 246 E4
WVILLE PO7 ... 255 M4

Mill Road (North) CHAR BH8 ... 323 K4
Mill Road (South) CHAR BH8 ... 323 K5
Mill Rythe La HISD PO11 ... 318 C1
Mills Rd NEND PO2 ... 296 E3
The Mills BKME/WDN BH12 ... 321 N5
Mill Stream Ferry FNM GU9 ... 96 E5
Millstream Cl AND SP10 ... 102 D4
CFDH BH17 ... 320 C5
ENEY PO4 ... 317 M2
WIMB BH21 ... 203 L5
Millstream Ri ROMY SO51 ... 204 B6
The Millstream HASM GU27 ... 156 D8
Mill St FHAM/STUB PO14 ... 293 N1
Millview ODIM RG29 ... 92 F1
Millvina Cl TOTT SO40 ... 245 M7
Mill Wy TOTT SO40 ... 246 C6
Millway Cl AND SP10 ... 102 C3
Millway Rd AND SP10 ... 102 C2
Millyford Br LYND SO43 ... 264 A6
Millyford Cl NMIL/BTOS BH25 ... 326 F7
Milne Cl FAWY SO45 ... 267 N8
Milner Ct WSHM SO15 ... 247 N3
Milne Rd CFDH BH17 ... 320 D3
Milner Pl FUFL SO22 ... 164 F9
Milner Rd WBNE BH4 ... 334 C4
Milnthorpe La FUFL SO22 ... 22 A6
The Milsons STOK SO20 ... 141 L6
Milton Av AND SP10 ... 102 B1
Milton Cl CHIN RG24 ... 69 M4
PSTN BH14 ... 321 M9
Milton Gra ASHV GU12 ... 76 F7
Milton Gn NMIL/BTOS BH25 * ... 327 K3
Milton Gv NMIL/BTOS BH25 ... 271 H9
NMIL/BTOS BH25 ... 327 J3
Milton Md NMIL/BTOS BH25 ... 327 H5
Milton Pde HORN PO8 ... 255 N9
Milton Park Av ENEY PO4 ... 317 J4
Milton Rd BMTH BH1 ... 334 C1
ELGH SO50 ... 207 K8
ENEY PO4 ... 317 J4
HORN PO8 ... 255 N9
PSTN BH14 ... 321 M9
WIMB BH21 ... 278 E8
WSHM SO15 ... 247 J9
WVILLE PO7 ... 275 M1
Milverton Cl
CHCH/BSGR BH23 ... 326 A6
Milverton Rd FUFL SO22 ... 22 A3
TOTT SO40 ... 246 E5
Milvil Rd LSOL/BMARY PO13 ... 314 C5
Mimosa Av WIMB BH21 ... 300 F5
Mimosa Cl BOR GU35 ... 154 D3
FHAM PO15 ... 271 L6
Mimosa Ct AND SP10 * ... 102 B3
Mimosa Dr ASHV GU12 ... 76 E8
Minchens La TADY RG26 ... 51 P2
Mincingfield La BPWT SO32 ... 232 A1
Minden Cl AND SP10 ... 82 D8
CHIN RG24 ... 69 J3
The Mindens TDWTH SP9 * ... 98 G3
Minden Wy FUFL SO22 ... 164 F9
Minehurst Rd FRIM GU16 ... 58 D3
Minerva Cl WVILLE PO7 ... 275 N8
Minerva Crs PSEA PO1 * ... 18 C5
Minerva Dr GPORT PO12 ... 315 M1
Ministry Rd STHA RG19 ... 31 M1
Minley Cl FARN GU14 ... 57 M9
Minley Ct HAV PO9 ... 277 H5
Minley Gv FLEETN GU51 ... 74 B4
Minley Rd BLKW GU17 ... 57 H6
FARN GU14 ... 57 K8
FLEETN GU51 ... 74 A1
Minorca Rd GPORT PO12 ... 13 J2
Minorca Av FRIM GU16 ... 59 K3
Minorca Rd FRIM GU16 ... 59 K4
Minores Rd TDWTH SP9 ... 79 J5
Minstead Av WEND SO18 ... 249 J3
Minstead Cl FUFL SO22 ... 164 E3
TADY RG26 ... 34 D8
Minstead Rd ENEY PO4 ... 317 K5
NBNE BH10 ... 322 C4
Minster Cl FHAM PO15 ... 272 A8
Minster Ct CBLY GU15 ... 57 N1
Minster La WINC SO23 ... 22 E5
Minster Wy WIMB BH21 * ... 280 E5
Minster Vw WIMB BH21 ... 278 E9
Mintern Cl ELGH SO50 ... 207 M8
Minterne Rd
CHAR BH8 ... 337 J1
MOOR/WNTN BH9 ... 322 G5
PSTN BH14 ... 333 L4
Minters Lepe WVILLE PO7 ... 275 N7
Mint Rd LISS GU33 ... 173 N9
Mirabella Cl ITCH SO19 ... 248 F9
Mirror Cl HLER SO31 ... 295 K2
Mislingford Rd BPWT SO32 ... 232 D2
Missenden Acres HEND SO30 ... 250 C3
Mission Rd BDST BH18 ... 320 C2
Misslebrook La NBAD SO52 ... 205 P9
Mistletoe Rd YTLY GU46 ... 56 E1
Mitchell Av HTWY RG27 ... 55 H8
Mitchell Cl AND SP10 ... 4 A3
FHAM PO15 ... 271 K5
ITCH SO19 ... 249 M8
NMIL/BTOS BH25 ... 327 J8
Mitchell Dr ELGH SO50 ... 206 D8
Mitchell Gdns BH/HW/K RG22 ... 89 N4
Mitchell Rd CFDH BH17 ... 321 H4
ELGH SO50 ... 206 D8
HAV PO9 ... 276 B7
WIMB BH21 ... 302 A1
Mitchells Cl ROMY SO51 ... 204 D6
RSAL SP5 ... 119 H8
Mitchell Wy HSEA PO3 ... 297 K6
WEND SO18 ... 229 H6
Mitford Rd NARL SO24 ... 145 N9
Mitre Copse ELGH SO50 ... 229 P2
Mizen Wy LSOL/BMARY PO13 ... 315 H2
Moat Cl FAWY SO45 ... 290 D6
TADY RG26 ... 51 P1
Moat Hl GPORT PO12 ... 315 H5
Moat La WEND SO18 ... 229 H9
Moat La NMIL/BTOS BH25 ... 327 L5
Mockbeggar La RGWD BH24 ... 260 E3
Moffat Rd CHCH/BSGR BH23 ... 336 D1
Moffatts Cl SHST GU47 ... 41 H6

Moggs Md EPSF GU31 ...... 215 N2
Mole CI FARN GU14 ...... 57 L7
Mole HI WVILLE PO7 ...... 275 P5
Molesworth Rd GPORT PO12 ...... 12 D3
Mollison Rd FHAM PO15 ...... 271 K4
Molyneux Rd
  NMIL/BTOS BH25 ...... 327 M4
Momford Rd FUFL SO22 ...... 183 K3
Monachus La HTWY RG27 ...... 55 J6
Monarch CI BH/HW/K RG22 ...... 89 L5
  HLER SO31 ...... 271 H8
  WVILLE PO7 ...... 275 J6
Monarch's Wy BPWT SO32 ...... 209 P8
  HAV PO9 ...... 257 H8
  HORN PO8 ...... 255 K2
  RWIN SO21 ...... 182 C8
  RWIN SO21 ...... 208 G1
Monarch Wy FUFL SO22 ...... 164 D9
  HEND SO30 ...... 249 P1
Monastery Rd WEND SO18 ...... 248 G4
Monckton Rd GPORT PO12 ...... 315 M7
  HSEA PO3 ...... 297 H7
Moneyer Rd ALDT GU11 ...... 249 L4
Moneyfield Av HSEA PO3 ...... 297 J9
Moneyfield La HSEA PO3 ...... 297 J7
Moneyfly Rd VWD BH31 ...... 259 H5
Mongers Piece CHIN RG24 ...... 30 A7
Monier Williams Rd
  RWIN SO21 ...... 104 D7
Moniton Est BH/HW/K RG22 * 68 E8
Monks Brook CI ELGH SO50 ...... 228 G3
Monks CI FARN GU14 ...... 58 B9
  FERN BH22 ...... 280 C9
  TDWTH SP9 ...... 78 G4
Monkshanger FNM GU9 ...... 96 E9
Monkshood CI
  CHCH/BSGR BH23 ...... 325 M6
Monks Wd PSF GU52 ...... 191 M9
Monks Orch PSF GU52 ...... 191 M9
Monks PI TOTT SO40 ...... 246 B5
Monks PI FLEETN GU51 ...... 74 A3
Monks Rd HLER SO31 ...... 269 K4
  WINC SO23 ...... 22 E2
Monks Wk CHAM PO6 ...... 290 A1
Monks Wk FNM GU9 ...... 116 T3
Monks Wy BWD BH11 ...... 301 L8
  ELGH SO50 ...... 229 H5
  FHAM/STUB PO14 ...... 293 P9
  WEND SO18 ...... 228 G3
Monks' Well RFNM GU10 ...... 117 J2
Monkswell Gn
  CHCH/BSGR BH23 ...... 325 H9
Monks Wd PSF GU52 ...... 191 M9
Monkswood CI NWBY RG14 ...... 24 A8
Monks Wood CI ROWN SO16 ...... 228 D6
Monks Wood Crs TADY RG26 ...... 34 C7
Monkton CI FERN BH22 ...... 302 D2
Monkton Crs
  BKME/WDN BH12 ...... 321 N4
Monkton La FNM GU9 ...... 96 E6
  TOTT SO40 ...... 246 B5
Monktons La THLE RG7 ...... 36 B1
Monknoworthy Dr RGWD BH24 ...... 281 M4
Monmouth CI CHFD SO53 ...... 206 D7
  RGWD BH24 ...... 282 E3
  VWD BH31 ...... 259 H6
Monmouth Dr VWD BH31 ...... 259 H6
Monmouth Rd NEND PO2 ...... 296 F7
Monmouth Sq FUFL SO22 ...... 164 D7
Monnow Gdns WEND SO18 ...... 249 K2
Monroe CI GPORT PO12 ...... 315 J5
Mons Barracks ALDT GU11 ...... 76 B7
Mons CI ALDT GU11 ...... 76 D5
Mons Ct WINC SO23 ...... 22 C4
Monks Staff Quarters
  ALDT GU11 * 76 C7
Montacute CI FARN GU14 ...... 58 C9
Montacute Wy WIMB BH21 ...... 300 C5
Montagu CI GPORT PO12 ...... 295 N9
Montague Av ITCH SO19 ...... 249 M8
Montague CI ITCH SO19 ...... 249 M8
Montague Gdns EPSF GU31 ...... 216 A2
Montague PI BSTK RG21 ...... 69 L2
Montague Rd BOSC BH5 ...... 335 P2
  NEND PO2 ...... 296 G8
Montague Ter NWBY RG14 ...... 16 F7
Montagu Rd
  CHCH/BSGR BH23 ...... 326 D8
Monteagle La YTLY GU46 ...... 40 C9
Montenay Dr LYMN SO41 ...... 227 P3
Monterey Dr HAV PO9 ...... 276 C6
  HLER SO31 ...... 270 G8
Montfort CI ROMY SO51 ...... 204 G6
Montfort Hts ROMY SO51 ...... 204 G6
Montfort Rd ROMY SO51 ...... 204 G7
Montgomerie Rd SSEA PO5 ...... 19 H5
Montgomery Av BWD BH11 ...... 322 G2
  TOTT SO40 ...... 246 B3
Montgomery CI FUFL SO22 ...... 183 L1
  SHST GU47 ...... 41 J6
Montgomery Rd FARN GU14 ...... 75 N1
  HAV PO9 ...... 15 H5
  LSOL/BMARY PO13 ...... 294 C5
  NWBY RG14 ...... 16 A7
  RAND SP11 ...... 82 F4
  WEND SO18 ...... 249 J3
Montgomery Wk WVILLE PO7 ...... 275 L5
Montgomery Wy CHFD SO53 ...... 228 D1
Montpelier CI HLER SO31 ...... 271 J7
Montrose Av
  FHAM/PORC PO16 ...... 274 A9
Montrose CI BOR GU35 ...... 154 A7
  FLEETN GU51 ...... 74 E4
  FRIM GU16 ...... 58 D3
  HEND SO30 ...... 250 E5
  VWD BH31 ...... 258 F4
Montrose Dr NBNE BH10 ...... 322 B5
Montserrat PI CHIN RG24 ...... 69 M2
Montserrat Rd CHIN RG24 ...... 69 M3
  LSOL/BMARY PO13 ...... 314 C2

Monument Cha BOR GU35 ...... 154 B7
Monument CI NWBY RG14 ...... 24 A8
Monument La LYMN SO41 ...... 329 N3
Monxton Rd RAND SP11 ...... 100 C9
  RAND SP11 ...... 101 N5
Moody Rd FHAM/STUB PO14 ...... 293 P8
Moon CI TOTT SO40 ...... 267 J1
Moonhills La BROC SO42 ...... 289 M7
Moonrakers Wy
  CHCH/BSGR BH23 ...... 326 A6
Moonscross Av TOTT SO40 ...... 246 D7
Moons HI RFNM GU10 ...... 116 B8
Moor CI BOR GU35 ...... 153 N5
  SHST GU47 ...... 41 M5
Moor Court La RWIN SO21 ...... 163 L4
Moorcroft Av
  CHCH/BSGR BH23 ...... 324 G5
Moorcroft CI RWIN SO21 ...... 125 M6
Moordown CI
  MOOR/WNTN BH9 ...... 322 C5
Moore Av BWD BH11 ...... 322 A4
Moore CI AND SP10 ...... 4 D1
  FLEETS GU51 ...... 74 D7
  NMIL/BTOS BH25 ...... 327 H6
  RFNM GU10 ...... 97 M3
Moore Crs HLER SO31 ...... 269 K4
Moore Gdns GPORT PO12 ...... 315 K4
Moore Rd CHOB/PIR GU24 ...... 59 N7
  FLEETS GU51 ...... 74 D7
Moorfield La HASM GU27 ...... 156 E8
Moorfield Gv
  MOOR/WNTN BH9 ...... 322 F5
Moorfields Rd CCLF BH13 ...... 333 P3
Moorfoot Gdns BH/HW/K RG22 ...... 68 C5
Moorgreen Pk HEND SO30 * 249 P1
Moorgreen Rd HAV PO9 ...... 276 G5
  HEND SO30 ...... 249 N2
Moorhams Av BH/HW/K RG22 ...... 89 L5
Moorhill Gdns WEND SO18 ...... 249 N4
Moorhill Rd HEND SO30 ...... 249 M3
  RGWD BH24 ...... 284 B8
Moorings CI PLE BH15 ...... 332 B2
The Moorings BSTK RG21 ...... 7 K5
  FHAM/PORC PO16 ...... 295 P1
  GSHT GU26 ...... 156 D2
Moorings Wy ENEY PO4 ...... 317 L2
Moorland Av
  NMIL/BTOS BH25 ...... 327 H7
Moorland CI FAWY SO45 ...... 267 P7
  HLER SO31 ...... 291 H5
Moorland Ga BMTH BH24 ...... 282 E4
Moorland Rd BMTH BH8 ...... 335 K2
  PSEA PO1 ...... 316 G2
Moorlands Crs WEND SO18 ...... 249 K3
Moorlands Ri FERN BH22 ...... 280 F6
Moorlands Rd BPWT SO32 ...... 232 E6
  CBLY GU15 ...... 57 P1
  FERN BH22 ...... 280 E7
  VWD BH31 ...... 259 N3
Moor Pk WILLE PO7 ...... 256 T9
Moor Park La FNM GU9 ...... 96 E8
Moor Park Wy FNM GU9 ...... 96 F9
Moor Rd BDST BH18 ...... 300 D8
  FARN GU14 ...... 75 P1
  FRIM GU16 ...... 58 E5
  HASM GU27 ...... 156 B8
  LISS GU33 ...... 173 N6
Moors CI CHCH/BSGR BH23 ...... 305 P9
  RWIN SO21 ...... 207 P4
Moorside CI BWD BH11 ...... 322 B4
  FARN GU14 ...... 57 P4
Moorside Rd BWD BH11 ...... 322 A4
  WINC SO23 ...... 280 E7
The Moors NTHA RG18 ...... 165 K5
  RFNM GU10 ...... 25 N4
  STHA RG19 ...... 97 L4
  STHA RG19 ...... 25 M5
Moortown Av CHAM PO6 ...... 275 L9
Moortown Dr WIMB BH21 ...... 301 K4
Moortown La RGWD BH24 ...... 282 F5
Moorvale Rd
  MOOR/WNTN BH9 ...... 322 G5
Moor Vw CHIN RG24 ...... 70 C5
Moor View Rd PLE BH15 ...... 320 G6
Moot CI AND SP10 ...... 82 F7
  RSAL SP5 ...... 199 L2
Moot Gdns RSAL SP5 ...... 199 K2
Mopley FAWY SO45 ...... 313 H1
Mopley CI FAWY SO45 ...... 313 H1
Morant Rd RGWD BH24 ...... 260 F9
Moraunt CI GPORT PO12 ...... 295 M9
Moraunt Dr
  FHAM/PORC PO16 ...... 295 M3
Moray Av SHST GU47 ...... 41 L7
Mordaunt Dr CWTH RG45 ...... 41 J3
Mordaunt Rd SHAM SO14 ...... 9 G1
Morden Av FERN BH22 ...... 302 C4
Moreland CI ALTN GU34 ...... 132 E7
Moreland Rd GPORT PO12 ...... 12 C1
Morelands Rd WVILLE PO7 ...... 275 N6
Morestead Rd WINC SO23 ...... 184 B1
Moreton CI FLEETS GU51 ...... 74 C8
Moreton Rd
  RFNM GU10 ...... 114 B1
Morgan La Fay Dr CHFD SO53 ...... 206 B6
Morgan Rd ENEY PO4 ...... 317 L4
  HEND SO30 ...... 250 D6
Morgans Dr FHAM/STUB PO14 ...... 294 A4
Morgan's La RSAL SP5 ...... 195 J8
Morgans Rise Rd RSAL SP5 ...... 199 P6
Morgans Vale Rd RSAL SP5 ...... 199 P7
Morgaston Rd TADY RG26 ...... 51 J6
Morland's Rd ALDT GU11 ...... 76 C7
Morley CI BOSC BH5 ...... 335 N1
  CHCH/BSGR BH23 ...... 326 A2
  ITCH SO19 ...... 249 H5
  YTLY GU46 ...... 40 G9

Morley College WINC SO23 * 22 E5
Morley Crs HORN PO8 ...... 256 A8
Morley Dr BPWT SO32 ...... 232 A4
Morley Gdns CHFD SO53 ...... 206 E5
Morley Rd BKME/WDN BH12 ...... 335 N1
  BSTK RG21 ...... 90 C2
  ENEY PO4 ...... 317 J6
  FNM GU9 ...... 116 C1
Morningside Av
  FHAM/PORC PO16 ...... 273 P9
Mornington CI AND SP10 ...... 102 E5
  TADY RG26 ...... 33 N5
Mornington Dr FUFL SO22 ...... 164 D5
Mornington Gdns BOR GU35 ...... 153 M5
Mornish Rd CCLF BH13 ...... 333 P1
Morpeth Av TOTT SO40 ...... 246 D3
Morris CI FAWY SO45 ...... 267 P6
Morris Dr BH/HW/K RG22 ...... 88 C6
Morrison Av
  BKME/WDN BH12 ...... 321 P6
Morris Rd CHIN RG24 ...... 69 P2
Morris Rd CFDH BH17 ...... 320 F4
  FARN GU14 ...... 76 A1
  WSHM SO15 ...... 20 B2
Morris St HTWY RG27 ...... 71 H4
Morse CI FAWY SO45 ...... 153 P7
Morse Rd BH/HW/K RG22 ...... 69 H8
Morshead Crs
  FHAM/PORC PO16 ...... 10 D2
Mortimer CI CHCH/BSGR BH23 ...... 325 L9
  HLER SO31 ...... 269 K4
  HTWY RG27 ...... 54 C9
  TOTT SO40 ...... 246 B2
  WINC SO23 ...... 22 A2
Mortimer Gdns TADY RG26 ...... 34 D7
Mortimer La ELGH SO50 ...... 230 D2
  THLE RG7 ...... 36 C6
Mortimer Dr ELGH SO50 ...... 230 D2
Mortimer La ELGH SO50 ...... 230 D2
Mortimer Wy NBAD SO52 ...... 227 K1
Mortimore Rd GPORT PO12 ...... 315 K2
Morton CI FHAM PO15 ...... 272 A8
Morval CI FAWY SO45 ...... 323 K6
Morval La BKME/WDN BH12 ...... 321 P5
Moselle CI FHAM PO15 ...... 271 P5
Mosaic CI ITCH SO19 ...... 249 P7
Moselle CI FRIM GU16 ...... 57 L8
Mosquito Wy FARN GU14 ...... 75 M2
Moss CI LISS GU33 ...... 192 E2
Mosscrop Ct BSTK RG21 * 69 K8
Mosse CI WHAM PO17 ...... 252 E8
Mossleigh Av ROWN SO16 ...... 227 K7
Mossley Av BKME/WDN BH12 ...... 321 P5
Moss Rd WINC SO23 ...... 21 K6
Mossley Rd FARN GU14 ...... 58 E5
Mossy Rd BH/HW/K RG22 ...... 88 E5
Mothecombe Wk HAV PO9 ...... 257 L5
Mothes House TADY RG26 ...... 34 D7
Mothes Grace CHIN RG24 ...... 68 G4
Mottisfont CI WSHM SO15 ...... 247 L5
Mottisfont Rd ELGH SO50 ...... 207 J9
Moulin Av SSEA PO5 ...... 316 G6
Moulsham Copse La YTLY GU46 ...... 40 C7
Moulsham La YTLY GU46 ...... 40 C6
Moulshay La HTWY RG27 ...... 52 D8
Mound CI GPORT PO12 ...... 316 A9
Mountain Ash CI WEND SO18 ...... 248 L4
Mountbatten Av ROMY SO51 ...... 204 D6
Mountbatten CI
  CHCH/BSGR BH23 ...... 337 L1
  LSOL/BMARY PO13 ...... 294 C5
  NWBY RG14 ...... 16 F1
Mountbatten Ct AND SP10 ...... 5 J3
  FUFL SO22 ...... 164 F4
Mountbatten PI WINC SO23 ...... 145 K8
Mountbatten PI SHST GU47 ...... 40 G5
Mountbatten Rd CCLF BH13 ...... 334 B5
  CHAR BH8 ...... 323 M5
  ELGH SO50 ...... 229 M8
  TOTT SO40 ...... 246 B3
Mountbatten Sq ENEY PO4 ...... 317 K6
Mountbatten Wy WSHM SO15 ...... 247 P6
Mount Carmel Rd RAND SP11 ...... 119 M4
Mount CI FUFL SO22 ...... 164 F14
Mount Dr CHFD SO53 ...... 206 D5
Mount Grace Dr FHAM 295 P1
Mounters La ALTN GU34 ...... 132 D8
Mountfield FAWY SO45 ...... 268 A6
Mount Grace Dr PSTN BH14 ...... 333 L4
Mount Hermon Rd
  RAND SP11 ...... 119 N3
Mount House CI FAWY SO45 ...... 268 T5
Mountjoy CI WIMB BH21 ...... 301 H3
Mount La ROMY SO51 ...... 178 F7
Mount Pleasant FNM GU9 ...... 96 A9
  HTWY RG27 ...... 55 J7
  RGWD BH24 ...... 241 P6
  ROMY SO51 * 204 C7
  SHST GU47 ...... 41 J5
  TADY RG26 ...... 34 B6
Mount Pleasant Dr CHAR BH8 ...... 323 M6
  CHCH/BSGR BH23 ...... 305 N7
Mount Pleasant La
  LYMN SO41 ...... 308 F8
Mount Pleasant Rd
  ALTN GU34 ...... 132 F7
  ASHV GU12 ...... 3 H3
  BOR GU35 ...... 154 C3
  GPORT PO12 ...... 12 C6
  PLE BH15 ...... 331 P3
  SHAM SO14 ...... 248 D4
Mount Rd BH/HW/K RG22 ...... 88 A3
  KSCL RG20 ...... 29 N7
  NTHA RG18 ...... 165 L4
  PSTN BH14 ...... 333 J5
Mount's La ALTN GU34 ...... 151 N4
Mountsom's La ALTN GU34 ...... 151 N4
Mounts Wy FLEETN GU51 ...... 73 P1

Mount Temple ROMY SO51 ...... 204 E6
The Mount BOR GU35 ...... 155 H2
  FLEETN GU51 ...... 74 D2
  HASM GU27 ...... 157 L3
  LSOL/BMARY PO13 ...... 295 J8
  NWBY RG14 * 16 E7
  RGWD BH24 ...... 283 K1
  ROWN SO16 ...... 247 L2
Mount Vw ALDT GU11 ...... 3 J2
  ELGH SO50 ...... 207 K9
Mountview Av
  FHAM/PORC PO16 ...... 274 A9
Mount View Rd FUFL SO22 ...... 164 A9
Mourne CI BH/HW/K RG22 ...... 68 E8
Mousehole La FAWY SO45 ...... 268 C7
  WEND SO18 ...... 249 H3
Mousehole Rd CHAM PO6 ...... 274 A9
Mowatt Rd GSHT GU26 ...... 156 C5
Mowbray Rd ITCH SO19 ...... 249 K7
Moxhams FBDG SP6 * 240 D2
Mozart CI BH/HW/K RG22 ...... 90 A3
Muccleshell CI HAV PO9 ...... 276 D5
Muddyford Rd RSAL SP5 ...... 196 F8
Mudeford CHCH/BSGR BH23 ...... 337 K1
Mudeford Green CI
  CHCH/BSGR BH23 ...... 337 K1
Mudeford La
  CHCH/BSGR BH23 ...... 325 J9
Mud La HTWY RG27 ...... 39 J5
Mulberry Av CHAM PO6 ...... 297 J2
  FHAM/STUB PO14 ...... 294 A8
Mulberry CI ASHV GU12 ...... 76 A8
  CWTH RG45 ...... 41 K2
  HEND SO30 ...... 249 M9
  SHST GU47 ...... 41 L6
Mulberry Cnr CHFD SO53 * 206 C9
Mulberry CI ALTN GU34 ...... 150 D5
  HEND SO30 ...... 249 M9
  HLER SO31 ...... 270 E5
Mulberry Rd FHAM PO15 ...... 272 A8
Mulberry Wk CHIN RG24 ...... 70 A1
  WSHM SO15 ...... 247 N3
Mulberry Wy CHIN RG24 ...... 70 A1
Mulfords HI TADY RG26 ...... 34 C5
Mulgrave Rd FARN GU14 ...... 58 E5
Mull CI DEAN RG23 ...... 88 E1
Mullen CI ITCH SO19 ...... 248 C7
Mullins CI BKME/WDN BH12 ...... 322 C7
  BSTK RG21 ...... 69 L4
Mullion CI CHAM PO6 ...... 296 D2
Mundays Rw HORN PO8 ...... 13 H1
Mundays Rw HORN PO8 ...... 256 C2
Munnings CI BSTK RG21 ...... 69 N9
Munnings Dr SHST GU47 ...... 41 L8
Munro Crs WSHM SO15 ...... 247 K4
Munster Rd NEND PO2 ...... 296 F7
  PSTN BH14 ...... 321 M9
Murefield Rd PSEA PO1 ...... 19 K2
Muriel Rd WVILLE PO7 ...... 275 N2
Murley Rd MOOR/WNTN BH9 ...... 322 C7
Murray CI AND SP10 ...... 102 D5
  FHAM PO15 ...... 272 A7
  ITCH SO19 ...... 249 N5
Murray Rd FARN GU14 ...... 75 M1
  HORN PO8 ...... 256 B5
Murray's La PSEA PO1 ...... 316 B2
Murray's Rd ALDT GU11 ...... 76 F9
Murrell Rd ASHV GU12 ...... 76 F9
Murrells La CBLY GU15 ...... 58 A2
Mursell Wy HLER SO31 ...... 269 N4
Muscliffe CI HAV PO9 ...... 277 H5
Muscliffe La
  MOOR/WNTN BH9 ...... 322 A5
Muscliffe Pk
  MOOR/WNTN BH9 ...... 323 J5
Muscliffe Rd
  MOOR/WNTN BH9 ...... 322 F7
Muscott CI TDWTH SP9 ...... 98 F3
Museum Hl HASM GU27 ...... 157 J7
Museum Rd PSEA PO1 ...... 18 E5
Musgrave CI BH/HW/K RG22 ...... 89 P5
Musgrove Gdns ALTN GU34 ...... 132 C5
Musket Copse CHIN RG24 ...... 70 B6
Mussett CI TOTT SO40 ...... 246 C4
Muss La STOK SO20 ...... 161 M4
Mustang Av FHAM PO15 ...... 271 N5
Myers CI BPWT SO32 ...... 232 F7
Myers Wy FRIM GU16 ...... 59 J3
Mylen Rd AND SP10 ...... 102 C2
Myllers Lond HTWY RG27 ...... 72 C3
My Lords La HISD PO11 ...... 319 H5
Myrtle Av FHAM/PORC PO16 ...... 295 N2
  TOTT SO40 ...... 246 B5
Myrtle CI BLKW GU17 ...... 57 L1
Myrtle Gv HSEA PO3 ...... 317 K2
Myrtle Rd FHAM/STUB PO14 ...... 323 J9
  ROWN SO16 ...... 227 M8
Mytchett Farm Pk
  FRIM GU16 ...... 76 F2
Mytchett Heath FRIM GU16 ...... 76 E3
Mytchett Lake Rd FRIM GU16 ...... 76 E4
Mytchett Place Rd FRIM GU16 ...... 76 E3
Mytchett Rd FRIM GU16 ...... 76 D2
Myvern CI FAWY SO45 ...... 290 H6

N

Nada Rd CHCH/BSGR BH23 ...... 325 P6
Nadder Rd TDWTH SP9 ...... 79 H5
Nailsworth Rd CHAM PO6 ...... 274 D9
Naini Tal Rd TDWTH SP9 ...... 78 G5
Nairn CI FRIM GU16 ...... 58 D3
Nairn Rd CCLF BH13 ...... 333 N4
  TWDS BH3 ...... 322 E9
Naish CI HAV PO9 ...... 276 D7
Naish Dr GPORT PO12 ...... 295 L8
Naish Est NMIL/BTOS BH25 ...... 326 F7
Naish Rd NMIL/BTOS BH25 ...... 326 F8
Namu Rd MOOR/WNTN BH9 ...... 322 E6
Nancy Rd PSEA PO1 ...... 316 G3
Nansen Av PLE BH15 ...... 320 F7
Napier CI ALDT GU11 ...... 76 D5
  CWTH RG45 ...... 41 K2
  LSOL/BMARY PO13 ...... 315 H3
Napier Crs FHAM PO15 ...... 272 A9
Napier La ASHV GU12 ...... 76 F8
Napier Rd CWTH RG45 ...... 41 K2
  HORN PO8 ...... 256 C5
  ITCH SO19 ...... 249 N6
  SSEA PO5 ...... 316 F6
Napier Wk AND SP10 ...... 5 J2
Napoleon Av FARN GU14 ...... 58 A7
Napoleon Dr DEAN RG23 ...... 88 F5
Narrow La RGWD BH24 ...... 283 H1
Narvik Rd NEND PO2 ...... 296 F5
Naseby Ri NWBY RG14 ...... 24 A2
Naseby Rd MOOR/WNTN BH9 ...... 322 G6
Nash CI FARN GU14 ...... 57 N9
  FAWY SO45 ...... 267 P8
Nashe CI FHAM PO15 ...... 272 B7
Nashe Wy FHAM PO15 ...... 272 A7
Nash Rd ODIM RG29 ...... 92 C7
Nash Rd FAWY SO45 ...... 267 P9
Nasmith CI GPORT PO12 ...... 315 H4
Natasha Gdns
  BKME/WDN BH12 ...... 321 L5
Nations HI WINC SO23 ...... 71 M9
Navarino Ct WINC SO41 * 329 M4
Navigator's Wy HEND SO30 ...... 250 C2
Navy Rd PSEA PO1 ...... 316 C2
Nea CI CHCH/BSGR BH23 ...... 325 P7
Neacroft CI NMIL/BTOS BH25 ...... 326 F7
Nea Dr CHCH/BSGR BH23 ...... 259 N5
Nea Rd CHCH/BSGR BH23 ...... 326 A7
Neath Rd BSTK RG21 ...... 7 J5
Neath Wy CHFD SO53 ...... 206 C8
Needles Point LYMN SO41 ...... 338 C2
Neelands Gv CHAM PO6 ...... 296 D2
Neilson CI CHFD SO53 ...... 206 B8
Nelson Av FHAM/PORC PO16 ...... 295 M2
  NEND PO2 ...... 296 F7
Nelson CI ASHV GU12 ...... 3 J4
  EMRTH PO10 ...... 299 N1
  FAWY SO45 ...... 290 E6
  FNM GU9 ...... 96 D3
  NMIL/BTOS BH25 ...... 327 H4
  ROMY SO51 ...... 204 D5
  STOK SO20 ...... 141 L5
Nelson Crs HORN PO8 ...... 256 C2
  FHAM/STUB PO14 ...... 294 D3
Nelson Dr CHCH/BSGR BH23 ...... 325 K9
Nelson Ga WSHM SO15 ...... 20 B2
Nelson PI FHAM PO15 ...... 272 N7
Nelson PI LYMN SO41 ...... 329 M4
Nelson Rd BKME/WDN BH12 ...... 334 B2
  ELGH SO50 ...... 206 C3
  FNM GU9 ...... 96 D5
  GPORT PO12 ...... 12 D3
  PSEA PO1 ...... 316 F1
  SSEA PO5 ...... 19 H7
  WINC SO23 ...... 23 J6
  WSHM SO15 ...... 247 N5
Nelson Wk AND SP10 ...... 5 J2
Nelson Wy CBLY GU15 ...... 57 N1
Nene CI AND SP10 ...... 5 H5
Nepaul Rd TDWTH SP9 ...... 78 G4
Nepean CI GPORT PO12 ...... 315 M7
Neptune Rd BOR GU35 ...... 154 B6
  FHAM PO15 ...... 272 A8
Neptune Wy SHAM SO14 ...... 248 D9
Nerissa CI WVILLE PO7 ...... 276 B2
Nerquis CI HORN PO8 ...... 256 F5
Nesbitt CI LSOL/BMARY PO13 ...... 294 F6
Netherfield CI ALTN GU34 ...... 132 C5
  HAV PO9 ...... 15 J7
Netherhall Gdns WBNE BH4 ...... 334 C3
Netherhill BPWT SO32 ...... 231 J9
Nether Hill La BPWT SO32 ...... 251 H1
Netherhouse Moor
  FLEETN GU51 ...... 74 A6
Netherton Rd GPORT PO12 ...... 315 K1
Nether Vell-Mead FLEETS GU52 ...... 74 B8
Netherwood PI WIMB BH21 ...... 278 C9
Netley CIiff HLER SO31 * 269 K5
Netley CI CHFD SO53 ...... 228 D1
  PLE BH15 ...... 321 J5
Netley Firs Rd ITCH SO19 ...... 249 P7
Netley Hill Est ITCH SO19 ...... 249 P7
Netley Lodge CI HLER SO31 ...... 269 L5
Netley Rd FHAM/STUB PO14 ...... 271 J9
  SSEA PO5 * 19 K5
Netley St FARN GU14 ...... 76 B4
Nettlebeds La NARL SO24 ...... 148 E6
Nettlecombe Av ENEY PO4 ...... 316 G7
Nettlestone Rd ENEY PO4 * 317 J1
Nettlestone HLER SO31 ...... 269 L3
Nettleton CI CFDH BH17 ...... 320 C5
Neuvic Wy WHCH RG28 ...... 85 M7
Nevada CI FARN GU14 ...... 75 L1
Neva Rd WEND SO18 ...... 249 H3
Neville Av FHAM/PORC PO16 ...... 295 N2
  HSEA PO3 ...... 90 D1
Neville Dr ROMY SO51 ...... 205 J4
  STHA RG19 ...... 25 P4
Neville Duke Rd FARN GU14 ...... 57 N5
Neville Gdns EMRTH PO10 ...... 277 L8
Neville Rd HSEA PO3 ...... 277 J4
Neville Shute Rd HSEA PO3 ...... 297 K4
Newall Rd RAND SP11 ...... 101 N3
Newark Rd BLKW GU17 ...... 56 H4
New Barn CI FLEETS GU51 ...... 74 A5
New Barn La ALTN GU34 ...... 132 D1
  RAND SP11 ...... 123 K1
Newbarn Rd EPSF GU31 ...... 237 J4
  HAV PO9 ...... 276 C7

374 New - Nut

Newbold Rd NWBY RG14 24 A2
Newbolt Cl HORN PO8 255 N8
NTHA RG18 25 M2
Newbolt Rd CHAM PO6 274 B9
New Borough Rd WIMB BH21 300 E2
New Br CHAR BH8 323 N4
Newbridge HLER SO31 269 L4
New Bridge La BSTK RG21 7 K5
Newbridge Rd TOTT SO40 224 F9
Newbridge Wy LYMN SO41 329 J6
New Brighton Rd
EMRTH PO10 277 M8
Newbroke Rd
LSOL/BMARY PO13 295 H9
Newburgh St WINC SO23 22 C3
Newbury Cl ELGH SO50 230 B2
Newbury Dr NBNE BH10 322 D6
Newbury Pl HLER SO31 270 F8
Newbury Rd AND SP10 82 E8
KSCL RG20 48 A2
RAND SP11 82 F4
WHCH RG28 85 L6
WSHM SO15 247 N2
Newbury St AND SP10 4 E4
WHCH RG28 85 L6
Newchurch Rd TADY RG26 34 B5
New Cliffe Gdns HEND SO30 250 B5
Newcomb Cl AND SP10 102 D5
Newcombe Rd FERN BH22 280 D6
SBNE BH6 324 C9
WSHM SO15 248 A5
Newcomen Rd NEND PO2 296 E7
Newcome Rd FNM GU9 96 E4
PSEA PO1 316 G2
New Cottages Lane End
RWIN SO21 * 186 A6
New Crs RAND SP11 79 N2
Newcroft Gdns
CHCH/BSGR BH23 324 E7
New Cut HISD PO11 298 F6
New Dawn Cl FARN GU14 75 L1
New Down Farm Cots
RWIN SO21 146 A1
New Down La WVILLE PO7 275 J8
New Dro RAND SP11 79 N2
Newenham Rd LYMN SO41 329 L5
New Farm Rd NARL SO24 167 N2
RWIN SO21 127 M5
Newfield Av FARN GU14 57 M7
Newfield Rd ASHV GU12 76 F6
LISS GU33 173 M9
New Forest Dr BROC SO42 286 D8
Newfoundland Dr PLE BH15 332 E1
Newfoundland Rd FRIM GU16 59 J5
Newgate La
FHAM/STUB PO14 294 E6
New Harbour Rd PLE BH15 332 D2
New Harbour Rd South
PLE BH15 332 D3
New House La RAND SP11 80 G4
New Inn Ct HLER SO31 270 E4
New Inn La BROC SO42 310 G3
TOTT SO40 245 H5
New Inn Rd TOTT SO40 245 H5
Newitt Pl ROWN SO16 228 B6
Newland Av GPORT PO12 12 A2
Newlands FHAM PO15 272 A9
FLEETS GU52 74 D6
Newlands Av WSHM SO15 247 N4
Newlands Cl CHFD SO53 206 A8
FAWY SO45 290 G9
YTLY GU46 40 E9
Newlands Copse FAWY SO45 291 H8
Newlands Dr ASHV GU12 76 G8
Newlands La WVILLE PO7 275 J2
Newlands Rd CBLY GU15 58 A4
CHCH/BSGR BH23 325 K8
FAWY SO45 290 G7
LTDN BH7 323 N9
NMIL/BTOS BH25 327 K6
WVILLE PO7 275 M5
New La HAV PO9 15 H4
LYMN SO41 339 J3
NMIL/BTOS BH25 327 H1
STOK SO20 161 M3
Newlease Rd WVILLE PO7 275 P5
Newlyn Wk ROMY SO51 204 E4
Newlyn Wy BKME/WDN BH12 321 N5
CHAM PO6 296 C2
Newman La ALTN GU34 133 H4
Newmans Cl FERN BH22 280 E4
WIMB BH21 300 F2
Newmans Copse Rd
TOTT SO40 246 E7
Newmans Ct FNM GU9 96 A5
Newmans Hl WHAM PO17 252 G3
Newman's La FERN BH22 280 C4
Newman St ROWN SO16 247 M3
Newmarket Cl ELGH SO50 230 D5
Newmer Ct HAV PO9 276 C4
New Merrifield WIMB BH21 278 G7
New Mill La HTWY RG27 39 H4
New Mill Rd HTWY RG27 39 H4
Newmorton Rd
MOOR/WNTN BH9 322 G3
Newney Cl NEND PO2 297 H5
Newnham Ct HAV PO9 * 277 H5
Newnham La CHIN RG24 70 E4
HTWY RG27 71 K3
Newnham Pk HTWY RG27 71 N4
Newnham Rd HTWY RG27 71 L4
New North Dr HTWY RG27 52 F6
New Odiham Rd ALTN GU34 132 D5
New Orch PLE BH15 332 D1
New Paddock Cl ALTN GU34 133 J3
New Pde NBNE BH10 * 322 E4
New Park Rd SBNE BH6 336 A2
Newport Cl CHFD SO53 206 C9
NWBY RG14 24 E3
Newport La ROMY SO51 180 F8
Newport Rd ASHV GU12 3 J5
GPORT PO12 315 K3
NWBY RG14 24 E3
New Quay Rd PLE BH15 332 C2
New Rd BKME/WDN BH12 321 M6
BLKW GU17 57 M1
BOR GU35 153 P7
BPWT SO32 232 B2
BPWT SO32 232 D8
BPWT SO32 233 P1
BSTK RG21 7 F6
CWTH RG45 41 K1
ELGH SO50 230 B2
EMRTH PO10 277 P7
FAWY SO45 290 D3
FBDG SP6 219 L3
FERN BH22 302 D3
FHAM/PORC PO16 11 F5
FLEETS GU52 74 E6
FUFL SO22 164 B1
HASM GU27 156 E8
HAV PO9 14 C4
HLER SO31 269 K4
HLER SO31 292 D1
HORN PO8 236 C7
HORN PO8 255 N5
HTWY RG27 39 P7
HTWY RG27 55 H7
HTWY RG27 71 P3
LYMN SO41 339 K2
NBNE BH10 322 E2
NEND PO2 316 G1
NWBY RG14 17 J6
ODIM RG29 72 B8
RFNM GU10 97 M5
RGWD BH24 260 F2
RGWD BH24 282 E5
ROMY SO51 180 B7
ROMY SO51 204 E5
RSAL SP5 223 N3
RWIN SO21 107 H8
RWIN SO21 207 P4
SHAM SO14 20 E3
SHST GU47 41 H6
STHA RG19 24 G8
STOK SO20 120 C9
TADY RG26 34 B7
THLE RG7 27 M7
TOTT SO40 246 A9
WIMB BH21 258 A3
New Rd East NEND PO2 297 H9
Newstead Rd SBNE BH6 336 B2
New St AND SP10 4 E3
BSTK RG21 6 E7
LYMN SO41 329 L3
PLE BH15 332 D1
RGWD BH24 282 E3
STOK SO20 141 L6
THLE RG7 36 F6
Newton Cl FHAM/STUB PO14 294 A5
RSAL SP5 201 J2
Newton La ALTN GU34 151 M8
ROMY SO51 204 C6
RSAL SP5 200 F5
Newton Morrell PSTN BH14 321 M9
Newton Pl LSOL/BMARY PO13 314 C1
Newton Rd CCLF BH13 333 N3
FARN GU14 58 C7
NMIL/BTOS BH25 327 K7
RWIN SO21 184 A7
WEND SO18 248 G2
Newton Vls RAND SP11 * 80 B2
Newton Wy RFNM GU10 97 L4
New Town FHAM/PORC PO16 295 P1
Newtown TADY RG26 34 B5
Newtown Cl AND SP10 102 C3
Newtown La HISD PO11 318 E4
RGWD BH24 260 G1
VWD BH31 258 F5
Newtown Rd ELGH SO50 207 J9
HLER SO31 292 C1
ITCH SO19 269 K2
LIPH GU30 175 J4
NWBY RG14 16 E6
ROMY SO51 203 H2
SHST GU47 41 J6
STHA RG19 24 D9
VWD BH31 258 G6
New Valley Rd LYMN SO41 338 F2
New Vls KSCL RG20 * 29 J3
Nexus Pk ASHV GU12 76 E4
Nicholas Cl CHCH/BSGR BH23 326 D5
Nicholas Crs FHAM PO15 10 C4
Nicholas Gdns NBNE BH10 322 C5
Nicholas Rd FAWY SO45 312 G1
Nicholl Pl LSOL/BMARY PO13 294 G7
Nichol Rd CHFD SO53 206 F4
Nicholson Cl CFDH BH17 320 G4
Nicholson Pl NARL SO24 167 N2
Nicholson Wk ROWN SO16 227 H6
Nicholson Wy HAV PO9 14 E2
Nichols Rd SHAM SO14 21 G2
Nickel Cl WINC SO23 23 H3
Nickel St SSEA PO5 19 F6
Nickleby Gdns TOTT SO40 245 P4
Nickleby Rd HORN PO8 236 B6
Nickson Cl CHFD SO53 206 D5
Nideggan Cl STHA RG19 25 N4
Nightingale Av ELGH SO50 228 F2
Nightingale Cl FARN GU14 57 K7
FUFL SO22 164 C9
GPORT PO12 315 K2
HAV PO9 276 G1
HLER SO31 269 P2
ROMY SO51 204 E6
VWD BH31 258 G5
Nightingale Ct EMRTH PO10 277 P6
Nightingale Crs BPWT SO32 252 D3
Nightingale Dr FRIM GU16 76 F1
TOTT SO40 246 A3
Nightingale Gdns CHIN RG24 68 F4
HTWY RG27 71 P3
SHST GU47 41 J6
Nightingale Gv WSHM SO15 247 N4
Nightingale La THLE RG7 27 M9
Nightingale Pk HAV PO9 15 K6
Nightingale Ri OVTN RG25 87 H4
Nightingale Rd ASHV GU12 77 H9
BOR GU35 154 B6
HLER SO31 269 P2
PSF GU32 215 K3
SSEA PO5 316 D6
The Nightingales NWBY RG14 17 F7
Nightingale Wk HLER SO31 269 L6
Nightjar Cl CFDH BH17 320 A4
HORN PO8 256 A5
RFNM GU10 95 M3
Night Owls STHA RG19 24 F8
Nile Rd SD/PW SO17 248 C1
Nile St EMRTH PO10 299 M1
Nimrod Dr LSOL/BMARY PO13 315 H2
Nimrod Wy WIMB BH21 279 P8
Nine Elms La WHAM PO17 273 J6
Ninian Cl ELGH SO50 230 C3
Ninian Park Rd HSEA PO3 297 J7
Niton Cl LSOL/BMARY PO13 294 G7
Noads Cl FAWY SO45 268 B8
Noads Wy FAWY SO45 268 A9
Nobbs La PSEA PO1 18 D5
Nobes Av LSOL/BMARY PO13 294 G6
Nobes Cl LSOL/BMARY PO13 295 H7
Noble Cl BWD BH11 321 P3
Noble Rd HEND SO30 250 D5
Nob's Crook RWIN SO21 208 A6
Noctule Ct WHAM PO17 272 B3
Noel Cl BROC SO42 286 G8
Noel Rd NBNE BH10 322 B6
Nogarth Cl ROMY SO51 204 F4
Nomad Cl WEND SO18 249 K2
The Nook ELGH SO50 207 K8
LSOL/BMARY PO13 295 J8
Noon Gdns VWD BH31 259 H4
Noon Hill Dr VWD BH31 259 H4
Noon Hill Rd VWD BH31 259 H4
Norbury Cl CHFD SO53 206 D6
Norbury Gdns HLER SO31 269 N8
Norcliffe Cl BWD BH11 322 B4
Norcliffe Rd SD/PW SO17 248 C3
Norden Cl BSTK RG21 7 F3
Nordik Gdns HEND SO30 250 C6
Nore Crs EMRTH PO10 277 K9
Nore Farm Av EMRTH PO10 277 K9
Noreuil Rd PSF GU32 215 K2
Norfolk Av CHCH/BSGR BH23 324 D6
Norfolk Rd WSHM SO15 247 P3
Norfolk St SSEA PO5 19 G6
Norgett Wy
FHAM/PORC PO16 295 M3
Norham Av ROWN SO16 247 N1
Norham Cl ROWN SO16 247 N1
Norland Rd ENEY PO4 * 316 G5
Norlands NTHA RG18 25 M2
Norlands Dr RWIN SO21 207 L1
Norley Cl HAV PO9 276 E5
Norleywood
CHCH/BSGR BH23 326 B7
Norleywood Rd LYMN SO41 310 B7
Norman Av BKME/WDN BH12 321 P6
Norman Cl BOR GU35 154 B5
FHAM/PORC PO16 295 P3
Norman Court La RAND SP11 102 D7
Normandy Cl FRIM GU16 59 K5
LYMN SO41 308 A4
ROWN SO16 227 H6
Normandy Common La
RGUW GU3 77 N8
Normandy Dr
CHCH/BSGR BH23 325 H8
Normandy Gdns GPORT PO12 315 K4
Normandy La LYMN SO41 329 M5
Normandy Rd NEND PO2 296 F5
Normandy St ALTN GU34 132 G5
Normandy Wy FBDG SP6 240 C1
TOTT SO40 247 K8
Norman Gdns
BKME/WDN BH12 321 P6
HEND SO30 250 A6
Normanhurst Av CHAR BH8 323 K6
Norman Rd FAWY SO45 291 H9
GPORT PO12 315 L3
HISD PO11 319 H6
SSEA PO5 316 G5
WINC SO23 164 G9
WSHM SO15 247 P6
Normanton Cl
CHCH/BSGR BH23 324 D6
Normanton Rd BSTK RG21 69 L4
Norman Wy HAV PO9 276 C8
Normay Ri NWBY RG14 30 B1
Normoor Rd THLE RG7 27 H6
Norn Hl BSTK RG21 7 H3
Norn Hill Cl BSTK RG21 7 H3
Norrie Ct CHIN RG24 68 F4
Norris Br FARN GU14 75 H4
Norris Cl BOR GU35 153 N7
RGWD BH24 281 L5
ROMY SO51 204 G3
Norris Gdns HAV PO9 15 J7
NMIL/BTOS BH25 327 J6
RWIN SO21 144 E4
Norris Hl WEND SO18 248 G2
Norris Hill Rd FLEETN GU51 74 G5
Norrish Rd BKME/WDN BH12 321 L7
Norset Rd FHAM PO15 272 A8
Northam Br SHAM SO14 248 E5
Northam Ms PSEA PO1 * 19 J2
Northampton La FAWY SO45 290 G9
Northam Rd SHAM SO14 21 F3
Northam St PSEA PO1 19 K2
Northanger Cl ALTN GU34 132 E5
Northarbour Rd CHAM PO6 296 F2
North Av FNM GU9 96 D4
NBNE BH10 322 D1
NEND PO2 296 G4
North Battery Rd NEND PO2 296 D7
North Bay EMRTH PO10 299 N6
Northbourne Av NBNE BH10 322 D3
Northbourne Cl FAWY SO45 268 C9
Northbourne Gdns
NBNE BH10 322 E2
Northbourne Pl NBNE BH10 322 D2
Northbrook Av WINC SO23 23 H5
Northbrook Cl PSEA PO1 316 F1
WINC SO23 23 J5
Northbrook Rd ALDT GU11 3 F6
BDST BH18 320 C2
SHAM SO14 21 G2
Northbrook St NWBY RG14 16 E1
North Charford Crossing
FBDG SP6 199 H9
North Charford Dro RSAL SP5 198 B6
North Cl FARN GU14 57 P5
GPORT PO12 315 K4
HAV PO9 15 H7
LYMN SO41 329 L3
ROMY SO51 204 G4
North Common La
LYMN SO41 308 F9
RSAL SP5 201 J7
Northcote Av NEND PO2 297 H9
Northcote Rd ASHV GU12 76 F5
CHAR BH8 9 J1
ENEY PO4 316 G5
FARN GU14 57 M7
SD/PW SO17 248 E1
North Crs HISD PO11 319 H5
Northcroft La NWBY RG14 16 C1
Northcroft Rd GPORT PO12 315 K2
Northcroft Ter NWBY RG14 16 D2
North Cross St GPORT PO12 13 H2
Northdene Rd CHFD SO53 206 E8
North Downs Wy RFNM GU10 96 G9
North Dr CHOB/PIR GU24 59 P7
FUFL SO22 164 C2
NMIL/BTOS BH25 306 F8
RGWD BH24 * 281 H9
North East Cl ITCH SO19 249 L6
North East Rd ITCH SO19 249 J7
North End Av NEND PO2 296 F7
North End Cl CHFD SO53 206 E9
North End Gv NEND PO2 296 F7
Northend La BPWT SO32 233 L2
North End La FBDG SP6 240 B7
NARL SO24 168 A8
Northern Access Rd
FAWY SO45 291 M7
Northern Anchorage
ITCH SO19 21 K6
Northern Av AND SP10 4 D2
NWBY RG14 24 D2
Northern Pde NEND PO2 296 F6
Northern Rd CHAM PO6 297 H3
FAWY SO45 291 N7
Northern Wy PSEA PO1 316 B1
Northerwood Av LYND SO43 264 E5
Northerwood Cl NBAD SO52 205 K9
Northey Rd SBNE BH6 324 C9
North Farm Rd FARN GU14 57 M5
Northfield OVTN RG25 86 G1
North Fld OVTN RG25 * 86 G2
Northfield Av
FHAM/STUB PO14 294 D2
Northfield Cl ASHV GU12 97 K2
BPWT SO32 231 N3
FLEETS GU52 * 74 E6
HORN PO8 256 C1
Northfield La ALTN GU34 132 C9
Northfield Pk
FHAM/PORC PO16 * 273 M9
Northfield Rd FLEETS GU52 74 E6
HTWY RG27 52 E4
LYMN SO41 339 H1
NTHA RG18 25 L3
RGWD BH24 260 E9
WEND SO18 229 H9
Northfields Farm La
WHAM PO17 252 E6
North Front SHAM SO14 20 E3
North Fryerne YTLY GU46 40 E6
Northgate Av NEND PO2 317 H1
Northgate La OVTN RG25 110 D1
North Gate Rd FARN GU14 76 A2
Northgate Wy BH/HW/K RG22 89 L5
North Greenlands LYMN SO41 329 J5
North Head LYMN SO41 338 D1
North Hl CHAM PO6 274 D8
FHAM/PORC PO16 11 G1
North Hill Cl FUFL SO22 164 G5
Northington Rd RWIN SO21 146 G7
Northlands Cl TOTT SO40 246 B3
Northlands Dr WINC SO23 165 H5
Northlands Gdns WSHM SO15 248 A4
Northlands Rd ELGH SO50 229 J1
ROMY SO51 204 G7
TOTT SO40 246 B3
WSHM SO15 248 A4
North La ASHV GU12 3 K1
BROC SO42 289 J4
EPSF GU31 215 L8
EPSF GU31 216 F8
HORN PO8 236 B6
RSAL SP5 159 H6
RSAL SP5 223 L5
Northleigh Cnr WEND SO18 * 228 G7
Northleigh La WIMB BH21 278 G9
North Ldg FBDG SP6 * 239 M3
North Lodge Rd PSTN BH14 321 N8
Northmead FARN GU14 58 A9
Northmead Dr CFDH BH17 320 B4
Northmere Dr
BKME/WDN BH12 321 P5
Northmere Rd
BKME/WDN BH12 321 N6
North Millers Dl CHFD SO53 206 C4
Northmore Cl HLER SO31 271 H5
Northmore Rd HLER SO31 271 H5
Northney La HISD PO11 299 J5
Northney Rd HISD PO11 298 G4
Northolt Gdns ROWN SO16 227 L8
Northover La LYMN SO41 307 N9
Northover Rd HSEA PO3 297 K9
LYMN SO41 328 G3
North Pde BOR GU35 153 P2
North Plumley Dro
RGWD BH24 259 M1
North Poulner Rd
RGWD BH24 260 F8
North Rd ASHV GU12 76 E8
BROC SO42 286 G8
FARN GU14 76 C5
FAWY SO45 267 P8
HORN PO8 256 C1
LTDN BH7 335 L1
PLE BH15 332 C1
PSF GU32 215 M1
PSTN BH14 321 J7
SD/PW SO17 248 E3
WHAM PO17 274 C8
WINC SO23 145 J8
North Rd East WHAM PO17 274 C4
North Rd West WHAM PO17 274 B4
North Shore Rd HISD PO11 318 D3
North Side RFNM GU10 97 N4
Northside La NARL SO24 168 G2
North Sq WHAM PO17 272 C3
North St EMRTH PO10 277 M9
GPORT PO12 13 H2
HAV PO9 14 B4
KSCL RG20 48 C3
LYMN SO41 329 J5
NARL SO24 168 E2
PLE BH15 332 E1
PSEA PO1 18 D2
North Street Ar HAV PO9 15 G4
North Stroud La PSF GU32 214 E3
North Trestle Rd FAWY SO45 291 K3
Northumberland Rd
BOR GU35 154 A7
SHAM SO14 21 H2
North Vw FUFL SO22 22 B3
North View Rd TADY RG26 34 E7
North Wallington
FHAM/PORC PO16 11 K3
North Walls WINC SO23 23 F3
North Warnborough St
ODIM RG29 72 A9
North Wy HAV PO9 14 E5
AND SP10 83 H9
Northway FHAM PO15 271 L7
NTHA RG18 25 M2
NWBY RG14 17 G4
Northways FHAM/STUB PO14 294 B7
North Weirs BROC SO42 286 D8
Northwick HTWY RG27 39 P7
Northwood Cl ROWN SO16 228 C6
Northwood Dr NWBY RG14 24 F3
Northwood La HISD PO11 298 G8
Northwood Rd NEND PO2 296 G5
Northwood Sq
FHAM/PORC PO16 11 G4
Nortoft Rd CHAR BH8 323 H9
Norton Cl CHCH/BSGR BH23 325 H8
ITCH SO19 248 G8
WHAM PO17 274 B4
WVILLE PO7 275 M3
Norton Dr FHAM/PORC PO16 10 E2
Norton Gdns
MOOR/WNTN BH9 322 E6
Norton Ride CHIN RG24 70 A5
Norton Rd CBLY GU15 59 H1
MOOR/WNTN BH9 322 E6
THLE RG7 37 P4
WHAM PO17 274 B4
Norton Wy PLE BH15 332 C2
Norton Welch Cl NBAD SO52 205 M9
Norway Rd HSEA PO3 297 H5
Norwich Av CBLY GU15 58 D2
WCLF BH2 8 A3
Norwich Av West WCLF BH2 334 D3
Norwich Cl BH/HW/K RG22 89 M4
HLER SO31 270 E6
Norwich Pl
LSOL/BMARY PO13 314 C1
Norwich Rd CHAM PO6 274 F9
WCLF BH2 8 B4
WEND SO18 249 H1
Norwood Pl BOSC BH5 335 P1
Nottingham Pl
LSOL/BMARY PO13 314 C1
Nouale La RGWD BH24 283 H2
Novello Cl BH/HW/K RG22 89 P4
Novello Gdns WVILLE PO7 275 N5
Noyce Dr ELGH SO50 230 D3
Noyce Gdns CHAR BH8 323 P5
Nuffield Dr SHST GU47 41 N5
Nuffield Rd CFDH BH17 320 F4
Nugee Ct CWTH RG45 41 J1
Nugent Rd SBNE BH6 336 D2
Nunns Pk RSAL SP5 201 K1
Nuns Rd WINC SO23 23 F1
Nuns Wk WINC SO23 23 F1
Nunton Dro RSAL SP5 198 B1
Nursery Cl CHIN RG24 70 B1
EMRTH PO10 277 M7
FLEETN GU51 74 G4
FRIM GU16 58 E6
HTWY RG27 71 P2
LSOL/BMARY PO13 294 F6
Nursery Fld LISS GU33 192 C3
Nursery Gdns CHFD SO53 228 E1
FUFL SO22 164 E7
HORN PO8 256 A6
ITCH SO19 249 K5
ROMY SO51 204 E6
Nursery Gv HEND SO30 250 C6
Nursery La FHAM/STUB PO14 294 A8
Nursery Rd ALTN GU34 132 G4
HAV PO9 276 C8
MOOR/WNTN BH9 322 G4
NARL SO24 168 A2
RGWD BH24 282 E3
WEND SO18 248 F2
Nursery Ter ODIM RG29 * 72 B8
Nursling Crs HAV PO9 276 G5
Nursling Gn CHAR BH8 323 K5
Nursling St ROWN SO16 226 G7
Nutash FHAM/STUB PO14 271 J6
Nutbane Cl AND SP10 102 B3
Nutbane La RAND SP11 81 M4
Nutbean La THLE RG7 38 C1
Nutbeem Rd ELGH SO50 229 J2
Nutbourne FNM GU9 96 E4
Nutbourne Rd CHAM PO6 297 M2
HISD PO11 319 L7
Nutburn Rd NBAD SO52 205 M8
Nutchers Dro STOK SO20 161 M4
Nutcombe La GSHT GU26 156 D4
Nutfield Ct ROWN SO16 227 J9
Nutfield Pl PSEA PO1 316 F2
Nutfield Rd ROWN SO16 227 H6
Nuthatch Cl BH/HW/K RG22 89 K4
CFDH BH17 320 B5
FERN BH22 280 B9
HAV PO9 277 H1
RFNM GU10 95 M4

Nutley Cl BOR GU35 154 A6
BWD BH11 301 P9
YTLY GU46 40 E9
Nutley La OVTN RG25 109 K1
Nutley Rd HAV PO9 276 D5
Nutley Wy BWD BH11 321 P1
Nutmeg Ct FARN GU14 57 K8
Nutsey Av TOTT SO40 246 B1
Nutsey La TOTT SO40 246 C1
Nutshalling Av ROWN SO16 227 J6
Nutshalling Cl TOTT SO40 246 A1
Nutshell La FNM GU9 96 C5
Nutwick Rd HAV PO9 277 H7
Nutwood Wy TOTT SO40 246 C1
Nyewood Av
FHAM/PORC PO16 273 P9
Nyria Wy GPORT PO12 13 G3

O

Oakapple Gdns CHAM PO6 297 N1
Oak Av CHCH/BSGR BH23 324 B7
SHST GU47 41 L5
Oak Bank AND SP10 4 D7
Oakbank Rd ELGH SO50 229 L1
ITCH SO19 248 F8
Oak Cl BPWT SO32 209 M8
BSTK RG21 7 K6
DEAN RG23 88 F2
FAWY SO45 268 A9
FERN BH22 302 E7
HORN PO8 255 N9
KSCL RG20 48 D3
LYND SO43 * 264 F6
OVTN RG25 86 G4
TADY RG26 33 N6
TDWTH SP9 79 J4
WSHM SO15 246 G4
Oak Coppice Cl ELGH SO50 230 A2
Oak Coppice Rd FHAM PO15 271 K2
Oak Cots HASM GU27 * 156 D7
Oak Ct FNM GU9 116 B1
LYMN SO41 * 329 J5
Oakcroft La FHAM/STUB PO14 294 A4
Oakdale Rd PLE BH15 320 G6
Oakdene ALTN GU34 132 E4
LSOL/BMARY PO13 295 H8
THLE RG7 27 J4
TOTT SO40 245 P4
Oakdene Cl WIMB BH21 278 F9
Oakdene Rd ENEY PO4 317 L4
Oakdown Rd
FHAM/STUB PO14 294 B6
Oak Dr ELGH SO50 230 C2
EPSF GU31 215 L4
NWBY RG14 16 C4
PLE BH15 332 F1
THLE RG7 27 H5
Oakenbrow FAWY SO45 267 P8
LYMN SO41 308 A5
Oaken Copse FLEETS GU52 74 E8
Oaken Copse Crs FARN GU14 58 A6
Oaken Gv NWBY RG14 24 A7
The Oakes FHAM/STUB PO14 293 P5
Oak Farm Cl BLKW GU17 41 K9
Oakfield Ct HAV PO9 * 277 H5
Oakfield Pl FARN GU14 57 K9
Oakfield Rd BLKW GU17 57 M1
PLE BH15 320 E6
TADY RG26 34 F5
TOTT SO40 245 H4
Oakfields ELGH SO50 207 J6
Oakfields Cl KSCL RG20 47 L1
Oak Gdns BWD BH11 322 B5
LYMN SO41 328 D6
Oak Gn ALTN GU34 * 150 D5
Oak Green Wy WEND SO18 249 J3
Oak Grove Crs CBLY GU15 41 N8
Oakgrove Rd ELGH SO50 229 N2
Oak Hanger Cl HTWY RG27 72 A3
Oakhanger Rd BOR GU35 153 K5
Oakhill HLER SO31 270 B1
Oak Hl NARL SO24 168 A2
Oakhill Cl CHFD SO53 206 G8
HLER SO31 270 B1
Oakhill Ct CHFD SO53 206 G7
Oakhill Rd BOR GU35 155 J3
Oakhurst GSHT GU26 156 C2
Oakhurst Cl FERN BH22 280 F7
HLER SO31 269 L4
Oakhurst Dr WVILLE PO7 276 A2
Oakhurst Gdns WVILLE PO7 275 K8
Oakhurst La FERN BH22 280 F7
Oakhurst Rd FERN BH22 280 F8
SD/PW SO17 228 C9
Oakhurst Wy HLER SO31 269 L4
Oakland Av FNM GU9 96 E4
Oakland Dr TOTT SO40 267 K1
Oakland Rd WHCH RG28 85 L6
Oaklands HASM GU27 157 H6
HTWY RG27 55 H8
LYMN SO41 329 M5
RWIN SO21 144 E4
YTLY GU46 40 E8
Oaklands Av TOTT SO40 246 D4
Oaklands Cl FBDG SP6 240 C1
FUFL SO22 164 C9
VWD BH31 258 E4
Oaklands Gdns
FHAM/STUB PO14 271 J9
Oaklands Gv HORN PO8 255 N8
Oaklands Rd HAV PO9 15 H5
PSF GU32 215 L1
The Oaklands CHFD SO53 228 D1
Oaklands Wy DEAN RG23 68 F6
FAWY SO45 267 N8
FHAM/STUB PO14 271 J9
ROWN SO16 228 B8
Oakland Ter HTWY RG27 55 J7
Oakland Wk FERN BH22 302 E7
Oak La RGWD BH24 282 F1
Oaklea ASHV GU12 76 F7
Oaklea Dr HTWY RG27 39 H4
Oaklea Gdns TADY RG26 52 C3
Oakleigh Crs TOTT SO40 246 C5
Oakleigh Dr RSAL SP5 223 M3
Oakleigh Gdns ROMY SO51 204 E6
Oakleigh Wy
CHCH/BSGR BH23 326 B8
Oakley Cl FAWY SO45 290 E5
Oakley Dr FLEETN GU51 74 D4
Oakley Hl WIMB BH21 300 F4
Oakley La DEAN RG23 88 E2
ROMY SO51 179 M2
WIMB BH21 301 H3
Oakley Rd BOR GU35 154 A3
CBLY GU15 58 A1
HAV PO9 276 D5
NWBY RG14 24 G3
ROMY SO51 179 L4
ROWN SO16 247 K3
TADY RG26 66 E1
WIMB BH21 300 F3
Oakley Straight WIMB BH21 300 G4
Oak Ldg HASM GU27 * 157 K9
Oakmead TADY RG26 51 P1
Oakmead Gdns BWD BH11 301 N9
Oakmeadow Cl EMRTH PO10 277 N7
Oakmead Rd CFDH BH17 320 B4
Oakmont Dr HORN PO8 255 P9
Oakmount Av CHFD SO53 206 F9
SD/PW SO17 248 C2
TOTT SO40 246 D3
Oakmount Rd CHFD SO53 206 F9
Oak Park Dr HAV PO9 15 H2
Oakridge Centre BSTK RG21 7 G1
Oak Ridge Cl NWBY RG14 24 B7
Oakridge Rd BSTK RG21 6 B1
WSHM SO15 247 H3
Oak Rd BPWT SO32 232 B4
CHAR BH8 323 J9
FARN GU14 76 B1
FAWY SO45 268 A9
FBDG SP6 239 M6
FHAM PO15 10 A4
HLER SO31 269 N2
HORN PO8 236 C7
ITCH SO19 248 F9
NMIL/BTOS BH25 327 L3
Oaks Coppice HORN PO8 256 A5
Oaks Dr RGWD BH24 281 K6
Oakshott Dr HAV PO9 276 G5
Oaks Md VWD BH31 * 258 F4
The Oaks ALTN GU34 150 B1
AND SP10 * 102 C2
FLEETN GU51 74 A3
HLER SO31 269 P2
ITCH SO19 249 H6
NWBY RG14 24 D8
TADY RG26 34 B6
VWD BH31 258 E3
YTLY GU46 40 E9
Oak St GPORT PO12 13 F2
Oakthorn Cl
LSOL/BMARY PO13 314 G2
Oaktree Av STHA RG19 32 E1
Oak Tree Cl ASHV GU12 76 E3
ASHV GU12 97 K3
BOR GU35 154 G4
RWIN SO21 207 P5
STOK SO20 123 L5
TADY RG26 34 C5
Oaktree Ct LYMN SO41 338 F2
Oak Tree Dr EMRTH PO10 277 L6
HTWY RG27 72 A2
LISS GU33 192 E2
Oak Tree Gdns HEND SO30 250 B5
Oak Tree La HASM GU27 156 C7
Oak Tree Rd BOR GU35 153 P7
STHA RG19 25 P5
WEND SO18 248 F2
Oaktrees ASHV GU12 97 M2
FNM GU9 96 B5
Oak Tree Ter AND SP10 * 4 E4
Oak Tree Vw FNM GU9 96 D5
Oak Tree Wy ELGH SO50 207 J8
Oaktree Wy SHST GU47 41 H5
Oak V HEND SO30 229 K9
Oakway ASHV GU12 97 K3
RFNM GU10 114 E6
Oakway Dr FRIM GU16 58 D4
Oakwood CHIN RG24 70 A1
FLEETS GU52 74 D8
Oakwood Av HAV PO9 276 B7
NMIL/BTOS BH25 327 L3
RWIN SO21 207 L2
Oakwood Cl CHFD SO53 206 F4
HLER SO31 292 D1
MOOR/WNTN BH9 323 H5
ROMY SO51 204 G4
RWIN SO21 207 L1
Oakwood Ct HEND SO30 249 N1
HTWY RG27 55 H8
Oakwood Dr ALTN GU34 * 132 E6
ROWN SO16 227 N7
Oakwood Rd ALTN GU34 132 D7
CHCH/BSGR BH23 326 A6
CHFD SO53 206 F5
HISD PO11 318 F5
MOOR/WNTN BH9 322 G5
NEND PO2 296 G5
Oakwood Wy HLER SO31 270 A7
Oasthouse Dr FLEETN GU51 56 F9
Oast House La FNM GU9 96 D6
Oast La ALDT GU11 97 H4
Oates Rd MOOR/WNTN BH9 322 E6
Oatfield Gdns TOTT SO40 246 A2
Oatlands ROMY SO51 204 D5
Oatlands Cl BPWT SO32 250 F2
Oatlands Rd BPWT SO32 250 F2
Oatsheaf Pde
FLEETN GU51 * 74 C4
Oban Cl DEAN RG23 88 E1
Oban Rd TWDS BH3 322 E8
O'Bee Gdns TADY RG26 33 P5
Obelisk Rd ITCH SO19 248 F9
Oberfield Rd BROC SO42 286 D7
Oberon Cl WVILLE PO7 276 A2
Ober Rd BROC SO42 286 E7
Oberursel Wy ALDT GU11 2 C2
Observer Dr STHA RG19 25 P5
Occupation La
FHAM/STUB PO14 293 L2
Oceana Crs BH/HW/K RG22 89 K7
Ocean Cl FHAM PO15 272 B8
Oceanic Wy TOTT SO40 247 M8
Ocean Pk HSEA PO3 * 297 K8
Ocean Rd FHAM/STUB PO14 294 D4
SHAM SO14 268 C1
Ocean Wy SHAM SO14 248 D9
Ochil Cl BH/HW/K RG22 68 E9
Ockendon Cl SSEA PO5 19 G5
Ocknell Gv FAWY SO45 267 N7
O'Connell Rd ELGH SO50 228 G2
O'Connor Rd ALDT GU11 76 C5
Octavia Gdns CHFD SO53 207 H6
Octavia Hl FUFL SO22 164 E9
Octavian Cl BH/HW/K RG22 89 M4
Octavia Rd WEND SO18 228 G8
Octavius Ct WVILLE PO7 276 B1
Oddfellows Rd NWBY RG14 16 D3
Odell Cl FHAM/PORC PO16 10 C1
Odette Gdns TADY RG26 34 C5
Odiham Cl ROWN SO16 227 K8
Odiham Rd HTWY RG27 73 H2
ODIM RG29 72 F5
RFNM GU10 95 K3
THLE RG7 37 P3
The Officers Quarters
GPORT PO12 315 P3
Officers Rw TADY RG26 52 C3
Oglander Rd WINC SO23 165 H5
Ogle Rd SHAM SO14 20 D4
O'Gorman Av FARN GU14 76 A2
Okeford Rd BDST BH18 320 D2
Okement Cl WEND SO18 249 K1
Okingham Cl SHST GU47 41 L5
Olaf Cl AND SP10 82 F7
Olave Cl LSOL/BMARY PO13 * 314 C2
Old Acre Rd ALTN GU34 132 E7
Old Agwi Rd FAWY SO45 291 K4
Old Barn Cl CHCH/BSGR BH23 324 B5
OVTN RG25 108 C1
RGWD BH24 282 G2
Oldbarn Cl TOTT SO40 246 A1
Old Barn Crs WVILLE PO7 254 E1
Old Barn Farm Rd
WIMB BH21 280 G4
Old Barn La RFNM GU10 137 H7
Old Barn Rd CHCH/BSGR BH23 324 B5
Old Basing Ml BSTK RG21 7 F5
Old Bath Rd NWBY RG14 24 B3
Old Beggarwood La
BH/HW/K RG22 89 L6
Oldberg Gdns BH/HW/K RG22 90 B3
Old Bisley Rd FRIM GU16 58 F3
Old Brickfield Rd ALDT GU11 97 H4
Old Brickyard Rd FBDG SP6 239 P1
Old Bridge House Rd
HLER SO31 270 B2
Old Bridge Rd ENEY PO4 316 G6
RFNM GU10 97 H7
SBNE BH6 324 B7
Oldbury Cl FRIM GU16 58 E5
Oldbury Ct ROWN SO16 247 H1
Oldbury Wy
FHAM/STUB PO14 294 A1
Old Canal ENEY PO4 * 317 K4
Old Canal Pl BSTK RG21 7 K5
Old Chapel La ASHV GU12 97 N1
Old Christchurch Rd BMTH BH1 8 D4
LYMN SO41 328 D6
Old Church La FNM GU9 116 D3
Old Coach Rd TDWTH SP9 99 K2
Old Coastguard Rd
CCLF BH13 333 K7
Old College Rd NWBY RG14 24 C3
Old Commercial Rd
NEND PO2 316 E1
Old Common HLER SO31 270 G6
Old Common Gdns
HLER SO31 270 G7
Old Common Rd BSTK RG21 69 N8
Old Common Wy RAND SP11 79 P1
Old Compton La FNM GU9 116 E1
Old Copse Rd HAV PO9 15 H3
Oldcorne Hollow YTLY GU46 40 B9
Old Cove Rd FLEETN GU51 74 E1
Old Cracknore Cl TOTT SO40 247 K9
Old Cricket Ms WSHM SO15 248 B3
Old Dairy Cl FLEETN GU51 74 D3
Old Down RWIN SO21 185 H7
Old Down Cl BH/HW/K RG22 89 L2
Old Down Rd AND SP10 4 A1
Olde Farm Dr BLKW GU17 41 J9
Oldenburg FHAM PO15 271 H2
Old English Dr AND SP10 82 D7
Old Farm Cl RGWD BH24 260 G8
Old Farm Dr WEND SO18 249 H1
Old Farm La EMRTH PO10 277 P7
FHAM/STUB PO14 294 A8
Old Farm Pl ASHV GU12 76 E7
Old Farm Rd PLE BH15 320 G6
Old Farm Wk LYMN SO41 329 K4
Old Farm Wy CHAM PO6 297 N2
Old Farnham La FNM GU9 116 C2
Old Field Cl BOR GU35 154 A6
Oldfield Vw HTWY RG27 55 H8
The Old Flour Ml
EMRTH PO10 * 299 N1
Old Forge End SHST GU47 41 J7
Old Forge Gdns STOK SO20 * 140 A9
Old Forge Rd WIMB BH21 279 P8
Old Foundry Ms HTWY RG27 71 P3
Old Frensham Rd RFNM GU10 116 D4
Old Garden Cl
FHAM/STUB PO14 271 J8
Old Gdns FUFL SO22 164 G5
Oldgate Gdns NEND PO2 * 297 H5
Old Gosport Rd
FHAM/PORC PO16 294 F1
Old Guildford Rd FRIM GU16 58 G8
Old Ham La WIMB BH21 279 L9
Old Haslemere Rd
HASM GU27 157 H8
Old Heath Wy FNM GU9 * 96 C4
Old Hillside Rd FUFL SO22 164 D6
The Old Hl RAND SP11 123 K2
Oldhouse La ROMY SO51 202 E6
The Old Iron Foundry
STOK SO20 161 L4
Old Ively Rd FARN GU14 75 H4
Old Ivy La WEND SO18 249 K1
Old Kempshott La
BH/HW/K RG22 68 D9
Old Kennels Cl FUFL SO22 183 J3
Old Kennels La FUFL SO22 183 J3
RWIN SO21 182 G5
Old Kiln Cl RFNM GU10 136 F7
Old Kiln La RFNM GU10 136 F7
Old La ALDT GU11 96 G4
ASHV GU12 76 D9
RFNM GU10 135 M5
STHA RG19 33 H5
Old Litten La PSF GU32 191 J3
Old London Rd STOK SO20 141 M5
Old Lyndhurst Rd TOTT SO40 244 F3
Old Magazine Cl TOTT SO40 247 K9
Old Manor Cl WIMB BH21 300 G1
Old Manor Farm HAV PO9 * 276 B9
Old Manor Wy CHAM PO6 297 K2
Old Market Rd CHAM PO6 297 H1
Old Market Sq BSTK RG21 7 F7
Old Micheldever Rd
RAND SP11 103 L5
Old Mill La EPSF GU31 191 P9
HORN PO8 255 K3
Old Mill Pl HASM GU27 156 E6
Old Mill Wy ROWN SO16 247 L2
Old Milton Gn
NMIL/BTOS BH25 327 H6
Old Milton Rd
NMIL/BTOS BH25 327 H6
Old Mulberry Cl NBNE BH10 322 A6
Old Newtown Rd NWBY RG14 16 D5
Old Odiham Rd ALTN GU34 132 E4
Old Orch PLE BH15 332 E2
Old Orchards LYMN SO41 329 M5
The Old Orch FNM GU9 115 P3
ODIM RG29 92 F7
Old Palace Farm STOK SO20 161 M5
Old Park Cl FNM GU9 96 A5
Old Park La FNM GU9 96 A8
STOK SO20 121 H5
Old Park Rd NARL SO24 169 H4
Old Parsonage Ct RWIN SO21 * 207 L2
Old Pasture Rd FRIM GU16 58 E2
Old Pharmacy Ct CWTH RG45 * 41 K2
Old Pines Cl FERN BH22 302 E4
Old Pond Cl CBLY GU15 58 A4
Old Portsmouth Rd CBLY GU15 58 F1
Old Potbridge Rd HTWY RG27 72 F3
Old Priory Cl HLER SO31 270 A8
Old Priory Rd SBNE BH6 336 D2
Old Pumphouse Cl
FLEETN GU51 74 E2
The Old Quarry HASM GU27 156 E9
Old Reading Rd BSTK RG21 7 G5
Old Rectory Cl EMRTH PO10 277 P7
Old Rectory Dr ASHV GU12 97 P1
Old Rectory Gdns FARN GU14 58 C9
RWIN SO21 165 L1
Old Rectory La RWIN SO21 184 A7
Old Rectory Ms PLE BH15 332 B1
Old Rectory Rd CHAM PO6 297 N1
Old Redbridge Rd
WSHM SO15 246 G3
Old Reservoir Rd CHAM PO6 297 M2
Old River WVILLE PO7 255 H8
Old Rd GPORT PO12 12 E4
ROMY SO51 204 E5
WIMB BH21 300 D1
The Old Rd CHAM PO6 297 H3
Old Romsey Rd TOTT SO40 244 E3
The Old Rope Wk PLE BH15 * 332 B2
Old St John's Ms
MOOR/WNTN BH9 322 F4
Old Salisbury La ROMY SO51 203 L4
Old Salisbury Rd RAND SP11 101 P7
ROMY SO51 225 L5
Old Sawmill Cl VWD BH31 258 D3
Old School Cl ASHV GU12 76 F9
FAWY SO45 290 D3
FERN BH22 302 C3
FLEETN GU51 * 74 D3
HLER SO31 269 L3
HTWY RG27 55 J7
Old School Dr HISD PO11 319 H6
Old School Gdns HEND SO30 249 N1
Old School La YTLY GU46 40 D8
Old School Pl STOK SO20 * 140 A9
Old School Rd HTWY RG27 71 M4
LISS GU33 192 D2
Old Shamblehurst La
HEND SO30 250 C1
Old Spring La BPWT SO32 232 F7
Old Stacks Gdns RGWD BH24 282 G3
Old Star PSEA PO1 18 C2
Old Station Ap WINC SO23 23 H5
Old Station Rd RWIN SO21 146 D9
Old Station Wy BOR GU35 153 M3
Old Stockbridge Rd
STOK SO20 120 B3
Old Stoke Rd RWIN SO21 145 H2
Old St FHAM/STUB PO14 293 N7
Old Thornford Rd STHA RG19 32 A1
Old Timbers HISD PO11 318 F5
Old Town Ms FNM GU9 * 96 A9
Old Tpk FHAM/PORC PO16 11 G2
Old Vicarage Cl NBNE BH10 322 E1
Old Vicarage La LYMN SO41 308 C7
STOK SO20 161 M4
The Old Vineries FBDG SP6 240 B2
Old Vyne La TADY RG26 50 A4
Old Wareham Rd
BKME/WDN BH12 321 J5
The Old Well Cl ITCH SO19 249 L8
Old Welmore YTLY GU46 40 F9
Old Winchester Hill La
BPWT SO32 212 B2
Old Winton Rd AND SP10 4 E6
Oldwood Cha FARN GU14 75 J1
Old Worting Rd
BH/HW/K RG22 68 F8
Old Wymering La CHAM PO6 296 G1
Oleander Cl HLER SO31 270 G5
Oleander Dr TOTT SO40 245 P2
Olive Crs FHAM/PORC PO16 295 P3
Olive Gv RAND SP11 119 N4
Olive Rd ROWN SO16 227 L8
Oliver Ri ALTN GU34 132 F5
Oliver Rd ENEY PO4 317 H5
LYMN SO41 329 J4
WEND SO18 228 F9
Oliver's Battery Crs
FUFL SO22 183 K2
Oliver's Battery Gdns
FUFL SO22 183 K3
Oliver's Battery Rd North
FUFL SO22 183 K1
Oliver's Battery Rd South
FUFL SO22 183 K3
Olivers Cl TADY RG26 52 B3
TOTT SO40 245 P4
Oliver's La TADY RG26 52 B1
Olivers Rd WIMB BH21 279 J8
Olivers Wk CHIN RG24 70 A5
Olivers Wy WIMB BH21 279 J8
Olivia Cl WVILLE PO7 276 A1
Olympic Wy ELGH SO50 230 A1
Omdurman Rd SD/PW SO17 248 C1
Omega Pk ALTN GU34 133 H6
Omega St SSEA PO5 19 J3
Omer's Ri THLE RG7 27 H4
Onibury Cl WEND SO18 249 J2
Onibury Rd WEND SO18 249 J2
Onslow Cl CHIN RG24 69 P3
Onslow Gdns WIMB BH21 278 F8
Onslow Rd SHAM SO14 248 C5
SSEA PO5 316 F7
Ontario Wy LIPH GU30 175 K4
Openfields BOR GU35 154 F2
Ophir Gdns CHAR BH8 335 H1
Ophir Rd CHAR BH8 335 H1
NEND PO2 296 F7
Oracle Dr WVILLE PO7 275 N7
Orange Gv LSOL/BMARY PO13 295 H8
RAND SP11 119 N4
Orange La STOK SO20 120 C7
Orange Rw EMRTH PO10 299 M1
Oratory Gdns CCLF BH13 333 P3
Orchard Av ELGH SO50 229 P3
PSTN BH14 333 H1
Orchard Cl ASHV GU12 76 F7
BLKW GU17 57 N4
BPWT SO32 250 F1
CHCH/BSGR BH23 324 E9
EPSF GU31 217 J9
FAWY SO45 291 K6
FBDG SP6 240 D1
FERN BH22 302 E3
FNM GU9 96 G5
GPORT PO12 295 L8
HASM GU27 156 E8
HISD PO11 318 F6
HORN PO8 256 C5
MIDH GU29 217 L9
NARL SO24 168 A3
NBAD SO52 205 K8
NWBY RG14 24 F2
RGWD BH24 282 E1
RWIN SO21 144 D4
RWIN SO21 207 P4
TOTT SO40 246 D6
Orchard Ct HEND SO30 250 E4
VWD BH31 258 G5
Orchard Dean NARL SO24 168 A1
Orchard Dr BOR GU35 154 D4
Orchard Dro ELGH SO50 * 230 D6
Orchard End RFNM GU10 115 P7
Orchardene NWBY RG14 24 E3
Orchard Flds FLEETN GU51 74 C3
Orchard Gdns ASHV GU12 3 J7
FBDG SP6 240 D2
Orchard Ga SHST GU47 41 J6
Orchard Gv FHAM/PORC PO16 295 L2
HORN PO8 255 P8
NMIL/BTOS BH25 327 J6
Orchard La ALTN GU34 132 G5
EMRTH PO10 299 N1
ROMY SO51 204 C6
SHAM SO14 21 F6
Orchardlea BPWT SO32 232 F9
Orchard Mt RGWD BH24 * 282 E1
Orchard Rd AND SP10 102 C1
BH/HW/K RG22 68 F8
ELGH SO50 230 C2
ENEY PO4 316 G4
FARN GU14 57 P9
FNM GU9 96 G5
GPORT PO12 315 P2
HAV PO9 15 G7
HISD PO11 318 G6
HLER SO31 270 F8
RSAL SP5 199 P6
RWIN SO21 144 D4
THLE RG7 36 A1
Orchard St WCLF BH2 8 C4
Orchards Wy HEND SO30 249 M2
SD/PW SO17 248 C1
Orchard Ter ALTN GU34 132 G5
The Orchard BPWT SO32 232 B5
BWD BH11 301 M7
CHAM PO6 297 H2
CHCH/BSGR BH23 305 N8
FAWY SO45 267 P7
HTWY RG27 71 P2
LYMN SO41 338 G2
OVTN RG25 86 G3
ROWN SO16 228 A3
STHA RG19 * 25 J4
TADY RG26 34 E6
TOTT SO40 * 245 K6
WVILLE PO7 255 H7
Orchard Wk FUFL SO22 164 E5
Orchard Wy ASHV GU12 3 J7
CBLY GU15 58 A3
FAWY SO45 268 A8
Orcheston Rd CHAR BH8 323 J9
Orchid Cl WHAM PO17 272 B3
Orchid Ct AND SP10 * 102 B4
Orchid Dr RAND SP11 79 P2

Orchid Wy CHCH/BSGR BH23 .... 324 G8
Ordnance Ct HSEA PO3 * 297 J4
Ordnance Rd ALDT GU11 .... 101 H1
Ordnance Rd RAND SP11 .... 13 G2
GPORT PO12 .... 13 G2
TDWTH SP9 .... 79 H5
WSHM SO15 .... 248 C5
Ordnance Rw PSEA PO1 .... 18 C3
Ordnance Wy TOTT SO40 .... 247 L8
Oregon Cl ITCH SO19 .... 249 J7
Orford Cl CHCH/BSGR BH23 .... 324 B3
Oriana Wy ROWN SO16 .... 226 C1
Oriel Dr FHAM/STUB PO14 ...... 291 J9
Oriel HI CLLF GU11 .... 58 C1
Oriel Rd NEND PO2 .... 296 F7
Orion Av GPORT PO12 .... 315 N1
Orion Cl FHAM/STUB PO14 ...... 227 K8
ROWN SO16 .... 227 K8
Orkney Cl CHIN RG24 .... 69 N3
ROWN SO16 .... 227 J8
Orkney Rd CHAM PO6 .... 275 H9
Ormesby Dr ROWN SO16 .... 206 D5
Ormond Cl ELGH SO50 .... 230 D1
Ormonde Gdns NWBY RG14 ..... 334 A4
Ormonde Rd CCLF BH13 .... 333 N6
Ormsby Rd STOK PO13 .... 19 H7
Orpen Rd ITCH SO19 .... 249 L8
Orpine Cl FHAM PO15 .... 271 M7
Orsmond Cl WVILLE PO7 .... 274 C4
Orwell Cl FARN GU14 .... 57 M6
Orwell Crs FHAM/STUB PO14 ... 271 J8
Orwell Rd EPSF GU51 .... 215 L3
Osborn Crs
   LSOL/BMARY PO13 .... 294 F5
Osborne Cl ALTN GU34 .... 132 D6
BSTK RG21 .... 6 C2
WVILLE PO7 .... 276 A3
Osborne Dr CHFD SO53 .... 206 G8
FLEETS GU52 .... 74 E5
Osborne Gdns ELGH SO50 .... 230 E2
Osborne Ms ELGH SO50 .... 207 K6
Osborne Pl WHAM PO17 .... 272 C5
Osborne Rd AND SP10 .... 4 B5
FARN GU14 .... 76 B4
GPORT PO12 .... 315 P9
HLER SO31 .... 312 C9
LSOL/BMARY PO13 .... 314 C2
MOOR/WNTN BH9 .... 322 E7
NMIL/BTOS BH25 .... 327 K4
PSF GU32 .... 215 M1
PSTN BH14 .... 321 K9
SSEA PO5 .... 316 E6
TOTT SO40 .... 246 E4
WINC SO23 .... 300 F1
Osborne Rd North
   SD/PW SO17 .... 248 E2
Osborne Rd South
   .... 248 E3
Osborne View Rd
   FHAM/STUB PO14 .... 295 N8
Osborn Rd FHAM/PORC PO16 .. 11 H5
FNM GU9 .... 96 D7
Osborn Rd South
   FHAM/PORC PO16 .... 11 G5
Osborn Rd FHAM/PORC PO16 .. 11 J6
Osborn Wy HTWY RG27 .... 72 A4
Osier Cl NEND PO2 .... 296 E7
Osier Rd PSF GU32 .... 215 K3
Oslands La HLER SO31 .... 270 D3
Osier Cl TADY RG26 .... 26 E2
Osprey Cl CHCH/BSGR BH23 ... 337 L1
ROWN SO16 .... 227 M7
Osprey Dr HISD PO11 .... 319 H5
Osprey Gdns ALDT GU11 .... 96 G4
   LSOL/BMARY PO13 .... 314 C2
Osprey Quay EMRTH PO10 ...... 299 P2
Osprey Rd BH/HW/K RG22 ...... 89 K2
Ossemsley South Dr
   NMIL/BTOS BH25 .... 306 G8
Osterley Cl HEND SO30 .... 248 C6
Osterly Rd ITCH SO19 .... 249 L6
The Ostlers LYMN SO41 .... 349 N3
Oswald Cl MOOR/WNTN BH9 .. 322 E5
Oswald Rd MOOR/WNTN BH9 . 322 E5
Othello Dr WVILLE PO7 .... 276 A2
Ottawa Dr LISS GU33 .... 175 K4
Otterbourne Crs HAV PO9 .... 276 D5
   TADY RG26 .... 34 C8
Otterbourne HI RWIN SO21 ...... 207 L4
Otterbourne Rd RWIN SO21 ..... 207 L3
Otterbourne Wk HTWY RG27 ... 52 C8
Otter Cl ASHV GU12 .... 76 C9
ELGH SO50 .... 230 A2
   LSOL/BMARY PO13 .... 315 H3
   VWD BH31 .... 258 C5
Otter Rd PLE BH15 .... 321 H6
Otters Wk NMIL/BTOS BH25 ... 327 L1
Ouse Cl CHFD SO53 .... 206 C5
Ouse Ct AND SP10 .... 82 D8
Outer Cir ROWN SO16 .... 227 L8
Outlands La HEND SO30 .... 251 K5
Outram Rd SSEA PO5 .... 19 K6
Oval Gdns GPORT PO12 .... 315 K5
Oval Rd ROMY SO51 .... 178 F6
The Oval AND SP10 * 82 D8
   LISS GU33 .... 192 D2
   TDWTH SP9 * 78 G6
Overbecks NWBY RG14 .... 24 C3
Overbridge Sq NWBY RG14 ..... 25 H4
Overbrook Wy NARL SO24 ...... 268 B8
Overbrook Wy NARL SO24 ...... 205 J8
Overbury Rd PSTN BH14 .... 321 J9
Overcliff Ri ROWN SO16 .... 228 A8
Overcombe Cl CFDH BH17 ...... 320 C2
Overdale Pl BOR GU35 * 114 A7
Overdale Ri FRIM GU16 .... 58 D2
Overdale Wk BOR GU35 .... 154 A7
Over Links Dr PSTN BH14 .... 333 M1
Overstand Crs LYMN SO41 ...... 338 C3
Overton Cl ALDT GU11 .... 97 J5
Overton Crs HAV PO9 .... 276 F1
Oviat Cl TOTT SO40 .... 245 P4
Ovington Av LTDN BH7 .... 324 A8
Ovington Gdns LTDN BH7 .... 324 A8

Owen Cl LSOL/BMARY PO13 ... 314 G1
Owen Rd ELGH SO50 .... 229 H2
   NWBY RG14 .... 24 E1
Owen's Rd FUFL SO22 .... 22 C1
Owen St ENEY PO4 .... 317 J6
Owletts Gv NWBY RG14 .... 24 E3
Owlsmoor Rd SHST GU47 .... 41 L6
Owls Rd BOSC BH5 .... 335 L3
   VWD BH31 .... 258 C5
Owslebury Bottom
   .... 184 Q9
Owslebury Gv HAV PO9 .... 276 F5
Oxburgh Cl ELGH SO50 .... 207 H8
Ox Dro RAND SP11 .... 79 P9
   RAND SP11 .... 83 L9
   RSAL SP5 .... 194 A1
   RWIN SO21 .... 144 C4
Ox Drove Ri RAND SP11 .... 83 M8
Oxdrove Wy OVTN RG25 .... 129 P3
   RWIN SO21 .... 146 B4
Oxenden Ct RFNM GU10 .... 97 L3
Oxenden Rd RFNM GU10 .... 97 L3
Oxendown BPWT SO32 .... 211 H9
Oxenham Mdw STOK SO20 ..... 120 C5
Oxey Cl NMIL/BTOS BH25 .... 327 J6
   SHAM SO14 .... 21 F2
Oxford Av SBNE BH6 .... 335 P1
   SHAM SO14 .... 21 F2
Oxford Cl FHAM/PORC PO16 .. 10 D3
Oxford La BPWT SO32 .... 233 K5
   BWD BH11 .... 322 A6
Oxford Ms SHAM SO14 * 21 F7
Oxford Rd CHAR BH8 .... 9 H2
   FARN GU14 .... 76 B3
   GPORT PO12 .... 315 K5
   NWBY RG14 .... 24 C3
   RWIN SO21 .... 125 L6
   SHAM SO14 .... 248 C4
   SHST GU47 .... 41 M4
   SSEA PO5 .... 316 C5
Oxford St NWBY RG14 .... 24 C3
   SHAM SO14 .... 21 F7
Oxford Ter LYMN SO41 * 308 C6
Oxlease Cl RWIN SO21 .... 204 E4
Oxlease La OVTN RG25 .... 110 C3
Oxleys Cl FHAM/STUB PO14 ... 293 P1
Oxted Ct ENEY PO4 .... 317 K3
Oyseil Gdns
   FHAM/PORC PO16 .... 275 K9
Oyster Cl BH/HW/K RG22 .... 89 L4
Oyster Est CHAM PO6 * 297 M3
Oyster Ms PSEA PO1 .... 18 C6
Oyster Quay CHAM PO6 .... 296 D5
   HLER SO31 .... 270 A8
Oyster St PSEA PO1 .... 18 C6
Ozier Rd WEND SO18 .... 249 J1

P

Pacific Cl SHAM SO14 .... 248 D9
Packenham Rd BSTK RG21 ...... 69 J8
Pack La BH/HW/K RG22 .... 89 L1
   DEAN RG23 .... 67 N9
Packridge La ROMY SO51 .... 227 K3
Packway FNM GU9 .... 116 D3
Padbury Cl NEND PO2 .... 297 H5
Paddington Cl BWD BH11 .... 321 M3
Paddington Gv BWD BH11 .... 321 N1
Paddington Rd NEND PO2 .... 297 H8
Paddison Ct STHA RG19 .... 25 P5
Paddock Cl BKME/WDN BH12 .. 321 K6
   RGWD BH24 .... 281 M5
   RWIN SO21 .... 144 F4
Paddock Ct HTWY RG27 * 55 H8
Paddock End WVILLE PO7 ...... 255 H6
Paddock Flds STOK SO20 .... 123 M4
Paddockfields CHIN RG24 .... 70 C5
Paddock Flds STOK SO20 .... 121 H5
Paddock Gdns LYMN SO41 ..... 329 K2
Paddock Gv VWD BH31 .... 258 C5
Paddock Rd BH/HW/K RG22 .... 68 G9
   NWBY RG14 .... 16 D6
The Paddocks FAWY SO45 ...... 291 K6
The Paddock BOR GU35 .... 154 F3
   BROC SO42 .... 286 F8
   ELGH SO50 .... 207 K7
   FBDG SP6 .... 241 J5
   FHAM/STUB PO14 .... 294 A5
   GPORT PO12 .... 12 A4
   GSHT GU26 .... 155 P4
   HTWY RG27 .... 156 F5
   KSCL RG20 .... 48 B3
   RFNM GU10 * 17 K3
   RFNM GU10 * 115 P6
   TOTT SO40 .... 245 K5
   WINC SO23 .... 165 K1
Paddock Wy HASM GU27 .... 157 M3
   LIPH GU30 .... 175 J2
   NARL SO24 .... 167 L8
   PSF GU32 .... 215 K3
Padnon Pl FHAM/PORC PO16 .. 294 F3
Padfield Cl SBNE BH6 .... 324 C9
Padget Rd RGWD BH24 .... 260 G9
Padnall Av HORN PO8 .... 256 A9
Padnall Rd HORN PO8 .... 256 B8
Padstow Pl FBDG SP6 .... 240 C3
Padwell Rd SD/PW SO17 .... 248 C4
Padwick Av CHAM PO6 .... 297 J1
Padwick Cl BSTK RG21 .... 69 K8
Padwick La THLE RG7 .... 26 A4
Padworth Rd THLE RG7 .... 26 A4
Pafferd Cl LSOL/BMARY PO13 . 314 G1
Paget Rd LSOL/BMARY PO13 .. 290 F7
Pages Ct BROC SO42 .... 310 G2
Pages La BROC SO42 .... 310 F3
Paget Cl TDWTH SP9 .... 78 F3
Paget Dr AND SP10 .... 279 J7
   WIMB BH21 .... 279 J7
Paget Rd BWD BH11 .... 322 A3
   GPORT PO12 .... 15 N3
Paget St SHAM SO14 .... 21 H6
Pagham Cl EMRTH PO10 .... 299 N1
Pagham Gdns HISD PO11 .... 319 N6
Paice La ALTN GU34 .... 149 P4

Paices HI THLE RG7 .... 34 B2
Paignton Av HSEA PO3 .... 297 J9
Paignton Rd ROWN SO16 .... 247 K3
Paimpol Pl ROMY SO51 * 254 F1
Pain's Rd SSEA PO5 .... 19 J5
Painswick Cl CHAM PO6 .... 296 E1
Painter Cl HSEA PO3 .... 297 K6
Painter Cl HSEA PO3 .... 297 K6
Painters Pightle HTWY RG27 ... 71 H3
Paisley Rd SBNE BH6 .... 336 A1
Pakenham Dr ALDT GU11 * 97 P2
Palace Cl STOK SO20 .... 161 L5
Palace Ga ODIM RG29 .... 72 C9
Palace Ms BPWT SO32 .... 289 K8
Palace Rd BROC SO42 .... 289 K8
Pakfrey Rd NBNE BH10 .... 232 A5
Pale La HTWY RG27 .... 55 J6
Palestine Rd RAND SP11 .... 119 M3
Palk Rd HAV PO9 .... 14 C5
Pallant Gdns
   FHAM/PORC PO16 .... 273 H8
The Pallant HAV PO9 .... 15 G5
Pallet Cl RWIN SO21 .... 207 P5
Pallot Cl HLER SO31 .... 269 P2
Palmer Dr AND SP10 .... 5 J4
Palmer Pl NMIL/BTOS BH25 ... 327 J3
Palmer Rd PLE BH15 .... 320 E2
Palmers Rd ELGH SO50 .... 230 D2
Palmer's La THLE RG7 .... 27 L5
Palmer's Rd EMRTH PO10 ...... 277 M9
Palmerston Av
   CHCH/BSGR BH23 .... 325 H6
   FHAM/PORC PO16 .... 11 H5
Palmerston Cl FARN GU14 ...... 75 L1
Palmerston Dr
   FHAM/STUB PO14 .... 294 E2
Palmerstone Ms BMTH BH1 .... 335 L1
Palmerston Rd BMTH BH1 .... 335 L1
   HISD PO11 .... 318 C4
   NEND PO2 .... 296 E7
   SHAM SO14 * 20 E3
   SSEA PO5 .... 316 E6
Palmerston St ROMY SO51 ..... 204 C6
Palmerston Wy GPORT PO12 .. 315 J6
Palmers Yd KSCL RG20 .... 31 M8
Palm Hall Cl WINC SO23 .... 23 J5
Palm Rd ROWN SO16 .... 227 K9
Palmyra Rd GPORT PO12 .... 315 K6
Pamber Heath Rd TADY RG26 .. 34 E6
Pamber Rd THLE RG7 .... 35 H5
Pamela Av CHAM PO6 .... 296 F1
Pamplyn Cl LYMN SO41 .... 329 J3
Pangbourne Av CHAM PO6 ..... 297 K2
Pangbourne Cl ITCH SO19 ...... 249 J7
Pankridge St RFNM GU10 .... 95 H4
Pannall Rd GPORT PO12 .... 315 L1
Pannells RFNM GU10 .... 116 D5
Panorama Rd CCLF BH13 .... 333 K8
Pans Cnr FERN BH22 * 302 F5
Pan's Gdns CBLY GU15 .... 58 E1
Pan St PSEA PO1 .... 19 H1
Pansy Rd ROWN SO16 .... 228 C8
Panton Rd CHFD SO53 .... 206 D7
Pantile Dr HTWY RG27 .... 72 B5
Pantiles BOR GU35 .... 155 J3
The Pantiles FBDG SP6 .... 240 B2
Pantings La KSCL RG20 .... 29 N8
Panton Cl EMRTH PO10 .... 277 L7
Panwell Rd WEND SO18 .... 249 J4
Papermakers OVTN RG25 .... 87 H4
Paper Mill La ALTN GU34 .... 132 C5
The Parade ASHV GU12 * 76 F8
   BSTK RG21 .... 7 H4
   FRIM GU16 .... 58 C5
   LSOL/BMARY PO13 * 294 F6
   NMIL/BTOS BH25 .... 327 L6
   PSEA PO1 * 18 D4
   TADY RG26 * 34 C5
Paradise La BPWT SO32 .... 252 C6
   EMRTH PO10 .... 277 P6
   TOTT SO40 .... 245 K5
Paradise St PLE BH15 * 332 D2
   PSEA PO1 .... 19 H2
Parchment St WINC SO23 .... 22 E4
The Parchment HAV PO9 .... 15 F6
Pardoe Cl HEND SO30 .... 250 C6
Pardown DEAN RG23 .... 88 F4
Parfitts Cl FNM GU9 .... 96 A9
Parham Dr ELGH SO50 .... 207 H9
Parham Rd GPORT PO12 .... 315 N2
   NBNE BH10 .... 322 C5
Parish Cl ASHV GU12 .... 97 P2
   SHAM SO14 .... 96 A5
Parish Rd FARN GU14 .... 76 A4
   PLE BH15 .... 320 C9
Park Ap WHAM PO17 .... 272 C5
Park Av CBLY GU15 .... 58 B1
   CHIN RG24 .... 70 C7
   LYMN SO41 .... 329 K3
   NBNE BH10 .... 322 C1
   NTHA RG18 .... 25 N3
   WINC SO23 .... 23 F7
   WVILLE PO7 .... 275 L7
Park Cl BOR GU35 .... 134 G8
   BROC SO42 .... 286 C7
   CHCH/BSGR BH23 .... 88 E1
   DEAN RG23 .... 88 E1
   FAWY SO45 .... 268 D6
   GPORT PO12 .... 15 L8
   HASM GU27 .... 157 L4
   LYMN SO41 .... 329 K3
   NMIL/BTOS BH25 .... 327 H8
   TOTT SO40 .... 115 J8
   TOTT SO40 .... 267 H1
   WINC SO23 .... 165 H5
Park Close Rd ALTN GU34 ...... 132 C4
Park Corner Rd HTWY RG27 ... 55 J6
Park Cottage Dr FHAM PO15 .. 271 M7
Park Crs EMRTH PO10 .... 277 K9
Park Dr BWD BH11 .... 258 E5
Park Dro STOK SO20 .... 120 E5
Park End NWBY RG14 .... 24 C5
Parker Cl HTWY RG27 .... 55 J4
Parker Ct GPORT PO12 .... 315 L8
Parker Gdns WVILLE PO7 .... 275 L8
Parker Rd MOOR/WNTN BH9 .. 322 F8
Parkers Cl RGWD BH24 .... 260 G9
   RSAL SP5 .... 199 J4

Park Farm Av FHAM PO15 ...... 272 A6
Park Farm Cl FHAM PO15 .... 272 B7
Park Farm Rd WVILLE PO7 ..... 275 M6
Parkfields YTLY GU46 .... 40 E9
Park Gdns BSTK RG21 .... 69 M9
Park Gln HLER SO31 .... 271 J6
Park Gv CHAM PO6 .... 297 H2
Park HI FLEETS GU52 .... 74 C8
Parkhill Cl BLKW GU17 .... 57 L1
Park Hill Cl FAWY SO45 .... 290 E6
Parkhill Rd BLKW GU17 .... 57 L1
Park Homer Dr WIMB BH21 .... 279 H8
Park Homer Rd WIMB BH21 .... 279 H7
Park House Farm Wy
   HAV PO9 .... 276 B6
Parkhurst Flds RFNM GU10 .... 136 F8
Park Lake Rd PLE BH15 .... 332 C1
Parkland Cl VWD BH31 .... 259 K6
Parkland Dr NMIL/BTOS BH25 .. 327 H7
Parkland Gv FNM GU9 .... 96 F3
Parklands HLER SO31 .... 270 G6
   WEND SO18 .... 248 G2
Parklands Av HORN PO8 .... 256 A6
Parklands Cl CHFD SO53 .... 205 P7
   GPORT PO12 .... 315 M2
Park La ALTN GU34 .... 114 A6
   BPWT SO32 .... 232 F4
   BROC SO42 .... 331 M1
   CHAM PO6 .... 297 J2
   CHIN RG24 .... 70 C7
   ELGH SO50 .... 207 K9
   EMRTH PO10 .... 277 P2
   FAWY SO45 .... 290 D5
   FBDG SP6 .... 239 M5
   RAND SP11 .... 100 A6
   RSAL SP5 .... 158 B7
   RWIN SO21 .... 165 L1
   RWIN SO21 .... 207 K4
   THLE RG7 .... 26 C8
   TOTT SO40 .... 246 G9
   WIMB BH21 .... 300 E1
   WVILLE PO7 .... 276 C2
Park Ms HLER SO31 .... 271 H5
   NARL SO24 .... 167 P1
Park Pde HAV PO9 .... 14 B4
Park Pl BLKW GU17 * 57 N2
   FLEETS GU52 .... 74 C7
Parkside ROWN SO16 .... 247 H5
   NBNE BH10 .... 322 E5
Parkside Gdns FUFL SO22 ...... 164 D5
Parkside La NARL SO24 .... 169 K5
Parkside Rd BSTK RG21 .... 25 N2
Parkstone Av ENEY PO4 .... 316 G7
   PSTN BH14 .... 321 L8
Parkstone Rd CBLY GU15 .... 58 B1
   PLE BH15 .... 9 G1
Parkstone Hts PSTN BH14 ...... 321 K7
   PSTN BH14 .... 169 N5
   WVILLE PO7 .... 275 L7
   PLE BH15 .... 320 G9
Park St BOR GU35 .... 154 A5
   GPORT PO12 .... 12 D1
   NWBY RG14 .... 24 D3
   ROWN SO16 .... 247 H3
Park Ter NWBY RG14 .... 24 C3
Park Terraces GPORT PO12 * .. 12 C2
The Park BPWT SO32 .... 233 L3
   NMIL/BTOS BH25 .... 326 E8
Park Vw HEND SO30 .... 250 E5
   HAV PO9 .... 207 K6
   THLE RG7 .... 36 B9
Park Ter NWBY RG14 .... 24 C3
Parkview Cl AND SP10 .... 82 C9
Parkville Rd ROWN SO16 .... 228 F8
Park Wk FHAM SO30 .... 20 E5
Park Wy FHAM/STUB PO14 .... 271 L4
Park Wy HAV PO9 .... 14 E5
Parkway Cl CBLY GU15 .... 58 B2
   CWTH RG45 .... 41 M2
   FHAM PO15 .... 271 L4
Parkway Dr CHAR BH8 .... 323 L7
Parkway Gdns CHFD SO53 ...... 206 F9

The Parkway
   LSOL/BMARY PO13 .... 294 F7
   ROWN SO16 .... 228 C2
Parkwood Cl CHIN RG24 .... 52 A9
Parkwood Rd BOSC BH5 .... 335 N2
   WIMB BH21 .... 300 E1
Parley Cl FERN BH22 .... 302 B7
Parley Cross FERN BH22 .... 302 E8
Parley La FERN BH22 .... 303 H8
Parley Rd MOOR/WNTN BH9 .. 322 G6
Parliamentary Rd
   CHOB/PIR GU24 .... 59 M7
Parliament Pl FUFL SO22 .... 183 L2
Parmiter Dr WIMB BH21 .... 300 C1
Parmiter Rd WIMB BH21 .... 300 C1
Parmiter Wy WIMB BH21 .... 300 C1
Parnell Cl ALDT GU11 .... 102 A1
Parnell La ROMY SO51 .... 180 D4
Parnell Rd ELGH SO50 .... 229 H2
Parr Rd CHAM PO6 .... 296 F1
Parr St PSTN BH14 .... 321 J8
Parry Cl CHAM PO6 .... 296 A1
Parry Rd ITCH SO19 .... 249 M7
Parsonage Barn La
   RGWD BH24 .... 282 C1
Parsonage Cl ALTN GU34 .... 151 M5
   PSF GU32 .... 191 P9
Parsonage Est EPSF GU31 ...... 217 J1
Parsonage La BPWT SO32 ...... 231 H6
Parsonage Park Dr FBDG SP6 .. 240 C1
Parsonage Rd BMTH BH1 .... 8 H2
   SHAM SO14 .... 21 J1
Parsonage Wy FRIM GU16 ...... 58 D4
Parsons Cl FLEETS GU52 .... 74 C7
   HSEA PO3 .... 297 H5
Parsons Fld SHST GU47 .... 41 J6
Parsons Gn HASM GU27 .... 157 H5
Part La THLE RG7 .... 38 A1
Partridge Cl BH/HW/K RG22 .... 89 K4
Partridge Cl CHCH/BSGR BH23 . 337 L1
   FHAM/PORC PO16 * 295 J1
   FRIM GU16 .... 58 D4
   RFNM GU10 .... 95 M3
   RWIN SO21 .... 123 K2
Partridge Down FUFL SO22 ..... 185 K3
Partridge Dr PSTN BH14 .... 333 K2
Partridge Gdns HORN PO8 ...... 256 A6
Partridge Gn ALTN GU34 .... 132 F4
   NMIL/BTOS BH25 .... 327 K1
Partridge HI RSAL SP5 .... 224 C1
Partridge Rd BROC SO42 .... 286 F9
   FAWY SO45 .... 268 B9
Partridge Wk PSTN BH14 .... 333 L2
Partry Cl CHFD SO53 .... 206 C5
Pascoe Cl PSTN BH14 .... 321 J8
Passage La HLER SO31 .... 270 B9
Passfield Av ELGH SO50 .... 228 G2
Passfield Cl ELGH SO50 .... 228 G2
Passfield La LIPH GU30 .... 154 F8
Passfield Wk HAV PO9 .... 277 H5
Passford HI LYMN SO41 .... 309 K9
Passingham Wk HORN PO8 ..... 256 A7
The Pastures
   FHAM/STUB PO14 .... 271 J6
   NARL SO24 .... 167 P9
   WINC SO23 .... 145 J7
   WVILLE PO7 .... 254 G8
Pat Bear Cl WSHM SO15 .... 246 C3
Patchway Dr
   FHAM/STUB PO14 .... 294 A1
Paternoster Rw WINC SO23 .... 23 F5
Paterson Cl BH/HW/K RG22 .... 89 N4
Paterson Rd LISS GU33 .... 173 P5
Pathfields Cl HASM GU27 .... 157 H5
The Pathfinders FARN GU14 .... 75 K1
Patricia Cl HEND SO30 .... 249 M1
Patricia Dr HEND SO30 .... 250 D4
Patrick's Cl LISS GU33 .... 192 G1
Patten Av YTLY GU46 .... 40 D9
Pattinson Crs RAND SP11 .... 101 N5
Pauet Cl ALDT GU11 .... 2 A6
Paulet Cl FLEETN GU51 .... 58 B8
   WEND SO18 .... 249 J2
Paulet Lacave Av ROWN SO16 . 227 H6
Paulet Pl CHIN RG24 .... 70 C6
Pauletts La TOTT SO40 .... 225 P9
Paul's Fld HTWY RG27 .... 39 P6
Paulsgrove Rd NEND PO2 .... 297 H9
Pauls La LYMN SO41 .... 308 D8
Paulson Cl CHFD SO53 .... 206 E5
Pauncefote Av BOSC BH5 .... 335 N1
Pauntley Rd
   CHCH/BSGR BH23 .... 337 J1
Pavan Gdns NBNE BH10 .... 322 B4
Pavilion Cl ELGH SO50 .... 230 C4
Pavilion Rd ALDT GU11 .... 96 E2
   WIMB BH21 .... 250 D5
The Pavilions End CBLY GU15 . 58 C2
Pavilions Wy GPORT PO12 ...... 13 G1
Pawley Cl RFNM GU10 .... 97 M4
Pawmers Md FLEETS GU52 ..... 74 B9
Paxton Cl HEND SO30 .... 250 C6
Paxton Rd FHAM/STUB PO14 .. 10 D6
Payne Cl FERN BH22 .... 280 E4
Paynes Hay Rd ROMY SO51 ... 180 F6
Paynes Hay Rd ROMY SO51 ... 140 A9
Payne's Rd WSHM SO15 .... 247 N5
Peabody Rd FARN GU14 .... 76 C3
Peace Cl CHCH/BSGR BH23 ... 311 N4
Peach Gv HAM PO17 * 119 N4
Peach Cv RAND SP11 .... 227 L8
Peach Tree Cl FARN GU14 ...... 57 P6
Peacock Cl FHAM/PORC PO16 .. 295 J1
Peacock La PSEA PO1 .... 18 D6
Peacock Pl WINC SO23 .... 148 B5
Peak Cl ROWN SO16 .... 247 K3
Peak Dr FHAM/STUB PO14 ..... 294 B1

Peake New Rd BPWT SO32 ...... 212 B5
Peakfield RFNM GU10 .... 136 C2
Peak La BPWT SO32 .... 209 N8
  WVILLE PO7 .... 254 G7
  FHAM/STUB PO14 .... 298 B2
Peak Rd HORN PO8 .... 286 A7
The Peak HAV PO9 .... 257 J9
Pealsham Gdns FBDG SP6 ...... 240 C1
Pearce Av PSTN BH14 .... 333 J2
Pearce Ct GPORT PO12 .... 15 F1
Pearces PI KSCL RG20 * 48 C3
Pearl Cl BKME/WDN BH12 ...... 334 E2
Pearl Gdns NBNE BH10 .... 322 C3
Pearl Rd NBNE BH10 .... 322 C3
Pearman Dr AND SP10 .... 5 J4
Pearson Av PSTN BH14 .... 321 K7
Pearson Gdns NBNE BH10 ...... 322 D1
Pearson La RWIN SO21 .... 183 N7
Peartree LYMN SO41 * 329 L5
Peartree Av ITCH SO19 .... 248 G7
Pear Tree Cl BOR GU35 .... 154 C4
  BPWT SO32 .... 250 F1
  CHCH/BSGR BH23 .... 305 L8
  FBDG SP6 .... 239 M5
Peartree La FHAM/STUB PO14 ... 294 B6
  ITCH SO19 .... 248 F7
Pear Tree Cl LYMN SO41 .... 329 L5
Pear Tree Dr RSAL SP5 .... 223 M4
Pear Tree La NWBY RG14 .... 27 F2
  RFNM GU10 .... 118 E4
Pear Tree Wy BSTK RG21 * 7 G1
Peat Moor Cl FLEETN GU51 ..... 74 B2
Peatmoor Cl FLEETN GU51 ...... 74 B2
Peatmore Dr CHOB/PIR GU24 .... 59 P7
Pebble Cl HISD PO11 .... 319 H6
Pebble Ct TOTT SO40 .... 247 K9
Pedemarsh Rd FHAM PO6 .... 296 F1
Pecche Pl CHIN RG24 .... 70 B3
Peckham Av NMIL/BTOS BH25 .... 327 J5
Peckham Cl HLER SO31 .... 271 J8
Peckmoor Dr NWBY RG14 .... 26 A4
Pedam Cl ENEY PO4 .... 317 J5
Pedlars Gv YTLY GU46 .... 40 F8
Peel Av FRIM GU16 .... 58 A2
Peel Cl BKME/WDN BH12 .... 321 L7
  BOR GU35 .... 153 P7
  ROMY SO51 .... 204 G4
  SSEA PO5 .... 258 E3
Peel Ct HTWY RG27 * 55 H7
Peel Gdns KSCL RG20 * 48 B2
Peel PI SSEA PO5 .... 19 G5
Peel Rd GPORT PO12 .... 13 F1
Peel St SHAM SO14 .... 21 J2
Peewit Hi HLER SO31 * 250 A8
Pegasus Av ASHV GU12 .... 76 D9
  LYMN SO41 .... 328 A5
Pegasus Cl HASM GU27 .... 156 C8
  HLER SO31 .... 269 P8
  LSOL/BMARY PO13 .... 315 H3
  ROWN SO16 .... 227 K8
  STHA RG19 .... 25 K3
Pegasus Rd FARN GU14 .... 57 N6
Peggotty PI SHST GU47 .... 41 M4
Pegler Wy CHIN RG24 .... 68 G4
Pelham Cl BOR GU35 .... 154 A7
  CHCH/BSGR BH23 .... 325 H9
  CHIN RG24 .... 70 C7
Pelham PI RFNM GU10 .... 116 A6
Pelham Rd GPORT PO12 .... 12 C1
  SSEA PO5 .... 19 H7
Pelhams Pk BWD BH11 * 322 C1
Pelican Cl FHAM PO15 .... 272 B8
Pelican Ct AND SP10 .... 4 E2
Pelican La NWBY RG14 .... 26 C5
Pelican Rd RGWD BH24 .... 282 C5
Pelican Rd FHAM/STUB PO14 .... 294 D4
  TADY RG26 .... 34 F4
Pelton Rd BSTK RG21 .... 6 B4
Pembers Cl ELGH SO50 .... 207 H8
Pemberton Rd LYND SO43 .... 264 C5
Pembrey Cl ROWN SO16 .... 227 K7
Pembridge Rd FBDG SP6 .... 239 M5
Pembroke Cl ELGH SO50 .... 207 H8
  PSEA PO1 .... 18 D6
  ROMY SO51 .... 204 D6
  RWIN SO21 .... 27 L4
  TOTT SO40 .... 246 E3
Pembroke Crs
  FHAM/STUB PO14 .... 293 N7
Pembroke Rd
  BKME/WDN BH12 .... 321 M5
  DEAN RG23 .... 68 E7
  FUFL SO22 .... 164 D2
  ITCH SO19 .... 249 K7
  NWBY RG14 .... 16 D1
  PSEA PO1 .... 18 D6
  WBNE BH4 .... 334 B4
Pembury Rd PI ASHV GU12 ...... 4 B5
Pembury Rd
  FHAM/STUB PO14 .... 294 B5
  HAV PO9 .... 15 J7
Pemerton Rd BSTK RG21 .... 7 H2
  FUFL SO22 .... 164 E4
Penarth Av CHAM PO6 .... 297 K1
Penarth Cl ITCH SO19 .... 249 L5
Penarth PI WINC SO23 * 22 E5
Pen Cl AND SP10 .... 5 H5
Pendennis Cl DEAN RG23 .... 68 E6
Pendennis Rd CHAM PO6 .... 296 B1
Pendle Cl ROWN SO16 .... 247 K3
Pendle Gn ROMY SO51 .... 158 C5
Pendleton Gdns FAWY SO45 ..... 290 C8
Pendragon Wy CBLY GU15 .... 59 J1
Pendula Wy ELGH SO50 .... 207 N8
Penelope Gdns HLER SO31 ...... 249 P9
Penfold Cft FNM GU9 .... 96 F7
Penfords Paddock
  BPSD SO32 .... 232 B5
Pengelly Av NBNE BH10 .... 322 E2
Pengilly Rd FNM GU9 .... 96 B9

Penhale Gdns
  FHAM/STUB PO14 .... 271 H9
Penhale Rd PSEA PO1 .... 316 C3
Penhale Wy TOTT SO40 .... 246 C6
Peninsula Rd FUFL SO22 .... 22 B6
Peninsula Sq WINC SO23 .... 22 C5
Penistone Cl ITCH SO19 .... 269 K1
Penjar Av WVILLE PO7 .... 275 L6
Penk Rdg HAV PO9 .... 297 P1
Pennant Hills HAV PO9 .... 276 B8
Pennant Pk
  FHAM/PORC PO16 * 11 J1
Pennant Wy
  CHCH/BSGR BH23 .... 325 K8
Pennard Wy CHFD SO53 .... 206 C9
Pennefather's Rd ALDT GU11 ... 75 N9
Pennerley Ct HAV PO9 .... 276 D3
Penner Rd HAV PO9 .... 298 D2
Penn Hill Av PSTN BH14 .... 321 M9
Pennine Gdns FAWY SO45 .... 267 P8
Pennine Rd ROWN SO16 .... 247 K4
Pennine Wk
  FHAM/STUB PO14 .... 294 C2
Pennine Wy BH/HW/K RG22 ...... 68 E9
  CHFD SO53 .... 206 F9
  FARN GU14 .... 57 M6
  LSOL/BMARY PO13 .... 314 E4
  SHST GU47 .... 41 M7
Pennings Rd TDWTH SP9 .... 78 C4
Pennington Cl FERN BH22 ...... 280 D8
  LYMN SO41 .... 329 J5
  RWIN SO21 .... 207 P5
Pennington Crs FERN BH22 ..... 280 D7
Pennington Dr LYMN SO41 ...... 329 H5
Pennington Rd FERN BH22 ...... 280 D8
Pennington Wy FHAM PO15 ...... 272 B7
Penn Rd NWBY RG14 .... 24 A2
Penns PI EPSF GU31 .... 216 B2
Penns Rd PSF GU32 .... 215 L1
Penns Wd FARN GU14 .... 76 F5
Penn Wy GPORT PO12 .... 315 J5
Pennycress HLER SO31 .... 270 E8
Penny Hedge
  NMIL/BTOS BH25 .... 327 K7
Penny La EMRTH PO10 .... 299 P1
  STOK SO20 .... 118 C1
Penny's WVILLE PO7 * 275 N7
Penny's Crs FBDG SP6 .... 220 D9
Penny's Hatch KSCL RG20 ...... 48 D3
Penny's La FBDG SP6 .... 240 D1
Penny St PSEA PO1 .... 18 C7
Pennywell Gdns
  NMIL/BTOS BH25 .... 327 M3
Penrhyn Av CHAM PO6 .... 297 K1
Penrhyn Cl ASHV GU12 .... 3 F5
Penrith Cl VWD BH31 .... 258 E5
Penrith Rd BOSC BH5 .... 335 N2
  BSTK RG21 .... 6 C7
Penrose Ct NEND PO2 .... 296 F7
  NWBY RG14 .... 24 C2
Penrose Gdns ASHV GU12 .... 76 F6
Penrose Rd FERN BH22 .... 302 D2
Penrose Wy ALTN GU34 .... 150 B6
Penryn Dr BOR GU35 .... 155 K3
Penshurst Rd FRIM GU16 .... 58 E5
Penshurst Wy ELGH SO50 .... 207 J7
The Pentagon FAWY SO45 .... 291 J7
Pentere Rd HORN PO8 .... 256 A6
Pentire Av WSHM SO15 .... 247 P1
Pentire Wy WSHM SO15 .... 247 P1
Pentland Cl BH/HW/K RG22 ..... 68 E9
  FAWY SO45 .... 267 P8
Pentland Ri
  FHAM/PORC PO16 .... 273 P9
Penton Cl HAV PO9 .... 277 H4
Penton La RAND SP11 .... 81 M5
Penton PI WINC SO23 * 23 H7
Penton Rd RWIN SO21 .... 184 A7
Penton Ter FHAM SO16 .... 241 H5
Penton Wy CHIN RG24 .... 69 L2
Pentridge Wy TOTT SO40 .... 246 B6
Penwood Gn HAV PO9 * 277 H5
Penwood Hts KSCL RG20 .... 29 P6
Penwood Rd HSEA PO3 .... 297 H4
Peperham Rd HASM GU27 .... 157 H5
Peper Harow HORN PO8 .... 256 B5
Peppard Cl WEND SO18 .... 249 J4
Peppercorn Wy HEND SO30 ...... 230 B9
Pepys Av ITCH SO19 .... 249 M6
Pepys Cl ENEY PO4 .... 317 H5
Peregrine Cl TOTT SO40 .... 246 A5
Peregrine Ri
  CHCH/BSGR BH23 .... 325 L9
The Peregrines
  FHAM/PORC PO16 .... 295 K1
Pergin Crs CFDH BH17 .... 320 D5
Pergin Wy CFDH BH17 .... 320 D5
Perham Crs RAND SP11 .... 80 A1
Perins Cl NARL SO24 .... 167 N3
Periwinkle Cl BOR GU35 .... 154 D3
Pern Dr HEND SO30 .... 250 C4
Peronne Cl HSEA PO3 .... 297 H4
Peronne Rd HSEA PO3 .... 297 H4
Peronne St ALDT GU11 * 2 B3
Perran Rd ROWN SO16 .... 247 H2
Perring Av FARN GU14 .... 57 M5
Perring Rd FARN GU14 .... 75 P3
Perry Dr FLEETN GU51 .... 74 A3
Perryfield Gdns LTDN BH7 ..... 323 P7
Perry Gdns PLE BH15 .... 332 B3
Perryhill Dr SHST GU47 .... 40 G5
Perry Wy BOR GU35 .... 154 G4
  FNM GU9 .... 96 B4

Perrywood Cl FAWY SO45 .... 290 E6
Perrywood Gdns TOTT SO40 ..... 245 P3
Perseus PI WVILLE PO7 .... 275 P7
Perseus Ter PSEA PO1 * 18 C5
Pershore Cl HLER SO31 .... 270 C7
Pershore Rd CHIN RG24 .... 69 L3
Persian Dr FHAM PO15 .... 271 H5
Persley Rd NBNE BH10 .... 322 D3
Perth Cl CHCH/BSGR BH23 ...... 324 C6
Perth Rd ENEY PO4 .... 317 K4
  LSOL/BMARY PO13 .... 295 H6
  RAND SP11 .... 79 N4
Pervin Rd CHAM PO6 .... 297 H2
Pestead La BPWT SO32 .... 233 N8
Peter Ashley Rd CHAM PO6 ..... 275 M9
Peterborough Ct
  LSOL/BMARY PO13 * 315 H3
Peterborough Rd CHAM PO6 ..... 274 C9
Peter Grant Wy FERN BH22 ..... 302 C3
Peterhouse Cl SHST GU47 ...... 41 N4
Peters Cl HLER SO31 .... 270 E7
Peterscroft Av TOTT SO40 ..... 265 N1
Petersfield DEAN RG23 .... 88 F3
Petersfield Cl CHIN RG24 ..... 69 N2
Petersfield Gn TDWTH SP9 ..... 78 G5
Petersfield Rd HORN PO8 ...... 236 E5
Petersfield PI LTDN BH7 ...... 323 P8
Petersfield Rd ALTN GU34 ..... 170 F5
  BOR GU35 .... 153 P6
  EPSF GU31 .... 215 K8
  HAV PO9 .... 15 G2
  LISS GU33 .... 173 K6
  LTDN BH7 .... 323 N9
  NARL SO24 .... 169 J3
  NARL SO24 .... 187 H2
  RWIN SO21 .... 165 P9
  WINC SO23 .... 23 J6
Petersham Cl WVILLE PO7 ...... 275 M1
Petersham La WIMB BH21 .... 278 G1
Petersham Rd CFDH BH17 .... 320 B8
Peters Rd FERN BH22 .... 302 F5
  HLER SO31 .... 271 K9
Petit Rd MOOR/WNTN BH9 .... 322 C4
Petrel Cft BH/HW/K RG22 ...... 89 K5
Petrel Rd LSOL/BMARY PO13 .... 294 F7
Petticoat La RSAL SP5 .... 200 A6
Pettinger Gdns SD/PW SO17 .... 248 F3
Petty Cl RWIN SO21 .... 204 E6
Pettycot Crs
  LSOL/BMARY PO13 .... 294 F6
Petty's Brook Rd CHIN RG24 ... 52 A9
Petunia Cl BH/HW/K RG22 ...... 89 L3
Petworth Cl BH/HW/K RG22 ..... 89 M5
  FRIM GU16 .... 58 E5
Petworth Gdns ELGH SO50 ...... 207 J8
  ROWN SO16 .... 227 M7
Petworth Rd HASM GU27 .... 157 J8
Pinehill Ri SHST GU47 .... 41 J6
Pinehill Rd BOR GU35 .... 154 B6
  CWTH RG45 .... 41 J4
Pineholt Cl RGWD BH24 .... 281 N4
Pinehurst TADY RG26 .... 44 F7
Pinehurst Av
  CHCH/BSGR BH23 .... 337 K1
  FARN GU14 .... 58 A7
Pinehurst Cl WVILLE PO7 ...... 256 C9
Pinehurst Cots FARN GU14 * ... 76 A5
Pinehurst Pk FERN BH22 .... 280 F9
Pinehurst Rd FERN BH22 .... 280 E9
Pinehurst Rd FARN GU14 .... 76 A6
  FERN BH22 .... 280 F8
  ROWN SO16 .... 228 B4
Pinelands Rd ROWN SO16 .... 228 B4
Pine Manor Rd RGWD BH24 ...... 281 K4
Pine Mount Rd CBLY GU15 ...... 50 G4
Pine Rdg NWBY RG14 .... 24 C2
Pine Ridge Dr RFNM GU10 ...... 116 B5
Pine Ridge Rd THLE RG7 .... 27 J4
Pine Rdg NWBY RG14 .... 24 C2
Pine Rd ALTN GU34 .... 150 B2
  CHFD SO53 .... 232 B4
  FBDG SP6 .... 239 M6
  MOOR/WNTN BH9 .... 322 F6
  ROMY SO51 .... 229 P8
  WIMB BH21 .... 300 A4
Pine Tree Cl WIMB BH21 .... 300 A4

Pilgrim Cl NMIL/BTOS BH25 .... 327 L3
Pilgrim Pk RGWD BH24 .... 282 C1
Pilgrim PI WEND SO18 .... 228 G1
Pilgrims Cl CHFD SO53 .... 205 K8
  FNM GU9 .... 116 A2
Pilgrims PI RGWD BH24 * 282 C1
Pilgrims Wy AGY SP10 .... 5 G1
  BOR GU35 .... 154 F3
  CFDH BH17 .... 320 C5
  FHAM/STUB PO14 .... 293 P8
Pilley Bailey LYMN SO41 ...... 309 N6
Pilley Hi LYMN SO41 .... 309 N6
Pilley St LYMN SO41 .... 309 N6
Pill Hi RSAL SP5 .... 201 J1
Pilning Cl FHAM/STUB PO14 .... 294 A1
Pilot Hight Rd BWD BH11 ...... 322 A4
Pilsdon Dr CFDH BH17 .... 320 C2
Pimpern Cl CFDH BH17 .... 320 C2
Pimpernel Cl HLER SO31 .... 270 E8
Pimpernel Wy CHIN RG24 .... 70 A5
Pinchcut THLE RG7 .... 27 J4
Pinchinglon La NWBY RG14 ..... 24 D8
Pindar Pl NWBY RG14 .... 25 H2
Pine Av BKME/WDN BH12 .... 321 P5
  SBNE BH6 .... 336 A2
Pine Bank GSHT GU26 .... 160 D1
Pinecliffe Av SBNE BH6 .... 336 A2
Pinecliffe Rd
  NMIL/BTOS BH25 .... 326 E8
Pinecliff Rd CCLF BH13 .... 334 A6
Pine Cl ASHV GU12 .... 41 M7
  CBLY GU15 .... 50 D5
  FAWY SO45 .... 268 B8
  FERN BH22 .... 302 C1
  NBAD SO52 .... 205 K8
  NMIL/BTOS BH25 .... 326 C7
  RSAL SP5 .... 199 P9
  RWIN SO21 .... 144 F4
  TOTT SO40 .... 246 A8
Pine Ct FRIM GU16 * 76 F1
Pine Crs CHCH/BSGR BH23 ...... 326 A8
  CHFD SO53 .... 205 K8
Pine Dr BLKW GU17 .... 57 M2
  CCLF BH13 .... 321 P9
  RGWD BH24 .... 281 M5
  THLE RG7 .... 27 H9
  WEND SO18 .... 249 N4
Pine Dr East WEND SO18 .... 249 N4
Pine End FERN BH22 .... 302 F5
Pinefield Rd WEND SO18 .... 249 H1
Pinefields Cl CWTH RG45 ...... 41 J1
Pine Glen Av FERN BH22 .... 280 E8
Pine Gv FLEETS GU52 .... 74 E7
  HAV PO9 .... 116 A4
  RFNM GU10 .... 116 E4
Pinegrove Rd ITCH SO19 .... 249 H8
Pinehill Rd BOR GU35 .... 154 B6

TADY RG26 .... 33 N5
Pinewood Crs FARN GU14 .... 57 K8
  FAWY SO45 .... 268 A5
Pinewood Dr FAWY SO45 .... 268 D8
  KSCL RG20 .... 30 F4
Pinewood Gdns FERN BH22 ...... 302 D1
Pinewood HI FLEETN GU51 ...... 74 D2
Pinewood Pk FARN GU14 .... 57 K6
  ITCH SO19 .... 249 P6
Pinewood Rd ASHV GU12 .... 77 J9
  CCLF BH13 .... 334 B5
  CHCH/BSGR BH23 .... 326 B6
  HAV PO9 .... 116 A4
  LYMN SO41 .... 327 P4
  RGWD BH24 .... 281 M5
Pinkerton Rd BH/HW/K RG22 .... 89 N1
Pinkney La LYND SO43 .... 264 C8
Pink Rd HAV PO9 .... 296 G9
Pinks Hi FHAM/PORC PO16 ...... 273 H8
Pinks La TADY RG26 .... 33 P5
Pinnell Cl BH/HW/K RG22 ...... 89 L5
Pinsley Dr WHAM PO17 .... 274 C4
Pintail Cl BH/HW/K RG22 ...... 89 K4
Pinto Cl FHAM PO15 .... 271 H5
Pipers Ash RGWD BH24 .... 282 C1
Pipers Cl TOTT SO40 .... 246 B5
Pipers Cft FLEETS GU52 .... 74 C8
Pipers Md HORN PO8 .... 236 A7
Pipers Patch FARN GU14 .... 58 A9
Piping Cl RWIN SO21 .... 207 P5
Pippin Cl CHCH/BSGR BH23 ..... 324 C5
  LYMN SO41 .... 329 L5
Pipsons Cl YTLY GU46 .... 25 L4
Pirbright Rd FARN GU14 .... 76 B1
  RGUW GU3 .... 77 L8
Pirelli Cl WSHM SO15 .... 20 C4
Pirelli Wy ELGH SO50 .... 229 J2
Pirrie Cl WSHM SO15 .... 20 C4
Pitcairn Cl CHIN RG24 .... 69 M2
Pitcairn Ms ENEY PO4 * 317 K6
Pitchponds Rd HLER SO31 ...... 292 C1
Pitcot La RWIN SO21 .... 209 H2
Pitcroft Cl FLEETN GU51 ...... 215 M8
Pitcroft Rd NEND PO2 .... 296 F6
Pitfield La THLE RG7 .... 35 P4
Pitfield Av HASM GU27 .... 156 C7
Pitfold Cl HASM GU27 .... 156 D7
Pither Rd ODIM RG29 .... 93 J3
Pithouse La CHCH/BSGR BH23 ... 305 P6
Pitman Cl BH/HW/K RG22 .... 89 M1
Pitmore La LYMN SO41 .... 308 D6
Pitmore Rd ELGH SO50 .... 207 K5
Pitreavie Rd CHAM PO6 .... 297 J3
Pittard Rd BSTK RG21 .... 6 A9
Pitter Cl FUFL SO22 .... 164 C2
Pitthall TADY RG26 * 49 L8
Pitt Hill La WVILLE PO7 ...... 255 H4
Pitt La RFNM GU10 .... 136 A3
Pittmore Rd
  CHCH/BSGR BH23 .... 324 C5
Pitt Rd WSHM SO15 .... 247 N5
Pitts Deep La LYMN SO41 ...... 330 C2
Pitts La AND SP10 .... 4 C7
Pitts PI NMIL/BTOS BH25 ...... 327 M5
Pitts Rd ALDT GU11 .... 76 A8
Pitt Wk AMSY SP4 .... 57 N8
Pitwines Cl PLE BH15 .... 332 F1
Pitymoor La WHAM PO17 .... 274 D1
Place Crs WVILLE PO7 .... 275 P5
Place House Cl FHAM PO15 ..... 272 A9
Place La RWIN SO21 .... 183 M6
Plaitford Gv HAV PO9 .... 276 C6
Plantagenet Crs BWD BH11 ..... 301 M8
Plantation LYMN SO41 .... 328 E7
Plantation Dr
  CHCH/BSGR BH23 .... 326 C5
  TOTT SO40 .... 267 J1
Plantation Rd AND SP10 .... 102 C3
  CFDH BH17 .... 320 E3
  CHCH/BSGR BH23 .... 303 P4
  LISS GU33 .... 192 F4
  ROMY SO51 .... 204 A4
  TADY RG26 .... 34 A4
Plantation Wy BOR GU35 .... 153 M8
Plant Park Rd RGWD BH24 ...... 282 A6
Plants Cl ASHV GU12 .... 3 L1
Pine Tree Cl WIMB BH21 .... 278 F9
Pine Tree Gdns HORN PO8 ...... 256 A9
Pine Tree Gln WBNE BH4 .... 334 C3
Pinetree Houses TDWTH SP9 * .. 79 J4
Pine Trees Cl
  FHAM/STUB PO14 .... 294 B1
Pinetree Wk CFDH BH17 .... 320 B4
Pine Vale Crs NBNE BH10 ...... 322 C5
Pine Vw BOR GU35 .... 155 J2
Pine View Cl FNM GU9 .... 96 G6
  HLER SO31 .... 157 H5
Pineview Cl HLER SO31 .... 270 A1
  RSAL SP5 .... 199 P9
Pine View Rd VWD BH31 .... 258 D3
Pine Wk AND SP10 .... 102 B4
  FERN BH22 .... 280 B6
  FLEETS GU52 .... 74 C7
  LISS GU33 .... 193 M9
  ROWN SO16 .... 228 B5
  VWD BH31 .... 258 H5
Pine Wy ROWN SO16 .... 228 B5
Pinewood CHIN RG24 * 69 P1
Pinewood Av HAV PO9 .... 276 D7
  ROWN SO16 .... 295 J8
  WIMB BH21 .... 300 B1
Pinewood Cl
  CHCH/BSGR BH23 .... 326 C5
  FHAM/STUB PO14 .... 294 B2
  NBNE BH10 .... 322 D3
  ROMY SO51 .... 204 G4
  SHST GU47 .... 40 G6
Platoff Rd LYMN SO41 .... 329 L1
Player Ct FBDG SP6 .... 220 D9
Players Crs TOTT SO40 .... 246 C6
Playfair Rd SSEA PO5 .... 19 J5
Playfields Dr
  BKME/WDN BH12 .... 321 N6
Playing Field Cl HASM GU27 ... 157 H5
Pleasance Wy
  NMIL/BTOS BH25 .... 327 H4
Pleasant Hi TADY RG26 .... 34 C6
Pleasant Rd TOTT SO40 .... 246 D8
Plecy Cl FERN BH22 .... 302 D5
Plemont Cl BKME/WDN BH12 ..... 321 N3
Plough Gdns STOK SO20 .... 160 A1
Plough La BPWT SO32 .... 253 N1
  HTWY RG27 .... 54 E2
Plough Rd YTLY GU46 .... 40 F7
Plough Wy FUFL SO22 .... 183 M2
Ploughmans Wy RFNM GU10 ...... 82 F9
  BH/HW/K RG22 .... 89 M1
  FHAM/STUB PO14 .... 293 P7
  ROWN SO16 .... 227 M7
Plover Dr LYMN SO41 .... 339 J2
Plover Cl BH/HW/K RG22 .... 89 K4
  FARN GU14 .... 57 N6
Plover Rd TOTT SO40 .... 246 A5
Plovers Down FUFL SO22 .... 183 K3
Plovers Rd HORN PO8 .... 256 A5
Plovers Wy ALTN GU34 .... 132 G3

PLPH Rd FAWY SO45 291 K4
Plumer Rd CFDH BH17 320 C3
LISS GU33 173 P4
Plumpton Gdns HSEA PO3 297 K6
Plumpton Gv WVILLE PO7 276 B1
Plumpton Rd NWBY RG14 17 J6
Plumpton Wy ALTN GU34 132 F7
Pluto Rd ELGH SO50 229 H1
Plymouth Dr
FHAM/STUB PO14 293 P7
Plymouth St SSEA PO5 19 H4
Poachers Fld ODIM RG29 92 G8
Pococks La LISS GU33 172 E8
Poets Wy FUFL SO22 164 E7
Poinsettia Cl FHAM PO15 271 L7
Pointout Cl ROWN SO16 228 A9
Pointout Rd ROWN SO16 228 A9
Poland La ODIM RG29 72 D6
Polden Cl FARN GU14 57 M6
Polesden Cl CHFD SO53 206 D5
Poles La LYMN SO41 329 L6
RWIN SO21 182 D8
Police Station La BPWT SO32 233 M3
Polkerris Wy FLEETS GU52 74 E8
Pollard Gv CBLY GU15 59 H1
Pollards Moor Rd TOTT SO40 244 G2
Polmear Cl FLEETS GU52 74 E8
The Polygon WSHM SO15 20 C2
Pomeroy Crs HEND SO30 250 B1
Pomona Cl FERN BH22 302 D2
Pompeys La WIMB BH21 302 A4
Pond Cl NMIL/BTOS BH25 327 J4
NWBY RG14 24 A8
OVTN RG25 86 C5
TOTT SO40 247 K9
Pond Cft YTLY GU46 40 F8
Pond Head WIMB BH21 279 J1
Pondhead Cl FAWY SO45 290 E6
Pond La HORN PO8 236 B6
RAND SP11 120 B1
RFNM GU10 136 C5
Pondpenny La FARN GU14 75 H3
Pond Piece WVILLE PO7 255 H8
Pond Rd BOR GU35 155 H4
FARN GU14 76 A2
HLER SO31 270 F4
TADY RG26 52 B3
Pondside La BPWT SO32 231 P4
Pondtail Cl FLEETN GU51 74 F4
Pondtail Gdns FLEETN GU51 74 F4
Pondtail Rd FLEETN GU51 74 F4
Pondview Cl FLEETN GU51 74 F2
Ponsonby Rd PSTN BH14 321 M8
Pook La HAV PO9 15 K7
WHAM PO17 272 F6
Pookles La ALTN GU34 133 N8
Pooksgreen TOTT SO40 247 H9
Poole Br PLE BH15 332 D2
Poole Hl WCLF BH2 8 B4
Poole La BWD BH11 301 P9
Poole Rd CCLF BH13 321 P8
ITCH SO19 248 G7
WBNE BH4 334 B2
WCLF BH2 8 A4
WIMB BH21 300 E1
Pool Rd HTWY RG27 55 H6
Poors Farm Rd CHIN RG24 70 F4
Popes Hl KSCL RG20 48 B3
Popes La BPWT SO32 209 J9
TOTT SO40 246 D4
Popes Md HASM GU27 157 H6
Popes Rd PLE BH15 320 F6
Popham Ct HAV PO9 276 C4
Popham La OVTN RG25 108 C2
Poplar Cl CHCH/BSGR BH23 305 N8
CHCH/BSGR BH23 326 D7
FRIM GU16 76 F1
HTWY RG27 52 E4
TADY RG26 33 N6
WIMB BH21 278 F9
Poplar Crs RGWD BH24 282 F2
Poplar Dr FHAM/STUB PO14 294 C1
TOTT SO40 267 H1
Poplar Gv HISD PO11 318 G4
Poplar La CHCH/BSGR BH23 305 N7
Poplar Pl NWBY RG14 24 D2
Poplar Rd ITCH SO19 249 H5
NMIL/BTOS BH25 327 M3
Poplars Cl FARN GU14 57 K8
The Poplars BPWT SO32 232 C9
Poplar Wk FNM GU9 96 D4
Poplar Wy HEND SO30 250 D5
NBAD SO52 205 K8
RGWD BH24 282 F2
Popley Wy CHIN RG24 69 J4
Poppy Cl AND SP10 102 A3
CHCH/BSGR BH23 325 M7
HLER SO31 270 F8
Poppyfields CHFD SO53 206 C7
Poppy Flds CHIN RG24 70 B4
Poppy Rd ROWN SO16 228 E7
Porchester Cl AND SP10 82 B8
Porchester Rd ITCH SO19 248 C8
NWBY RG14 16 E6
Porlock Cl STHA RG19 * 25 N5
Porlock Rd ROWN SO16 246 G2
Portacre Ri BSTK RG21 69 J9
Portal Cl RAND SP11 101 P3
Portal Rd ELGH SO50 229 M1
ITCH SO19 249 K7
LSOL/BMARY PO13 294 G6
TOTT SO40 246 B4
WINC SO23 23 H7
Portarlington Cl WBNE BH4 334 D4
Portarlington Rd WBNE BH4 334 C3
Portchester Hts
FHAM/PORC PO16 273 P9
Portchester La WHAM PO17 273 P7
Portchester Pl CHAR BH8 335 H1
Portchester Ri ELGH SO50 207 J6
Portchester Rd
FHAM/PORC PO16 295 L1
NEND PO2 296 G9
Portelet Cl BKME/WDN BH12 321 M3
Portelet Pl HEND SO30 250 C6
Porteous Crs CHFD SO53 207 H7
Porter Cl ODIM RG29 * 93 J3
Porter End NWBY RG14 17 H7
Porter Rd BH/HW/K RG22 90 B2
CFDH BH17 320 D5
Portersbridge St ROMY SO51 204 C6
Porters Cl AND SP10 102 B1
OVTN RG25 109 H1
Porters La SHAM SO14 20 D7
WIMB BH21 279 L8
Portesham Gdns
MOOR/WNTN BH9 323 H3
Portesham Wy CFDH BH17 320 C1
Portfield Cl CHCH/BSGR BH23 324 E7
Portfield Rd
CHCH/BSGR BH23 324 E8
Port Hamble HLER SO31 * 270 A7
Portiswood Cl TADY RG26 34 E6
Portland Dr FLEETS GU52 74 C8
GPORT PO12 315 H5
Portland Gv AND SP10 4 D4
Portland Rd
MOOR/WNTN BH9 322 G7
SSEA PO5 316 E6
WVILLE PO7 275 N3
Portland's Cl PSF GU32 191 P9
Portland Sq LISS GU33 192 D2
Portland St PSEA PO1 18 E3
SHAM SO14 20 D4
Portland Ter FNM GU9 * 96 D7
SHAM SO14 20 D4
SSEA PO5 * 316 E6
Port La RWIN SO21 182 D7
Portman Crs BOSC BH5 335 P2
Portman Rd LTDN BH7 335 M1
Portman Ter BOSC BH5 * 335 P2
Portmore Cl BDST BH18 300 D7
Portobello Gv
FHAM/PORC PO16 273 P9
Port Royal St SSEA PO5 * 19 K3
Portsdown Av CHAM PO6 297 L1
Portsdown Hill Rd CHAM PO6 275 H9
FHAM/PORC PO16 273 L8
Portsdown Rd CHAM PO6 296 A1
Portside Cl TOTT SO40 247 L8
Portsmouth Cl ALTN GU34 132 D8
Portsmouth Crs
BH/HW/K RG22 68 G9
Portsmouth Rd BPWT SO32 209 H9
CBLY GU15 58 F1
CHAM PO6 297 H3
ELGH SO50 208 C7
FRIM GU16 58 C4
GSHT GU26 155 P9
HLER SO31 270 A1
HORN PO8 256 B6
ITCH SO19 248 F8
LIPH GU30 174 C4
LSOL/BMARY PO13 314 D4
Portsmouth Wk
BH/HW/K RG22 89 P1
Portsmouth Wy
BH/HW/K RG22 89 P1
Portsview Av
FHAM/PORC PO16 295 P1
Portsview Gdns
FHAM/PORC PO16 273 P9
Portswood Av SD/PW SO17 248 D3
Portswood Dr
MOOR/WNTN BH9 322 G3
Portswood Pk SD/PW SO17 248 D3
Portswood Rd HAV PO9 276 D4
NEND PO2 296 G4
SD/PW SO17 248 D3
Portview Rd WEND SO18 249 H1
Port Wy CHAM PO6 296 D3
Portway TADY RG26 33 N5
THLE RG7 37 P4
Portway Cl AND SP10 102 B2
WEND SO18 249 K4
Portway Pl DEAN RG23 68 E7
Posbrooke Rd ENEY PO4 317 J4
Posbrook La
FHAM/STUB PO14 293 L4
Postern Cl FHAM/PORC PO16 295 P1
Post Horn La HTWY RG27 53 M8
Posting House Ms NWBY RG14 24 B3
Post Office La OVTN RG25 109 H1
RDGW/BURGH RG30 27 L2
RGWD BH24 281 N4
Post Office Rd WCLF BH2 8 D4
WVILLE PO7 275 L5
Potbridge Rd ODIM RG29 72 E4
Pot La CHIN RG24 70 G4
Potley Hill Rd YTLY GU46 40 G9
Potteries La FRIM GU16 76 E1
The Potteries FARN GU14 57 L7
FHAM/PORC PO16 11 H2
Potterne Wy WIMB BH21 258 G6
Potterne Wood Cl VWD BH31 259 J6
Potters Crs ASHV GU12 76 G9
Potters Fld LISS GU33 192 E2
Potters Ga FNM GU9 96 A9
Potters Heron Cl ROMY SO51 206 A2
Potters Heron La ROMY SO51 206 A2
Potters La HTWY RG27 52 G2
Potters Wy PSTN BH14 333 L1
Pottery Cl RFNM GU10 115 P4
Pottery Dro STOK SO20 120 A7
Pottery La RFNM GU10 115 P4
Pottery Rd PSTN BH14 333 J1
Poulner Cl ITCH SO19 269 J1
Poulner Ct HAV PO9 276 C4
Poulner Hl RGWD BH24 283 H1
Poulner Pk RGWD BH24 260 G9
Poultons Cl OVTN RG25 86 C5
Poultons Rd OVTN RG25 86 G4
Pound Cl BOR GU35 154 C3
LSOL/BMARY PO13 295 H9
NARL SO24 130 B7
PLE BH15 321 H7
RGWD BH24 282 E1
STOK SO20 120 C7
TADY RG26 51 P2
Pound Cots BPWT SO32 211 N8
Pound Ga ALTN GU34 132 G4
Pound Gate Dr
FHAM/STUB PO14 271 J9
Pound Hl NARL SO24 167 P1
ROMY SO51 202 C8
Pound La BPWT SO32 211 P8
FBDG SP6 219 H7
KSCL RG20 30 D8
NWBY RG14 24 A3
PLE BH15 320 G7
RGWD BH24 284 A8
ROMY SO51 202 C8
ROMY SO51 205 M3
STHA RG19 25 K4
TOTT SO40 245 J1
TOTT SO40 246 C8
Pound Lea HISD PO11 318 G3
Pound Meadow HTWY RG27 52 F5
WHCH RG28 85 M6
Pound Rd ASHV GU12 3 G4
CHAM PO6 274 D8
HLER SO31 269 N1
LYMN SO41 329 H4
OVTN RG25 87 H4
STOK SO20 120 C7
WINC SO23 145 K8
Pound St NWBY RG14 16 D4
WEND SO18 249 J4
Pound Tree Rd SHAM SO14 20 E4
Poveys Md KSCL RG20 48 D3
Powell Crs TOTT SO40 246 D6
Powell Rd PSTN BH14 321 K9
Power Rd PSEA PO1 316 G2
Powerscourt Rd NEND PO2 296 G9
NMIL/BTOS BH25 326 F8
Powis Cl NMIL/BTOS BH25 327 K4
Powlingbroke HTWY RG27 72 C3
Poyle Rd RFNM GU10 97 N4
Poyner Cl FHAM/PORC PO16 11 G4
Poynings Crs BSTK RG21 90 E1
Poynings Pl PSEA PO1 18 D6
Poynters Cl AND SP10 82 D9
Poyntz Rd OVTN RG25 86 G3
Prancing Horse Cl STHA RG19 25 P4
The Precinct CHFD SO53 * 206 E7
FAWY SO45 290 E5
GPORT PO12 * 13 H2
HISD PO11 * 318 G5
WVILLE PO7 275 N3
Precosa Rd HEND SO30 250 E6
Prelate Wy FHAM/STUB PO14 271 J8
Premier Pde WEND SO18 * 229 H9
Premier Wy ROMY SO51 205 H8
Prentice Cl FARN GU14 58 A5
Prescelly Cl BH/HW/K RG22 68 E8
Preshaw Cl ROWN SO16 227 N8
Preston La CHCH/BSGR BH23 325 H4
Preston Pl NWBY RG14 24 G2
Preston Rd NEND PO2 297 H8
PLE BH15 320 E6
Preston Wy CHCH/BSGR BH23 325 P7
Prestwick La HASM GU27 157 M3
Prestwood Cl
NMIL/BTOS BH25 327 H6
Prestwood Rd HEND SO30 250 C5
Pretoria Cl LISS GU33 173 P5
Pretoria Rd ENEY PO4 317 H5
HEND SO30 250 B6
RAND SP11 80 B2
Pricketts Hl BPWT SO32 252 D4
Prideaux-Brune Av
LSOL/BMARY PO13 294 G5
Priest Croft Dr FAWY SO45 290 G7
Priest Down BH/HW/K RG22 89 L6
Priestfields FHAM/STUB PO14 271 J8
Priestlands ROMY SO51 204 C5
Priestlands Cl TOTT SO40 245 N5
Priestlands La LYMN SO41 329 J4
Priestlands Rd LYMN SO41 329 J4
Priest La CHCH/BSGR BH23 304 F9
CHOB/PIR GU24 59 P1
Priestley Cl TOTT SO40 246 B4
Priestley Rd CHIN RG24 69 H5
NBNE BH10 322 B6
Priestwood Cl WEND SO18 249 M4
Primate Rd FHAM/STUB PO14 271 K8
Prime One AND SP10 * 103 J1
Primrose Cl CHFD SO53 206 B9
HEND SO30 250 C6
LSOL/BMARY PO13 294 G4
Primrose Dr HTWY RG27 55 H6
Primrose Gdns BH/HW/K RG22 89 M6
CFDH BH17 320 B3
FARN GU14 75 M1
Primrose La LISS GU33 193 H2
RSAL SP5 199 N7
Primrose Rd RAND SP11 79 P1
ROWN SO16 228 C8
Primrose Wy
CHCH/BSGR BH23 325 N7
HLER SO31 270 F8
ROMY SO51 204 G5
SHST GU47 41 J5
WIMB BH21 300 A6
Primula Rd BOR GU35 154 B5
Prince Albert Gdns AND SP10 4 B5
Prince Albert Rd ENEY PO4 317 J5
Prince Alfred St GPORT PO12 12 D4
Prince Charles Crs FARN GU14 58 A5
Prince Cl AND SP10 83 H9
Prince Dr SHST GU47 41 H5
Prince George's St HAV PO9 15 G5
Prince George St HAV PO9 15 G5
PSEA PO1 18 D2
Prince Hold Rd STHA RG19 25 K4
Prince of Wales Av
WSHM SO15 247 L3
Prince of Wales Cl
WVILLE PO7 * 276 A3
Prince of Wales Rd
GPORT PO12 13 F2
WBNE BH4 334 B2
Prince Rd FHAM/STUB PO14 294 D3
ROWN SO16 227 J5
Prince's Av ALDT GU11 76 B7
Princes Blds WINC SO23 * 23 F4
Princes Cl BOR GU35 153 P7
BPWT SO32 231 P4
RSAL SP5 200 A6
Princes Ct SHAM SO14 21 J1
Princes' Crs BH/HW/K RG22 69 H9
Princes Dr WVILLE PO7 276 A1
Princes Hl RSAL SP5 200 A6
Princes Pl FUFL SO22 183 N1
Prince's Pl NMIL/BTOS BH25 327 L4
Princes Pl PSEA PO1 * 316 F1
Princes Rd FERN BH22 302 D3
PSF GU32 215 K1
ROMY SO51 204 C5
WSHM SO15 247 P5
Princess Av CHCH/BSGR BH23 324 F9
Princess Cl HEND SO30 249 N1
Princess Crs LYND SO43 265 H4
Princess Dr ALTN GU34 132 D6
Princess Gdns HORN PO8 256 B4
Princess Louise Sq ALTN GU34 132 D8
Princess Mary Gdns
RAND SP11 79 P1
Princess Rd BKME/WDN BH12 334 A2
TOTT SO40 245 P9
WBNE BH4 334 B2
Prince's St PSEA PO1 316 F1
Princes St SHAM SO14 21 J1
Princes Wy ALDT GU11 2 D2
Pringles Cl FERN BH22 302 E3
Pringles Dr FERN BH22 302 E3
Prinstead Cl WINC SO23 * 165 J9
Prinsted Crs CHAM PO6 297 M2
Prinsted Wk
FHAM/STUB PO14 294 B1
Prior Croft Cl CBLY GU15 58 F1
Priors Barton WINC SO23 183 P1
Priors Cl CHCH/BSGR BH23 325 N8
FARN GU14 58 A5
KSCL RG20 48 C3
Priorsdean Av HSEA PO3 317 J2
Priorsdean Crs HAV PO9 14 C1
Priors Dean Rd FUFL SO22 164 E3
Priors Keep FLEETS GU52 74 E4
Prior's La BLKW GU17 41 H9
Priors Rd CFDH BH17 320 C4
TADY RG26 34 B5
Priors Wk WIMB BH21 278 D9
Priors Wy FUFL SO22 183 K3
The Priors Wy NARL SO24 * 170 C5
Priors Wd CWTH RG45 40 E2
HASM GU27 156 E7
Priory Av SD/PW SO17 248 F2
Priory Cl BPWT SO32 231 P4
FLEETN GU51 74 A4
SD/PW SO17 248 F2
Priory Ct CBLY GU15 * 41 N9
Priory Crs ENEY PO4 317 J4
Priory Gdns CHIN RG24 70 C5
FHAM/PORC PO16 295 N1
WVILLE PO7 275 N1
Priory La HTWY RG27 55 H9
RFNM GU10 136 D1
WHCH RG28 86 A4
Priory Pl STHA RG19 24 E9
Priory Quay
CHCH/BSGR BH23 * 336 G1
Priory Rd ELGH SO50 229 H3
ENEY PO4 317 J6
FERN BH22 280 G9
FHAM PO15 272 B8
GPORT PO12 295 M9
HLER SO31 269 K4
NWBY RG14 16 E6
SD/PW SO17 248 E3
WCLF BH2 8 C5
WHAM PO17 274 C4
Priory St FARN GU14 58 C9
The Priory BPWT SO32 231 P5
Priory View Pl
MOOR/WNTN BH9 322 G4
Priory View Rd
CHCH/BSGR BH23 324 G5
MOOR/WNTN BH9 322 G4
Pritchard Cl STHA RG19 24 G8
Private Rd LYMN SO41 329 L2
Privet La RAND SP11 80 F7
Privet Rd BOR GU35 154 D3
MOOR/WNTN BH9 322 E7
Privett Cl CHIN RG24 70 B4
Privett Pl GPORT PO12 315 J4
Privett Rd FHAM PO15 272 A8
LSOL/BMARY PO13 314 G5
PSF GU32 190 D4
WVILLE PO7 275 M7
Prochurch Rd HORN PO8 256 B7
Proctor Cl ITCH SO19 249 M6
Proctor Dr LSOL/BMARY PO13 314 E4
NBAD SO52 227 K1
Proctor La PSEA PO1 317 H3
Promenade CCLF BH13 333 P4
The Promenade EMRTH PO10 299 M2
FAWY SO45 268 C5
NEND PO2 * 296 F8
Propeller Rd FARN GU14 76 A2
Propsperous St PLE BH15 332 E2
Prospect Av FARN GU14 58 A7
Prospect La HAV PO9 277 H5
Prospect Pl CHFD SO53 206 E7
FAWY SO45 268 C5
NWBY RG14 16 E5
Prospect Rd ASHV GU12 76 F7
FARN GU14 57 P9
NARL SO24 167 N3
PSEA PO1 316 E1
RFNM GU10 115 N7
Protea Gdns
FHAM/STUB PO14 293 M1
Provene Cl BPWT SO32 232 C8
Provene Gdns BPWT SO32 232 B8
Providence Hl HLER SO31 250 A9
Providence Pk ROWN SO16 228 B7
Provident Wy BSTK RG21 6 E5
Provost St FBDG SP6 240 D3
Prowse Cl LSOL/BMARY PO13 314 C1
Pruetts La LISS GU33 192 D5
Prunus Cl FERN BH22 302 B1
ROWN SO16 227 N7
Prunus Dr FERN BH22 302 B1
Puckridge Gate Rd ALDT GU11 75 L6
Puckridge Hill Rd ALDT GU11 75 M7
Puckshott Wy HASM GU27 157 J5
Pudbrooke Gdns HEND SO30 250 B3
Pudding La WINC SO23 165 J3
Puddleslosh La FBDG SP6 220 B9
Puddletown Crs CFDH BH17 321 H2
Puffers Wy NWBY RG14 16 A3
Puffin Cl BH/HW/K RG22 89 K5
ROWN SO16 227 M7
Puffin Crs FHAM/STUB PO14 293 P5
Puffin Gdns
LSOL/BMARY PO13 294 F6
Puffin Wk HORN PO8 255 M7
Pug's Hole RSAL SP5 159 H7
Pulens Crs EPSF GU31 216 A1
Pulens La EPSF GU31 215 P1
Pullman Ct FERN BH22 280 D7
Pullman Wy RGWD BH24 282 E3
Pump La HORN PO8 256 A6
LSOL/BMARY PO13 294 G8
Punsholt La NARL SO24 188 G3
Purbeck Av PLE BH15 332 A2
Purbeck Dr FHAM/STUB PO14 294 B1
VWD BH31 258 F5
Purbeck Rd NMIL/BTOS BH25 326 F8
WCLF BH2 8 B4
Purbrook Cl ROWN SO16 227 N8
Purbrook Gdns WVILLE PO7 275 L5
Purbrook Heath Rd
WVILLE PO7 275 H5
Purbrook Rd PSEA PO1 316 G3
TADY RG26 34 B6
Purbrook Wy HAV PO9 276 B6
WVILLE PO7 275 P6
Purcell Cl BH/HW/K RG22 90 B2
WVILLE PO7 275 N5
Purcell Rd ITCH SO19 249 M8
Purchase Rd
BKME/WDN BH12 322 C8
Purewell CHCH/BSGR BH23 325 H9
Purewell Cl CHCH/BSGR BH23 325 J9
Purewell Cross Rd
CHCH/BSGR BH23 325 H8
Purkess Cl CHFD SO53 206 F6
Purkiss Cl TOTT SO40 245 J6
Purley Wy FRIM GU16 58 D5
ROMY SO51 224 B1
Purlieu La FBDG SP6 221 K9
Purmerend Cl FARN GU14 57 K8
The Purrocks PSF GU32 191 M9
Purslane Gdns FHAM PO15 271 M7
Purvis Gdns ITCH SO19 249 K9
Pussex La CHCH/BSGR BH23 303 N8
Putmans La EPSF GU31 216 D7
Puttenham Rd CHIN RG24 70 B1
RFNM GU10 97 P7
Puttocks Cl HASM GU27 156 C8
Pycroft Cl HISD PO11 299 J6
ITCH SO19 249 H6
Pye La WIMB BH21 238 E4
WIMB BH21 300 D1
Pyestock Crs FARN GU14 57 J9
Pye St PSEA PO1 316 E2
Pyland's La HLER SO31 250 B8
Pyle Cl HORN PO8 256 A7
Pyle Hl NWBY RG14 17 H6
Pylewell Rd FAWY SO45 268 C5
Pyotts Copse CHIN RG24 70 B3
Pyotts Ct CHIN RG24 70 B3
Pyotts Hl CHIN RG24 70 B3
Pyramid Pk HAV PO9 298 E2
Pyrford Cl GPORT PO12 315 J5
WVILLE PO7 255 M9
Pyrford Ms LYMN SO41 329 L5
Pytchley Cl FHAM/STUB PO14 293 N7

Q

The Quadrangle ELGH SO50 207 J9
The Quadrant ASHV GU12 76 F8
Quail Wy HORN PO8 256 A5
Quantock Cl BH/HW/K RG22 68 E9
Quantock Rd ROWN SO16 247 J3
The Quantocks FAWY SO45 267 P8
STHA RG19 25 N5
Quarely Rd HAV PO9 276 C4
Quarrington Cl STHA RG19 25 P5
Quarry La YTLY GU46 40 F9
Quarry Rd WIMB BH21 279 J7
WINC SO23 23 H6
Quarters Rd FARN GU14 76 B2
Quartremaine Rd HSEA PO3 297 K6
Quater Deck Av NEND PO2 296 D8
Quavey Rd RSAL SP5 200 A7
Quay Hvn HLER SO31 270 D2
Quay La GPORT PO12 13 J2
Quayle Dr BWD BH11 301 P7
Quay Point CHAM PO6 * 296 E1
Quay Rd CHCH/BSGR BH23 324 F9
Quayside HEND SO30 * 250 G5
Quayside Rd FAWY SO45 291 P8
WEND SO18 248 F4
Quayside Wk TOTT SO40 247 K8
Quay St FHAM/PORC PO16 11 J6
LYMN SO41 329 M3
The Quay PLE BH15 332 E2
Quebec Cl LIPH GU30 175 K4
Quebec Gdns BLKW GU17 57 L1
HLER SO31 269 P1
Queen Anne Dr WIMB BH21 300 G6
Queen Anne's Dr HAV PO9 276 C8
Queen Anne's Ga FNM GU9 96 D4
Queen Elizabeth Av
LYMN SO41 329 K3
Queen Elizabeth Cl ASHV GU12 97 N1
Queen Elizabeth Dr ALDT GU11 2 C3
Queen Katherine Rd
LYMN SO41 329 M4
Queen Mary Av BSTK RG21 7 F3
CBLY GU15 41 P9
MOOR/WNTN BH9 322 F5
Queen Mary Cl FLEETN GU51 74 C2
Queen Mary Rd
FHAM/PORC PO16 295 P2
Queen Rd FHAM/STUB PO14 294 D3
Queen's Av ALDT GU11 75 P9
Queens Av AND SP10 4 B4

Queen's Av CHCH/BSGR BH23.....336 F1
Queensbury Pl BLKW GU17.....57 K2
Queens Cl FARN GU14.....76 A4
Queens Cl FAWY SO45.....268 C7
  FERN BH22.....280 D8
  LSOL/BMARY PO13 *.....314 C2
  RAND SP11.....79 P1
Queens Ct FHAM GU9.....96 B4
Queens Crs FHAM/STUB PO14...294 B6
  HORN PO8.....256 B4
  SSEA PO5.....19 H7
Queensfield OVTN RG25.....109 H1
Queens Gdns FBDG SP6.....240 D1
  BH44.....334 D2
Queen's Gate FARN GU14.....76 A5
Queens Gv NMIL/BTOS BH25...327 L3
Queens Gv SSEA PO5.....316 E6
Queens Gv WVILLE PO7.....275 M5
Queensland Rd LTDN BH1.....335 N1
Queens La FNM GU9.....96 B4
Queensmead
  CHCH/BSGR BH23.....324 E6
  FARN GU14.....58 A9
Queen's Pole LYND SO43.....264 F5
Queen's Pl AYND SO52.....327 L3
  WVILLE PO7.....275 N5
Queen's Park Av CHAR BH8.....323 J7
Queen's Park Gdns CHAR BH8..323 J8
Queen's Park Rd CHAR BH8.....323 K8
Queen's Park South Dr
  CHAR BH8.....323 K8
Queen's Park West Dr
  CHAR BH8.....323 J8
Queen's Pl SSEA PO5.....19 H7
Queen's Ride NBAD SO52.....205 J9
Queens Rd ALDT GU11.....2 B4
  ALTN GU34.....132 E6
Queen's Rd BSTK RG21.....6 B5
Queen's Rd CBLY GU15.....58 A1
Queen's Rd CHCH/BSGR BH23..325 J9
  CHFD SO53.....206 F4
Queens Rd FARN GU14.....76 B3
Queen's Rd FHAM/PORC PO16..11 C6
  FLEETS GU52.....74 D6
  FUFL SO22.....164 E8
  GPORT PO12.....12 E1
  HLER SO31.....292 C1
Queens Rd KSCL RG20.....48 D3
  LIPH GU30.....174 D4
  LSOL/BMARY PO13.....314 D4
  LYND SO43.....264 C5
Queen's Rd NEND PO2.....296 C9
  NWBY RG14.....17 C4
Queen's Rd ODIM RG29.....72 B9
Queen's Rd PSEA PO1.....316 B2
Queen's Rd PSF GU32.....215 K1
Queen's Rd PSTN BH14.....321 M8
  RAND SP11.....79 N1
  WCLF BH2.....334 D3
Queens Rd WHCH RG28.....85 M8
Queen's Ter SHAM SO14.....21 F7
  SSEA PO5.....19 G7
Queensway FRIM GU16.....58 F6
  HISD PO11.....298 C6
  NMIL/BTOS BH25.....326 C4
  RGWD BH24.....282 F2
The Queensway
  FHAM/PORC PO16.....295 M1
Queenswood Av CHAR BH8.....323 L6
Queenswood Dr FERN BH22....302 D1
Queen Victoria Ct FARN GU14...58 A8
Queenwood Av STOK SO20.....159 F3
Queenwood Rd STOK SO20.....160 A1
Quennells HI HORN GU10.....115 N4
Querida Cl HLER SO31.....270 D2
Quilter Cl ITCH SO19.....249 M7
Quilter Rd BH/HW/K GU22.....89 N2
Quince La WIMB BH21.....278 F8
Quince Tree Wy HTWY RG27....72 A3
Quintin Cl CHCH/BSGR BH23...326 B7
Quinton Cl SSEA PO5.....19 J4
Quinton Flds EMRTH PO10.....277 N7
Quintrell Av
  FHAM/PORC PO16.....295 L1
Quob Farm Cl HEND SO30.....229 N9
Quob La HEND SO30.....229 N9
The Quomp RGWD BH24.....282 E2

R

Racecourse Rd NWBY RG14.....17 G5
Racecourse Vw LYND SO43.....264 F4
Rachel Cl ELGH SO50.....230 B2
Rack Cl AND SP10.....4 E4
Rackclose Rd ALTN GU34.....132 E6
Rackfield HASM GU27.....156 C6
Rackstraw Rd SHST GU47.....41 L5
Racton Av CHAM PO6.....297 K2
Racton Rd EMRTH PO10.....277 M7
Radar Rd FARN GU14.....75 L3
Radcliffe Cl FRIM GU16.....58 E6
Radcliffe Rd SHAM SO14.....21 H1
Radcliffe Rd
  FHAM/PORC PO16.....11 K3
Radford Cl FHAM GU9.....96 E6
Radford Gdns BH/HW/K RG22..79 K5
Radipole Rd CFDH BH17.....321 H2
Radleigh Gdns TOTT SO40.....245 P3
Radnor Rd HEND SO30.....250 C2
Radnor St SSEA PO5.....19 H4

Radstock Rd ITCH SO19.....248 G8
Radway Crs WSHM SO15.....247 P3
Radway Rd WSHM SO15.....247 P3
Raeburn Cl NARL SO24.....187 H1
Raeburn Dr HEND SO30.....250 C4
Raeburn Wy SHST GU47.....41 L8
Rae Rd FARN GU14.....76 A2
Raf Gate Rd FARN GU14.....76 A3
Ragdale THLE RG7.....27 J4
Raglan Cl ASHV GU12.....3 H5
  CHFD SO53.....206 B9
  FRIM GU16.....58 E5
Raglan Gdns BWD BH11.....322 A5
Raglan St STHA RG19.....19 J3
Ragmore La PSF GU32.....190 E1
Rails La HISD PO11.....319 H6
Railway Triangle CHAM PO6 *..297 K3
Railway Vw PSEA PO1.....19 J2
Rainbow Cl CHIN RG24.....70 D7
Rainham Cl BH/HW/K RG22.....89 K4
Rakemakers ALTN GU34.....133 K2
Rake Rd LIPH GU30.....195 P4
  LISS GU33.....192 E2
Raleigh Cl CHCH/BSGR BH23 ..337 K1
  NMIL/BTOS BH25.....327 H4
Raleigh Rd RFNM GU10.....126 D9
Raleigh Wy FRIM GU16.....58 E2
Raley Rd HLER SO31.....270 C8
Ralph La ROMY SO51.....204 E4
Ralph La WSHM SO15.....247 J4
Ram Aly STHA RG19.....32 F6
Ramalley La CHFD SO53.....206 D6
Rambler Dr
  LSOL/BMARY PO13.....314 C2
Ramblers Wy WVILLE PO7.....276 B1
Ramillies Cl RAND SP11.....76 D5
Ramillies Rd ALDT GU11.....76 C7
Ramley Rd LYMN SO41.....328 F2
Rampart Gdns HSEA PO3.....297 H4
Rampart Rd WEND SO18.....248 F4
Rampart Wy GPORT PO12.....13 J4
The Rampart LYMN SO41.....329 K2
Rampton La THLE RG7.....26 D9
Rampton's Meadow
  TADY RG26.....34 E7
Ramsay PI LSOL/BMARY PO13..294 C7
Ramsay Rd WINC SO23.....145 K9
Ramsdale Av HAV PO9.....276 C5
Ramsdean Rd PSF GU32.....214 D4
Ramsdell CI TADY RG26.....34 C7
Ramsdell Rd FLEETN GU51.....73 H9
  TADY RG26.....50 E4
Ramsey Rd HISD PO11.....318 G5
Ramshill EPSF GU31.....215 N1
Ramshill Rd OVTN RG25.....108 C1
Rances Wy FUFL SO22.....183 N1
Randall Cl TOTT SO40.....246 A1
Randall Rd CHFD SO53.....206 F3
Randalls La RGWD BH24.....283 P4
Randell Cl BLKW GU17.....57 M4
Randolph Dr FARN GU14.....75 K1
Randolph Rd BMTH BH1.....335 L2
  NEND PO2.....296 C6
  PSTN BH14.....321 L7
Randolph St WSHM SO15.....247 N4
Ranelagh Gdns WSHM SO15...248 A4
Ranelagh Rd
  CHCH/BSGR BH23.....326 B8
  HAV PO9.....14 C5
  NEND PO2.....296 E8
  WINC SO23.....164 F9
Ranfurly Gdns FAWY SO45.....268 A8
Range Gdns ITCH SO19.....249 K8
Range Gn NEND PO2.....296 E6
Range Rd CBLY GU15.....11 N7
Range Vw SHST GU47.....41 M6
Rankine Cl FNM GU9.....76 B1
Rannoch Cl FHAM PO15.....10 A2
Ransome Cl FHAM/STUB PO14..293 M2
Ranvilles La FHAM/STUB PO14..294 A4
Rapallo Cl FARN GU14.....58 B9
Raphael Cl BSTK RG21.....69 N9
Rapson Cl CHAM PO6.....274 E9
Rareridge La BPWT SO32.....232 B4
Rasset Md FLEETS GU52.....74 B9
Ratcliffe Rd FARN GU14.....57 N5
  FAWY SO45.....268 B9
  NEND PO2.....250 C4
Rathdora Ms HLER SO31.....269 P7
Ratlake La RWIN SO21.....206 B1
Rattigan Gdns FHAM PO15.....271 J2
Ravel Cl BH/HW/K RG22.....90 A2
Ravelin Cl FLEETN GU51.....56 C9
  RFNM GU10.....95 H6
Raven Rd HTWY RG27.....71 P3
  SHAM SO14.....21 G1
Ravens Cl WSHM SO15.....41 N8
Ravenscourt Rd LYMN SO41....329 K4
  SBNE BH6.....336 A1
Ravenscroft HTWY RG27.....72 B3
Ravens Cft HTWY RG27 *.....72 B3
Ravenscroft Cl ASHV GU12.....77 H9
  HLER SO31.....269 P1
Ravensdale Cl
  BKME/WDN BH12.....321 L6
Raven Sq ALTN GU34.....132 F3
Ravens Wy LYMN SO41.....338 C2
Ravenswood Av CWTH RG45...40 F1
Ravensworth Rd THLE RG7.....26 G9
Raven Wy CHCH/BSGR BH23...337 L1
Ravine Rd BOSC BH5.....335 P2
  CCLF BH13.....333 P3
Rawlings Ct RAND SP11.....79 P1
Rawlings Rd HTWY RG27.....72 A1

Rawlinson Rd ALDT GU11.....76 B6
Rawson Rd NEND PO2.....41 N8
Rayngnoldes FLEETS GU52.....74 B9
Rayleigh Rd BSTK RG21.....6 D6
Raymond Cl FAWY SO45.....290 F6
  HEND SO30.....229 P9
  VWD BH31.....259 H4
Raymond Rd CHAM PO6.....274 A9
  WSHM SO15.....247 P4
Rayners Gdns ROWN SO16.....228 F8
Rayne's Meadow CHIN RG24....70 B4
Raynes Rd LSOL/BMARY PO13..314 D4
Rays Cl TADY RG26.....34 C6
Reading Dr North HTWY RG27..38 G9
Reading Rd BLKW GU17.....57 J1
  CHIN RG24.....69 N4
  FARN GU14.....76 B3
  HTWY RG27.....52 E5
  HTWY RG27.....71 P2
  THLE RG7.....27 J5
  THLE RG7.....34 G1
  YTLY GU46.....40 C7
Reading Rd North
  CBLY GU15.....74 A2
Reading Road Rbt CHIN RG24..69 N4
Reading Rd South
  CBLY GU15.....74 C4
Readon Cl EPSF GU31.....215 N1
Read's Fld ALTN GU34.....150 C6
Rebbeck Rd LTDN BH1.....335 N1
Rebecca Cl FLEETS GU52.....74 B9
The Recess ELGH SO50.....207 K8
Record Rd EMRTH PO10.....277 L9
Recreation Rd FARN GU14.....57 N4
Recreation Rd ALDT GU11.....5 F7
  BKME/WDN BH12.....321 N6
  ODIM RG29.....93 J1
  RAND SP11.....79 P1
  RFNM GU10.....115 N7
  THLE RG7.....27 J5
Rectory Av CHAM PO6.....279 P5
Rectory CI FHAM/STUB PO14...294 A6
  GPORT PO12.....12 B6
  NWBY RG14.....16 C4
  SHST GU47.....40 G6
  TADY RG26.....34 D8
Rectory Ct HEND SO30.....250 C4
Rectory Gdns HTWY RG27.....52 F5
Rectory La RSAL SP5.....177 M3
Rectory La BPWT SO32.....211 N8
  FBDG SP6.....220 F3
  ODIM RG29.....155 L9
  RWIN SO21.....114 F6
  RWIN SO21.....146 F8
  STOK SO20.....160 A1
  TADY RG26.....48 F6
Rectory PI RAND SP11.....79 N1
Rectory Rd DEAN RG23.....88 C2
  FARN GU14.....58 B9
  HAV PO9.....15 F7
  HTWY RG27.....71 P4
  PLE BH15.....320 E6
  THLE RG7.....26 B8
Reculver Wy AND SP10.....82 B9
Redan Cl CHCH/BSGR BH23.....326 B8
Redan Gdns ASHV GU12.....3 G3
Redan Hill Est ASHV GU12 *.....3 H3
The Redan GPORT PO12.....315 N7
Red Barn Av
  FHAM/PORC PO16.....273 N9
Red Barn La FHAM PO15.....272 C6
Redbreast Rd
  MOOR/WNTN BH9.....322 C4
Redbreast Rd North
  MOOR/WNTN BH9.....322 G4
Redbridge Cswy ROWN SO16...246 F3
Redbridge Dr AND SP10.....4 A6
Redbridge Gv HAV PO9.....14 B1
Redbridge Hl ROWN SO16.....247 K2
Redbridge La CHIN RG24.....69 P7
  ROWN SO16.....246 F1
Redbridge Rd WSHM SO15.....247 H3
Redbrook Ter FBDG SP6 *.....240 E4
Red Bushes Cl ALTN GU34.....150 D4
Redcar Av HSEA PO3.....297 J8
Redcliffe Cl CHCH/BSGR BH23..324 G5
Redcote Cl WEND SO18.....248 A9
Redcotts La WIMB BH21.....278 D9
Redcotts Rd WIMB BH21.....278 D9
Redcroft La HLER SO31.....270 A1
Redenham Dro RAND SP11.....80 G3
Redes Cl HTWY RG27.....72 C3
Redfield Ct NWBY RG14.....16 D3
Redfields La FLEETS GU52.....74 C9
The Redfords TOTT SO40.....246 C2
Redhearne Flds RFNM GU10...136 E7
Red HI ALTN GU34.....150 C3
  HTWY RG27.....54 D4
Redhill Av MOOR/WNTN BH9...322 E3
Redhill Cl NBNE BH10 *.....322 E5
Redhill Crs MOOR/WNTN BH9..322 F4
Redhill Dr NBNE BH10.....322 E5
Red Hill Crs ROWN SO16.....228 A8
Red Hill Wy ROWN SO16.....228 A8
Redhoave Rd CFDH BH17.....320 G3
Red House Ct EPSF GU31.....217 K1
Redhouse Park Gdns
  GPORT PO12.....315 J2
Redlands BKME/WDN BH12....321 P7
Redlands Dr ITCH SO19.....249 H5
Redlands Gv ENEY PO4.....317 L4
Redlynch La RSAL SP5.....170 E1
Red La BOR GU35.....155 J1
  OVTN RG25.....107 H2
  RSAL SP5.....159 H8
Red Leaves BPWT SO32.....252 C1

Red Lion La BSTK RG21.....7 F7
  HAV PO9.....116 B1
  OVTN RG25.....86 C5
Red Ldg CHFD SO53.....228 D1
Redlynch Cl HAV PO9.....277 N5
Redmans Vw VWD BH31.....258 D4
Redmayne Cl CBLY GU15.....59 H1
Redmill Dr CHCH/BSGR BH23..314 C1
Rednoor Cl ITCH SO19.....249 H5
Red Oaks RFNM GU10 *.....115 N7
Red Oaks Cl FERN BH22.....302 B1
Red Oaks Dr HLER SO31.....271 H5
Redon Wy AND SP10.....4 A1
Red Post La RAND SP11.....101 L2
Red Rice Rd RAND SP11.....102 A9
Redrise Cl FAWY SO45.....290 C6
Redshank Cl CFDH BH17.....320 B3
Redshank Ct STHA RG19.....25 K4
Redshank Rd HORN PO8.....256 A4
Redvers Buller Rd ALDT GU11...76 B5
Redvers Rd CHCH/BSGR BH23..325 J8
Redward Rd ROWN SO16.....227 K7
Redwing Ct ENEY PO4.....317 L3
Redwing Gdns TOTT SO40.....246 A3
Redwing Rd BH/HW/K RG22.....89 K4
  HORN PO8.....256 C7
Redwood Cl FAWY SO45.....267 N7
  HEND SO30.....249 L1
  LYMN SO41.....329 J2
  RGWD BH24.....282 F2
Redwood Dr CBLY GU15.....324 D7
  FHAM/PORC PO16.....295 N1
Redwood Gdns TOTT SO40.....246 A4
Redwood Gv ALTN GU34.....131 J9
Redwood Wy FLEETS GU52.....74 C9
  ROWN SO16.....228 C6
Reed Cl ALDT GU11.....76 C6
Reed Dr TOTT SO40.....247 K9
Reeder Cl FBDG SP6.....240 C2
Reedling Dr ENEY PO4.....317 L3
Reed Meadow CI WVILLE PO7 *..276 A4
Reeds La LISS GU33.....174 A9
Reed's Pl GPORT PO12.....315 L3
Reeds Rd RFNM GU10.....116 D9
The Reeds Rd RFNM GU10.....116 D9
Reed Wk NWBY RG14.....24 F3
Rees Rd RWIN SO21.....144 D6
Reeves Cl ROMY SO51.....224 E1
Reeves Rd ASHV GU12.....3 H4
Reeves Wy HLER SO31.....269 P1
Regal Cl CHAM PO6.....297 H1
Regency Crs
  CHCH/BSGR BH23.....324 D7
Regency Pl WVILLE PO7.....275 N4
Regency Pl FLEET GU51.....74 D4
  RWIN SO21.....207 L1
Regent Cl BSTK RG21.....7 G3
Regent Ct LTDN BH7.....323 M7
Regent Ms PSF GU32.....215 K1
Regent Pl SSEA PO5.....19 F7
Regent Rd CHFD SO53.....206 D8
Regents Ct HAV PO9.....298 F1
Regents Cl RWIN SO21.....16 D1
Regents Ga HLER SO31.....270 E5
Regent's Gv ROWN SO16.....207 M1
Regent's Park Gdns
  WSHM SO15.....247 M4
Regent's Park Rd WSHM SO15..247 L4
Regent St PSHT GU47.....41 K6
Regent St FLEETN GU51.....74 D4
Regent Wy CHCH/BSGR BH23..324 F9
  FRIM GU16.....58 E4
Regiment Cl FARN GU14 *.....75 K1
Reginald Rd ENEY PO4.....317 J5
Regnum Dr NWBY RG14.....24 E2
Reid St CHCH/BSGR BH23.....324 E8
Relay Rd WVILLE PO7.....275 M2
Rembrandt Cl BSTK RG21.....69 N9
Remembrance Gdns
  CHIN RG24.....69 P2
Rempstone Rd WIMB BH21.....300 F4
Renault Dr BDST BH18.....320 C3
Renda Rd FAWY SO45.....290 E5
Renoir Cl BSTK RG21.....69 N9
Renouf Cl LYMN SO41.....329 J4
Renown Cl CHIN RG24.....52 A9
Renton Cl GPORT PO12.....315 J4
Renown Gdns HORN PO8.....256 C7
Repton Cl BSTK RG21.....7 M3
Repton Gdns HORN PO8.....256 C7
Reservoir La HEND SO30.....250 A5
  PSF GU32.....191 M9
Rest-a-Wyle Av HISD PO11.....318 G3
Restormel Cl DEAN RG23.....68 E6
Retreat Rd WIMB BH21.....300 F1
The Retreat ELGH SO50.....207 K9
  SSEA PO5.....19 H7
Retford Rd SHST GU47.....40 C6
Reuben's Crs TADY RG26.....34 C7
Revelstoke Av FARN GU14.....58 A7
Revenge Cl ENEY PO4.....317 L2
Rewlands Dr FUFL SO22.....164 D3
Reynards Cl TADY RG26.....34 D7
Reynolds Cl BSTK RG21.....69 N8
Reynolds Ct ROMY SO51.....230 A2
Reynolds Gn SHST GU47.....41 L8
Reynolds Rd ELGH SO50.....230 A2
  WSHM SO15.....247 N1
Reynolds St FLEETN GU51.....56 D9
Reynties Aly ODIM RG29.....155 L9
Rhine Banks FARN GU14.....57 L8
Rhinefield Cl BROC SO42.....286 C7
  ELGH SO50.....229 P2
  HAV PO9.....277 H1
Rhinefield Ornamental Dr
  BROC SO42.....285 P4
Rhinefield Rd BROC SO42.....286 D7

NMIL/BTOS BH25.....306 G6
Rhiners Cl LYMN SO41.....308 E5
Rhodes Sq AND SP10.....82 G8
Rhododendron Rd FRIM GU16...58 G5
Rhyll Gdns ALDT GU11.....2 B5
Rhyme Hall Ms FAWY SO45.....291 K6
Ribble Cl BDST BH18.....320 C2
  CHFD SO53.....206 C8
Ribble Ct AND SP10 *.....82 G9
  ROWN SO16.....247 J2
Ribble Pl FARN GU14.....57 M7
Ribble Wy BSTK RG21.....7 J6
Ricardo Crs CHCH/BSGR BH23..325 L9
Ricardo Wy LYMN SO41.....309 K9
Richard Cl FLEETS GU51.....74 B5
Richard Gv GPORT PO12.....295 L8
Richards Cl ASHV GU12 *.....76 F7
  HLER SO31.....271 H7
Richards Fld CHIN RG24.....70 B2
Richardson Ct TADY RG26.....52 A2
Richardson Dr FHAM PO15.....272 B8
Richborough Dr AND SP10.....82 A9
Richmans Rd HEND SO30.....250 C5
Richlans Rd AND STHA RG19...25 K4
Richmond Cl BOR GU35.....154 A7
  CHFD SO53.....206 D4
  FARN GU14.....75 L1
  FLEETS GU52.....74 C6
  FRIM GU16.....58 E4
Richmond Ct STHA RG19.....32 F1
  TOTT SO40.....245 P2
Richmond Crs TDWTH SP9.....79 J5
Richmond Dr HISD PO11.....318 D4
Richmond Gdns BMTH BH1.....8 E3
  SD/PW SO17.....248 D2
  WVILLE PO7.....275 L5
Richmond Hl BMTH BH1.....8 D4
Richmond Hill Dr WCLF BH2.....8 D3
Richmond Hill Rbt WCLF BH2....8 D4
Richmond La ROMY SO51.....204 E4
Richmond Pk RWIN SO21.....207 M1
Richmond Park Av CHAR BH8..323 H8
Richmond Park Cl
  CHAR BH8.....323 K9
Richmond Park Crs CHAR BH8..323 J8
Richmond Park Rd CHAR BH8..323 J8
Richmond Pl PSEA PO1.....18 E3
  SSEA PO5.....316 E6
Richmond Ri
  FHAM/PORC PO16.....273 N9
Richmond Rd BSTK RG21.....6 D5
  GPORT PO12.....12 A3
  LSOL/BMARY PO13.....314 B2
  PSTN BH14.....321 L8
  SHST GU47.....41 M6
  SSEA PO5.....316 F6
  WIMB BH21.....300 F1
  WSHM SO15.....247 N5
Richmond Ter SSEA PO5 *.....316 E6
Richmond Wood Rd
  CHAR BH8.....323 H8
Richville Rd ROWN SO16.....247 L3
Ridding Cl WSHM SO15.....247 N2
Riddings La STHA RG19.....32 F4
Riders La HAV PO9.....276 E6
Rideway Cl CBLY GU15.....58 A1
Ridge Cl BH/HW/K RG22.....89 N1
  HORN PO8.....256 C8
Ridge Common La PSF GU32....191 J8
Ridgefield Gdns
  CHCH/BSGR BH23.....325 P7
Ridge La HEND SO30.....251 K8
  HTWY RG27.....71 L3
  ROMY SO51.....225 P4
  TOTT SO40.....246 A6
Ridgemoor La PLE BH15.....320 A9
Ridgemount Av ROWN SO16...228 B7
Ridgemount Gdns ROWN SO16..228 C7
Ridges Cl RAND SP11.....83 H3
The Ridge RSAL SP5.....199 P3
Ridge Top La HAV PO9.....190 D8
Ridgeway BDST BH18.....300 D9
  FERN BH22.....302 B2
  FUFL SO22.....183 L1
Ridgeway Cl CHAM PO6.....274 D9
  CHFD SO53.....206 G8
  ELGH SO50.....230 C1
Ridgeway La LYMN SO41.....330 K4
The Ridgeway ALTN GU34.....132 F7
  FHAM/PORC PO16.....273 J9
Ridgewood Cl FRIM GU16.....59 J2
Ridgway HAV PO9.....14 B6
Ridgway Hill Rd FNM GU9.....116 C2
Ridgway Pde FNM GU9 *.....116 C2
Ridgway Rd FNM GU9.....116 C2
The Ridings BPWT SO32.....232 C8
  ELGH SO50.....230 A2
  FERN BH22.....58 G2
  LISS GU33.....193 F2
  NEND PO2.....297 H6
Ridley Cl FAWY SO45.....290 E5
  FLEETS GU52.....74 C5
Ridleys Piece ODIM RG29.....92 C7
Ridout Cl NBNE BH10.....322 C1
Rigby Rd SD/PW SO17.....248 D3
Rigby Rd SD/PW SO17.....248 D3
Riggs Gdns BWD BH11.....321 P2
Rigler Rd PLE BH15.....332 C2
Riley La FARN GU14.....70 C5
Riley Rd HAV PO9.....144 F6
Rimbault Cl ALDT GU11.....76 C5
Rimbury Wy
  CHCH/BSGR BH23.....324 E7
Rimes's La TADY RG26.....34 M8
Rimmington Rd HORN PO8.....255 N8
Rindle Cl FARN GU14.....77 H7
Ringbury LYMN SO41.....329 K1
Ringlet Wy WINC SO23.....123 K4
Ringsgreen La PSF GU32.....190 G3
Ringshall Gdns TADY RG26.....51 P2
The Ring ROWN SO16.....228 A5
Ringway East BSTK RG21.....7 H1
Ringway North BSTK RG21.....69 H5

Ringway South BSTK RG21 69 M9
Ringway West BSTK RG21 69 H9
Ringwood Dr NBAD SO52 205 J8
Ringwood Rd
BKME/WDN BH12 321 K4
BLKW GU17 41 K8
CHCH/BSGR BH23 304 E8
CHCH/BSGR BH23 325 N1
ENEY PO4 317 K5
FARN GU14 58 B6
FBDG SP6 239 N7
FERN BH22 302 B5
PSTN BH14 321 H6
TOTT SO40 245 L5
WIMB BH21 280 D1
Ripley Gv HSEA PO3 297 J9
Ripley Ter HTWY RG27 52 B8
Ripon Cl CBLY GU15 59 J2
Ripon Ct LSOL/BMARY PO13 * 315 H3
Ripon Gdns WVILLE PO7 276 B1
Ripon Rd BLKW GU17 57 H5
MOOR/WNTN BH9 322 G7
Ripplesmore Cl SHST GU47 41 J6
Ripplewood TOTT SO40 267 L1
Ripstone Gdns SD/PW SO17 228 D9
The Rise BROC SO42 286 F8
CWTH RG45 40 G1
EWKG RG40 39 K4
THLE RG7 * 36 B1
WVILLE PO7 275 M8
Ritchie Ct ITCH SO19 249 K7
Ritchie Pl FERN BH22 280 D5
Ritchie Rd BWD BH11 322 B3
Rival Moor Rd EPSF GU31 215 P3
River Cl ALTN GU34 150 C6
WIMB BH21 278 E8
Riverdale RFNM GU10 115 N3
Riverdale Av WVILLE PO7 276 A3
Riverdale Cl FBDG SP6 240 D1
Riverdale La
CHCH/BSGR BH23 324 E9
Riverdene Pl WEND SO18 248 F3
River Gdns LYMN SO41 339 H2
River Gn HLER SO31 270 A8
Riverhead NARL SO24 168 F3
Riverhead Cl ENEY PO4 317 K3
River La FHAM PO15 272 A4
RFNM GU10 115 N3
Riverlea Rd CHCH/BSGR BH23 324 E9
Rivermead Cl ROMY SO51 204 B6
Rivermead Gdns
CHCH/BSGR BH23 324 C5
Rivermead Rd CBLY GU15 58 A3
Rivermede BOR GU35 154 B4
River Pde AND SP10 * 82 G9
River Pk NWBY RG14 17 H1
River Rd FBDG SP6 241 H1
YTLY GU46 40 C7
River Rw FNM GU9 115 P2
Rivers Cl FARN GU14 76 D3
Riversdale Cl ITCH SO19 268 G1
Riversdale Rd SBNE BH6 336 E2
Riverside ELGH SO50 229 M1
NBNE BH10 * 322 F3
RGWD BH24 282 D3
WHCH RG28 * 85 L6
Riverside Av
FHAM/PORC PO16 273 H7
LTDN BH7 323 P5
Riverside Cl CHIN RG24 70 C5
FARN GU14 57 N8
LISS GU33 192 D2
OVTN RG25 87 H3
TOTT SO40 245 J5
Riverside Gdns ROMY SO51 204 C7
Riverside Gn STOK SO20 161 M4
Riverside La SBNE BH6 336 D1
Riverside Ms WHAM PO17 * 252 E8
Riverside Pl FBDG SP6 240 D2
Riverside Rd FERN BH22 280 D7
SBNE BH6 336 D1
Riverside Wy CBLY GU15 57 P2
Riversmeet RFNM GU10 117 J6
Rivers Reach LYMN SO41 * 329 M4
River's St SSEA PO5 19 J4
River St EMRTH PO10 277 P6
Riverview TOTT SO40 246 D6
River View Cl STOK SO20 123 K5
River View Rd WEND SO18 248 F1
River Wk NWBY RG14 24 F3
WEND SO18 228 G9
River Wy AND SP10 82 F9
CHCH/BSGR BH23 324 B6
HAV PO9 15 H2
R L Stevenson Av WBNE BH4 334 B3
Roads Hl HORN PO8 255 P2
Road Vw NEND PO2 296 E9
Robert Cecil Av WEND SO18 228 G8
Robert Mays Rd ODIM RG29 93 J1
Roberts Cl LYMN SO41 328 E6
WHAM PO17 252 E7
WINC SO23 145 J7
Robertsfield STHA RG19 25 J4
Roberts La CFDH BH17 320 C5
Robertson Cl ALTN GU34 132 D8
NWBY RG14 24 E7
Robertson Rd NARL SO24 167 P3
Robertson Wy ASHV GU12 97 M2
Roberts Rd ASHV GU12 3 K4
CBLY GU15 41 P8
CFDH BH17 320 D3
FAWY SO45 268 B6
GPORT PO12 315 K2
LISS GU33 173 P5
LTDN BH7 323 N9
RWIN SO21 124 F1
TOTT SO40 246 D6
WSHM SO15 247 P6
Robert Wy FRIM GU16 76 E1
Robert Whitworth Dr
ROMY SO51 204 D4
Robina Cl WVILLE PO7 276 A3
Robin Cl ALTN GU34 132 G3
ASHV GU12 76 E6
BH/HW/K RG22 89 L3
THLE RG7 * 27 K4
Robin Crs NMIL/BTOS BH25 326 F2
Robin Gdns CHCH/BSGR BH23 324 E7
HORN PO8 255 M7
TOTT SO40 246 A3
Robin Gv NMIL/BTOS BH25 327 H5
Robin Hill Dr CBLY GU15 58 F2
Robin Hood Cl FARN GU14 57 P6
Robinia Gn ROWN SO16 227 N7
Robin La SHST GU47 41 K6
Robins Cl FHAM/STUB PO14 294 A6
NWBY RG14 24 C8
Robins Grove Crs YTLY GU46 40 C8
Robins Meadow
FHAM/STUB PO14 271 J9
Robinson Rd
FHAM/STUB PO14 293 P8
Robinson Wy BOR GU35 154 B6
HSEA PO3 297 L6
Robin Sq ELGH SO50 228 E3
Robins Wy CHCH/BSGR BH23 337 M1
Robinswood Dr FERN BH22 280 D9
Robin Wy AND SP10 82 F9
Rochester Cl BH/HW/K RG22 89 M3
Rochester Ct
LSOL/BMARY PO13 * 315 H3
Rochester Gv FLEETN GU51 74 C4
Rochester Rd BWD BH11 322 B3
ENEY PO4 317 H5
Rochester St SHAM SO14 21 J3
Rochford Rd BSTK RG21 6 C6
CHAM PO6 296 F1
Rockall Cl ROWN SO16 227 J7
Rockbourne Cl HAV PO9 276 C6
Rockbourne Gdns
NMIL/BTOS BH25 326 F7
Rockbourne La FBDG SP6 219 L5
Rockbourne Rd FUFL SO22 164 E3
HTWY RG27 52 C8
Rockdale Dr GSHT GU26 156 C2
Rockery Cl FAWY SO45 267 N6
The Rockery FARN GU14 75 L1
Rocket Rd FARN GU14 75 L3
Rock Farm Wy HISD PO11 318 F4
Rockfield Wy SHST GU47 * 41 L6
Rockford Cl SBNE BH6 336 D3
Rock Gdns ALDT GU11 2 B4
Rockingham Rd NWBY RG14 16 C3
Rockingham Wy
FHAM/PORC PO16 295 M1
Rock La RFNM GU10 116 A5
Rockleigh Dr TOTT SO40 246 B7
Rockleigh Rd ROWN SO16 227 P9
Rockley Rd PLE BH15 332 A1
Rockmoor La RAND SP11 43 J3
Rockram Cl TOTT SO40 245 H4
Rockram Gdns FAWY SO45 267 N7
Rockrose Ct RAND SP11 79 P2
Rockrose Wy CHAM PO6 274 C8
Rockstone La SHAM SO14 248 C5
Rockstone Pl WSHM SO15 248 B5
Rockville Dr WVILLE PO7 275 N3
Rodbourne Cl LYMN SO41 328 D7
Rodfield La RWIN SO21 185 P3
Roding Cl BSTK RG21 7 J6
Rodlease La LYMN SO41 309 L6
Rodmel Ct FARN GU14 76 D3
Rodney Cl BKME/WDN BH12 322 A7
LSOL/BMARY PO13 314 G2
Rodney Ct AND SP10 5 K2
Rodney Dr CHCH/BSGR BH23 325 K9
Rodney Rd ENEY PO4 317 H3
Rodney Wy HORN PO8 256 B5
Rodway WIMB BH21 300 E1
Rodwell Cl NBNE BH10 322 C1
Roebuck Av FHAM PO15 272 B5
WHAM PO17 272 C3
Roebuck Cl CHAM PO6 297 H2
NMIL/BTOS BH25 327 K4
Roebuck Dr GPORT PO12 315 N1
Roebuts Cl NWBY RG14 16 C7
Roedeer Copse HASM GU27 156 D7
Roe Downs Rd ALTN GU34 150 A2
Roentgen Rd CHIN RG24 69 P5
Roeshot Crs
CHCH/BSGR BH23 326 A6
Roewood Cl FAWY SO45 290 E6
Roewood Rd FAWY SO45 290 E6
Rogate Gdns
FHAM/PORC PO16 273 N9
Roger Penny Wy FBDG SP6 221 L9
RSAL SP5 222 B6
Rogers Cl ELGH SO50 207 N9
GPORT PO12 315 M2
Rogers Ct ALTN GU34 132 F5
Rogers Md HISD PO11 298 F6
Rogers Rd ELGH SO50 207 N9
Rokeby Cl NWBY RG14 24 D8
Roke La ODIM RG29 93 P4
Roker Wy ELGH SO50 230 B3
Rokes Pl YTLY GU46 40 B8
Roland Cl HORN PO8 256 B5
Rollesbrook Gdns WSHM SO15 20 A1
Rollestone Rd FAWY SO45 290 F7
Rolling Mill Ms ELGH SO50 229 H2
Rolls Dr SBNE BH6 336 F2
Roman Cl CHFD SO53 206 G6
Roman Dr ROWN SO16 228 A5
Roman Gdns FAWY SO45 267 P9
Roman Gn WVILLE PO7 254 G7
Roman Gv FHAM/PORC PO16 295 P3
Roman Hts WIMB BH21 300 A5
Roman Ride CWTH RG45 40 E1
Roman Rd BDST BH18 300 A9
CHIN RG24 68 F4
DEAN RG23 68 E6
FAWY SO45 267 P9
ROWN SO16 228 A3
RSAL SP5 138 A9
RWIN SO21 184 A8
STOK SO20 141 J5
WHCH RG28 64 G5
Romans Fld THLE RG7 35 J6
Romans Ga TADY RG26 34 G5
Romans' Rd WINC SO23 22 D7
Roman Wy AND SP10 82 F7
DEAN RG23 68 D7
FAWY SO45 267 P9
FNM GU9 96 E7
HAV PO9 276 C8
NTHA RG18 25 K3
RWIN SO21 124 G1
The Romany FARN GU14 75 H3
Romford Rd HLER SO31 292 D1
Romill Cl HEND SO30 229 K9
Romney Cl NBNE BH10 * 322 E4
Romney Rd FARN GU14 75 M3
NBNE BH10 322 E3
Romsey Av FHAM/PORC PO16 295 L1
HSEA PO3 317 K2
Romsey Cl ALDT GU11 97 J5
BLKW GU17 41 K8
CHIN RG24 69 K3
ELGH SO50 229 J1
Romsey Rd ELGH SO50 229 J1
FUFL SO22 22 A5
HORN PO8 256 C1
LYND SO43 264 F4
RAND SP11 122 G1
ROMY SO51 179 L9
ROMY SO51 202 E9
ROWN SO16 227 H7
RSAL SP5 201 L1
STOK SO20 139 L1
STOK SO20 161 J7
TOTT SO40 244 F3
Romyns Ct FHAM/STUB PO14 10 C6
Rookcliff Wy LYMN SO41 338 F2
Rookery Av FHAM PO15 271 H3
Rookery Gra HLER SO31 271 H3
Rookery La FBDG SP6 220 D3
STOK SO20 160 B1
The Rookery EMRTH PO10 277 N9
WHCH RG28 85 L6
Rookes Cl HORN PO8 256 B5
Rookes La LYMN SO41 329 K5
Rooke's Wy NTHA RG18 25 H3
Rook Hill Rd
CHCH/BSGR BH23 325 M9
Rook La RWIN SO21 126 G6
Rookley HLER SO31 269 L3
Rooksbridge FAWY SO45 267 N7
Rooksbury Cft HAV PO9 276 G5
Rooksbury Rd AND SP10 102 C4
Rooksdown Av CHIN RG24 68 F4
Rooksdown La CHIN RG24 68 F3
Rooks Down Rd FUFL SO22 183 M1
Rooksfield KSCL RG20 31 M4
Rooksnest La HUNG RG17 28 B1
Rooksway Gv
FHAM/PORC PO16 295 K1
Rookswood ALTN GU34 132 F4
Rookswood Cl HTWY RG27 72 A3
Rookwood Av SHST GU47 41 M5
Rookwood Cl ELGH SO50 207 K7
Rookwood Gdns FBDG SP6 240 B2
Rookwood La NARL SO24 149 M8
Rookwood Vw WVILLE PO7 255 H6
Roosevelt Crs BWD BH11 322 B1
Rope Hl LYMN SO41 309 K7
Rope Quays GPORT PO12 13 H1
Rope Wk STHA RG19 25 M4
The Rope Wk
FHAM/PORC PO16 * 294 F1
Ropley Cl ITCH SO19 269 J2
TADY RG26 34 B7
Ropley Rd ALTN GU34 170 G2
HAV PO9 277 H5
LTDN BH7 324 A8
Rorkes Drift FRIM GU16 58 E9
Rosamund Av WIMB BH21 300 G4
Rosary Gdns YTLY GU46 * 40 E8
Roscrea Cl SBNE BH6 336 F2
Roscrea Dr SBNE BH6 336 F2
Rosebank Cl ROWN SO16 227 J7
TADY RG26 34 C6
Rosebank Ldg ROWN SO16 * 227 J7
Rosebay Cl ELGH SO50 230 C6
Rosebay Ct WVILLE PO7 275 P5
Rosebay Gdns HTWY RG27 72 B2
Roseberry Cl BH/HW/K RG22 89 M6
Rosebery Av CHAM PO6 297 J2
Rosebery Cl VWD BH31 259 J5
Rosebery Crs ELGH SO50 207 K7
Rosebery Rd BOSC BH5 335 N1
NARL SO24 167 P2
Rosebud Av
MOOR/WNTN BH9 322 G5
Rosebury Av FAWY SO45 268 C9
Rose Cl BH/HW/K RG22 89 M3
FAWY SO45 268 C8
HEND SO30 250 C3
Rosecrae Cl NMIL/BTOS BH25 327 H3
Rose Crs PLE BH15 321 H6
Rosedale ASHV GU12 3 H3
Rosedale Av ROMY SO51 204 E6
Rosedale Cl CHCH/BSGR BH23 325 J9
FHAM/STUB PO14 293 M1
Rosedale Gdns STHA RG19 25 M5
Rosedene Gdns FLEETN GU51 74 C2
Rosedene La SHST GU47 41 L7
The Rose Est HTWY RG27 * 72 A4
Rose Gdns FARN GU14 75 L1
MOOR/WNTN BH9 322 G5
Rose Hl HORN PO8 256 A5
Rosehill Cl CHCH/BSGR BH23 * 305 M7
Rosehill Dr CHCH/BSGR BH23 305 M7
Rosehip Cl ELGH SO50 230 A3
Rosehip Wy CHIN RG24 70 A5
Rose Hodson Pl DEAN RG23 68 F5
Roselands HEND SO30 249 M3
HORN PO8 256 A6
Roselands Cl ELGH SO50 230 B1
Roselands Gdns SD/PW SO17 248 C1
Roseleigh Dr TOTT SO40 246 C5
Rosemary Av ASHV GU12 76 F4
Rosemary Cl FARN GU14 57 L8
Rosemary Dr TADY RG26 34 C8
Rosemary Gdns
BKME/WDN BH12 321 K5
BLKW GU17 41 K9
FHAM PO15 271 K2
HEND SO30 250 C6
NTHA RG18 25 P3
Rosemary La BLKW GU17 41 K8
PSEA PO1 18 C3
RFNM GU10 115 N6
Rosemary Price Ct
HEND SO30 * 250 C3
Rosemary Rd
BKME/WDN BH12 321 L5
Rosemary Wy HORN PO8 256 B7
Rosemoor Gdns NWBY RG14 24 F3
Rosemoor Gv CHFD SO53 206 D4
Rosemount Rd WBNE BH4 334 B4
Rosendale Rd CHFD SO53 206 F9
Rose Rd SHAM SO14 248 C3
TOTT SO40 246 E5
The Rosery GPORT PO12 315 M7
Rosetta Rd ENEY PO4 317 K4
Rose Wk FLEETN GU51 74 C2
Rosewall Rd ROWN SO16 227 K9
Rosewarne Ct WINC SO23 22 E2
Rosewood CHIN RG24 * 69 P1
LSOL/BMARY PO13 295 J8
Rosewood Gdns HORN PO8 236 C7
NMIL/BTOS BH25 327 H3
TOTT SO40 267 L1
Rosewood Rd BOR GU35 154 D3
Rosewood Ter TDWTH SP9 * 79 J4
Rosina Cl WVILLE PO7 276 B2
Roslin Rd TWDS BH3 322 E8
Roslin Rd South TWDS BH3 322 D8
Rosoman Rd ITCH SO19 249 H7
Rossan Av HLER SO31 292 D2
Ross Cl BSTK RG21 90 C1
Ross Gdns BWD BH11 301 L8
ROWN SO16 247 L1
Ross Glades TWDS BH3 322 E9
Rossington Av WEND SO18 249 H4
Rossington Wy WEND SO18 249 H4
Rossini Cl BH/HW/K RG22 90 A3
Rossiters Quay
CHCH/BSGR BH23 324 G9
Rossley Cl CHCH/BSGR BH23 326 A5
Rosslyn Cl NBAD SO52 205 L9
Ross Ms HLER SO31 * 269 J4
Rossmore Gdns ALDT GU11 2 A5
Rossmore Rd
BKME/WDN BH12 321 M5
Ross Rd RGWD BH24 260 G9
Ross Wy LSOL/BMARY PO13 314 D1
Rostron Cl WEND SO18 229 J9
Rosyth Rd WEND SO18 249 H4
Rotary Cl WIMB BH21 279 H7
Rotary Ct HLER SO31 269 K4
Rotary Wy STHA RG19 25 N6
Rothay Ct BSTK RG21 7 J6
Rothbury Cl ITCH SO19 * 249 J7
TOTT SO40 246 B2
Rothbury Pk
NMIL/BTOS BH25 327 K5
Rotherbank Farm La
LISS GU33 173 M9
Rother Cl EPSF GU31 216 A1
SHST GU47 41 K6
WEND SO18 249 K2
Rothercombe La PSF GU32 214 G1
Rother Dl ITCH SO19 249 N8
Rotherfield Rd BOSC BH5 335 P3
CHCH/BSGR BH23 326 C6
Rother Rd FARN GU14 57 M7
Rotherwick Cl HAV PO9 277 H5
Rotherwick La HTWY RG27 53 J5
Rotherwick Rd TADY RG26 34 C7
Rothesay Dr
CHCH/BSGR BH23 326 A8
Rothesay Rd GPORT PO12 315 L1
TWDS BH3 322 C9
Rothsbury Dr CHFD SO53 206 D7
Rothschild Cl ITCH SO19 268 G1
Rothville Pl CHFD SO53 206 D3
Rothwell Cl CHAM PO6 274 C9
Rotten Green Rd HTWY RG27 56 B7
Rotten Hl WHCH RG28 86 E5
Rotterdam Dr
CHCH/BSGR BH23 325 H8
Rotunda Est ALDT GU11 3 G3
Roughdown La FAWY SO45 290 E8
Roumelia La BOSC BH5 335 L2
The Roundabouts LISS GU33 192 E1
Roundaway La RAND SP11 81 L1
Round Cl YTLY GU46 40 G9
Round End NWBY RG14 30 C1
Roundhaye Rd BWD BH11 301 P8
Round Hl FBDG SP6 240 D2
Roundhill Cl WEND SO18 249 J2
Roundhouse Dr TOTT SO40 245 P5
Roundhouse Meadow
EMRTH PO10 299 N2
Roundhuts Ri WINC SO23 23 K4
Roundmead Rd BSTK RG21 6 C7
Roundway WVILLE PO7 275 P2
Roundway Ct AND SP10 102 C2
Roundways BWD BH11 * 321 P1
Rounton Rd FLEETS GU52 74 D7
Routs Wy ROWN SO16 227 J5
Rowallan Av
LSOL/BMARY PO13 294 F8
Rowan Av HORN PO8 256 B9
Rowan Cha RFNM GU10 116 A5
Rowan Cl BPWT SO32 232 F8
CHCH/BSGR BH23 325 P7
FLEETN GU51 74 F3
HLER SO31 269 P2
LSOL/BMARY PO13 314 D3
LYMN SO41 308 B7
RGWD BH24 281 K5
ROMY SO51 204 G7
ROWN SO16 227 K9
RWIN SO21 144 F4
TOTT SO40 246 B5
Rowan Ct ENEY PO4 317 H4
TDWTH SP9 * 79 H4
Rowan Dl FLEETS GU52 74 C7
Rowan Dr CFDH BH17 320 A3
CHCH/BSGR BH23 325 P7
NWBY RG14 24 D2
VWD BH31 259 H6
Rowan Gdns HEND SO30 250 D5
Rowan Rd HAV PO9 277 H7
TADY RG26 34 D7
Rowans Cl FARN GU14 57 M4
Rowanside Cl BOR GU35 155 K4
Rowans Pk LYMN SO41 329 K4
The Rowans GSHT GU26 156 C3
TOTT SO40 267 K1
Rowan Tree Cl LISS GU33 192 E2
Rowan Wy FHAM/STUB PO14 294 A1
RDGW/BURGH RG30 27 K3
Rowbarrow Cl CFDH BH17 320 G2
Rowborough Rd WEND SO18 249 H3
Rowbury Rd HAV PO9 276 D4
Rowcroft Cl ASHV GU12 76 F6
Rowdell Cots NARL SO24 169 M2
Rowden Cl ROMY SO51 224 E2
Rowe Ashe Wy HLER SO31 270 F7
Rowe Gdns BKME/WDN BH12 321 P5
Rowena Rd SBNE BH6 336 D1
Rowes La LYMN SO41 310 F9
Rowhay La BPWT SO32 209 J8
Rowhill Av ALDT GU11 2 B6
Rowhill Crs ALDT GU11 2 B7
Rowhill Dr FAWY SO45 267 N7
Rowhills Cl FNM GU9 2 B7
Rowin Cl HISD PO11 319 K6
Rowland Av PLE BH15 320 G6
Rowland Rd CHAM PO6 274 A9
FHAM PO15 10 C4
Rowlands Av WVILLE PO7 275 N1
Rowlands Castle Rd
HORN PO8 256 D5
Rowlands Cl CHFD SO53 206 C9
Rowland's Cl THLE RG7 35 K1
Rowlands Hl WIMB BH21 278 E9
Rowlands Wk WEND SO18 249 J1
Rowlett Rd LYMN SO41 329 L4
Rowley Cl HEND SO30 250 F3
Rowley Dr HEND SO30 250 F3
Rowlings Rd FUFL SO22 164 E4
Rowner Cl LSOL/BMARY PO13 294 G8
Rowner La LSOL/BMARY PO13 294 G8
Rowner Rd
LSOL/BMARY PO13 294 F8
Rownhams Cl ROWN SO16 227 J6
Rownhams La NBAD SO52 227 K3
ROWN SO16 227 K5
Rownhams Pk ROWN SO16 * 227 J4
Rownhams Rd CHAR BH8 323 J4
HAV PO9 276 D5
NBAD SO52 227 L1
ROWN SO16 247 K1
Rownhams Rd North
ROWN SO16 227 K7
Rownhams Wy ROWN SO16 227 J6
Rowse Cl ROMY SO51 204 D4
The Row RSAL SP5 200 A6
Row Wood La
LSOL/BMARY PO13 294 F8
Roxbee Cox Rd FLEETN GU51 75 H3
Roxburgh Cl CBLY GU15 59 H1
Roxburghe Cl BOR GU35 154 A6
Royal Albert Wk ENEY PO4 * 316 G6
Royal Clarence Yd
GPORT PO12 * 315 P2
Royal Cl BH/HW/K RG22 89 L6
Royal Crescent Rd SHAM SO14 21 G7
The Royal Crs TDWTH SP9 79 H4
Royal Dr BOR GU35 154 B2
Royale Cl ALDT GU11 3 H7
Royal Gdns HAV PO9 276 G1
Royal Ga ENEY PO4 317 K6
Royal Huts Av GSHT GU26 156 E1
Royal Oak Cl YTLY GU46 40 F8
Royal Oak Rd NBNE BH10 322 C2
Royal Sovereign Av
FHAM/STUB PO14 294 D4
The Royal FRIM GU16 59 J6
Royal Wy WVILLE PO7 276 A3
Royce Cl AND SP10 101 P1
Royden La LYMN SO41 309 K6
Roydon Cl FUFL SO22 183 M1
Roy's Cl RAND SP11 79 P1
Roy's La BPWT SO32 253 N1
Royster Cl CFDH BH17 320 E3
Royston Av ELGH SO50 207 J8
Royston Cl SD/PW SO17 248 D1
Royston Dr WIMB BH21 278 F9
Royston Pl NMIL/BTOS BH25 327 K7
Rozeldene GSHT GU26 156 D2
Rozelle Cl FUFL SO22 164 B2
Rozelle Rd PSTN BH14 321 L8
Rubens Cl BSTK RG21 90 F1
NMIL/BTOS BH25 327 J3
Ruby Cl TOTT SO40 245 P2
Ruby Rd ITCH SO19 249 J5
Rudd Hall Ri CBLY GU15 58 C2
Rudd La ROMY SO51 180 B6
Rudgwick Cl
FHAM/PORC PO16 295 M1
Rudland Cl STHA RG19 25 N5
Rudmore Sq NEND PO2 296 E9
Ruffield Cl FUFL SO22 164 D4
Rufford Cl ELGH SO50 207 J7
FLEETS GU52 74 D6
Rufford Gdns SBNE BH6 336 C1
Rufus Cl CHFD SO53 206 G5
ROWN SO16 227 H6
Rufus Gdns TOTT SO40 246 A4
Rugby Cl SHST GU47 41 M5
Rugby Rd CFDH BH17 320 C3
SSEA PO5 316 G4
Rumbridge Gdns TOTT SO40 246 E4
Rumbridge St TOTT SO40 246 D5
Rune Dr AND SP10 82 D7
Runfold St George
RFNM GU10 97 H6
Runnymede FHAM PO15 272 B6
HEND SO30 249 M2
Runnymede Av BWD BH11 301 M7
Runnymede Ct HEND SO30 249 M2
Runton Rd BKME/WDN BH12 321 P7
The Runway
CHCH/BSGR BH23 325 M8
Runwick La RFNM GU10 115 K2
Rupert Rd NWBY RG14 24 C7
Rural Cl FNM GU9 115 P4
Rushden Wy FNM GU9 96 D4
Rushes Farm PSF GU32 * 215 L1
Rushes Rd PSF GU32 215 L1

The Rushes *BSTK* RG21 .... 7 K6
  TOTT SO40 .... 247 K9
Rushfield Rd *LISS* SG33 .... 192 D3
Rushford Warren
  CHCH/BSGR BH23 .... 337 K2
Rushington Av *TOTT* SO40 .... 246 D5
Rushington La *TOTT* SO40 .... 246 C6
Rushmere La *WVILLE* PO7 .... 254 F2
Rushmere Rd *SBNE* BH6 .... 324 A8
Rushmoor Cl *FLEETS* GU52 .... 74 D5
Rushmoor Rd *ALDT* GU11 .... 75 M9
Rushpole Ct *FAWY* SO45 .... 267 N7
Rushton Crs *TWDS* BH3 .... 322 F9
Ruskin Av *MOOR/WNTN* BH9 .... 323 H4
Ruskin Cl *BSTK* RG21 .... 69 N9
Ruskin Ct *CWTH* RG45 * 40 G2
Ruskin Rd *ELGH* SO50 .... 207 J8
  ENEY PO4 .... 317 J4
Ruskin Wy *HORN* PO8 .... 255 P7
Rusland Cl *CHFD* SO53 .... 206 D6
Russell Cotes Rd *BMTH* BH1 .... 9 F5
Russell Cl *BLKW* GU17 .... 41 L9
Russell Dr *CHCH/BSGR* BH23 .... 325 H9
  ROMY SO51 .... 179 K6
Russell Gdns *RGWD* BH24 .... 281 P4
Russell Pl *FHAM/PORC* PO16 .... 11 F5
  SD/PW SO17 .... 248 D2
Russell Rd *BDST* BH18 .... 69 L9
  HAV PO9 .... 15 G2
  LSOL/BMARY PO13 .... 314 D3
  NWBY RG14 .... 16 B3
  WINC SO23 .... 165 H5
Russell St *GPORT* PO12 .... 315 L2
  SHAM SO14 .... 21 F6
Russell Wy *EPSF* GU31 .... 215 N3
Russel Rd *BH10* 322 A3
Russet Cl *FERN* BH22 .... 302 D2
  LYMN SO41 .... 329 M5
  NARL SO24 .... 167 P3
  RFNM GU10 .... 97 L4
Russet Gdns *CBLY* GU15 .... 52 B7
  EMRTH PO10 .... 299 P1
Russet Gld *THLE* RG7 .... 27 J1
Russett Cl *BPWT* SO32 .... 232 F8
Russett Rd *ALTN* GU34 .... 132 C6
Russetts Dr *FLEETN* GU51 .... 74 C4
Rustan Cl *ELGH* SO50 .... 230 D2
  HEND SO30 .... 250 B5
Rustic Gln *FLEETS* GU52 .... 74 C7
Ruth Cl *FARN* GU14 .... 57 K8
Rutherford Cl *KSCL* RG20 .... 45 N1
Rutherford Rd *CHIN* RG24 .... 69 N4
Rutland Cl *ALDT* GU11 .... 2 D1
Rutland Gdns *HLER* SO31 .... 270 A4
Rutland Rd *CHCH/BSGR* BH23 .... 324 D6
  MOOR/WNTN BH9 .... 323 H7
Rutland Wy *WEND* SO18 .... 249 J2
Ruxley Cl *FAWY* SO45 .... 290 E5
Ryall Rd *CFDH* BH17 .... 320 F3
Ryan Cl *FERN* BH22 .... 302 C1
Ryan Gdns *FERN* BH22 .... 302 C1
Ryan Mt *SHST* GU47 .... 41 H6
Rycroft Meadow
  BH/HW/K RG22 .... 89 L7
Rydal Cl *BH/HW/K* RG22 .... 89 L7
  BOR GU35 .... 154 A3
  CHAM PO6 .... 274 D9
  CHCH/BSGR BH23 .... 324 B5
  FARN GU14 .... 75 L1
Rydal Dr *FLEETS* GU52 .... 74 C7
  NTHA RG18 .... 25 K3
Rydal Rd *GPORT* PO12 .... 295 L9
Ryde Pl *LSOL/BMARY* PO13 .... 314 E4
Ryde Ter *SHAM* SO14 .... 21 H6
Ryebeck Rd *FLEETS* GU52 .... 74 D7
Rye Cl *CHFD* SO53 .... 206 B7
  FARN GU14 .... 58 A5
  FLEETN GU51 .... 56 F8
Ryecroft *HAV* PO9 .... 277 H9
  FHAM/STUB PO14 .... 271 J8
Rye Cft *FLEETS* GU52 .... 74 B8
Ryecroft Av *BWD* BH11 .... 301 N8
Ryecroft Gdns *BLKW* GU17 .... 57 M1
Rye Dl *TOTT* SO40 .... 246 A8
Ryedown La *ROMY* SO51 .... 203 J9
Ryefield Cl *EPSF* GU31 .... 216 A2
Ryeland Cl *FLEETN* GU51 * 56 F8
Ryelaw Rd *FLEETS* GU52 .... 74 D7
Rye Paddock La *FAWY* SO45 .... 291 K5
Rykmansford Rd *FLEETN* GU51 .... 56 B9
Rylandes Cl *ROWN* SO16 .... 227 K7
Ryle Rd *FNM* GU9 .... 116 B2
Ryon Cl *AND* SP10 .... 82 E7
Ryves Av *YTLY* GU46 .... 40 B9

St Alban's Av *CHAR* BH8 .... 323 H8
St Albans Ct
  LSOL/BMARY PO13 * 315 H3
St Alban's Crs *CHAR* BH8 .... 323 H8
St Alban's Rd *CHAR* BH8 .... 323 H8
St Albans Rd *ENEY* PO4 .... 317 H5
  HAV PO9 .... 15 J1
  SHAM SO14 .... 21 H2
St Aldhelm's Cl *CCLF* BH13 .... 321 P9
St Aldhelm's Rd *CCLF* BH13 .... 321 P8
St Alphege Gdns *AND* SP10 .... 82 D8
St Andrew Cl *HORN* PO8 .... 256 C1
St Andrews Cl *NBAD* SO52 .... 205 J8
  ROMY SO51 .... 180 B8
St Andrews Pk *ELGH* SO50 .... 230 C6
St Andrews Rd *BDST* BH18 .... 300 C8
  BH/HW/K RG22 .... 68 D3
  BOR GU35 .... 153 N6
St Andrew's Rd *CHAM* PO6 .... 297 P1
  GPORT PO12 .... 12 D3
  HISD PO11 .... 319 H6
St Andrews Rd *SHAM* SO14 .... 20 E2
  SSEA PO5 .... 18 B4
  TDWTH SP9 .... 78 C5
St Andrew's Wy *FNM* GU16 .... 58 E6
St Anne's Av *ENEY* PO4 .... 317 J6
St Annes Cl *FUFL* SO22 .... 183 L1
  RAND SP11 .... 122 D1
St Anne's Gdns *ITCH* SO19 .... 248 G9
St Annes Gdns *LYMN* SO41 .... 329 K4
St Annes La *BPWT* SO32 .... 252 B4
St Anne's Rd *ITCH* SO19 .... 248 G9
St Ann's Cl *AND* SP10 .... 4 B6
St Ann's Crs *GPORT* PO12 .... 315 L2
St Ann's Rd *HORN* PO8 .... 256 C4
St Anthony's Rd *WCLF* BH2 .... 334 F1
St Aubin's Av *ITCH* SO19 .... 249 J6
St Aubins Cl *HISD* PO11 .... 318 D5
St Aubin's Pk *HISD* PO11 * 332 D1
St Aubyns La *RGWD* BH24 .... 261 J9
St Augustine Gdns
  SD/PW SO17 .... 248 F2
St Augustine Rd *ENEY* PO4 .... 317 H5
St Augustine's Cl *ASHV* GU12 * 97 K2
St Augustin's Rd *WCLF* BH2 .... 334 F1
St Austell Cl *ELGH* SO50 .... 229 N1
St Barbara's Cl *FARN* GU26 .... 52 C3
St Barbara Wy *NEND* PO2 .... 297 H5
St Bartholomew Gdns
  SSEA PO5 .... 19 K6
St Benedict's Cl *ALDT* GU11 .... 2 D5
St Birinus Gdns *AND* SP10 .... 82 D8
St Birstan Gdns *AND* SP10 .... 82 D9
St Blaize Rd *ROMY* SO51 .... 204 F5
St Bonnet Dr *BPWT* SO32 .... 232 A4
St Brelades Av
  BKME/WDN BH12 .... 321 M3
St Catherines *WIMB* BH21 .... 300 E1
St Catherine's Hl *THLE* RG7 .... 35 M1
St Catherines Rd *ELCH* SO50 .... 207 J8
St Catherines Rd *FRIM* GU16 .... 58 F4
St Catherine's Rd *HISD* PO11 .... 318 C5
  SBNE BH6 .... 336 C3
  WEND SO18 .... 248 G2
  WINC SO23 .... 23 H7
St Catherines's Wy
  CHCH/BSGR BH23 .... 324 B4
St Catherine St *SSEA* PO5 .... 18 D6
St Catherines Vw *HEND* SO30 .... 250 A5
St Catherines Wy
  FHAM/PORC PO16 .... 273 J9
St Catherines Wd *CBLY* GU15 .... 58 B1
St Chad's Av *NEND* PO2 .... 296 G7
St Christopher Av
  FHAM/PORC PO16 .... 11 H2
St Christophers Cl *ASHV* GU12 .... 3 K2
  BH/HW/K RG22 .... 68 F9
  HASM GU27 * 156 F7
St Christopher's Pl *FARN* GU14 .... 75 N1
  HASM GU27 * 156 F7
  HAV PO9 .... 276 C7
St Clair Rd *CCLF* BH13 .... 333 N5
St Clares Av *HAV* PO9 .... 276 D5
St Cleeve Wy *FERN* BH22 .... 302 C5
St Clements Cl *ROMY* SO51 .... 204 D5
St Clements Gdns *BMTH* BH1 .... 335 K1
St Clement's Rd *BMTH* BH1 .... 335 K1
St Clement's Rd *BDST* BH18 .... 321 K5
St Clement St *WINC* SO23 .... 22 D5
St Colman's Av *CHAM* PO6 .... 297 J1
St Contest Wy *TOTT* SO40 .... 267 K2
St Cross Rd *FNM* GU9 .... 96 C8
  FRIM GU16 .... 58 F6
  HAV PO9 .... 95 H6
  WINC SO23 .... 164 G9
St Cuthberts Cl *HLER* SO31 .... 271 H6
St Cuthberts La *HLER* SO31 .... 271 H6
St David's Cl *FARN* GU14 .... 57 N5
  FNM GU9 .... 96 E4
St Davids Cl *ODIM* RG29 .... 93 J1
St David's Cl *TOTT* SO40 .... 246 A2
St Davids Ct
  LSOL/BMARY PO13 * 314 G2
St David's Rd *BH/HW/K* RG22 .... 69 H9
St Davids Rd *HLER* SO31 .... 270 F7
St David's Rd *HORN* PO8 .... 256 C7
  NWBY RG14 .... 16 C4
St Davids Rd *SSEA* PO5 .... 19 K5
St Denys Rd *SD/PW* SO17 .... 248 D2
St Dominic Cl *FARN* GU14 .... 57 P5
St Donats Pl *NWBY* RG14 * 16 E4
St Edmondsbury Ct
  LSOL/BMARY PO13 * 315 H3
St Edmund Cl
  FHAM/STUB PO14 .... 271 H9
St Edmund's Rd *ROWN* SO16 .... 227 M8
St Edward's Rd *GPORT* PO12 .... 12 D3
St Edwards Rd *SSEA* PO5 .... 269 K5
  SSEA PO5 .... 18 C7
St Elizabeth's Av *WEND* SO18 .... 249 K4
St Evox Cl *ROWN* SO16 .... 227 K7
St Faith's Cl *GPORT* PO12 .... 12 A1

St Faiths Rd *PSEA* PO1 .... 19 H1
St Faith's Rd *WINC* SO23 .... 183 P1
St Francis Av *WEND* SO18 .... 249 K3
St Francis Cl *FAWY* SO45 .... 312 C1
St Francis Ct *NEND* PO2 * 296 G5
St Francis Pl *HAV* PO9 .... 14 D1
St Francis Rd *FAWY* SO45 .... 312 C1
  GPORT PO12 .... 315 N7
St Gabriels Lea *CHIN* RG24 .... 70 B1
St Gabriel's Rd *WEND* SO18 .... 249 K4
St George Cl *HLER* SO31 .... 269 P1
St Georges *PLE* BH15 * 332 D2
St George's Av
  BKME/WDN BH12 .... 321 K4
  CHAR BH8 .... 323 J7
  HAV PO9 .... 277 H9
  NWBY RG14 .... 16 E4
St George's Cl *CHAR* BH8 .... 323 J7
  CHCH/BSGR BH23 .... 325 P7
  FNM GU9 * 97 H5
St Georges Cl *TDWTH* SP9 .... 78 C6
St Georges Ct
  FHAM/PORC PO16 .... 294 F1
St Georges Dr *BWD* BH11 .... 321 M1
  CHCH/BSGR BH23 .... 305 M7
St Georges Dr *FERN* BH22 .... 302 C4
St Georges Ms *FNM* GU9 * 96 B8
St George's Rd *ASHV* GU12 .... 3 F5
  CHAM PO6 .... 297 H1
  ENEY PO4 .... 317 J6
St Georges Rd *FBDG* SP6 .... 240 D1
  FNM GU9 .... 97 H5
St George's Rd *FNM* GU9 .... 116 D1
  HISD PO11 .... 318 B5
St Georges Rd *HLER* SO31 .... 270 F7
St Georges Rd *PSEA* PO1 .... 18 D4
St Georges Rd *TDWTH* SP9 .... 78 C5
St Georges Rd East *ASHV* GU12 .... 3 G4
St Georges Sq *PSEA* PO1 * 18 D5
St Georges St *SHAM* SO14 .... 21 F5
St George's St *WINC* SO23 .... 22 E4
St Georges Wk *GPORT* PO12 .... 13 G1
St Georges Yd *FNM* GU9 .... 96 B9
St Giles Cl *WINC* SO23 .... 23 H5
St Giles Hl *WINC* SO23 .... 23 H5
St Giles Wy *HORN* PO8 .... 256 C1
St Helena Gdns *WEND* SO18 .... 229 H9
St Helena Wy
  FHAM/PORC PO16 .... 295 N1
St Helen's Cl *ENEY* PO4 .... 317 H6
St Helens Crs *SHST* GU47 .... 41 H6
St Helens Pde *ENEY* PO4 .... 316 G7
St Helens Rd *GPORT* PO12 .... 315 J5
St Helen's Rd *HISD* PO11 .... 318 D5
St Helier Rd *BKME/WDN* BH12 .... 321 M3
  GPORT PO12 .... 295 N1
St Hellen's Rd *CHAM* PO6 .... 297 P1
St Hermans Rd *HISD* PO11 .... 319 J6
St Hilda Av *HORN* PO8 .... 256 C1
St Hubert Rd *AND* SP10 .... 102 C3
  HORN PO8 .... 256 C1
St Ives End La *RGWD* BH24 .... 281 N5
St Ives Gdns *WCLF* BH2 .... 334 F1
St Ives Pk *RGWD* BH24 .... 281 N4
St Ives Wd *RGWD* BH24 .... 281 P4
St James' Av *FNM* GU9 .... 96 D7
St James Cl *HORN* PO8 .... 236 C8
  PLE BH15 .... 332 C6
  TADY RG26 .... 52 C4
St James' La *FUFL* SO22 .... 22 B5
St James Pk *NBAD* SO52 .... 206 C5
St James' Rd *EMRTH* PO10 .... 277 M9
St James Rd *FERN* BH22 .... 302 A2
St James Rd *FNM* GU9 .... 96 D7
St James's Park Rd
  ROWN SO16 .... 247 N1
St James's Rd *SSEA* PO5 .... 19 G5
  WSHM SO15 .... 247 N2
St James's Sq *BOSC* BH5 .... 335 N1
St James St *RAND* SP11 .... 79 N1
St James' Ter *FNM* GU9 .... 96 C8
St James Wy *WINC* SO23 .... 22 C5
St James' Wy
  FHAM/PORC PO16 .... 295 P1
St John Cl *TADY* RG26 .... 52 B3
St John's Av *WVILLE* PO7 .... 275 N7
St John's Cl *GPORT* PO12 .... 315 K3
St Johns Cl *HISD* PO11 .... 318 E5
  NEND PO2 .... 72 A3
St John's Cl *WIMB* BH21 .... 300 F1
St Johns Cl *FARN* GU14 * 57 L8
  TOTT SO40 .... 267 K1
St Johns Dr *TOTT* SO40 .... 267 J1
St John's Gdns
  MOOR/WNTN BH9 .... 322 F6
St Johns Gdns *ROMY* SO51 .... 204 D5
St Johns Glebe *ROWN* SO16 .... 227 K6
St Johns Gv *FNM* GU9 .... 116 B3
St John's Hl *WIMB* BH21 .... 278 F9
St Johns North *WINC* SO23 .... 23 G5
St John's Piece *DEAN* RG23 .... 88 F3
St John's Rd *AND* SP10 .... 4 E3
  CHAM PO6 .... 297 J1
  CHCH/BSGR BH23 .... 324 E9
  DEAN RG23 .... 88 F1
  ELGH SO50 .... 207 K9
  FARN GU14 .... 58 A7
  FARN GU14 .... 57 M9
  HAV PO9 .... 276 C6
  HEND SO30 .... 250 A7
  HLER SO31 .... 271 H8
St Johns Rd *HTWY* RG27 .... 55 J8
  NMIL/BTOS BH25 .... 307 J9
St John's Rd *NWBY* RG14 .... 16 E5
  PLE BH15 .... 320 F8
  SHST GU47 .... 41 J7
  STHA RG19 .... 25 M4
  THLE RG7 .... 35 H1
  WINC SO23 .... 23 H4

St Johns South *WINC* SO23 .... 23 G5
St Johns Sq *GPORT* PO12 * 315 M3
St John's St *FAWY* SO45 .... 268 C6
  WINC SO23 .... 23 G4
St Joseph's Crs *CHIN* RG24 .... 70 A2
St Joseph's Ms *SSEA* PO5 * 19 H6
St Joseph's Rd *ASHV* GU12 .... 2 E5
  FERN BH22 .... 302 D5
St Just Cl *AMSY* SP4 .... 118 D4
St Lawrence Cl *HEND* SO30 .... 250 D1
St Lawrence Rd *ALTN* GU34 .... 132 F5
  ELGH SO50 .... 21 G7
  SHAM SO14 .... 21 G7
St Ledger's Pl *CHAR* BH8 * 323 K9
St Ledger's Rd *CHAR* BH8 .... 323 K8
St Leger Ct *NWBY* RG14 * 34 B3
St Leonards Cl *FHAM* PO15 .... 271 L7
  RWIN SO21 .... 144 E4
St Leonard's Rd *CHAR* BH8 .... 323 J7
St Leonards Rd *LYMN* SO41 .... 310 F9
St Leonards Rd *WINC* SO23 .... 23 J7
St Leonards Wy *RGWD* BH24 .... 281 K4
St Lukes Cl *BH/HW/K* RG22 .... 89 N1
St Luke's Rd *GPORT* PO12 .... 315 L2
  TWDS BH3 .... 322 F8
St Maradox La
  MOOR/WNTN BH9 .... 322 F5
St Margaret's Av
  CHCH/BSGR BH23 .... 324 E9
St Margarets Cl *WEND* SO18 .... 249 K4
St Margaret's Hl *WIMB* BH21 .... 278 C9
St Margarets La
  FHAM/STUB PO14 .... 271 L9
  HISD PO11 .... 318 C5
St Margaret's Rd *NBNE* BH10 .... 322 B5
  PLE BH15 .... 320 E8
St Marks Cl *CHFD* SO53 .... 207 H4
  FARN GU14 .... 76 B3
St Mark's Ct *GPORT* PO12 .... 315 L7
St Marks Cl *STHA* RG19 .... 25 M4
  TADY RG26 .... 52 B3
St Marks Pl *FNM* GU9 * 96 B4
St Mark's Rd *BWD* BH11 .... 322 B4
  GPORT PO12 .... 315 L7
St Marks Rd *LYMN* SO41 .... 328 A5
St Martin's Cl *HASM* GU27 .... 157 H6
St Martin's Ct *PSEA* PO1 .... 18 D5
St Martins Cl *ROWN* SO16 .... 227 J9
  WINC SO23 .... 23 H4
St Marys *AND* SP10 .... 328 A5
St Marys Cl *LYMN* SO41 .... 328 A5
St Marys Cl *SHST* GU47 .... 41 K6
St Mary's Ct *BSTK* RG21 .... 7 G6
  TADY RG26 .... 52 C3
St Mary's Meadow
  RAND SP11 .... 101 N6
St Marys Pl *FNM* GU9 * 96 C8
St Mary's Pl *NWBY* RG14 .... 16 C4
  SHAM SO14 .... 21 K2
St Mary's Rd *ASHV* GU12 .... 76 F7
  BMTH BH1 .... 323 K9
  ELGH SO50 .... 207 M9
  FERN BH22 .... 302 D3
  FHAM/STUB PO14 .... 294 A5
  HISD PO11 .... 318 F5
  HLER SO31 .... 269 L4
  HTWY RG27 .... 55 H8
  KSCL RG20 .... 48 C3
  LISS GU33 .... 192 D2
  NWBY RG14 .... 24 D3
  PLE BH15 .... 320 F9
St Marys Rd *PSEA* PO1 .... 317 H2
St Mary St *SHAM* SO14 .... 21 F1
  THLE RG7 .... 27 J9
St Mary's Ter *SHAM* SO14 .... 184 A8
St Mary St *FUFL* SO22 .... 183 M1
St Mary's Wy *THLE* RG7 .... 27 K4
St Matthews Cl *GPORT* PO12 .... 13 H1
St Matthew's Cl *SHAM* SO14 .... 21 F2
St Matthew's Rd *CHAM* PO6 .... 297 H1
St Matthews Rd *FUFL* SO22 .... 164 E5
St Merrin's Cl *NBNE* BH10 .... 322 C3
St Michaels Av *TDWTH* SP9 .... 78 C6
St Michaels Cl *FAWY* SO45 .... 290 G8
  FLEETN GU51 .... 74 F4
St Michael's Cl *OVTN* RG25 .... 108 C1
St Michael's Cl *PLE* BH15 .... 320 A9
  VWD BH31 .... 258 F5
St Michael's Gdns *WINC* SO23 .... 274 D9
St Michael's Gv
  FHAM/STUB PO14 .... 294 D5
St Michaels La *THLE* RG7 .... 26 F2
St Michael's Pl *WCLF* BH2 .... 8 A9
St Michaels Rd *ASHV* GU12 .... 3 F5
  BH/HW/K RG22 .... 68 F7
  FARN GU14 .... 58 A7
  HAV PO9 .... 276 C6
  HEND SO30 .... 250 A7
  HLER SO31 .... 270 F8
St Michaels Rd *NWBY* RG14 .... 16 C4
  SHAM SO14 .... 19 F4
  SHST GU47 .... 40 G6
St Michael's Rd *TOTT* SO40 .... 246 C5
  WINC SO23 .... 22 D6
St Michaels Wy *HORN* PO8 .... 256 C1
St Monica Rd *ITCH* SO19 .... 249 J8
St Neot's Rd *HTWY* RG27 .... 39 J7

St Nicholas Av
  LSOL/BMARY PO13 .... 314 G1
St Nicholas Cl *FLEETN* GU51 .... 74 C5
  RAND SP11 .... 80 B1
St Nicholas Ct *BH/HW/K* RG22 .... 68 G6
St Nicholas Ri *WINC* SO23 .... 165 J1
St Nicholas Rd *HAV* PO9 .... 14 A1
  NWBY RG14 .... 16 D3
St Nicholas St *PSEA* PO1 .... 18 D6
St Osmund's Rd *PSTN* BH14 .... 321 J1
St Patricks Av *TWDS* BH3 .... 78 F6
St Patrick's La *LISS* GU33 .... 192 C7
St Patrick's Rd *BH/HW/K* RG22 .... 69 H9
St Pauls Cl *RFNM* GU10 .... 97 M4
St Paul's Hl *FUFL* SO22 .... 22 C3
St Pauls La *BMTH* BH1 .... 9 H2
St Pauls Pl *CHAR* BH8 .... 9 H2
St Paul's Rd *BH/HW/K* RG22 .... 69 H9
St Pauls Rd *CHAR* BH8 .... 9 H1
St Paul's Rd *HLER* SO31 .... 270 E4
St Pauls Rd *SSEA* PO5 .... 19 F4
St Pauls Sq *SSEA* PO5 * 19 F5
St Peter's Av *HISD* PO11 .... 299 J7
St Peters Cl *BPWT* SO32 .... 251 K3
St Peter's Rd *RAND* SP11 .... 102 F3
  STHA RG19 .... 32 A4
St Peters Cl *SSEA* PO5 .... 98 C3
St Peter's Gdns *RFNM* GU10 .... 115 P4
  YTLY GU46 .... 40 C9
St Peters Gv *SSEA* PO5 .... 19 G6
St Peters Md *ASHV* GU12 .... 97 P1
St Peters Pk *ALDT* GU11 .... 96 E5
St Peter's Rd *BH/HW/K* RG22 .... 68 F9
  BMTH BH1 * 9 G3
  HISD PO11 .... 299 J7
  PSF GU32 .... 215 M2
  PSTN BH14 .... 321 J8
St Peters Rbt *BMTH* BH1 * 9 F3
St Peter's Sq *EMRTH* PO10 .... 299 M1
St Peter's St *BPWT* SO32 .... 232 A4
St Peter St *WINC* SO23 .... 22 E4
St Philip's Wy *WEND* SO18 .... 249 K4
St Pirans Av *HSEA* PO3 .... 317 J1
St Richards Gdns
  WVILLE PO7 * 275 L5
St Ronan's Av *ENEY* PO4 .... 316 G6
St Ronan's Rd *ENEY* PO4 .... 316 G6
St Sebastian Crs
  FHAM/PORC PO16 .... 11 H1
St Simon Cl *HLER* SO31 .... 271 H7
St Simon's Rd *SSEA* PO5 .... 316 F6
St Stephens Cl *HASM* GU27 .... 157 H6
St Stephens La *VWD* BH31 .... 258 G4
St Stephen's Rd *FUFL* SO22 .... 164 E5
  NEND PO2 .... 296 G9
  WCLF BH2 .... 8 A3
St Stephen's Wy *WCLF* BH2 .... 8 A3
St Swithin Cl *GPORT* PO12 .... 56 C9
St Swithin Wy *AND* SP10 .... 82 D9
St Swithun Cl *BPWT* SO32 .... 231 P4
St Swithun's Cl *ROMY* SO51 .... 205 H4
St Swithun's Rd *BMTH* BH1 .... 9 J1
  NEND PO2 .... 297 H7
St Swithun's Rd South
  CHAR BH8 .... 9 J2
St Swithuns Ter *WINC* SO23 * 22 C6
St Swithun St *WINC* SO23 .... 22 C6
St Theresas Cl *HAV* PO9 .... 14 A2
St Thomas Av *HISD* PO11 .... 318 D4
St Thomas' Cl *BSTK* RG21 .... 6 D2
St Thomas Ct
  FHAM/PORC PO16 .... 11 J2
St Thomas Pk *LYMN* SO41 .... 329 K3
St Thomas's Cl *NBNE* BH10 .... 322 D5
St Thomas's Ct *PSEA* PO1 .... 18 D5
St Thomas's Rd *GPORT* PO12 .... 295 M9
  PSEA PO1 .... 18 C6
St Thomas St *WINC* SO23 .... 22 D6
St Tristan Cl *HLER* SO31 .... 271 H7
St Ursula Gv *SSEA* PO5 .... 19 J6
St Valerie Rd *GPORT* PO12 .... 12 D5
  WCLF BH2 .... 334 F1
St Vigor Wy *RWIN* SO21 .... 207 B8
St Vincent Crs *HORN* PO8 .... 256 B5
St Vincent Rd *GPORT* PO12 .... 315 N2
  SSEA PO5 .... 316 F6
St Vincent St *PSEA* PO1 * 19 F4
St Winifred's Rd *ROWN* SO16 .... 247 N1
  WCLF BH2 .... 334 F1
Salamanca *CWTH* RG45 .... 40 F1
Salcombe Av *HSEA* PO3 .... 297 J8
Salcombe Cl *CHFD* SO53 .... 206 C5
Salcombe Crs *TOTT* SO40 .... 246 C5
Salcombe Rd *NWBY* RG14 .... 16 A5
  TOTT SO40 .... 246 C5
  WSHM SO15 .... 247 N4
Salcot Rd *WINC* SO23 .... 165 H5
Salem St *WSHM* SO15 .... 247 N2
Salerno Cl *ALDT* GU11 .... 2 D2
Salerno Dr *GPORT* PO12 .... 315 K4
Salerno Rd *NEND* PO2 .... 296 F5
  ROWN SO16 .... 227 N8
Salesian Vw *FARN* GU14 .... 76 D4
Salet Wy *WVILLE* PO7 .... 276 B1
Salisbury Cl *ALTN* GU34 .... 132 C7
  ELGH SO50 .... 207 J8
  ODIM RG29 .... 93 J1
Salisbury Gdns *FRIM* GU16 .... 76 F1
Salisbury Gv *FRIM* GU16 .... 76 F1
Salisbury La *STOK* SO20 .... 120 C8
Salisbury Rd *AND* SP10 .... 102 B4
  ASHV GU12 .... 97 J1
  BLKW GU17 .... 41 K9
  BMTH BH1 .... 335 L2
  CHAM PO6 .... 297 J2
  CHCH/BSGR BH23 .... 324 F1
  ENEY PO4 .... 317 H6
  FBDG SP6 .... 220 G2
  FBDG SP6 .... 240 E1
  NARL SO24 .... 167 P2
  PSTN BH14 .... 321 L1
  RAND SP11 .... 101 N9

S

Sabre Ct *ALDT* GU11 .... 2 A3
Sabre Rd *EMRTH* PO10 .... 299 N6
Sackville St *SSEA* PO5 .... 19 G5
Saddleback Wy *FLEETN* GU51 .... 56 E9
Saddle Cl *WIMB* BH21 .... 279 L8
Saddler Cnr *SHST* GU47 .... 41 J7
Saddlers Cl *ELGH* SO50 .... 207 J7
  FBDG SP6 .... 240 D2
  RWIN SO21 .... 145 J1
Saddlers Scarp *CSHT* GU26 .... 155 P4
Saddlewood *CBLY* GU15 .... 58 B1
Sadlers La *FAWY* SO45 .... 268 C5
Sadlers Wk *EMRTH* PO10 .... 299 N1
Saffron Ct *CHIN* RG24 .... 52 A9
  FBDG SP6 .... 240 D2
Saffron Dr *CHCH/BSGR* BH23 .... 325 M7
Saffron Wy *BWD* BH11 .... 321 M1
Sage Cl *WVILLE* PO7 .... 276 A4
Sagecroft Rd *NTHA* RG18 .... 25 N2
Sages La *ALTN* GU34 .... 189 L1
Sailor's La *BPWT* SO32 .... 210 G6
Sailors La *MFD/CHID* GU8 .... 137 M7
Sainfoin La *DEAN* RG23 .... 88 F3
Sainsbury Cl *AND* SP10 .... 4 A7
St Agatha's Rd *HLER* SO31 .... 270 A6

RAND SP11 .... 119 N3
RGWD BH24 .... 260 D3
ROMY BH24 .... 282 D1
ROMY SO51 .... 202 A2
ROMY SO51 .... 224 C1
ROMY SO51 .... 225 J4
ROWN SO16 .... 228 C9
RSAL SP5 .... 199 J4
STOK SO20 .... 139 M5
TDWTH SP9 .... 98 C5
TOTT SO40 .... 246 C1
Salisbury Road Ar
TOTT SO40 .... 246 D2
Salisbury St FBDG SP6 .... 240 D2
WSHM SO15 .... 20 D1
Salisbury Ter FRIM GU16 .... 76 F1
LSOL/BMARY PO13 .... 314 D3
Salmon Dr ELGH SO50 .... 229 P2
Salmond Rd RAND SP11 .... 101 P2
Salmon Rd ALDT GU11 .... 76 C7
Salmons Rd ODIM RG29 .... 93 J1
Salterns Av ENEY PO4 .... 317 K3
Salterns Cl HISD PO11 .... 319 J5
Salterns Est
FHAM/PORC PO16 .... 294 F2
Salterns La FAWY SO45 .... 291 K5
FHAM/PORC PO16 .... 294 F2
HISD PO11 .... 319 H5
HLER SO31 .... 270 A4
Salterns Rd FHAM/STUB PO14 .... 293 P9
PSTN BH14 .... 321 J9
Salterns Wy PSTN BH14 .... 321 J9
Salter Rd CCLF BH13 .... 333 K8
Salters Acres FUFL SO22 .... 164 D4
Salters Heath Rd TADY RG26 .... 50 E8
Salters La FUFL SO22 .... 164 C5
Saltgrass La LYMN SO41 .... 339 K3
The Saltings CHAM PO6 .... 298 F3
Salt La BPWT SO32 .... 210 C2
Saltmarsh La HISD PO11 .... 318 E3
Saltmarsh Rd SHAM SO14 .... 21 H7
Saltmead SD/PW SO17 .... 248 E1
Salt Meat La GPORT PO12 .... 315 P2
Saltram Rd FARN GU14 .... 76 D2
Salvia Cl WVILLE PO7 .... 276 A4
Salwey Rd HEND SO30 .... 250 D6
Samarkand Cl CBLY GU15 .... 58 C1
Samber Cl LYMN SO41 .... 329 J3
Sampan Cl HLER SO31 .... 270 E9
Samphire Cl LYMN SO41 .... 329 K2
Samples Wy CFDH BH17 .... 321 H4
Sampson Rd
FHAM/STUB PO14 .... 294 D3
PSEA PO1 .... 18 B1
Samson Cl LSOL/BMARY PO13 .... 315 H1
Samuel Rd PSEA PO1 .... 317 H2
Sam Whites Hl RAND SP11 .... 102 C6
San Carlos Ap ALDT GU11 .... 3 J2
Sancreed Rd
BKME/WDN BH12 .... 321 N5
Sanctuary Pl HTWY RG27 .... 55 J6
Sandbanks Dr BH/HW/K RG22 .... 89 M4
Sandbanks Rd PLE BH15 .... 321 H9
Sandbourne Rd PLE BH15 .... 320 F8
WBNE BH4 .... 334 B5
Sand Cl ROMY SO51 .... 224 E1
Sandcroft Cl GPORT PO12 .... 315 J5
Sandcotes Rd PSTN BH14 .... 321 L9
Sanderling Rd ENEY PO4 .... 317 L3
Sanderlings RGWD BH24 .... 282 G3
The Sanderlings HISD PO11 .... 318 C6
Sandford Av GPORT PO12 .... 315 H4
Sandford Cl KSCL RG20 .... 48 E1
MOOR/WNTN BH9 .... 323 J4
Sandford Ct ALDT GU11 .... 2 A4
TADY RG26 .... 34 B6
Sandford Wy BDST BH18 .... 320 B1
Sand HI FARN GU14 .... 36 E6
Sandhill La LSOL/BMARY PO13 .... 314 E2
Sandhills Cl CFDH BH17 .... 320 F2
Sandhurst Dr WIMB BH21 .... 280 C2
Sandhurst La BLKW GU17 .... 41 J8
Sandhurst Rd CWTH RG45 .... 41 J3
WSHM SO15 .... 20 B1
YTLY GU46 .... 40 F8
San Diego Rd GPORT PO12 .... 315 M2
Sandisplatt FHAM/STUB PO14 .... 294 A1
Sandle Copse FBDG SP6 .... 239 P2
Sandleford La STHA RG19 .... 24 E9
Sandleford Lodge Pk
STHA RG19 .... 24 D8
Sandleford Pde NWBY RG14 * 24 D8
Sandleford Rd NWBY RG14 .... 276 D3
Sandleheath Rd FBDG SP6 .... 239 M4
Sandlewood Cl HORN PO8 .... 236 C7
TOTT SO40 .... 246 A3
Sandmartin Cl
NMIL/BTOS BH25 .... 327 H8
Sandown Cl ALTN GU34 .... 132 C7
BLKW GU17 .... 41 L9
GPORT PO12 .... 315 J5
Sandown Crs ALDT GU11 .... 3 G4
Sandown Dr FRIM GU16 .... 58 C3
Sandown Rd CHAM PO6 .... 296 C2
WSHM SO15 .... 247 M2
Sandown Wy NWBY RG14 .... 17 J6
Sandpiper Cl CFDH BH17 .... 320 B3
HORN PO8 .... 256 A4
TOTT SO40 .... 267 J1
Sandpiper Rd ROWN SO16 .... 227 L7
Sandpit La LYMN SO41 .... 331 H2
THLE RG7 .... 38 E1
Sandport Gv
FHAM/PORC PO16 .... 295 M2
Sandringham Cl ALTN GU34 .... 132 D6
CHFD SO53 .... 206 B9
MOOR/WNTN BH9 .... 323 H3
Sandringham Gdns
MOOR/WNTN BH9 .... 323 H3
Sandringham La PSEA PO1 * 316 G3
Sandringham Rd
FHAM/STUB PO14 .... 293 P1
PSEA PO1 .... 316 G3

PSF GU32 .... 215 M1
PSTN BH14 .... 321 K9
WEND SO18 .... 248 G2
Sandringham Wy FRIM GU16 .... 58 E5
Sandrock HASM GU27 .... 157 H7
Sandrock Hill Rd RFNM GU10 .... 115 P4
Sandsbury La PSF GU32 .... 191 J9
Sands Cl RFNM GU10 .... 97 K9
Sands Rd RFNM GU10 .... 97 J9
The Sands BOR GU35 .... 153 M6
Sandy Brow WVILLE PO7 .... 275 M6
Sandy Cl EPSF GU31 .... 216 A2
WIMB BH21 .... 279 J6
Sandycroft HLER SO31 .... 292 D1
Sandy Down LYMN SO41 .... 309 H4
Sandy Field Crs HORN PO8 .... 255 N8
Sandy Hill Rd FNM GU9 .... 96 A4
Sandyhurst Cl CFDH BH17 .... 320 E3
Sandy La BPWT SO32 .... 252 A3
CHCH/BSGR BH23 .... 324 C5
ELGH SO50 .... 230 B2
FARN GU14 .... 57 K7
FHAM/STUB PO14 .... 293 M1
FLEETS GU52 .... 74 D8
CSHT GU26 .... 156 E3
HASM GU27 .... 156 M8
HTWY RG27 .... 55 J8
LISS GU33 .... 193 J3
LYND SO43 .... 264 F6
NBAD SO52 .... 205 M8
RFNM GU10 .... 116 C9
RGWD BH24 .... 281 M5
ROMY SO51 .... 204 E2
RSAL SP5 .... 200 A6
SBNE BH6 .... 335 P1
SHST GU47 .... 40 C5
TADY RG26 .... 54 E6
WIMB BH21 .... 258 E8
WIMB BH21 .... 279 J6
Sandy Mead Rd CHAR BH8 .... 319 L6
Sandy Plot CHCH/BSGR BH23 .... 324 C6
Sandy Point Rd HISD PO11 .... 319 L7
Sandys Cl BH/HW/K RG22 .... 69 H9
Sandys Rd BH/HW/K RG22 .... 69 H8
Sandy Wy NBNE BH10 .... 322 C4
Sankey La FLEETN GU51 .... 56 C9
Sanross Cl FHAM/STUB PO14 .... 293 N8
Santina Cl FNM GU9 .... 96 D3
Saor Ms AND SP10 .... 4 B3
Sapley La OVTN RG25 .... 86 C4
The Saplings FAWY SO45 .... 290 D4
Sapphire Cl GPORT PO12 .... 315 M1
WVILLE PO7 * 276 A3
Sapphire Rdg WVILLE PO7 .... 276 A3
Saracen Cl LYMN SO41 .... 323 J6
Saracens Rd CHFD SO53 .... 207 H6
Sarah Cl LTDN PO7 .... 323 P7
Sarah Sands Cl
CHCH/BSGR BH23 .... 325 H7
Sarah Wy FARN GU14 .... 58 A9
Sargood Cl STHA RG19 .... 25 P5
Sarisbury Cl TADY RG26 .... 34 B6
Sark Rd BKME/WDN BH12 .... 321 M4
Sarnia Ct ROWN SO16 .... 227 J9
Sarson Cl RAND SP11 .... 101 H3
Sarson La RAND SP11 .... 101 H3
Sartoris Cl HLER SO31 .... 270 D9
Sarum Av FERN BH22 .... 280 E5
Sarum Ct FUFL SO22 .... 164 D8
STOK SO20 .... 120 D9
TDWTH SP9 .... 98 F2
Sarum HI BSTK RG21 .... 6 C7
Sarum Rd CHFD SO53 .... 206 C7
FUFL SO22 .... 164 E8
TADY RG26 .... 34 B5
Sarum St PLE BH15 * 332 D2
Sarum Vw FUFL SO22 .... 164 C9
Sarum Wk LYMN SO41 .... 329 K1
Satchell La HLER SO31 .... 270 A7
Saturn Cl ROWN SO16 .... 227 K8
Saufland Dr
CHCH/BSGR BH23 .... 325 P7
Saufland Pl CHCH/BSGR BH23 .... 325 P7
Saunders Cl
LSOL/BMARY PO13 .... 314 E1
Saunders Gdn TADY RG26 .... 34 C6
Saunders La ROMY SO51 .... 179 K9
Saunders Ms ENEY PO4 .... 317 K6
Saunton Gdns FARN GU14 .... 57 P7
Savernake Cl
LSOL/BMARY PO13 .... 295 H7
ROMY SO51 .... 204 F4
Savile Crs BOR GU35 .... 154 A5
Saville Gdns FHAM/PORC PO16 .... 207 M8
Savoy Cl AND SP10 .... 4 E5
Savoy Cv BLKW GU17 .... 57 L2
The Sawmills BPWT SO32 .... 231 H7
Sawyer Cl FUFL SO22 .... 164 C6
Sawyers Ley THLE RG7 .... 27 M7
Saxby Cl THLE RG7 .... 27 K4
Saxholm Cl ROWN SO16 .... 228 B6
Saxholm Dr ROWN SO16 .... 228 B6
Saxholm Wy ROWN SO16 .... 228 B6
Saxley Ct HAV PO9 .... 276 C4
Saxonbury Rd SBNE BH6 .... 324 C9
Saxon Cl FHAM/PORC PO16 .... 295 J8
HLER SO31 .... 270 E9
HORN PO8 .... 236 C8
Saxon Ct AND SP10 .... 82 E8
ELGH SO50 .... 205 N7
STHA RG19 .... 25 K4
Saxon Cft FNM GU9 .... 5 J5
Saxonford Rd
CHCH/BSGR BH23 .... 325 N8
Saxon Gdns HEND SO30 .... 250 A6
Saxonhurst Cl RSAL SP5 .... 199 L6
Saxonhurst Gdns NBNE BH10 .... 322 D3
Saxonhurst Rd NBNE BH10 .... 322 D3
Saxon King Gdns SBNE BH6 .... 336 F2
Saxon Leas RSAL SP5 .... 158 B1
Saxon Mdw PI LYMN SO41 .... 329 K1
Saxon Rd FAWY SO45 .... 291 N8
STOK SO20 .... 120 G4
WINC SO23 .... 22 E2

WSHM SO15 .... 247 P6
Saxon Wy AND SP10 .... 82 D8
CHIN RG24 .... 70 A5
FBDG SP6 .... 239 N6
ROMY SO51 .... 204 F6
Saxony Crs RWIN SO21 .... 163 K5
Saxton La HASM GU27 .... 156 D6
Sayers Cl FRIM GU16 .... 58 D1
NWBY RG14 .... 24 E7
Sayers Rd ELGH SO50 .... 229 M2
Sbac Tr ALDT GU11 .... 75 M6
Scafell Av FHAM/STUB PO14 .... 294 B1
Scallows La ROMY SO51 .... 202 D8
Scamblers Md RAND SP11 .... 81 M8
Scantabout Av CHFD SO53 .... 206 C6
Scarf Rd CFDH BH17 .... 321 H5
Scarlatti Rd BH/HW/K RG22 .... 90 B3
Scarlet Oaks CBLY GU15 .... 58 D2
Scarlett's Ct ALDT GU11 .... 75 P9
Scholars' Wk CHAM PO6 .... 297 L2
School Cl CHFD SO53 .... 206 D8
LYMN SO41 .... 329 J5
RAND SP11 .... 43 H8
School Flds BOR GU35 .... 134 F8
School Hill NTHA RG18 .... 233 N6
CWTH RG45 .... 41 L2
RFNM GU10 .... 97 P7
RFNM GU10 .... 115 P4
SHST GU47 .... 41 P5
School La BWD BH11 .... 322 B2
CHCH/BSGR BH23 .... 306 A4
CHFD SO53 .... 206 D9
EMRTH PO10 .... 299 M1
HLER SO31 .... 270 A9
LISS GU33 .... 193 L2
LYMN SO41 .... 309 M8
LYMN SO41 .... 328 E9
LYMN SO41 .... 329 L3
NARL SO24 .... 168 C2
PLE BH15 .... 320 E7
PSF GU32 .... 191 N8
RFNM GU10 .... 114 F5
RFNM GU10 .... 116 D4
RGUW GU3 .... 77 L8
RGWD BH24 .... 281 N4
RWIN SO21 .... 163 M8
STOK SO20 .... 120 F9
STOK SO20 .... 139 P9
THLE RG7 .... 27 H5
THLE RG7 .... 35 J5
THLE RG7 .... 38 B5
WIMB BH21 .... 278 D9
WIMB BH21 .... 280 F7
WINC SO23 .... 165 J2
WVILLE PO7 .... 254 F6
YTLY GU46 .... 40 C8
School Rd BWD BH11 .... 322 B2
CHCH/BSGR BH23 .... 306 A4
FAWY SO45 .... 291 J6
GPORT PO12 .... 295 K8
GSHT GU26 .... 156 A2
HLER SO31 .... 270 A2
RDGW/BURGH RG30 .... 27 L1
RFNM GU10 .... 115 N7
ROMY SO51 .... 204 G4
RSAL SP5 .... 200 B9
RSAL SP5 .... 223 L4
RWIN SO21 .... 183 P8
THLE RG7 .... 26 B6
THLE RG7 .... 38 B2
TOTT SO40 .... 246 E5
WHAM PO17 .... 252 B8
Schooner Wy ENEY PO4 .... 317 L2
HLER SO31 .... 270 E9
Schroeder Cl BSTK RG21 .... 90 C7
Schubert Rd BH/HW/K RG22 .... 90 A3
The Scimitars
FHAM/STUB PO14 .... 293 P6
Scivier's La BPWT SO32 .... 231 J2
Scotland Cl ASHV GU12 .... 76 F7
ROMY SO51 .... 230 E2
Scotland Farm Rd ASHV GU12 .... 76 F7
Scotland Hl SHST GU47 .... 41 H6
Scotland La HASM GU27 .... 156 C8
RSAL SP5 .... 201 J6
Scotlands Cl HASM GU27 .... 156 C8
Scotlands Dr HASM GU27 .... 156 C8
Scotney Ct HAV PO9 .... 277 H4
Scots Cl HTWY RG27 .... 72 B2
Scott Cl AND SP10 .... 103 J1
BKME/WDN BH12 .... 321 P4
FHAM/STUB PO14 .... 294 A5
RWIN SO21 .... 208 A5
STOK SO20 .... 161 M5
Scotter Rd ELGH SO50 .... 229 M1
LTDN PO7 * 335 P1
Scott-Paine Dr FAWY SO45 .... 268 D6
Scott Rd BKME/WDN BH12 .... 321 P3
ELGH SO50 .... 229 H2
HSEA PO3 .... 297 H4
ITCH SO19 .... 269 H1
PSEA PO1 .... 18 B1
Scotts CI RSAL SP5 .... 199 H5
Scotts Ct FARN GU14 .... 58 A6
Scott's Gn CHCH/BSGR BH23 .... 325 K7
Scotts Hills La
CHCH/BSGR BH23 .... 325 H9
Scratchface La HAV PO9 .... 275 P6
WVILLE PO7 .... 275 P6
Scrubbs La HASM GU27 .... 168 D4
Scullards La SHAM SO14 .... 20 D4
Scures Rd HTWY RG27 .... 71 N3
Seabird Wy FHAM/PORC PO16 .... 294 F2
Seabourne Pl BOR GU35 .... 335 P1
Seabourne Rd LTDN BH7 .... 335 H1
Sea Breeze Gdns ENEY PO4 .... 317 L5
Seabreeze Wy LYMN SO41 .... 328 A9
Seacole Gdns ROWN SO16 .... 247 N2
Seacombe Gn ROWN SO16 .... 247 H2
Seacombe Rd CCLF BH13 .... 333 K8
Sea Crest Rd
LSOL/BMARY PO13 .... 314 D3

Seacroft Av NMIL/BTOS BH25 .... 326 G7
Seafarers Wk HISD PO11 .... 319 M7
Seafield Cl NMIL/BTOS BH25 .... 327 H8
Seafield Dr SBNE BH6 .... 324 C9
Seafield Park Rd
FHAM/STUB PO14 .... 293 P8
Seafield Rd CHCH/BSGR BH23 .... 325 N9
FHAM/PORC PO16 .... 295 M2
HSEA PO3 .... 297 J8
NMIL/BTOS BH25 .... 326 G7
ROWN SO16 .... 247 H1
SBNE BH6 .... 336 D2
Seafields EMRTH PO10 .... 299 L1
Seafire Rd CHCH/BSGR BH23 .... 325 P2
Seafire Wy ALDT GU11 .... 75 M5
Seaford Cl HLER SO31 .... 269 P1
Seagarth La ROWN SO16 .... 227 P9
Seager's Ct PSEA PO1 .... 18 B6
Seager Wy PLE BH15 .... 332 F1
Seagrim Rd CHAR BH8 .... 323 J4
Sea Grove Av HISD PO11 .... 318 G6
Seagrove Rd NEND PO2 .... 296 F8
Seagull Cl BH/HW/K RG22 .... 89 M4
ENEY PO4 .... 317 L2
Seagull La EMRTH PO10 .... 277 M9
Seagull Rd CHAR BH8 .... 323 J6
The Seagulls
LSOL/BMARY PO13 .... 314 E4
Seahorse Wk GPORT PO12 .... 13 H1
Sea Kings FHAM/STUB PO14 .... 293 P7
Sea La LSOL/BMARY PO13 .... 294 A9
Sealark Rd GPORT PO12 .... 315 M1
Seale La RFNM GU10 .... 97 K7
Seale Rd MFD/CHID GU8 .... 117 P3
Seaman's La LYND SO43 .... 244 B7
Seamead FHAM/STUB PO14 .... 294 A9
Sea Mill Gdns PSEA PO1 .... 18 D3
Seamoor La WBNE BH4 .... 334 B3
Seamoor Rd WBNE BH4 .... 334 B3
Searing Wy TADY RG26 .... 34 B5
Searle Cl FUFL SO22 .... 116 C2
Searles Cl NARL SO24 .... 168 A2
Searles HI RWIN SO21 .... 184 A8
Searl's La HTWY RG27 .... 54 A9
Sea Rd BOSC BH5 .... 335 L2
ITCH SO19 .... 248 F7
NMIL/BTOS BH25 .... 326 C7
Seathrift Cl
LSOL/BMARY PO13 .... 314 C2
Seaton Av HSEA PO3 .... 297 J9
Seaton Cl CHCH/BSGR BH23 .... 326 D7
FHAM/STUB PO14 .... 294 A7
LYMN SO41 .... 329 L2
WEND SO18 .... 249 L2
Seaton Rd CHCH/BSGR BH23 .... 326 D7
Seatown Cl CFDH BH17 .... 321 J3
Sea Vw LYMN SO41 * 308 B8
Seaview Av
FHAM/PORC PO16 .... 274 A9
Seaview Est HLER SO31 .... 269 K5
Sea View Rd
BKME/WDN BH12 .... 321 J7
CHAM PO6 .... 297 L1
Seaview Rd CHCH/BSGR BH23 .... 326 E6
HISD PO11 .... 319 J5
NMIL/BTOS BH25 .... 326 F8
SBNE BH6 .... 335 P2
Seaward Av ITCH SO19 .... 248 G7
NMIL/BTOS BH25 .... 327 K7
Seaway NMIL/BTOS BH25 .... 325 N9
Seaway Av CHCH/BSGR BH23 .... 325 N9
Seaway Crs ENEY PO4 .... 317 L4
Seaway Gv FHAM/PORC PO16 .... 295 N3
Seaweed Cl ITCH SO19 .... 248 F7
Seawinds LYMN SO41 .... 338 D1
Sebastian Gv WVILLE PO7 .... 276 A2
Sebastopol Rd ALDT GU11 .... 3 F3
Second Av CHAM PO6 .... 297 N2
HAV PO9 .... 15 K4
THLE RG7 .... 34 D4
WSHM SO15 .... 247 H4
Second Marine Av
NMIL/BTOS BH25 .... 327 J9
Second St FAWY SO45 .... 290 C1
Second St East STHA RG19 .... 31 M1
Second St West KSCL RG20 .... 31 L2
Sedbergh Rd ROWN SO16 .... 247 H2
Seddon Cl NMIL/BTOS BH25 .... 327 K7
Sedgefield Cl CHAM PO6 .... 296 B1
TOTT SO40 .... 246 A3
Sedgefield Rd NWBY RG14 .... 17 J7
Sedge Gv NTHA RG18 .... 25 P3
Sedgeley Gv GPORT PO12 .... 295 L9
Sedgemead HLER SO31 .... 269 K5
Sedgemoor FAWY SO45 .... 58 A6
Sedgewick Cl
LSOL/BMARY PO13 .... 294 C9
Sedgewick Rd ELGH SO50 .... 229 M1
ITCH SO19 .... 249 L6
Sedgley Cl SSEA PO5 .... 19 J5
Sedgley Rd MOOR/WNTN BH9 .... 322 F7
Seebys Oak SHST GU47 .... 41 L8
Seeviours Ct WHCH RG28 .... 85 L6
Segars La WIMB SO21 .... 183 P9
Segensworth Rd FHAM PO15 .... 271 M7
Selangor Av EMRTH PO10 .... 277 K9
Selborne Av HAV PO9 .... 276 D5
WEND SO18 .... 249 L3
Selborne Cl BLKW GU17 .... 41 K8
PSF GU32 .... 191 N9
Selborne Gdns FNM GU9 .... 116 A3
GPORT PO12 .... 315 L4
Selborne PI FUFL SO22 .... 183 M1
Selborne Rd ALTN GU34 .... 132 E8
FUFL SO22 .... 183 M1
Selbourne Dr ELGH SO50 .... 207 J9
Selborne Rd HAV PO9 .... 14 E6
WEND SO18 .... 246 B3
Selbourne Ter PSEA PO1 .... 316 G5
Selby Cl BDST BH18 .... 320 C1
Selby Wk CHIN RG24 .... 69 L3

Seldon Cl FUFL SO22 .... 183 K2
Seldown PLE BH15 .... 320 F9
Seldown Br PLE BH15 .... 332 F1
Seldown La PLE BH15 .... 320 F9
Seldown Rd PLE BH15 .... 320 F9
Selfridge Av ENEY PO4 .... 317 P3
Selfridge Cl ENEY PO4 .... 317 P3
Selfridge Cl SBNE BH6 .... 336 F5
Selhurst Wy ELGH SO50 .... 230 C3
Seliot Cl PLE BH15 .... 320 F9
Selkirk Cl WIMB SO21 .... 300 C4
Sellwood Rd HLER SO31 .... 269 L4
Sellwood Wy
NMIL/BTOS BH25 .... 326 F7
Selman Cl FAWY SO45 .... 268 C6
Selsdon Av ROMY SO51 .... 204 F5
Selsey Gv ENEY PO4 .... 317 J6
GPORT PO12 .... 295 K9
Selsey Cl HISD PO11 .... 319 M6
ROWN SO16 .... 227 P9
Selsmore Av HISD PO11 .... 319 J6
Selsmore Rd HISD PO11 .... 318 G5
Selwood Pk NBNE BH10 * 302 C9
Selworth La BPWT SO32 .... 233 M9
Selworthy Cl PSTN BH14 .... 333 J1
Selwyn Dr YTLY GU46 .... 40 C8
Selwyn Gdns ELGH SO50 .... 207 J8
Sengana Cl HEND SO30 .... 250 D5
Seniac Rd ROMY SO51 .... 204 F6
Sennen Pl CHAM PO6 .... 296 C2
Sentinel Cl WVILLE PO7 .... 276 B1
Sepen Meade FLEETS GU52 .... 74 B8
Seps 4 Rd FAWY SO45 .... 291 K5
September Cl HEND SO30 .... 249 M2
Serle Cl TOTT SO40 .... 245 P4
Serle Gdns TOTT SO40 .... 246 B5
Sermon Rd FUFL SO22 .... 164 C6
Serpentine Rd
FHAM/PORC PO16 .... 11 G2
PLE BH15 .... 320 E9
SSEA PO5 .... 316 D6
WVILLE PO7 .... 275 L7
Setley Gdns CHAR BH8 .... 323 L4
Seton Dr HTWY RG27 .... 71 N4
Setters Cl RWIN SO21 .... 207 P5
Set Thorns Rd LYMN SO41 .... 308 C6
Settle Cl ROWN SO16 .... 247 M3
Settlers Cl PSEA PO1 .... 19 J1
The Sett YTLY GU46 .... 40 C9
Sevenoaks Dr LTDN BH7 .... 323 N7
Sevenoaks Rd FHAM/PORC PO16 .... 296 C1
Seventh St STHA RG19 .... 31 L1
The Severals CHIN RG24 .... 69 H1
Severn Cl CHAM PO6 .... 274 D9
NTHA RG18 .... 25 L2
SHST GU47 .... 41 K6
Severn Ct AND SP10 .... 82 G9
Severn Gdns DEAN RG23 .... 88 F2
Severn Rd FARN GU14 .... 57 M7
FERN BH22 .... 302 G2
ROWN SO16 .... 247 J3
Severn Wy BSTK RG21 .... 7 K6
HEND SO30 .... 249 M1
Seville Crs AND SP10 .... 5 G2
Seward Av ROMY SO51 .... 204 G5
Seward Rd FAWY SO45 .... 268 D7
Seymour Cl CHFD SO53 .... 206 C8
NEND PO2 .... 316 F1
TOTT SO40 .... 246 A2
Seymour Gdns RGWD BH24 .... 260 F9
Seymour La NBAD SO52 .... 205 K9
Seymour Pl ODIM RG29 .... 72 D9
Seymour Rd BH/HW/K RG22 .... 89 N1
BOR GU35 .... 155 K4
LSOL/BMARY PO13 .... 314 D4
RGWD BH24 .... 260 F9
ROWN SO16 .... 227 N9
Shackleton Cl ASHV GU12 .... 76 E9
Shackleton Rd
LSOL/BMARY PO13 .... 295 H3
Shackleton Sq AND SP10 * 305 M7
CHCH/BSGR BH23 .... 305 M7
Shadwell Rd NEND PO2 .... 296 G5
Shady Nook FNM GU9 .... 96 B5
Shaftesbury Av CHFD SO53 .... 206 E9
SD/PW SO17 .... 248 D2
WVILLE PO7 .... 275 M6
Shaftesbury Cl FERN BH22 .... 280 F9
Shaftesbury Mt BLKW GU17 .... 57 K2
Shaftesbury Rd CHAR BH8 .... 323 J9
FERN BH22 .... 280 F9
PLE BH15 .... 320 F9
SSEA PO5 .... 316 E6
Shaftesbury St FBDG SP6 .... 240 C2
Shaftsbury Rd ASHV GU12 .... 12 E3
Shaggs Meadow LYND SO43 .... 264 E5
Shakespeare Av CHIN RG24 .... 69 M4
ELGH SO50 .... 207 H8
NTHA RG18 .... 25 M3
PSEA PO1 .... 316 G2
SBNE BH6 .... 324 B8
WIMB BH21 .... 278 E8
Shakespeare Dr TOTT SO40 .... 246 B1
Shakespeare Gdns FARN GU14 .... 57 L8
HORN PO8 .... 255 N8
Shakespeare Rd CHIN RG24 .... 69 M4
ELGH SO50 .... 207 H8
ITCH SO19 .... 10 C2
PSEA PO1 .... 18 G3
Shalbourne Rd GPORT PO12 .... 315 L1
Shalcombe HLER SO31 .... 269 L3
Shalden Cl ROWN SO16 .... 227 M8
Shalden La ALTN GU34 .... 131 P2
Shalden Rd ASHV GU12 .... 13 K8
Shaldon Rd HAV PO9 .... 277 H4
Shaldon Wy FLEETN GU51 .... 74 A4
Shales Rd WEND SO18 .... 248 E3
Shallow La LYMN SO41 .... 309 K8
The Shallows FBDG SP6 .... 250 C2
Shamblehurst La HEND SO30 .... 250 C2
Shamblehurst La North
HEND SO30 .... 230 D9
Shamblehurst La South
HEND SO30 .... 250 C2
Shamrock Cl FRIM GU16 .... 58 C5
Shamrock Quay SHAM SO14 * 248 F5
Shamrock Rd ITCH SO19 .... 248 G8
Shamrock Wy FAWY SO45 .... 268 C5

Shanklin Av *ASHV* GU12 ...... 3 J5
Shanklin Crs *WSHM* SO15 ...... 247 P2
Shanklin Rd *ENEY* PO4 ...... 316 G4
WSHM SO15 ...... 247 P1
Shannon Cl *FHAM* PO15 ...... 272 B8
Shannon Ct *AND* SP10 ...... 82 C9
Shannon Rd
FHAM/STUB PO14 ...... 293 P5
Shapland Av *BWD* BH11 ...... 301 N8
Shappen Hill La *RGWD* BH24 ...... 284 B7
Shapton Cl *FAWY* SO45 ...... 290 D5
Shard Cl *VWD* BH31 ...... 258 C4
Sharf Rd *BKME/WDN* BH12 ...... 322 A8
Sharlands Cl *BDST* BH18 ...... 320 D1
Sharlands Rd
FHAM/STUB PO14 ...... 294 E3
Sharon Rd *HEND* SO30 ...... 249 L1
Sharpley Cl *FBDG* SP6 ...... 220 C9
Sharpness Cl
FHAM/STUB PO14 * 294 A1
Sharps Rd *HAV* PO9 ...... 277 H5
Sharvells Rd *LYMN* SO41 ...... 338 F1
Shavard La *BPWT* SO32 ...... 211 P8
Shaves La *NMIL/BTOS* BH25 ...... 327 J2
Shaw Br *NWBY* RG14 * 24 E2
Shaw Cl *AND* SP10 ...... 102 A2
TOTT SO40 ...... 246 B4
WEND SO18 ...... 249 J1
Shaw Farm Rd *NWBY* RG14 ...... 24 E2
Shawfield La *ASHV* GU12 ...... 97 M1
Shawfield Rd *ASHV* GU12 ...... 97 M2
HAV PO9 ...... 15 J7
Shawford Cl *ROWN* SO16 ...... 228 A8
Shawford Gdns *CHAR* BH8 ...... 323 K5
Shawford Dr *HAV* PO9 ...... 276 C5
Shawford Rd *CHAR* BH8 ...... 323 K4
RWIN SO21 ...... 183 P8
Shaw HI *NWBY* RG14 ...... 24 E2
Shaw La *TADY* RG26 ...... 34 A8
Shaw Pk *CWTH* RG45 ...... 41 J3
Shaw Pightle *HTWY* RG27 ...... 71 N3
Shaw Rd *NWBY* RG14 ...... 24 E3
RCWD BH24 ...... 260 G8
Shaws Wk *AND* SP10 ...... 4 D5
Shayer Rd *WSHM* SO15 ...... 247 N2
Sheardley La *BPWT* SO32 ...... 234 B4
Shearer Rd *PSEA* PO1 ...... 316 C1
Shear HI *EPSF* GU31 ...... 191 P9
Shears Brook Cl
CHCH/BSGR BH23 ...... 305 M7
Shears Rd *ELGH* SO50 ...... 229 N1
Shearwater Av
FHAM/PORC PO16 ...... 295 J1
Shearwater Cl
LSOL/BMARY PO13 ...... 294 F7
Shearwater Dr *FHAM* PO16 ...... 297 P2
Sheep Dro *STOK* SO20 ...... 139 L4
Sheep Fair *AND* SP10 ...... 5 G4
Sheep Fair Cl *AND* SP10 ...... 5 G4
Sheephatch La *RFNM* GU10 ...... 117 H5
Sheephouse *FNM* GU9 ...... 116 C2
Sheep Pond La *BPWT* SO32 ...... 233 J1
Sheep St *PSF* GU32 ...... 215 M2
Sheepwash La *KSCL* RG20 ...... 30 E4
TADY RG26 ...... 50 F7
WVILLE PO7 ...... 275 H2
Sheffield Cl *ELGH* SO50 ...... 207 M8
FARN GU14 ...... 57 N9
Sheffield Ct
LSOL/BMARY PO13 * 314 G2
Sheffield Rd *PSEA* PO1 ...... 316 C5
Shelbourne Cl *CHAR* BH8 ...... 323 K9
Shelbourne Rd *CHAR* BH8 ...... 323 J9
Sheldon's La *HTWY* RG27 ...... 71 N3
Sheldon's Rd *HTWY* RG27 ...... 71 P3
Sheldrake Gdns *LYMN* SO41 ...... 328 B3
ROWN SO16 ...... 227 M7
Sheldrake Rd
CHCH/BSGR BH23 ...... 337 L1
Shelford Rd *ENEY* PO4 ...... 317 K3
Shellcroft *HLER* SO31 ...... 292 D1
Shelley Av *CHAM* PO6 ...... 274 A9
Shelley Cl *BMTH* BH1 ...... 335 L1
CHCH/BSGR BH23 ...... 325 N8
CHIN RG24 ...... 69 M4
FLEETN GU51 ...... 74 D4
FUFL SO22 ...... 164 E7
RCWD BH24 ...... 281 L4
Shelley Gdns *BMTH* BH1 ...... 335 L1
HORN PO8 ...... 255 N8
Shelley La *ROMY* SO51 ...... 225 L3
Shelley Rd *BKME/WDN* BH12 ...... 321 N7
BMTH BH1 ...... 335 L1
ELGH SO50 ...... 229 K5
ITCH SO19 ...... 249 M5
NTHA RG18 ...... 25 M3
TOTT SO40 ...... 246 B1
Shelley Rd East *BMTH* BH1 ...... 335 L1
Shelleys La *ALTN* GU34 ...... 133 L8
Shelley Wy *YTLY* GU46 ...... 40 C9
Shell La *ALTN* GU34 ...... 171 J4
Shelly Ri *FARN* GU14 ...... 57 N7
Shelton Rd *SBNE* BH6 ...... 324 A9
Shenley Cl *FHAM* PO15 ...... 272 A8
Shenstone Ct
NMIL/BTOS BH25 ...... 327 J6
Shepards Ct *FHAM/STUB* PO14.. 294 A1
Shepherd Cl
CHCH/BSGR BH23 ...... 306 F6
Shepherd & Flock Rbt
FNM GU9 ...... 96 F7
Shepherd Rd *FUFL* SO22 ...... 183 K2
TOTT SO40 ...... 245 H5
Shepherds Down *NARL* SO24 ...... 167 P3
Shepherds Hey Rd *TOTT* SO40 ...... 245 P3
Shepherds HI *HASM* GU27 ...... 157 H7
Shepherds La *RGWD* BH24 ...... 260 A4
Shepherds La *RGWD* BH24 ...... 259 N4
...... 183 H8
Shepherds Purse Cl
FNM GU9 ...... 96 F7
Shepherds Ri *RAND* SP11 ...... 43 H8

Shepherds Rd *TOTT* SO40 ...... 245 H5
WINC SO23 ...... 23 K4
Shepherds Rw *AND* SP10 ...... 5 G5
Shepherds Spring La *AND* SO14.. 4 D3
Shepherds Wk *FARN* GU14 ...... 57 M6
Shepherds Wy *CWTH* RG45 ...... 40 F2
LIPH GU30 ...... 175 L4
LTDN BH7 ...... 323 N8
LYMN SO41 ...... 328 C6
RFNM GU10 ...... 117 J6
ROWN SO16 ...... 226 G7
Shephrs Farm La
BPWT SO32 ...... 211 J9
Sheppard Cl *HORN* PO8 ...... 256 A5
WHCH RG28 ...... 85 L7
Sheppard Rd *BSTK* RG21 ...... 90 C1
Sheppards Fld *WIMB* BH21 ...... 278 D8
Sheppard Sq *AND* SP10 * 82 G9
Shepton Br *BROC* SO42 ...... 288 F4
Sheraton Av *BH/HW/K* RG22 ...... 89 M4
Sheraton Cl *BLKW* GU17 * 57 M1
Sherborn Crs *CFDN* BH17 ...... 321 H3
Sherborne Cl *ELCH* SO50 ...... 207 H7
Sherborne Dr *FERN* BH22 ...... 302 D4
Sherborne Rd *BSTK* RG21 ...... 6 C2
CHIN RG24 ...... 69 J2
FARN GU14 ...... 76 C4
SD/PW SO17 ...... 248 D1
Sherborne Wy *HEND* SO30 ...... 250 C5
Sherbrooke Cl
LSOL/BMARY PO13 ...... 314 E2
WINC SO23 ...... 145 K8
Sherecroft Gdns *HEND* SO30 ...... 251 H4
Sherfield Av *HAV* PO9 ...... 276 C5
Sherfield Cl *CHAR* BH8 ...... 323 K5
Sherfield English La *RSAL* SP5 ...... 234 F5
Sherfield Rd *TADY* RG26 ...... 52 A2
Sheridan Cl *ALDT* GU11 ...... 2 E6
FUFL SO22 ...... 183 L1
Sheridan Crs *TADY* RG26 ...... 33 P5
Sheridan Gdns *FHAM* PO15 ...... 271 J2
TOTT SO40 ...... 246 B4
Sheridan Rd *FRIM* GU16 ...... 58 C5
Sheringham Rd
BKME/WDN BH12 ...... 321 P7
CHAM PO6 * 274 F9
Sherington Cl *FARN* GU14 ...... 58 A7
Sherley Gn *HLER* SO31 ...... 269 P1
Sherlock Lea *HTWY* RG27 ...... 39 P7
Shermin's Bank
CHCH/BSGR BH23 ...... 323 J7
Sherrardmead *NWBY* RG14 ...... 24 E2
Sherrin Cl *PLE* BH15 ...... 320 F7
Sherringham Cl *FAWY* SO45 ...... 291 K6
Sherrington Wy
BH/HW/K RG22 ...... 90 B1
Sherwin Crs *FARN* GU14 ...... 58 A5
Sherwin Wk *GPORT* PO12 ...... 12 A5
Sherwood Av *FERN* BH22 ...... 302 C5
HEND SO30 ...... 250 C7
PSTN BH14 ...... 333 H1
Sherwood Cl *BH/HW/K* RG22 ...... 89 N5
CHCH/BSGR BH23 ...... 324 D8
LISS GU33 ...... 173 M8
ROWN SO16 ...... 228 A9
Sherwood Dr *VWD* BH31 ...... 259 H4
Sherwood Gdns *HLER* SO31 ...... 270 E6
Sherwood Rd *CHFD* SO53 ...... 206 B4
GPORT PO12 ...... 12 B2
Sherwood Ter *ALTN* GU34 * 132 C6
Sherwood Wy *FAWY* SO45 ...... 312 G1
Shetland Cl *CHAM* PO6 ...... 275 H9
TOTT SO40 ...... 245 P3
Shetland Ri *FHAM* PO15 ...... 271 H4
Shetland Rd *CHIN* RG24 ...... 69 M3
Shetland Vw *VWD* BH31 ...... 258 G4
Shetland Wy *FLEETN* GU51 ...... 56 E4
Shildon Cl *CBLY* GU15 ...... 59 J2
Shillinglee *WVILLE* PO7 ...... 275 N7
Shillingstone Dr
MOOR/WNTN BH9 ...... 323 H4
Shillingstone Gdns
BKME/WDN BH12 ...... 321 P5
Shillito Rd *BKME/WDN* BH12 ...... 321 N8
Shinewell Gdns *ROWN* SO16 ...... 247 J3
Shingle Bank Dr *LYMN* SO41 ...... 338 C2
Ship Aly *FARN* GU14 ...... 58 B7
Shipbuilding Rd *PSEA* PO1 ...... 316 B2
Shipcote La *BPWT* SO32 ...... 232 A2
Ship La *FARN* GU14 ...... 58 B7
Ship Leopard St *PSEA* PO1 ...... 18 C3
Shipley Cl *ALTN* GU34 ...... 132 C4
Shipley Ct *LIPH* GU30 ...... 175 J4
Shipley Rd *RWIN* SO21 ...... 160 C9
Shipton Wy *BH/HW/K* RG22 ...... 89 N1
Shire Av *FLEETN* GU51 ...... 74 F1
Shire Ct *FHAM* PO15 ...... 271 H3
WVILLE PO7 ...... 276 B1
Shires Cl *RGWD* BH24 ...... 282 E5
Shires Copse *SBNE* BH6 ...... 336 D5
Shires Wy *YTLY* GU46 ...... 40 E6
Shirley Av *ENEY* PO4 ...... 317 L4
WINC SO23 ...... 23 F5
Shirley Cl *CHCH/BSGR* BH23 ...... 305 M7
FERN BH22 ...... 302 E1
Shirley High St *ROWN* SO16 ...... 247 M3
Shirley Holms *LYMN* SO41 ...... 309 H7
Shirley Park Rd *ROWN* SO16 ...... 247 M3
Shirley Rd *BKME/WDN* BH12 ...... 321 K6
MOOR/WNTN BH9 ...... 323 H8
SSEA PO5 ...... 316 C6
WSHM SO15 ...... 322 G6
Shirley Towers *WSHM* SO15 * 247 N3
Shoddesden La *RAND* SP11 ...... 80 C5
Shoe La *ALDT* GU11 ...... 75 P6
BPWT SO32 ...... 209 N7
Sholing Cl *HAV* PO9 ...... 276 D4
Sholing Rd *ITCH* SO19 ...... 248 G7
Shooters Hill Cl *ITCH* SO19 ...... 249 K8
Shooters Wy *BSTK* RG21 ...... 7 G2
Shop La *WHAM* PO17 ...... 253 P8
Shoot La *LSOL/BMARY* PO13 ...... 314 D1
Shop La *HLER* SO31 ...... 249 N9
NWBY RG14 ...... 24 C1
Shore Av *ENEY* PO4 ...... 317 K2

Shore Cl *LYMN* SO41 ...... 338 G2
Shore Crs *BPWT* SO32 ...... 232 B5
Shorefield Crs *LYMN* SO41 ...... 338 F1
Shorefield Rd *LYMN* SO41 ...... 327 P9
TOTT SO40 ...... 247 K9
Shorefield Wy *LYMN* SO41 ...... 338 F1
Shorehaven *CHAM* PO6 ...... 296 B1
Shore Rd *BPWT* SO32 ...... 232 B5
Shore Rd *CCLF* BH13 ...... 333 M5
FAWY SO45 ...... 268 D6
Shore Sq *NEND* PO2 ...... 296 D2
PSTN BH14 ...... 333 M5
Shorewell *HLER* SO31 ...... 269 L5
Shorewood Cl *HLER* SO31 ...... 270 G9
Short Cl *BKME/WDN* BH12 ...... 322 A7
Short Dale Rd *ALDT* GU11 ...... 97 J5
Shortfield Rd *RFNM* GU10 ...... 116 C9
Shortheath Crest *FNM* GU9 ...... 116 A4
Shortheath La *THLE* RG7 ...... 26 F4
Short HI *ROMY* SO51 ...... 204 G4
RSAL SP5 ...... 223 K4
Short La *FAWY* SO45 ...... 101 N1
Short Rd *FHAM/STUB* PO14 ...... 295 N7
Short Rw *PSEA* PO1 ...... 18 D1
Shorts Cl *CHCH/BSGR* BH23 ...... 324 C6
Shorts Rd *ELGH* SO50 ...... 230 B2
Short St *ALDT* GU11 ...... 2 D2
.... 79 P1
Shortwoodcopse La
DEAN RG23 ...... 89 K6
Shotterfield Ter *LISS* GU33 ...... 192 D2
Shottermill Pk *HASM* GU27 ...... 156 D6
Shotters Hill Cl *HEND* SO30 ...... 249 M2
Shotters La *ALTN* GU34 ...... 154 C1
Shottsford Rd *PLE* BH15 ...... 320 E7
Shotts La *LYMN* SO41 ...... 330 A3
Shraveshill Cl *TOTT* SO40 ...... 246 B2
The Shrave *ALTN* GU34 ...... 150 F4
Shrewsbury Ter *NWBY* RG14 * .. 16 B5
Shrivenham Cl *STHA* SO47 ...... 41 L6
Shrubbery Cl
FHAM/PORC PO16 ...... 295 N2
The Shrubbery *FARN* GU14 ...... 75 L1
GPORT PO12 ...... 315 K1
Shrubb's Av *LYMN* SO41 ...... 328 A5
Shrubbs Hill Gdns *LYND* SO43 ...... 264 F6
Shrubbs Hill Rd *LYND* SO43 ...... 264 F6
Shrubbs La *RFNM* GU10 ...... 115 P6
Shrubland Ct *WEND* SO18 ...... 249 K3
Shyshack La *TADY* RG26 ...... 33 P5
Sian Cl *FLEETS* GU52 ...... 74 E7
Sibelius Cl *BH/HW/K* RG22 ...... 90 A4
Sibland Cl *FHAM/STUB* PO14 ...... 294 B1
Sickle Rd *HASM* GU27 ...... 156 E8
Sickles La *BOR* GU35 ...... 134 F7
Sickles Rd *BOR* GU35 ...... 134 E5
Sidbury Circular Rd
TDWTH SP9 ...... 78 F4
Sidbury Hts *TDWTH* SP9 ...... 78 C3
Sidbury Hill Av *TDWTH* SP9 ...... 78 G3
Siddal Cl *ITCH* SO19 ...... 249 L8
Sidestrand Rd *ALDT* GU11 ...... 75 M5
The Sidings *ALDT* GU11 ...... 24 K7
HLER SO31 ...... 269 M5
RSAL SP5 ...... 199 L5
Sidlaw Cl *BH/HW/K* RG22 ...... 68 D9
Sidlaws Rd *FARN* GU14 ...... 57 L6
Sidlesham Cl *HIGD* PO11 ...... 316 A8
Sidmouth Av *HASM* PO25 ...... 297 J9
Sidmouth Rd *AND* SP10 ...... 5 H4
Sidney St *LYMN* SO41 ...... 328 A5
Silchester Cl *AND* SP10 ...... 82 C9
WCLF BH2 ...... 334 F1
Silchester Pl *WINC* SO23 ...... 22 E2
Silchester Rd *CHAM* PO6 ...... 274 E9
HASM PO3 ...... 317 K1
TADY RG26 ...... 34 C5
Silkin Gdns *TOTT* SO40 ...... 246 B5
Silk Mill La *OVTN* RG25 ...... 86 F3
Silkstead Av *HAV* PO9 ...... 276 F4
Silkstead La *RWIN* SO21 ...... 183 H9
Silkweavers Rd *AND* SP10 ...... 4 E3
Sillen La *FBDG* SP6 ...... 195 P6
Silver Birch Av
FHAM/STUB PO14 ...... 10 A7
Silver Birch Cl
BKME/WDN BH12 ...... 334 A2
FLEETS GU52 ...... 74 C7
LISS GU33 ...... 192 E2
Silverbirch Rd *AND* SP10 ...... 102 C2
Silver Birch Wy *FHAM* PO15 ...... 271 K2
Silverdale *FLEETS* GU52 ...... 74 D6
NMIL/BTOS BH25 ...... 327 K6
Silverdale Cl *HLER* SO31 ...... 270 G9
Silverdale Ct *WVILLE* PO7 ...... 255 L9
Silverdale Crs *FBDG* SP6 ...... 239 N5
Silverdale Dr *WVILLE* PO7 ...... 255 L9
Silverdale Rd *TADY* RG26 ...... 34 C5
WINC SO23 ...... 248 A4
Silver Dr *FRIM* GU16 ...... 59 J2
Silverglades *YTLY* GU46 ...... 39 P7
Silver HI *SHST* GU47 ...... 41 M6
WINC SO23 ...... 23 F5
Silver La *THLE* RG7 ...... 26 C7
Silverlock Cl *NEND* PO2 ...... 295 N1
Silverlock Pl *EMRTH* PO10 * 277 P5
Silver Park Cl *FLEETS* GU52 ...... 74 E6
Silversands Gdns *HISD* PO11 ...... 319 H6
Silvers End *FAWY* SO45 ...... 268 C9
Silver St *CHCH/BSGR* BH23 ...... 324 F9
LSOL/BMARY PO13 ...... 314 F5
LYMN SO41 ...... 264 D5
SSEA PO5 ...... 19 F6
Silvers Wd *TOTT* SO40 ...... 246 A2
Silverthorne Wy *WVILLE* PO7 ...... 275 M4
Silvertrees *EMRTH* PO10 ...... 277 M8
Silver Trees *FHAM* PO15 ...... 271 K2
Silvertrees *HLER* SO31 ...... 270 E5
Silverweed Cl *CHFD* SO53 ...... 206 B6
Silverweed Ct *FUFL* SO22 ...... 183 M1
WIMB BH21 ...... 300 F3
Silvester Cl *BSTK* RG21 ...... 7 K2
Silvester Rd *HORN* PO8 ...... 255 N9
Silvester Wy *FLEETS* GU52 ...... 74 B8
Silwood Cl *FUFL* SO22 ...... 164 E6
Simmonds Cl *PLE* BH15 ...... 320 F7

Simmons Cl *HEND* SO30 ...... 250 C3
Simmons Gn *HISD* PO11 ...... 319 J5
Simms Farm La *THLE* RG7 ...... 35 N1
Simnel St *SHAM* SO14 ...... 20 D6
Simonds Ct *WINC* SO23 ...... 165 H5
Simonds Rd *RAND* SP11 ...... 79 N4
Simons Cl *CHIN* RG24 ...... 69 P2
Simons Rd *WEND* SO18 ...... 249 N4
Simpson Cl *FHAM/PORC* PO16.. 295 N1
Simpson Rd *NEND* PO2 ...... 296 E8
Sims Cl *TADY* RG26 ...... 52 C3
Sinah La *HISD* PO11 ...... 318 D5
Sinclair Rd *ROWN* SO16 ...... 227 L7
Sine Cl *FARN* GU14 ...... 58 A5
Singleton Dr *NBNE* BH10 ...... 322 C5
Singleton Gdns *HORN* PO8 ...... 236 D8
Singleton Wy *TOTT* SO40 ...... 245 P3
Sinhurst Rd *CBLY* GU15 ...... 58 A1
Sir Christopher Cl *FAWY* SO45.. 268 D6
Sirdar Rd *SD/PW* SO17 ...... 228 E9
Sir Galahad Rd *CHFD* SO53 ...... 206 B7
Sir George's Rd *WSHM* SO15 ...... 247 P5
Sir Lancelot Cl *CHFD* SO53 ...... 206 B7
Sir Richard's Ride *HTWY* RG27.. 55 K1
Siskin Cl *BPWT* SO32 ...... 231 N4
FERN BH22 ...... 302 B1
ROWN SO16 ...... 227 L7
Siskin Rd *ENEY* PO4 ...... 317 L3
Sissinghurst Cl *ITCH* SO19 ...... 269 J1
Sissinghurst Rd
FHAM/PORC PO16 ...... 295 L2
Six Oaks Rd *NBAD* SO52 ...... 205 L8
Sixpenny Cl *BKME/WDN* BH12.. 321 P5
Sixth Av *CHAM* PO6 ...... 296 C1
Sixth St *STHA* RG19 ...... 31 L1
Sizer Wy *FAWY* SO45 ...... 267 M7
Skates La *TADY* RG26 ...... 34 E9
Skew Rd *FHAM/PORC* PO16 ...... 275 N8
RAND SP11 ...... 80 A2
WHAM PO17 ...... 273 N8
Skinner St *PLE* BH15 ...... 332 E2
Skipper Cl *TOTT* SO40 ...... 247 L8
Skipper Wy
LSOL/BMARY PO13 ...... 314 D3
Skippetts La East *BSTK* RG21 ...... 90 E1
Skippetts La West
BH/HW/K RG22 ...... 90 D1
Skipton Cl *BDST* BH18 ...... 320 C2
Skipton Rd *CHFD* SO53 ...... 206 B9
Skye Cl *CHAM* PO6 ...... 275 H9
Sky End La *LYMN* SO41 ...... 328 A5
Skylark Cl *BH/HW/K* RG22 ...... 89 K4
Skylark Ct *ENEY* PO4 ...... 317 L3
Skylark Mdw *FHAM* PO15 ...... 271 M5
Skylings *NWBY* RG14 ...... 24 C3
Skys Wood Rd *CHFD* SO53 ...... 206 B6
Slab La *RDWN* SO21 ...... 224 D1
RSAL SP5 ...... 199 L6
Slade Cl *LYMN* SO41 ...... 328 A4
Slade La *EPSF* GU31 ...... 216 G1
Slades Hill *FAWY* SO45 ...... 289 H2
Slades La *NBNE* BH10 ...... 322 C7
Slade's La *NBNE* BH10 ...... 322 C7
Slater Ap *NEND* PO2 ...... 296 C9
Slater Cl *TOTT* SO40 ...... 245 P3
Sleepbrook Cl *VWD* BH31 ...... 258 E4
Sleepers Delle Gdns *FUFL* SO22.. 22 A7
Sleepers Hill *FUFL* SO22 ...... 164 E9
Sleepers Hill Gdns
FUFL SO22 * 164 E9
Slepe Crs *BKME/WDN* BH12 ...... 321 P4
Slessor Cl *RAND* SP11 ...... 101 P5
Slim Cl *ALDT* GU11 ...... 76 D6
Slindon Cl *HORN* PO8 ...... 256 D7
Slindon Gdns *HAV* PO9 ...... 15 G6
Slindon St *PSEA* PO1 ...... 19 H2
Slingsby Cl *PSEA* PO1 ...... 18 F5
Slinn Rd *CHCH/BSGR* BH23 ...... 325 J8
Slipper Mi *EMRTH* PO10 * 299 N2
Slipper Rd *EMRTH* PO10 ...... 299 N2
Slip Wy *PLE* BH15 ...... 332 D1
The Slipway *CHAM* PO6 * 296 B2
Sloane Av *FAWY* SO45 ...... 290 F5
Sloane Ct *FAWY* SO45 ...... 290 F5
Sloane Pk *BPWT* SO32 ...... 252 B4
Sloe Tree Cl *HLER* SO31 ...... 271 J8
Small Cl *EPSF* GU31 ...... 191 N9
Smallfield Dr *HTWY* RG27 ...... 72 B3
Smallridge *KSCL* RG20 ...... 30 B2
Smannell Rd *AND* SP10 ...... 82 F8
Smay Down La *MARL* SN8 ...... 42 A2
Smeaton Rd *AND* SP10 ...... 81 P9
Smeeton Rd
LSOL/BMARY PO13 ...... 314 D2
Smith Cl *FAWY* SO45 ...... 291 H7
Smithe Cl *ELGH* SO50 ...... 229 J1
Smithfield La *RFNM* GU10 ...... 136 A3
Smithfield Pl
MOOR/WNTN BH9 ...... 322 F6
Smith's Fld *ROMY* SO51 ...... 205 J2
Smith's La *BPWT* SO32 ...... 252 D3
Smith's Md *OVTN* RG25 ...... 108 D1
Smithson Cl *BKME/WDN* BH12.. 322 B7
Smith St *GPORT* PO12 ...... 12 B2
Smithy Cl *ALTN* GU34 ...... 133 K2
Smithy La *NMIL/BTOS* BH25 ...... 349 K1
The Smithy *TADY* RG26 ...... 52 A2
Smugglers La *CFDH* BH17 ...... 320 C9
Smugglers La North
CHCH/BSGR BH23 ...... 306 A6
Smugglers La South
CHCH/BSGR BH23 ...... 325 N6
Smugglers' Wy *RFNM* GU10 ...... 117 L2
Smugglers Wood Rd
CHCH/BSGR BH23 ...... 325 N6
Smythe Rd *ITCH* SO19 ...... 249 M8
Snailing La *LISS* GU33 ...... 172 C9
Snails La *RGWD* BH24 ...... 260 E7
Snailslynch *FNM* GU9 ...... 96 D9
Snakemoor La *BPWT* SO32 ...... 230 E7

Snapdragon Cl *HLER* SO31 ...... 270 F8
Snape Cl *LSOL/BMARY* PO13 .... 294 G9
Snellgrove Cl *TOTT* SO40 ...... 246 A1
Snellgrove Pl *TOTT* SO40 ...... 246 A1
Snoddington Rd *TDWTH* SP9 ...... 99 M3
Snode HI *ALTN* GU34 ...... 132 A6
Snooks La *LYMN* SO41 ...... 328 C8
Snowberry Crs *HAV* PO9 ...... 277 H7
Snowdon Dr *STHA* SO19 ...... 25 N5
Snowdon Dr
FHAM/STUB PO14 ...... 294 C1
NBNE BH10 ...... 322 C2
WBNE BH4 ...... 334 C2
Snowdrop Cl *BH/HW/K* RG22 ...... 89 L3
HLER SO31 ...... 270 F8
Snowdrop Gdns
CHCH/BSGR BH23 ...... 325 M6
Snowhill *WHAM* PO17 * 273 P4
Soake Rd *WVILLE* PO7 ...... 255 P8
Soalwood La *PSF* GU32 ...... 190 F5
Soame's La *NARL* SO24 ...... 169 P4
Sobers Sq *AND* SP10 ...... 82 G8
Soberton Rd *CHAR* BH8 ...... 323 K8
HAV PO9 ...... 14 C6
Soke HI *NARL* SO24 ...... 149 P8
Soke La *THLE* RG7 ...... 34 F7
The Soke *NARL* SO24 ...... 148 A9
Solartron Rd *FARN* GU14 ...... 76 A1
Solby's Rd *PLE* BH15 ...... 6 C6
Soldridge Cl *HAV* PO9 ...... 277 H4
Soldridge Rd *ALTN* GU34 ...... 148 P5
Solent Av *ALTN* SO19 ...... 249 N5
LYMN SO41 ...... 329 M4
Solent Cl *CHFD* SO53 ...... 206 C7
LYMN SO41 ...... 329 M4
Solent Dr *BH/HW/K* RG22 ...... 89 M4
ENEY PO4 ...... 317 K4
FAWY SO45 ...... 268 B6
HISD PO11 ...... 318 F6
HLER SO31 ...... 292 D3
NMIL/BTOS BH25 ...... 327 J6
RAND SP11 ...... 43 G7
Solent Mdw *HLER* SO31 ...... 293 J2
Solent Ms *NMIL/BTOS* BH25 ...... 327 J6
Solent Rd Coast 297 L1
CHCH/BSGR BH23 ...... 326 D5
FAWY SO45 ...... 290 A1
FHAM/STUB PO14 ...... 293 N8
HAV PO9 ...... 14 C6
SBNE BH6 ...... 336 E3
WSHM SO15 ...... 20 A5
Solent Twentyseven
CHAM PO6 ...... 297 L3
Solent Vw *FHAM/PORC* PO16.. 273 H9
Solent Wy *BROC* SO42 ...... 289 L9
BROC SO42 ...... 311 K8
CHAM PO6 ...... 297 N4
ENEY PO4 ...... 317 K6
FAWY SO45 ...... 290 C2
FHAM/STUB PO14 ...... 293 J6
HAV PO9 ...... 14 C6
ITCH SO19 ...... 268 G2
LSOL/BMARY PO13 ...... 314 B1
LYMN SO41 ...... 329 N9
LYMN SO41 ...... 339 J3
PLE BH15 ...... 18 C5
Solly Cl *BKME/WDN* BH12 ...... 321 N5
Solomons La *BPWT* SO32 ...... 252 D1
Solona Cl *CHFD* SO53 ...... 207 H6
Somborne Dr *HAV* PO9 ...... 276 C5
Somborne Park Rd
STOK SO20 ...... 141 P7
Somerby Rd *PLE* BH15 ...... 320 F6
Somerford Av
CHCH/BSGR BH23 ...... 325 M7
Somerford Cl *ITCH* SO19 ...... 249 J5
Somerford Rd
CHCH/BSGR BH23 ...... 325 J8
Somerford Wy
CHCH/BSGR BH23 ...... 325 J8
Somerley Rd
MOOR/WNTN BH9 ...... 322 G8
Somerley Vw *RGWD* BH24 ...... 282 E1
Somers Cl *FUFL* SO22 ...... 188 V4
Somerset Av *RGWD* BH24 ...... 154 A5
WEND SO18 ...... 249 L4
Somerset Crs *CHFD* SO53 ...... 228 G1
Somerset Rd
CHCH/BSGR BH23 ...... 324 C8
FARN GU14 ...... 76 B3
LTDN BH7 ...... 335 M1
SD/PW SO17 ...... 248 E1
SSEA PO5 ...... 316 F7
Somerset Ter *WSHM* SO15 ...... 247 N5
Somers Rd *SSEA* PO5 ...... 34 P5
Somers Rd North *PSEA* PO1 ...... 19 K3
Somerton Av *WEND* SO18 ...... 249 K4
Somerton *NMIL/BTOS* BH25.. 327 J4
Somerton Gv *STHA* SO19 ...... 25 M5
Somervell Cl *GPORT* PO12 ...... 12 A7
Somervell Dr
FHAM/PORC PO16 ...... 10 E2
Somerville Cl *AND* SP10 ...... 5 J2
Somerville Crs *YTLY* GU46 ...... 40 F8
Somerville Rd *RGWD* BH24 ...... 282 C1
WCLF BH2 ...... 8 A4
Somme Rd *RAND* SP11 ...... 145 K7
Sonnet Wy *WVILLE* PO7 ...... 276 B2
Sonning Cl *BH/HW/K* RG22 ...... 89 K4
Sonninge Cl *FLEETS* GU52 ...... 74 B8
Soper Gv *BSTK* RG21 ...... 6 E3
Sopers La *CFDH* BH17 ...... 320 E9
CHCH/BSGR BH23 ...... 324 E9
Sopers Rw *CHIN* RG24 * 70 B6
Sopley Cl *NMIL/BTOS* BH25 ...... 326 F1
Sopley Ct *HAV* PO9 ...... 15 K4
Sopwith Cl *WIMB* BH21 ...... 300 G3
Sopwith Pk *AND* SP10 ...... 101 P1
Sopwith Rd *ELGH* SO50 ...... 229 H1
Sopwith Wy *HLER* SO31 ...... 270 E2
Sorrel Cl *FARN* GU14 ...... 57 K8
CHAR BH8 ...... 324 C4
ROMY SO51 ...... 204 G4
THLE RG7 ...... 27 K4
WVILLE PO7 ...... 276 A4

Sorrel Dr FHAM PO15 ...... 271 K3
Sorrel Gdns BDST BH18 ...... 320 B2
Sorrell CI HLER SO31 ...... 270 F8
Sorrell's CI CHIN RG24 ...... 70 A1
Sorrel Wy CHCH/BSGR BH23.. 325 M7
Sotherington La ALTN GU34 .... 172 E1
Southampton CI BLKW GU17 ... 41 K8
Southampton HI
  FHAM/STUB PO14 ...... 271 M9
Southampton Rd BROC SO42 .. 308 C5
  CHAM PO6 ...... 296 B1
  ELGH SO50 ...... 229 J4
  FAWY SO45 ...... 268 A6
  FBDG SP6 ...... 240 F2
  FHAM PO15 ...... 271 K8
  FHAM/PORC PO16 ...... 11 G4
  HLER SO31 ...... 271 J5
  LYMN SO41 ...... 309 H5
  LYND SO43 ...... 265 J4
  RGWD BH24 ...... 282 E1
  ROMY SO51 ...... 204 E7
  TOTT SO40 ...... 244 B3
Southampton St FARN GU14.... 76 A4
South Atlantic Dr ALDT GU11 .... 3 H1
South Av FAWY SO45 ...... 290 E4
  FNM GU9 ...... 96 D5
  NEND PO2 ...... 296 D5
  NMIL/BTOS BH25 ...... 327 K5
South Baddesey Rd
  LYMN SO41 ...... 329 P3
South Bay EMRTH PO10...... 299 N6
South Beta Rd FARN GU14 ...... 76 A2
Southbourne Av CHAM PO6 .... 297 K2
  EMRTH PO10 ...... 299 P1
Southbourne Coast Rd
  SBNE BH6...... 336 C5
Southbourne Gv BOSC BH5...... 335 P2
Southbourne Overcliff Dr
  SBNE BH6...... 336 A3
Southbourne Rd FAWY SO45 .. 290 E5
  LYMN SO41 ...... 329 J4
  SBNE BH6...... 336 A2
Southbrook CI CFDH BH17 ...... 321 J2
  HAV PO9 ...... 202 F1
Southbrook Cots RWIN SO21 .. 127 H6
Southbrook PI RWIN SO21...... 126 C6
Southbrook Rd HAV PO9 ...... 298 F2
  WSHM SO15 ...... 20 A3
Southby Dr FLEETN GU51 ...... 74 E3
South Charford Dro RSAL SP5. 198 B7
Southcliff LSOL/BMARY PO13 .. 314 C1
Southcliffe Rd
  CHCH/BSGR BH23 ...... 325 M9
  NMIL/BTOS BH25 ...... 326 F7
Southcliff Rd SHAM SO14 ...... 248 C4
South Cliff Rd WCLF BH2 ...... 8 B6
South CI GPORT PO12 ...... 315 K6
  HAV PO9 ...... 15 H7
  NARL SO24 ...... 167 N2
  ROMY SO51 ...... 204 G4
Southcote Rd BMTH BH1...... 9 K1
South Ct HLER SO31 ...... 269 N8
Southcroft Rd GPORT PO12 ... 315 K5
South Cross St GPORT PO12.... 13 H2
Southdene Rd CHFD SO53...... 206 E8
Southdown Rd CHAM PO6 ...... 297 J1
  HORN PO8 ...... 236 C9
  RWIN SO21 ...... 183 M8
  RG19 ...... 25 J4
  TADY RG26 ...... 34 B5
Southdowns NARL SO24 ...... 148 A7
South Downs Wy NARL SO24.. 186 E9
  WINC SO23 ...... 23 H7
Southdown Vw WVILLE PO7 .... 255 L9
Southdown Wy FERN BH22 ...... 280 F8
South Dr CHOB/PIR GU24 ...... 59 P7
  FUFL SO22 ...... 164 B3
  HTWY RG27 ...... 52 E6
  RGWD BH24 * 303 H1
  TDWTH SP9 ...... 78 C7
South East Crs ITCH SO19 ...... 249 J7
South East Rd ITCH SO19 ...... 249 J7
Southend NTHA RG18 ...... 25 M1
South End CI RWIN SO21 ...... 182 D7
Southend La BPWT SO32 ...... 245 P5
South End Rd ABP SO21 ...... 102 F4
Southend Rd BSTK RG21 ...... 6 C6
Southern Av FERN BH22...... 280 G8
Southernhay WVILLE PO7...... 255 M7
Southern Haye HTWY RG27 .... 55 H8
Southernhay Rd VWD BH31.... 259 H4
Southern La NMIL/BTOS BH25.. 327 H7
Southern Oaks
  NMIL/BTOS BH25 ...... 327 H6
Southern Rd BOR GU35...... 335 P1
  BSTK RG21 ...... 69 L8
  HEND SO30 ...... 249 M1
  LYMN SO41 ...... 329 K3
  SBNE BH6...... 336 A2
  WSHM SO15 ...... 20 A4
Southern Wy FARN GU14...... 76 C1
  FNM GU9 ...... 116 C1
Southey Rd CHCH/BSGR BH23 .. 325 K7
Southfield RGWD BH24...... 282 E3
Southfield Ms RGWD BH24 .... 284 C2
Southfields CI BPWT SO32...... 232 A4
South Front SHAM SO14...... 21 D5
Southgate St WINC SO23 ...... 22 D6
Southgate Vls WINC SO23 * 22 D6
South Gv FLEETN GU51...... 56 F9
  LYMN SO41 ...... 329 M4
South Ham Rd BH/HW/K WGT.. 233 L4
South HI RPWT SO32...... 195 K3
  FBDG SP6 ...... 239 N5
  OVTN RG25 ...... 92 C6
South Hurst BOR GU35...... 154 A7
Southill Av BKME/WDN BH12.. 321 L6
Southill Gdns
  MOOR/WNTN BH9 ...... 322 C6
Southill Rd BKME/WDN BH12.. 321 L6
  MOOR/WNTN BH9 ...... 322 C6
Southington CI OVTN RG25 .... 86 E3
Southington La OVTN RG25.... 86 F5

South Kinson Dr BWD BH11.... 322 A3
Southlands CHIN RG24...... 69 P1
Southlands CI ASHV GU12...... 97 N2
Southlands Av SBNE BH6...... 336 D2
Southlands Rd ASHV GU12 ...... 97 N2
South La ASHV GU12 ...... 97 P2
  EPSH GU31 ...... 215 K9
  HORN PO8 ...... 236 B6
  RSAL SP5 ...... 199 J6
  RSAL SP5 ...... 223 L5
South Loading Rd
  GPORT PO12 * 13 H2
South Ldg FHAM PO15...... 271 P9
South Meadow CWTH RG45 .... 41 L3
Southmead Rd ALDT GU11 ...... 3 F6
  FHAM PO15 ...... 271 P9
South Millers Dl CHFD SO53 .. 206 D6
South Mill Rd WSHM SO15 .... 247 K4
Southmoor La HAV PO9 ...... 298 D2
South Normandy PSEA PO1 .... 18 D5
South Pde ENEY PO4...... 316 F7
  TOTT SO40 ...... 246 D3
South Park Rd
  BKME/WDN BH12 ...... 322 A7
South PI LSOL/BMARY PO13 .. 314 E4
South Rdg ODIM RG29 ...... 93 L1
South Rd ASHV GU12 ...... 335 L1
  BMTH BH1 ...... 274 C8
  CHAM PO6 ...... 297 M2
  CWTH RG45 ...... 41 M3
  HISD PO11 ...... 318 F5
  HORN PO8 ...... 256 C2
  KSCL RG20 ...... 48 D3
  LIPH GU30 ...... 175 K6
  NARL SO24 ...... 167 N2
  PLE BH15 ...... 332 E1
  PSEA PO1 ...... 316 G1
  SD/PW SO17 ...... 248 E3
  STOK SO20 ...... 160 B2
  WHAM PO17 ...... 274 C4
Southrope Gn OVTN RG25 .... 111 L3
Southsea Ter SSEA PO5 ...... 19 F7
South Side RFNM GU10 ...... 97 M4
Southside Rd RAND SP11...... 104 D5
South Sp CHAM PO6 ...... 274 D8
South St AND SP10...... 4 D5
  ELGH SO50 ...... 229 J4
  EMRTH PO10 ...... 299 M1
  FARN GU14 ...... 76 D3
  FAWY SO45 ...... 268 C7
  FHAM/STUB PO14 ...... 293 M1
  FNM GU9 ...... 96 C9
  GPORT PO12 ...... 12 E3
  HAV PO9 ...... 14 C5
  LYMN SO41 ...... 329 J5
  NARL SO24 ...... 169 M5
  SSEA PO5 ...... 19 F6
South Sway La LYMN SO41 .... 328 D7
South Ter PSEA PO1 ...... 18 C2
South Town Rd ALTN GU34 .... 150 A3
South Trestle Rd FAWY SO45.. 291 L4
South Vw FUFL SO22 ...... 22 B4
South View CI RWIN SO21...... 125 M6
Southview Cots HTWY RG27 *.. 71 N4
South View Cots WHCH RG28.. 86 A4
Southview Gdns AND SP10...... 4 E6
South View Gdns NWBY RG14 *.. 24 E5
Southview Ri ALTN GU34...... 132 E4
Southview Rd BOR GU35 ...... 155 J3
South View Rd
  CHCH/BSGR BH23 ...... 324 E9
  FUFL SO22 ...... 183 K2
  WSHM SO15 ...... 247 P3
South View Ter HAMP SP11 .... 84 C3
Southville Rd BOSC BH5...... 335 P1
South Wk ASHV GU12 ...... 97 N4
Southwalk CI TDWTH SP9 ...... 79 J5
  YTLY GU46 ...... 40 D8
South Wy AND SP10...... 83 J9
Southway CBLY GU15...... 58 A1
  FHAM PO15 ...... 271 L7
Southways BROC SO42...... 294 B7
South Weirs BROC SO42 ...... 308 D1
South Western Crs
  PSTN BH14 ...... 333 K1
Southwick Av
  FHAM/PORC PO16 ...... 274 A9
Southwick CI FUFL SO22 ...... 164 E3
Southwick Ct
  FHAM/STUB PO14 ...... 294 E3
Southwick Hill Rd CHAM PO6 .. 274 C9
Southwick PI SBNE BH6 ...... 324 A8
Southwick Rd CHAM PO6 ...... 274 E8
  SBNE BH6...... 324 A9
  WHAM PO17 ...... 252 G8
  WVILLE PO7 ...... 254 G7
Southwood Av
  CHCH/BSGR BH23 ...... 326 C6
  SBNE BH6...... 336 A2
Southwood CI
  CHCH/BSGR BH23 ...... 326 C6
  FERN BH22 ...... 302 C5
Southwood Crs FARN GU14 .... 75 L1
South Wood Gdns HLER SO31.. 270 F7
Southwood Gdns THLE RG7 .... 27 J4
Southwood La FLEETN GU51.... 75 N1
Southwood Rd ALTN GU34 .... 132 B1
  BLKW GU17 ...... 56 F4
  FARN GU14 ...... 57 M9
  HISD PO11 ...... 319 J6
  NEND PO2 ...... 296 C5
Sovereign Av GPORT PO12 .... 315 N1
Sovereign CI LTDN BH7 ...... 325 M7
  TOTT SO40 ...... 245 P3
Sovereign Crs
  FHAM/STUB PO14 ...... 270 G9
Sovereign Dr ENEY PO4...... 317 L3
  HEND SO30 ...... 250 D5

Sovereign La WVILLE PO7 ...... 275 N7
Sovereign Wy ELGH SO50...... 207 H7
Sowcroft La ODIM RG29 ...... 112 C5
Sowden CI HEND SO30 ...... 250 B4
Sowley La LYMN SO41 ...... 330 E2
Spackman CI STHA RG19...... 25 N5
Spain La ALTN GU34 ...... 110 C7
The Spain PSF GU32...... 215 L2
Spalding Rd ITCH SO19 ...... 249 M6
Spa Meadow CI STHA RG19.... 24 F7
Spaniard's La ROMY SO51...... 226 D1
Sparkford CI FUFL SO22 ...... 22 B7
  LTDN BH7 ...... 323 P7
Sparkford Rd FUFL SO22 ...... 22 B7
Spa Rd SHAM SO14 ...... 20 D5
Sparrow CI HORN PO8...... 255 P7
Sparrow Ct
  LSOL/BMARY PO13 ...... 314 D1
Sparrowgrove RWIN SO21 .... 207 L1
Sparrowhawk CI HSEA PO3 .... 297 J5
  RFNM GU10 ...... 95 P5
Sparrow Sq ELGH SO50...... 228 F2
Sparsholt CI HAV PO9 ...... 276 C5
Sparsholt Rd FUFL SO22 ...... 163 M9
  ITCH SO19 ...... 269 H2
  RWIN SO21 ...... 182 D3
Spartan CI EMRTH PO10 ...... 299 N6
  FHAM/STUB PO14 ...... 294 A4
Spartina Dr LYMN SO41...... 329 L1
Sparvells HTWY RG27 ...... 39 P6
Spats La BOR GU35...... 135 P9
Speakers Corner Rbt
  SHAM SO14 ...... 20 E5
Spear Rd SHAM SO14...... 248 C3
Speckled Wood Rd CHIN RG24.. 69 L3
Specks La ENEY PO4 ...... 317 J4
Speedwell CI HLER SO31 ...... 270 F8
Speedwell Dr
  CHCH/BSGR BH23 ...... 325 M7
Speen Hill CI NWBY RG14 ...... 24 B3
Speen La NWBY RG14 ...... 24 B3
Speen Lodge Ct NWBY RG14 .. 24 B3
Speen PI NWBY RG14...... 24 B3
Speggs Wk HEND SO30 ...... 250 C5
Spetham HI WVILLE PO7 ...... 294 C1
Spencer CI ALTN GU34 ...... 150 C5
  FLEETS GU52...... 74 F7
  FRIM GU52 ...... 58 D7
  HISD PO11 * 318 G5
  TADY RG26 ...... 34 F5
Spencer Ct FHAM/STUB PO14 .. 294 C7
Spencer Dr
  LSOL/BMARY PO13 ...... 314 D3
Spencer Gdns HORN PO8 ...... 255 N8
Spencer Rd BMTH BH1...... 335 J2
  CCLF BH13 ...... 333 N5
  ELGH SO50 ...... 228 G8
  EMRTH PO10 ...... 277 L6
  ENEY PO4 ...... 317 H6
  NMIL/BTOS BH25 ...... 327 J4
  NWBY RG14 ...... 24 E5
Spenlow CI NEND PO2 ...... 296 F9
Spenser CI ALTN GU34 ...... 132 C4
  HLER SO31 ...... 292 D1
Sperrin CI BH/HW/K RG22...... 68 E9
Spetisbury CI
  MOOR/WNTN BH9 ...... 323 H4
  ROWN SO16 ...... 82 G9
Spicer La AND SP10 ...... 301 N8
Spicers ALTN GU34 ...... 132 G6
Spicer's HI TOTT SO40 ...... 246 D6
Spicer St PSEA PO1 * 19 H1
Spicer's Wy TOTT SO40 ...... 246 C5
Spicewood FHAM PO15 ...... 92 M8
Spiers CI TADY RG26...... 34 E6
Spiers La NARL SO24 ...... 148 B2
Spinacre NMIL/BTOS BH25 .. 327 K7
Spindle CI BDST BH18 ...... 320 B2
Spindle Warren HAV PO9 ...... 277 J7
Spindlewood CI
  NMIL/BTOS BH25 ...... 327 J6
  ROWN SO16 ...... 228 C6
Spindlewood Wy TOTT SO40 .. 267 K2
Spinnaker CI HISD PO11...... 318 E4
  LSOL/BMARY PO13 ...... 315 H1
Spinnaker Dr NEND PO2...... 296 F5
Spinnaker Gra HISD PO11 ...... 299 J5
Spinnaker Vw HAV PO9 ...... 276 A9
Spinners CI FERN BH22 ...... 280 E8
Spinney CI HORN PO8 ...... 255 N8
  RGWD BH24 ...... 281 K5
Spinney DI FAWY SO45 ...... 268 D8
Spinney Gdns CHIN RG24...... 68 G4
Spinney Rd RAND SP11 ...... 79 N1
The Spinney FERN BH22 ...... 302 D3
The Spinney ELGH SO50...... 230 A2
  FHAM/PORC PO16 ...... 275 K9
  FLEETN GU51...... 74 A4
  GSHT GU26 ...... 155 P4
  HASM GU27 * 156 C8
  HORN PO8 ...... 256 A5
  HTWY RG27 ...... 52 B7
  LSOL/BMARY PO13 ...... 295 H8
  NARL SO24 ...... 187 N1
  RGWD BH24 ...... 281 M3
  ROWN SO16 ...... 228 G6
  TOTT SO40 ...... 185 L7
  WVILLE PO7 ...... 255 H8
  YTLY GU46 ...... 40 D7
Spinney Wk WEND SO18 ...... 229 H9
Spinney Wy NMIL/BTOS BH25.. 327 J1
Spitalfields Rd ALTN GU34 .... 132 F5
Spitalhatch ALTN GU34...... 133 H6
Spitfire End WINC SO23 ...... 165 L7
Spitfire La SO30 ...... 140 E4
Spitfire Loop WEND SO18...... 229 H5
Spitfire Rd WINC SO23 ...... 75 M4
  HLER SO31 ...... 269 P7
Spithead Av GPORT PO12...... 315 N7
Spittlefields RGWD BH24 ...... 282 F2
Spoil La RFNM GU10 ...... 97 M4
Spokane CI ALDT GU11 ...... 2 C6
Spouts La ROMY SO51 ...... 202 D7

Sprat's Hatch La HTWY RG27 .. 73 J7
Spray Leaze RAND SP11 ...... 80 B1
Spreadbury Dr FLEETN GU51 .. 74 C1
Sprents La OVTN RG25...... 87 H4
Spriggs CI STHA RG19...... 25 N5
Springbank Rd LTDN BH7 ...... 323 M7
Spring CI CHIN RG24 ...... 68 G1
  ELGH SO50 ...... 230 C2
  ITCH SO19 ...... 249 H7
  VWD BH31 ...... 258 F5
Spring Crs SD/PW SO17 ...... 248 D3
Springcroft
  LSOL/BMARY PO13 ...... 294 F4
Springcross Av BLKW GU17 .... 57 L2
Springdale Av BDST BH18...... 300 B8
Springdale Gv WIMB BH21 .... 300 A9
Springfarm Rd HASM GU27.... 156 D8
Springfield DEAN RG23 ...... 88 F1
Springfield Av
  CHCH/BSGR BH23 ...... 324 B5
  FAWY SO45 ...... 290 F5
  HTWY RG27 ...... 55 H6
  SBNE BH6...... 336 E2
Springfield CI AND SP10...... 5 J3
  HAV PO9 ...... 276 B8
  LYMN SO41 ...... 329 N4
  VWD BH31 ...... 258 F5
  WHAM PO17 ...... 252 E7
Springfield Crs PSTN BH14 .... 321 K8
  RSAL SP5 ...... 199 P8
Springfield Dr TOTT SO40 ...... 246 C5
Springfield Gdns
  NMIL/BTOS BH25 ...... 327 M5
Springfield Gv FAWY SO45 .... 290 F5
Springfield La FLEETN GU51.... 74 B3
  NWBY RG14 ...... 24 D7
Springfield PI CHIN RG24 * 70 C5
Springfield Rd ASHV GU12 .... 76 F7
  PSTN BH14 ...... 321 J7
  TADY RG26 ...... 34 F5
  VWD BH31 ...... 258 F5
Springfields WIMB BH21 ...... 278 G2
Springfields CI RWIN SO21 .... 207 P4
Springfield Wy
  FHAM/STUB PO14 ...... 294 A8
Springford CI ROWN SO16 .... 227 M8
Springford Crs ROWN SO16.... 227 M8
Springford Gdns ROWN SO16.. 227 M8
Springford Rd ROWN SO16.... 227 M8
Spring Garden La GPORT PO12.. 13 F1
Spring Gdns
  BKME/WDN BH12 ...... 321 M7
  EMRTH PO10 ...... 299 M1
  EWKG RG40 * 40 A1
  FARN GU14 ...... 57 D6
  HEND SO30 ...... 250 D3
  KSCL RG20 ...... 30 A3
  NARL SO24 ...... 167 N3
  NBAD SO52 ...... 205 K8
  PSEA PO1 ...... 19 F5
Spring Gv HLER SO31 ...... 270 A1
Spring Hill La RAND SP11 ...... 84 D2
Springhill Rd CHFD SO53...... 206 E7
Spring Hills ITCH SO19 ...... 249 L7
Springholm CI FNM GU9 ...... 97 H5
Spring House CI RWIN SO21 .. 208 A4
Spring House La RWIN SO21 .. 207 P4
Springlake Est ASHV GU12 * .. 76 D9
Spring La BPWT SO32 ...... 232 F7
  ELGH SO50 ...... 229 M1
  FNM GU9 ...... 96 A4
  KSCL RG20 ...... 30 C3
  NMIL/BTOS BH25 ...... 327 M5
  RWIN SO21 ...... 207 P4
  THLE RG7 ...... 27 J8
  THLE RG7 ...... 37 N1
Spring La West FNM GU9...... 96 A5
Springles La FHAM PO15...... 271 N5
Spring Ms AND SP10 ...... 4 E2
Spring PI ROMY SO51...... 204 C6
Spring Rd BMTH BH1...... 335 J1
  FAWY SO45 ...... 268 C6
  HLER SO31 ...... 270 F4
  ITCH SO19 ...... 249 H8
  LYMN SO41 ...... 329 N4
The Springs THLE RG7 ...... 36 C6
Spring St PSEA PO1...... 19 G2
The Spring WVILLE PO7 ...... 255 H8
Spring V BPWT SO32 ...... 232 E7
  HORN PO8 ...... 256 B7
Springvale Av LTDN BH7...... 323 M7
  WINC SO23 ...... 165 J1
Springvale Rd FUFL SO22 ...... 164 C5
  WINC SO23 ...... 165 J2
Springwater CI BWD BH11 .... 322 A4
Springwater Rd BWD BH11.... 322 A4
Spring Wy NARL SO24 ...... 167 P3
Springwell La HTWY RG27 .... 55 J5
Springwood Av WVILLE PO7 .. 255 N8
Spring Wood La THLE RG7...... 27 J5
Spring Woods FLEETS GU52.... 74 C5
  SHST GU47 ...... 41 K5
Spruce Av BOR GU35...... 153 N5
  WVILLE PO7 ...... 276 A3
Spruce CI AND SP10 ...... 320 A3
  CFDH BH17 ...... 320 A3
  HLER SO31 ...... 292 D1
  NARL SO24 ...... 144 F3
Spruce Dr ITCH SO19 ...... 249 N6
  WIMB BH21 ...... 245 P5
Spruce Wy FLEETN GU51...... 74 C8
Spur CI WIMB BH21 ...... 279 L8
Spurcroft Rd STHA RG19...... 25 N5
Spurgeon Rd LTDN BH7 ...... 323 P9
Spur Hill Av PSTN BH14 ...... 321 M9
Spurlings Rd WHAM PO17...... 273 H1
Spur Rd CHAM PO6 ...... 297 H1
  PSTN BH14 ...... 321 M9
  WVILLE PO7 ...... 275 N3
Spurs Ct ALDT GU11...... 2 A3
The Spur GPORT PO12 ...... 315 K6
  WIMB BH21 ...... 252 E7
Spybush La NARL SO24 ...... 147 P2

Square CI WIMB BH21 * 301 P2
Squarefield Gdns HTWY RG27.. 72 B2
The Square BSTK RG21 * 7 H4
  EMRTH PO10 ...... 277 P7
  EPSF GU31 ...... 216 P9
  FAWY SO45 ...... 291 K6
  GPORT PO12 ...... 295 M9
  HLER SO31 ...... 270 A8
  ITCH SO19 ...... 175 J5
  LYMN SO41 ...... 329 J4
  PSF GU32 ...... 215 M2
  RGWD BH24 ...... 281 H9
  ROMY SO51 ...... 203 H1
  SHAM SO14 ...... 20 D3
  STHA RG19 ...... 31 M2
  STOK SO20 ...... 139 P2
  WHAM PO17 ...... 252 E8
  WINC SO23 ...... 22 E5
Squarey CI RSAL SP5 ...... 199 K7
Squires Hill La RFNM GU10 .... 117 J5
Squires Wk ITCH SO19 ...... 268 C1
Squirrel CI ELGH SO50...... 229 P2
  HLER SO31 ...... 271 J5
  SHST GU47 ...... 41 J6
Squirrel Dr DEAN RG23 ...... 89 K7
  ITCH SO19 ...... 249 J8
Squirrel La FARN GU14 ...... 57 P8
Squirrels CI CHCH/BSGR BH23.. 324 B5
Squirrels Drey CWTH RG45 .... 40 C1
Squirrels Wk FAWY SO45...... 268 B8
Stable CI RAND SP11 ...... 79 N2
  FHAM/STUB PO14 ...... 271 K8
  HTWY RG27 ...... 71 N5
  THLE RG7 ...... 27 J4
Stable Rd NWBY RG14 ...... 24 E2
Stable Rd BOR GU35...... 153 P2
Stables Rd TDWTH SP9...... 78 G7
Stable Wy YTLY GU46...... 40 E7
Stacey CI FARN GU14...... 57 P8
Stacey CI BKME/WDN BH12.. 321 L5
Stacey Ct HAV PO9 ...... 276 D3
Stacey Gdns CHAR BH8...... 323 M5
Stafford Rd BMTH BH1...... 9 G3
  PSF GU32 ...... 215 L2
  WSHM SO15 ...... 247 P4
Staff Rd ASHV GU12 ...... 3 J3
  ROMY SO51 ...... 179 P6
Stagbrake CI FAWY SO45...... 290 D6
Stag CI ELGH SO50...... 229 P2
  NMIL/BTOS BH25 ...... 326 C3
Stag Dr HEND SO30 ...... 250 D3
Stag Gates FAWY SO45 ...... 290 G8
Stag HI BH/HW/K RG22 ...... 89 P1
Stagshorn Rd HORN PO8...... 256 C4
Stag Oak La CHIN RG24 ...... 51 P9
Stagswood VWD BH31...... 258 D4
Stag Wy FHAM PO15 ...... 272 B5
Stainer CI ITCH SO19 ...... 249 M8
Stainers La RWIN SO21 ...... 144 D4
Staith CI ITCH SO19 ...... 249 L6
Stake La FARN GU14 ...... 57 P9
Stakes Hill Rd WVILLE PO7...... 275 N3
Stakes La BPWT SO32 ...... 231 L1
Stake's CI BPWT SO32 ...... 210 D6
Stakes Rd WVILLE PO7...... 275 L6
Stalbridge Dr FERN BH22...... 302 D4
Stalbridge Rd CFDH BH17 .... 320 C5
Stalham Rd BKME/WDN BH12.. 321 H4
Stallard CI EMRTH PO10 ...... 277 L9
Stallards La RGWD BH24 ...... 282 D2
Stalybridge CI HLER SO31...... 270 C4
Stamford Av FRIM GU16 ...... 58 E4
Stamford Rd ENEY PO4 ...... 317 H4
Stamford St SBNE BH6...... 336 B1
Stamford St PSEA PO1 ...... 19 K1
Stamford Wy ELGH SO50...... 230 C3
Stamshaw Rd NEND PO2 ...... 296 F8
Stanbridge La NARL SO24 ...... 205 P2
Stanbridge Rd HAV PO9 ...... 15 K1
Stanbury CI RAND SP11 ...... 100 E2
Stanbury Rd RAND SP11...... 100 D1
Stancomb Broad La
  ALTN GU34 ...... 149 M6
Standard La ALTN GU34...... 112 C9
  ALTN GU34 ...... 149 N5
Standard Wy
  FHAM/PORC PO16 ...... 11 J2
Standen Rd ROWN SO16...... 226 C7
Standford HI BOR GU35...... 154 D7
Standford La BOR GU35...... 154 D5
Standford St SHAM SO14...... 21 H5
Standing HI RSAL SP5...... 158 F7
Stanfield TADY RG26...... 34 C6
Stanfield Rd
  BKME/WDN BH12 ...... 321 M5
  CHCH/BSGR BH23 ...... 302 C2
  MOOR/WNTN BH9 ...... 322 E7
Stanford CI CHAM PO6 ...... 296 F1
Stanford Ct HAV PO9...... 277 H5
Stanford Gdns LYMN SO41 .... 329 K5
Stanford Ri LYMN SO41 ...... 308 B6
Stanford Rd BH/HW/K RG22.... 89 N3
Stanham CI RWIN SO21 ...... 144 E6
Stanhope Rd CBLY GU15...... 57 N1
  PSEA PO1 ...... 19 G2
Stanier Wy HEND SO30 ...... 250 C1
Stanley Av HSEA PO3...... 297 K9
Stanley CI FHAM PO15 ...... 10 A5
  GPORT PO12 ...... 295 L8
  VWD BH31 ...... 258 C5
Stanley Dr FARN GU14...... 75 K1
Stanley Green Crs PLE BH15 .. 320 D7
Stanley Green Rd PLE BH15.... 320 C7
Stanley HI CHOB/PIR GU24.... 59 P8
Stanley La SSEA PO5...... 316 E6
Stanley Rd BMTH BH1...... 335 J1
  CHCH/BSGR BH23 ...... 326 C7
  EMRTH PO10 ...... 299 N1
  FAWY SO45 ...... 290 F5
  LYMN SO41 ...... 329 M5
  NEND PO2 ...... 296 D5
  NWBY RG14 ...... 17 G4
  PLE BH15 ...... 332 E2
  SD/PW SO17 ...... 248 E2
  TOTT SO40 ...... 246 B2
Stanley St SSEA PO5...... 316 E6

Stanmore Gdns THLE RG7 35 N1
Stanmore La FUFL SO22 164 D9
Stannington Cl
NMIL/BTOS BH25 327 J5
Stannington Crs TOTT SO40 246 D3
Stannington Wy TOTT SO40 246 D3
Stanpit CHCH/BSGR BH23 337 J1
Stanstead Rd ELGH SO50 207 H9
Stansted Cl HAV PO9 257 J9
Stansted Crs HAV PO9 277 H4
Stansted Rd SSEA PO5 19 K5
Stanswood Rd FAWY SO45 313 K4
HAV PO9 276 D4
Stanton Dr FLEETN GU51 74 B4
Stanton Rd NBNE BH10 322 C5
PSF GU32 215 L1
WSHM SO15 247 K4
Stapehill Crs WIMB BH21 279 K9
Stapehill Rd WIMB BH21 301 N3
Staple Ash La PSF GU32 190 C7
Staple Cl WVILLE PO7 275 M1
Staple Close La PLE BH15 320 E6
Staple Cross WHAM PO17 273 M2
Staplecross La
CHCH/BSGR BH23 325 H7
Stapleford Av FERN BH22 302 F2
Stapleford Cl ROMY SO51 204 F3
Stapleford La BPWT SO32 230 F7
Staple Gdns WINC SO23 22 D4
Staplehurst Cl ITCH SO19 269 J1
Staplers Reach
LSOL/BMARY PO13 294 F8
Stapleton Rd HSEA PO3 297 J9
Staplewood La TOTT SO40 266 F3
Stapley La NARL SO24 169 N5
Stares Cl LSOL/BMARY PO13 314 G1
Star Hl HTWY RG27 55 L4
RFNM GU10 136 D7
Star Hill Dr RFNM GU10 136 D7
Starina Gdns WVILLE PO7 276 B2
Star La ASHV GU12 97 M1
KSCL RG20 29 N8
RGWD BH24 282 D2
Starlight Farm Cl VWD BH31 259 H3
Starling Cl BH/HW/K RG22 89 K3
Starling Sq ELGH SO50 228 F2
Starting Gates NWBY RG14 17 J6
The Starting Ga NWBY RG14 17 J5
Statham Sq AND SP10 82 G8
Station Ap ALTN GU34 150 C5
AND SP10 4 A3
ASHV GU12 76 F5
BDST BH18 300 C9
BLKW GU17 57 M1
EMRTH PO10 * 277 M9
NARL SO24 168 A2
NWBY RG14 16 E3
PSEA PO1 18 C3
RAND SP11 119 P2
Station Cl RWIN SO21 166 D1
WHAM PO17 252 E7
Station Hl ELGH SO50 229 K1
FNM GU9 96 C9
HEND SO30 251 J4
HLER SO31 270 B3
OVTN RG25 87 H1
RWIN SO21 166 D1
WINC SO23 22 D3
Station La CHFD SO53 206 E7
Station Rd ALDT GU11 3 F2
ALTN GU34 132 G5
BOR GU35 153 P3
BPWT SO32 232 A5
BPWT SO32 233 N5
CHAM PO6 297 L3
CHCH/BSGR BH23 324 E8
CHCH/BSGR BH23 326 A4
DEAN RG23 88 D1
EPSF GU31 215 M1
FARN GU14 58 A9
FBDG SP6 239 M5
FERN BH22 280 D7
FHAM/PORC PO16 295 P1
GPORT PO12 315 K1
HISD PO11 318 E4
HLER SO31 269 K4
HSEA PO3 297 J9
HTWY RG27 71 P3
HTWY RG27 73 J3
ITCH SO19 249 H8
KSCL RG20 29 N4
LIPH GU30 175 J5
LISS GU33 192 D2
LYMN SO41 308 A7
NARL SO24 168 A1
NMIL/BTOS BH25 327 J5
NWBY RG14 16 E4
OVTN RG25 87 H3
OVTN RG25 90 D4
PLE BH15 332 C2
PSF GU32 212 E1
PSF GU32 215 L1
PSTN BH14 321 K9
RAND SP11 119 P2
RFNM GU10 114 F8
RGWD BH24 284 F9
ROMY SO51 204 C6
ROWN SO16 226 E8
STHA RG19 25 N4
STOK SO20 120 C8
STOK SO20 123 K6
TDWTH SP9 79 H6
THLE RG7 36 D1
VWD BH31 258 D3
WHAM PO17 252 E7
WHCH RG28 85 L5
WIMB BH21 300 F2
WINC SO23 22 C3
WSHM SO15 246 G3
Station Rd East ASHV GU12 76 E5
Station Rd North TOTT SO40 * 246 E4
Station Rd South TOTT SO40 * 246 E4
Station Rd West ASHV GU12 76 E5
Station St LYMN SO41 329 M3
PSEA PO1 19 G2
Station Ter WIMB BH21 300 F2
Station Vw ASHV GU12 76 F4
Station Yd FBDG SP6 239 L5
Staunton Av HISD PO11 318 D5
Staunton Rd HAV PO9 14 D4
Staunton St PSEA PO1 316 E2
Staunton Wy EPSF GU31 237 H3
HAV PO9 14 D3
HORN PO8 236 F4
Stavedown Rd RWIN SO21 144 D4
Stead Cl HISD PO11 319 H5
Stedman Rd BOSC BH5 335 P1
Steele Cl CHFD SO53 206 F9
Steele's Rd ALDT GU11 76 A8
Steels Dro FBDG SP6 221 J5
Steels La FBDG SP6 219 J8
Steel St SSEA PO5 19 F6
Steep Cl FHAM/PORC PO16 * 273 N9
Steepdene PSTN BH14 321 K9
Steeple Cl CFDH BH17 320 F1
Steeple Dr ALTN GU34 132 F5
Steepleton Rd BDST BH18 320 E1
Steeple Wy FHAM/STUB PO14 271 K7
Steerforth Cl NEND PO2 316 F1
Steerforth Copse SHST GU47 41 M4
Steinbeck Cl FHAM PO15 271 J2
Stem La NMIL/BTOS BH25 326 G4
Stenbury Dr OVTN RG25 129 M1
Stenbury Wy HLER SO31 269 L3
Stenhurst Rd PLE BH15 320 G6
Stephen Cl HORN PO8 256 B9
Stephendale Rd FNM GU9 96 D7
Stephen Langton Dr
BWD BH11 301 M8
Stephen Martin Gdns
FBDG SP6 240 C1
Stephen Rd FHAM PO15 10 D5
Stephen's Cl THLE RG7 27 H9
Stephens Firs THLE RG7 26 G9
Stephenson Cl AND SP10 102 A1
GPORT PO12 12 A7
NTHA RG18 25 N3
Stephenson Ct NWBY RG14 24 C3
Stephenson Rd BSTK RG21 69 H6
FHAM PO15 271 L8
TOTT SO40 246 B1
Stephenson Wy HEND SO30 230 B9
Stephens Rd TADY RG26 34 D6
Stephen's Rd THLE RG7 27 H9
Steplake Rd ROMY SO51 202 D6
Step Ter FUFL SO22 22 B4
Sterling Gdns SHST GU47 41 M6
Sterling Pk AND SP10 102 A1
Sterte Av PLE BH15 320 D8
Sterte Av West PLE BH15 320 D8
Sterte Cl PLE BH15 320 E8
Sterte Esp PLE BH15 320 E8
Sterte Rd PLE BH15 320 E8
Steuart Rd WEND SO18 248 F4
Stevens Dro STOK SO20 160 G2
Stevens Gn RAND SP11 84 C2
Stevens Hl YTLY GU46 40 F9
Stevenson Crs PSTN BH14 321 M9
Stevenson Rd RWIN SO21 104 E8
SBNE BH6 336 E3
Stevensons Cl WIMB BH21 300 E1
Steventon Rd OVTN RG25 108 C1
WEND SO18 249 L4
Stewards Ri RFNM GU10 115 P3
Stewart Cl CHAR BH8 335 J1
Stewart Rd CHAR BH8 335 J1
CHIN RG24 69 P3
Stewarts Gn WVILLE PO7 234 E9
Stewarts Wy FERN BH22 302 E1
Steyning Ter HAV PO9 * 15 G4
St Grgs Crs FBDG SP6 240 D1
Stibbs Wy CHCH/BSGR BH23 305 N7
Stickle Down FRIM GU16 59 J5
Stile Gdns HASM GU27 156 F7
Stiles Dr AND SP10 5 J4
Stillions Cl ALTN GU34 132 G6
Still Mdw HLER SO31 270 G8
Stillmore Rd BWD BH11 321 M1
Stillwater Pk RGWD BH24 * 260 G8
Stillwell Cl YTLY GU46 40 F8
Stinchar Dr CHFD SO53 206 C8
Stinsford Cl
MOOR/WNTN BH9 323 H3
Stinsford Rd CFDH BH17 320 F3
Stirling Av WVILLE PO7 275 P3
Stirling Cl ASHV GU12 76 E7
FARN GU14 75 P1
FRIM GU16 58 D3
NMIL/BTOS BH25 327 K4
TOTT SO40 246 E2
Stirling Crs HEND SO30 250 C2
TOTT SO40 246 E3
Stirling Rd TWDS BH3 322 E8
Stirling St NEND PO2 296 F9
Stirling Wy ALDT GU11 75 L5
CHCH/BSGR BH23 325 M9
NTHA RG18 25 M3
Stirrup Cl NWBY RG14 24 E8
WIMB BH21 279 L8
Stoatley Hollow HASM GU27 156 F5
Stoatley Ri HASM GU27 156 F5
Stoatley River HASM GU27 156 F5
Stoborough Dr BDST BH18 320 C2
Stockbridge Cl CFDH BH17 321 K2
CHIN RG24 52 C9
HAV PO9 277 H5
Stockbridge Dr ALDT GU11 97 J5
Stockbridge Rd FLEETN GU51 56 A9
OVTN RG25 108 C3
RAND SP11 121 N6
ROMY SO51 180 A7
RWIN SO21 125 L5
RWIN SO21 143 K8
STOK SO20 161 M4
Stockbridge Wy YTLY GU46 56 E1
Stocker Cl BSTK RG21 90 C1
Stocker Pl LSOL/BMARY PO13 295 H7
Stockers Av FUFL SO22 164 E6
Stockheath La HAV PO9 14 D2
Stockheath Rd HAV PO9 276 E6
Stockheath Wy HAV PO9 15 G1
Stockholm Dr HEND SO30 250 B6
Stock La RSAL SP5 201 L6
Stockley Cl FAWY SO45 290 E6
Stock's La BPWT SO32 212 C9
Stocks La PSF GU32 189 J5
Stockton Av FLEETN GU51 74 C2
Stockton Cl HEND SO30 250 D4
Stockton Pk FLEETN GU51 74 C2
Stockwood Wy FNM GU9 96 F4
Stoddart Av ITCH SO19 249 H5
Stodham La LISS GU33 192 C6
Stoke Charity Rd RWIN SO21 145 H5
Stoke Common Rd
ELGH SO50 207 N8
Stoke Gdns GPORT PO12 12 E3
Stoke Ga RAND SP11 62 F8
Stoke Hts ELGH SO50 230 B1
Stoke Hl RAND SP11 62 E9
Stoke Hills FNM GU9 96 C8
Stoke La RAND SP11 62 D7
Stoken La HTWY RG27 54 E6
Stoke Pde GPORT PO12 * 12 E3
Stoke Park Dr ELGH SO50 207 M9
Stoke Park Rd ELGH SO50 207 M9
Stoke Rd GPORT PO12 12 D3
RAND SP11 83 J4
ROWN SO16 247 L2
WINC SO23 165 H4
Stokes Av PLE BH15 320 E8
Stokesay Cl FAWY SO45 290 C1
Stokes Bay Rd GPORT PO12 315 K6
Stokes La TADY RG26 33 M5
Stokesway GPORT PO12 * 12 E3
Stoke Wood Cl ELGH SO50 230 B2
Stoke Wood Rd TWDS BH3 322 F8
Stonechat Cl EPSF GU31 216 A3
FERN BH22 280 B9
Stonechat Dr TOTT SO40 245 P3
Stonechat Rd HORN PO8 256 A5
Stone Cl AND SP10 102 C4
RSAL SP5 158 B1
Stonecrop Cl BDST BH18 320 A2
Stone Crop Cl HLER SO31 270 E9
Stonedene Cl BOR GU35 155 J4
Stone Gdns CHAR BH8 323 N5
Stoneham Cemetery Rd
WEND SO18 229 H8
Stoneham Cl PSF GU32 215 K1
ROWN SO16 228 F7
Stoneham La ELGH SO50 228 G5
ROWN SO16 228 F7
Stoneham Pk PSF GU32 215 K1
Stoneham Wy ROWN SO16 228 G7
Stonehill Pk BOR GU35 155 J4
Stonehill Rd BOR GU35 155 K4
Stonehills FAWY SO45 291 L7
Stonehouse Ri FRIM GU16 58 D4
Stonehouse Rd LIPH GU30 175 L3
Stone La GPORT PO12 12 D3
WIMB BH21 278 C8
Stoneleigh Av LYMN SO41 327 P3
Stoneleigh Cl
FHAM/PORC PO16 295 M1
Stoneleigh Ct FRIM GU16 58 E4
Stoners Cl LSOL/BMARY PO13 294 F6
Stone Sq HAV PO9 276 F6
Stone St ASHV GU12 97 K3
SSEA PO5 19 F6
Stone Ter RWIN SO21 * 207 K4
Stoney Bottom GSHT GU26 156 B2
Stoney Cl YTLY GU46 56 E1
Stoney Croft Ri CHFD SO53 228 E2
Stoney Cross RAND SP11 79 P1
Stoneyfields FNM GU9 116 E1
Stoney La ALTN GU34 150 C4
FUFL SO22 164 E5
NTHA RG18 24 G1
STHA RG19 25 P4
Stony La CHCH/BSGR BH23 324 G8
FBDG SP6 218 G8
PSEA PO1 18 C1
Stony La South
CHCH/BSGR BH23 324 G9
Stonymoor Cl FAWY SO45 290 E6
Stookes Wy YTLY GU46 56 C1
Stopples La LYMN SO41 327 P3
Storrington Rd HORN PO8 236 D7
Story La BDST BH18 300 D9
Stourbank Rd
CHCH/BSGR BH23 324 E9
Stourcliffe Av SBNE BH6 336 A2
Stour Cl EPSF GU31 215 L3
WEND SO18 229 J9
WIMB BH21 301 M1
Stourcroft Dr
CHCH/BSGR BH23 324 B5
Stourfield Rd BOSC BH5 335 P2
Stourhead Cl AND SP10 102 C3
FARN GU14 58 C9
Stourpaine Rd CFDH BH17 320 F2
Stour Pk NBNE BH10 * 322 E1
Stour Rd CHAR BH8 323 K9
CHCH/BSGR BH23 324 E8
DEAN RG23 88 F2
Stourvale Av
CHCH/BSGR BH23 324 B7
Stourvale Gdns CHFD SO53 206 F8
Stourvale Pl BOSC BH5 335 P1
Stourvale Rd SBNE BH6 335 P1
Stour Valley Wy NBNE BH10 322 E1
Stour View Gdns WIMB BH21 300 A4
Stour Wk CHAR BH8 323 K3
Stour Wy CHCH/BSGR BH23 324 B5
Stourwood Av SBNE BH6 336 A2
Stourwood Rd SBNE BH6 336 B2
Stouts La CHCH/BSGR BH23 305 M7
Stovold's Wy ALDT GU11 2 B6
Stow Crs FHAM PO15 272 B8
Stowe Cl HEND SO30 250 D2
Stowe Rd ENEY PO4 317 K4
Stradbrook
LSOL/BMARY PO13 294 F8
Stragwyne Cl NBAD SO52 205 J8
The Straight Mile ROMY SO51 205 J4
Strand SHAM SO14 20 E5
Stranding St ELGH SO50 229 H1
Strand St PLE BH15 332 D2
The Strand HISD PO11 319 J7
Strategic Pk HEND SO30 * 249 P4
Stratfield Av TADY RG26 34 C7
Stratfield Dr CHFD SO53 206 D4
Stratfield Pk WVILLE PO7 * 275 L2
Stratfield Pl NMIL/BTOS BH25 326 G4
Stratfield Rd BSTK RG21 69 K4
Stratfield Saye Rd TADY RG26 36 B9
Stratford Pl ELGH SO50 207 K9
LYMN SO41 329 K2
Stratford Rd ASHV GU12 76 E4
WVILLE PO7 276 A2
Strathfield Rd AND SP10 102 D5
Strathmore Dr VWD BH31 258 G4
Strathmore Rd GPORT PO12 13 F2
MOOR/WNTN BH9 322 G3
Stratton Cl CHAM PO6 296 E1
RWIN SO21 127 N5
Stratton La RWIN SO21 127 N4
Stratton Pk BH/HW/K RG22 89 M1
Stratton Rd BSTK RG21 90 B1
MOOR/WNTN BH9 323 J3
WINC SO23 23 H6
WSHM SO15 247 N2
Stratton Wk FARN GU14 57 P6
Strauss Rd BH/HW/K RG22 89 N3
Stravinsky Rd BH/HW/K RG22 90 B3
Strawberry Ct FRIM GU16 59 J5
Strawberry Flds BROC SO42 311 H2
HEND SO30 250 A5
TADY RG26 52 A2
THLE RG7 36 A1
Strawberry Hl HLER SO31 270 F7
NWBY RG14 24 C3
Strawberry Md ELGH SO50 230 B3
Stream Farm Cl RFNM GU10 116 D3
Streamleaze
FHAM/STUB PO14 271 J9
Streamside FLEETN GU51 74 D4
Stream Valley Rd RFNM GU10 116 C4
Street End HTWY RG27 55 N9
NBAD SO52 205 M8
Streets La RGWD BH24 282 G5
The Street ALTN GU34 134 C2
CHIN RG24 70 B6
FLEETN GU51 74 A7
HTWY RG27 53 M8
ODIM RG29 92 F1
ODIM RG29 93 K8
RFNM GU10 97 M6
RFNM GU10 115 N4
RFNM GU10 136 C2
ROMY SO51 202 D4
RSAL SP5 201 J1
TADY RG26 51 N3
THLE RG7 36 A1
Streetway Rd RAND SP11 119 N3
Strete Mt CHCH/BSGR BH23 * 325 J8
Stride Av HSEA PO3 317 K2
Strides La RGWD BH24 282 D2
Strides Wy TOTT SO40 245 P4
Strode Gdns RGWD BH24 281 P4
Strode Rd NEND PO2 296 E7
Strokins Rd KSCL RG20 48 C2
Strongs Cl ROMY SO51 204 F5
Stroud Cl CHIN RG24 69 P2
TADY RG26 34 E5
WIMB BH21 279 J8
Strouden Av CHAR BH8 323 H6
Strouden Cl HAV PO9 276 D3
Stroud End PSF GU32 215 H1
Strouden Rd
MOOR/WNTN BH9 322 G6
Stroud Gdns
CHCH/BSGR BH23 325 J9
Stroud Gn NWBY RG14 17 G5
Stroud Green La
FHAM/STUB PO14 294 B4
Stroud La BLKW GU17 57 H2
CHCH/BSGR BH23 325 J9
FLEETN GU51 73 P7
Stroudley Av CHAM PO6 297 L3
Stroudley Rd CHIN RG24 69 P5
Stroudley Wy HEND SO30 250 D1
Stroud Park Av
CHCH/BSGR BH23 325 J9
Stroudwood La BPWT SO32 230 G1
Stroudwood Rd HAV PO9 15 H1
Struan Cl RGWD BH24 281 M3
Struan Ct RGWD BH24 281 N3
Struan Dr RGWD BH24 281 M3
Struan Gdns RGWD BH24 281 M3
Stuart Cl FARN GU14 57 P8
FHAM/STUB PO14 294 A7
Stuart Crs FUFL SO22 183 N1
Stuart Rd CHCH/BSGR BH23 326 D7
Stubbington Av BOR GU35 153 P7
NEND PO2 296 G8
Stubbington Gn
FHAM/STUB PO14 294 A6
Stubbington La
FHAM/STUB PO14 294 A9
Stubbington Wy ELGH SO50 230 D3
Stubbs Ct AND SP10 4 B1
Stubbs Court Ct AND SP10 4 B1
Stubbs Dro HEND SO30 250 D4
Stubbs Folly SHST GU47 41 L7
Stubbs Moor Rd FARN GU14 57 N8
Stubbs Rd BSTK RG21 90 E1
ITCH SO19 249 L9
Stuckton Rd FBDG SP6 240 E3
Studland Cl ROWN SO16 247 H2
Studland Dr LYMN SO41 338 E1
Studland Rd
LSOL/BMARY PO13 314 C2
ROWN SO16 247 H2
WBNE BH4 334 C5
Studley Av FAWY SO45 290 E6
Studley Cl CHCH/BSGR BH23 326 E7
Studley Ct NMIL/BTOS BH25 326 F7
Stukeley Rd BSTK RG21 69 J8
Sturdee Cl FRIM GU16 58 D4
Sturminster Rd
MOOR/WNTN BH9 323 H3
Sturt Av HASM GU27 156 E8
Sturt Rd FNM GU9 96 B4
FRIM GU16 58 E8
Sudbury Rd CHAM PO6 296 F1
Suetts La BPWT SO32 232 D5
Suffolk Av CHCH/BSGR BH23 324 D5
WSHM SO15 247 P4
Suffolk Cl CHFD SO53 228 E2
WIMB BH21 279 L8
Suffolk Ct FRIM GU16 59 J5
Suffolk Dr CHFD SO53 228 E2
FHAM PO15 271 H3
Suffolk Rd AND SP10 4 B6
ENEY PO4 317 J5
WCLF BH2 334 D3
Suffolk Rd South WCLF BH2 334 D2
Sulhamstead Rd THLE RG7 26 E1
Sullivan Cl CHAM PO6 296 A1
FARN GU14 57 P9
Sullivan Rd BH/HW/K RG22 90 A2
CBLY GU15 41 P9
ITCH SO19 249 M8
Sullivan Wy WVILLE PO7 275 N5
Sultan Rd EMRTH PO10 277 M9
NEND PO2 316 F1
Sumar Cl FHAM/STUB PO14 294 B4
Summercroft Wy FERN BH22 280 E6
Summer Down La DEAN RG23 67 K7
Summerfield Cl
CHCH/BSGR BH23 324 G5
Summer Field Cl WIMB BH21 301 J1
Summerfield Gdns
ROWN SO16 228 F7
Summerfield La RFNM GU10 116 A8
Summerfields CHIN RG24 52 B9
HLER SO31 271 H9
LTDN BH7 323 M8
Summer Flds VWD BH31 258 F6
Summerhill Rd HORN PO8 255 P8
Summerlands Rd ELGH SO50 230 C2
Summerlands Wk HAV PO9 * 277 H5
Summer La BROC SO42 290 A8
Summerleigh Wk
FHAM/STUB PO14 294 B4
Summerplug THLE RG7 35 P1
Summers Av BWD BH11 322 B1
Summers La
CHCH/BSGR BH23 325 H6
Summers St SHAM SO14 248 D5
Summertrees Ct
NMIL/BTOS BH25 327 M3
Summit Av FARN GU14 75 K1
Summit Wy WEND SO18 249 H2
Sumner Rd EPSF GU31 215 K8
FNM GU9 96 C8
Sunbeam Wy GPORT PO12 12 D5
Sun Brow HASM GU27 156 E8
Sunbury Cl BOR GU35 154 B5
BWD BH11 322 A1
Sunbury Ct FHAM PO15 272 C6
Sunderland Dr
CHCH/BSGR BH23 325 M8
Sunderland Gdns NWBY RG14 24 A5
Sunderland Pl NTHA RG18 25 M3
Sunderton La HORN PO8 236 C7
Sundew Cl CHCH/BSGR BH23 325 N6
NMIL/BTOS BH25 327 M3
Sundew Rd BDST BH18 320 A2
Sundridge Cl CHAM PO6 296 G1
Sunflower Cl BH/HW/K RG22 89 L4
Sun Gdns THLE RG7 27 J6
Sun Hill Crs NARL SO24 168 A3
Sun La NARL SO24 168 A3
THLE RG7 37 N4
Sunley Cl NWBY RG14 24 A9
Sunlight Gdns FHAM PO15 10 B3
Sunningdale FAWY SO45 268 B8
Sunningdale Cl ELGH SO50 229 P2
LSOL/BMARY PO13 294 G8
Sunningdale Crs NBNE BH10 322 C3
Sunningdale Gdns
WEND SO18 249 K4
Sunningdale Rd
FHAM/PORC PO16 295 P2
HSEA PO3 317 J2
Sunnybank RAND SP11 101 L4
Sunnybank Ms ASHV GU12 * 76 G9
Sunnybank Rd FARN GU14 57 L7
WIMB BH21 279 K8
Sunnydell La FNM GU9 116 A4
Sunnydown Rd FUFL SO22 183 J3
Sunnyfield Ri HLER SO31 270 A1
Sunnyfield Rd
NMIL/BTOS BH25 327 J7
Sunnyheath HAV PO9 14 D1
Sunny Hill Rd ALDT GU11 96 D1
BKME/WDN BH12 321 M7
Sunnyhill Rd SBNE BH6 335 P1
Sunnylands Av SBNE BH6 336 D2
Sunny Md DEAN RG23 88 F3
Sunnymead Dr WVILLE PO7 255 L9
Sunnymoor Rd BWD BH11 322 A6
Sunnyside FLEETN GU51 74 B2
KSCL RG20 * 48 B4
Sunnyside Cl AND SP10 82 B9
Sunnyside Rd
BKME/WDN BH12 321 M6
BOR GU35 155 K4
Sunnyview Cl ASHV GU12 3 J4
Sunny Wk PSEA PO1 18 B2
Sunny Wy TOTT SO40 246 D4
Sun Ray Est SHST GU47 40 G6
Sunridge Cl BKME/WDN BH12 322 A9
Sunset Av TOTT SO40 246 C3
Sunset Rd TOTT SO40 246 C3
Sunshine Av HISD PO11 319 H6
Sun St PSEA PO1 18 D3
Suntrap Gdns HISD PO11 * 319 H6
Sunvale Av HASM GU27 156 C7
Sunvale Cl HASM GU27 156 C7
ITCH SO19 249 K8
Sunwood Rd HAV PO9 276 D5
Surbiton Rd ELGH SO50 207 K8
Surrey Av CBLY GU15 57 P1
Surrey Cl CHCH/BSGR BH23 324 D5
TOTT SO40 246 B6
Surrey Gdns WBNE BH4 334 C2
Surrey Rd BKME/WDN BH12 334 A1
CHFD SO53 228 E1
ITCH SO19 248 F9
WBNE BH4 334 B2
Surrey Rd South WBNE BH4 334 C2
Surrey St PSEA PO1 19 G2

Sussex Border Pth
EMRTH PO10 .... 299 M6
EPSF GU31 .... 216 F3
LIPH GU30 .... 174 F7
Sussex CI AND/WNTN BH9 .. 323 H5
FLEETN GU51 .... 56 G9
Sussex PI SSEA PO5 * 19 G7
Sussex Rd CHFD S053 .... 228 F1
EPSF GU31 .... 215 N3
SHAM S014 .... 20 E4
Sussex St WINC S023 .... 22 D5
Sussex Ter SSEA PO5 .... 19 G7
Sutcliffe Sq AND SP10 * 82 C8
Sutherland Av BDST BH18 .. 300 A8
Sutherland CI BOR GU35 .. 154 A7
ROMY S051 .... 208 G4
Sutherland Ct AND SP10 .... 4 B1
Sutherland Rd ENEY PO4 .. 316 C5
ROWN S016 .... 227 K7
Sutherlands NWBY RG14 .. 24 B8
Sutherlands Ct CHFD S053 .. 206 E7
Sutherlands Wy CHFD S053 .. 206 D6
Sutton CI CFDH BH17 .... 321 J2
HORN PO8 .... 255 M8
HSEA PO3 .... 297 K5
Sutton Fld BOR GU35 .... 153 P7
Sutton Gdns WINC S023 .. 22 E4
Sutton Park CI RWIN S021 .. 125 L5
Sutton PI BROC S042 .... 286 C8
Sutton Rd BSTK RG21 .... 6 E2
HORN PO8 .... 255 M8
MOOR/WNTN BH9 .. 323 H6
NWBY RG14 .... 24 A2
TOTT S040 .... 258 D2
Sutton Wood La NARL S024 .. 149 H8
Swains CI TADY RG26 .... 34 C6
Swains Rd TADY RG26 .... 34 C6
Swaledale Gdns FLEETN GU51 .. 56 E9
Swale Dr CHFD S053 .... 206 C6
Swale Rd FARN GU14 .... 57 L7
Swallow CI ALTN GU34 .... 132 C3
BH/HW/K RG22 .... 89 K3
CFDH BH17 .... 320 B4
HAV PO9 .... 15 K2
TDWTH SP9 .... 79 H5
TOTT S040 .... 245 P5
YTLY GU46 .... 40 C8
Swallow Ct
LSOL/BMARY PO13 .... 314 D1
Swallow Dr LYMN S041 .... 339 H2
Swallowfields AND SP10 .. 82 F9
Swallow Sq ELGH S050 .... 228 E2
Swallow Wy WIMB BH21 .. 279 J6
Swallow Wd FHAM/PORC PO16 .. 11 G1
Swanage CI ITCH S019 .... 248 G8
Swanage Rd
LSOL/BMARY PO13 .... 314 C2
Swan Barn Rd HASM GU27 .. 157 J7
Swan CI EMRTH PO10 .... 299 N2
HLER S031 .... 270 D3
Swancote FHAM/PORC PO16 .. 295 K1
Swan Ct AND SP10 .... 4 E4
HTWY RG27 .... 55 J7
NWBY RG14 .... 24 C5
Swan La SHST GU47 .... 41 J8
WINC S023 .... 22 D3
Swanley CI ELGH S050 .... 207 J8
Swan Md RGWD BH24 .... 282 C3
Swan Ms ODIM RG29 .... 72 D8
Swanmore Av ITCH S019 .. 249 K8
Swanmore CI FUFL S022 .. 164 D3
LTDN BH7 .... 323 P8
Swanmore Rd BPWT S032 .. 232 D5
HAV PO9 .... 276 D3
Swansbury Dr CHAR BH8 .. 323 N5
Swan St KSCL RG20 .... 48 B4
PSF GU32 .... 215 L2
Swans Wk HISD PO11 .... 319 J5
Swanton CI FHAM/STUB PO14 .. 294 B6
Swanton Gdns CHFD S053 * .. 206 D6
Swan Wy FLEETN GU51 .... 74 A5
Swanwick La HLER S031 .... 270 D2

Swordfish Dr
CHCH/BSGR BH23 .... 325 M8
Swordfish Wy FARN GU14 .. 75 M5
Sword Sands Rd HSEA PO3 .. 317 L1
Swordsman's Rd FHAM GU16 .. 59 J4
Sycamore Av CHFD S053 .. 206 B8
Sycamore CI CFDH BH17 .. 320 B3
CHCH/BSGR BH23 .... 324 B7
FHAM/STUB PO14 .... 271 J9
FRIM GU16 .... 58 D4
HLER S031 .... 269 P2
HORN PO8 .... 256 C7
HORN PO8 .... 255 N8
LSOL/BMARY PO13 .... 295 J8
LYMN S041 .... 338 F1
NBAD S052 .... 205 K8
RDCW/BURGH RG30 .... 27 K2
SHST GU47 * 41 J7
TDWTH SP9 .... 79 J3
Sycamore Crs FLEETN GU51 .. 74 B6
Sycamore Dr ASHV GU12 .. 76 E5
FAWY S045 .... 290 D4
FRIM GU16 .... 58 D8
HISD PO11 .... 318 E4
RFNM GU10 .... 116 A4
WINC S023 .... 145 J8
Sycamore PI WIMB BH21 .. 279 M9
Sycamore Ri NWBY RG14 .. 24 F1
Sycamore Rd BPWT S032 .. 232 C5
FARN GU14 .... 76 C1
FAWY S045 .... 268 B7
LYMN S041 .... 327 P5
ROWN S016 .... 247 L1
The Sycamores BLKW GU17 .. 41 J9
FARN GU14 .... 76 C1
Sycamore Wk AND SP10 .. 102 B3
Sydenham Ter PSEA PO1 .. 19 K3
The Sydings NWBY RG14 .. 24 A2
Sydling CI CFDH BH17 .... 321 K2
Sydmanton CI ROMY S051 .. 204 E7
Sydmonton Ct HAV PO9 .. 277 H4
Sydney Av HLER S031 .... 269 N7
Sydney CI STHA RG19 * .. 25 P4
Sydney Loader PI BDST BH18 .. 41 H8
Sydney Rd BDST BH18 .... 320 C1
BOR GU35 .... 154 A5
CHCH/BSGR BH23 .... 324 C6
ELGH S050 .... 207 M9
GPORT PO12 .... 12 D2
WSHM S015 .... 247 M2
Sydney Smith Av FARN GU14 .. 76 A3
Syers Rd LISS GU33 .... 192 D2
Sylmor Gdns
MOOR/WNTN BH9 .. 323 H5
Sylvan Av ITCH S019 .... 249 L5
Sylvan CI LYMN S041 .... 328 B5
RGWD BH24 .... 281 K5
Sylvan Dr NBAD S052 .... 205 K9
Sylvan La HLER S031 .... 269 P9
Sylvan Rd BKME/WDN BH12 .. 321 K6
The Sylvans FAWY S045 .... 267 P7
Sylvan Vw WVILLE PO7 .... 275 P4
Sylvan Wy FLEETS GU51 .... 74 C7
Sylvester CI NWBY RG14 .... 24 E2
Sylvia CI BSTK RG21 .... 69 K9
Sylvia Crs TOTT S040 .... 246 C2
Symes Rd ROMY S051 .... 204 F6
Symonds CI CHFD S053 .... 206 C9
Symonds St WINC S023 .... 22 E6
Sympson Rd TADY RG26 .... 34 E1
Syon CI PFARN GU14 .... 58 C9
Sywell Crs HSEA PO3 .... 297 K5

T

Tadburn CI CHFD S053 .... 206 F8
Tadburn Gn ROMY S051 .... 204 C7
Tadburn Rd ROMY S051 .... 204 E7
Tadden Wk BDST BH18 .... 320 B2
Tadfield Rd ROMY S051 .... 204 E6
Tadham PI STHA RG19 .... 25 M5
Tadley CI FLEETN GU51 * 56 A8
Tadley Common Rd TADY RG26 .. 34 D5
Tadley HI TADY RG26 .... 34 D6
Tadpole La WHAM PO17 .... 252 A5
Tagdell La HORN PO8 .... 255 P5
Taiping Rd STOK S020 .... 120 C4
Tait CI CFDH BH17 .... 320 C5
Tait PI LSOL/BMARY PO13 .. 295 H8
Talavera CI CWTH RG45 .... 40 F2
Talbot Av TWDS SN3 .... 322 E8
Talbot CI FRIM GU16 .... 58 D9
HAV PO9 .... 14 A2
NWBY RG14 .... 24 B2
ROWN S016 .... 246 B1
Talbot Dr BKME/WDN BH12 .. 322 B7
CHCH/BSGR BH23 .... 326 B5
Talbot Hill Rd
MOOR/WNTN BH9 .. 322 D7
Talbot Mdw BKME/WDN BH12 .. 322 B7
Talbot Ms BH10 .... 322 B6
Talbot Ri NBNE BH10 .... 322 B6
Talbot Rd ENEY PO4 .... 316 C4
FAWY S045 .... 267 P9
FHAM PO15 .... 271 L8
HAV PO9 .... 14 B2
MOOR/WNTN BH9 .. 322 D7
Talgarth Dr FARN GU14 .... 58 C9
Talisman CI CWTH RG45 .... 40 E1
Talland Rd FHAM/STUB PO14 .. 271 H9
Tallis Gdns BH/HW/K RG22 .. 90 A2
Talmey CI CHIN RG24 .... 69 P1
Tamar CI FERN BH22 .... 302 C3
FHAM/PORC PO16 .... 273 L9
Tamar Down WVILLE PO7 .. 276 A3
Tamar Dr DEAN S053 .... 88 F2
Tamar Gdns WEND S018 .. 249 K1
Tamar Gv FAWY S045 .... 268 A7
Tamarisk CI BH/HW/K RG22 .. 89 N6

ENEY PO4 .... 317 L5
FHAM/STUB PO14 .... 294 A9
WVILLE PO7 .... 276 A5
Tamarin Gdns WEND S018 .. 248 G3
Tamarisk Rd HEND S030 .. 250 B4
Tamella Rd HEND S030 .... 250 E5
Tammys Turn
FHAM/STUB PO14 .... 293 P1
Tamorisk Dr TOTT S040 .. 246 A5
Tamworth Dr FLEETN GU51 .. 56 E9
Tamworth PI GPORT PO12 .. 12 C4
Tamworth Rd HEND S030 .. 317 J2
Tanfield La WHAM PO17 .. 252 C9
Tanfield Pk WHAM PO17 .. 252 D8
Tangier CI ALDT GU11 .... 2 B3
Tangier La BPWT S032 .... 231 M5
Tangier Rd PSEA PO3 .... 317 J1
Tanglewood CI FHAM/PORC PO16 .. 10 E1
TOTT S040 .... 267 L1
Tanglewood La WVILLE PO7 .. 275 L6
Tangley Wk HAV PO9 * 277 H5
Tangmere CI
CHCH/BSGR BH23 .... 325 M9
Tangmere Dr ROWN S016 .. 227 K8
Tangyes CI FHAM/STUB PO14 .. 294 B6
Tanhouse CI HEND S030 .. 250 C6
Tanhouse La ALTN GU34 .. 132 C5
HEND S030 .... 250 D7
Tan Howse CI LTDN BH7 .. 323 P7
Tankerdale La LISS GU33 .. 192 A6
Tanker Rd FARN GU14 .... 76 A3
Tankerton CI CHAM PO6 .. 296 C1
Tankerville Rd ITCH S019 .. 248 F8
Tanner La GU15 .... 41 N9
The Tanneries
FHAM/STUB PO14 * 293 N1
HAV PO9 * 14 E6
Tanners Brook Wy
WSHM S015 .... 247 K5
Tanners CI ROWN S016 .. 227 M8
THLE RG7 .... 27 H6
Tanners La FBDG SP6 .... 219 M9
FHAM/STUB PO14 .... 294 C5
HASM GU27 .... 157 H6
LYMN S041 .... 330 E3
Tanner's La WVILLE PO7 .. 255 H6
Tanners Rdg WVILLE PO7 .. 275 N7
Tanners Rd NBAD S052 .. 205 L9
The Tanners
FHAM/STUB PO14 .... 293 J1
Tanner St WINC S023 .... 23 F5
Tanners Wy DEAN RG23 .. 88 F1
Tansy CI WVILLE PO7 .... 276 A4
Tansy Meadow CHFD S053 .. 206 D4
The Tanyards CHFD S053 .. 206 D4
Taplin Dr HEND S030 .... 250 C3
Taplings CI WINC S023 .. 164 E4
Taplings Rd FUFL S022 .. 164 E4
Taplin's Farm La HTWY RG27 .. 73 K1
Taranto Rd ROWN S016 .. 227 N8
Tarbat Ct SHST GU47 .... 41 L6
Tarbery Crs HORN PO8 .. 256 C4
Target Rd NEND PO2 .... 296 D9
Tariff Wy CHCH/BSGR BH23 .. 305 K7
Tarius CI LSOL/BMARY PO13 .. 295 H7
Tarleton Rd CHAM PO6 .. 274 D9
Tarn CI FARN GU14 .... 75 M2
Tarn Howes CI STHA RG19 .. 25 N4
Tarn La NWBY RG14 .... 16 C7
Tarn Ri HORN PO8 .... 256 C1
Tarn Rd GSHT GU26 .... 156 C2
Tarragon CI FARN GU14 .... 57 K9
Tarragon Wy THLE RG7 .... 27 H4
Tarrant CI CFDH BH17 .. 320 C2
Tarrant Gdns HAV PO9 .. 14 C2
Tarrant Rd MOOR/WNTN BH9 .. 323 H4
Taskers Dr RAND SP11 .. 102 A5
Tasman CI CHCH/BSGR BH23 .. 324 D7
SHAM S014 .... 248 D9
Tasmania CI CHIN RG24 .. 69 M2
Taswell Rd SSEA PO5 .... 316 F6
Tanberry Gv THLE RG7 .... 27 J1
Tate Rd WSHM S015 .... 246 G3
Tattenham Rd BROC S042 .. 286 F9
Tattershall Crs
FHAM/PORC PO16 .... 295 M2
Tatwin CI ITCH S019 .... 249 M6
Tatwin Crs ITCH S019 .... 249 M6
Taunton Dr WEND S018 .. 249 K4
Tavells La TOTT S040 .... 267 J1
Tavell's La TOTT S040 .... 267 J1
Taverner CI BSTK RG21 .. 7 J2
PLE BH15 .... 331 N3
Taverners CI ITCH S019 .. 249 M8
Tavistock CI ROMY S051 .. 204 F4
Tavistock Gdns FARN GU14 .. 58 A6
HAV PO9 .... 15 K6
Tavistock Rd FLEETN GU51 .. 74 A3
Taw CI CHFD S053 .... 206 D6
Taw Dr CHFD S053 .... 206 D6
Tawny Owl CI
FHAM/STUB PO14 .... 293 P5
Tawny Rw SHST GU47 * 41 L6
Tawny Gv THLE RG7 .... 27 J4
Tay CI FARN GU14 .... 57 M7
Taylor Dr CHAR BH8 .... 323 K3
TADY RG26 .... 52 B3
Taylor Rd ALDT GU11 .... 76 C5
Taylor's Bids Pd ENEY PO4 .. 316 E3
Taylors Ct BOR GU35 .... 154 C3
Taylors La BOR GU35 .... 154 C3
Tay La NWBY RG14 .... 31 J1
Teachers Wy FAWY S045 .. 290 C5
Teal CI FHAM/PORC PO16 .. 11 G5
HORN PO8 .... 256 A6
TOTT S040 .... 246 A4
Teal Crs BH/HW/K RG22 .. 89 K4

Teasel CI RAND SP11 .... 79 P2
Teasel Wy FERN BH22 .... 280 E8
Teazle CI EPSF GU31 .... 216 A3
Tebourba Dr GPORT PO12 .. 12 A5
Tebourba Wy WSHM S015 .. 247 K4
Technology Rd CFDH BH17 .. 320 C4
Ted Bates Rd SHAM S014 .. 21 H6
Tedder CI BWD BH11 .... 322 B4
RAND SP11 .... 101 P3
Tedder Rd BWD BH11 .... 322 B4
LSOL/BMARY PO13 .... 295 H6
WEND S018 .... 248 A9
Tedder Wy TOTT S040 .... 246 B4
Teddington Rd ENEY PO4 .. 317 J4
Tees CI CHFD S053 .... 206 C6
FARN GU14 .... 57 M7
Tees Farm Rd RWIN S021 .. 207 P5
Teg Down Meads FUFL S022 .. 164 C6
Tegg Down Rd NARL S024 .. 169 H4
Teignmouth Rd GPORT PO12 .. 315 K1
HSEA PO3 .... 297 J9
Tekels Wy CBLY GU15 .... 58 D2
Telconia CI BOR GU35 .... 155 K4
Telegraph La ALTN GU34 .. 147 L8
Telegraph Rd HEND S030 .. 249 N5
Telegraph Wy RWIN S021 .. 166 A8
Telephone Rd ENEY PO4 .. 316 G4
Telford CI NWBY RG14 .... 24 C3
Telford Gdns HEND S030 .. 250 D1
Telford PI LYMN S041 .... 339 H2
Telford Rd BSTK RG21 .... 69 H5
NEND PO2 .... 296 C6
WIMB BH21 .... 280 A9
Telford Wy HLER S031 .... 271 J5
NEND PO2 .... 296 C6
Tempest Av WVILLE PO7 .. 276 B1
Templar Av FNM GU9 .... 116 B2
Templar CI SHST GU47 .... 41 H6
Templars Mede CHFD S053 .. 228 D1
Templars Wy CHFD S053 .. 206 B9
Telscombe Rd ELGH S050 .. 229 H9
Temple Gdns CHFD S053 .. 249 H9
Temple La PSF GU32 .... 213 M5
Templemere
FHAM/STUB PO14 .... 294 A2
Temple Ms BMTH BH1 * .. 323 K9
Temple PI LYMN S041 * 74 B7
Templer CI BWD BH11 .... 321 P3
Temple Rd ITCH S019 .... 249 H9
Temple's CI RFNM GU10 .. 117 J1
Temple St PSEA PO1 .... 19 H1
Templeton CI NEND PO2 * .. 296 C6
Tenby G WEND S018 .... 249 J5
Tenby Dr CHFD S053 .... 206 C9
Tenby Rd FRIM GU16 .... 58 F5
Tench Wy ROMY S051 .... 204 D5
Tennyson CI BPWT S032 .. 232 C4
FARN GU14 .... 58 C7
Tennyson Crs WVILLE PO7 .. 275 M1
Tennyson Gdns
FHAM/PORC PO16 .... 10 E4
MOOR/WNTN BH9 .. 322 F5
NEND PO2 .... 297 H9
NTHA RG18 .... 25 M3
PSTN BH14 .... 321 J9
SD/PW S017 .... 248 D3
TOTT S040 .... 246 B1
WIMB BH21 .... 280 A9
Tennyson's La HASM GU27 .. 157 K9
Tennyson's Rdg HASM GU27 .. 157 J8
Tennyson Wy BH/HW/K RG22 .. 69 H9
Tensing CI FHAM/PORC PO16 .. 10 E1
Tensing Rd CHCH/BSGR BH23 .. 325 J8
Tenterton Av ITCH S019 .. 269 K6
Terence Av CFDH BH17 .. 320 E5
Terminus Ter SHAM S014 .. 21 F7
Tern CI BH/HW/K RG22 .. 89 K4
FAWY S045 .... 268 D8
Tern Wk ENEY PO4 .... 317 K5
Terrace Rd WCLF BH2 .... 8 C4
The Terrace CBLY GU15 .... 41 N9
FARN GU14 * 76 C1
Terrier CI HEND S030 .... 230 C9
Terriote CI CHFD S053 .... 206 E6
Terry CI BH/HW/K RG22 .... 89 K7
Tesimond Dr YTLY GU46 .... 40 B9
Testbourne Av TOTT S040 .. 246 B4
Testbourne CI TOTT S040 .. 246 B4
Testbourne Rd OVTN RG25 .. 85 M8
Test CI EPSF GU31 .... 215 L3
Testcombe Rd GPORT PO12 .. 12 B5
Test Ct AND SP10 .... 82 G9
Testlands Av ROWN S016 .. 227 H9
Test La ROWN S016 .... 246 F2
Test Ms WHCH RG28 .... 85 L6
Test Mills ROMY S051 * .. 204 C6
Test Ri STOK S020 .... 123 L6
Test Rd SHAM S014 .... 268 D2
WHCH RG28 .... 85 L7
Test Wy BSTK RG21 .... 7 J6
RAND SP11 .... 94 B1
ROMY S051 .... 179 M7
Testwood Av TOTT S040 .. 246 B2
Testwood Crs TOTT S040 .. 231 P8
Testwood La TOTT S040 .. 246 B2
Testwood PI TOTT S040 .. 246 B3
Testwood Rd HAV PO9 .. 295 M5
WSHM S015 .... 247 M5
Tethering Dro FBDG SP6 .. 217 P4
Tetney CI ROWN S016 .... 227 J9
Teviot Rd CHFD S053 .... 206 C8
Tewkesbury Av FHAM PO15 .. 272 A7
GPORT PO12 .... 315 J1
Tewkesbury CI CHAM PO6 .. 299 L2
CHIN RG24 .... 69 L3
Texas Dr FUFL S022 .... 183 K4
Thackeray Ms
FHAM/PORC PO16 .... 11 J5

Thackeray Rd SD/PW S017 .. 248 D3
Thackham's La HTWY RG27 .. 54 E8
The Thakerays STHA RG19 .. 25 N5
Thames CI FARN GU14 .... 57 M7
FERN BH22 .... 302 G2
WEND S018 .... 229 K9
Thames Ct BSTK RG21 .... 7 J5
Thames Dr FHAM PO15 .... 272 B6
Thamesmead CI GPORT PO12 .. 315 K1
Thames Ms PLE BH15 * 332 D2
Thames Rd NTHA RG18 .... 25 L2
Thames St PLE BH15 .... 332 D2
Thatched Cottage Pk
LYND S043 * 265 H4
Thatchers La
CHCH/BSGR BH23 .... 305 H7
LYMN S041 .... 310 D8
Theal CI SHST GU47 .... 41 J8
Theale Rd RDCW/BURGH RG30 .. 27 K1
Theatre Ms SSEA PO5 .... 316 F6
Theatre Rd FARN GU14 .... 76 A4
The Itchen Br SHAM S014 .. 21 K7
Theobalds Wy FRIM GU16 .. 59 H2
Theobold Rd
CHCH/BSGR BH23 .... 303 N8
Theseus Rd
LSOL/BMARY PO13 .... 314 A3
Thetchers CI NMIL/BTOS BH25 .. 327 K2
Thetford Gdns CHFD S053 .. 206 C5
Thetford Rd
BKME/WDN BH12 .... 321 P6
GPORT PO12 .... 315 K1
Thibet Rd SHST GU47 .... 41 K6
The Thicket
FHAM/PORC PO16 .... 273 K9
LSOL/BMARY PO13 .... 295 J8
ROMY S051 .... 204 C7
SSEA PO5 * 19 J7
WVILLE PO7 .... 275 M8
Third Av CHAM PO6 .... 296 C1
HAV PO9 .... 15 J4
WSHM S015 .... 247 K5
Third St East STHA RG19 .. 31 M1
Thirlmere ELGH S050 .... 229 H2
Thirlmere CI BOR GU35 .. 154 A3
FARN GU14 .... 57 M9
FHAM/STUB PO14 .... 294 B5
Thirlmere Rd FLEETS GU52 .. 74 B7
Thirlmere Rd RWIN S016 .. 247 J1
Thirlstane Firs CHFD S053 .. 206 D9
Thirsk Ct ASHV GU12 .... 3 K2
Thirt Wy STOK S020 .... 123 N8
Thistlebarrow Rd LTDN BH7 .. 323 L9
Thistle CI CHCH/BSGR BH23 .. 325 N7
Thistledown HORN PO8 .... 256 B6
Thistledown AND SP10 .... 102 C1
Thistledowne Gdns
EMRTH PO10 .... 299 P1
Thistle Bd CHFD S053 .... 206 B8
HEND S030 .... 250 B5
Thomas CI TOTT S040 .... 246 B5
Thomas Grant Av
GPORT PO12 .... 315 P2
Thomas Lewis Wy
SHAM S014 .... 248 D3
Thomas Merriman Ct
NWBY RG14 * 16 E3
Thomas Rd NBAD S052 .. 205 L9
Thompson Dr STHA RG19 .. 25 P5
Thompson's La RWIN S021 .. 208 F6
Thorburn Cha SHST GU47 .. 41 M8
Thoresby CI NMIL/BTOS BH25 .. 326 B5
Thornbrake Rd GPORT PO12 .. 13 F4
Thornbury Av FAWY S045 .. 290 C9
WSHM S015 .... 248 A4
Thornbury CI CWTH RG45 .. 41 J1
FHAM/STUB PO14 .... 294 A1
Thornbury Hts CHFD S053 .. 207 H4
Thornbury Rd SBNE BH6 .. 336 E2
Thornbury Wd CHFD S053 .. 207 H4
Thorncliffe CI NEND PO2 .. 297 H5
Thorn Ct ALTN GU34 .... 150 D5
ELGH S050 .... 207 J7
EPSF GU31 .... 216 A3
RFNM GU10 .... 115 P6
Thorncombe CI CFDH BH17 .. 320 E4
MOOR/WNTN BH9 .. 323 H3
Thorn CI ALTN GU34 .... 150 C6
Thorn Crs ALTN GU34 .... 150 C6
Thorncroft Rd PSEA PO1 .. 316 C3
Thorndike CI ROWN S016 .. 247 L1
Thorn Dr ALTN GU34 .... 150 C5
Thorne CI VWD BH31 .... 258 E3
Thorne Rd KSCL RG20 .... 48 C3
Thornes CI ROWN S016 .... 246 G2
Thorne Wy WIMB BH21 .... 280 A8
Thorney La FHAM/STUB PO14 .. 294 B1
Thorney Rd EMRTH PO10 .. 299 P2
Thorney Vw HISD PO11 * .. 299 J3
Thornfield Dr
CHCH/BSGR BH23 .... 326 B6
Thornford Rd STHA RG19 .. 32 A1
Thorngate Rd RSAL SP5 * .. 159 F7
Thorngate Wy GPORT PO12 .. 13 H2
Thornham La EMRTH PO10 .. 299 P5
Thornham Rd
NMIL/BTOS BH25 .... 327 M4
Thornhill Av ITCH S019 .... 249 M5
Thornhill CI FAWY S045 .. 291 H7
Thornhill Crs ALDT GU11 .. 2 D5
Thornhill Park Rd WEND S018 .. 249 M4
Thornhill Rd ALDT GU11 .. 76 C3
FAWY S045 .... 291 H7
ROWN S016 .... 227 P8
Thornleigh Rd ITCH S019 .. 248 G9
Thornley Rd NBNE BH10 .. 322 D3
RFNM GU10 .... 115 P5
Thorns La LYMN S041 .... 331 K1
Thornton Av HLER S031 .. 270 C9

Thornton Cl TADY RG26.......52 C3
  WVILLE PO7..........275 K8
Thornton End ALTN GU34...135 J3
Thornton Rd GPORT PO12....295 M9
Thornycroft Av ITCH SO19....248 F9
Thornycroft Cl NWBY RG14...17 H2
Thornycroft La BH/HW/K RG22..68 G7
Thornycroft Rbt BSTK RG21...69 H7
Thornyhurst Rd FRIM GU16...35 P8
Thorold Rd CHFD SO53........206 G4
  FNM GU9.......96 C8
  WEND SO18.......248 G2
Thorpe Gdns ALTN GU34.....132 D5
Threadgill Wy TDWTH SP9....98 E3
Three Acre Dr
  NMIL/BTOS BH25........327 H7
Three Acre Rd NWBY RG14...24 C7
Three Acres WVILLE PO7......20 A2
Three Castles Pth CWTH RG45...41 M3
  HTWY RG27.......39 K9
  NARL SO24.......130 A8
  ODIM RG25.......72 C7
  OVTN RG25........91 P4
  OVTN RG25........110 E9
  RWIN SO21.......147 H8
  WINC SO23.......137 N6
Three Cross Rd FERN BH22...280 E4
Threefield La SHAM SO14.....21 F6
Three Firs Wy THLE RG7......26 G6
Three Horse Shoes La
  NARL SO24.........188 G4
Three Lions Cl WIMB BH21...278 D9
Three Oaks ITCH SO19......249 N6
Three Stiles Rd FNM GU9....95 P8
Three Tun Cl PSEA PO1......18 D3
Three Ways Cl
  FHAM/STUB PO14......294 B4
Thresher Cl WVILLE PO7.....276 C1
Threshers Cnr FLEETN GU51...54 C8
Throgmorton Rd YTLY GU46...40 F9
Throop Cl CHAR BH8.........325 N5
Throop Rd CHAR BH8.........323 L3
Throopside Av
  MOOR/WNTN BH9.......323 K3
Thrush Cl BH/HW/K RG22....89 K3
  THLE RG7.......27 K4
Thrush Rd BKME/WDN BH12...321 L3
Thrush Wk HORN PO8........255 N7
Thruxton Ct ITCH SO19.......248 G6
Thruxton Rd HAV PO9.......276 C5
Thuillier Rd RWIN SO21......104 E8
Thumwood CHIN RG24.......70 A1
Thundery Hl RFNM GU10.....97 M7
Thurbans Rd FNM GU9......116 A3
Thurbern Rd NEND PO2......246 D2
Thurmell Cl WEND SO18......250 C7
Thurmell Cl HEND SO30.....250 C7
Thurmell Wk HEND SO30.....250 C7
Thurmond Crs FUFL SO22....164 D9
Thurmond Rd FUFL SO22....164 D9
Thursby Rd CHCH/BSGR BH23..326 B5
Thursley Rd RFNM GU10.....137 J6
Thurston Cl CHFD SO53.......206 F6
Thurstons ALTN GU34.......134 C3
Thwaite Rd BKME/WDN BH12..334 D1
Thyme Av FHAM PO15........271 K2
Thyme Cl CHIN RG24........52 A8
Thyme Ct FARN GU14.........57 N8
Tiberius Cl DEAN RG23........68 F5
Tiberius Rd AND SP10........82 F8
Tichborne Cl BLKW GU17......41 L9
Tichborne Down NARL SO24...167 P4
Tichborne Gv HAV PO9.......276 D5
Tichborne Pl ASHV GU12......3 K7
Tichborne Rd ELGH SO50....229 H4
  WEND SO18.......249 M3
Tichborne Wy
  LSOL/BMARY PO13.......295 H8
Tichfield Cl FRIM GU16.......58 E2
Tickleford Dr ITCH SO19......269 J1
Tickner Cl HEND SO30.......250 E6
Ticonderoga Gdns
  ITCH SO19.......268 C1
Tidemill Cl CHCH/BSGR BH23..324 E7
Tides Reach WEND SO18.....133 J8
Tides Wy TOTT SO40........247 K9
Tideway Gdns ENEY PO4.....317 L4
Tidworth Rd AMSY SP4......98 B4
  HAV PO9.......276 F6
Tiffany Cl LYMN SO41.......327 P3
Tiffield Ct HSEA PO3.......297 L5
Tiger Moth Cl
  LSOL/BMARY PO13.......314 C2
Tiger Rd PSEA PO1.......316 B1
Tigwells Fld ODIM RG29......92 C7
Tilbrook Rd WSHM SO15....247 L3
Tilburg Rd CHCH/BSGR BH23..326 B5
Tilbury's Ct BOR GU35......154 A5
Tilden Rd RWIN SO21.......183 L9
Tile Barn Cl FARN GU14......57 P7
Tilebarn La BROC SO42.......308 F2
Tilford Rd FNM GU9.......116 D1
  HORN PO8.......139 J6
  RFNM GU10.......137 J6
Tilford St RFNM GU10.......117 K4
Tillingdon Gdns HORN PO8...236 D8
Tilmore Gdns PSF GU32.....191 M9
Tilmore Rd PSF GU32.......215 L1
Tilney Cl ALTN GU34.......132 C6
Timber Bank FRIM GU16......58 F8
Timber Cl FNM GU9 *.......96 B9
Timbercroft Cl ALTN GU34...150 B7
Timberlake WVILLE PO7.....275 M6
Timberlake La HASM GU27...156 E7
The Timbers FHAM PO15....272 A9
Timor Cl CHIN RG24.........52 A5
  FHAM PO15.......271 H2
Timothy Cl NBNE BH10......322 D2
Timothys Fld RAND SP11.....101 M7
Timsbury Crs HAV PO9.......14 D2
Timsbury Dr ROWN SO16....247 K1
Timson Cl TOTT SO40.......246 A5

Tincleton Gdns
  MOOR/WNTN BH9.......323 H3
Tindale Rd ROWN SO16......247 J1
Tinker Aly WEND SO18........229 J5
Tinley Gdns ODIM RG29......72 E9
Tinneys Cl RSAL SP5........199 P9
Tintagel Cl AND SP10........82 E8
  DEAN RG23.......68 F6
  ROWN SO16.......227 N6
Tintagel Dr FRIM GU16......58 E4
Tintagel Wy CHAM PO6......296 D2
Tintern Cl CHAM PO6.......274 B9
  CHIN RG24.......69 J4
Tintern Gv WSHM SO15.......20 A2
Tintern Rd GPORT PO12......12 B2
Tipner Gn NEND PO2.......296 E6
Tipner La NEND PO2.......296 D6
Tipner Rd NEND PO2.......296 E7
Tippet Gdns BH/HW/K RG22...90 B5
Tiptoe Rd NMIL/BTOS BH25...307 L7
Tiptree Cl ELGH SO50.......207 J8
Tisbury Ct FLEETN GU51......74 B1
Tisted Ct HAV PO9 *.......277 H5
Titchfield Cl FHAM PO14....34 D7
Titchfield Gra FHAM PO15...271 L7
Titchfield Hl
  FHAM/STUB PO14.......293 N1
Titchfield Pk Rd FHAM PO15..272 A2
Titchfield Rd
  FHAM/STUB PO14.......294 A5
Tithe Barn LYMN SO41.......329 L2
Tithelands La NARL SO24....188 B2
Tithe Md ROMY SO51.......204 D4
Tithe Meadow BH/HW/K RG22..89 N6
The Tithe WVILLE PO7.......275 P6
Tithewood Cl CHFD SO53....206 D3
Tithing Rd FLEETN GU51.....56 C9
Tittymouse La RAND SP11....81 J9
Titus Gdns WVILLE PO7.....276 A2
Tiverton Rd DEAN RG23......68 E7
Tivoli Cl CHFD SO53.......207 H6
Toad La BLKW GU17........57 M1
Tobago Cl CHIN RG24......69 L3
Tobruk Cl RAND SP11.......57 M4
Tobruk Rd RAND SP11.......79 M5
Toby St ENEY PO4.......19 H1
Todber Cl BWD BH11........321 M1
Todmore LISS GU33........173 L4
Tokar St ENEY PO4.......317 J6
Tokio Rd HSEA PO3........297 J8
Toledo Gv AND SP10.......5 C1
Tolefrey Gdns CHFD SO53...206 B7
Tolland Cl NEND PO2.......321 N4
Tolbar Wy HEND SO30......250 A2
Tollerford Rd CFDH BH17....320 F2
Tollgate CHFD SO53........228 D9
Tollgate Cl DEAN RG23......67 N9
Tollgate Rd AND SP10.......102 C1
  HLER SO31.......270 D2
The Tollgate FHAM/PORC PO16..11 H3
Tollway CHIN RG24.......70 B1
Tolpuddle Gdns
  MOOR/WNTN BH9.......323 H3
Tolpuddle Wy YTLY GU46....40 G9
Tolstoi Rd PSTN BH14.......321 J6
Tomkyns Cl CHFD SO53.....206 B7
Tomlin Cl ITCH SO19.......25 P5
Tomlins Av FRIM GU16.......58 C3
Tomlins Cl TADY RG26.......54 C7
Tomlinscote Wy FRIM GU16..58 C3
Tommy Green Wk ELGH SO50..229 H1
Toms La RGWD BH24........261 L2
Tonbridge St SSEA PO5......316 E6
Tonge Rd BWD BH11.......322 B1
Tongham Mdw RFNM GU10...97 K6
Tongham Rd ALDT GU11.....97 K6
  RFNM GU10.......97 J3
Tonnant Cl FHAM/STUB PO14..294 B8
Toogoods Wy ROWN SO16...227 H7
Toomer Cl FAWY SO45.......291 H7
Toomers Wnf NWBY RG14 *..14 B2
Toothill Rd ROMY SO51.....158 E8
Topaz Dr AND SP10.......102 B2
Topaz Gv WVILLE PO7......276 A2
Topiary Gdns HLER SO31....271 H6
The Topiary CHIN RG24.....70 B4
  PSTN BH14.......75 M1
  PSTN BH14.......321 H7
Toplady Hl FNM GU9.......96 H6
Top La RGWD BH24.......282 E2
Torbay Rd PSTN BH14......321 L9
Torberry Dr EPSF GU31.....215 P3
Torbryan Cl CHIN RG24.....50 C8
Tor Cl FHAM/PORC PO16....273 J9
  PSTN BH14.......75 P7
Torcross Cl ITCH SO19......248 G9
Torfrida Ct ENEY PO4.......317 L5
Tormead FAWY SO45........268 A7
Torna Gv NBAD SO52.......205 H6
Toronto Pl GPORT PO12.....12 D1
Toronto Rd HSEA PO3......316 C1
Torquay Av GPORT PO12.....295 L9
  WSHM SO15.......247 P3
Torque Cl ITCH SO19........249 N7
Torridge Gdns WEND SO18..229 J3
Torrington Cl BOR GU35....154 D3
  ITCH SO19.......249 N7
Torrington Rd NEND PO2....296 G6
Tor Rd FNM GU9.......95 P9
Tortworth Cl
  FHAM/STUB PO14.......294 B1
Tor Wy EPSF GU31.......215 N2
Torwood Gdns ELGH SO50..229 P2
Tosson Cl ROWN SO16......247 J3
Totland Cl FARN GU14......57 P7
  ROWN SO16.......247 J3
Totland Rd CHAM PO6......296 G2
  LSOL/BMARY PO13.......314 G7
Totmel Rd CFDH BH17......321 J2
Totnes Cl ELGH SO50.......207 H8
Tottehale Cl NBAD SO52....227 K1
Tottenham Rd PSEA PO1....52 A1

Tottenham Rd PSEA PO1....316 G2
Tottenham Wk SHST GU47...41 L5
Totterdown THLE RG7.......27 H6
Totters La ODIM RG29.......72 E5
Totton By-Pass TOTT SO40..246 E5
Tournai Cl ALDT GU11.......76 D5
Tournerbury La HISD PO11...318 C4
Tourney Rd BWD BH11......301 M7
Tovey Cl AND SP10.......9 K2
Tovey Pl WINC SO23.......145 K8
Tower Cl AND SP10.......82 B8
  GPORT PO12.......315 H7
Tower Gdns HAV PO9.......298 F3
Tower Hl FARN GU14.......75 P1
Tower La ELGH SO50.......229 L2
Tower Pl HEND SO30.......249 M2
Tower Rd BMTH BH1........335 L1
  CCLF BH13.......334 B5
  GSHT GU26.......183 H5
  WINC SO23.......23 D3
Tower Rd West CCLF BH13...334 A5
Towers Dr CWTH RG45......41 J2
Tower St ALTN GU34.......132 E7
  EMRTH PO10.......299 N1
  PSEA PO1.......18 B6
  WINC SO23.......22 D4
Town Centre East Jct
  CHIN RG24.......69 P6
Town Cl NARL SO24.......169 N3
Towngate Br PLE BH15......332 E1
Towngate Ms RGWD BH24 *..282 E3
Town Hall Rd HAV PO9......15 G6
Townhill Wy WEND SO18....249 J3
Town La PSF GU32.......191 P9
Town Mill La WHCH RG28....85 M6
Town Mill Rd NWBY RG14....16 E2
Town Quay SHAM SO14......248 B9
Townsend Cl BDST RG21.....6 B7
  BWD BH11.......322 B1
Townsend La FBDG SP6.....195 N5
Townsville Rd
  MOOR/WNTN BH9.......323 H5
Towpath Md ENEY PO4......317 L4
Toynbee Cl ELGH SO50......229 J1
Toynbee Rd ELGH SO50.....229 J1
Tozer Cl BWD BH11.......321 P2
Trade St KSCL RG20.......29 L6
Trafalgar Cl CHFD SO53....206 D8
Trafalgar Ct
  FHAM/STUB PO14.......294 D2
  FNM GU9.......116 B1
Trafalgar Pl PSEA PO1......316 C2
Trafalgar Ri HORN PO8.......236 B7
Trafalgar Rd
  MOOR/WNTN BH9.......322 F8
  WSHM SO15.......247 N5
Trafalgar Sq GPORT PO12...315 M3
Trafalgar St WINC SO23.....22 D5
Trafalgar Wy CBLY GU15....57 N1
  FAWY SO45.......268 D9
Trafalgar Vls FARN GU14....57 K9
Trafford Rd FRIM GU16......58 D5
Trafford Wy ELGH SO50.....230 B3
Trajan Wk AND SP10 *.......82 F8
Trampers La WHAM PO17...275 L1
Tranby Rd SSEA PO5.......19 J7
Tranmere Cl LYMN SO41....329 N5
Tranmere Rd ENEY PO4.....317 K4
Transport Rd FARN GU14....76 A3
Travellers Cnr THLE RG7....35 M1
Travellers End FUFL SO22...164 E6
Travis La SHST GU47.......41 K7
Treadwheel Rd HORN PO8...256 C5
Treagore Rd TOTT SO40......246 A2
Trearnan Cl ROWN SO16....247 K3
Treble Cl FUFL SO22.......183 K2
Trebor Av FNM GU9.......116 C3
Tredegar Rd ENEY PO4......317 H5
Tredenham Cl FARN GU14...76 B4
Tree Av HASM GU27.......156 E5
Treebys Cl CHCH/BSGR BH23..325 N5
Treeside Av TOTT SO40......246 F4
Treeside Dr FNM GU9.......116 A3
Treeside Rd WSHM SO15....247 N3
Tree Side Wy WVILLE PO7...275 N1
Trefoil Cl HTWY RG27.......55 H6
  WVILLE PO7.......275 P3
Trefoil Wy
  CHCH/BSGR BH23.......325 N7
Tregaron Av CHAM PO6.....297 K2
Tregolls Dr FARN GU14......76 B1
Tregonwell Rd WCLF BH2...8 B3
Trellis Dr CHIN RG24.......70 B4
Teloar Rd HISD PO11.......319 L7
Treloyhan Cl CHFD SO53...206 F9
Tremayne Wk CBLY GU15...59 H9
Tremona Cl ROWN SO16....247 M2
Tremona Rd ROWN SO16....247 M1
Trenchard Rd RAND SP11...101 P3
Trenchmead Gdns CHIN RG24..69 L4
Trenley Cl FAWY SO45.......290 C6
Trent Cl FARN GU14.......57 J7
  WEND SO18.......249 H2
Trent Crs NTHA RG18.......25 L2
Trentham Av LTDN BH7......323 P7
Trentham Cl LTDN BH7......323 P7
Trentham Ct CHAM PO6.....296 E6
Trent Rd WEND SO18.......249 H2
Trent Wy BSTK RG21.......7 K6
  FERN BH22.......302 C2
  HEND SO30.......249 M1
Tresham Crs YTLY GU46.....40 B8
Tresillian Gdns WEND SO18..229 K9
Tresillian Wy
  CHCH/BSGR BH23.......326 D5
Trevis Rd ENEY PO4.......317 L4
Trevone Cl TOTT SO40......265 M3
Trevor Rd ENEY PO4.......316 G5
Trevose Cl CHFD SO53......206 B7
  LSOL/BMARY PO13.......294 G8
Trevose Crs CHFD SO53.....206 B7
Trevose Wy FHAM/STUB PO14..293 H9
Triangle La FHAM/STUB PO14..293 L6

The Triangle
  NMIL/BTOS BH25 *.......326 E8
  NWBY RG14.......16 E4
  RSAL SP5.......201 K1
  WCLF BH2.......8 B4
  WEND SO18 *.......248 G2
Tribe Rd GPORT PO12......12 B1
Tricketts La FERN BH22.....302 F2
Trigon Rd PLE BH15.......320 F5
Trimaran Cl HLER SO31......70 B7
Trimaran Rd HLER SO31.....270 E9
Trimmer's Cl FNM GU9......96 C4
Trimmer's Ct PSEA PO1.....18 B5
Trimmers Fld FNM GU9....116 E1
Trimm's Dro FBDG SP6.....221 J4
Trims Ct OVTN RG25.......91 N1
Trinidad Cl CHIN RG24......69 L3
Trinidad Crs BKME/WDN BH12..321 L4
Trinity Cl GPORT PO12.....13 H5
Trinity Flds FNM GU9......96 H5
Trinity Gdns FHAM/PORC PO16..11 F5
  WINC SO23.......23 H4
Trinity Gn GPORT PO12.....13 J3
Trinity Hl ALTN GU34......130 C9
  FNM GU9.......96 A5
Trinity Ri RAND SP11.......81 H8
Trinity Rd ALTN GU34......130 C8
  BMTH BH1.......9 G5
  SHAM SO14.......21 F2
Trinity St FHAM/PORC PO16..11 C5
Tristan Cl FAWY SO45......313 N1
Tristram Cl CHFD SO53.....206 A7
Trithan Cl FHAM PO15......272 B8
Triumph Rd FHAM/STUB PO14..294 D4
Troak Cl CHCH/BSGR BH23..325 J7
Trojan Wy WVILLE PO7.....275 P7
Troon Crs CHAM PO6.......275 L9
Troon Rd BDST RG21.......88 B2
Trosnant Rd HAV PO9......14 D5
Trotsford Meadow BLKW GU17..57 K1
Trotts Cl TOTT SO40.......246 C7
Trotwood Cl SHST GU47.....41 M4
Trout Rd HASM GU27.......156 D7
Trowbridge Cl ROWN SO16..227 J6
Trowe's La THLE RG7.......37 J4
Trueman Sq AND SP10.....82 G8
Truman Rd BWD BH11.....322 B1
Trunk Rd FARN GU14......57 K9
Truro Cl LSOL/BMARY PO13 *..314 G2
Truro Ri BH/HW/K RG22....89 M3
Truro Rd BDST RG21.......88 B2
Trurol Rd CHFD SO53.......206 B1
Truscott Av MOOR/WNTN BH9..322 G8
Trussell Cl FUFL SO22.......164 E4
Trussell Crs FUFL SO22......164 E4
Trust Cl HTWY RG27.......71 N5
Tryplets FLEETS GU52.......74 A9
Tubb's La KSCL RG20.......29 N8
Tuckers Cl CHAM PO6......297 K3
Tucks Cl CHCH/BSGR BH23..305 L7
Tuckton Cl SBNE BH6......336 B2
Tuckton Rd SBNE BH6......336 B2
Tudor Av BMTH PO10......277 L6
Tudor Cl FBDG SP6.......239 N6
  GSHT GU26.......156 C3
  HISD PO11.......318 F6
  TADY RG26.......51 M3
  TOTT SO40.......246 A3
Tudor Crs CHAM PO6.......297 H3
Tudor Dr YTLY GU46.......56 E1
Tudor Gdns HEND SO30.....250 A6
  RDST BH18.......309 D9
  NWBY RG14.......17 F5
Tudor Wy FLEETS GU52.....74 D8
  WINC SO23.......145 J8
Tudor Wood Cl ROWN SO16..228 B8
Tuffin Cl ROWN SO16......226 C7
Tukes Av LSOL/BMARY PO13..296 C6
Tulip Cl BH/HW/K RG22.....89 L4
Tulip Gdns HAV PO9.......276 C8
  HLER SO31.......270 F7
Tulls La BOR GU35.......154 E6
Tulip Rd ROWN SO16......228 E8
Tumbler La LIPH GU30......175 J2
Tumbledown Cl ITCH SO19..249 J1
Tumulus Cl ITCH SO19.....249 P7
Tunball La MARL SN8.......42 B6
Tunbridge Cres LIPH GU30...175 J3
Tunbridge La LIPH GU30....175 J4
Tunnel La CHAM PO6......75 M3
Tunstall Rd CHAM PO6......274 F9
  ITCH SO19.......249 N7
Tunworth Cl FLEETN GU51...56 B9
Tunworth Ct HAV PO9......277 H5
  TADY RG26.......34 D7
Tunworth Ms TADY RG26....54 C5
Tunworth Rd OVTN RG25....91 N1
Turbary Gdns TADY RG26....34 C5
Turbary Rd BKME/WDN BH12..321 M5
  FERN BH22.......302 F1
Turgis Rd FLEETN GU51.....56 B9
Turin Cl AND SP10.......82 F7
Turks La PSTN BH14.......333 J2
Turk's La THLE RG7.......35 N2
Turk St ALTN GU34.......132 F6
Turnberry Cl
  CHCH/BSGR BH23.......324 D9
Turnberry Dr BH/HW/K RG22..89 L6
Turner Av LSOL/BMARY PO13..295 J9
Turner Cl BSTK RG21.......69 P8
Turner Ct AND SP10.......4 B1
Turner Rd AND SP10.......41 L8
Turner Roadwingield St
  PSEA PO1.......316 F1
Turners Av FLEETN GU51.....56 B9
Turners Dr STHA RG19......25 P4
Turners Farm Crs LYMN SO41..328 F4
Turner's Green La HTWY RG27..55 P9

Turners Wy FLEETN GU51....74 A1
The Turnery STHA RG19.....25 M4
Turnfields STHA RG19.......25 N4
Turnilc Lt RAND SP11 *.....82 F4
Turnpike Cros CHIN RG25...87 H3
Turnpike Down WINC SO23..23 K4
Turnpike Rd NWBY RG14....24 G5
Turnpike Wy DEAN RG23....88 E1
  HEND SO30.......250 A5
Turnstone End YTLY GU46...40 C8
Turnstone Gdns ROWN SO16..227 M7
Turnworth Cl BDST RG18...320 E1
Turtle Cl FHAM/STUB PO14..293 P5
Tuscan Wk CHFD SO53......206 G4
Tuscany Wy WVILLE PO7....276 A2
  YTLY GU46.......56 D1
The Tussocks TOTT SO40....247 K9
Tutland Rd NBAD SO52.....205 K9
Tutor Cl HLER SO31.......269 P7
Tutts La ROMY SO51.......202 E8
Tweedale Rd
  MOOR/WNTN BH9.......323 J4
Tweed Cl CHFD SO53.......206 C6
  FARN GU14.......57 M7
Tweed La LYMN SO41.......309 K8
Tweedsmuir Cl BH/HW/K RG22..68 E8
Twelve Acre Crs FARN GU14..75 L1
Twemlow Av PSTN BH14....333 H1
Tweseldown Rd FLEETS GU52..74 E8
Twiggs End Cl HLER SO31...270 F6
Twiggs La TOTT SO40.......267 H4
Twinley La WHCH RG28.....86 A3
Twin Oaks Cl BDST BH18....320 C1
Twisell Thorne FLEETS GU52..74 B8
Twittens Wy HAV PO9......15 G6
Two Gate La OVTN RG25....87 H4
Two Rivers Wy NWBY RG14..24 G4
Twyford Av NEND PO2......296 F8
  WSHM SO15.......247 N2
Twyford Cl CHAR BH8......323 K5
  FLEETS GU52.......56 B8
Twyford Dr
  LSOL/BMARY PO13.......314 D2
Twyford La RFNM GU10.....116 B8
Twyford Rd ELGH SO50.....207 K7
Twyford Wy CFDH BH17....321 J2
Twynes Meadow HTWY RG27..72 C3
Twynham Av
  CHCH/BSGR BH23.......324 E9
Twynham Cl RSAL SP5.....199 K7
Twynham Rd SBNE BH6.....336 C2
Twynhams Hl BPWT SO32...252 E3
Twynhams NWBY RG14.....24 B8
Tyfield CHIN RG24.......69 H1
Tylers Cl LYMN SO41.......329 K2
The Tyleshades ROMY SO51..204 E1
Tylney La HTWY RG27.......71 L3
Tylney Vw HTWY RG27......71 P4
Tyrrston Meadow LIPH GU30..175 J1
Tyndalls GSHT GU26.......156 E1
Tyne Cl CHFD SO53.......206 C8
  FARN GU14.......57 M7
Tynedale Cl GPORT PO12...295 K9
  MOOR/WNTN BH9.......323 J3
Tyneham Av
  BKME/WDN BH12.......321 K4
Tyne Wy HEND SO30.......249 N1
  NTHA RG18.......25 L2
Tyrells Cl AND SP10.......5 G4
Tyrells La RGWD BH24......284 A5
Tyrrell Gdns CHAR BH8.....323 N5
Tyrrells Ct CHCH/BSGR BH23..305 M7
Tyrrell Rd CHFD SO53......206 C8
Tyseley Rd SSEA PO5.......19 H4
Tytherley Gn CHAR BH8....323 K5
Tytherley Rd RSAL SP5.....158 D1
  WEND SO18.......249 L3

U

Ubsdell Cl NMIL/BTOS BH25..327 J4
Uddens Dr WIMB BH21......299 M6
Ufton Br THLE RG7.......26 B1
Ufton La THLE RG7.......26 A1
Ullswater Av FARN GU14....75 M1
  WEND SO18.......249 K2
Ullswater Cl BOR GU35.....154 B3
  FNM GU9.......96 A5
  STHA RG19.......25 K4
Ullswater Ct ASHV GU12 *..76 E7
Ullswater Gv NARL SO24....168 A3
Ullswater Rd WEND SO18...247 J2
  WIMB BH21.......300 C8
Undercliff Dr BMTH BH1....9 G5
Undercliff Rd BOSC BH5....335 L3
Underdown Av WVILLE PO7..275 M8
Underhill La FNM GU9......116 A1
Undershore LYMN SO41....309 N6
Undershore Rd LYMN SO41..330 A3
Underwood Cl ASHV GU12...97 L2
Underwood Ct CFDH BH17..320 A3
  ROWN SO16.......228 A8
Underwood Rd ELGH SO50..207 M9
  HASM GU27.......156 E6
  ROWN SO16.......228 A8
Unicorn Rd
  LSOL/BMARY PO13.......314 B1
  PSEA PO1.......316 D2
Union Cl SHST GU47.......41 M4
Union La BPWT SO32.......233 L2
  KSCL RG20.......48 C2
Union Pl PSEA PO1.......19 K1
Union Ri LISS GU33.......174 A5
Union Rd FNM GU9.......96 C9
  HAV PO9.......15 H6
  HAV PO9.......14 C5
  SHAM SO14.......21 H1
Union St ALDT GU11.......3 E4
  AND SP10.......4 E4
  CHOB/PIR GU24.......59 M7
  FARN GU14.......57 P9

FHAM/PORC PO16 .... 11 K6
PSEA PO1 .... 18 D2
WINC SO23 .... 23 G4
University Crs SD/PW SO17.. 228 D9
University Pkwy ROWN SO16 .. 227 N5
University Rd SD/PW SO17.. 228 C9
Unwin Cl ITCH SO19 .... 268 F1
Upfallow CHIN RG24 .... 70 B5
Up Gn HTWY RG27 .... 40 A8
Upham St BPWT SO32 .... 209 J9
Uphill Rd FUFL SO22 .... 164 C2
Upland La LISS GU33 .... 172 F8
Uplands Av NMIL/BTOS BH25.. 327 J7
Uplands Cl FERN BH22 .... 280 C9
HASM GU27 .... 157 J5
SHST SU47 .... 41 J6
Uplands Crs FHAM/PORC PO16.. 11 G8
Uplands Gdns CHIN BH8.. 323 J5
Uplands La ALTN GU34 .... 150 B7
Uplands Rd CHAM PO6 .... 275 L9
CHAR BH8 .... 323 J5
FERN BH22 .... 280 C9
FNM GU9 .... 116 C2
FUFL SO22 .... 164 F4
HAV PO9 .... 257 J9
WVILLE PO7 .... 254 D5
Uplands Wy Cl CFDH BH17.. 321 J2
Uplyme Cl CFDH BH17 .... 321 J2
Upmill Cl HEND SO30 .... 229 K9
Upnor Cl RAND SO11 .... 79 M4
Upper Arundel St PSEA PO1 .. 19 H2
Upper Banister St
WSHM SO15 .... 248 B5
Upper Barn Copse ELGH SO50.. 208 B9
Upper Bere Wd WVILLE PO7 .. 275 P4
Upper Bourne La RFNM GU10.. 116 A5
Upper Bourne V RFNM GU10.. 116 A5
Upper Broadmoor Rd
CWTH RG45 .... 41 K1
Upper Brook Dr HLER SO31.. 270 E8
Upper Brook St WINC SO23 .. 22 E4
Upper Brownhill Rd
ROWN SO16 .... 227 K9
Upper Bugle St SHAM SO14.... 20 D6
Upper Chestnut Dr BSTK RG21.. 69 J9
Upper Chobham Rd CBLY GU15.. 58 F2
Upper Church La FNM GU9.. 96 B9
Upper Church Rd BPWT SO32.. 252 C4
Upper Common Rd
LYMN SO41 .... 328 F4
Upper Cornaway La
FHAM/PORC PO16 .... 295 M1
Upper Crabbick La
WVILLE PO7 .... 254 E6
Upper Crescent Rd
NBAD SO52 .... 205 K9
Upper Deacon Rd ITCH SO19.. 249 K5
Upper Dro AND SP10 .... 102 A2
Upper Elms Rd ALDT GU11 .... 2 D4
Upper Farm Rd DEAN RG23.. 88 E3
Upper Froyle Dr
FLEETN GU51 * 74 B1
Upper Golf Links Rd
BDST BH18 .... 300 D8
Upper Gordon Rd
CHCH/BSGR BH23 .... 326 C6
Upper Grove Rd FAWY SO45.. 291 M8
Upper Hale Rd FNM GU9 .... 96 B4
Upper Heyshott EPSF GU31.. 215 N2
Upper High St WINC SO23 .... 22 E5
Upper Hinton Rd BMTH BH1.. 8 E4
Upper House Ct WHAM PO17.. 252 D8
Upper Lamborough La
NARL SO24 .... 168 B9
Upper Lanham La NARL SO24.. 148 C1
Upper Market St ELGH SO50.. 229 K1
Upper Md STOK SO20 .... 121 H5
Upper Mead Cl ELGH SO50 .. 230 D2
Upper Moors Rd RWIN SO21.. 207 P5
Upper Mt HASM GU27 .... 157 L4
LISS GU33 .... 192 C3
Upper Mullin's La FAWY SO45.. 268 A7
Upper Neatham Mill La
ALTN GU34 .... 133 J3
Upper New Rd HEND SO30 .. 249 M2
Upper Northam Cl
HEND SO30 .... 250 A5
Upper Northam Dr
HEND SO30 .... 249 N5
Upper Northam Rd
HEND SO30 .... 250 B5
Upper Norwich Rd WCLF BH2.. 8 A4
Upper Old Pk La FNM GU9 .. 95 P6
Upper Old St
FHAM/STUB PO14 .... 293 P5
Upper Piece WVILLE PO7 .... 255 J8
Upper Pinewood Rd
ASHV GU12 .... 77 H9
Upper St Helens Rd
HEND SO30 .... 250 B7
Upper St Michael's Gv
FHAM/STUB PO14 .... 294 D1
Upper St Michael's Rd
ALDT GU11 * 3 F6
Upper School Dr HASM GU27.. 156 E8
Upper Shaftesbury Av
SD/PW SO17 .... 248 D1
Upper Shirley Av WSHM SO15.. 247 N2
Upper Soldridge Rd
ALTN GU34 .... 149 N6
Upper South Vw FNM GU9.. 96 C8
Upper Spinney HLER SO31 .. 292 C1
Upper St FLEETN GU51 .... 74 C3
Upper Terrace Rd FARN GU14.. 75 P4
WCLF BH2 .... 8 C4
Upper Toothill Rd ROMY SO51.. 187 G5
Upper Union Ter ALDT GU11 .. 2 D5
Upper Verran Rd CBLY GU15.. 58 C2
Upper Wardown EPSF GU31.. 215 P1
Upper Wy FNM GU9 .... 116 B2
Upper Weston La ITCH SO19.. 249 J9
Upper Weybourne La
FNM GU9 .... 96 D3
Upper Whf FHAM/PORC PO16.. 11 J7
Upper Wield Dr FLEETS GU52.. 74 B9
Uppleby Rd BKME/WDN BH12.. 321 L7

Upron Field Cl BH/HW/K RG22.. 89 M4
Up St OVTN RG25 .... 108 C1
Upton Cl FARN GU14 .... 76 C1
HAV PO9 .... 276 D5
Upton Crs BSTK RG21 .... 6 D1
ROWN SO16 .... 226 C5
Upton Grey Cl FUFL SO22 .. 164 E4
Upton Grey Rd ODIM RG29.. 92 E1
OVTN RG25 .... 92 D2
Upton La ROWN SO16 .... 226 F7
Upton Rd CFDH BH17 .... 320 B5
Upton Wy BDST BH18 .... 320 A9
Upwey Av PLE BH15 .... 320 A9
Urquhart Rd STHA RG19 .... 25 P6
Usborne Cl LSOL/BMARY PO13.. 314 D3
Utrecht Ct CHCH/BSGR BH23.. 325 H8
Uxbridge Cl HLER SO31 .... 270 F4

V

Vadne Gdns GPORT PO12 *.. 315 M2
Vaggs La LYMN SO41 .... 307 M9
Vale Cl RFNM GU10 .... 116 C6
Vale Dr WEND SO18 .... 249 H2
Vale Gv GPORT PO12 .... 315 L1
Valencia Cl CHCH/BSGR BH23.. 324 B5
Valencia Wy AND SP10 .... 96 E1
Valentine Av ITCH SO19 .... 249 L8
Valentine Cl FNM GU9 .... 116 A4
Valentine Ct WVILLE PO7 .. 276 A2
Valentine La FHAM PO15 .... 272 A7
Valerian Av FHAM PO15 .... 271 M7
Valerian Cl ELGH SO50 .... 230 C5
Valerian Rd HEND SO30 .... 250 C5
Vale Rd ASHV GU12 .... 76 F5
BMTH BH1 .... 335 K2
CBLY GU15 .... 57 P1
PSTN BH14 .... 321 N8
RSAL SP5 .... 199 P7
WINC SO23 .... 23 J7
The Vale DEAN RG23 .... 88 C2
FAWY SO45 .... 268 B7
HLER SO31 .... 271 H8
HORN PO8 .... 256 C2
SSEA PO5 .... 316 E6
Valetta Pk EMRTH PO10 .... 299 L1
Valette Rd MOOR/WNTN BH9.. 322 C4
Vale View Dr THLE RG7 .... 37 J1
Valeview Pk LYMN SO41 * .. 307 P9
Vale Wy WINC SO23 .... 145 J7
Vale Wood Dr RFNM GU10.. 116 C6
Vale Wood La GU26 .... 156 E1
Valewood Rd HASM GU27 .. 157 H9
Valiant Gdns NEND PO2 .... 296 F5
Valiant Wy CHCH/BSGR BH23.. 325 M8
FARN GU14 .... 75 L4
Valley Cl CHCH/BSGR BH23.. 324 C4
FAWY SO45 .... 290 C8
RSAL SP5 .... 199 P7
RWIN SO21 .... 207 P5
WVILLE PO7 .... 275 L7
Valleydene FAWY SO45 .... 268 B8
Valley Hi FUFL SO22 .... 164 D2
Valley La CHCH/BSGR BH23.. 306 A4
RFNM GU10 .... 116 C4
Valley Park CI CHCH/BSGR BH23.. 258 D9
SBNE BH6 .... 336 E6
Valley Rd CHAR BH8 .... 323 H4
CHFD SO53 .... 206 C6
FRIM GU16 .... 58 C5
FUFL SO22 .... 164 C2
NWBY RG14 .... 16 A7
THLE RG7 .... 27 J1
TOTT SO40 .... 246 D6
Valley Side LIPH GU30 .... 175 J3
The Valley FUFL SO22 .... 164 E9
Valley Vw
BKME/WDN BH12 .... 322 B8
SHST GU47 .... 41 H7
Valley Wy TADY RG26 .... 34 F5
Vallis Cl PLE BH15 .... 332 F2
Valmeade Cl HTWY RG27 .. 72 A3
Valsheda Dr
FHAM/STUB PO14 .... 293 P8
Vampire Wy FARN GU14 .... 75 K1
Vanburgh Gdns
BH/HW/K RG22 .... 89 M4
Vanburgh Wy CHFD SO53 .. 206 D4
Van Dyck Cl BSTK RG21 .... 69 P8
Vanguard Hi FUFL SO22 .. 164 D1
Vanguard Rd CHAR BH8 .... 323 L6
GPORT PO12 .... 295 N9
PLE BH15 .... 332 E1
WEND SO18 .... 249 J3
Vanners La KSCL RG20 .... 29 L1
Vanstone Rd
LSOL/BMARY PO13 .... 295 H9
Vantage Wy
BKME/WDN BH12 .... 321 K2
Vardy Cl ITCH SO19 .... 249 M8
Varna Rd BOR GU35 .... 154 B5
WSHM SO15 .... 247 N6
Varndell Rd HTWY RG27 .... 71 N3
Varney Cl FARN GU14 .... 57 M8
Varos Cl GPORT PO12 .... 315 L2
Vaudrey Cl WSHM SO15 .... 247 N2
Vaughan Cl ITCH SO19 .... 249 N6
Vaughan Rd FAWY SO45 .... 267 N6
Vaughans ALTN GU34 .... 132 C6
Vauxhall Wy PSF GU32 .... 215 L2
Veal's La TOTT SO40 .... 267 M3
Vear's La RWIN SO21 .... 208 A5
Vecta Cl CHCH/BSGR BH23.. 325 N9
Vectis Cl ALTN GU34 .... 150 C6
Vectis Rd GPORT PO12 .... 315 J3
NMIL/BTOS BH25 .... 326 F8
Vectis Wy CHAM PO6 .... 297 H2
Velder Av ENEY PO4 .... 317 J3
Veldene Av ENEY SO16 .... 246 C2
Velmead Cl FLEETS GU52 .. 74 E5
Velmead Rd FLEETS GU52 .. 74 D5
Velmore Rd CHFD SO53 .... 206 D9
Velsheda Ct FAWY SO45 .... 268 C5

Velvet Lawn Rd
NMIL/BTOS BH25 .... 327 H3
Venator PI WIMB BH21 .... 278 E8
Venerable Rd
FHAM/STUB PO14 .... 294 E4
Vengeance Rd
LSOL/BMARY PO13 .... 314 C1
Venice Cl WVILLE PO7 .... 276 A2
Venice Ct AND SP10 .... 82 C8
Venison Ter STOK SO20 * .. 140 A9
Venning Av AND SP10 .... 82 B8
Venning Av BH11 .... 301 N8
Ventnor Rd ENEY PO4 .... 316 C4
Ventor Gv AND SP10 .... 294 F6
Ventnor Ter ASHV GU12 .... 3 H5
Ventnor Wy
FHAM/PORC PO16 .... 273 J9
Ventry Cl BKME/WDN BH12.. 321 P8
Venture Ct HSEA PO3 .... 297 J4
Venture Rd ROWN SO16 .... 227 P3
Venture Sidings ENEY PO4 * 316 G4
Verbena Crs HORN PO8 .... 256 B7
Verbena Wy HEND SO30 .... 250 C5
Verdi Cl BH/HW/K RG22 .... 89 P7
Verdon Av HLER SO31 .... 269 N7
Verdun Wy AND SP10 .... 82 D8
Verger Cl FHAM/STUB PO14.. 271 J7
Verge Wk ALDT GU11 .... 96 C4
Verica Gdns TADY RG26 .... 34 F4
Verity Crs CFDH BH17 .... 321 H5
Verity Sq AND SP10 .... 81 N8
Vermont Cl ROWN SO16 .... 228 B8
Vernalls Cl NBNE BH10 .... 322 D1
Vernalls Ct NMIL/BTOS BH25.. 327 L2
Vernalls Gdns NBNE BH10 .. 322 D2
Verner Cl BOR GU35 .... 154 C2
Verne Rd VWD BH31 .... 258 C5
The Verne FLEETS GU52 .... 74 D7
Verney Cl BWD BH11 .... 322 B4
Verney Rd BWD BH11 .... 322 A4
Vernham Rd FUFL SO22 .... 164 E5
Vernon La CHCH/BSGR BH23.. 325 N5
Vernon Av ENEY PO4 .... 317 J4
Vernon Cl GPORT PO12 .... 12 B1
Vernon Hl BPWT SO32 .... 232 A2
Vernon Ms ENEY PO4 .... 317 J3
Vernon Rd GPORT PO12 .... 12 B1
HSEA PO3 .... 297 J7
Verona Av SBNE BH6 .... 336 B1
Verona Rd CHFD SO53 .... 206 C6
Veronica Cl BH/HW/K RG22.. 89 L4
Veronica Dr FLEETN GU51 .. 74 A7
Verran Rd CBLY GU15 .... 58 C2
Verulam Pl BMTH BH1 .... 8 D3
Verulam Rd PSTN BH14 .... 321 H8
SHAM SO14 .... 248 D4
Verwood Crs SBNE BH6 .... 336 E2
Verwood Rd HAV PO9 .... 277 H4
VWD BH31 .... 259 N9
WIMB BH21 .... 258 A5
Veryan FHAM/STUB PO14 .. 10 A6
Vesey Cl FARN GU14 .... 57 P8
Vespasian Gdns CHIN RG24.. 68 F4
Vespasian Rd AND SP10 .... 82 F7
WEND SO18 .... 248 F2
Vespasian Wy CHFD SO53.. 206 G7
Vesta Wy CHFD SO53 .... 206 G6
Vestry Cl AND SP10 .... 4 B4
Vetch Cl CHCH/BSGR BH23.. 325 M7
Vetch Flds HTWY RG27 .... 72 B3
Viables Cl BSTK RG21 .... 90 D2
Viables Rd BH/HW/K RG22.. 90 B2
Vian Cl LSOL/BMARY PO13.. 294 G5
Vian Rd WVILLE PO7 .... 275 M4
Vicarage Cl FNM GU9 .... 116 D5
Vicarage Dr HEND SO30 .... 250 B6
Vicarage Gdns FLEETS GU52.. 74 C8
GSHT GU26 .... 156 B2
LYMN SO41 .... 328 A5
Vicarage Hl ALTN GU34 .... 132 F6
SBNE BH6 .... 336 G2
Vicarage La ALTN GU34 .... 132 F6
AND SP10 .... 55 J8
BPWT SO32 .... 251 J3
FHAM/STUB PO14 .... 294 A6
FNM GU9 .... 116 D3
HTWY RG27 .... 72 D5
LYMN SO41 .... 328 A5
NARL SO24 .... 169 L3
TOTT SO40 .... 245 L2
WVILLE PO7 .... 234 F9
YTLY GU46 .... 41 K3
Vicarage Rd RSAL SP5 .... 199 P7
Vicarage Rd ALTN GU34 .... 132 E7
BLKW GU17 .... 57 M1
MOOR/WNTN BH9 .... 322 E6
PLE BH15 .... 320 E7
SSEA PO5 .... 18 E7
TOTT SO40 .... 267 K1
VWD BH31 .... 258 F3
YTLY GU46 .... 40 D7
Vicarage Wy
CHCH/BSGR BH23 .... 325 H5
Vice La LYND SO43 .... 224 A8
Viceroy Rd ITCH SO19 .... 249 J8
Vickers Cl CHAR BH8 .... 323 P5
Vickery Wy CHCH/BSGR BH23.. 325 M7
Victena Rd ELGH SO50 .... 230 C2
Victoria Av CBLY GU15 .... 49 M2
HISD PO11 * 318 F5
MOOR/WNTN BH9 .... 322 E6
PSEA PO1 .... 18 E7
WVILLE PO7 .... 275 K7
Victoria Cl ALDT GU11 .... 3 H4
ITCH SO19 .... 255 J4
Victoria Ct AND SP10 .... 4 C5
Victoria Dr BLKW GU17 .... 57 K1
Victoria Gdns FARN GU14 .. 57 K9
FBDG SP6 .... 240 B2
FERN BH22 .... 280 C2
FLEETS GU51 * 74 C3
NWBY RG14 .... 16 E3
RWIN SO21 .... 133 P2
Victoria Gld HLER SO31 .... 269 L5
Victoria Gv NWBY RG14 .... 17 G4

SSEA PO5 .... 19 K7
Victoria Hill Rd FLEETN GU51.. 74 B3
Victoria Ms FLEETS GU51 *.. 74 B3
LYMN SO41 * 329 M3
Victoria Pde FLEETN GU51 *.. 74 C3
WHAM PO17 .... 272 C3
Victoria Park Rd
MOOR/WNTN BH9 .... 322 E6
Victoria Pl BH/HW/K RG22 *.. 68 E8
CHAR BH8 .... 335 J1
GPORT PO12 * 12 D3
LYMN SO41 .... 329 L5
RAND SP11 * 62 B5
ROMY SO51 .... 204 C6
WIMB BH21 .... 278 D9
Victoria Rd ALDT GU11 .... 2 E3
ALTN GU34 .... 132 F5
BKME/WDN BH12 .... 321 L5
BMTH BH1 .... 335 J1
BPWT SO32 .... 231 P4
CHCH/BSGR BH23 .... 337 J1
ELGH SO50 .... 207 K8
EMRTH PO10 .... 277 L9
FARN GU14 .... 58 A9
FBDG SP6 .... 240 B2
FERN BH22 .... 302 D2
FLEETN GU51 * 74 B3
FNM GU9 .... 96 D6
HISD PO11 .... 298 F7
HLER SO31 .... 269 J4
ITCH SO19 .... 268 E1
LYMN SO41 .... 338 F2
PSEA PO1 .... 316 B2
SHST GU47 .... 41 K6
THLE RG7 .... 27 H9
WIMB BH21 .... 278 C9
WINC SO23 .... 22 D2
WVILLE PO7 .... 275 N3
Victoria Rd East ALTN GU34.. 132 C5
Victoria Rd North SSEA PO5.. 19 K5
Victoria Sq LSOL/BMARY PO13.. 314 C2
Victoria St BSTK RG21 .... 6 E7
GPORT PO12 .... 12 E1
PSEA PO1 .... 316 E1
SHAM SO14 .... 21 J3
Victoria Ter CHAM PO6 *.. 297 H2
Victor Rd ALDT GU11 .... 75 L5
CHFD SO53 .... 206 B7
ITCH SO19 .... 247 N5
WIMB BH21 .... 278 C9
Victory Av ROWN SO16 .... 226 A5
Victory Cl CHFD SO53 .... 206 D8
WIMB BH21 .... 281 H5
Victory Ct FAWY SO45 .... 268 D8
Victory Cr AND SP10 * 4 C5
Victory Rd FHAM/STUB PO14.. 294 B7
NEND PO2 .... 296 F7
WSHM SO15 .... 247 M5
Victory Rbt BSTK RG21 .... 6 D5
Victory Sq WSHM SO15 .... 247 M5
Vigo La YTLY GU46 .... 56 D2
Vigo Rd AND SP10 .... 5 F3
Viking Cl FAWY SO45 .... 291 H9
FHAM/STUB PO14 .... 293 P6
ROWN SO16 .... 226 B2
SBNE BH6 .... 336 E2
The Vikings ROMY SO51 .... 204 F6
Viking Wy AND SP10 .... 82 F7
CHCH/BSGR BH23 .... 337 L1
HORN PO8 .... 236 C9
SBNE BH6 .... 336 E2
Villeneuve St George's Wy
ELGH SO50 .... 228 G1
Villa Gdns WVILLE PO7 .... 275 N2
Village Cl FHAM/STUB PO14.. 294 A7
Village Rd GPORT PO12 .... 315 K6
Village St ALTN GU34 .... 111 J7
PSF GU32 .... 191 P8
STOK SO20 .... 123 L5
The Village EWKG RG40 .... 39 P3
RSAL SP5 .... 159 H7
Village Wy YTLY GU46 .... 40 E7
Ville De Paris Rd
FHAM/STUB PO14 .... 294 E4
Villette Cl CHCH/BSGR BH23.. 324 E6
Villiers Rd FAWY SO45 .... 290 B1
SSEA PO5 .... 316 E6
Vimoutiers Ct FBDG SP6 .. 240 C2
Vince Cl BWD BH11 .... 322 B2
Vincent Av ROWN SO16 .... 247 N1
Vincent Cl NMIL/BTOS BH25.. 327 J5
Vincent Gv FHAM/PORC PO16.. 295 N2
Vincent Rd NMIL/BTOS BH25.. 327 H4
NTHA RG18 .... 25 P3
WSHM SO15 .... 247 N5
Vincent's Gv WSHM SO15 .. 247 N5
Vincents Wk SHAM SO14 .. 20 E4
Vindomis Cl ALTN GU34 .... 133 K2
Vine Cl ALDT GU11 .... 3 G8
HLER SO31 .... 75 P6
LTDN BH7 .... 323 N8
RFNM GU10 .... 116 A6
Vine Coppice WVILLE PO7.. 275 N6
Vine Farm Cl
BKME/WDN BH12 .... 322 C7
Vine Farm Rd
BKME/WDN BH12 .... 322 C7
Vinegar Hl LYMN SO41 .... 338 C1
Vine Rd BMTH BH1 .... 278 A9
Vine House Cl FHAM/STUB PO14.. 10 A5
Vineries Cl WIMB BH21 .... 279 H8
The Vineries WIMB BH21 .... 279 H8
Vine Rd ROWN SO16 .... 227 L9
Vinery Gdns ROWN SO16 .. 247 N1
Vineside ELGH SO50 .... 206 A8
Vine St RFNM GU10 .... 116 A5
Vine Tree Cl TADY RG26 .... 34 E7
Vineyard Cl ITCH SO19 .... 248 A5
Vineyard Cl ITCH SO19 .... 268 B1

The Vineyards NBAD SO52.. 205 L9
Viney Av ROMY SO51 .... 204 F5
Viney Rd LYMN SO41 .... 329 L6
Vinnells La PSF GU32 .... 188 F7
Vinneys Cl CHCH/BSGR BH23.. 324 C5
Vinns La OVTN RG25 .... 86 F4
Vinson Rd LISS GU33 .... 192 C2
Violet Av FHAM/STUB PO14.. 293 P7
Violet Cl BH/HW/K RG22 .... 89 L4
CHFD SO53 .... 206 C7
Violet Gv NTHA RG18 .... 25 P2
Violet La NMIL/BTOS BH25.. 327 J9
TADY RG26 .... 33 M8
Violet Rd ROWN SO16 .... 228 C8
Virginia Cl BKME/WDN BH12.. 321 L5
VWD BH31 .... 259 J6
Virginia Gdns FARN GU14 .. 76 B2
Viscount Cl ASHV GU12 .... 76 F5
Viscount Dr CHCH/BSGR BH23.. 325 M9
Viscount Wk BWD BH11 .... 301 L8
Vita Rd NEND PO2 .... 296 C6
Vitre Gdns LYMN SO41 .... 329 L5
Vivaldi Cl BH/HW/K RG22 .. 90 A4
Vivian Cl FLEETS GU52 .... 74 E6
Vivian Rd BSTK RG21 .... 7 H1
Vixen Cl FHAM/STUB PO14.. 293 P7
Vixen Dr ASHV GU12 .... 76 D9
Vixen Wk NMIL/BTOS BH25.. 327 K2
Vockins Cl TDWTH SP9 .... 78 C3
Vokes Cl ITCH SO19 .... 249 K6
Vulcan Cl WSHM SO15 .... 247 K5
Vulcan Rd WSHM SO15 .... 247 K5
Vyne Cl ALTN GU34 .... 132 F5
Vyne Meadow CHIN RG24 .. 51 J9
Vyne Rd BSTK RG21 .... 6 E3
CHIN RG24 .... 51 J9
Vyse La SHAM SO14 * 20 D7

W

Wade Court Rd HAV PO9 .. 15 H7
Wade La HAV PO9 .... 298 C2
Wade Rd CHIN RG24 .... 69 P4
Wadham SHST GU47 .... 41 N5
Wadham Rd NEND PO2 .... 296 F7
Wadhurst Gdns ITCH SO19.. 268 A2
Wadhurst Rd HEND SO30.. 250 C5
Wadmore Cl CHAR BH8 .. 324 A5
Wadwick Bottom RAND SP11.. 63 J9
Waggoners Wy GSHT GU26.. 155 P4
Waggoners Wells Rd
GSHT GU26 .... 155 P6
Wagner Cl BH/HW/K RG22.. 90 A3
Wagon La HTWY RG27 .... 72 A2
Wagtail Cl NMIL/BTOS BH25.. 327 H5
Wagtail Dr NMIL/BTOS BH25.. 327 H5
Wagtail Wy FHAM/PORC PO16.. 295 K1
Wainscott Rd ENEY PO4 .... 317 J6
Wainsford Cl LYMN SO41 *.. 328 E7
Wainsford Plantation
LYMN SO41 .... 328 E7
Wainsford Rd LYMN SO41 .. 328 E5
Wainwright Cl CHAM PO6 .. 297 L3
Wait End Rd WVILLE PO7 .. 275 N4
Wakefield Av
FHAM/PORC PO16 .... 10 D1
NBNE BH10 .... 322 E2
Wakefield Ct WEND SO18 .. 249 J2
Wakefield Rd WEND SO18 .. 249 J2
Wakeford Cl TADY RG26 .... 34 E5
Wakeford Ct TADY RG26 .... 34 E5
Wakeford Pl HLER SO31 .... 270 E9
Wakefords Copse FLEETS GU52.. 74 E9
Wakefords Cnr FLEETS GU52 *.. 74 E8
Wakefords Pk FLEETS GU52.. 74 E9
Wakefords Wy HAV PO9 .. 277 H5
Wakely Gdns BWD BH11 .. 322 A2
Wakely Rd BWD BH11 .... 322 B2
Walberton Av CHAM PO6 .. 297 J1
Walburton Wy HORN PO8.. 236 D8
Walcote Av CFDH BH17 .... 320 E2
Waldegrave Cl ITCH SO19.. 268 F1
Waldegrave Pl NWBY RG14 *.. 16 E2
Walden Cots BDGW GU9 .. 77 M9
Walden Gdns HORN PO8 .. 255 N2
Walden Rd NEND PO2 .... 296 F7
Waldtch Gdns CFDH BH17.. 320 E2
Waldon Gdns WEND SO18.. 249 K1
Waldorf Hts BLKW GU17 .. 57 K2
Waldren Cl PLE BH15 .... 332 F1
Waleron Rd FLEETN GU51.. 56 C9
Wales St WINC SO23 .... 23 G4
Walford Av NTHA RG18 .... 25 P3
Walford Cl WIMB BH21 .... 278 E8
Walford Gdns WIMB BH21.. 278 D8
Walford Rd CHAM PO6 .... 296 E1
Walhampton Hl LYMN SO41.. 329 M2
Walker Pl HLER SO31 .... 269 P8
LSOL/BMARY PO13 .... 295 H8
Walker Rd NEND PO2 .... 296 F7
Walkers La North FAWY SO45.. 291 H8
Walkers La South FAWY SO45.. 313 H1
Walker's La FAWY SO45 .... 311 J8
Walkford
CHCH/BSGR BH23 .... 326 E5
Walkford Wy
CHCH/BSGR BH23 .... 326 D6
Walking Field La PLE BH15.. 332 F1
The Walk FUFL SO22 * 183 N1
Walkwood Av LTDN BH7 .. 323 P7
Wallace La BROC SO42 .... 348 C2
Wallington Gdns GU11 .... 3 G1
Wallisdean Av FARN GU14 .. 57 K9
ITCH SO19 .... 269 H1
NEND PO2 .... 297 H9
Wallis Av ALDT GU11 .... 2 A1
Walldown Rd BOR GU35 .. 158 D3
The Walled Gdns ODIM RG29 *.. 92 G8
Walled Meadow AND SP10 .. 5 H4
Waller Rd NWBY RG14 .... 25 H2

Wallington Ct
FHAM/STUB PO14 294 D3
Wallington Dr CHFD SO53 206 C5
Wallington Hl
FHAM/PORC PO16 11 J4
Wallington Orch
FHAM/PORC PO16 * 273 H7
Wallington Rd NEND PO2 297 H8
Wallington Shore Rd
FHAM/PORC PO16 11 K4
Wallington Wy
FHAM/PORC PO16 11 J4
Wallins Copse CHIN RG24 70 A2
Walliscott Rd BWD BH11 322 A6
Wallisdean Av
FHAM/STUB PO14 294 D1
HSEA PO3 317 K1
Wallisdown Rd
BKME/WDN BH12 321 M2
Wallis Dr TADY RG26 52 C3
Wallis Gdns WVILLE PO7 275 N1
Wallis Rd BSTK RG21 69 L9
NBNE BH10 322 B6
WVILLE PO7 275 N1
Wall La THLE RG7 35 K4
Wallop Dr BH/HW/K RG22 89 L5
Wallop Dro STOK SO20 139 L4
Wallop Rd STOK SO20 120 A5
Walmer Cl CWTH RG45 41 K1
ELGH SO50 207 J6
FRIM GU16 58 E6
Walmer Rd PSEA PO1 316 G3
Walnut Av WEND SO18 228 G7
Walnut Cl ALDT GU11 2 E7
ALTN GU34 132 F4
CHFD SO53 206 E3
NMIL/BTOS BH25 327 H4
ROWN SO16 247 K2
YTLY GU46 56 E1
Walnut Dr FHAM/STUB PO14 293 P7
Walnut Gv FUFL SO22 164 E6
ROWN SO16 247 K3
The Walnuts FLEETS GU52 74 A7
Walnut Tree Cl HISD PO11 318 F5
RWIN SO21 144 E4
Walnut Tree Rd AND SP10 4 A6
Walnut Wy BSTK RG21 7 G1
Walnwright Gdns HEND SO30 230 C9
Walpole Gdns HTWY RG27 55 J7
Walpole La HLER SO31 270 E3
Walpole Rd BMTH BH1 335 K1
FUFL SO22 183 L1
GPORT PO12 13 F2
Walrus Rd FARN GU14 75 L4
Walsall Rd HSEA PO3 317 J2
Walsford Rd WBNE BH4 334 C1
Walsingham Cl CHAM PO6 * 274 F9
Walsingham Dene LTDN BH7 323 M7
Walsingham Gdns
WEND SO18 228 G9
Waltham Cl BPWT SO32 233 L2
FHAM/PORC PO16 273 N8
SHST GU47 41 L5
Waltham Ct OVTN RG25 87 H3
Waltham Crs ROWN SO16 227 N8
Waltham La OVTN RG25 87 K6
Waltham Rd LTDN BH7 323 P8
OVTN RG25 87 H4
Waltham St SSEA PO5 19 F4
Walton Cl BH/HW/K RG22 90 A2
FLEETN GU51 74 C4
GPORT PO12 12 B3
WVILLE PO7 275 N5
Walton Ct FHAM PO15 272 B6
Walton Pl FUFL SO22 183 M1
Walton Rd CHAM PO6 297 K4
GPORT PO12 12 B3
ITCH SO19 249 M7
NBNE BH10 322 C5
PLE BH15 321 J6
Waltons Av FAWY SO45 290 F5
Walton Wy NWBY RG14 24 F3
Walworth Rd AND SP10 5 J1
RAND SP11 83 K9
Walworth Rbt AND SP10 5 J1
Wandesford Pl GPORT PO12 295 L8
Wandle Cl ASHV GU12 97 N2
Wandsdyke Cl FRIM GU16 58 E5
Wangfield La BPWT SO32 251 J2
Wansbeck Cl CHFD SO53 206 D8
Wansey Gdns NWBY RG14 24 G2
Wanstead Cl RGWD BH24 260 F9
Wantage Rd SHST GU47 41 L6
Wapiti Wy FARN GU14 75 L4
Warbler Cl HORN PO8 256 A4
ROWN SO16 227 M6
Warbleton Rd CHIN RG24 70 B1
Warblington Av HAV PO9 277 H9
Warblington Cl CHFD SO53 228 D1
TADY RG26 34 D7
Warblington Rd EMRTH PO10 299 L2
Warblington St PSEA PO1 18 D5
Warborne La LYMN SO41 309 M8
Warbrook Ct HAV PO9 277 H5
Warbrook La HTWY RG27 39 K6
Warburton Cl ITCH SO19 249 N7
Warburton Rd CFDH BH17 320 G4
ITCH SO19 249 M6
Ward Cl AND SP10 82 E9
Ward Crs EMRTH PO10 277 N7
Warden Cl HEND SO30 249 M2
Wardens Cl HISD PO11 318 F3
Wardle Rd ELGH SO50 207 M6
Ward Rd ENEY PO4 317 J6
Wardroom Rd NEND PO2 296 D8
Warehouse Rd STHA RG19 31 L1
Warfield Av WVILLE PO7 275 N3
Warfield Crs WVILLE PO7 275 N3
Wargrove Dr SHST GU47 41 L6
Warland Wy WIMB BH21 300 A6
Warlock Cl ITCH SO19 249 M8
Warmwell Cl CFDH BH17 321 H2
Warner Cl CHIN RG24 69 L2
Warner Ct AND SP10 4 B4
Warner Ms HEND SO30 250 G4
Warnes La RGWD BH24 284 B7
Warnford Cl GPORT PO12 12 A3
Warnford Crs HAV PO9 276 D5
Warnford Rd BPWT SO32 233 N1
LTDN BH7 323 P8
Warren Av CHCH/BSGR BH23 337 K1
CHFD SO53 206 G8
ENEY PO4 317 K3
ROWN SO16 247 L1
Warren Cl BOR GU35 153 M6
CHFD SO53 206 G8
FLEETS GU52 74 E5
HISD PO11 318 C4
HTWY RG27 55 J8
RGWD BH24 282 B4
ROWN SO16 247 L1
SHST GU47 41 H6
THLE RG7 27 J5
Warren Cnr RFNM GU10 95 L4
Warren Crs ROWN SO16 247 L1
Warren Dr RAND SP11 101 M7
RGWD BH24 282 B4
Warren Edge Cl SBNE BH6 336 D3
Warren Edge Rd SBNE BH6 336 D3
Warren La BROC SO42 311 P8
EWKG RG40 39 P1
PSF GU32 191 J1
RGWD BH24 282 B4
RWIN SO21 185 L6
Warren Pk LYMN SO41 328 A9
Warren Pl TOTT SO40 246 A1
Warren Ri FRIM GU16 58 D2
Warren Rd LISS GU33 173 M8
NWBY RG14 24 A9
PSTN BH14 321 M8
WBNE BH4 334 B4
WINC SO23 23 K3
Warrens La RSAL SP5 199 J1
The Warren ALDT GU11 2 C4
FAWY SO45 290 D4
FNM GU9 96 E3
TADY RG26 34 B6
Warren Wk FERN BH22 302 B1
Warrington Ms ALDT GU11 96 E3
Warrior Cl CHFD SO53 206 D9
Warrys Cl FAWY SO45 290 C1
Warsash Cl HAV PO9 276 E4
Warsash Gv
LSOL/BMARY PO13 294 F7
Warsash Rd HLER SO31 270 C9
Warspite Cl NEND PO2 296 F5
Warton Cl BROC SO42 310 G2
Warton Rd BSTK RG21 7 G3
Warwick Av NMIL/BTOS BH25 327 K4
Warwick Cl ALDT GU11 3 H7
CBLY GU15 58 G2
CHFD SO53 206 C9
LSOL/BMARY PO13 314 E4
Warwick Crs SSEA PO5 19 H5
Warwick Dr NWBY RG14 17 H6
Warwick Pl ROMY SO51 224 E1
Warwick Rd ASHV GU12 76 E3
DEAN RG23 68 F6
FARN GU14 75 L4
LTDN BH7 335 N1
PSTN BH14 321 L9
TOTT SO40 246 D3
WSHM SO15 247 P1
Warwick Wy WHAM PO17 * 252 E7
Wasdale Cl HORN PO8 256 C1
SHST GU47 41 L4
Wash Brook HTWY RG27 71 P2
Washbrook Rd CHAM PO6 296 F1
Washford La BOR GU35 154 C4
Washington Av BMTH BH1 323 K9
Washington Rd EMRTH PO10 277 M9
NEND PO2 296 F9
Wash Water KSCL RG20 30 A3
Watchetts Dr CBLY GU15 58 B3
Watchetts Lake Cl CBLY GU15 58 C2
Watchetts Rd CBLY GU15 58 A2
Watchmoor Point CBLY GU15 * 58 A1
Watchmoor Rd CBLY GU15 57 P2
Watcombe Rd SBNE BH6 336 B1
Waterbeech Dr HEND SO30 250 C3
Waterberry Dr WVILLE PO7 275 L1
Waterbrook Rd ALTN GU34 133 H5
Watercress Meadow
NARL SO24 167 N3
Waterditch Rd
CHCH/BSGR BH23 325 K4
Water End La CHIN RG24 70 G5
Waterford Cl LYMN SO41 329 M4
PSTN BH14 333 J1
Waterford Gdns
CHCH/BSGR BH23 326 C8
Waterford La LYMN SO41 329 M4
Waterford Pl
CHCH/BSGR BH23 326 C8
Waterford Rd
CHCH/BSGR BH23 326 D7
Waterhouse Cl RWIN SO21 184 A7
Waterhouse La WSHM SO15 247 M5
Waterhouse Md SHST GU47 41 L7
Waterhouse Wy WSHM SO15 247 M4
Wateridge Rd BSTK RG21 69 M4
Water La FARN GU14 57 P6
FAWY SO45 268 A8
FNM GU9 96 F7
NARL SO24 168 F3
RAND SP11 102 D6
SBNE BH6 324 B8
STHA RG19 24 F7
TOTT SO40 246 B3
WINC SO23 23 G4
Waterlily Cl BSTK RG21 7 K6
Waterlock Gdns ENEY PO4 317 M4
Waterloo Av DEAN RG23 68 F5
Waterloo Cl HORN PO8 255 M8
Waterloo Ct AND SP10 4 D5
Waterloo Pl CWTH RG45 * 41 J2
Waterloo Rd ASHV GU12 3 H5
CFDH BH17 320 E4
CWTH RG45 41 H2
GPORT PO12 315 N7
HAV PO9 15 G4
LYMN SO41 329 M3
MOOR/WNTN BH9 322 F8
WSHM SO15 247 P5
Waterloo St SSEA PO5 19 G4
Waterloo Ter WSHM SO15 20 D1
Waterloo Wy RGWD BH24 282 E3
Watermain Rd
CHCH/BSGR BH23 303 N3
Waterman Cl BOR GU35 154 C6
Watermans La FAWY SO45 268 A9
The Watermeadows
AND SP10 102 D5
Watermead Rd CHAM PO6 297 N2
Watermill Rd
CHCH/BSGR BH23 324 E7
Watermills Cl AND SP10 102 D4
Water Rede FLEETS GU52 74 B9
Water Ridges DEAN RG23 88 F3
Water's Edge HEND SO30 250 B5
Waters Edge Gdns
EMRTH PO10 299 M1
Watersedge Rd CHAM PO6 296 C1
Waters Gn BROC SO42 286 G7
Waters Green Ct BROC SO42 286 G7
Watership Dr RGWD BH24 283 H3
Waterside CHCH/BSGR BH23 337 K2
Waterside Cl BOR GU35 154 B4
RGWD BH24 260 F9
Waterside Ct ALTN GU34 132 G5
FLEETN GU51 74 E1
Waterside Gdns
FHAM/PORC PO16 273 H8
Waterside La
FHAM/PORC PO16 296 A3
Waterside Ms FLEETN GU51 74 E1
Waterside Rd ROMY SO51 204 E4
Waterside Sq FAWY SO45 268 B5
Watersmeet
FHAM/PORC PO16 294 F3
The Waters WHAM PO17 272 C5
Waterston Cl CFDH BH17 320 F3
Watertower Wy CHIN RG24 68 G4
Water Tower Rd BDST BH18 300 E9
Water Wy BSTK RG21 7 K6
Waterworks Rd CHAM PO6 297 M1
PSF GU32 191 N8
RWIN SO21 207 L1
Watery La AND SP10 5 F1
CHCH/BSGR BH23 325 L6
FLEETS GU52 74 B9
KSCL RG20 28 G1
Watkin Rd BOSC BH5 335 M2
HEND SO30 250 D1
Watland Cl WVILLE PO7 275 N4
Watley Cl ROWN SO16 227 H7
Watley La RWIN SO21 163 N3
RWIN SO21 208 D2
Watling End BH/HW/K RG22 89 M4
Watson Acre AND SP10 102 C2
Watson Wk TOTT SO40 246 A4
Watson Wy DEAN RG23 68 G5
Watt Cl AND SP10 102 A1
Watton Cl CHAR BH8 323 N5
Watton La BPWT SO32 233 P2
Watton Rd FAWY SO45 290 E5
Wattons La RGWD BH24 304 A2
Watts Cl ROWN SO16 247 J1
Watts Common Rd ALDT GU11 75 M5
Watts Rd FARN GU14 57 N8
HEND SO30 250 C4
PSEA PO1 316 F1
Wavecrest Cl TOTT SO40 247 K8
Wavell Av CFDH BH17 320 C3
Wavell Cl BH/HW/K RG22 90 A1
Wavell Rd BWD BH11 322 B3
LSOL/BMARY PO13 295 H6
TDWTH SP9 78 F3
WEND SO18 249 J4
Wavell Wy FUFL SO22 183 L1
Wavendon Av
NMIL/BTOS BH25 326 G7
Waveney Cl
LSOL/BMARY PO13 314 D2
Waveney Gn ROWN SO16 247 J2
Waverley Av BSTK RG21 90 C1
FLEETN GU51 74 C1
HLER SO31 269 L4
Waverley Cl CBLY GU15 58 E1
FBDG SP6 220 D9
FNM GU9 * 96 D9
ODIM RG29 72 E9
ROMY SO51 204 F4
Waverley Ct HLER SO31 269 L5
Waverley Crs PLE BH15 320 F7
Waverley Dr ASHV GU12 76 F6
RWIN SO21 144 F4
Waverley Gdns ASHV GU12 76 F6
Waverley Gv ENEY PO4 316 G6
Waverley La FNM GU9 116 E1
Waverley Rd CHAM PO6 297 L1
FARN GU14 76 C1
FBDG SP6 220 D9
NMIL/BTOS BH25 327 K5
SSEA PO5 316 G6
WSHM SO15 247 P6
The Waverleys NTHA RG18 25 N3
Wayfarer Cl ENEY PO4 * 317 L3
HLER SO31 270 F9
Wayfarers LSOL/BMARY PO13 315 H1
Wayfarer's Wk BPWT SO32 233 K3
DEAN RG23 88 C5
EMRTH PO10 299 L2
HAV PO9 14 A4
HUNG RG17 28 C7
NARL SO24 186 G8
OVTN RG25 66 C2
OVTN RG25 88 A2
OVTN RG25 108 G7
WHCH RG28 64 E1
WVILLE PO7 254 G4
WVILLE PO7 275 H4
Wayground Rd WIMB BH21 300 A4
Waylands Pl HEND SO30 250 B7
Wayman Rd FARN GU14 57 M5
WIMB BH21 300 A7
Wayne Rd BKME/WDN BH12 321 K6
Waynflete Cl BPWT SO32 232 A4
Waynflete La FNM GU9 95 P9
Waynflete Pl FUFL SO22 164 E9
Ways End CBLY GU15 58 D1
Wayside HLER SO31 270 D2
Wayside Cl LYMN SO41 338 G1
Wayside Rd DEAN RG23 68 E7
RGWD BH24 281 L8
SBNE BH6 336 C2
Wayte St CHAM PO6 297 H2
Waytown Cl CFDH BH17 320 F3
Weald Cl HLER SO31 270 G6
Weale Ct BSTK RG21 6 E3
Weardale Rd CHFD SO53 206 F9
Weatherby Gdns HTWY RG27 55 J7
Weathermore La ALTN GU34 150 E6
Weaver Moss SHST GU47 41 J7
Weavers Cl AND SP10 4 E3
FERN BH22 280 E8
Weavers Down LIPH GU30 * 174 E4
Weavers Gdns FNM GU9 115 P3
Weavers Gn HAV PO9 277 J7
Weavers La STOK SO20 120 G4
Weavers Piece HTWY RG27 * 53 M8
Weavers Pl CHFD SO53 206 D5
Weavers Wk NWBY RG14 * 16 E1
Weavills Rd ELGH SO50 230 A2
Webb Cl CHIN RG24 69 P2
HISD PO11 318 G6
Webb La HISD PO11 318 G6
Webb Rd FHAM/PORC PO16 295 P3
Webbs Cl RGWD BH24 281 K3
Webbs Farm Cl WHCH RG28 85 L8
Webbs Gn BPWT SO32 233 M9
Webburn Gdns WEND SO18 229 J9
Webster Rd FUFL SO22 164 C6
MOOR/WNTN BH9 322 G4
Wedderburn Av
BH/HW/K RG22 89 M6
Wedgewood Cl FAWY SO45 290 E5
Wedgewood Gdns
CHCH/BSGR BH23 305 N7
Wedgewood Wy HORN PO8 255 N8
Wedgwood Dr PSTN BH14 333 J1
Wedman's La HTWY RG27 53 N6
Wedmore Cl FUFL SO22 183 J3
Weeke Cl RSAL SP5 199 H6
Weeke Manor Cl FUFL SO22 164 E5
Weevil La GPORT PO12 315 P3
Weir Av FARN GU14 75 P1
Weir Cl FARN GU14 75 P1
Weir Rd FLEETN GU51 75 H2
HTWY RG27 54 G9
The Weirs WINC SO23 23 G6
The Weir WHCH RG28 85 L8
Welbeck Av SD/PW SO17 248 D1
Welbeck Cl FARN GU14 57 N9
Welch Rd ENEY PO4 316 G6
GPORT PO12 315 L1
Welch Wy ROWN SO16 227 J7
Welchwood Cl HORN PO8 255 P5
Weldon Av BWD BH11 301 N8
Weldon Cl FLEETS GU52 74 E7
Welland Gdns WEND SO18 249 K1
Welland Gn ROWN SO16 247 J3
Welland Rd WIMB BH21 300 F1
Wellands Rd LYND SO43 264 G5
Wella Rd BH/HW/K RG22 90 B1
Wellbrooke Gdns CHFD SO53 206 D6
Wellburn Cl SHST GU47 41 J7
Well Cl CBLY GU15 58 A1
NMIL/BTOS BH25 326 G6
OVTN RG25 108 C1
Well Copse Cl HORN PO8 256 C2
Weller Dr CBLY GU15 58 B2
Wellers Cl TOTT SO40 245 P4
Wellesley Av
CHCH/BSGR BH23 325 M8
Wellesley Cl ASHV GU12 76 E5
WVILLE PO7 275 N3
Wellesley Dr CWTH RG45 40 F1
Wellesley Gdn FNM GU9 96 C4
Wellesley Ga ASHV GU12 * 3 F4
Wellesley Rd ALDT GU11 75 L9
AND SP10 102 E4
FARN GU14 75 L4
RFNM GU10 137 H3
Well House Cl FBDG SP6 219 P1
Well House La FUFL SO22 164 F2
HTWY RG27 38 E3
Wellhouse Rd ALTN GU34 131 P7
Wellington Av ALDT GU11 2 B2
BOR GU35 153 P6
CHCH/BSGR BH23 325 N8
FLEETN GU51 74 E2
WEND SO18 249 K4
Wellington Cl FAWY SO45 267 P9
HORN PO8 256 D5
NWBY RG14 24 F2
SHST GU47 41 K6
Wellington Ct HEND SO30 249 L1
Wellington Crs TADY RG26 33 N5
Wellington Dr
LSOL/BMARY PO13 314 E3
Wellington Gdns ALDT GU11 * 2 B4
Wellington Gv
FHAM/PORC PO16 295 N2
Wellingtonia Av EWKG RG40 40 C2
Wellington La FNM GU9 96 D4
Wellington Pk HEND SO30 250 A2
Wellington Pl ASHV GU12 76 E8
LYMN SO41 * 329 M3
Wellington Rd AND SP10 4 A2
CHAR BH8 334 G1
CWTH RG45 41 K2
PSTN BH14 321 L9
SHST GU47 41 J6
WEND SO18 248 F1
Wellington St ALDT GU11 2 E2
SSEA PO5 19 G4
Wellington Ter DEAN RG23 68 F5
SHST GU47 41 K6
Wellington Wy FARN GU14 75 L5
WVILLE PO7 275 N3
Well La ALTN GU34 113 P4
BPWT SO32 232 F5
FBDG SP6 241 J1
HASM GU27 157 J7
HLER SO31 270 A8
ODIM RG29 113 P2
PLE BH15 320 E8
Wellmans Meadow KSCL RG20 48 B2
Well Meadow HAV PO9 276 E4
NWBY RG14 24 E2
Wellowbrook Cl CHFD SO53 206 C7
Wellow Cl HAV PO9 14 C2
WEND SO18 249 L4
Wellow Dro ROMY SO51 202 E6
Wellow Gdns
FHAM/STUB PO14 271 J8
Wellow Wood Rd ROMY SO51 202 D5
Well Rd RFNM GU10 94 G5
Wells Cl HSEA PO3 317 K2
Wells Cots FNM GU9 116 A3
Wells La RGUW GU3 77 P8
Wellsmoor FHAM/STUB PO14 271 J7
Wells Pl ELGH SO50 229 J2
Wells's La WHCH RG28 85 K7
Wellstead Wy HEND SO30 250 B1
Well St KSCL RG20 46 F1
Wellswood Gdns HAV PO9 257 J8
Wellsworth La HAV PO9 257 J8
Wellworthy Rd LYMN SO41 329 K1
The Welsh Dr HTWY RG27 39 H9
Welsh La THLE RG7 37 M4
Welshman's Rd THLE RG7 35 J1
Welton Ct BSTK RG21 6 C5
Wembley Gv CHAM PO6 297 K3
Wendan Rd NWBY RG14 16 D7
Wendover Cl
NMIL/BTOS BH25 327 H6
Wendover Dr FRIM GU16 59 H2
Wendover Rd HAV PO9 14 D4
Wendys Crs FERN BH22 * 302 F5
Wenlock Wy STHA RG19 25 N5
Wensley Gdns EMRTH PO10 277 M7
Wentwood Gdns
NMIL/BTOS BH25 327 M5
Wentworth Av BOSC BH5 335 N2
Wentworth Cl ASHV GU12 76 F5
BOSC BH5 335 N3
FNM GU9 96 F5
YTLY GU46 40 E9
Wentworth Ct NWBY RG14 17 G5
Wentworth Crs ASHV GU12 76 F6
BH/HW/K RG22 89 L6
Wentworth Dr BDST BH18 300 C8
CHCH/BSGR BH23 324 D9
HORN PO8 256 B4
Wentworth Gdns ALTN GU34 132 E5
FAWY SO45 290 F7
ITCH SO19 269 K1
Wentworth Gra FUFL SO22 22 B7
Wentworth Gv FAWY SO45 290 F6
Wescott Wy BWD BH11 301 N9
Wesermarsch Rd HORN PO8 256 A7
Wesley Cl CHAR BH8 335 J1
ITCH SO19 249 M7
Wesley Gv HSEA PO3 297 H6
Wesley Rd BKME/WDN BH12 321 L7
WIMB BH21 278 F9
WINC SO23 145 K9
Wessex Av NMIL/BTOS BH25 327 J5
ODIM RG29 93 K2
Wessex Cl BSTK RG21 69 K9
CHCH/BSGR BH23 325 N8
FAWY SO45 291 H8
LSOL/BMARY PO13 314 E2
Wessex Ct ITCH SO19 249 J7
Wessex Crs ODIM RG29 93 K2
Wessex Dr FUFL SO22 164 F5
ODIM RG29 93 K2
Wessex Est RGWD BH24 282 F1
Wessex Gdns AND SP10 4 B3
FHAM/PORC PO16 295 M2
ROMY SO51 204 F6
Wessex Ga CHAR BH8 323 J9
Wessex La WEND SO18 228 F8
Wessex Pl FNM GU9 116 C1
Wessex Rd FARN GU14 75 M2
HORN PO8 236 C9
PSTN BH14 321 J9
RGWD BH24 282 F1
Wessex Wy LTDN BH7 323 M7
RWIN SO21 208 A5
WCLF BH2 8 B2
West Av FNM GU9 96 D5
WIMB BH21 280 D1
West Bargate SHAM SO14 20 D5
West Battery Rd NEND PO2 296 D8
West Bay Rd WSHM SO15 247 P7
Westbeams Rd LYMN SO41 308 B6
Westborn Rd
FHAM/PORC PO16 11 H5
West Borough WIMB BH21 278 D9
Westbourne Ar WBNE BH4 * 334 B3
Westbourne Av EMRTH PO10 277 N8
FAWY SO45 290 E5
Westbourne Cl EMRTH PO10 277 N8
WBNE BH4 334 C3
Westbourne Crs SD/PW SO17 248 C2
Westbourne Park Rd
WBNE BH4 334 B4
Westbourne Rd EMRTH PO10 277 N7
NEND PO2 297 H9
SHST GU47 41 M7
Westbourne Ter NWBY RG14 * 24 C3
Westbroke Gdns ROMY SO51 204 D4
Westbrook Cl AND SP10 4 D5
West Brook Cl DEAN RG23 88 F3
Westbrook Cl HLER SO31 270 G5
NBNE BH10 322 D5
Westbrooke Cl HORN PO8 256 A5
Westbrooke Rd ALTN GU34 132 E6
Westbrook Gv WVILLE PO7 275 M5
Westbrook Hl MFD/CHID GU8 117 P6
Westbrook Rd
FHAM/PORC PO16 295 P3
Westbrook Wy WEND SO18 228 F8
Westburn Flds ALTN GU34 114 A6
Westbury Av FLEETN GU51 74 G4
Westbury Cl CHAM PO6 274 D9
CHCH/BSGR BH23 305 L9
FLEETN GU51 74 F4
NMIL/BTOS BH25 327 J7
Westbury Ct HEND SO30 250 B6
Westbury Gdns FLEETN GU51 74 G4
FNM GU9 96 E7

Westbury Pth
FHAM/PORC PO16 ... **11** H5
Westbury Rd
FHAM/PORC PO16 ... **11** H5
RGWD BH24 ... **282** F2
WSHM SO15 ... **247** K4
Westbury Wy *ASHV* GU12 ... **3** K2
West Butts St *PLE* BH15 ... **332** D1
Westby Rd *BOSC* BH5 ... **335** L2
Westcliff Cl
LSOL/BMARY PO13 ... **314** C1
West Cliff Gdns *WCLF* BH2 ... **8** B6
Westcliff Ms *ITCH* SO19 ... **248** F8
West Cl *FNM* GU9 ... **96** D4
LYMN SO41 ... **329** H5
SBNE BH6 * ... **336** E2
VWD BH31 ... **258** D4
West Common *FAWY* SO45 ... **312** F1
Westcot Rd *FAWY* SO45 ... **290** D6
Westcroft Pde
NMIL/BTOS BH25 * ... **327** K5
Westcroft Pk *BDST* BH18 ... **300** E9
Westcroft Rd *GPORT* PO12 ... **315** K3
Westdeane Ct *BSTK* RG21 ... **6** B7
West Dean Rd *RSAL* SP5 ... **158** F6
Westdown Rd *BWD* BH11 ... **322** A2
West Downs Cl
FHAM/PORC PO16 ... **272** E6
West Dr *ELGH* SO50 ... **207** M9
RGWD BH24 ... **303** H1
West End *CHIN* RG24 ... **50** G8
West End Cl *FUFL* SO22 ... **22** B4
West End Gv *FNM* GU9 ... **96** A9
West End La *ALTN* GU34 ... **149** L4
RFNM GU10 ... **115** N9
West End Rd *WEND* SO18 ... **249** K3
THLE RG7 ... **35** M1
Westend Rd *WEND* SO18 ... **249** J4
West End Ter *FUFL* SO22 ... **22** B4
Westerdale *STHA* RG19 ... **25** M4
Westerdale Dr *FRIM* GU16 ... **58** G2
Westerham Cl *CHAM* PO6 ... **296** G1
Westerham Rd *CCLF* BH13 ... **334** B3
Westering *ROMY* SO51 ... **204** F4
Westerley Cl *HLER* SO31 * ... **270** E9
Western Av *AND* SP10 ... **4** C5
CCLF BH13 ... **333** N1
EMRTH PO10 ... **299** K1
NBNE BH10 ... **322** D3
NMIL/BTOS BH25 ... **326** F7
NWBY RG14 ... **24** B3
WSHM SO15 ... **247** K5
Western Cl *NBNE* BH10 ... **322** D2
Western District Cut
WSHM SO15 ... **247** P4
Western End *NWBY* RG14 ... **16** A4
Western Esp *WSHM* SO15 ... **20** B3
Western La *ODIM* RG29 ... **93** K1
Western Pde *EMRTH* PO10 ... **299** L2
ITCH SO19 ... **268** G2
SSEA PO5 ... **19** F7
Western Rd *ALDT* GU11 ... **2** A4
AND SP10 ... **4** C5
BOR GU35 ... **153** P2
CCLF BH13 ... **333** P3
CHAM PO6 ... **296** F2
CHFD SO53 ... **206** G4
FAWY SO45 ... **291** P9
FHAM/PORC PO16 ... **11** G6
FUFL SO22 ... **22** B3
HAV PO9 ... **14** D4
HEND SO30 ... **249** M2
LISS GU33 ... **120** D7
LYMN SO41 ... **329** K3
Western Wy *BH/HW/K* RG22 ... **89** P1
FHAM/PORC PO16 ... **11** F6
PSEA PO1 ... **316** B2
Westfield Av
FHAM/STUB PO14 ... **294** D1
HISD PO11 ... **318** E5
Westfield Cl *ELGH* SO50 ... **230** C5
HLER SO31 ... **269** N8
West Field Cl *TADY* RG26 ... **34** E6
Westfield Cl *WIMB* BH21 ... **278** D9
Westfield Common
HLER SO31 ... **269** M8
Westfield Crs *CHFD* SO53 ... **228** E1
NTHA RG18 ... **25** L3
Westfield Dr *BPWT* SO32 ... **253** H1
Westfield Dro *NARL* SO24 ... **186** E6
Westfield Gdns
CHCH/BSGR BH23 ... **325** M6
LYMN SO41 ... **328** E6
Westfield La *RFNM* GU10 ... **115** N4
Westfield Oaks *HISD* PO11 ... **318** F5
Westfield Rd *BSTK* RG21 ... **69** M9
CBLY GU15 ... **58** A3
CHFD SO53 ... **228** E1
ENEY PO4 ... **317** J5
FUFL SO22 ... **164** C2
GPORT PO12 ... **315** K3
LYMN SO41 ... **329** M5
NTHA RG18 ... **25** K2
SBNE BH6 ... **336** C2
TOTT SO40 ... **246** D3
West Field Rd *WINC* SO23 ... **145** K8
Westfield Rd *WSHM* SO15 ... **247** L4
Westfield Wy *NWBY* RG14 ... **16** A4
West Fryerne *YTLY* GU46 ... **40** E7
Westgate *FHAM/STUB* PO14 ... **294** A8
Westgate Cl *DEAN* RG23 * ... **68** E7
Westgate Ms *HEND* SO30 ... **249** N2
Westgate Pk *WBNE* BH4 ... **334** B3
Westgate Rd *NWBY* RG14 ... **16** A4
Westgate St *SHAM* SO14 ... **20** D7
Westglade *FARN* GU14 ... **57** L9
West Gn *YTLY* GU46 ... **40** C7
West Green Rd *HTWY* RG27 ... **54** E7
Westgrove *FBDG* SP6 ... **240** C2
West Ham Cl *BH/HW/K* RG22 ... **68** F8
Westham Cl *CFDH* BH17 ... **320** G1
West Ham La *BH/HW/K* RG22 ... **68** E8
West Haye Rd *HISD* PO11 ... **319** K7
West Hayes *LYMN* SO41 ... **329** M4
Westheath Rd *BDST* BH18 ... **300** D9
West Heath Rd *FARN* GU14 ... **57** N9
West Hl *FUFL* SO22 * ... **22** B4
West Hill Dr *FAWY* SO45 ... **268** B5
FUFL SO22 ... **22** A4
West Hill Gdns *FLEETN* GU51 ... **74** A2
West Hill Pk *FUFL* SO22 ... **164** E7
West Hill Pl *WCLF* BH2 ... **8** B4
West Hill Rd *WCLF* BH2 ... **8** B5
West Hill Rd North
RWIN SO21 ... **144** F3
West Hill Rd South
RWIN SO21 ... **144** F4
West Hoe La *BPWT* SO32 ... **232** D4
West Horton Cl *ELGH* SO50 ... **229** P2
West Horton La *ELGH* SO50 ... **229** P3
West Howe Cl *BWD* BH11 ... **322** A3
The West Hundreds
FLEETN GU51 ... **74** A1
Westland *NTHA* RG18 ... **25** L3
Westland Dr
LSOL/BMARY PO13 ... **314** E3
WVILLE PO7 ... **275** N6
Westland Gdns *GPORT* PO12 ... **12** A5
Westlands Ct
CHCH/BSGR BH23 ... **305** L8
Westlands Dr *CCLF* BH13 ... **333** P3
Westlands Gv
FHAM/PORC PO16 ... **295** N2
Westlands Rd *NWBY* RG14 ... **17** F7
West La *CHCH/BSGR* BH23 ... **305** K8
HISD PO11 ... **318** E4
LYMN SO41 ... **328** E6
NBAD SO52 ... **205** J8
Westley Cl *FUFL* SO22 ... **164** E6
Westley Court Rd *RWIN* SO21 ... **163** K3
Westley Gv *FHAM/STUB* PO14 ... **10** C7
Westley La *RWIN* SO21 ... **163** M2
Westlyn Rd *TADY* RG26 ... **34** F5
Westman Rd *FUFL* SO22 ... **164** E5
West Marlands Rd *SHAM* SO14 ... **20** D3
Westmead *FARN* GU14 ... **76** A1
West Md *FNM* GU9 * ... **96** B9
Westmead Cl *HISD* PO11 ... **318** D5
Westmead Dr *NWBY* RG14 ... **24** C7
West Mills *NWBY* RG14 ... **16** D2
West Mills Rd *FBDG* SP6 ... **240** C2
West Mills Yd *NWBY* RG14 * ... **16** D2
Westminister Rd *LYMN* SO41 ... **338** E2
Westminster Cl *BH/HW/K* RG22 ... **89** M4
FLEETN GU51 ... **74** D2
Westminster Gdns
FHAM/STUB PO14 ... **271** J7
Westminster Ga *FUFL* SO22 ... **183** K1
Westminster Rd *CCLF* BH13 ... **334** B5
Westminster Rd East
CCLF BH13 ... **334** B5
West Moors Rd *FERN* BH22 ... **302** D1
WIMB BH21 ... **280** E2
Westmorland Dr *CBLY* GU15 ... **58** G2
Westmorland Wy *CHFD* SO53 ... **206** G8
Weston Av *ENEY* PO4 ... **317** K4
Weston Cl *ITCH* SO19 ... **269** H1
Weston Ct *RAND* SP11 ... **82** F3
Weston Crs *WEND* SO18 ... **249** L4
Weston Down Rd *RWIN* SO21 ... **126** E4
Weston Dr *BMTH* BH1 ... **9** J3
Weston Grove Rd *ITCH* SO19 ... **248** F9
Weston La *ITCH* SO19 ... **268** G1
PSF GU32 ... **215** H5
ROWN SO16 ... **226** E8
RSAL SP5 ... **158** A2
Weston Rd *ELGH* SO50 ... **229** J1
EPSF GU31 ... **215** N2
OVTN RG25 ... **92** A8
WIMB BH21 ... **279** H7
West Overcliff Dr *WBNE* BH4 ... **334** C4
Westover La *RGWD* BH24 ... **282** B3
Westover Rd *BMTH* BH1 ... **8** E4
FLEETN GU51 ... **74** E3
HSEA PO3 ... **297** J9
LYMN SO41 ... **338** G2
ROWN SO16 ... **246** F3
West Pk *RAND* SP11 ... **81** H5
West Park Dr *FBDG* SP6 ... **219** K7
West Park La *FBDG* SP6 ... **219** J7
West Park Rd *WSHM* SO15 ... **20** C3
West Portway *AND* SP10 ... **81** P9
West Quay Rd *PLE* BH15 ... **332** D1
WSHM SO15 ... **20** A4
Westray Cl *BSTK* RG21 ... **7** J2
Westridge *KSCL* RG20 ... **45** M1
West Rdg *RFNM* GU10 * ... **97** M6
Westridge Rd *SD/PW* SO17 ... **248** D2
West Ring *RFNM* GU10 ... **97** M4
West Rd *BOSC* BH5 ... **335** N1
CHCH/BSGR BH23 ... **305** L8
EMRTH PO10 ... **299** L1
FARN GU14 ... **57** P5
FAWY SO45 ... **267** P9
HEND SO30 ... **249** P5
ITCH SO19 ... **248** G9
LYMN SO41 ... **338** D1
RWIN SO21 ... **124** F2
SHAM SO14 ... **248** C9
WHAM PO17 ... **274** C4
West Rw *WIMB* BH21 ... **300** D1
Westrow Gdns *WSHM* SO15 ... **248** A4
Westrow Rd *WSHM* SO15 ... **248** A4
Westside *AMSY* SP4 ... **118** A5
Westside Cl *BH/HW/K* RG22 ... **68** G9
Westside Vw *WVILLE* PO7 ... **275** L1
West St *AND* SP10 ... **4** D4
BPWT SO32 ... **233** M7
EMRTH PO10 ... **299** M1
FAWY SO45 ... **268** B5
FBDG SP6 ... **240** C2
FHAM/PORC PO16 ... **11** F6
FHAM/PORC PO16 ... **295** P1
FHAM/STUB PO14 ... **293** M1
FNM GU9 ... **115** P1
HASM GU27 ... **157** H7
HAV PO9 ... **14** C5
KSCL RG20 ... **46** D1
NARL SO24 ... **168** A1
NWBY RG14 ... **16** D1
ODIM RG29 ... **93** J1
PLE BH15 ... **332** D1
PSEA PO1 ... **18** B6
RGWD BH24 ... **282** C2
SHAM SO14 ... **20** D6
TADY RG26 ... **34** D6
WHAM PO17 ... **274** A4
WIMB BH21 ... **300** D1
WVILLE PO7 ... **254** E2
West Street Cl *TADY* RG26 ... **34** D6
West Undercliff Prom
WCLF BH2 ... **8** C6
West Vw *BOR* GU35 * ... **153** N7
West View Dr *STOK* SO20 ... **123** L6
Westview Gdns *AND* SP10 ... **4** D6
West View Rd *BOR* GU35 ... **155** K4
CHCH/BSGR BH23 ... **325** J9
Westview Rd *FUFL* SO22 ... **164** B5
West View Rd *PLE* BH15 ... **320** E8
Westward Rd *HEND* SO30 ... **250** C3
Westway *FHAM* PO15 ... **271** L7
West Wy *AND* SP10 ... **5** J1
BDST BH18 ... **320** B1
LYMN SO41 ... **329** J5
MOOR/WNTN BH9 ... **323** H5
West Way Cl
MOOR/WNTN BH9 ... **323** H6
Westways *FHAM/STUB* PO14 ... **294** B7
HAV PO9 ... **297** P1
Westways Cl *ROWN* SO16 ... **227** H7
Westwood Av *FERN* BH22 ... **302** C2
Westwood Cl *EMRTH* PO10 ... **277** N7
Westwood Gdns *CHFD* SO53 ... **206** G5
Westwood Ho *HTWY* RG27 ... **39** N6
Westwood Pk
NMIL/BTOS BH25 * ... **326** G2
Westwood Rd *HLER* SO31 ... **269** K3
LYND SO43 ... **264** F4
NEND PO2 ... **296** G5
NWBY RG14 ... **17** H7
SD/PW SO17 ... **248** C3
Westwood Vw *NARL* SO24 ... **187** J5
Wetherby Cl *BDST* BH18 ... **320** C2
Wetherby Gdns *AND* SP10 ... **82** C9
FARN GU14 ... **76** B4
TOTT SO40 ... **246** A3
Wetherdown *EPSF* GU31 ... **215** N2
Wey Bank *RFNM* GU10 ... **114** G7
Weybank Cl *FNM* GU9 ... **96** C8
Weybridge Cl *HLER* SO31 ... **270** F4
Weybridge Md *YTLY* GU46 ... **40** F7
Weybrook Ct *CHIN* RG24 ... **50** G9
Wey Cl *ASHV* GU12 ... **97** N2
Weycombe Rd *HASM* GU27 ... **157** H5
Weydon Farm La *FNM* GU9 ... **116** B2
Weydon Hill Cl *FNM* GU9 ... **116** B2
Weydon Hill Rd *FNM* GU9 ... **116** B2
Weydon La *FNM* GU9 ... **116** A2
Weydon Mill La *FNM* GU9 ... **116** B1
Weydown Rd *HASM* GU27 ... **156** G6
Wey Gdns *HASM* GU27 ... **156** E8
Wey Hl *HASM* GU27 ... **156** F7
Weyhill Cl *FHAM/PORC* PO16 ... **273** N9
HAV PO9 ... **276** D5
TADY RG26 ... **34** C7
Weyhill Gdns *RAND* SP11 ... **81** K9
Weyhill Rd *AND* SP10 ... **4** A5
RAND SP11 ... **81** K9
Weyland Cl *LIPH* GU30 ... **175** K2
Wey Lodge Cl *LIPH* GU30 ... **175** L3
Weyman's Av *NBNE* BH10 ... **322** C1
Weymans Dr *NBNE* BH10 ... **322** C1
Weymouth Av *GPORT* PO12 ... **295** K9
Weymouth Rd *NEND* PO2 * ... **296** F8
PSTN BH14 ... **321** L7
Weyside Pk *ALTN* GU34 * ... **133** H4
Weysprings *HASM* GU27 ... **156** E6
Weysprings Cl *BSTK* RG21 ... **7** J5
Weywood Cl *FNM* GU9 ... **96** F4
Weywood La *FNM* GU9 ... **96** E4
Whaddon Cha
FHAM/STUB PO14 ... **293** P7
Whaddon Ct *HAV* PO9 ... **276** C4
Whaddon La *RWIN* SO21 ... **208** G5
Whale Island Wy *NEND* PO2 ... **296** E8
Whalesmead Cl *ELGH* SO50 ... **229** P3
Whalesmead Rd *ELGH* SO50 ... **229** P3
Whaley Rd *NEND* PO2 ... **296** D8
Wharf Cl *BKME/WDN* BH12 ... **321** N6
Wharfdale Rd
BKME/WDN BH12 ... **321** M6
Wharfenden Wy *FRIM* GU16 ... **58** E7
Wharf Hl *WINC* SO23 ... **23** G7
Wharf Rd *ASHV* GU12 ... **76** F8
FRIM GU16 ... **58** E7
ITCH SO19 ... **248** F8
NEND PO2 ... **296** E9
NWBY RG14 ... **16** E1
Wharf St *NWBY* RG14 ... **16** E2
The Wharf *NWBY* RG14 * ... **17** F2
Wharf Wy *FRIM* GU16 ... **58** E7
Wharncliffe Gdns
CHCH/BSGR BH23 ... **326** C8
Wharncliffe Rd *BMTH* BH1 ... **335** K2
CHCH/BSGR BH23 ... **326** C8
ITCH SO19 ... **248** F8
Whartons La *TOTT* SO40 ... **246** A7
Whatleigh Cl *PLE* BH15 ... **332** E2
Wheat Cl *CHFD* SO53 ... **206** B7
Wheatcroft Dr *WEND* SO18 ... **249** K2
Wheatcroft Rd
LSOL/BMARY PO13 ... **314** D2
Wheatear Dr *EPSF* GU31 ... **216** A3
Wheatears Dr *ROMY* SO51 ... **224** E1
Wheatland Cl *FUFL* SO22 ... **183** M1
Wheatlands
FHAM/STUB PO14 ... **271** J6
Wheatlands Av *HISD* PO11 ... **319** L7
Wheatlands Crs *HISD* PO11 ... **319** L7
Wheatley La *BOR* GU35 ... **134** E4
Wheatley Rd *ALDT* GU11 ... **2** C2
Wheaton Rd *LTDN* BH7 ... **335** N1
Wheatsheaf Ct *HEND* SO30 ... **250** B5
Wheatsheaf Dr *HORN* PO8 ... **255** M8
Wheatsheaf La *NWBY* RG14 ... **24** E3
Wheatstone Rd *ENEY* PO4 ... **316** G5
Wheeler Cl *GPORT* PO12 ... **315** M2
THLE RG7 ... **27** K4
WHCH RG28 ... **85** M7
Wheelers Green Wy
STHA RG19 ... **25** P5
Wheelers Hl *HTWY* RG27 ... **72** B3
Wheelers La *BWD* BH11 ... **301** L8
Wheelers Meadow
HLER SO31 ... **269** N1
Wheelers Wk *FAWY* SO45 ... **290** G9
Wheelers Yd *RWIN* SO21 * ... **125** L5
Wheelhouse Pk *NBAD* SO52 * ... **206** C4
Wheelwrights La *GSHT* GU26 ... **155** P4
Wheely Down Rd *BPWT* SO32 ... **211** L1
Whernside Cl *ROWN* SO16 ... **247** K3
Wherwell Ct *HAV* PO9 ... **277** H5
Whetstone Rd *FARN* GU14 ... **57** K9
Whichers Cl *HAV* PO9 ... **277** H2
Whichers Gate Rd *HAV* PO9 ... **277** H2
Whimbrel Cl *ENEY* PO4 ... **317** L3
Whinchat Cl *FHAM* PO15 ... **272** A6
HTWY RG27 ... **55** H6
ROWN SO16 ... **227** M6
Whincroft Cl *FERN* BH22 ... **302** E1
Whincroft Dr *FERN* BH22 ... **302** E1
Whinfield Rd *FAWY* SO45 ... **268** A9
Whin Holt *FLEETS* GU52 ... **74** D6
Whins Cl *CBLY* GU15 ... **58** A1
Whins Dr *CBLY* GU15 ... **58** A1
Whinwhistle Rd *ROMY* SO51 ... **225** H2
Whippingham Cl *CHAM* PO6 ... **296** F1
Whistler Cl *BSTK* RG21 ... **69** N9
Whistler Gv *SHST* GU47 ... **41** L8
Whistler Rd *ITCH* SO19 ... **249** L8
Whistlers La *THLE* RG7 ... **35** J5
Whitaker Crs *LYMN* SO41 ... **329** J4
Whitakers Ct *NTHA* RG18 ... **25** L3
Whitby Av *BDST* BH18 ... **320** C2
Whitby Cl *CHCH/BSGR* BH23 ... **324** B3
FARN GU14 ... **76** D3
Whitby Crs *BDST* BH18 ... **320** C2
Whitby Rd *LYMN* SO41 ... **338** E2
Whitchurch Av *BDST* BH18 ... **320** E1
Whitchurch Cl *ALDT* GU11 ... **97** K5
Whitchurch Ct *ITCH* SO19 ... **249** H8
Whitchurch Rd *FLEETN* GU51 ... **74** B1
Whitcombe Cl *TOTT* SO40 ... **246** C4
Whitcombe Gdns *HSEA* PO3 ... **317** H2
Whiteacres Cl *GPORT* PO12 ... **315** M3
White Acres Rd *FRIM* GU16 ... **58** E9
White Av *LISS* GU33 ... **173** P5
White Barn Crs *LYMN* SO41 ... **328** A4
Whitebeam Cl *BH/HW/K* RG22 ... **68** D8
FHAM/STUB PO14 ... **10** A7
HORN PO8 ... **256** C6
RWIN SO21 ... **208** A5
Whitebeam Gdns *FARN* GU14 ... **75** K1
White Beam Ri *HORN* PO8 ... **236** C7
Whitebeam Rd *HEND* SO30 ... **250** D4
Whitebeam Wy *NBAD* SO52 ... **205** L8
VWD BH31 ... **259** H5
Whitechimney Rw
EMRTH PO10 ... **277** P7
White City *CWTH* RG45 ... **41** L1
Whitecliff Crs *PSTN* BH14 ... **333** J1
Whitecliffe Av *HSEA* PO3 ... **317** J1
Whitecliff Rd *PSTN* BH14 ... **333** H1
White Cliff Rd *PSTN* BH14 ... **333** J1
White Cl *PLE* BH15 ... **321** J5
White Cloud Pk *ENEY* PO4 ... **317** H5
White Cottage Cl *FNM* GU9 ... **96** D5
Whitecroft *FAWY* SO45 * ... **268** C8
Whitecross Cl *CFDH* BH17 ... **320** G1
Whitecross Gdns *NEND* PO2 ... **297** H6
Whitedell La *WHAM* PO17 ... **273** H6
White Dirt La *HORN* PO8 ... **256** B1
Whitedown *ALTN* GU34 ... **132** E7
Whitedown La *ALTN* GU34 ... **132** C7
Whitedown Rd *TADY* RG26 ... **34** A6
White Farm Cl *NBNE* BH10 ... **322** D7
Whitefield Rd *FAWY* SO45 ... **290** E6
NMIL/BTOS BH25 ... **327** J4
PSTN BH14 ... **333** J1
White Gates *BPWT* SO32 ... **231** H7
Whitehall *CHCH/BSGR* BH23 ... **336** F1
Whitehall Rd *STOK* SO20 ... **162** B1
Whitehart Flds *RGWD* BH24 ... **282** G1
White Hart La *BSTK* RG21 ... **7** G7
FHAM/PORC PO16 ... **295** M2
TADY RG26 ... **50** B5
TOTT SO40 ... **244** F3
White Hart Ms *LIPH* GU30 ... **175** J5
White Hart Rd *ELGH* SO50 ... **230** C3
GPORT PO12 ... **12** D4
PSEA PO1 ... **18** C6
Whitehaven
FHAM/PORC PO16 ... **295** M2
HORN PO8 ... **256** D5
Whitehayes Cl
CHCH/BSGR BH23 ... **325** H5
Whitehayes Rd
CHCH/BSGR BH23 ... **324** G6
Whitehead Cl *CHIN* RG24 ... **70** A5
White Heather Ct *FAWY* SO45 ... **268** C4
White Hl *KSCL* RG20 ... **46** C3
KSCL RG20 ... **47** L2
ODIM RG29 ... **93** M8
OVTN RG25 ... **48** A7
Whitehill La *NARL* SO24 ... **168** C3
Whitehill Rd *BOR* GU35 ... **154** C7
Whitehorn Dr *RSAL* SP5 ... **223** M3
White Horse Dr *PLE* BH15 ... **320** E7
White Horse La *EWKG* RG40 ... **39** M1
WVILLE PO7 ... **255** J5
White House Cl *BH/HW/K* RG22 ... **89** P1
Whitehouse Cl *FARN* GU14 ... **58** A7
Whitehouse Gdns *PSF* GU32 ... **191** L9
White House Gdns
WSHM SO15 ... **247** L5
YTLY GU46 ... **40** D7
Whitehouse Rd *WIMB* BH21 ... **300** F3
White House Wk *FNM* GU9 ... **96** D4
White Knights
NMIL/BTOS BH25 ... **327** H8
White Ladies Cl *HAV* PO9 ... **15** H6
Whitelands *CHCH/BSGR* BH23 ... **305** P5
Whitelands Rd *NTHA* RG18 ... **25** M3
White La *ODIM* RG29 ... **92** D1
RWIN SO21 ... **184** A6
TADY RG26 ... **67** H6
Whitelaw Rd *WSHM* SO15 ... **247** M4
Whiteleaf La *WVILLE* PO7 ... **234** E5
Whitelegg Wy *NBNE* BH10 ... **322** E2
Whiteley La *HLER* SO31 ... **271** J1
Whiteley Village
FHAM PO15 * ... **271** L2
Whiteley Wy *FHAM* PO15 ... **271** K4
White Lion Wk *GPORT* PO12 ... **13** H1
White Lion Wy *YTLY* GU46 ... **40** E7
White Lodge Gdns
FHAM/PORC PO16 ... **272** C6
Whitemoor La *ROMY* SO51 ... **225** L8
Whitemoor Rd *BROC* SO42 ... **286** D7
Whitenap Cl *ROMY* SO51 ... **204** F7
Whitenap La *ROMY* SO51 ... **204** G7
White Oak Wy *RAND* SP11 ... **102** A6
White Post La *RFNM* GU10 ... **116** A6
White Rd *CBLY* GU15 ... **41** N8
ELGH SO50 ... **207** M9
White Rose La *FNM* GU9 ... **116** B3
Whites Cl *HTWY* RG27 ... **71** N3
Whites Hl *RWIN* SO21 ... **208** F1
White's Hl *THLE* RG7 ... **26** G3
Whiteshoot *RSAL* SP5 ... **200** B9
STOK SO20 ... **140** A9
Whiteshoot Hl *RSAL* SP5 ... **200** A9
Whiteshute La *WINC* SO23 ... **183** N1
Whites La *FAWY* SO45 ... **291** K6
Whites Pl *GPORT* PO12 ... **315** M3
Whites Rd *FARN* GU14 ... **76** D3
White's Rd *ITCH* SO19 ... **249** J6
Whitestar Pl *SHAM* SO14 ... **21** G6
Whitestone Cl *ROWN* SO16 ... **247** K3
Whitestones *BH/HW/K* RG22 ... **89** N5
White Swan Rd *PSEA* PO1 ... **19** F3
Whites Wy *HEND* SO30 ... **250** B1
Whitethorn Cl *ASHV* GU12 ... **97** P2
Whitethorn Rd *HISD* PO11 ... **319** H5
White Tree Cl *ELGH* SO50 ... **230** D4
Whitewater Ri *FAWY* SO45 ... **268** B8
HTWY RG27 ... **72** B2
Whitewater Rd *FLEETN* GU51 ... **56** C9
ODIM RG29 ... **72** B8
Whiteway Ms *HLER* SO31 ... **270** D9
Whiteways *WIMB* BH21 ... **278** G8
The White Wy *BPWT* SO32 ... **211** L6
Whitewood *CHIN* RG24 ... **70** A1
Whitfield Cl *HASM* GU27 ... **157** H4
Whitfield Pk *RGWD* BH24 ... **281** P4
Whitfield Rd *HASM* GU27 ... **157** H5
Whitgift Cl *BH/HW/K* RG22 ... **89** M6
Whithedwood Av
WSHM SO15 ... **247** P3
Whithers La *BROC* SO42 ... **310** G2
Whitlet Cl *FNM* GU9 ... **116** B1
Whitley Cl *EMRTH* PO10 ... **277** P5
Whitley Rd *HORN* PO8 ... **255** P5
YTLY GU46 ... **56** E1
Whitley Wy *FARN* GU14 ... **75** M3
NMIL/BTOS BH25 ... **327** K2
Whitmarsh La *CHIN* RG24 ... **70** C1
Whitmead La *RFNM* GU10 ... **117** K6
Whitmoor Vale Rd *GSHT* GU26 ... **155** N1
Whitmore Cl *SHST* GU47 ... **41** L6
Whitmore Gn *FNM* GU9 ... **96** E5
Whitmore La *WIMB* BH21 ... **258** A3
Whitmore V *GSHT* GU26 ... **155** N2
Whitmore Vale Rd *GSHT* GU26 ... **156** A1
Whitney Rd *CHIN* RG24 ... **69** P5
Whitsbury Cl *CHAR* BH8 ... **323** K5
Whitsbury Rd *FBDG* SP6 ... **240** D1
HAV PO9 ... **276** C5
Whitstable Rd *CHAM* PO6 ... **296** C1
Whittington Cl *FAWY* SO45 ... **268** B8
Whittington Ct *EMRTH* PO10 ... **299** M1
Whittle Av *FHAM* PO15 ... **271** J5
Whittle Cl *ASHV* GU12 ... **76** E7
SHST GU47 ... **41** H5
Whittle Crs *FARN* GU14 ... **57** N6
Whittle Rd *AND* SP10 ... **101** P1
WIMB BH21 ... **279** P7
Whittles Wy *PLE* BH15 ... **332** D1
Whitwell *HLER* SO31 ... **269** L3
Whitwell Rd *ENEY* PO4 ... **316** G7
Whitworth Cl *GPORT* PO12 ... **12** B2
Whitworth Crs *WEND* SO18 ... **248** F3
Whitworth Rd *GPORT* PO12 ... **12** B2
NEND PO2 ... **297** H9
WEND SO18 ... **248** F3
Whynot La *AND* SP10 ... **102** C2
Whyte Cl *FAWY* SO45 ... **290** D6
Whyteways *ELGH* SO50 ... **207** H9
Wick Dr *NMIL/BTOS* BH25 ... **326** G5
Wicket Hl *RFNM* GU10 ... **116** A4
Wicket Rd *NBNE* BH10 ... **322** C2
The Wicket *FAWY* SO45 ... **268** B8
Wickfield Av
CHCH/BSGR BH23 ... **324** F9
Wickfield Cl *CHCH/BSGR* BH23 ... **324** F9
Wickham Cl *ALTN* GU34 ... **132** D7
FLEETS GU52 ... **74** B7
TADY RG26 ... **34** C6
Wickham Pl *FLEETS* GU52 ... **74** B6
Wickham Rd *BPWT* SO32 ... **233** L8
FHAM/PORC PO16 ... **11** G1
FLEETS GU52 ... **74** B6
WHAM PO17 ... **272** F5
Wickham St *PSEA* PO1 ... **18** C2
Wickham Wy *HTWY* RG27 ... **52** C8
Wick Hill La *EWKG* RG40 ... **40** B1
Wick La *RSAL* SP5 ... **198** E5
SBNE BH6 ... **336** E1
Wicklea Rd *SBNE* BH6 ... **336** F2
Wicklow Cl *BH/HW/K* RG22 ... **68** E9
Wicklow Dr *CHFD* SO53 ... **206** C8
Wickmeads Rd *SBNE* BH6 ... **336** E2
Wickor Cl *EMRTH* PO10 ... **277** N8
Wickor Wy *EMRTH* PO10 ... **277** M7
Wick Point Ms
CHCH/BSGR BH23 ... **336** F1
Wicor Mill La
FHAM/PORC PO16 ... **295** M3
Wicor Pth *FHAM/PORC* PO16 ... **296** A3
Widbury Rd *LYMN* SO41 ... **329** J5
Widden Cl *LYMN* SO41 ... **308** B6
Widdicombe Av *PSTN* BH14 ... **333** N1
Widecombe Dr *FAWY* SO45 ... **268** A6
Wide La *WEND* SO18 ... **228** F7
Wide Lane Cl *BROC* SO42 ... **286** F8

Widgeon Cl GPORT PO12 .... 315 M1
ROWN SO16 .... 227 M6
Widgeons ALTN GU34 .... 132 F4
Widget Cl BWD BH11 .... 322 B5
Widlers La BPWT SO32 .... 209 L7
Widley Ct FHAM/STUB PO14 .... 294 D3
Widley Court Dr CHAM PO6 .... 297 J2
Widley Gdns WVILLE PO7 .... 295 M7
Widley Rd CHAM PO6 .... 297 J1
NEND PO2 .... 296 E7
Widley Wk CHAM PO6 .... 275 J6
Widmore Rd BH/HW/K RG22 .... 89 L1
Widworthy Dr BDST BH18 .... 300 B8
Wield Cl HAV PO9 .... 276 C6
Wield Rd ALTN GU34 .... 149 P1
NARL SO24 .... 130 D6
Wigan Crs HAV PO9 .... 276 B8
Wigan Rd FARN GU14 .... 75 L4
Wights Wk BMTH RG22 .... 89 M4
Wight Wk FERN BH22 .... 302 E6
Wigmore Rd TADY RG26 .... 34 A5
Wigwam Crs GPORT PO12 .... 315 N7
SSEA PO5 .... 19 G6
Wilby La HSEA PO3 .... 297 L5
Wild Arum Wy CHFD SO53 .... 206 B9
Wildburn Cl TOTT SO40 .... 246 A1
Wild Cherry Wy CHFD SO53 .... 206 C7
Wilde Cl TOTT SO40 .... 270 F7
Wildern Cl HLER SO31 .... 270 F7
Wildern Ct HEND 250 B3
Wilderness Hts WEND SO18 .... 249 L2
Wilderness Rd HEND SO30 .... 250 C5
Wilders Cl FRIM GU16 .... 58 C2
Wilderton Rd CCLF BH13 .... 321 P9
Wilderton Rd West
CCLF BH13 .... 321 P8
Wildfell Cl CHCH/BSGR BH23 .... 324 L6
Wild Flower Dr FHAM PO15 .... 271 L7
Wildground La FAWY SO45 .... 268 C9
Wild Herons HTWY RG27 .... 72 B3
Wildmoor La HTWY RG27 .... 52 D7
Wildown Gdns SBNE BH6 .... 336 E3
Wildown Rd SBNE BH6 .... 336 E3
Wild Ridings
FHAM/STUB PO14 .... 293 J7
Wild Rose Crs HLER SO31 .... 270 E8
Wildwood Dr TADY RG26 .... 33 N5
Wildwood Gdns YTLY GU46 .... 49 K5
Wilfred Rd BOSC BH5 .... 335 M2
Wilkins Cl HORN PO8 .... 236 B6
Wilkinson Dr CHAR BH8 .... 323 N5
Wilks Cl ROWN SO16 .... 226 C7
Willems Av ALDT GU11 .... 2 B2
Willersley Cl CHAM PO6 .... 274 E9
Willett Rd WIMB BH21 .... 300 B3
Will Hall Cl ALTN GU34 .... 132 C8
William Cl CHCH/BSGR BH23 .... 326 C5
FHAM/STUB PO14 .... 294 B8
STHA RG19 .... 25 N5
William Farthing Cl ALDT GU11 .... 2 D3
William Macleod Wy
NARL SO24 .... 247 L3
William Price Gdns
FHAM/PORC PO16 .... 11 G3
William Rd HSEA PO3 .... 297 K6
LYMN SO41 .... 329 L2
Williams Cl FAWY SO45 .... 290 F6
LSOL/BMARY PO13 .... 315 H1
RAND SP11 .... 79 N1
Williams Rd HSEA PO3 .... 297 K6
William St FLEETN GU51 .... 74 F5
William Wy ALTN GU34 .... 132 C4
Willis Av NBAD SO52 .... 205 M9
Willis La ALTN GU34 .... 132 E5
Willis Rd GPORT PO12 .... 13 F2
PSEA PO1 .... 19 G2
ROWN SO16 .... 228 F7
Willis Wy PLE BH15 .... 320 D7
Willis Waye WINC SO23 .... 165 K1
Willoughby Cl ALTN GU34 .... 132 E5
Willoughby Wy DEAN RG23 .... 68 G6
Willow Av FBDG SP6 .... 240 C1
Willow Cl BOR GU35 .... 154 B5
FRIM GU16 .... 58 D9
HAV PO9 .... 15 H6
HEND SO30 .... 249 N1
LIPH GU30 .... 175 L4
NWBY RG14 .... 16 D6
RDGW/BURGH RG30 .... 27 K2
ROWD BH24 .... 281 K5
Willow Crt FRIM GU16 .... 58 C4
ROWN SO16 .... 227 L9
Willow Crs FARN GU14 .... 58 A8
Willowdale Rd PSF GU32 .... 214 F1
Willowdene Cl HAV PO9 .... 276 B6
NMIL/BTOS BH25 .... 327 L4
Willow Dr EPSF GU31 .... 215 M4
RGWD BH24 .... 280 D4
TOTT SO40 .... 267 K2
WIMB BH21 .... 279 J8
Willow Flds ASHV GU12 .... 97 P2
Willowford YTLY GU46 .... 40 E8
Willow Gdns EMRTH PO10 .... 277 P6
LIPH GU30 .... 175 L4
NBAD SO52 .... 205 K8
Willow Gn RWIN SO21 .... 208 A5
Willow Gv GU34 .... 4 B6
ELGH SO50 .... 230 D2
Willow Herb Cl HLER SO31 .... 270 E8
Willow La BLKW GU17 .... 49 M2
CHCH/BSGR BH23 .... 305 P5
Willow Md CHAM PO6 .... 300 B3
Willowmead Cl NWBY RG14 .... 30 B1
Willow Ms TDWTH SP9 .... 79 J4
Willow Pk ASHV GU12 .... 97 M1
PSTN BH14 * 321 H9
Willow Pl GPORT PO12 .... 315 M3
Willow Rd BPWT SO32 .... 232 F8
KSCL RG20 .... 31 L4
LISS GU33 .... 192 D2
TADY RG26 .... 34 C6
Willows End SHST GU47 .... 41 J6

The Willows AND SP10 .... 4 A7
CHFD SO53 * 228 E1
FNM GU10 .... 97 J7
WVILLE PO7 .... 254 C7
Willow Tree Gdns
FHAM/STUB PO14 .... 10 A7
Willow Tree Ri BWD BH11 .... 322 B5
Willow Tree Wk ITCH SO19 .... 249 K8
Willow Wk NMIL/BTOS BH25 .... 327 K8
Willow Wy ASHV GU12 .... 97 L3
CHCH/BSGR BH23 .... 336 E1
DEAN RG23 .... 68 G5
FERN BH22 .... 302 D1
FNM GU9 .... 96 D5
HTWY RG27 .... 52 E4
SHST GU47 .... 40 G5
STOK SO20 .... 121 H5
Willow Wood Rd HISD PO11 .... 318 C5
Wills Rd BKME/WDN BH12 .... 321 P8
Wills Wy ROMY SO51 .... 204 E7
Willwood Cl CFDH BH17 .... 320 C1
Willymington Cl WEND SO18 .... 231 M8
Wilmot Cl ELGH SO50 .... 207 N8
Wilmott Cl GPORT PO12 .... 315 K3
Wilmott La GPORT PO12 .... 315 K3
Wilmott Wy DEAN RG23 .... 68 G6
Wilmur Wy PLE BH15 .... 58 E2
Wilsom Cl ALTN GU34 .... 132 E2
Wilsom Rd ALTN GU34 .... 133 H6
Wilsom Gv SSEA PO5 .... 19 K6
Wilson Rd ASHV GU12 .... 97 K2
BMTH BH1 .... 335 K1
FERN 75 N1
NEND PO2 .... 296 E7
PSTN BH14 .... 321 L8
Wilsons Rd BOR GU35 .... 155 J3
Wilson St SHAM SO14 .... 21 J2
Wilton Av WSHM SO15 .... 248 A5
Wilton Cl CHCH/BSGR BH23 .... 324 B6
GPORT PO12 .... 315 K4
Wilton Crs FARN GU14 .... 76 C1
Wilton Crs WSHM SO15 .... 247 P2
Wilton Dr HORN PO8 .... 256 A6
Wilton Gdns NMIL/BTOS BH25 .... 327 H4
WSHM SO15 .... 247 P2
Wilton Rd CBLY GU15 .... 58 A2
SSEA PO5 .... 316 E6
Wilton St CBLY GU15 .... 58 A2
LTDN BH7 .... 335 M1
WSHM SO15 .... 247 P3
Wilton Ter SSEA PO5 .... 316 F6
Wiltshire Crs DEAN RG23 .... 68 D9
Wiltshire Gdns
CHCH/BSGR BH23 .... 305 K8
Wiltshire Rd
CHCH/BSGR BH23 .... 305 K8
CHFD SO53 .... 228 C1
Wiltshire St SSEA PO5 .... 19 F4
HAV PO9 .... 276 C6
Wilverley Av CHAR BH8 .... 323 M5
Wilverley Pl FAWY SO45 .... 290 C8
Wilverley Rd BROC SO42 .... 286 F8
CHCH/BSGR BH23 .... 325 L7
NMIL/BTOS BH25 .... 307 H5
Wimbledon Park Rd
SSEA PO5 .... 316 F6
Wimborne Rd BWD BH11 .... 301 P7
ENEY PO4 .... 19 J8
PLE BH15 .... 320 E6
TWDS BH3 .... 322 F8
WCLF BH2 .... 8 B1
Wimborne Rd East
WIMB BH21 .... 302 A2
Wimborne Rd West
WIMB BH21 .... 301 J1
Wimpole St PSEA PO1 .... 19 K1
Wimpson Gdns ROWN SO16 .... 247 K2
Wimpson La ROWN SO16 .... 247 J3
Wincanton Cl ALTN GU34 .... 132 C7
Wincanton Wy WVILLE PO7 .... 276 B1
Winchcombe Cl FLEETN GU51 .... 74 D3
Winchcombe Rd BSTK RG21 .... 6 C7
CHAM PO6 .... 274 D9
NWBY RG14 .... 17 F3
Winchester By-Pass
FUFL SO22 .... 144 E9
RWIN SO21 .... 125 K7
WINC SO23 .... 165 K4
Winchester Cl HLER SO31 .... 269 K4
Winchester Ct
LSOL/BMARY PO13 * 315 H3
Winchester Gdns AND SP10 .... 102 E4
Winchester Hl ROMY SO51 .... 204 D6
RWIN SO21 .... 125 L6
Winchester Rd ALTN GU34 .... 132 E8
ALTN GU34 .... 150 A7
ALTN GU34 .... 151 L1
AND SP10 .... 4 E7
ASHV GU12 .... 76 F9
BPWT SO32 .... 230 E9
BPWT SO32 .... 231 K1
BPWT SO32 .... 252 C3
CHFD SO53 .... 206 F7
DEAN RG23 .... 89 J7
ELGH SO50 .... 208 B7
KSCL RG20 .... 48 B6
NARL SO24 .... 167 M2
NARL SO24 .... 169 L1
NEND PO2 .... 296 F1
NMIL/BTOS BH25 .... 327 L2
PSF GU32 .... 190 B8
PSF GU32 .... 215 J1
RAND SP11 .... 137 H2
ROMY SO51 .... 205 J1
ROWN SO16 .... 247 L2
RWIN SO21 .... 127 H8
STOK SO20 .... 123 M4
STOK SO20 .... 161 N4
WHAM PO17 .... 252 D6
WHCH RG28 .... 85 L8
Winchester Road Rbt
BH/HW/K RG22 .... 69 J9
Winchester St AND SP10 .... 4 E5
BSTK RG21 .... 6 E7

FARN GU14 .... 76 B4
HEND SO30 .... 250 G3
OVTN RG25 .... 87 H5
WHCH RG28 .... 85 L7
WSHM SO15 .... 20 D1
Winchester Wy BLKW GU17 .... 41 K8
TOTT SO40 .... 246 A4
Winchfield Cl FLEETN GU51 .... 74 B1
ITCH SO19 .... 250 B2
Winchfield Ct HTWY RG27 .... 73 M3
Winchfield Rd HAV PO9 .... 276 C6
Wincombe Cl FERN BH22 .... 302 D5
Wincombe Dr FERN BH22 .... 302 D4
Windbury Rd ROWN SO16 .... 247 J1
Windermere Av
BH/HW/K RG22 .... 89 L1
FHAM/STUB PO14 .... 294 B5
ROWN SO16 .... 247 H1
Windermere Cl FARN GU14 .... 75 M1
Windermere Ct ASHV GU12 * 76 E8
Windermere Gdns NARL SO24 .... 168 A3
TOTT SO40 .... 246 C3
Windermere Rd BOR GU35 .... 154 A3
NEND PO2 .... 297 H6
TWDS BH3 .... 308 D8
WEND SO18 .... 249 K2
Windermere Wy FNM GU9 .... 96 A5
STHA RG19 .... 25 K4
Windfield Dr ROMY SO51 .... 204 F5
Windham Rd BMTH BH1 .... 335 J1
Winding Wood Dr CBLY GU15 .... 58 C4
Windmill Ct HORN PO8 .... 236 C7
LYMN SO41 .... 338 C1
Windmill Copse FAWY SO45 .... 268 B9
Windmill Cnr THLE RG7 .... 27 J9
Windmill Dr BOR GU35 .... 155 J2
Windmill Fld WVILLE PO7 .... 255 J7
Windmill Flds ALTN GU34 .... 150 C5
Windmill Gv
FHAM/PORC PO16 .... 295 M3
Windmill Hl ALTN GU34 .... 132 C7
Windmill La HLER SO31 .... 250 K8
RAND SP11 .... 61 P5
RAND SP11 .... 102 A6
RGWD BH24 .... 282 B5
Windmill Rd ASHV GU12 .... 3 H4
THLE RG7 .... 27 J9
The Windmills ALTN GU34 * 132 D6
Windover Cl ITCH SO19 .... 249 L5
Windrush Cl BSTK RG21 .... 7 K6
Windrush Gdns WVILLE PO7 .... 275 M3
Windrush Hts SHST GU47 .... 41 J6
Windrush Rd ROWN SO16 .... 247 J2
Windrush Wy FAWY SO45 .... 268 B9
Windsor Cl ALTN GU34 .... 132 D6
FARN GU14 .... 57 P9
LYMN SO41 .... 327 N3
RGWD BH24 .... 281 M4
Windsor Crs ELGH SO50 .... 207 M9
NWBY RG14 .... 17 J2
Windsor Ga FARN GU14 .... 57 P9
Windsor Gdns HAV PO9 .... 276 A3
Windsor La SSEA PO5 .... 19 H5
Windsor Pk CBLY GU15 .... 58 B2
Windsor Rd ALTN GU34 .... 132 F7
BH/HW/K RG22 .... 89 L5
Windsor Ga ELGH SO50 .... 207 J7
NWBY RG14 .... 16 A2
Windsor Rd NWBY RG14 .... 17 J7
Windsor Ride CBLY GU15 .... 41 P6
Windsor Ri NWBY RG14 .... 17 J7
Windsor Rd ALTN GU34 .... 150 C4
FARN GU14 .... 57 P9
LYMN SO41 .... 327 N3
RGWD BH24 .... 281 M4
Windsor Wk BOR GU35 .... 154 C3
Windsor Wy ALDT GU11 .... 3 F5
FBDG SP6 .... 239 N5
FRIM GU16 .... 58 E5
Windwhistle La RSAL SP5 .... 176 B7
Winfield Wy EMRTH PO10 .... 277 M6
Winfrith Crs
BKME/WDN BH12 .... 321 N4
Wingate Dr WBLKW GU17 .... 227 H7
Wingate Ct ALDT GU11 .... 2 C2
Wingate Rd GPORT PO12 .... 295 K8
ODIM RG29 .... 93 K8
TOTT SO40 .... 246 B3
Wingfield Av
CHCH/BSGR BH23 .... 325 P6
PLE BH15 .... 320 F6
Wingfield Gdns FRIM GU16 .... 59 J2
Wingfield St PSEA PO1 .... 316 F1
Wingrove Rd TOTT SO40 .... 246 A8
Wings Cl FNM GU9 .... 96 B5
Wings Rd FNM GU9 .... 96 B5
Winifred Cl ELGH SO50 .... 230 C1
Winifred Rd PLE BH15 .... 320 C7
WVILLE PO7 .... 275 N2
Winkfield Row HORN PO8 .... 256 A6
Winklebury Wy DEAN RG23... .... 68 E7
Winkton Cl CHCH/BSGR BH23 .... 324 C4
HAV PO9 .... 14 C2
Winkworth La THLE RG7 .... 34 D4
Winkworth Pl FNM GU9 * 96 E3
Winnall Ct WINC SO23 .... 23 K2
Winnall Manor Rd WINC SO23 .... 23 J3
Winnall Valley Rd WINC SO23 .... 23 J3
Winnards Ct FERN BH22 .... 302 E6
Winnards La HLER SO31 .... 270 D7
Winners Enclosure
CHCH/BSGR BH23 .... 230 D5
Winnham Dr
FHAM/PORC PO16 .... 273 J9
Winnington FHAM PO15 .... 272 B6
Winnipeg Cl LIPH GU30 .... 175 N4
Winn Rd SD/PW SO17 .... 248 C3
Winscombe Av HORN PO8 .... 256 A9

WSHM SO15 .... 247 N4
Wolsey Wy LYMN SO41 .... 338 C1
Wolsingham Wy STHA RG19 .... 25 N5
Wolterton Rd
BKME/WDN BH12 .... 334 A1
Wolverley Ct ROWN SO16 .... 247 P1
Wolversdene Cl AND SP10 .... 5 G6
Wolversdene Gdns AND SP10 .... 5 H6
Wolversdene Rd AND SP10 .... 5 G6
Wolverton La HAV PO9 .... 49 J4
Wolverton Rd HAV PO9 .... 276 C5
LTDN BH7 .... 335 M1
SHAM SO14 * 21 H2
Wolverton Wy SHAM SO14 .... 49 J3
Wolverton Townsend
TADY RG26 .... 49 K3
Wolverton Wy SHAM SO14 .... 21 G2
Wolvesey Pl CHFD SO53 .... 206 C9
Wolvesey Ter WINC SO23 .... 23 G7
Wonderholme Pde
NBNE BH10 * 322 B5
Wonston Cl ROWN SO21 .... 125 M6
Wonston Ct HAV PO9 .... 277 J4
Wonston La RWIN SO21 .... 144 D1
Wonston Rd ROWN SO16 .... 227 M8
Woodacore Gdns NTHA RG18 .... 16 B3
The Woodbarn FNM GU9 * 116 C1
Woodberry La HAV PO9 .... 277 K1
Woodbind Wk SHST GU47 .... 270 F8
Woodbine Cl SHST GU47 .... 41 K7
Woodbourne Cl FNM GU9 .... 96 E4
Woodbourne Cl FHAM PO15 .... 272 B9
LISS GU33 .... 192 C2
YTLY GU46 .... 40 E8
Woodbridge Rd BLKW GU17 .... 41 K8
Woodbury BROC SO42 .... 286 D8
Woodbury Av CHAR BH8 .... 323 M5
HAV PO9 .... 298 F1
PSF GU32 .... 191 J3
Woodbury Cl
CHCH/BSGR BH23 .... 324 C4
Woodby Cg HORN PO8 .... 255 P6
Wood Cl BH/HW/K RG22 .... 89 M5
ITCH SO19 .... 249 L8
Woodcock La LYMN SO41 .... 328 N4
Woodcocks Crs LTDN BH7 .... 323 N8
Woodcot Crs HAV PO9 .... 276 C4
Woodcote La FLEETN GU51 .... 74 A4
Woodcote Rd BPWT SO32 .... 209 N6
Woodcote Rd SD/PW SO17 .... 228 E8
Woodcot Gdns FARN GU14 .... 57 L9
Woodcot Ter ASHV GU12 .... 3 K6
Woodcroft DEAN RG23 .... 88 F5
Woodcroft La HORN PO8 .... 255 N7
Woodcut Rd RFNM GU10 .... 115 P5
Woodcutters Dr HORN PO8 .... 255 N7
Wood End CHIN RG24 .... 69 P1
CWTH RG45 .... 41 P4
Woodend FARN GU14 .... 76 C1
Woodend Rd FRIM GU16 .... 59 H6
MOOR/WNTN BH9 .... 322 E8
Wood End Rd RGWD BH24 .... 283 J4
Wood End Wy CHFD SO53 .... 206 C6
Wooden House La LYMN SO41 .... 330 B2
Woodfern CFDH BH17 .... 241 H1
Woodfield Av CHAM PO6 .... 298 E8
Woodfield Av ALTN GU34 * 133 N8
Wood Field CHIN RG24 .... 70 A1
Woodfield Dr FUFL SO22 .... 164 C9
Woodfield Gdns
CHCH/BSGR BH23 .... 325 P6
Woodfield Park Rd
EMRTH PO10 .... 277 P9
Woodford Ri CHIN RG24 .... 70 A1
Woodford Rd BMTH BH1 .... 322 A2
Woodford Rd RGWD BH24 .... 282 F2
Woodford St BMTH BH24 .... 9 K2
Woodgarston Dr
BH/HW/K RG22 .... 89 L5
Woodgate La HISD PO9 .... 299 L5
Woodgate FLEETN GU51 .... 74 F1
Wood Glade Cl TOTT SO40 .... 267 K1
Woodgreen Av HAV PO9 .... 14 C3
Woodgreen Dr BWD BH11 .... 301 M9
Woodgreen Rd FUFL SO22 .... 164 E3
Woodhall Wy FHAM PO15 .... 10 B1
Woodhayes Av
CHCH/BSGR BH23 .... 326 A5
Wood Hill La ODIM RG29 .... 93 K7
Woodhouse La HAV PO9 .... 257 J7
HEND SO30 .... 250 C5
HORN PO8 .... 256 G5
STHA RG19 .... 33 H3
Woodhouse Rd HORN PO8 .... 256 F4
Woodington Cl HAV PO9 .... 256 C4
Woodington Rd ROMY SO51 .... 203 J9
Woodland Av HISD PO11 .... 299 J8
Woodland Cl ROMY SO51 .... 225 H2
VWD BH31 .... 258 E3
WEND SO18 .... 249 M4
Woodland Crs FARN GU14 .... 58 B7
Woodland Dr RFNM GU10 .... 116 B4
RSAL SP5 .... 158 A1
TADY RG26 .... 52 C3
Woodland Dro RWIN SO21 .... 208 A2
Woodland Ms NEND SO30 .... 249 M2
Woodland Rd FLEETS GU52 .... 74 B7
Woodlands CHIN RG24 .... 70 A1
FHAM/PORC PO16 .... 273 H8
FLEETN GU51 .... 74 C2
KSCL RG20 .... 29 P7
LYMN SO41 .... 328 A4
OVTN RG25 .... 85 N6
YTLY GU46 .... 40 G8
Woodlands Av EMRTH PO10 .... 277 L7
FNM GU9 .... 96 E4
PLE BH15 .... 320 B9
THLE RG7 .... 27 J3
Woodlands Cl ASHV GU12 .... 76 F7
BLKW GU17 .... 57 M4
CHCH/BSGR BH23 .... 305 L8

CHFD SO53..... 206 F3
FAWY SO45..... 268 A9
HLER SO31..... 270 F4
LSOL/BMARY PO13..... 314 G2
Woodlands Ct FAWY SO45..... 268 A9
SHST GU47..... 41 N5
Woodlands Ct PLE BH15..... 320 A9
Woodlands Dr HLER SO31..... 269 M4
TOTT SO40..... 245 K7
Woodlands Dro TOTT SO40..... 245 M8
Woodlands Gv WVILLE PO7..... 275 M5
Woodlands La HASM GU27..... 156 E6
HISD PO11..... 318 E3
LISS GU33..... 192 F4
Woodlands Rd BROC SO42..... 308 F1
FARN 57 L7
NMIL/BTOS BH25..... 326 G8
TADY RG26..... 33 N5
TOTT SO40..... 245 L7
The Woodlands BOR GU35..... 154 A7
WINC SO23..... 165 K1
Woodlands Wk BLKW GU17..... 57 M4
Woodlands Wy AND SP10..... 5 G4
HAV PO9..... 276 F6
HLER SO31..... 269 P2
NBAD SO52..... 205 J9
NMIL/BTOS BH25..... 327 K1
RGWD BH24..... 281 M5
WSHM SO15..... 248 B3
Woodland Vw HLER SO31..... 269 P2
HORN PO8..... 255 P5
Woodland Wk ASHV GU12..... 76 C9
BOSC BH5..... 335 N2
FERN BH22..... 302 F1
Woodland Wy
CHCH/BSGR BH23..... 325 P7
LYMN SO41..... 338 F2
Wood La BWD BH11..... 301 N7
FARN 75 P1
FLEETN GU51..... 74 F5
HTWY RG27..... 71 K7
LYMN SO41..... 338 F1
NARL SO24..... 187 P1
RFNM GU10..... 97 P7
WHAM PO17..... 274 C5
Woodlane CI NARL SO24..... 187 P1
Woodlark Gdns EPSF GU31..... 216 A2
Wood Lawn CI
NMIL/BTOS BH25..... 327 H6
Woodlea CI FUFL SO22..... 164 F5
Woodlea Gdns HEND SO30..... 249 N2
Woodlea Wy ROMY SO51..... 206 B3
Woodleaze CI BDST BH18..... 300 D7
Woodleigh CI HAV PO9..... 277 J7
Woodleigh Rd FLEETN GU51..... 74 D4
Woodley CI ROWN SO16..... 204 G3
Woodley Gdns LYMN SO41..... 329 K2
Woodley La ROMY SO51..... 204 E4
Woodley Rd GPORT PO12..... 12 E3
ITCH SO19..... 248 F8
Woodley Wy ROWN SO16..... 204 G3
Woodling Crs FBDG SP6..... 241 H1
Woodlinken CI VWD BH31..... 259 H6
Woodlinken Dr VWD BH31..... 259 H6
Woodlinken Wy VWD BH31..... 259 J6
Wood Ldg TOTT SO40..... 245 P2
Woodmancote La CRWN PO4..... 317 J4
Woodman Fld OVTN RG25..... 92 C5
Woodmans La THLE RG7..... 27 H4
Woodmere Cft BH/HW/K RG22..... 89 K4
Woodmill La WEND SO18..... 228 F9
Woodmoor SSEA PO5..... 19 H7
Woodpecker CI BH/HW/K RG22..... 89 K4
BOR GU35..... 154 A6
HAV PO9..... 15 K5
RFNM GU10..... 95 M3
VWD BH31..... 258 F5
Woodpecker Copse
HLER SO31..... 271 H7
Woodpecker Dr CFDH BH17..... 320 A4
TOTT SO40..... 267 J1
Woodpeckers WINC SO23..... 165 H5
Woodpeckers Dr FUFL SO22..... 164 D5
Woodpecker Wy ELGH SO50..... 228 F2
HSEA PO3..... 197 J5
Wood Rdg RWIN RG14..... 24 A8
Wood Rd CBLY GU15..... 58 A4
FNM GU9..... 96 C4
TOTT SO40..... 245 P9
Woodroffe Dr BH/HW/K RG22..... 89 P1
Woodrow WVILLE PO7..... 254 C7
Woodruff CI
CHCH/BSGR BH23..... 325 N7
Woodrush Crs HLER SO31..... 270 E8

Woodsedge WVILLE PO7..... 276 A4
Woodside BLKW GU17..... 57 K2
CBLY GU15..... 41 N7
LSOL/BMARY PO13..... 294 F4
NWBY RG14..... 24 A8
ROWN SO16..... 228 A2
Woodside Av ELGH SO50..... 228 A2
LYMN SO41..... 329 L1
Woodside CI BOR GU35..... 154 A5
FERN BH22..... 302 E2
LYMN SO41..... 329 L5
THLE RG7..... 27 J9
TOTT SO40..... 267 J1
Woodside Crs BOR GU35..... 154 A5
ROWN SO16..... 227 P2
Woodside Gdns CHIN RG24..... 52 A9
FLEETN GU51..... 74 F2
TOTT SO40..... 246 A8
Woodside La ALTN GU34..... 151 H4
LYMN SO41..... 329 L5
NMIL/BTOS BH25..... 327 L2
Woodside Pk BOR GU35..... 154 A5
Woodside Rd BOSC BH5..... 335 P2
ELGH SO50..... 206 G9
FARN GU14..... 75 N5
FERN BH22..... 302 E2
FNM GU9..... 96 E4
NBAD SO52..... 205 K9
PSTN BH14..... 321 L9
SD/PW SO17..... 248 D3
Woodside Wy HEND SO30..... 250 A6
Woods La OVTN RG25..... 90 B4
Woods Vw HORN PO8..... 256 A6
Woodstock CI
FHAM/STUB PO14..... 10 A5
HEND SO30..... 250 D6
Woodstock Dr SD/PW SO17..... 248 C2
Woodstock La RGWD BH24..... 282 E2
Woodstock Md BH/HW/K RG22..... 89 M5
Woodstock Rd
CHCH/BSGR BH23..... 325 H5
GPORT PO12..... 12 E3
HAV PO9..... 202 E9
PSTN BH14..... 333 J1
Woodstocks FARN GU14..... 58 B7
Wood St ASHV GU12..... 76 F6
Woods View Rd
MOOR/WNTN BH9..... 322 D7
Woodthorpe Gdns HLER SO31..... 270 F4
Woodvale FHAM PO15..... 272 B8
Woodvale Gdns
NMIL/BTOS BH25..... 327 L3
Wood Vw WIMB BH21..... 279 J6
Woodview CI ROWN SO16..... 228 C6
Woodville CI BLKW GU17..... 41 J9
Woodville Dr PSEA PO1..... 18 E6
Woodville Rd FAWY SO45..... 291 K6
HAV PO9..... 276 B8
Woodward CI GPORT PO12..... 315 K4
Woofferton Rd CHAM PO6..... 276 C9
Wooldridge Crs ODIM RG29..... 93 J3
Woolfield La ALTN GU34..... 190 B3
Woolford CI FUFL SO22..... 164 D9
Woolfords La MFD/CHID GU8..... 137 N2
Woolford Wy DEAN RG23..... 68 G6
Wool Gv AND SP10..... 5 G5
Woollards Rd ASHV GU12..... 76 F8
Woolley Sq AND SP10..... 82 C8
Woolmead Rd FNM GU9..... 96 C9
The Woolmead FNM GU9 *..... 96 C9
Woolmer CI HAV PO9..... 277 H5
Woolmer Hill Rd HASM GU27..... 156 B6
Woolmer La LIPH GU30..... 155 K8
RGWD BH24..... 260 E8
Woolmer Rd LISS GU33..... 173 N4
Woolmer St EMRTH PO10..... 277 L6
Woolmer Wy BOR GU35..... 155 P6
Woolner Av CHAM PO6..... 297 J1
PSF GU32..... 215 M1
Wool Rd BKME/WDN BH12..... 321 K4
Wools Br WIMB BH21..... 281 J3
Woolsbridge Rd RGWD BH24..... 281 L5
Woolslope CI FERN BH22..... 280 E8
Woolslope Gdns FERN BH22..... 280 E8
Woolslope Rd FERN BH22..... 280 E8
Woolston Rd HAV PO9..... 276 C4
ITCH SO19..... 269 K2
Woolton Lodge Gdns
KSCL RG20..... 29 N4
Woolven Ct PSTN BH14..... 321 J7
Woolwich CI HLER SO31..... 249 P9
Wooteys Wy ALTN GU34..... 132 F4
Wootton HLER SO31..... 269 L3
Wootton Farm Rd
NMIL/BTOS BH25..... 306 G6
Wootton Gdns BMTH BH1..... 9 F5
Wootton Mt BMTH BH1..... 9 G3
Wootton Rd
LSOL/BMARY PO13..... 314 G2

LYMN SO41..... 307 M8
Wootton Rough
NMIL/BTOS BH25..... 307 K8
Wootton St CHAM PO6..... 297 H2
Worbarrow Gdns
BKME/WDN BH12..... 321 L4
Worcester Av BH/HW/K RG22..... 89 M3
Worcester CI FARN GU14..... 58 A6
SSEA PO5..... 19 H5
Worcester Ct
LSOL/BMARY PO13..... 314 G2
Worcester PI ITCH SO19..... 249 K9
Wordsworth Av CHAM PO6..... 274 A9
CHAR BH8..... 323 L6
YTLY GU46..... 56 C7
Wordsworth CI BPWT SO32..... 232 C4
CHIN RG24..... 69 M4
FUFL SO22..... 164 E7
Wordsworth PI FHAM PO15..... 271 J1
Wordsworth Rd NTHA RG18..... 25 M3
WSHM SO15..... 247 N2
Worgret Rd PLE BH15..... 320 F5
Workhouse La PSF GU32..... 213 M4
Workman's La HLER SO31..... 292 E4
Workshop Rd WHAM PO17..... 274 C8
Wordham HI ALTN GU34..... 133 H8
Worley Wy FERN BH22..... 280 C5
Wormersley Rd STHA RG19..... 24 C7
Worrell Dr BKME/WDN BH12..... 321 L4
Worrell Sq AND SP10 *..... 82 G8
Worsam Ct BH/HW/K RG22..... 68 E8
Worsley Rd FRIM GU16..... 58 C5
SSEA PO5..... 19 H7
Worsley St ENEY PO4..... 317 J6
Worthing Rd SSEA PO5..... 316 F6
Worthington Crs PSTN BH14..... 321 J9
Worthy CI HAV PO9 *..... 277 H5
Worthy La WINC SO23..... 22 D2
Worthy Rd NMIL/BTOS BH25..... 327 J4
Worting Rd BH/HW/K RG22..... 68 F8
DEAN RG23..... 68 B8
Wortley Rd CHCH/BSGR BH23..... 326 C8
Wote St BSTK RG21..... 7 F7
Wouldham CI RAND SP11..... 79 H4
Wraxhall CI CFDH BH17..... 320 F3
Wraysbury Park Dr
EMRTH PO10..... 276 C7
Wrecclesham HI RFNM GU10..... 115 M5
Wrecclesham Rd FNM GU9..... 115 P2
Wrekin CI BH/HW/K RG22..... 68 E9
The Wrekin FARN GU14..... 76 D3
Wren CI ALTN GU34..... 132 C4
CHCH/BSGR BH23..... 337 M1
FUFL SO22..... 183 M1
NMIL/BTOS BH25 *..... 327 H5
RGWD BH24..... 282 C3
THLE RG7..... 27 K4
Wren CI ASHV GU12..... 76 C8
Wren Crs BKME/WDN BH12..... 334 B1
Wren Gdns FBDG SP6..... 239 P5
Wren Rd ELGH SO50..... 228 C3
Wrexham Av CI FARN GU14..... 57 N6
FHAM/PORC PO16..... 295 K1
Wrexham Gv HORN PO8..... 256 B9
Wright CI FHAM PO15..... 271 M4
Wrights CI RWIN SO21..... 144 E4
Wright's HI ITCH SO19..... 249 J9
Wrights Wk HLER SO31..... 269 P1
Wrights Wy RWIN SO21..... 144 E4
Wroxham Rd
BKME/WDN BH12..... 321 P7
Wryneck CI ROWN SO16..... 227 M6
Wulwyn Side CWTH RG45 *..... 41 H1
Wychbury CI HISD PO11..... 318 C6
Wych La LSOL/BMARY PO13..... 294 F5
Wychwood CI ASHV GU12..... 97 M1
WCLF BH2..... 8 C1
Wychwood Dr FAWY SO45..... 312 C1
WCLF BH2..... 334 F1
Wychwood PI FUFL SO22..... 164 D5
Wyck La ALTN GU34..... 151 H2
Wycliffe Rd MOOR/WNTN BH9..... 322 F7
WEND SO18..... 249 J2
Wycote Rd
LSOL/BMARY PO13..... 294 F5
Wye Ct AND SP10..... 82 C9
Wyeford CI HAV PO9..... 277 H4
Wyelands Av WIMB BH21..... 279 M9
Wyke Av ASHV GU12..... 77 J9
Wykeham CI CFDH BH17..... 320 G4
SSEA PO5..... 19 K4
Wykeham Ct ODIM RG29..... 93 K3
Wykeham Dr DEAN RG23..... 68 D6
Wykeham Fld WHAM PO17..... 252 B8

Wykeham Pk RWIN SO21 *..... 166 B8
Wykeham PI FUFL SO22..... 183 M1
Wykeham Rd FNM GU9..... 96 C8
HLER SO31..... 269 K4
Wykeham Rd..... 296 C8
Wykwood LIPH GU30..... 175 L3
Wylde Green La LISS GU33..... 192 E1
Wylds La PSF GU32..... 215 J5
Wylye CI WEND SO18..... 229 K9
Wylye Rd TDWTH SP9..... 79 H4
Wymering CI FARN GU14..... 76 C1
Wymering La CHAM PO6..... 296 C1
Wymering Manor CI
CHAM PO6 *..... 296 C1
Wymering Rd NEND PO2..... 296 C9
Wyncombe La BOSC BH5..... 335 P1
Wyndcliffe Rd ENEY PO4..... 316 G5
Wyndham CI
CHCH/BSGR BH23..... 326 D5
HORN PO8..... 256 B7
YTLY GU46..... 40 E7
Wyndham Ms AMSY SP4..... 118 A5
Wyndham Ms PSEA PO1..... 18 D6
Wyndham PI WSHM SO15..... 20 B2
Wyndham Rd AND SP10..... 102 D5
CHCH/BSGR BH23..... 326 D5
NWBY RG14..... 24 C2
PSTN BH14..... 321 K9
Wyndham St ASHV GU12..... 3 H4
Wynfields FRIM GU16..... 76 E1
Wynford Rd
MOOR/WNTN BH9..... 322 C3
PSTN BH14..... 321 L9
Wynne CI BDST BH18..... 300 B9
Wynne Gdns FLEETS GU52..... 74 E7
Wynsdale Cha AND SP11..... 292 C2
Wynter CI ITCH SO19..... 249 K3
Wynton Wy FHAM PO15..... 272 A7
Wynyards Gap NBAD SO52..... 205 K9
Wyre CI CHFD SO53..... 206 C8
Wyvern CI ASHV GU12 *..... 76 E7
BKME/WDN BH12..... 321 M5
CHFD SO53..... 206 F7

Y

Yachtsman CI HLER SO31..... 270 B2
Yaldhurst Ct HAV PO9..... 277 H4
Yaldhurst La LYMN SO41..... 329 K8
Yale CI SHST GU47..... 41 N4
Yapton St PSEA PO1..... 19 G2
Yarborough Rd SSEA PO5..... 19 C7
Yardlea CI HAV PO9..... 277 H1
Yardley CI HSEA PO3..... 297 L5
Yardley Rd HEND SO30..... 250 B6
Yarmley La RSAL SP5..... 158 A1
Yarmouth CI
BKME/WDN BH12..... 334 A1
Yarmouth Gdns WSHM SO15..... 247 M2
Yarmouth Rd
BKME/WDN BH12..... 321 P6
Yarnhams CI ALTN GU34..... 150 C6
Yarrell Cft LYMN SO41..... 329 H4
Yarrell Md LYMN SO41..... 329 H3
Yarrow CI CHCH/BSGR BH23..... 325 M7
NTHA RG18..... 25 N2
Yarrow Rd BKME/WDN BH12..... 321 P7
Yarrow Wy HLER SO31..... 270 E8
Yateley CI HAV PO9..... 276 C5
Yateley Rd YTLY GU46..... 40 C7
Yatesbury CI FNM GU9..... 115 P3
Yates Copse NWBY RG14..... 25 H2
Yaverland Rd SSEA PO5..... 269 L4
Yeatminster Rd CFDH BH17..... 321 H2
Yellowhammer Rd
BH/HW/K RG22..... 89 K5
Yellowhammers ALTN GU34..... 132 F3
Yelverton Av HAV PO9..... 318 G6
Yelverton Rd BMTH BH1..... 8 B2
Yeo Ct ENEY PO4..... 317 L5
Yeomanry CI STHA RG19..... 25 P5
Yeomans CI FARN GU14..... 57 P8
LIPH GU30..... 97 M3
Yeomans PI BOR GU35..... 154 F3
Yeomans Rd CHAR BH8..... 323 K5
Yeomans Wy CHAR BH8..... 323 L4
Yeovil Cha WEND SO18..... 249 K3
Yeovil CI FARN GU14..... 76 C3

Yeovil Rd SHST GU47..... 41 M5
Yeovilton CI LYMN SO41..... 328 E6
Yerville Gdns LYMN SO41..... 327 P4
Yetminster Rd FARN GU14..... 76 C3
Yew CI KSCL RG20..... 48 D3
Yew Ga NWBY RG14..... 24 C1
Yew La NMIL/BTOS BH25..... 327 L3
Yew Rd WEND SO18..... 249 J3
Yewside LSOL/BMARY PO13..... 295 H8
Yew Tree Av HORN PO8..... 256 D4
Yew Tree Av HORN PO8..... 256 B8
Yewtree CI FAWY SO45..... 290 C1
Yew Tree CI DEAN RG23..... 88 F3
ELGH SO50..... 230 C1
HAV PO9..... 75 K1
HEND SO30..... 250 B5
RAND SP11..... 102 E9
RSAL SP5..... 158 A1
TADY RG26..... 52 B3
WIMB BH21..... 278 F9
Yew Tree End HEND SO30 *..... 249 N2
Yew Tree Dr FHAM PO15..... 271 H3
Yew Tree Gdns RGWD BH24..... 282 E3
WVILLE PO7..... 254 C7
Yew Tree La ROWN SO16..... 226 C9
Yewtree La ROWN SO16..... 226 G9
Yew Tree La RSAL SP5..... 159 J4
Yew Tree PI LISS GU33..... 192 E2
Yew Tree Rd HISD PO11..... 298 C9
Yew Tree Wk FRIM GU16..... 58 G4
Yockley CI CBLY GU15..... 59 J2
Yoells Crs HORN PO8..... 255 P5
Yoells La HORN PO8..... 255 P5
Yokesford HI ROMY SO51..... 180 C9
Yolland CI FNM GU9..... 96 C4
Yonge CI ELGH SO50..... 229 K1
York Av NMIL/BTOS BH25..... 327 L3
York Bldgs SHAM SO14..... 20 E5
York CI BDST BH18..... 320 C2
BH/HW/K RG22..... 89 M3
BOR GU35..... 154 A6
CHCH/BSGR BH23..... 324 D8
CHFD SO53..... 206 B9
NWBY RG14..... 24 C2
PSF GU32..... 215 K2
SHAM SO14..... 21 K1
TOTT SO40..... 246 E3
York Crs ALDT GU11..... 3 C4
LSOL/BMARY PO13..... 314 E4
Yorkdale HLER SO31..... 270 C7
York Dro RSAL SP5..... 223 L4
WEND SO18..... 249 K4
Yorke St SSEA PO5..... 19 F5
Yorke Wy HLER SO31..... 269 N7
York Gdns FHAM/PORC PO16..... 295 P5
York Ga HTWY RG27..... 55 H8
York Ms ALTN GU34..... 132 C5
York PI LTDN BH7..... 335 N1
PSEA PO1..... 18 E1
York Rd ALDT GU11..... 2 C5
ASHV GU12..... 76 F9
BDST BH18..... 320 C3
BMTH BH1..... 9 J2
ELGH SO50..... 229 J3
FARN GU14..... 116 C2
FNM GU9..... 96 C4
WSHM SO15..... 247 N4
York Terrace La CBLY GU15 *..... 41 P9
Yorktown Rd SHST GU47..... 41 J7
York Wy SHST GU47..... 41 H6
Yorkwood LISS GU33..... 192 D2
Young Cr STHA RG19..... 24 G7
Youngs Dr ASHV GU12..... 97 M1
Youngs Paddock RSAL SP5..... 158 B1
Youngs Rd ALTN GU34..... 132 F5
BWD BH11..... 322 A2
Yves Ms SSEA PO5..... 316 F6

Z

Zamek CI BWD BH11..... 322 A2
Zetland Rd CHAM PO6..... 297 M2
GPORT PO12..... 12 C1
Zeus La WVILLE PO7..... 275 P7
Zinnia CI BH/HW/K RG22..... 89 L5
NBNE BH10..... 322 D5
Zion Rd RAND SP11..... 119 M4
Zouch Av TDWTH SP9..... 78 F4
Zouch CI TDWTH SP9..... 78 G4
Zouch Farm Rd TDWTH SP9..... 78 G4

Index - featured places

The AA - Fanum House
BSTK RG21..... 7 K4
Abbey Business Park
FNM GU9..... 116 F2
Abbey Chiropractic Clinic
ROMY SO51..... 204 C6
Abbey House
WINC SO23..... 23 F5
The Abbey School
FNM GU9..... 116 D1
Abbotsford Farm
Business Centre
ALTN GU34..... 150 D5
Abbotswood School
TOTT SO40..... 246 B4
Abbotts Ann Primary School
RAND SP11..... 101 M6
ABC Cinema
BMTH BH1..... 8 E4

Abro Industrial Estate
ALDT GU11..... 76 C9
Acorn Business Centre
BKME/WDN BH12..... 321 K5
CHAM PO6..... 296 C1
Action Stations
PSEA PO1..... 18 C2
Ad Astra First School
CFDH BH17..... 321 H2
Addington Clinic
BWD BH11..... 322 B2
Admiral Lord Nelson
School
HSEA PO3..... 297 K8
Adventure Wonderland
CHCH/BSGR BH23..... 303 L9
Aeropark Business
Park
FARN GU14..... 75 N4

AFC Bournemouth
(Fitness First Stadium)
LTDN BH7..... 323 M9
AFC Newbury
NWBY RG14..... 17 G1
Airborne Forces Museum
ALDT GU11..... 75 P7
Airfield Industrial Estate
CFDH BH17..... 321 H2
Albany Business Centre
WHAM PO17..... 272 F3
Albany Park Industrial Estate
FRIM GU16..... 58 A4
Albert Road Cemetery
HEND SO30..... 250 B6
Alder Hills Industrial Park
BKME/WDN BH12..... 321 P5
Aldermoor Health Centre
ROWN SO16..... 227 N8

Alderney
Community Hospital
BKME/WDN BH12..... 321 L3
Aldershot Centre for Health
ALDT GU11..... 75 P9
Aldershot Garrison
Sports Centre
ALDT GU11..... 76 B6
Aldershot Military Cemetery
ALDT GU11..... 76 C9
Aldershot Military Museum
ALDT GU11..... 76 B5
Aldershot Military Stadium
ALDT GU11..... 76 B6
Aldershot Outpatients
Department
ALDT GU11..... 3 F1
Aldershot Town FC
ALDT GU11..... 3 H3

Aldworth Science College
BH/HW/K RG22..... 89 P1
Alexander Barracks
CHOB/PIR GU24..... 59 N7
Alexander House
Business Centre
ALDT GU11..... 3 F3
Allbrook School
ELGH SO50..... 207 K6
Allenbourn Middle School
WIMB BH21..... 278 E8
All Hallows
Catholic School
FNM GU9..... 96 F4
Allington Manor
Business Centre
ELGH SO50..... 229 N5
All Saints CE Infant School
RFNM GU10..... 117 J7

All Saints CE Junior School
FLEETN GU51 .... **74** A4
All Saints CE Primary School
RSAL SP5 .... **201** K2
All Saints CE (VC)
Primary School
WINC SO23 .... **23** H7
Alpha Business Park
SHAM SO14 .... **248** D4
Alpine Snowsports
Dry Ski Slope
ALDT GU11 .... **76** B8
Alresford County
Junior School
NARL SO24 .... **168** A2
Alresford Golf Club
NARL SO24 .... **167** P4
Alton Business Centre
ALTN GU34 .... **133** H6
Alton Cemetery
ALTN GU34 .... **132** F4
Alton College
ALTN GU34 .... **132** F4
Alton Community Centre
ALTN GU34 .... **132** F4
Alton Community Hospital
ALTN GU34 .... **132** D8
Alton Convent School
ALTN GU34 .... **132** G3
Alton County Infant School
ALTN GU34 .... **132** G3
Alton Golf Club
ALTN GU34 .... **112** E9
Alton Grange Hotel
ALTN GU34 .... **133** H4
Alton Health Centre
ALTN GU34 .... **132** G5
Alton House Hotel
ALTN GU34 .... **132** G5
Alton Sports Centre
ALTN GU34 .... **132** D8
Alton Town FC
ALTN GU34 .... **133** H4
Alton Town RFC
ALTN GU34 .... **133** H4
Alverstoke CE Junior School
GPORT PO12 .... **12** A5
Alverstoke Infant School
GPORT PO12 .... **12** A7
Ambassador Industrial Estate
CHCH/BSGR BH23 .... **325** L9
Amery Hill Secondary School
ALTN GU34 .... **132** F5
Amesbury School
GSHT GU26 .... **156** D4
Amey Industrial Estate
PSF GU32 .... **215** L2
AMF Bowling
WEND SO18 .... **249** J5
AMF Bowling & Bingo
PSEA PO1 .... **19** H2
Ampfield Par 3 Golf Club
ROMY SO51 .... **205** N2
Ampfield Primary School
ROMY SO51 .... **205** N1
Amport CE J & I School
RAND SP11 .... **100** C5
Anchor Business Centre
CHDS SO53 .... **206** D7
Andover Athletics Club
AND SP10 .... **82** A9
Andover Cemetery
AND SP10 .... **4** E5
Andover CE Primary School
AND SP10 .... **4** E5
Andover FC
AND SP10 .... **82** A9
Andover Golf Club
AND SP10 .... **102** E4
Andover Leisure Centre
AND SP10 .... **4** D3
Andover Museum & the
Museum of the Iron Age
AND SP10 .... **4** E3
Andover Road Retail Park
FUFL SO22 .... **22** C2
Andrews Endowed CE
Primary School
ALTN GU34 .... **133** J5
Anglo-Swiss Hotel
BMTH BH1 .... **9** H3
Annie Lawson School
NWBY RC14 .... **16** B4
Ann's Hill Cemetery
GPORT PO12 .... **315** K3
Ansells Farm
Community Centre
FLEETN GU51 .... **56** F9
Anstey County Junior School
ALTN GU34 .... **132** F5
Antelope Inn Hotel
PLE BH15 .... **332** D2
Anton County Infant School
AND SP10 .... **102** E4
Anton Junior School
AND SP10 .... **102** E4
Anton Trading Estate
AND SP10 .... **4** C7
The Anvil Concert Hall
BSTK RG21 .... **6** E5
Apollo Cinema
FHAM/PORC PO16 .... **11** H6
Apollo Hotel
CHIN RG24 .... **69** J4
Apple Industrial Estate
WEND SO18 .... **271** J5
Applemore College
FAWY SO45 .... **267** N8
Applemore
Recreation Centre
FAWY SO45 .... **267** N7
Ardglen Industrial Estate
WHCH RG28 .... **85** K6
Argyle Community Centre
SHAM SO14 .... **21** F2
The Ark School
THLE RG7 .... **26** B6

Arlington Hotel
WCLF BH2 .... **8** E5
Army Golf Club
ALDT GU11 .... **75** M6
Army Medical
Services Museum
ASHV GU12 .... **76** G3
Army Training Regiment
CHOB/PIR GU24 .... **59** P7
Arndale Court Hotel
PLE BH15 .... **320** E9
The Arnewood School
NMIL/BTOS BH25 .... **327** H5
Arnhem Barracks
ALDT GU11 .... **75** P9
Arrow Industrial Estate
FARN GU14 .... **75** N2
The Arts Institute of
Bournemouth
BKME/WDN BH12 .... **322** C7
Art Space School
PSEA PO1 .... **316** E1
Arundel Court J & I School
PSEA PO1 .... **19** K1
Arundel Tower
WSHM SO15 .... **20** D5
Ashdown Leisure Centre
CFDH BH17 .... **321** H3
Ashdown Technology College
CFDH BH17 .... **320** G3
Ashford Hangers National
Nature Reserve
PSF GU32 .... **191** L4
Ashford Hill Primary School
* STHA* RG19 .... **33** H5
Ash Grange CP School
ASHV GU12 .... **97** P1
Ashley Heath
Industrial Estate
WIMB BH21 .... **281** J2
Ashley Infant School
NMIL/BTOS BH25 .... **327** N4
Ashley Junior School
NMIL/BTOS BH25 .... **327** L4
Ash Manor School
ASHV GU12 .... **97** N3
Ashurst Hospital
TOTT SO40 .... **265** P1
Ash Vale Health Centre
ASHV GU12 .... **76** G8
The Atherly & Grove Place
Preparatory School
ROWN SO16 .... **226** F6
Avenue Clinic
WSHM SO15 .... **20** C1
The Avenue Shopping Centre
WCLF BH2 .... **8** C3
Avington Park
RWIN SO21 .... **166** D2
Avonbourne Girls School
LTDN BH7 .... **323** N8
Avondale Lawn Tennis Club
RFNM GU10 .... **74** C9
Avon Heath Country Park
RGWD BH24 .... **281** N6
The Avonmouth Hotel
CHCH/BSGR BH23 .... **337** L1
Avon Trading Park
CHCH/BSGR BH23 .... **324** E7
Awbridge Primary School
ROMY SO51 .... **179** K9
Back of Beyond Touring Park
RGWD BH24 .... **281** J8
Baddesley Park
Industrial Estate
NBAD SO52 .... **205** M9
Baden Powell & St Peters
CE Middle School
PSTN BH14 .... **321** K9
Badshot Lea Village
Infant School
FNM GU9 .... **96** G5
Balksbury Hill
Industrial Estate
RAND SP11 .... **102** C5
The Balksbury J & I School
AND SP10 .... **102** B4
Ballard College
NMIL/BTOS BH25 .... **327** J4
Balmer Lawn Hotel
BROC SO42 .... **286** G6
Banister Infant School
WSHM SO15 .... **248** N4
The Banks Medical Centre
TWDS BH3 .... **322** E8
Bar End Industrial Estate
WINC SO23 .... **184** B1
Barfield School
RFNM GU10 .... **97** H8
Barford Park Trout Farm
RSAL SP5 .... **199** K2
Bargate Museum
SHAM SO14 .... **20** D5
Bargate Shopping Centre
SHAM SO14 .... **20** E5
Barncroft Infant School
HAV PO9 .... **14** B1
Barncroft Junior School
HAV PO9 .... **276** C6
Barratt Industrial Park
FHAM PO15 .... **271** J5
Bartley CE Junior School
TOTT SO40 .... **245** H4
Bartley Lodge Hotel
TOTT SO40 .... **244** F4
Bartley Wood
Business Park (East)
HTWY RG27 .... **72** B4
Bartley Wood
Business Park (West)
HTWY RG27 .... **72** A4
Barton Industrial Estate
NARL SO24 .... **130** B8
Barton-on-Sea Golf Club
NMIL/BTOS BH25 .... **327** L8
Barton Peveril College
ELGH SO50 .... **229** H3

Barton Stacey CE
Primary School
RWIN SO21 .... **124** G1
Bashley Park
NMIL/BTOS BH25 .... **307** K9
Basing House
CHIN RG24 .... **70** B6
Basingstoke Aquadrome
DEAN RG23 .... **68** F7
Basingstoke Business Centre
BH/HW/K RG22 .... **90** A1
Basingstoke College of
Technology
BSTK RG21 .... **6** C6
FLEETN GU51 .... **74** C3
Basingstoke Country Hotel
HTWY RG27 .... **71** M5
Basingstoke Crematorium
OVTN RG25 .... **108** A3
Basingstoke Golf Club
DEAN RG23 .... **89** K6
Basingstoke Leisure Park
BH/HW/K RG22 .... **68** G7
Basingstoke Planet Ice
DEAN RG23 .... **68** F7
Basingstoke RFC
BH/HW/K RG22 .... **89** M2
Basingstoke Sports Centre
BSTK RG21 .... **6** E5
Basingstoke Town FC
BH/HW/K RG22 .... **90** A1
Bassett Green
Primary School
ROWN SO16 .... **228** D8
Baycroft School
FHAM/STUB PO14 .... **294** B7
Bay House School
GPORT PO12 .... **315** J6
Bay View Court Hotel
BMTH BH1 .... **9** K4
BBC South TV & Radio Solent
WSHM SO15 .... **20** C2
Beacon Hill National
Nature Reserve
BPWT SO32 .... **211** K2
Bearwood CP School
BWD BH11 .... **301** L7
Bearwood Medical Centre
BWD BH11 .... **301** M8
Beaucroft
Foundation School
WIMB BH21 .... **278** G8
Beaulieu Abbey
BROC SO42 .... **289** K7
Beaulieu Hotel
BROC SO42 .... **266** C9
Beaulieu National
Motor Museum
BROC SO42 .... **289** J7
Beaulieu Primary School
BROC SO42 .... **289** K8
Beaumont Junior School
ALDT GU11 .... **2** A3
Beaver Industrial Estate
CHCH/BSGR BH23 .... **325** J3
LIPH GU30 .... **175** K5
Bedales School
PSF GU32 .... **191** L7
Bedenham Primary School
LSOL/BMARY PO13 .... **294** C6
Beechnut Industrial Estate
ASHV GU12 .... **3** G4
Beechwood Junior School
WEND SO18 .... **249** H4
The Beggarwood Surgery
DEAN RG23 .... **89** K6
Belbins Business Park
ROMY SO51 .... **204** E2
Belgrave Industrial Estate
SD/PW SO17 .... **248** L1
Bellemoor Secondary School
ROWN SO16 .... **247** P1
Belle Vue Infant School
ASHV GU12 .... **3** K3
Bell Inn Hotel
LYND SO43 .... **244** A2
Belvedere Hotel
BMTH BH1 .... **9** F4
Benridge Business Park
CFDH BH17 .... **320** C4
Bentley CE Primary School
RFNM GU10 .... **114** F5
Bentley Industrial Centre
RFNM GU10 .... **114** E6
Bentley Trimmings
Business Park
RFNM GU10 .... **114** F5
Bentworth CE Primary School
ALTN GU34 .... **131** J4
Berrywood Business Village
HEND SO30 .... **230** B9
Berrywood Primary School
HEND SO30 .... **250** D2
Best Western
Botleigh Grange Hotel
HEND SO30 .... **250** D3
Best Western Crown Hotel
LYND SO43 .... **264** F5
Best Western
East Anglia Hotel
WBNE BH4 .... **334** D5
Best Western
Forest Lodge Hotel
LYND SO43 .... **264** F4
Best Western
Mansion House Hotel
PLE BH15 .... **332** D1
Best Western
the Connaught Hotel
WCLF BH2 .... **8** B5
Best Western
Waterford Lodge Hotel
CHCH/BSGR BH23 .... **325** M4
Bethany CE Junior School
BMTH BH1 .... **335** L1
Bevois Town Primary School
SHAM SO14 .... **248** C4

Bicknell Special School
LTDN BH7 .... **323** N8
Bidbury J & I School
HAV PO9 .... **14** B4
Bilton Industrial Estate
CHIN RG24 .... **69** P3
Binsted CE Primary School
RFNM GU10 .... **134** B2
Binswood View
Business Centre
BOR GU35 .... **153** J4
Birchwood Medical Centre
CFDH BH17 .... **320** B4
Birdworld &
Underwaterworld
RFNM GU10 .... **115** K7
Bishop Challoner RC School
BH/HW/K RG22 .... **68** F9
The Bishop of Winchester
Comprehensive School
CHAR BH8 .... **323** K6
Bishops Green
Farm Camp Site
KSCL RG20 .... **31** M4
Bishops Palace
WINC SO23 .... **23** F6
Bishops Waltham
Infant School
BPWT SO32 .... **232** B4
Bishop's Waltham Palace
BPWT SO32 .... **232** A5
Bishopswood Golf Club
TADY RG26 .... **34** A7
Bishopswood J & I Schools
TADY RG26 .... **34** C7
Bitterne CE (Controlled)
Junior School
ITCH SO19 .... **249** H5
Bitterne CE Infant School
ITCH SO19 .... **249** H5
Bitterne Health Centre
WEND SO18 .... **249** J4
Bitterne Leisure Centre
WEND SO18 .... **249** J4
Bitterne Manor
Primary School
WEND SO18 .... **248** F4
Bitterne Park Clinic
WEND SO18 .... **248** F3
Bitterne Park J & I School
WEND SO18 .... **248** F1
Bitterne Park
Secondary School
WEND SO18 .... **248** G1
Blackbrook Business Park
FHAM PO15 .... **10** A5
Blackbushe Airport
BLKW GU17 .... **56** B3
Blackbushe Business Park
YTLY GU46 .... **56** D1
Black Dam Nature Reserve
BSTK RG21 .... **69** P8
Blackdown Barracks
FRIM GU16 .... **59** J7
Blackfield Cemetery
FAWY SO45 .... **290** G9
Blackfield Health Centre
FAWY SO45 .... **290** F7
Blackfield Primary School
FAWY SO45 .... **290** G8
Blackmoor Golf Club
BOR GU35 .... **153** M7
Blacknest Industrial Park
ALTN GU34 .... **134** C2
Blackwater & Hawley
Leisure Centre
BLKW GU17 .... **57** L2
Blackwater Industrial Estate
BLKW GU17 .... **41** M9
Blackwater Trading Estate
ASHV GU12 .... **97** K3
Bleach's Yard
Industrial Estate
LIPH GU30 .... **175** K5
Blue Reef Aquarium
SSEA PO5 .... **316** E7
The Boatyard
Industrial Estate
FHAM/PORC PO16 .... **294** E1
Bohunt Manor
LIPH GU30 .... **175** J4
Bohunt School
LIPH GU30 .... **175** J3
Boldrewood Centre
ROWN SO16 .... **228** B9
Bone lane Industrial Area
NWBY RC14 .... **17** K1
Bordon Infant School
BOR GU35 .... **153** P4
Bordon Trading Estate
BOR GU35 .... **153** M3
Boscombe Dental
Health Centre
LTDN BH7 .... **335** M1
Boscombe Manor
Medical Centre
BOSC BH5 .... **335** M2
Boscombe Pier
BOSC BH5 .... **335** L4
Bosmere Junior School
HAV PO9 .... **15** F6
Botley CE Primary School
HEND SO30 .... **250** F4
Boundary Oak School
WHAM PO17 .... **272** G5
Bourne Hall Hotel
WCLF BH2 .... **8** C6
Bourne Mill Industrial Estate
FNM GU9 .... **96** E8
Bournemouth
Business Centre
CHAR BH8 .... **9** H2
Bournemouth Crematorium
CHAR BH8 .... **323** J6
Bournemouth
International Airport
CHCH/BSGR BH23 .... **303** M8

Bournemouth
International Centre
WCLF BH2 .... **8** D6
Bournemouth
Jewish Day School
BMTH BH1 .... **9** F3
Bournemouth Learning
Support Centre
NBNE BH10 .... **322** C6
Bournemouth
Nuffield Hospital
CHAR BH8 .... **334** G1
Bournemouth Pier
.... **8** E6
The Bournemouth
& Poole College
BMTH BH1 .... **9** H3
PSTN BH14 .... **321** H8
Bournemouth School
CHAR BH8 .... **323** J6
Bournemouth School
for Girls
CHAR BH8 .... **323** J5
Bournemouth Sports Club
CHCH/BSGR BH23 .... **303** J7
Bournemouth University
BKME/WDN BH12 .... **322** C7
The Bourne School
RFNM GU10 .... **116** D3
Bourne Tennis Club
FNM GU9 .... **116** C2
Bourne Valley Business Park
BKME/WDN BH12 .... **334** A1
Bowlplex
BH/HW/K RG22 .... **68** F7
PSEA PO1 .... **18** C4
Boyatt Shopping Centre
ELGH SO50 .... **207** J8
Boyatt Wood
Industrial Estate
ELGH SO50 .... **207** H9
Bradbury Centre &
Rosewood School
ROWN SO16 .... **227** N3
Braishfield Primary School
ROMY SO51 .... **181** H3
Brambles Farm
Industrial Estate
WVILLE PO7 .... **275** M2
Bramley CE J & I School
TADY RG26 .... **52** A1
Bramshaw Golf Club
LYND SO43 .... **244** A2
Branksome Cemetery
BKME/WDN BH12 .... **321** L5
Branksome Heath
Middle School
BKME/WDN BH12 .... **321** L6
Bransgore CE
Primary School
CHCH/BSGR BH23 .... **305** N8
Bratley Arch
LYND SO43 .... **262** G3
Braxton Gardens
LYMN SO41 .... **328** E7
Breamore CE Primary School
FBDC SP6 .... **220** F4
Breamore House &
Countryside Museum
FBDC SP6 .... **220** E1
Briar Park Business Centre
CHCH/BSGR BH23 .... **324** E8
Brickfield Trading Estate
CHFD SO53 .... **206** D8
Brick Kiln Industrial Estate
TADY RG26 .... **34** D5
Brickyards Industrial Estate
PSF GU32 .... **191** N5
Bridge House Hotel
FERN BH22 .... **302** B9
Bridgemary
Community School
LSOL/BMARY PO13 .... **294** G7
The Bridge Shopping Centre
PSEA PO1 .... **19** K2
Bridge Stones Gasworks
ALDT GU11 .... **76** D8
Brighton Hill
Community College
BH/HW/K RG22 .... **89** P2
Brighton Hill Retail Park
BH/HW/K RG22 .... **90** A1
Bristow Infant School
CBLY GU15 .... **58** A3
Broadlands
ROMY SO51 .... **204** C3
Broadmarsh Business &
Innovation Centre
HAV PO9 .... **14** A7
Broadmoor CP School
CWTH RG45 .... **41** L2
Broadmoor Hospital
CWTH RG45 .... **41** M1
Broadstone Cemetery
BDST BH18 .... **300** E8
Broadstone (Dorset)
Golf Club
BDST BH18 .... **300** C2
Broadstone First School
BDST BH18 .... **300** D8
Broadstone Leisure Centre
BDST BH18 .... **300** D8
Broadstone Middle School
BDST BH18 .... **300** E8
Brockenhurst CE
Primary School
BROC SO42 .... **286** F4
Brockenhurst College
BROC SO42 .... **286** G7
CHCH/BSGR BH23 .... **325** H9
Brockenhurst Manor
Golf Club
BROC SO42 .... **308** G2
Brockhurst Infant School
GPORT PO12 .... **315** K1
Brockhurst Junior School
GPORT PO12 .... **315** L2

Brockhurst Medical Centre
GPORT PO12 .... **315** K1
Brockwood Park School
NARL SO24 .... **188** A5
Brokenford Business Centre
TOTT SO40 .... **246** D5
Brookes Hill Industrial Estate
TOTT SO40 .... **225** P8
Brookfield Community School
HLER SO31 .... **270** E6
Brookfield Hotel
EMRTH PO10 .... **277** K9
Brookham School
LIPH GU30 .... **175** M5
Brook Park Estate
WIMB BH21 .... **300** C2
The Brooks Shopping Centre
WINC SO23 .... **22** E4
The Brook Trading Estate
ASHV GU12 .... **76** D9
Brookvale Hall
BSTK RG21 .... **6** C6
Brookway Industrial Estate
NWBY RG14 .... **24** C5
Brookwood Industrial Estate
ELGH SO50 .... **229** J1
Broughton Primary School
STOK SO20 .... **140** A9
Browning Barracks
ALDT GU11 .... **75** P7
Brownsea Island (NT)
CCLF BH13 .... **332** G7
Brownsea Open Air Theatre
CCLF BH13 .... **333** H7
Broxhead Trading Estate
BOR GU35 .... **154** C2
Brune Park Community School
LSOL/BMARY PO13 .... **295** J9
Buckholme Towers School
PSTN BH14 .... **321** J9
Buckland Medical Centre
NEND PO2 .... **296** F9
Bucklers Hard Village & Maritime Museum
BROC SO42 .... **311** P4
Budds Lane Trading Estate
ROMY SO51 .... **204** B4
The Bungate School & Sixth Form Centre
FBDG SP6 .... **220** D9
Burghclere Primary School
KSCL RG20 .... **30** F8
Burghfield Health Centre
THLE RG7 .... **27** K4
Burghfield St Marys Primary School
RDGW/BURGH RG30 .... **27** L1
Buriton Business Park
EPSF GU31 .... **215** J6
Buriton Primary School
EPSF GU31 .... **215** K8
Burley Court Hotel
BMTH BH1 .... **9** G4
Burley Golf Club
RGWD BH24 .... **284** D7
Burley Manor Hotel
RGWD BH24 .... **284** C5
Burley Primary School
RGWD BH24 .... **284** C6
Burnham Copse J & I Schools
TADY RG26 .... **34** B5
Burrfields Retail Park
HSEA PO3 .... **297** L8
Burridge Social & Sports Club
HLER SO31 .... **251** H9
Bursledon CE J & I School
HLER SO31 .... **270** A2
Bursledon Windmill Museum
HLER SO31 .... **250** A9
Burton CE Primary School
CHCH/BSGR BH23 .... **324** G4
Burton Medical Centre
CHCH/BSGR BH23 .... **325** H5
Buryfields Infant School
ODIM RG29 .... **93** L1
Bury Hill
RAND SP11 .... **102** B6
Business Aviation Centre
FARN GU14 .... **75** N5
The Business Centre Morgans Vale
RSAL SP5 .... **199** P6
Busketts Lawn Hotel
TOTT SO40 .... **245** L8
Butser Ancient Farm
HORN PO8 .... **236** G7
Butser Hill National Nature Reserve
EPSF GU31 .... **214** F8
The Butts CP School
ALTN GU34 .... **132** D7
Byngs Business Park
WVILLE PO7 .... **255** K9
Cabot Business Village
CFDH BH17 .... **320** D4
Cadland Primary School
FAWY SO45 .... **290** E6
Calleva Atrebatum Roman Town
THLE RG7 .... **35** M4
Calleva Business Park
THLE RG7 .... **33** P4
Calmore Industrial Estate
TOTT SO40 .... **246** C1
Calmore J & I School
TOTT SO40 .... **246** A2
Calmore Sports Club
TOTT SO40 .... **245** N1
Calshot Castle
FAWY SO45 .... **292** B8
Calthorpe Park School
FLEETN GU51 .... **73** P4
Camberley CC
CBLY GU15 .... **58** C2

Camberley Health Centre
CBLY GU15 .... **58** A2
Camberley Heath Golf Club
CBLY GU15 .... **58** F1
Camberley RFC
CBLY GU15 .... **58** B2
Camberley Town FC
CBLY GU15 .... **58** A2
Cameleon Theatre
WSHM SO15 .... **247** H6
Camelsdale County First School
HASM GU27 .... **156** E8
Camera Obscura
WCLF BH2 .... **8** C4
Campana Finishing School
RFNM GU10 .... **116** G1
Campbell Court Industrial Estate
TADY RG26 .... **52** B3
Camp Road Industrial Estate
FARN GU14 .... **76** B4
Cams Hall Estate Golf Club
FHAM/PORC PO16 .... **295** H2
Cams Hill School
FHAM/PORC PO16 .... **295** J1
Canada House Business Centre
NMIL/BTOS BH25 .... **327** L5
Canford Heath First School
CFDH BH17 .... **320** C5
Canford Heath Middle School
CFDH BH17 .... **320** F5
Canford Magna Golf Club
WIMB BH21 .... **301** M5
Canford School
WIMB BH21 .... **301** J3
Cannons Health Club
NWBY RG14 .... **24** G5
Cantell Maths & Computing College
ROWN SO16 .... **228** C7
Capitol School of English
MOOR/WNTN BH9 .... **322** E8
Careys Manor Hotel
BROC SO42 .... **286** G7
Carnegie Library
PSEA PO1 .... **316** G2
Carnival Hall
BSTK RG21 .... **69** K8
Carrington House Hotel
BMTH BH1 .... **335** K3
Cartel Business Centre
CHIN RG24 .... **69** P4
Carter Community Sports College
PLE BH15 .... **332** B1
Carvers Trading Estate
RGWD BH24 .... **282** E2
Carwarden House School
CBLY GU15 .... **58** F2
Casa dei Cesari Hotel
YTLY GU46 .... **56** F1
Cascades Shopping Centre
PSEA PO1 .... **19** G1
Castle CP School
FHAM/PORC PO16 .... **295** P2
Castledown School
RAND SP11 .... **79** L2
Castle Hill Infant School
DEAN RG23 .... **68** E7
Castle Industrial Park
NWBY RG14 .... **24** C1
Castle Trading Estate
FHAM/PORC PO16 .... **296** A2
Catchcold Tower
SHAM SO14 .... **20** D5
Cathedral Church of St Thomas of Canterbury
PSEA PO1 .... **18** C6
Cathedral Discovery Centre
PSEA PO1 .... **19** F1
Catherine Corbett Clinic
HAV PO9 .... **15** G5
Catherington CE (Controlled) Infant School
HORN PO8 .... **256** B2
Cenotaph
WSHM SO15 .... **20** D2
Central Estate
ALDT GU11 .... **3** F4
Central Hall
SHAM SO14 .... **21** G5
Central Health Clinic
SHAM SO14 .... **20** E2
Central Industrial Estate
HAV PO9 .... **14** E6
Central Trading Estate
WEND SO18 .... **21** J4
Centurion Industrial Park
WEND SO18 .... **248** E4
Chalcroft Distribution Park
HEND SO30 .... **230** A7
Chalk Ridge Primary School
BH/HW/K RG22 .... **90** A2
Chalwyn Industrial Estate
BKME/WDN BH12 .... **321** J5
Chamberlayne Park School
ITCH SO19 .... **269** J1
Chandler's Ford Industrial Estate
CHFD SO53 .... **206** E8
Chandlers Ford Infant School
CHFD SO53 .... **206** F6
The Chantry Centre
AND SP10 .... **4** D4
Chapel of St Johns Hospital
WINC SO23 .... **23** F5
Charles Dickens' Birthplace Museum
PSEA PO1 .... **316** E1
Charles Dickens J & I School
PSEA PO1 .... **316** E2

Charles Kingsleys CE Primary School
HTWY RG27 .... **39** M6
Charlton House School
WEND SO18 .... **249** H3
Charlton Sports & Leisure Centre
AND SP10 .... **82** A9
Charris Camping & Caravan Park
WIMB BH21 .... **300** A3
Chase Community Hospital
BOR GU35 .... **154** A6
Chawton Primary School
ALTN GU34 .... **151** L1
Cheam School
STHA RG19 .... **32** A6
Cherbourg Primary School
ELGH SO50 .... **229** J3
The Cheriton Brewhouse
NARL SO24 .... **186** G1
Cheriton Primary School
NARL SO24 .... **167** P9
Cherry Wood Primary School
FAWY SO45 .... **57** P7
Chesil Theatre
WINC SO23 .... **23** G6
Chevron Business Park
FAWY SO45 .... **290** D3
Chewton Glen Hotel
NMIL/BTOS BH25 .... **326** E7
Chilworth Golf Club
ROWN SO16 .... **227** M1
Chilworth Manor Hotel
ROWN SO16 .... **227** N3
Chineham Business Park
CHIN RG24 .... **51** P9
Chineham Park Primary School
CHIN RG24 .... **69** N4
Chineham Shopping Centre
CHIN RG24 .... **70** A3
Chine Hotel
BMTH BH1 .... **335** K3
Cholderton Rare Breeds Farm
AMSY SP4 .... **98** B9
Christchurch Castle & Norman House
CHCH/BSGR BH23 .... **324** G9
Christchurch Hospital
CHCH/BSGR BH23 .... **324** D6
Christchurch J & I School
CHCH/BSGR BH23 .... **324** E8
Christchurch Medical Centre
CHCH/BSGR BH23 .... **325** J8
Christchurch Priory
CHCH/BSGR BH23 .... **324** G9
Christchurch Rowing Club
HAV PO9 .... **277** J7
Christchurch Ski & Leisure Centre
CHCH/BSGR BH23 .... **303** P5
Christ's Hospital
WINC SO23 .... **22** D6
Christ the King Catholic Primary School
BWD BH11 .... **322** A2
Church Cottage
BSTK RG21 .... **6** E6
Church Crookham Junior School
FLEETS GU52 .... **74** D8
Churchers College
EPSF GU31 .... **215** N1
Churchers College Junior Department
PSF GU32 .... **215** L2
Church Grange & Bramblys Grange Health Centre
BSTK RG21 .... **6** D7
Churchill Yard Industrial Estate
WVILLE PO7 .... **275** N1
Cineworld
SHAM SO14 .... **248** D9
City Business Centre
WINC SO23 .... **22** E3
City Grove Trading Estate
ELGH SO50 .... **206** G9
City Industrial Park
WSHM SO15 .... **20** A5
City Museum & Records Office
PSEA PO1 .... **18** E5
The City of Portsmouth Boys School
NEND PO2 .... **296** G5
City of Portsmouth Girls School
PSEA PO1 .... **316** G1
City of Portsmouth Sports Club
NEND PO2 .... **296** F6
Civic Gateway
BSTK RG21 .... **7** F7
Civil Service Sports Ground
HSEA PO3 .... **297** J6
NBNE BH10 .... **302** C9
Clanfield Junior School
HORN PO8 .... **236** B5
Clarence Pier & Amusement Centre
SSEA PO5 .... **316** C6
Clarendon J & I School
TDWTH SP9 .... **79** H4
Clatford CE J & I School
RAND SP11 .... **102** E9
Clayfields Sports Centre
ELGH SO50 .... **267** P6
Clayhall Military Cemetery
GPORT PO12 .... **12** D7
Clayton Barracks
ALDT GU11 .... **76** C8
Cliddesden Primary School
OVTN RG25 .... **90** C6

Cliff Court Hotel
WCLF BH2 .... **8** A5
Cliffdale Primary School
NEND PO2 .... **297** H7
Cliffeside Hotel
BMTH BH1 .... **9** J4
Cloud Hotel
BROC SO42 .... **286** G7
The Club at Meyrick Park
WCLF BH2 .... **8** B1
Cluster Industrial Estate
ENEY PO4 .... **317** J5
The Coast Clinic
FAWY SO45 .... **291** K6
Coastguard Office
PLE BH15 .... **332** D2
Cody Technology Park
FARN GU14 .... **75** K4
Cogdean Elms Industrial Estate
WIMB BH21 .... **300** A4
Colden Common Primary School
ELGH SO50 .... **207** P4
Colehill First School
WIMB BH21 .... **279** K8
Coliseum Business Centre
CBLY GU15 .... **57** P2
College Park Infant School
NEND PO2 .... **297** H7
College Town J & I School
SHST GU47 .... **41** M6
Collingwood Business Park
FHAM/STUB PO14 .... **294** E3
Colthrop Business Park
STHA RG19 .... **25** P4
Coltwood Business Centre
ALDT GU11 .... **3** F3
Commercial Business Centre
CHFD SO53 .... **206** E7
Common Marsh
STOK SO20 .... **141** K7
Compton Acres Gardens
PSTN BH14 .... **333** N3
Compton CE Primary School
RWIN SO21 .... **183** M6
Compton Place Business Centre
CBLY GU15 .... **57** P1
Concorde Club & Hotel
ELGH SO50 .... **228** G4
The Connaught School
ASHV GU12 .... **97** L4
Continental Ferry Port
NEND PO2 .... **296** E9
Cooper Dean Pavilion
BMTH BH1 .... **9** F1
Copnor Bridge Business Centre
NEND PO2 .... **317** H1
Copnor J & I School
HSEA PO3 .... **297** J8
Copythorne CE Infant School
TOTT SO40 .... **245** H1
Corfe Hills School
BDST BH18 .... **300** B7
Corhampton Golf Club
BPWT SO32 .... **211** J9
Corn Exchange
NWBY RG14 .... **16** E2
Corpus Christi Catholic Primary School
BOSC BH5 .... **335** M1
Corpus Christi RC (Aided) Primary School
NEND PO2 .... **296** F7
Cosham Health Centre
CHAM PO6 .... **297** H2
Costello Technical College
CHAM PO6 .... **7** H7
Cottage Grove Primary School
SSEA PO5 .... **19** H6
Courthill First School
PSTN BH14 .... **321** M8
Court Lane J & I School
CHAM PO6 .... **297** J2
Court Moor School
FLEETS GU52 .... **74** C6
Cove CC
FARN GU14 .... **57** M9
Cove Infant School
FARN GU14 .... **57** M7
Cove Junior School
FARN GU14 .... **57** M8
Cove School
FARN GU14 .... **57** M8
Cowplain Community School
WVILLE PO7 .... **255** N9
Coxlease School
LYND SO43 .... **264** F8
Coxmoor Farm Light Industrial Estate
RFNM GU10 .... **94** F1
Cracknore Industrial Park
TOTT SO40 .... **267** J1
Cranbourne Business & Enterprise College
BSTK RG21 .... **69** J9
Craneswater Junior School
ENEY PO4 .... **317** H6
Crane Valley Golf Club
WIMB BH21 .... **258** B3
The Crescent Primary School
ELGH SO50 .... **229** J1
Crestwood College of Business & Enterprise
ELGH SO50 .... **207** H8
Crickade College
AND SP10 .... **4** D3
Crickade Theatre
AND SP10 .... **4** C3
Crofton Anne Dale J & I School
FHAM/STUB PO14 .... **293** P7

Crofton Hammond Infant School
FHAM/STUB PO14 .... **294** A7
Crofton Hammond Junior School
FHAM/STUB PO14 .... **294** A7
Crofton School
FHAM/STUB PO14 .... **294** C7
Crondall Primary School
RFNM GU10 .... **95** H5
Crookham CE Infant School
FLEETS GU52 .... **74** C8
The Crookhorn Community School
WVILLE PO7 .... **275** P6
Cross Farm Infant School
FRIM GU16 .... **58** D7
Crow Arch Lane Industrial Estate
RGWD BH24 .... **282** F4
Crown Heights
BSTK RG21 .... **7** F5
Crowthorne CE Primary School
CWTH RG45 .... **41** J1
Cumberland Business Centre
BMTH BH1 .... **19** K3
Cumberland Hotel
BMTH BH1 .... **9** J4
Cumberland Infant School
ENEY PO4 .... **317** J5
Cupernham J & I School
ROMY SO51 .... **204** F4
Curdridge Primary School
BPWT SO32 .... **251** K2
Curtis Museum
ALTN GU34 .... **132** F6
Custom House
PLE BH15 .... **332** D2
Dalkeith Arcade
BMTH BH1 .... **8** E3
Danebury Ring
STOK SO20 .... **121** L9
Daneshill East Industrial Estate
CHIN RG24 .... **69** P5
Daneshill House School
HTWY RG27 .... **53** L1
Daneshill West Industrial Estate
CHIN RG24 .... **69** N4
Danesmead Community Centre
BSTK RG21 .... **69** M4
David Hart Business Centre
RSAL SP5 .... **199** J5
Days Inn Hotel
FLEETN GU51 .... **56** A9
D-Day Museum & Overlord Embroidery
SSEA PO5 .... **316** E7
Deacon Trading Estate
ELGH SO50 .... **229** L2
Deanery Campus
SHAM SO14 .... **21** G5
The Deanery
WINC SO23 .... **22** E6
Deane's Almshouses
BSTK RG21 .... **69** L8
Dean Farm Estate
WHAM PO17 .... **272** E5
Dean Farm Golf Club
BOR GU35 .... **134** F9
Deer Park Farm Industrial Estate
ELGH SO50 .... **230** E3
Delta Business Park
FHAM/PORC PO16 .... **294** F2
Denmark Road Medical Centre
MOOR/WNTN BH9 .... **322** F6
Denmead Cemetery
WVILLE PO7 .... **255** H6
Denmead Health Centre
WVILLE PO7 .... **255** H6
Denmead Infant School
WVILLE PO7 .... **255** J7
Denmead Junior School
WVILLE PO7 .... **255** H7
Denvale Trading Park
NWBY RG14 .... **24** G5
Derry Down Health Clinic
RAND SP11 .... **84** C2
The Derwent Hospital
LTDN BH7 .... **323** N6
De Vere Grand Harbour Hotel
WSHM SO15 .... **20** C6
De Vere Royal Bath Hotel
BMTH BH1 .... **9** F5
Devonshire Infant School
ENEY PO4 .... **317** H4
Devon Towers Hotel
WCLF BH2 .... **8** C5
Dibden Golf Centre
FAWY SO45 .... **267** N5
Dibles Park
HLER SO31 .... **270** E9
Ditcham Park School
EPSF GU31 .... **237** M4
Dockyard Apprentice Exhibition
PSEA PO1 .... **18** B2
Dogmersfield CE Primary School
HTWY RG27 .... **73** M5
The Dolphin Shopping Centre & Sports Centre
PLE BH15 .... **332** F1
Dolphin Swimming Pool
PLE BH15 .... **332** F1
The Donald Burrell Centre
CHIN RG24 .... **68** G4
Dorset Heavy Horse Centre
WIMB BH21 .... **238** D9
Dorset Medical Centre
SHAM SO14 .... **20** E3

Dorset Police
Eastern Division
FERN BH22 .... 280 B8
The Dorset Racquets &
Health Club
CFDH BH17 .... 320 D4
Dove House School
BSTK RG21 .... 7 F2
Down Grange Athletics Track
BH/HW/K RG22 .... 89 M2
Down House
RSAL SP5 .... 199 P5
Downton CE Primary School
RSAL SP5 .... 199 J5
Downton Industrial Estate
RSAL SP5 .... 199 J5
Drewitts Industrial Estate
BWD BH11 .... 321 N2
Droxford Cemetery
BPWT SO32 .... 233 M2
Droxford Junior School
BPWT SO32 .... 233 L3
Duck's Nest Long Barrow
FBDG SP6 .... 197 J2
Dudmoor Farm Golf Course
CHCH/BSGR BH23 .... 324 E3
Dudsbury Golf Club
FERN BH22 .... 302 C7
Dukes Mill
ROMY SO51 .... 204 C6
Dummer Golf Club
OVTN RG25 .... 89 J3
Dumpton School
WIMB BH21 .... 278 F6
Dunannie School
PSF GU32 .... 191 L8
Dunces Arch
LYND SO43 .... 265 J4
Dunhurst School
PSF GU32 .... 191 L8
Dunwood Manor Golf Club
ROMY SO51 .... 203 K3
Durley CE Primary School
BPWT SO32 .... 230 C6
Durley Grange Hotel
WCLF BH2 .... 8 B4
Durley Hall Hotel
WBNE BH4 .... 334 D4
Durlston Court School
NMIL/BTOS BH25 .... 327 J7
Eagle House School
SHST GU47 .... 41 H4
East Berkshire Golf Club
CWTH RG45 .... 40 F1
East Cemetery Littledown
LTDN BH7 .... 323 M9
East Cliff Lift
BMTH BH1 .... 9 H5
Eastern Industrial Centre
CHAM PO6 .... 297 L3
East Horton Golf Centre
ELGH SO50 .... 230 F2
Eastleigh Cemetery
ELGH SO50 .... 207 H9
Eastleigh College
ELGH SO50 .... 229 J3
Eastleigh College of
Further Education
ELGH SO50 .... 229 H2
Eastleigh FC
ELGH SO50 .... 228 G5
Eastleigh Health Centre
ELGH SO50 .... 229 J1
Eastleigh Museum
ELGH SO50 .... 229 J2
Eastleigh RFC
ELGH SO50 .... 229 L1
Eastney Beam Engine House
ENEY PO4 .... 317 L5
Eastney Health Centre
ENEY PO4 .... 317 J5
Eastney Swimming Baths
ENEY PO4 .... 317 L6
Easton Lane Business Park
WINC SO23 .... 23 J3
Eastrop Community Centre
BSTK RG21 .... 7 K5
East Shore School
ENEY PO4 .... 317 K2
East Street Shopping Centre
SHAM SO14 .... 21 F5
Eblojake Industrial Estate
VWD BH31 .... 259 J6
The Eddie Read Swimming
& Diving Complex
WSHM SO15 .... 20 C6
Edgebarrow School
CWTH RG45 .... 41 J3
Edgebarrow Sports Centre
CWTH RG45 .... 41 J3
Edgeborough School
RFNM GU10 .... 116 C7
The Edge Sports Centre
HASM GU27 .... 156 C5
Education Other than
at School
GPORT PO12 .... 13 H6
Eelmoor Road Depot
Trading Estate
FARN GU14 .... 75 P2
Eggars School
ALTN GU34 .... 133 H3
Eling Cemetery
TOTT SO40 .... 246 F6
Eling Infant School
TOTT SO40 .... 246 E5
Elizabeth Barracks
CHOB/PIR GU24 .... 59 M7
Elizabeth House Hotel
WSHM SO15 .... 248 B3
The Elizabeth Johnson
Organisation
LIPH GU30 .... 154 E8
Elliott Industrial Park
ASHV GU12 .... 97 L1
Elmhurst Business Park
GPORT PO12 .... 12 D2

Elmrise CP School
BWD BH11 .... 301 P9
Elson County Infant School
GPORT PO12 .... 295 L9
Elson County Junior School
GPORT PO12 .... 295 L9
Elstead Hotel
BMTH BH1 .... 9 K2
Elvetham Heath Local
Nature Reserve
FLEETN GU51 .... 56 C9
Elvetham Heath Primary
School *FLEETN* GU51 .... 74 A1
The Elvetham
HTWY RG27 .... 55 M8
Embley Park
Industrial Estate
ROMY SO51 .... 203 L6
The Emmanuel CE VA
Middle School
VWD BH31 .... 258 E5
Empire Cinema
BKME/WDN BH12 .... 321 J5
Emsworth Museum
EMRTH PO10 .... 299 M1
Emsworth Primary School
EMRTH PO10 .... 277 L9
Enterprise Industrial Estate
ASHV GU12 .... 76 E5
HORN PO8 .... 256 C3
Enterprise Park
VWD BH31 .... 259 J6
The Epiphany CE
Primary School
MOOR/WNTN BH9 .... 323 H3
Esseborne Manor Hotel
RAND SP11 .... 62 F2
Everest Community College
CHIN RG24 .... 69 K3
Eversley CC
HTWY RG27 .... 40 A6
Exbury Gardens & Railway
FAWY SO45 .... 312 C3
Exbury House
FAWY SO45 .... 312 C3
Experimental
Horticulture Station
LYMN SO41 .... 328 G7
Explosion! Museum of
Naval Firepower
GPORT PO12 .... 315 P1
Express by Holiday Inn
HEND SO30 .... 249 N2
PSEA PO1 .... 18 C4
Fairfax Industrial Estate
ASHV GU12 .... 97 L1
Fairfield Infant School
HAV PO9 .... 15 H5
Fairfields Arts Centre
BSTK RG21 .... 69 L8
Fairfields Primary School
BSTK RG21 .... 69 L8
Fairisle Infant School
ROWN SO16 .... 227 J8
Fairisle Junior School
ROWN SO16 .... 227 J8
Fairlands Montessori
School
BPWT SO32 .... 252 C4
Fair Oak Cemetery
ELGH SO50 .... 230 C3
Fair Oak Infant School
ELGH SO50 .... 230 C3
Fair Oak Junior School
ELGH SO50 .... 230 C3
Fairway Business Centre
HSEA PO3 .... 297 L6
Fairway House (NHS)
HLER SO31 .... 270 F2
Fairways School
CHIN RG24 .... 68 F3
Falcon Hotel
FARN GU14 .... 76 B3
Falkland Memorial
NWBY RG14 .... 24 A9
Falkland Primary School
NWBY RG14 .... 24 A9
Falkland St Gabriels School
KSCL RG20 .... 30 C1
Fareham College
FHAM/STUB PO14 .... 10 C6
Fareham Leisure Centre
FHAM/PORC PO16 .... 11 F4
Fareham Megabowl
FHAM/STUB PO14 .... 294 F4
Fareham Shopping Centre
FHAM/PORC PO16 .... 11 J5
Fareham Town Quay
FHAM/PORC PO16 .... 11 H7
Farleigh School
RAND SP11 .... 121 P1
Farley Hill Primary School
THLE RG7 .... 38 F1
Farley Mount
Country Park
RWIN SO21 .... 163 K7
Farlington Marshes
RSPB Reserve
HSEA PO3 .... 297 N5
The Farmhouse Hotel
HSEA PO3 .... 297 L8
Farnborough
Aerospace Centre
FARN GU14 .... 75 N4
Farnborough Airport
FARN GU14 .... 75 N3
Farnborough
Business Centre
FARN GU14 .... 75 N2
Farnborough Central
FARN GU14 .... 76 B2
Farnborough College
of Technology
FARN GU14 .... 76 B2
Farnborough Gate
Retail Park
FARN GU14 .... 58 B6

Farnborough Grange
Infant School
FARN GU14 .... 57 P5
Farnborough Hill School
FARN GU14 .... 58 B7
Farnborough
Recreation Centre
FARN GU14 .... 76 A1
Farnborough RFC
FARN GU14 .... 57 P7
Farnborough
Sixth Form College
FARN GU14 .... 58 A6
Farnborough Town FC
FARN GU14 .... 57 P5
Farnham Adult
Education Centre
FNM GU9 .... 96 B9
Farnham Bowling Club
FNM GU9 .... 96 B8
Farnham Business Centre
FNM GU9 .... 96 C8
Farnham Business Park
FNM GU9 .... 116 A1
Farnham Castle Keep
FNM GU9 .... 116 A1
Farnham Cemetery
FNM GU9 .... 116 A1
Farnham College
FNM GU9 .... 116 C1
Farnham Golf Club
RFNM GU10 .... 97 K9
Farnham Health Centre
FNM GU9 .... 96 C9
Farnham Heath End School
FNM GU9 .... 96 E5
Farnham Hospital
FNM GU9 .... 96 B8
Farnham Museum
FNM GU9 .... 96 A9
Farnham Park Golf Club
FNM GU9 .... 96 B7
Farnham Retail Park
FNM GU9 .... 96 B8
Farnham Trading Estate
FNM GU9 .... 96 F7
Farringdon Horticulture Estate
ALTN GU34 .... 151 K6
Fawley Business Centre
FAWY SO45 .... 291 J6
Fawley Infant School
FAWY SO45 .... 291 J6
Fawley Oil Refinery
FAWY SO45 .... 291 H5
Fenwick Hospital
LYND SO43 .... 264 E4
Ferndown First School
FERN BH22 .... 302 C3
Ferndown Forest Golf Club
FERN BH22 .... 280 C8
Ferndown Golf Club
FERN BH22 .... 302 E4
Ferndown Industrial Estate
WIMB BH21 .... 279 P8
Ferndown Medical Centre
FERN BH22 .... 302 D3
Ferndown Middle School
FERN BH22 .... 302 D3
Ferndown Sports Centre
FERN BH22 .... 302 B2
Ferndown Upper School
FERN BH22 .... 302 B2
Ferneham Hall
FHAM/PORC PO16 .... 11 H5
Fernhill Primary School
FARN GU14 .... 57 N4
Fernhill School
FARN GU14 .... 57 N4
Fernhill Tutors
FLEETN GU51 .... 56 F9
Fernhurst Junior School
ENEY PO4 .... 317 H4
Fernside Business Park
WIMB BH21 .... 302 A1
Ferry Terminal
LYMN SO41 .... 329 N4
SHAM SO14 .... 248 B9
Festival Place
Shopping Centre
BSTK RG21 .... 6 E6
The Fieldgate Centre
KSCL RG20 .... 48 B3
Finchampstead CE
Primary School
EWKG RG40 .... 39 P3
Finchampstead Sports Club
EWKG RG40 .... 39 P5
Finkley Down Farm Park
RAND SP11 .... 83 J8
Finns Industrial Park
NWBY RG14 .... 94 F1
Fir Tree Primary School
NWBY RG14 .... 25 H3
Firvale Respite Centre
CHIN RG24 .... 68 G3
Flagship Portsmouth
PSEA PO1 .... 316 A2
Flanders Industrial Park
HEND SO30 .... 250 B3
Fleet Business Park
FLEETS GU52 .... 74 E9
Fleet Community Centre
FLEETN GU51 .... 74 B5
Fleet Community Hospital
FLEETN GU51 .... 74 B2
Fleet CC
FLEETN GU51 .... 74 B4
Fleet Infant School
FLEETS GU52 .... 74 E5
Fleetsbridge Business Centre
CFDH BH17 .... 320 D5
Fleetspoint Business Centre
PLE BH15 .... 320 D7
Fleet Sports Ground
FLEETN GU51 .... 18 E4
Fleet Town FC
FLEETN GU51 .... 74 B4

Fleming Park Golf Club
ELGH SO50 .... 228 G1
Fleming Park Leisure Centre
ELGH SO50 .... 228 C1
Flying Bull Primary School
NEND PO2 .... 296 F9
Focus 303 Business Centre
AND SP10 .... 5 K1
Folly Farm Touring
Caravan Park
RWIN SO21 .... 143 K9
Folly Hill Infant School
FNM GU9 .... 96 A5
Fordingbridge Business Park
FBDG SP6 .... 240 A2
Fordingbridge Hospital
FBDG SP6 .... 240 D2
Fordingbridge J & I School
FBDG SP6 .... 240 D3
Forest Edge School
TOTT SO40 .... 246 C4
Forest Edge Touring Park
BROC SO42 .... 281 K7
Forest Park Hotel
BROC SO42 .... 286 E7
The Forest Shopping Centre
BOR GU35 .... 154 B5
Forres Sandle Manor School
FBDG SP6 .... 240 B1
Fort Blockhouse
GPORT PO12 .... 13 J6
Fort Brockhurst
GPORT PO12 .... 295 K8
Fort Cumberland
ENEY PO4 .... 317 N5
Fort Fareham
FHAM/STUB PO14 .... 294 E3
Fort Fareham
Industrial Estate
FHAM/STUB PO14 .... 294 E3
Fort Hill Community School
DEAN RG23 .... 68 F6
Fort Monckton
GPORT PO12 .... 315 N8
Fort Purbrook
CHAM PO6 .... 275 M9
Fort Southwick
WHAM PO17 .... 274 B8
Fort Wallington
Industrial Estate
FHAM/PORC PO16 .... 273 H8
Fort Widley
CHAM PO6 .... 275 M8
Fosters Business Park
HTWY RG27 .... 71 L5
Foundry Lane
Primary School
WSHM SO15 .... 247 M4
Four Lanes Infant &
Community Junior School
CHIN RG24 .... 70 A1
Four Seasons Hotel
HTWY RG27 .... 73 K8
Foxhills Infant School
TOTT SO40 .... 246 B7
Foxhills Junior School
TOTT SO40 .... 246 A7
Francis Avenue
Industrial Estate
BWD BH11 .... 321 M1
Francis Baily Primary School
NTHA RG18 .... 25 P4
Fratton Community Centre
PSEA PO1 .... 316 G2
Fratton Industrial Estate
ENEY PO4 .... 317 H3
Fred Woolley House
(Hospital)
ROWN SO16 .... 228 D4
Freegrounds County
J & I School
HEND SO30 .... 250 D5
Freemantle Business Centre
WSHM SO15 .... 247 N6
Freemantle CE (Controlled)
Infant School
WSHM SO15 .... 247 N5
Frensham Common &
Country Park
RFNM GU10 .... 136 E3
Frensham Heights School
RFNM GU10 .... 116 A8
Frensham Pond Hotel
RFNM GU10 .... 136 C5
Frensham Pond
Sailing Club
RFNM GU10 .... 136 C4
Friarsgate Medical Centre
WINC SO23 .... 23 F5
Friends Meeting House
WINC SO23 .... 23 F6
Frimley Business Park
FARN GU14 .... 58 A5
Frimley CE Junior School
FRIM GU16 .... 58 D6
Frimley Green Medical Centre
FRIM GU16 .... 58 E7
Frimley Park Hospital
CBLY GU15 .... 58 C3
Frobisher Industrial Centre
ROMY SO51 .... 204 C4
Frogmore Community School
YTLY GU46 .... 40 G9
Frogmore County
Infant School
BLKW GU17 .... 57 J1
Frogmore Junior School
BLKW GU17 .... 41 J9
Front Lawn Junior School
HAV PO9 .... 276 F5
Froxfield Endowed
Infant School
PSF GU32 .... 190 E4
Fryern Infant School
CHFD SO53 .... 206 G7
Furzeley Golf Club
WVILLE PO7 .... 255 H9

Furzey Gardens
LYND SO43 .... 244 A8
The Gantry Arts Centre
WSHM SO15 .... 20 B3
Carderobe Tower
WSHM SO15 .... 20 C6
Garland Junior School
THLE RG7 .... 27 J4
Garrison Theatre
TDWTH SP7 .... 78 F5
Gaston's Wood
Industrial Estate
CHIN RG24 .... 69 N3
Gatcombe Park
Primary School
NEND PO2 .... 297 H5
The George Hotel
ODIM RG22 .... 72 D9
George Street School
Branch Clinic
NEND PO2 .... 317 H1
Giant's Grave
FBDG SP6 .... 198 A8
Gilbert White's House & the
Oates Museum
ALTN GU34 .... 152 C8
Gillies Health Centre
BH/HW/K RG22 .... 89 P3
Glenfield Infant School
WEND SO18 .... 249 H4
Glenhurst School
HAV PO9 .... 15 H5
Glenmoor School for Girls
NBNE BH10 .... 322 D6
Glenwood School
EMRTH PO10 .... 277 L9
Goldsmith Infant School
ENEY PO4 .... 316 G4
Gomer J & I School
GPORT PO12 .... 315 J5
Goodway Sea School
GPORT PO12 .... 295 M9
Gordleton Industrial Estate
LYMN SO41 .... 328 F2
Gordleton Industrial Estate
LYMN SO41 .... 328 E2
Gore Road Industrial Estate
NMIL/BTOS BH25 .... 327 H5
Gosport Airfield
FHAM/STUB PO14 .... 294 C8
Gosport Health Centre
GPORT PO12 .... 12 A3
Gosport Museum
GPORT PO12 .... 13 G2
Gosport & Stokes Bay
Golf Club
GPORT PO12 .... 315 N7
Gosport War Memorial
Hospital
GPORT PO12 .... 12 A3
Grange Community
Junior School
FARN GU14 .... 57 N5
The Grange
Comprehensive School
CHCH/BSGR BH23 .... 325 J8
Grange Farm Business Park
BPWT SO32 .... 252 A3
Grange J & I School
LSOL/BMARY PO13 .... 314 C1
Grange Road Business Centre
CHCH/BSGR BH23 .... 325 L7
The Grange
NARL SO24 .... 147 K3
Grateley Business Park
RAND SP11 .... 119 N2
Grateley House School
RAND SP11 .... 120 B1
Grateley Primary School
RAND SP11 .... 120 B1
Gravatom Business Centre
BPWT SO32 .... 231 P4
Grayshott CE Primary School
GSHT GU26 .... 156 A2
Grayshott Clinic
GSHT GU26 .... 156 A1
Grayswood CE Infant School
HASM GU27 .... 157 L3
Great Binfields
Primary School
CHIN RG24 .... 70 A3
Greatbridge Business Park
ROMY SO51 .... 204 B4
The Great Hall
WINC SO23 .... 22 C5
Greatham Primary School
LISS GU33 .... 173 L5
Great Oaks School
ROWN SO16 .... 228 A8
Great Salterns Public
Golf Club
HSEA PO3 .... 297 K8
Greenfields Junior School
HTWY RG27 .... 55 H8
Greenham Court
Primary School
NWBY RG14 .... 24 D4
Greenham Road Retail Park
NWBY RG14 .... 17 F4
Greenhill Farm Camping &
Caravan Park
RSAL SP5 .... 223 P2
Green Pastures Farm
ROMY SO51 .... 225 L8
The Gregg School
WEND SO18 .... 229 J9
Gresham Industrial Estate
ASHV GU12 .... 97 L1
Grey House
Preparatory School
HTWY RG27 .... 55 J7
Greywell Shopping Centre
HAV PO9 .... 276 F5
Griffin Industrial Park
TOTT SO40 .... 226 B9
Grosvenor Casino
WSHM SO15 .... 20 B5

Grosvenor Hotel
STOK SO20 ...... 141 L5
Grovebell Industrial Estate
FNM GU9 ...... 115 P3
Grove CP School
FRIM GU16 ...... 58 D3
Grove Farm Meadow
Holiday Caravan Park
CHCH/BSGR BH23 ...... 324 A6
Grove House Business Centre
CHIN RG24 ...... 70 A4
Groveley Business Centre
CHCH/BSGR BH23 ...... 325 J9
Grove Park Business &
Enterprise Company
ITCH SO19 ...... 249 K9
Grove Park Industrial Estate
ALTN GU34 ...... 133 H5
The Guard Room
FUFL SO22 ...... 22 C4
Guildford Road
Industrial Estate
FNM GU9 ...... 96 D8
Guillemont County
Junior School
BLKW GU17 ...... 57 K7
Gundrymoor Trading Estate
WIMB BH21 ...... 280 E4
Gunwharf Quays Retail &
Leisure Park
PSEA PO1 ...... 18 B4
Hackwood House
OVTN RG25 ...... 90 F3
Hackwood Medical Centre
BSTK RG21 ...... 6 D6
Hale Primary School
FBDG SP6 ...... 221 N1
ROMY SO51 ...... 96 B4
Halterworth Primary School
ROMY SO51 ...... 204 G6
Hamble Community
Sport College
HLER SO31 ...... 269 N4
Hamble Court Business Park
HLER SO31 ...... 269 N7
Hambledon CC
WVILLE PO7 ...... 234 G2
Hambledon Infant School
WVILLE PO7 ...... 234 F9
Hambledon Vineyard &
Winepress
WVILLE PO7 ...... 234 F9
Hamble Primary School
HLER SO31 ...... 269 N6
Hamilton Business Park
NMIL/BTOS BH25 ...... 326 C5
Hammond Industrial Estate
FHAM/STUB PO14 ...... 294 B8
Hampreston CE First School
WIMB BH21 ...... 301 N2
Hampshire Brewery
HORN PO8 ...... 256 D4
ROMY SO51 ...... 204 C4
Hampshire CCC
(The Rose Bowl)
HEND SO30 ...... 249 P2
The Hampshire Clinic
CHIN RG24 ...... 69 P6
Hampshire Collegiate School
ROMY SO51 ...... 203 L7
The Hampshire Court Hotel
CHIN RG24 ...... 70 A3
Hampshire Golf Club
RAND SP11 ...... 102 F8
Hampshire International
Business Park
CHIN RG24 ...... 51 P9
Hampshire Records Office
WINC SO23 ...... 22 D3
Hampshire Tennis &
Health Club
HEND SO30 ...... 249 P3
Hamptworth Golf &
Country Club
RSAL SP5 ...... 201 J9
Hamworthy
Community Clinic
PLE BH15 ...... 320 A9
Hamworthy First School
PLE BH15 ...... 332 B2
Hamworthy Middle School
PLE BH15 ...... 332 B2
Handy Cross
RGWD BH24 ...... 262 B7
Hankley Common Golf Club
RFHM GU10 ...... 117 K9
Harbour Heights Hotel
CCLF BH13 ...... 333 N5
Harbour Lights Picture House
SHAM SO14 ...... 248 D9
The Harbour School
NEND PO2 ...... 296 D6
Harbridge School
RGWD BH24 ...... 260 B2
The Hard Interchange Bus &
Coach Station
PSEA PO1 ...... 18 B3
Hardley School & Sixth Form
FAWY SO45 ...... 290 E4
Harefield Clinic
WEND SO18 ...... 249 J4
Harefield Primary School
WEND SO18 ...... 249 K3
Harestock Primary School
FUFL SO22 ...... 164 E4
Harewood Forest
Industrial Estate
RAND SP11 ...... 104 A7
Harlington Centre
FLEETN GU51 ...... 74 C4
Harness House (NHS)
CHIN RG24 ...... 68 G4
Harrison Primary School
FHAM/PORC PO16 ...... 11 H4
Harrow Way
Community School
AND SP10 ...... 82 B9

Harrow Wood Farm
Caravan Park
CHCH/BSGR BH23 ...... 305 N8
Hartley Park Farm
Business Centre
ALTN GU34 ...... 152 C4
Hartley Wintney CC
HTWY RG27 ...... 55 J7
Hartley Wintney Golf Club
HTWY RG27 ...... 55 K6
Hart Plain Infant School
HORN PO8 ...... 255 N9
Hart Plain Junior School
WVILLE PO7 ...... 255 N9
Hart Shopping Centre
FLEETN GU51 ...... 74 C3
Hart Sports Centre
FLEETN GU51 ...... 73 P4
Haselworth CP School
GPORT PO12 ...... 12 D4
Haslemere Hall
HASM GU27 ...... 157 H6
Haslemere Hospital &
Health Centre
HASM GU27 ...... 157 J6
Haslemere Museum
HASM GU27 ...... 157 J6
Hassocks Wood
Industrial Estate
CHIN RG24 ...... 69 P5
Hatch Warren Infant School
BH/HW/K RG22 ...... 89 N4
Hatch Warren Primary School
BH/HW/K RG22 ...... 89 N4
Hatch Warren Retail Park
BH/HW/K RG22 ...... 89 L5
Hatherden CE Primary School
RAND SP11 ...... 82 A2
Havant Arts Centre
HAV PO9 ...... 15 G6
Havant Business Centre
HAV PO9 ...... 14 C7
Havant Cemetery
HAV PO9 ...... 15 H4
Havant Indoor Bowls Centre
HAV PO9 ...... 15 F3
Havant Leisure Centre
HAV PO9 ...... 15 G3
Havant Museum
HAV PO9 ...... 15 H6
Havant Retail Park
HAV PO9 ...... 276 B9
Havant RFC
HAV PO9 ...... 14 C3
Havant Sixth Form College
HAV PO9 ...... 14 E2
Havant Sports Club
HAV PO9 ...... 15 F4
Havant War Memorial
Hospital
HAV PO9 ...... 14 E4
Havant & Waterlooville FC
HAV PO9 ...... 276 C3
Havelock Community Centre
EPSF PO4 ...... 316 G5
Haven Hotel
CCLF BH15 ...... 333 K8
The Hawk Conservancy Trust
RAND SP11 ...... 101 H3
Hawley CP School
BLKW GU17 ...... 57 M2
Hawley Lane
Industrial Estate
FARN GU14 ...... 58 A5
Hawley Place School
FLEETS GU52 ...... 57 M4
Haweswood First School
WIMB BH21 ...... 279 J8
Hayling Billy Business Centre
HISD PO11 ...... 318 D4
Hayling Golf Club
HISD PO11 ...... 318 C5
Hayling Island Health Centre
HISD PO11 ...... 318 G5
The Hayling School
HISD PO11 ...... 318 G3
Haymarket Theatre
BSTK RG21 ...... 6 E7
Haymoor Middle School
CFDH BH17 ...... 320 C3
Hayward Business Centre
HAV PO9 ...... 15 K1
Hazel Wood Infant School
TOTT SO40 ...... 246 A4
Headlands Business Park
RGWD BH24 ...... 260 E8
Headley Park Country Club
BOR GU35 ...... 135 M8
Headway Place
CHIN RG24 ...... 68 F3
Heatherlands First School
BKME/WDN BH12 ...... 321 M7
Heather Ridge County
Infant School
CBLY GU15 ...... 59 J1
Heatherside Infant School
FLEETS GU52 ...... 74 D5
Heatherside Junior School
FLEETS GU52 ...... 74 C4
Heatherview Medical Centre
BKME/WDN BH12 ...... 322 A8
Heathfield Junior School
ITCH SO19 ...... 249 L9
Heathfield School
FHAM/STUB PO14 ...... 294 A1
Heathlands Cemetery
YTLY GU46 ...... 56 F1
Heathlands Hotel
BMTH BH1 ...... 9 H4
Heathlands Primary School
BWD BH11 ...... 322 A4
Hedge End Business Centre
HEND SO30 ...... 250 B2
Hedge End Retail Park
HEND SO30 ...... 250 A4
Helix Business Park
CBLY GU15 ...... 58 A2

Henry Beaufort School
FUFL SO22 ...... 164 F3
Henry Cort
Community School
FHAM PO15 ...... 272 A7
Henry Tyndale School
FNM GU9 ...... 58 B7
Herbert Day Hospital
WBNE BH4 ...... 334 B4
Hermitage Hotel
WCLF BH2 ...... 8 E5
The Herne Farm
Leisure Centre
EPSF GU31 ...... 215 N1
The Herne Junior School
EPSF GU31 ...... 215 N1
The Herons Swimming &
Fitness Centre
HASM GU27 ...... 156 E7
Highbury College
CHAM PO6 ...... 297 J4
PSEA PO1 ...... 19 H2
PSEA PO1 ...... 316 D2
Highbury Primary School
CHAM PO6 ...... 297 J3
Highclere Castle & Gardens
KSCL RG20 ...... 46 A3
Highcliffe Castle
CHCH/BSGR BH23 ...... 326 A8
Highcliffe Castle Golf Club
CHCH/BSGR BH23 ...... 326 A8
Highcliffe Medical Centre
CHCH/BSGR BH23 ...... 337 M1
Highcliffe St Mark
Primary School
CHCH/BSGR BH23 ...... 326 C6
Highcliffe School
CHCH/BSGR BH23 ...... 325 P6
Highcliff Marriott Hotel
WCLF BH2 ...... 8 C6
Highcroft Industrial Estate
HORN PO8 ...... 256 C3
Highfield CE (Aided)
Primary School
SD/PW SO17 ...... 228 C9
Highfield House Hotel
SD/PW SO17 ...... 248 D1
Highfield School
LIPH GU30 ...... 175 M5
Highgrove Industrial Park
HSEA PO3 ...... 297 K6
Highland Road Cemetery
ENEY PO4 ...... 317 H6
Highlands Medical Centre
FHAM PO15 ...... 272 B8
Hightown Industrial Estate
RGWD BH24 ...... 282 F3
Hightown Primary School
ITCH SO19 ...... 249 N7
Hillbourne Community
First School
CFDH BH17 ...... 320 C2
Hillbourne Middle School
BDST BH18 ...... 320 C2
Hill Cottage Farm Touring
Caravan Park
FBDG SP6 ...... 239 N3
Hill Farm Caravan Park
ROMY SO51 ...... 202 F2
Hill Head Preparatory School
FHAM/STUB PO14 ...... 293 P8
Hill House School
LYMN SO41 ...... 309 K7
Hill Park Clinic
FHAM PO15 ...... 10 B1
Hillside First School
VWD BH31 ...... 258 F3
Hillside Industrial Estate
FNM GU9 ...... 256 C3
Hillview Business Centre
NBNE BH10 ...... 322 E4
Hilsea Lines Business Park
HSEA PO3 ...... 297 J5
Hiltingbury Junior School
CHFD SO53 ...... 206 E4
Hinton Ampner
NARL SO24 ...... 187 K2
Hinton Ampner Garden (NT)
NARL SO24 ...... 187 K3
Hinton Firs Hotel
BMTH BH1 ...... 9 K4
HM Prison
FUFL SO22 ...... 22 A4
HSEA PO3 ...... 317 H2
HMS Nelson
PSEA PO1 ...... 18 E1
HMS Temeraire
PSEA PO1 ...... 18 E4
HMS Victory
PSEA PO1 ...... 18 B3
HMS Warrior
PSEA PO1 ...... 18 B3
Hockley Golf Club
RWIN SO21 ...... 184 A4
Hogs Back Brewery
RFNM GU10 ...... 97 M6
Holbrook Primary School
LSOL/BMARY PO13 ...... 294 G6
Holbrook Recreation Centre
LSOL/BMARY PO13 ...... 295 J8
Hollybrook Cemetery
ROWN SO16 ...... 227 N9
Hollybrook Infant School
ROWN SO16 ...... 227 P9
Hollybrook Junior School
ROWN SO16 ...... 227 P9
Hollybush Industrial Park
ALDT GU11 ...... 76 D7
Hollycombe Steam
Collection
LIPH GU30 ...... 175 M8
Holly Hill Cemetery
HLER SO31 ...... 270 E6
Holly Lodge Primary School
ASHV GU12 ...... 76 E4
Holtwater School
BOR GU35 ...... 154 D4

The Holme Primary School
BOR GU35 ...... 154 E2
Holt Heath National
Nature Reserve
WIMB BH21 ...... 279 P1
Holy Cross Hospital
HASM GU27 ...... 156 E6
Holy Family Catholic
Primary School
ROWN SO16 ...... 247 H1
Holy Ghost Chapel Ruins
BSTK RG21 ...... 6 E4
Home Farm Business Centre
ROMY SO51 ...... 178 E1
Homefield House
CHIN RG24 ...... 68 F4
Hones Yard Business Park
FNM GU9 ...... 96 D9
Hook Bowling Club
HTWY RG27 ...... 71 N3
Hook Community Centre
HTWY RG27 ...... 72 A3
Hook Junior School
HTWY RG27 ...... 72 A3
Hook with Warsash CE
Primary School
HLER SO31 ...... 292 D1
Hope Lodge School
WEND SO18 ...... 248 G4
Hordle CE Primary School
LYMN SO41 ...... 328 A4
Hordle House School
LYMN SO41 ...... 338 C1
Hordle Walhampton School
LYMN SO41 ...... 329 N1
Horizon West Industrial Estate
NWBY RG14 ...... 24 G4
Horndean CE Junior School
HORN PO8 ...... 256 C4
Horndean FC
HORN PO8 ...... 256 C4
Horndean Health Centre
HORN PO8 ...... 256 C4
Horndean Infant School
HORN PO8 ...... 256 C4
Horndean Technology
College
HORN PO8 ...... 256 B4
Horris Hill School
KSCL RG20 ...... 30 D3
Horse Power, the King's
Royal Hussars
WINC SO23 ...... 22 C5
Hoskins Place
Industrial Estate
CBLY GU15 ...... 58 A2
Hospital of St Cross
WINC SO23 ...... 183 P2
Hotel Collingwood
WCLF BH2 ...... 8 C5
Hotel du Vin
WINC SO23 ...... 22 D5
Hotel Miramar
BMTH BH1 ...... 9 G4
Hotel Piccadilly
BMTH BH1 ...... 9 G4
Houghton Lodge & Garden
STOK SO20 ...... 141 H9
Houndmills Industrial Estate
BSTK RG21 ...... 69 H6
Hounsdown Business Park
TOTT SO40 ...... 246 D7
Hounsdown School
TOTT SO40 ...... 246 D7
Hughes Business Centre
CHCH/BSGR BH23 ...... 325 L8
Hulbert Junior School
WVILLE PO7 ...... 275 P4
Hurlands Business Centre
FNM GU9 ...... 96 F7
Hursley Cemetery
RWIN SO21 ...... 182 E7
Hurstbourne Tarrant CE
J & I School
RAND SP11 ...... 62 B6
Hurst Castle
LYMN SO41 ...... 339 N6
The Hurst Community
College
TADY RG26 ...... 33 N4
Hurst Leisure Centre
TADY RG26 ...... 33 N5
Hyde Primary School
FBDG SP6 ...... 241 H6
Hythe Medical Centre
FAWY SO45 ...... 268 B8
Hythe Primary School
FAWY SO45 ...... 268 C6
Ibis Hotel
PSEA PO1 ...... 19 G4
Ibsley Common (NT)
RGWD BH24 ...... 261 J1
Icknield School
AND SP10 ...... 82 G9
Iford Bridge Club
CHCH/BSGR BH23 ...... 324 B7
Iford Golf Centre
LTDN BH7 ...... 324 A5
IKEA Store
(opens Spring 2009)
WSHM SO15 ...... 20 C5
Innkeeper's Lodge
CBLY GU15 ...... 58 D2
CHAR BH8 ...... 323 N6
FLEETN GU51 ...... 57 H9
HAV PO9 ...... 277 H2
NEND PO2 ...... 297 H5
Institute of Health &
Community Studies
CHAR BH8 ...... 9 H3
Intec Business Park
CHIN RG24 ...... 69 P4
INTECH - Family
Science Centre
RWIN SO21 ...... 166 A8
The Irish Centre
BSTK RG21 ...... 69 L8

Isle of Wight
Car Ferry Terminal
PSEA PO1 ...... 18 C5
Itchen Abbas CP School
RWIN SO21 ...... 166 E1
Itchen College
ITCH SO19 ...... 249 J6
Itchen Valley Brewery
NARL SO24 ...... 167 P3
Itchen Valley Country Park
HEND SO30 ...... 229 L7
Jane Austen's House
ALTN GU34 ...... 132 D9
WINC SO23 ...... 22 E6
Jellicoe Theatre
PSTN BH14 ...... 321 H7
The Jigsaw School
FRIM GU16 ...... 76 D1
J M L Trading Estate
WSHM SO15 ...... 20 A3
John Arlott Pavilion
BSTK RG21 ...... 69 M8
The John Hanson
Community School
AND SP10 ...... 102 A3
John Keble CE
Primary School
RWIN SO21 ...... 182 D8
John Neame Swimming Pool
PSTN BH14 ...... 321 K8
John Pounds Community
Centre PSEA PO1 ...... 18 G2
John Rankin Infant School
NWBY RG14 ...... 24 A7
John Rankin Junior School
NWBY RG14 ...... 24 A7
Jubilee Business Centre
WVILLE PO7 ...... 275 M2
Jurys Inn
WSHM SO15 ...... 20 E1
Kanes Hill Primary School
ITCH SO19 ...... 249 N5
Kempshott Infant School
BH/HW/K RG22 ...... 89 L3
Kempshott Junior School
BH/HW/K RG22 ...... 89 L3
Kemps Quay Industrial Park
ITCH SO19 ...... 248 F4
Kemp Welch Leisure Centre
BKME/WDN BH12 ...... 321 M4
Kendall Court Business Park
CBLY GU15 ...... 57 N1
Kennet Leisure Centre
STHA RG19 ...... 25 P4
Kennet School
STHA RG19 ...... 25 P4
Kennet Shopping Centre
NWBY RG14 ...... 16 E2
Kenwood Business Park
HAV PO9 ...... 15 K2
The Kerridge
Industrial Estate
ALTN GU34 ...... 132 G5
Kimpton CE J & i School
RAND SP11 ...... 100 D1
King Alfreds Statue
WINC SO23 ...... 23 G5
King Edward VI School
WSHM SO15 ...... 248 A3
Kingfisher Court
Industrial Estate
NWBY RG14 ...... 24 G4
King Richard
Secondary School
CHAM PO6 ...... 296 B1
The Kings Centre
ALDT GU11 ...... 2 E2
Kingsclere Business Park
KSCL RG20 ...... 48 B3
Kingsclere Cemetery
KSCL RG20 ...... 48 A3
Kingsclere CE Primary School
KSCL RG20 ...... 48 C3
Kingsclere Health Centre
KSCL RG20 ...... 48 B3
Kings Copse Primary School
HEND SO30 ...... 250 C6
Kings Court School
HORN PO8 ...... 256 D2
Kings Furlong Infant School
BSTK RG21 ...... 69 J8
Kings Furlong Junior School
BSTK RG21 ...... 69 J8
Kingsgrove Industrial Estate
FARN GU14 ...... 75 P1
The Kings Head Hotel
WIMB BH21 ...... 278 D3
Kings High School
NBNE BH10 ...... 322 C4
Kings International College
CBLY GU15 ...... 58 B3
Kingsland Centre
STHA RG19 ...... 25 N4
Kingsland Industrial Estate
CHIN RG24 ...... 69 P3
Kingsland Market
SHAM SO14 ...... 21 F4
Kingsleigh Primary School
NBNE BH10 ...... 322 C4
Kingsley Business Park
BOR GU35 ...... 134 G8
Kingsmead Shopping Centre
FARN GU14 ...... 76 A1
King's Park Athletics Centre
BMTH BH1 ...... 323 J4
Kings Park
Community Hospital
LTDN BH7 ...... 323 M9
Kings Park Primary School
BMTH BH1 ...... 323 L9
The Kings Primary School
HEND SO30 ...... 229 N9
Kings Road Industrial Estate
HASM GU27 ...... 156 F7
The King's Royal Hussars
Regimental Museum
WINC SO23 ...... 22 C4

Kings School
  BSTK RG21 .... 6 D7
  FUFL SO22 .... 164 C9
The Kings School Senior
  ELGH SO50 .... 230 B4
Kings Somborne CE
  Primary School
  STOK SO20 .... 161 L5
Kings Theatre
  SSEA PO5 .... 19 K7
Kingston Cemetery
  PSEA PO1 .... 317 H1
Kingston Great Common
  National Nature Reserve
  RGWD BH24 .... 283 L7
Kingstons Industrial Estate
  ASHV GU12 .... 97 L1
Kingsworthy Primary School
  WINC SO23 .... 165 K1
Kin Hon Clinic
  PSEA PO1 .... 19 F4
Kinson Cemetery
  BWD BH11 .... 322 B3
Kinson Pottery
  Industrial Estate
  PSTN BH14 .... 321 H6
Kinson Primary School
  BWD BH11 .... 322 B2
Kinson Road Medical Centre
  NBNE BH10 .... 322 C1
Kinson Swimming Pool
  BWD BH11 .... 322 B3
Knighton Heath Golf Club
  BWD BH11 .... 321 L1
Knighton Heath
  Industrial Estate
  BWD BH11 .... 321 N1
Knights Enham Junior School
  AND SP10 .... 82 E8
Knightwood Lodge Hotel
  LYND SO43 .... 265 H4
Knightwood Primary School
  CHFD SO53 .... 206 B6
Knoll Gardens & Nursery
  WIMB BH21 .... 279 P9
Ladle Hill
  (Unfinished Hill Fort)
  KSCL RG20 .... 46 G7
Lainston House Hotel
  RWIN SO21 .... 163 P3
Lake Road Health Centre
  PSEA PO1 .... 316 G2
Lakeside Business Park
  SHST GU47 .... 41 H7
Lakeside Country Club
  FRIM GU16 .... 58 F7
Lakeside International Hotel
  FRIM GU16 .... 58 F7
Lakeside Primary School
  FRIM GU16 .... 58 E4
Lakeside School
  CHFD SO53 .... 207 H5
Landford CE Primary School
  RSAL SP5 .... 201 M9
Land Registry
  PSEA PO1 .... 19 F3
Langrish House Hotel
  PSF GU32 .... 214 C2
Langrish Primary School
  PSF GU32 .... 214 G2
Langside School
  BKME/WDN BH12 .... 322 A7
Langstone Infant School
  HSEA PO3 .... 317 J2
Langstone Junior School
  HSEA PO3 .... 317 J1
Langtry Manor
  Lovenest of a King Hotel
  BMTH BH1 .... 335 J3
Lankhills School
  WINC SO23 .... 22 D1
Lansdowne Clinic
  BMTH BH1 .... 334 C1
Lasham Airfield
  ALTN GU34 .... 111 M7
Leckford Golf Club
  STOK SO20 .... 141 N2
Lee-on-the-Solent Golf Club
  LSOL/BMARY PO13 .... 294 E9
Leeland CE Infant School
  GPORT PO12 .... 12 C2
Leesland CE Junior School
  GPORT PO12 .... 12 C2
Leigh House Hospital
  CHFD SO53 .... 206 D5
Lepe Country Park
  FAWY SO45 .... 313 K6
Lido Sports Club
  WINC SO23 .... 22 E2
Lifeboat Museum
  PLE BH15 .... 332 E2
The Lighthouse
  PLE BH15 .... 329 P9
Lilliput CE First School
  PSTN BH14 .... 333 L3
Limington House School
  BH/HW/K RG22 .... 68 G9
Liners Industrial Estate
  WSHM SO15 .... 247 N5
Linsford Business Park
  FRIM GU16 .... 76 E1
Linwood School
  TWDS BH3 .... 322 G8
Lion & Lamb Yard
  Shopping Centre
  FNM GU9 .... 96 B8
Liphook CE Junior School
  LIPH GU30 .... 175 H3

Liphook Golf Club
  LIPH GU30 .... 175 H8
Liphook Infant School
  LIPH GU30 .... 175 H3
Lismoyne Hotel
  FLEETN GU51 .... 74 C3
Liss Business Centre
  LISS GU33 .... 192 C1
Liss J & I School
  LISS GU33 .... 192 E3
Littledown Leisure Centre
  LTDN BH7 .... 323 N7
Littleton Barrows
  FUFL SO22 .... 164 C1
Local Education Office
  HAV PO9 .... 15 H2
Lockerley CE J & I School
  ROMY SO51 .... 178 C5
Locks Heath J & I School
  HLER SO31 .... 270 C9
Loddon Centre
  CHIN RG24 .... 69 P4
The Loddon School
  HTWY RG27 .... 52 E8
London Road
  Industrial Estate
  NWBY RG14 .... 17 C1
Longbridge Industrial Estate
  SHAM SO14 .... 21 J7
The Long Curtain
  (Old Town Defences)
  PSEA PO1 .... 18 D7
Longdown Activity Farm
  TOTT SO40 .... 246 B9
Longfleet CE
  Combined School
  PLE BH15 .... 320 F8
Long Meadow
  IndustrialEstate
  WIMB BH21 .... 280 F2
Longparish Primary School
  LGPR SP11 .... 104 D6
Longspee School
  CFDH BH17 .... 320 F5
Long Sutton CE
  Primary School
  ODIM RG29 .... 93 K8
Lordshill Health Centre
  ROWN SO16 .... 227 K8
Lord Wandsworth College
  ODIM RG29 .... 93 L9
Lord Wilson School
  HLER SO31 .... 270 F6
Lower William Street
  Industrial Estate
  SHAM SO14 .... 248 F5
Lucia Foster Welch College
  SHAM SO14 .... 21 G7
Ludgershall Castle
  Primary School
  RAND SP11 .... 80 A1
Ludgershall Sports Club
  RAND SP11 .... 79 N1
Ludlow Infant School
  ITCH SO19 .... 248 G8
Ludlow Junior School
  ITCH SO19 .... 248 G7
Ludshott Common (NT)
  GSHT GU26 .... 155 N5
Lulworth Business Centre
  TOTT SO40 .... 246 C1
Lydlynch Infant School
  TOTT SO40 .... 246 C4
Lymington Barn
  Industrial Estate
  ALTN GU34 .... 150 B5
Lymington Community
  Centre Cinema
  LYMN SO41 .... 329 L3
Lymington Community
  Hospital
  LYMN SO41 .... 329 L2
Lymington Hospital
  LYMN SO41 .... 329 K3
Lymington J & I School
  LYMN SO41 .... 329 K3
Lymington Recreation Centre
  LYMN SO41 .... 329 J4
Lyndhurst Junior
  Foundation School
  NEND PO2 .... 297 H8
Lyndhurst Park Hotel
  LYND SO43 .... 264 G5
Lyon Way Industrial Estate
  FRIM GU16 .... 58 B4
Lysses House Hotel
  FHAM/PORC PO16 .... 11 K4
Lythe Hill Hotel & Spa
  HASM GU27 .... 157 N3
Lytton Lawn Touring Park
  LYMN SO41 .... 328 C6
Macdonald Botley Park Hotel,
  Golf & Country Club
  BPWT SO32 .... 250 F1
Macdonald
  Elmers Court Hotel
  LYMN SO41 .... 329 P4
The Maemar Hotel
  WCLF BH2 .... 8 B5
Magdalen Hill Cemetery
  RWIN SO21 .... 165 P8
Magpies Sports Club
  WIMB BH21 .... 280 C1
Mainline Business Centre
  LISS GU33 .... 192 D2
The Malls Shopping Centre
  BSTK RG21 .... 6 E5
Malvern Business Centre
  ROWN SO16 .... 247 P1
Mannings Heath Retail Park
  BKME/WDN BH12 .... 321 J4
Manor Farm Business Centre
  HLER SO31 .... 97 M5
Manor Farm Country Park
  HLER SO31 .... 250 C8
Manor Field Junior School
  BH/HW/K RG22 .... 90 A4

Manor Infant School
  FARN GU14 .... 57 N7
  FAWY SO45 .... 290 E4
  PSEA PO1 .... 316 G2
Manor Park Industrial Estate
  ASHV GU12 .... 3 H4
Manorside Combined School
  BKME/WDN BH12 .... 321 N3
Mansbridge Primary School
  WEND SO18 .... 228 G8
Mansel Infant School
  ROWN SO16 .... 246 G1
Mansel Junior School
  ROWN SO16 .... 247 H1
Mansfield Business Park
  ALTN GU34 .... 150 B5
Mansfield Hotel
  WCLF BH2 .... 8 B6
Maple Business Park
  WIMB BH21 .... 279 P7
Maple Ridge School
  BSTK RG21 .... 6 D2
Marchwood CE Infant School
  TOTT SO40 .... 267 J2
Marchwood Industrial Park
  TOTT SO40 .... 247 L8
Marchwood Junior School
  TOTT SO40 .... 267 K1
Marchwood Priory Hospital
  TOTT SO40 .... 267 L3
Market Quay
  FHAM/PORC PO16 .... 11 H6
The Mark Way School
  AND SO10 .... 5 H3
Marlands Shopping Centre
  SHAM SO14 .... 20 D3
Marlborough County
  Infant School
  ALDT GU11 .... 76 B5
Marnel Infants School
  CHIN RG24 .... 69 M3
Marnel Junior School
  CHIN RG24 .... 69 M3
Marriott Meon Valley Hotel
  & Country Club
  BPWT SO32 .... 252 B3
Marsham Court Hotel
  BMTH BH1 .... 9 G5
Marsh Farm Business Centre
  RFNM GU10 .... 95 H2
Marwell Hotel
  RWIN SO21 .... 208 E6
Marwell Zoological Park
  RWIN SO21 .... 208 F5
Marycourt School
  GPORT PO12 .... 315 L7
Mary Hare Primary School
  STHA RG19 .... 25 H7
Mary Rose Museum
  PSEA PO1 .... 18 B2
Mary Rose Shiphall
  PSEA PO1 .... 18 B1
Mason Moore Primary School
  ROWN SO16 .... 247 J3
Master Builders House Hotel
  BROC SO42 .... 311 P3
Matbro Industrial Estate
  RAND SP11 .... 103 P7
Maternity Hospital
  Basingstoke
  CHIN RG24 .... 68 G4
Mayfield Avenue
  Industrial Park
  RAND SP11 .... 80 G9
Mayfield School
  ALTN GU34 .... 133 H4
Mayfield Secondary School
  NEND PO2 .... 296 C7
Mayflower Memorial
  SHAM SO14 .... 20 D7
Mayflower Theatre
  SHAM SO14 .... 20 B2
Mayhill Junior School
  ODIM RG29 .... 93 L1
May's Bounty (Basingstoke
  & North Hants CC)
  BSTK RG21 .... 69 L9
Maycree Infant School
  SHAM SO14 .... 248 D5
Mayville High School
  ENEY PO4 .... 316 F6
Meadowlands Infant School
  HORN PO8 .... 255 N6
Meadowlands Junior School
  HORN PO8 .... 255 N6
The Meadows Hospital
  HLER SO31 .... 270 F5
The Meadows
  SHST GU47 .... 41 M9
Medina Primary School
  CHAM PO6 .... 296 G2
Medstead Cemetery
  ALTN GU34 .... 150 A2
Megabowl
  BKME/WDN BH12 .... 321 K3
Mengham Infant School
  HISD PO11 .... 318 G4
Mengham Junior School
  HISD PO11 .... 318 G4
Meoncross School
  FHAM/STUB PO14 .... 294 B5
Meon Infant School
  ENEY PO4 .... 317 K4
Meon Junior School
  ENEY PO4 .... 317 K3
Meonstoke CE School
  BPWT SO32 .... 211 N9
Mercure Bush Hotel
  FNM GU9 .... 96 C9
Mercure Wessex Hotel
  WINC SO23 .... 22 E5
Merdon Junior School
  CHFD SO53 .... 206 F6
Meredith Infant School
  NEND PO2 .... 296 G9
Meridian Shopping Centre
  HAV PO9 .... 15 F5

Meridian TV Studios
  SHAM SO14 .... 248 G5
Merley Court
  WIMB BH21 .... 300 D4
Merley First School
  WIMB BH21 .... 300 F4
Merton Junior School
  CHIN RG24 .... 69 K4
Micheldever Primary School
  RWIN SO21 .... 126 G6
Middle Hill Health Clinic
  ALDT GU11 .... 2 E1
Middle Park Medical Centre
  HAV PO9 .... 276 C6
Middle Wallop Airfield
  STOK SO20 .... 121 H7
Mid Hants Railway
  (Watercress Line)
  NARL SO24 .... 168 B2
Milestones - Hampshire's
  Living History
  BH/HW/K RG22 .... 69 H7
Milford CE Primary School
  LYMN SO41 .... 328 E9
Millbrook Cemetery
  WSHM SO15 .... 247 K4
Millbrook Clinic
  ROWN SO16 .... 247 K3
Millbrook Community School
  ROWN SO16 .... 227 J9
Millbrook Secondary School
  ROWN SO16 .... 227 J9
Millbrook Trading Estate
  WSHM SO15 .... 247 H4
Mill Chase
  Community School
  BOR GU35 .... 154 C5
Mill House Business Centre
  ITCH SO19 .... 248 F7
Mill Lane Industrial Estate
  ALTN GU34 .... 133 H5
Mill Rythe Holiday Village
  HISD PO11 .... 319 J2
Mill Rythe J & I School
  HISD PO11 .... 319 H2
Millstream Trading Estate
  RGWD BH24 .... 282 E4
Milton Business Centre
  NMIL/BTOS BH25 .... 326 G5
Milton Cemetery
  ENEY PO4 .... 317 J3
Miltoncross
  Secondary School
  HSEA PO3 .... 317 J3
Milton Park J & I School
  ENEY PO4 .... 317 K4
MLS International College
  BMTH BH1 .... 8 D5
Moniton Trading Estate
  DEAN RG23 .... 68 E2
Monks Brook Industrial Park
  CHFD SO53 .... 206 D8
Montacute Special School
  CFDH BH17 .... 320 E2
Montagu Arms Hotel
  BROC SO42 .... 289 K8
The Montague Hotel
  WCLF BH2 .... 8 A5
Moordown Medical Centre
  MOOR/WNTN BH9 .... 322 F4
Moorgreen Hospital
  HEND SO30 .... 249 P1
Moorhill House Hotel
  RGWD BH24 .... 284 C8
Moorings Way Infant School
  ENEY PO4 .... 317 L2
Moorlands College
  CHCH/BSGR BH23 .... 324 F1
Moorlands Infant School
  WEND SO18 .... 249 J2
Moors Valley Country Park
  RGWD BH24 .... 281 L2
Moors Valley Golf Club
  RGWD BH24 .... 259 K9
More House School
  RFNM GU10 .... 116 C8
Moreland Primary School
  NMIL/BTOS BH25 .... 327 L4
Morgans Vale & Woodfalls
  CE Primary School
  RSAL SP5 .... 199 P6
Mortimer Arms Hotel
  ROMY SO51 .... 225 L7
Mortimer St John's
  Infant School
  THLE RG7 .... 35 P1
Mortimer St Marys CE
  Junior School
  THLE RG7 .... 36 C1
Mortimers Farm
  Industrial Estate
  ROMY SO51 .... 225 L6
Mottisfont Abbey &
  Garden (NT)
  ROMY SO51 .... 179 M3
Mountbatten
  Business Centre
  WSHM SO15 .... 247 P6
Mountbatten Business Park
  CHAM PO6 .... 297 L3
Mountbatten Centre
  Athletics Track
  NEND PO2 .... 296 F6
Mountbatten School
  ROMY SO51 .... 204 G7
The Mount Hospital
  ELGH SO50 .... 207 M8
Mount Pleasant
  Industrial Estate
  SHAM SO14 .... 248 D4
Mount Pleasant
  School
  SHAM SO14 .... 248 D4
Moyles Court School
  RGWD BH24 .... 260 G4
Mrs Blands Infant School
  THLE RG7 .... 27 H5

Mudeford Infant School
  CHCH/BSGR BH23 .... 325 J9
Mudeford Junior School
  CHCH/BSGR BH23 .... 325 K9
Murrell Green Business Park
  HTWY RG27 .... 72 D2
Muscliff Primary School
  MOOR/WNTN BH9 .... 323 J3
Museum of Archaeology
  SHAM SO14 .... 248 C9
Museum of Army Flying
  STOK SO20 .... 120 G6
Mylen Road Business Centre
  AND SP10 .... 102 C2
Mytchett Primary School
  FRIM GU16 .... 58 E9
The Naked Man
  RGWD BH24 .... 285 K9
Natural History Museum &
  Butterfly House
  ENEY PO4 .... 317 H7
Natural Training &
  Therapy Centre
  VWD BH31 .... 258 F3
Nelson Industrial Park
  HEND SO30 .... 250 B2
Nest Business Park
  HAV PO9 .... 277 H6
Netley Abbey
  HLER SO31 .... 269 J4
Netley Abbey J & I School
  HLER SO31 .... 269 K5
Netley Marsh CE
  Infant School
  TOTT SO40 .... 245 N4
Neville Lovett Community
  School
  FHAM/STUB PO14 .... 294 C1
Newbridge Junior School
  NEND PO2 .... 317 H1
Newbury Business Park
  NWBY RG14 .... 24 F3
Newbury Bus Station
  NWBY RG14 .... 16 E3
Newbury College
  NWBY RG14 .... 24 D8
Newbury & Crookham
  Golf Club
  STHA RG19 .... 25 H8
Newbury Hockey & CC
  NWBY RG14 .... 16 C1
Newbury Manor Hotel
  NWBY RG14 .... 24 G4
Newbury Racecourse
  NWBY RG14 .... 17 K4
Newbury Retail Park
  NWBY RG14 .... 24 E8
Newbury RFC
  NWBY RG14 .... 24 C9
New College Swimming Pool
  WSHM SO15 .... 248 B4
New Fields Business Park
  CFDH BH17 .... 320 F4
New Forest Golf Club
  LYND SO43 .... 265 H4
New Forest Museum &
  Visitor Centre
  LYND SO43 .... 264 G5
The New Forest Otter, Owl
  & Wildlife Park
  TOTT SO40 .... 266 G2
New Greenham Park
  Leisure Centre
  STHA RG19 .... 31 M1
New Horizons College
  SBNE SH6 .... 336 E3
Newlands CP School
  YTLY GU46 .... 40 D9
The New Medical Centre
  CHCH/BSGR BH23 .... 305 L7
New Milton J & I School
  NMIL/BTOS BH25 .... 327 J6
New Milton
  Recreation Centre
  NMIL/BTOS BH25 .... 327 H5
New Milton Sports Club
  NMIL/BTOS BH25 .... 327 L4
New Park Manor Hotel
  BROC SO42 .... 286 F4
Newport Junior School
  ASHV GU12 .... 3 K5
New Scotland Hill
  Primary School
  SHST GU47 .... 41 H4
New Street FC
  RAND SP11 .... 82 B6
New Theatre Royal
  PSEA PO1 .... 19 F3
The Newton Health Clinic
  SHAM SO14 .... 248 C5
Newton Tony CE
  Primary School
  AMSY SP4 .... 118 D4
Newtown Business Park
  BKME/WDN BH12 .... 321 K5
Newtown Soberton
  Infant School
  WHAM PO17 .... 253 M5
New Westcliff Hotel
  WCLF BH2 .... 8 A5
The Nightingale
  Primary School
  ELGH SO50 .... 228 T3
No. 6 Cinema
  PSEA PO1 .... 18 B2
Noadswood School
  FAWY SO45 .... 268 A8
Nomansland & Hamptworth
  CE Primary School
  RSAL SP5 .... 223 K4
Norn Court
  Preparatory School
  RSAL SP5 .... 158 G5
Norman Gate School
  AND SP10 .... 5 H3
Northam Business Centre
  SHAM SO14 .... 248 E5

Northam Community Centre
 SHAM SO14 .... 21 J2
North Baddesley Infant School
 NBAD SO52 .... 205 M9
North Baddesley Junior School
 NBAD SO52 .... 205 M9
Northbrook Industrial Estate
 ROWN SO16 .... 247 N1
North Cemetery Charminster
 CHAR BH20 .... 323 J6
Northcroft Leisure Centre
 NWBY RG14 .... 16 B1
Northern County J & I School
 FHAM/PORC PO16 .... 273 N9
Northern Parade Clinic
 NEND PO2 .... 296 G5
Northern Parade J & I School
 NEND PO2 .... 296 G6
North Farnborough County Infant School
 FARN GU14 .... 58 C8
North Hampshire Hospital
 CHIN RG24 .... 69 H4
North Hants Golf Club
 FLEETN GU51 .... 56 D9
North Lodge Industrial Park
 LIPH GU30 .... 175 L7
North Solent National Nature Reserve
 BROC SO42 .... 312 A2
Northtown Trading Estate
 ASHV GU12 .... 97 L2
North Waltham Business Centre
 OVTN RG25 .... 88 F9
North Waltham Primary School
 OVTN RG25 .... 108 C1
Norton Park Hotel
 RWIN SO21 .... 125 M2
Norwood Primary School
 ELGH SO50 .... 229 J1
Novotel
 WSHM SO15 .... 20 A4
Nuffield Industrial Estate
 CFDH BH17 .... 320 E4
Nuffield Theatre
 SD/PW SO17 .... 228 C9
Nursling CE Primary School
 ROWN SO16 .... 227 H7
Nursling Industrial Estate
 ROWN SO16 .... 226 F8
Oakdene Forest Park
 RGWD BH24 .... 303 H1
Oak Farm Community Park
 FARN GU14 .... 57 P7
Oakfield Primary School
 TOTT SO40 .... 246 C2
Oakhurst First School
 FERN BH22 .... 280 F7
Oaklands Catholic School
 WVILLE PO7 .... 275 P5
Oaklands Community School
 ROWN SO16 .... 227 K7
Oaklands Swimming Pool
 ROWN SO16 .... 227 J7
Oakley CE Junior School
 DEAN RG23 .... 88 E2
Oakley County Infant School
 DEAN RG23 .... 88 E2
Oakley Shopping Centre
 WIMB BH21 .... 300 G4
Oak Lodge School
 FAWY SO45 .... 267 N7
Oakmead College of Technology
 BWD BH11 .... 301 N9
Oakmeadians RFC
 WCLF BH2 .... 334 E1
Oak Meadow Early Years & Family Centre
 FHAM PO15 .... 272 A7
Oak Meadow Primary School
 FHAM PO15 .... 272 A7
Oak Park Golf Club
 RFNM GU10 .... 95 J5
Oakridge Infant School
 BSTK RG21 .... 6 C1
Oakridge Junior School
 BSTK RG21 .... 6 C1
Oakridge West Community Centre
 BSTK RG21 .... 6 D1
Oakwood Infant School
 HTWY RG27 .... 55 H9
Oakwood Junior School
 ROWN SO16 .... 227 M7
Oatlands House Health Clinic
 WSHM SO15 .... 247 N2
Oceanarium
 WCLF BH2 .... 8 E6
Ocean View Hotel
 BMTH BH1 .... 9 K4
Odeon Cinema
 CHAM PO6 .... 296 D3
 BMTH BH1 .... 8 E4
 DEAN RG23 .... 68 G7
 NEND PO2 .... 296 F8
Odeon Leisure World
 WSHM SO15 .... 20 B5
Odiham Airfield
 ODIM RG29 .... 93 K4
Odiham Castle
 ODIM RG29 .... 72 A8
Odiham Cemetery
 ODIM RG29 .... 93 L1
Odiham Cottage Hospital
 ODIM RG29 .... 93 L1
The Odiham Health Centre
 ODIM RG29 .... 72 C9
O Jays Industrial Park
 HSEA PO3 .... 297 J7
Old Basing Infant School
 CHIN RG24 .... 70 C6

Old Hambledonians CC
 PSF GU32 .... 235 N2
The Old Hop Kiln
 FNM GU9 .... 116 B1
Old House Hotel
 WHAM PO17 .... 252 E8
Old Thorns Golf & Country Club
 LIPH GU30 .... 174 E4
Old Thorns Hotel
 LIPH GU30 .... 174 E4
Old Town First School
 PLE BH15 .... 332 E1
Old Turnpike Business Park
 FHAM/PORC PO16 .... 11 H5
Olivers Battery Primary School
 FUFL SO22 .... 183 L3
The Omni Business Centre
 ALTN GU34 .... 133 H6
Orchard Infant School
 FAWY SO45 .... 268 A8
Orchard Lea Infant School
 FHAM PO15 .... 272 B6
Orchard Lea Junior School
 FHAM PO15 .... 272 C6
Ordnance Survey Office
 ROWN SO16 .... 247 K1
Oriel Business Park
 ALTN GU34 .... 133 H5
Orion Business Centre
 WEND SO18 .... 228 G7
Ormonde House Hotel
 LYND SO43 .... 265 H5
The Osborn Clinic
 FHAM/PORC PO16 .... 11 J5
Otterbourne CE Primary School
 RWIN SO21 .... 207 K3
Our Lady & St Joseph Catholic Primary School
 LYMN SO41 .... 328 G3
Our Ladys Preparatory School
 CWTH RG45 .... 41 H1
Overton CE Primary School
 OVTN RG25 .... 86 F2
Overton Community Centre
 OVTN RG25 .... 86 G3
Owlsmoor Primary School
 SHST GU47 .... 41 M5
Owslebury CP School
 RWIN SO21 .... 208 G1
Padnell Infant School
 HORN PO8 .... 256 A8
Padnell Junior School
 HORN PO8 .... 256 B8
Padworth College
 THLE RG7 .... 26 A6
Palace House
 BROC SO42 .... 289 K7
Palmers Road Industrial Estate
 EMRTH PO10 .... 277 N9
Palmerston Business Park
 FHAM/STUB PO14 .... 294 E2
Pamphill First School
 WIMB BH21 .... 278 A8
Paramount Basingstoke Country Hotel
 HTWY RG27 .... 71 M5
Park Community School
 HAV PO9 .... 276 C5
Park Crematorium
 ASHV GU12 .... 97 K5
Park Farm Industrial Estate
 FRIM GU16 .... 58 B4
Park Gate Business Centre
 HLER SO31 .... 270 C4
Park Gate Primary School
 HLER SO31 .... 271 H5
Park House Primary School
 HAV PO9 .... 276 C5
Park House School
 NWBY RG14 .... 24 B9
Parklands Business Park
 WVILLE PO7 .... 255 H8
Parklands Hospital
 CHIN RG24 .... 68 G3
Park Lane Medical Centre
 HAV PO9 .... 14 B1
The Park School
 CHAR BH8 .... 323 K9
Parkstone Cemetery
 PSTN BH14 .... 333 K1
Parkstone Golf Club
 PSTN BH14 .... 333 M1
Parkstone Grammar School
 CFDH BH17 .... 320 E3
Parkstone Health Centre
 PSTN BH14 .... 321 L7
Park View Infant School
 RWIN SO21 .... 89 M1
Park View Junior School
 BH/HW/K RG22 .... 89 M1
Parkway Retail Park
 CHAR BH8 .... 9 J1
Parley First School
 FERN BH22 .... 302 D5
Parley Golf Course
 CHCH/BSGR BH23 .... 303 K9
Parley Sports Club
 FERN BH22 .... 302 F7
Parsonage Farm Infant School
 FARN GU14 .... 57 K8
Parsons Down Infant School
 STHA RG19 .... 25 L4
Parsons Down Junior School
 STHA RG19 .... 25 K4
Passfield Mill Business Park
 LIPH GU30 .... 154 E7
Passford House Hotel
 LYMN SO41 .... 308 G3
Paulsgrove Industrial Centre
 CHAM PO6 .... 296 D1

Paulsgrove Primary School
 CHAM PO6 .... 296 D1
Paultons Golf Centre
 ROMY SO51 .... 225 L6
Paultons Park
 ROMY SO51 .... 225 K6
Pavilion Theatre
 BMTH BH1 .... 8 E5
Peacock Trading Estate
 ELGH SO50 .... 206 G9
Peel Common Infant School
 FHAM/STUB PO14 .... 294 E7
Peel Common Junior School
 LSOL/BMARY PO13 .... 294 E7
Pegham Industrial Park
 FHAM PO15 .... 271 P4
Penhale Infant School
 PSEA PO1 .... 316 C3
Penn Hill Clinic
 PSTN BH14 .... 321 N9
Pennington J & I School
 LYMN SO41 .... 329 J4
Perins Community School
 NARL SO24 .... 167 P2
Petersfield Business Park
 PSF GU32 .... 215 K2
Petersfield Cemetery
 PSF GU32 .... 191 M9
Petersfield Community Hospital
 PSF GU32 .... 215 L2
Petersfield Golf Club
 LISS GU33 .... 192 A6
Petersfield Infant School
 PSF GU32 .... 215 M2
Petersfield RFC
 EPSF GU31 .... 216 B1
The Petersfield School
 PSF GU32 .... 215 L3
Petersfield Swimming Pool
 EPSF GU31 .... 215 N2
Petersfield Town FC
 EPSF GU31 .... 215 N1
Petersgate Infant School
 HORN PO8 .... 256 C8
Peter Symonds College
 FUFL SO22 .... 22 C1
Philip Green Memorial School
 WIMB BH21 .... 238 A1
The Phoenix Cinema
 ROWN SO16 .... 228 B9
Phoenix Industrial Park
 ELGH SO50 .... 229 L2
Pierrepointe School
 RFNM GU10 .... 116 E9
Pier Theatre
 WCLF BH2 .... 8 E7
The Pilgrims School
 WINC SO23 .... 23 F6
The Pilgrims Way Primary School
 FNM GU9 .... 116 B2
Pine Ridge Golf Club
 FRIM GU16 .... 59 J3
Pinewood Infant School
 FARN GU14 .... 57 L6
Pipers Wood Industrial Park
 WVILLE PO7 .... 275 L2
Pirbright Camp
 CHOB/PIR GU24 .... 59 N6
The Plague Monument
 FUFL SO22 .... 22 C4
Planet Ice
 LSOL/BMARY PO13 .... 295 J8
Plaza Theatre
 ROMY SO51 .... 204 D6
Pokesdown Primary School
 BOSC BH5 .... 335 P1
Polygon School
 WSHM SO15 .... 20 B2
Polymonds Tower
 SHAM SO14 .... 20 E5
The Pompey Centre
 PSEA PO1 .... 317 H3
Poole Crematorium
 CFDH BH17 .... 300 F8
Poole Freight Ferry Terminal
 PLE BH15 .... 332 D3
Poole Grammar School
 CFDH BH17 .... 320 F2
Poole High School
 PLE BH15 .... 320 F9
Poole Hospital
 PLE BH15 .... 320 F9
Poole Passenger Ferry Terminal
 PLE BH15 .... 332 D3
Poole Pottery
 PLE BH15 .... 332 E2
Poole Stadium (Speedway Track & Football Stadium)
 PLE BH15 .... 332 C2
Popham Airfield
 RWIN SO21 .... 107 L5
Popham Beacons
 RWIN SO21 .... 107 J6
Popley Fields Community Centre
 CHIN RG24 .... 69 M2
Porchester Cemetery
 FHAM/PORC PO16 .... 296 A3
Porchester RFC
 SBNE BH6 .... 324 C9
Portchester Castle
 FHAM/PORC PO16 .... 296 A3
Portchester Community School
 FHAM/PORC PO16 .... 295 N2
Portchester Crematorium
 FHAM/PORC PO16 .... 273 M9
Portchester Health Centre
 FHAM/PORC PO16 .... 295 P1
Portfield School
 LTDN BH7 .... 323 N8
Portchester School
 CHCH/BSGR BH23 .... 303 H8

Portsdown Primary School
 CHAM PO6 .... 297 H1
Portsea Clinic
 PSEA PO1 .... 18 D3
Portsmouth College
 HSEA PO3 .... 317 L1
Portsmouth Deaf Association Centre
 PSEA PO1 .... 19 K2
Portsmouth FC (Fratton Park)
 ENEY PO4 .... 317 H3
Portsmouth Fish Market
 PSEA PO1 .... 18 C5
Portsmouth Golf Club
 WVILLE PO7 .... 275 N8
Portsmouth Grammar Junior School
 PSEA PO1 .... 18 E5
Portsmouth Grammar School
 PSEA PO1 .... 18 D5
Portsmouth High School
 SSEA PO5 .... 19 F7
 SSEA PO5 .... 316 E6
Portsmouth Historic Dockyard
 PSEA PO1 .... 18 A2
Portsmouth Indoor Tennis Centre
 CHAM PO6 .... 18 E4
Portsmouth Marriott Hotel
 CHAM PO6 .... 296 E2
Portsmouth Natural Health Centre
 PSEA PO1 .... 19 F5
Portsmouth RFC
 HSEA PO3 .... 297 J5
Portsmouth University
 PSEA PO1 .... 18 D3
Portswood Primary School
 SD/PW SO17 .... 248 E1
Portuguese Fireplace
 LYND SO43 .... 263 P6
Portway Industrial Estate
 AND SP10 .... 82 B9
 AND SP10 .... 102 A1
Portway Infant School
 AND SP10 .... 102 A2
Portway Junior School
 AND SP10 .... 102 A2
Potley Hill Primary School
 YTLY GU46 .... 41 H9
Potters Gate CE Primary School
 FNM GU9 .... 96 A9
Potters Industrial Park
 FLEETS GU52 .... 74 F7
Potters International Hotel
 ALDT GU11 .... 75 N8
Poulner J & I School
 RGWD BH24 .... 260 G8
Premier Business Centre
 FHAM/STUB PO14 .... 294 F4
Premier Business Park
 FHAM/STUB PO14 .... 10 A7
Premier Inn
 BH/HW/K RG22 .... 68 G7
 CFDH BH17 .... 320 C4
 CHAM PO6 .... 296 D1
 CHCH/BSGR BH23 .... 324 D8
 ELGH SO50 .... 325 L7
 ELGH SO50 .... 228 C1
 FARN GU14 .... 75 M1
 HAV PO9 .... 302 G1
 HAV PO9 .... 276 B9
 HLER SO31 .... 271 J6
 OVTN RG25 .... 108 D5
 PLE BH15 .... 320 D8
 ROMY SO51 .... 225 M5
 ROWN SO16 .... 227 K4
 SHAM SO14 .... 21 F3
 SHST GU47 .... 41 L7
 SSEA PO5 .... 316 C6
Preston Candover CE Primary School
 OVTN RG25 .... 129 M1
Preston House
 OVTN RG25 .... 109 M9
Preymead Industrial Estate
 FNM GU9 .... 97 H4
Priestlands School
 LYMN SO41 .... 329 K5
Priest's House Museum & Garden
 WIMB BH21 .... 300 E1
Prince Consort's Library
 ALDT GU11 .... 75 N9
Princes Hall
 ALDT GU11 .... 2 D2
Princes Mead School
 RWIN SO21 .... 165 M1
Princes Mead Shopping Centre
 FARN GU14 .... 76 A1
Princess Anne Hospital
 ROWN SO16 .... 227 M9
The Princess Royal Barracks
 FRIM GU16 .... 59 J6
The Priory CE VA Primary School
 CHCH/BSGR BH23 .... 324 F9
Priory College
 SSEA PO5 .... 316 G4
Priory Industrial Park
 CHCH/BSGR BH23 .... 325 M8
The Priory Primary School
 TADY RG26 .... 50 F3
Prospect Business Centre
 NSEA SO24 .... 167 P3
Purbeck Pottery
 PLE BH15 .... 332 D2
Purbrook CC
 WVILLE PO7 .... 275 K6
Purbrook J & I School
 WVILLE PO7 .... 275 M5
Purbrook Park School
 WVILLE PO7 .... 275 M7

The Pyramids Leisure Centre
 SSEA PO5 .... 316 F7
The Quadrant Centre
 BMTH BH1 .... 8 E3
Quality Hotel
 AND SP10 .... 5 H6
 AND SP10 .... 9 G4
Quarley Hill
 RAM SP11 .... 99 N9
Quarterdeck Hotel
 PSTN BH14 .... 321 H9
Quayside Education Centre
 GPORT PO12 .... 315 M2
Queen Alexandra Hospital
 CHAM PO6 .... 275 H9
Queen Elizabeth Country Park
 HORN PO8 .... 236 G1
Queen Elizabeths Leisure Centre
 WIMB BH21 .... 278 B8
Queen Elizabeths School
 WIMB BH21 .... 278 B8
Queen Mary's College
 BSTK RG21 .... 69 L9
Queens Hotel
 SSEA PO5 .... 316 D6
Queens Inclosure Primary School
 WVILLE PO7 .... 276 A1
Queen's Park Golf Club
 CHAR BH8 .... 323 K8
Queens Park Infant School
 CHAR BH8 .... 323 J6
Queens Park Junior School
 CHAR BH8 .... 323 H6
Quilley School of Engineering
 ELGH SO50 .... 229 H3
Raceview Business Centre
 NWBY RG14 .... 17 H3
Rachel Madocks School
 HORN PO8 .... 255 N7
Railway Triangle Industrial Estate
 CHAM PO6 .... 297 K3
Rake Business Park
 LISS GU33 .... 193 J2
Rake CE First School
 LISS GU33 .... 193 K1
Ramada Hotel
 RFNM GU10 .... 97 N6
Ramalley Cemetery
 CHFD SO53 .... 206 D6
Ranvilles Infant School
 FHAM/STUB PO14 .... 294 A1
Ranvilles Junior School
 FHAM/STUB PO14 .... 294 A1
Redan Road Cemetery
 ASHV GU12 .... 3 J2
Red Barn CP School
 FHAM/PORC PO16 .... 295 M1
Redbridge Community School
 ROWN SO16 .... 246 G3
Redbridge Primary School
 WSHM SO15 .... 247 H3
Redfields Business Park
 FLEETS GU52 .... 95 J1
Red Funnel Ferry Terminal
 SHAM SO14 .... 248 B9
Red House Museum & Gardens
 CHCH/BSGR BH23 .... 336 C1
Redlands Primary School
 FHAM/PORC PO16 .... 294 E2
Red Lion Hotel
 BSTK RG21 .... 7 F6
Redlynch CE Primary School
 RSAL SP5 .... 200 B8
Red Shoot Brewery
 RGWD BH24 .... 261 M3
Red Shoot Camping Park
 RGWD BH24 .... 261 M2
Redwood Park Secondary School
 CHAM PO6 .... 297 K3
Regency Park Hotel
 NTHA RG18 .... 25 L1
The Regent Centre
 CHCH/BSGR BH23 .... 324 F9
Regents Park Girls School
 ROWN SO16 .... 247 L3
Rex Industrial Estate
 CHFD SO53 .... 206 E8
Rhinefield House Hotel
 BROC SO42 .... 285 P5
Richmond Court Business Centre
 CHAR BH8 .... 323 H9
Riders J & I School
 HAV PO9 .... 276 D5
Ridgemede Junior School
 BPWT SO32 .... 232 B2
The Ridgeway Centre
 BH/HW/K RG22 .... 68 E9
The Ridgeway Community School
 FNM GU9 .... 116 C3
Ringwood Brewery
 RGWD BH24 .... 282 D3
Ringwood CE Infant School
 RGWD BH24 .... 282 E2
Ringwood Junior School
 RGWD BH24 .... 282 E2
Ringwood Recreation Centre
 RGWD BH24 .... 282 E2
Ringwood Road Retail Park
 BWD BH11 .... 321 N1
Ringwood Secondary School
 RGWD BH24 .... 282 E2
Ringwood Trading Estate
 RGWD BH24 .... 282 E5
Ringwood Waldorf School
 RGWD BH24 .... 282 B5
Riverpark Industrial Estate
 NWBY RG14 .... 17 J1

River Park Leisure Centre WINC SO23 ... 23 F2
Riverside Business Park FNM GU9 ... 96 C8
LYMN SO41 ... 329 M3
Riverside Holidays HLER SO31 ... 270 A6
Riverside Park Industrial Estate FNM GU9 ... 96 D8
WIMB BH21 ... 300 F2
Riverside School WVILLE PO7 ... 275 P7
Riverwey Industrial Park ALTN GU34 ... 133 H5
The Riviera Hotel WBNE BH4 ... 334 C5
RNLI Headquarters PLE BH15 ... 332 D1
Robert Mays School ODIM RG29 ... 72 B9
Robert Sandilands Primary School NWBY RG14 ... 24 B3
Rockbourne Roman Villa FBDG SP6 ... 219 M5
Rockford Common (NT) RCWD BH24 ... 261 K5
Rogate CE Primary School EPSF GU31 ... 217 K1
Romans Business Park FNM GU9 ... 96 D8
Romans Country House Hotel THLE RG7 ... 35 J6
Roman Way Primary School AND SP10 ... 82 F7
Romsey Abbey CE (Aided) Primary School ROMY SO51 ... 204 B6
Romsey CC ROMY SO51 ... 204 D7
Romsey Golf Club ROWN SO16 ... 226 G5
Romsey Hospital ROMY SO51 ... 204 E6
Romsey Industrial Estate ROMY SO51 ... 204 C4
Romsey Infant School ROMY SO51 ... 204 D6
Romsey Junior School ROMY SO51 ... 204 E5
Romsey RFC ROMY SO51 ... 204 D7
The Romsey School ROMY SO51 ... 204 C5
Romsey Sports Centre ROMY SO51 ... 204 C5
Romsey Town FC ROMY SO51 ... 204 D7
Rookesbury Park School WHAM PO17 ... 253 H7
Rookwood School AND SP10 ... 102 C3
Rosemary Medical Centre BKME/WDN BH12 ... 321 K5
Rossmore Community College BKME/WDN BH12 ... 321 M4
Rowlands Castle Golf Club HAV PO9 ... 257 H9
Rowledge CE (Controlled) Primary School RFNM GU10 ... 115 M7
Rowner Health Centre LSOL/BMARY PO13 ... 294 G9
Rowner Infant School LSOL/BMARY PO13 ... 295 H8
Rowner Junior School LSOL/BMARY PO13 ... 295 H8
Rowner Swimming Centre LSOL/BMARY PO13 ... 314 G2
Rownhams House Industrial Estate ROWN SO16 ... 227 J6
Rownhams St Johns CE Primary School ROWN SO16 ... 227 J6
Royal Armouries Fort Nelson WHAM PO17 ... 273 M7
Royal Army Medical Corps ALDT GU11 ... 76 C8
Royal Beach Hotel ENEY PO4 ... 316 C2
Royal Bournemouth Hospital LTDN BH7 ... 323 P6
Royal Exeter Hotel WCLF BH2 ... 8 D5
Royal Hampshire County Hospital FUFL SO22 ... 164 E8
Royal Hampshire Regiment Museum & Memorial Garden WINC SO23 ... 22 D5
Royal Hospital Haslar GPORT PO12 ... 13 H6
The Royal Junior School CSHT GU26 ... 156 C4
Royal Logistic Corps Museum FNM GU16 ... 59 J5
The Royal Marines Museum ENEY PO4 ... 317 K6
Royal Military Academy CBLY GU15 ... 41 P7
Royal Naval Memorial PSEA PO5 ... 316 D6
Royal Naval Museum PSEA PO1 ... 18 A2
Royal Navy Submarine Museum GPORT PO12 ... 13 J5
Royal Pier SHAM SO14 ... 248 B9
The Royal School HASM GU27 ... 156 C3
Royal South Hants Hospital SHAM SO14 ... 21 F1

Royal Victoria Country Park HLER SO31 ... 269 L6
Royal Winchester Golf Club FUFL SO22 ... 164 C8
Rucstall Community Centre BSTK RG21 ... 69 N9
Rucstall J & I School BSTK RG21 ... 69 N9
Rufus Stone LYND SO43 ... 244 A6
Rural Life Centre RFNM GU10 ... 116 F7
Rushington Business Park TOTT SO40 ... 246 C6
Russell Cotes Art Gallery & Museum BMTH BH1 ... 9 F5
St Albans CE Primary School HAV PO9 ... 15 J1
St Albans Medical Centre CHAR BH8 ... 323 H7
St Aldhelms CE Combined School BKME/WDN BH12 ... 322 A9
St Andrews CE Infant School FNM GU9 ... 96 B9
St Annes Catholic Primary School BH/HW/K RG22 ... 68 G9
St Annes Catholic School WSHM SO15 ... 248 B5
St Anns Hospital CCLF BH13 ... 333 N5
St Anthonys Catholic Primary School FHAM/STUB PO14 ... 271 K8
St Augustines Primary School FRIM GU16 ... 58 E3
St Barbe Museum & Visitor Centre LYMN SO41 ... 329 L3
St Bartholomews Primary School HASM GU27 ... 157 H5
St Bartholomews School NWBY RG14 ... 16 B6
St Bede CE Primary School WINC SO23 ... 23 F3
St Bedes Catholic Primary School CHIN RG24 ... 69 K3
St Bernadettes Catholic Primary School FARN GU14 ... 57 P8
St Catherines Catholic Primary School WIMB BH21 ... 279 J8
St Catherines Hill Nature Reserve WINC SO23 ... 184 A2
St Christophers Hospital FHAM/PORC PO16 ... 11 J2
St Clements & St John CE Infant School BMTH BH1 ... 335 K1
St Denys Primary School WSHM SO17 ... 248 E2
St Edmunds Catholic Secondary School PSEA PO1 ... 19 J2
St Edmunds School GSHT GU26 ... 156 C2
St Edwards Comprehensive School PLE BH15 ... 321 H5
St Edwards School ROMY SO51 ... 202 A4
St Faiths CE Primary School WINC SO23 ... 183 P1
St Francis Primary School CHFD SO53 ... 206 C8
St Francis Special School FHAM/STUB PO14 ... 294 A1
St George RC Boys School ROWN SO16 ... 228 F6
St Georges Business Centre PSEA PO1 ... 18 D4
St Georges Primary School PSEA PO1 ... 18 C2
St Georges Hospital CBLY GU15 ... 58 A2
St Georges Industrial Estate CBLY GU15 ... 58 A2
ENEY PO4 ... 317 J3
St Georges University School of Medicine WINC SO23 ... 22 E4
St Ives First School RCWD BH24 ... 281 N4
St Ives School HASM GU27 ... 157 K5
St James CE First School FBDG SP6 ... 239 N5
St James CE Primary School EMRTH PO10 ... 277 M8
HEND SO30 ... 249 P1
St James CE VA Primary School LTDN BH7 ... 323 P9
St James Hospital ENEY PO4 ... 317 K3
St Johns Almshouses WINC SO23 ... 23 G5
St Johns Cathedral PSEA PO1 ... 316 C2
St Johns Catholic Primary School PSEA PO1 ... 19 J2
St Johns CE First School WIMB BH21 ... 300 F1
St Johns CE Infant School RFNM GU10 ... 136 E8
St Johns CE Primary School BSTK RG21 ... 69 K9
GPORT PO12 ... 315 M1

St Johns CE VA Primary School MOOR/WNTN BH9 ... 322 F6
St Johns College SSEA PO5 ... 19 J7
St John's Cross RAND SP11 ... 101 N8
St Johns Infant School SHAM SO14 ... 20 D7
St Johns Primary School Rowlands Castle HAV PO9 ... 277 H2
St Johns RC Cathedral PSEA PO1 ... 19 F2
St John the Baptist CE Primary School BPWT SO32 ... 252 C1
FHAM/STUB PO14 ... 271 J1
St John the Baptist RC J & I School AND SP10 ... 102 B3
St John the Evangelist Infant School NWBY RG14 ... 16 D6
St Joseph RC Primary School NWBY RG14 ... 24 E3
St Josephs Catholic Combined School BKME/WDN BH12 ... 321 N5
St Josephs Catholic Primary School ALDT GU11 ... 2 E7
St Josephs Primary School CHCH/BSGR BH23 ... 325 L7
St Judes CE (Controlled) Primary School FERN ... 18 E6
St Judes Primary School FHAM/STUB PO14 ... 10 B6
St Jude's Youth Centre SSEA PO5 ... 19 F6
St Katharines CE VA Primary School SBNE BH6 ... 336 F2
St Lawrence CE (Controlled) Primary School ALTN GU34 ... 132 E5
St Leonards Community Hospital RCWD BH24 ... 281 J8
St Leonards Farm Caravan & Camping Park FERN BH22 ... 302 C1
St Leonards Hotel RCWD BH24 ... 281 L6
St Lukes CE Primary School LYMN SO41 ... 308 B6
St Lukes CE Secondary School SSEA PO5 ... 19 H3
St Lukes CE VA Primary School MOOR/WNTN BH9 ... 322 F7
St Marks CE Junior School WSHM SO15 ... 247 P4
St Marks CE Primary School FARN GU14 ... 76 C4
St Marks CE VA Primary School NBNE BH10 ... 322 C6
St Marks Primary School BH/HW/K RG22 ... 89 M5
St Martins East Woodhay CE Primary School KSCL RG20 ... 29 H7
St Martins School TWDS BH3 ... 322 F9
St Mary Bourne Primary School RAND SP11 ... 84 B1
St Mary Extra Cemetery ITCH SO19 ... 249 K9
St Mary Magdalen Almshouses WINC SO23 ... 23 G6
St Marys Catholic Combined School PLE BH15 ... 320 G7
St Marys CE (Aided) Infant School RFNM GU10 ... 136 D2
St Marys CE (Controlled) Primary School SHAM SO14 ... 21 G3
St Marys CE First School CHIN RG24 ... 280 D6
St Marys CE Junior School CHIN RG24 ... 70 C6
St Mary's Church Centre BSTK RG21 ... 7 G6
St Marys College WEND SO18 ... 248 G3
St Marys CP School GPORT PO12 ... 315 L3
St Marys Hospital ENEY PO4 ... 317 H3
St Michael & All Angels Infant School LYND SO43 ... 264 F5
St Michaels Abbey FARN GU14 ... 58 B8
St Michaels CE Infant School ALDT GU11 ... 3 G7
St Michaels CE Junior School ALDT GU11 ... 3 H7
St Michaels CE Middle School WIMB BH21 ... 278 C7
St Michaels CE Primary School SHST GU47 ... 40 F6
St Michaels CE VC Primary School WCLF BH2 ... 8 A4
St Michael's Hospice CHIN RG24 ... 69 H3
St Michaels School KSCL RG20 ... 30 E8

St Monica Infant School ITCH SO19 ... 249 J8
St Monica Junior School ITCH SO19 ... 249 J8
St Neots School HTWY RG27 ... 39 J6
St Nicholas School FLEETS GU51 ... 95 J1
St Nicolas CE Junior School NWBY RG14 ... 16 D4
St Omer Barracks ALDT GU11 ... 76 C8
St Patricks Catholic Primary School FARN GU14 ... 58 C9
ITCH SO19 ... 248 G8
St Pauls Catholic VA Primary School CHAM PO6 ... 296 D1
St Pauls CE Infant School RFNM GU10 ... 97 N4
St Peters Catholic Primary School WVILLE PO7 ... 275 P5
St Peters CE (Aided) Primary School FNM GU9 ... 115 P3
St Peters CE Junior School FARN GU14 ... 58 B9
YTLY GU46 ... 40 E8
St Peter's Church BMTH BH1 ... 9 H4
St Peters CE Primary School RAND SP11 ... 81 H4
St Peters RC Primary School FUFL SO22 ... 183 K1
St Peters School LTDN BH7 ... 323 P7
SBNE BH6 ... 336 D2
St Polycarps Catholic Primary School FNM GU9 ... 96 D9
St Swithuns RC (Aided) Primary School SSEA PO5 ... 316 G6
St Swithuns School RWIN SO21 ... 165 L7
St Swithun upon Kingsgate WINC SO23 ... 22 E6
St Swithun Wells CHFD SO53 ... 206 F8
St Thomas Clinic LYMN SO41 ... 329 L4
St Thomas Garnets School LTDN BH7 ... 335 N1
St Thomas Infant School KSCL RG20 ... 29 M6
St Thomas Mores RC Primary School HAV PO9 ... 14 B2
St Vincent College GPORT PO12 ... 315 M3
St Walburgas Catholic Primary School MOOR/WNTN BH9 ... 323 H6
St Winifreds School SD/PW SO17 ... 248 C2
Salesian College FARN GU14 ... 76 C3
Salterns Harbourside Hotel PSTN BH14 ... 333 K3
Salterns School TOTT SO40 ... 246 E3
Salto Gym Club AND SP10 ... 82 B9
Sammy Miller Motorcycle Museum NMIL/BTOS BH25 ... 326 C2
Sampson Business Park CBLY GU15 ... 58 A2
The Samuel Cody School FARN GU14 ... 76 A5
Sandbanks Business Centre CCLF BH13 ... 333 K8
Sandbanks Hotel CCLF BH13 ... 333 N6
Sandford Springs Golf Club TADY RG26 ... 48 F3
Sandham Memorial Chapel (NT) KSCL RG20 ... 30 D8
Sandhurst School SHST GU47 ... 41 L5
Sandhurst Sports Centre SHST GU47 ... 41 L6
Sandhurst Sports Club SHST GU47 ... 41 K7
Sandringham Infant School FRIM GU16 ... 58 E6
Sandy Balls Holiday Centre FBDG SP6 ... 241 H1
Sarisbury CE Junior School HLER SO31 ... 270 C5
Sarisbury Infant School HLER SO31 ... 270 E6
Sarum Road Hospital FUFL SO22 ... 164 D8
Saxon Centre CHCH/BSGR BH23 ... 324 F8
Saxon Shore Infant School CHAM PO6 ... 296 A1
Saxon Square Shopping Centre CHCH/BSGR BH23 ... 324 F9
Saxon Wood School CHIN RG24 ... 68 E4
Scantabout Primary School CHFD SO53 ... 207 H6
Screen Cinema WINC SO23 ... 22 D6
Seacrest Hotel SSEA PO5 ... 316 F7
Seaview Business Centre BKME/WDN BH12 ... 321 K6
Sea Vixen Industrial Estate CHCH/BSGR BH23 ... 325 L8

Selborne Primary School ALTN GU34 ... 152 C8
Shakespeare Business Centre ELGH SO50 ... 207 K9
Shakespeare Infant School ELGH SO50 ... 207 J9
Shakespeare Junior School ELGH SO50 ... 207 J8
Shamblehurst Primary School HEND SO30 ... 250 C3
Shannon Retail Park ELGH SO50 ... 206 G9
Sharps Copse Primary School HAV PO9 ... 277 H5
Shawcross Industrial Park HEND PO3 ... 297 J4
Shaw cum Donnington Primary School NWBY RG14 ... 24 D1
Shawfield Primary School ASHV GU12 ... 76 F9
Shedfield Road Cemetery BPWT SO32 ... 252 C4
Sheet CP School PSF GU32 ... 191 P8
Sheiling School RGWD BH24 ... 282 A3
Shelley Museum ... 335 M2
Shepherds Down Special School RWIN SO21 ... 183 J8
Shepherds Spring Infant School AND SP10 ... 82 F6
Shepherds Spring Junior School AND SP10 ... 82 F6
Sherborne St John CE Primary School CHIN RG24 ... 51 H9
Sherbourne House School CHFD SO53 ... 206 F5
Sherfield on Loddon CC HTWY RG27 ... 52 E5
Sherfield School HTWY RG27 ... 52 E5
Shipton Bellinger Primary School TDWTH SP9 ... 98 F2
Shirley Business Park WSHM SO15 ... 247 P5
The Shirley Health Centre WSHM SO15 ... 247 N4
Shirley J & I School WSHM SO15 ... 247 N2
Shirley Swimming Pool WSHM SO15 ... 247 N4
Shirley Warren Primary School ROWN SO16 ... 247 L1
Sholing J & I School ITCH SO19 ... 249 J6
Sholing Technology College ITCH SO19 ... 249 H7
Shottermill Infant School HASM GU27 ... 156 E6
Sidings Industrial Estate HLER SO31 ... 269 M5
Silchester CE Primary School THLE RG7 ... 35 J5
Silver Business Park CHCH/BSGR BH23 ... 325 K8
Simcoe Clinic WSHM SO15 ... 248 A4
Sinclair Primary School ROWN SO16 ... 227 L7
The Sir Harold Hillier Gardens ROMY SO51 ... 205 H1
Siskin J & I School LSOL/BMARY PO13 ... 315 H2
Skyline Plaza BSTK RG21 ... 7 F5
Smannell & Enham CE Primary School RAND SP11 ... 83 H4
Solatron Retail Park FARN GU14 ... 75 P7
Solent Business Centre WSHM SO15 ... 247 M5
Solent Hotel & Spa FHAM PO15 ... 271 K3
Solent Industrial Centre WSHM SO15 ... 247 N4
Solent Industrial Estate HEND SO30 ... 250 B2
Solent Infant School CHAM PO6 ... 297 M1
Solent Junior School CHAM PO6 ... 297 M1
Solent Meads Golf Centre SBNE BH6 ... 336 F2
Solent Peoples Theatre ITCH SO19 ... 249 J8
Solent Sky Museum SHAM SO14 ... 21 H7
Somerford Business Park CHCH/BSGR BH23 ... 325 L8
Somerford Primary & Community School CHCH/BSGR BH23 ... 325 J8
Somers Park Primary School SSEA PO5 ... 19 J3
Somers Town Health Centre SSEA PO5 ... 19 J4
Sopley Primary School CHCH/BSGR BH23 ... 304 G7
Southampton Cemetery WSHM SO15 ... 248 A3
Southampton City Art Gallery WSHM SO15 ... 20 D2
Southampton City College SHAM SO14 ... 21 G5
Southampton FC (St Mary's Stadium) SHAM SO14 ... 21 H3

Southampton
General Hospital
ROWN SO16 .... 227 M9
Southampton Institute &
Millais Gallery
SHAM SO14 .... 20 E2
Southampton
International Airport
WEND SO18 .... 229 H6
Southampton Maritime
Museum
SHAM SO14 .... 20 D7
Southampton Municipal
Golf Course
ROWN SO16 .... 228 A6
Southampton
Oceanography Centre
SHAM SO14 .... 268 D1
Southampton Park Hotel
SHAM SO14 .... 20 C1
Southampton
Solent University
SHAM SO14 .... 20 E3
Southampton Sports Centre
ROWN SO16 .... 227 P8
Southampton Sports Club
ROWN SO16 .... 246 G1
Southampton Super Bowl
SHAM SO14 .... 247 K4
South Baddesley
Primary School
LYMN SO41 .... 330 B1
Southbourne Surgery
SBNE BH6 .... 336 A1
South Downs College
WVILLE PO7 .... 276 A7
Southdowns Country Hotel
EPSF GU31 .... 217 N5
Southern Electric Museum
CHCH/BSGR BH23 .... 324 F8
South Farnborough County
Junior School
FARN GU14 .... 76 C2
South Farnborough
Infant School
FARN GU14 .... 76 C4
South Farnham School
FNM GU9 .... 116 E1
South Ham Medical Centre
BH/HW/K RG22 .... 68 F9
South Hampshire
Industrial Park
TOTT SO40 .... 226 B9
South Hants Country Club
WHAM PO17 .... 273 L1
Southlands School
LYMN SO41 .... 309 L9
South Parade Pier
ENEY PO4 .... 316 C7
Southsea Castle
SSEA PO5 .... 316 E7
Southsea Community Centre
SSEA PO5 .... 19 F5
Southsea
Hovercraft Terminal
SSEA PO5 .... 316 C6
Southsea Infant School
SSEA PO5 .... 316 G6
Southsea Skate Park
SSEA PO5 .... 316 E7
South View Cemetery
BSTK RG21 .... 6 D4
South View Infant School
BSTK RG21 .... 7 G1
Southwick Park Golf Club
WHAM PO17 .... 274 C5
South Winchester Golf Club
FUFL SO22 .... 183 J2
South Wonston
Primary School
RWIN SO21 .... 144 E4
Southwood Golf Club
FARN GU14 .... 75 M2
Southwood Infant School
FARN GU14 .... 75 L1
Sovereign Business Centre
PLE BH15 .... 320 D6
Sovereign Business Park
PLE BH15 .... 320 D6
Sovereign Centre
BMTH BH1 .... 335 L1
Sparsholt CE Primary School
RWIN SO21 .... 165 N4
Sparsholt College Hampshire
RWIN SO21 .... 165 K3
Spectrum Sports Club
SBNE BH6 .... 336 A2
Speenhamland
Primary School
NWBY RG14 .... 24 C3
Spinnaker Tower
PSEA PO1 .... 18 B4
Spinners Garden & Nursery
LYMN SO41 .... 309 L7
Spitbank Fort
SSEA PO5 .... 316 D9
Splashdown
BKME/WDN BH12 .... 321 J3
Springdale First School
BDST BH18 .... 300 A9
Springfield School
CHAM PO6 .... 297 L2
Springhill Catholic
Primary School
WSHM SO15 .... 248 A5
Springlake Country Club
ALDT GU11 .... 76 D8
Springwell School
HLER SO31 .... 269 J5
Spurcroft Primary School
STHA RG19 .... 25 N5
Spurlings Industrial Estate
WHAM PO17 .... 273 H7
Square Tower
PSEA PO1 .... 18 B7
SS Shieldhall
SHAM SO14 .... 248 D9

Staffwise Business Centre
CHAM PO6 .... 297 H3
Stag Business Park
RGWD BH24 .... 282 E4
Stakes Hill Infant School
WVILLE PO7 .... 275 P4
Stamshaw Infant School
NEND PO2 .... 296 F7
Stamshaw Junior School
NEND PO2 .... 296 E6
Stamshaw & Tipner
Leisure Centre
NEND PO2 .... 296 E7
Stanbridge Earls School
ROMY SO51 .... 203 P2
Stanley Casino
SHAM SO14 .... 21 G7
Stanley Green First School
PLE BH15 .... 320 E6
Stanley Green
Industrial Estate
PLE BH15 .... 320 D7
Stanmore Primary School
FUFL SO22 .... 185 N1
Stanton Industrial Estate
WSHM SO15 .... 247 L4
Stanton Road
Industrial Estate
WSHM SO15 .... 247 L4
Stanwell House Hotel
LYMN SO41 .... 329 M4
Stapehill Abbey
WIMB BH21 .... 279 N9
Station Industrial Estate
FLEETN GU51 .... 74 E1
Station Theatre
HISD PO11 .... 318 D4
Staunton Country Park
HAV PO9 .... 276 F2
Staunton Park
Community School
HAV PO9 .... 277 H3
Steep School
PSF GU32 .... 191 L7
The Stepping Stone School
GSHT GU26 .... 156 E2
Sterling Industrial Estate
NWBY RG14 .... 17 G3
Sterte Industrial Estate
PLE BH15 .... 320 D8
Stockbridge Primary School
STOK SO20 .... 141 M5
Stockton House School
FLEETN GU51 .... 74 C2
Stoke Hill Infant School
ELGH SO50 .... 229 N1
Stoke Park Junior School
ELGH SO50 .... 229 N2
Stokes Bay
Mobile Home Park
GPORT PO12 .... 315 H6
Stokes Bay
ROWN SO16 .... 228 D6
Stone Lane Industrial Estate
WIMB BH21 .... 278 C8
Stourfield Infant School
SBNE BH6 .... 324 B9
Strouden Park
Medical Centre
CHAR BH8 .... 323 L6
The Stroud School
ROMY SO51 .... 205 J5
Stubbs Industrial Estate
ALDT GU11 .... 76 D7
Studland Industrial Estate
KSCL RG20 .... 29 J2
Sulhamstead & Ufton Nervet
Primary School
THLE RG7 .... 26 E3
Suncliff Hotel
BMTH BH1 .... 9 J4
Sundridge School
HORN PO8 .... 255 P9
Sun Hill Junior School
NARL SO24 .... 168 A3
Sun Valley Business Park
WINC SO23 .... 23 K2
Swan Centre
ELGH SO50 .... 229 K2
Swan Hotel
NARL SO24 .... 168 A1
Swanmore Business Park
BPWT SO32 .... 232 D7
Swanmore CE
Primary School
BPWT SO32 .... 232 F6
Swanmore College
of Technology
BPWT SO32 .... 232 E7
Swanwick Business Park
HLER SO31 .... 270 D3
Swanwick Lodge
HLER SO31 .... 270 F3
Sway Manor Restaurant
& Hotel
LYMN SO41 .... 308 B7
Sway Park Industrial Estate
LYMN SO41 .... 308 A6
Swaythling Clinic
SD/PW SO17 .... 228 E9
Swaythling Primary School
SD/PW SO17 .... 228 D9
Sylvan First School
BKME/WDN BH12 .... 321 K6
Tadley Community
Primary School
TADY RG26 .... 34 D8
Tadley Learning Centre
TADY RG26 .... 34 C5
Tadley Swimming Pool
TADY RG26 .... 34 D7
Talavera Junior School
ALDT GU11 .... 2 E1
Talbot Combined School
BKME/WDN BH12 .... 322 B7
Talbot Heath School
WBNE BH4 .... 334 C1

Talbot House Preparatory
School
MOOR/WNTN BH9 .... 322 E7
Talbot Medical Centre
BWD BH11 .... 322 A6
Talisman Business Centre
HLER SO31 .... 271 H4
The Tanneries
Industrial Estate
HAV PO9 .... 14 E6
Tanners Brook J & I School
WSHM SO15 .... 247 K4
Taro Leisure Centre
EPSF GU31 .... 216 B2
Tatchbury Manor House
TOTT SO40 .... 245 M2
Tatchbury Mount Hospital
TOTT SO40 .... 245 N1
Tauntons College
WSHM SO15 .... 248 A2
Tavistock Infant School
FLEETN GU51 .... 74 A4
Tempus Business Centre
BSTK RG21 .... 6 A2
Terminus Industrial Estate
PSEA PO1 .... 19 J3
Testbourne Community
School
WHCH RG28 .... 85 M8
Test Valley Business Centre
ROWN SO16 .... 246 F1
Test Valley Business Park
NBAD SO52 .... 205 L7
Test Valley Golf Club
OVTN RG25 .... 107 H2
Test Valley School
STOK SO20 .... 141 J5
Testwood School
TOTT SO40 .... 246 D2
Thatcham Bowling Club
NTHA RG18 .... 25 N3
Thatcham Park CE
Primary School
NTHA RG18 .... 25 N2
Theatre Royal
WINC SO23 .... 22 D3
Thistle Hotel
PLE BH15 .... 332 E2
Thornden School
CHFD SO53 .... 205 H5
Thorney Island
Primary School
EMRTH PO10 .... 299 N6
Thornford Park Track
STHA RG19 .... 25 P9
Thorngate Hall
GPORT PO12 .... 12 A3
Thorngrove School
KSCL RG20 .... 29 M7
Thornhill Clinic
ITCH SO19 .... 249 M5
Thornhill Primary School
ITCH SO19 .... 249 L6
Thornycroft Industrial Estate
BH/HW/K RG22 .... 69 H6
Three Counties
Education Trust
RFNM GU10 .... 116 D4
Three Legged Cross
First School
WIMB BH21 .... 258 B3
Thruxton Aerodrome &
Motor Racing Circuit
RAND SP11 .... 100 B2
Thruxton Industrial Estate
RAND SP11 .... 100 B3
Tidworth College
TDWTH SP9 .... 79 H5
Tidworth Garrison Golf Club
TDWTH SP9 .... 78 E7
Tidworth Leisure Centre
TDWTH SP9 .... 79 H5
Tidworth Military Cemetery
TDWTH SP9 .... 78 C1
Tiptoe Primary School
LYMN SO41 .... 307 M8
Titanic Memorial
WSHM SO15 .... 20 D2
Titchfield Abbey
FHAM PO15 .... 271 N8
Titchfield Cemetery
FHAM/STUB PO14 .... 293 M2
Titchfield Primary School
FHAM/STUB PO14 .... 271 M9
Tivoli Theatre
WIMB BH21 .... 278 D9
Tomlinscote School & Sixth
Form College
FRIM GU16 .... 58 E3
Totally Tennis
BSTK RG21 .... 69 M9
Totton College
TOTT SO40 .... 246 B3
Totton Recreation Centre
TOTT SO40 .... 246 A3
Tower Hill Primary School
FARN GU14 .... 75 N1
Tower House Hotel
WCLF BH2 .... 8 B6
Tower Industrial Estate
ELGH SO50 .... 229 L2
Tower Park
BKME/WDN BH17 .... 321 K3
Towngate Shopping Centre
PLE BH15 .... 332 E1
Town Hall Annexe
WCLF BH2 .... 8 C2
Townhill Infant School
WEND SO18 .... 249 J1
Townhill Junior School
WEND SO18 .... 249 J1
Townhill Park Health Clinic
WEND SO18 .... 249 J1
Town Quay
SHAM SO14 .... 20 D6
Townsend Primary School
CHAR BH8 .... 323 N5

Trafalgar School at Downton
RSAL SP5 .... 199 J6
Tralee Hotel
WCLF BH2 .... 8 C6
Travel Interchange
Superstore
CHAR BH8 .... 9 H1
Travelodge
ALTN GU34 .... 150 A6
BH/HW/K RG22 .... 89 P2
CBLY GU15 .... 49 N9
ELGH SO50 .... 207 K7
EMRTH PO10 .... 277 L8
KSCL RG20 .... 30 C7
LIPH GU30 .... 174 G2
LYND SO43 .... 243 N7
NEND PO2 .... 296 F9
RGWD BH24 .... 281 L6
RWIN SO21 .... 104 F8
RWIN SO21 .... 125 K5
SHAM SO14 .... 248 C4
Treadgolds Museum
PSEA PO1 .... 18 D2
Treloar School
ALTN GU34 .... 113 P8
Triakes Country Park
SHST GU47 .... 40 G7
Trinity Business Centre
TOTT SO40 .... 246 C1
Trinity CE VA First School
VWD BH31 .... 258 F2
Trinity Church Hall
BSTK RG21 .... 6 E7
Trinity Industrial Estate
WIMB BH21 .... 300 G2
WSHM SO15 .... 247 K4
Trinity School & Performing
Arts College
NWBY RG14 .... 24 E2
Trojans Sports Club
ELGH SO50 .... 228 E5
Trosnant Primary & Infant
School
HAV PO9 .... 14 E1
Trouville Hotel
WCLF BH2 .... 8 D5
Tudor House Museum
SHAM SO14 .... 20 D6
Tudor Merchants Hall
SHAM SO14 .... 20 D6
Tunworth House
OVTN RG25 .... 91 M3
Turbary Retail Park
BWD BH11 .... 321 M1
Turnpike Business Park
FHAM/PORC PO16 .... 11 H3
Tweseldown
Infant School
FLEETS GU52 .... 74 E8
Twin Oaks Medical Centre
CHCH/BSGR BH23 .... 305 M8
Two Riversmeet
Leisure Centre
CHCH/BSGR BH23 .... 324 C9
Twyford St Mary's CE
Primary School
RWIN SO21 .... 183 P8
Twyford School
RWIN SO21 .... 184 A8
Twynham School
CHCH/BSGR BH23 .... 324 E9
Tylney Hall Hotel
HTWY RG27 .... 71 L1
Tylney Park Golf Club
HTWY RG27 .... 53 L9
Tyrrells Ford
Country House Hotel
CHCH/BSGR BH23 .... 304 D4
Uddens Trading Estate
WIMB BH21 .... 279 N8
Ullswater Hotel
WCLF BH2 .... 8 A6
Unicorn Trading Estate
HASM GU27 .... 156 C6
United Services RFC
PSEA PO1 .... 18 E3
University College
Winchester
FUFL SO22 .... 164 E8
University College
Winchester (Chute House)
WINC SO23 .... 6 D5
University College for
Creative Arts
FNM GU9 .... 96 A9
University of Portsmouth
ENEY PO4 .... 317 H6
HISD PO11 .... 317 H4
PSEA PO1 .... 18 E5
SSEA PO5 .... 19 F7
University of Southampton
SD/PW SO17 .... 248 C1
SHAM SO14 .... 248 B4
University of Southampton
(Winchester School of Art)
WINC SO23 .... 23 G3
Upham CE Primary School
BPWT SO32 .... 209 L8
Uplands CP School
SHST GU47 .... 41 J6
Uplands Primary School
FHAM/PORC PO16 .... 10 E2
Uplands School
PSTN BH14 .... 321 L9
Upper Hale Cemetery
FNM GU9 .... 96 B4
Upton Country Park
CFDH BH17 .... 320 A6
Upton Grey House
OVTN RG25 .... 92 A5
Valentine Infant School
ITCH SO19 .... 249 L8
Velmead Community Centre
FLEETN GU51 .... 74 A8
Venture Industrial Park
HSEA PO3 .... 297 J4
LSOL/BMARY PO13 .... 295 H6

Vermont School
ROWN SO16 .... 228 A8
Vernham Dean School
RAND SP11 .... 43 H8
Verwood CE First School
VWD BH31 .... 258 E5
Verwood Industrial Estate
VWD BH31 .... 258 G4
Verwood Leisure Centre
VWD BH31 .... 258 F4
Viables Craft Centre
BH/HW/K RG22 .... 90 C2
Viables Industrial Estate
BH/HW/K RG22 .... 90 B3
Vicarage Farm Business Park
ELGH SO50 .... 208 C8
Vicarage Lane Clinic
HASM GU27 .... 156 E7
Vickers Business Centre
BSTK RG21 .... 69 H4
Victoria Cottage Hospital
EMRTH PO10 .... 277 M9
Victoria Education Centre
CCLF BH13 .... 321 P8
Victoria Park Swimming
Centre
PSEA PO1 .... 19 F2
Victoria Road Cemetery
FARN GU14 .... 58 A9
Victoria Stadium
PSEA PO1 .... 18 A5
Victory Business Centre
PSEA PO1 .... 316 G3
Victory Retail Park
PSEA PO1 .... 316 E1
Victory Trading Estate
HSEA PO3 .... 297 K7
Vigo J & I School
AND SP10 .... 5 H2
Vistarama Balloon
BMTH BH1 .... 8 D4
Vue Cinema
BSTK RG21 .... 7 F5
PSEA PO1 .... 18 C4
The Vyne Community School
BSTK RG21 .... 6 E2
The Vyne (NT)
CHIN RG24 .... 51 L7
Waite End Primary School
WVILLE PO7 .... 275 N4
Walford Mill Medical Centre
WIMB BH21 .... 278 D8
Wallisdean Infant School
FHAM/STUB PO14 .... 10 C7
Wallisdean Junior School
FHAM/STUB PO14 .... 10 C7
Walloji J & I School
STOK SO20 .... 120 F9
Walsh Memorial CE
Infant School
ASHV GU12 .... 97 M2
Waltham Business Park
BPWT SO32 .... 232 E8
Walworth Road
Industrial Estate
AND SP10 .... 83 H9
Warblington Cemetery
HAV PO9 .... 299 N2
Warblington
Secondary School
HAV PO9 .... 15 K5
War Memorial Hospital
AND SP10 .... 82 C9
Warren Avenue
Industrial Estate
ENEY PO4 .... 317 K3
Warren Park Primary School
HAV PO9 .... 276 D3
Warrior Business Centre
CHAM PO6 .... 297 N2
Warsash Maritime Academy
HLER SO31 .... 292 C2
The Watchetts Junior School
CBLY GU15 .... 58 B3
Waterfront Business Park
FLEETN GU51 .... 74 E2
The Waterfront Complex
WCLF BH2 .... 8 E5
Waterfront Museum
PLE BH15 .... 332 D2
The Waterloo Hotel
CWTH RG45 .... 41 H1
Waterloo Industrial Estate
HEND SO30 .... 250 B2
Waterlooville Cemetery
WVILLE PO7 .... 275 N3
Waterlooville Golf Club
HORN PO8 .... 256 D5
Waterlooville Health Centre
WVILLE PO7 .... 255 M9
The Waterside Health Centre
FAWY SO45 .... 268 C8
Waterside Medical Centre
GPORT PO12 .... 13 H1
Waterside Primary School
FAWY SO45 .... 268 D7
Watersplash Hotel
BROC SO42 .... 286 F8
The Wavell School
ALDT GU11 .... 76 A5
Waverley Abbey CE School
RFNM GU10 .... 117 J5
Waverley Abbey House
RFNM GU10 .... 117 H2
Wea Clovelly Centre
SHAM SO14 .... 21 F1
Webb Peploe House Surgery
LYMN SO41 .... 329 L4
Weeke Primary School
FUFL SO22 .... 164 G5
Wellington Arms Hotel
HTWY RG27 .... 37 J9
Wellington Business Park
CWTH RG45 .... 40 F2

Wellington College
 CWTH RG45 .... 41 H2
Wellington Country Park
 THLE RG7 .... 38 A4
Wellingtonia Avenue
 (Arboretum)
 CWTH RG45 .... 40 D2
Wellington Monument
 HTWY RG27 .... 37 N6
Wellington Shopping Centre
 ALDT GU11 .... 2 E3
Wellington Sports Centre
 CWTH RG45 .... 40 G2
Wellington Sports Club
 ELGH SO50 .... 228 F5
Wellow Golf Club
 ROMY SO51 .... 203 L9
Wellow Primary School
 ROMY SO51 .... 224 F1
Wentworth College
 BOSC BH5 .... 335 N2
Wessex Complementary
 Medical Centre
 SBNE BH6 .... 336 C1
Wessex Gate Retail Park
 PLE BH15 .... 320 D6
Wessex Hotel
 WCLF BH2 .... 8 B5
Wessex Nuffield Hospital
 CHFD SO53 .... 207 H4
Wessex Road Surgery
 PSTN BH14 .... 321 J9
Wessex Superbowl
 BKME/WDN BH12 .... 321 P8
 HAV PO9 .... 276 B9
Wessex Tutors
 WSHM SO15 .... 20 A2
West Berkshire
 Community Hospital
 NTHA RG18 .... 25 H3
West Berkshire Museum
 NWBY RG14 .... 16 E2
Westbourne CP School
 EMRTH PO10 .... 277 P6
Westbourne Medical Centre
 WBNE BH4 .... 334 C2
West Canford Heath
 Medical Centre
 CFDH BH17 .... 320 F3
West End Infant School
 ALDT GU11 .... 2 C4
Western Community Hospital
 ROWN SO16 .... 247 L2
Western Downland CE
 Primary School
 FBDG SP6 .... 219 M3
Western Primary School
 FUFL SO22 .... 164 E7
Westfield Hall Hotel
 ENEY PO4 .... 317 H6
Westfield Industrial Estate
 GPORT PO12 .... 315 K4
 HORN PO8 .... 256 D4
Westfield Junior School
 CHAM PO6 .... 296 A1
Westfields Infant School
 YTLY GU46 .... 40 C9
Westfields Junior School
 YTLY GU46 .... 40 C9
The Westgate Museum
 WINC SO23 .... 22 C4
The Westgate School
 FUFL SO22 .... 164 E6
West Green House
 Gardens (NT)
 HTWY RG27 .... 54 D8

Westhill Cemetery
 FUFL SO22 .... 22 B5
West Hill Park School
 FHAM/STUB PO14 .... 293 L1
West Hoe Cemetery
 BPWT SO32 .... 232 D4
West Howe Clinic
 BWD BH11 .... 322 A4
West Howe Industrial Estate
 BWD BH11 .... 321 N1
Westlands Medical Centre
 FHAM/PORC PO16 .... 295 N2
West March Business Centre
 AND SP10 .... 82 F9
West Moors Middle School
 FERN BH22 .... 280 F8
Weston Park Boys School
 ITCH SO19 .... 269 K1
Weston Park Infant School
 ITCH SO19 .... 269 J1
Weston Park Junior School
 ITCH SO19 .... 269 J1
Weston Shore Infant School
 ITCH SO19 .... 269 N2
Westover Hall Hotel
 LYMN SO41 .... 338 F2
Westover Primary School
 HSEA PO3 .... 297 K9
West Point Business Park
 AND SP10 .... 102 C2
West Portway
 Industrial Estate
 AND SP10 .... 101 N1
West Quay Retail Park
 WSHM SO15 .... 20 B4
West Quay Shopping Centre
 WSHM SO15 .... 20 C4
West Tytherley
 Primary School
 RSAL SP5 .... 159 H7
Westwood Business Park
 TOTT SO40 .... 246 D1
Weybourne County
 Infant School
 FNM GU9 .... 96 E5
Weybrook Park Golf Club
 CHIN RG24 .... 68 F3
Weydon School
 RFNM GU10 .... 115 P3
Weydown Industrial Estate
 HASM GU27 .... 157 H6
Weyford Infant School
 BOR GU35 .... 154 C4
Weyford Junior School
 BOR GU35 .... 154 C4
Weyhill Business Park
 RAND SP11 .... 81 H9
Wherwell J & I School
 RAND SP11 .... 123 M2
Whitchurch Cemetery
 WHCH RG28 .... 85 K7
Whitchurch CE
 Primary School
 WHCH RG28 .... 85 M7
Whitchurch Medical Centre
 WHCH RG28 .... 85 K6
Whitchurch Silk Mill
 WHCH RG28 .... 85 L7
Whitedown Special School
 ALTN GU34 .... 132 D7
Whitehall Hotel
 WCLF BH2 .... 8 D4
White Hart Industrial Estate
 BLKW GU17 .... 41 M9
Whitehill Cemetery
 BOR GU35 .... 154 D5

Whitelands Park
 Primary School
 NTHA RG18 .... 25 M2
Whiteley Primary School
 FHAM PO15 .... 271 J3
Whiteley Village
 Outlet Shopping
 FHAM PO15 .... 271 L2
Whitewater CE
 Primary School
 HTWY RG27 .... 53 M8
Whitley Ridge
 Country House Hotel
 BROC SO42 .... 287 K7
Wick 1 Industrial Estate
 NMIL/BTOS BH25 .... 326 G5
Wick 2 Industrial Estate
 NMIL/BTOS BH25 .... 326 G5
Wickham CE
 Primary School
 WHAM PO17 .... 252 E7
Wickham Park Golf Club
 WHAM PO17 .... 252 C7
Wickham Road Cemetery
 FHAM/PORC PO16 .... 11 H1
Wickham Vineyard
 BPWT SO32 .... 251 P4
Wicor CP School
 FHAM/PORC PO16 .... 295 L1
Widern Clinic
 HEND SO30 .... 250 C4
Widern School
 HEND SO30 .... 250 C3
Wildground Infant School
 FAWY SO45 .... 268 B9
Wildground Junior School
 FAWY SO45 .... 268 B9
Wilksworth Farm
 Caravan Park
 WIMB BH21 .... 278 D6
William Cobbett
 Junior School
 FNM GU9 .... 96 E5
William Gilpin CE
 Primary School
 LYMN SO41 .... 309 M7
Williams Industrial Park
 NMIL/BTOS BH25 .... 326 G5
Willink Leisure Centre
 THLE RG7 .... 27 H5
Willink School
 THLE RG7 .... 27 H5
Willis Museum
 BSTK RG21 .... 7 F7
Willment Marine &
 Business Park
 ITCH SO19 .... 248 F6
Wimbledon Park
 Sports Centre
 SSEA PO5 .... 316 F6
Wimborne First School
 WIMB BH21 .... 278 D8
Wimborne Hospital
 WIMB BH21 .... 278 C9
Wimborne Industrial Estate
 WIMB BH21 .... 278 E9
Wimborne J & I School
 ENEY PO4 .... 317 J4
Wimborne Market
 WIMB BH21 .... 300 F1
Wimborne Minster
 WIMB BH21 .... 300 D1
Wimborne RFC
 WIMB BH21 .... 300 G1
Wimborne Town FC
 WIMB BH21 .... 278 C9

The Winchcombe School
 NWBY RG14 .... 24 D2
Winchelsea Special School
 BKME/WDN BH12 .... 321 M3
Winchester
 Agricultural Museum
 WINC SO23 .... 22 E2
Winchester Cathedral
 WINC SO23 .... 22 E5
Winchester City FC
 WINC SO23 .... 23 F1
Winchester City Mill (NT)
 WINC SO23 .... 23 G5
Winchester College
 WINC SO23 .... 22 E7
The Winchester Hotel
 WINC SO23 .... 22 D1
Winchester
 Lawn Tennis Club
 FUFL SO22 .... 164 E5
Winchester RFC
 WINC SO23 .... 23 G1
Winchester Road
 Industrial Estate
 BH/HW/K RG22 .... 90 B1
The Winchester Royal Hotel
 WINC SO23 .... 22 E4
Winklebury Centre
 DEAN RG23 .... 68 F7
Winklebury
 Football Complex
 DEAN RG23 .... 68 G7
Winklebury Infant School
 DEAN RG23 .... 68 G6
Winklebury Medical Centre
 DEAN RG23 .... 68 F6
Winnall CP School
 WINC SO23 .... 23 J4
Winnall Farm
 Industrial Estate
 WINC SO23 .... 23 H3
Winnall Trading Estate
 WINC SO23 .... 23 J2
Winter Gardens Theatre
 WCLF BH2 .... 8 C5
Winterslow CE
 Primary School
 RSAL SP5 .... 158 A1
Winton Primary School
 MOOR/WNTN BH9 .... 322 E5
Winton School
 AND SP10 .... 5 J3
 NBNE BH10 .... 322 D6
Wispers School
 HASM GU27 .... 157 H4
Wokefield Park Golf Club
 THLE RG7 .... 27 N7
Wolverdene School
 AND SP10 .... 5 F6
Wolvesey Castle
 WINC SO23 .... 23 F6
Woodcote Primary School
 LSOL/BMARY PO13 .... 294 F5
Woodhill Preparatory School
 CHFD SO53 .... 206 F6
 HEND SO30 .... 250 F4
Woodland Park
 RFNM GU10 .... 135 K1
Woodlands Business Village
 BSTK RG21 .... 7 J3
Woodlands
 Community School
 WEND SO18 .... 249 L3
Woodlands
 Education Centre
 HORN PO8 .... 255 M7

The Woodlands Lodge Hotel
 TOTT SO40 .... 245 K8
Woodlea Primary School
 BOR GU35 .... 154 A7
Wooldings Vineyard
 WHCH RG28 .... 85 P2
Woolmer Hill Athletics Track
 HASM GU27 .... 156 C5
Woolmer Hill
 Technology College
 HASM GU27 .... 156 C6
Woolsbridge
 Industrial Estate
 WIMB BH21 .... 281 H3
Woolsbridge Manor Farm
 Caravan Park
 WIMB BH21 .... 281 H3
Woolsbridge
 Small Business Centre
 WIMB BH21 .... 280 G3
Wooltston Infant School
 ITCH SO19 .... 248 G9
Woolston School
 Language College
 ITCH SO19 .... 249 H8
Woolton Hill Junior School
 KSCL RG20 .... 29 M6
Wootey Junior School
 ALTN GU34 .... 132 F3
Wordsworth House
 ROWN SO16 .... 247 M1
Wordsworth Infant School
 WSHM SO15 .... 247 M2
Worldham Golf Course
 ALTN GU34 .... 133 J7
Worting Road Cemetery
 BH/HW/K RG22 .... 69 J8
Wyke CP School
 RGUW GU3 .... 77 L8
Wykeham Gallery
 STOK SO20 .... 141 L5
Wykeham House School
 FHAM/PORC PO16 .... 11 K5
Wykeham Industrial Estate
 WINC SO23 .... 23 J1
Wynford Farm
 Industrial Estate
 ROMY SO51 .... 204 D1
Wyvern Technology College
 ELGH SO50 .... 230 C3
Yateley Common
 Country Park
 YTLY GU46 .... 56 G2
Yateley Health Centre
 YTLY GU46 .... 40 E8
Yateley Infant School
 YTLY GU46 .... 40 E8
Yateley Manor School
 YTLY GU46 .... 40 E7
Yateley School
 YTLY GU46 .... 40 D9
Yeoman Industrial Park
 ROWN SO16 .... 246 F1
Yeomans Industrial Park
 CHAR BH8 .... 323 L4
York Town Industrial Estate
 CBLY GU15 .... 41 P9
Youngs Industrial Estate
 THLE RG7 .... 34 A2
YYS Business Park
 BKME/WDN BH12 .... 321 L5
Zouch Primary School
 TDWTH SP9 .... 78 F3

Acknowledgements

Schools address data provided by Education Direct.

Petrol station information supplied by Johnsons.

Garden centre information provided by:

Garden Centre Association ● Britains best garden centres

🌿 Wyevale Garden Centres

The statement on the front cover of this atlas is sourced, selected and quoted
from a reader comment and feedback form received in 2004

Speed camera locations

Speed camera locations provided in association with RoadPilot Ltd

SPEED READING

RoadPilot is the developer of one of the largest and most accurate databases of speed camera locations in the UK and Europe. It has provided the speed camera information in this atlas. RoadPilot is the UK's pioneer and market leader in GPS (Global Positioning System) road safety technologies.

microGo (pictured right) is RoadPilot's latest in-car speed camera location system. It improves road safety by alerting you to the location of accident black spots,

fixed and mobile camera sites. RoadPilot's microGo does not jam police lasers and is therefore completely legal.

RoadPilot's database of fixed camera locations has been compiled with the full co-operation of regional police forces and the Safety Camera Partnerships.

For more information on RoadPilot's GPS road safety products, please visit **www.roadpilot.com** or telephone 0870 240 1701

GPS Antenna
microGo is directional, it only alerts you to cameras on your side of the road

Visual Countdown
To camera location

Your Speed
The speed you are travelling when approaching camera

Camera Types Located
Gatso, Specs, Truvelo, TSS/DS5, Traffipax, mobile camera sites, accident black spots, congestion charges, tolls

Voice Warnings
Only if you are exceeding the speed limit at the camera

ALARM MODE

Plug and Go
Easy to move from vehicle to vehicle

64 Colour Options
To match vehicle's illumination

Speed Limit at Camera
Screen turns red as additional visual alert

Single Button Operation
For easy access to speed display, camera warning, rescue me location, trip computer, congestion charge, max speed alarm, date and time

RoadPilot

AA **Street by Street** QUESTIONNAIRE

Dear Atlas User
Your comments, opinions and recommendations are very important to us.
So please help us to improve our street atlases by taking a few minutes
to complete this simple questionnaire.

You do not need a stamp (unless posted outside the UK). If you do not want to remove
this page from your street atlas, then photocopy it or write your answers on a plain sheet
of paper.

Send to: Marketing Assistant, AA Publishing, 14th Floor Fanum House,
Freepost SCE 4598, Basingstoke RG21 4GY

ABOUT THE ATLAS...

Please state which city / town / county you bought:

_____

Where did you buy the atlas? (City, Town, County)

_____

For what purpose? (please tick all applicable)

To use in your local area ☐   **To use on business or at work** ☐

Visiting a strange place ☐   **In the car** ☐   **On foot** ☐

Other (please state)

_____

Have you ever used any street atlases other than AA Street by Street?

Yes ☐   **No** ☐

If so, which ones?

_____

Is there any aspect of our street atlases that could be improved?
(Please continue on a separate sheet if necessary)

_____
_____
_____
_____
_____

Please list the features you found most useful:

_____
_____
_____

Please list the features you found least useful:

_____
_____
_____

LOCAL KNOWLEDGE...

Local knowledge is invaluable. Whilst every attempt has been made to make the information contained in this atlas as accurate as possible, should you notice any inaccuracies, please detail them below (if necessary, use a blank piece of paper) or e-mail us at _streetbystreet@theAA.com_

_____
_____
_____

ABOUT YOU...

Name (Mr/Mrs/Ms) _____
Address _____
                                    Postcode _____
Daytime tel no _____
E-mail address _____

Which age group are you in?

Under 25 ☐   25-34 ☐   35-44 ☐   45-54 ☐   55-64 ☐   65+ ☐

Are you an AA member?   YES ☐   NO ☐

Do you have Internet access?   YES ☐   NO ☐

Thank you for taking the time to complete this questionnaire. Please send it to us as soon as possible, and remember, you do not need a stamp (unless posted outside the UK).

We may use information we hold about you to telephone or email you about other products and services offered by the AA, we do NOT disclose this information to third parties.

Please tick here if you do not wish to hear about products and services from the AA. ☐